CRIME IN THE UNITED STATES

CRIME IN THE UNITED STATES

2019

13th EDITION

EDITED BY SHANA HERTZ HATTIS

Bernan Press

Lanham • Boulder • New York • London

Published by Bernan Press
An imprint of The Rowman & Littlefield Publishing Group, Inc.
4501 Forbes Boulevard, Suite 200, Lanham, Maryland 20706
www.rowman.com
800-462-6420

6 Tinworth Street, London, SE11 5AL, UK

ISBN: 978-1-64143-348-8
eISBN: 978-1-64143-349-5

∞™ The paper used in this publication meets the minimum requirements
of American National Standard for Information Sciences—Permanence
of Paper for Printed Library Materials, ANSI/NISO Z39.48-1992.

CONTENTS

SECTION I

SUMMARY OF THE UNIFORM CRIME REPORTING (UCR) PROGRAM

SECTION I: SUMMARY OF THE UNIFORM CRIME REPORTING (UCR) PROGRAM

Bernan Press is proud to present its 13th edition of *Crime in the United States*. This title was formerly published by the Federal Bureau of Investigation (FBI), but is no longer available in printed form from the government. This edition contains final data from 2017, the most current year for which data is available.

This section describes the history of the UCR program, which collects the data used in *Crime in the United States*. It also examines the best way to use the data in this publication.

Currently, the UCR program includes four data collections:

- National Incident-Based Reporting System (NIBRS)— Provides detailed incident information on 52 offenses including the victims, offenders, and property stolen, recovered, or damaged. In addition, NIBRS collects arrest data for those offenses plus 10 others.

- Summary Reporting System (SRS)—Furnishes aggregate offense counts for 10 Part I offenses and arrest data for an additional 20 offenses. The historic data collection will give way to make UCR a NIBRS-only data collection by January 1, 2021.

- Law Enforcement Officers Killed and Assaulted (LEOKA) Program—Offers information about officers who were killed or assaulted while performing their duties. The information is published and used to help agencies develop polices to improve officer safety. More information about LEOKA and the accompanying data is available in Bernan Press's *Justice Statistics: An Extended Look at Crime in the United States*.

- Hate Crime Statistics Program—Provides information on crimes motivated by offenders' bias against race, gender, gender identity, religion, disability, sexual orientation, and ethnicity. These data are also collected via NIBRS.

About the UCR Program

The UCR program's primary objective is to generate reliable information for use in law enforcement administration, operation, and management; however, over the course of the program, its data has stood out as one of the country's leading social indicators.

The UCR program is a nationwide, cooperative statistical effort of more than 18,000 city, university and college, county, state, tribal, and federal law enforcement agencies voluntarily reporting data on crimes brought to their attention. Since 1930, the FBI has administered the UCR program and continued to assess and monitor the nature and type of crime in the nation. Criminologists, sociologists, legislators, municipal planners, the media, and other students of criminal justice use the data for varied research and planning purposes.

Note for Users

It is important for UCR data users to remember that the FBI's primary objective is to generate a reliable set of crime statistics for use in law enforcement administration, operation, and management. The FBI does not provide a ranking of agencies; instead, it provides alphabetical tabulations of states, metropolitan statistical areas, cities with over 10,000 inhabitants, suburban and rural counties, and selected colleges and universities. Law enforcement officials use these data for their designed purposes. Additionally, the public relies on these data for information about the fluctuations in levels of crime from year to year, while criminologists, sociologists, legislators, city planners, media outlets, and other students of criminal justice use them for a variety of research and planning purposes. Since crime is a sociological phenomenon influenced by a variety of factors, the FBI discourages data users from ranking agencies and using the data as a measurement of the effectiveness of law enforcement.

To ensure that data are uniformly reported, the FBI provides contributing law enforcement agencies with a handbook that explains how to classify and score offenses and provides uniform crime offense definitions. Acknowledging that offense definitions may vary from state to state, the FBI cautions agencies to report offenses according to the guidelines provided in the handbook, rather than by local or state statutes. Most agencies make a good faith effort to comply with established guidelines.

The UCR program publishes the statistics most commonly requested by data users. More information regarding the availability of UCR program data is available by telephone at (304) 625-4830, or by e-mail at ucr@fbi.gov. Data requests via e-mail cannot be processed without the requester's full name, mailing address, and contact telephone number.

Variables Affecting Crime: Caution Against Ranking

Until data users examine all the variables that affect crime in a town, city, county, state, region, or college or university, they can make no meaningful comparisons. In each edition of *Crime in the United States*, many entities—including news media, tourism agencies, and other organizations with an interest in crime in the nation—use reported figures to compile rankings of cities and counties. However, these rankings are merely a quick choice made by that data user; they provide no insight into the many variables that mold the crime in a particular town, city, county, state, or region. Consequently, these rankings may lead to simplistic and/or incomplete analyses, which can create misleading perceptions and thus adversely affect cities, counties, and their residents.

Considering Other Characteristics of a Jurisdiction

To assess criminality and law enforcement's response from jurisdiction to jurisdiction, data users must consider many variables, some of which (despite having significant impact on crime) are not readily measurable or applicable among all locales. Geographic and demographic factors specific to each jurisdiction must be considered and applied in order to make an accurate and complete assessment of crime in that jurisdiction. Several sources of information are available to help the researcher explore the variables that affect crime in a particular locale. The U.S. Census Bureau data, for example, can help the user better understand the makeup of a locale's population. The transience of the population, its racial and ethnic makeup, and its composition by age and gender, educational levels, and prevalent family structures are all key factors in assessing and understanding crime.

Local chambers of commerce, planning offices, and similar entities provide information regarding the economic and cultural makeup of cities and counties. Understanding a jurisdiction's industrial/economic base, its dependence upon neighboring jurisdictions, its transportation system, its economic dependence on nonresidents (such as tourists and convention attendees), and its proximity to military installations, correctional institutions, and other types of facilities all contribute to accurately gauging and interpreting the crime known to and reported by law enforcement.

The strength (including personnel and other resources) and aggressiveness of a jurisdiction's law enforcement agency are also key factors in understanding the nature and extent of crime occurring in that area. Although information pertaining to the number of sworn and civilian employees can be found in this publication, it cannot be used alone as an assessment of the emphasis that a community places on enforcing the law. For example, one city may report more crime than another comparable city because its law enforcement agency identifies more offenses. Attitudes of citizens toward crime and their crime reporting practices—especially for minor offenses—also have an impact on the volume of crimes known to police.

Making Valid Crime Assessments

It is essential for all data users to become as well educated as possible about understanding and quantifying the nature and extent of crime in the United States and in the jurisdictions represented by law enforcement contributors to the UCR program. Valid assessments are possible only with careful study and analysis of the various unique conditions that affect each local law enforcement jurisdiction.

Some factors that are known to affect the volume and type of crime occurring from place to place are:

- Population density and degree of urbanization

- Variations in composition of population, particularly in the concentration of youth

- Stability of the population with respect to residents' mobility, commuting patterns, and transient factors

- Modes of transportation and highway systems

- Economic conditions, including median income, poverty level, and job availability

- Cultural factors and educational, recreational, and religious characteristics

- Family conditions, with respect to divorce and family cohesiveness

- Climate

- Effective strength of law enforcement agencies

- Administrative and investigative emphases of law enforcement

- Policies of other components of the criminal justice system (that is, prosecutorial, judicial, correctional, and probational policies)

- Residents' attitudes toward crime

- Crime reporting practices of residents

Although many of the listed factors equally affect the crime of a particular area, the UCR program makes no attempt to relate them to the data presented. **The data user is therefore cautioned against comparing statistical data of individual reporting units from cities, counties, metropolitan areas, states, or colleges or universities solely on the basis on their population coverage or student enrollment.** Until data users examine all the variables that affect crime in a town, city, county, state, region, or college or university, they can make no meaningful comparisons.

Historical Background

Since 1930, the FBI has administered the UCR program; the agency continues to assess and monitor the nature and type of crime in the nation. Data users look to the UCR program for various research and planning purposes.

Recognizing a need for national crime statistics, the International Association of Chiefs of Police (IACP) formed the Committee on Uniform Crime Records in the 1920s to develop a system of uniform crime statistics. After studying state criminal codes and making an evaluation of the recordkeeping practices in use, the committee completed a plan for crime reporting that became the foundation of the UCR program in 1929. The plan included standardized offense definitions for seven main offense classifications known as Part I crimes to gauge fluctuations in the overall volume and rate of crime. Developers also instituted the Hierarchy Rule as the main reporting procedure for what is now known as the Summary Reporting System of the UCR program.

Seven main offense classifications, known as Part I crimes, were chosen to gauge the state of crime in the nation. These seven offense classifications included the violent crimes of murder and nonnegligent manslaughter, rape, robbery, and aggravated assault; also included were the property crimes of burglary, larceny-theft, and motor vehicle theft. By congressional mandate, arson was added as the eighth Part I offense category. Data collection for arson began in 1979.

During the early planning of the program, it was recognized that the differences among criminal codes precluded a mere aggregation of state statistics to arrive at a national total. Also, because of the variances in punishment for the same offenses in different states, no distinction between felony and misdemeanor crimes was possible. To avoid these problems and provide nationwide uniformity in crime reporting, standardized offense definitions were developed. Law enforcement agencies use these to submit data without regard for local statutes. UCR program offense definitions can be found in Appendix I.

In January 1930, 400 cities (representing 20 million inhabitants in 43 states) began participating in the UCR program. Congress enacted Title 28, Section 534, of the *United States Code* that same year, which authorized the attorney general to gather crime information. The attorney general, in turn, designated the FBI to serve as the national clearinghouse for the collected crime data. Since then, data based on uniform classifications and procedures for reporting have been obtained annually from the nation's law enforcement agencies.

Advisory Groups

Providing vital links between local law enforcement and the FBI for the UCR program are the Criminal Justice Information Systems Committees of the IACP and the National Sheriffs' Association (NSA). The IACP represents the thousands of police departments nationwide, as it has since the program began. The NSA encourages sheriffs throughout the country to participate fully in the program. Both committees serve the program in advisory capacities.

In 1988, a Data Providers' Advisory Policy Board was established. This board operated until 1993, when it combined with the National Crime Information Center Advisory Policy Board to form a single Advisory Policy Board (APB) to address all FBI criminal justice information services. The current APB works to ensure continuing emphasis on UCR-related issues. The Association of State Uniform Crime Reporting Programs (ASUCRP) focuses on UCR issues within individual state law enforcement associations and also promotes interest in the UCR program. These organizations foster widespread and responsible use of uniform crime statistics and lend assistance to data contributors.

Redesign of UCR

Although UCR data collection was originally conceived as a tool for law enforcement administration, the data were widely used by other entities involved in various forms of social planning by the 1980s. Recognizing the need for more detailed crime statistics, law enforcement called for a thorough evaluative study to modernize the UCR program. The FBI formulated a comprehensive three-phase redesign effort. The Bureau of Justice Statistics (BJS) agency in the Department of Justice responsible for funding criminal justice information projects, agreed to underwrite the first two phases. These phases were conducted by an independent contractor and structured to determine what, if any, changes should be made to the current program. The third phase would involve implementation of the changes identified.

The final report, the *Blueprint for the Future of the Uniform Crime Reporting Program,* was released in the summer of 1985. It specifically outlined recommendations for an expanded, improved UCR program to meet future informational needs. There were three recommended areas of enhancement to the UCR program:

- Offenses and arrests would be reported using an incident-based system

- Data would be collected on two levels. Agencies in level one would report important details about those offenses comprising the Part I crimes, their victims, and arrestees. Level two would consist of law enforcement agencies covering populations of more than 100,000 and a sampling of smaller agencies that would collect expanded detail on all significant offenses

- A quality assurance program would be introduced

In January 1986, Phase III of the redesign effort began, guided by the general recommendations set forth in the *Blueprint*. The FBI selected an experimental site to implement the redesigned program, while contractors developed new data guidelines and system specifications. Upon selecting the South Carolina Law Enforcement Division (SLED), which enlisted the cooperation of nine local law enforcement agencies, the FBI developed automated data capture specifications to adapt the SLED's state system to the national UCR program's standards, and the BJS funded the revisions. The pilot demonstration ran from March 1 through September 30, 1987, and resulted in further refinement of the guidelines and specifications.

From March 1 through March 3, 1988, the FBI held a national UCR conference to present the new system to law enforcement and to obtain feedback on its acceptability. Attendees of the conference passed three overall recommendations without dissent: first, that there be established a new, incident-based national crime reporting system; second, that the FBI manage this program, and third, that an Advisory Policy Board composed of law enforcement executives be formed to assist in directing and implementing the new program. Furthermore, attendees recommended that the implementation of national incident-based reporting proceed at a pace commensurate with the resources and limitations of contributing law enforcement agencies.

Establishing the NIBRS

From March 1988 through January 1989, the FBI developed and assumed management of the UCR program's National Incident-Based Reporting System (NIBRS), and by April 1989, the first test of NIBRS data was submitted to the national UCR program. Over the next few years, the national UCR program published information about the redesigned program in five documents:

- *Uniform Crime Reporting Handbook*, NIBRS Edition (1992) provides a nontechnical program overview focusing on definitions, policies, and procedures of the IBRS

- *Data Submission Specifications* (May 1992) is used by local and state systems personnel, who are responsible

for preparing magnetic media for submission to the FBI

- *Approaches to Implementing an Incident-Based System* (July 1992) is a guide for system designers

- *Error Message Manual* (revised December 1999) contains designations of mandatory and optional data elements, data element edits, and error messages

- *Data Collection Guidelines* (revised August 2000) contains a system overview and descriptions of the offense codes, reports, data elements, and data values used in the system

As more agencies inquired about the NIBRS, the FBI, in May 2002, made the *Handbook for Acquiring a Records Management System (RMS) That Is Compatible with the NIBRS* available to agencies considering or developing automated incident-based records management systems. The handbook, developed under the sponsorship of the FBI and the BJS, provides instructions for planning and conducting a system acquisition and offers guidelines on preparing an agency for conversion to the new system and to the NIBRS.

Originally designed with 52 data elements, the redesigned NIBRS captures up to 57 data elements via 6 types of data segments: administrative, offense, victim property, offender, and arrestee. Although, in the late 1980s, the FBI committed to hold all changes to the NIBRS in abeyance until a substantial amount of contributors implemented the system, modifications have been necessary. The system's flexibility has allowed the collection of four additional pieces of information to be captured within an incident: bias-motivated offenses (1990), the presence of gang activity (1997), data for law enforcement officers killed and assaulted (2003), and data on cargo theft (2005). The system has also allowed the addition of new codes to further specify location types and property types (2010).

The FBI began accepting NIBRS data from a handful of agencies in January 1989. As more contributing law enforcement agencies become educated about the rich data available through incident-based reporting and as resources permit, more agencies are implementing the NIBRS. Based on the 2012 data submissions, 15 states submit all their data via the NIBRS and 32 state UCR Programs are certified for NIBRS participation.

Suspension of the *Crime Index* and the *Modified Crime Index*

In June 2004, the CJIS APB approved discontinuing the use of the *Crime Index* in the UCR program and its publications and directed the FBI to publish a violent crime total and a property crime total. The *Crime Index*, first published in *Crime in the United States* in 1960, was the title used for a simple aggregation of the seven main offense classifications (Part I offenses) in the Summary Reporting System. The Modified Crime Index was the number of Crime Index offenses plus arson.

For several years, the CJIS Division studied the appropriateness and usefulness of these indices and brought the matter before many advisory groups including the UCR Subcommittee of the CJIS APB, the ASUCRP, and a meeting of leading criminologists and sociologists hosted by the BJS. In short, the *Crime Index* and the *Modified Crime Index* were not true indicators of the degrees of criminality because they were always driven upward by the offense with the highest number, typically larceny-theft. The sheer volume of those offenses overshadowed more serious but less frequently committed offenses, creating a bias against a jurisdiction with a high number of larceny-thefts but a low number of other serious crimes such as murder and rape.

Recent Developments in UCR Program

In the fall of 2011, the APB recommended, and FBI Director Robert Mueller III approved, changing the definition of rape. Since 1929, in the SRS, rape had been defined as "the carnal knowledge of a female forcibly and against her will," (*UCR Handbook*, 2004, p.19). Beginning with the 2013 data collection, the SRS definition for the violent crime of rape will be: "Penetration, no matter how slight, of the vagina or anus with any body part or object, or oral penetration by a sex organ of another person, without the consent of the victim." This definition can be found in the *Summary Reporting System [SRS] User Manual*, Version 1.0, dated June 20, 2013. The FBI is developing reporting options for law enforcement agencies to meet this requirement, which will be built into the redeveloped data collection system.

In addition to approving the new definition of rape for the SRS, the APB and Director Mueller approved removing the word "forcible" from the name of the offense and also replacing the phrase "against the person's will" with "without the consent of the victim" in other sex-related offenses in the SRS, the NIBRS, the Hate Crime Statistics Program, and Cargo Theft.

In response to a directive by the U.S. Government's Office of Management and Budget, the national UCR Program has expanded its data collection categories for race from four (White, Black, American Indian or Alaska Native, and Asian or Other Pacific Islander) to five (White, Black or African American, American Indian or Alaska Native, Asian, and Native Hawaiian or Other Pacific Islander). Also, the ethnicity categories have changed from "Hispanic" to "Hispanic or Latino" and from "Non-Hispanic" to "Not Hispanic or Latino." These changes are reflected in data presented for 2012.

The national UCR Program staff continues to develop data collection methods to comply with both the William Wilberforce Trafficking Victims Protection Reauthorization Act of 2008 and the Matthew Shepard and James Byrd, Jr. Hate Crime Prevention Act of 2009. As a result, the FBI will begin accepting data on human trafficking as well as data on crimes motivated by "gender and gender identity" bias and "crimes committed by, and crimes directed against, juveniles" from contributors in January 2013.

UCR Redevelopment Project Update

To streamline the program's database management and quality control activities, the FBI created the UCR Redevelopment Project (UCRRP). The UCRRP's goal is to improve the efficiency, usability, and maintainability of the UCR Program's submission processes, databases, and quality control activities. Through the UCRRP, the UCR Program will improve customer service by decreasing the time it takes to analyze data and by decreasing the time needed to release and publish crime data. The program will also enhance its external data query tool so that the public can view and analyze more published UCR data from the Internet.

Another major goal of the UCRRP is to reduce, to the point of elimination, the exchange of printed materials between submitting agencies and the FBI. Beginning with the 2013 data collections, all data was to be submitted electronically, and after July 2013, the UCR Program no longer accepted paper submissions or the electronic submission of documents (for example, Portable Document Format files). The UCRRP has begun working with agencies to help them adopt electronic submissions via the NIBRS, electronic SRS, or Extensible Markup Language.

Uniform Crime Reporting Program
Changes Definition of Rape

For the first time in the more than 80-year history of the Uniform Crime Reporting (UCR) Program, the FBI has changed the definition of a Part 1 offense. In December 2011, then FBI Director Robert S. Mueller, III, approved revisions to the UCR Program's definition of rape as recommended by the FBI's Criminal Justice Information Services (CJIS) Division Advisory Policy Board (APB), which is made up of representatives from all facets of law enforcement.

Beginning in 2013, rape is defined for Summary UCR purposes as, "Penetration, no matter how slight, of the vagina or anus with any body part or object, or oral penetration by a sex organ of another person, without the consent of the victim." The new definition updated the 80-year-old historical definition of rape which was "carnal knowledge of a female forcibly and against her will." Effectively, the revised definition expands rape to include both male and female victims and offenders, and reflects the various forms of sexual penetration understood to be rape, especially nonconsenting acts of sodomy, and sexual assaults with objects. Beginning in 2017, only this revised definition of rape was used.

"This new, more inclusive definition will provide us with a more accurate understanding of the scope and volume of these crimes," said Attorney General Eric Holder. Proponents of the new definition and of the omission of the term "forcible" say that the changes broaden the scope of the previously narrow definitions by capturing (1) data without regard to gender, (2) the penetration of any bodily orifice, penetration by any object or body part, and (3) offenses in which physical force is not involved. Now, for example, instances in which offenders use drugs or alcohol or incidents in which offenders sodomize victims of the same gender will be counted as rape for statistical purposes.

It has long been the UCR Program's mission to collect and publish data regarding the scope and nature of crime in the nation, including those for rape. Since the FBI began collecting data using the revised definition of rape in January 2013, program officials expected that the number of reported rapes would rise. According to David Cuthbertson, former FBI Assistant Director of the CJIS Division, "As we implement this change, the FBI is confident that the number of victims of this heinous crime will be more accurately reflected in national crime statistics."

Expanded Offense Tables

Expanded offense data are the details of the various offenses that the Uniform Crime Reporting Program collects beyond the count of how many crimes law enforcement agencies report. These details may include the type of weapon used in a crime, the type or value of items stolen, and so forth. Expanded homicide data provide supplemental details about murders such as the age, sex, and race of both the victim and the offender, the weapon used in the homicide, the circumstances surrounding the offense, and the relationship of the victim to the offender. In addition, expanded data includes trends (for example, 2-year comparisons) and rates per 100,000 inhabitants.

Expanded offense data, including expanded homicide data, are information collected in addition to the reports of the number of crimes known. As a result, law enforcement agencies can report an offense without providing the supplemental data about that offense. These additional tables can be found at https://ucr.fbi.gov/crime-in-the-u.s/2017/crime-in-the-u.s.-2017/topic-pages/expanded-offense.

About the Editor

Shana Hertz Hattis is a consulting writer-editor for Bernan Press. She holds a master of science in education degree in from Northwestern University and a bachelor's degree in journalism from the same university. She has previously edited *Vital Statistics of the United States: Births, Life Expectancy, Deaths, and Selected Health Data* and several volumes of *Crime in the United States* for Bernan.

SECTION II

OFFENSES KNOWN TO POLICE

VIOLENT CRIME

- MURDER

- RAPE

- ROBBERY

- AGGRAVATED ASSAULT

PROPERTY CRIME

- BURGLARY

- LARCENY-THEFT

- MOTOR VEHICLE THEFT

- ARSON

VIOLENT CRIME

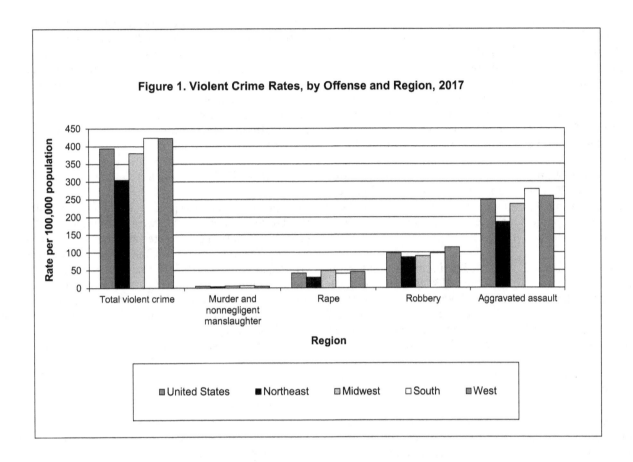

Figure 1. Violent Crime Rates, by Offense and Region, 2017

Definition

Violent crime consists of four offenses: murder and non-negligent manslaughter, rape, robbery, and aggravated assault. According to the Uniform Crime Reporting (UCR) program, run by the Federal Bureau of Investigation (FBI), violent crimes involve either the use of force or the threat of force.

Data Collection

The data presented in *Crime in the United States* reflect the Hierarchy Rule, which counts only the most serious offense in a multiple-offense criminal incident. In descending order of severity, the violent crimes are murder and nonnegligent manslaughter, rape, robbery, and aggravated assault; these are followed by the property crimes of burglary, larceny-theft, and motor vehicle theft. Arson is also considered a property crime, but the Hierarchy Rule does not apply to the arson offense. In cases in which arson occurs in conjunction with another violent or property crime, the arson and the additional crime are reported. More information on the expanded violent crime tables (which are available online but not included in this publication) can be found in Section I.

IMPORTANT NOTE: RAPE DATA

In 2016, the FBI UCR Program initiated the collection of rape data within the Summary Reporting System under a revised definition. The changes bring uniformity to the offense in both the Summary Reporting System (SRS) and the National Incident-Based Reporting System (NIBRS) by capturing data (1) without regard to gender, (2) including penetration of any bodily orifice by any object or body part, and (3) including offenses where physical force is not involved. The term "forcible" was removed, and the definition changed to the revised UCR definition below.

- Legacy UCR definition of rape: The carnal knowledge of a female forcibly and against her will. Use of this definition was discontinued in 2017.

- Revised UCR definition of rape (now called "rape," as it is the only definition in use): Penetration, no matter how slight, of the vagina or anus with any body part or object, or oral penetration by a sex organ of another person, without the consent of the victim.

National Volume, Trends, and Rate

In 2017, an estimated 1,247,321 violent crimes occurred in the United States, a decrease of 0.2 percent from the 2016 estimate. An estimated 382.9 violent crimes were committed per 100,000 inhabitants in 2017, a decline of 0.9 percent since 2016. Aggravated assaults accounted for 65.0 percent of violent crimes, the highest percentage of violent crimes reported to law enforcement. Robbery accounted for 25.6 percent of violent crimes, and murder accounted for 1.4 percent of violent crimes. (Table 1)

Occurrences of murder and robbery incidents decreased from 2016 to 2017, with murder decreasing by 0.7 percent and robbery by 4.0 percent. Rape (revised definition) increased 2.5 percent and aggravated assault increased 1.0 percent. (Tables 1 and 1A)

In longer-term trends, the 2017 estimated violent crime total was 6.8 percent below the 2013 level and 10.6 percent below the 2008 level. The 5-year and 10-year trend data also showed that the violent crime rate increased 3.7 percent between 2013 and 2017 and decreased 16.5 percent between 2008 and 2017. (Tables 1 and 1A)

In 2017, offenders used firearms in 72.6 percent of the nation's murders, 40.6 percent of robberies, and 26.3 percent of aggravated assaults. Although the largest percentage of murders were committed with firearms, weapons such as clubs and blunt objects accounted for more aggravated assaults (31.1 percent) than any other type of weapon. (Weapons data are not collected for rape offenses.) (Expanded Homicide Table 7, Expanded Offense Robbery Table 3, and Expanded Aggravated Assault Table; see <https://ucr.fbi.gov/crime-in-the-u.s/2017/crime-in-the-u.s.-2017/topic-pages/expanded-offense> for more information)

Many violent crimes are committed by people in known relationships. Figure 2 shows the number of murder victims who knew their offender. In the figure, the relationship categories of husband and wife include common-law spouses and ex-spouses. The categories of mother, father, sister, brother, son, and daughter include stepparents, stepchildren, and stepsiblings. The category of "acquaintance" includes homosexual relationships and the composite category of other known-to-victim offenders.

Regional Offense Trends and Rate

The UCR program divides the United States into four regions: the Northeast, the South, the Midwest, and the West. (More details concerning geographic regions are provided in Appendix IV.) The population distribution of the regions can be found in Table 3, and the estimated volume and rate of violent crime by region are provided in Table 4.

THE NORTHEAST

The Northeast accounted for an estimated 17.3 percent of the nation's population in 2017 and an estimated 13.4 percent of its violent crimes. The estimated number of violent crimes decreased 3.6 percent from 2016 to 2017. Murder decreased 1.0 percent in the Northeast. However, rape increased 0.6 percent. Robberies declined 8.0 percent. Aggravated assaults decreased 2.1 percent from 2016. In 2017, there were an estimated 304.7 violent crimes per 100,000 inhabitants. (Tables 3 and 4)

THE MIDWEST

With an estimated 20.9 percent of the total population of the United States, the Midwest accounted for 20.2 percent of the nation's estimated number of violent crimes in 2017. The region had a 0.2 percent increase in violent crime from 2016 to 2017. The estimated number of aggravated assaults increased 1.7 percent, while the estimated number of robberies fell 4.9 percent and the estimated number of murders fell 1.1 percent. The estimated number of rapes increased 3.4 percent. The rate of violent crime per 100,000 inhabitants in the Midwest was 380.7, a decrease of 0.1 percent from 2016 to 2017. (Tables 3 and 4)

THE SOUTH

The South, the nation's most populous region, accounted for 38.0 percent of the nation's population in 2017. Approximately 40.8 percent of violent crimes in 2017 occurred in the South. Violent crime decreased 0.8 percent, while the estimated number of murders fell 1.2 percent and the estimated number of rapes rose 0.8 percent. Robberies dropped 6.3 percent, while aggravated assault increased by 1.1 percent. The estimated rate of violent crime in the South was 423.8 incidents per 100,000 inhabitants in 2017. (Tables 3 and 4)

THE WEST

With 23.8 percent of the nation's population in 2017, the West also accounted for an estimated 25.5 percent of the nation's violent crime. Violent crime in the West decreased 0.3 percent from 2016 to 2017. Murders rose 2.4 percent, rapes increased 5.1 percent, robberies increased 2.4 percent, and aggravated assault increased 1.9 percent. The region's violent crime rate in 2017 was 423.1 per 100,000 inhabitants. (Tables 3 and 4)

Community Types

The UCR program aggregates crime data into three community types: metropolitan statistical areas (MSAs), cities outside MSAs, and nonmetropolitan counties outside MSAs. Appendix IV provides additional information regarding community types. In 2017, approximately 85.7 percent of the nation's population lived in MSAs. Residents of cities outside MSAs accounted for 5.8 percent of the country's population, and residents living in non-metropolitan counties accounted for 8.4 percent of the population. (Table 2)

In the areas reporting violent crimes to the UCR Program, approximately 89.2 percent of these crimes occurred in MSAs, while 6.0 percent occurred in cities outside MSAs and 4.1 percent occurred in nonmetropolitan counties. By community type, the violent crime rates were estimated at 412.3 incidents per 100,000 inhabitants in MSAs, 402.5 incidents per 100,000 inhabitants in cities outside MSAs, and 201.6 incidents per 100,000 inhabitants in nonmetropolitan counties. (Table 2)

Population Groups: Trends and Rates

In the UCR program, data are also aggregated into population groups; these groups are described in more detail in Appendix IV. The nation's cities had an overall increase of 0.1 percent in the estimated number of violent crimes from 2016 to 2017. By city population group, cities with 500,000 to 999,999 inhabitants had the largest percentage increase in the estimated number of violent crimes (2.3 percent). Cities with 1 million or more inhabitants had the largest decrease in violent crimes at 0.7 percent. (Table 12)

The law enforcement agencies in the nation's cities collectively reported a rate of 469.6 violent crimes per 100,000 inhabitants in 2017. Law enforcement agencies in the subset of cities with 500,000 to 999,999 inhabitants reported the highest violent crime rate, 870.0 violent crimes per 100,000 inhabitants; the violent crime rate for all cities with 250,000 or more inhabitants was 768.5 per 100,000 inhabitants. Agencies in cities with 10,000 to 24,999 inhabitants reported the lowest violent crime rate (269.5 incidents per 100,000 inhabitants). Law enforcement agencies in the nation's metropolitan counties reported a collective violent crime rate of 262.9 per 100,000 inhabitants, while agencies in nonmetropolitan counties reported a collective rate of 206.7 violent crimes per 100,000 inhabitants. (Table 16)

MURDER

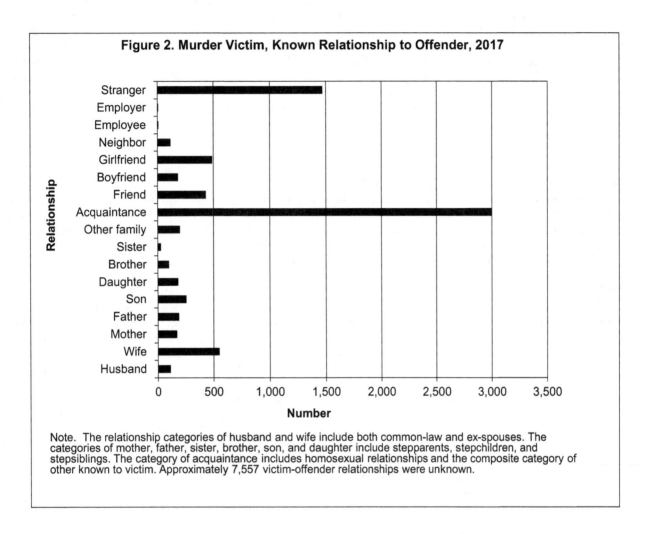

Figure 2. Murder Victim, Known Relationship to Offender, 2017

Note. The relationship categories of husband and wife include both common-law and ex-spouses. The categories of mother, father, sister, brother, son, and daughter include stepparents, stepchildren, and stepsiblings. The category of acquaintance includes homosexual relationships and the composite category of other known to victim. Approximately 7,557 victim-offender relationships were unknown.

Definition

The UCR program defines murder and non-negligent manslaughter as the willful (non-negligent) killing of one human being by another. The classification of this offense is based solely on police investigation, rather than on the determination of a court, medical examiner, coroner, jury, or other judicial body. The UCR program does not include the following situations under this offense classification: deaths caused by negligence, suicide, or accident; justifiable homicides; and attempts to murder or assaults to murder, which are considered aggravated assaults.

Data Collection/Supplementary Homicide Reports (SHR)

The UCR program's *Supplementary Homicide Report* (SHR) provides information about murder victims and offenders by age, sex, and race; the types of weapons used in the murders; the relationships of the victims to the offenders; and the circumstances surrounding the incident. Law enforcement agencies are asked to complete an SHR for each murder reported to the UCR program. Data from SHRs can be viewed in the Expanded Homicide Data section, found on the FBI Web site: https://ucr.fbi.gov/crime-in-the-u.s/2017/crime-in-the-u.s.-2017/topic-pages/expanded-offense. More information on these reports and the expanded homicide tables can be found in Section I. Highlights from these tables have been included below.

National Volume, Trends, and Rates

An estimated 17,284 persons were murdered nationwide in 2017. This number was a 0.7 percent decrease from the 2016 estimate, a 20.7 percent increase from the 2013 figure, and a 5.0 percent increase from the 2008 estimate. The 2017 murder rate, 5.3 offenses per 100,000 inhabitants, was a 1.4 percent decrease from the 2016 rate. Murder accounted for 1.3 percent of the overall estimated number of violent crimes in 2017. (Tables 1 and 1A)

Regional Offense Trends and Rates

The UCR program divides the United States into four regions: the Northeast, the South, the Midwest, and the West. (More details concerning geographic regions are provided in Appendix IV.) In 2017, 45.9 percent of murders were reported in the South, the country's most populous region. The Midwest reported 22.6 percent of all murders, while the West reported 20.2 percent and the Northeast reported 11.3 percent. (Table 3)

THE NORTHEAST

In 2017, the Northeast accounted for an estimated 17.3 percent of the nation's population and 11.3 percent of its estimated number of murders. With an estimated 1,957 murders, the Northeast saw a 1.0 percent decrease from its 2016 figure. The offense rate for the Northeast was 3.5 murders per 100,000 inhabitants. (Tables 3 and 4)

THE MIDWEST

The Midwest accounted for an estimated 20.9 percent of the nation's total population and 22.6 percent of the country's estimated number of murders in 2017. The Midwest reported an estimated 3,914 murders in 2017. The region experienced a rate of 5.7 murders per 100,000 inhabitants in 2017, below its 2016 rate of 5.8. (Tables 3 and 4)

THE SOUTH

The South accounted for an estimated 38.0 percent of the nation's population in 2017 and 45.9 percent of the nation's murders, the highest proportion among the four regions. The estimated 7,928 murders represented a 1.2 percent decrease from the 2016 figure. The region's estimated rate of 6.4 murders per 100,000 inhabitants represented a decrease of 2.2 percent from the estimated rate for 2016. (Tables 3 and 4)

THE WEST

The West accounted for an estimated 23.8 percent of the nation's population and 20.2 percent of the estimated number of murders in 2017. The West experienced an estimated 3,485 murders, a 0.9 percent increase from the 2016 estimate. The region's murder rate was 4.5 per 100,000 inhabitants. (Tables 3 and 4)

Community Types

The UCR program aggregates data for three community types: metropolitan statistical areas (MSAs), cities outside MSAs, and nonmetropolitan counties outside MSAs. (See Appendix IV for definitions.) In 2017, MSAs accounted for 85.7 percent of the nation's population and 89.8 percent of the estimated total number of murders. MSAs experienced a rate of 5.6 murders per 100,000 inhabitants in 2017. Cities outside MSAs accounted for 5.8 percent of the U.S. population and (with an estimated 803 murders) accounted for 4.6 percent of the estimated murders in the nation. The murder rate for cities outside MSAs was 4.2 per 100,000 inhabitants. In 2017, approximately 8.4 percent of the nation's population lived in nonmetropolitan counties outside MSAs. An estimated 956 murders took place in these counties, accounting for 5.5 percent of the nation's estimated total. (Table 2)

Population Groups: Trends and Rates

The UCR program uses the following population group designations in its data presentations: cities (grouped according to population size) and counties (classified as either metropolitan or nonmetropolitan). A breakdown of these classifications is provided in Appendix IV.

From 2016 to 2017, the nation's cities experienced a 1.6 percent increase in homicides. Four city groups experienced an increase (6.8 percent in cities with 100,000 to 249,999 inhabitants, 7.2 percent in cities with 50,000 to 99,999 inhabitants, 4.3 percent in cities from 25,000 to 49,999 inhabitants and 12.7 percent in cities with less than 10,000 inhabitants). The city groups with decreases in homicides were cities with 1,000,000 or more inhabitants (8.1 percent) and cities with 10,000 to 24,999 inhabitants (1.3 percent). Metropolitan counties experienced a decrease in homicides of 5.7 percent from 2016 to 2017, while nonmetropolitan counties experienced a decrease of 9.1 percent. (Table 12)

In 2017, cities collectively had a rate of 6.2 murders per 100,000 inhabitants. Cities with 500,000 to 999,999 inhabitants had the highest murder rate (13.4 murders per 100,000 inhabitants). Cities with 10,000 to 24,999 inhabitants had the lowest murder rate, with 3.1 murders per 100,000 inhabitants. The homicide rate for metropolitan counties was 3.6 murders per 100,000 inhabitants, while the rate for nonmetropolitan counties was 3.5 murders per 100,000 inhabitants. Suburban areas had a homicide rate of 3.2 per 100,000 inhabitants. (Table 16)

Supplementary Homicide Reports Data

VICTIMS/OFFENDERS

Based on 2017 supplemental homicide data (where the ages, sexes, or races of the murder victims were identified), 90.9 percent of victims were over 18 years of age, 19.8 percent were under 22 years of age, 8.0 percent were under 18 years of age, and the age of 0.1 percent of the victims was unknown. Of the 15,129 murder victims represented in the 2017 expanded tables whose gender was identified, 78.4 percent were male. Concerning race, 43.5 percent of victims were White, 51.9 percent were Black, and 3.0 percent were of other races. Race was unknown for 423 victims. For murders in which the gender of the offender was identified, 88.1 percent were males; the sex of offenders for 29.8 percent of homicides was unknown. For the offenders for whom race was identified, 54.2 percent were Black, 43.1 percent were White, and 2.6 percent were other races; 5,368 offenders were of unknown race. (Expanded Homicide Data Tables 1, 2, and 3)

VICTIM-OFFENDER RELATIONSHIPS

For incidents in which the victim-offender relationship was specified (including the designation of "unknown"), 12.3 percent of victims were slain by family members, 9.7 percent were murdered by strangers, and 28.0 percent were killed by acquaintances (neighbor, friend, boyfriend, employer, etc.). The victim-offender relationship was unknown in 50.0 percent of incidents. (Expanded Homicide Data Table 10)

CIRCUMSTANCES/WEAPONS

Concerning the known circumstances surrounding murders, and including murders with unknown circumstances, 39.0 percent of victims were murdered during arguments (including romantic triangles) and brawls in 2017. Felony circumstances (rape, robbery, burglary, etc.) accounted for 24.7 percent of murders. Circumstances were unknown for 40.2 percent of reported homicides. Of the homicides for which the type of weapon was specified, 72.6 percent involved the use of firearms. Of the identified firearms used, handguns comprised 64.0 percent of the total. (Expanded Homicide Data Tables 8 and 12)

Justifiable Homicide

Certain willful killings must be reported as justifiable, or excusable, homicide. In the UCR program, justifiable homicide is defined as, and is limited to, the following:

- The killing of a felon by a peace officer in the line of duty

- The killing of a felon, during the commission of a felony, by a private citizen

Because these killings are determined by law enforcement investigation to be justifiable, they are tabulated separately from murder and nonnegligent manslaughter. Law enforcement reported 782 justifiable homicides in 2017. Of those, law enforcement officers justifiably killed 429 individuals, and private citizens justifiably killed 353 individuals. (Expanded Homicide Data Tables 14 and 15)

RAPE

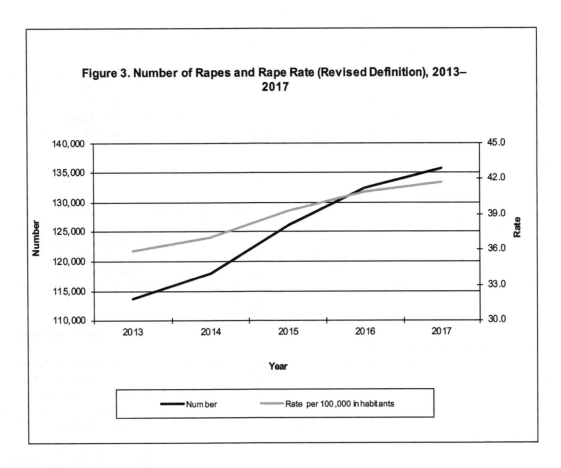

Figure 3. Number of Rapes and Rape Rate (Revised Definition), 2013–2017

Definition

In 2013, the FBI UCR Program initiated collection of rape data under a revised definition within the Summary Reporting System. Previously, offense data for forcible rape was collected under the legacy UCR definition: the carnal knowledge of a female forcibly and against her will. Beginning with the 2013 data year, the term "forcible" was removed from the offense title, and the definition was changed. The revised UCR definition of rape is: Penetration, no matter how slight, of the vagina or anus with any body part or object, or oral penetration by a sex organ of another person, without the consent of the victim. Attempts or assaults to commit rape are also included; however, statutory rape and incest are excluded.

In 2016, the FBI Director approved the recommendation to discontinue the reporting of rape data using the UCR legacy definition beginning in 2017. However, to maintain the 20-year trend in Table 1, national estimates for rape under the legacy definition are provided along with estimates under the revised definition for 2017. In these notes, the data, unless otherwise specified, is derived from the current definition in use by the FBI.

DATA COLLECTION

The UCR Program counts one offense for each victim of a rape, attempted rape, or assault with intent to rape, regardless of the victim's age. Non-consensual sexual relations involving a familial member is considered rape, not incest. All other crimes of a sexual nature are considered to be Part II offenses; as such, the UCR Program collects only arrest data for those crimes. The offense of statutory rape, in which no force is used but the female victim is under the age of consent, is included in the arrest total for the sex offenses category.

National Volume, Trends, and Rates

In 2017, the estimated number of rapes (revised definition), 135,755, increased 2.5 percent from the 2016 estimate. The estimated volume of rapes in 2017 was 19.4 percent higher than in the 2013 estimate. (Tables 1 and 1A)

Regional Offense Trends and Rates

The UCR program divides the United States into four regions: the Northeast, the South, the Midwest, and the

West. (More details concerning geographic regions are provided in Appendix IV) Regional analysis offers estimates of the volume of female rapes, the percent change from the previous year's estimate, and the rate of rape per 100,000 female inhabitants in each region.

NORTHEAST

The Northeast made up 17.3 percent of the U.S. population in 2017. An estimated 16,863 rapes—12.4 percent of the national total—occurred in the Northeast. This was an increase of 0.6 percent from the 2016 estimated figure. (Tables 3 and 4)

MIDWEST

The Midwest accounted for 20.9 percent of the U.S. population in 2017. Of all the rapes in the nation, 24.6 percent occurred in the Midwest in 2017. The 2017 estimate (33,370 rapes) represented an increase of 3.4 percent from the 2016 estimate. (Tables 3 and 4)

SOUTH

The South, the nation's most populous region, accounted for an estimated 38.0 percent of the nation's population in 2017; the region also accounted for an estimated 37.0 percent of the nation's estimated number of rapes. An estimated 50,249 female victims reported rape in the South in 2017, up 0.8 percent from 2016. (Tables 3 and 4)

WEST

The West accounted for 23.8 percent of the nation's population in 2017. The region also accounted for 26.0 percent of the nation's total number of estimated rapes with an estimated 33,273 offenses. The West saw a 5.1 percent increase in rapes from 2016 to 2017. (Tables 3 and 4)

Community Types

Using the U.S. Office of Management and Budget's designations, the UCR program aggregates crime data by type of community in which the offenses occur: metropolitan statistical areas (MSAs), cities outside MSAs, and nonmetropolitan counties outside MSAs. (Appendix IV provides more detailed information about community types.)

MSAS

In 2017, MSAs accounted for 85.7 percent of the nation's population and 85.0 percent of the nation's estimated number of rapes (legacy definition). An estimated 115,398 females were forcibly raped in metropolitan areas. (Table 2)

CITIES OUTSIDE MSAS

Cities outside MSAs are mostly incorporated areas that are served by city law enforcement agencies. Although accounting for only 5.8 percent of the U.S. population in 2017, cities outside MSAs accounted for 7.6 percent of the nation's estimated rapes (10,286 estimated offenses). (Table 2)

NONMETROPOLITAN COUNTIES

In 2017, approximately 8.4 percent of the nation's population lived in nonmetropolitan counties outside MSAs (counties made up of mostly non-incorporated areas that are served by noncity law enforcement agencies). Collectively, these areas had an estimated 10,071 rapes, representing 7.4 percent of the nation's estimated total. (Table 2)

Population Groups: Trends and Rates

The UCR program uses the following population group designations in its data presentations: cities (grouped according to population size) and counties (classified as either metropolitan or nonmetropolitan). A breakdown of these classifications is provided in Appendix IV.

From 2016 to 2017, the nation's cities experienced a 3.9 percent increase in rapes (see table notes for classification details). Cities with 25,000 to 49,999 inhabitants experienced the greatest increase (4.5 percent). Metropolitan counties experienced a 3.4 percent increase from 2016 to 2017, while nonmetropolitan counties experienced an increase of 0.6 percent. (Table 12)

In 2017, cities collectively had a rate of 42.4 rapes per 100,000 inhabitants. Cities with 250,000 or more inhabitants had the highest rate of rape (59.7 rapes per 100,000 inhabitants). Cities with 25,000 to 49,999 inhabitants had the lowest rate, with 35.0 rapes per 100,000 inhabitants. The rape rate for metropolitan counties was 32.5 per 100,000 inhabitants, and for nonmetropolitan counties, it was 39.2 per 100,000 inhabitants. Suburban areas had a rape rate of 32.1 per 100,000 inhabitants. (Table 16)

ROBBERY

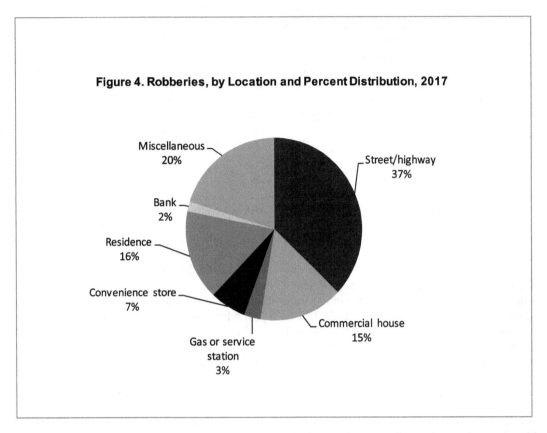

Figure 4. Robberies, by Location and Percent Distribution, 2017

- Miscellaneous 20%
- Street/highway 37%
- Bank 2%
- Residence 16%
- Convenience store 7%
- Commercial house 15%
- Gas or service station 3%

Definition

The UCR program defines robbery as the taking or attempt to take anything of value from the care, custody, or control of a person or persons by force or threat of force or violence and/or by putting the victim in fear.

National Volume, Trends, and Rates

In 2017, the estimated robbery total (319,356) decreased 4.0 percent from the 2016 estimate. The 5-year robbery trend (2013 data compared with 2017 data) showed a decrease of 7.5 percent. The 2017 estimated robbery rate (98.0 per 100,000 inhabitants) showed a decrease of 4.7 percent when compared with the 2016 rate. (Tables 1 and 1A)

Regional Offense Trends and Rates

The UCR program divides the United States into four regions: the Northeast, the South, the Midwest, and the West. (More details concerning geographic regions are provided in Appendix IV.)

NORTHEAST

The Northeast, with an estimated 17.3 percent of the nation's population in 2017, accounted for 15.3 percent

of the nation's estimated number of robberies. The estimated number of robberies decreased 8.0 percent from 2016. The rate for this region was 86.3 robberies per 100,000 inhabitants, down from 94.0 robberies per 100,000 inhabitants in 2016. (Tables 3 and 4)

MIDWEST

The Midwest accounted for 20.9 percent of the total population of the United States and 19.1 percent of its estimated number of robberies in 2017. An estimated 61,004 robberies occurred in the Midwest in 2017, a 4.9 percent decrease from the estimated figure from 2016. The region's robbery rate was 89.5 robberies per 100,000 inhabitants in 2017. (Tables 3 and 4)

SOUTH

The South, the nation's most highly populated region, accounted for an estimated 38.0 percent of the nation's population and 38.0 percent of the nation's estimated number of robberies in 2017. Robberies accounted for an estimated 121,290 violent crimes in this region in 2017, representing a 6.3 percent decrease from the 2016 figure. The 2017 robbery rate in the South was 98.1 per 100,000 inhabitants, down 7.2 percent from 2016. (Tables 3 and 4)

WEST

The West was home to an estimated 23.8 percent of the nation's population and accounted for 27.7 percent of the nation's estimated number of robberies in 2017. The estimated number of robberies (88,348) in the region in 2017 represented a 2.4 percent increase from the 2016 figure. The rate of robberies per 100,000 inhabitants in the West was 114.1, a 1.4 percent increase from the 2016 rate. (Tables 3 and 4)

Community Types

The UCR program aggregates data for three community types: metropolitan statistical areas (MSAs), cities outside MSAs, and nonmetropolitan counties outside MSAs. MSAs include a central city or urbanized area with at least 50,000 inhabitants, as well as the county that contains the principal city and other adjacent counties that have, as defined by the U.S. Office of Management and Budget, a high degree of social and economic integration as measured through commuting. Cities outside MSAs are mostly incorporated areas, and nonmetropolitan counties are made up of mostly unincorporated areas served by non-city law enforcement.

In 2017, MSAs were home to an estimated 85.7 percent of the nation's population, and 96.3 percent of the nation's estimated number of robberies took place in these areas. Robberies in MSAs occurred at a rate of 110.1 per 100,000 inhabitants. Cities outside MSAs accounted for 5.8 percent of the U.S. population and accounted for 2.7 percent of the estimated number of robberies in the nation. The robbery rate for cities outside MSAs was 45.6 per 100,000 inhabitants. Nonmetropolitan counties made up 8.4 percent of the nation's estimated population and 1.0 percent of the nation's estimated robberies, at a rate of 11.5 robberies per 100,000 inhabitants. (Table 2)

Population Groups: Trends and Rates

The national UCR program aggregates data by various population groups, which include cities, metropolitan counties, and nonmetropolitan counties. A definition of these groups can be found in Appendix IV. The number of robberies in cities as a whole decreased by 4.0 percent between 2016 and 2017. Among the population groups and subsets labeled *city*, those cities with under 10,000 inhabitants had the greatest decrease in the number of robberies (7.5 percent). Nonmetropolitan counties had a 4.4 percent decrease in the estimated number of robberies, and metropolitan counties showed a 6.0 percent decrease. The number of robberies in suburban areas fell 5.3 percent. (Table 12)

Among the population groups, the nation's cities collectively had a rate of 101.2 robberies per 100,000 inhabitants. Of the population groups and subsets designated *city*, those with 500,000 to 999,999 inhabitants had the highest rate (272.6 per 100,000 inhabitants), while those with fewer than 10,000 inhabitants had the lowest rate (39.9 per 100,000 inhabitants) of robberies. Of the two county groups, metropolitan counties had a rate of 47.1 robberies per 100,000 inhabitants, while nonmetropolitan counties had a rate of 11.0 robberies per 100,000 inhabitants. Suburban areas had a robbery rate of 49.4 per 100,000 inhabitants, down from the 2016 rate of 55.9. (Table 16)

Offense Analysis

The UCR program collects supplemental data about robberies to document the use of weapons, the dollar loss associated with the offense, and the location types.

ROBBERY BY WEAPON

Firearms were used in 40.5 percent of robberies in 2017. Offenders used knives or cutting instruments in 8.1 percent of these crimes. (Table 19)

LOSS BY DOLLAR VALUE

Based on the supplemental reports from law enforcement agencies, the average loss per robbery was $1,373. Average dollar losses were the highest for banks, which suffered an average loss of $3,483 per offense. Gas and service stations lost an average of $1,087 per offense. Commercial houses, which include supermarkets, department stores, and restaurants, had average losses of $1,284 per offense. An average of $1,732 was taken from residences. An average of $957 was lost in each offense against convenience stores. (Table 23)

ROBBERY TRENDS BY LOCATION

Among the location types, street/highway robberies had the greatest percentage decrease from 2016 to 2017, declining 8.1 percent. Robberies that occurred at convenience stores increased 5.6 percent, while those that occurred at banks decreased 7.1 percent. The number of robberies that occurred at commercial houses increased 0.1 percent, the same percentage increase as 2016, while those that occurred at gas or service stations increased 3.3 percent. (Table 23)

By location type, the greatest proportion of robberies in 2017 occurred on streets and highways (37.2 percent). Robbers targeted commercial houses in 15.5 percent of offenses and struck residences in 16.0 percent of offenses. Convenience stores accounted for 6.6 percent of robberies, followed by gas and service stations (3.0 percent) and banks (1.7 percent). (Table 23)

AGGRAVATED ASSAULT

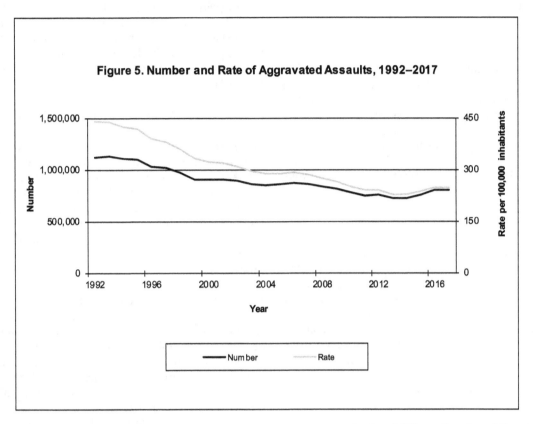

Figure 5. Number and Rate of Aggravated Assaults, 1992–2017

Definition

The UCR program defines aggravated assault as an unlawful attack by one person upon another for the purpose of inflicting severe or aggravated bodily injury. This type of assault is usually accompanied by the use of a weapon or by other means likely to produce death or great bodily harm. Attempted aggravated assaults that involve the display or threat of a gun, knife, or other weapon are included in this crime category because serious personal injury would likely result if these assaults were completed. When aggravated assault and larceny-theft occur together, the offense falls under the category of robbery.

National Volume, Trends, and Rates

In 2017, estimated occurrences of aggravated assaults totaled 810,825, a 1.0 percent increase from the 2016 figure and a 3.9 percent decline when compared with the estimate for 2008. The estimated rate of aggravated assault in 2017 was 248.9 per 100,000 inhabitants, a 10.6 percent decrease from 2008. (Tables 1 and 1A)

Among the four types of violent crime offenses (murder, rape, robbery, and aggravated assault), aggravated assault typically has the highest rate of occurrence. This trend continued in 2017. (Table 1)

Regional Offense Trends and Rates

The UCR program divides the United States into four regions: the Northeast, the South, the Midwest, and the West. (More details concerning geographic regions are provided in Appendix IV.)

NORTHEAST

The region with the smallest proportion of the nation's population (an estimated 17.3 percent in 2017) also accounted for the smallest proportion of the nation's estimated number of aggravated assaults (12.9 percent). Occurrences of aggravated assault decreased 2.1 percent from 2016 to 2017, dropping to an estimated 104,508 incidents. The region continued to have the lowest aggravated assault rate in the nation, at 185.1 incidents per 100,000 inhabitants. (Tables 3 and 4)

MIDWEST

With 20.9 percent of the nation's total population in 2017, the Midwest accounted for approximately 19.9 percent of the nation's estimated number of aggravated assaults. Occurrences of this offense increased 1.7 percent from the estimated total for 2016, rising to an estimated 161,278 incidents. The region's aggravated assault rate, at 236.5 incidents per 100,000 inhabitants, represented a 1.4 percent increase from the 2016 rate. (Tables 3 and 4)

SOUTH

The South, the nation's most highly populated region, accounted for an estimated 28.0 percent of the nation's population in 2017 and the largest amount of the nation's estimated number of aggravated assaults (42.5 percent). From 2016 to 2017, the estimated number of aggravated assaults increased 1.1 percent to a total of 344,643 incidents. The rate of aggravated assaults increased nominally to 278.7 incidents per 100,000 inhabitants. (Tables 3 and 4)

WEST

In 2017, the West was home to an estimated 23.8 percent of the nation's population. The region accounted for 24.7 percent of the nation's estimated number of aggravated assaults. From 2016 to 2017, the estimated number of offenses increased 1.9 percent to 200,396 incidents. The rate, estimated at 258.9 offenses per 100,000 inhabitants, represented a 0.9 percent increase from the rate in 2016. (Tables 3 and 4)

Community Types

The UCR program aggregates data for three community types: metropolitan statistical areas (MSAs), cities outside MSAs, and nonmetropolitan counties outside MSAs. MSAs include a central city or urbanized area with at least 50,000 inhabitants, as well as the county that contains the principal city and other adjacent counties that have a high degree of social and economic integration as measured through commuting. Cities outside MSAs are mostly incorporated areas, and nonmetropolitan counties are made up of mostly unincorporated areas. (For additional information about community types, see Appendix IV.)

In 2017, 85.7 percent of the nation's population lived in MSAs, where the rate of aggravated assault was an estimated 255.3 per 100,000 inhabitants. Cities outside MSAs (with 5.8 percent of the U.S. population) had the highest rate of aggravated assault at 298.7 offenses per 100,000 inhabitants. Nonmetropolitan counties accounted for 8.4 percent of the U.S. population and had an offense rate of 149.9 aggravated assaults per 100,000 inhabitants. (Table 2)

Population Groups: Trends and Rates

From 2016 to 2017, the number of aggravated assaults increased or remained static for all cities. Cities with 500,000 to 999,999 inhabitants experienced the greatest increase (3.8 percent). In metropolitan counties, the number of aggravated assaults changed by less than one-tenth of one percent; in nonmetropolitan counties, this number increased 1.8 percent. Aggravated assaults in suburban areas increased 0.4 percent from 2016 to 2017. (Table 12)

Aggravated assault occurred at an estimated rate of 252.4 offenses per 100,000 inhabitants nationwide. The collective rate for cities was 288.3 aggravated assaults per 100,000 inhabitants. Among city population groups and subsets, rates ranged from a high of 521.0 offenses per 100,000 inhabitants (in cities with 500,000 to 999,999 inhabitants) to a low of 180.5 offenses per 100,000 inhabitants (in cities with 10,000 to 24,999 inhabitants). The aggravated assault rate was 180.9 in metropolitan counties and 154.9 in nonmetropolitan counties. It was 169.1 in suburban areas. (Table 16)

Offense Analysis

AGGRAVATED ASSAULT BY WEAPON

Of the aggravated assault offenses for which law enforcement agencies provided expanded data in 2017, 25.4 percent involved personal weapons (such as hands, feet, and fists); 26.3 percent were committed with firearms; 17.2 percent involved knives or other cutting instruments; and 31.1 percent involved other weapons. (Table 19)

PROPERTY CRIME

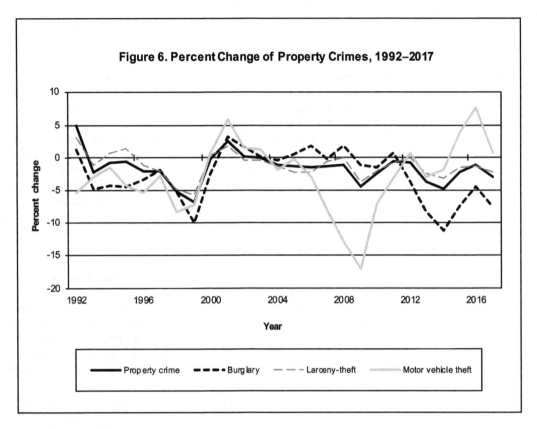

Figure 6. Percent Change of Property Crimes, 1992–2017

Definition

The UCR program's definition of property crime includes the offenses of burglary, larceny-theft, motor vehicle theft, and arson. The object of theft-type offenses is the taking of money or property without the use of force or threat of force against the victims. Property crime includes arson because the offense involves the destruction of property; however, arson victims may be subjected to force. Because of limited participation and the varying collection procedures conducted by local law enforcement agencies, only limited data are available for arson. Arson statistics are included in the trend, clearance, and arrest tables in *Crime in the United States*, but they are not included in any estimated volume data. More information on the expanded arson tables (which are available online but not included in this publication) can be found in Section I.

Data Collection

The data presented in *Crime in the United States* reflect the Hierarchy Rule, which counts only the most serious offense in a multiple-offense criminal incident. In descending order of severity, the violent crimes are murder and nonnegligent manslaughter, rape, robbery, and aggravated assault; these are followed by the property crimes of burglary, larceny-theft, and motor vehicle theft. The Hierarchy Rule does not apply to the offense of arson.

National Volume, Trends, and Rates

An estimated 7,694,086 property crimes were committed in the United States in 2017, representing a 3.0 percent decrease from the 2016 (2-year trend) estimate, an 11.1 percent decrease from the 2013 (5-year trend) estimate, and a 21.3 percent decrease from the 2008 (10-year trend) estimate. (Tables 1 and 1A)

From 2016 to 2017, motor vehicle theft increased 0.8 percent; from 2013 to 2017, it increased 10.4 percent, and from 2008 to 2017, it decreased 19.4 percent. Larceny-theft decreased 16.2 percent from 2008 to 2017, 8,3 percent from 2013 to 2017, and 2.2 percent from 2016 to 2017. Burglary declined 37.1 percent from 2008, 27.4 percent from 2013, and 7.6 percent from 2016. (Tables 1 and 1A)

The estimated property crime rate per 100,000 inhabitants in 2017 was 2,632.2 incidents per 100,000 people, a 3.6 percent decrease from the 2016 rate, a 13.6 percent decrease from the 2013 rate, and a 26.5 percent decrease from the 2008 rate. The rate of burglaries per 100,000 residents fell 41.3 percent from 2008 to 2017. The motor vehicle theft rates per 100,000 residents fell 24.7 percent from 2008 to 2017. (Tables 1 and 1A)

Regional Offense Trends and Rates

The UCR program separates the United States into four regions: the Northeast, the Midwest, the South, and the West. (Geographic breakdowns can be found in Appendix IV.) Property crime data collected by the UCR program and aggregated by region reflected the following results.

NORTHEAST

The Northeast region accounted for 17.3 percent of the nation's population in 2017. The region also accounted for 11.4 percent of the nation's estimated number of property crimes in 2017. Law enforcement in the Northeast saw a 3.0 percent decrease in the estimated number of property crimes from 2016 to 2017. The property crime rate for the Northeast, estimated at 1,558.6 incidents per 100,000 inhabitants, was 3.2 percent less than the 2016 rate. (Tables 3 and 4)

MIDWEST

The Midwest, with 20.9 percent of the U.S. population in 2017, accounted for 19.6 percent of the nation's estimated number of property crimes. Law enforcement in the Midwest saw the number of property crimes decrease 2.8 percent from 2016 to 2017. The rate of property crime in the Midwest in 2017, estimated at 2,207.8 incidents per 100,000 inhabitants, represented a 3.1 percent decrease from the 2016 rate. (Tables 3 and 4)

SOUTH

The South, the nation's most populous region, accounted for 38.0 percent of the U.S. population in 2017. The region also accounted for an estimated 41.9 percent of the nation's property crimes. The South experienced a 3.6 percent decrease in its estimated number of property crimes from 2016 to 2017. The 2017 property crime rate, an estimated 2,609.9 incidents per 100,000 inhabitants, dropped 4.6 percent from the 2016 rate. (Tables 3 and 4)

WEST

In 2017, the West accounted for 23.8 percent of the nation's population. The West also accounted for 27.0 percent of the nation's estimated number of property crimes. From 2016 to 2017, the estimated number of property crimes in this region decreased 2.0 percent. The estimated property crime rate in the West in 2017, 2,688.6 incidents per

100,000 inhabitants, was a 2.9 percent decrease from the 2016 rate. (Tables 3 and 4)

Community Types

The UCR program aggregates data by three community types: metropolitan statistical areas (MSAs), cities outside metropolitan areas, and nonmetropolitan counties. (Additional in-depth information regarding community types can be found in Appendix IV.) In 2017, 85.7 percent of the U.S. population lived in MSAs. The property crime rate for MSAs was 2,441.7 per 100,000 inhabitants. Cities outside metropolitan areas, which accounted for 5.8 percent of the total population in 2017, had a property crime rate of 2,896.7 per 100,000 inhabitants. Nonmetropolitan counties, with 8.4 percent of the nation's population in 2017, had a property crime rate of 1,183.1 per 100,000 inhabitants. (Table 2)

Population Groups: Trends and Rates

The UCR program organizes the agencies that contribute data into population groups, which include cities, metropolitan counties, and nonmetropolitan counties. (Appendix IV provides further details about these groups.) From 2016 to 2017, law enforcement in the nation's cities collectively reported a 2.6 percent decrease in the number of property crimes. All city groups experienced decreases in the number of property crimes; cities with 25,000 to 49,999 residents had the greatest decline, 4.4 percent. Metropolitan counties also experienced a decrease of 4.3 percent from 2016 to 2017, while property crime in nonmetropolitan counties dropped 3.9 percent. (Table 12)

The nation's cities collectively had a property crime rate of 2,771.5 incidents per 100,000 inhabitants in 2017. Nonmetropolitan counties had a rate of 1,201.8 incidents per 100,000 inhabitants, and metropolitan counties had a rate of 1,633.0 incidents per 100,000 inhabitants. The rate was 1,837.3 in suburban areas. (Table 16)

Offense Analysis

The estimated dollar loss attributing to property crimes, not including arson, in 2017 was $15.3 billion. Among the individual property crime categories, the dollar losses were an estimated $3.4 billion for burglary, $5.6 billion for larceny-theft, and nearly $6.0 billion for motor vehicle theft. In 2017, the average dollar value per motor vehicle stolen in the United States was $7,708. The average dollar value of property taken during burglaries was $2,416, and during larceny-thefts, $1,007. (Tables 1 and 23) Arson had an average dollar loss of $15,573. Arsons of industrial/manufacturing structures had the highest average dollar loss ($54,517), followed by "other commercial" structures ($38,326). (Expanded Arson Table 2)

BURGLARY

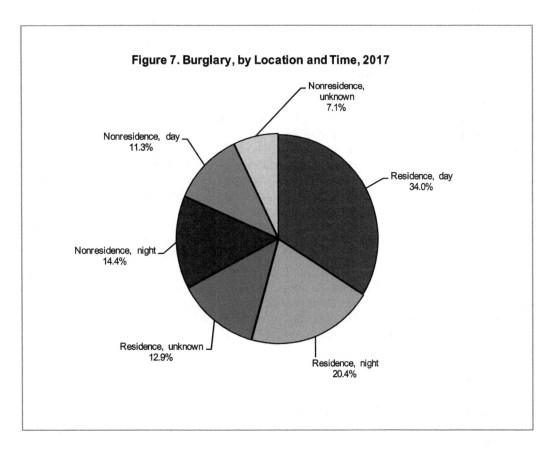

Figure 7. Burglary, by Location and Time, 2017

- Nonresidence, unknown 7.1%
- Nonresidence, day 11.3%
- Nonresidence, night 14.4%
- Residence, unknown 12.9%
- Residence, night 20.4%
- Residence, day 34.0%

Definition

The UCR program defines burglary as the unlawful entry of a structure to commit a felony or theft. To classify an offense as a burglary, the use of force to gain entry need not have occurred. The program has three subclassifications for burglary: forcible entry, unlawful entry where no force is used, and attempted forcible entry. The UCR definition of "structure" includes, but is not limited to, apartments, barns, house trailers or houseboats (when used as permanent dwellings), offices, railroad cars (but not automobiles), stables, and vessels (such as ships).

National Volume, Trends, and Rate

In 2017, there were an estimated 1,401,840 burglaries—a decrease of 7.6 percent when compared with 2016 data. There was a decrease of 27.4 percent in the number of burglaries in 2017 when compared with the 2013 estimate, and a decrease of 37.1 percent when compared with the 2008 estimate. Burglary accounted for 18.2 percent of the estimated number of property crimes committed in 2017. The burglary rate for the United States in 2017 was 430.4 incidents per 100,000 inhabitants, an 8.2 percent decrease from the 2016 rate. (Tables 1 and 1A)

Regional Offense Trends and Rates

The UCR program divides the United States into four regions: the Northeast, the Midwest, the South, and the West. (Details regarding these regions can be found in Appendix IV.) An analysis of burglary data by region showed the following details.

NORTHEAST

In 2017, 17.3 percent of the nation's population lived in the Northeast. This region accounted for 9.1 percent of the estimated total number of burglary offenses in the nation in 2017. The region's burglary rate, an estimated 322.7 offenses per 100,000 inhabitants, represented a decrease of 13.3 percent from the 2016 rate. (Tables 3 and 4)

MIDWEST

The Midwest accounted for 20.9 percent of the nation's population in 2017. This region accounted for 19.6 percent of the nation's estimated number of burglaries. In this region, the estimated number of burglaries dropped 13.81 percent from 2016 to 2017. The Midwest had a burglary rate of 488.5 offenses per 100,000 inhabitants, a 14.0 percent decrease from the 2016 rate. (Tables 3 and 4)

SOUTH

The South, the nation's most highly populated region (38.0 percent of all inhabitants), had the most burglaries in 2017 (an estimated 800,905); however, this represented an 8.2 percent drop from its estimate in 2016. With 38.0 percent of the nation's population, this region accounted for 44.9 percent of all burglaries in the United States. The estimated rate of burglary in the South was 668.7 incidents per 100,000 inhabitants, a 9.2 percent decrease from the 2016 rate. (Tables 3 and 4)

WEST

The West accounted for 23.8 percent of the nation's population in 2017. This region accounted for an estimated 26.3 percent of the nation's burglaries. The region's burglary rate was 554.4, an 11.7 percent increase from the 2016 rate. The total number of burglaries (416,814) represented a 10.7 percent decrease from the 2016 estimate. (Tables 3 and 4)

Community Types

The UCR program aggregates data by three community types: metropolitan statistical areas (MSAs), cities outside MSAs, and nonmetropolitan counties. (See Appendix IV for more information regarding community types.) In 2017, 85.7 percent of the U.S. population lived in MSAs, and an estimated 85.0 percent of all burglaries occurred in this type of community. Inhabitants of cities outside MSAs accounted for 5.8 percent of the total population in 2017 and 7.7 percent of the estimated number of burglaries; nonmetropolitan counties, with 8.4 percent of the U.S. population, accounted for 7.3 percent of all burglaries. The burglary rates per 100,000 inhabitants were 426.8 in MSAs, 564.1 in cities outside MSAs, and 373.6 in nonmetropolitan counties. (Table 2)

Population Groups: Trends and Rates

In addition to analyzing data by region and community type, the UCR program aggregates crime statistics by population groups. Cities are categorized into six groups based on the number of inhabitants; counties are categorized into two groups, metropolitan and nonmetropolitan. (Appendix IV offers further details regarding these population groups.)

An examination of data from law enforcement agencies showed that the nation's cities experienced a collective 6.9 percent decrease in burglaries from 2016 to 2017. Burglaries decreased in all city groups and subsets, with cities of 25,000 to 49,999 inhabitants posting the greatest decrease (9.8 percent). The volume of burglaries decreased 10.8 percent in metropolitan counties, 5.8 percent in nonmetropolitan counties, and 10.0 percent in suburban areas. (Table 12)

The UCR program calculates burglary rates for population groups from the information provided by participating agencies that submitted all 12 months of offense data for the year. In 2017, the nation's cities had 465.3 offenses per 100,000 inhabitants. Cities with 500,000 to 999,999 inhabitants had the highest burglary rate at 742.0 incidents per 100,000 inhabitants. Cities with 10,000 to 24,999 inhabitants had the lowest burglary rate—372.4 incidents per 100,000 inhabitants. Metropolitan counties had a rate of 344.6 per 100,000 inhabitants, and nonmetropolitan counties had a rate of 369.8 per 100,000 inhabitants. The rate in suburban areas was 329.8 per 100,000 inhabitants. (Table 16)

Offense Analysis

The UCR program requests that participating law enforcement agencies provide details regarding the nature of burglaries in their jurisdictions, such as type of entry, type of structure, time of day, and dollar loss associated with each offense.

Of all burglaries in 2017, 57.5 percent involved forcible entry, 36.2 percent were unlawful entries (without force), and 6.3 percent comprised forcible entry attempts. (Table 19)

Victims of burglary offenses suffered an estimated $3.4 billion in lost property in 2017; overall, the average dollar loss per burglary offense was $2,416. (Tables 1 and 23)

As in the past, burglars targeted residences more often than nonresidential structures. In 2017, burglaries of residential properties accounted for 67.2 percent of all burglary offenses. Of the burglaries for which time of day could be established, most burglaries of residences (34.0 percent of all reported burglaries) occurred during the day, while most burglaries of nonresidential structures (14.4 percent of all reported burglaries) occurred at night. (Table 23)

LARCENY-THEFT

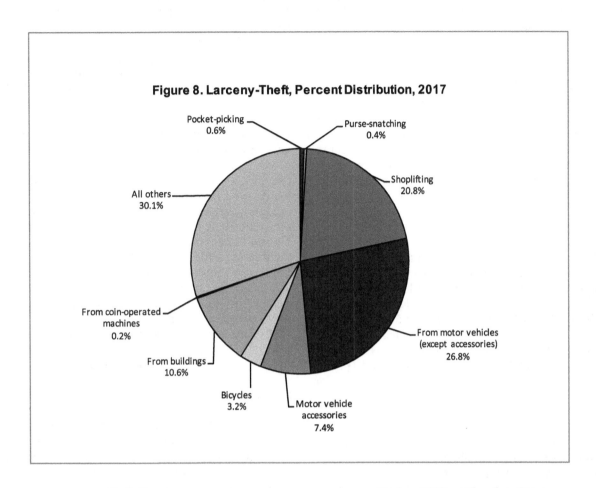

Figure 8. Larceny-Theft, Percent Distribution, 2017

- Pocket-picking 0.6%
- Purse-snatching 0.4%
- Shoplifting 20.8%
- All others 30.1%
- From motor vehicles (except accessories) 26.8%
- From coin-operated machines 0.2%
- From buildings 10.6%
- Bicycles 3.2%
- Motor vehicle accessories 7.4%

Definition

The UCR program defines larceny-theft as the unlawful taking, carrying, leading, or riding away of property from the possession or constructive possession of another. Examples are thefts of bicycles, motor vehicle parts and accessories, shoplifting, pocket picking, or the stealing of any property or article not taken by force and violence or by fraud. Attempted larcenies are included. Embezzlement, confidence games, forgery, check fraud, and so on, are excluded from this category.

National Volume, Trends, and Rates

Larceny-thefts accounted for an estimated 71.7 percent of property crimes in 2017—an estimated 5,519,107 larceny-thefts nationwide. The estimated number of larceny-thefts declined 2.2 from 2016 to 2017. The 2017 estimate showed a 13.6 percent decline compared with the 2008 estimate. The trend data also showed decreases in the larceny-theft rates per 100,000 inhabitants during these periods. The rate of larceny-thefts declined 2.9 percent from 2016 to 2017 and 21.8 percent from 2008 to 2017. (Tables 1 and 1A)

Regional Offense Trends and Rates

The UCR program defines four regions within the United States: the Northeast, the Midwest, the South, and the West. (See Appendix IV for a geographical description of each region.)

NORTHEAST

The Northeast was the region with the smallest proportion (17.3 percent) of the U.S. population in 2017. The region also experienced the fewest larceny-thefts in the country, accounting for only 12.6 percent of all larceny-thefts. The estimated number of offenses in 2017 (695,447) represented a 1.9 percent decline from 2016, and the estimated rate—1,231.5 incidents per 100,000 inhabitants—represented a 2.1 percent decline. (Tables 3 and 4)

MIDWEST

With 20.9 percent of the U.S. population in 2017, the Midwest accounted for an estimated 19.8 percent of the nation's larceny-thefts (the same proportion as in 2016). The estimated number of offenses (1,092,608) declined

2.1 percent compared with the 2016 data, and the estimated rate of occurrences (1,602.5 incidents per 100,000 inhabitants) declined 2.4 percent. (Tables 3 and 4)

SOUTH

With nearly two-fifths of the U.S. population in 2017 (38.0 percent), the South had the nation's highest proportion of larceny-theft offenses: an estimated 42.1 percent. (Estimated offenses in this region totaled 2,323,145, a 2.9 percent decrease from the 2016 estimate. The South's larceny-theft rate—estimated at 1,878.7 offenses per 100,000 inhabitants—decreased 3.9 percent from the 2016 estimate. (Tables 3 and 4)

WEST

In 2017, an estimated 23.8 percent of the U.S. population lived in the West. This region was also where 25.5 percent of the nation's estimated number of larceny-thefts took place. Occurrences of larceny-theft decreased 1.3 percent from 2016 to 2017 to an estimated total of 1,407,907 offenses. The region's larceny-theft rate, estimated at 1,818.8 offenses per 100,000 inhabitants, was a decrease of 2.3 percent from the 2016 rate. (Tables 3 and 4)

Community Types

The UCR program aggregates data for three community types: metropolitan statistical areas (MSAs), cities outside MSAs, and nonmetropolitan counties outside MSAs. MSAs include a central city or urbanized area with at least 50,000 inhabitants, as well as the county that contains the principal city and other adjacent counties that share a high degree of social and economic integration as measured through commuting. Cities outside MSAs are mostly incorporated areas, and nonmetropolitan counties are composed of unincorporated areas. (See Appendix IV for more information regarding community types.)

In 2017, MSAs were home to an estimated 85.7 percent of the nation's population and experienced 89.0 percent of the nation's larceny-theft incidents. Cities outside MSAs accounted for 5.8 percent of the U.S. population and 7.5 percent of larceny-theft offenses. Nonmetropolitan counties, which were home to 8.4 percent of the nation's population, accounted for 3.5 percent of the estimated number of larceny-theft offenses. The larceny-theft rates per 100,000 inhabitants were 1,759.3 in MSAs, 2,172.9 in cities outside MSAs, and 702.9 in nonmetropolitan counties. (Table 2)

Population Groups: Trends and Rates

In cities, collectively, occurrences of larceny-theft decreased 2.0 percent between 2016 and 2017. Cities with 25,000 to 49,999 inhabitants experienced the greatest decrease (3.8 percent). Larceny-theft continued to show decline in counties and suburban areas—nonmetropolitan counties experienced the greatest drop in larceny thefts, decreasing 4.6 percent, followed by suburban areas and metropolitan counties, with larceny-theft decreasing 3.0 and 2.8 percent, respectively. (Table 12)

Based on reports of larceny-theft offenses from U.S. law enforcement agencies that submitted 12 months of complete data for 2017, this offense occurred at a rate of 1,706.7 offenses per 100,000 inhabitants. The collective rate for cities was 2,021.3 offenses per 100,000 inhabitants. Among city population groups and subsets, cities with 500,000 to 999,000 inhabitants had the highest larceny-theft rate, 2,871.2 incidents per 100,000 inhabitants. Cities with 10,000 to 24,999 inhabitants had the lowest rate, at 1,750.6. In metropolitan counties, the rate was 1,122.6 incidents per 100,000 inhabitants; in nonmetropolitan counties, the rate was 721.6 incidents per 100,000 inhabitants. The rate in suburban areas was 1,349.8 incidents per 100,000 inhabitants. (Table 16)

Offense Analysis

DISTRIBUTION

Table 23 provides a further breakdown of larceny-theft offenses, including shoplifting, thefts from buildings, thefts of motor vehicle accessories, thefts of bicycles, thefts from coin-operated machines, purse snatching, and pocket picking. The "all other" category, which includes the less-defined types of larceny-theft, accounted for 30.1 percent of all offenses in 2017.

LOSS BY DOLLAR VALUE

Larceny-theft offenses cost victims an estimated $5.6 billion dollars in 2017. The average value of property stolen was $1,007 per offense, $66 more than in 2016. Larceny-theft from buildings had the highest average dollar loss per offense at $1,381. Thefts from motor vehicles (except accessories) had an average dollar loss of $879 per offense; thefts of motor vehicle accessories, $505; purse snatching, $564; pocket picking, $648; thefts from coin-operated machines, $538; thefts of bicycles, $477; and shoplifting, $260. (Tables 1 and 23)

Offenses in which the stolen property was valued at more than $200 accounted for 45.9 percent of all larceny-thefts in 2017. Table 23 provides further analysis, including the average dollar value per offense of all offenses in the overall category of property crime. (Table 23)

MOTOR VEHICLE THEFT

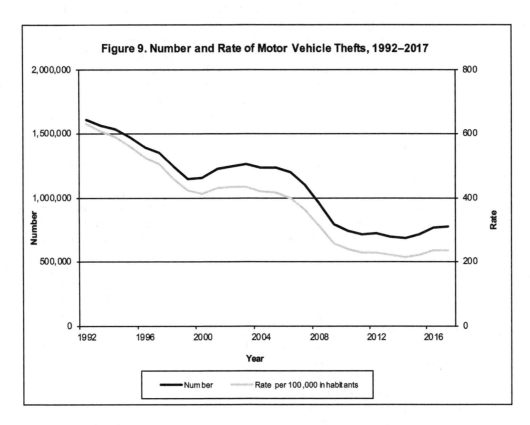

Figure 9. Number and Rate of Motor Vehicle Thefts, 1992–2017

Definition

The UCR program defines motor vehicle theft as the theft or attempted theft of a motor vehicle. The offense includes the stealing of automobiles, trucks, buses, motorcycles, snowmobiles, etc. The taking of a motor vehicle for temporary use by a person or persons with lawful access is excluded.

National Volume, Trends, and Rates

In 2017, an estimated 773,139 motor vehicle thefts took place in the United States. The estimated number of motor vehicle thefts increased 0.8 percent when compared with data from 2016 and increased 10.4 percent when compared with 2013 figures, but decreased 19.4 percent when compared with 2008 figures. (Tables1 and 1A)

The estimated rate of motor vehicle theft in 2017 was 237.4 incidents per 100,000 inhabitants. The 2017 rate was less than one-tenth of one percent different than the 2016 rate, 7.3 percent higher than the 2013 rate, and 24.7 percent lower than the 2008 rate. (Tables 1 and 1A)

Regional Offense Trends and Rates

In order to analyze crime by geographic area, the UCR program divides the United States into four regions: the Northeast, the Midwest, the South, and the West. (Appendix IV provides a map delineating the regions.)

This section provides a regional overview of motor vehicle theft.

NORTHEAST

The Northeast accounted for an estimated 17.3 percent of the nation's population in 2017. The region also accounted for an estimated 7.3 percent of its motor vehicle thefts. An estimated 56,799 motor vehicle thefts occurred in the Northeast in 2017, a 0.2 percent drop in occurrences from 2016. The estimated rate of 100.6 motor vehicle thefts per 100,000 inhabitants in the Northeast in 2017 represented a 0.4 percent decline from the 2016 rate. (Tables 3 and 4)

MIDWEST

An estimated 20.9 percent of the country's population resided in the Midwest in 2017. The region accounted for 17.8 percent of the nation's motor vehicle thefts. The Midwest had an estimated 137,260 motor vehicle thefts in 2017, an increase of 4.1 percent from the previous year's total. The motor vehicle theft rate was estimated at 201.3 motor vehicles stolen per 100,000 inhabitants, an increase of 3.8 percent from the 2016 rate. (Tables 3 and 4)

SOUTH

The South, the nation's most populous region, was home to an estimated 38.0 percent of the U.S. population in

2017 and accounted for 35.5 percent of the nation's motor vehicle thefts. The estimated 274,677 motor vehicle thefts in the South was up 1.9 percent from the 2016 estimate. Motor vehicles in the South were stolen at an estimated rate of 222.1 offenses per 100,000 inhabitants in 2017, a rate that was 0.9 percent higher than the 2016 rate. (Tables 3 and 4)

WEST

With approximately 23.8 percent of the U.S. population in 2017, the West accounted for the highest percentage (39.4 percent) of all motor vehicle thefts in the nation in 2017. An estimated 304,403 motor vehicle thefts occurred in this region. This number represented a 1.5 percent decrease from the previous year's estimate. The region's 2017 rate of 393.2 motor vehicles stolen per 100,000 inhabitants was 2.4 percent lower than the 2016 rate. (Tables 3 and 4)

Community Types

The UCR program aggregates data by three community types: metropolitan statistical areas (MSAs), cities outside MSAs, and nonmetropolitan counties. MSAs are areas that include a principal city or urbanized area with at least 50,000 inhabitants and the county that contains the principal city and other adjacent counties that have, as defined by the U.S. Office of Management and Budget, a high degree of economic and social integration.

In 2017, the vast majority (85.7 percent) of the U.S. population resided in MSAs, where approximately 92.3 percent of motor vehicle thefts occurred. For 2017, the UCR program estimated an overall rate of 255.5 motor vehicles stolen per 100,000 MSA inhabitants. Cities outside MSAs accounted for 3.9 percent of motor vehicle thefts, and nonmetropolitan counties accounted for 3.8 percent of motor vehicle thefts. The UCR program estimated a 2017 rate of 159.7 motor vehicles stolen for every 100,000 inhabitants in cities outside MSAs (unchanged from 2016), and a rate of 106.6 motor vehicles stolen per 100,000 inhabitants in nonmetropolitan counties. (Table 2)

Population Groups: Trends and Rates

The UCR program aggregates data by various population groups, which include cities, metropolitan counties, and nonmetropolitan counties. (A definition of these groups can be found in Appendix IV.)

In cities, collectively, the number of motor vehicle thefts increased 0.5 percent from 2016 to 2017. Cities with 1,000,000 or more residents experienced the greatest decline at 2.4 percent, while cities with under 10,000 residents experienced the greatest increase at 4.1 percent. Nonmetropolitan counties experienced an increase of 8.2 percent, suburban areas experienced an increase of 1.0 percent, and metropolitan counties experienced an increase of 0.5 percent. (Table 12)

In 2017, cities had a collective motor vehicle theft rate of 284.9 per 100,000 inhabitants. Among the population groups and subsets, cities with 500,000 to 999,999 inhabitants experienced the highest rate of motor vehicle thefts with 534.0 motor vehicle thefts per 100,000 inhabitants. Conversely, the nation's smallest cities, those with populations under 10,000, had the lowest rate of motor vehicle theft with 143.7 incidents per 100,000 in population. Within the county groups, metropolitan counties had a rate of 165.8 motor vehicles stolen per 100,000 inhabitants, while nonmetropolitan counties had a rate of 110.4 incidents per 100,000 inhabitants. Suburban areas had a rate of 157.7 per 100,000 inhabitants. (Table 16)

Offense Analysis

Based on the reports of law enforcement agencies, the UCR program estimated the combined value of motor vehicles stolen nationwide in 2017 at nearly $6.0 billion. In 2017, the average dollar value per motor vehicle stolen in the United States was $7,708. (Tables 1 and 23) Automobiles were, by far, the most frequently stolen vehicles, accounting for 75.4 percent of all vehicles stolen. Trucks and buses accounted for 15.1 percent of stolen vehicles, and other vehicles accounted for 9.5 percent of stolen vehicles. (Expanded Motor Vehicle Theft Table)

By type of vehicle, automobiles were stolen at a rate of 185.6 cars per 100,000 inhabitants in 2017. Trucks and buses were stolen at a rate of 37.1 vehicles per 100,000 inhabitants, and other types of vehicles were stolen at a rate of 23.4 vehicles per 100,000 inhabitants. (Table 19)

ARSON

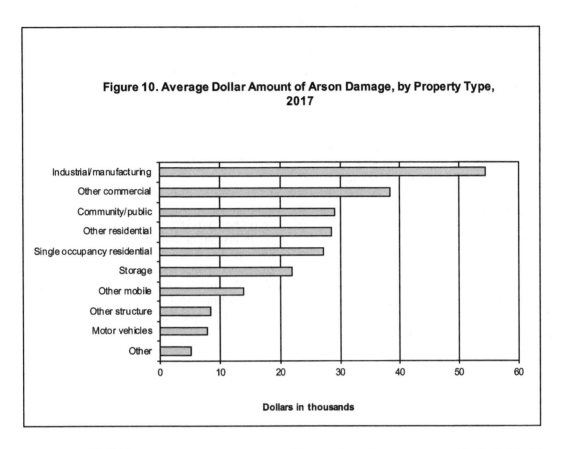

Figure 10. Average Dollar Amount of Arson Damage, by Property Type, 2017

Definition

The UCR program defines arson as any willful or malicious burning or attempt to burn (with or without intent to defraud) a dwelling house, public building, motor vehicle, aircraft, or personal property of another, etc.

Data Collection

Only fires that investigators determined were willfully set (not fires labeled as "suspicious" or "of unknown origin") are included in this arson data collection. Points to consider regarding arson statistics include:

National offense rates per 100,000 inhabitants (found in Tables 1, 2, and 4) do not include arson data; the FBI presents rates for arson separately. Arson rates are calculated based upon data received from all law enforcement agencies that provide the UCR program with data for 12 complete months.

Arson data collection does not include estimates for arson, because the degree of reporting arson offenses varies from agency to agency. Because of this unevenness of reporting, arson offenses are excluded from Tables 1 through 7, all of which contain offense estimations.

The number of arsons reported by individual law enforcement agencies is available in Tables 8 through 11. Arson trend data (which indicate year-to-year changes) can be found in Tables 12 through 15.

Population Groups: Trends and Rates

The number of arsons reported in cities 2017 was 0.3 percent higher than the number reported in 2016. Among the population groups labeled *city*, the subset with 500,000 to 999,999 inhabitants reported the largest increase (11.0 percent). Cities with under 10,000 inhabitants reported the largest year-to-year decrease, 4.3 percent. Agencies in the nation's metropolitan counties reported an 8.3 percent decrease in the number of arsons, while those in nonmetropolitan counties reported a 6.4 percent decrease from 2016 to 2017. Those in suburban areas reported a 6.9 percent decline. (Table 12)

Arson rates in this paragraph were based on information received from 14,813 agencies that provided 12 months of complete arson data to the UCR program. An examination of data indicated that in 2017, the highest rate among city groups and subsets—27.0 arsons per 100,000 inhabitants—was reported in cities with 500,000 to 999,999 inhabitants. Cities with 10,000 to 24,999 inhabitants had the lowest rate of arson at 9.5 per 100,000 inhabitants. Metropolitan counties had 9.6 arsons per 100,000 inhabitants, and nonmetropolitan counties had 9.3 arsons per 100,000 inhabitants, the lowest of all the population groups. The rate in suburban areas was 9.6 arsons per 100,000 inhabitants. (Expanded Arson Table 1)

Offense Analysis

The UCR program breaks down arson offenses into three property categories: structural, mobile, and other. In addition, the structural property type is broken down into seven types of structures, and the mobile property type consists of two subgroupings. The program also collects information on the estimated dollar value of the damaged property.

Property Type

Arsons for the structural property type consisted of 45.0 percent of arsons, while arsons for the mobile property type comprised 24.5 percent of arsons and 30.5 percent of arsons involved other types of property (such as crops, timber, fences, etc.). Of the arsons involving structures, 61.9 percent involved residential properties. Of the residential arsons, 73.4 percent were single-occupancy residences. Approximately 13.1 percent of structures were not in use when the arson occurred. Mobile arsons accounted for 24.2 percent of all arsons. Within this category, 94.4 percent of offenses involved the burning of motor vehicles. (Table 15 and Expanded Arson Table 2)

DOLLAR LOSS

In monetary terms, the average dollar loss in 2017 for arson was $15,573. The average dollar loss for a structural arson was $26,785. Within the structural arson category, the industrial/manufacturing subcategory had the highest average dollar loss at $54,517. Within that same category, single-occupancy dwellings had an average dollar loss of $27,168. Mobile property had an average dollar loss of $8,175. Other property types had an average dollar loss of $5,039. (Expanded Arson Table 2)

Table 1. Crime in the United States, by Volume and Rate Per 100,000 Inhabitants, 1998–2017

(Number, rate per 100,000 population.)

Year	Population[1]	Violent crime[2]		Murder and nonnegligent manslaughter		Rape (revised definition)[3]		Rape (legacy definition)[4]		Robbery		Aggravated assault	
		Number	Rate	Number	Rate	Number	Rate	Number	Rate	Number	Rate	Number	Rate
1998	270,248,003	1,533,887	567.6	16,974	6.3	X	X	93,144	34.5	447,186	165.5	976,583	361.4
1999	272,690,813	1,426,044	523.0	15,522	5.7	X	X	89,411	32.8	409,371	150.1	911,740	334.3
2000	281,421,906	1,425,486	506.5	15,586	5.5	X	X	90,178	32.0	408,016	145.0	911,706	324.0
2001[5]	285,317,559	1,439,480	504.5	16,037	5.6	X	X	90,863	31.8	423,557	148.5	909,023	318.6
2002	287,973,924	1,423,677	494.4	16,229	5.6	X	X	95,235	33.1	420,806	146.1	891,407	309.5
2003	290,788,976	1,383,676	475.8	16,528	5.7	X	X	93,883	32.3	414,235	142.5	859,030	295.4
2004	293,656,842	1,360,088	463.2	16,148	5.5	X	X	95,089	32.4	401,470	136.7	847,381	288.6
2005	296,507,061	1,390,745	469.0	16,740	5.6	X	X	94,347	31.8	417,438	140.8	862,220	290.8
2006	299,398,484	1,435,123	479.3	17,309	5.8	X	X	94,472	31.6	449,246	150.0	874,096	292.0
2007	301,621,157	1,422,970	471.8	17,128	5.7	X	X	92,160	30.6	447,324	148.3	866,358	287.2
2008	304,059,724	1,394,461	458.6	16,465	5.4	X	X	90,750	29.8	443,563	145.9	843,683	277.5
2009	307,006,550	1,325,896	431.9	15,399	5.0	X	X	89,241	29.1	408,742	133.1	812,514	264.7
2010	309,330,219	1,251,248	404.5	14,722	4.8	X	X	85,593	27.7	369,089	119.3	781,844	252.8
2011	311,587,816	1,206,005	387.1	14,661	4.7	X	X	84,175	27.0	354,746	113.9	752,423	241.5
2012	313,873,685	1,217,057	387.8	14,856	4.7	X	X	85,141	27.1	355,051	113.1	762,009	242.8
2013	316,497,531	1,168,298	369.1	14,319	4.5	113,695	35.9	82,109	25.9	345,093	109.0	726,777	229.6
2014	318,907,401	1,153,022	361.6	14,164	4.4	118,027	37.0	84,864	26.6	322,905	101.3	731,089	229.2
2015	320,896,618	1,199,310	373.7	15,883	4.9	126,134	39.3	91,261	28.4	328,109	102.2	764,057	238.1
2016[6]	323,405,935	1,250,162	386.6	17,413	5.4	132,414	40.9	96,970	30.0	332,797	102.9	802,982	248.3
2017	325,719,178	1,247,321	382.9	17,284	5.3	135,755	41.7	99,856	30.7	319,356	98.0	810,825	248.9

Table 1. Crime in the United States, by Volume and Rate Per 100,000 Inhabitants, 1998–2017—Continued

(Number, rate per 100,000 population.)

Year	Property crime		Burglary		Larceny-theft		Motor vehicle theft	
	Number	Rate	Number	Rate	Number	Rate	Number	Rate
1998	10,951,827	4052.5	2,332,735	863.2	7,376,311	2729.5	1,242,781	459.9
1999	10,208,334	3743.6	2,100,739	770.4	6,955,520	2550.7	1,152,075	422.5
2000	10,182,584	3618.3	2,050,992	728.8	6,971,590	2477.3	1,160,002	412.2
2001[5]	10,437,189	3658.1	2,116,531	741.8	7,092,267	2485.7	1,228,391	430.5
2002	10,455,277	3630.6	2,151,252	747.0	7,057,379	2450.7	1,246,646	432.9
2003	10,442,862	3591.2	2,154,834	741.0	7,026,802	2416.5	1,261,226	433.7
2004	10,319,386	3514.1	2,144,446	730.3	6,937,089	2362.3	1,237,851	421.5
2005	10,174,754	3431.5	2,155,448	726.9	6,783,447	2287.8	1,235,859	416.8
2006	10,019,601	3346.6	2,194,993	733.1	6,626,363	2213.2	1,198,245	400.2
2007	9,882,212	3276.4	2,190,198	726.1	6,591,542	2185.4	1,100,472	364.9
2008	9,774,152	3214.6	2,228,887	733.0	6,586,206	2166.1	959,059	315.4
2009	9,337,060	3041.3	2,203,313	717.7	6,338,095	2064.5	795,652	259.2
2010	9,112,625	2945.9	2,168,459	701.0	6,204,601	2005.8	739,565	239.1
2011	9,052,743	2905.4	2,185,140	701.3	6,151,095	1974.1	716,508	230.0
2012	9,001,992	2868.0	2,109,932	672.2	6,168,874	1965.4	723,186	230.4
2013	8,651,892	2733.6	1,932,139	610.5	6,019,465	1901.9	700,288	221.3
2014	8,209,010	2574.1	1,713,153	537.2	5,809,054	1821.5	686,803	215.4
2015	8,024,115	2500.5	1,587,564	494.7	5,723,488	1783.6	713,063	222.2
2016[6]	7,928,530	2451.6	1,516,405	468.9	5,644,835	1745.4	767,290	237.3
2017	7,694,086	2362.2	1,401,840	430.4	5,519,107	1694.4	773,139	237.4

Note: Although arson data are included in the trend and clearance tables, sufficient data are not available to estimate totals for this offense. Therefore, no arson data are published in this table.

X = Not applicable.   1 Populations are U.S. Census Bureau provisional estimates as of July 1 for each year except 2000 and 2010, which are decennial census counts.   2 The violent crime figures include the offenses of murder, rape (legacy definition), robbery, and aggravated assault.   3 The figures shown in this column for the offense of rape were estimated using the revised Uniform Crime Reporting Program's (UCR) definition of rape.   4 The figures shown in this column for the offense of rape were estimated using the legacy UCR definition of rape.   5 The murder and nonnegligent homicides that occurred as a result of the events of September 11, 2001, are not included in this table.   6 The crime figures have been adjusted.

Table 1A. Crime in the United States, Percent Change in Volume and Rate Per 100,000 Inhabitants for 2 Years, 5 Years, and 10 Years, 2008–2017

(Percent change.)

Years	Violent crime		Murder and nonnegligent manslaughter		Rape (revised definition)[2]		Rape (legacy definition)[3]		Robbery		Aggravated assault		Property crime		Burglary		Larceny-theft		Motor vehicle theft	
	Number[1]	Rate	Number	Rate	Number	Rate	Number	Rate	Number	Rate	Number	Rate	Number	Rate	Number	Rate	Number	Rate	Number	Rate
2008–2017	-10.6	-16.5	+5.0	-2.0	X	X	+10.0	+2.7	-28.0	-32.8	-3.9	-10.3	-21.3	-26.5	-37.1	-41.3	-16.2	-21.8	-19.4	-24.7
2013–2017	+6.8	+3.7	+20.7	+17.3	+19.4	+16.0	+21.6	+18.2	-7.5	-10.1	+11.6	+8.4	-11.1	-13.6	-27.4	-29.5	-8.3	-10.9	+10.4	+7.3
2016–2017	-0.2	-0.9	-0.7	-1.4	+2.5	+1.8	+3.0	+2.2	-4.0	-4.7	+1.0	+0.3	-3.0	-3.6	-7.6	-8.2	-2.2	-2.9	+0.8	*

X = Not applicable.   * = Less than one-tenth of one percent.   1 The violent crime figures include the offenses of murder, rape (legacy definition), robbery, and aggravated assault.   2 The figures shown in this column for the offense of rape were estimated using the revised UCR definition of rape.   3 The figures shown in this column for the offense of rape were estimated using the legacy UCR definition of rape.

Table 2. Crime in the United States, by Community Type, 2017

(Number, percent, rate per 100,000 population.)

Area	Population[1]	Violent crime[2]	Murder and nonnegligent manslaughter	Rape[3]	Robbery	Aggravated assault	Property crime	Burglary	Larceny-theft	Motor vehicle theft
United States	325,719,178	1,283,220	17,284	135,755	319,356	810,825	7,694,086	1,401,840	5,519,107	773,139
Rate per 100,000 inhabitants	X	394.0	5.3	41.7	98.0	248.9	2,362.2	430.4	1,694.4	237.4
Metropolitan Statistical Areas	279,216,046									
Area actually reporting[4]	98.6	1,144,183	15,447	114,398	306,096	708,242	6,755,487	1,180,576	4,865,847	709,064
Estimated total	100.0	1,151,205	15,525	115,398	307,506	712,776	6,817,490	1,191,830	4,912,206	713,454
Rate per 100,000 inhabitants	X	412.3	5.6	41.3	110.1	255.3	2,441.7	426.8	1,759.3	255.5
Cities Outside Metropolitan Areas	19,049,382									
Area actually reporting[4]	91.6	70,441	727	9,449	7,702	52,563	500,733	96,127	376,596	28,010
Estimated total	100.0	76,671	803	10,286	8,687	56,895	551,797	107,449	413,927	30,421
Rate per 100,000 inhabitants	X	402.5	4.2	54.0	45.6	298.7	2,896.7	564.1	2,172.9	159.7
Nonmetropolitan Counties	27,453,750									
Area actually reporting[4]	92.6	52,011	881	9,426	2,893	38,811	301,897	93,599	180,793	27,505
Estimated total	100.0	55,344	956	10,071	3,163	41,154	324,799	102,561	192,974	29,264
Rate per 100,000 inhabitants	X	201.6	3.5	36.7	11.5	149.9	1,183.1	373.6	702.9	106.6

Note: Although arson data are included in the trend and clearance tables, sufficient data are not available to estimate totals for this offense. Therefore, no arson data are published in this table.
X = Not applicable.   1 Population figures are U.S. Census Bureau provisional estimates as of July 1, 2017.   2 The violent crime figures include the offenses of murder, rape (revised definition), robbery, and aggravated assault.   3 The figures shown in this column for the offense of rape were estimated using the revised Uniform Crime Reporting definition of rape.   4 Although arson data are included in the trend and clearance tables, sufficient data are not available to estimate totals for this offense. Therefore, no arson data are published in this table.

Table 3. Crime in the United States, Population and Offense Distribution, by Region, 2017

(Percent distribution.)

Region	Population	Violent crime	Murder and nonnegligent manslaughter	Rape (revised definition)[1]	Robbery	Aggravated assault	Property crime	Burglary	Larceny-theft	Motor vehicle theft
United States[2]	100.0	100.0	100.0	100.0	100.0	100.0	100.0	100.0	100.0	100.0
Northeast	17.3	13.4	11.3	12.4	15.3	12.9	11.4	9.1	12.6	7.3
Midwest	20.9	20.2	22.6	24.6	19.1	19.9	19.6	19.6	19.8	17.8
South	38.0	40.8	45.9	37.0	38.0	42.5	41.9	44.9	42.1	35.5
West	23.8	25.5	20.2	26.0	27.7	24.7	27.0	26.3	25.5	39.4

Note: Although arson data are included in the trend and clearance tables, sufficient data are not available to estimate totals for this offense. Therefore, no arson data are published in this table.

1 The figures shown in the rape column were calculated using the revised Uniform Crime Reporting (UCR) definition of rape.   2 Because of rounding, the percentages may not add to 100.0.

Table 4. Crime in the United States,[1] by Region, Geographic Division, and State, 2016–2017

(Number, rate per 100,000 population, percent.)

Area	Population[2]	Violent crime[3]		Murder and nonnegligent manslaughter		Rape[4]		Robbery	
		Number	Rate	Number	Rate	Number	Rate	Number	Rate
United States[5,6]									
2016	323,405,935	1,285,606	397.5	17,413	5.4	132,414	40.9	332,797	102.9
2017	325,719,178	1,283,220	394.0	17,284	5.3	135,755	41.7	319,356	98.0
Percent change	0.7	-0.2	-0.9	-0.7	-1.4	+2.5	+1.8	-4.0	-4.7
Northeast									
2016	56,359,360	178,406	316.6	1,977	3.5	16,763	29.7	52,958	94.0
2017	56,470,581	172,042	304.7	1,957	3.5	16,863	29.9	48,714	86.3
Percent change	0.2	-3.6	-3.8	-1.0	-1.2	+0.6	+0.4	-8.0	-8.2
New England									
2016	14,757,573	41,841	283.5	296	2.0	4,569	31.0	9,394	63.7
2017	14,810,001	40,519	273.6	346	2.3	4,833	32.6	8,918	60.2
Percent change	0.4	-3.2	-3.5	+16.9	+16.5	+5.8	+5.4	-5.1	-5.4
Connecticut									
2016	3,587,685	8,169	227.7	79	2.2	791	22.0	2,711	75.6
2017	3,588,184	8,180	228.0	102	2.8	837	23.3	2,813	78.4
Percent change	*	+0.1	+0.1	+29.1	+29.1	+5.8	+5.8	+3.8	+3.7
Maine									
2016	1,330,232	1,649	124.0	20	1.5	413	31.0	268	20.1
2017	1,335,907	1,617	121.0	23	1.7	473	35.4	249	18.6
Percent change	0.4	-1.9	-2.4	+15.0	+14.5	+14.5	+14.0	-7.1	-7.5
Massachusetts									
2016	6,823,721	25,975	380.7	135	2.0	2,141	31.4	5,365	78.6
2017	6,859,819	24,560	358.0	173	2.5	2,197	32.0	4,871	71.0
Percent change	0.5	-5.4	-5.9	+28.1	+27.5	+2.6	+2.1	-9.2	-9.7
New Hampshire									
2016	1,335,015	2,668	199.8	19	1.4	609	45.6	431	32.3
2017	1,342,795	2,668	198.7	14	1.0	663	49.4	419	31.2
Percent change	0.6	0.0	-0.6	-26.3	-26.7	+8.9	+8.2	-2.8	-3.3
Rhode Island									
2016	1,057,566	2,529	239.1	29	2.7	445	42.1	541	51.2
2017	1,059,639	2,460	232.2	20	1.9	445	42.0	474	44.7
Percent change	0.2	-2.7	-2.9	-31.0	-31.2	0.0	-0.2	-12.4	-12.6
Vermont									
2016	623,354	851	136.5	14	2.2	170	27.3	78	12.5
2017	623,657	1,034	165.8	14	2.2	218	35.0	92	14.8
Percent change	*	+21.5	+21.4	0.0	*	+28.2	+28.2	+17.9	+17.9
Middle Atlantic									
2016	41,601,787	136,565	328.3	1,681	4.0	12,194	29.3	43,564	104.7
2017	41,660,580	131,523	315.7	1,611	3.9	12,030	28.9	39,796	95.5
Percent change	0.1	-3.7	-3.8	-4.2	-4.3	-1.3	-1.5	-8.6	-8.8
New Jersey									
2016	8,978,416	21,861	243.5	378	4.2	1,454	16.2	8,940	99.6
2017	9,005,644	20,604	228.8	324	3.6	1,505	16.7	7,895	87.7
Percent change	0.3	-5.7	-6.0	-14.3	-14.5	+3.5	+3.2	-11.7	-12.0
New York									
2016	19,836,286	74,315	374.6	629	3.2	6,281	31.7	22,310	112.5
2017	19,849,399	70,799	356.7	548	2.8	6,324	31.9	20,108	101.3
Percent change	0.1	-4.7	-4.8	-12.9	-12.9	+0.7	+0.6	-9.9	-9.9
Pennsylvania									
2016	12,787,085	40,389	315.9	674	5.3	4,459	34.9	12,314	96.3
2017	12,805,537	40,120	313.3	739	5.8	4,201	32.8	11,793	92.1
Percent change	0.1	-0.7	-0.8	+9.6	+9.5	-5.8	-5.9	-4.2	-4.4
Midwest									
2016	67,978,168	258,949	380.9	3,956	5.8	32,271	47.5	64,138	94.4
2017	68,179,351	259,566	380.7	3,914	5.7	33,370	48.9	61,004	89.5
Percent change	0.3	+0.2	-0.1	-1.1	-1.4	+3.4	+3.1	-4.9	-5.2
East North Central									
2016	46,798,649	181,827	388.5	3,019	6.5	22,479	48.0	49,524	105.8
2017	46,885,244	180,826	385.7	2,859	6.1	23,210	49.5	46,605	99.4
Percent change	0.2	-0.6	-0.7	-5.3	-5.5	+3.3	+3.1	-5.9	-6.1
Illinois									
2016	12,835,726	56,054	436.7	1,061	8.3	5,003	39.0	17,829	138.9
2017	12,802,023	56,180	438.8	997	7.8	5,556	43.4	17,567	137.2
Percent change	-0.3	+0.2	+0.5	-6.0	-5.8	+11.1	+11.3	-1.5	-1.2
Indiana									
2016	6,634,007	26,516	399.7	431	6.5	2,449	36.9	7,291	109.9
2017	6,666,818	26,598	399.0	397	6.0	2,625	39.4	6,600	99.0
Percent change	0.5	+0.3	-0.2	-7.9	-8.3	+7.2	+6.7	-9.5	-9.9
Michigan									
2016	9,933,445	45,782	460.9	612	6.2	7,268	73.2	7,123	71.7
2017	9,962,311	44,826	450.0	569	5.7	7,031	70.6	6,488	65.1
Percent change	0.3	-2.1	-2.4	-7.0	-7.3	-3.3	-3.5	-8.9	-9.2
Ohio									
2016	11,622,554	35,759	307.7	683	5.9	5,754	49.5	12,574	108.2
2017	11,658,609	34,683	297.5	710	6.1	5,859	50.3	11,605	99.5
Percent change	0.3	-3.0	-3.3	+4.0	+3.6	+1.8	+1.5	-7.7	-8.0

Table 4. Crime in the United States,[1] by Region, Geographic Division, and State, 2016–2017—Continued

(Number, rate per 100,000 population, percent.)

Area	Aggravated assault Number	Rate	Property crime Number	Rate	Burglary Number	Rate	Larceny-theft Number	Rate	Motor vehicle theft Number	Rate
United States[9,8]										
2016	802,982	248.3	7,928,530	2,451.6	1,516,405	468.9	5,644,835	1,745.4	767,290	237.3
2017	810,825	248.9	7,694,086	2,362.2	1,401,840	430.4	5,519,107	1,694.4	773,139	237.4
Percent change	+1.0	+0.3	-3.0	-3.6	-7.6	-8.2	-2.2	-2.9	+0.8	*
Northeast										
2016	106,708	189.3	907,781	1,610.7	142,092	252.1	708,772	1,257.6	56,917	101.0
2017	104,508	185.1	880,154	1,558.6	127,908	226.5	695,447	1,231.5	56,799	100.6
Percent change	-2.1	-2.3	-3.0	-3.2	-10.0	-10.2	-1.9	-2.1	-0.2	-0.4
New England										
2016	27,582	186.9	242,151	1,640.9	41,835	283.5	182,176	1,234.5	18,140	122.9
2017	26,422	178.4	228,293	1,541.5	36,958	249.5	173,101	1,168.8	18,234	123.1
Percent change	-4.2	-4.5	-5.7	-6.1	-11.7	-12.0	-5.0	-5.3	+0.5	+0.2
Connecticut										
2016	4,588	127.9	64,875	1,808.3	10,107	281.7	47,642	1,327.9	7,126	198.6
2017	4,428	123.4	63,509	1,769.9	8,890	247.8	47,310	1,318.5	7,309	203.7
Percent change	-3.5	-3.5	-2.1	-2.1	-12.0	-12.1	-0.7	-0.7	+2.6	+2.6
Maine										
2016	948	71.3	21,908	1,646.9	4,001	300.8	17,131	1,287.8	776	58.3
2017	872	65.3	20,133	1,507.1	3,334	249.6	16,006	1,198.1	793	59.4
Percent change	-8.0	-8.4	-8.1	-8.5	-16.7	-17.0	-6.6	-7.0	+2.2	+1.8
Massachusetts										
2016	18,334	268.7	106,430	1,559.7	19,204	281.4	79,155	1,160.0	8,071	118.3
2017	17,319	252.5	98,575	1,437.0	17,089	249.1	73,946	1,078.0	7,540	109.9
Percent change	-5.5	-6.0	-7.4	-7.9	-11.0	-11.5	-6.6	-7.1	-6.6	-7.1
New Hampshire										
2016	1,609	120.5	20,323	1,522.3	2,989	223.9	16,454	1,232.5	880	65.9
2017	1,572	117.1	18,555	1,381.8	2,574	191.7	15,066	1,122.0	915	68.1
Percent change	-2.3	-2.9	-8.7	-9.2	-13.9	-14.4	-8.4	-9.0	+4.0	+3.4
Rhode Island										
2016	1,514	143.2	18,910	1,788.1	3,650	345.1	14,157	1,338.6	1,103	104.3
2017	1,521	143.5	18,561	1,751.6	3,217	303.6	13,861	1,308.1	1,483	140.0
Percent change	+0.5	+0.3	-1.8	-2.0	-11.9	-12.0	-2.1	-2.3	+34.5	+34.2
Vermont										
2016	589	94.5	9,705	1,556.9	1,884	302.2	7,637	1,225.1	184	29.5
2017	710	113.8	8,960	1,436.7	1,854	297.3	6,912	1,108.3	194	31.1
Percent change	+20.5	+20.5	-7.7	-7.7	-1.6	-1.6	-9.5	-9.5	+5.4	+5.4
Middle Atlantic										
2016	79,126	190.2	665,630	1,600.0	100,257	241.0	526,596	1,265.8	38,777	93.2
2017	78,086	187.4	651,861	1,564.7	90,950	218.3	522,346	1,253.8	38,565	92.6
Percent change	-1.3	-1.5	-2.1	-2.2	-9.3	-9.4	-0.8	-0.9	-0.5	-0.7
New Jersey										
2016	11,089	123.5	138,012	1,537.2	25,229	281.0	101,459	1,130.0	11,324	126.1
2017	10,880	120.8	140,086	1,555.5	23,891	265.3	104,025	1,155.1	12,170	135.1
Percent change	-1.9	-2.2	+1.5	+1.2	-5.3	-5.6	+2.5	+2.2	+7.5	+7.1
New York										
2016	45,095	227.3	305,224	1,538.7	39,850	200.9	250,990	1,265.3	14,384	72.5
2017	43,819	220.8	300,555	1,514.2	35,002	176.3	252,143	1,270.3	13,410	67.6
Percent change	-2.8	-2.9	-1.5	-1.6	-12.2	-12.2	+0.5	+0.4	-6.8	-6.8
Pennsylvania										
2016	22,942	179.4	222,394	1,739.2	35,178	275.1	174,147	1,361.9	13,069	102.2
2017	23,387	182.6	211,220	1,649.4	32,057	250.3	166,178	1,297.7	12,985	101.4
Percent change	+1.9	+1.8	-5.0	-5.2	-8.9	-9.0	-4.6	-4.7	-0.6	-0.8
Midwest										
2016	158,584	233.3	1,549,241	2,279.0	301,149	443.0	1,116,188	1,642.0	131,904	194.0
2017	161,278	236.5	1,505,278	2,207.8	275,410	403.9	1,092,608	1,602.5	137,260	201.3
Percent change	+1.7	+1.4	-2.8	-3.1	-8.5	-8.8	-2.1	-2.4	+4.1	+3.8
East North Central										
2016	106,805	228.2	1,034,821	2,211.2	208,077	444.6	742,456	1,586.5	84,288	180.1
2017	108,152	230.7	984,783	2,100.4	185,412	395.5	713,795	1,522.4	85,576	182.5
Percent change	+1.3	+1.1	-4.8	-5.0	-10.9	-11.1	-3.9	-4.0	+1.5	+1.3
Illinois										
2016	32,161	250.6	263,256	2,051.0	48,193	375.5	195,196	1,520.7	19,867	154.8
2017	32,060	250.4	257,497	2,011.4	43,459	339.5	193,157	1,508.8	20,881	163.1
Percent change	-0.3	-0.1	-2.2	-1.9	-9.8	-9.6	-1.0	-0.8	+5.1	+5.4
Indiana										
2016	16,345	246.4	168,460	2,539.3	33,567	506.0	120,454	1,815.7	14,439	217.7
2017	16,976	254.6	161,132	2,416.9	30,140	452.1	115,591	1,733.8	15,401	231.0
Percent change	+3.9	+3.3	-4.3	-4.8	-10.2	-10.7	-4.0	-4.5	+6.7	+6.1
Michigan										
2016	30,779	309.9	190,249	1,915.2	39,738	400.0	130,249	1,311.2	20,262	204.0
2017	30,738	308.5	179,318	1,800.0	35,641	357.8	124,104	1,245.7	19,573	196.5
Percent change	-0.1	-0.4	-5.7	-6.0	-10.3	-10.6	-4.7	-5.0	-3.4	-3.7
Ohio										
2016	16,748	144.1	300,945	2,589.3	67,081	577.2	214,102	1,842.1	19,762	170.0
2017	16,509	141.6	282,034	2,419.1	58,573	502.4	203,208	1,743.0	20,253	173.7
Percent change	-1.4	-1.7	-6.3	-6.6	-12.7	-13.0	-5.1	-5.4	+2.5	+2.2

Table 4. Crime in the United States,[1] by Region, Geographic Division, and State, 2016–2017—Continued

(Number, rate per 100,000 population, percent.)

Area	Population[2]	Violent crime[3]		Murder and nonnegligent manslaughter		Rape[4]		Robbery	
		Number	Rate	Number	Rate	Number	Rate	Number	Rate
Wisconsin									
2016	5,772,917	17,716	306.9	232	4.0	2,005	34.7	4,707	81.5
2017	5,795,483	18,539	319.9	186	3.2	2,139	36.9	4,345	75.0
Percent change	0.4	+4.6	+4.2	-19.8	-20.1	+6.7	+6.3	-7.7	-8.1
West North Central									
2016	21,179,519	77,122	364.1	937	4.4	9,792	46.2	14,614	69.0
2017	21,294,107	78,740	369.8	1,055	5.0	10,160	47.7	14,399	67.6
Percent change	0.5	+2.1	+1.5	+12.6	+12.0	+3.8	+3.2	-1.5	-2.0
Iowa									
2016	3,130,869	9,170	292.9	73	2.3	1,278	40.8	1,150	36.7
2017	3,145,711	9,230	293.4	104	3.3	1,234	39.2	1,253	39.8
Percent change	0.5	+0.7	+0.2	+42.5	+41.8	-3.4	-3.9	+9.0	+8.4
Kansas									
2016	2,907,731	11,665	401.2	132	4.5	1,618	55.6	1,757	60.4
2017	2,913,123	12,030	413.0	160	5.5	1,627	55.9	1,785	61.3
Percent change	0.2	+3.1	+2.9	+21.2	+21.0	+0.6	+0.4	+1.6	+1.4
Minnesota									
2016	5,525,050	13,365	241.9	101	1.8	2,349	42.5	3,730	67.5
2017	5,576,606	13,291	238.3	113	2.0	2,385	42.8	3,621	64.9
Percent change	0.9	-0.6	-1.5	+11.9	+10.8	+1.5	+0.6	-2.9	-3.8
Missouri									
2016	6,091,176	31,720	520.8	538	8.8	2,557	42.0	6,576	108.0
2017	6,113,532	32,420	530.3	600	9.8	2,729	44.6	6,351	103.9
Percent change	0.4	+2.2	+1.8	+11.5	+11.1	+6.7	+6.3	-3.4	-3.8
Nebraska									
2016	1,907,603	5,661	296.8	49	2.6	1,108	58.1	946	49.6
2017	1,920,076	5,873	305.9	43	2.2	1,191	62.0	968	50.4
Percent change	0.6	+3.7	+3.1	-12.2	-12.8	+7.5	+6.8	+2.3	+1.7
North Dakota									
2016	755,548	1,905	252.1	16	2.1	356	47.1	181	24.0
2017	755,393	2,125	281.3	10	1.3	399	52.8	183	24.2
Percent change	*	+11.5	+11.6	-37.5	-37.5	+12.1	+12.1	+1.1	+1.1
South Dakota									
2016	861,542	3,636	422.0	28	3.2	526	61.1	274	31.8
2017	869,666	3,771	433.6	25	2.9	595	68.4	238	27.4
Percent change	0.9	+3.7	+2.7	-10.7	-11.5	+13.1	+12.1	-13.1	-14.0
South[5,6]									
2016	122,423,457	528,273	431.5	8,027	6.6	49,829	40.7	129,408	105.7
2017	123,658,624	524,110	423.8	7,928	6.4	50,249	40.6	121,290	98.1
Percent change	1.0	-0.8	-1.8	-1.2	-2.2	+0.8	-0.2	-6.3	-7.2
South Atlantic[5,6]									
2016	63,991,523	259,114	404.9	4,126	6.4	22,502	35.2	66,916	104.6
2017	64,705,532	251,287	388.4	3,995	6.2	22,003	34.0	61,622	95.2
Percent change	1.1	-3.0	-4.1	-3.2	-4.2	-2.2	-3.3	-7.9	-8.9
Delaware									
2016	952,698	4,859	510.0	58	6.1	311	32.6	1,359	142.6
2017	961,939	4,361	453.4	54	5.6	334	34.7	1,082	112.5
Percent change	1.0	-10.2	-11.1	-6.9	-7.8	+7.4	+6.4	-20.4	-21.1
District of Columbia[5]									
2016	684,336	8,236	1,203.5	136	19.9	533	77.9	3,500	511.4
2017	693,972	6,974	1,004.9	116	16.7	444	64.0	2,623	378.0
Percent change	1.4	-15.3	-16.5	-14.7	-15.9	-16.7	-17.9	-25.1	-26.1
Florida									
2016	20,656,589	88,700	429.4	1,111	5.4	7,598	36.8	20,175	97.7
2017	20,984,400	85,625	408.0	1,057	5.0	7,940	37.8	18,597	88.6
Percent change	1.6	-3.5	-5.0	-4.9	-6.3	+4.5	+2.9	-7.8	-9.3
Georgia									
2016	10,313,620	40,268	390.4	682	6.6	3,381	32.8	12,114	117.5
2017	10,429,379	37,258	357.2	703	6.7	2,718	26.1	10,044	96.3
Percent change	1.1	-7.5	-8.5	+3.1	+1.9	-19.6	-20.5	-17.1	-18.0
Maryland									
2016	6,024,752	29,019	481.7	536	8.9	1,827	30.3	10,815	179.5
2017	6,052,177	30,273	500.2	546	9.0	1,691	27.9	11,200	185.1
Percent change	0.5	+4.3	+3.8	+1.9	+1.4	-7.4	-7.9	+3.6	+3.1
North Carolina[6]									
2016	10,156,689	37,767	371.8	678	6.7	2,847	28.0	9,336	91.9
2017	10,273,419	37,364	363.7	591	5.8	2,715	26.4	9,350	91.0
Percent change	1.1	-1.1	-2.2	-12.8	-13.8	-4.6	-5.7	+0.1	-1.0
South Carolina									
2016	4,959,822	25,137	506.8	358	7.2	2,491	50.2	4,071	82.1
2017	5,024,369	25,432	506.2	390	7.8	2,504	49.8	3,870	77.0
Percent change	1.3	+1.2	-0.1	+8.9	+7.5	+0.5	-0.8	-4.9	-6.2
Virginia									
2016	8,414,380	18,495	219.8	482	5.7	2,830	33.6	4,826	57.4
2017	8,470,020	17,632	208.2	453	5.3	2,862	33.8	4,332	51.1
Percent change	0.7	-4.7	-5.3	-6.0	-6.6	+1.1	+0.5	-10.2	-10.8
West Virginia									
2016	1,828,637	6,633	362.7	85	4.6	684	37.4	720	39.4
2017	1,815,857	6,368	350.7	85	4.7	795	43.8	524	28.9
Percent change	-0.7	-4.0	-3.3	0.0	+0.7	+16.2	+17.0	-27.2	-26.7

Table 4. Crime in the United States,[1] by Region, Geographic Division, and State, 2016–2017—Continued

(Number, rate per 100,000 population, percent.)

Area	Aggravated assault		Property crime		Burglary		Larceny-theft		Motor vehicle theft	
	Number	Rate	Number	Rate	Number	Rate	Number	Rate	Number	Rate
Wisconsin										
2016	10,772	186.6	111,911	1,938.6	19,498	337.7	82,455	1,428.3	9,958	172.5
2017	11,869	204.8	104,802	1,808.3	17,599	303.7	77,735	1,341.3	9,468	163.4
Percent change	+10.2	+9.8	-6.4	-6.7	-9.7	-10.1	-5.7	-6.1	-4.9	-5.3
West North Central										
2016	51,779	244.5	514,420	2,428.9	93,072	439.4	373,732	1,764.6	47,616	224.8
2017	53,126	249.5	520,495	2,444.3	89,998	422.6	378,813	1,779.0	51,684	242.7
Percent change	+2.6	+2.0	+1.2	+0.6	-3.3	-3.8	+1.4	+0.8	+8.5	+8.0
Iowa										
2016	6,669	213.0	65,888	2,104.5	15,306	488.9	45,580	1,455.8	5,002	159.8
2017	6,639	211.0	66,855	2,125.3	15,078	479.3	46,198	1,468.6	5,579	177.4
Percent change	-0.4	-0.9	+1.5	+1.0	-1.5	-2.0	+1.4	+0.9	+11.5	+11.0
Kansas										
2016	8,158	280.6	82,293	2,830.1	14,759	507.6	60,119	2,067.6	7,415	255.0
2017	8,458	290.3	81,593	2,800.9	13,931	478.2	59,816	2,053.3	7,846	269.3
Percent change	+3.7	+3.5	-0.9	-1.0	-5.6	-5.8	-0.5	-0.7	+5.8	+5.6
Minnesota										
2016	7,185	130.0	117,723	2,130.7	18,582	336.3	90,421	1,636.6	8,720	157.8
2017	7,172	128.6	122,212	2,191.5	18,787	336.9	93,446	1,675.7	9,979	178.9
Percent change	-0.2	-1.1	+3.8	+2.9	+1.1	+0.2	+3.3	+2.4	+14.4	+13.4
Missouri										
2016	22,049	362.0	170,661	2,801.8	31,716	520.7	120,649	1,980.7	18,296	300.4
2017	22,740	372.0	173,253	2,833.9	30,081	492.0	123,251	2,016.0	19,921	325.9
Percent change	+3.1	+2.8	+1.5	+1.1	-5.2	-5.5	+2.2	+1.8	+8.9	+8.5
Nebraska										
2016	3,558	186.5	43,197	2,264.5	6,459	338.6	32,009	1,678.0	4,729	247.9
2017	3,671	191.2	43,663	2,274.0	6,472	337.1	31,988	1,666.0	5,203	271.0
Percent change	+3.2	+2.5	+1.1	+0.4	+0.2	-0.4	-0.1	-0.7	+10.0	+9.3
North Dakota										
2016	1,352	178.9	17,451	2,309.7	3,248	429.9	12,249	1,621.2	1,954	258.6
2017	1,533	202.9	16,602	2,197.8	2,942	389.5	11,887	1,573.6	1,773	234.7
Percent change	+13.4	+13.4	-4.9	-4.8	-9.4	-9.4	-3.0	-2.9	-9.3	-9.2
South Dakota										
2016	2,808	325.9	17,207	1,997.2	3,002	348.4	12,705	1,474.7	1,500	174.1
2017	2,913	335.0	16,317	1,876.2	2,707	311.3	12,227	1,405.9	1,383	159.0
Percent change	+3.7	+2.8	-5.2	-6.1	-9.8	-10.7	-3.8	-4.7	-7.8	-8.7
South[5,6]										
2016	341,009	278.5	3,348,650	2,735.3	685,526	560.0	2,393,605	1,955.2	269,519	220.2
2017	344,643	278.7	3,227,423	2,609.9	629,601	509.1	2,323,145	1,878.7	274,677	222.1
Percent change	+1.1	+0.1	-3.6	-4.6	-8.2	-9.1	-2.9	-3.9	+1.9	+0.9
South Atlantic[5,6]										
2016	165,570	258.7	1,693,453	2,646.4	329,778	515.3	1,234,149	1,928.6	129,526	202.4
2017	163,667	252.9	1,620,766	2,504.8	295,702	457.0	1,195,134	1,847.0	129,930	200.8
Percent change	-1.1	-2.2	-4.3	-5.3	-10.3	-11.3	-3.2	-4.2	+0.3	-0.8
Delaware										
2016	3,131	328.6	26,370	2,767.9	5,028	527.8	19,812	2,079.6	1,530	160.6
2017	2,891	300.5	23,477	2,440.6	3,970	412.7	18,138	1,885.6	1,369	142.3
Percent change	-7.7	-8.6	-11.0	-11.8	-21.0	-21.8	-8.4	-9.3	-10.5	-11.4
District of Columbia[5]										
2016	4,067	594.3	32,377	4,731.2	2,361	345.0	27,089	3,958.4	2,927	427.7
2017	3,791	546.3	29,729	4,283.9	1,809	260.7	25,333	3,650.4	2,587	372.8
Percent change	-6.8	-8.1	-8.2	-9.5	-23.4	-24.4	-6.5	-7.8	-11.6	-12.8
Florida										
2016	59,816	289.6	553,812	2,681.0	100,325	485.7	410,352	1,986.5	43,135	208.8
2017	58,031	276.5	527,220	2,512.4	88,853	423.4	395,453	1,884.5	42,914	204.5
Percent change	-3.0	-4.5	-4.8	-6.3	-11.4	-12.8	-3.6	-5.1	-0.5	-2.1
Georgia										
2016	24,091	233.6	307,305	2,979.6	62,715	608.1	218,127	2,114.9	26,463	256.6
2017	23,793	228.1	298,298	2,860.2	55,374	530.9	216,661	2,077.4	26,263	251.8
Percent change	-1.2	-2.3	-2.9	-4.0	-11.7	-12.7	-0.7	-1.8	-0.8	-1.9
Maryland										
2016	15,841	262.9	139,716	2,319.0	24,832	412.2	100,995	1,676.3	13,889	230.5
2017	16,836	278.2	134,496	2,222.3	23,508	388.4	97,420	1,609.7	13,568	224.2
Percent change	+6.3	+5.8	-3.7	-4.2	-5.3	-5.8	-3.5	-4.0	-2.3	-2.8
North Carolina[6]										
2016	24,906	245.2	277,765	2,734.8	72,082	709.7	190,377	1,874.4	15,306	150.7
2017	24,708	240.5	261,486	2,545.3	64,786	630.6	180,902	1,760.9	15,798	153.8
Percent change	-0.8	-1.9	-5.9	-6.9	-10.1	-11.1	-5.0	-6.1	+3.2	+2.0
South Carolina										
2016	18,217	367.3	161,534	3,256.9	33,149	668.4	114,455	2,307.6	13,930	280.9
2017	18,668	371.5	160,575	3,195.9	31,306	623.1	115,012	2,289.1	14,257	283.8
Percent change	+2.5	+1.2	-0.6	-1.9	-5.6	-6.8	+0.5	-0.8	+2.3	+1.0
Virginia										
2016	10,357	123.1	157,292	1,869.3	20,159	239.6	127,285	1,512.7	9,848	117.0
2017	9,985	117.9	151,855	1,792.9	18,468	218.0	123,215	1,454.7	10,172	120.1
Percent change	-3.6	-4.2	-3.5	-4.1	-8.4	-9.0	-3.2	-3.8	+3.3	+2.6
West Virginia										
2016	5,144	281.3	37,282	2,038.8	9,127	499.1	25,657	1,403.1	2,498	136.6
2017	4,964	273.4	33,630	1,852.0	7,628	420.1	23,000	1,266.6	3,002	165.3
Percent change	-3.5	-2.8	-9.8	-9.2	-16.4	-15.8	-10.4	-9.7	+20.2	+21.0

Table 4. Crime in the United States,[1] by Region, Geographic Division, and State, 2016–2017—Continued

(Number, rate per 100,000 population, percent.)

Area	Population[2]	Violent crime[3]		Murder and nonnegligent manslaughter		Rape[4]		Robbery	
		Number	Rate	Number	Rate	Number	Rate	Number	Rate
East South Central									
2016	18,931,477	87,200	460.6	1,404	7.4	7,748	40.9	18,320	96.8
2017	19,029,020	87,888	461.9	1,439	7.6	7,714	40.5	17,108	89.9
Percent change	0.5	+0.8	+0.3	+2.5	+2.0	-0.4	-0.9	-6.6	-7.1
Alabama									
2016	4,860,545	25,878	532.4	407	8.4	1,915	39.4	4,687	96.4
2017	4,874,747	25,551	524.2	404	8.3	2,028	41.6	4,217	86.5
Percent change	0.3	-1.3	-1.6	-0.7	-1.0	+5.9	+5.6	-10.0	-10.3
Kentucky									
2016	4,436,113	10,452	235.6	265	6.0	1,748	39.4	3,371	76.0
2017	4,454,189	10,056	225.8	263	5.9	1,661	37.3	2,958	66.4
Percent change	0.4	-3.8	-4.2	-0.8	-1.2	-5.0	-5.4	-12.3	-12.6
Mississippi									
2016	2,985,415	8,411	281.7	237	7.9	1,282	42.9	2,433	81.5
2017	2,984,100	8,526	285.7	245	8.2	1,091	36.6	2,071	69.4
Percent change	*	+1.4	+1.4	+3.4	+3.4	-14.9	-14.9	-14.9	-14.8
Tennessee									
2016	6,649,404	42,459	638.5	495	7.4	2,803	42.2	7,829	117.7
2017	6,715,984	43,755	651.5	527	7.8	2,934	43.7	7,862	117.1
Percent change	1.0	+3.1	+2.0	+6.5	+5.4	+4.7	+3.6	+0.4	-0.6
West South Central									
2016	39,500,457	181,959	460.7	2,497	6.3	19,579	49.6	44,172	111.8
2017	39,924,072	184,935	463.2	2,494	6.2	20,532	51.4	42,560	106.6
Percent change	1.1	+1.6	+0.6	-0.1	-1.2	+4.9	+3.8	-3.6	-4.7
Arkansas									
2016	2,988,231	16,563	554.3	217	7.3	2,214	74.1	2,125	71.1
2017	3,004,279	16,671	554.9	258	8.6	2,053	68.3	1,935	64.4
Percent change	0.5	+0.7	+0.1	+18.9	+18.3	-7.3	-7.8	-8.9	-9.4
Louisiana									
2016	4,686,157	26,477	565.0	555	11.8	1,819	38.8	5,575	119.0
2017	4,684,333	26,092	557.0	582	12.4	1,867	39.9	5,358	114.4
Percent change	*	-1.5	-1.4	+4.9	+4.9	+2.6	+2.7	-3.9	-3.9
Oklahoma									
2016	3,921,207	17,855	455.3	247	6.3	2,100	53.6	3,174	80.9
2017	3,930,864	17,934	456.2	242	6.2	2,142	54.5	3,000	76.3
Percent change	0.2	+0.4	+0.2	-2.0	-2.3	+2.0	+1.7	-5.5	-5.7
Texas									
2016	27,904,862	121,064	433.8	1,478	5.3	13,446	48.2	33,298	119.3
2017	28,304,596	124,238	438.9	1,412	5.0	14,470	51.1	32,267	114.0
Percent change	1.4	+2.6	+1.2	-4.5	-5.8	+7.6	+6.1	-3.1	-4.5
West									
2016	76,644,950	319,978	417.5	3,453	4.5	33,551	43.8	86,293	112.6
2017	77,410,622	327,502	423.1	3,485	4.5	35,273	45.6	88,348	114.1
Percent change	1.0	+2.4	+1.3	+0.9	-0.1	+5.1	+4.1	+2.4	+1.4
Mountain									
2016	23,811,346	102,680	431.2	1,125	4.7	13,278	55.8	21,713	91.2
2017	24,158,117	105,943	438.5	1,220	5.1	13,868	57.4	21,876	90.6
Percent change	1.4	+3.2	+1.7	+8.4	+6.9	+4.4	+2.9	+0.8	-0.7
Arizona									
2016	6,908,642	32,542	471.0	389	5.6	3,304	47.8	7,045	102.0
2017	7,016,270	35,644	508.0	416	5.9	3,581	51.0	7,440	106.0
Percent change	1.5	+9.5	+7.9	+6.9	+5.3	+8.4	+6.7	+5.6	+4.0
Colorado									
2016	5,530,105	19,030	344.1	189	3.4	3,635	65.7	3,525	63.7
2017	5,607,154	20,638	368.1	221	3.9	3,858	68.8	3,838	68.4
Percent change	1.4	+8.4	+7.0	+16.9	+15.3	+6.1	+4.7	+8.9	+7.4
Idaho									
2016	1,680,026	3,876	230.7	49	2.9	719	42.8	213	12.7
2017	1,716,943	3,888	226.4	32	1.9	707	41.2	196	11.4
Percent change	2.2	+0.3	-1.8	-34.7	-36.1	-1.7	-3.8	-8.0	-10.0
Montana									
2016	1,038,656	3,886	374.1	37	3.6	598	57.6	268	25.8
2017	1,050,493	3,961	377.1	41	3.9	613	58.4	295	28.1
Percent change	1.1	+1.9	+0.8	+10.8	+9.6	+2.5	+1.4	+10.1	+8.8
Nevada									
2016	2,939,254	19,924	677.9	228	7.8	1,729	58.8	6,338	215.6
2017	2,998,039	16,667	555.9	274	9.1	1,890	63.0	4,841	161.5
Percent change	2.0	-16.3	-18.0	+20.2	+17.8	+9.3	+7.2	-23.6	-25.1
New Mexico									
2016	2,085,432	14,585	699.4	139	6.7	1,527	73.2	2,737	131.2
2017	2,088,070	16,359	783.5	148	7.1	1,259	60.3	3,722	178.3
Percent change	0.1	+12.2	+12.0	+6.5	+6.3	-17.6	-17.7	+36.0	+35.8
Utah									
2016	3,044,321	7,406	243.3	74	2.4	1,560	51.2	1,528	50.2
2017	3,101,833	7,410	238.9	73	2.4	1,697	54.7	1,468	47.3
Percent change	1.9	+0.1	-1.8	-1.4	-3.2	+8.8	+6.8	-3.9	-5.7
Wyoming									
2016	584,910	1,431	244.7	20	3.4	206	35.2	59	10.1
2017	579,315	1,376	237.5	15	2.6	263	45.4	76	13.1
Percent change	-1.0	-3.8	-2.9	-25.0	-24.3	+27.7	+28.9	+28.8	+30.1

Table 4. Crime in the United States,[1] by Region, Geographic Division, and State, 2016–2017—Continued

(Number, rate per 100,000 population, percent.)

Area	Aggravated assault		Property crime		Burglary		Larceny-theft		Motor vehicle theft	
	Number	Rate	Number	Rate	Number	Rate	Number	Rate	Number	Rate
East South Central										
2016	59,728	315.5	514,692	2,718.7	119,073	629.0	354,409	1,872.1	41,210	217.7
2017	61,627	323.9	518,062	2,722.5	115,098	604.9	356,724	1,874.6	46,240	243.0
Percent change	+3.2	+2.7	+0.7	+0.1	-3.3	-3.8	+0.7	+0.1	+12.2	+11.6
Alabama										
2016	18,869	388.2	143,259	2,947.4	34,045	700.4	97,498	2,005.9	11,716	241.0
2017	18,902	387.8	144,160	2,957.3	31,477	645.7	99,842	2,048.1	12,841	263.4
Percent change	+0.2	-0.1	+0.6	+0.3	-7.5	-7.8	+2.4	+2.1	+9.6	+9.3
Kentucky										
2016	5,068	114.2	97,713	2,202.7	20,932	471.9	66,833	1,506.6	9,948	224.3
2017	5,174	116.2	94,833	2,129.1	20,195	453.4	64,394	1,445.7	10,244	230.0
Percent change	+2.1	+1.7	-2.9	-3.3	-3.5	-3.9	-3.6	-4.0	+3.0	+2.6
Mississippi										
2016	4,459	149.4	82,521	2,764.1	23,489	786.8	54,725	1,833.1	4,307	144.3
2017	5,119	171.5	81,581	2,733.9	24,710	828.1	52,240	1,750.6	4,631	155.2
Percent change	+14.8	+14.9	-1.1	-1.1	+5.2	+5.2	-4.5	-4.5	+7.5	+7.6
Tennessee										
2016	31,332	471.2	191,199	2,875.4	40,607	610.7	135,353	2,035.6	15,239	229.2
2017	32,432	482.9	197,488	2,940.6	38,716	576.5	140,248	2,088.3	18,524	275.8
Percent change	+3.5	+2.5	+3.3	+2.3	-4.7	-5.6	+3.6	+2.6	+21.6	+20.4
West South Central										
2016	115,711	292.9	1,140,505	2,887.3	236,675	599.2	805,047	2,038.1	98,783	250.1
2017	119,349	298.9	1,088,595	2,726.7	218,801	548.0	771,287	1,931.9	98,507	246.7
Percent change	+3.1	+2.0	-4.6	-5.6	-7.6	-8.5	-4.2	-5.2	-0.3	-1.3
Arkansas										
2016	12,007	401.8	98,092	3,282.6	23,814	796.9	67,091	2,245.2	7,187	240.5
2017	12,425	413.6	92,489	3,078.6	21,862	727.7	63,374	2,109.5	7,253	241.4
Percent change	+3.5	+2.9	-5.7	-6.2	-8.2	-8.7	-5.5	-6.0	+0.9	+0.4
Louisiana										
2016	18,528	395.4	154,511	3,297.2	34,689	740.2	109,492	2,336.5	10,330	220.4
2017	18,285	390.3	157,712	3,366.8	34,265	731.5	112,485	2,401.3	10,962	234.0
Percent change	-1.3	-1.3	+2.1	+2.1	-1.2	-1.2	+2.7	+2.8	+6.1	+6.2
Oklahoma										
2016	12,334	314.5	118,010	3,009.5	29,376	749.2	76,358	1,947.3	12,276	313.1
2017	12,550	319.3	113,066	2,876.4	28,608	727.8	72,207	1,836.9	12,251	311.7
Percent change	+1.8	+1.5	-4.2	-4.4	-2.6	-2.9	-5.4	-5.7	-0.2	-0.4
Texas										
2016	72,842	261.0	769,892	2,759.0	148,796	533.2	552,106	1,978.5	68,990	247.2
2017	76,089	268.8	725,328	2,562.6	134,066	473.7	523,221	1,848.5	68,041	240.4
Percent change	+4.5	+3.0	-5.8	-7.1	-9.9	-11.2	-5.2	-6.6	-1.4	-2.8
West										
2016	196,681	256.6	2,122,858	2,769.7	387,638	505.8	1,426,270	1,860.9	308,950	403.1
2017	200,396	258.9	2,081,231	2,688.6	368,921	476.6	1,407,907	1,818.8	304,403	393.2
Percent change	+1.9	+0.9	-2.0	-2.9	-4.8	-5.8	-1.3	-2.3	-1.5	-2.4
Mountain										
2016	66,564	279.5	676,849	2,842.5	123,130	517.1	475,693	1,997.8	78,026	327.7
2017	68,979	285.5	668,772	2,768.3	121,086	501.2	467,137	1,933.7	80,549	333.4
Percent change	+3.6	+2.1	-1.2	-2.6	-1.7	-3.1	-1.8	-3.2	+3.2	+1.8
Arizona										
2016	21,804	315.6	207,317	3,000.8	38,216	553.2	150,618	2,180.1	18,483	267.5
2017	24,207	345.0	204,515	2,914.9	37,627	536.3	147,830	2,107.0	19,058	271.6
Percent change	+11.0	+9.3	-1.4	-2.9	-1.5	-3.1	-1.9	-3.4	+3.1	+1.5
Colorado										
2016	11,681	211.2	152,146	2,751.2	23,825	430.8	108,680	1,965.2	19,641	355.2
2017	12,721	226.9	151,483	2,701.6	22,831	406.9	106,809	1,904.9	21,861	389.9
Percent change	+8.9	+7.4	-0.4	-1.8	-4.2	-5.6	-1.7	-3.1	+11.3	+9.8
Idaho										
2016	2,895	172.3	29,357	1,747.4	6,318	376.1	20,962	1,247.7	2,077	123.6
2017	2,953	172.0	28,079	1,635.4	5,655	329.4	20,278	1,181.1	2,146	125.0
Percent change	+2.0	-0.2	-4.4	-6.4	-10.5	-12.4	-3.3	-5.3	+3.3	+1.1
Montana										
2016	2,983	287.2	28,156	2,710.8	3,966	381.8	21,427	2,063.0	2,763	266.0
2017	3,012	286.7	27,225	2,591.6	3,615	344.1	21,018	2,000.8	2,592	246.7
Percent change	+1.0	-0.2	-3.3	-4.4	-8.9	-9.9	-1.9	-3.0	-6.2	-7.2
Nevada										
2016	11,629	395.6	75,922	2,583.0	18,816	640.2	43,949	1,495.2	13,157	447.6
2017	9,662	322.3	78,322	2,612.4	20,049	668.7	45,461	1,516.4	12,812	427.3
Percent change	-16.9	-18.5	+3.2	+1.1	+6.6	+4.5	+3.4	+1.4	-2.6	-4.5
New Mexico										
2016	10,182	488.2	81,930	3,928.7	17,280	828.6	52,907	2,537.0	11,743	563.1
2017	11,230	537.8	82,306	3,941.7	17,917	858.1	52,617	2,519.9	11,772	563.8
Percent change	+10.3	+10.2	+0.5	+0.3	+3.7	+3.6	-0.5	-0.7	+0.2	+0.1
Utah										
2016	4,244	139.4	90,561	2,974.8	12,938	425.0	68,261	2,242.2	9,362	307.5
2017	4,172	134.5	86,238	2,780.2	11,817	381.0	64,892	2,092.1	9,529	307.2
Percent change	-1.7	-3.5	-4.8	-6.5	-8.7	-10.4	-4.9	-6.7	+1.8	-0.1
Wyoming										
2016	1,146	195.9	11,460	1,959.3	1,771	302.8	8,889	1,519.7	800	136.8
2017	1,022	176.4	10,604	1,830.4	1,593	275.0	8,232	1,421.0	779	134.5
Percent change	-10.8	-10.0	-7.5	-6.6	-10.1	-9.2	-7.4	-6.5	-2.6	-1.7

Table 4. Crime in the United States,[1] by Region, Geographic Division, and State, 2016–2017—Continued

(Number, rate per 100,000 population, percent.)

Area	Population[2]	Violent crime[3]		Murder and nonnegligent manslaughter		Rape[4]		Robbery	
		Number	Rate	Number	Rate	Number	Rate	Number	Rate
Pacific									
2016	52,833,604	217,298	411.3	2,328	4.4	20,273	38.4	64,580	122.2
2017	53,252,505	221,559	416.1	2,265	4.3	21,405	40.2	66,472	124.8
Percent change	0.8	+2.0	+1.2	-2.7	-3.5	+5.6	+4.8	+2.9	+2.1
Alaska									
2016	741,522	5,966	804.6	52	7.0	1,053	142.0	850	114.6
2017	739,795	6,133	829.0	62	8.4	863	116.7	951	128.5
Percent change	-0.2	+2.8	+3.0	+19.2	+19.5	-18.0	-17.9	+11.9	+12.1
California									
2016	39,296,476	174,796	444.8	1,930	4.9	13,702	34.9	54,789	139.4
2017	39,536,653	177,627	449.3	1,830	4.6	14,721	37.2	56,622	143.2
Percent change	0.6	+1.6	+1.0	-5.2	-5.8	+7.4	+6.8	+3.3	+2.7
Hawaii									
2016	1,428,683	3,452	241.6	35	2.4	601	42.1	985	68.9
2017	1,427,538	3,577	250.6	39	2.7	567	39.7	1,077	75.4
Percent change	-0.1	+3.6	+3.7	+11.4	+11.5	-5.7	-5.6	+9.3	+9.4
Oregon[6]									
2016	4,085,989	10,983	268.8	116	2.8	1,784	43.7	2,307	56.5
2017	4,142,776	11,674	281.8	104	2.5	1,999	48.3	2,432	58.7
Percent change	1.4	+6.3	+4.8	-10.3	-11.6	+12.1	+10.5	+5.4	+4.0
Washington									
2016	7,280,934	22,101	303.5	195	2.7	3,133	43.0	5,649	77.6
2017	7,405,743	22,548	304.5	230	3.1	3,255	44.0	5,390	72.8
Percent change	1.7	+2.0	+0.3	+17.9	+16.0	+3.9	+2.1	-4.6	-6.2
Puerto Rico									
2016	3,406,520	7,643	224.4	679	19.9	169	5.0	3,201	94.0
2017	3,337,177	7,762	232.6	679	20.3	209	6.3	3,055	91.5
Percent change	-2.1	+1.6	+3.7	0.0	+2.1	+23.7	+26.2	-4.6	-2.6

Table 4. Crime in the United States,[1] by Region, Geographic Division, and State, 2016–2017—Continued

(Number, rate per 100,000 population, percent.)

Area	Aggravated assault		Property crime		Burglary		Larceny-theft		Motor vehicle theft	
	Number	Rate	Number	Rate	Number	Rate	Number	Rate	Number	Rate
Pacific										
2016	130,117	246.3	1,446,009	2,736.9	264,508	500.6	950,577	1,799.2	230,924	437.1
2017	131,417	246.8	1,412,459	2,652.4	247,835	465.4	940,770	1,766.6	223,854	420.4
Percent change	+1.0	+0.2	-2.3	-3.1	-6.3	-7.0	-1.0	-1.8	-3.1	-3.8
Alaska										
2016	4,011	540.9	24,876	3,354.7	4,053	546.6	17,766	2,395.9	3,057	412.3
2017	4,257	575.4	26,204	3,542.1	4,171	563.8	17,775	2,402.7	4,258	575.6
Percent change	+6.1	+6.4	+5.3	+5.6	+2.9	+3.2	+0.1	+0.3	+39.3	+39.6
California										
2016	104,375	265.6	1,002,070	2,550.0	188,304	479.2	637,010	1,621.0	176,756	449.8
2017	104,454	264.2	987,114	2,496.7	176,690	446.9	642,033	1,623.9	168,391	425.9
Percent change	+0.1	-0.5	-1.5	-2.1	-6.2	-6.7	+0.8	+0.2	-4.7	-5.3
Hawaii										
2016	1,831	128.2	42,353	2,964.5	5,983	418.8	30,871	2,160.8	5,499	384.9
2017	1,894	132.7	40,392	2,829.5	5,549	388.7	29,574	2,071.7	5,269	369.1
Percent change	+3.4	+3.5	-4.6	-4.6	-7.3	-7.2	-4.2	-4.1	-4.2	-4.1
Oregon[6]										
2016	6,776	165.8	121,716	2,978.9	16,919	414.1	91,507	2,239.5	13,290	325.3
2017	7,139	172.3	123,722	2,986.5	17,705	427.4	88,877	2,145.3	17,140	413.7
Percent change	+5.4	+3.9	+1.6	+0.3	+4.6	+3.2	-2.9	-4.2	+29.0	+27.2
Washington										
2016	13,124	180.3	254,994	3,502.2	49,249	676.4	173,423	2,381.9	32,322	443.9
2017	13,673	184.6	235,027	3,173.6	43,720	590.4	162,511	2,194.4	28,796	388.8
Percent change	+4.2	+2.4	-7.8	-9.4	-11.2	-12.7	-6.3	-7.9	-10.9	-12.4
Puerto Rico										
2016	3,594	105.5	35,201	1,033.3	8,251	242.2	23,163	680.0	3,787	111.2
2017	3,819	114.4	31,176	934.2	7,949	238.2	19,633	588.3	3,594	107.7
Percent change	+6.3	+8.5	-11.4	-9.6	-3.7	-1.7	-15.2	-13.5	-5.1	-3.1

Note: Although arson data are included in the trend and clearance tables, sufficient data are not available to estimate totals for this offense. Therefore, no arson data are published in this table.
* = Less than one-tenth of 1 percent.
1 The previous year's crime figures have been adjusted.   2 Population figures are U.S. Census Bureau provisional estimates as of July 1, 2017.   3 The violent crime figures include the offenses of murder, rape (revised definition), robbery, and aggravated assault.   4 The figures shown in this column for the offense of rape were estimated using the revised Uniform Crime Reporting (UCR) definition of rape. See chapter notes for more detail.   5 Includes offenses reported by the Metro Transit Police and the District of Columbia Fire and Emergency Medical Services: Arson Investigation Unit.   6 This state's agencies submitted rape data according to the legacy UCR definition of rape.

Table 5. Crime, by State and Area, 2017

(Number, percent, rate per 100,000 population.)

Area	Population	Violent crime[1]	Murder and nonnegligent manslaughter	Rape (revised definition)[2]	Robbery	Aggravated assault	Property crime	Burglary	Larceny-theft	Motor vehicle theft
Alabama										
Metropolitan statistical area	3,732,789									
Area actually reporting	99.0%	20,396	337	1,535	3,706	14,818	114,790	24,598	79,734	10,458
Estimated total	100.0%	20,585	340	1,548	3,738	14,959	116,031	24,809	80,666	10,556
Cities outside metropolitan areas	518,602									
Area actually reporting	94.3%	3,526	38	264	366	2,858	19,732	3,964	14,367	1,401
Estimated total	100.0%	3,715	40	277	385	3,013	20,642	4,169	15,000	1,473
Nonmetropolitan counties	623,356									
Area actually reporting	92.9%	1,162	22	189	87	864	6,954	2,321	3,879	754
Estimated total	100.0%	1,251	24	203	94	930	7,487	2,499	4,176	812
State total	4,874,747	25,551	404	2,028	4,217	18,902	144,160	31,477	99,842	12,841
Rate per 100,000 inhabitants		524.2	8.3	41.6	86.5	387.8	2,957.3	645.7	2,048.1	263.4
Alaska										
Metropolitan statistical area	348,650									
Area actually reporting	100.0%	3,859	38	418	830	2,573	18,698	2,453	12,750	3,495
Cities outside metropolitan areas	127,272									
Area actually reporting	97.2%	1,035	6	212	81	736	4,079	635	3,170	274
Estimated total	100.0%	1,064	6	218	83	757	4,197	653	3,262	282
Nonmetropolitan counties	263,873									
Area actually reporting	100.0%	1,210	18	227	38	927	3,309	1,065	1,763	481
State total	739,795	6,133	62	863	951	4,257	26,204	4,171	17,775	4,258
Rate per 100,000 inhabitants		829.0	8.4	116.7	128.5	575.4	3,542.1	563.8	2,402.7	575.6
Arizona										
Metropolitan statistical area	6,665,732									
Area actually reporting	99.6%	30,336	376	3,300	7,300	19,360	194,978	35,203	141,758	18,017
Estimated total	100.0%	30,412	376	3,310	7,316	19,410	195,650	35,305	142,278	18,067
Cities outside metropolitan areas	125,031									
Area actually reporting	96.9%	4,644	34	253	89	4,268	6,746	1,590	4,420	736
Estimated total	100.0%	4,790	35	261	92	4,402	6,958	1,640	4,559	759
Nonmetropolitan counties	225,507									
Area actually reporting	100.0%	442	5	10	32	395	1,907	682	993	232
State total	7,016,270	35,644	416	3,581	7,440	24,207	204,515	37,627	147,830	19,058
Rate per 100,000 inhabitants		508.0	5.9	51.0	106.0	345.0	2,914.9	536.3	2,107.0	271.6
Arkansas										
Metropolitan statistical area	1,870,966									
Area actually reporting	99.3%	11,887	171	1,250	1,614	8,852	64,624	14,487	44,777	5,360
Estimated total	100.0%	11,939	171	1,258	1,617	8,893	64,898	14,566	44,946	5,386
Cities outside metropolitan areas	515,402									
Area actually reporting	90.4%	2,565	46	396	252	1,871	16,666	4,271	11,542	853
Estimated total	100.0%	2,846	51	446	279	2,070	18,442	4,726	12,772	944
Nonmetropolitan counties	617,911									
Area actually reporting	93.5%	1,756	34	320	36	1,366	8,551	2,402	5,286	863
Estimated total	100.0%	1,886	36	349	39	1,462	9,149	2,570	5,656	923
State total	3,004,279	16,671	258	2,053	1,935	12,425	92,489	21,862	63,374	7,253
Rate per 100,000 inhabitants		554.9	8.6	68.3	64.4	413.6	3,078.6	727.7	2,109.5	241.4
California										
Metropolitan statistical area	38,706,996									
Area actually reporting	99.9%	173,634	1,778	14,252	56,127	101,477	968,957	171,705	631,712	165,540
Estimated total	100.0%	173,659	1,778	14,254	56,135	101,492	969,133	171,737	631,828	165,568
Cities outside metropolitan areas	263,117									
Area actually reporting	100.0%	1,641	13	182	296	1,150	9,240	1,950	6,070	1,220
Nonmetropolitan counties	566,540									
Area actually reporting	100.0%	2,327	39	285	191	1,812	8,741	3,003	4,135	1,603
State total	39,536,653	177,627	1,830	14,721	56,622	104,454	987,114	176,690	642,033	168,391
Rate per 100,000 inhabitants		449.3	4.6	37.2	143.2	264.2	2,496.7	446.9	1,623.9	425.9
Colorado										
Metropolitan statistical area	4,904,129									
Area actually reporting	99.9%	19,312	209	3,531	3,742	11,830	137,837	20,399	96,472	20,966
Estimated total	100.0%	19,326	209	3,533	3,743	11,841	138,023	20,421	96,613	20,989
Cities outside metropolitan areas	339,363									
Area actually reporting	96.6%	801	5	202	77	517	9,686	1,394	7,772	520
Estimated total	100.0%	829	5	209	80	535	10,024	1,443	8,043	538
Nonmetropolitan counties	363,662									
Area actually reporting	96.2%	465	7	112	14	332	3,305	913	2,071	321
Estimated total	100.0%	483	7	116	15	345	3,436	949	2,153	334
State total	5,607,154	20,638	221	3,858	3,838	12,721	151,483	22,813	106,809	21,861
Rate per 100,000 inhabitants		368.1	3.9	68.8	68.4	226.9	2,701.6	406.9	1,904.9	389.9
Connecticut										
Metropolitan statistical area	2,967,056									
Area actually reporting	100.0%	7,739	95	732	2,745	4,167	59,420	8,014	44,567	6,839
Cities outside metropolitan areas	112,933									
Area actually reporting	100.0%	125	1	24	22	78	1,532	206	1,215	111
Nonmetropolitan counties	508,195									
Area actually reporting	100.0%	316	6	81	46	183	2,557	670	1,528	359
State total	3,588,184	8,180	102	837	2,813	4,428	63,509	8,890	47,310	7,309
Rate per 100,000 inhabitants		228.0	2.8	23.3	78.4	123.4	1,769.9	247.8	1,318.5	203.7

Table 5. Crime, by State and Area, 2017—Continued

(Number, percent, rate per 100,000 population.)

Area	Population	Violent crime[1]	Murder and nonnegligent manslaughter	Rape (revised definition)[2]	Robbery	Aggravated assault	Property crime	Burglary	Larceny-theft	Motor vehicle theft
Delaware										
Metropolitan statistical area	961,939									
Area actually reporting	100.0%	4,361	54	334	1,082	2,891	23,476	3,970	18,137	1,369
Cities outside metropolitan areas	None									
Nonmetropolitan counties	None									
Area actually reporting	100.0%	0	0	0	0	0	1	0	1	0
State total	961,939	4,361	54	334	1,082	2,891	23,477	3,970	18,138	1,369
Rate per 100,000 inhabitants		453.4	5.6	34.7	112.5	300.5	2,440.6	412.7	1,885.6	142.3
District of Columbia[3]										
Metropolitan statistical area	693,972									
Area actually reporting	100.0%	6,974	116	444	2,623	3,791	29,729	1,809	25,333	2,587
Cities outside metropolitan areas	None									
Nonmetropolitan counties	None									
District total	693,972	6,974	116	444	2,623	3,791	29,729	1,809	25,333	2,587
Rate per 100,000 inhabitants		1,004.9	16.7	64.0	378.0	546.3	4,283.9	260.7	3,650.4	372.8
Florida										
Metropolitan statistical area	20,272,180									
Area actually reporting	99.9%	82,152	1,013	7,675	18,321	55,143	512,472	84,699	385,742	42,031
Estimated total	100.0%	82,182	1,013	7,678	18,329	55,162	512,696	84,730	385,916	42,050
Cities outside metropolitan areas	148,666									
Area actually reporting	96.5%	908	13	41	128	726	4,826	1,069	3,474	283
Estimated total	100.0%	940	13	42	133	752	5,002	1,108	3,601	293
Nonmetropolitan counties	563,554									
Area actually reporting	100.0%	2,503	31	220	135	2,117	9,522	3,015	5,936	571
State total	20,984,400	85,625	1,057	7,940	18,597	58,031	527,220	88,853	395,453	42,914
Rate per 100,000 inhabitants		408.0	5.0	37.8	88.6	276.5	2,512.4	423.4	1,884.5	204.5
Georgia										
Metropolitan statistical area	8,648,476									
Area actually reporting	98.7%	31,624	611	2,270	9,098	19,645	250,990	44,839	182,264	23,887
Estimated total	100.0%	31,963	617	2,294	9,194	19,858	253,813	45,376	184,272	24,165
Cities outside metropolitan areas	644,485									
Area actually reporting	89.3%	2,543	43	190	607	1,703	23,153	4,446	17,875	832
Estimated total	100.0%	2,843	48	208	680	1,907	25,928	4,979	20,017	932
Nonmetropolitan counties	1,136,418									
Area actually reporting	93.9%	2,303	36	203	160	1,904	17,421	4,712	11,614	1,095
Estimated total	100.0%	2,452	38	216	170	2,028	18,557	5,019	12,372	1,166
State total	10,429,379	37,258	703	2,718	10,044	23,793	298,298	55,374	216,661	26,263
Rate per 100,000 inhabitants		357.2	6.7	26.1	96.3	228.1	2,860.2	530.9	2,077.4	251.8
Hawaii										
Metropolitan statistical area	1,156,252									
Area actually reporting	100.0%	2,886	34	380	975	1,497	33,206	4,237	24,556	4,413
Cities outside metropolitan areas	None									
Nonmetropolitan counties	271,286									
Area actually reporting	100.0%	691	5	187	102	397	7,186	1,312	5,018	856
State total	1,427,538	3,577	39	567	1,077	1,894	40,392	5,549	29,574	5,269
Rate per 100,000 inhabitants		250.6	2.7	39.7	75.4	132.7	2,829.5	388.7	2,071.7	369.1
Idaho										
Metropolitan statistical area	1,262,172									
Area actually reporting	100.0%	3,067	20	563	170	2,314	22,617	4,422	16,514	1,681
Cities outside metropolitan areas	185,424									
Area actually reporting	95.9%	407	6	63	18	320	2,943	587	2,180	176
Estimated total	100.0%	425	6	66	19	334	3,070	612	2,274	184
Nonmetropolitan counties	269,347									
Area actually reporting	95.1%	377	6	74	7	290	2,275	591	1,417	267
Estimated total	100.0%	396	6	78	7	305	2,392	621	1,490	281
State total	1,716,943	3,888	32	707	196	2,953	28,079	5,655	20,278	2,146
Rate per 100,000 inhabitants		226.4	1.9	41.2	11.4	172.0	1,635.4	329.4	1,181.1	125.0
Illinois										
Metropolitan statistical area	11,331,892									
Area actually reporting	97.1%	51,775	951	4,759	17,115	28,950	230,153	37,601	172,871	19,681
Estimated total	100.0%	52,451	958	4,868	17,292	29,333	235,187	38,399	176,814	19,974
Cities outside metropolitan areas	826,086									
Area actually reporting	83.5%	2,219	15	378	202	1,624	14,323	2,828	10,981	514
Estimated total	100.0%	2,661	18	455	242	1,946	17,164	3,389	13,159	616
Nonmetropolitan counties	644,045									
Area actually reporting	89.8%	955	19	205	30	701	4,621	1,501	2,859	261
Estimated total	100.0%	1,068	21	233	33	781	5,146	1,671	3,184	291
State total	12,802,023	56,180	997	5,556	17,567	32,060	257,497	43,459	193,157	20,881
Rate per 100,000 inhabitants		438.8	7.8	43.4	137.2	250.4	2,011.4	339.5	1,508.8	163.1
Indiana										
Metropolitan statistical area	5,204,012									
Area actually reporting	85.1%	22,751	357	1,992	6,157	14,245	126,203	23,313	90,351	12,539
Estimated total	100.0%	24,167	370	2,212	6,390	15,195	137,437	25,342	98,436	13,659
Cities outside metropolitan areas	521,675									
Area actually reporting	66.3%	814	6	87	99	622	9,615	1,356	7,640	619
Estimated total	100.0%	1,237	9	140	149	939	14,509	2,046	11,529	934

Table 5. Crime, by State and Area, 2017—Continued

(Number, percent, rate per 100,000 population.)

Area	Population	Violent crime[1]	Murder and nonnegligent manslaughter	Rape (revised definition)[2]	Robbery	Aggravated assault	Property crime	Burglary	Larceny-theft	Motor vehicle theft
Nonmetropolitan counties	941,131									
Area actually reporting	55.8%	646	10	132	34	470	5,127	1,536	3,140	451
Estimated total	100.0%	1,194	18	273	61	842	9,186	2,752	5,626	808
State total	6,666,818	26,598	397	2,625	6,600	16,976	161,132	30,140	115,591	15,401
Rate per 100,000 inhabitants		399.0	6.0	39.4	99.0	254.6	2,416.9	452.1	1,733.8	231.0
Iowa										
Metropolitan statistical area	1,875,128									
Area actually reporting	98.4%	5,814	79	768	1,098	3,869	47,559	9,932	33,401	4,226
Estimated total	100.0%	5,885	79	780	1,103	3,923	48,116	10,045	33,812	4,259
Cities outside metropolitan areas	599,405									
Area actually reporting	94.3%	2,343	13	307	132	1,891	13,785	3,177	9,759	849
Estimated total	100.0%	2,484	14	325	140	2,005	14,614	3,368	10,346	900
Nonmetropolitan counties	671,178									
Area actually reporting	99.3%	855	11	128	10	706	4,096	1,653	2,026	417
Estimated total	100.0%	861	11	129	10	711	4,125	1,665	2,040	420
State total	3,145,711	9,230	104	1,234	1,253	6,639	66,855	15,078	46,198	5,579
Rate per 100,000 inhabitants		293.4	3.3	39.2	39.8	211.0	2,125.3	479.3	1,468.6	177.4
Kansas										
Metropolitan statistical area	1,983,302									
Area actually reporting	98.0%	9,009	126	1,241	1,554	6,088	59,437	9,265	43,779	6,393
Estimated total	100.0%	9,097	127	1,253	1,562	6,155	60,179	9,382	44,337	6,460
Cities outside metropolitan areas	599,197									
Area actually reporting	95.3%	2,092	23	298	192	1,579	16,577	3,109	12,542	926
Estimated total	100.0%	2,191	24	309	201	1,657	17,393	3,262	13,159	972
Nonmetropolitan counties	330,624									
Area actually reporting	96.9%	719	9	63	21	626	3,896	1,247	2,248	401
Estimated total	100.0%	742	9	65	22	646	4,021	1,287	2,320	414
State total	2,913,123	12,030	160	1,627	1,785	8,458	81,593	13,931	59,816	7,846
Rate per 100,000 inhabitants		413.0	5.5	55.9	61.3	290.3	2,800.9	478.2	2,053.3	269.3
Kentucky										
Metropolitan statistical area	2,621,479									
Area actually reporting	100.0%	7,663	175	876	2,586	4,026	71,161	13,555	49,835	7,771
Cities outside metropolitan areas	542,756									
Area actually reporting	100.0%	915	20	206	247	442	13,481	2,757	9,686	1,038
Nonmetropolitan counties	1,289,954									
Area actually reporting	100.0%	1,478	68	579	125	706	10,191	3,883	4,873	1,435
State total	4,454,189	10,056	263	1,661	2,958	5,174	94,833	20,195	64,394	10,244
Rate per 100,000 inhabitants		225.8	5.9	37.3	66.4	116.2	2,129.1	453.4	1,445.7	230.0
Louisiana										
Metropolitan statistical area	3,929,950									
Area actually reporting	97.1%	22,131	539	1,662	4,971	14,959	135,775	28,709	97,204	9,862
Estimated total	100.0%	22,555	547	1,690	5,038	15,280	138,987	29,388	99,555	10,044
Cities outside metropolitan areas	249,151									
Area actually reporting	85.6%	1,691	12	69	206	1,404	9,884	2,459	7,129	296
Estimated total	100.0%	1,977	14	81	241	1,641	11,552	2,874	8,332	346
Nonmetropolitan counties	505,232									
Area actually reporting	97.0%	1,513	20	93	77	1,323	6,958	1,943	4,460	555
Estimated total	100.0%	1,560	21	96	79	1,364	7,173	2,003	4,598	572
State total	4,684,333	26,092	582	1,867	5,358	18,285	157,712	34,265	112,485	10,962
Rate per 100,000 inhabitants		557.0	12.4	39.9	114.4	390.3	3,366.8	731.5	2,401.3	234.0
Maine										
Metropolitan statistical area	793,252									
Area actually reporting	100.0%	949	6	273	189	481	12,182	1,815	9,917	450
Cities outside metropolitan areas	255,603									
Area actually reporting	100.0%	355	4	103	35	213	5,022	716	4,138	168
Nonmetropolitan counties	287,052									
Area actually reporting	100.0%	313	13	97	25	178	2,929	803	1,951	175
State total	1,335,907	1,617	23	473	249	872	20,133	3,334	16,006	793
Rate per 100,000 inhabitants		121.0	1.7	35.4	18.6	65.3	1,507.1	249.6	1,198.1	59.4
Maryland										
Metropolitan statistical area	5,901,111									
Area actually reporting	100.0%	29,897	545	1,666	11,135	16,551	131,261	22,726	95,128	13,407
Cities outside metropolitan areas	52,511									
Area actually reporting	100.0%	255	0	17	46	192	2,048	388	1,569	91
Nonmetropolitan counties	98,555									
Area actually reporting	100.0%	121	1	8	19	93	1,187	394	723	70
State total	6,052,177	30,273	546	1,691	11,200	16,836	134,496	23,508	97,420	13,568
Rate per 100,000 inhabitants		500.2	9.0	27.9	185.1	278.2	2,222.3	388.4	1,609.7	224.2
Massachusetts										
Metropolitan statistical area	6,760,988									
Area actually reporting	97.8%	23,749	171	2,099	4,786	16,693	95,258	16,466	71,455	7,337
Estimated total	100.0%	24,170	173	2,143	4,852	17,002	97,138	16,785	72,877	7,476
Cities outside metropolitan areas	91,409									
Area actually reporting	84.9%	327	0	46	16	265	1,220	258	908	54
Estimated total	100.0%	385	0	54	19	312	1,437	304	1,069	64

Table 5. Crime, by State and Area, 2017—Continued

(Number, percent, rate per 100,000 population.)

Area	Population	Violent crime[1]	Murder and nonnegligent manslaughter	Rape (revised definition)[2]	Robbery	Aggravated assault	Property crime	Burglary	Larceny-theft	Motor vehicle theft
Nonmetropolitan counties	7,422									
Area actually reporting	98.8%	5	0	0	0	5	0	0	0	0
Estimated total	100.0%	5	0	0	0	5	0	0	0	0
State total	6,859,819	24,560	173	2,197	4,871	17,319	98,575	17,089	73,946	7,540
Rate per 100,000 inhabitants		358.0	2.5	32.0	71.0	252.5	1,437.0	249.1	1,078.0	109.9
Michigan										
Metropolitan statistical area	8,164,062									
Area actually reporting	99.8%	40,088	528	5,351	6,359	27,850	156,823	31,228	107,009	18,586
Estimated total	100.0%	40,136	528	5,361	6,366	27,881	157,112	31,273	107,231	18,608
Cities outside metropolitan areas	588,043									
Area actually reporting	98.0%	1,688	12	584	72	1,020	10,765	1,316	9,108	341
Estimated total	100.0%	1,723	12	598	73	1,040	10,980	1,342	9,290	348
Nonmetropolitan counties	1,210,206									
Area actually reporting	99.6%	2,955	29	1,068	49	1,809	11,178	3,013	7,551	614
Estimated total	100.0%	2,967	29	1,072	49	1,817	11,226	3,026	7,583	617
State total	9,962,311	44,826	569	7,031	6,488	30,738	179,318	35,641	124,104	19,573
Rate per 100,000 inhabitants		450.0	5.7	70.6	65.1	308.5	1,800.0	357.8	1,245.7	196.5
Minnesota										
Metropolitan statistical area	4,335,177									
Area actually reporting	100.0%	11,571	105	1,895	3,514	6,057	103,177	15,151	79,289	8,737
Cities outside metropolitan areas	557,001									
Area actually reporting	99.2%	1,077	5	294	79	699	12,204	1,667	9,934	603
Estimated total	100.0%	1,085	5	296	80	704	12,299	1,680	10,011	608
Nonmetropolitan counties	684,428									
Area actually reporting	100.0%	635	3	194	27	411	6,736	1,956	4,146	634
State total	5,576,606	13,291	113	2,385	3,621	7,172	122,212	18,787	93,446	9,979
Rate per 100,000 inhabitants		238.3	2.0	42.8	64.9	128.6	2,191.5	336.9	1,675.7	178.9
Mississippi										
Metropolitan statistical area	1,382,070									
Area actually reporting	82.8%	3,251	113	386	1,010	1,742	33,658	7,787	23,607	2,264
Estimated total	100.0%	3,633	124	429	1,088	1,992	38,696	8,952	27,189	2,555
Cities outside metropolitan areas	582,548									
Area actually reporting	43.1%	1,197	22	135	315	725	11,667	3,450	7,761	456
Estimated total	100.0%	2,790	51	326	731	1,682	27,061	8,002	18,001	1,058
Nonmetropolitan counties	1,019,482									
Area actually reporting	31.4%	636	22	81	79	454	4,972	2,437	2,215	320
Estimated total	100.0%	2,103	70	336	252	1,445	15,824	7,756	7,050	1,018
State total	2,984,100	8,526	245	1,091	2,071	5,119	81,581	24,710	52,240	4,631
Rate per 100,000 inhabitants		285.7	8.2	36.6	69.4	171.5	2,733.9	828.1	1,750.6	155.2
Missouri										
Metropolitan statistical area	4,571,538									
Area actually reporting	99.9%	27,993	535	2,278	6,095	19,085	141,180	23,237	100,277	17,666
Estimated total	100.0%	27,996	535	2,278	6,095	19,088	141,230	23,244	100,315	17,671
Cities outside metropolitan areas	659,462									
Area actually reporting	99.2%	2,323	23	278	202	1,820	21,999	3,593	17,220	1,186
Estimated total	100.0%	2,340	23	279	204	1,834	22,169	3,621	17,353	1,195
Nonmetropolitan counties	882,532									
Area actually reporting	99.7%	2,077	42	171	52	1,812	9,820	3,205	5,564	1,051
Estimated total	100.0%	2,084	42	172	52	1,818	9,854	3,216	5,583	1,055
State total	6,113,532	32,420	600	2,729	6,351	22,740	173,253	30,081	123,251	19,921
Rate per 100,000 inhabitants		530.3	9.8	44.6	103.9	372.0	2,833.9	492.0	2,016.0	325.9
Montana										
Metropolitan statistical area	370,184									
Area actually reporting	100.0%	1,426	13	208	171	1,034	14,098	1,694	11,002	1,402
Cities outside metropolitan areas	225,508									
Area actually reporting	99.5%	1,238	12	234	101	891	6,820	803	5,482	535
Estimated total	100.0%	1,243	12	235	101	895	6,851	807	5,507	537
Nonmetropolitan counties	454,801									
Area actually reporting	99.9%	1,291	16	170	23	1,082	6,269	1,113	4,504	652
Estimated total	100.0%	1,292	16	170	23	1,083	6,276	1,114	4,509	653
State total	1,050,493	3,961	41	613	295	3,012	27,225	3,615	21,018	2,592
Rate per 100,000 inhabitants		377.1	3.9	58.4	28.1	286.7	2,591.6	344.1	2,000.8	246.7
Nebraska										
Metropolitan statistical area	1,253,777									
Area actually reporting	99.4%	4,759	37	853	897	2,972	33,109	4,542	24,048	4,519
Estimated total	100.0%	4,768	37	856	897	2,978	33,202	4,556	24,117	4,529
Cities outside metropolitan areas	338,896									
Area actually reporting	92.8%	740	3	235	57	445	7,711	1,255	6,037	419
Estimated total	100.0%	802	3	258	61	480	8,312	1,353	6,507	452
Nonmetropolitan counties	327,403									
Area actually reporting	90.2%	272	3	68	9	192	1,938	508	1,230	200
Estimated total	100.0%	303	3	77	10	213	2,149	563	1,364	222
State total	1,920,076	5,873	43	1,191	968	3,671	43,663	6,472	31,988	5,203
Rate per 100,000 inhabitants		305.9	2.2	62.0	50.4	191.2	2,274.0	337.1	1,666.0	271.0
Nevada										
Metropolitan statistical area	2,724,009									
Area actually reporting	100.0%	15,990	260	1,773	4,806	9,151	74,017	18,877	42,781	12,359

Table 5. Crime, by State and Area, 2017—Continued

(Number, percent, rate per 100,000 population.)

Area	Population	Violent crime[1]	Murder and nonnegligent manslaughter	Rape (revised definition)[2]	Robbery	Aggravated assault	Property crime	Burglary	Larceny-theft	Motor vehicle theft
Cities outside metropolitan areas	48,711									
Area actually reporting	100.0%	236	6	44	17	169	1,377	330	932	115
Nonmetropolitan counties	225,319									
Area actually reporting	100.0%	441	8	73	18	342	2,928	842	1,748	338
State total	2,998,039	16,667	274	1,890	4,841	9,662	78,322	20,049	45,461	12,812
Rate per 100,000 inhabitants		555.9	9.1	63.0	161.5	322.3	2,612.4	668.7	1,516.4	427.3
New Hampshire										
Metropolitan statistical area	844,743									
Area actually reporting	99.3%	1,728	9	378	312	1,029	10,940	1,439	8,935	566
Estimated total	100.0%	1,736	9	380	313	1,034	11,008	1,447	8,992	569
Cities outside metropolitan areas	452,773									
Area actually reporting	91.6%	804	5	241	95	463	6,579	933	5,345	301
Estimated total	100.0%	882	5	267	104	506	7,185	1,019	5,837	329
Nonmetropolitan counties	45,279									
Area actually reporting	93.9%	46	0	14	2	30	340	101	223	16
Estimated total	100.0%	50	0	16	2	32	362	108	237	17
State total	1,342,795	2,668	14	663	419	1,572	18,555	2,574	15,066	915
Rate per 100,000 inhabitants		198.7	1.0	49.4	31.2	117.1	1,381.8	191.7	1,122.0	68.1
New Jersey										
Metropolitan statistical area	9,005,644									
Area actually reporting	100.0%	20,604	324	1,505	7,895	10,880	140,086	23,891	104,025	12,170
Cities outside metropolitan areas	None									
Nonmetropolitan counties	None									
State total	9,005,644	20,604	324	1,505	7,895	10,880	140,086	23,891	104,025	12,170
Rate per 100,000 inhabitants		228.8	3.6	16.7	87.7	120.8	1,555.5	265.3	1,155.1	135.1
New Mexico										
Metropolitan statistical area	1,392,948									
Area actually reporting	100.0%	12,153	102	898	3,409	7,744	63,392	12,665	40,610	10,117
Cities outside metropolitan areas	398,213									
Area actually reporting	95.9%	2,620	28	208	249	2,135	14,711	3,696	9,903	1,112
Estimated total	100.0%	2,734	29	220	260	2,225	15,333	3,852	10,322	1,159
Nonmetropolitan counties	296,909									
Area actually reporting	97.4%	1,433	17	136	52	1,228	3,488	1,364	1,641	483
Estimated total	100.0%	1,472	17	141	53	1,261	3,581	1,400	1,685	496
State total	2,088,070	16,359	148	1,259	3,722	11,230	82,306	17,917	52,617	11,772
Rate per 100,000 inhabitants		783.5	7.1	60.3	178.3	537.8	3,941.7	858.1	2,519.9	563.8
New York										
Metropolitan statistical area	18,471,765									
Area actually reporting	99.3%	67,860	522	5,260	19,828	42,250	274,714	31,348	230,558	12,808
Estimated total	100.0%	68,039	523	5,291	19,872	42,353	276,293	31,528	231,892	12,873
Cities outside metropolitan areas	506,148									
Area actually reporting	97.0%	1,221	11	269	181	760	15,094	1,514	13,362	218
Estimated total	100.0%	1,260	11	278	187	784	15,569	1,562	13,782	225
Nonmetropolitan counties	871,486									
Area actually reporting	100.0%	1,500	14	755	49	682	8,693	1,912	6,469	312
State total	19,849,399	70,799	548	6,324	20,108	43,819	300,555	35,002	252,143	13,410
Rate per 100,000 inhabitants		356.7	2.8	31.9	101.3	220.8	1,514.2	176.3	1,270.3	67.6
North Carolina[4]										
Metropolitan statistical area	8,060,478									
Area actually reporting	96.9%	30,308	445	2,144	8,045	19,674	204,202	46,533	144,865	12,804
Estimated total	100.0%	30,803	450	2,184	8,154	20,015	209,340	47,782	148,496	13,062
Cities outside metropolitan areas	650,145									
Area actually reporting	89.5%	3,393	67	214	749	2,363	25,304	6,399	17,799	1,106
Estimated total	100.0%	3,778	75	225	837	2,641	28,282	7,152	19,894	1,236
Nonmetropolitan counties	1,562,796									
Area actually reporting	95.3%	2,652	63	291	342	1,956	22,746	9,390	11,926	1,430
Estimated total	100.0%	2,783	66	306	359	2,052	23,864	9,852	12,512	1,500
State total	10,273,419	37,364	591	2,715	9,350	24,708	261,486	64,786	180,902	15,798
Rate per 100,000 inhabitants		363.7	5.8	26.4	91.0	240.5	2,545.3	630.6	1,760.9	153.8
North Dakota										
Metropolitan statistical area	376,890									
Area actually reporting	100.0%	1,193	4	226	143	820	10,148	1,567	7,708	873
Cities outside metropolitan areas	195,777									
Area actually reporting	99.6%	746	4	131	35	576	4,719	944	3,150	625
Estimated total	100.0%	748	4	131	35	578	4,739	948	3,163	628
Nonmetropolitan counties	182,726									
Area actually reporting	100.0%	184	2	42	5	135	1,715	427	1,016	272
State total	755,393	2,125	10	399	183	1,533	16,602	2,942	11,887	1,773
Rate per 100,000 inhabitants		281.3	1.3	52.8	24.2	202.9	2,197.8	389.5	1,573.6	234.7
Ohio										
Metropolitan statistical area	9,298,408									
Area actually reporting	93.2%	30,217	628	4,676	10,754	14,159	227,171	47,926	161,354	17,891
Estimated total	100.0%	31,168	642	4,891	11,034	14,601	239,845	49,912	171,437	18,496
Cities outside metropolitan areas	1,044,126									
Area actually reporting	80.3%	1,609	29	439	338	803	22,829	3,952	18,105	772
Estimated total	100.0%	2,007	36	550	421	1,000	28,425	4,921	22,543	961

Table 5. Crime, by State and Area, 2017—Continued

(Number, percent, rate per 100,000 population.)

Area	Population	Violent crime[1]	Murder and nonnegligent manslaughter	Rape (revised definition)[2]	Robbery	Aggravated assault	Property crime	Burglary	Larceny-theft	Motor vehicle theft
Nonmetropolitan counties	1,316,075									
Area actually reporting	93.9%	1,412	30	389	141	852	12,918	3,510	8,661	747
Estimated total	100.0%	1,508	32	418	150	908	13,764	3,740	9,228	796
State total	11,658,609	34,683	710	5,859	11,605	16,509	282,034	58,573	203,208	20,253
Rate per 100,000 inhabitants		297.5	6.1	50.3	99.5	141.6	2,419.1	502.4	1,743.0	173.7
Oklahoma										
Metropolitan statistical area	2,655,595									
Area actually reporting	100.0%	13,871	206	1,629	2,697	9,339	81,976	20,294	52,055	9,627
Cities outside metropolitan areas	710,875									
Area actually reporting	99.8%	2,998	28	389	265	2,316	23,644	5,703	16,208	1,733
Estimated total	100.0%	3,002	28	389	265	2,320	23,683	5,712	16,235	1,736
Nonmetropolitan counties	564,394									
Area actually reporting	97.9%	1,039	8	121	37	873	7,254	2,548	3,836	870
Estimated total	100.0%	1,061	8	124	38	891	7,407	2,602	3,917	888
State total	3,930,864	17,934	242	2,142	3,000	12,550	113,066	28,608	72,207	12,251
Rate per 100,000 inhabitants		456.2	6.2	54.5	76.3	319.3	2,876.4	727.8	1,836.9	311.7
Oregon										
Metropolitan statistical area	3,476,871									
Area actually reporting	99.1%	9,804	88	1,681	2,244	5,791	106,699	14,322	77,116	15,261
Estimated total	100.0%	9,878	89	1,701	2,257	5,831	107,527	14,417	77,746	15,364
Cities outside metropolitan areas	311,774									
Area actually reporting	85.1%	857	3	135	122	597	9,390	1,519	6,996	875
Estimated total	100.0%	1,009	4	160	143	702	11,040	1,786	8,225	1,029
Nonmetropolitan counties	354,131									
Area actually reporting	82.1%	636	9	104	26	497	4,231	1,233	2,385	613
Estimated total	100.0%	787	11	138	32	606	5,155	1,502	2,906	747
State total	4,142,776	11,674	104	1,999	2,432	7,139	123,722	17,705	88,877	17,140
Rate per 100,000 inhabitants		281.8	2.5	48.3	58.7	172.3	2,986.5	427.4	2,145.3	413.7
Pennsylvania										
Metropolitan statistical area	11,340,583									
Area actually reporting	99.6%	37,306	693	3,610	11,526	21,477	193,204	28,135	152,753	12,316
Estimated total	100.0%	37,390	693	3,613	11,547	21,537	193,907	28,218	153,344	12,345
Cities outside metropolitan areas	675,346									
Area actually reporting	96.0%	1,524	20	134	149	1,221	8,478	1,280	6,974	224
Estimated total	100.0%	1,585	21	137	155	1,272	8,829	1,333	7,263	233
Nonmetropolitan counties	789,608									
Area actually reporting	100.0%	1,145	25	451	91	578	8,484	2,506	5,571	407
State total	12,805,537	40,120	739	4,201	11,793	23,387	211,220	32,057	166,178	12,985
Rate per 100,000 inhabitants		313.3	5.8	32.8	92.1	182.6	1,649.4	250.3	1,297.7	101.4
Puerto Rico										
Metropolitan statistical area	3,190,926									
Area actually reporting	100.0%	7,509	658	201	3,001	3,649	30,209	7,606	19,045	3,558
Cities outside metropolitan areas	146,251									
Area actually reporting	100.0%	253	21	8	54	170	967	343	588	36
Total	3,337,177	7,762	679	209	3,055	3,819	31,176	7,949	19,633	3,594
Rate per 100,000 inhabitants		232.6	20.3	6.3	91.5	114.4	934.2	238.2	588.3	107.7
Rhode Island										
Metropolitan statistical area	1,059,639									
Area actually reporting	100.0%	2,436	19	432	473	1,512	18,507	3,217	13,809	1,481
Cities outside metropolitan areas	None									
Nonmetropolitan counties	None									
Area actually reporting	100.0%	24	1	13	1	9	54	0	52	2
State total	1,059,639	2,460	20	445	474	1,521	18,561	3,217	13,861	1,483
Rate per 100,000 inhabitants		232.2	1.9	42.0	44.7	143.5	1,751.6	303.6	1,308.1	140.0
South Carolina										
Metropolitan statistical area	4,279,294									
Area actually reporting	99.1%	21,049	312	2,109	3,344	15,284	134,276	24,630	97,240	12,406
Estimated total	100.0%	21,216	313	2,127	3,369	15,407	135,417	24,831	98,083	12,503
Cities outside metropolitan areas	203,970									
Area actually reporting	97.0%	1,861	25	133	270	1,433	10,587	2,175	7,930	482
Estimated total	100.0%	1,919	26	137	278	1,478	10,918	2,243	8,178	497
Nonmetropolitan counties	541,105									
Area actually reporting	99.2%	2,279	51	238	221	1,769	14,130	4,199	8,684	1,247
Estimated total	100.0%	2,297	51	240	223	1,783	14,240	4,232	8,751	1,257
State total	5,024,369	25,432	390	2,504	3,870	18,668	160,575	31,306	115,012	14,257
Rate per 100,000 inhabitants		506.2	7.8	49.8	77.0	371.5	3,195.9	623.1	2,289.1	283.8
South Dakota										
Metropolitan statistical area	420,832									
Area actually reporting	98.9%	1,632	13	323	174	1,122	9,862	1,536	7,410	916
Estimated total	100.0%	1,638	13	324	174	1,127	9,929	1,548	7,460	921
Cities outside metropolitan areas	219,744									
Area actually reporting	91.2%	1,742	6	192	48	1,496	4,830	793	3,712	325
Estimated total	100.0%	1,914	7	213	53	1,641	5,297	870	4,071	356
Nonmetropolitan counties	229,090									
Area actually reporting	74.7%	159	4	39	8	108	815	216	520	79
Estimated total	100.0%	219	5	58	11	145	1,091	289	696	106

Table 5. Crime, by State and Area, 2017—Continued

(Number, percent, rate per 100,000 population.)

Area	Population	Violent crime[1]	Murder and nonnegligent manslaughter	Rape (revised definition)[2]	Robbery	Aggravated assault	Property crime	Burglary	Larceny-theft	Motor vehicle theft
State total	869,666	3,771	25	595	238	2,913	16,317	2,707	12,227	1,383
Rate per 100,000 inhabitants		433.6	2.9	68.4	27.4	335.0	1,876.2	311.3	1,405.9	159.0
Tennessee										
Metropolitan statistical area	5,208,587									
Area actually reporting	100.0%	37,597	479	2,443	7,498	27,177	163,250	30,730	117,262	15,258
Cities outside metropolitan areas	515,162									
Area actually reporting	100.0%	3,238	25	255	247	2,711	19,530	3,503	14,723	1,304
Nonmetropolitan counties	992,235									
Area actually reporting	100.0%	2,920	23	236	117	2,544	14,708	4,483	8,263	1,962
State total	6,715,984	43,755	527	2,934	7,862	32,432	197,488	38,716	140,248	18,524
Rate per 100,000 inhabitants		651.5	7.8	43.7	117.1	482.9	2,940.6	576.5	2,088.3	275.8
Texas										
Metropolitan statistical area	25,244,087									
Area actually reporting	99.5%	114,973	1,309	13,086	31,501	69,077	671,216	119,385	487,397	64,434
Estimated total	100.0%	115,298	1,311	13,133	31,573	69,281	673,378	119,794	488,952	64,632
Cities outside metropolitan areas	1,446,994									
Area actually reporting	96.5%	5,463	40	668	522	4,233	33,073	7,568	23,758	1,747
Estimated total	100.0%	5,655	41	695	539	4,380	34,188	7,824	24,561	1,803
Nonmetropolitan counties	1,613,515									
Area actually reporting	99.1%	3,254	59	635	154	2,406	17,597	6,388	9,618	1,591
Estimated total	100.0%	3,285	60	642	155	2,428	17,762	6,448	9,708	1,606
State total	28,304,596	124,238	1,412	14,470	32,267	76,089	725,328	134,066	523,221	68,041
Rate per 100,000 inhabitants		438.9	5.0	51.1	114.0	268.8	2,562.6	473.7	1,848.5	240.4
Utah										
Metropolitan statistical area	2,773,185									
Area actually reporting	99.4%	6,689	67	1,536	1,444	3,642	79,982	10,796	60,188	8,998
Estimated total	100.0%	6,719	67	1,544	1,450	3,658	80,375	10,856	60,471	9,048
Cities outside metropolitan areas	149,804									
Area actually reporting	87.2%	330	3	80	10	237	2,927	442	2,290	195
Estimated total	100.0%	378	3	92	11	272	3,357	507	2,626	224
Nonmetropolitan counties	178,844									
Area actually reporting	87.3%	274	3	54	6	211	2,186	396	1,566	224
Estimated total	100.0%	313	3	61	7	242	2,506	454	1,795	257
State total	3,101,833	7,410	73	1,697	1,468	4,172	86,238	11,817	64,892	9,529
Rate per 100,000 inhabitants		238.9	2.4	54.7	47.3	134.5	2,780.2	381.0	2,092.1	307.2
Vermont										
Metropolitan statistical area	218,089									
Area actually reporting	100.0%	389	3	97	44	245	3,779	580	3,157	42
Cities outside metropolitan areas	202,042									
Area actually reporting	100.0%	394	2	82	34	276	3,551	623	2,864	64
Nonmetropolitan counties	203,526									
Area actually reporting	100.0%	251	9	39	14	189	1,630	651	891	88
State total	623,657	1,034	14	218	92	710	8,960	1,854	6,912	194
Rate per 100,000 inhabitants		165.8	2.2	35.0	14.8	113.8	1,436.7	297.3	1,108.3	31.1
Virginia										
Metropolitan statistical area	7,428,019									
Area actually reporting	99.9%	15,710	387	2,444	4,087	8,792	136,379	15,520	111,704	9,155
Estimated total	100.0%	15,714	387	2,445	4,088	8,794	136,408	15,523	111,728	9,157
Cities outside metropolitan areas	256,861									
Area actually reporting	99.4%	710	26	90	157	437	6,832	951	5,550	331
Estimated total	100.0%	714	26	90	158	440	6,876	957	5,586	333
Nonmetropolitan counties	785,140									
Area actually reporting	100.0%	1,204	40	327	86	751	8,571	1,988	5,901	682
State total	8,470,020	17,632	453	2,862	4,332	9,985	151,855	18,468	123,215	10,172
Rate per 100,000 inhabitants		208.2	5.3	33.8	51.1	117.9	1,792.9	218.0	1,454.7	120.1
Washington										
Metropolitan statistical area	6,668,792									
Area actually reporting	99.9%	20,983	209	2,944	5,200	12,630	217,244	39,445	150,755	27,044
Estimated total	100.0%	20,983	209	2,944	5,200	12,630	217,252	39,446	150,761	27,045
Cities outside metropolitan areas	304,884									
Area actually reporting	96.0%	1,005	9	214	143	639	11,533	2,059	8,314	1,160
Estimated total	100.0%	1,045	9	221	149	666	12,014	2,145	8,661	1,208
Nonmetropolitan counties	432,067									
Area actually reporting	100.0%	520	12	90	41	377	5,761	2,129	3,089	543
State total	7,405,743	22,548	230	3,255	5,390	13,673	235,027	43,720	162,511	28,796
Rate per 100,000 inhabitants		304.5	3.1	44.0	72.8	184.6	3,173.6	590.4	2,194.4	388.8
West Virginia										
Metropolitan statistical area	1,123,324									
Area actually reporting	86.3%	3,837	59	494	413	2,871	22,338	5,066	15,252	2,020
Estimated total	100.0%	4,244	62	558	443	3,181	25,592	5,687	17,609	2,296
Cities outside metropolitan areas	186,093									
Area actually reporting	59.6%	359	5	42	29	283	2,086	351	1,608	127
Estimated total	100.0%	620	8	88	49	475	3,502	589	2,700	213
Nonmetropolitan counties	506,440									
Area actually reporting	97.1%	1,459	15	143	31	1,270	4,405	1,313	2,613	479
Estimated total	100.0%	1,504	15	149	32	1,308	4,536	1,352	2,691	493

Table 5. Crime, by State and Area, 2017—Continued

(Number, percent, rate per 100,000 population.)

Area	Population	Violent crime[1]	Murder and nonnegligent manslaughter	Rape (revised definition)[2]	Robbery	Aggravated assault	Property crime	Burglary	Larceny-theft	Motor vehicle theft
State total	1,815,857	6,368	85	795	524	4,964	33,630	7,628	23,000	3,002
Rate per 100,000 inhabitants		350.7	4.7	43.8	28.9	273.4	1,852.0	420.1	1,266.6	165.3
Wisconsin										
Metropolitan statistical area	4,296,895									
Area actually reporting	99.3%	16,336	171	1,625	4,234	10,306	84,396	14,034	61,746	8,616
Estimated total	100.0%	16,365	171	1,632	4,237	10,325	84,630	14,080	61,920	8,630
Cities outside metropolitan areas	655,239									
Area actually reporting	99.7%	1,299	7	284	87	921	13,535	1,593	11,496	446
Estimated total	100.0%	1,303	7	285	87	924	13,578	1,598	11,533	447
Nonmetropolitan counties	843,349									
Area actually reporting	100.0%	871	8	222	21	620	6,594	1,921	4,282	391
State total	5,795,483	18,539	186	2,139	4,345	11,869	104,802	17,599	77,735	9,468
Rate per 100,000 inhabitants		319.9	3.2	36.9	75.0	204.8	1,808.3	303.7	1,341.3	163.4
Wyoming										
Metropolitan statistical area	178,138									
Area actually reporting	100.0%	465	6	94	55	310	4,881	784	3,678	419
Cities outside metropolitan areas	245,155									
Area actually reporting	95.7%	563	3	107	18	435	4,400	555	3,598	247
Estimated total	100.0%	589	3	112	19	455	4,597	580	3,759	258
Nonmetropolitan counties	156,022									
Area actually reporting	88.9%	285	5	49	2	229	1,002	204	707	91
Estimated total	100.0%	322	6	57	2	257	1,126	229	795	102
State total	579,315	1,376	15	263	76	1,022	10,604	1,593	8,232	779
Rate per 100,000 inhabitants		237.5	2.6	45.4	13.1	176.4	1,830.4	275.0	1,421.0	134.5

Note: Although arson data are included in the trend and clearance tables, sufficient data are not available to estimate totals for this offense. Therefore, no arson data are published in this table.
1 The violent crime figures include the offenses of murder, rape (revised definition), robbery, and aggravated assault.   2 The figures shown in the rape (revised definition) column were estimated using the revised Uniform Crime Reporting (UCR) definition of rape. See chapter notes for more detail.   3 Includes offenses reported by the Metro Transit Police and the Arson Investigation Unit of the District of Columbia Fire and Emergency Medical Services.   4 This state's agencies submitted rape data according to the legacy UCR definition of rape.

Table 6. Crime in the United States, by Selected Metropolitan Statistical Area, 2017

(Number, percent, rate per 100,000 population.)

Area	Population	Violent crime	Murder and nonnegligent manslaughter	Rape[1]	Robbery	Aggravated assault	Property crime	Burglary	Larceny-theft	Motor vehicle theft
Abilene, TX MSA[2, 3]	170,995									
Includes Callahan, Jones, and Taylor Counties										
City of Abilene[2, 3]	122,981	636	4	100	138	394			2,605	260
Total area actually reporting	100.0%	753	7	120	143	483			2,938	301
Rate per 100,000 inhabitants		440.4	4.1	70.2	83.6	282.5			1,718.2	176.0
Akron, OH MSA[4]	703,907									
Includes Portage[4] and Summit Counties										
City of Akron	197,412	1,377	42	209	395	731	8,360	2,301	5,304	755
Total area actually reporting	96.3%	1,911	51	335	494	1,031	17,340	3,681	12,587	1,072
Estimated total	100.0%	1,952	52	344	506	1,050	17,886	3,764	13,024	1,098
Rate per 100,000 inhabitants		277.3	7.4	48.9	71.9	149.2	2,541.0	534.7	1,850.2	156.0
Albany, GA MSA	151,534									
Includes Baker, Dougherty, Lee, Terrell, and Worth Counties										
City of Albany	73,209	827	22	27	152	626	4,116	879	3,048	189
Total area actually reporting	96.0%	1,079	23	55	186	815	5,773	1,229	4,289	255
Estimated total	100.0%	1,101	23	57	192	829	5,966	1,259	4,436	271
Rate per 100,000 inhabitants		726.6	15.2	37.6	126.7	547.1	3,937.1	830.8	2,927.4	178.8
Albany, OR MSA[2]	124,014									
Includes Linn County[2]										
City of Albany[2]	53,701	56	0	8	20	28	1,406	158	1,137	111
Total area actually reporting	100.0%	196	2	41	26	127	3,159	489	2,368	302
Rate per 100,000 inhabitants		158.0	1.6	33.1	21.0	102.4	2,547.3	394.3	1,909.5	243.5
Albany-Schenectady-Troy, NY MSA	885,673									
Includes Albany, Rensselaer, Saratoga, Schenectady, and Schoharie Counties										
City of Albany	98,174	876	8	54	247	567	3,394	432	2,853	109
City of Schenectady	64,710	577	2	58	141	376	2,057	348	1,534	175
City of Troy	49,644	351	6	31	114	200	1,732	370	1,272	90
Total area actually reporting	100.0%	2,579	18	361	640	1,560	17,312	2,279	14,376	657
Rate per 100,000 inhabitants		291.2	2.0	40.8	72.3	176.1	1,954.7	257.3	1,623.2	74.2
Albuquerque, NM MSA	915,069									
Includes Bernalillo, Sandoval, Torrance, and Valencia Counties										
City of Albuquerque	561,375	7,686	70	473	2,930	4,213	41,350	6,996	26,670	7,684
Total area actually reporting	100.0%	9,928	81	607	3,180	6,060	50,319	9,056	32,128	9,135
Rate per 100,000 inhabitants		1,084.9	8.9	66.3	347.5	662.2	5,498.9	989.7	3,511.0	998.3
Alexandria, LA MSA	154,181									
Includes Grant and Rapides Parishes										
City of Alexandria	47,860	690	17	9	129	535	4,197	987	2,953	257
Total area actually reporting	85.8%	1,047	20	28	154	845	6,774	1,652	4,731	391
Estimated total	100.0%	1,124	21	33	167	903	7,345	1,777	5,142	426
Rate per 100,000 inhabitants		729.0	13.6	21.4	108.3	585.7	4,763.9	1,152.5	3,335.0	276.3
Allentown-Bethlehem-Easton, PA-NJ MSA	838,894									
Includes Warren County, NJ and Carbon, Lehigh, and Northampton Counties, PA										
City of Allentown, PA	120,823	557	16	70	269	202	3,302	634	2,362	306
City of Bethlehem, PA	75,336	594	0	29	61	504	1,359	187	1,124	48
Total area actually reporting	99.2%	1,980	26	176	496	1,282	13,889	1,934	11,166	789
Estimated total	100.0%	1,992	26	177	499	1,290	13,984	1,945	11,246	793
Rate per 100,000 inhabitants		237.5	3.1	21.1	59.5	153.8	1,667.0	231.9	1,340.6	94.5
Altoona, PA MSA	124,337									
Includes Blair County										
City of Altoona	44,366	120	0	33	31	56	918	167	708	43
Total area actually reporting	100.0%	252	0	67	41	144	1,765	249	1,447	69
Rate per 100,000 inhabitants		202.7	0.0	53.9	33.0	115.8	1,419.5	200.3	1,163.8	55.5
Amarillo, TX MSA	264,936									
Includes Armstrong, Carson, Oldham, Potter, and Randall Counties										
City of Amarillo	200,993	1,518	16	183	237	1,082	8,787	1,684	6,113	990
Total area actually reporting	100.0%	1,680	17	220	243	1,200	9,507	1,840	6,584	1,083
Rate per 100,000 inhabitants		634.1	6.4	83.0	91.7	452.9	3,588.4	694.5	2,485.1	408.8
Ames, IA MSA	98,260									
Includes Story County										
City of Ames	67,461	124	1	49	23	51	1,392	248	1,087	57
Total area actually reporting	93.1%	162	1	62	25	74	1,777	322	1,381	74
Estimated total	100.0%	178	1	65	26	86	1,901	347	1,473	81
Rate per 100,000 inhabitants		181.2	1.0	66.2	26.5	87.5	1,934.7	353.1	1,499.1	82.4
Anchorage, AK MSA	313,465									
Includes Anchorage Municipality and Matanuska-Susitna Borough										

Table 6. Crime in the United States, by Selected Metropolitan Statistical Area, 2017—Continued

(Number, percent, rate per 100,000 population.)

Area	Population	Violent crime	Murder and nonnegligent manslaughter	Rape[1]	Robbery	Aggravated assault	Property crime	Burglary	Larceny-theft	Motor vehicle theft
City of Anchorage	296,188	3,564	27	391	778	2,368	16,041	2,216	10,721	3,104
Total area actually reporting	100.0%	3,645	28	392	789	2,436	17,057	2,283	11,495	3,279
Rate per 100,000 inhabitants		1,162.8	8.9	125.1	251.7	777.1	5,441.4	728.3	3,667.1	1,046.0
Ann Arbor, MI MSA	368,898									
Includes Washtenaw County										
City of Ann Arbor	121,930	259	0	57	53	149	2,108	278	1,731	99
Total area actually reporting	100.0%	1,206	11	233	179	783	6,029	864	4,753	412
Rate per 100,000 inhabitants		326.9	3.0	63.2	48.5	212.3	1,634.3	234.2	1,288.4	111.7
Anniston-Oxford-Jacksonville, AL MSA	113,915									
Includes Calhoun County										
City of Anniston	21,955	754	14	47	71	622	1,352	542	700	110
City of Oxford	16,937	48	1	0	7	40	884	94	756	34
City of Jacksonville	12,573	113	2	10	12	89	489	137	325	27
Total area actually reporting	99.3%	976	17	71	98	790	3,242	955	2,095	192
Estimated total	100.0%	980	17	71	99	793	3,267	959	2,114	194
Rate per 100,000 inhabitants		860.3	14.9	62.3	86.9	696.1	2,867.9	841.9	1,855.8	170.3
Appleton, WI MSA	235,528									
Includes Calumet and Outagamie Counties										
City of Appleton	74,660	203	1	39	17	146	1,155	136	996	23
Total area actually reporting	100.0%	331	2	55	30	244	2,905	340	2,479	86
Rate per 100,000 inhabitants		140.5	0.8	23.4	12.7	103.6	1,233.4	144.4	1,052.5	36.5
Asheville, NC MSA[4]	457,928									
Includes Buncombe, Haywood, Henderson, and Madison Counties[4]										
City of Asheville[4]	90,103		7		181	363	4,248	733	3,191	324
Total area actually reporting	99.2%		16		275	712	9,645	2,492	6,410	743
Estimated total	100.0%		16		277	718	9,745	2,510	6,488	747
Rate per 100,000 inhabitants			3.5		60.5	156.8	2,128.1	548.1	1,416.8	163.1
Athens-Clarke County, GA MSA	207,610									
Includes Clarke, Madison, Oconee, and Oglethorpe Counties										
City of Athens-Clarke County	124,903	519	6	57	123	333	3,930	683	3,017	230
Total area actually reporting	100.0%	639	7	72	135	425	5,345	922	4,133	290
Rate per 100,000 inhabitants		307.8	3.4	34.7	65.0	204.7	2,574.5	444.1	1,990.8	139.7
Atlanta-Sandy Springs-Roswell, GA MSA	5,882,917									
Includes Barrow, Bartow, Butts, Carroll, Cherokee, Clayton, Cobb, Coweta, Dawson, DeKalb, Douglas, Fayette, Forsyth, Fulton, Gwinnett, Haralson, Heard, Henry, Jasper, Lamar, Meriwether, Morgan, Newton, Paulding, Pickens, Pike, Rockdale, Spalding, and Walton Counties										
City of Atlanta	481,343	4,504	79	282	1,413	2,730	22,991	3,390	16,304	3,297
City of Sandy Springs	107,740	126	0	12	56	58	2,263	377	1,708	178
City of Roswell	95,602	108	2	15	32	59	1,616	229	1,278	109
City of Alpharetta	66,711	34	0	1	22	11	1,187	96	1,056	35
City of Marietta	61,646	215	4	14	102	95	2,209	327	1,700	182
Total area actually reporting	98.5%	21,357	392	1,514	6,715	12,736	166,368	27,784	120,804	17,780
Estimated total	100.0%	21,627	397	1,534	6,791	12,905	168,586	28,218	122,365	18,003
Rate per 100,000 inhabitants		367.6	6.7	26.1	115.4	219.4	2,865.7	479.7	2,080.0	306.0
Atlantic City-Hammonton, NJ MSA	271,486									
Includes Atlantic County										
City of Atlantic City	38,601	425	13	24	227	161	1,732	319	1,298	115
City of Hammonton	14,370	17	0	0	3	14	177	37	134	6
Total area actually reporting	100.0%	847	21	54	344	428	6,943	1,230	5,435	278
Rate per 100,000 inhabitants		312.0	7.7	19.9	126.7	157.7	2,557.4	453.1	2,001.9	102.4
Auburn-Opelika, AL MSA	162,152									
Includes Lee County										
City of Auburn	64,831	217	4	17	30	166	1,711	156	1,454	101
City of Opelika	30,476	223	5	21	47	150	1,399	220	1,091	88
Total area actually reporting	100.0%	895	12	64	99	720	4,388	681	3,379	328
Rate per 100,000 inhabitants		552.0	7.4	39.5	61.1	444.0	2,706.1	420.0	2,083.8	202.3
Augusta-Richmond County, GA-SC MSA[5]	600,734									
Includes Burke, Columbia, Lincoln, McDuffie, and Richmond Counties, GA and Aiken and Edgefield Counties, SC										
Total area actually reporting	96.6%	1,800	39	190	419	1,152				1,330
Estimated total	100.0%	1,891	40	199	432	1,220				1,386
Rate per 100,000 inhabitants		314.8	6.7	33.1	71.9	203.1				230.7
Austin-Round Rock, TX MSA[2]	2,115,140									
Includes Bastrop, Caldwell, Hays, Travis, and Williamson Counties										
City of Austin	971,949	4,032	25	834	987	2,186	31,001	4,380	24,542	2,079
City of Round Rock	124,617	169	2	33	44	90	2,701	232	2,405	64

Table 6. Crime in the United States, by Selected Metropolitan Statistical Area, 2017—Continued

(Number, percent, rate per 100,000 population.)

Area	Population	Violent crime	Murder and nonnegligent manslaughter	Rape[1]	Robbery	Aggravated assault	Property crime	Burglary	Larceny-theft	Motor vehicle theft
Total area actually reporting	99.9%	6,476	52	1,345	1,316	3,763	49,566	7,377	38,969	3,220
Estimated total	100.0%	6,479	52	1,345	1,317	3,765	49,588	7,380	38,986	3,222
Rate per 100,000 inhabitants		306.3	2.5	63.6	62.3	178.0	2,344.4	348.9	1,843.2	152.3
Bakersfield, CA MSA	891,188									
Includes Kern County										
City of Bakersfield	381,154	1,827	41	92	753	941	15,507	3,667	9,063	2,777
Total area actually reporting	100.0%	4,989	89	307	1,297	3,296	28,933	7,429	15,605	5,899
Rate per 100,000 inhabitants		559.8	10.0	34.4	145.5	369.8	3,246.6	833.6	1,751.0	661.9
	2,811,573									
Baltimore-Columbia-Towson, MD MSA	2,811,573									
Includes Anne Arundel, Baltimore, Carroll, Harford, Howard, and Queen Anne's Counties and Baltimore City										
City of Baltimore	613,217	12,430	342	382	5,879	5,827	30,220	8,041	17,008	5,171
Total area actually reporting	100.0%	22,001	413	1,048	8,454	12,086	76,837	14,673	53,711	8,453
Rate per 100,000 inhabitants		782.5	14.7	37.3	300.7	429.9	2,732.9	521.9	1,910.4	300.7
Bangor, ME MSA	151,887									
Includes Penobscot County										
City of Bangor	31,814	48	1	8	14	25	1,209	181	1,004	24
Total area actually reporting	100.0%	100	2	29	21	48	2,413	386	1,950	77
Rate per 100,000 inhabitants		65.8	1.3	19.1	13.8	31.6	1,588.7	254.1	1,283.8	50.7
Barnstable Town, MA MSA	214,183									
Includes Barnstable County										
City of Barnstable	44,142	197	1	18	13	165	547	79	446	22
Total area actually reporting	100.0%	761	3	91	39	628	2,930	731	2,078	121
Rate per 100,000 inhabitants		355.3	1.4	42.5	18.2	293.2	1,368.0	341.3	970.2	56.5
Baton Rouge, LA MSA	836,722									
Includes Ascension, East Baton Rouge, East Feliciana, Iberville, Livingston, Pointe Coupee, St. Helena, West Baton Rouge, and West Feliciana Parishes										
City of Baton Rouge	227,403	2,335	87	100	868	1,280	12,721	3,226	8,504	991
Total area actually reporting	99.7%	4,565	140	240	1,211	2,974	32,865	6,853	24,185	1,827
Estimated total	100.0%	4,575	140	241	1,212	2,982	32,946	6,868	24,248	1,830
Rate per 100,000 inhabitants		546.8	16.7	28.8	144.9	356.4	3,937.5	820.8	2,898.0	218.7
Battle Creek, MI M.S.A	134,442									
Includes Calhoun County										
City of Battle Creek	60,852	580	3	73	72	432	2,251	501	1,656	94
Total area actually reporting	99.9%	920	4	147	99	670	3,977	811	2,994	172
Estimated total	100.0%	920	4	147	99	670	3,978	811	2,995	172
Rate per 100,000 inhabitants		684.3	3.0	109.3	73.6	498.4	2,958.9	603.2	2,227.7	127.9
Bay City, MI MSA	104,519									
Includes Bay County										
City of Bay City	33,286	242	1	57	35	149	998	223	716	59
Total area actually reporting	100.0%	385	2	117	48	218	1,992	398	1,486	108
Rate per 100,000 inhabitants		368.4	1.9	111.9	45.9	208.6	1,905.9	380.8	1,421.8	103.3
Beaumont-Port Arthur, TX MSA[3]	410,600									
Includes Hardin, Jefferson, Newton, and Orange Counties										
City of Beaumont	118,456	1,259	16	86	304	853	5,136	1,259	3,472	405
City of Port Arthur	55,583	378	6	15	110	247	2,031	767	1,111	153
Total area actually reporting	99.9%	2,263	27	151	509	1,576			6,995	959
Estimated total	100.0%	2,264	27	151	509	1,577			7,004	960
Rate per 100,000 inhabitants		551.4	6.6	36.8	124.0	384.1			1,705.8	233.8
Beckley, WV MSA	119,499									
Includes Fayette and Raleigh Counties										
City of Beckley	16,862	117	1	22	19	75	1,006	172	791	43
Total area actually reporting	95.7%	360	6	51	36	267	2,466	564	1,720	182
Estimated total	100.0%	372	6	53	37	276	2,624	587	1,845	192
Rate per 100,000 inhabitants		311.3	5.0	44.4	31.0	231.0	2,195.8	491.2	1,543.9	160.7
Bellingham, WA MSA	220,105									
Includes Whatcom County										
City of Bellingham	88,652	258	2	56	73	127	4,151	552	3,435	164
Total area actually reporting	100.0%	496	4	121	96	275	6,526	1,116	5,080	330
Rate per 100,000 inhabitants		225.3	1.8	55.0	43.6	124.9	2,964.9	507.0	2,308.0	149.9
Bend-Redmond, OR MSA	185,760									
Includes Deschutes County										
City of Bend	93,786	154	0	33	24	97	1,960	177	1,680	103
City of Redmond	29,870	82	0	16	11	55	933	114	740	79
Total area actually reporting	100.0%	325	0	71	39	215	3,700	462	2,996	242
Rate per 100,000 inhabitants		175.0	0.0	38.2	21.0	115.7	1,991.8	248.7	1,612.8	130.3

Table 6. Crime in the United States, by Selected Metropolitan Statistical Area, 2017—Continued

(Number, percent, rate per 100,000 population.)

Area	Population	Violent crime	Murder and nonnegligent manslaughter	Rape[1]	Robbery	Aggravated assault	Property crime	Burglary	Larceny-theft	Motor vehicle theft
Billings, MT MSA	171,334									
Includes Carbon, Golden Valley, and Yellowstone Counties										
City of Billings	111,317	549	2	76	87	384	6,076	783	4,451	842
Total area actually reporting	100.0%	680	4	96	92	488	7,156	951	5,229	976
Rate per 100,000 inhabitants		396.9	2.3	56.0	53.7	284.8	4,176.6	555.1	3,051.9	569.6
Binghamton, NY MSA	243,440									
Includes Broome and Tioga Counties										
City of Binghamton	45,399	362	4	42	90	226	1,983	370	1,557	56
Total area actually reporting	99.7%	743	4	179	138	422	5,284	865	4,248	171
Estimated total	100.0%	744	4	179	138	423	5,295	866	4,258	171
Rate per 100,000 inhabitants		305.6	1.6	73.5	56.7	173.8	2,175.1	355.7	1,749.1	70.2
Bismarck, ND MSA	131,352									
Includes Burleigh, Morton, Oliver, and Sioux Counties										
City of Bismarck	74,397	256	0	45	33	178	2,438	322	1,884	232
Total area actually reporting	100.0%	423	1	85	34	303	3,538	522	2,634	382
Rate per 100,000 inhabitants		322.0	0.8	64.7	25.9	230.7	2,693.5	397.4	2,005.3	290.8
Bloomington, IL MSA	189,116									
Includes DeWitt and McLean Counties										
City of Bloomington	78,203	343	3	73	45	222	1,334	220	1,037	77
Total area actually reporting	93.1%	525	5	135	67	318	2,753	424	2,212	117
Estimated total	100.0%	553	5	139	75	334	2,963	455	2,379	129
Rate per 100,000 inhabitants		292.4	2.6	73.5	39.7	176.6	1,566.8	240.6	1,258.0	68.2
Bloomington, IN MSA	167,618									
Includes Monroe and Owen Counties										
City of Bloomington	85,121	443	2	78	52	311	2,584	478	1,940	166
Total area actually reporting	87.6%	524	2	102	62	358	3,875	644	2,969	262
Estimated total	100.0%	554	2	107	66	379	4,108	698	3,121	289
Rate per 100,000 inhabitants		330.5	1.2	63.8	39.4	226.1	2,450.8	416.4	1,862.0	172.4
Bloomsburg-Berwick, PA MSA	84,669									
Includes Columbia and Montour Counties										
City of Bloomsburg Town	14,542	35	0	6	2	27	175	35	138	2
City of Berwick	10,080	22	1	2	2	17	195	23	167	5
Total area actually reporting	99.1%	164	1	45	6	112	960	150	787	23
Estimated total	100.0%	165	1	45	6	113	970	151	796	23
Rate per 100,000 inhabitants		194.9	1.2	53.1	7.1	133.5	1,145.6	178.3	940.1	27.2
Boise City, ID MSA	710,265									
Includes Ada, Boise, Canyon, Gem, and Owyhee Counties										
City of Boise	225,677	630	2	144	51	433	5,517	736	4,435	346
Total area actually reporting	100.0%	1,669	7	341	105	1,216	12,514	2,240	9,271	1,003
Rate per 100,000 inhabitants		235.0	1.0	48.0	14.8	171.2	1,761.9	315.4	1,305.3	141.2
Boston-Cambridge-Newton, MA-NH MSA	4,839,029									
Includes the Metropolitan Divisions of Boston, MA; Cambridge-Newton-Framingham, MA; and Rockingham County-Strafford County, NH										
City of Boston, MA	682,903	4,570	57	290	1,404	2,819	14,266	2,109	10,952	1,205
City of Cambridge, MA	111,707	313	2	17	101	193	2,031	252	1,685	94
City of Newton, MA	89,736	49	0	5	5	39	576	87	471	18
City of Framingham, MA	72,153	235	0	14	20	201	748	132	549	67
City of Waltham, MA	63,413	98	1	16	14	67	609	118	447	44
Total area actually reporting	98.6%	14,587	124	1,319	3,162	9,982	62,474	9,085	48,476	4,913
Estimated total	100.0%	14,775	125	1,339	3,191	10,120	63,317	9,227	49,115	4,975
Rate per 100,000 inhabitants		305.3	2.6	27.7	65.9	209.1	1,308.5	190.7	1,015.0	102.8
Boston, MA MD	2,014,011									
Includes Norfolk, Plymouth, and Suffolk Counties										
Total area actually reporting	97.1%	8,539	76	695	2,076	5,692	30,242	4,338	23,540	2,364
Estimated total	100.0%	8,706	77	713	2,102	5,814	30,985	4,464	24,102	2,419
Rate per 100,000 inhabitants		432.3	3.8	35.4	104.4	288.7	1,538.5	221.6	1,196.7	120.1
Cambridge-Newton-Framingham, MA MD	2,390,681									
Includes Essex and Middlesex Counties										
Total area actually reporting	99.7%	5,404	43	448	988	3,925	26,985	4,140	20,527	2,318
Estimated total	100.0%	5,424	43	450	991	3,940	27,075	4,155	20,595	2,325
Rate per 100,000 inhabitants		226.9	1.8	18.8	41.5	164.8	1,132.5	173.8	861.5	97.3
Rockingham County-Strafford County, NH MD	434,337									
Includes Rockingham and Strafford Counties										
Total area actually reporting	99.8%	644	5	176	98	365	5,247	607	4,409	231
Estimated total	100.0%	645	5	176	98	366	5,257	608	4,418	231
Rate per 100,000 inhabitants		148.5	1.2	40.5	22.6	84.3	1,210.4	140.0	1,017.2	53.2
Bowling Green, KY MSA	173,283									
Includes Allen, Butler, Edmonson, and Warren Counties										

Table 6. Crime in the United States, by Selected Metropolitan Statistical Area, 2017—Continued

(Number, percent, rate per 100,000 population.)

Area	Population	Violent crime	Murder and nonnegligent manslaughter	Rape[1]	Robbery	Aggravated assault	Property crime	Burglary	Larceny-theft	Motor vehicle theft
City of Bowling Green	66,317	225	4	61	82	78	3,089	436	2,476	177
Total area actually reporting	100.0%	295	5	86	93	111	4,201	799	3,129	273
Rate per 100,000 inhabitants		170.2	2.9	49.6	53.7	64.1	2,424.4	461.1	1,805.7	157.5
Bremerton-Silverdale, WA MSA	267,867									
Includes Kitsap County										
City of Bremerton	41,173	216	3	26	29	158	1,670	264	1,206	200
Total area actually reporting	100.0%	685	11	132	67	475	6,178	1,196	4,406	576
Rate per 100,000 inhabitants		255.7	4.1	49.3	25.0	177.3	2,306.4	446.5	1,644.8	215.0
Bridgeport-Stamford-Norwalk, CT MSA	930,673									
Includes Fairfield County										
City of Bridgeport	146,110	1,315	21	77	565	652	3,416	548	2,152	716
City of Stamford	130,189	292	0	30	91	171	1,986	241	1,488	257
City of Norwalk	88,849	255	3	11	40	201	1,505	160	1,188	157
City of Danbury	85,614	163	1	19	71	72	1,105	90	942	73
City of Stratford	52,263	89	2	10	50	27	1,117	137	826	154
Total area actually reporting	100.0%	2,298	28	181	889	1,200	13,459	1,713	9,951	1,795
Rate per 100,000 inhabitants		246.9	3.0	19.4	95.5	128.9	1,446.2	184.1	1,069.2	192.9
Brownsville-Harlingen, TX MSA[2]	424,158									
Includes Cameron County										
City of Brownsville	185,216	476	5	79	133	259	5,176	661	4,374	141
City of Harlingen	65,617	233	0	18	32	183	2,693	523	2,079	91
Total area actually reporting	100.0%	1,324	8	226	191	899	11,131	1,790	8,991	350
Rate per 100,000 inhabitants		312.1	1.9	53.3	45.0	211.9	2,624.3	422.0	2,119.7	82.5
Brunswick, GA MSA	117,664									
Includes Brantley, Glynn, and McIntosh Counties										
City of Brunswick	16,500	170	4	10	44	112	866	265	557	44
Total area actually reporting	100.0%	418	13	29	91	285	3,617	990	2,428	199
Rate per 100,000 inhabitants		355.2	11.0	24.6	77.3	242.2	3,074.0	841.4	2,063.5	169.1
Buffalo-Cheektowaga-Niagara Falls, NY MSA	1,134,907									
Includes Erie and Niagara Counties										
City of Buffalo	256,169	2,611	40	142	857	1,572	9,827	2,356	6,638	833
City of Cheektowaga Town	77,576	187	1	14	82	90	2,296	300	1,908	88
City of Niagara Falls	48,385	544	3	36	150	355	2,336	458	1,738	140
Total area actually reporting	100.0%	4,264	49	336	1,318	2,561	24,807	4,645	18,741	1,421
Rate per 100,000 inhabitants		375.7	4.3	29.6	116.1	225.7	2,185.8	409.3	1,651.3	125.2
Burlington, NC MSA[4]	161,435									
Includes Alamance County[4]										
City of Burlington[4]	52,986		4		114	381	2,016	502	1,402	112
Total area actually reporting	100.0%		4		152	525	3,550	927	2,444	179
Rate per 100,000 inhabitants			2.5		94.2	325.2	2,199.0	574.2	1,513.9	110.9
Burlington-South Burlington, VT MSA	218,089									
Includes Chittenden, Franklin, and Grand Isle Counties										
City of Burlington	42,230	132	1	21	11	99	1,164	223	941	0
City of South Burlington	19,146	37	0	16	5	16	510	47	463	0
Total area actually reporting	100.0%	389	3	97	44	245	3,779	580	3,157	42
Rate per 100,000 inhabitants		178.4	1.4	44.5	20.2	112.3	1,732.8	265.9	1,447.6	19.3
California-Lexington Park, MD MSA	113,700									
Includes St. Mary's County										
Total area actually reporting	100.0%	214	1	22	47	144	1,973	479	1,444	50
Rate per 100,000 inhabitants		188.2	0.9	19.3	41.3	126.6	1,735.3	421.3	1,270.0	44.0
Cape Coral-Fort Myers, FL MSA	742,930									
Includes Lee County										
City of Cape Coral	184,346	235	3	16	41	175	2,888	570	2,148	170
City of Fort Myers	79,918	752	10	53	187	502	2,207	374	1,607	226
Total area actually reporting	100.0%	2,297	45	249	541	1,462	11,268	2,294	8,018	956
Rate per 100,000 inhabitants		309.2	6.1	33.5	72.8	196.8	1,516.7	308.8	1,079.2	128.7
Cape Girardeau, MO-IL MSA	97,715									
Includes Alexander County, IL and Bollinger and Cape Girardeau Counties, MO										
City of Cape Girardeau, MO	39,887	234	5	24	51	154	1,523	252	1,189	82
Total area actually reporting	100.0%	378	5	36	55	282	2,277	452	1,714	111
Rate per 100,000 inhabitants		386.8	5.1	36.8	56.3	288.6	2,330.2	462.6	1,754.1	113.6
Carson City, NV MSA	54,994									
Includes Carson City										
Total area actually reporting	100.0%	198	1	0	18	179	908	175	649	84
Rate per 100,000 inhabitants		360.0	1.8	0.0	32.7	325.5	1,651.1	318.2	1,180.1	152.7
Casper, WY MSA	80,644									
Includes Natrona County										
City of Casper	60,034	91	1	29	14	47	1,727	318	1,281	128

Table 6. Crime in the United States, by Selected Metropolitan Statistical Area, 2017—Continued

(Number, percent, rate per 100,000 population.)

Area	Population	Violent crime	Murder and nonnegligent manslaughter	Rape[1]	Robbery	Aggravated assault	Property crime	Burglary	Larceny-theft	Motor vehicle theft
Total area actually reporting	100.0%	177	1	54	20	102	2,109	407	1,524	178
Rate per 100,000 inhabitants		219.5	1.2	67.0	24.8	126.5	2,615.2	504.7	1,889.8	220.7
Cedar Rapids, IA MSA	269,046									
Includes Benton, Jones, and Linn Counties										
City of Cedar Rapids	131,878	370	6	34	121	209	4,952	929	3,681	342
Total area actually reporting	99.1%	580	8	70	138	364	6,439	1,350	4,636	453
Estimated total	100.0%	585	8	71	138	368	6,484	1,359	4,669	456
Rate per 100,000 inhabitants		217.4	3.0	26.4	51.3	136.8	2,410.0	505.1	1,735.4	169.5
Chambersburg-Waynesboro, PA MSA	154,614									
Includes Franklin County										
City of Chambersburg	20,757	56	2	4	19	31	601	72	512	17
City of Waynesboro	10,889	15	0	2	5	8	236	37	193	6
Total area actually reporting	100.0%	200	2	48	41	109	2,140	374	1,704	62
Rate per 100,000 inhabitants		129.4	1.3	31.0	26.5	70.5	1,384.1	241.9	1,102.1	40.1
Champaign-Urbana, IL MSA	239,744									
Includes Champaign, Ford, and Piatt Counties										
City of Champaign	87,543	634	5	83	109	437	2,623	446	2,054	123
City of Urbana	42,091	142	0	25	48	69	1,421	252	1,142	27
Total area actually reporting	99.0%	1,011	6	154	194	657	5,527	1,029	4,300	198
Estimated total	100.0%	1,016	6	155	195	660	5,565	1,035	4,330	200
Rate per 100,000 inhabitants		423.8	2.5	64.7	81.3	275.3	2,321.2	431.7	1,806.1	83.4
Charleston, WV MSA[5]	215,067									
Includes Boone, Clay, and Kanawha Counties										
City of Charleston	48,788	572	10	57	84	421	3,516	736	2,427	353
Total area actually reporting	91.6%	1,178	20	132	108	918				933
Estimated total	100.0%	1,225	20	140	112	953				966
Rate per 100,000 inhabitants		569.6	9.3	65.1	52.1	443.1				449.2
Charleston-North Charleston, SC MSA[5]	778,783									
Includes Berkeley,[5] Charleston, and Dorchester Counties										
City of Charleston	136,845	388	6	50	100	232	3,144	399	2,442	303
City of North Charleston	111,305	1,026	35	74	305	612	6,291	919	4,687	685
Total area actually reporting	99.4%	3,190	64	301	668	2,157			15,340	2,043
Estimated total	100.0%	3,209	64	303	671	2,171			15,466	2,054
Rate per 100,000 inhabitants		412.1	8.2	38.9	86.2	278.8			1,985.9	263.7
Charlotte-Concord-Gastonia, NC-SC MSA[4]	2,524,068									
Includes Cabarrus, Gaston, Iredell, Lincoln, Mecklenburg, Rowan, and Union Counties, NC[4] and Chester, Lancaster, and York Counties, SC										
City of Charlotte-Mecklenburg, NC[4]	914,609		86		2,017	3,965	34,894	6,416	25,856	2,622
City of Concord, NC[4]	91,756		1		31	62	1,791	293	1,433	65
City of Gastonia, NC[4]	76,191		4		158	405	3,714	587	2,865	262
City of Rock Hill, SC	74,053	469	9	51	95	314	3,007	365	2,506	136
Total area actually reporting	97.7%	10,337	132	534	2,864	6,807	68,955	13,155	51,285	4,515
Estimated total	100.0%	10,506	134	549	2,904	6,919	70,683	13,456	52,631	4,596
Rate per 100,000 inhabitants		416.2	5.3	21.8	115.1	274.1	2,800.4	533.1	2,085.2	182.1
Charlottesville, VA MSA	233,192									
Includes Albemarle, Buckingham, Fluvanna, Greene, and Nelson Counties and Charlottesville City										
City of Charlottesville	47,446	185	3	31	22	129	1,036	145	820	71
Total area actually reporting	100.0%	409	11	103	43	252	3,147	395	2,535	217
Rate per 100,000 inhabitants		175.4	4.7	44.2	18.4	108.1	1,349.5	169.4	1,087.1	93.1
Chattanooga, TN-GA MSA	556,437									
Includes Catoosa, Dade, and Walker Counties, GA and Hamilton, Marion, and Sequatchie Counties, TN										
City of Chattanooga, TN	178,753	1,905	31	120	330	1,424	10,700	1,540	7,818	1,342
Total area actually reporting	100.0%	3,101	37	202	426	2,436	18,886	3,182	13,510	2,194
Rate per 100,000 inhabitants		557.3	6.6	36.3	76.6	437.8	3,394.1	571.9	2,427.9	394.3
Cheyenne, WY MSA	97,494									
Includes Laramie County										
City of Cheyenne	64,730	209	2	29	34	144	2,265	264	1,817	184
Total area actually reporting	100.0%	288	5	40	35	208	2,772	377	2,154	241
Rate per 100,000 inhabitants		295.4	5.1	41.0	35.9	213.3	2,843.3	386.7	2,209.4	247.2
Chicago-Naperville-Elgin, IL-IN-WI MSA[3, 4]	9,525,454									
Includes the Metropolitan Divisions of Chicago-Naperville-Arlington Heights, IL; Elgin, IL; Gary, IN; and Lake County-Kenosha County, IL-WI										
City of Chicago, IL	2,706,171	29,737	653	1,762	11,887	15,435	88,324	12,912	63,834	11,578
City of Naperville, IL	147,934	136	1	22	33	80	1,716	129	1,540	47

Table 6. Crime in the United States, by Selected Metropolitan Statistical Area, 2017—Continued

(Number, percent, rate per 100,000 population.)

Area	Population	Violent crime	Murder and nonnegligent manslaughter	Rape[1]	Robbery	Aggravated assault	Property crime	Burglary	Larceny-theft	Motor vehicle theft
City of Elgin, IL	112,767	224	2	38	56	128	1,579	195	1,310	74
City of Gary, IN	75,808	471	48	32	192	199	2,581	678	1,481	422
City of Arlington Heights, IL	75,586	44	0	9	14	21	654	77	550	27
City of Evanston, IL	74,947	122	1	3	40	78	1,769	284	1,422	63
City of Schaumburg, IL	74,471	79	2	13	31	33	1,244	92	1,103	49
City of Skokie, IL	64,167	185	2	20	40	123	1,546	212	1,279	55
City of Des Plaines, IL	58,089	61	1	7	10	43	565	79	454	32
City of Hoffman Estates, IL	51,704	50	0	8	14	28	466	50	386	30
Total area actually reporting	97.3%		888	3,498	15,738		188,541	27,131	143,546	17,864
Estimated total	100.0%		895	3,574	15,877		192,857	27,767	146,931	18,159
Rate per 100,000 inhabitants			9.4	37.5	166.7		2,024.6	291.5	1,542.5	190.6
Chicago-Naperville-Arlington Heights, IL MD	7,313,953									
Includes Cook, DuPage, Grundy, Kendall, McHenry, and Will Counties										
Total area actually reporting	98.3%	37,400	780	2,888	14,501	19,231	154,261	22,184	116,450	15,627
Estimated total	100.0%	37,672	784	2,929	14,576	19,383	156,316	22,487	118,084	15,745
Rate per 100,000 inhabitants		515.1	10.7	40.0	199.3	265.0	2,137.2	307.5	1,614.5	215.3
Elgin, IL MD	639,123									
Includes DeKalb and Kane Counties										
Total area actually reporting	98.3%	1,145	11	200	214	720	8,115	985	6,792	338
Estimated total	100.0%	1,169	11	204	221	733	8,296	1,012	6,936	348
Rate per 100,000 inhabitants		182.9	1.7	31.9	34.6	114.7	1,298.0	158.3	1,085.2	54.4
Gary, IN MD[3,4]	700,701									
Includes Jasper, Lake, Newton, and Porter Counties										
Total area actually reporting	87.8%		73	141	637		14,518	2,131	10,968	1,419
Estimated total	100.0%		75	161	674		16,060	2,358	12,147	1,555
Rate per 100,000 inhabitants			10.7	23.0	96.2		2,292.0	336.5	1,733.5	221.9
Lake County-Kenosha County, IL-WI M.D.	871,677									
Includes Lake County, IL and Kenosha County, WI										
Total area actually reporting	96.2%	1,561	24	269	386	882	11,647	1,831	9,336	480
Estimated total	100.0%	1,633	25	280	406	922	12,185	1,910	9,764	511
Rate per 100,000 inhabitants		187.3	2.9	32.1	46.6	105.8	1,397.9	219.1	1,120.1	58.6
Chico, CA MSA	227,777									
Includes Butte County										
City of Chico	92,459	413	2	85	63	263	3,593	531	2,615	447
Total area actually reporting	100.0%	921	7	182	143	589	7,280	1,599	4,740	941
Rate per 100,000 inhabitants		404.3	3.1	79.9	62.8	258.6	3,196.1	702.0	2,081.0	413.1
Cincinnati, OH-KY-IN MSA[2,4]	2,177,816									
Includes Dearborn, Ohio, and Union Counties, IN; Boone, Bracken, Campbell, Gallatin, Grant, Kenton, and Pendleton Counties, KY; and Brown, Butler, Clermont, Hamilton, and Warren Counties, OH										
City of Cincinnati, OH	299,116	2,833	70	292	1,196	1,275	15,105	3,448	10,172	1,485
Total area actually reporting	94.9%	5,598	109	970	2,006	2,513	51,309	9,555	38,380	3,374
Estimated total	100.0%	5,770	111	1,001	2,045	2,613	53,156	9,874	39,779	3,503
Rate per 100,000 inhabitants		264.9	5.1	46.0	93.9	120.0	2,440.8	453.4	1,826.6	160.8
Clarksville, TN-KY MSA	286,499									
Includes Christian and Trigg Counties, KY and Montgomery County, TN										
City of Clarksville, TN	153,294	956	14	80	127	735	4,411	743	3,427	241
Total area actually reporting	100.0%	1,198	15	122	176	885	7,045	1,396	5,229	420
Rate per 100,000 inhabitants		418.2	5.2	42.6	61.4	308.9	2,459.0	487.3	1,825.1	146.6
Cleveland, TN MSA	122,405									
Includes Bradley and Polk Counties										
City of Cleveland	44,778	390	1	27	53	309	2,515	369	1,921	225
Total area actually reporting	100.0%	641	4	41	62	534	3,875	701	2,713	461
Rate per 100,000 inhabitants		523.7	3.3	33.5	50.7	436.3	3,165.7	572.7	2,216.4	376.6
Cleveland-Elyria, OH MSA[2,3,4]	2,057,704									
Includes Cuyahoga, Geauga, Lake,[3,4] Lorain, and Medina Counties										
City of Cleveland	385,351	5,999	107	497	2,697	2,698	18,944	5,853	9,696	3,395
City of Elyria	53,586	191	3	39	64	85	1,146	248	842	56
Total area actually reporting	89.1%		143	812	3,480		38,814	9,416	24,784	4,614
Estimated total	100.0%		148	888	3,584		43,432	10,118	28,483	4,831
Rate per 100,000 inhabitants			7.2	43.2	174.2		2,110.7	491.7	1,384.2	234.8
Coeur d'Alene, ID MSA[3]	158,326									
Includes Kootenai County[3]										
City of Coeur d'Alene	51,364	197	4	49	11	133	1,142	180	901	61
Total area actually reporting	100.0%	380	5	82	21	272			2,347	156
Rate per 100,000 inhabitants		240.0	3.2	51.8	13.3	171.8			1,482.4	98.5
College Station-Bryan, TX MSA[2]	259,198									
Includes Brazos, Burleson, and Robertson[2] Counties										

Table 6. Crime in the United States, by Selected Metropolitan Statistical Area, 2017—Continued

(Number, percent, rate per 100,000 population.)

Area	Population	Violent crime	Murder and nonnegligent manslaughter	Rape[1]	Robbery	Aggravated assault	Property crime	Burglary	Larceny-theft	Motor vehicle theft
City of College Station	115,357	230	1	53	49	127	2,304	300	1,887	117
City of Bryan	84,438	363	4	53	69	237	2,028	348	1,557	123
Total area actually reporting	99.1%	734	8	136	128	462	5,474	903	4,283	288
Estimated total	100.0%	740	8	137	129	466	5,528	911	4,325	292
Rate per 100,000 inhabitants		285.5	3.1	52.9	49.8	179.8	2,132.7	351.5	1,668.6	112.7
Colorado Springs, CO MSA	720,520									
Includes El Paso and Teller Counties										
City of Colorado Springs	472,958	2,479	29	489	482	1,479	15,214	2,508	10,571	2,135
Total area actually reporting	99.9%	3,110	33	620	534	1,923	18,822	3,097	13,184	2,541
Estimated total	100.0%	3,111	33	620	534	1,924	18,840	3,099	13,198	2,543
Rate per 100,000 inhabitants		431.8	4.6	86.0	74.1	267.0	2,614.8	430.1	1,831.7	352.9
Columbia, MO MSA	179,032									
Includes Boone County										
City of Columbia	122,585	610	9	115	117	369	3,597	505	2,826	266
Total area actually reporting	100.0%	735	10	128	129	468	4,672	641	3,673	358
Rate per 100,000 inhabitants		410.5	5.6	71.5	72.1	261.4	2,609.6	358.0	2,051.6	200.0
Columbia, SC MSA[5]	826,594									
Includes Calhoun, Fairfield, Kershaw, Lexington,[5] Richland, and Saluda Counties										
City of Columbia	134,957	991	10	66	273	642	7,134	954	5,389	791
Total area actually reporting	100.0%	4,620	59	372	808	3,381		4,831		3,425
Rate per 100,000 inhabitants		558.9	7.1	45.0	97.8	409.0		584.4		414.4
Columbus, GA-AL MSA	311,195									
Includes Russell County, AL and Chattahoochee, Harris, Marion, and Muscogee Counties, GA										
City of Columbus, GA	198,832	1,303	35	71	394	803	8,820	2,131	5,985	704
Total area actually reporting	96.3%	1,605	44	126	470	965	10,877	2,659	7,304	914
Estimated total	100.0%	1,640	45	128	480	987	11,157	2,714	7,500	943
Rate per 100,000 inhabitants		527.0	14.5	41.1	154.2	317.2	3,585.2	872.1	2,410.1	303.0
Columbus, IN MSA[4]	82,293									
Includes Bartholomew County										
City of Columbus[4]	47,322		1		18	4	1,904	202	1,537	165
Total area actually reporting	100.0%	108	2	26	42	38	2,545	358	1,924	263
Rate per 100,000 inhabitants		131.2	2.4	31.6	51.0	46.2	3,092.6	435.0	2,338.0	319.6
Columbus, OH MSA	2,070,524									
Includes Delaware, Fairfield, Franklin, Hocking, Licking, Madison, Morrow, Perry, Pickaway, and Union Counties										
City of Columbus	872,205	4,478	142	919	1,963	1,454	34,408	7,111	23,121	4,176
Total area actually reporting	93.9%	5,836	161	1,310	2,369	1,996	56,924	10,722	41,013	5,189
Estimated total	100.0%	6,018	164	1,351	2,421	2,082	59,333	11,122	42,904	5,307
Rate per 100,000 inhabitants		290.7	7.9	65.2	116.9	100.6	2,865.6	537.2	2,072.1	256.3
Corpus Christi, TX MSA	458,865									
Includes Aransas, Nueces, and San Patricio Counties										
City of Corpus Christi	329,256	2,313	21	232	470	1,590	11,739	2,232	8,776	731
Total area actually reporting	100.0%	2,900	30	289	520	2,061	15,495	3,202	11,368	925
Rate per 100,000 inhabitants		632.0	6.5	63.0	113.3	449.2	3,376.8	697.8	2,477.4	201.6
Corvallis, OR MSA	90,142									
Includes Benton County										
City of Corvallis	57,576	75	2	20	13	40	1,440	153	1,229	58
Total area actually reporting	100.0%	125	3	34	19	69	2,115	226	1,803	86
Rate per 100,000 inhabitants		138.7	3.3	37.7	21.1	76.5	2,346.3	250.7	2,000.2	95.4
Crestview-Fort Walton Beach-Destin, FL MSA	273,416									
Includes Okaloosa and Walton Counties										
City of Crestview	24,022	117	0	17	16	84	868	189	605	74
City of Fort Walton Beach	22,413	73	1	14	16	42	617	92	460	65
Total area actually reporting	99.7%	904	7	117	93	687	5,970	1,216	4,336	418
Estimated total	100.0%	907	7	117	94	689	5,993	1,219	4,354	420
Rate per 100,000 inhabitants		331.7	2.6	42.8	34.4	252.0	2,191.9	445.8	1,592.4	153.6
Cumberland, MD-WV MSA	98,718									
Includes Allegany County, MD and Mineral County, WV										
City of Cumberland, MD	19,842	150	1	7	41	101	1,240	248	976	16
Total area actually reporting	100.0%	280	2	24	62	192	2,518	535	1,923	60
Rate per 100,000 inhabitants		283.6	2.0	24.3	62.8	194.5	2,550.7	541.9	1,948.0	60.8
Dallas-Fort Worth-Arlington, TX MSA[2, 3]	7,365,764									
Includes the Metropolitan Divisions of Dallas-Plano-Irving and Fort Worth-Arlington										
City of Dallas	1,338,551	10,369	167	831	4,377	4,994	42,634	9,874	24,847	7,913
City of Fort Worth	873,069	4,891	70	569	1,286	2,966	28,072	5,116	20,250	2,706
City of Arlington[2]	397,377	2,054	19	254	576	1,205	12,707	1,801	9,546	1,360

Table 6. Crime in the United States, by Selected Metropolitan Statistical Area, 2017—Continued

(Number, percent, rate per 100,000 population.)

Area	Population	Violent crime	Murder and nonnegligent manslaughter	Rape[1]	Robbery	Aggravated assault	Property crime	Burglary	Larceny-theft	Motor vehicle theft
City of Plano	290,413	435	15	81	119	220	5,035	728	3,968	339
City of Irving	242,062	549	8	54	228	259	6,147	969	4,467	711
City of Denton	136,836	416	1	120	94	201	3,091	426	2,367	298
City of Richardson	115,824	193	3	25	97	68	2,295	389	1,717	189
Total area actually reporting	99.9%	27,188	380	3,485	8,869	14,454			122,870	20,323
Estimated total	100.0%	27,204	380	3,487	8,873	14,464			122,971	20,333
Rate per 100,000 inhabitants		369.3	5.2	47.3	120.5	196.4			1,669.5	276.0
Dallas-Plano-Irving, TX MD[2,3]	4,887,235									
Includes Collin, Dallas, Denton, Ellis, Hunt, Kaufman, and Rockwall Counties										
Total area actually reporting	99.9%	17,925	262	2,194	6,547	8,922			75,859	14,516
Estimated total	100.0%	17,938	262	2,196	6,550	8,930			75,944	14,524
Rate per 100,000 inhabitants		367.0	5.4	44.9	134.0	182.7			1,553.9	297.2
Fort Worth-Arlington, TX MD[2]	2,478,529									
Includes Hood,[2] Johnson, Parker, Somervell, Tarrant, and Wise Counties										
Total area actually reporting	99.9%	9,263	118	1,291	2,322	5,532	63,640	10,822	47,011	5,807
Estimated total	100.0%	9,266	118	1,291	2,323	5,534	63,661	10,825	47,027	5,809
Rate per 100,000 inhabitants		373.9	4.8	52.1	93.7	223.3	2,568.5	436.8	1,897.4	234.4
Includes Lawrence and Morgan Counties										
City of Decatur	55,836	112	0	7	25	80	2,451	434	1,883	134
Total area actually reporting	98.4%	246	2	36	40	168	3,660	791	2,631	238
Estimated total	100.0%	256	2	37	42	175	3,750	809	2,697	244
Rate per 100,000 inhabitants		166.9	1.3	24.1	27.4	114.1	2,445.5	527.6	1,758.8	159.1
Dalton, GA MSA	144,348									
Includes Murray and Whitfield Counties										
City of Dalton	34,228	108	0	16	17	75	981	126	782	73
Total area actually reporting	99.6%	315	2	38	23	252	2,941	566	2,147	228
Estimated total	100.0%	318	2	38	24	254	2,965	569	2,166	230
Rate per 100,000 inhabitants		220.3	1.4	26.3	16.6	176.0	2,054.1	394.2	1,500.5	159.3
Danville, IL MSA	77,582									
Includes Vermilion County										
City of Danville	31,368	546	10	36	88	412	1,833	456	1,306	71
Total area actually reporting	98.4%	696	10	87	96	503	2,651	728	1,817	106
Estimated total	100.0%	699	10	87	97	505	2,671	731	1,833	107
Rate per 100,000 inhabitants		901.0	12.9	112.1	125.0	650.9	3,442.8	942.2	2,362.7	137.9
Daphne-Fairhope-Foley, AL MSA	212,998									
Includes Baldwin County										
City of Daphne	26,669	34	0	1	9	24	556	74	464	18
City of Fairhope	20,180	52	0	6	4	42	606	89	490	27
City of Foley	18,032	47	0	4	9	34	782	65	693	24
Total area actually reporting	100.0%	532	4	42	54	432	4,662	716	3,694	252
Rate per 100,000 inhabitants		249.8	1.9	19.7	25.4	202.8	2,188.8	336.2	1,734.3	118.3
Davenport-Moline-Rock Island, IA-IL MSA	382,517									
Includes Henry, Mercer, and Rock Island Counties, IL and Scott County, IA										
City of Davenport, IA	103,063	750	13	90	203	444	5,249	1,108	3,586	555
City of Moline, IL	42,042	224	0	31	20	173	1,363	234	1,083	46
City of Rock Island, IL	38,079	133	3	5	10	115	1,060	198	754	108
Total area actually reporting	96.0%	1,520	18	212	266	1,024	10,659	2,175	7,613	871
Estimated total	100.0%	1,546	18	217	270	1,041	10,839	2,217	7,740	882
Rate per 100,000 inhabitants		404.2	4.7	56.7	70.6	272.1	2,833.6	579.6	2,023.4	230.6
Dayton, OH MSA[4]	802,856									
Includes Greene, Miami, and Montgomery Counties										
City of Dayton	140,171	1,232	30	122	393	687	6,083	1,779	3,688	616
Total area actually reporting	96.9%	2,326	42	439	722	1,123	19,998	4,079	14,356	1,563
Estimated total	100.0%	2,363	43	447	733	1,140	20,504	4,156	14,761	1,587
Rate per 100,000 inhabitants		294.3	5.4	55.7	91.3	142.0	2,553.9	517.7	1,838.6	197.7
Decatur, AL MSA	151,897									
Includes Lawrence and Morgan Counties										
City of Decatur	54,958	199	9	20	53	117	2,284	431	1,680	173
Total area actually reporting	99.3%	463	11	45	61	346	3,423	791	2,345	287
Estimated total	100.0%	468	11	45	62	350	3,460	797	2,373	290
Rate per 100,000 inhabitants		308.1	7.2	29.6	40.8	230.4	2,277.9	524.7	1,562.2	190.9
Decatur, IL MSA	105,916									
Includes Macon County										
City of Decatur	72,153	443	10	52	106	275	2,394	731	1,571	92
Total area actually reporting	99.0%	503	10	66	113	314	2,818	818	1,896	104
Estimated total	100.0%	505	10	66	114	315	2,836	821	1,910	105
Rate per 100,000 inhabitants		476.8	9.4	62.3	107.6	297.4	2,677.6	775.1	1,803.3	99.1
Deltona-Daytona Beach-Ormond Beach, FL MSA	647,702									
Includes Flagler and Volusia Counties										
City of Daytona Beach	67,564	748	12	23	82	631	3,819	497	3,027	295

Table 6. Crime in the United States, by Selected Metropolitan Statistical Area, 2017—Continued

(Number, percent, rate per 100,000 population.)

Area	Population	Violent crime	Murder and nonnegligent manslaughter	Rape[1]	Robbery	Aggravated assault	Property crime	Burglary	Larceny-theft	Motor vehicle theft
City of Ormond Beach	42,625	202	0	10	25	167	1,386	280	1,003	103
Total area actually reporting	100.0%	2,298	32	136	340	1,790	16,087	2,655	12,258	1,174
Rate per 100,000 inhabitants		354.8	4.9	21.0	52.5	276.4	2,483.7	409.9	1,892.5	181.3
Denver-Aurora-Lakewood, CO MSA[3]	2,895,448									
Includes Adams, Arapahoe, Broomfield, Clear Creek, Denver, Douglas, Elbert, Gilpin, Jefferson, and Park Counties										
City of Denver	706,616	4,774	59	699	1,232	2,784	25,912	4,331	16,021	5,560
City of Aurora	368,018	2,239	30	319	679	1,211	11,054	1,671	7,194	2,189
City of Lakewood	156,344	1,007	5	151	208	643	7,596	911	5,492	1,193
City of Broomfield	68,158	84	1	23	7	53	1,790	197	1,400	193
Total area actually reporting	99.9%	11,976	133	2,102	2,694	7,047			58,868	15,209
Estimated total	100.0%	11,985	133	2,104	2,695	7,053			58,944	15,222
Rate per 100,000 inhabitants		413.9	4.6	72.7	93.1	243.6			2,035.7	525.7
Detroit-Warren-Dearborn, MI MSA	4,309,631									
Includes the Metropolitan Divisions of Detroit-Dearborn-Livonia and Warren-Troy-Farmington Hills										
City of Detroit	670,792	13,796	267	697	2,639	10,193	30,458	8,258	14,045	8,155
City of Warren	135,303	681	7	125	97	452	2,900	659	1,804	437
City of Dearborn	93,889	256	0	38	51	167	2,272	218	1,776	278
City of Livonia	93,603	108	0	16	16	76	1,431	165	1,137	129
City of Troy	84,086	55	0	14	6	35	1,275	94	1,114	67
City of Farmington Hills	81,359	93	1	15	16	61	915	119	719	77
City of Southfield	73,324	151	1	18	37	95	2,032	315	1,454	263
City of Taylor	60,882	348	4	39	58	247	1,480	326	973	181
City of Pontiac	59,731	644	4	61	97	482	1,510	468	820	222
City of Novi	59,895	43	0	11	6	26	617	42	543	32
Total area actually reporting	100.0%	23,445	339	2,277	4,040	16,789	83,845	17,022	53,177	13,646
Rate per 100,000 inhabitants		544.0	7.9	52.8	93.7	389.6	1,945.5	395.0	1,233.9	316.6
Detroit-Dearborn-Livonia, MI MD	1,742,865									
Includes Wayne County										
Total area actually reporting	100.0%	17,965	304	1,257	3,360	13,044	51,921	11,710	29,411	10,800
Rate per 100,000 inhabitants		1,030.8	17.4	72.1	192.8	748.4	2,979.1	671.9	1,687.5	619.7
Warren-Troy-Farmington Hills, MI MD	2,566,766									
Includes Lapeer, Livingston, Macomb, Oakland, and St. Clair Counties										
Total area actually reporting	100.0%	5,480	35	1,020	680	3,745	31,924	5,312	23,766	2,846
Rate per 100,000 inhabitants		213.5	1.4	39.7	26.5	145.9	1,243.7	207.0	925.9	110.9
Dothan, AL MSA	148,079									
Includes Geneva, Henry, and Houston Counties										
City of Dothan	67,653	572	6	35	67	464	2,686	615	1,875	196
Total area actually reporting	99.4%	841	8	66	87	680	4,079	946	2,822	311
Estimated total	100.0%	845	8	66	88	683	4,107	951	2,843	313
Rate per 100,000 inhabitants		570.6	5.4	44.6	59.4	461.2	2,773.5	642.2	1,919.9	211.4
Dover, DE MSA	177,027									
Includes Kent County										
City of Dover	38,084	264	4	14	38	208	1,671	52	1,558	61
Total area actually reporting	100.0%	757	6	81	108	562	4,058	534	3,379	145
Rate per 100,000 inhabitants		427.6	3.4	45.8	61.0	317.5	2,292.3	301.6	1,908.7	81.9
Dubuque, IA MSA	97,394									
Includes Dubuque County										
City of Dubuque	58,674	166	2	40	16	108	1,606	333	1,210	63
Total area actually reporting	100.0%	188	2	50	16	120	1,805	398	1,329	78
Rate per 100,000 inhabitants		193.0	2.1	51.3	16.4	123.2	1,853.3	408.6	1,364.6	80.1
Duluth, MN-WI MSA	280,022									
Includes Carlton and St. Louis Counties, MN and Douglas County, WI										
City of Duluth, MN	86,306	279	1	31	66	181	3,819	506	3,091	222
Total area actually reporting	100.0%	565	4	100	89	372	8,421	1,263	6,644	514
Rate per 100,000 inhabitants		201.8	1.4	35.7	31.8	132.8	3,007.3	451.0	2,372.7	183.6
Durham-Chapel Hill, NC MSA[4]	569,875									
Includes Chatham, Durham, Orange and Person Counties[4]										
City of Durham[4]	269,088		23		852	1,257	10,296	2,334	7,200	762
City of Chapel Hill[4]	59,553		1		40	38	1,284	251	980	53
Total area actually reporting	100.0%		31		1,003	1,679	16,298	3,967	11,324	1,007
Rate per 100,000 inhabitants			5.4		176.0	294.6	2,859.9	696.1	1,987.1	176.7
East Stroudsburg, PA MSA	165,582									
Includes Monroe County										
Total area actually reporting	100.0%	428	8	73	71	276	3,213	587	2,534	92
Rate per 100,000 inhabitants		258.5	4.8	44.1	42.9	166.7	1,940.4	354.5	1,530.4	55.6
Eau Claire, WI MSA[3]	167,499									
Includes Chippewa and Eau Claire[3] Counties										

Table 6. Crime in the United States, by Selected Metropolitan Statistical Area, 2017—Continued

(Number, percent, rate per 100,000 population.)

Area	Population	Violent crime	Murder and nonnegligent manslaughter	Rape[1]	Robbery	Aggravated assault	Property crime	Burglary	Larceny-theft	Motor vehicle theft
City of Eau Claire	68,687	162	1	32	44	85	2,000	385	1,531	84
Total area actually reporting	100.0%		3	55	52		3,158	576	2,433	149
Rate per 100,000 inhabitants			1.8	32.8	31.0		1,885.4	343.9	1,452.5	89.0
El Centro, CA MSA	181,724									
Includes Imperial County										
City of El Centro	44,458	185	4	15	45	121	1,820	409	1,285	126
Total area actually reporting	95.9%	628	7	45	87	489	4,836	1,293	3,017	526
Estimated total	100.0%	653	7	47	95	504	5,012	1,325	3,133	554
Rate per 100,000 inhabitants		359.3	3.9	25.9	52.3	277.3	2,758.0	729.1	1,724.0	304.9
Elizabethtown-Fort Knox, KY MSA	149,535									
Includes Hardin, Larue, and Meade Counties										
City of Elizabethtown	30,065	61	1	11	13	36	469	169	244	56
Total area actually reporting	100.0%	169	5	31	37	96	1,810	519	1,098	193
Rate per 100,000 inhabitants		113.0	3.3	20.7	24.7	64.2	1,210.4	347.1	734.3	129.1
Elmira, NY MSA	86,084									
Includes Chemung County										
City of Elmira	27,740	80	2	2	29	47	863	126	717	20
Total area actually reporting	100.0%	143	4	28	32	79	1,417	185	1,198	34
Rate per 100,000 inhabitants		166.1	4.6	32.5	37.2	91.8	1,646.1	214.9	1,391.7	39.5
El Paso, TX MSA	847,071									
Includes El Paso and Hudspeth Counties										
City of El Paso	688,667	2,609	19	371	400	1,819	12,526	1,297	10,429	800
Total area actually reporting	100.0%	3,018	21	441	432	2,124	14,287	1,604	11,784	899
Rate per 100,000 inhabitants		356.3	2.5	52.1	51.0	250.7	1,686.6	189.4	1,391.1	106.1
Enid, OK MSA	62,575									
Includes Garfield County										
City of Enid	51,257	174	0	34	21	119	1,751	417	1,242	92
Total area actually reporting	100.0%	189	0	36	21	132	1,890	458	1,328	104
Rate per 100,000 inhabitants		302.0	0.0	57.5	33.6	210.9	3,020.4	731.9	2,122.3	166.2
Erie, PA MSA	275,639									
Includes Erie County										
City of Erie	98,071	306	6	32	98	170	2,258	531	1,619	108
Total area actually reporting	100.0%	643	12	66	114	451	4,907	911	3,814	182
Rate per 100,000 inhabitants		233.3	4.4	23.9	41.4	163.6	1,780.2	330.5	1,383.7	66.0
Eugene, OR MSA[2]	372,953									
Includes Lane County										
City of Eugene	168,310	651	3	101	177	370	6,276	1,129	4,602	545
Total area actually reporting	99.1%	1,235	8	172	249	806	11,248	1,925	8,349	974
Estimated total	100.0%	1,242	8	174	250	810	11,334	1,935	8,414	985
Rate per 100,000 inhabitants		333.0	2.1	46.7	67.0	217.2	3,039.0	518.8	2,256.0	264.1
Evansville, IN-KY MSA	317,010									
Includes Posey, Vanderburgh, and Warrick Counties, IN and Henderson County, KY										
City of Evansville	119,371	825	20	75	185	545	5,979	863	4,641	475
Total area actually reporting	98.0%	1,167	26	117	231	793	8,672	1,442	6,569	661
Estimated total	100.0%	1,185	26	119	235	805	8,831	1,460	6,698	673
Rate per 100,000 inhabitants		373.8	8.2	37.5	74.1	253.9	2,785.7	460.6	2,112.9	212.3
Fairbanks, AK MSA	35,185									
Includes Fairbanks North Star Borough										
City of Fairbanks	32,937	205	10	24	40	131	1,493	164	1,121	208
Total area actually reporting	100.0%	214	10	26	41	137	1,641	170	1,255	216
Rate per 100,000 inhabitants		608.2	28.4	73.9	116.5	389.4	4,663.9	483.2	3,566.9	613.9
Fargo, ND-MN MSA	239,227									
Includes Clay County, MN and Cass County, ND										
City of Fargo, ND	123,430	497	3	83	68	343	3,870	593	2,975	302
Total area actually reporting	100.0%	670	4	133	85	448	5,755	902	4,370	483
Rate per 100,000 inhabitants		280.1	1.7	55.6	35.5	187.3	2,405.7	377.0	1,826.7	201.9
Farmington, NM MSA	112,964									
Includes San Juan County										
City of Farmington	40,940	519	3	62	54	400	1,971	492	1,326	153
Total area actually reporting	100.0%	1,250	5	133	66	1,046	3,144	792	2,110	242
Rate per 100,000 inhabitants		1,106.5	4.4	117.7	58.4	926.0	2,783.2	701.1	1,867.9	214.2
Fayetteville, NC MSA[4]	383,425									
Includes Cumberland and Hoke Counties[4]										
City of Fayetteville[4]	205,432		24		292	1,105	8,811	1,818	6,578	415
Total area actually reporting	96.5%		31		347	1,243	11,022	2,464	8,084	474
Estimated total	100.0%		31		356	1,265	11,401	2,533	8,378	490
Rate per 100,000 inhabitants			8.1		92.8	329.9	2,973.5	660.6	2,185.0	127.8
Flagstaff, AZ MSA	141,844									
Includes Coconino County										

Table 6. Crime in the United States, by Selected Metropolitan Statistical Area, 2017—Continued

(Number, percent, rate per 100,000 population.)

Area	Population	Violent crime	Murder and nonnegligent manslaughter	Rape[1]	Robbery	Aggravated assault	Property crime	Burglary	Larceny-theft	Motor vehicle theft
City of Flagstaff	72,388	307	7	35	57	208	2,729	161	2,486	82
Total area actually reporting	100.0%	545	11	78	62	394	3,944	356	3,455	133
Rate per 100,000 inhabitants		384.2	7.8	55.0	43.7	277.8	2,780.5	251.0	2,435.8	93.8
Flint, MI MSA	406,927									
Includes Genesee County										
City of Flint	96,605	1,879	37	104	272	1,466	2,632	961	1,397	274
Estimated total	100.0%	2,902	48	293	412	2,149	7,752	1,901	5,274	577
Rate per 100,000 inhabitants		713.2	11.8	72.0	101.2	528.1	1,905.0	467.2	1,296.1	141.8
Florence, SC MSA	206,228									
Includes Darlington and Florence Counties										
City of Florence	38,449	487	5	27	61	394	2,728	353	2,242	133
Total area actually reporting	98.2%	1,707	48	111	208	1,340	8,997	1,981	6,454	562
Estimated total	100.0%	1,724	48	113	211	1,352	9,127	1,999	6,557	571
Rate per 100,000 inhabitants		836.0	23.3	54.8	102.3	655.6	4,425.7	969.3	3,179.5	276.9
Florence-Muscle Shoals, AL MSA	146,328									
Includes Colbert and Lauderdale Counties										
City of Florence	40,059	189	1	30	40	118	1,703	319	1,239	145
City of Muscle Shoals	13,939	81	1	3	5	72	637	121	458	58
Total area actually reporting	99.8%	488	2	68	65	353	3,601	749	2,499	353
Estimated total	100.0%	489	2	68	65	354	3,611	751	2,506	354
Rate per 100,000 inhabitants		334.2	1.4	46.5	44.4	241.9	2,467.7	513.2	1,712.6	241.9
Fond du Lac, WI MSA	102,243									
Includes Fond du Lac County										
City of Fond du Lac	42,929	110	1	28	19	62	901	82	788	31
Total area actually reporting	100.0%	148	2	42	19	85	1,225	150	1,027	48
Rate per 100,000 inhabitants		144.8	2.0	41.1	18.6	83.1	1,198.1	146.7	1,004.5	46.9
Fort Collins, CO MSA	345,764									
Includes Larimer County										
City of Fort Collins	167,633	369	6	45	42	276	4,250	457	3,586	207
Total area actually reporting	100.0%	829	6	147	76	600	7,755	937	6,394	424
Rate per 100,000 inhabitants		239.8	1.7	42.5	22.0	173.5	2,242.9	271.0	1,849.2	122.6
Fort Smith, AR-OK MSA	281,048									
Includes Crawford and Sebastian Counties, AR and Le Flore and Sequoyah Counties, OK										
City of Fort Smith, AR	88,437	787	7	71	107	602	4,511	832	3,345	334
Total area actually reporting	99.7%	1,419	10	160	128	1,121	8,268	1,837	5,857	574
Estimated total	100.0%	1,423	10	161	128	1,124	8,289	1,842	5,872	575
Rate per 100,000 inhabitants		506.3	3.6	57.3	45.5	399.9	2,949.3	655.4	2,089.3	204.6
Fort Wayne, IN MSA[4, 5]	434,895									
Includes Allen, Wells, and Whitley Counties										
City of Fort Wayne	266,259	952	37	136	299	480	8,466	1,308	6,626	532
Total area actually reporting	92.7%	1,176	39	180	337	620		1,565		640
Estimated total	100.0%	1,233	39	187	347	660		1,648		687
Rate per 100,000 inhabitants		283.5	9.0	43.0	79.8	151.8		378.9		158.0
Fresno, CA MSA	986,951									
Includes Fresno County										
City of Fresno	526,371	2,974	56	174	958	1,786	20,220	3,649	13,782	2,789
Total area actually reporting	100.0%	5,747	85	336	1,214	4,112	30,470	6,757	19,322	4,391
Rate per 100,000 inhabitants		582.3	8.6	34.0	123.0	416.6	3,087.3	684.6	1,957.7	444.9
Gadsden, AL MSA	102,194									
Includes Etowah County										
City of Gadsden	35,665	613	3	23	63	524	2,641	497	1,914	230
Total area actually reporting	93.6%	800	6	41	68	685	3,648	780	2,528	340
Estimated total	100.0%	834	7	44	73	710	3,864	817	2,690	357
Rate per 100,000 inhabitants		816.1	6.8	43.1	71.4	694.8	3,781.0	799.5	2,632.2	349.3
Gainesville, FL MSA	284,282									
Includes Alachua and Gilchrist Counties										
City of Gainesville	132,777	952	4	164	176	608	4,778	500	3,915	363
Total area actually reporting	99.3%	1,670	9	249	296	1,116	7,465	1,158	5,779	528
Estimated total	100.0%	1,678	9	250	298	1,121	7,524	1,166	5,825	533
Rate per 100,000 inhabitants		590.3	3.2	87.9	104.8	394.3	2,646.7	410.2	2,049.0	187.5
Gainesville, GA MSA	199,799									
Includes Hall County										
City of Gainesville	40,836	157	2	19	34	102	1,404	209	1,091	104
Total area actually reporting	100.0%	442	5	71	70	296	3,654	622	2,663	369
Rate per 100,000 inhabitants		221.2	2.5	35.5	35.0	148.1	1,828.8	311.3	1,332.8	184.7
Gettysburg, PA MSA	102,366									
Includes Adams County										
City of Gettysburg	7,716	37	0	4	7	26	136	15	120	1
Total area actually reporting	100.0%	144	1	27	14	102	770	130	603	37
Rate per 100,000 inhabitants		140.7	1.0	26.4	13.7	99.6	752.2	127.0	589.1	36.1

Table 6. Crime in the United States, by Selected Metropolitan Statistical Area, 2017—Continued

(Number, percent, rate per 100,000 population.)

Area	Population	Violent crime	Murder and nonnegligent manslaughter	Rape[1]	Robbery	Aggravated assault	Property crime	Burglary	Larceny-theft	Motor vehicle theft
Glens Falls, NY MSA	126,220									
Includes Warren and Washington Counties										
City of Glens Falls	14,268	29	2	1	3	23	190	28	156	6
Total area actually reporting	98.0%	179	5	77	13	84	1,372	200	1,134	38
Estimated total	100.0%	182	5	77	14	86	1,409	204	1,166	39
Rate per 100,000 inhabitants		144.2	4.0	61.0	11.1	68.1	1,116.3	161.6	923.8	30.9
Goldsboro, NC MSA[4]	124,619									
Includes Wayne County[4]										
City of Goldsboro[4]	35,824		10		75	184	1,796	337	1,399	60
Total area actually reporting	97.7%		11		113	339	3,515	997	2,310	208
Estimated total	100.0%		11		115	344	3,595	1,012	2,372	211
Rate per 100,000 inhabitants			8.8		92.3	276.0	2,884.8	812.1	1,903.4	169.3
Grand Forks, ND-MN MSA	101,846									
Includes Polk County, MN and Grand Forks County, ND										
City of Grand Forks, ND	58,090	183	0	29	32	122	1,720	265	1,331	124
Total area actually reporting	100.0%	252	1	51	35	165	2,450	394	1,910	146
Rate per 100,000 inhabitants		247.4	1.0	50.1	34.4	162.0	2,405.6	386.9	1,875.4	143.4
Grand Junction, CO MSA	150,129									
Includes Mesa County										
City of Grand Junction	62,352	361	2	71	25	263	2,849	356	2,324	169
Total area actually reporting	99.2%	610	4	137	41	428	4,405	680	3,407	318
Estimated total	100.0%	613	4	138	41	430	4,438	684	3,432	322
Rate per 100,000 inhabitants		408.3	2.7	91.9	27.3	286.4	2,956.1	455.6	2,286.0	214.5
Grand Rapids-Wyoming, MI MSA	1,059,630									
Includes Barry, Kent, Montcalm, and Ottawa Counties										
City of Grand Rapids	197,868	1,408	12	141	351	904	4,102	763	2,976	363
City of Wyoming	76,153	356	3	74	83	196	1,666	235	1,221	210
Total area actually reporting	99.6%	3,422	30	828	554	2,010	16,004	2,762	12,232	1,010
Estimated total	100.0%	3,433	30	830	556	2,017	16,070	2,772	12,283	1,015
Rate per 100,000 inhabitants		324.0	2.8	78.3	52.5	190.3	1,516.6	261.6	1,159.2	95.8
Grants Pass, OR MSA[2]	86,520									
Includes Josephine County[2]										
City of Grants Pass	38,082	103	0	17	15	71	1,627	156	1,264	207
Total area actually reporting	100.0%	191	5	28	18	140	2,044	265	1,415	364
Rate per 100,000 inhabitants		220.8	5.8	32.4	20.8	161.8	2,362.5	306.3	1,635.5	420.7
Great Falls, MT MSA	81,700									
Includes Cascade County										
City of Great Falls	59,167	246	3	20	30	193	3,023	284	2,539	200
Total area actually reporting	100.0%	275	5	23	30	217	3,166	315	2,636	215
Rate per 100,000 inhabitants		336.6	6.1	28.2	36.7	265.6	3,875.2	385.6	3,226.4	263.2
Greeley, CO MSA	301,211									
Includes Weld County										
City of Greeley	105,906	449	5	75	57	312	2,714	428	2,020	266
Total area actually reporting	99.6%	769	9	113	85	562	5,205	848	3,812	545
Estimated total	100.0%	772	9	114	85	564	5,239	852	3,838	549
Rate per 100,000 inhabitants		256.3	3.0	37.8	28.2	187.2	1,739.3	282.9	1,274.2	182.3
Green Bay, WI MSA[2]	320,287									
Includes Brown, Kewaunee, and Oconto Counties										
City of Green Bay	105,331	498	0	76	65	357	2,147	321	1,738	88
Total area actually reporting	91.2%	687	0	127	73	487	4,180	530	3,509	141
Estimated total	100.0%	712	0	133	75	504	4,366	571	3,642	153
Rate per 100,000 inhabitants		222.3	0.0	41.5	23.4	157.4	1,363.2	178.3	1,137.1	47.8
Greensboro-High Point, NC MSA[4]	763,106									
Includes Guilford, Randolph, and Rockingham Counties[4]										
City of Greensboro[4]	290,051		46		664	1,394	10,332	2,062	7,424	846
City of High Point[4]	112,368		20		206	530	4,161	754	3,127	280
Total area actually reporting	99.5%		83		1,017	2,448	21,988	4,800	15,692	1,496
Estimated total	100.0%		83		1,020	2,455	22,100	4,820	15,779	1,501
Rate per 100,000 inhabitants			10.9		133.7	321.7	2,896.1	631.6	2,067.7	196.7
Greenville, NC MSA[4]	179,034									
Includes Pitt County[4]										
City of Greenville[4]	92,630		4		154	420	3,394	724	2,566	104
Total area actually reporting	97.5%		5		195	611	5,090	1,218	3,691	181
Estimated total	100.0%		5		198	619	5,218	1,241	3,791	186
Rate per 100,000 inhabitants			2.8		110.6	345.7	2,914.5	693.2	2,117.5	103.9
Greenville-Anderson-Mauldin, SC MSA	896,199									
Includes Anderson, Greenville, Laurens, and Pickens Counties										

Table 6. Crime in the United States, by Selected Metropolitan Statistical Area, 2017—Continued

(Number, percent, rate per 100,000 population.)

Area	Population	Violent crime	Murder and nonnegligent manslaughter	Rape[1]	Robbery	Aggravated assault	Property crime	Burglary	Larceny-theft	Motor vehicle theft
City of Greenville	68,922	415	4	28	91	292	2,831	393	2,281	157
City of Anderson	27,728	181	2	14	20	145	1,666	229	1,310	127
City of Mauldin	25,535	65	1	5	12	47	409	45	332	32
City of Easley	21,107	125	0	8	15	102	1,308	127	1,117	64
Total area actually reporting	100.0%	4,363	47	466	591	3,259	27,798	5,315	19,862	2,621
Rate per 100,000 inhabitants		486.8	5.2	52.0	65.9	363.6	3,101.8	593.1	2,216.2	292.5
Gulfport-Biloxi-Pascagoula, MS MSA[4]	393,581									
Includes Hancock, Harrison, and Jackson Counties										
City of Gulfport	72,792	299	10	26	82	181	3,662	562	2,897	203
City of Biloxi	46,263	178	1	39	74	64	2,963	871	1,933	159
City of Pascagoula	21,928	72	0	25	22	25	1,450	246	1,135	69
Total area actually reporting	93.2%	884	21	143	242	478	14,458	2,909	10,603	946
Estimated total	100.0%	935	22	146	255	512	15,221	3,070	11,174	977
Rate per 100,000 inhabitants		237.6	5.6	37.1	64.8	130.1	3,867.3	780.0	2,839.1	248.2
Hagerstown-Martinsburg, MD-WV MSA	264,967									
Includes Washington County, MD and Berkeley County, WV										
City of Hagerstown, MD	40,568	249	8	18	119	104	1,036	244	668	124
City of Martinsburg, WV	17,761	84	1	12	20	51	804	93	690	21
Total area actually reporting	100.0%	784	12	76	194	502	4,391	940	3,144	307
Rate per 100,000 inhabitants		295.9	4.5	28.7	73.2	189.5	1,657.2	354.8	1,186.6	115.9
Hammond, LA MSA	131,701									
Includes Tangipahoa Parish										
City of Hammond	20,712	308	2	24	64	218	2,006	655	1,272	79
Total area actually reporting	96.6%	1,173	12	79	225	857	5,665	1,709	3,577	379
Estimated total	100.0%	1,193	12	80	228	873	5,831	1,739	3,706	386
Rate per 100,000 inhabitants		905.8	9.1	60.7	173.1	662.9	4,427.5	1,320.4	2,813.9	293.1
Hanford-Corcoran, CA MSA	149,193									
Includes Kings County										
City of Hanford	55,789	284	2	28	54	200	1,359	197	916	246
City of Corcoran	22,345	78	1	9	10	58	383	101	222	60
Total area actually reporting	100.0%	754	9	88	104	553	2,935	620	1,786	529
Rate per 100,000 inhabitants		505.4	6.0	59.0	69.7	370.7	1,967.3	415.6	1,197.1	354.6
Harrisburg-Carlisle, PA MSA	571,453									
Includes Cumberland, Dauphin, and Perry Counties										
City of Harrisburg	48,804	564	13	50	178	323	1,494	348	963	183
City of Carlisle	19,233	35	1	5	12	17	370	33	332	5
Total area actually reporting	98.6%	1,598	25	266	365	942	8,576	1,337	6,853	386
Estimated total	100.0%	1,612	25	267	368	952	8,691	1,351	6,949	391
Rate per 100,000 inhabitants		282.1	4.4	46.7	64.4	166.6	1,520.9	236.4	1,216.0	68.4
Harrisonburg, VA MSA	133,939									
Includes Rockingham County and Harrisonburg City										
City of Harrisonburg	53,717	128	3	24	12	89	897	115	739	43
Total area actually reporting	100.0%	194	4	49	14	127	1,498	222	1,190	86
Rate per 100,000 inhabitants		144.8	3.0	36.6	10.5	94.8	1,118.4	165.7	888.5	64.2
Hartford-West Hartford-East Hartford, CT MSA	1,015,610									
Includes Hartford, Middlesex, and Tolland Counties										
City of Hartford	122,891	1,343	29	45	465	804	4,907	738	3,490	679
City of West Hartford	62,812	67	0	1	61	5	1,859	150	1,588	121
City of East Hartford	50,067	133	1	24	55	53	1,231	188	883	160
City of Middletown	46,363	49	0	6	8	35	730	68	591	71
Total area actually reporting	100.0%	2,511	40	248	888	1,335	22,946	3,009	17,487	2,450
Rate per 100,000 inhabitants		247.2	3.9	24.4	87.4	131.4	2,259.3	296.3	1,721.8	241.2
Hilton Head Island-Bluffton-Beaufort, SC MSA[5]	216,071									
Includes Beaufort[5] and Jasper Counties										
City of Bluffton	20,024	41	0	6	5	30	330	33	275	22
City of Beaufort	13,612	92	1	3	21	67	667	98	536	33
Total area actually reporting	100.0%	815	13	109	112	581				308
Rate per 100,000 inhabitants		377.2	6.0	50.4	51.8	268.9				142.5
Homosassa Springs, FL MSA	144,428									
Includes Citrus County										
Total area actually reporting	100.0%	399	3	42	40	314	2,037	431	1,472	134
Rate per 100,000 inhabitants		276.3	2.1	29.1	27.7	217.4	1,410.4	298.4	1,019.2	92.8
Hot Springs, AR MSA	97,820									
Includes Garland County										
City of Hot Springs	36,956	218	8	20	59	131	2,518	838	1,514	166
Total area actually reporting	100.0%	514	8	48	69	389	4,130	1,514	2,318	298
Rate per 100,000 inhabitants		525.5	8.2	49.1	70.5	397.7	4,222.0	1,547.7	2,369.7	304.6
Houma-Thibodaux, LA MSA	211,101									
Includes Lafourche and Terrebonne Parishes										
City of Houma	34,083	123	2	20	18	83	1,245	168	1,027	50

Table 6. Crime in the United States, by Selected Metropolitan Statistical Area, 2017—Continued

(Number, percent, rate per 100,000 population.)

Area	Population	Violent crime	Murder and nonnegligent manslaughter	Rape[1]	Robbery	Aggravated assault	Property crime	Burglary	Larceny-theft	Motor vehicle theft
City of Thibodaux	14,617	61	1	3	14	43	578	89	468	21
Total area actually reporting	100.0%	685	10	67	68	540	5,731	997	4,488	246
Rate per 100,000 inhabitants		324.5	4.7	31.7	32.2	255.8	2,714.8	472.3	2,126.0	116.5
Houston-The Woodlands-Sugar Land, TX MSA[2,5]	6,914,428									
Includes Austin, Brazoria, Chambers, Fort Bend, Galveston, Harris, Liberty, Montgomery,[5] and Waller Counties										
City of Houston	2,338,235	25,609	269	1,366	9,773	14,201	96,532	17,108	67,828	11,596
City of Sugar Land	89,790	71	0	15	36	20	1,289	158	1,075	56
City of Baytown	76,704	288	6	38	108	136	2,678	506	1,846	326
City of Conroe	85,534	249	4	54	65	126	1,931	276	1,479	176
Total area actually reporting	99.9%	40,846	438	2,938	14,152	23,318			132,783	
Estimated total	100.0%	41,008	440	2,958	14,187	23,423			133,368	
Rate per 100,000 inhabitants		593.1	6.4	42.8	205.2	338.8			1,928.8	
Huntington-Ashland, WV-KY-OH MSA[4]	357,503									
Includes Boyd and Greenup Counties, KY; Lawrence County OH; and Cabell, Lincoln, Putnam, and Wayne Counties, WV										
City of Huntington, WV	47,933	428	16	54	120	238	2,082	599	1,303	180
City of Ashland, KY	20,927	39	0	11	3	25	864	113	698	53
Total area actually reporting	81.8%	925	26	141	162	596	6,693	1,525	4,556	612
Estimated total	100.0%	1,097	28	167	173	729	7,842	1,775	5,344	723
Rate per 100,000 inhabitants		306.9	7.8	46.7	48.4	203.9	2,193.5	496.5	1,494.8	202.2
Huntsville, AL MSA	454,756									
Includes Limestone and Madison Counties										
City of Huntsville	195,173	1,766	22	172	360	1,212	9,232	1,428	6,758	1,046
Total area actually reporting	100.0%	2,532	33	256	441	1,802	14,229	2,550	10,229	1,450
Rate per 100,000 inhabitants		556.8	7.3	56.3	97.0	396.3	3,128.9	560.7	2,249.3	318.9
Idaho Falls, ID MSA	145,276									
Includes Bonneville, Butte, and Jefferson Counties										
City of Idaho Falls	60,727	215	2	30	8	175	1,122	366	671	85
Total area actually reporting	100.0%	347	2	50	10	285	1,870	600	1,126	144
Rate per 100,000 inhabitants		238.9	1.4	34.4	6.9	196.2	1,287.2	413.0	775.1	99.1
Indianapolis-Carmel-Anderson, IN MSA[2,4]	2,026,454									
Includes Boone, Brown, Hamilton, Hancock, Hendricks, Johnson, Madison, Marion, Morgan, Putnam, and Shelby Counties										
City of Indianapolis	870,788	11,616	156	668	3,485	7,307	38,418	8,945	24,569	4,904
City of Carmel	93,098	17	0	6	6	5	695	61	596	38
City of Anderson	54,959	260	1	82	101	76	2,418	408	1,786	224
Total area actually reporting	87.7%	13,657	164	923	3,878	8,692	55,047	10,992	37,679	6,376
Estimated total	100.0%	14,074	169	979	3,943	8,983	58,410	11,643	40,041	6,726
Rate per 100,000 inhabitants		694.5	8.3	48.3	194.6	443.3	2,882.4	574.6	1,975.9	331.9
Iowa City, IA MSA	171,405									
Includes Johnson and Washington Counties										
City of Iowa City	75,519	156	4	25	46	81	1,767	310	1,376	81
Total area actually reporting	100.0%	447	4	93	72	278	3,468	586	2,747	135
Rate per 100,000 inhabitants		260.8	2.3	54.3	42.0	162.2	2,023.3	341.9	1,602.6	78.8
Jackson, MI MSA	158,563									
Includes Jackson County										
City of Jackson	32,822	371	7	58	55	251	1,371	211	1,052	108
Total area actually reporting	98.7%	803	12	158	78	555	3,442	569	2,658	215
Estimated total	100.0%	809	12	159	79	559	3,479	575	2,686	218
Rate per 100,000 inhabitants		510.2	7.6	100.3	49.8	352.5	2,194.1	362.6	1,694.0	137.5
Jackson, MS MSA[4]	579,463									
Includes Copiah, Hinds, Madison,[4] Rankin, Simpson, and Yazoo Counties										
City of Jackson[4]	168,397		60		542	591	7,449	2,006	4,696	747
Total area actually reporting	76.4%	1,733	68	147	617	901	11,062	2,637	7,497	928
Estimated total	100.0%	1,957	75	166	666	1,050	14,139	3,335	9,710	1,094
Rate per 100,000 inhabitants		337.7	12.9	28.6	114.9	181.2	2,440.0	575.5	1,675.7	188.8
Jackson, TN MSA	129,687									
Includes Chester, Crockett, and Madison Counties										
City of Jackson	67,031	655	7	28	91	529	2,917	497	2,271	149
Total area actually reporting	100.0%	907	8	41	104	754	3,729	744	2,772	213
Rate per 100,000 inhabitants		699.4	6.2	31.6	80.2	581.4	2,875.4	573.7	2,137.5	164.2
Jacksonville, FL MSA	1,505,471									
Includes Baker, Clay, Duval, Nassau, and St. Johns Counties										
City of Jacksonville	894,638	5,648	109	538	1,376	3,625	31,551	5,646	22,980	2,925
Total area actually reporting	100.0%	7,239	123	724	1,600	4,792	41,816	7,661	30,548	3,607
Rate per 100,000 inhabitants		480.8	8.2	48.1	106.3	318.3	2,777.6	508.9	2,029.1	239.6

Table 6. Crime in the United States, by Selected Metropolitan Statistical Area, 2017—Continued

(Number, percent, rate per 100,000 population.)

Area	Population	Violent crime	Murder and nonnegligent manslaughter	Rape[1]	Robbery	Aggravated assault	Property crime	Burglary	Larceny-theft	Motor vehicle theft
Janesville-Beloit, WI MSA	161,894									
Includes Rock County										
City of Janesville	64,257	170	2	45	30	93	1,948	308	1,572	68
City of Beloit	36,724	156	1	32	34	89	1,114	211	863	40
Total area actually reporting	100.0%	391	4	105	70	212	3,774	664	2,966	144
Rate per 100,000 inhabitants		241.5	2.5	64.9	43.2	130.9	2,331.2	410.1	1,832.1	88.9
Jefferson City, MO MSA[3]	151,721									
Includes Callaway, Cole, Moniteau, and Osage Counties										
City of Jefferson City	42,989	152	4	16	38	94	1,254	164	1,032	58
Total area actually reporting	100.0%		6	57	47		2,757	512	2,080	165
Rate per 100,000 inhabitants			4.0	37.6	31.0		1,817.2	337.5	1,370.9	108.8
Johnson City, TN MSA	202,495									
Includes Carter, Unicoi, and Washington Counties										
City of Johnson City	67,193	267	2	26	42	197	2,831	377	2,296	158
Total area actually reporting	100.0%	663	8	54	65	536	5,653	958	4,342	353
Rate per 100,000 inhabitants		327.4	4.0	26.7	32.1	264.7	2,791.7	473.1	2,144.3	174.3
Johnstown, PA MSA	133,419									
Includes Cambria County										
City of Johnstown	20,946	157	9	10	27	111	634	190	419	25
Total area actually reporting	99.1%	246	11	27	40	168	1,835	345	1,435	55
Estimated total	100.0%	247	11	27	40	169	1,852	347	1,449	56
Rate per 100,000 inhabitants		185.1	8.2	20.2	30.0	126.7	1,388.1	260.1	1,086.1	42.0
Jonesboro, AR MSA	131,530									
Includes Craighead and Poinsett Counties										
City of Jonesboro	76,188	400	13	54	62	271	3,124	1,239	1,728	157
Total area actually reporting	92.8%	560	16	84	67	393	4,221	1,441	2,532	248
Estimated total	100.0%	597	16	89	69	423	4,406	1,500	2,638	268
Rate per 100,000 inhabitants		453.9	12.2	67.7	52.5	321.6	3,349.8	1,140.4	2,005.6	203.8
Joplin, MO MSA	178,239									
Includes Jasper and Newton Counties										
City of Joplin	52,412	317	3	44	61	209	3,729	487	2,918	324
Total area actually reporting	100.0%	713	5	92	81	535	6,971	1,020	5,370	581
Rate per 100,000 inhabitants		400.0	2.8	51.6	45.4	300.2	3,911.0	572.3	3,012.8	326.0
Kahului-Wailuku-Lahaina, HI MSA	165,868									
Includes Kalawao and Maui Counties										
Total area actually reporting	100.0%	446	2	95	67	282	5,729	906	4,016	807
Rate per 100,000 inhabitants		268.9	1.2	57.3	40.4	170.0	3,454.0	546.2	2,421.2	486.5
Kalamazoo-Portage, MI MSA	339,412									
Includes Kalamazoo and Van Buren Counties										
City of Kalamazoo	76,263	913	10	130	152	621	3,174	710	2,132	332
City of Portage	48,876	108	0	31	14	63	1,468	186	1,223	59
Total area actually reporting	99.7%	1,697	16	313	239	1,129	8,991	1,897	6,381	713
Estimated total	100.0%	1,699	16	313	239	1,131	9,006	1,899	6,393	714
Rate per 100,000 inhabitants		500.6	4.7	92.2	70.4	333.2	2,653.4	559.5	1,883.6	210.4
Kankakee, IL MSA	109,501									
Includes Kankakee County										
City of Kankakee	26,265	210	6	35	68	101	1,049	198	800	51
Total area actually reporting	91.5%	360	7	56	100	197	2,143	390	1,657	96
Estimated total	100.0%	380	7	59	106	208	2,294	412	1,777	105
Rate per 100,000 inhabitants		347.0	6.4	53.9	96.8	190.0	2,095.0	376.3	1,622.8	95.9
Kennewick-Richland, WA MSA	289,723									
Includes Benton and Franklin Counties										
City of Kennewick	81,499	213	1	30	59	123	2,228	307	1,732	189
City of Richland	56,151	102	0	19	14	69	1,321	184	1,086	51
Total area actually reporting	100.0%	594	2	85	123	384	5,926	1,040	4,383	503
Rate per 100,000 inhabitants		205.0	0.7	29.3	42.5	132.5	2,045.4	359.0	1,512.8	173.6
Killeen-Temple, TX MSA	440,220									
Includes Bell, Coryell, and Lampasas Counties										
City of Killeen	145,912	1,118	18	151	313	636	4,109	1,140	2,403	566
City of Temple	74,794	238	5	63	65	105	2,130	409	1,483	238
Total area actually reporting	99.3%	1,860	33	296	442	1,089	10,247	2,391	6,864	992
Estimated total	100.0%	1,868	33	297	444	1,094	10,316	2,401	6,918	997
Rate per 100,000 inhabitants		424.3	7.5	67.5	100.9	248.5	2,343.4	545.4	1,571.5	226.5
Kingsport-Bristol-Bristol, TN-VA MSA	306,090									
Includes Hawkins and Sullivan Counties, TN and Scott and Washington Counties and Bristol City, VA										
City of Kingsport, TN	52,810	381	3	17	58	303	2,884	377	2,303	204
City of Bristol, TN	27,176	110	2	14	8	86	915	137	704	74
City of Bristol, VA	16,795	54	0	15	3	36	562	86	428	48

Table 6. Crime in the United States, by Selected Metropolitan Statistical Area, 2017—Continued

(Number, percent, rate per 100,000 population.)

Area	Population	Violent crime	Murder and nonnegligent manslaughter	Rape[1]	Robbery	Aggravated assault	Property crime	Burglary	Larceny-theft	Motor vehicle theft
Total area actually reporting	100.0%	1,086	16	125	88	857	7,630	1,339	5,633	658
Rate per 100,000 inhabitants		354.8	5.2	40.8	28.7	280.0	2,492.7	437.5	1,840.3	215.0
Kingston, NY MSA	179,106									
Includes Ulster County										
City of Kingston	23,110	73	1	5	22	45	449	53	392	4
Total area actually reporting	100.0%	287	2	64	39	182	2,257	307	1,885	65
Rate per 100,000 inhabitants		160.2	1.1	35.7	21.8	101.6	1,260.1	171.4	1,052.4	36.3
Knoxville, TN MSA	875,281									
Includes Anderson, Blount, Campbell, Grainger, Knox, Loudon, Morgan, Roane, and Union Counties										
City of Knoxville	187,539	1,676	33	145	371	1,127	10,211	1,665	7,510	1,036
Total area actually reporting	100.0%	3,852	60	311	528	2,953	22,730	4,387	15,953	2,390
Rate per 100,000 inhabitants		440.1	6.9	35.5	60.3	337.4	2,596.9	501.2	1,822.6	273.1
Kokomo, IN MSA	82,647									
Includes Howard County										
City of Kokomo	57,758	417	6	36	48	327	1,669	413	1,169	87
Total area actually reporting	98.7%	487	6	41	48	392	1,871	473	1,291	107
Estimated total	100.0%	490	6	41	49	394	1,898	476	1,313	109
Rate per 100,000 inhabitants		592.9	7.3	49.6	59.3	476.7	2,296.5	575.9	1,588.7	131.9
La Crosse-Onalaska, WI-MN MSA	137,553									
Includes Houston County, MN and La Crosse County, WI										
City of La Crosse, WI	52,234	140	0	29	35	76	2,167	365	1,746	56
City of Onalaska, WI	18,847	15	0	4	0	11	532	26	495	11
Total area actually reporting	100.0%	213	1	38	36	138	3,242	495	2,665	82
Rate per 100,000 inhabitants		154.8	0.7	27.6	26.2	100.3	2,356.9	359.9	1,937.4	59.6
Lafayette, LA MSA[3,5]	493,395									
Includes Acadia,[3] Iberia, Lafayette, St. Martin, and Vermilion Parishes										
City of Lafayette	128,691	721	22	21	175	503	5,863	1,011	4,555	297
Total area actually reporting	85.2%	1,915	39	101	320	1,455		2,957		
Estimated total	100.0%	2,169	44	119	361	1,645		3,371		
Rate per 100,000 inhabitants		439.6	8.9	24.1	73.2	333.4		683.2		
Lafayette-West Lafayette, IN MSA	219,515									
Includes Benton, Carroll, and Tippecanoe Counties										
City of Lafayette	72,274	364	4	43	80	237	2,637	573	1,903	161
City of West Lafayette	46,541	49	0	8	5	36	466	49	397	20
Total area actually reporting	85.9%	488	5	68	93	322	3,940	789	2,926	225
Estimated total	100.0%	542	5	75	102	360	4,389	871	3,248	270
Rate per 100,000 inhabitants		246.9	2.3	34.2	46.5	164.0	1,999.4	396.8	1,479.6	123.0
Lake Charles, LA MSA[2]	207,792									
Includes Calcasieu and Cameron Parishes										
City of Lake Charles	77,647	638	9	45	146	438	3,524	1,836	1,429	259
Total area actually reporting	96.9%	1,239	21	101	203	914	9,209	3,403	5,230	576
Estimated total	100.0%	1,268	22	103	207	936	9,449	3,446	5,417	586
Rate per 100,000 inhabitants		610.2	10.6	49.6	99.6	450.5	4,547.3	1,658.4	2,606.9	282.0
Lake Havasu City-Kingman, AZ MSA[6]	205,868									
Includes Mohave County										
City of Lake Havasu City	53,937	120	0	21	6	93	1,164	245	848	71
City of Kingman	29,181	131	2	12	15	102	1,445	237	1,119	89
Total area actually reporting	97.7%		8	59	75		6,514	1,620	4,355	539
Estimated total	100.0%		8	61	78		6,644	1,640	4,455	549
Rate per 100,000 inhabitants			3.9	29.6	37.9		3,227.3	796.6	2,164.0	266.7
Lakeland-Winter Haven, FL MSA	679,166									
Includes Polk County										
City of Lakeland	107,927	307	1	73	89	144	4,021	574	3,237	210
City of Winter Haven	39,859	192	0	30	24	138	1,112	177	862	73
Total area actually reporting	100.0%	1,936	12	206	289	1,429	13,312	2,585	9,739	988
Rate per 100,000 inhabitants		285.1	1.8	30.3	42.6	210.4	1,960.1	380.6	1,434.0	145.5
Lancaster, PA MSA	541,945									
Includes Lancaster County										
City of Lancaster	59,199	530	5	97	141	287	1,999	205	1,689	105
Total area actually reporting	100.0%	1,126	15	198	241	672	7,196	959	5,923	314
Rate per 100,000 inhabitants		207.8	2.8	36.5	44.5	124.0	1,327.8	177.0	1,092.9	57.9
Lansing-East Lansing, MI MSA	478,097									
Includes Clinton, Eaton, and Ingham Counties										
City of Lansing	116,302	1,321	14	108	238	961	3,549	883	2,267	399
City of East Lansing	48,920	82	0	22	16	44	781	106	538	137
Total area actually reporting	100.0%	2,068	22	351	335	1,360	9,336	1,906	6,660	770
Rate per 100,000 inhabitants		432.5	4.6	73.4	70.1	284.5	1,952.7	398.7	1,393.0	161.1

Table 6. Crime in the United States, by Selected Metropolitan Statistical Area, 2017—Continued

(Number, percent, rate per 100,000 population.)

Area	Population	Violent crime	Murder and nonnegligent manslaughter	Rape[1]	Robbery	Aggravated assault	Property crime	Burglary	Larceny-theft	Motor vehicle theft
Laredo, TX MSA	274,365									
Includes Webb County										
City of Laredo	260,669	839	10	114	154	561	6,474	874	5,430	170
Total area actually reporting	100.0%	890	10	125	156	599	6,715	931	5,610	174
Rate per 100,000 inhabitants		324.4	3.6	45.6	56.9	218.3	2,447.5	339.3	2,044.7	63.4
Las Vegas-Henderson-Paradise, NV MSA	2,203,346									
Includes Clark County										
City of Las Vegas Metropolitan Police Department	1,627,244	10,071	205	1,296	3,436	5,134	47,896	13,102	26,608	8,186
City of Henderson	299,285	554	10	86	240	218	5,486	1,089	3,756	641
Total area actually reporting	100.0%	13,395	238	1,543	4,286	7,328	61,236	16,496	34,468	10,272
Rate per 100,000 inhabitants		607.9	10.8	70.0	194.5	332.6	2,779.2	748.7	1,564.3	466.2
Lawton, OK MSA	126,813									
Includes Comanche and Cotton Counties										
City of Lawton	94,134	831	8	83	131	609	3,618	1,207	2,097	314
Total area actually reporting	100.0%	856	8	94	132	622	4,037	1,322	2,369	346
Rate per 100,000 inhabitants		675.0	6.3	74.1	104.1	490.5	3,183.4	1,042.5	1,868.1	272.8
Lebanon, PA MSA	139,840									
Includes Lebanon County										
City of Lebanon	25,771	89	2	6	34	47	538	126	389	23
Total area actually reporting	95.9%	250	3	34	50	163	1,775	303	1,416	56
Estimated total	100.0%	260	3	35	52	170	1,856	313	1,484	59
Rate per 100,000 inhabitants		185.9	2.1	25.0	37.2	121.6	1,327.2	223.8	1,061.2	42.2
Lewiston, ID-WA MSA	63,349									
Includes Nez Perce County, ID and Asotin County, WA										
City of Lewiston, ID	33,029	53	2	11	4	36	943	188	687	68
Total area actually reporting	100.0%	100	2	19	12	67	1,564	331	1,140	93
Rate per 100,000 inhabitants		157.9	3.2	30.0	18.9	105.8	2,468.9	522.5	1,799.6	146.8
Lewiston-Auburn, ME MSA	107,554									
Includes Androscoggin County										
City of Lewiston	36,067	98	0	24	31	43	788	164	582	42
City of Auburn	22,931	40	0	14	10	16	712	55	646	11
Total area actually reporting	100.0%	169	0	57	45	67	1,885	304	1,508	73
Rate per 100,000 inhabitants		157.1	0.0	53.0	41.8	62.3	1,752.6	282.6	1,402.1	67.9
Lexington-Fayette, KY MSA[3]	512,740									
Includes Bourbon, Clark, Fayette, Jessamine, Scott, and Woodford Counties										
City of Lexington	322,332	1,131	29	200	547	355	12,191	2,087	8,831	1,273
Total area actually reporting	100.0%	1,401	34	260	656	451		3,109		1,634
Rate per 100,000 inhabitants		273.2	6.6	50.7	127.9	88.0		606.4		318.7
Lima, OH MSA[4]	103,577									
Includes Allen County										
City of Lima	37,220	275	5	52	81	137	1,982	569	1,334	79
Total area actually reporting	93.9%	326	6	72	96	152	3,145	804	2,230	111
Estimated total	100.0%	336	6	74	99	157	3,276	824	2,335	117
Rate per 100,000 inhabitants		324.4	5.8	71.4	95.6	151.6	3,162.9	795.5	2,254.4	113.0
Little Rock-North Little Rock-Conway, AR MSA	741,067									
Includes Faulkner, Grant, Lonoke, Perry, Pulaski, and Saline Counties										
City of Little Rock	199,314	3,256	55	175	502	2,524	13,817	2,378	10,309	1,130
City of North Little Rock	66,938	530	9	19	124	378	2,764	541	1,875	348
City of Conway	66,299	315	1	41	63	210	2,314	331	1,835	148
Total area actually reporting	100.0%	5,918	87	453	849	4,529	30,296	5,909	21,646	2,741
Rate per 100,000 inhabitants		798.6	11.7	61.1	114.6	611.1	4,088.2	797.4	2,920.9	369.9
Logan, UT-ID MSA	138,078									
Includes Franklin County, ID and Cache County, UT										
City of Logan, UT	51,059	48	1	23	1	23	678	94	547	37
Total area actually reporting	100.0%	110	4	55	4	47	1,251	207	945	99
Rate per 100,000 inhabitants		79.7	2.9	39.8	2.9	34.0	906.0	149.9	684.4	71.7
Longview, TX MSA	217,681									
Includes Gregg, Rusk, and Upshur Counties										
City of Longview	80,334	388	6	61	97	224	2,735	599	1,900	236
Total area actually reporting	98.0%	909	12	115	128	654	5,361	1,328	3,575	458
Estimated total	100.0%	921	12	117	131	661	5,461	1,343	3,652	466
Rate per 100,000 inhabitants		423.1	5.5	53.7	60.2	303.7	2,508.7	617.0	1,677.7	214.1
Longview, WA MSA	105,944									
Includes Cowlitz County										
City of Longview	37,424	112	2	46	21	43	1,360	262	956	142
Total area actually reporting	100.0%	259	3	96	31	129	2,698	564	1,867	267
Rate per 100,000 inhabitants		244.5	2.8	90.6	29.3	121.8	2,546.6	532.4	1,762.3	252.0

Table 6. Crime in the United States, by Selected Metropolitan Statistical Area, 2017—Continued

(Number, percent, rate per 100,000 population.)

Area	Population	Violent crime	Murder and nonnegligent manslaughter	Rape[1]	Robbery	Aggravated assault	Property crime	Burglary	Larceny-theft	Motor vehicle theft
Los Angeles-Long Beach-Anaheim, CA MSA[2]	13,375,094									
Includes the Metropolitan Divisions of Anaheim-Santa Ana-Irvine and Los Angeles-Long Beach-Glendale										
City of Los Angeles	4,007,147	30,507	281	2,455	10,814	16,957	101,618	16,668	65,757	19,193
City of Long Beach	471,397	3,101	22	203	1,237	1,639	12,598	2,765	7,104	2,729
City of Anaheim	353,400	1,253	10	115	480	648	9,296	1,351	6,393	1,552
City of Santa Ana	335,699	1,640	21	188	605	826	7,017	929	4,108	1,980
City of Irvine	276,115	169	2	46	55	66	3,635	627	2,814	194
City of Glendale	202,381	274	3	32	127	112	3,118	498	2,303	317
City of Torrance	147,482	267	0	36	116	115	3,206	557	2,213	436
City of Pasadena	142,891	574	8	51	202	313	2,946	745	1,842	359
City of Orange	141,130	218	4	12	64	138	2,584	489	1,754	341
City of Costa Mesa	113,267	361	1	61	128	171	4,298	620	3,158	520
City of Burbank	104,622	253	0	20	86	147	2,944	355	2,344	245
City of Carson	92,992	475	8	20	166	281	2,250	479	1,261	510
City of Santa Monica	92,935	705	3	54	241	407	4,374	648	3,462	264
City of Newport Beach	86,910	124	0	31	21	72	2,123	361	1,630	132
City of Tustin	81,246	132	3	11	47	71	1,949	288	1,484	177
City of Monterey Park	61,210	112	1	10	55	46	1,613	439	955	219
City of Gardena	60,249	393	4	16	218	155	1,393	353	678	362
City of Arcadia	58,883	110	0	7	56	47	1,534	485	957	92
City of Fountain Valley	56,704	68	0	3	28	37	1,581	238	1,199	144
Total area actually reporting	100.0%	66,435	642	5,129	23,584	37,080	314,350	57,168	200,941	56,241
Rate per 100,000 inhabitants		496.7	4.8	38.3	176.3	277.2	2,350.3	427.4	1,502.4	420.5
Anaheim-Santa Ana-Irvine, CA MD	3,195,538									
Includes Orange County										
Total area actually reporting	100.0%	7,627	62	830	2,495	4,240	65,638	10,196	46,607	8,835
Rate per 100,000 inhabitants		238.7	1.9	26.0	78.1	132.7	2,054.1	319.1	1,458.5	276.5
Los Angeles-Long Beach-Glendale, CA MD[2]	10,179,556									
Includes Los Angeles County										
Total area actually reporting	100.0%	58,808	580	4,299	21,089	32,840	248,712	46,972	154,334	47,406
Rate per 100,000 inhabitants		577.7	5.7	42.2	207.2	322.6	2,443.2	461.4	1,516.1	465.7
Louisville/Jefferson County, KY-IN MSA[4]	1,291,962									
Includes Clark, Floyd, Harrison, Scott, and Washington Counties, IN and Bullitt, Henry, Jefferson, Oldham, Shelby, Spencer, and Trimble Counties, KY										
City of Louisville Metro, KY	684,362	4,428	109	175	1,326	2,818	28,211	5,623	18,724	3,864
Total area actually reporting	91.4%	5,164	121	273	1,544	3,226	38,015	7,312	25,744	4,959
Estimated total	100.0%	5,396	123	299	1,590	3,384	39,982	7,608	27,239	5,135
Rate per 100,000 inhabitants		417.7	9.5	23.1	123.1	261.9	3,094.7	588.9	2,108.3	397.5
Lynchburg, VA MSA	261,147									
Includes Amherst, Appomattox, Bedford, and Campbell Counties and Bedford and Lynchburg Cities										
City of Lynchburg	80,890	287	4	33	42	208	1,886	224	1,522	140
Total area actually reporting	100.0%	502	7	78	66	351	3,995	544	3,156	295
Rate per 100,000 inhabitants		192.2	2.7	29.9	25.3	134.4	1,529.8	208.3	1,208.5	113.0
Macon-Bibb County, GA MSA	228,963									
Includes Bibb, Crawford, Jones, Monroe, and Twiggs Counties										
Total area actually reporting	99.6%	1,057	33	73	328	623	9,076	2,108	6,317	651
Estimated total	100.0%	1,060	33	73	329	625	9,113	2,113	6,346	654
Rate per 100,000 inhabitants		463.0	14.4	31.9	143.7	273.0	3,980.1	922.9	2,771.6	285.6
Madera, CA MSA	155,133									
Includes Madera County										
City of Madera	64,939	378	4	32	107	235	1,702	336	967	399
Total area actually reporting	100.0%	891	7	56	145	683	3,484	941	1,830	713
Rate per 100,000 inhabitants		574.3	4.5	36.1	93.5	440.3	2,245.8	606.6	1,179.6	459.6
Madison, WI MSA	656,500									
Includes Columbia, Dane, Green, and Iowa Counties										
City of Madison	255,850	958	11	95	212	640	6,811	927	5,452	432
Total area actually reporting	100.0%	1,501	15	193	301	992	11,988	1,712	9,552	724
Rate per 100,000 inhabitants		228.6	2.3	29.4	45.8	151.1	1,826.0	260.8	1,455.0	110.3
Manchester-Nashua, NH MSA	410,406									
Includes Hillsborough County										
City of Manchester	110,655	745	2	92	174	477	2,905	491	2,229	185
City of Nashua	88,102	150	1	53	30	66	1,190	115	1,003	72
Total area actually reporting	98.7%	1,084	4	202	214	664	5,693	832	4,526	335
Estimated total	100.0%	1,091	4	204	215	668	5,751	839	4,574	338
Rate per 100,000 inhabitants		265.8	1.0	49.7	52.4	162.8	1,401.3	204.4	1,114.5	82.4
Manhattan, KS MSA	97,562									
Includes Pottawatomie and Riley Counties										

Table 6. Crime in the United States, by Selected Metropolitan Statistical Area, 2017—Continued

(Number, percent, rate per 100,000 population.)

Area	Population	Violent crime	Murder and nonnegligent manslaughter	Rape[1]	Robbery	Aggravated assault	Property crime	Burglary	Larceny-theft	Motor vehicle theft
Total area actually reporting	100.0%	277	2	60	24	191	1,801	301	1,395	105
Rate per 100,000 inhabitants		283.9	2.0	61.5	24.6	195.8	1,846.0	308.5	1,429.9	107.6
Mankato-North Mankato, MN MSA	100,926									
Includes Blue Earth and Nicollet Counties										
City of Mankato	42,047	107	0	24	17	66	1,301	183	1,067	51
City of North Mankato	13,664	16	0	2	1	13	162	32	119	11
Total area actually reporting	100.0%	166	0	49	20	97	1,856	312	1,451	93
Rate per 100,000 inhabitants		164.5	0.0	48.6	19.8	96.1	1,839.0	309.1	1,437.7	92.1
Mansfield, OH MSA	120,919									
Includes Richland County										
City of Mansfield	46,507	248	7	45	75	121	2,392	569	1,745	78
Total area actually reporting	99.3%	324	7	69	97	151	3,971	897	2,944	130
Estimated total	100.0%	325	7	69	97	152	3,990	900	2,959	131
Rate per 100,000 inhabitants		268.8	5.8	57.1	80.2	125.7	3,299.7	744.3	2,447.1	108.3
McAllen-Edinburg-Mission, TX MSA[2]	861,327									
Includes Hidalgo County										
City of McAllen	144,162	208	7	27	49	125	4,007	185	3,776	46
City of Edinburg	89,595	299	2	51	44	202	3,373	472	2,793	108
City of Mission	84,511	98	0	27	30	41	2,005	231	1,700	74
Total area actually reporting	99.3%	2,506	38	411	361	1,696	21,519	3,229	17,509	781
Estimated total	100.0%	2,523	38	414	365	1,706	21,656	3,249	17,615	792
Rate per 100,000 inhabitants		292.9	4.4	48.1	42.4	198.1	2,514.3	377.2	2,045.1	92.0
Medford, OR MSA	219,042									
Includes Jackson County										
City of Medford	82,792	376	4	33	98	241	4,936	489	4,145	302
Total area actually reporting	100.0%	714	7	80	139	488	8,526	1,161	6,783	582
Rate per 100,000 inhabitants		326.0	3.2	36.5	63.5	222.8	3,892.4	530.0	3,096.7	265.7
Memphis, TN-MS-AR MSA[4]	1,346,961									
Includes Crittenden County, AR; Benton, DeSoto, Marshall, Tate, and Tunica[4] Counties, MS; and Fayette, Shelby, and Tipton Counties, TN										
City of Memphis, TN	652,765	13,077	181	590	3,457	8,849	41,110	9,532	27,576	4,002
Total area actually reporting	97.1%	15,677	219	796	3,855	10,807	56,258	13,098	38,180	4,980
Estimated total	100.0%	15,737	220	803	3,865	10,849	56,959	13,270	38,659	5,030
Rate per 100,000 inhabitants		1,168.3	16.3	59.6	286.9	805.4	4,228.7	985.2	2,870.1	373.4
Merced, CA MSA	270,396									
Includes Merced County										
City of Merced	83,180	563	8	28	158	369	2,668	472	1,706	490
Total area actually reporting	100.0%	1,557	19	64	274	1,200	7,148	1,607	4,383	1,158
Rate per 100,000 inhabitants		575.8	7.0	23.7	101.3	443.8	2,643.5	594.3	1,621.0	428.3
Miami-Fort Lauderdale-West Palm Beach, FL MSA	6,167,945									
Includes the Metropolitan Divisions of Fort Lauderdale-Pompano Beach-Deerfield Beach, Miami-Miami Beach-Kendall, and West Palm Beach-Boca Raton-Delray Beach										
City of Miami	463,009	3,338	52	105	978	2,203	18,586	2,440	14,311	1,835
City of Fort Lauderdale	180,972	1,072	15	81	429	547	10,006	1,657	7,424	925
City of West Palm Beach	109,459	906	25	66	322	493	5,275	847	3,907	521
City of Pompano Beach	111,027	958	8	61	410	479	5,330	898	3,624	808
City of Miami Beach	92,571	884	4	101	308	471	7,587	706	6,431	450
City of Boca Raton	98,069	223	1	27	81	114	2,503	435	1,871	197
City of Deerfield Beach	80,552	324	3	35	111	175	2,360	328	1,771	261
City of Delray Beach	68,533	409	2	36	93	278	2,587	366	1,949	272
City of Jupiter	65,311	103	4	14	22	63	1,210	133	1,019	58
Total area actually reporting	100.0%	28,261	375	2,005	8,229	17,652	189,749	25,852	145,685	18,212
Rate per 100,000 inhabitants		458.2	6.1	32.5	133.4	286.2	3,076.4	419.1	2,362.0	295.3
Fort Lauderdale-Pompano Beach-Deerfield Beach, FL MD	1,942,468									
Includes Broward County										
Total area actually reporting	100.0%	7,546	95	581	2,523	4,347	57,397	8,191	43,253	5,953
Rate per 100,000 inhabitants		388.5	4.9	29.9	129.9	223.8	2,954.8	421.7	2,226.7	306.5
Miami-Miami Beach-Kendall, FL MD	2,756,549									
Includes Miami-Dade County										
Total area actually reporting	100.0%	14,460	188	874	4,032	9,366	92,712	11,628	72,384	8,700
Rate per 100,000 inhabitants		524.6	6.8	31.7	146.3	339.8	3,363.3	421.8	2,625.9	315.6
West Palm Beach-Boca Raton-Delray Beach, FL MD	1,468,928									
Includes Palm Beach County										
Total area actually reporting	100.0%	6,255	92	550	1,674	3,939	39,640	6,033	30,048	3,559
Rate per 100,000 inhabitants		425.8	6.3	37.4	114.0	268.2	2,698.6	410.7	2,045.6	242.3
Midland, MI MSA	83,632									
Includes Midland County										
City of Midland	42,131	53	1	25	1	26	508	54	444	10

Table 6. Crime in the United States, by Selected Metropolitan Statistical Area, 2017—Continued

(Number, percent, rate per 100,000 population.)

Area	Population	Violent crime	Murder and nonnegligent manslaughter	Rape[1]	Robbery	Aggravated assault	Property crime	Burglary	Larceny-theft	Motor vehicle theft
Total area actually reporting	100.0%	113	1	44	1	67	822	121	677	24
Rate per 100,000 inhabitants		135.1	1.2	52.6	1.2	80.1	982.9	144.7	809.5	28.7
Midland, TX MSA	172,994									
Includes Martin and Midland Counties										
City of Midland	138,954	377	2	37	59	279	2,677	431	2,026	220
Total area actually reporting	98.2%	462	2	39	79	342	3,368	543	2,503	322
Estimated total	100.0%	470	2	40	81	347	3,437	553	2,557	327
Rate per 100,000 inhabitants		271.7	1.2	23.1	46.8	200.6	1,986.8	319.7	1,478.1	189.0
Milwaukee-Waukesha-West Allis, WI MSA	1,575,520									
Includes Milwaukee, Ozaukee, Washington, and Waukesha Counties										
City of Milwaukee	595,168	9,507	118	434	2,919	6,036	22,569	5,518	11,548	5,503
City of Waukesha	72,565	119	0	43	25	51	1,007	126	845	36
City of West Allis	60,043	205	2	26	82	95	2,044	324	1,536	184
Total area actually reporting	100.0%	10,721	124	644	3,301	6,652	40,111	7,429	26,095	6,587
Rate per 100,000 inhabitants		680.5	7.9	40.9	209.5	422.2	2,545.9	471.5	1,656.3	418.1
Minneapolis-St. Paul-Bloomington, MN-WI MSA	3,597,545									
Includes Anoka, Carver, Chisago, Dakota, Hennepin, Isanti, Le Sueur, Mille Lacs, Ramsey, Scott, Sherburne, Sibley, Washington, and Wright Counties, MN and Pierce and St. Croix Counties, WI										
City of Minneapolis, MN	418,971	4,614	42	514	1,819	2,239	19,446	3,762	13,296	2,388
City of St. Paul, MN	306,696	1,996	22	217	697	1,060	10,935	2,274	6,577	2,084
City of Bloomington, MN	85,704	140	1	43	33	63	2,590	175	2,282	133
City of Plymouth, MN	78,356	63	0	16	15	32	964	181	755	28
City of Eagan, MN	66,805	58	2	18	14	24	1,270	100	1,128	42
City of Eden Prairie, MN	64,429	32	2	7	9	14	824	56	739	29
Total area actually reporting	99.9%	10,178	95	1,557	3,301	5,225	86,492	12,701	66,076	7,715
Estimated total	100.0%	10,182	95	1,558	3,302	5,227	86,540	12,706	66,117	7,717
Rate per 100,000 inhabitants		283.0	2.6	43.3	91.8	145.3	2,405.5	353.2	1,837.8	214.5
Missoula, MT MSA	117,150									
Includes Missoula County										
City of Missoula	73,304	352	2	71	45	234	3,342	325	2,843	174
Total area actually reporting	100.0%	471	4	89	49	329	3,776	428	3,137	211
Rate per 100,000 inhabitants		402.0	3.4	76.0	41.8	280.8	3,223.2	365.3	2,677.8	180.1
Mobile, AL MSA[7]	414,842									
Includes Mobile County										
City of Mobile[7]	248,431	1,839	50	142	440	1,207	13,549	3,023	9,267	1,259
Total area actually reporting	99.5%	2,558	64	178	568	1,748	18,832	4,476	12,462	1,894
Estimated total	100.0%	2,568	64	179	570	1,755	18,897	4,487	12,511	1,899
Rate per 100,000 inhabitants		619.0	15.4	43.1	137.4	423.1	4,555.2	1,081.6	3,015.8	457.8
Modesto, CA MSA	545,448									
Includes Stanislaus County										
City of Modesto	213,677	2,074	20	110	519	1,425	8,465	1,188	5,865	1,412
Total area actually reporting	100.0%	3,300	41	196	905	2,158	16,789	2,774	10,781	3,234
Rate per 100,000 inhabitants		605.0	7.5	35.9	165.9	395.6	3,078.0	508.6	1,976.5	592.9
Monroe, LA MSA[2]	179,088									
Includes Ouachita and Union Parishes										
City of Monroe[2]	49,354	1,098	13	35	214	836	4,063	848	3,011	204
Total area actually reporting	95.6%	1,640	17	66	272	1,285	8,231	2,217	5,580	434
Estimated total	100.0%	1,675	18	68	277	1,312	8,521	2,269	5,806	446
Rate per 100,000 inhabitants		935.3	10.1	38.0	154.7	732.6	4,758.0	1,267.0	3,242.0	249.0
Monroe, MI MSA	149,119									
Includes Monroe County										
City of Monroe	19,868	107	1	25	9	72	389	54	303	32
Total area actually reporting	97.3%	362	3	110	30	219	2,119	477	1,471	171
Estimated total	100.0%	373	3	112	32	226	2,188	488	1,524	176
Rate per 100,000 inhabitants		250.1	2.0	75.1	21.5	151.6	1,467.3	327.3	1,022.0	118.0
Montgomery, AL MSA	373,522									
Includes Autauga, Elmore, Lowndes, and Montgomery Counties										
City of Montgomery	199,099	1,277	38	52	346	841	8,800	2,129	5,827	844
Total area actually reporting	99.0%	1,794	50	111	436	1,197	13,068	2,997	8,844	1,227
Estimated total	100.0%	1,813	50	113	439	1,211	13,192	3,018	8,937	1,237
Rate per 100,000 inhabitants		485.4	13.4	30.3	117.5	324.2	3,531.8	808.0	2,392.6	331.2
Morgantown, WV MSA	138,881									
Includes Monongalia and Preston Counties										
City of Morgantown	31,215	83	0	10	16	57	480	88	369	23
Total area actually reporting	88.4%	354	0	46	36	272	1,523	331	1,105	87
Estimated total	100.0%	393	0	52	41	300	2,018	403	1,497	118
Rate per 100,000 inhabitants		283.0	0.0	37.4	29.5	216.0	1,453.0	290.2	1,077.9	85.0

Table 6. Crime in the United States, by Selected Metropolitan Statistical Area, 2017—Continued

(Number, percent, rate per 100,000 population.)

Area	Population	Violent crime	Murder and nonnegligent manslaughter	Rape[1]	Robbery	Aggravated assault	Property crime	Burglary	Larceny-theft	Motor vehicle theft
Morristown, TN MSA	118,061									
Includes Hamblen and Jefferson Counties										
City of Morristown	29,774	222	2	12	23	185	1,387	210	1,066	111
Total area actually reporting	100.0%	477	3	34	39	401	3,031	599	2,176	256
Rate per 100,000 inhabitants		404.0	2.5	28.8	33.0	339.7	2,567.3	507.4	1,843.1	216.8
Mount Vernon-Anacortes, WA MSA	125,204									
Includes Skagit County										
City of Mount Vernon	35,085	82	3	15	23	41	1,302	234	947	121
City of Anacortes	16,838	19	0	4	0	15	470	64	386	20
Total area actually reporting	100.0%	262	10	47	51	154	4,076	794	2,988	294
Rate per 100,000 inhabitants		209.3	8.0	37.5	40.7	123.0	3,255.5	634.2	2,386.5	234.8
Muncie, IN MSA	115,406									
Includes Delaware County										
City of Muncie	68,814	246	3	38	85	120	2,491	422	1,794	275
Total area actually reporting	100.0%	324	5	50	95	174	3,080	536	2,204	340
Rate per 100,000 inhabitants		280.7	4.3	43.3	82.3	150.8	2,668.8	464.4	1,909.8	294.6
Muskegon, MI MSA	174,084									
Includes Muskegon County										
City of Muskegon	38,375	229	3	29	55	142	2,059	395	1,467	197
Total area actually reporting	100.0%	702	9	150	118	425	5,838	909	4,562	367
Rate per 100,000 inhabitants		403.3	5.2	86.2	67.8	244.1	3,353.6	522.2	2,620.6	210.8
Myrtle Beach-Conway-North Myrtle Beach, SC-NC MSA[4]	462,909									
Includes Brunswick County, NC[4] and Horry County, SC										
City of Myrtle Beach, SC	33,167	523	5	60	146	312	4,331	378	3,608	345
City of Conway, SC	23,806	142	2	21	18	101	936	100	769	67
City of North Myrtle Beach, SC	16,422	72	0	22	13	37	1,278	197	976	105
Total area actually reporting	98.2%	1,901	28	354	328	1,191	16,469	2,872	12,262	1,335
Estimated total	100.0%	1,924	28	356	334	1,206	16,708	2,914	12,449	1,345
Rate per 100,000 inhabitants		415.6	6.0	76.9	72.2	260.5	3,609.3	629.5	2,689.3	290.6
Napa, CA MSA	142,919									
Includes Napa County										
City of Napa	80,958	272	1	39	43	189	1,353	338	828	187
Total area actually reporting	100.0%	597	1	60	61	475	2,225	560	1,384	281
Rate per 100,000 inhabitants		417.7	0.7	42.0	42.7	332.4	1,556.8	391.8	968.4	196.6
Naples-Immokalee-Marco Island, FL MSA	373,775									
Includes Collier County										
City of Naples	22,244	23	1	3	3	16	389	57	323	9
City of Marco Island	18,089	11	0	2	0	9	122	16	97	9
Total area actually reporting	100.0%	996	7	82	155	752	4,392	712	3,447	233
Rate per 100,000 inhabitants		266.5	1.9	21.9	41.5	201.2	1,175.0	190.5	922.2	62.3
Nashville-Davidson–Murfreesboro–Franklin, TN MSA	1,902,780									
Includes Cannon, Cheatham, Davidson, Dickson, Hickman, Macon, Maury, Robertson, Rutherford, Smith, Sumner, Trousdale, Williamson, and Wilson Counties										
City of Nashville Metropolitan	674,942	7,682	110	492	2,046	5,034	25,769	4,261	18,943	2,565
City of Murfreesboro	136,102	735	3	89	144	499	4,339	522	3,548	269
City of Franklin	76,995	146	1	18	14	113	1,048	78	940	30
Total area actually reporting	100.0%	11,890	149	894	2,486	8,361	48,684	7,912	36,448	4,324
Rate per 100,000 inhabitants		624.9	7.8	47.0	130.7	439.4	2,558.6	415.8	1,915.5	227.2
New Bern, NC MSA[4]	126,212									
Includes Craven, Jones, and Pamlico Counties[4]										
City of New Bern[4]	30,191		1		47	92	1,005	198	792	15
Total area actually reporting	88.7%		3		72	188	2,589	853	1,659	77
Estimated total	100.0%		3		78	207	2,860	923	1,846	91
Rate per 100,000 inhabitants			2.4		61.8	164.0	2,266.0	731.3	1,462.6	72.1
New Haven-Milford, CT MSA	801,867									
Includes New Haven County										
City of New Haven	129,953	1,100	7	52	378	663	5,211	840	3,728	643
City of Milford	54,265	24	0	1	18	5	967	92	809	66
Total area actually reporting	100.0%	2,465	23	200	856	1,386	19,355	2,776	14,223	2,356
Rate per 100,000 inhabitants		307.4	2.9	24.9	106.8	172.8	2,413.7	346.2	1,773.7	293.8
New Orleans-Metairie, LA MSA[2]	1,276,063									
Includes Jefferson, Orleans, Plaquemines, St. Bernard, St. Charles, St. James, St. John the Baptist, and St. Tammany Parishes										
City of New Orleans	397,447	4,457	157	575	1,308	2,417	16,867	2,229	12,107	2,531
Total area actually reporting	100.0%	7,197	218	762	1,920	4,297	37,620	5,483	28,314	3,823
Rate per 100,000 inhabitants		564.0	17.1	59.7	150.5	336.7	2,948.1	429.7	2,218.9	299.6

Table 6. Crime in the United States, by Selected Metropolitan Statistical Area, 2017—Continued

(Number, percent, rate per 100,000 population.)

Area	Population	Violent crime	Murder and nonnegligent manslaughter	Rape[1]	Robbery	Aggravated assault	Property crime	Burglary	Larceny-theft	Motor vehicle theft
New York-Newark-Jersey City, NY-NJ-PA MSA	20,306,398									
Includes the Metropolitan Divisions of Dutchess County-Putnam County, NY; Nassau County-Suffolk County, NY; Newark, NJ-PA; and New York-Jersey City-White Plains, NY-NJ										
City of New York, NY	8,616,333	46,433	292	2,375	13,995	29,771	124,815	11,104	107,976	5,735
City of Newark, NJ	283,673	2,543	77	116	1,070	1,280	6,794	1,202	3,200	2,392
City of Jersey City, NJ	267,906	1,365	21	123	534	687	4,841	1,119	3,231	491
City of White Plains, NY	58,461	103	0	9	26	68	982	34	916	32
City of New Brunswick, NJ	57,481	360	4	22	191	143	1,341	253	1,001	87
City of Lakewood Township, NJ	102,759	95	1	4	30	60	931	216	689	26
Total area actually reporting	99.8%	67,519	571	4,002	21,803	41,143	270,484	30,904	221,682	17,898
Estimated total	100.0%	67,600	571	4,012	21,826	41,191	271,205	30,986	222,294	17,925
Rate per 100,000 inhabitants		332.9	2.8	19.8	107.5	202.8	1,335.6	152.6	1,094.7	88.3
Dutchess County-Putnam County, NY MD	393,569									
Includes Dutchess and Putnam Counties										
Total area actually reporting	99.2%	628	5	127	122	374	4,124	507	3,529	88
Estimated total	100.0%	634	5	128	124	377	4,173	513	3,570	90
Rate per 100,000 inhabitants		161.1	1.3	32.5	31.5	95.8	1,060.3	130.3	907.1	22.9
Nassau County-Suffolk County, NY MD	2,863,520									
Includes Nassau and Suffolk Counties										
Total area actually reporting	98.8%	3,270	39	146	1,094	1,991	31,111	2,731	26,639	1,741
Estimated total	100.0%	3,327	39	153	1,110	2,025	31,624	2,789	27,075	1,760
Rate per 100,000 inhabitants		116.2	1.4	5.3	38.8	70.7	1,104.4	97.4	945.5	61.5
Newark, NJ-PA MD	2,523,572									
Includes Essex, Hunterdon, Morris, Somerset, Sussex, and Union Counties, NJ and Pike County, PA										
Total area actually reporting	100.0%	6,636	126	420	2,933	3,157	36,319	6,019	24,558	5,742
Rate per 100,000 inhabitants		263.0	5.0	16.6	116.2	125.1	1,439.2	238.5	973.1	227.5
New York-Jersey City-White Plains, NY-NJ MD	14,525,737									
Includes Bergen, Hudson, Middlesex, Monmouth, Ocean, and Passaic Counties, NJ and Bronx, Kings, New York, Orange, Queens, Richmond, Rockland, and Westchester Counties, NY										
Total area actually reporting	99.9%	56,985	401	3,309	17,654	35,621	198,930	21,647	166,956	10,327
Estimated total	100.0%	57,003	401	3,311	17,659	35,632	199,089	21,665	167,091	10,333
Rate per 100,000 inhabitants		392.4	2.8	22.8	121.6	245.3	1,370.6	149.1	1,150.3	71.1
Niles-Benton Harbor, MI MSA	153,925									
Includes Berrien County										
City of Niles	11,202	67	1	16	9	41	265	57	169	39
City of Benton Harbor	9,899	218	3	23	36	156	392	131	228	33
Total area actually reporting	100.0%	763	8	159	93	503	3,034	622	2,213	199
Rate per 100,000 inhabitants		495.7	5.2	103.3	60.4	326.8	1,971.1	404.1	1,437.7	129.3
North Port-Sarasota-Bradenton, FL MSA	805,941									
Includes Manatee and Sarasota Counties										
City of North Port	65,498	110	1	26	8	75	788	136	633	19
City of Sarasota	57,383	323	1	26	87	209	1,964	270	1,582	112
City of Bradenton	56,821	298	4	27	59	208	1,444	199	1,166	79
City of Venice	22,762	28	0	4	1	23	305	44	249	12
Total area actually reporting	100.0%	2,853	32	267	440	2,114	14,371	2,440	11,192	739
Rate per 100,000 inhabitants		354.0	4.0	33.1	54.6	262.3	1,783.1	302.8	1,388.7	91.7
Norwich-New London, CT MSA	176,834									
Includes New London County										
City of Norwich	39,393	103	0	21	33	49	601	134	428	39
City of New London	26,880	132	4	24	33	71	741	98	541	102
Total area actually reporting	100.0%	397	4	83	95	215	3,239	418	2,620	201
Rate per 100,000 inhabitants		224.5	2.3	46.9	53.7	121.6	1,831.7	236.4	1,481.6	113.7
Ocala, FL MSA	353,029									
Includes Marion County										
City of Ocala	59,731	468	4	54	117	293	3,172	482	2,537	153
Total area actually reporting	100.0%	1,388	17	143	253	975	8,071	1,947	5,435	689
Rate per 100,000 inhabitants		393.2	4.8	40.5	71.7	276.2	2,286.2	551.5	1,539.5	195.2
Ocean City, NJ MSA	94,353									
Includes Cape May County										
City of Ocean City	11,281	12	1	3	2	6	385	34	350	1
Total area actually reporting	100.0%	192	2	18	42	130	2,696	468	2,164	64
Rate per 100,000 inhabitants		203.5	2.1	19.1	44.5	137.8	2,857.4	496.0	2,293.5	67.8
Odessa, TX MSA	160,996									
Includes Ector County										
City of Odessa	121,194	912	7	78	101	726	3,219	560	2,386	273
Total area actually reporting	100.0%	1,079	12	85	121	861	4,734	858	3,411	465
Rate per 100,000 inhabitants		670.2	7.5	52.8	75.2	534.8	2,940.4	532.9	2,118.7	288.8

Table 6. Crime in the United States, by Selected Metropolitan Statistical Area, 2017—Continued

(Number, percent, rate per 100,000 population.)

Area	Population	Violent crime	Murder and nonnegligent manslaughter	Rape[1]	Robbery	Aggravated assault	Property crime	Burglary	Larceny-theft	Motor vehicle theft
Ogden-Clearfield, UT MSA	664,366									
Includes Box Elder, Davis, Morgan, and Weber Counties										
City of Ogden	87,323	463	6	49	91	317	3,794	546	2,780	468
City of Clearfield	30,994	41	1	7	9	24	615	73	492	50
Total area actually reporting	98.1%	1,055	15	253	167	620	13,618	1,970	10,461	1,187
Estimated total	100.0%	1,078	15	258	172	633	13,923	2,018	10,677	1,228
Rate per 100,000 inhabitants		162.3	2.3	38.8	25.9	95.3	2,095.7	303.7	1,607.1	184.8
Oklahoma City, OK MSA	1,385,915									
Includes Canadian, Cleveland, Grady, Lincoln, Logan, McClain, and Oklahoma Counties										
City of Oklahoma City	648,260	5,104	81	474	1,120	3,429	24,326	6,105	15,421	2,800
Total area actually reporting	100.0%	6,907	105	806	1,439	4,557	40,163	9,656	26,316	4,191
Rate per 100,000 inhabitants		498.4	7.6	58.2	103.8	328.8	2,897.9	696.7	1,898.8	302.4
Olympia-Tumwater, WA MSA	279,936									
Includes Thurston County										
City of Olympia	51,923	256	1	42	67	146	2,171	371	1,596	204
City of Tumwater	22,961	71	1	13	10	47	691	142	453	96
Total area actually reporting	100.0%	756	9	121	137	489	7,164	1,542	4,909	713
Rate per 100,000 inhabitants		270.1	3.2	43.2	48.9	174.7	2,559.2	550.8	1,753.6	254.7
Omaha-Council Bluffs, NE-IA MSA	933,488									
Includes Harrison, Mills, and Pottawattamie Counties, IA and Cass, Douglas, Sarpy, Saunders, and Washington Counties, NE										
City of Omaha, NE	449,388	2,909	31	410	625	1,843	17,437	2,088	11,849	3,500
City of Council Bluffs, IA	62,549	150	1	24	62	63	3,717	435	2,853	429
Total area actually reporting	99.2%	3,573	35	556	741	2,241	25,674	3,317	17,906	4,451
Estimated total	100.0%	3,589	35	559	742	2,253	25,810	3,343	18,007	4,460
Rate per 100,000 inhabitants		384.5	3.7	59.9	79.5	241.4	2,764.9	358.1	1,929.0	477.8
Orlando-Kissimmee-Sanford, FL MSA	2,502,951									
Includes Lake, Orange, Osceola, and Seminole Counties										
City of Orlando	283,982	2,113	23	183	605	1,302	15,490	2,388	11,715	1,387
City of Kissimmee	71,130	350	7	32	88	223	2,104	314	1,633	157
City of Sanford	59,457	415	9	53	95	258	2,476	398	1,944	134
Total area actually reporting	99.9%	11,100	125	1,179	2,353	7,443	69,377	12,859	51,177	5,341
Estimated total	100.0%	11,108	125	1,180	2,355	7,448	69,433	12,867	51,220	5,346
Rate per 100,000 inhabitants		443.8	5.0	47.1	94.1	297.6	2,774.0	514.1	2,046.4	213.6
Oshkosh-Neenah, WI MSA	170,405									
Includes Winnebago County										
City of Oshkosh	66,652	157	0	4	28	125	1,363	177	1,116	70
City of Neenah	25,983	50	0	7	2	41	496	40	444	12
Total area actually reporting	100.0%	292	0	32	32	228	2,737	351	2,264	122
Rate per 100,000 inhabitants		171.4	0.0	18.8	18.8	133.8	1,606.2	206.0	1,328.6	71.6
Owensboro, KY MSA	118,539									
Includes Daviess, Hancock, and McLean Counties										
City of Owensboro	59,576	178	3	46	52	77	2,597	390	1,964	243
Total area actually reporting	100.0%	196	4	52	53	87	3,073	538	2,239	296
Rate per 100,000 inhabitants		165.3	3.4	43.9	44.7	73.4	2,592.4	453.9	1,888.8	249.7
Oxnard-Thousand Oaks-Ventura, CA MSA	852,923									
Includes Ventura County										
City of Oxnard	209,513	908	15	65	430	398	5,328	787	3,848	693
City of Thousand Oaks	129,240	172	2	44	35	91	1,687	269	1,305	113
City of Ventura	110,006	460	2	63	111	284	3,638	585	2,717	336
City of Camarillo	67,714	107	1	8	42	56	1,086	182	826	78
Total area actually reporting	100.0%	2,239	26	270	730	1,213	15,985	2,612	11,764	1,609
Rate per 100,000 inhabitants		262.5	3.0	31.7	85.6	142.2	1,874.1	306.2	1,379.3	188.6
Palm Bay-Melbourne-Titusville, FL MSA	586,851									
Includes Brevard County										
City of Palm Bay	111,275	561	7	41	50	463	2,120	445	1,524	151
City of Melbourne	82,013	670	4	63	121	482	3,399	548	2,679	172
City of Titusville	46,425	289	1	35	55	198	1,631	387	1,071	173
Total area actually reporting	100.0%	2,703	25	235	396	2,047	14,264	2,651	10,588	1,025
Rate per 100,000 inhabitants		460.6	4.3	40.0	67.5	348.8	2,430.6	451.7	1,804.2	174.7
Total area actually reporting	100.0%	649	17	60	142	430	3,382	1,281	1,867	234
Rate per 100,000 inhabitants		685.4	18.0	63.4	150.0	454.1	3,571.5	1,352.8	1,971.6	247.1
Panama City, FL MSA	203,139									
Includes Bay and Gulf Counties										
City of Panama City	38,135	332	5	4	53	270	2,352	395	1,752	205
Total area actually reporting	100.0%	943	11	82	106	744	6,994	1,291	5,204	499
Rate per 100,000 inhabitants		464.2	5.4	40.4	52.2	366.3	3,443.0	635.5	2,561.8	245.6
Parkersburg-Vienna, WV MSA	90,643									
Includes Wirt and Wood Counties										

Table 6. Crime in the United States, by Selected Metropolitan Statistical Area, 2017—Continued

(Number, percent, rate per 100,000 population.)

Area	Population	Violent crime	Murder and nonnegligent manslaughter	Rape[1]	Robbery	Aggravated assault	Property crime	Burglary	Larceny-theft	Motor vehicle theft
City of Parkersburg	30,475	221	4	26	11	180	1,431	413	905	113
City of Vienna	10,409	22	0	3	0	19	352	25	318	9
Total area actually reporting	96.7%	388	8	48	11	321	2,288	609	1,506	173
Estimated total	100.0%	395	8	49	12	326	2,379	622	1,578	179
Rate per 100,000 inhabitants		435.8	8.8	54.1	13.2	359.7	2,624.6	686.2	1,740.9	197.5
Pensacola-Ferry Pass-Brent, FL MSA	493,108									
Includes Escambia and Santa Rosa Counties										
City of Pensacola	54,072	319	0	29	69	221	2,073	302	1,680	91
Total area actually reporting	100.0%	2,003	24	246	337	1,396	12,076	2,400	9,027	649
Rate per 100,000 inhabitants		406.2	4.9	49.9	68.3	283.1	2,449.0	486.7	1,830.6	131.6
Peoria, IL MSA	375,998									
Includes Marshall, Peoria, Stark, Tazewell, and Woodford Counties										
City of Peoria	114,157	867	12	65	281	509	4,810	1,119	3,357	334
Total area actually reporting	89.6%	1,421	14	189	321	897	8,311	1,931	5,872	508
Estimated total	100.0%	1,488	14	203	333	938	8,785	2,036	6,212	537
Rate per 100,000 inhabitants		395.7	3.7	54.0	88.6	249.5	2,336.4	541.5	1,652.1	142.8
Philadelphia-Camden-Wilmington, PA-NJ-DE-MD MSA	6,095,755									
Includes the Metropolitan Divisions of Camden, NJ; Montgomery County-Bucks County-Chester County, PA; Philadelphia, PA; and Wilmington, DE-MD-NJ										
City of Philadelphia, PA	1,575,595	14,930	316	1,182	6,026	7,406	48,268	6,590	36,195	5,483
City of Camden County Police Department, NJ	74,299	1,462	23	75	410	954	2,526	583	1,393	550
City of Wilmington, DE	71,552	1,142	34	33	381	694	3,550	705	2,413	432
Total area actually reporting	99.9%	26,128	496	2,024	9,313	14,295	125,286	18,104	97,216	9,966
Estimated total	100.0%	26,131	496	2,024	9,314	14,297	125,306	18,106	97,233	9,967
Rate per 100,000 inhabitants		428.7	8.1	33.2	152.8	234.5	2,055.6	297.0	1,595.1	163.5
Camden, NJ MD	1,256,928									
Includes Burlington, Camden, and Gloucester Counties										
Total area actually reporting	100.0%	3,283	52	273	1,024	1,934	24,128	4,530	18,097	1,501
Rate per 100,000 inhabitants		261.2	4.1	21.7	81.5	153.9	1,919.6	360.4	1,439.8	119.4
Montgomery County-Bucks County-Chester County, PA MD	1,972,157									
Includes Bucks, Chester, and Montgomery Counties										
Total area actually reporting	99.9%	2,513	33	307	714	1,459	25,532	2,636	21,847	1,049
Estimated total	100.0%	2,516	33	307	715	1,461	25,552	2,638	21,864	1,050
Rate per 100,000 inhabitants		127.6	1.7	15.6	36.3	74.1	1,295.6	133.8	1,108.6	53.2
Philadelphia, PA MD	2,140,093									
Includes Delaware and Philadelphia Counties										
Total area actually reporting	100.0%	17,041	361	1,277	6,635	8,768	58,080	7,840	44,059	6,181
Rate per 100,000 inhabitants		796.3	16.9	59.7	310.0	409.7	2,713.9	366.3	2,058.7	288.8
Wilmington, DE-MD-NJ MD	726,577									
Includes New Castle County, DE; Cecil County, MD; and Salem County, NJ										
Total area actually reporting	100.0%	3,291	50	167	940	2,134	17,546	3,098	13,213	1,235
Rate per 100,000 inhabitants		452.9	6.9	23.0	129.4	293.7	2,414.9	426.4	1,818.5	170.0
Phoenix-Mesa-Scottsdale, AZ MSA	4,737,604									
Includes Maricopa and Pinal Counties										
City of Phoenix	1,644,177	12,511	157	1,142	3,293	7,919	60,353	12,801	39,899	7,653
City of Mesa	492,268	2,047	23	252	454	1,318	10,692	1,878	7,930	884
City of Scottsdale	251,840	396	5	103	100	188	5,470	878	4,346	246
City of Tempe	186,086	883	5	151	229	498	7,669	1,076	6,120	473
Total area actually reporting	99.9%	22,288	271	2,364	5,322	14,331	133,339	24,504	95,496	13,339
Estimated total	100.0%	22,293	271	2,365	5,323	14,334	133,380	24,510	95,528	13,342
Rate per 100,000 inhabitants		470.6	5.7	49.9	112.4	302.6	2,815.3	517.4	2,016.4	281.6
Pine Bluff, AR MSA	90,789									
Includes Cleveland, Jefferson, and Lincoln Counties										
City of Pine Bluff	43,040	795	22	34	133	606	2,378	812	1,282	284
Total area actually reporting	100.0%	914	27	55	143	689	3,200	1,107	1,717	376
Rate per 100,000 inhabitants		1,006.7	29.7	60.6	157.5	758.9	3,524.7	1,219.3	1,891.2	414.1
Pittsburgh, PA MSA	2,341,460									
Includes Allegheny, Armstrong, Beaver, Butler, Fayette, Washington, and Westmoreland Counties										
City of Pittsburgh	305,932	2,008	55	90	802	1,061	9,528	1,610	7,238	680
Total area actually reporting	99.3%	6,485	127	479	1,672	4,207	36,609	5,972	28,841	1,796
Estimated total	100.0%	6,514	127	482	1,679	4,226	36,833	5,999	29,029	1,805
Rate per 100,000 inhabitants		278.2	5.4	20.6	71.7	180.5	1,573.1	256.2	1,239.8	77.1
Pittsfield, MA MSA	126,293									
Includes Berkshire County										
City of Pittsfield	42,546	375	4	50	43	278	1,092	399	656	37

Table 6. Crime in the United States, by Selected Metropolitan Statistical Area, 2017—Continued

(Number, percent, rate per 100,000 population.)

Area	Population	Violent crime	Murder and nonnegligent manslaughter	Rape[1]	Robbery	Aggravated assault	Property crime	Burglary	Larceny-theft	Motor vehicle theft
Total area actually reporting	90.3%	669	4	89	59	517	2,162	679	1,416	67
Estimated total	100.0%	705	4	93	65	543	2,320	706	1,535	79
Rate per 100,000 inhabitants		558.2	3.2	73.6	51.5	430.0	1,837.0	559.0	1,215.4	62.6
Pocatello, ID MSA	85,293									
Includes Bannock County										
City of Pocatello	54,800	243	1	13	9	220	1,609	295	1,194	120
Total area actually reporting	100.0%	257	1	13	12	231	2,077	339	1,601	137
Rate per 100,000 inhabitants		301.3	1.2	15.2	14.1	270.8	2,435.1	397.5	1,877.1	160.6
Portland-South Portland, ME MSA[2]	533,811									
Includes Cumberland, Sagadahoc, and York Counties										
City of Portland	67,079	186	2	48	55	81	1,767	166	1,504	97
City of South Portland	25,679	56	0	4	13	39	578	78	481	19
Total area actually reporting	100.0%	680	4	187	123	366	7,884	1,125	6,459	300
Rate per 100,000 inhabitants		127.4	0.7	35.0	23.0	68.6	1,476.9	210.7	1,210.0	56.2
Portland-Vancouver-Hillsboro, OR-WA MSA[2,5]	2,462,322									
Includes Clackamas, Columbia,[2] Multnomah, Washington, and Yamhill Counties, OR and Clark and Skamania Counties, WA										
City of Portland, OR	649,408	3,349	24	438	1,045	1,842	36,867	4,735	24,837	7,295
City of Vancouver, WA	176,884	652	9	154	122	367	5,469	749	3,657	1,063
City of Hillsboro, OR	107,433	268	1	80	60	127	2,144	209	1,714	221
City of Beaverton, OR	98,897	172	1	60	32	79	1,760	157	1,396	207
Total area actually reporting	98.8%	6,911	64	1,418	1,673	3,756			49,367	12,728
Estimated total	100.0%	6,974	65	1,432	1,685	3,792			49,932	12,820
Rate per 100,000 inhabitants		283.2	2.6	58.2	68.4	154.0			2,027.8	520.6
Port St. Lucie, FL MSA	473,556									
Includes Martin and St. Lucie Counties										
City of Port St. Lucie	188,652	186	2	13	31	140	2,126	309	1,730	87
Total area actually reporting	100.0%	1,106	13	156	195	742	7,964	1,450	6,114	400
Rate per 100,000 inhabitants		233.6	2.7	32.9	41.2	156.7	1,681.7	306.2	1,291.1	84.5
Prescott, AZ MSA	227,836									
Includes Yavapai County										
City of Prescott	42,975	157	0	11	15	131	903	121	757	25
Total area actually reporting	100.0%	701	4	75	43	579	4,197	768	3,184	245
Rate per 100,000 inhabitants		307.7	1.8	32.9	18.9	254.1	1,842.1	337.1	1,397.5	107.5
Providence-Warwick, RI-MA MSA	1,619,966									
Includes Bristol County, MA and Bristol, Kent, Newport, Providence, and Washington Counties, RI										
City of Providence, RI	179,854	960	12	104	255	589	5,925	1,013	4,332	580
City of Warwick, RI	81,617	97	1	27	12	57	1,383	173	1,149	61
Total area actually reporting	99.5%	4,756	32	637	1,002	3,085	27,304	4,963	20,182	2,159
Estimated total	100.0%	4,777	32	639	1,005	3,101	27,402	4,980	20,256	2,166
Rate per 100,000 inhabitants		294.9	2.0	39.4	62.0	191.4	1,691.5	307.4	1,250.4	133.7
Provo-Orem, UT MSA	616,739									
Includes Juab and Utah Counties										
City of Provo	117,540	148	1	52	29	66	2,036	155	1,764	117
City of Orem	99,045	69	0	14	22	33	2,016	191	1,696	129
Total area actually reporting	100.0%	492	7	163	92	230	9,436	1,051	7,857	528
Rate per 100,000 inhabitants		79.8	1.1	26.4	14.9	37.3	1,530.0	170.4	1,274.0	85.6
Pueblo, CO MSA	165,456									
Includes Pueblo County										
City of Pueblo	110,872	1,167	10	199	219	739	6,838	1,376	4,234	1,228
Total area actually reporting	100.0%	1,201	11	200	226	764	8,004	1,562	5,072	1,370
Rate per 100,000 inhabitants		725.9	6.6	120.9	136.6	461.8	4,837.5	944.1	3,065.5	828.0
Punta Gorda, FL MSA	182,274									
Includes Charlotte County										
City of Punta Gorda	19,181	16	0	0	5	11	246	23	208	15
Total area actually reporting	100.0%	376	1	33	28	314	2,299	391	1,781	127
Rate per 100,000 inhabitants		206.3	0.5	18.1	15.4	172.3	1,261.3	214.5	977.1	69.7
Racine, WI MSA[2]	195,139									
Includes Racine County										
City of Racine[2]	77,371	520	1	61	122	336	1,762	417	1,216	129
Total area actually reporting	100.0%	673	2	79	143	449	2,961	579	2,197	185
Rate per 100,000 inhabitants		344.9	1.0	40.5	73.3	230.1	1,517.4	296.7	1,125.9	94.8
Rapid City, SD MSA	146,750									
Includes Custer, Meade, and Pennington Counties										
City of Rapid City	74,986	480	6	101	68	305	2,872	466	2,102	304
Total area actually reporting	99.7%	705	7	173	72	453	3,865	685	2,795	385
Estimated total	100.0%	705	7	173	72	453	3,870	686	2,799	385
Rate per 100,000 inhabitants		480.4	4.8	117.9	49.1	308.7	2,637.1	467.5	1,907.3	262.4

Table 6. Crime in the United States, by Selected Metropolitan Statistical Area, 2017—Continued

(Number, percent, rate per 100,000 population.)

Area	Population	Violent crime	Murder and nonnegligent manslaughter	Rape[1]	Robbery	Aggravated assault	Property crime	Burglary	Larceny-theft	Motor vehicle theft
Reading, PA MSA	415,562									
Includes Berks County										
City of Reading	87,487	624	9	60	219	336	2,106	631	1,278	197
Total area actually reporting	100.0%	1,077	13	149	295	620	6,124	1,245	4,510	369
Rate per 100,000 inhabitants		259.2	3.1	35.9	71.0	149.2	1,473.7	299.6	1,085.3	88.8
Redding, CA MSA	179,818									
Includes Shasta County										
City of Redding	92,127	654	2	64	150	438	3,841	690	2,360	791
Total area actually reporting	100.0%	1,225	6	118	177	924	5,645	1,249	3,175	1,221
Rate per 100,000 inhabitants		681.2	3.3	65.6	98.4	513.9	3,139.3	694.6	1,765.7	679.0
Reno, NV MSA	465,669									
Includes Storey and Washoe Counties										
City of Reno	248,531	1,674	19	142	382	1,131	7,669	1,347	4,890	1,432
Total area actually reporting	100.0%	2,397	21	230	502	1,644	11,873	2,206	7,664	2,003
Rate per 100,000 inhabitants		514.7	4.5	49.4	107.8	353.0	2,549.7	473.7	1,645.8	430.1
Riverside-San Bernardino-Ontario, CA MSA[2]	4,572,004									
Includes Riverside and San Bernardino Counties										
City of Riverside	328,023	1,669	12	166	544	947	10,032	1,673	6,629	1,730
City of San Bernardino	217,259	2,805	34	158	877	1,736	8,403	2,136	3,990	2,277
City of Ontario[2]	174,724	683	8	136	220	319	4,473	720	2,842	911
City of Corona	169,164	223	1	36	107	79	3,297	561	2,177	559
City of Victorville	123,284	862	14	54	267	527	3,318	830	1,839	649
City of Temecula	115,220	117	1	5	38	73	2,614	353	2,011	250
City of Chino	89,420	227	3	10	87	127	2,142	443	1,405	294
City of Redlands	71,707	216	1	36	69	110	2,629	426	1,910	293
Total area actually reporting	100.0%	17,525	209	1,396	5,208	10,712	113,833	23,358	69,876	20,599
Rate per 100,000 inhabitants		383.3	4.6	30.5	113.9	234.3	2,489.8	510.9	1,528.3	450.5
Roanoke, VA MSA	314,169									
Includes Botetourt, Craig, Franklin, and Roanoke Counties and Roanoke and Salem Cities										
City of Roanoke	100,027	402	16	41	79	266	4,493	487	3,719	287
Total area actually reporting	100.0%	722	26	113	121	462	7,507	863	6,147	497
Rate per 100,000 inhabitants		229.8	8.3	36.0	38.5	147.1	2,389.5	274.7	1,956.6	158.2
Rochester, MN MSA	218,186									
Includes Dodge, Fillmore, Olmsted, and Wabasha Counties										
City of Rochester	115,228	224	1	61	46	116	2,143	288	1,757	98
Total area actually reporting	100.0%	318	1	86	51	180	2,855	423	2,278	154
Rate per 100,000 inhabitants		145.7	0.5	39.4	23.4	82.5	1,308.5	193.9	1,044.1	70.6
Rochester, NY MSA	1,081,106									
Includes Livingston, Monroe, Ontario, Orleans, Wayne, and Yates Counties										
City of Rochester	208,591	1,872	27	141	707	997	7,934	1,337	5,981	616
Total area actually reporting	99.6%	3,052	40	467	951	1,594	20,785	3,039	16,662	1,084
Estimated total	100.0%	3,059	40	468	953	1,598	20,843	3,046	16,711	1,086
Rate per 100,000 inhabitants		283.0	3.7	43.3	88.2	147.8	1,927.9	281.7	1,545.7	100.5
Rockford, IL MSA	337,935									
Includes Boone and Winnebago Counties										
City of Rockford	146,768	2,331	18	113	427	1,773	5,236	1,383	3,403	450
Total area actually reporting	99.0%	2,762	21	194	471	2,076	8,148	1,991	5,580	577
Estimated total	100.0%	2,769	21	195	473	2,080	8,204	1,999	5,625	580
Rate per 100,000 inhabitants		819.4	6.2	57.7	140.0	615.5	2,427.7	591.5	1,664.5	171.6
Rocky Mount, NC MSA[4]	146,800									
Includes Edgecombe and Nash Counties[4]										
City of Rocky Mount[4]	55,098		15		95	270	1,984	554	1,310	120
Total area actually reporting	94.2%		22		130	371	3,230	1,043	2,017	170
Estimated total	100.0%		22		136	385	3,471	1,087	2,204	180
Rate per 100,000 inhabitants			15.0		92.6	262.3	2,364.4	740.5	1,501.4	122.6
Rome, GA MSA	96,700									
Includes Floyd County										
City of Rome	36,366	205	3	6	32	164	1,480	268	1,151	61
Total area actually reporting	100.0%	322	5	21	43	253	2,898	566	2,161	171
Rate per 100,000 inhabitants		333.0	5.2	21.7	44.5	261.6	2,996.9	585.3	2,234.7	176.8
Sacramento–Roseville–Arden-Arcade, CA MSA	2,318,414									
Includes El Dorado, Placer, Sacramento, and Yolo Counties										
City of Sacramento	499,997	3,378	39	99	1,100	2,140	14,683	2,888	9,077	2,718
City of Roseville	135,028	237	0	27	87	123	3,322	389	2,623	310
City of Folsom	78,155	64	0	21	21	22	1,229	257	847	125
Total area actually reporting	100.0%	8,977	99	614	2,568	5,696	52,147	9,747	34,682	7,718
Rate per 100,000 inhabitants		387.2	4.3	26.5	110.8	245.7	2,249.3	420.4	1,495.9	332.9
Saginaw, MI MSA	191,556									
Includes Saginaw County										
City of Saginaw	48,589	762	15	50	75	622	913	383	455	75

Table 6. Crime in the United States, by Selected Metropolitan Statistical Area, 2017—Continued

(Number, percent, rate per 100,000 population.)

Area	Population	Violent crime	Murder and nonnegligent manslaughter	Rape[1]	Robbery	Aggravated assault	Property crime	Burglary	Larceny-theft	Motor vehicle theft
Total area actually reporting	100.0%	1,214	19	131	127	937	3,165	802	2,199	164
Rate per 100,000 inhabitants		633.8	9.9	68.4	66.3	489.2	1,652.3	418.7	1,148.0	85.6
Salem, OR MSA[4]	423,228									
Includes Marion[4] and Polk Counties										
City of Salem	169,565	641	6	44	167	424	7,195	897	5,437	861
Total area actually reporting	100.0%	1,186	14	115	265	792	12,931	1,732	9,521	1,678
Rate per 100,000 inhabitants		280.2	3.3	27.2	62.6	187.1	3,055.3	409.2	2,249.6	396.5
Salinas, CA MSA	437,962									
Includes Monterey County										
City of Salinas	158,313	1,021	28	71	358	564	4,795	964	2,589	1,242
Total area actually reporting	100.0%	1,802	43	168	547	1,044	10,043	1,937	6,026	2,080
Rate per 100,000 inhabitants		411.5	9.8	38.4	124.9	238.4	2,293.1	442.3	1,375.9	474.9
Salisbury, MD-DE MSA	404,765									
Includes Sussex County, DE and Somerset, Wicomico, and Worcester Counties, MD										
City of Salisbury, MD	33,558	326	7	21	94	204	1,784	273	1,443	68
Total area actually reporting	100.0%	1,592	16	192	320	1,064	10,313	2,001	7,973	339
Rate per 100,000 inhabitants		393.3	4.0	47.4	79.1	262.9	2,547.9	494.4	1,969.8	83.8
Salt Lake City, UT MSA[2]	1,203,339									
Includes Salt Lake and Tooele[2] Counties										
City of Salt Lake City	194,968	1,713	10	334	508	861	15,694	1,884	11,924	1,886
Total area actually reporting	99.9%	4,821	44	999	1,169	2,609	53,353	7,123	39,225	7,005
Estimated total	100.0%	4,821	44	999	1,169	2,609	53,363	7,124	39,233	7,006
Rate per 100,000 inhabitants		400.6	3.7	83.0	97.1	216.8	4,434.6	592.0	3,260.3	582.2
San Angelo, TX MSA	121,144									
Includes Irion and Tom Green Counties										
City of San Angelo	101,931	282	3	74	40	165	4,499	802	3,425	272
Total area actually reporting	100.0%	303	4	92	41	166	4,912	977	3,631	304
Rate per 100,000 inhabitants		250.1	3.3	75.9	33.8	137.0	4,054.7	806.5	2,997.3	250.9
San Antonio-New Braunfels, TX MSA[2,3]	2,476,620									
Includes Atascosa, Bandera, Bexar, Comal, Guadalupe, Kendall, Medina, and Wilson Counties										
City of San Antonio	1,520,712	10,759	124	1,270	2,298	7,067	73,676	11,722	55,090	6,864
City of New Braunfels	76,993	193	1	33	29	130	1,321	221	952	148
Total area actually reporting	99.9%	12,972	159	1,741	2,659	8,413			68,938	8,439
Estimated total	100.0%	12,976	159	1,742	2,660	8,415			68,960	8,441
Rate per 100,000 inhabitants		523.9	6.4	70.3	107.4	339.8			2,784.4	340.8
San Diego-Carlsbad, CA MSA	3,350,968									
Includes San Diego County										
City of San Diego	1,424,116	5,221	35	559	1,410	3,217	26,246	3,817	17,294	5,135
City of Carlsbad	115,344	247	0	30	46	171	2,209	432	1,638	139
Total area actually reporting	100.0%	11,296	81	1,098	3,013	7,104	56,816	9,134	37,951	9,731
Rate per 100,000 inhabitants		337.1	2.4	32.8	89.9	212.0	1,695.5	272.6	1,132.5	290.4
San Francisco-Oakland-Hayward, CA MSA[3]	4,732,078									
Includes the Metropolitan Divisions of Oakland-Hayward-Berkeley, San Francisco-Redwood City-South San Francisco, and San Rafael										
City of San Francisco	881,255	6,301	56	367	3,220	2,658	54,356	4,935	44,587	4,834
City of Oakland	424,915	5,521	69	400	2,676	2,376	25,422	2,622	17,305	5,495
City of Hayward	161,417	563	5	70	306	182	5,023	482	2,740	1,801
City of Berkeley	122,687	666	1	83	364	218	6,020	843	4,556	621
City of San Leandro	91,386	524	2	21	292	209	3,715	460	2,369	886
City of Redwood City	86,353	209	0	57	61	91	1,390	177	1,053	160
City of San Ramon	76,325	56	0	8	30	18	974	126	768	80
City of Pleasanton	84,440	99	0	13	53	33	1,661	137	1,406	118
City of Walnut Creek	69,953	105	1	2	39	63	2,304	243	1,871	190
City of South San Francisco	67,533	234	1	31	72	130	1,605	214	1,184	207
City of San Rafael	59,144	194	0	21	89	84	1,627	271	1,091	265
Total area actually reporting	100.0%	22,554	199	1,848	10,314	10,193		19,501		25,398
Rate per 100,000 inhabitants		476.6	4.2	39.1	218.0	215.4		412.1		536.7
Oakland-Hayward-Berkeley, CA MD[3]	2,817,472									
Includes Alameda and Contra Costa Counties										
Total area actually reporting	100.0%	13,753	132	1,104	6,317	6,200		11,086		18,442
Rate per 100,000 inhabitants		488.1	4.7	39.2	224.2	220.1		393.5		654.6
San Francisco-Redwood City-South San Francisco, CA MD	1,652,939									
Includes San Francisco and San Mateo Counties										
Total area actually reporting	100.0%	8,338	63	698	3,848	3,729	70,395	7,474	56,440	6,481
Rate per 100,000 inhabitants		504.4	3.8	42.2	232.8	225.6	4,258.8	452.2	3,414.5	392.1
San Rafael, CA MD	261,667									
Includes Marin County										
Total area actually reporting	100.0%	463	4	46	149	264	5,006	941	3,590	475
Rate per 100,000 inhabitants		176.9	1.5	17.6	56.9	100.9	1,913.1	359.6	1,372.0	181.5

Table 6. Crime in the United States, by Selected Metropolitan Statistical Area, 2017—Continued
(Number, percent, rate per 100,000 population.)

Area	Population	Violent crime	Murder and nonnegligent manslaughter	Rape[1]	Robbery	Aggravated assault	Property crime	Burglary	Larceny-theft	Motor vehicle theft
San Jose-Sunnyvale-Santa Clara, CA MSA	2,000,325									
Includes San Benito and Santa Clara Counties										
City of San Jose	1,037,529	4,188	32	571	1,376	2,209	25,323	3,926	13,329	8,068
City of Sunnyvale	154,919	182	1	29	56	96	2,682	512	1,872	298
City of Santa Clara	127,538	214	2	35	82	95	3,618	408	2,810	400
City of Mountain View	81,525	150	1	14	44	91	1,982	290	1,590	102
City of Milpitas	79,503	114	2	12	58	42	1,978	235	1,447	296
City of Palo Alto	67,441	90	0	11	39	40	1,783	214	1,478	91
City of Cupertino	60,970	77	2	9	21	45	970	164	756	50
Total area actually reporting	100.0%	6,178	48	827	1,931	3,372	45,510	6,972	28,107	10,431
Rate per 100,000 inhabitants		308.8	2.4	41.3	96.5	168.6	2,275.1	348.5	1,405.1	521.5
San Luis Obispo-Paso Robles-Arroyo Grande, CA MSA[5]	284,792									
Includes San Luis Obispo County[5]										
City of San Luis Obispo	47,934	178	0	44	23	111	1,782	172	1,516	94
City of Paso Robles	32,266	35	0	3	6	26	920	126	731	63
City of Arroyo Grande	18,239	32	0	3	5	24	311	53	226	32
Total area actually reporting	100.0%		2	96	85		5,812	1,038	4,345	429
Rate per 100,000 inhabitants			0.7	33.7	29.8		2,040.8	364.5	1,525.7	150.6
Santa Cruz-Watsonville, CA MSA	276,313									
Includes Santa Cruz County										
City of Santa Cruz	65,132	409	1	57	103	248	3,684	412	2,911	361
City of Watsonville	54,226	298	1	41	69	187	1,711	251	995	465
Total area actually reporting	100.0%	1,056	3	156	232	665	8,947	1,235	6,445	1,267
Rate per 100,000 inhabitants		382.2	1.1	56.5	84.0	240.7	3,238.0	447.0	2,332.5	458.5
Santa Fe, NM MSA	149,636									
Includes Santa Fe County										
City of Santa Fe	84,358	289	4	36	56	193	3,178	1,228	1,736	214
Total area actually reporting	100.0%	482	5	42	71	364	4,061	1,639	2,171	251
Rate per 100,000 inhabitants		322.1	3.3	28.1	47.4	243.3	2,713.9	1,095.3	1,450.9	167.7
Santa Maria-Santa Barbara, CA MSA	449,405									
Includes Santa Barbara County										
City of Santa Maria	107,424	476	3	58	155	260	2,354	446	1,231	677
City of Santa Barbara	92,508	377	0	67	80	230	2,499	327	1,968	204
Total area actually reporting	100.0%	1,532	8	257	327	940	8,742	1,663	5,825	1,254
Rate per 100,000 inhabitants		340.9	1.8	57.2	72.8	209.2	1,945.2	370.0	1,296.2	279.0
Santa Rosa, CA MSA	505,613									
Includes Sonoma County										
City of Santa Rosa	176,361	722	5	109	126	482	3,245	525	2,309	411
Total area actually reporting	100.0%	2,025	12	298	277	1,438	7,586	1,399	5,358	829
Rate per 100,000 inhabitants		400.5	2.4	58.9	54.8	284.4	1,500.4	276.7	1,059.7	164.0
Savannah, GA MSA[3]	390,752									
Includes Bryan, Chatham, and Effingham Counties										
City of Savannah-Chatham Metropolitan	242,941	1,124	35	100	381	608	8,336	1,335	6,061	940
Total area actually reporting	100.0%	1,534	38	130	440	926			8,601	1,142
Rate per 100,000 inhabitants		392.6	9.7	33.3	112.6	237.0			2,201.1	292.3
Scranton–Wilkes-Barre–Hazleton, PA MSA	554,189									
Includes Lackawanna, Luzerne, and Wyoming Counties										
City of Scranton	77,499	198	1	22	90	85	1,698	351	1,215	132
City of Wilkes-Barre	40,418	251	2	12	104	133	1,101	225	816	60
City of Hazleton	24,549	91	1	7	26	57	304	82	191	31
Total area actually reporting	98.5%	1,407	22	127	338	920	8,692	1,524	6,752	416
Estimated total	100.0%	1,422	22	128	342	930	8,813	1,538	6,854	421
Rate per 100,000 inhabitants		256.6	4.0	23.1	61.7	167.8	1,590.3	277.5	1,236.8	76.0
Seattle-Tacoma-Bellevue, WA MSA[3,4]	3,872,207									
Includes the Metropolitan Divisions of Seattle-Bellevue-Everett and Tacoma-Lakewood										
City of Seattle	721,365	4,564	27	266	1,515	2,756	37,934	7,805	26,499	3,630
City of Tacoma	213,504	1,737	10	171	403	1,153	11,901	2,073	7,742	2,086
City of Bellevue	143,703	144	0	24	55	65	4,175	592	3,274	309
City of Everett	110,040	497	5	52	131	309	5,099	869	3,292	938
City of Kent	128,990	465	7	70	203	185	6,928	948	4,666	1,314
City of Renton	102,470	328	3	45	113	167	5,128	607	3,640	881
City of Auburn[3]	78,718	376	3	64	117	192			2,124	653
City of Lakewood	61,080	425	4	54	89	278	2,793	488	1,927	378
City of Redmond	63,889	96	2	11	33	50	2,077	271	1,695	111
Total area actually reporting	100.0%	13,695	115	1,451	3,955	8,174			94,652	18,627
Rate per 100,000 inhabitants		353.7	3.0	37.5	102.1	211.1			2,444.4	481.0
Seattle-Bellevue-Everett, WA MD[3,4]	2,996,781									
Includes King[4] and Snohomish Counties										
Total area actually reporting	100.0%	9,645	91	1,005	3,087	5,462			74,313	13,991
Rate per 100,000 inhabitants		321.8	3.0	33.5	103.0	182.3			2,479.8	466.9
Tacoma-Lakewood, WA MD[3]	875,426									

Table 6. Crime in the United States, by Selected Metropolitan Statistical Area, 2017—Continued

(Number, percent, rate per 100,000 population.)

Area	Population	Violent crime	Murder and nonnegligent manslaughter	Rape[1]	Robbery	Aggravated assault	Property crime	Burglary	Larceny-theft	Motor vehicle theft
Includes Pierce County										
Total area actually reporting	100.0%	4,050	24	446	868	2,712			20,339	4,636
Rate per 100,000 inhabitants		462.6	2.7	50.9	99.2	309.8			2,323.3	529.6
Sebastian-Vero Beach, FL MSA	154,339									
Includes Indian River County										
City of Sebastian	25,277	48	0	3	8	37	381	51	312	18
City of Vero Beach	17,015	46	0	10	7	29	490	94	376	20
Total area actually reporting	100.0%	457	3	39	51	364	2,884	532	2,189	163
Rate per 100,000 inhabitants		296.1	1.9	25.3	33.0	235.8	1,868.6	344.7	1,418.3	105.6
Sebring, FL MSA	101,583									
Includes Highlands County										
City of Sebring	10,679	68	2	5	12	49	538	129	395	14
Total area actually reporting	100.0%	329	7	38	42	242	2,665	693	1,863	109
Rate per 100,000 inhabitants		323.9	6.9	37.4	41.3	238.2	2,623.5	682.2	1,834.0	107.3
Sheboygan, WI MSA	115,448									
Includes Sheboygan County										
City of Sheboygan	48,595	161	0	40	12	109	821	90	698	33
Total area actually reporting	100.0%	211	2	66	14	129	1,416	170	1,202	44
Rate per 100,000 inhabitants		182.8	1.7	57.2	12.1	111.7	1,226.5	147.3	1,041.2	38.1
Sherman-Denison, TX MSA	129,343									
Includes Grayson County										
City of Sherman	42,122	158	2	20	35	101	1,306	287	942	77
City of Denison	23,814	107	4	18	15	70	525	115	340	70
Total area actually reporting	97.1%	375	6	64	52	253	2,509	606	1,664	239
Estimated total	100.0%	385	6	66	54	259	2,596	619	1,731	246
Rate per 100,000 inhabitants		297.7	4.6	51.0	41.7	200.2	2,007.1	478.6	1,338.3	190.2
Shreveport-Bossier City, LA MSA	439,907									
Includes Bossier, Caddo, De Soto, and Webster Parishes										
City of Shreveport	193,937	1,850	52	152	498	1,148	10,813	2,256	7,673	884
City of Bossier City	69,632	535	4	48	79	404	3,283	451	2,549	283
Total area actually reporting	100.0%	2,670	62	218	598	1,792	16,859	3,438	12,082	1,339
Rate per 100,000 inhabitants		606.9	14.1	49.6	135.9	407.4	3,832.4	781.5	2,746.5	304.4
Sierra Vista-Douglas, AZ MSA	124,671									
Includes Cochise County										
City of Sierra Vista	42,859	191	0	24	23	144	1,287	225	998	64
City of Douglas	16,443	41	1	0	3	37	657	94	549	14
Total area actually reporting	89.6%	466	1	38	35	392	2,721	392	2,185	144
Estimated total	100.0%	504	1	42	43	418	3,071	445	2,456	170
Rate per 100,000 inhabitants		404.3	0.8	33.7	34.5	335.3	2,463.3	356.9	1,970.0	136.4
Sioux City, IA-NE-SD MSA	168,938									
Includes Plymouth and Woodbury Counties, IA; Dakota and Dixon Counties, NE; and Union County, SD										
City of Sioux City, IA	82,879	360	2	56	71	231	3,561	612	2,660	289
Total area actually reporting	98.5%	488	3	73	80	332	4,634	802	3,420	412
Estimated total	100.0%	492	3	74	80	335	4,671	809	3,447	415
Rate per 100,000 inhabitants		291.2	1.8	43.8	47.4	198.3	2,764.9	478.9	2,040.4	245.7
Sioux Falls, SD MSA	259,149									
Includes Lincoln, McCook, Minnehaha, and Turner Counties										
City of Sioux Falls	177,888	801	4	121	100	576	5,083	655	3,959	469
Total area actually reporting	99.3%	918	6	146	102	664	5,870	833	4,517	520
Estimated total	100.0%	921	6	147	102	666	5,895	837	4,536	522
Rate per 100,000 inhabitants		355.4	2.3	56.7	39.4	257.0	2,274.8	323.0	1,750.3	201.4
South Bend-Mishawaka, IN-MI MSA[5]	321,506									
Includes St. Joseph County, IN and Cass County, MI										
City of South Bend, IN	101,857	1,064	15	93	345	611	5,100	1,192	3,440	468
City of Mishawaka, IN[5]	48,749	105	3	8	54	40		275		
Total area actually reporting	96.9%	1,389	23	166	435	765		2,028		
Estimated total	100.0%	1,417	23	170	440	784		2,056		
Rate per 100,000 inhabitants		440.7	7.2	52.9	136.9	243.9		639.5		
Spokane-Spokane Valley, WA MSA	563,140									
Includes Pend Oreille, Spokane, and Stevens Counties										
City of Spokane	217,066	1,360	6	238	229	887	15,697	2,221	11,739	1,737
City of Spokane Valley	97,430	200	2	48	29	121	4,417	606	3,376	435
Total area actually reporting	99.9%	1,814	15	365	286	1,148	25,182	4,069	18,499	2,614
Estimated total	100.0%	1,814	15	365	286	1,148	25,190	4,070	18,505	2,615
Rate per 100,000 inhabitants		322.1	2.7	64.8	50.8	203.9	4,473.1	722.7	3,286.0	464.4
Springfield, IL MSA	210,042									
Includes Menard and Sangamon Counties										

Table 6. Crime in the United States, by Selected Metropolitan Statistical Area, 2017—Continued

(Number, percent, rate per 100,000 population.)

Area	Population	Violent crime	Murder and nonnegligent manslaughter	Rape[1]	Robbery	Aggravated assault	Property crime	Burglary	Larceny-theft	Motor vehicle theft
City of Springfield	115,568	1,219	11	93	251	864	5,496	1,210	3,973	313
Total area actually reporting	96.2%	1,462	13	135	266	1,048	6,599	1,506	4,682	411
Estimated total	100.0%	1,480	13	138	271	1,058	6,730	1,525	4,786	419
Rate per 100,000 inhabitants		704.6	6.2	65.7	129.0	503.7	3,204.1	726.0	2,278.6	199.5
Springfield, MA MSA	631,954									
Includes Hampden and Hampshire Counties										
City of Springfield	154,562	1,351	14	73	380	884	4,594	1,183	2,902	509
Total area actually reporting	97.5%	3,138	22	312	637	2,167	13,512	2,875	9,609	1,028
Estimated total	100.0%	3,184	22	317	644	2,201	13,718	2,910	9,765	1,043
Rate per 100,000 inhabitants		503.8	3.5	50.2	101.9	348.3	2,170.7	460.5	1,545.2	165.0
Springfield, MO MSA	462,905									
Includes Christian, Dallas, Greene, Polk, and Webster Counties										
City of Springfield	168,654	2,258	14	352	382	1,510	14,932	2,236	10,727	1,969
Total area actually reporting	100.0%	2,672	23	431	412	1,806	19,826	3,241	14,171	2,414
Rate per 100,000 inhabitants		577.2	5.0	93.1	89.0	390.1	4,283.0	700.1	3,061.3	521.5
Springfield, OH MSA	134,569									
Includes Clark County										
City of Springfield	58,843	370	9	25	177	159	4,024	1,040	2,691	293
Total area actually reporting	94.7%	393	9	32	180	172	4,883	1,269	3,281	333
Estimated total	100.0%	403	9	34	183	177	5,030	1,291	3,399	340
Rate per 100,000 inhabitants		299.5	6.7	25.3	136.0	131.5	3,737.9	959.4	2,525.8	252.7
State College, PA MSA	162,798									
Includes Centre County										
City of State College	58,169	44	0	7	9	28	616	45	566	5
Total area actually reporting	100.0%	152	3	56	19	74	1,685	173	1,490	22
Rate per 100,000 inhabitants		93.4	1.8	34.4	11.7	45.5	1,035.0	106.3	915.2	13.5
Staunton-Waynesboro, VA MSA	121,588									
Includes Augusta County and Staunton and Waynesboro Cities										
City of Staunton	24,423	35	0	7	8	20	551	77	456	18
City of Waynesboro	22,004	40	0	13	10	17	528	46	459	23
Total area actually reporting	100.0%	170	1	48	23	98	1,975	334	1,507	134
Rate per 100,000 inhabitants		139.8	0.8	39.5	18.9	80.6	1,624.3	274.7	1,239.4	110.2
St. Cloud, MN MSA	197,461									
Includes Benton and Stearns Counties										
City of St. Cloud	67,911	256	3	62	49	142	2,789	330	2,278	181
Total area actually reporting	100.0%	361	4	93	53	211	4,515	579	3,662	274
Rate per 100,000 inhabitants		182.8	2.0	47.1	26.8	106.9	2,286.5	293.2	1,854.5	138.8
St. Joseph, MO-KS MSA	126,515									
Includes Doniphan County, KS and Andrew, Buchanan, and DeKalb Counties, MO										
City of St. Joseph, MO	76,435	438	7	37	98	296	5,146	737	3,633	776
Total area actually reporting	99.4%	524	8	42	104	370	5,827	907	4,067	853
Estimated total	100.0%	525	8	42	104	371	5,847	910	4,082	855
Rate per 100,000 inhabitants		415.0	6.3	33.2	82.2	293.2	4,621.6	719.3	3,226.5	675.8
St. Louis, MO-IL MSA[2,5,6]	2,813,173									
Includes Bond, Calhoun, Clinton, Jersey, Macoupin, Madison, Monroe, and St. Clair Counties, IL and Franklin, Jefferson, Lincoln, St. Charles, St. Louis, and Warren Counties and St. Louis City, MO										
City of St. Louis, MO	310,284	6,461	205	289	1,944	4,023	18,745	3,138	12,894	2,713
City of St. Charles, MO	69,804	158	2	23	35	98	1,765	181	1,450	134
Total area actually reporting	97.9%		352	1,069	3,395		67,670	11,354	49,545	6,771
Estimated total	100.0%		354	1,088	3,428		68,598	11,496	50,276	6,826
Rate per 100,000 inhabitants			12.6	38.7	121.9		2,438.5	408.6	1,787.2	242.6
Stockton-Lodi, CA MSA[2]	740,904									
Includes San Joaquin County										
City of Stockton[2]	309,566	4,379	55	154	1,208	2,962	11,229	2,140	7,040	2,049
City of Lodi	65,042	323	1	13	127	182	1,681	347	985	349
Total area actually reporting	100.0%	5,991	68	247	1,671	4,005	21,751	3,925	13,965	3,861
Rate per 100,000 inhabitants		808.6	9.2	33.3	225.5	540.6	2,935.7	529.8	1,884.9	521.1
Sumter, SC MSA	107,470									
Includes Sumter County										
City of Sumter	40,747	333	5	13	63	252	1,839	354	1,411	74
Total area actually reporting	100.0%	736	8	36	99	593	3,812	990	2,575	247
Rate per 100,000 inhabitants		684.8	7.4	33.5	92.1	551.8	3,547.0	921.2	2,396.0	229.8
Syracuse, NY MSA	656,920									
Includes Madison, Onondaga, and Oswego Counties										
City of Syracuse	143,069	1,009	20	98	284	607	4,817	1,145	3,301	371

Table 6. Crime in the United States, by Selected Metropolitan Statistical Area, 2017—Continued

(Number, percent, rate per 100,000 population.)

Area	Population	Violent crime	Murder and nonnegligent manslaughter	Rape[1]	Robbery	Aggravated assault	Property crime	Burglary	Larceny-theft	Motor vehicle theft
Total area actually reporting	100.0%	1,759	26	353	386	994	13,478	2,300	10,506	672
Rate per 100,000 inhabitants		267.8	4.0	53.7	58.8	151.3	2,051.7	350.1	1,599.3	102.3
Tallahassee, FL MSA	382,480									
Includes Gadsden, Jefferson, Leon, and Wakulla Counties										
City of Tallahassee	192,455	1,503	17	190	348	948	9,428	1,519	7,165	744
Total area actually reporting	99.2%	2,316	25	286	409	1,596	13,446	2,521	9,957	968
Estimated total	100.0%	2,327	25	287	412	1,603	13,532	2,533	10,024	975
Rate per 100,000 inhabitants		608.4	6.5	75.0	107.7	419.1	3,538.0	662.3	2,620.8	254.9
Tampa-St. Petersburg-Clearwater, FL MSA	3,083,660									
Includes Hernando, Hillsborough, Pasco, and Pinellas Counties										
City of Tampa	384,360	1,785	39	121	406	1,219	6,702	1,235	4,900	567
City of St. Petersburg	263,712	1,842	20	136	499	1,187	11,373	1,772	8,623	978
City of Clearwater	115,295	578	3	85	141	349	3,652	494	2,909	249
City of Largo	83,728	365	1	71	97	196	2,856	310	2,315	231
Total area actually reporting	100.0%	10,273	111	1,137	2,104	6,921	64,807	10,650	49,151	5,006
Rate per 100,000 inhabitants		333.1	3.6	36.9	68.2	224.4	2,101.6	345.4	1,593.9	162.3
Texarkana, TX-AR MSA	150,196									
Includes Little River and Miller Counties, AR and Bowie County, TX										
City of Texarkana, TX	37,882	478	3	31	86	358	1,889	311	1,457	121
Total area actually reporting	100.0%	939	11	86	150	692	4,748	1,032	3,391	325
Rate per 100,000 inhabitants		625.2	7.3	57.3	99.9	460.7	3,161.2	687.1	2,257.7	216.4
The Villages, FL MSA	130,154									
Includes Sumter County										
Total area actually reporting	100.0%	305	6	24	24	251	1,158	310	782	66
Rate per 100,000 inhabitants		234.3	4.6	18.4	18.4	192.8	889.7	238.2	600.8	50.7
Toledo, OH MSA[2,5]	606,018									
Includes Fulton, Lucas, and Wood Counties										
City of Toledo[2,5]	277,116		35		780	1,834	11,095	3,103	7,247	745
Total area actually reporting	94.9%		38		856	2,016	16,670	3,890	11,830	950
Estimated total	100.0%		39		870	2,038	17,309	3,987	12,342	980
Rate per 100,000 inhabitants			6.4		143.6	336.3	2,856.2	657.9	2,036.6	161.7
Topeka, KS MSA	232,643									
Includes Jackson, Jefferson, Osage, Shawnee, and Wabaunsee Counties										
City of Topeka	126,624	777	27	56	269	425	6,494	1,001	4,725	768
Total area actually reporting	98.0%	952	32	83	283	554	8,126	1,340	5,862	924
Estimated total	100.0%	962	32	85	284	561	8,223	1,352	5,938	933
Rate per 100,000 inhabitants		413.5	13.8	36.5	122.1	241.1	3,534.6	581.1	2,552.4	401.0
Trenton, NJ MSA	373,064									
Includes Mercer County										
City of Trenton	84,231	1,083	23	63	343	654	2,193	792	1,035	366
Total area actually reporting	100.0%	1,387	27	96	451	813	6,996	1,543	4,822	631
Rate per 100,000 inhabitants		371.8	7.2	25.7	120.9	217.9	1,875.3	413.6	1,292.5	169.1
Tucson, AZ MSA	1,021,012									
Includes Pima County										
City of Tucson	532,323	4,268	46	498	1,431	2,293	27,956	4,424	21,125	2,407
Total area actually reporting	99.4%	5,078	64	612	1,657	2,745	39,956	6,517	30,246	3,193
Estimated total	100.0%	5,095	64	614	1,661	2,756	40,107	6,540	30,363	3,204
Rate per 100,000 inhabitants		499.0	6.3	60.1	162.7	269.9	3,928.2	640.5	2,973.8	313.8
Tulsa, OK MSA	989,910									
Includes Creek, Okmulgee, Osage, Pawnee, Rogers, Tulsa, and Wagoner Counties										
City of Tulsa	404,868	4,214	70	423	964	2,757	22,088	5,574	13,054	3,460
Total area actually reporting	100.0%	5,600	90	655	1,098	3,757	33,968	8,320	20,791	4,857
Rate per 100,000 inhabitants		565.7	9.1	66.2	110.9	379.5	3,431.4	840.5	2,100.3	490.7
Tuscaloosa, AL MSA	243,131									
Includes Hale, Pickens, and Tuscaloosa Counties										
City of Tuscaloosa	101,124	474	9	54	168	243	4,174	814	3,161	199
Total area actually reporting	99.0%	853	16	87	211	539	6,863	1,460	4,983	420
Estimated total	100.0%	865	16	88	213	548	6,940	1,473	5,041	426
Rate per 100,000 inhabitants		355.8	6.6	36.2	87.6	225.4	2,854.4	605.8	2,073.4	175.2
Twin Falls, ID MSA	108,516									
Includes Jerome and Twin Falls Counties										
City of Twin Falls	48,912	210	0	44	9	157	1,287	196	1,006	85
Total area actually reporting	100.0%	344	0	65	17	262	1,976	435	1,375	166
Rate per 100,000 inhabitants		317.0	0.0	59.9	15.7	241.4	1,820.9	400.9	1,267.1	153.0
Tyler, TX MSA	227,621									
Includes Smith County										

Table 6. Crime in the United States, by Selected Metropolitan Statistical Area, 2017—Continued

(Number, percent, rate per 100,000 population.)

Area	Population	Violent crime	Murder and nonnegligent manslaughter	Rape[1]	Robbery	Aggravated assault	Property crime	Burglary	Larceny-theft	Motor vehicle theft
City of Tyler	106,115	464	6	65	60	333	3,337	446	2,745	146
Total area actually reporting	99.9%	802	9	116	85	592	5,618	1,152	4,076	390
Estimated total	100.0%	802	9	116	85	592	5,622	1,153	4,079	390
Rate per 100,000 inhabitants		352.3	4.0	51.0	37.3	260.1	2,469.9	506.5	1,792.0	171.3
Urban Honolulu, HI MSA	990,384									
Includes Honolulu County										
Total area actually reporting	100.0%	2,440	32	285	908	1,215	27,477	3,331	20,540	3,606
Rate per 100,000 inhabitants		246.4	3.2	28.8	91.7	122.7	2,774.4	336.3	2,073.9	364.1
Utica-Rome, NY MSA	293,570									
Includes Herkimer and Oneida Counties										
City of Utica	60,395	337	3	42	78	214	1,986	376	1,543	67
City of Rome	32,200	71	1	10	13	47	563	109	440	14
Total area actually reporting	99.1%	839	5	237	114	483	5,047	816	4,076	155
Estimated total	100.0%	843	5	237	115	486	5,084	820	4,108	156
Rate per 100,000 inhabitants		287.2	1.7	80.7	39.2	165.5	1,731.8	279.3	1,399.3	53.1
Valdosta, GA MSA	145,652									
Includes Brooks, Echols, Lanier, and Lowndes Counties										
City of Valdosta	56,729	215	10	17	47	141	3,485	554	2,699	232
Total area actually reporting	99.4%	439	11	39	69	320	5,259	1,023	3,859	377
Estimated total	100.0%	442	11	39	70	322	5,294	1,028	3,886	380
Rate per 100,000 inhabitants		303.5	7.6	26.8	48.1	221.1	3,634.7	705.8	2,668.0	260.9
Vallejo-Fairfield, CA MSA	444,232									
Includes Solano County										
City of Vallejo	122,174	1,048	15	93	390	550	4,597	2,445	1,181	971
City of Fairfield	116,372	546	10	40	181	315	3,252	545	2,174	533
Total area actually reporting	100.0%	2,112	30	179	701	1,202	12,004	3,660	6,337	2,007
Rate per 100,000 inhabitants		475.4	6.8	40.3	157.8	270.6	2,702.2	823.9	1,426.5	451.8
Victoria, TX MSA	100,898									
Includes Goliad and Victoria Counties										
City of Victoria	68,544	217	4	48	49	116	2,436	646	1,680	110
Total area actually reporting	100.0%	339	6	85	57	191	3,126	941	2,026	159
Rate per 100,000 inhabitants		336.0	5.9	84.2	56.5	189.3	3,098.2	932.6	2,008.0	157.6
Vineland-Bridgeton, NJ MSA	153,970									
Includes Cumberland County										
City of Vineland	60,477	298	2	24	93	179	2,414	472	1,883	59
City of Bridgeton	24,937	272	5	22	147	98	994	245	710	39
Total area actually reporting	100.0%	802	11	70	300	421	5,472	1,109	4,213	150
Rate per 100,000 inhabitants		520.9	7.1	45.5	194.8	273.4	3,553.9	720.3	2,736.2	97.4
Virginia Beach-Norfolk-Newport News, VA-NC MSA[4]	1,733,006									
Includes Currituck and Gates Counties, NC[4] and Gloucester, Isle of Wight, James City, Mathews, and York Counties and Chesapeake, Hampton, Newport News, Norfolk, Poquoson, Portsmouth, Suffolk, Virginia Beach, and Williamsburg Cities, VA										
City of Virginia Beach, VA	454,353	625	14	102	272	237	8,790	754	7,577	459
City of Norfolk, VA	245,190	1,363	36	135	371	821	9,192	1,156	7,318	718
City of Newport News, VA	181,738	907	24	93	239	551	5,528	829	4,211	488
City of Hampton, VA	134,929	407	17	26	185	179	4,364	551	3,481	332
City of Portsmouth, VA	95,100	677	17	36	224	400	5,447	1,160	3,903	384
Total area actually reporting	99.3%	5,717	137	597	1,633	3,350	45,489	5,952	36,587	2,950
Estimated total	100.0%	5,732	137	598	1,635	3,362	45,642	6,007	36,675	2,960
Rate per 100,000 inhabitants		330.8	7.9	34.5	94.3	194.0	2,633.7	346.6	2,116.3	170.8
Visalia-Porterville, CA MSA	462,877									
Includes Tulare County										
City of Visalia	132,143	457	9	81	144	223	4,396	839	2,953	604
City of Porterville	59,245	247	4	10	58	175	1,535	338	925	272
Total area actually reporting	100.0%	1,665	33	162	386	1,084	11,770	2,367	7,184	2,219
Rate per 100,000 inhabitants		359.7	7.1	35.0	83.4	234.2	2,542.8	511.4	1,552.0	479.4
Waco, TX MSA[2]	266,886									
Includes Falls and McLennan Counties										
City of Waco	135,997	690	5	117	108	460	4,889	957	3,741	191
Total area actually reporting	92.3%	1,169	5	210	143	811	7,037	1,345	5,383	309
Estimated total	100.0%	1,225	5	218	156	846	7,435	1,417	5,674	344
Rate per 100,000 inhabitants		459.0	1.9	81.7	58.5	317.0	2,785.8	530.9	2,126.0	128.9
Walla Walla, WA MSA	64,684									
Includes Columbia and Walla Walla Counties										
City of Walla Walla	32,189	140	1	31	24	84	1,131	148	917	66
Total area actually reporting	100.0%	217	1	48	26	142	1,707	259	1,323	125
Rate per 100,000 inhabitants		335.5	1.5	74.2	40.2	219.5	2,639.0	400.4	2,045.3	193.2

Table 6. Crime in the United States, by Selected Metropolitan Statistical Area, 2017—Continued

(Number, percent, rate per 100,000 population.)

Area	Population	Violent crime	Murder and nonnegligent manslaughter	Rape[1]	Robbery	Aggravated assault	Property crime	Burglary	Larceny-theft	Motor vehicle theft
Warner Robins, GA MSA	191,962									
Includes Houston, Peach, and Pulaski Counties										
City of Warner Robins	75,323	385	5	34	132	214	4,107	805	3,072	230
Total area actually reporting	100.0%	722	12	46	187	477	7,153	1,313	5,434	406
Rate per 100,000 inhabitants		376.1	6.3	24.0	97.4	248.5	3,726.3	684.0	2,830.8	211.5
Washington-Arlington-Alexandria, DC-VA-MD-WV MSA[2]	6,207,972									
Includes the Metropolitan Divisions of Silver Spring-Frederick-Rockville, MD and Washington-Arlington-Alexandria, DC-VA-MD-WV										
City of Washington, D.C.	693,972	6,584	116	443	2,351	3,674	28,843	1,808	24,490	2,545
City of Alexandria, VA	158,256	262	6	16	102	138	2,482	163	2,046	273
City of Frederick, MD	70,860	468	1	28	87	352	1,298	148	1,107	43
Total area actually reporting	99.9%	16,953	280	1,782	5,895	8,996	108,091	9,688	89,168	9,235
Estimated total	100.0%	16,973	280	1,785	5,897	9,011	108,355	9,726	89,378	9,251
Rate per 100,000 inhabitants		273.4	4.5	28.8	95.0	145.2	1,745.4	156.7	1,439.7	149.0
Silver Spring-Frederick-Rockville, MD MD[2]	1,304,678									
Includes Frederick and Montgomery[2] Counties										
Total area actually reporting	100.0%	2,166	17	283	777	1,089	17,090	1,874	14,288	928
Rate per 100,000 inhabitants		166.0	1.3	21.7	59.6	83.5	1,309.9	143.6	1,095.1	71.1
Washington-Arlington-Alexandria, DC-VA-MD-WV MD	4,903,294									
Includes District of Columbia; Calvert, Charles, and Prince George's Counties, MD; Arlington, Clarke, Culpeper, Fairfax, Fauquier, Loudoun, Prince William, Rappahannock, Spotsylvania, Stafford, and Warren Counties and Alexandria, Fairfax, Falls Church, Fredericksburg, Manassas, and Manassas Park Cities, VA; and Jefferson County, WV										
Total area actually reporting	99.8%	14,787	263	1,499	5,118	7,907	91,001	7,814	74,880	8,307
Estimated total	100.0%	14,807	263	1,502	5,120	7,922	91,265	7,852	75,090	8,323
Rate per 100,000 inhabitants		302.0	5.4	30.6	104.4	161.6	1,861.3	160.1	1,531.4	169.7
Waterloo-Cedar Falls, IA MSA	170,137									
Includes Black Hawk, Bremer, and Grundy Counties										
City of Waterloo	67,855	341	5	34	53	249	1,927	532	1,253	142
City of Cedar Falls	41,744	86	1	27	6	52	822	128	666	28
Total area actually reporting	94.0%	517	6	77	62	372	3,226	833	2,184	209
Estimated total	100.0%	541	6	81	64	390	3,412	871	2,321	220
Rate per 100,000 inhabitants		318.0	3.5	47.6	37.6	229.2	2,005.4	511.9	1,364.2	129.3
Watertown-Fort Drum, NY MSA	113,858									
Includes Jefferson County										
City of Watertown	25,746	139	1	39	16	83	1,054	153	880	21
Total area actually reporting	99.1%	234	4	84	23	123	2,003	291	1,665	47
Estimated total	100.0%	235	4	84	23	124	2,019	293	1,678	48
Rate per 100,000 inhabitants		206.4	3.5	73.8	20.2	108.9	1,773.3	257.3	1,473.8	42.2
Wausau, WI MSA	135,895									
Includes Marathon County										
City of Wausau	38,832	123	0	32	14	77	736	90	620	26
Total area actually reporting	100.0%	217	4	58	18	137	1,442	195	1,206	41
Rate per 100,000 inhabitants		159.7	2.9	42.7	13.2	100.8	1,061.1	143.5	887.4	30.2
Weirton-Steubenville, WV-OH MSA	118,293									
Includes Jefferson County, OH and Brooke and Hancock Counties, WV										
City of Weirton, WV	18,870	21	0	3	5	13	188	39	134	15
City of Steubenville, OH	17,979	49	3	4	11	31	1,132	89	1,021	22
Total area actually reporting	84.8%	133	4	21	21	87	1,681	228	1,385	68
Estimated total	100.0%	167	4	27	28	108	2,131	294	1,744	93
Rate per 100,000 inhabitants		141.2	3.4	22.8	23.7	91.3	1,801.5	248.5	1,474.3	78.6
Wenatchee, WA MSA	119,117									
Includes Chelan and Douglas Counties										
City of Wenatchee	34,191	73	1	18	16	38	818	123	647	48
Total area actually reporting	100.0%	140	2	35	25	78	2,068	417	1,513	138
Rate per 100,000 inhabitants		117.5	1.7	29.4	21.0	65.5	1,736.1	350.1	1,270.2	115.9
Wheeling, WV-OH MSA	141,891									
Includes Belmont County, OH and Marshall and Ohio Counties, WV										
City of Wheeling, WV	27,196	332	2	15	31	284	584	153	407	24
Total area actually reporting	83.7%	465	5	42	38	380	1,467	314	1,063	90
Estimated total	100.0%	515	5	51	45	414	1,904	396	1,386	122
Rate per 100,000 inhabitants		363.0	3.5	35.9	31.7	291.8	1,341.9	279.1	976.8	86.0
Wichita, KS MSA[3]	646,209									
Includes Butler, Harvey, Kingman, Sedgwick,[3] and Sumner Counties										

Table 6. Crime in the United States, by Selected Metropolitan Statistical Area, 2017—Continued

(Number, percent, rate per 100,000 population.)

Area	Population	Violent crime	Murder and nonnegligent manslaughter	Rape[1]	Robbery	Aggravated assault	Property crime	Burglary	Larceny-theft	Motor vehicle theft
City of Wichita	391,084	3,998	35	382	599	2,982	21,649	3,281	15,890	2,478
Total area actually reporting	99.4%	4,671	44	486	645	3,496			19,971	2,896
Estimated total	100.0%	4,680	44	488	646	3,502			20,036	2,903
Rate per 100,000 inhabitants		724.2	6.8	75.5	100.0	541.9			3,100.5	449.2
Wichita Falls, TX MSA[2]	150,431									
Includes Archer, Clay, and Wichita Counties										
City of Wichita Falls	104,706	374	4	78	127	165	3,257	725	2,294	238
Total area actually reporting	97.7%	491	6	103	132	250	4,020	926	2,784	310
Estimated total	100.0%	501	6	105	134	256	4,098	938	2,844	316
Rate per 100,000 inhabitants		333.0	4.0	69.8	89.1	170.2	2,724.2	623.5	1,890.6	210.1
Williamsport, PA MSA	115,169									
Includes Lycoming County										
City of Williamsport	28,743	107	2	12	27	66	880	119	741	20
Total area actually reporting	100.0%	211	2	29	35	145	1,887	292	1,557	38
Rate per 100,000 inhabitants		183.2	1.7	25.2	30.4	125.9	1,638.5	253.5	1,351.9	33.0
Wilmington, NC MSA[4]	287,932									
Includes New Hanover and Pender Counties[4]										
City of Wilmington[4]	119,422		18		195	535	4,318	998	3,039	281
Total area actually reporting	99.1%		25		257	706	7,883	1,793	5,700	390
Estimated total	100.0%		25		259	710	7,955	1,806	5,756	393
Rate per 100,000 inhabitants			8.7		90.0	246.6	2,762.8	627.2	1,999.1	136.5
Winchester, VA-WV MSA	136,089									
Includes Frederick County and Winchester City, VA and Hampshire County, WV										
City of Winchester, VA	27,715	115	0	36	25	54	688	81	584	23
Total area actually reporting	84.3%	217	0	77	43	97	1,907	239	1,578	90
Estimated total	100.0%	277	1	86	46	144	2,214	319	1,769	126
Rate per 100,000 inhabitants		203.5	0.7	63.2	33.8	105.8	1,626.9	234.4	1,299.9	92.6
Worcester, MA-CT MSA	865,611									
Includes Windham County, CT and Worcester County, MA										
City of Worcester, MA	185,107	1,345	5	42	324	974	4,047	866	2,784	397
Total area actually reporting	94.7%	2,986	10	279	475	2,222	11,051	2,055	8,198	798
Estimated total	100.0%	3,118	11	293	496	2,318	11,636	2,154	8,641	841
Rate per 100,000 inhabitants		360.2	1.3	33.8	57.3	267.8	1,344.3	248.8	998.3	97.2
Yakima, WA MSA	251,281									
Includes Yakima County										
City of Yakima	94,375	593	13	70	150	360	4,306	901	2,841	564
Total area actually reporting	100.0%	893	22	105	211	555	8,128	1,760	5,230	1,138
Rate per 100,000 inhabitants		355.4	8.8	41.8	84.0	220.9	3,234.6	700.4	2,081.3	452.9
York-Hanover, PA MSA	445,423									
Includes York County										
City of York	43,857	472	14	10	191	257	1,288	251	885	152
City of Hanover	15,606	36	0	2	10	24	378	32	340	6
Total area actually reporting	100.0%	1,098	23	108	301	666	6,492	860	5,294	338
Rate per 100,000 inhabitants		246.5	5.2	24.2	67.6	149.5	1,457.5	193.1	1,188.5	75.9
Yuba City, CA MSA	172,545									
Includes Sutter and Yuba Counties										
City of Yuba City	67,042	255	0	23	82	150	2,207	380	1,448	379
Total area actually reporting	100.0%	667	4	55	146	462	4,919	1,160	2,785	974
Rate per 100,000 inhabitants		386.6	2.3	31.9	84.6	267.8	2,850.9	672.3	1,614.1	564.5
Yuma, AZ MSA	206,897									
Includes Yuma County										
City of Yuma	95,522	491	5	49	90	347	2,595	502	1,874	219
Total area actually reporting	100.0%	725	17	74	106	528	4,307	1,046	2,837	424
Rate per 100,000 inhabitants		350.4	8.2	35.8	51.2	255.2	2,081.7	505.6	1,371.2	204.9
Aguadilla-Isabela, Puerto Rico MSA	302,615									
Includes Aguada, Aguadilla, Anasco, Isabela, Lares, Moca, Rincon, San Sebastian, and Utuado Municipios										
Total area actually reporting	100.0%	495	19	15	96	365	1,857	715	1,062	80
Rate per 100,000 inhabitants		163.6	6.3	5.0	31.7	120.6	613.7	236.3	350.9	26.4
Arecibo, Puerto Rico MSA	181,643									
Includes Arecibo, Camuy, Hatillo, and Quebradillas Municipios										
Total area actually reporting	100.0%	321	15	9	92	205	1,180	319	760	101
Rate per 100,000 inhabitants		176.7	8.3	5.0	50.6	112.9	649.6	175.6	418.4	55.6
Guayama, Puerto Rico MSA	76,166									
Includes Arroyo, Guayama, and Patillas Municipios										
Total area actually reporting	100.0%	175	14	3	24	134	501	203	282	16
Rate per 100,000 inhabitants		229.8	18.4	3.9	31.5	175.9	657.8	266.5	370.2	21.0

Table 6. Crime in the United States, by Selected Metropolitan Statistical Area, 2017—Continued

(Number, percent, rate per 100,000 population.)

Area	Population	Violent crime	Murder and nonnegligent manslaughter	Rape[1]	Robbery	Aggravated assault	Property crime	Burglary	Larceny-theft	Motor vehicle theft
Mayaguez, Puerto Rico MSA	91,557									
Includes Hormigueros and Mayaguez Municipios										
Total area actually reporting	100.0%	163	10	6	45	102	820	165	617	38
Rate per 100,000 inhabitants		178.0	10.9	6.6	49.1	111.4	895.6	180.2	673.9	41.5
Ponce, Puerto Rico MSA	300,843									
Includes Guanica, Guyanilla, Juana Diaz, Penuelas, Ponce, Villalba, and Yauco Municipios										
Total area actually reporting	100.0%	834	52	16	179	587	2,289	522	1,674	93
Rate per 100,000 inhabitants		277.2	17.3	5.3	59.5	195.1	760.9	173.5	556.4	30.9
San German, Puerto Rico MSA	126,097									
Includes Cabo Rojo, Lajas, Sabana Grande, and San German Municipios										
Total area actually reporting	100.0%	141	9	5	19	108	459	158	281	20
Rate per 100,000 inhabitants		111.8	7.1	4.0	15.1	85.6	364.0	125.3	222.8	15.9
San Juan-Carolina-Caguas, Puerto Rico MSA	2,112,005									
Includes Aguas Buenas, Aibonito, Barceloneta, Barranquitas, Bayamon, Caguas, Canovanas, Carolina, Catano, Cayey, Ceiba, Ciales, Cidra, Comerio, Corozal, Dorado, Fajardo, Florida, Guaynabo, Gurabo, Humacao, Juncos, Las Piedras, Loiza, Luquillo, Manati, Maunabo, Morovis, Naguabo, Naranjito, Orocovis, Rio Grande, San Juan, San Lorenzo, Toa Alta, Toa Baja, Trujillo Alto, Vega Alta, Vega Baja, and Yabucoa Municipios										
Total area actually reporting	100.0%	5,380	539	147	2,546	2,148	23,103	5,524	14,369	3,210
Rate per 100,000 inhabitants		254.7	25.5	7.0	120.5	101.7	1,093.9	261.6	680.3	152.0

1 The figures shown in this column for the offense of rape were reported using only the revised Uniform Crime Reporting (UCR) definition of rape. See the chapter notes for further explanation.   2 Because of changes in the state/local agency's reporting practices, figures are not comparable to previous years' data.   3 The FBI determined that the agency's data were overreported. Consequently, those data are not included in this table.   4 One or more agency(s) wihin this Metropolitan Statistical Area submitted rape data classified according to the legacy UCR definition. See the chapter notes for further explanation.   5 The FBI determined that the agency's data were underreported. Consequently, those data are not included in this table.   6 The FBI determined that the agency did not follow national UCR Program guidelines for reporting an offense. Consequently, this figure is not included in this table.   7 The population for the city of Mobile, Alabama, includes 55,819 inhabitants from the jurisdiction of the Mobile County Sheriff's Department.

Table 7. Offense Analysis, United States, 2013–2017

(Number.)

Classification	2013	2014	2015	2016[1]	2017[1]
Murder	14,319	14,164	15,883	17,413	17,284
Rape[2]	113,695	118,027	126,134	132,414	135,755
Robbery[3]	345,093	322,905	328,109	332,797	319,356
By location					
Street/highway	146,499	132,269	130,724	129,337	118,719
Commercial house	45,760	45,273	47,229	50,785	49,462
Gas or service station	8,354	8,072	8,916	9,708	9,566
Convenience store	17,103	17,380	18,661	20,656	20,967
Residence	57,372	54,120	54,142	55,102	51,062
Bank	6,512	5,939	5,691	5,914	5,420
Miscellaneous	63,495	59,853	62,747	61,296	64,161
Burglary[3]	1,932,139	1,713,153	1,587,564	1,516,405	1,401,840
By location					
Residence (dwelling)	1,428,448	1,253,915	1,136,664	1,054,470	942,734
Residence, night	395,604	349,441	328,736	311,805	286,338
Residence, day	756,617	669,364	594,668	543,930	476,123
Residence, unknown	276,227	235,111	213,260	198,735	180,273
Nonresidence (store, office, etc.)	503,691	459,238	450,900	461,935	459,106
Nonresidence, night	206,031	188,010	189,167	199,741	201,548
Nonresidence, day	183,380	167,749	159,177	159,630	157,915
Nonresidence, unknown	114,280	103,480	102,556	102,564	99,643
Larceny-theft (except motor vehicle theft)[3]	6,019,465	5,809,054	5,723,488	5,644,835	5,519,107
By type					
Pocket-picking	32,426	31,213	31,208	27,648	31,060
Purse-snatching	25,867	23,479	23,144	22,671	21,985
Shoplifting	1,199,157	1,247,199	1,276,575	1,179,137	1,146,216
From motor vehicles (except accessories)	1,405,858	1,332,924	1,373,720	1,477,587	1,479,321
Motor vehicle accessories	439,151	408,545	399,452	415,590	407,468
Bicycles	212,889	209,762	205,600	184,546	174,997
From buildings	740,092	712,073	664,381	605,765	587,261
From coin-operated machines	15,906	13,328	13,020	12,349	12,028
All others	1,948,120	1,830,531	1,736,388	1,719,542	1,658,771
By value					
Under $50	1,857,474	1,815,113	1,832,128	1,861,970	1,815,743
$50 to $200	1,342,473	1,306,350	1,278,027	1,221,246	1,170,907
Over $200	2,819,518	2,687,591	2,613,333	2,561,619	2,532,457
Motor vehicle theft	700,288	686,803	713,063	767,290	773,139

1 The crime figures have been adjusted.   2 The figures shown for this offense of rape were estimated using the revised Uniform Crime Reporting (UCR) definition of rape. See chapter notes for more detail.   3 Because of rounding, the number of offenses may not add to the total.

Table 8. Offenses Known to Law Enforcement, by Selected State and City, 2017

(Number.)

State/city	Population	Violent crime	Murder and nonnegligent manslaughter	Rape (revised definition)[1]	Robbery	Aggravated assault	Property crime	Burglary	Larceny-theft	Motor vehicle theft	Arson[2]
ALABAMA											
Abbeville	2,590	12	0	2	0	10	66	13	47	6	
Adamsville	4,334	25	1	1	6	17	261	42	204	15	
Alabaster	33,253	74	0	0	5	69	527	44	462	21	
Albertville	21,588	22	0	7	7	8	648	145	413	90	
Alexander City	14,744	255	3	7	15	230	551	107	398	46	
Aliceville	2,337	9	0	0	0	9	16	4	11	1	
Andalusia	8,958	83	0	5	8	70	468	62	385	21	
Anniston	21,955	754	14	47	71	622	1,352	542	700	110	
Arab	8,380	46	0	6	3	37	521	79	406	36	
Ashford	2,151	7	0	0	0	7	15	2	13	0	
Ashland	1,961	53	0	1	1	51	56	11	42	3	
Athens	26,004	13	1	0	12	0	695	86	597	12	
Atmore	9,994	111	2	2	19	88	431	102	314	15	
Auburn	64,831	217	4	17	30	166	1,711	156	1,454	101	
Bay Minette	9,483	82	1	4	3	74	339	69	250	20	
Bayou La Batre	2,499	39	0	4	2	33	255	64	164	27	
Bessemer	26,360	787	10	25	117	635	2,581	495	1,867	219	
Boaz	9,748	77	0	3	2	72	333	53	241	39	
Brent	4,916	20	0	3	1	16	163	29	124	10	
Brewton	5,436	38	0	5	2	31	165	20	135	10	
Brookwood	1,827	10	0	3	0	7	89	26	54	9	
Butler	1,755	8	0	2	1	5	30	7	18	5	
Camp Hill	969	5	1	1	0	3	27	11	15	1	
Carrollton	974	1	0	0	0	1	20	5	15	0	
Centre	3,566	25	0	2	2	21	191	17	165	9	
Chatom	1,221	9	0	2	1	6	27	8	17	2	
Chickasaw	5,879	45	0	4	6	35	289	94	174	21	
Childersburg	4,970	78	1	4	2	71	185	29	143	13	
Citronelle	3,882	14	0	2	0	12	46	11	31	4	
Clayton	2,888	4	0	0	1	3	23	7	15	1	
Coaling	1,640	11	1	3	0	7	55	17	33	5	
Columbiana	4,605	64	0	0	2	62	106	28	75	3	
Cordova	2,001	3	0	1	0	2	24	6	12	6	
Crossville	1,837	2	0	0	0	2	20	2	16	2	
Cullman	15,613	22	1	8	1	12	614	70	505	39	
Dadeville	3,113	21	1	1	4	15	119	22	95	2	
Daleville	5,068	13	0	1	0	12	147	20	117	10	
Daphne	26,669	34	0	1	9	24	556	74	464	18	
Dauphin Island	1,265	1	0	0	0	1	62	8	50	4	
Decatur	54,958	199	9	20	53	117	2,284	431	1,680	173	
Demopolis	6,949	40	2	0	6	32	146	28	110	8	
Dora	1,933	8	0	3	1	4	110	12	89	9	
Dothan	68,894	582	6	36	68	472	2,735	626	1,909	200	
Double Springs	1,046	1	0	0	0	1	20	5	15	0	
Douglas	764	10	0	1	0	9	65	21	39	5	
East Brewton	2,405	18	0	1	0	17	62	11	46	5	
Eclectic	1,030	7	0	0	0	7	38	8	30	0	
Elba	3,884	8	0	1	2	5	114	51	61	2	
Enterprise	28,239	105	1	10	11	83	767	141	578	48	
Eufaula	12,295	74	0	5	19	50	502	100	380	22	
Eutaw	2,722	29	1	1	6	21	58	17	36	5	
Evergreen	3,653	53	1	5	6	41	189	53	124	12	
Fairfield	10,759	205	8	8	74	115	738	193	445	100	
Fairhope	20,180	52	0	6	4	42	606	89	490	27	
Falkville	1,257	10	0	0	0	10	45	12	25	8	
Fayette	4,402	15	0	6	1	8	88	5	78	5	
Flomaton	1,403	12	2	1	0	9	48	15	29	4	
Florence	40,059	189	1	30	40	118	1,703	319	1,239	145	
Foley	18,032	47	0	4	9	34	782	65	693	24	
Fultondale	9,207	48	0	3	7	38	381	40	315	26	
Fyffe	1,017	2	0	0	0	2	34	4	27	3	
Gadsden	35,665	613	3	23	63	524	2,641	497	1,914	230	
Geneva	4,419	24	0	3	4	17	174	32	129	13	
Georgiana	1,640	6	0	0	1	5	22	3	17	2	
Geraldine	898	1	0	0	0	1	13	2	8	3	
Glencoe	5,130	8	0	2	1	5	108	27	74	7	
Grant	909	7	0	1	1	5	32	5	24	3	
Greenville	7,724	78	1	0	7	70	363	44	307	12	
Guin	2,293	6	0	0	2	4	48	10	33	5	
Gulf Shores	11,905	40	1	8	1	30	578	76	474	28	
Hackleburg	1,470	1	0	1	0	0	22	5	15	2	
Haleyville	4,059	23	0	6	0	17	186	44	133	9	
Hamilton	6,714	27	0	2	3	22	220	48	155	17	
Hanceville	3,317	9	0	4	0	5	92	13	68	11	
Harpersville	1,684	13	0	3	0	10	37	8	24	5	
Hartford	2,640	23	0	1	2	20	79	10	66	3	
Hartselle	14,503	22	0	1	1	20	311	35	260	16	
Headland	4,777	3	0	1	1	1	78	11	61	6	
Helena	18,965	16	0	2	0	14	93	6	79	8	
Hokes Bluff	4,275	4	1	0	0	3	53	15	31	7	
Hoover	85,634	82	2	17	33	30	978	213	701	64	2
Hueytown	15,472	89	2	8	11	68	557	78	453	26	
Huntsville	195,173	1,766	22	172	360	1,212	9,232	1,428	6,758	1,046	

Table 8. Offenses Known to Law Enforcement, by Selected State and City, 2017—Continued

(Number.)

State/city	Population	Violent crime	Murder and nonnegligent manslaughter	Rape (revised definition)[1]	Robbery	Aggravated assault	Property crime	Burglary	Larceny-theft	Motor vehicle theft	Arson[2]
Irondale	12,362	54	2	1	4	47	394	89	261	44	
Jackson	4,858	33	0	5	2	26	198	43	147	8	
Jacksonville	12,573	113	2	10	12	89	489	137	325	27	
Jasper	13,940	106	1	7	27	71	919	149	714	56	
Kimberly	3,009	7	0	1	1	5	17	5	9	3	
Kinston	539	2	0	0	1	1	26	6	17	3	
Lanett	6,383	88	2	13	17	56	472	105	322	45	
Leeds	11,964	83	0	4	12	67	429	59	339	31	
Leesburg	1,005	4	0	1	0	3	46	18	21	7	
Leighton	703	4	0	1	0	3	36	16	17	3	
Level Plains	1,994	12	0	0	0	12	67	23	39	5	
Linden	1,968	5	0	0	0	5	25	5	17	3	
Lineville	2,293	13	0	0	1	12	30	8	19	3	
Lipscomb	2,121	13	0	1	1	11	68	35	27	6	
Littleville	976	1	0	0	0	1	17	1	15	1	
Livingston	3,454	40	0	1	1	38	67	5	54	8	
Loxley	2,091	18	1	0	3	14	129	21	92	16	
Madison	48,777	177	2	22	24	129	931	143	723	65	
Margaret	4,668	6	0	2	0	4	32	8	15	9	
McIntosh	223	3	0	1	0	2	35	4	28	3	
Midfield	5,141	64	3	3	21	37	292	110	164	18	
Midland City	2,396	9	0	1	1	7	91	31	55	5	
Millbrook	15,537	45	2	9	11	23	602	86	480	36	
Mobile[3]	248,431	1,839	50	142	440	1,207	13,549	3,023	9,267	1,259	57
Montevallo	6,793	21	1	4	4	12	154	30	114	10	
Montgomery	199,099	1,277	38	52	346	841	8,800	2,129	5,827	844	
Moody	13,007	63	1	4	4	54	219	28	160	31	
Morris	1,946	4	0	1	0	3	52	11	32	9	
Moulton	3,323	9	0	1	2	6	64	26	33	5	
Moundville	2,438	2	0	1	0	1	37	7	29	1	
Muscle Shoals	13,939	81	1	3	5	72	637	121	458	58	
New Brockton	1,159	1	0	0	0	1	25	8	14	3	
New Hope	2,802	4	0	0	0	4	48	10	30	8	
Newton	1,450	1	0	0	0	1	71	15	39	17	
Northport	25,337	47	0	5	14	28	655	82	556	17	
Notasulga	832	10	0	1	1	8	35	21	13	1	
Odenville	3,765	25	0	4	0	21	41	6	28	7	
Ohatchee	1,135	1	0	0	0	1	36	14	22	0	
Oneonta	6,721	11	0	2	3	6	250	30	203	17	
Opelika	30,476	223	5	21	47	150	1,399	220	1,091	88	
Opp	6,573	28	0	0	2	26	140	38	98	4	
Orange Beach	6,073	11	0	1	0	10	189	18	165	6	
Owens Crossroads	1,908	5	0	0	0	5	53	8	41	4	
Oxford	21,084	60	1	0	9	50	1,101	117	942	42	
Ozark	14,559	156	3	11	5	137	682	107	544	31	
Parrish	955	5	0	0	0	5	49	11	28	10	
Pelham	23,310	33	0	5	8	20	504	35	430	39	
Pell City	13,978	55	0	15	10	30	481	60	390	31	
Phenix City	37,841	251	9	47	73	122	1,488	366	949	173	
Piedmont	4,633	22	0	3	1	18	177	52	110	15	
Pine Hill	904	13	3	0	1	9	36	13	22	1	
Pleasant Grove	10,191	11	0	1	0	10	164	37	116	11	
Prattville	35,858	85	4	12	32	37	1,280	132	1,025	123	
Prichard	22,119	404	9	11	96	288	1,359	441	746	172	
Ragland	1,707	0	0	0	0	0	11	2	7	2	
Rainsville	5,025	13	0	1	0	12	103	31	60	12	
Red Bay	3,112	8	0	1	0	7	60	7	45	8	
Reform	1,603	7	0	0	2	5	11	4	6	1	
Riverside	2,333	7	0	1	0	6	53	15	31	7	
Robertsdale	6,112	38	0	4	4	30	287	37	235	15	
Russellville	9,810	33	1	9	1	22	310	79	205	26	
Saraland	13,999	45	0	4	3	38	614	74	496	44	
Sardis City	1,782	5	0	0	0	5	48	11	32	5	
Satsuma	6,198	2	0	0	0	2	50	9	34	7	
Scottsboro	14,660	192	0	9	4	179	586	83	465	38	
Sheffield	9,022	67	0	9	11	47	329	73	223	33	
Slocomb	1,952	10	0	3	0	7	47	15	31	1	
Snead	842	7	0	0	0	7	44	10	22	12	
Southside	8,630	15	0	1	0	14	105	20	74	11	
Spanish Fort	8,584	32	0	2	3	27	326	16	304	6	
Springville	4,280	28	0	0	0	28	63	3	58	2	
Sulligent	1,838	8	0	1	2	5	67	16	46	5	
Sumiton	2,390	5	1	0	1	3	94	8	81	5	
Summerdale	1,314	8	0	0	0	8	85	15	55	15	
Talladega	15,356	136	1	5	21	109	831	217	560	54	
Tallassee	4,748	43	0	5	3	35	270	39	199	32	
Tarrant	6,249	106	4	4	25	73	337	92	213	32	
Thomasville	3,971	22	0	1	0	21	116	19	88	9	
Trinity	2,176	4	0	3	0	1	29	12	8	9	
Troy	19,360	222	1	5	23	193	979	193	735	51	
Tuscaloosa	101,124	474	9	54	168	243	4,174	814	3,161	199	
Tuscumbia	8,407	29	0	8	3	18	270	48	197	25	
Tuskegee	8,549	83	3	7	22	51	352	137	179	36	

Table 8. Offenses Known to Law Enforcement, by Selected State and City, 2017—Continued

(Number.)

State/city	Population	Violent crime	Murder and nonnegligent manslaughter	Rape (revised definition)[1]	Robbery	Aggravated assault	Property crime	Burglary	Larceny-theft	Motor vehicle theft	Arson[2]
Union Springs	3,714	42	0	1	10	31	144	50	80	14	
Uniontown	2,342	20	0	0	2	18	62	26	29	7	
Valley	9,363	65	0	11	13	41	633	112	452	69	
Vance	1,500	3	0	0	0	3	35	14	18	3	
Vestavia Hills	34,781	24	1	1	3	19	425	53	342	30	
Warrior	3,195	14	0	1	1	12	49	8	35	6	
Wedowee	804	8	0	2	0	6	50	14	33	3	
West Blocton	1,259	16	0	4	2	10	55	15	34	6	
Wetumpka	8,501	41	2	2	5	32	350	31	308	11	
Winfield	4,510	18	0	4	1	13	168	33	120	15	
Woodstock	1,594	2	0	0	0	2	51	11	34	6	
ALASKA											
Anchorage	296,188	3,564	27	391	778	2,368	16,041	2,216	10,721	3,104	62
Bethel	6,426	91	1	31	14	45	75	35	28	12	1
Bristol Bay Borough	874	0	0	0	0	0	15	3	3	9	0
Cordova	2,199	0	0	0	0	0	29	3	24	2	0
Craig	1,235	5	0	0	0	5	15	4	10	1	0
Dillingham	2,369	39	0	10	3	26	60	18	34	8	0
Fairbanks	32,937	205	10	24	40	131	1,493	164	1,121	208	6
Haines	2,472	7	0	3	0	4	18	4	14	0	0
Homer	5,735	11	0	5	1	5	211	24	178	9	0
Juneau	32,344	303	1	50	46	206	1,683	326	1,262	95	8
Kenai	7,852	35	0	16	1	18	441	41	360	40	2
Ketchikan	8,230	34	1	19	0	14	341	25	298	18	0
Kodiak	6,198	60	0	15	4	41	211	20	180	11	0
Kotzebue	3,251	121	0	16	3	102	178	34	123	21	3
Nome	3,829	59	0	7	0	52	27	8	16	3	0
North Pole	2,248	5	0	1	1	3	66	6	58	2	1
North Slope Borough	9,539	173	2	15	1	155	88	19	59	10	3
Palmer	7,184	20	1	1	4	14	244	19	208	17	0
Petersburg	3,108	4	0	2	1	1	106	16	88	2	0
Seward	2,806	11	0	0	0	11	61	14	43	4	0
Sitka	8,736	14	1	0	1	12	163	12	145	6	1
Skagway	1,100	0	0	0	0	0	16	2	13	1	0
Soldotna	4,693	33	0	16	6	11	233	16	205	12	1
Unalaska	4,449	15	0	0	0	15	29	6	21	2	0
Valdez	3,842	12	0	5	0	7	51	4	44	3	0
Wasilla	10,093	54	0	0	5	49	464	40	377	47	1
Wrangell	2,395	8	0	2	0	6	28	1	22	5	0
ARIZONA											
Apache Junction	40,672	80	3	0	9	68	965	184	680	101	8
Avondale	84,041	257	6	27	97	127	3,347	480	2,633	234	20
Buckeye	67,147	32	4	3	15	10	1,152	148	940	64	3
Bullhead City[4]	40,039		2	5	30		1,480	338	994	148	3
Camp Verde	11,299	33	0	0	2	31	288	63	196	29	1
Chandler	249,355	647	5	130	142	370	5,809	784	4,653	372	
Clarkdale	4,304	8	0	0	2	6	86	39	39	8	0
Coolidge	12,645	39	1	3	6	29	530	76	427	27	3
Cottonwood	12,116	49	0	1	4	44	380	42	314	24	1
Douglas	16,443	41	1	0	3	37	657	94	549	14	0
Eagar	5,001	12	0	0	1	11	46	12	33	1	1
El Mirage	35,611	85	1	21	22	41	1,005	458	443	104	2
Eloy	17,552	90	1	4	5	80	508	154	326	28	8
Flagstaff	72,388	307	7	35	57	208	2,729	161	2,486	82	36
Florence	25,623	19	0	0	0	19	123	20	94	9	0
Gilbert	242,090	207	5	39	51	112	3,355	466	2,754	135	30
Glendale	249,273	1,217	12	97	481	627	11,293	1,589	8,541	1,163	48
Globe	7,349	126	1	2	7	116	554	89	409	56	1
Goodyear	79,419	210	2	27	28	153	2,280	346	1,817	117	0
Holbrook	5,077	44	1	0	4	39	255	50	189	16	3
Jerome	457	2	0	0	0	2	13	6	7	0	0
Kearny	2,096	6	0	0	0	6	28	15	10	3	0
Kingman	29,181	131	2	12	15	102	1,445	237	1,119	89	15
Lake Havasu City	53,937	120	0	21	6	93	1,164	245	848	71	23
Marana	45,123	40	2	7	15	16	1,184	90	1,056	38	5
Maricopa	47,466	91	1	10	14	66	604	87	473	44	2
Mesa	492,268	2,047	23	252	454	1,318	10,692	1,878	7,930	884	23
Miami	1,774	31	0	0	2	29	92	53	33	6	7
Nogales	19,878	43	0	0	1	42	573	68	385	120	0
Oro Valley	44,251	17	0	2	4	11	626	81	531	14	1
Page	7,632	64	0	4	1	59	372	34	320	18	2
Paradise Valley	14,629	6	0	2	1	3	222	63	155	4	0
Parker	3,022	7	0	0	0	7	119	40	70	9	2
Patagonia	872	0	0	0	0	0	2	0	2	0	0
Payson	15,504	58	0	4	3	51	556	158	362	36	3
Peoria	165,889	414	4	66	78	266	3,385	533	2,615	237	7
Phoenix	1,644,177	12,511	157	1,142	3,293	7,919	60,353	12,801	39,899	7,653	190
Pima	2,527	3	0	0	0	3	51	13	35	3	1
Pinetop-Lakeside	4,392	35	0	1	2	32	162	43	114	5	0
Prescott	42,975	157	0	11	15	131	903	121	757	25	2
Prescott Valley	43,891	86	0	20	8	58	941	99	824	18	6

Table 8. Offenses Known to Law Enforcement, by Selected State and City, 2017—Continued

(Number.)

State/city	Population	Violent crime	Murder and nonnegligent manslaughter	Rape (revised definition)[1]	Robbery	Aggravated assault	Property crime	Burglary	Larceny-theft	Motor vehicle theft	Arson[2]
Safford	9,617	23	0	0	1	22	363	45	301	17	2
Sahuarita	29,373	28	0	10	3	15	328	36	277	15	3
San Luis	32,823	44	0	3	6	35	523	122	325	76	2
Scottsdale	251,840	396	5	103	100	188	5,470	878	4,346	246	23
Show Low	11,163	60	0	6	4	50	434	63	355	16	3
Sierra Vista	42,859	191	0	24	23	144	1,287	225	998	64	7
Snowflake-Taylor	10,025	45	0	0	1	44	237	71	150	16	14
Somerton	15,082	19	0	0	1	18	160	39	96	25	5
Springerville	2,000	9	0	0	0	9	15	4	10	1	0
St. Johns	3,581	11	0	1	1	9	54	20	33	1	0
Superior	3,026	7	0	0	0	7	105	20	82	3	14
Surprise	135,345	120	2	18	47	53	2,421	228	2,018	175	6
Tempe	186,086	883	5	151	229	498	7,669	1,076	6,120	473	20
Thatcher	5,054	1	0	0	0	1	85	14	71	0	1
Tolleson	7,289	68	0	5	30	33	773	250	453	70	3
Tucson	532,323	4,268	46	498	1,431	2,293	27,956	4,424	21,125	2,407	156
Wickenburg	6,979	20	0	5	1	14	142	31	96	15	0
Willcox	3,471	45	0	0	1	44	161	9	146	6	1
Williams	3,181	30	1	5	0	24	87	16	71	0	1
Winslow	9,764	67	1	2	10	54	795	117	638	40	1
Yuma	95,522	491	5	49	90	347	2,595	502	1,874	219	34
ARKANSAS											
Alexander	2,810	23	3	5	3	12	51	12	36	3	1
Alma	5,699	51	0	11	3	37	344	50	280	14	0
Altus	720	1	0	0	0	1	13	6	7	0	0
Amity	698	3	0	0	0	3	3	1	1	1	0
Arkadelphia	10,810	58	0	6	5	47	367	23	334	10	0
Ashdown	4,433	16	2	2	1	11	185	41	135	9	0
Atkins	3,065	13	0	8	0	5	95	27	66	2	1
Austin	4,091	8	0	3	0	5	21	5	15	1	0
Bald Knob	2,908	11	0	2	1	8	121	38	80	3	0
Barling	4,820	26	0	5	1	20	91	9	76	6	1
Batesville	10,806	30	0	14	1	15	215	24	176	15	1
Bay	1,819	4	0	1	0	3	31	5	24	2	0
Bearden	874	1	0	0	0	1	17	7	10	0	0
Beebe	8,258	35	0	5	4	26	375	53	305	17	2
Bella Vista	28,721	72	0	19	3	50	166	33	125	8	0
Benton	36,702	144	0	16	20	108	1,430	228	1,079	123	2
Bentonville	49,301	69	0	16	8	45	865	104	723	38	1
Berryville	5,390	20	1	12	2	5	220	54	163	3	2
Bethel Heights	2,564	2	0	0	0	2	23	4	10	9	0
Black Rock	615	1	0	0	0	1	3	1	2	0	0
Blytheville	14,184	109	9	2	19	79	921	179	727	15	0
Bono	2,304	11	0	1	0	10	32	8	20	4	0
Booneville	3,886	11	0	6	1	4	154	30	116	8	1
Bradford	759	2	0	0	0	2	29	13	15	1	0
Brinkley	2,740	62	0	5	6	51	141	37	94	10	3
Brookland	3,353	6	0	2	0	4	105	14	88	3	0
Bryant	20,593	59	0	9	5	45	990	57	870	63	1
Bull Shoals	1,944	10	0	0	0	10	31	15	12	4	0
Cabot	26,118	57	1	20	5	31	406	92	280	34	0
Caddo Valley	599	5	1	0	1	3	32	6	22	4	1
Camden	11,069	166	0	13	11	142	436	126	289	21	6
Cammack Village	742	1	0	0	0	1	17	1	13	3	1
Caraway	1,275	0	0	0	0	0	14	2	11	1	0
Carlisle	2,164	2	0	0	0	2	64	10	53	1	0
Cave Springs	4,031	5	0	4	0	1	30	14	14	2	0
Centerton	13,521	44	0	22	0	22	150	40	102	8	0
Charleston	2,457	10	0	5	0	5	32	0	31	1	0
Cherokee Village	4,639	5	0	0	0	5	86	37	47	2	3
Clarksville	9,581	47	0	22	1	24	325	24	289	12	1
Clinton	2,505	6	0	1	0	5	36	10	26	0	0
Concord	236	0	0	0	0	0	0	0	0	0	0
Conway	66,299	315	1	41	63	210	2,314	331	1,835	148	8
Corning	3,078	7	0	0	0	7	27	10	15	2	0
Cotter	944	2	0	0	1	1	21	7	11	3	0
Crossett	5,069	29	0	2	6	21	225	86	135	4	0
Damascus	378	0	0	0	0	0	10	2	8	0	0
Dardanelle	4,578	25	0	9	3	13	111	42	56	13	1
Decatur	1,803	13	0	9	0	4	28	10	17	1	0
Dell	201	0	0	0	0	0	2	0	2	0	0
De Queen	6,555	16	0	4	1	11	146	40	96	10	1
Dermott	2,711	5	0	1	0	4	29	24	3	2	0
Des Arc	1,617	3	0	1	0	2	18	4	12	2	0
De Valls Bluff	577	1	0	0	0	1	3	3	0	0	0
De Witt	3,120	19	1	2	0	16	121	44	75	2	5
Diaz	1,219	3	0	1	0	2	17	6	6	5	0
Dover	1,404	3	0	0	0	3	25	6	19	0	0
Dumas	4,226	18	1	1	2	14	83	35	45	3	0
Dyer	864	2	0	1	0	1	13	6	7	0	0
El Dorado	18,257	206	5	11	17	173	838	385	409	44	9
Elkins	3,018	4	0	2	0	2	26	5	20	1	0

Table 8. Offenses Known to Law Enforcement, by Selected State and City, 2017—Continued

(Number.)

State/city	Population	Violent crime	Murder and nonnegligent manslaughter	Rape (revised definition)[1]	Robbery	Aggravated assault	Property crime	Burglary	Larceny-theft	Motor vehicle theft	Arson[2]
England	2,741	19	0	1	0	18	87	33	48	6	0
Etowah	318	1	0	0	0	1	9	2	7	0	0
Eudora	2,048	9	0	3	0	6	50	19	23	8	0
Eureka Springs	2,074	10	0	1	1	8	119	42	71	6	1
Fairfield Bay	2,232	5	0	2	1	2	68	19	48	1	0
Farmington	6,949	24	3	8	2	11	99	23	72	4	0
Fayetteville	85,592	515	1	91	71	352	4,064	463	3,257	344	12
Flippin	1,338	3	0	0	0	3	60	4	55	1	0
Fordyce	3,904	45	1	4	7	33	196	48	141	7	1
Fort Smith	88,437	787	7	71	107	602	4,511	832	3,345	334	14
Gassville	2,140	3	0	0	0	3	50	12	36	2	1
Gentry	3,777	10	0	7	0	3	24	4	19	1	0
Gosnell	3,175	17	0	1	1	15	77	24	53	0	3
Gravette	3,295	13	0	5	0	8	70	6	60	4	1
Greenbrier	5,488	2	0	0	0	2	23	0	18	5	1
Green Forest	2,784	14	0	3	0	11	46	6	38	2	0
Greenland	1,405	11	0	3	1	7	29	2	23	4	0
Greenwood	9,409	15	0	5	0	10	39	14	21	4	0
Greers Ferry	859	0	0	0	0	0	17	3	9	5	0
Gurdon	2,126	13	0	1	0	12	41	11	25	5	0
Guy	775	1	0	1	0	0	2	2	0	0	0
Hamburg	2,719	9	0	2	0	7	30	19	11	0	0
Hampton	1,249	7	0	0	0	7	17	7	10	0	0
Hardy	768	1	0	0	0	1	22	11	10	1	0
Harrisburg	2,315	10	0	0	0	10	71	14	51	6	0
Harrison	13,208	80	1	18	7	54	512	90	394	28	9
Hazen	1,388	4	0	1	0	3	12	7	5	0	0
Heber Springs	7,071	16	0	6	1	9	271	47	207	17	1
Helena-West Helena	10,609	118	8	10	15	85	451	167	260	24	9
Higginson	668	0	0	0	0	0	1	0	1	0	0
Highfill	659	1	0	0	0	1	2	1	1	0	0
Highland	1,071	4	0	0	0	4	17	5	12	0	0
Hope	9,859	118	1	10	12	95	472	81	365	26	1
Hot Springs	36,956	218	8	20	59	131	2,518	838	1,514	166	3
Hoxie	2,661	6	0	1	0	5	16	4	10	2	0
Hughes	1,278	5	0	0	0	5	23	8	14	1	0
Jacksonville	28,540	261	3	22	33	203	1,271	288	870	113	5
Johnson	3,681	7	0	3	1	3	71	27	37	7	0
Jonesboro	76,188	400	13	54	62	271	3,124	1,239	1,728	157	12
Judsonia	2,002	1	0	0	0	1	46	13	27	6	0
Keiser	676	2	0	0	0	2	3	2	1	0	0
Kensett	1,647	3	1	0	1	1	20	5	13	2	0
Lake City	2,462	4	1	2	0	1	29	10	18	1	1
Lakeview	722	0	0	0	0	0	9	4	4	1	0
Lake Village	2,357	10	0	2	3	5	76	18	58	0	1
Lamar	1,680	3	0	0	0	3	24	6	16	2	0
Lavaca	2,418	6	0	0	0	6	21	3	16	2	0
Leachville	1,800	2	0	0	0	2	32	12	19	1	1
Lewisville	1,134	2	0	0	0	2	21	7	12	2	0
Lincoln	2,455	29	0	5	0	24	55	11	40	4	0
Little Flock	2,842	6	2	0	0	4	38	11	25	2	0
Little Rock	199,314	3,256	55	175	502	2,524	13,817	2,378	10,309	1,130	51
Lonoke	4,234	38	0	3	2	33	119	26	87	6	5
Lowell	9,220	18	0	5	0	13	124	45	70	9	0
Luxora	1,059	2	0	0	1	1	2	0	2	0	1
Magnolia	11,568	55	0	3	14	38	635	423	195	17	1
Malvern	11,007	44	1	7	5	31	411	134	257	20	4
Mammoth Spring	959	1	0	0	0	1	1	0	1	0	0
Marianna	3,521	29	2	3	11	13	189	75	108	6	1
Marion	12,356	133	1	7	19	106	413	81	309	23	1
Marked Tree	2,496	14	0	2	1	11	66	22	41	3	1
Marmaduke	1,240	10	1	1	0	8	29	8	20	1	2
Marvell	990	5	0	2	1	2	21	5	14	2	0
Maumelle	18,278	37	0	1	3	33	369	74	270	25	1
Mayflower	2,469	15	0	1	0	14	106	40	60	6	0
McCrory	1,554	15	0	4	0	11	12	6	4	2	1
McRae	663	2	0	1	0	1	13	3	9	1	0
Mena	5,624	7	0	2	0	5	220	24	186	10	0
Menifee	312	1	0	1	0	0	1	0	1	0	0
Mineral Springs	1,159	0	0	0	0	0	11	2	9	0	0
Monette	1,573	3	0	0	0	3	37	19	18	0	0
Monticello	9,775	37	1	7	11	18	298	76	204	18	3
Morrilton	6,715	10	1	2	1	6	391	49	330	12	3
Mountainburg	623	5	0	4	0	1	33	9	22	2	1
Mountain Home	12,347	25	0	14	1	10	439	49	374	16	0
Mountain View	2,880	12	0	1	0	11	69	11	53	5	0
Mulberry	1,641	9	0	1	0	8	64	11	52	1	0
Murfreesboro	1,571	2	0	2	0	0	30	10	20	0	0
Nashville	4,480	13	1	7	1	4	187	22	160	5	3
Norfork	497	0	0	0	0	0	2	0	2	0	0
North Little Rock	66,938	530	9	19	124	378	2,764	541	1,875	348	15
Ola	1,227	6	0	2	0	4	15	5	8	2	0
Osceola	6,984	155	6	4	16	129	420	201	205	14	1

Table 8. Offenses Known to Law Enforcement, by Selected State and City, 2017—Continued

(Number.)

State/city	Population	Violent crime	Murder and nonnegligent manslaughter	Rape (revised definition)[1]	Robbery	Aggravated assault	Property crime	Burglary	Larceny-theft	Motor vehicle theft	Arson[2]
Ozark	3,555	20	0	4	1	15	124	40	72	12	2
Paragould	28,588	163	0	39	14	110	1,454	261	1,071	122	1
Paris	3,443	28	1	1	1	25	123	37	78	8	2
Pea Ridge	5,506	19	0	4	0	15	98	16	81	1	2
Perryville	1,415	5	0	0	0	5	63	14	46	3	0
Piggott	3,574	6	0	0	0	6	75	21	53	1	2
Pine Bluff	43,040	795	22	34	133	606	2,378	812	1,282	284	51
Plumerville	796	5	0	1	0	4	8	2	6	0	0
Pocahontas	6,447	18	0	2	0	16	283	46	227	10	1
Pottsville	3,146	10	0	3	1	6	39	9	26	4	0
Prairie Grove	5,511	15	0	3	0	12	127	17	108	2	1
Quitman	730	1	0	0	0	1	27	2	21	4	0
Ravenden	447	2	0	0	0	2	3	0	3	0	0
Redfield	1,547	8	0	1	1	6	22	7	10	5	0
Rison	1,258	1	0	1	0	0	23	8	13	2	0
Rogers	66,626	266	0	101	17	148	2,006	198	1,671	137	4
Rose Bud	482	0	0	0	0	0	10	3	7	0	0
Russellville	29,786	154	0	23	9	122	1,069	148	820	101	1
Salem	1,622	4	0	0	1	3	22	4	16	2	0
Shannon Hills	3,958	8	0	0	0	8	27	5	14	8	0
Sheridan	4,866	10	1	1	1	7	196	38	150	8	0
Sherwood	30,830	171	3	15	22	131	1,313	436	787	90	3
Siloam Springs	16,680	65	2	13	3	47	537	118	385	34	1
Stamps	1,493	1	0	0	1	0	6	0	4	2	0
Star City	2,131	16	0	2	3	11	73	25	41	7	1
Stuttgart	8,882	65	1	11	6	47	336	75	246	15	2
Sulphur Springs	534	2	0	0	0	2	16	7	8	1	0
Swifton	739	1	0	1	0	0	8	1	7	0	0
Texarkana	30,334	240	2	12	44	182	1,355	287	988	80	4
Trumann	7,104	48	0	12	2	34	313	76	216	21	3
Tuckerman	1,722	4	0	1	0	3	31	9	18	4	0
Tyronza	739	0	0	0	0	0	7	1	5	1	0
Van Buren	23,456	97	0	10	8	79	704	227	448	29	1
Vilonia	4,595	4	0	3	0	1	89	34	53	2	0
Waldron	3,331	12	0	6	1	5	158	38	110	10	6
Walnut Ridge	4,638	13	0	2	0	11	78	19	57	2	2
Ward	5,007	62	1	19	0	42	123	39	77	7	0
Warren	5,719	32	1	9	3	19	124	63	54	7	1
West Fork	2,588	4	0	2	0	2	36	3	30	3	1
West Memphis	25,126	447	7	35	103	302	1,301	380	819	102	10
White Hall	5,009	4	1	1	0	2	59	13	42	4	1
Wilson	847	2	0	0	0	2	16	4	12	0	0
Wynne	8,033	51	0	10	3	38	281	59	211	11	2
CALIFORNIA											
Adelanto	33,693	238	2	28	48	160	578	190	290	98	13
Agoura Hills	20,814	16	0	2	4	10	278	71	187	20	4
Alameda	79,761	253	0	16	133	104	2,347	219	1,725	403	25
Albany	19,880	36	0	1	28	7	523	77	383	63	3
Alhambra	85,865	172	4	17	89	62	1,877	363	1,244	270	12
Aliso Viejo	51,984	44	0	4	8	32	394	62	299	33	3
Alturas	2,491	39	2	2	3	32	129	31	88	10	2
American Canyon	20,593	49	0	5	14	30	413	85	272	56	2
Anaheim	353,400	1,253	10	115	480	648	9,296	1,351	6,393	1,552	45
Anderson	10,281	43	0	6	3	34	492	124	267	101	4
Angels Camp	3,779	7	0	1	0	6	57	13	36	8	0
Antioch	112,252	607	10	51	230	316	3,838	589	2,261	988	75
Apple Valley	73,105	231	4	19	63	145	1,565	299	986	280	7
Arcadia	58,883	110	0	7	56	47	1,534	485	957	92	0
Arcata	18,054	64	1	7	20	36	705	107	487	111	17
Arroyo Grande	18,239	32	0	3	5	24	311	53	226	32	2
Artesia	16,933	103	2	2	31	68	460	153	236	71	2
Arvin	21,390	229	6	8	23	192	453	72	242	139	5
Atascadero	30,661	107	0	8	18	81	518	96	395	27	3
Atherton	7,256	4	0	3	0	1	75	12	61	2	0
Atwater	29,442	188	0	7	23	158	951	185	649	117	7
Auburn	14,069	54	2	5	5	42	271	58	175	38	3
Avalon	3,773	20	0	4	0	16	58	13	35	10	0
Avenal	12,054	66	1	8	5	52	149	62	65	22	4
Azusa	50,202	147	1	16	44	86	1,203	251	729	223	14
Bakersfield	381,154	1,827	41	92	753	941	15,507	3,667	9,063	2,777	269
Baldwin Park	76,636	348	3	26	89	230	1,405	290	788	327	6
Banning	31,247	151	3	14	17	117	667	254	255	158	0
Barstow	24,028	302	2	17	97	186	988	318	484	186	13
Bear Valley	5,497	5	0	3	0	2	59	11	47	1	0
Beaumont	46,856	182	1	18	19	144	872	195	561	116	2
Bell	35,925	228	0	17	78	133	652	153	348	151	0
Bellflower	77,984	363	5	16	158	184	1,988	418	1,065	505	13
Bell Gardens	42,930	100	2	5	47	46	749	87	342	320	6
Belmont	27,285	39	1	4	7	27	377	49	296	32	8
Belvedere	2,131	0	0	0	0	0	11	0	11	0	0
Benicia	28,370	28	0	6	12	10	472	129	273	70	1
Berkeley	122,687	666	1	83	364	218	6,020	843	4,556	621	30

Table 8. Offenses Known to Law Enforcement, by Selected State and City, 2017—Continued

(Number.)

State/city	Population	Violent crime	Murder and nonnegligent manslaughter	Rape (revised definition)[1]	Robbery	Aggravated assault	Property crime	Burglary	Larceny-theft	Motor vehicle theft	Arson[2]
Beverly Hills	34,781	118	0	10	50	58	1,819	402	1,318	99	6
Big Bear	5,270	52	1	8	4	39	178	49	112	17	3
Biggs	1,700	17	0	2	0	15	26	7	12	7	0
Bishop	3,767	44	0	10	5	29	296	68	217	11	0
Blythe	19,572	62	0	13	16	33	805	264	492	49	27
Bradbury	1,084	1	0	0	1	0	7	3	4	0	0
Brawley	26,342	176	0	11	12	153	892	146	680	66	16
Brea	43,000	114	2	8	39	65	1,440	180	1,160	100	1
Brentwood	62,120	157	0	11	45	101	1,489	273	1,084	132	5
Brisbane	4,764	12	0	0	5	7	128	67	49	12	1
Broadmoor	4,438	21	0	2	5	14	77	28	37	12	0
Buellton	5,139	6	0	0	2	4	76	14	55	7	0
Buena Park	83,552	292	1	9	96	186	2,814	299	2,115	400	15
Burbank	104,622	253	0	20	86	147	2,944	355	2,344	245	16
Burlingame	30,551	74	1	19	17	37	895	119	670	106	4
Calabasas	24,295	30	0	14	9	7	330	63	248	19	2
Calexico	40,499	89	0	3	21	65	1,280	486	581	213	38
California City	13,753	88	1	3	16	68	341	180	122	39	2
Calimesa	8,737	12	1	0	6	5	248	42	175	31	0
Calistoga	5,336	9	0	0	0	9	79	25	46	8	0
Camarillo	67,714	107	1	8	42	56	1,086	182	826	78	6
Campbell	41,192	102	1	19	27	55	1,340	247	917	176	12
Canyon Lake	11,227	16	0	0	0	16	115	22	65	28	2
Capitola	10,222	34	1	5	14	14	622	50	540	32	6
Carlsbad	115,344	247	0	30	46	171	2,209	432	1,638	139	18
Carmel	3,918	6	0	1	1	4	111	33	77	1	0
Carpinteria	13,791	34	0	5	10	19	282	58	195	29	1
Carson	92,992	475	8	20	166	281	2,250	479	1,261	510	21
Cathedral City	54,506	137	2	14	49	72	769	176	340	253	6
Central Marin	35,060	46	1	8	15	22	892	252	599	41	1
Ceres	48,673	227	1	20	75	131	1,601	314	879	408	10
Cerritos	50,809	127	2	4	71	50	2,268	561	1,511	196	3
Chico	92,459	413	2	85	63	263	3,593	531	2,615	447	157
Chino	89,420	227	3	10	87	127	2,142	443	1,405	294	6
Chino Hills	79,480	70	0	12	19	39	1,362	323	936	103	5
Chowchilla	18,174	62	0	1	11	50	453	150	208	95	6
Chula Vista	271,109	808	2	62	304	440	3,883	640	2,482	761	23
Citrus Heights	88,126	349	2	50	102	195	2,782	462	1,964	356	11
Claremont	36,246	74	0	9	30	35	940	279	593	68	6
Clayton	12,173	8	0	0	5	3	113	14	91	8	0
Clearlake	15,018	144	1	17	37	89	621	214	273	134	17
Cloverdale	8,830	27	0	9	2	16	143	23	109	11	5
Clovis	108,419	243	0	44	61	138	2,895	453	2,234	208	8
Coachella	45,646	128	0	3	41	84	1,141	182	775	184	4
Coalinga	16,371	124	0	9	10	105	210	50	147	13	3
Colma	1,520	21	0	0	11	10	369	62	290	17	0
Colton	55,127	245	4	6	115	120	1,439	264	828	347	7
Colusa	5,930	5	0	1	3	1	91	26	52	13	0
Commerce	12,994	106	1	6	40	59	1,174	131	698	345	4
Compton	97,728	1,164	21	33	441	669	2,583	411	1,402	770	54
Concord	129,789	462	5	63	163	231	4,419	448	3,212	759	27
Corcoran	22,345	78	1	9	10	58	383	101	222	60	0
Corning	7,511	25	0	1	5	19	286	79	172	35	2
Corona	169,164	223	1	36	107	79	3,297	561	2,177	559	19
Coronado	26,294	29	0	4	5	20	366	27	311	28	2
Costa Mesa	113,267	361	1	61	128	171	4,298	620	3,158	520	12
Cotati	7,485	49	0	6	7	36	94	18	62	14	0
Covina	48,674	172	2	22	51	97	1,180	283	712	185	4
Crescent City	6,529	38	0	0	11	27	228	30	192	6	1
Cudahy	24,146	74	0	3	29	42	214	41	93	80	5
Culver City	39,440	183	0	1	131	51	1,886	208	1,570	108	1
Cupertino	60,970	77	2	9	21	45	970	164	756	50	10
Cypress	49,064	69	0	5	21	43	726	142	495	89	3
Daly City	107,355	265	0	52	90	123	1,561	202	1,156	203	12
Dana Point	34,123	64	0	6	22	36	515	85	399	31	1
Danville	45,088	16	0	1	6	9	353	55	272	26	2
Davis	68,540	94	0	17	35	42	1,619	269	1,221	129	8
Delano	52,639	248	6	10	32	200	1,314	219	647	448	39
Del Mar	4,398	12	0	1	0	11	146	38	95	13	0
Del Rey Oaks	1,694	1	0	0	1	0	57	16	36	5	0
Desert Hot Springs	28,717	292	7	18	56	211	784	341	189	254	3
Diamond Bar	56,996	57	0	5	25	27	1,043	381	592	70	2
Dinuba	24,387	194	1	7	18	168	563	93	385	85	9
Dixon	20,049	39	0	2	5	32	373	38	281	54	14
Dorris	899	1	0	0	0	1	30	15	13	2	0
Dos Palos	5,291	59	2	4	1	52	171	50	103	18	3
Downey	113,511	382	3	23	182	174	3,222	591	1,866	765	9
Duarte	21,877	64	2	2	18	42	352	72	225	55	2
Dublin	62,235	85	0	9	23	53	1,195	117	970	108	1
Dunsmuir	1,569	9	0	2	1	6	36	14	19	3	0
East Palo Alto	29,933	125	0	14	60	51	466	96	293	77	8
Eastvale	62,422	55	0	1	24	30	1,319	211	938	170	2
El Cajon	104,447	429	1	48	163	217	2,330	414	1,502	414	12

Table 8. Offenses Known to Law Enforcement, by Selected State and City, 2017—Continued

(Number.)

State/city	Population	Violent crime	Murder and nonnegligent manslaughter	Rape (revised definition)[1]	Robbery	Aggravated assault	Property crime	Burglary	Larceny-theft	Motor vehicle theft	Arson[2]
El Centro	44,458	185	4	15	45	121	1,820	409	1,285	126	11
El Cerrito	25,704	168	1	2	93	72	1,341	164	1,100	77	5
Elk Grove	172,620	560	3	39	99	419	2,245	366	1,668	211	6
El Monte	116,168	451	5	43	183	220	2,816	687	1,431	698	13
El Segundo	16,932	40	1	4	21	14	687	183	423	81	0
Emeryville	11,971	151	1	5	105	40	2,084	66	1,833	185	6
Encinitas	63,722	106	0	13	23	70	925	208	651	66	2
Escalon	7,587	34	0	3	1	30	172	45	109	18	0
Escondido	152,845	576	3	51	174	348	2,605	427	1,780	398	29
Etna	713	2	0	0	0	2	3	1	1	1	0
Eureka	27,230	244	2	31	85	126	1,400	285	888	227	27
Exeter	10,533	24	1	4	6	13	239	55	152	32	1
Fairfax	7,623	4	0	0	1	3	94	10	78	6	2
Fairfield	116,372	546	10	40	181	315	3,252	545	2,174	533	32
Farmersville	10,760	34	0	2	6	26	172	32	105	35	2
Ferndale	1,372	2	0	1	0	1	15	1	12	2	0
Fillmore	15,708	30	0	6	5	19	119	24	83	12	5
Firebaugh	8,436	27	0	3	2	22	96	14	64	18	4
Folsom	78,155	64	0	21	21	22	1,229	257	847	125	15
Fontana	211,782	714	9	62	206	437	3,736	563	2,292	881	13
Fort Bragg	7,289	47	1	7	2	37	341	59	262	20	1
Fort Jones	684	2	0	0	0	2	7	3	4	0	0
Fortuna	12,154	49	0	5	15	29	519	101	374	44	4
Foster City	34,808	43	0	10	4	29	349	53	272	24	4
Fountain Valley	56,704	68	0	3	28	37	1,581	238	1,199	144	3
Fowler	6,475	22	0	4	0	18	101	48	35	18	1
Fremont	236,368	431	2	68	187	174	5,083	673	3,545	865	26
Fresno	526,371	2,974	56	174	958	1,786	20,220	3,649	13,782	2,789	217
Fullerton	141,637	293	1	63	98	131	3,952	293	3,273	386	30
Galt	25,971	91	0	4	15	72	595	74	451	70	6
Gardena	60,249	393	4	16	218	155	1,393	353	678	362	9
Garden Grove	175,466	602	5	22	220	355	4,348	840	2,851	657	22
Gilroy	56,163	208	1	32	81	94	1,648	213	1,144	291	8
Glendale	202,381	274	3	32	127	112	3,118	498	2,303	317	13
Glendora	52,133	129	0	15	33	81	1,533	248	1,180	105	3
Goleta	31,000	51	1	3	18	29	451	101	318	32	3
Gonzales	8,508	10	0	2	4	4	64	17	36	11	0
Grand Terrace	12,584	32	0	8	9	15	283	83	169	31	0
Grass Valley	12,947	76	2	0	9	65	750	125	515	110	3
Greenfield	17,603	102	2	7	18	75	214	49	86	79	14
Gridley	6,588	104	0	6	3	95	188	38	133	17	2
Grover Beach	13,720	39	1	7	7	24	246	43	161	42	0
Guadalupe	7,360	4	0	1	0	3	55	12	29	14	1
Gustine	5,865	33	0	1	1	31	85	26	43	16	1
Hanford	55,789	284	2	28	54	200	1,359	197	916	246	21
Hawaiian Gardens	14,505	86	0	1	30	55	324	78	161	85	0
Hawthorne	88,664	587	5	25	275	282	2,273	408	1,350	515	16
Hayward	161,417	563	5	70	306	182	5,023	482	2,740	1,801	37
Healdsburg	11,915	19	0	2	4	13	221	38	156	27	0
Hemet	85,166	457	4	25	133	295	3,103	703	1,868	532	10
Hercules	25,570	30	0	6	12	12	378	66	269	43	0
Hermosa Beach	19,836	28	0	4	7	17	590	116	426	48	3
Hesperia	94,292	380	2	38	97	243	2,117	452	1,230	435	25
Hidden Hills	1,937	1	0	0	0	1	12	4	7	1	0
Highland	55,229	186	4	13	74	95	1,082	250	609	223	17
Hillsborough	11,531	8	0	4	0	4	70	28	38	4	0
Hollister	38,310	132	1	18	33	80	396	71	252	73	5
Holtville	6,519	25	1	5	1	18	65	10	49	6	0
Hughson	7,552	2	0	0	1	1	101	15	74	12	0
Huntington Beach	202,244	461	2	75	95	289	4,285	617	3,283	385	32
Huntington Park	59,004	427	4	42	197	184	1,817	210	903	704	12
Huron	6,973	66	3	6	6	51	54	16	24	14	29
Imperial	17,629	11	1	0	2	8	61	14	36	11	1
Imperial Beach	27,593	133	1	5	34	93	364	69	211	84	1
Indian Wells	5,408	1	0	0	0	1	159	51	103	5	0
Indio	90,055	639	3	39	119	478	2,287	449	1,483	355	6
Industry	204	73	1	5	36	31	928	151	629	148	6
Inglewood	110,811	785	13	46	389	337	2,760	492	1,466	802	20
Ione	6,915	3	0	0	0	3	61	4	50	7	1
Irvine	276,115	169	2	46	55	66	3,635	627	2,814	194	10
Irwindale	1,436	12	1	0	7	4	212	56	121	35	0
Isleton	841	5	1	0	0	4	6	3	3	0	0
Jackson	4,683	21	0	2	2	17	129	37	76	16	3
Jurupa Valley	104,922	272	5	19	82	166	2,661	368	1,591	702	5
Kensington	5,397	3	0	1	1	1	49	13	29	7	1
Kerman	14,760	49	0	9	8	32	343	92	221	30	2
King City	14,037	57	3	9	2	43	196	71	72	53	2
Kingsburg	11,874	35	0	2	4	29	254	108	109	37	4
La Canada Flintridge	20,480	16	0	1	6	9	287	105	162	20	0
Lafayette[5]	26,492	7	0	2	4	1		41		19	1
Laguna Beach	23,261	100	0	10	14	76	559	124	369	66	1
Laguna Hills	31,715	44	1	5	18	20	467	117	301	49	4
Laguna Niguel	65,700	54	1	7	11	35	573	95	428	50	1

Table 8. Offenses Known to Law Enforcement, by Selected State and City, 2017—Continued

(Number.)

State/city	Population	Violent crime	Murder and nonnegligent manslaughter	Rape (revised definition)[1]	Robbery	Aggravated assault	Property crime	Burglary	Larceny-theft	Motor vehicle theft	Arson[2]
Laguna Woods	16,305	4	0	1	0	3	127	22	90	15	1
La Habra	61,878	137	1	9	46	81	1,251	197	869	185	3
La Habra Heights	5,426	4	0	1	1	2	95	29	60	6	1
Lake Elsinore	66,136	177	1	12	57	107	2,145	299	1,507	339	1
Lake Forest	84,224	133	0	19	24	90	757	166	504	87	2
Lakeport	4,775	28	0	3	6	19	242	58	160	24	0
Lake Shastina	2,562	1	0	0	0	1	21	7	11	3	0
Lakewood	81,317	318	3	13	151	151	2,422	438	1,725	259	4
La Mesa	60,425	160	3	11	50	96	1,193	177	823	193	7
La Mirada	49,328	104	2	7	34	61	906	143	625	138	1
Lancaster	160,653	1,219	15	80	337	787	3,318	935	1,733	650	40
La Palma	15,811	19	0	0	7	12	363	140	190	33	1
La Puente	40,467	148	0	14	43	91	444	92	190	162	3
La Quinta	41,528	67	0	8	32	27	1,197	168	963	66	0
La Verne	32,613	92	0	11	27	54	766	137	563	66	3
Lawndale	33,205	178	2	3	66	107	433	75	214	144	2
Lemon Grove	27,113	171	1	4	55	111	618	93	422	103	0
Lemoore	25,999	141	3	20	21	97	434	93	267	74	4
Lincoln	47,741	44	2	19	6	17	605	108	435	62	3
Lindsay	13,513	45	2	0	13	30	273	58	149	66	7
Livermore	90,485	166	0	30	48	88	1,977	191	1,510	276	22
Livingston	14,117	54	0	2	12	40	285	95	154	36	6
Lodi	65,042	323	1	13	127	182	1,681	347	985	349	8
Loma Linda	24,265	39	0	6	12	21	610	112	401	97	1
Lomita	20,764	56	1	3	13	39	402	90	241	71	1
Lompoc	43,948	243	2	34	37	170	974	225	598	151	8
Long Beach	471,397	3,101	22	203	1,237	1,639	12,598	2,765	7,104	2,729	127
Los Alamitos	11,671	16	0	5	10	1	202	73	105	24	0
Los Altos	30,816	10	0	3	2	5	321	87	215	19	3
Los Altos Hills	8,579	2	0	1	0	1	59	22	36	1	4
Los Angeles	4,007,147	30,507	281	2,455	10,814	16,957	101,618	16,668	65,757	19,193	1,414
Los Banos	37,910	138	2	6	41	89	1,073	217	695	161	8
Los Gatos	30,720	14	0	3	4	7	431	70	319	42	0
Lynwood	71,453	458	8	16	220	214	1,681	293	688	700	22
Madera	64,939	378	4	32	107	235	1,702	336	967	399	16
Malibu	12,918	38	0	8	6	24	366	78	255	33	0
Mammoth Lakes	7,956	27	0	5	5	17	147	21	115	11	0
Manhattan Beach	35,843	71	0	11	36	24	875	179	625	71	3
Manteca	78,564	256	4	18	89	145	2,240	302	1,616	322	14
Marina	22,030	54	0	7	14	33	405	72	288	45	2
Martinez	38,619	54	0	7	20	27	619	78	318	223	0
Marysville	12,275	95	1	6	20	68	508	107	265	136	14
Maywood	27,671	115	2	8	39	66	364	68	157	139	3
McFarland	14,882	67	2	16	5	44	179	54	82	43	12
Mendota	11,459	74	0	5	7	62	124	38	59	27	1
Menifee	90,403	123	3	8	43	69	1,972	326	1,373	273	2
Menlo Park	34,195	53	0	15	15	23	656	95	527	34	0
Merced	83,180	563	8	28	158	369	2,668	472	1,706	490	92
Mill Valley	14,423	9	0	0	3	6	211	36	163	12	0
Milpitas	79,503	114	2	12	58	42	1,978	235	1,447	296	4
Mission Viejo	96,928	101	1	13	26	61	969	158	733	78	1
Modesto	213,677	2,074	20	110	519	1,425	8,465	1,188	5,865	1,412	63
Monrovia	37,214	66	2	12	26	26	848	120	645	83	2
Montague	1,392	9	1	2	0	6	18	10	6	2	0
Montclair	39,318	230	1	25	85	119	1,534	284	870	380	15
Montebello	63,473	203	2	9	82	110	1,644	665	519	460	103
Monterey	28,584	125	0	17	58	50	1,206	162	964	80	5
Monterey Park	61,210	112	1	10	55	46	1,613	439	955	219	4
Monte Sereno	3,583	0	0	0	0	0	11	3	8	0	0
Moorpark	36,813	48	0	8	9	31	332	55	257	20	4
Moraga	17,653	6	0	1	3	2	128	29	89	10	1
Moreno Valley	207,418	798	9	26	352	411	6,356	1,148	4,050	1,158	14
Morgan Hill	45,277	72	0	1	18	53	722	92	507	123	2
Morro Bay	10,716	22	0	2	4	16	197	35	152	10	3
Mountain View	81,525	150	1	14	44	91	1,982	290	1,590	102	6
Mount Shasta	3,276	17	1	2	1	13	66	8	48	10	1
Murrieta	113,016	80	1	14	33	32	1,582	254	1,143	185	8
Napa	80,958	272	1	39	43	189	1,353	338	828	187	1
National City	61,574	296	3	23	109	161	1,157	132	667	358	11
Needles	5,011	37	0	4	4	29	178	57	104	17	9
Nevada City	3,157	8	0	0	2	6	117	22	67	28	0
Newark	46,360	88	1	15	48	24	1,498	201	1,041	256	3
Newman	11,271	13	0	0	4	9	142	46	70	26	0
Newport Beach	86,910	124	0	31	21	72	2,123	361	1,630	132	6
Norco	26,654	69	1	5	17	46	688	124	472	92	0
Norwalk	106,278	437	5	17	133	282	1,956	418	1,123	415	7
Novato	56,698	92	1	5	26	60	927	145	689	93	2
Oakdale	22,886	31	0	7	6	18	586	104	400	82	3
Oakland	424,915	5,521	69	400	2,676	2,376	25,422	2,622	17,305	5,495	196
Oakley	41,509	52	1	4	12	35	489	79	302	108	2
Oceanside	176,815	694	9	69	165	451	4,088	592	3,000	496	22
Ojai	7,603	4	0	2	0	2	45	11	33	1	0
Ontario[6]	174,724	683	8	136	220	319	4,473	720	2,842	911	29

Table 8. Offenses Known to Law Enforcement, by Selected State and City, 2017—Continued

(Number.)

State/city	Population	Violent crime	Murder and nonnegligent manslaughter	Rape (revised definition)[1]	Robbery	Aggravated assault	Property crime	Burglary	Larceny-theft	Motor vehicle theft	Arson[2]
Orange	141,130	218	4	12	64	138	2,584	489	1,754	341	19
Orange Cove	9,674	58	5	0	6	47	95	20	52	23	0
Orinda	19,760	10	0	1	6	3	153	53	94	6	1
Orland	7,624	24	1	2	2	19	132	38	71	23	2
Oroville	19,091	124	0	16	40	68	1,427	259	970	198	12
Oxnard	209,513	908	15	65	430	398	5,328	787	3,848	693	43
Pacifica	39,353	86	1	17	20	48	528	100	383	45	3
Pacific Grove	15,716	16	0	8	0	8	324	55	249	20	0
Palmdale	158,094	681	4	37	218	422	2,659	613	1,611	435	29
Palm Desert	52,845	91	0	3	30	58	2,076	424	1,536	116	1
Palm Springs	48,193	290	5	40	94	151	1,963	436	1,277	250	3
Palo Alto	67,441	90	0	11	39	40	1,783	214	1,478	91	6
Palos Verdes Estates	13,611	3	0	1	2	0	125	43	77	5	0
Paradise	26,610	88	0	16	9	63	295	127	131	37	2
Paramount	55,041	324	6	8	125	185	1,613	283	892	438	6
Parlier	15,289	106	1	8	16	81	258	90	83	85	21
Pasadena	142,891	574	8	51	202	313	2,946	745	1,842	359	42
Paso Robles	32,266	35	0	3	6	26	920	126	731	63	4
Patterson	21,994	46	0	3	9	34	513	50	327	136	2
Perris	77,626	192	2	4	66	120	1,877	270	1,104	503	7
Petaluma	60,957	233	1	32	40	160	946	170	712	64	9
Pico Rivera	63,746	236	1	19	75	141	1,432	250	853	329	5
Piedmont	11,464	14	0	7	3	4	174	60	98	16	0
Pinole	19,449	66	0	5	31	30	968	93	789	86	3
Pismo Beach	8,291	42	0	3	4	35	393	88	283	22	1
Pittsburg	71,944	341	7	34	121	179	1,766	299	876	591	28
Placentia	52,437	89	1	1	25	62	864	187	563	114	2
Placerville	10,732	29	0	6	9	14	279	57	176	46	1
Pleasant Hill	35,136	83	0	10	34	39	1,739	158	1,451	130	9
Pleasanton	84,440	99	0	13	53	33	1,661	137	1,406	118	5
Pomona	153,066	853	18	88	344	403	4,484	718	2,516	1,250	26
Porterville	59,245	247	4	10	58	175	1,535	338	925	272	3
Port Hueneme	22,374	39	2	4	14	19	396	65	287	44	6
Poway	50,438	58	0	8	13	37	576	136	389	51	3
Rancho Cordova	73,607	305	1	17	85	202	1,410	285	899	226	1
Rancho Cucamonga	178,308	329	1	46	118	164	4,180	814	2,998	368	7
Rancho Mirage	18,347	28	0	0	13	15	572	121	411	40	0
Rancho Palos Verdes	42,563	33	0	5	7	21	446	152	259	35	0
Rancho Santa Margarita	49,144	32	0	4	6	22	328	45	265	18	4
Red Bluff	14,169	160	0	29	31	100	960	156	698	106	10
Redding	92,127	654	2	64	150	438	3,841	690	2,360	791	9
Redlands	71,707	216	1	36	69	110	2,629	426	1,910	293	20
Redondo Beach	68,051	176	0	18	62	96	1,570	358	1,042	170	0
Redwood City	86,353	209	0	57	61	91	1,390	177	1,053	160	18
Reedley	25,794	100	0	5	14	81	369	147	148	74	9
Rialto	103,980	399	2	28	150	219	1,684	475	596	613	3
Richmond	110,804	1,014	10	49	392	563	4,128	698	2,199	1,231	42
Ridgecrest	28,873	155	0	19	13	123	518	136	309	73	9
Rio Dell	3,414	6	0	1	0	5	44	8	24	12	1
Rio Vista	8,870	41	0	1	4	36	94	40	45	9	0
Ripon	15,659	13	0	7	4	2	286	28	241	17	0
Riverbank	24,669	40	0	1	21	18	562	73	431	58	2
Riverside	328,023	1,669	12	166	544	947	10,032	1,673	6,629	1,730	73
Rocklin	63,735	66	0	14	29	23	1,135	211	813	111	10
Rohnert Park	42,922	218	0	29	21	168	832	110	610	112	7
Rolling Hills	1,891	0	0	0	0	0	6	1	5	0	0
Rolling Hills Estates	8,259	12	0	2	1	9	153	42	103	8	2
Rosemead	54,615	173	1	12	59	101	1,327	330	719	278	7
Roseville	135,028	237	0	27	87	123	3,322	389	2,623	310	33
Ross	2,475	2	0	0	1	1	37	8	29	0	0
Sacramento	499,997	3,378	39	99	1,100	2,140	14,683	2,888	9,077	2,718	209
Salinas	158,313	1,021	28	71	358	564	4,795	964	2,589	1,242	24
San Bernardino	217,259	2,805	34	158	877	1,736	8,403	2,136	3,990	2,277	67
San Bruno	43,274	121	1	13	51	56	1,117	126	904	87	4
San Clemente	65,596	91	0	9	37	45	812	173	574	65	4
Sand City	392	10	0	0	5	5	132	10	119	3	0
San Diego	1,424,116	5,221	35	559	1,410	3,217	26,246	3,817	17,294	5,135	158
San Dimas	34,499	67	0	5	24	38	735	158	500	77	4
San Fernando	24,899	120	3	9	34	74	360	85	184	91	1
San Francisco	881,255	6,301	56	367	3,220	2,658	54,356	4,935	44,587	4,834	303
San Gabriel	40,531	114	1	3	40	70	666	199	407	60	3
Sanger	25,126	110	2	12	15	81	489	173	240	76	2
San Jacinto	47,932	114	3	2	55	54	1,605	343	1,005	257	1
San Jose	1,037,529	4,188	32	571	1,376	2,209	25,323	3,926	13,329	8,068	173
San Juan Capistrano	36,532	82	0	12	16	54	448	103	313	32	3
San Leandro	91,386	524	2	21	292	209	3,715	460	2,369	886	20
San Luis Obispo	47,934	178	0	44	23	111	1,782	172	1,516	94	12
San Marcos	97,290	195	0	25	54	116	1,136	202	784	150	4
San Marino	13,402	14	0	0	6	8	255	127	126	2	0
San Mateo	105,090	268	0	19	64	185	2,125	706	1,231	188	8
San Pablo	30,781	178	2	7	103	66	1,040	129	547	364	8
San Rafael	59,144	194	0	21	89	84	1,627	271	1,091	265	19
San Ramon	76,325	56	0	8	30	18	974	126	768	80	7

Table 8. Offenses Known to Law Enforcement, by Selected State and City, 2017—Continued

(Number.)

State/city	Population	Violent crime	Murder and nonnegligent manslaughter	Rape (revised definition)[1]	Robbery	Aggravated assault	Property crime	Burglary	Larceny-theft	Motor vehicle theft	Arson[2]
Santa Ana	335,699	1,640	21	188	605	826	7,017	929	4,108	1,980	60
Santa Barbara	92,508	377	0	67	80	230	2,499	327	1,968	204	23
Santa Clara	127,538	214	2	35	82	95	3,618	408	2,810	400	7
Santa Clarita	216,350	352	4	40	122	186	3,081	674	1,997	410	13
Santa Cruz	65,132	409	1	57	103	248	3,684	412	2,911	361	30
Santa Fe Springs	18,339	106	0	4	48	54	1,048	183	688	177	6
Santa Maria	107,424	476	3	58	155	260	2,354	446	1,231	677	11
Santa Monica	92,935	705	3	54	241	407	4,374	648	3,462	264	25
Santa Paula	30,496	103	2	7	18	76	434	84	308	42	2
Santa Rosa	176,361	722	5	109	126	482	3,245	525	2,309	411	22
Santee	58,563	155	0	11	43	101	866	109	665	92	1
Saratoga	30,886	33	2	3	6	22	192	94	81	17	4
Sausalito	7,155	14	0	0	3	11	231	37	187	7	0
Scotts Valley	11,985	14	0	6	4	4	227	40	167	20	0
Seal Beach	24,495	45	0	2	19	24	643	92	503	48	1
Seaside	34,519	92	1	8	31	52	513	81	360	72	1
Sebastopol	7,725	20	0	5	3	12	129	39	81	9	1
Selma	24,817	292	3	12	17	260	873	300	411	162	7
Shafter	19,284	43	0	7	11	25	473	117	242	114	11
Sierra Madre	11,080	8	0	1	1	6	108	43	61	4	2
Signal Hill	11,757	63	1	5	34	23	749	93	521	135	2
Simi Valley	126,635	184	0	32	39	113	1,824	331	1,355	138	7
Solana Beach	13,542	13	0	3	4	6	229	68	142	19	0
Soledad	25,560	50	2	3	7	38	170	47	76	47	3
Solvang	5,899	7	0	1	1	5	85	21	62	2	0
Sonoma	11,120	31	0	5	7	19	186	36	146	4	1
Sonora	4,811	33	0	9	7	17	324	56	239	29	7
South El Monte	21,012	121	2	4	35	80	684	169	314	201	9
South Gate	95,717	674	6	41	223	404	3,131	507	1,691	933	14
South Lake Tahoe	21,768	58	0	12	8	38	482	129	280	73	1
South Pasadena	25,961	18	1	2	9	6	504	130	315	59	2
South San Francisco	67,533	234	1	31	72	130	1,605	214	1,184	207	8
Stallion Springs	2,644	4	0	0	0	4	10	0	10	0	0
Stanton	38,767	142	1	17	37	87	649	130	384	135	4
St. Helena	6,210	11	0	5	1	5	93	33	52	8	2
Stockton[6]	309,566	4,379	55	154	1,208	2,962	11,229	2,140	7,040	2,049	208
Suisun City	29,738	101	3	8	38	52	689	110	490	89	8
Sunnyvale	154,919	182	1	29	56	96	2,682	512	1,872	298	19
Susanville	14,414	209	0	9	11	189	314	102	197	15	7
Sutter Creek	2,517	4	0	0	0	4	61	8	47	6	1
Taft	9,393	83	0	5	7	71	405	77	287	41	0
Tehachapi	12,210	49	1	4	8	36	223	57	130	36	4
Temecula	115,220	117	1	5	38	73	2,614	353	2,011	250	2
Temple City	36,500	54	2	3	20	29	552	258	257	37	0
Thousand Oaks	129,240	172	2	44	35	91	1,687	269	1,305	113	12
Tiburon	9,210	3	0	0	1	2	86	16	70	0	0
Torrance	147,482	267	0	36	116	115	3,206	557	2,213	436	12
Tracy	90,263	193	3	27	77	86	2,179	201	1,616	362	11
Truckee	16,429	19	0	4	0	15	165	40	98	27	4
Tulare	63,349	254	2	22	66	164	1,703	284	1,008	411	15
Tulelake	988	2	0	0	0	2	1	1	0	0	0
Turlock	73,488	447	4	24	142	277	2,296	382	1,471	443	35
Tustin	81,246	132	3	11	47	71	1,949	288	1,484	177	9
Twentynine Palms	26,210	40	2	2	6	30	326	142	139	45	8
Ukiah	15,859	121	0	14	20	87	335	59	234	42	13
Union City	76,311	255	1	15	83	156	1,686	216	1,114	356	4
Upland	77,154	232	7	25	101	99	2,071	586	1,194	291	6
Vacaville	99,293	198	1	20	56	121	2,108	186	1,742	180	17
Vallejo	122,174	1,048	15	93	390	550	4,597	2,445	1,181	971	60
Ventura	110,006	460	2	63	111	284	3,638	585	2,717	336	17
Vernon	113	35	0	0	20	15	424	60	229	135	5
Victorville	123,284	862	14	54	267	527	3,318	830	1,839	649	42
Villa Park	5,933	2	0	0	0	2	74	35	35	4	1
Visalia	132,143	457	9	81	144	223	4,396	839	2,953	604	16
Vista	103,004	370	4	38	104	224	1,494	310	889	295	9
Walnut	30,189	43	0	12	8	23	485	232	221	32	2
Walnut Creek	69,953	105	1	2	39	63	2,304	243	1,871	190	2
Waterford	8,928	16	0	1	2	13	120	26	55	39	0
Watsonville	54,226	298	1	41	69	187	1,711	251	995	465	14
Weed	2,605	23	0	0	0	23	95	23	62	10	0
West Covina	108,128	275	0	31	144	100	2,733	502	1,821	410	10
West Hollywood	37,093	254	1	29	122	102	1,705	234	1,367	104	2
Westlake Village	8,476	14	0	1	4	9	208	48	155	5	0
Westminster	91,863	281	4	23	132	122	2,825	443	1,987	395	14
Westmorland	2,276	5	0	0	0	5	21	9	10	2	0
West Sacramento	53,703	199	7	19	79	94	1,138	201	756	181	21
Wheatland	3,831	6	0	0	2	4	37	10	22	5	1
Whittier	87,141	300	5	15	137	143	2,507	420	1,774	313	6
Wildomar	36,683	56	0	2	15	39	683	128	430	125	1
Williams	5,201	11	0	3	5	3	75	34	32	9	2
Willits	4,870	57	0	4	5	48	61	11	25	25	0
Windsor	27,679	61	0	15	6	40	279	40	219	20	2
Winters	7,235	14	0	0	1	13	131	26	93	12	2

Table 8. Offenses Known to Law Enforcement, by Selected State and City, 2017—Continued

(Number.)

State/city	Population	Violent crime	Murder and nonnegligent manslaughter	Rape (revised definition)[1]	Robbery	Aggravated assault	Property crime	Burglary	Larceny-theft	Motor vehicle theft	Arson[2]
Woodlake	7,678	27	1	1	2	23	122	20	86	16	4
Woodland	59,676	187	0	21	38	128	1,861	326	1,306	229	35
Yorba Linda	68,889	45	0	9	5	31	714	185	482	47	5
Yountville	3,020	1	0	0	0	1	42	7	33	2	0
Yreka	7,564	51	1	5	2	43	213	57	113	43	1
Yuba City	67,042	255	0	23	82	150	2,207	380	1,448	379	15
Yucaipa	53,614	74	0	12	23	39	927	202	590	135	5
Yucca Valley	21,806	65	0	9	18	38	444	148	244	52	2
COLORADO											
Alamosa	10,025	46	0	8	6	32	721	125	582	14	6
Arvada	119,346	193	0	39	44	110	3,302	337	2,521	444	19
Aspen	6,906	2	0	2	0	0	292	30	246	16	1
Ault	1,710	2	0	0	0	2	2	1	1	0	0
Aurora	368,018	2,239	30	319	679	1,211	11,054	1,671	7,194	2,189	68
Avon	6,551	20	0	7	2	11	117	8	104	5	0
Basalt	3,933	0	0	0	0	0	23	2	19	2	0
Bayfield	2,677	3	0	0	1	2	36	9	26	1	0
Black Hawk	129	4	0	3	0	1	216	5	198	13	0
Bow Mar	982	0	0	0	0	0	5	1	3	1	0
Breckenridge	4,959	5	0	1	0	4	174	32	136	6	1
Brighton	39,099	188	0	38	24	126	1,307	145	956	206	8
Broomfield	68,158	84	1	23	7	53	1,790	197	1,400	193	9
Brush	5,397	6	0	5	0	1	69	15	50	4	0
Buena Vista	2,815	1	0	0	0	1	42	3	37	2	0
Burlington	4,178	11	0	2	0	9	69	2	64	3	1
Calhan	797	3	0	1	0	2	10	1	9	0	0
Canon City	16,723	73	1	16	6	50	650	110	488	52	7
Carbondale	6,844	17	0	7	1	9	108	10	93	5	1
Castle Rock	59,337	54	0	26	10	18	969	120	797	52	2
Center	2,232	2	0	0	0	2	53	23	27	3	0
Cherry Hills Village	6,685	2	0	0	1	1	25	5	17	3	0
Colorado Springs	472,958	2,479	29	489	482	1,479	15,214	2,508	10,571	2,135	115
Columbine Valley	1,432	1	0	0	0	1	11	4	5	2	0
Commerce City	56,469	314	4	54	39	217	1,843	240	1,287	316	25
Cortez	9,095	15	0	3	4	8	288	2	283	3	0
Craig	8,869	17	0	7	2	8	202	25	168	9	1
Crested Butte	1,626	14	0	0	0	14	15	2	13	0	1
Cripple Creek	1,173	6	0	0	1	5	94	13	76	5	0
Dacono	5,261	6	0	0	2	4	29	10	15	4	0
Delta	8,925	8	0	2	1	5	396	85	292	19	1
Denver	706,616	4,774	59	699	1,232	2,784	25,912	4,331	16,021	5,560	129
Dillon	970	2	0	0	1	1	28	5	21	2	0
Durango	18,801	44	0	2	7	35	708	62	598	48	3
Eagle	6,780	10	0	3	0	7	94	9	81	4	2
Eaton	5,212	2	0	0	0	2	42	4	34	4	0
Edgewater	5,350	11	0	1	4	6	346	25	270	51	0
Erie	23,660	12	2	0	3	7	200	27	160	13	3
Estes Park	6,435	19	0	6	0	13	59	16	41	2	0
Evans	22,153	68	1	5	12	50	458	90	317	51	8
Federal Heights	12,624	77	1	9	12	55	541	63	346	132	2
Firestone	13,416	9	0	0	1	8	119	20	83	16	2
Florence	3,953	4	0	0	0	4	53	4	40	9	0
Fort Collins	167,633	369	6	45	42	276	4,250	457	3,586	207	14
Fort Lupton	8,057	9	0	4	1	4	91	12	65	14	2
Fort Morgan	11,347	44	0	25	2	17	318	46	250	22	2
Fountain	29,203	149	0	29	14	106	781	115	566	100	5
Fowler	1,139	2	0	0	0	2	8	2	4	2	0
Fraser/Winter Park	2,293	5	0	3	0	2	55	6	47	2	0
Frederick	12,850	7	0	0	0	7	58	6	48	4	1
Frisco	3,154	4	0	2	2	0	60	13	44	3	2
Fruita	12,971	25	0	6	3	16	172	36	131	5	2
Garden City	270	4	0	0	1	3	21	2	14	5	1
Glendale	5,362	46	0	9	17	20	781	41	690	50	3
Glenwood Springs	10,073	27	0	7	4	16	457	35	405	17	0
Golden	20,948	23	1	7	3	12	600	62	485	53	3
Granby	1,929	1	0	0	0	1	40	7	31	2	0
Grand Junction	62,352	361	2	71	25	263	2,849	356	2,324	169	32
Greeley	105,906	449	5	75	57	312	2,714	428	2,020	266	23
Gunnison	6,326	16	0	6	0	10	131	15	106	10	0
Haxtun	912	0	0	0	0	0	6	1	5	0	0
Hayden	1,887	3	0	0	1	2	33	7	26	0	0
Holyoke	2,195	3	1	0	0	2	10	1	8	1	0
Hotchkiss	912	0	0	0	0	0	21	10	11	0	0
Hugo	748	3	0	3	0	0	7	1	5	1	0
Idaho Springs	1,751	15	0	2	3	10	69	5	58	6	4
Ignacio	728	0	0	0	0	0	3	1	1	1	0
Johnstown	16,552	3	0	2	0	1	171	18	131	22	0
Kersey	1,616	3	0	0	0	3	6	1	3	2	0
Kiowa	745	0	0	0	0	0	0	0	0	0	0
Lafayette	28,939	66	0	24	7	35	711	65	607	39	3
La Junta	6,900	35	0	15	1	19	404	78	300	26	1
Lakeside	8	1	0	0	1	0	248	2	246	0	0

Table 8. Offenses Known to Law Enforcement, by Selected State and City, 2017—Continued

(Number.)

State/city	Population	Violent crime	Murder and nonnegligent manslaughter	Rape (revised definition)[1]	Robbery	Aggravated assault	Property crime	Burglary	Larceny-theft	Motor vehicle theft	Arson[2]
Lakewood	156,344	1,007	5	151	208	643	7,596	911	5,492	1,193	24
Lamar	7,468	1	0	0	1	0	70	15	55	0	0
La Salle	2,153	1	0	0	0	1	50	4	41	5	0
Leadville	2,711	4	0	0	0	4	26	3	23	0	1
Limon	1,967	2	0	0	1	1	5	0	4	1	0
Littleton	47,112	48	0	18	15	15	1,429	262	996	171	5
Log Lane Village	863	4	0	0	0	4	4	0	3	1	1
Lone Tree	13,638	22	0	0	6	16	892	51	833	8	2
Longmont	93,979	331	4	108	26	193	2,318	307	1,776	235	60
Louisville	21,224	18	0	5	5	8	85	37	32	16	3
Loveland	78,671	249	0	64	26	159	1,888	199	1,581	108	15
Mancos	1,482	0	0	0	0	0	7	1	6	0	1
Manitou Springs	5,364	12	0	2	0	10	85	19	57	9	1
Meeker	2,336	4	0	1	0	3	35	4	30	1	0
Milliken	6,870	16	0	2	0	14	42	7	34	1	0
Monte Vista	4,235	10	0	0	3	7	239	62	170	7	0
Montrose	19,346	44	1	7	4	32	946	132	735	79	2
Monument	6,644	3	0	0	0	3	175	17	146	12	0
Mountain View	531	1	0	0	1	0	19	4	12	3	0
Mountain Village	1,432	1	0	0	0	1	16	0	15	1	0
Mount Crested Butte	839	1	0	1	0	0	11	0	10	1	0
Nederland	1,548	3	0	0	0	3	23	3	19	1	1
New Castle	4,798	5	0	2	0	3	47	5	38	4	0
Northglenn	39,520	152	0	30	13	109	1,384	130	909	345	8
Oak Creek	920	0	0	0	0	0	8	4	3	1	0
Olathe	1,803	2	1	1	0	0	28	10	16	2	0
Ouray	1,038	0	0	0	0	0	21	3	16	2	0
Pagosa Springs	1,858	11	0	1	1	9	79	1	75	3	1
Palisade	2,645	8	0	3	1	4	58	14	41	3	0
Parachute	1,119	20	0	5	0	15	78	35	36	7	1
Parker	52,179	77	0	16	8	53	784	117	616	51	6
Platteville	3,854	4	0	4	0	0	54	9	42	3	0
Pueblo	110,872	1,167	10	199	219	739	6,838	1,376	4,234	1,228	50
Rangely	2,359	2	0	0	0	2	4	0	3	1	0
Rifle	9,724	31	0	12	3	16	305	24	267	14	2
Salida	5,642	5	0	1	1	3	171	15	145	11	1
Severance	4,177	4	0	1	0	3	25	7	18	0	0
Sheridan	6,103	43	1	5	11	26	555	44	428	83	1
Silt	3,116	6	0	1	0	5	27	3	19	5	0
Silverthorne	4,615	16	0	3	1	12	112	10	97	5	1
Snowmass Village	2,913	2	0	0	0	2	14	0	13	1	0
Steamboat Springs	12,799	22	0	10	2	10	294	28	252	14	1
Sterling	13,955	61	1	14	3	43	453	84	349	20	4
Telluride	2,481	1	0	0	0	1	58	0	58	0	0
Thornton[5]	139,825	490	5	150	72	263			3,028	739	28
Timnath	3,806	0	0	0	0	0	150	24	121	5	0
Trinidad	7,961	31	0	3	14	14	458	104	340	14	2
Vail	5,516	6	0	0	0	6	247	23	209	15	0
Walsh	506	0	0	0	0	0	0	0	0	0	0
Westminster	115,155	275	4	68	46	157	3,668	446	2,489	733	12
Wheat Ridge	31,567	134	0	30	14	90	1,541	153	1,105	283	11
Windsor	23,523	5	0	1	1	3	269	27	226	16	5
Woodland Park	7,424	18	0	2	2	14	181	23	153	5	0
Wray	2,369	0	0	0	0	0	5	1	3	1	0
Yuma	3,593	1	0	0	0	1	12	3	8	1	1
CONNECTICUT											
Ansonia	18,647	22	0	6	3	13	353	21	283	49	1
Avon	18,397	2	0	0	2	0	166	10	141	15	0
Berlin	20,601	27	0	1	6	20	400	65	310	25	0
Bethel	19,796	9	0	2	3	4	171	20	147	4	2
Bloomfield	20,667	36	0	10	10	16	575	48	461	66	7
Branford	28,027	16	0	0	7	9	555	33	476	46	0
Bridgeport	146,110	1,315	21	77	565	652	3,416	548	2,152	716	14
Bristol	60,090	61	1	13	25	22	1,025	146	752	127	6
Brookfield	17,203	3	0	0	1	2	122	15	95	12	0
Canton	10,285	2	0	0	1	1	65	10	52	3	0
Cheshire	29,282	3	0	0	0	3	175	16	145	14	0
Clinton	12,915	18	0	5	1	12	314	55	255	4	2
Coventry	12,431	4	0	1	2	1	106	30	69	7	0
Cromwell	13,953	10	0	2	3	5	261	8	226	27	0
Danbury	85,614	163	1	19	71	72	1,105	90	942	73	1
Darien	21,910	3	0	0	1	2	273	22	225	26	0
Derby	12,586	42	1	2	16	23	306	35	238	33	1
East Hampton	12,855	5	0	0	2	3	61	10	48	3	0
East Hartford	50,067	133	1	24	55	53	1,231	188	883	160	3
East Haven	28,739	41	0	6	23	12	607	75	462	70	0
Easton	7,570	0	0	0	0	0	10	3	6	1	0
East Windsor	11,383	13	0	1	8	4	303	52	234	17	2
Enfield	44,321	79	0	6	21	52	797	171	566	60	0
Fairfield	61,402	23	0	2	9	12	915	110	703	102	0
Farmington	25,551	19	0	4	7	8	537	40	464	33	0
Glastonbury	34,606	24	0	5	7	12	505	74	389	42	0

Table 8. Offenses Known to Law Enforcement, by Selected State and City, 2017—Continued

(Number.)

State/city	Population	Violent crime	Murder and nonnegligent manslaughter	Rape (revised definition)[1]	Robbery	Aggravated assault	Property crime	Burglary	Larceny-theft	Motor vehicle theft	Arson[2]
Granby	11,241	0	0	0	0	0	89	9	76	4	0
Greenwich	62,531	21	1	2	12	6	471	87	311	73	0
Groton	9,093	17	0	3	5	9	170	60	106	4	1
Groton Long Point	506	0	0	0	0	0	6	1	5	0	0
Groton Town	29,524	36	0	8	7	21	464	48	403	13	3
Guilford	22,259	5	0	3	0	2	264	26	230	8	0
Hamden	61,042	183	1	4	26	152	1,175	88	989	98	4
Hartford	122,891	1,343	29	45	465	804	4,907	738	3,490	679	87
Ledyard	14,889	15	0	3	2	10	92	5	75	12	2
Madison	18,130	0	0	0	0	0	86	15	61	10	0
Manchester	57,808	108	2	26	38	42	1,489	148	1,226	115	3
Meriden	59,417	223	2	29	58	134	1,432	277	980	175	10
Middlebury	7,651	5	0	1	4	0	89	12	61	16	0
Middletown	46,363	49	0	6	8	35	730	68	591	71	0
Milford	54,265	24	0	1	18	5	967	92	809	66	3
Monroe	19,682	10	0	2	4	4	151	20	111	20	0
Naugatuck	31,310	36	0	10	9	17	448	66	353	29	1
New Britain	72,442	269	4	39	91	135	2,087	357	1,342	388	22
New Canaan	20,364	2	0	1	0	1	128	16	97	15	0
New Haven	129,953	1,100	7	52	378	663	5,211	840	3,728	643	32
Newington	30,402	41	2	11	10	18	937	60	797	80	3
New London	26,880	132	4	24	33	71	741	98	541	102	2
New Milford	26,993	26	0	11	4	11	273	6	247	20	2
Newtown	27,908	11	0	6	3	2	95	14	75	6	1
North Branford	14,163	6	0	2	0	4	176	28	136	12	0
North Haven	23,646	17	0	2	7	8	464	71	352	41	0
Norwalk	88,849	255	3	11	40	201	1,505	160	1,188	157	5
Norwich	39,393	103	0	21	33	49	601	134	428	39	8
Old Saybrook	10,070	2	0	0	0	2	82	6	72	4	0
Orange	13,904	7	0	1	4	2	362	19	326	17	1
Plainfield	15,011	12	0	6	0	6	68	14	49	5	0
Plainville	17,669	35	0	8	0	27	599	61	513	25	0
Plymouth	11,671	7	0	0	2	5	150	38	96	16	1
Portland	9,324	8	0	0	0	8	103	12	80	11	0
Putnam	9,293	26	0	4	3	19	116	24	86	6	1
Redding	9,223	4	0	1	0	3	72	14	54	4	0
Ridgefield	25,127	0	0	0	0	0	110	3	91	16	0
Rocky Hill	20,189	5	0	3	0	2	290	33	225	32	0
Seymour	16,555	12	0	2	4	6	127	25	92	10	0
Shelton	41,625	28	0	3	7	18	396	81	259	56	1
Simsbury	24,559	4	0	0	2	2	164	15	133	16	0
Southington	43,769	31	0	8	16	7	732	101	572	59	8
South Windsor[5]	25,740	14	0	4	5	5	443	60	350	33	
Stamford	130,189	292	0	30	91	171	1,986	241	1,488	257	5
Stonington	18,666	17	0	1	3	13	240	36	198	6	1
Stratford	52,263	89	2	10	50	27	1,117	137	826	154	3
Suffield	15,602	3	0	1	0	2	109	40	56	13	0
Thomaston	7,548	6	0	0	2	4	116	24	82	10	1
Torrington	34,372	56	1	6	9	40	558	73	448	37	1
Trumbull	36,265	55	0	12	27	16	848	83	708	57	1
Vernon	29,142	22	0	3	8	11	365	75	261	29	0
Wallingford	44,577	25	0	1	4	20	618	112	473	33	0
Waterbury	107,924	544	11	51	255	227	4,136	690	2,619	827	13
Waterford	19,034	31	0	1	10	20	405	17	376	12	2
Watertown	21,672	19	0	0	3	16	313	47	243	23	0
West Hartford	62,812	67	0	1	61	5	1,859	150	1,588	121	5
West Haven	54,342	142	1	24	34	83	1,152	120	917	115	7
Weston	10,320	4	0	0	0	4	37	1	32	4	0
Westport	28,079	5	0	2	1	2	298	29	233	36	0
Wethersfield	26,116	30	1	8	12	9	386	55	247	84	4
Willimantic	17,768	30	0	10	14	6	203	60	118	25	2
Wilton	18,643	4	0	1	2	1	143	14	123	6	0
Winchester	10,677	11	0	7	2	2	121	18	99	4	0
Windsor	28,836	21	0	6	9	6	798	58	684	56	0
Windsor Locks	12,513	10	0	4	1	5	195	41	120	34	0
Wolcott	16,632	5	0	2	2	1	278	67	183	28	0
Woodbridge	8,816	3	0	0	2	1	82	12	58	12	0
DELAWARE											
Bethany Beach	1,218	3	0	0	2	1	78	9	67	2	0
Blades	1,404	7	0	1	5	1	25	3	20	2	0
Bridgeville	2,345	6	0	2	1	3	38	9	29	0	0
Camden	3,492	16	0	0	7	9	181	7	174	0	0
Cheswold	1,435	8	0	1	1	6	31	10	20	1	0
Clayton	3,198	13	0	0	0	13	28	2	26	0	0
Dagsboro	895	4	0	0	0	4	21	3	17	1	0
Delaware City	1,750	9	0	2	1	6	54	11	40	3	0
Delmar	1,794	8	0	2	1	5	56	10	45	1	2
Dewey Beach	386	7	0	0	1	6	30	0	29	1	0
Dover	38,084	264	4	14	38	208	1,671	52	1,558	61	9
Ellendale	430	2	0	1	1	0	5	2	2	1	0
Elsmere	6,102	16	0	0	2	14	114	29	72	13	0
Felton	1,426	1	0	1	0	0	31	3	28	0	0

Table 8. Offenses Known to Law Enforcement, by Selected State and City, 2017—Continued

(Number.)

State/city	Population	Violent crime	Murder and nonnegligent manslaughter	Rape (revised definition)[1]	Robbery	Aggravated assault	Property crime	Burglary	Larceny-theft	Motor vehicle theft	Arson[2]
Fenwick Island	434	0	0	0	0	0	28	19	9	0	0
Frankford	969	1	0	1	0	0	13	4	8	1	0
Frederica	838	1	0	0	1	0	3	0	3	0	0
Georgetown	7,338	45	0	10	14	21	422	71	344	7	0
Greenwood	1,105	4	0	0	1	3	25	9	16	0	0
Harrington	3,699	21	0	0	4	17	120	17	99	4	0
Kenton	268	0	0	0	0	0	1	0	1	0	0
Laurel	4,238	54	0	3	12	39	180	38	132	10	0
Lewes	3,131	4	0	1	0	3	77	13	62	2	0
Middletown	21,213	75	0	6	25	44	459	54	391	14	0
Milford	11,223	103	1	9	23	70	645	80	552	13	0
Millsboro	4,366	15	0	2	5	8	184	10	173	1	1
Milton	2,932	7	0	4	1	2	46	8	37	1	0
Newark	33,722	96	1	11	34	50	666	71	569	26	2
New Castle	5,362	18	0	0	7	11	228	20	195	13	0
Newport	1,049	5	0	0	4	1	27	4	20	3	0
Ocean View	2,117	4	0	1	0	3	27	7	20	0	0
Rehoboth Beach	1,516	10	0	1	4	5	144	11	130	3	1
Seaford	7,880	59	0	3	20	36	446	51	389	6	1
Selbyville	2,466	13	0	3	3	7	56	13	38	5	0
Smyrna	11,593	63	0	7	12	44	279	43	227	9	2
South Bethany	518	0	0	0	0	0	17	5	12	0	1
Viola	173	0	0	0	0	0	0	0	0	0	0
Wilmington	71,552	1,142	34	33	381	694	3,550	705	2,413	432	2
Wyoming	1,516	8	0	1	0	7	13	3	9	1	0
DISTRICT OF COLUMBIA											
Washington	693,972	6,584	116	443	2,351	3,674	28,843	1,808	24,490	2,545	
FLORIDA											
Alachua	10,037	40	0	4	6	30	266	45	211	10	2
Altamonte Springs	43,833	136	1	16	29	90	1,369	147	1,147	75	2
Apalachicola	2,345	3	0	0	0	3	5	1	4	0	0
Apopka	50,833	225	1	22	51	151	1,881	350	1,387	144	2
Arcadia	7,992	71	5	4	6	56	175	82	83	10	1
Atlantic Beach	13,589	52	0	3	7	42	356	55	269	32	0
Atlantis	2,141	2	0	0	1	1	53	2	47	4	0
Auburndale	15,903	35	0	1	12	22	502	79	403	20	0
Aventura	38,039	60	0	4	29	27	1,942	90	1,790	62	4
Bal Harbour Village	3,114	2	0	0	0	2	81	8	70	3	0
Bartow	19,889	98	0	15	13	70	660	106	521	33	2
Bay Harbor Islands	6,049	8	0	1	3	4	49	3	37	9	1
Belleair	4,048	2	0	1	1	0	101	11	80	10	0
Belleair Beach	1,634	1	0	0	0	1	25	8	13	4	0
Belleair Bluffs	2,125	2	0	0	2	0	32	3	26	3	0
Belle Glade	19,280	238	3	8	26	201	887	184	627	76	4
Belle Isle	6,973	10	0	3	2	5	92	22	56	14	0
Belleview	4,926	36	1	3	10	22	285	91	187	7	1
Biscayne Park	3,218	9	0	0	3	6	97	26	60	11	0
Blountstown	2,499	9	0	0	1	8	47	8	39	0	0
Boca Raton	98,069	223	1	27	81	114	2,503	435	1,871	197	1
Bonifay	2,742	9	0	0	1	8	23	3	14	6	0
Bowling Green	2,904	5	0	0	0	5	58	18	36	4	0
Boynton Beach	76,845	445	9	15	175	246	3,176	384	2,454	338	6
Bradenton	56,821	298	4	27	59	208	1,444	199	1,166	79	5
Bradenton Beach	1,278	2	0	1	1	0	28	4	24	0	0
Brooksville	8,047	55	0	4	7	44	306	29	268	9	0
Bunnell	2,900	30	1	1	3	25	115	13	92	10	0
Cape Coral	184,346	235	3	16	41	175	2,888	570	2,148	170	2
Carrabelle	2,742	0	0	0	0	0	33	16	16	1	0
Casselberry	27,218	148	1	12	24	111	999	128	828	43	8
Center Hill	1,423	0	0	0	0	0	3	0	3	0	0
Chattahoochee	3,082	11	2	2	0	7	52	15	24	13	0
Chiefland	2,222	3	0	0	0	3	227	130	94	3	0
Chipley	3,576	9	0	0	1	8	137	13	121	3	0
Clearwater	115,295	578	3	85	141	349	3,652	494	2,909	249	16
Clermont	34,412	95	1	6	22	66	823	167	621	35	2
Clewiston	7,735	35	0	0	4	31	211	56	141	14	0
Cocoa	18,265	219	1	11	55	152	956	165	728	63	7
Cocoa Beach	11,851	80	0	6	3	71	516	61	425	30	0
Coconut Creek	60,533	81	3	12	15	51	1,153	162	859	132	3
Cooper City	36,694	22	0	6	3	13	537	67	421	49	1
Coral Gables	51,487	75	3	4	22	46	1,358	176	1,106	76	2
Coral Springs	131,558	249	0	47	68	134	2,609	249	2,149	211	3
Crescent City	1,544	5	0	0	2	3	56	13	40	3	0
Crestview	24,022	117	0	17	16	84	868	189	605	74	6
Cross City	1,706	11	0	0	0	11	29	11	14	4	0
Cutler Bay	45,458	115	1	9	39	66	1,288	186	1,032	70	1
Dade City	7,214	70	0	7	11	52	307	52	239	16	2
Dania Beach	31,718	220	1	18	75	126	1,129	177	852	100	6
Davenport	4,201	3	0	0	0	3	61	16	40	5	0
Davie	103,555	244	0	33	82	129	2,722	267	2,168	287	13
Daytona Beach	67,564	748	12	23	82	631	3,819	497	3,027	295	6

Table 8. Offenses Known to Law Enforcement, by Selected State and City, 2017—Continued

(Number.)

State/city	Population	Violent crime	Murder and nonnegligent manslaughter	Rape (revised definition)[1]	Robbery	Aggravated assault	Property crime	Burglary	Larceny-theft	Motor vehicle theft	Arson[2]
Daytona Beach Shores	4,518	14	1	1	1	11	193	29	146	18	0
Deerfield Beach	80,552	324	3	35	111	175	2,360	328	1,771	261	1
De Funiak Springs	6,489	23	1	2	5	15	111	13	94	4	0
Deland	32,406	184	2	0	44	138	1,129	187	844	98	1
Delray Beach	68,533	409	2	36	93	278	2,587	366	1,949	272	1
Doral	60,239	66	1	6	9	50	1,756	160	1,465	131	2
Dunedin	36,559	53	0	12	17	24	648	79	537	32	1
Dunnellon	1,815	1	0	0	1	0	96	26	67	3	0
Eatonville	2,297	40	1	4	5	30	117	16	93	8	1
Edgewater	22,301	28	1	0	7	20	474	100	344	30	4
Edgewood	2,914	5	1	1	0	3	46	15	27	4	0
El Portal	2,493	5	0	0	4	1	73	28	35	10	0
Eustis	21,161	54	0	6	25	23	639	115	481	43	1
Fellsmere	5,608	8	0	0	2	6	98	24	70	4	0
Fernandina Beach	12,606	28	0	5	1	22	260	42	204	14	1
Flagler Beach	5,087	6	1	1	1	3	87	22	61	4	0
Florida City	12,215	278	2	3	78	195	968	83	821	64	0
Fort Lauderdale	180,972	1,072	15	81	429	547	10,006	1,657	7,424	925	15
Fort Myers	79,918	752	10	53	187	502	2,207	374	1,607	226	5
Fort Pierce	45,858	312	8	30	78	196	1,460	261	1,079	120	12
Fort Walton Beach	22,413	73	1	14	16	42	617	92	460	65	1
Fruitland Park	6,435	15	0	3	0	12	104	26	75	3	0
Gainesville	132,777	952	4	164	176	608	4,778	500	3,915	363	12
Golden Beach	976	0	0	0	0	0	15	5	9	1	0
Graceville	2,202	1	0	0	0	1	57	21	31	5	0
Greenacres City	40,417	159	2	16	44	97	958	115	771	72	4
Green Cove Springs	7,800	43	0	13	8	22	128	22	94	12	0
Groveland	13,267	42	0	5	6	31	207	67	129	11	0
Gulf Breeze	6,586	12	0	1	2	9	130	21	107	2	0
Gulfport	12,473	38	1	4	10	23	540	90	401	49	1
Gulf Stream	860	0	0	0	0	0	28	2	24	2	0
Haines City	23,968	29	0	2	7	20	518	72	422	24	0
Hallandale Beach	39,896	227	3	17	70	137	1,340	183	1,049	108	1
Hialeah	238,260	473	6	33	154	280	5,274	593	3,996	685	24
Hialeah Gardens	24,192	33	0	1	11	21	495	45	371	79	3
Highland Beach	3,797	2	0	1	0	1	38	5	27	6	0
High Springs	6,046	14	0	2	3	9	67	17	46	4	0
Hillsboro Beach	2,025	1	0	0	1	0	24	5	18	1	0
Holly Hill	12,226	32	0	6	7	19	600	84	475	41	1
Hollywood	153,893	445	8	27	176	234	4,661	722	3,434	505	9
Holmes Beach	4,364	7	1	1	0	5	53	15	35	3	0
Homestead	69,276	671	1	25	251	394	2,482	420	1,883	179	9
Howey-in-the-Hills	1,195	2	0	0	0	2	12	5	7	0	0
Hypoluxo	2,763	8	0	3	2	3	73	5	59	9	0
Indialantic	2,919	4	0	0	1	3	72	13	56	3	2
Indian Creek Village	92	0	0	0	0	0	2	1	1	0	0
Indian Harbour Beach	8,649	9	1	1	2	5	142	12	127	3	0
Indian River Shores	4,286	0	0	0	0	0	11	2	9	0	0
Indian Rocks Beach	4,351	6	0	5	1	0	92	12	75	5	0
Indian Shores	3,766	3	0	0	0	3	32	3	26	3	1
Jacksonville	894,638	5,648	109	538	1,376	3,625	31,551	5,646	22,980	2,925	96
Jacksonville Beach	23,740	143	2	29	33	79	1,029	105	842	82	2
Jasper	4,156	10	0	1	4	5	77	15	58	4	0
Jennings	873	1	0	0	0	1	0	0	0	0	0
Juno Beach	3,629	3	0	0	0	3	62	6	55	1	1
Jupiter	65,311	103	4	14	22	63	1,210	133	1,019	58	5
Jupiter Inlet Colony	462	1	0	0	0	1	1	0	0	1	0
Jupiter Island	916	0	0	0	0	0	9	1	8	0	0
Kenneth City	5,125	20	0	7	3	10	135	15	114	6	3
Key Biscayne	13,127	2	0	0	0	2	153	9	132	12	0
Key Colony Beach	861	0	0	0	0	0	15	2	13	0	0
Key West	27,399	101	3	8	15	75	809	107	622	80	0
Kissimmee	71,130	350	7	32	88	223	2,104	314	1,633	157	8
Lady Lake	15,151	21	0	0	2	19	254	26	193	35	0
Lake Alfred	5,899	1	0	0	0	1	69	18	51	0	0
Lake City	12,326	177	3	8	26	140	924	137	759	28	1
Lake Clarke Shores	3,611	4	0	0	1	3	67	16	47	4	0
Lake Hamilton	1,409	9	0	0	1	8	57	8	43	6	1
Lake Helen	2,758	0	0	0	0	0	31	7	24	0	0
Lakeland	107,927	307	1	73	89	144	4,021	574	3,237	210	3
Lake Mary	16,636	53	0	9	5	39	255	31	209	15	0
Lake Park	8,668	111	0	9	37	65	708	62	600	46	0
Lake Placid	2,272	11	0	2	1	8	87	14	71	2	0
Lake Wales	16,150	53	0	4	10	39	452	59	364	29	1
Lake Worth	38,305	494	6	43	213	232	1,508	360	974	174	7
Lantana	11,322	71	0	8	24	39	591	66	460	65	0
Largo	83,728	365	1	71	97	196	2,856	310	2,315	231	4
Lauderdale-by-the-Sea	6,589	12	0	1	5	6	120	16	94	10	0
Lauderdale Lakes	35,144	302	2	14	93	193	1,350	238	982	130	2
Lauderhill	72,406	664	18	20	187	439	2,773	439	1,956	378	6
Lawtey	716	3	0	0	0	3	2	1	1	0	0
Leesburg	22,763	234	5	21	78	130	1,319	256	977	86	3
Lighthouse Point	11,277	14	1	0	6	7	223	23	184	16	0

Table 8. Offenses Known to Law Enforcement, by Selected State and City, 2017—Continued

(Number.)

State/city	Population	Violent crime	Murder and nonnegligent manslaughter	Rape (revised definition)[1]	Robbery	Aggravated assault	Property crime	Burglary	Larceny-theft	Motor vehicle theft	Arson[2]
Live Oak	6,984	45	0	0	5	40	129	69	49	11	0
Longboat Key	7,400	2	2	0	0	0	59	8	51	0	0
Longwood	15,254	45	1	6	5	33	427	95	304	28	1
Lynn Haven	21,262	40	0	5	1	34	458	66	360	32	1
Madeira Beach	4,437	10	0	5	2	3	162	15	141	6	0
Madison	2,823	57	0	1	6	50	148	48	94	6	0
Maitland	17,830	35	0	5	6	24	389	66	295	28	1
Manalapan	466	3	0	0	1	2	25	5	14	6	0
Mangonia Park	2,009	45	2	2	7	34	244	21	200	23	1
Marco Island	18,089	11	0	2	0	9	122	16	97	9	0
Margate	58,649	119	0	4	40	75	1,046	188	735	123	0
Marianna	9,346	98	1	1	6	90	169	54	108	7	2
Mascotte	5,613	25	1	0	3	21	88	18	64	6	0
Medley	844	16	0	0	0	16	217	27	154	36	0
Melbourne	82,013	670	4	63	121	482	3,399	548	2,679	172	11
Melbourne Beach	3,306	3	0	0	1	2	41	6	32	3	0
Melbourne Village	708	1	0	0	0	1	11	0	11	0	0
Mexico Beach	1,211	5	0	0	0	5	74	17	56	1	0
Miami	463,009	3,338	52	105	978	2,203	18,586	2,440	14,311	1,835	73
Miami Beach	92,571	884	4	101	308	471	7,587	706	6,431	450	2
Miami Gardens	114,008	896	19	18	246	613	3,722	492	2,811	419	13
Miami Lakes	31,110	32	0	3	9	20	613	49	485	79	0
Miami Shores	10,808	25	0	3	12	10	567	74	441	52	1
Miami Springs	14,529	38	0	1	12	25	456	58	339	59	1
Midway	3,301	4	0	2	0	2	24	5	15	4	0
Milton	10,011	24	1	4	8	11	196	52	134	10	0
Minneola	11,370	27	0	5	8	14	126	33	83	10	0
Miramar	141,328	408	3	33	92	280	2,246	292	1,694	260	3
Monticello	2,385	11	0	0	1	10	55	24	29	2	0
Mount Dora	14,104	80	2	7	19	52	412	139	264	9	0
Naples	22,244	23	1	3	3	16	389	57	323	9	0
Neptune Beach	7,388	7	1	0	0	6	175	18	148	9	0
New Port Richey	16,388	139	0	12	22	105	535	106	401	28	4
New Smyrna Beach	26,230	102	2	3	5	92	748	149	547	52	2
Niceville	15,380	16	0	1	1	14	250	46	196	8	0
North Bay Village	8,463	14	0	2	1	11	136	10	97	29	0
North Lauderdale	44,137	231	4	24	63	140	966	201	639	126	1
North Miami	62,543	481	4	30	188	259	2,618	395	1,895	328	4
North Miami Beach	44,269	305	1	15	113	176	1,814	245	1,400	169	5
North Palm Beach	13,160	17	0	1	5	11	136	19	99	18	0
North Port	65,498	110	1	26	8	75	788	136	633	19	1
North Redington Beach	1,485	2	0	2	0	0	13	2	11	0	0
Oakland	2,949	9	0	1	0	8	63	22	38	3	0
Oakland Park	44,814	275	1	24	84	166	1,776	308	1,313	155	4
Ocala	59,731	468	4	54	117	293	3,172	482	2,537	153	10
Ocean Ridge	1,946	2	0	1	0	1	44	10	31	3	0
Ocoee	46,501	131	0	13	30	88	1,362	270	1,036	56	2
Okeechobee	5,701	3	1	0	0	2	286	26	246	14	0
Oldsmar	14,527	13	1	4	4	4	295	43	241	11	0
Opa Locka	16,668	325	4	9	87	225	944	162	659	123	6
Orange City	11,478	51	1	6	10	34	741	68	644	29	3
Orange Park	8,848	30	0	1	3	26	111	27	79	5	1
Orlando	283,982	2,113	23	183	605	1,302	15,490	2,388	11,715	1,387	22
Ormond Beach	42,625	202	0	10	25	167	1,386	280	1,003	103	4
Oviedo	40,391	79	1	22	7	49	408	97	303	8	1
Pahokee	6,149	75	1	11	3	60	230	40	176	14	3
Palatka	10,439	77	0	5	30	42	537	81	417	39	2
Palm Bay	111,275	561	7	41	50	463	2,120	445	1,524	151	7
Palm Beach	8,779	10	0	2	0	8	103	17	76	10	0
Palm Beach Gardens	54,677	66	2	9	28	27	1,464	143	1,259	62	2
Palm Beach Shores	1,253	6	0	0	1	5	43	23	19	1	0
Palmetto	13,581	89	1	8	19	61	395	69	309	17	1
Palmetto Bay	24,755	56	0	1	18	37	778	101	644	33	0
Palm Springs	24,300	137	1	13	37	86	1,006	145	785	76	1
Panama City	38,135	332	5	4	53	270	2,352	395	1,752	205	5
Panama City Beach	12,987	109	1	12	13	83	938	122	811	5	3
Parker	4,667	25	0	9	3	13	145	36	99	10	0
Parkland	32,951	22	0	2	4	16	261	36	185	40	0
Pembroke Park	6,347	76	2	3	31	40	294	67	210	17	3
Pembroke Pines	170,923	321	1	27	85	208	3,725	361	3,054	310	6
Pensacola	54,072	319	0	29	69	221	2,073	302	1,680	91	4
Perry	7,051	87	0	11	11	65	234	66	159	9	0
Pinellas Park	52,635	229	2	31	53	143	2,408	277	2,014	117	5
Plantation	93,995	231	1	8	89	133	3,087	381	2,441	265	0
Plant City	38,798	206	0	16	38	152	1,275	237	948	90	11
Pompano Beach	111,027	958	8	61	410	479	5,330	898	3,624	808	8
Ponce Inlet	3,253	0	0	0	0	0	51	6	38	7	0
Port Orange	61,892	32	1	0	5	26	1,550	193	1,252	105	1
Port Richey	2,836	14	0	2	2	10	160	11	145	4	1
Port St. Joe	3,479	17	0	1	2	14	58	22	32	4	0
Port St. Lucie	188,652	186	2	13	31	140	2,126	309	1,730	87	1
Punta Gorda	19,181	16	0	0	5	11	246	23	208	15	0
Quincy	7,623	83	1	4	18	60	287	96	180	11	0

Table 8. Offenses Known to Law Enforcement, by Selected State and City, 2017—Continued

(Number.)

State/city	Population	Violent crime	Murder and nonnegligent manslaughter	Rape (revised definition)[1]	Robbery	Aggravated assault	Property crime	Burglary	Larceny-theft	Motor vehicle theft	Arson[2]
Redington Beaches	1,493	0	0	0	0	0	12	1	11	0	0
Riviera Beach	34,536	473	11	19	72	371	1,400	236	995	169	8
Rockledge	27,432	81	1	6	9	65	472	76	355	41	3
Royal Palm Beach	38,676	78	0	7	20	51	785	61	663	61	0
Safety Harbor	17,732	19	1	7	3	8	249	32	189	28	0
Sanford	59,457	415	9	53	95	258	2,476	398	1,944	134	2
Sanibel	7,505	5	0	2	0	3	56	9	47	0	0
Sarasota	57,383	323	1	26	87	209	1,964	270	1,582	112	2
Satellite Beach	10,954	8	0	3	1	4	94	14	71	9	0
Sea Ranch Lakes	740	0	0	0	0	0	19	0	19	0	0
Sebastian	25,277	48	0	3	8	37	381	51	312	18	0
Sebring	10,679	68	2	5	12	49	538	129	395	14	2
Seminole	18,542	37	0	6	15	16	624	41	554	29	1
Sewall's Point	2,212	0	0	0	0	0	14	6	8	0	0
South Bay	5,152	41	1	3	4	33	149	28	111	10	1
South Daytona	12,882	44	0	1	11	32	366	108	224	34	1
South Miami	12,291	59	0	5	9	45	619	120	473	26	0
South Palm Beach	1,447	0	0	0	0	0	12	3	6	3	0
South Pasadena	5,137	3	0	0	1	2	149	7	137	5	0
Southwest Ranches	7,990	10	0	1	2	7	128	13	99	16	0
Springfield	9,593	31	1	5	2	23	370	62	274	34	0
Starke	5,413	42	0	0	4	38	179	26	137	16	1
St. Augustine	14,500	100	1	6	23	70	512	87	397	28	0
St. Augustine Beach	7,117	11	0	2	1	8	151	19	129	3	0
St. Cloud	49,791	86	1	21	8	56	592	101	466	25	2
St. Pete Beach	9,727	13	0	4	1	8	349	40	291	18	1
St. Petersburg	263,712	1,842	20	136	499	1,187	11,373	1,772	8,623	978	48
Stuart	16,800	59	0	12	8	39	587	82	489	16	1
Sunny Isles Beach	22,290	23	0	4	7	12	344	20	286	38	2
Sunrise	95,342	216	5	8	69	134	2,787	234	2,306	247	1
Surfside	5,849	6	0	0	2	4	96	8	81	7	0
Sweetwater	20,824	37	0	1	10	26	564	51	461	52	0
Tallahassee	192,455	1,503	17	190	348	948	9,428	1,519	7,165	744	12
Tamarac	65,988	137	1	12	63	61	1,543	251	1,140	152	1
Tampa	384,360	1,785	39	121	406	1,219	6,702	1,235	4,900	567	39
Tarpon Springs	25,104	86	0	17	16	53	588	62	505	21	3
Tavares	16,274	35	1	1	8	25	279	104	163	12	0
Temple Terrace	26,854	77	0	7	25	45	635	142	455	38	0
Tequesta	6,049	4	0	0	0	4	80	56	20	4	0
Titusville	46,425	289	1	35	55	198	1,631	387	1,071	173	7
Treasure Island	6,977	17	0	4	5	8	225	28	191	6	1
Umatilla	3,808	5	0	1	1	3	91	23	63	5	0
Valparaiso	5,081	8	0	0	0	8	52	18	27	7	0
Venice	22,762	28	0	4	1	23	305	44	249	12	5
Vero Beach	17,015	46	0	10	7	29	490	94	376	20	0
Village of Pinecrest	19,644	20	0	2	6	12	471	76	381	14	0
Virginia Gardens	2,487	5	0	0	1	4	51	3	44	4	0
Wauchula	4,920	18	0	1	3	14	119	42	72	5	0
Welaka	681	1	0	0	0	1	7	4	3	0	0
Wellington	65,156	115	1	11	25	78	1,076	79	885	112	6
West Melbourne	21,808	42	0	2	12	28	592	80	485	27	1
West Miami	7,742	4	0	1	1	2	106	22	76	8	0
Weston	70,796	41	0	10	9	22	456	59	347	50	3
West Palm Beach	109,459	906	25	66	322	493	5,275	847	3,907	521	27
West Park	15,272	145	2	7	24	112	495	88	348	59	1
White Springs	775	9	0	1	1	7	28	8	16	4	0
Wildwood	7,810	44	1	2	6	35	186	68	107	11	0
Williston	2,758	18	0	0	2	16	105	11	87	7	0
Wilton Manors	12,861	63	0	0	29	34	484	100	348	36	0
Windermere	3,400	2	0	0	1	1	45	25	19	1	0
Winter Garden	43,295	146	0	9	19	118	1,126	140	929	57	5
Winter Haven	39,859	192	0	30	24	138	1,112	177	862	73	1
Winter Park	30,602	88	1	15	18	54	955	158	747	50	6
Winter Springs	35,995	45	0	7	8	30	348	74	245	29	0
Zephyrhills	15,145	44	0	1	5	38	758	110	611	37	3
GEORGIA											
Abbeville	2,736	4	0	0	0	4	9	6	3	0	0
Acworth	22,747	40	0	7	6	27	579	43	513	23	0
Adairsville	4,844	6	0	1	1	4	131	14	100	17	0
Adel	5,359	33	1	2	14	16	363	70	281	12	0
Alamo	3,437	2	0	0	0	2	21	6	14	1	0
Alapaha	661	1	0	0	0	1	2	0	2	0	0
Albany	73,209	827	22	27	152	626	4,116	879	3,048	189	28
Alma	3,570	25	0	3	4	18	234	61	161	12	1
Alpharetta	66,711	34	0	1	22	11	1,187	96	1,056	35	1
Alto	1,163	0	0	0	0	0	10	0	10	0	0
Aragon	1,241	2	0	0	0	2	6	4	0	2	0
Arcade	1,811	6	0	0	0	6	30	7	19	4	0
Arlington	1,365	14	1	5	1	7	32	8	22	2	0
Ashburn	3,674	29	0	2	5	22	123	19	95	9	3
Athens-Clarke County	124,903	519	6	57	123	333	3,930	683	3,017	230	13
Atlanta	481,343	4,504	79	282	1,413	2,730	22,991	3,390	16,304	3,297	74

Table 8. Offenses Known to Law Enforcement, by Selected State and City, 2017—Continued

(Number.)

State/city	Population	Violent crime	Murder and nonnegligent manslaughter	Rape (revised definition)[1]	Robbery	Aggravated assault	Property crime	Burglary	Larceny-theft	Motor vehicle theft	Arson[2]
Attapulgus	429	0	0	0	0	0	3	0	3	0	0
Auburn	7,698	11	2	2	2	5	140	27	99	14	0
Avondale Estates	3,183	6	0	0	1	5	50	9	37	4	0
Bainbridge	12,208	47	1	6	10	30	379	92	270	17	4
Baldwin	3,308	9	0	1	1	7	46	8	38	0	1
Ball Ground	2,003	0	0	0	0	0	16	2	13	1	0
Barnesville	6,696	24	0	1	1	22	289	44	232	13	0
Baxley	4,752	48	1	2	4	41	327	109	211	7	0
Berlin	560	0	0	0	0	0	0	0	0	0	0
Blackshear	3,620	39	1	0	4	34	210	28	176	6	0
Blairsville	569	1	0	0	1	0	19	3	16	0	0
Blakely	4,649	37	0	2	3	32	96	37	56	3	0
Bloomingdale	2,729	0	0	0	0	0	55	10	35	10	0
Blue Ridge	1,400	11	0	0	3	8	17	4	12	1	0
Blythe	689	1	0	0	0	1	7	2	5	0	0
Bowdon	2,106	4	0	1	1	2	60	13	47	0	0
Braselton	10,761	12	0	3	2	7	94	24	62	8	0
Braswell	391	0	0	0	0	0	0	0	0	0	0
Bremen	6,453	20	0	2	5	13	291	36	238	17	0
Brookhaven	52,973	188	1	18	90	79	1,461	298	1,038	125	7
Brooklet	1,547	2	0	0	0	2	3	0	3	0	0
Brunswick	16,500	170	4	10	44	112	866	265	557	44	2
Buchanan	1,148	0	0	0	0	0	58	13	42	3	0
Buena Vista	2,132	5	0	0	0	5	40	7	33	0	0
Butler	1,854	4	0	1	1	2	13	2	10	1	0
Byron	5,228	4	0	0	2	2	188	41	137	10	0
Cairo	9,558	33	1	1	6	25	346	57	282	7	0
Calhoun	16,557	56	1	4	8	43	538	121	401	16	2
Camilla	5,176	11	0	1	6	4	196	40	144	12	0
Canon	804	0	0	0	0	0	0	0	0	0	0
Canton	26,897	67	2	10	15	40	698	69	599	30	0
Carrollton	26,951	146	0	14	38	94	1,163	149	961	53	1
Cartersville	20,918	78	0	10	10	58	967	157	753	57	0
Cave Spring	1,145	8	0	1	0	7	19	13	6	0	1
Cedartown	9,806	37	0	5	8	24	468	108	328	32	0
Centerville	7,689	27	0	0	3	24	387	37	343	7	0
Chamblee	28,558	135	3	9	49	74	951	124	749	78	0
Chattahoochee Hills	2,877	2	0	0	1	1	44	10	31	3	0
Clarkesville	1,777	14	1	0	0	13	65	11	54	0	0
Clarkston	12,849	77	1	8	36	32	506	151	314	41	0
Claxton	2,284	6	0	0	2	4	92	21	69	2	0
Clayton	2,285	4	0	1	0	3	65	7	58	0	0
Cleveland	3,912	17	0	6	1	10	224	28	190	6	0
Cochran	5,029	22	0	2	6	14	164	32	126	6	0
College Park	15,134	222	9	11	85	117	1,125	169	727	229	2
Columbus	198,832	1,303	35	71	394	803	8,820	2,131	5,985	704	35
Commerce	6,826	33	1	0	1	31	198	31	156	11	1
Conyers	16,034	110	1	14	30	65	791	105	625	61	4
Coolidge	529	1	0	0	1	0	0	0	0	0	0
Cordele	10,812	47	3	5	9	30	578	165	383	30	1
Cornelia	4,282	10	0	1	1	8	224	19	199	6	2
Covington	14,122	69	4	11	21	33	813	89	675	49	0
Cumming	6,365	12	0	3	2	7	299	50	233	16	0
Cuthbert	3,635	0	0	0	0	0	39	7	32	0	0
Dallas	13,373	18	2	3	5	8	275	51	204	20	0
Dalton	34,228	108	0	16	17	75	981	126	782	73	4
Danielsville	588	0	0	0	0	0	11	0	10	1	0
Darien	1,830	1	0	0	0	1	74	26	46	2	0
Davisboro	1,659	0	0	0	0	0	1	0	1	0	0
Dawson	4,249	24	0	3	4	17	125	26	93	6	0
Decatur	23,378	40	0	2	27	11	531	63	441	27	1
Demorest	2,094	1	0	0	0	1	20	5	14	1	0
Dillard	336	0	0	0	0	0	0	0	0	0	0
Doerun	769	0	0	0	0	0	0	0	0	0	0
Donalsonville	2,635	11	0	0	6	5	58	14	39	5	1
Doraville	10,593	61	1	1	31	28	565	62	432	71	0
Douglasville	33,640	244	0	14	51	179	2,099	212	1,802	85	2
Dublin	16,086	103	3	5	32	63	707	139	538	30	0
Duluth	29,795	33	2	3	18	10	557	79	445	33	1
Dunwoody	49,321	63	1	6	22	34	2,003	136	1,775	92	2
East Ellijay	561	1	0	0	0	1	135	4	128	3	0
Eastman	5,093	35	0	3	5	27	471	86	371	14	0
East Point	35,740	467	8	23	222	214	4,136	483	3,160	493	0
Eatonton	6,568	40	0	1	11	28	189	44	143	2	0
Elberton	4,397	23	0	4	2	17	252	72	174	6	1
Ellaville	1,856	3	0	1	0	2	17	7	10	0	0
Ellijay	1,705	6	0	0	0	6	62	6	54	2	0
Emerson	1,579	10	0	0	1	9	73	13	55	5	0
Enigma	1,300	3	0	1	0	2	20	10	6	4	0
Ephesus	418	0	0	0	0	0	0	0	0	0	0
Eton	896	0	0	0	0	0	14	4	10	0	2
Fairburn	14,370	47	0	6	12	29	778	135	572	71	1
Fairmount	741	0	0	0	0	0	7	0	5	2	0

Table 8. Offenses Known to Law Enforcement, by Selected State and City, 2017—Continued

(Number.)

State/city	Population	Violent crime	Murder and nonnegligent manslaughter	Rape (revised definition)[1]	Robbery	Aggravated assault	Property crime	Burglary	Larceny-theft	Motor vehicle theft	Arson[2]
Fayetteville	17,749	34	0	1	18	15	468	32	422	14	1
Fitzgerald	8,902	53	2	3	11	37	494	122	355	17	0
Flowery Branch	7,317	2	0	0	0	2	128	8	119	1	0
Folkston	4,795	16	0	0	0	16	82	30	47	5	0
Forest Park	19,948	131	4	10	57	60	1,122	221	762	139	3
Forsyth	4,169	25	0	1	7	17	140	16	119	5	0
Fort Oglethorpe	9,935	55	0	2	8	45	643	57	564	22	0
Fort Valley	8,465	86	0	3	15	68	318	86	218	14	0
Franklin	959	1	0	0	0	1	34	1	32	1	0
Franklin Springs	1,160	2	0	1	1	0	7	0	7	0	0
Gainesville	40,836	157	2	19	34	102	1,404	209	1,091	104	13
Garden City[5]	8,932	157	2	5	25	125			341	5	1
Glennville	5,086	4	0	0	3	1	121	28	88	5	1
Gordon	1,943	6	0	0	1	5	37	11	23	3	0
Graham	300	0	0	0	0	0	6	2	4	0	0
Grantville	3,226	5	0	0	0	5	52	12	35	5	0
Greenville	852	3	0	1	1	1	14	3	8	3	0
Griffin	22,878	204	2	3	45	154	1,337	257	1,029	51	2
Grovetown	13,841	9	0	2	2	5	261	85	163	13	0
Guyton	1,928	8	0	0	2	6	42	6	35	1	0
Hagan	967	1	0	0	0	1	5	3	2	0	0
Hampton	7,623	16	1	4	3	8	91	6	76	9	1
Hapeville	6,665	52	1	2	33	16	780	67	612	101	0
Harlem	3,077	0	0	0	0	0	28	0	27	1	0
Hartwell	4,511	23	1	0	6	16	250	44	198	8	0
Hazlehurst	4,178	7	0	1	1	5	225	33	186	6	0
Helen	547	7	0	1	0	6	70	4	63	3	0
Hephzibah	3,879	1	0	0	1	0	64	20	44	0	1
Hiawassee	921	5	0	1	2	2	33	5	25	3	0
Hiram	3,954	10	0	2	2	6	383	20	338	25	0
Hoboken	525	0	0	0	0	0	2	2	0	0	0
Hogansville	3,157	12	0	3	3	6	87	22	63	2	0
Holly Springs	11,653	12	1	1	1	9	144	12	125	7	0
Homeland	855	0	0	0	0	0	0	0	0	0	0
Homerville	2,451	23	0	1	3	19	119	17	97	5	0
Irwinton	565	0	0	0	0	0	0	0	0	0	0
Ivey	911	0	0	0	0	0	11	3	8	0	0
Jackson	5,071	16	0	1	5	10	164	19	140	5	0
Jasper	3,841	5	0	2	2	1	329	24	293	12	0
Jefferson	10,658	17	1	0	6	10	175	44	121	10	0
Jesup	10,170	36	0	0	9	27	651	100	519	32	1
Johns Creek	85,048	25	0	2	10	13	575	83	474	18	1
Jonesboro	4,731	22	0	2	4	16	164	24	124	16	0
Kennesaw	34,154	72	0	17	19	36	480	49	408	23	1
Kingsland	16,852	42	1	0	8	33	371	95	251	25	0
Kingston	657	0	0	0	0	0	6	0	6	0	0
LaGrange	30,981	110	1	3	52	54	1,563	258	1,234	71	4
Lake City	2,811	15	0	0	7	8	157	23	115	19	0
Lakeland	3,284	29	0	6	5	18	74	21	46	7	1
Lake Park	724	1	0	0	1	0	20	8	11	1	0
Lavonia	2,170	29	0	0	2	27	100	4	95	1	0
Lawrenceville	31,183	73	2	6	37	28	947	161	740	46	1
Leary	573	0	0	0	0	0	0	0	0	0	0
Leslie	380	0	0	0	0	0	4	0	4	0	0
Lilburn	12,844	36	1	1	19	15	479	66	391	22	0
Lithonia	2,098	12	1	1	5	5	95	24	55	16	0
Locust Grove	6,028	6	0	3	3	0	418	47	357	14	0
Loganville	11,887	14	0	1	2	11	321	30	270	21	1
Lookout Mountain	1,573	0	0	0	0	0	15	2	9	4	0
Louisville	2,366	12	0	0	6	6	95	37	58	0	0
Ludowici	2,244	6	0	0	0	6	23	12	8	3	0
Lumber City	1,255	0	0	0	0	0	2	0	1	1	0
Lumpkin	1,083	0	0	0	0	0	0	0	0	0	0
Lyons	4,365	28	1	2	11	14	189	65	121	3	0
Madison	4,072	15	0	0	3	12	171	26	139	6	0
Manchester	4,034	18	0	0	2	16	81	22	55	4	0
Marietta	61,646	215	4	14	102	95	2,209	327	1,700	182	4
Marshallville	1,292	1	0	0	0	1	9	1	7	1	0
Maysville	1,901	2	0	1	1	0	9	1	7	1	0
McDonough	24,278	72	0	7	28	37	700	93	560	47	0
McIntyre	611	1	0	0	0	1	12	6	6	0	0
McRae-Helena	8,295	11	0	0	3	8	143	35	106	2	0
Metter	4,066	20	1	2	7	10	135	24	105	6	3
Midville	262	0	0	0	0	0	0	0	0	0	0
Midway	1,983	6	0	0	3	3	40	7	27	6	0
Milledgeville	19,051	53	0	8	13	32	697	158	519	20	3
Millen	2,853	33	0	1	0	32	114	41	66	7	0
Milton	39,388	9	0	3	3	3	298	40	247	11	0
Molena	371	1	0	0	0	1	0	0	0	0	0
Monroe	13,579	109	3	3	23	80	636	120	487	29	0
Montezuma	3,095	23	2	0	5	16	109	24	78	7	0
Morrow	7,400	32	1	5	22	4	716	80	563	73	0
Moultrie	14,365	72	2	4	34	32	830	133	669	28	1

Table 8. Offenses Known to Law Enforcement, by Selected State and City, 2017—Continued

(Number.)

State/city	Population	Violent crime	Murder and nonnegligent manslaughter	Rape (revised definition)[1]	Robbery	Aggravated assault	Property crime	Burglary	Larceny-theft	Motor vehicle theft	Arson[2]
Mountain City	1,073	0	0	0	0	0	0	0	0	0	0
Mount Airy	1,302	0	0	0	0	0	3	0	1	2	0
Mount Zion	1,772	5	0	0	0	5	6	1	5	0	0
Nahunta	1,047	3	0	1	1	1	7	0	7	0	0
Nashville	4,849	18	0	6	1	11	197	50	143	4	0
Newnan	38,825	235	1	5	24	205	1,022	154	800	68	4
Norcross	17,060	80	2	8	20	50	522	118	351	53	0
Norman Park	968	1	0	0	1	0	15	7	8	0	0
Oak Park	476	1	0	0	0	1	21	1	17	3	0
Ocilla	3,630	14	0	0	4	10	80	9	68	3	3
Oglethorpe	1,174	9	0	0	1	8	25	14	10	1	0
Omega	1,228	4	0	2	0	2	49	10	38	1	0
Oxford	2,239	0	0	0	0	0	36	4	28	4	0
Palmetto	4,744	13	0	1	6	6	116	40	63	13	0
Patterson	758	0	0	0	0	0	0	0	0	0	0
Peachtree City	35,300	14	0	1	7	6	591	25	488	78	1
Pelham	3,607	9	0	0	3	6	65	23	33	9	0
Pembroke	2,539	4	0	0	0	4	71	20	51	0	0
Pine Lake	767	1	0	0	0	1	31	5	23	3	0
Pine Mountain	1,385	7	0	1	2	4	43	9	31	3	0
Plains	727	2	0	0	0	2	3	0	3	0	0
Pooler	24,601	25	0	3	8	14	876	100	713	63	0
Porterdale	1,506	5	0	0	4	1	19	7	7	5	0
Port Wentworth	8,452	22	1	1	4	16	151	22	108	21	1
Powder Springs	15,127	47	1	3	13	30	342	52	277	13	0
Quitman	3,884	45	0	3	8	34	277	54	209	14	
Remerton	1,122	12	0	4	2	6	65	18	40	7	
Reynolds	1,016	0	0	0	0	0	3	1	0	2	
Rincon	10,101	12	0	2	2	8	351	21	321	9	0
Ringgold	4,403	17	0	1	3	13	164	19	131	14	0
Riverdale	16,435	87	4	2	31	50	1,130	159	884	87	0
Rochelle	1,101	2	0	0	2	0	28	10	18	0	0
Rockmart	4,317	30	0	1	9	20	366	109	244	13	0
Rome	36,366	205	3	6	32	164	1,480	268	1,151	61	7
Roswell	95,602	108	2	15	32	59	1,616	229	1,278	109	1
Sale City	343	0	0	0	0	0	1	0	1	0	0
Sandersville	5,669	26	0	0	12	14	216	27	183	6	0
Sandy Springs	107,740	126	0	12	56	58	2,263	377	1,708	178	10
Sardis	971	6	0	0	0	6	37	15	18	4	0
Savannah-Chatham Metro-politan	242,941	1,124	35	100	381	608	8,336	1,335	6,061	940	18
Screven	778	3	0	1	0	2	23	3	19	1	
Senoia	4,283	0	0	0	0	0	39	10	28	1	0
Shiloh	462	0	0	0	0	0	0	0	0	0	0
Smyrna	57,576	172	3	4	35	130	1,544	156	1,162	226	
Snellville	19,982	39	0	2	11	26	697	53	612	32	
Social Circle	4,490	6	1	0	0	5	85	21	61	3	0
Sparks	1,994	8	0	1	1	6	83	27	53	3	1
Sparta	1,264	9	0	0	2	7	26	8	17	1	0
Springfield	4,308	4	0	0	0	4	78	40	38	0	0
Statesboro	31,937	125	3	16	50	56	962	190	736	36	3
Stone Mountain	6,413	47	1	1	11	34	210	45	134	31	1
Summerville	4,337	0	0	0	0	0	48	0	47	1	
Suwanee	20,186	32	0	4	14	14	520	65	433	22	0
Swainsboro	7,522	74	3	3	7	61	347	28	313	6	0
Sylvania	2,514	4	0	0	1	3	96	31	61	4	0
Talbotton	834	1	0	0	0	1	11	2	7	2	0
Tallapoosa	3,189	9	0	0	1	8	79	21	54	4	1
Temple	4,403	11	0	1	3	7	132	24	98	10	0
Tennille	1,914	7	0	0	1	6	36	12	22	2	
Thomasville	18,866	29	0	2	14	13	992	216	755	21	1
Thunderbolt	2,710	2	0	0	2	0	56	13	34	9	0
Tifton	16,908	199	3	16	50	130	1,105	142	922	41	6
Toccoa	8,392	37	0	0	9	28	538	46	484	8	
Trenton	2,248	1	0	0	0	1	46	6	39	1	0
Tunnel Hill	878	0	0	0	0	0	24	0	23	1	
Tybee Island	3,134	4	0	0	1	3	152	11	137	4	
Tyrone	7,260	12	0	0	9	3	63	5	57	1	0
Union City	21,160	259	5	9	81	164	2,315	255	1,724	336	8
Valdosta	56,729	215	10	17	47	141	3,485	554	2,699	232	16
Vidalia	10,743	66	1	3	12	50	643	108	522	13	1
Vienna	3,652	10	0	1	2	7	89	12	75	2	
Villa Rica	15,398	67	1	3	11	52	553	61	463	29	3
Warner Robins	75,323	385	5	34	132	214	4,107	805	3,072	230	17
Warrenton	1,786	10	0	0	1	9	55	11	42	2	
Warwick	407	0	0	0	0	0	4	1	3	0	0
Watkinsville	2,866	3	0	0	1	2	42	2	39	1	0
Waverly Hall	763	1	0	0	0	1	3	1	1	1	0
Waynesboro	5,669	50	1	2	12	35	218	38	165	15	1
West Point	3,821	31	2	2	4	23	203	48	150	5	0
Whitesburg	607	3	0	0	0	3	28	7	21	0	
Willacoochee	1,367	2	0	0	2	0	32	11	21	0	0
Winder	16,006	142	0	6	13	123	483	78	386	19	

Table 8. Offenses Known to Law Enforcement, by Selected State and City, 2017—Continued

(Number.)

State/city	Population	Violent crime	Murder and nonnegligent manslaughter	Rape (revised definition)[1]	Robbery	Aggravated assault	Property crime	Burglary	Larceny-theft	Motor vehicle theft	Arson[2]
Winterville	1,210	2	0	0	2	0	9	5	4	0	0
Woodland	351	0	0	0	0	0	0	0	0	0	0
Woodstock	32,293	35	1	2	7	25	601	50	530	21	0
Wrens	2,020	13	0	0	3	10	83	28	50	5	0
HAWAII											
Honolulu	990,384	2,440	32	285	908	1,215	27,477	3,331	20,540	3,606	327
IDAHO											
Aberdeen	1,910	1	0	0	0	1	23	9	13	1	0
American Falls	4,286	14	0	0	1	13	39	10	28	1	0
Bellevue	2,315	2	0	0	0	2	9	4	5	0	0
Blackfoot	11,870	41	1	5	1	34	340	85	238	17	1
Boise	225,677	630	2	144	51	433	5,517	736	4,435	346	41
Bonners Ferry	2,574	5	0	0	0	5	31	2	28	1	0
Buhl	4,326	14	0	1	0	13	71	21	41	9	2
Caldwell	54,345	139	0	6	6	127	1,060	286	628	146	8
Coeur d'Alene	51,364	197	4	49	11	133	1,142	180	901	61	18
Emmett	6,747	23	0	5	0	18	87	15	68	4	4
Fruitland	5,205	3	0	2	0	1	38	17	20	1	0
Garden City	11,708	66	0	7	7	52	347	61	265	21	2
Gooding	3,481	14	0	1	1	12	29	13	13	3	0
Hailey	8,267	13	0	0	0	13	44	14	27	3	1
Homedale	2,577	11	0	1	2	8	49	8	33	8	0
Idaho Falls	60,727	215	2	30	8	175	1,122	366	671	85	7
Jerome	11,380	27	0	8	4	15	250	60	172	18	2
Kamiah	1,292	3	0	0	1	2	9	3	3	3	0
Ketchum	2,760	5	0	2	0	3	29	1	23	5	0
Kimberly	3,812	4	0	1	0	3	46	21	21	4	1
Lewiston	33,029	53	2	11	4	36	943	188	687	68	4
McCall	3,338	9	0	5	1	3	60	15	45	0	0
Meridian	99,241	149	0	46	11	92	1,489	216	1,218	55	8
Middleton	7,486	7	0	3	0	4	63	26	35	2	0
Montpelier	2,492	3	0	1	0	2	60	4	53	3	0
Moscow	25,576	34	0	8	5	21	633	86	528	19	2
Mountain Home	13,772	31	0	7	1	23	227	39	175	13	1
Nampa	93,064	264	4	70	21	169	2,455	461	1,718	276	13
Orofino[5]	3,039	8	1	0	0	7			33	3	0
Osburn	1,500	5	0	1	0	4	21	9	11	1	0
Parma	2,101	1	0	0	0	1	34	18	13	3	1
Payette	7,405	18	0	2	0	16	144	24	108	12	4
Pocatello	54,814	243	1	13	9	220	1,609	295	1,194	120	7
Post Falls	32,583	65	0	5	4	56	736	93	605	38	3
Preston	5,372	10	3	1	1	5	58	29	27	2	2
Rathdrum	8,113	16	0	3	0	13	89	21	59	9	1
Rexburg	28,698	11	0	3	0	8	176	34	137	5	0
Rigby	4,078	6	0	1	1	4	65	6	56	3	0
Rupert	5,849	13	0	2	0	11	93	19	70	4	0
Shelley	4,329	3	0	1	0	2	80	12	48	20	0
Soda Springs	2,970	3	0	1	1	1	20	5	14	1	0
Spirit Lake	2,207	2	0	0	0	2	31	3	27	1	0
St. Anthony	3,493	5	0	0	0	5	31	4	25	2	0
Sun Valley	1,441	2	0	1	0	1	7	3	4	0	0
Twin Falls	48,912	210	0	44	9	157	1,287	196	1,006	85	7
Wendell	2,700	1	0	0	0	1	25	9	12	4	0
ILLINOIS											
Addison	36,883	41	2	8	11	20	566	85	454	27	1
Albany	879	4	0	4	0	0	6	3	3	0	0
Aledo	3,496	0	0	0	0	0	25	2	22	1	0
Alexis	794	0	0	0	0	0	16	13	3	0	0
Algonquin	31,096	21	0	5	3	13	375	28	338	9	2
Alsip	19,137	20	1	0	19	0	486	72	365	49	3
Altamont	2,292	2	0	0	0	2	25	8	16	1	0
Alton	26,693	169	1	22	34	112	1,064	214	784	66	9
Amboy	2,308	2	0	1	1	0	40	5	35	0	0
Anna	4,244	11	0	3	0	8	121	20	98	3	2
Annawan	851	1	0	0	0	1	22	3	19	0	0
Antioch	14,242	27	0	4	5	18	190	24	163	3	0
Arlington Heights	75,586	44	0	9	14	21	654	77	550	27	6
Aroma Park	698	0	0	0	0	0	17	5	12	0	0
Arthur	2,265	2	0	0	0	2	10	2	8	0	0
Ashland	1,224	0	0	0	0	0	22	14	5	3	0
Ashton	898	0	0	0	0	0	3	2	1	0	0
Assumption	1,094	2	0	0	0	2	14	8	6	0	0
Athens	1,944	0	0	0	0	0	12	3	9	0	0
Auburn	4,741	12	0	2	2	8	49	16	32	1	0
Aurora	201,599	521	6	57	108	350	2,665	366	2,123	176	20
Aviston	2,119	1	0	0	0	1	4	2	2	0	0
Bannockburn	1,573	0	0	0	0	0	18	2	16	0	0
Barrington	10,309	8	0	3	0	5	108	8	94	6	1
Barrington Hills	4,221	0	0	0	0	0	24	4	18	2	0
Barry	1,260	0	0	0	0	0	14	7	7	0	0

Table 8. Offenses Known to Law Enforcement, by Selected State and City, 2017—Continued

(Number.)

State/city	Population	Violent crime	Murder and nonnegligent manslaughter	Rape (revised definition)[1]	Robbery	Aggravated assault	Property crime	Burglary	Larceny-theft	Motor vehicle theft	Arson[2]
Bartlett	41,167	19	1	4	6	8	214	20	187	7	7
Bartonville	6,311	21	0	7	1	13	183	25	146	12	0
Batavia	26,425	33	0	7	6	20	415	8	400	7	1
Beardstown	5,582	58	0	0	0	58	161	43	117	1	1
Bedford Park	581	25	1	1	12	11	275	15	247	13	0
Beecher	4,459	3	0	1	0	2	47	2	43	2	0
Belgium	393	0	0	0	0	0	2	0	2	0	0
Belleville	41,511	212	1	34	57	120	1,386	325	987	74	13
Belvidere	24,991	69	1	11	9	48	354	58	281	15	3
Bensenville	18,353	25	1	13	5	6	265	28	213	24	0
Berkeley	5,138	11	0	3	5	3	89	8	72	9	0
Berwyn	55,594	141	1	21	57	62	1,117	218	779	120	5
Bethalto	9,296	4	0	0	1	3	166	30	130	6	0
Blandinsville	606	1	0	0	0	1	3	1	2	0	0
Bloomingdale	22,075	16	0	2	9	5	585	29	551	5	1
Bloomington	78,203	343	3	73	45	222	1,334	220	1,037	77	7
Blue Island	23,348	161	1	16	47	97	420	64	282	74	2
Bluffs	666	0	0	0	0	0	9	5	4	0	0
Bolingbrook	74,692	140	1	34	27	78	735	69	596	70	4
Bourbonnais	18,474	43	0	10	12	21	232	31	195	6	0
Bradley	15,405	47	0	0	12	35	465	37	420	8	0
Braidwood	6,145	3	1	1	0	1	39	7	32	0	0
Bridgeview	16,213	61	1	9	17	34	339	27	291	21	0
Brighton	2,173	5	0	0	0	5	13	3	7	3	0
Broadview	7,807	38	1	11	18	8	382	21	338	23	1
Brookfield	18,715	12	0	5	4	3	228	34	188	6	0
Brookport	919	4	0	1	1	2	18	8	10	0	0
Buffalo Grove	41,323	10	0	1	5	4	222	24	194	4	14
Bunker Hill	1,702	4	0	0	0	4	18	4	13	1	0
Burbank	28,876	59	0	2	18	39	306	43	245	18	1
Burr Ridge	10,813	9	0	1	2	6	125	19	97	9	1
Byron	3,604	0	0	0	0	0	42	5	35	2	0
Cahokia	14,105	67	3	8	33	23	613	160	410	43	6
Calumet City	36,663	237	4	21	146	66	1,083	223	688	172	15
Cambridge	2,089	0	0	0	0	0	19	6	12	1	0
Campton Hills	11,342	0	0	0	0	0	18	5	13	0	0
Canton	13,996	33	0	9	2	22	243	34	201	8	0
Carbondale	26,127	135	4	33	35	63	868	143	698	27	17
Carlinville	5,585	13	0	3	1	9	184	30	150	4	1
Carlyle	3,195	5	0	0	0	5	49	2	46	1	0
Carol Stream	40,118	53	0	8	19	26	355	29	309	17	1
Carpentersville	38,380	33	0	5	16	12	747	58	665	24	1
Carrollton	2,411	7	0	2	0	5	45	14	30	1	0
Carterville	5,900	14	0	2	1	11	53	23	25	5	0
Carthage	2,537	1	0	1	0	0	24	2	21	1	0
Cary	17,768	21	0	5	3	13	65	19	46	0	2
Catlin	1,971	0	0	0	0	0	4	0	4	0	0
Centralia	12,496	183	0	24	37	122	491	131	326	34	7
Centreville	4,988	45	2	3	15	25	222	69	111	42	1
Chadwick	518	0	0	0	0	0	9	3	6	0	0
Champaign	87,543	634	5	83	109	437	2,623	446	2,054	123	10
Channahon	12,603	9	0	6	3	0	56	7	40	9	0
Charleston	21,016	44	2	4	1	37	113	35	72	6	0
Chatham	12,592	13	0	6	1	6	104	23	80	1	0
Chenoa	3,167	3	0	2	0	1	19	5	14	0	0
Cherry Valley	3,075	7	0	1	1	5	202	6	192	4	0
Chester	8,559	13	0	3	0	10	24	8	13	3	0
Chicago	2,706,171	29,737	653	1,762	11,887	15,435	88,324	12,912	63,834	11,578	514
Chicago Heights	29,967	282	9	32	118	123	702	218	363	121	9
Chicago Ridge	14,222	18	0	2	5	11	452	20	409	23	1
Chillicothe	6,225	20	0	3	0	17	123	11	109	3	0
Christopher	2,746	9	0	0	0	9	25	10	15	0	1
Cicero	82,779	301	6	37	146	112	1,840	434	1,245	161	18
Clarendon Hills	8,689	11	0	0	2	9	47	8	31	8	1
Coal City	5,409	7	0	1	0	6	29	6	21	2	0
Coal Valley	3,721	7	0	0	0	7	22	6	15	1	0
Cobden	1,119	7	0	0	0	7	10	2	7	1	0
Colfax	1,032	2	0	0	0	2	12	2	9	1	0
Collinsville	24,487	55	1	14	12	28	610	85	507	18	3
Columbia	10,369	8	0	0	0	8	73	16	55	2	1
Cortland	4,331	3	0	0	0	3	57	8	49	0	0
Country Club Hills	16,651	73	1	9	32	31	502	61	403	38	8
Countryside	5,951	5	0	0	1	4	207	9	186	12	0
Cowden	572	3	0	0	0	3	2	0	2	0	0
Crest Hill	21,223	55	0	16	15	24	235	46	168	21	0
Crete	8,151	23	0	4	7	12	138	20	111	7	1
Creve Coeur	5,192	43	1	6	1	35	85	17	66	2	0
Crystal Lake	40,228	53	2	11	9	31	586	39	540	7	1
Danvers	1,121	1	0	0	0	1	1	0	1	0	0
Danville	31,368	546	10	36	88	412	1,833	456	1,306	71	9
Darien	22,081	14	0	0	5	9	242	25	202	15	2
Decatur	72,153	443	10	52	106	275	2,394	731	1,571	92	30
Deer Creek	670	0	0	0	0	0	2	1	1	0	0

Table 8. Offenses Known to Law Enforcement, by Selected State and City, 2017—Continued

(Number.)

State/city	Population	Violent crime	Murder and nonnegligent manslaughter	Rape (revised definition)[1]	Robbery	Aggravated assault	Property crime	Burglary	Larceny-theft	Motor vehicle theft	Arson[2]
Deerfield	19,126	5	0	1	2	2	130	21	101	8	0
De Kalb	43,043	189	1	40	30	118	1,323	156	1,130	37	7
Delavan	1,625	3	0	0	0	3	47	13	30	4	5
De Pue	1,710	0	0	0	0	0	17	3	14	0	0
De Soto	1,559	7	0	1	1	5	15	6	9	0	0
Des Plaines	58,089	61	1	7	10	43	565	79	454	32	2
Diamond	2,461	0	0	0	0	0	3	2	1	0	0
Divernon	1,139	1	0	0	0	1	5	0	5	0	0
Dixon	15,044	28	0	17	1	10	317	28	280	9	0
Downers Grove	49,563	35	0	8	11	16	634	84	528	22	2
Dupo	3,848	6	0	0	1	5	96	19	70	7	0
Du Quoin	5,808	22	0	2	1	19	70	21	49	0	1
Earlville	1,606	0	0	0	0	0	31	6	24	1	0
East Alton	6,116	32	1	13	3	15	182	31	141	10	0
East Dubuque	1,620	4	0	1	0	3	19	6	10	3	0
East Dundee	3,239	6	0	0	3	3	63	8	52	3	0
East Hazel Crest	1,530	3	0	0	2	1	42	20	16	6	0
East Moline	21,106	82	1	22	11	48	478	105	337	36	4
East Peoria	22,856	97	0	25	10	62	684	164	504	16	2
East St. Louis	26,927	741	30	43	97	571	590	173	273	144	14
Edwardsville	25,190	23	0	0	5	18	270	35	220	15	0
Effingham	12,710	18	0	5	1	12	379	54	311	14	1
Elburn	5,782	2	0	1	0	1	15	1	13	1	0
Elgin	112,767	224	2	38	56	128	1,579	195	1,310	74	8
Elizabeth	735	3	1	0	0	2	3	0	2	1	0
Elk Grove Village	32,894	35	2	0	5	28	419	42	339	38	1
Elmhurst	46,763	34	0	3	9	22	554	56	474	24	1
Elmwood	2,073	0	0	0	0	0	27	11	16	0	0
Elmwood Park	24,581	59	0	6	17	36	301	44	238	19	1
El Paso	2,773	4	0	1	0	3	29	4	22	3	0
Elwood	2,252	0	0	0	0	0	38	4	28	6	0
Energy	1,141	0	0	0	0	0	13	1	11	1	0
Erie	1,526	1	0	1	0	0	3	0	3	0	0
Essex	761	0	0	0	0	0	0	0	0	0	0
Eureka	5,393	21	0	3	1	17	55	8	42	5	0
Evanston	74,947	122	1	3	40	78	1,769	284	1,422	63	8
Evergreen Park	19,600	48	1	4	20	23	596	25	563	8	0
Fairbury	3,577	13	0	2	0	11	33	8	23	2	0
Fairfield	5,004	7	0	1	0	6	108	13	93	2	3
Fairmont City	2,458	2	0	1	1	0	23	6	13	4	0
Fairmount	604	0	0	0	0	0	0	0	0	0	0
Fairview Heights	16,618	47	0	5	5	37	720	60	633	27	0
Farmersville	689	0	0	0	0	0	1	0	1	0	0
Farmington	2,293	6	0	0	1	5	43	7	36	0	0
Findlay	644	0	0	0	0	0	4	1	3	0	0
Fisher	1,943	1	0	0	0	1	16	3	13	0	0
Fithian	458	0	0	0	0	0	1	0	1	0	0
Flora	4,870	3	0	0	0	3	106	13	92	1	0
Flossmoor	9,347	13	0	7	3	3	206	20	181	5	0
Forest Park	13,950	75	1	13	32	29	455	62	321	72	0
Forest View	682	2	0	0	0	2	40	3	21	16	0
Fox Lake	10,432	31	0	3	5	23	260	41	205	14	0
Fox River Grove	4,628	8	0	0	2	6	44	6	35	3	0
Frankfort	19,034	7	0	1	0	6	157	15	131	11	1
Franklin Grove	948	2	0	2	0	0	5	2	3	0	0
Freeburg	4,211	2	0	0	0	2	40	2	36	2	0
Freeport	24,196	59	2	25	13	19	820	146	662	12	6
Fulton	3,309	1	0	0	0	1	48	12	36	0	0
Galena	3,229	6	0	1	0	5	43	8	35	0	0
Galesburg	30,759	96	0	16	7	73	549	110	423	16	4
Geneseo	6,511	7	0	2	0	5	62	15	46	1	1
Geneva	21,941	9	0	3	2	4	181	30	149	2	3
Genoa	5,196	4	0	0	0	4	64	8	54	2	0
Georgetown	3,286	14	0	0	1	13	83	25	54	4	0
Germantown	1,286	2	0	0	0	2	8	0	7	1	0
Gibson City	3,372	6	0	1	0	5	24	8	16	0	0
Gifford	1,097	0	0	0	0	0	4	1	3	0	0
Gilberts	7,869	1	0	0	0	1	57	5	49	3	0
Gilman	1,718	2	0	0	1	1	65	7	57	1	0
Girard	2,008	8	0	0	0	8	9	2	7	0	1
Glasford	991	0	0	0	0	0	0	0	0	0	0
Glen Carbon	12,984	7	1	0	3	3	90	16	70	4	2
Glencoe	8,922	3	0	1	2	0	67	8	52	7	0
Glendale Heights	34,128	26	2	0	9	15	442	28	388	26	2
Glen Ellyn	28,083	20	0	4	7	9	342	30	299	13	0
Glenview	47,944	35	0	2	9	24	568	93	456	19	1
Glenwood	8,897	13	1	0	5	7	60	24	31	5	1
Godley	712	1	0	1	0	0	5	3	1	1	0
Golf	494	0	0	0	0	0	0	0	0	0	0
Goodfield	1,004	0	0	0	0	0	77	0	77	0	0
Grafton	635	2	0	0	0	2	12	6	6	0	0
Grand Ridge	525	0	0	0	0	0	2	0	2	0	0
Grandview	1,420	5	0	0	0	5	25	10	14	1	0

Table 8. Offenses Known to Law Enforcement, by Selected State and City, 2017—Continued

(Number.)

State/city	Population	Violent crime	Murder and nonnegligent manslaughter	Rape (revised definition)[1]	Robbery	Aggravated assault	Property crime	Burglary	Larceny-theft	Motor vehicle theft	Arson[2]
Granite City	28,755	217	1	27	33	156	908	289	525	94	22
Grantfork	327	0	0	0	0	0	2	0	1	1	0
Grayslake	20,818	23	1	5	7	10	208	28	174	6	2
Grayville	1,616	10	0	0	0	10	37	4	30	3	0
Greenfield	982	5	0	0	0	5	28	10	17	1	0
Greenup	1,485	0	0	0	0	0	18	5	13	0	0
Greenville	6,713	7	0	0	0	7	102	5	91	6	0
Gurnee	30,902	47	1	18	10	18	1,199	69	1,104	26	1
Hainesville	3,660	7	1	1	2	3	44	7	37	0	1
Hampshire	6,367	16	1	1	1	13	29	6	22	1	0
Hampton	1,812	1	0	0	0	1	49	30	17	2	0
Hanover Park	38,053	40	0	7	7	26	236	36	186	14	3
Harrisburg	8,775	100	1	7	7	85	297	103	188	6	0
Hartford	1,370	4	0	2	1	1	23	1	22	0	0
Harvard	9,067	11	1	6	1	3	73	8	64	1	1
Harwood Heights	8,538	12	0	0	3	9	158	11	137	10	0
Havana	2,988	17	0	8	0	9	60	13	44	3	0
Hawthorn Woods	8,234	2	0	1	0	1	20	3	15	2	0
Hazel Crest	13,871	74	0	5	53	16	333	103	164	66	1
Henning	242	0	0	0	0	0	0	0	0	0	0
Henry	2,291	9	0	2	0	7	35	5	28	2	1
Herrin	13,020	30	1	4	12	13	478	135	304	39	3
Herscher	1,536	0	0	0	0	0	2	1	1	0	0
Hickory Hills	13,980	26	1	9	7	9	138	10	111	17	1
Highland	9,809	8	0	0	0	8	43	11	30	2	0
Highland Park	29,618	15	0	2	3	10	341	40	275	26	1
Highwood	5,307	3	0	1	1	1	45	8	35	2	0
Hillsboro	6,052	20	0	4	0	16	52	10	40	2	4
Hillsdale	503	0	0	0	0	0	2	2	0	0	0
Hillside	8,066	17	0	1	6	10	280	27	233	20	0
Hinckley	2,055	3	0	0	0	3	9	1	8	0	0
Hinsdale	17,765	6	1	3	1	1	118	22	84	12	0
Hodgkins	1,840	3	0	0	0	3	250	2	244	4	0
Hoffman Estates	51,704	50	0	8	14	28	466	50	386	30	1
Homer	1,176	0	0	0	0	0	2	0	2	0	0
Homer Glen	24,516	4	0	2	2	0	135	8	124	3	0
Hometown	4,289	5	0	0	3	2	28	2	26	0	0
Homewood	19,150	40	0	8	21	11	781	44	713	24	0
Hoopeston	5,106	46	0	15	2	29	187	65	112	10	1
Hudson	1,837	1	0	0	0	1	6	3	3	0	0
Huntley	27,002	5	0	0	2	3	168	19	143	6	0
Ina	2,335	1	0	0	0	1	4	0	4	0	0
Indian Head Park	3,799	0	0	0	0	0	17	1	13	3	0
Indianola	266	0	0	0	0	0	0	0	0	0	0
Island Lake	8,076	5	0	4	1	0	51	9	42	0	0
Itasca	8,739	6	0	2	4	0	63	13	46	4	0
Jacksonville	18,615	73	0	6	8	59	669	93	557	19	4
Jerseyville	8,315	19	1	6	0	12	136	36	92	8	0
Johnsburg	6,251	3	0	0	0	3	128	8	115	5	0
Joliet	148,342	540	15	67	159	299	2,625	446	2,014	165	79
Jonesboro	1,738	1	0	0	0	1	15	2	13	0	0
Kankakee	26,265	210	6	35	68	101	1,049	198	800	51	10
Kansas	729	2	0	0	0	2	7	2	5	0	0
Kenilworth	2,522	1	0	0	1	0	24	3	20	1	0
Kewanee	12,386	49	1	20	0	28	473	37	431	5	0
Kildeer	4,072	1	0	0	0	1	17	3	13	1	0
Kincaid	1,405	3	0	1	0	2	21	4	13	4	0
Kingston	1,160	1	0	0	0	1	4	3	0	1	0
Kirkland	1,730	3	0	1	0	2	14	3	11	0	0
Lacon	1,797	1	0	0	0	1	16	8	7	1	0
La Grange	15,617	17	0	1	4	12	175	17	153	5	0
La Grange Park	13,465	7	0	0	1	6	58	9	45	4	0
La Harpe	1,190	3	0	1	0	2	13	5	7	1	0
Lake Bluff	5,664	3	0	1	2	0	72	10	56	6	0
Lake in the Hills	28,798	25	2	14	2	7	61	12	46	3	4
Lakemoor	5,969	0	0	0	0	0	41	1	40	0	0
Lake Villa	8,800	15	0	3	2	10	70	11	54	5	1
Lakewood	3,878	2	0	1	0	1	13	1	12	0	0
Lake Zurich	20,012	7	0	2	0	5	317	17	296	4	3
Lansing	28,039	99	0	13	66	20	1,948	225	1,628	95	3
La Salle	9,134	4	0	0	0	4	134	34	97	3	1
Lebanon	4,427	6	0	4	0	2	48	23	22	3	1
Lemont	17,035	5	0	3	1	1	104	25	74	5	0
Lenzburg	483	0	0	0	0	0	3	3	0	0	0
Le Roy	3,547	5	0	0	1	4	35	10	24	1	0
Libertyville	20,412	18	0	0	1	17	287	20	258	9	0
Lincoln	13,887	43	0	0	6	37	321	65	246	10	0
Lincolnshire	7,259	5	0	2	0	3	27	10	17	0	0
Lincolnwood	12,515	20	1	0	5	14	531	106	402	23	1
Lindenhurst	14,362	14	0	10	0	4	65	10	52	3	0
Lisle	22,999	8	0	2	4	2	160	19	131	10	1
Litchfield	6,761	8	0	1	0	7	237	36	191	10	3
Loami	750	0	0	0	0	0	14	7	7	0	0

Table 8. Offenses Known to Law Enforcement, by Selected State and City, 2017—Continued

(Number.)

State/city	Population	Violent crime	Murder and nonnegligent manslaughter	Rape (revised definition)[1]	Robbery	Aggravated assault	Property crime	Burglary	Larceny-theft	Motor vehicle theft	Arson[2]
Lockport	25,280	7	0	3	1	3	213	20	187	6	0
Lombard	43,885	38	0	5	12	21	943	79	845	19	3
Loves Park	23,317	81	1	12	7	61	494	107	371	16	2
Lovington	1,086	3	0	0	0	3	6	1	4	1	0
Lyons	10,601	11	0	1	2	8	88	9	67	12	2
Machesney Park	22,772	51	0	10	5	36	540	75	448	17	3
Macomb	18,200	56	0	12	5	39	262	62	190	10	2
Mahomet	8,441	3	0	0	1	2	54	7	43	4	0
Malta	1,151	0	0	0	0	0	4	0	4	0	0
Manhattan	7,625	5	0	1	0	4	35	2	33	0	0
Maple Park	1,303	0	0	0	0	0	12	0	12	0	0
Marengo	7,406	5	0	2	1	2	72	8	63	1	0
Marine	924	2	0	0	0	2	9	2	4	3	0
Marissa	1,814	22	0	1	0	21	69	28	39	2	0
Maroa	1,714	4	0	0	0	4	42	15	27	0	0
Marquette Heights	2,703	2	0	1	0	1	8	3	5	0	0
Marseilles	4,893	6	1	1	0	4	97	27	65	5	0
Marshall	3,870	3	0	0	1	2	36	5	30	1	0
Martinsville	1,128	0	0	0	0	0	11	1	10	0	0
Maryville	7,968	12	0	0	2	10	67	6	57	4	0
Mascoutah	8,034	6	0	3	0	3	50	7	43	0	0
Matteson	19,107	160	0	12	19	129	518	52	429	37	0
Mattoon	17,942	81	0	21	4	56	310	68	242	0	2
Maywood	23,697	202	10	16	103	73	546	112	341	93	5
McCook	228	0	0	0	0	0	15	2	11	2	0
McCullom Lake	1,006	0	0	0	0	0	0	0	0	0	0
McHenry	26,540	51	0	25	3	23	395	25	362	8	0
McLean	802	1	0	0	0	1	5	2	3	0	0
Melrose Park	25,195	71	2	7	17	45	295	55	197	43	0
Mendota	7,124	9	0	1	0	8	128	22	101	5	0
Merrionette Park	1,860	1	0	0	0	1	58	18	38	2	0
Metropolis	6,238	42	0	8	9	25	379	64	299	16	3
Midlothian	14,678	34	0	0	19	15	343	56	258	29	10
Milan	5,017	21	0	4	2	15	131	24	106	1	0
Milledgeville	968	3	0	2	0	1	4	0	4	0	0
Millstadt	3,859	3	0	2	0	1	22	3	19	0	0
Minier	1,208	3	0	1	0	2	19	7	12	0	0
Minonk	2,029	8	0	3	0	5	19	3	14	2	0
Mokena	20,321	14	0	4	2	8	299	20	267	12	0
Moline	42,042	224	0	31	20	173	1,363	234	1,083	46	7
Momence	3,155	9	0	1	2	6	47	11	31	5	0
Monee	5,064	8	1	2	3	2	68	31	33	4	0
Monmouth	9,172	36	1	6	0	29	178	36	129	13	3
Montgomery	19,720	31	1	7	2	21	364	33	317	14	4
Monticello	5,591	5	0	1	0	4	32	5	27	0	0
Morris	14,640	19	0	3	4	12	297	39	254	4	0
Morrison	4,092	10	1	2	0	7	102	4	93	5	6
Morton	16,287	22	0	9	1	12	144	54	82	8	0
Morton Grove	23,220	17	0	1	6	10	308	70	224	14	0
Mount Carmel	6,950	27	0	1	2	24	215	36	177	2	0
Mount Carroll	1,593	0	0	0	0	0	13	6	6	1	0
Mount Morris	2,829	1	0	0	0	1	13	1	12	0	0
Mount Olive	1,985	4	0	0	0	4	17	5	10	2	0
Mount Prospect	54,162	25	0	3	7	15	567	51	499	17	1
Mount Pulaski	1,506	0	0	0	0	0	0	0	0	0	0
Mount Vernon	15,117	182	2	17	22	141	404	157	230	17	12
Mount Zion	5,857	11	0	3	1	7	44	7	37	0	1
Moweaqua	1,723	0	0	0	0	0	14	2	12	0	0
Mundelein	31,547	17	0	7	3	7	244	27	208	9	2
Murphysboro	7,637	47	0	3	5	39	252	76	172	4	0
Naperville	147,934	136	1	22	33	80	1,716	129	1,540	47	8
Neoga	1,605	6	0	0	0	6	17	7	10	0	0
New Athens	1,914	3	0	2	0	1	24	10	13	1	0
New Baden	3,280	2	0	0	0	2	22	0	22	0	5
New Berlin	1,345	0	0	0	0	0	14	3	11	0	0
New Lenox	26,529	36	0	12	6	18	302	22	269	11	5
Newton	2,780	0	0	0	0	0	32	7	21	4	0
Nokomis	2,140	6	0	0	0	6	63	9	49	5	0
Normal	54,540	128	1	42	20	65	1,040	106	912	22	1
Norridge	14,484	11	0	0	6	5	303	37	255	11	0
Norris City	1,240	15	0	0	0	15	9	2	7	0	0
North Aurora	17,542	30	0	6	8	16	280	23	251	6	0
Northbrook	33,452	10	0	2	5	3	377	32	337	8	0
North Chicago	29,553	93	2	21	20	50	61	30	24	7	0
Northfield	5,459	4	0	0	0	4	84	14	63	7	0
Northlake	12,401	18	0	1	10	7	294	16	263	15	2
North Riverside	6,585	16	0	0	8	8	457	15	439	3	0
North Utica	1,337	1	0	0	0	1	3	1	1	1	0
Oak Brook	8,099	3	0	0	1	2	593	9	575	9	0
Oakbrook Terrace	2,162	8	0	3	1	4	121	7	107	7	0
Oak Forest	27,761	42	0	8	15	19	314	54	234	26	1
Oak Lawn	56,178	97	2	6	41	48	673	89	570	14	4
Oak Park	51,753	178	1	8	134	35	1,453	311	1,034	108	2

Table 8. Offenses Known to Law Enforcement, by Selected State and City, 2017—Continued
(Number.)

State/city	Population	Violent crime	Murder and nonnegligent manslaughter	Rape (revised definition)[1]	Robbery	Aggravated assault	Property crime	Burglary	Larceny-theft	Motor vehicle theft	Arson[2]
Oakwood	1,495	2	0	1	0	1	14	6	8	0	0
Oblong	1,414	3	0	2	0	1	16	8	8	0	1
O'Fallon	29,085	54	0	11	8	35	605	80	512	13	3
Oglesby	3,591	2	0	0	0	2	36	8	28	0	0
Okawville	1,382	4	0	1	0	3	22	7	14	1	0
Olney	8,928	34	0	6	1	27	362	55	295	12	4
Onarga	1,294	1	0	0	0	1	0	0	0	0	0
Oregon	3,517	14	0	6	0	8	93	10	79	4	0
Orion	1,806	0	0	0	0	0	5	2	2	1	0
Orland Park	59,227	35	1	4	7	23	1,094	20	1,059	15	0
Oswego	35,273	22	0	13	4	5	353	23	319	11	1
Ottawa	18,209	36	0	1	6	29	352	53	292	7	2
Palatine	68,792	41	0	12	10	19	573	31	513	29	1
Palestine	1,313	8	0	3	0	5	22	5	17	0	1
Palos Heights	12,423	5	1	0	3	1	121	10	107	4	0
Palos Hills	17,396	10	0	2	1	7	96	14	70	12	0
Palos Park	4,837	1	0	0	1	0	23	5	17	1	0
Pana	5,518	11	0	0	1	10	87	23	59	5	0
Paris	8,352	46	0	3	4	39	115	51	53	11	4
Park City	7,314	10	0	5	0	5	107	17	70	20	0
Park Forest	21,750	67	1	15	27	24	328	70	217	41	3
Park Ridge	37,492	15	0	1	9	5	278	57	212	9	3
Pawnee	2,685	0	0	0	0	0	2	0	2	0	0
Paxton	4,274	20	0	1	3	16	57	17	39	1	1
Pekin	32,866	124	0	18	10	96	506	128	358	20	8
Peoria	114,157	867	12	65	281	509	4,810	1,119	3,357	334	44
Peoria Heights	5,913	24	1	4	5	14	179	35	121	23	3
Peotone	4,132	6	0	1	1	4	39	2	35	2	0
Peru	9,829	19	0	6	5	8	156	27	126	3	0
Phoenix	1,942	14	0	0	2	12	39	13	20	6	0
Pierron	547	0	0	0	0	0	0	0	0	0	0
Pinckneyville	5,366	5	0	0	0	5	26	11	13	2	0
Pingree Grove	8,005	4	0	2	0	2	32	1	30	1	1
Pittsfield	4,452	5	0	1	0	4	53	10	43	0	0
Plainfield	43,450	55	1	12	13	29	327	25	281	21	2
Plano	11,438	3	0	3	0	0	110	13	92	5	2
Pleasant Hill	936	0	0	0	0	0	2	1	1	0	0
Pleasant Plains	798	2	0	0	0	2	2	0	2	0	0
Polo	2,209	5	0	0	2	3	39	5	34	0	1
Pontiac	11,813	40	0	0	10	30	177	33	139	5	1
Pontoon Beach	5,572	8	0	1	2	5	95	22	65	8	0
Posen	5,920	18	1	1	7	9	195	30	144	21	0
Potomac	704	1	0	1	0	0	4	2	2	0	0
Princeton	7,550	10	0	0	3	7	133	23	108	2	0
Prophetstown	1,978	0	0	0	0	0	0	0	0	0	0
Prospect Heights	16,237	16	0	2	3	11	102	15	77	10	0
Quincy	40,506	233	0	44	19	170	1,194	222	930	42	7
Raleigh	343	1	0	0	0	1	10	2	8	0	0
Rankin	525	0	0	0	0	0	0	0	0	0	0
Rantoul	12,791	41	0	8	17	16	315	79	220	16	4
Red Bud	3,536	9	0	0	0	9	22	3	16	3	0
Richmond	1,899	4	0	0	1	3	39	12	26	1	0
Richton Park	13,542	41	0	6	23	12	369	60	269	40	2
Ridge Farm	833	1	0	0	0	1	4	1	3	0	0
Riverdale	13,371	120	2	8	76	34	341	104	188	49	1
River Forest	11,073	21	1	1	9	10	282	39	237	6	2
River Grove	10,114	7	1	0	0	6	137	24	105	8	0
Riverside	8,726	13	0	2	0	11	95	5	87	3	1
Riverton	3,429	12	0	0	1	11	72	15	53	4	1
Riverwoods	3,633	3	0	3	0	0	19	3	15	1	0
Robbins	5,479	32	1	2	9	20	55	20	15	20	0
Rochester	3,772	11	0	2	0	9	17	4	10	3	0
Rockdale	1,935	1	0	0	0	1	15	1	11	3	0
Rock Falls	8,927	18	0	1	2	15	100	32	66	2	0
Rockford	146,770	2,331	18	113	427	1,773	5,236	1,383	3,403	450	58
Rock Island	38,079	133	3	5	10	115	1,060	198	754	108	3
Rockton	7,469	5	0	2	0	3	117	6	111	0	0
Rolling Meadows	24,005	22	0	4	7	11	335	28	294	13	1
Romeoville	39,710	58	1	13	15	29	555	53	477	25	2
Roscoe	10,478	3	0	0	0	3	90	20	68	2	0
Roselle	22,824	13	0	5	4	4	169	27	132	10	2
Rosemont	4,162	33	0	5	7	21	388	5	375	8	27
Round Lake	18,382	19	0	4	2	13	105	20	78	7	0
Round Lake Beach	27,710	44	0	7	3	34	559	37	508	14	2
Round Lake Heights	2,701	5	0	0	1	4	23	3	19	1	0
Round Lake Park	7,532	15	0	0	0	15	63	22	40	1	0
Roxana	1,463	6	0	2	0	4	30	8	19	3	1
Royalton	1,122	1	0	0	0	1	3	1	2	0	0
Ruma	313	0	0	0	0	0	2	0	2	0	0
Rushville	2,875	5	0	1	0	4	32	3	28	1	0
Salem	7,202	28	0	4	2	22	391	78	306	7	0
Sandoval	1,211	10	0	2	2	6	43	9	27	7	30
Sandwich	7,349	9	0	0	1	8	37	2	34	1	0

Table 8. Offenses Known to Law Enforcement, by Selected State and City, 2017—Continued

(Number.)

State/city	Population	Violent crime	Murder and nonnegligent manslaughter	Rape (revised definition)[1]	Robbery	Aggravated assault	Property crime	Burglary	Larceny-theft	Motor vehicle theft	Arson[2]
San Jose	604	1	0	1	0	0	0	0	0	0	0
Sauget	150	1	0	0	1	0	46	6	31	9	0
Sauk Village	10,418	72	1	4	30	37	179	49	91	39	3
Schaumburg	74,471	79	2	13	31	33	1,244	92	1,103	49	0
Schiller Park	11,674	25	1	7	4	13	169	23	126	20	0
Seneca	2,267	7	0	0	0	7	57	6	51	0	0
Sesser	1,883	10	2	2	2	4	54	17	36	1	0
Shannon	699	0	0	0	0	0	0	0	0	0	0
Shawneetown	1,143	4	0	0	0	4	22	9	10	3	0
Sherman	4,777	1	0	1	0	0	43	5	38	0	0
Shiloh	13,094	15	1	5	2	7	174	51	119	4	1
Shorewood	17,171	18	0	6	4	8	141	15	117	9	0
Sidell	576	0	0	0	0	0	0	0	0	0	0
Silvis	7,596	39	0	5	2	32	323	70	244	9	0
Skokie	64,167	185	2	20	40	123	1,546	212	1,279	55	6
Sleepy Hollow	3,333	2	0	1	0	1	8	0	8	0	0
Smithton	3,766	0	0	0	0	0	14	0	14	0	0
Somonauk	1,879	0	0	0	0	0	13	4	9	0	1
South Barrington	4,973	3	0	0	2	1	67	5	60	2	0
South Beloit	7,613	8	0	0	1	7	118	20	94	4	1
South Chicago Heights	4,095	8	0	0	3	5	157	8	140	9	0
South Elgin	22,504	30	0	9	7	14	184	22	160	2	2
South Holland	21,782	92	1	13	59	19	563	103	373	87	2
South Pekin	1,108	2	0	0	0	2	19	4	13	2	0
South Roxana	1,975	8	0	3	4	1	30	10	17	3	0
Springfield	115,568	1,219	11	93	251	864	5,496	1,210	3,973	313	50
Spring Grove	5,657	2	1	1	0	0	27	2	23	2	0
Spring Valley	5,216	5	0	1	0	4	78	15	61	2	0
Stanford	577	0	0	0	0	0	4	3	1	0	0
St. Anne	1,201	2	0	0	1	1	28	5	23	0	0
St. Charles	32,780	56	2	3	6	45	268	31	223	14	2
Steger	9,436	27	0	6	11	10	291	47	231	13	1
St. Elmo	1,381	2	0	0	0	2	24	9	12	3	0
Sterling	14,823	33	0	14	3	16	559	74	454	31	3
Stickney	6,710	7	0	1	6	0	71	5	59	7	0
Stockton	1,747	6	1	2	1	2	37	4	32	1	0
Streator	13,049	36	0	22	1	13	348	35	293	20	7
Sullivan	4,479	16	0	1	1	14	37	2	33	2	0
Summit	11,358	27	2	3	9	13	170	15	116	39	3
Sumner	3,166	1	0	0	0	1	12	2	9	1	0
Swansea	13,484	25	0	13	3	9	179	32	130	17	1
Sycamore	17,925	31	1	11	2	17	142	23	116	3	2
Taylorville	10,668	3	0	1	0	2	220	30	175	15	0
Thayer	670	1	0	0	0	1	2	1	1	0	0
Thomasboro	1,113	2	0	0	0	2	25	3	20	2	0
Thornton	2,474	4	0	0	1	3	46	10	33	3	0
Tilton	2,562	9	0	2	1	6	76	13	61	2	0
Tinley Park	56,823	57	0	4	18	35	675	77	557	41	3
Tolono	3,433	11	0	0	0	11	31	6	24	1	1
Toluca	1,307	1	0	0	0	1	13	2	11	0	0
Tonica	726	0	0	0	0	0	2	0	1	1	0
Tower Lakes	1,245	0	0	0	0	0	5	0	5	0	0
Trenton	2,641	1	0	1	0	0	17	3	14	0	0
Troy	10,125	15	0	1	2	12	60	15	40	5	0
Tuscola	4,377	20	0	0	1	19	68	20	43	5	0
Urbana	42,091	142	0	25	48	69	1,421	252	1,142	27	13
Valmeyer	1,257	1	0	0	0	1	9	0	9	0	0
Vernon Hills	26,547	10	0	3	4	3	469	20	438	11	1
Vienna	1,748	1	0	1	0	0	5	0	3	2	0
Villa Park	21,857	29	0	3	11	15	219	22	176	21	0
Viola	903	0	0	0	0	0	0	0	0	0	0
Virden	3,371	18	0	6	0	12	74	18	55	1	1
Walnut	1,326	0	0	0	0	0	5	2	3	0	0
Warren	1,340	1	0	1	0	0	4	1	3	0	0
Warrensburg	1,143	2	0	0	1	1	9	1	8	0	0
Warrenville	13,255	8	0	4	0	4	89	11	71	7	0
Washington	17,136	9	0	3	2	4	157	39	116	2	0
Washington Park	3,917	37	1	1	6	29	53	11	24	18	4
Watseka	4,961	8	1	1	2	4	133	18	104	11	1
Waukegan	88,017	361	6	18	138	199	1,988	442	1,487	59	11
Waverly	1,240	1	0	0	0	1	8	4	4	0	0
Wayne	2,432	0	0	0	0	0	3	0	3	0	0
Wenona	972	3	0	0	0	3	9	3	6	0	0
Westchester	16,536	24	0	1	17	6	271	69	193	9	2
West Chicago	27,219	28	0	7	9	12	314	51	248	15	1
West City	648	3	0	0	0	3	70	3	67	0	0
West Dundee	7,365	5	0	4	0	1	124	4	117	3	0
Western Springs	13,464	6	0	0	3	3	101	8	88	5	0
West Frankfort	7,971	3	0	0	3	0	208	74	122	12	0
Westmont	24,781	15	0	7	4	4	287	32	244	11	2
Westville	3,036	7	0	3	0	4	45	22	21	2	0
Wheaton	53,444	38	1	12	4	21	493	54	427	12	6
Wheeling	38,419	38	0	9	6	23	337	40	285	12	0

Table 8. Offenses Known to Law Enforcement, by Selected State and City, 2017—Continued

(Number.)

State/city	Population	Violent crime	Murder and nonnegligent manslaughter	Rape (revised definition)[1]	Robbery	Aggravated assault	Property crime	Burglary	Larceny-theft	Motor vehicle theft	Arson[2]
White Hall	2,328	5	0	2	1	2	29	9	20	0	1
Willowbrook	8,542	5	0	3	1	1	123	11	103	9	0
Willow Springs	5,645	1	0	0	0	1	19	3	15	1	0
Wilmette	27,242	4	0	2	0	2	349	43	292	14	1
Wilmington	5,681	13	0	1	2	10	48	6	39	3	0
Winfield	9,718	4	0	1	0	3	87	7	77	3	0
Winnebago	2,986	6	0	2	1	3	36	7	28	1	0
Winnetka	12,451	7	0	0	1	6	144	17	112	15	0
Winthrop Harbor	6,777	2	0	0	0	2	33	7	23	3	3
Witt	854	0	0	0	0	0	4	0	4	0	0
Wood Dale	13,817	11	0	3	5	3	193	17	167	9	0
Woodridge	33,553	39	2	9	13	15	382	84	272	26	1
Wood River	10,187	31	0	6	10	15	401	59	325	17	2
Woodstock	25,127	24	1	5	4	14	398	27	367	4	0
Worth	10,662	16	0	0	6	10	110	24	69	17	1
Yates City	659	1	0	0	0	1	8	3	5	0	0
Yorkville	19,155	10	0	5	1	4	165	17	143	5	1
Zion	23,969	121	1	21	26	73	621	122	458	41	3
INDIANA											
Albion	2,316	10	0	2	0	8	29	2	22	5	
Alexandria	5,004	9	0	6	2	1	100	30	64	6	0
Anderson	54,959	260	1	82	101	76	2,418	408	1,786	224	
Aurora	3,678	25	0	3	0	22	143	7	129	7	0
Bargersville	7,441	9	0	0	1	8	126	14	100	12	0
Batesville	6,705	16	0	2	1	13	97	14	77	6	1
Bedford	13,330	11	1	3	2	5	337	32	278	27	1
Beech Grove[7]	14,831		0		12	5	338	51	223	64	0
Berne[7]	4,118		0		0	0	16	2	12	2	1
Bloomington	85,121	443	2	78	52	311	2,584	478	1,940	166	13
Bluffton[8]	10,011	7	0	6	0	1		23		9	0
Boonville	6,176	35	0	6	3	26	185	23	150	12	
Bremen[7]	4,547		0		0	14	61	22	31	8	0
Brownsburg[7]	26,030		1		6	39	298	22	254	22	0
Carmel	93,098	17	0	6	6	5	695	61	596	38	0
Cedar Lake[7]	12,286		0		2	7	198	40	145	13	
Charlestown[7]	8,248		0		1	47	128	22	101	5	
Chesterton	13,497	8	1	2	0	5	117	18	87	12	
Clarksville	21,948	109	0	3	18	88	1,199	66	1,010	123	
Clinton	4,782	24	0	0	0	24	155	23	127	5	0
Columbus[7]	47,322		1		18	4	1,904	202	1,537	165	4
Crawfordsville	16,011	76	0	2	5	69	411	75	319	17	1
Crown Point	29,399	10	0	2	6	2	333	21	296	16	
Cumberland	5,649	16	0	2	8	6	156	18	127	11	
Danville[7]	9,783		0		0	37	115	15	83	17	0
Decatur	9,541	10	0	5	1	4	137	9	122	6	0
Dyer	15,869	4	0	0	3	1	135	25	93	17	0
East Chicago	28,210	188	4	9	95	80	975	165	705	105	3
Edinburgh	4,592	20	0	0	5	15	493	34	458	1	1
Elkhart[7]	52,330		5		71	471	1,837	334	1,314	189	
Ellettsville	6,682	9	0	0	1	8	124	21	90	13	1
Elwood	8,386	12	0	8	2	2	221	42	165	14	3
Evansville	119,371	825	20	75	185	545	5,979	863	4,641	475	39
Fairmount	2,782	10	0	1	0	9	7	6	1	0	0
Fishers	92,367	43	1	14	9	19	855	69	751	35	2
Fort Wayne	266,259	952	37	136	299	480	8,466	1,308	6,626	532	94
Frankfort	15,873	15	0	7	2	6	501	71	406	24	0
Franklin	25,060	127	0	8	7	112	851	76	755	20	0
Gary	75,808	471	48	32	192	199	2,581	678	1,481	422	51
Gas City	5,828	4	0	0	1	3	176	46	128	2	0
Goshen[7]	33,195		1		18	7	1,118	193	852	73	2
Greenfield	21,872	94	0	12	3	79	413	63	315	35	
Greenwood	57,484	298	1	0	21	276	1,862	111	1,624	127	5
Griffith	16,149	25	0	3	10	12	355	28	306	21	0
Hagerstown	1,702	6	0	1	0	5	10	2	8	0	0
Hammond	76,550	486	12	32	180	262	2,996	508	2,162	326	32
Hartford City	5,873	7	0	0	1	6	47	7	37	3	0
Highland	22,577	36	0	0	19	17	735	69	632	34	1
Hobart	28,066	93	1	5	13	74	1,169	98	1,015	56	
Huntingburg	6,143	20	0	0	1	19	55	13	36	6	0
Indianapolis	870,788	11,616	156	668	3,485	7,307	38,418	8,945	24,569	4,904	256
Jasper	15,577	35	0	3	1	31	160	7	143	10	0
Jeffersonville	47,459	67	0	17	32	18	1,435	184	1,070	181	3
Kendallville[7]	9,915		0		2	50	226	31	162	33	0
Knox	3,580	4	0	0	0	4	196	10	183	3	0
Kokomo	57,758	417	6	36	48	327	1,669	413	1,169	87	5
Lafayette	72,274	364	4	43	80	237	2,637	573	1,903	161	8
Lake Station	11,852	15	2	1	6	6	332	60	246	26	5
La Porte[6]	21,681	103	0	8	17	78	552	105	428	19	1
Lawrenceburg	4,955	29	1	8	2	18	129	5	112	12	
Ligonier	4,420	1	0	1	0	0	37	5	24	8	0
Linton	5,221	4	0	0	2	2	147	7	134	6	
Logansport	17,700	24	1	6	6	11	660	100	535	25	4

Table 8. Offenses Known to Law Enforcement, by Selected State and City, 2017—Continued

(Number.)

State/city	Population	Violent crime	Murder and nonnegligent manslaughter	Rape (revised definition)[1]	Robbery	Aggravated assault	Property crime	Burglary	Larceny-theft	Motor vehicle theft	Arson[2]
Lowell	9,552	2	0	0	0	2	6	1	5	0	0
Marion	28,385	97	0	10	32	55	1,057	152	821	84	6
Merrillville[5]	34,999		2	3	35		1,286	64	1,100	122	1
Mishawaka[8]	48,749	105	3	8	54	40		275			5
Mooresville	9,709	7	0	1	1	5	280	22	236	22	0
Muncie	68,814	246	3	38	85	120	2,491	422	1,794	275	
Munster	22,701	23	0	4	18	1	458	33	405	20	0
Nappanee[7]	6,800		0		0	5	103	33	61	9	0
New Haven	15,481	38	1	4	13	20	335	40	266	29	1
New Whiteland	6,117	1	0	0	0	1	39	35	0	4	0
Noblesville[7]	61,527		0		4	25	810	75	687	48	0
North Vernon	6,837	18	0	0	3	15	177	19	158	0	0
Peru[7]	11,009		0		5	41	436	60	362	14	0
Plainfield	32,067	85	0	5	6	74	856	66	713	77	2
Plymouth	9,936	6	0	0	4	2	272	29	223	20	1
Porter	4,843	9	0	3	1	5	39	6	30	3	0
Portland	6,154	14	0	4	0	10	88	1	83	4	
Rushville[7]	6,022		0		1	2	232	45	178	9	0
Scottsburg[7]	6,669		0		4	4	307	50	252	5	0
Sellersburg	8,836	7	0	0	1	6	86	21	51	14	0
Seymour	19,604	66	0	8	8	50	732	94	572	66	1
Shelbyville[7]	19,047		0		4	207	533	73	423	37	0
South Bend	101,857	1,064	15	93	345	611	5,100	1,192	3,440	468	37
South Whitley[7]	1,733		0		0	0	8	1	7	0	0
Speedway	12,150	38	0	1	23	14	499	64	398	37	1
St. John	17,128	2	0	0	1	1	143	21	109	13	0
Tell City	7,319	5	0	4	0	1	131	16	104	11	0
Tipton	5,094	8	0	1	0	7	77	12	53	12	2
Valparaiso	33,329	48	0	8	9	31	504	52	431	21	
Vincennes	17,847	24	1	5	11	7	1,022	188	741	93	4
Warsaw[7]	14,850		2		7	65	613	65	527	21	
Waterloo	2,250	10	0	0	0	10	66	11	41	14	0
Westfield	38,542	22	0	0	8	14	391	27	348	16	1
West Lafayette	46,541	49	0	8	5	36	466	49	397	20	0
Whitestown[6]	7,464	14	0	0	2	12	139	16	108	15	
Whiting[7]	4,805		0		8	6	102	7	92	3	0
Winchester	4,718	1	0	0	0	1	193	30	158	5	0
IOWA											
Adel[5]	4,397	14	0	1	0	13			79	10	1
Albia	3,787	10	0	1	1	8	45	9	34	2	0
Algona	5,509	15	0	1	0	14	27	6	18	3	0
Altoona	18,556	24	0	1	3	20	545	45	477	23	2
Ames	67,461	124	1	49	23	51	1,392	248	1,087	57	0
Anamosa	5,411	11	0	0	0	11	99	19	77	3	0
Ankeny	61,090	130	0	23	10	97	831	143	650	38	5
Atlantic	6,588	23	0	2	2	19	131	28	94	9	1
Audubon	1,939	8	0	4	0	4	17	1	16	0	0
Bettendorf	36,133	54	0	4	9	41	650	134	470	46	4
Blue Grass	1,743	7	0	2	1	4	11	2	8	1	1
Boone	12,607	64	0	1	1	62	161	43	104	14	0
Buffalo	1,297	3	0	1	0	2	9	0	8	1	0
Burlington	25,227	234	2	14	16	202	985	240	671	74	16
Carroll	9,920	2	0	0	1	1	168	53	103	12	2
Cedar Falls	41,744	86	1	27	6	52	822	128	666	28	2
Cedar Rapids	131,878	370	6	34	121	209	4,952	929	3,681	342	14
Centerville	5,316	19	0	1	0	18	289	153	122	14	4
Charles City	7,425	14	1	6	2	5	159	29	126	4	1
Cherokee	4,954	15	0	1	0	14	29	4	25	0	0
Clarinda	5,353	17	0	4	0	13	157	40	104	13	1
Clear Lake	7,559	28	0	1	0	27	151	31	109	11	0
Clinton	25,532	295	0	32	21	242	1,255	277	874	104	11
Clive	17,913	14	0	2	0	12	272	38	211	23	4
Colfax	2,034	4	0	1	0	3	31	5	22	4	0
Coralville	20,652	47	0	14	18	15	753	118	621	14	0
Council Bluffs	62,549	150	1	24	62	63	3,717	435	2,853	429	16
Cresco	3,799	0	0	0	0	0	21	5	15	1	0
Creston	7,829	13	0	0	0	13	165	24	134	7	3
Davenport	103,063	750	13	90	203	444	5,249	1,108	3,586	555	23
Decorah	7,883	4	0	0	0	4	84	6	71	7	2
Denison	8,304	15	0	3	0	12	65	14	47	4	0
Des Moines	217,277	1,456	28	73	364	991	9,589	2,388	5,941	1,260	42
De Witt	5,218	18	0	1	2	15	82	23	57	2	0
Dubuque	58,674	166	2	40	16	108	1,606	333	1,210	63	15
Dyersville	4,217	6	0	0	0	6	36	9	26	1	0
Eldridge	6,406	6	0	0	0	6	50	20	18	12	0
Emmetsburg	3,736	8	0	3	0	5	33	8	25	0	2
Estherville	5,877	31	0	7	0	24	68	28	40	0	2
Evansdale	4,792	27	0	3	2	22	131	62	61	8	1
Fairfield	10,337	16	0	5	0	11	338	111	211	16	2
Forest City	3,993	8	0	1	0	7	20	10	10	0	0
Fort Dodge	24,331	151	1	22	18	110	1,075	137	880	58	15
Fort Madison	10,525	66	0	14	5	47	351	26	292	33	2

Table 8. Offenses Known to Law Enforcement, by Selected State and City, 2017—Continued

(Number.)

State/city	Population	Violent crime	Murder and nonnegligent manslaughter	Rape (revised definition)[1]	Robbery	Aggravated assault	Property crime	Burglary	Larceny-theft	Motor vehicle theft	Arson[2]
Glenwood	5,315	17	0	5	0	12	111	43	63	5	0
Grinnell	9,141	75	0	7	2	66	229	55	162	12	3
Grundy Center	2,683	7	0	2	0	5	13	2	6	5	0
Hampton	4,202	6	0	0	0	6	12	2	8	2	0
Harlan	4,904	8	0	1	0	7	5	2	3	0	1
Hawarden	2,524	6	0	2	0	4	20	9	9	2	0
Humboldt	4,538	2	0	0	0	2	47	3	41	3	0
Independence	6,027	12	0	2	2	8	117	38	73	6	1
Indianola	15,953	90	2	13	0	75	359	70	263	26	3
Iowa City	75,519	156	4	25	46	81	1,767	310	1,376	81	5
Jefferson	4,140	15	0	1	0	14	164	45	116	3	0
Johnston	21,816	32	1	4	7	20	242	32	199	11	0
Keokuk	10,376	90	1	5	3	81	656	202	400	54	2
Le Claire	4,012	9	0	0	0	9	20	5	13	2	1
Le Mars	9,955	9	0	3	0	6	158	36	111	11	2
Lisbon	2,219	6	0	0	0	6	31	21	9	1	0
Manchester	5,032	20	0	4	1	15	110	26	78	6	2
Maquoketa	5,954	15	1	1	2	11	176	43	131	2	1
Marion	39,050	68	1	11	13	43	623	141	446	36	10
Mason City	27,327	43	3	9	11	20	834	196	601	37	5
Monticello	3,843	25	0	0	0	25	78	13	59	6	0
Mount Pleasant	8,349	13	0	0	0	13	211	59	143	9	1
Mount Vernon	4,436	6	0	3	0	3	32	4	27	1	0
Muscatine	23,940	194	0	18	6	170	479	84	358	37	13
New Hampton	3,401	5	0	1	0	4	24	4	17	3	1
Newton	14,999	71	0	9	2	60	499	146	335	18	0
North Liberty	19,491	56	0	11	5	40	190	40	147	3	0
Norwalk	10,874	9	0	1	1	7	90	13	69	8	0
Oelwein	5,999	19	0	3	2	14	129	34	88	7	2
Ogden	1,989	9	0	2	0	7	27	10	17	0	0
Onawa	2,848	11	0	1	0	10	58	18	34	6	3
Orange City	6,199	8	0	1	1	6	32	8	23	1	0
Osage	3,623	15	0	0	0	15	36	14	19	3	0
Osceola	5,051	8	0	1	0	7	92	26	61	5	0
Oskaloosa	11,525	46	0	4	3	39	242	58	175	9	2
Ottumwa	24,397	143	0	23	13	107	1,294	287	918	89	22
Pella	10,240	19	0	5	0	14	135	26	96	13	0
Perry	7,824	16	0	1	1	14	247	105	131	11	1
Pleasant Hill	9,910	24	2	3	0	19	339	82	219	38	0
Polk City	4,616	6	0	0	0	6	21	5	15	1	1
Prairie City	1,718	1	0	0	0	1	12	6	6	0	0
Red Oak	5,437	40	0	11	0	29	190	58	124	8	3
Rock Valley	3,788	4	1	3	0	0	10	5	4	1	1
Sac City	2,086	3	0	3	0	0	25	6	18	1	0
Sergeant Bluff	4,606	12	0	0	1	11	25	5	17	3	0
Sheldon	5,102	15	0	2	0	13	92	31	54	7	0
Sigourney	1,976	5	0	1	0	4	31	4	25	2	0
Sioux Center	7,578	2	0	1	0	1	21	1	20	0	1
Sioux City	82,879	360	2	56	71	231	3,561	612	2,660	289	16
Spencer	11,125	15	0	14	0	1	230	42	175	13	2
Spirit Lake	5,124	20	0	0	0	20	105	15	84	6	0
Storm Lake	10,790	71	0	15	0	56	282	49	227	6	3
Story City	3,406	5	0	1	0	4	29	9	18	2	0
Tama	2,825	22	0	4	0	18	22	10	10	2	0
Tipton	3,217	9	0	4	1	4	28	16	11	1	2
Toledo	2,163	6	0	0	0	6	25	6	16	3	1
Urbandale	43,637	115	0	10	8	97	538	139	352	47	5
Vinton	5,125	20	0	1	0	19	52	11	39	2	1
Walcott	1,639	1	0	0	0	1	11	2	6	3	0
Washington	7,451	62	0	7	0	55	128	15	109	4	0
Waterloo	67,855	341	5	34	53	249	1,927	532	1,253	142	19
Waukee	20,359	31	0	9	1	21	238	48	152	38	2
Webster City	7,708	15	0	2	0	13	98	30	59	9	0
West Branch	2,365	5	0	0	0	5	5	2	2	1	0
West Burlington	2,935	5	0	0	1	4	219	14	197	8	0
Williamsburg	3,197	4	1	0	0	3	21	9	9	3	0
Windsor Heights	5,001	14	0	3	2	9	217	20	196	1	3
Winterset	5,282	17	0	2	0	15	64	14	47	3	0
KANSAS											
Abilene	6,407	7	0	2	0	5	95	13	79	3	0
Altamont	1,036	5	0	1	0	4	8	0	8	0	0
Alta Vista	419	0	0	0	0	0	0	0	0	0	0
Andale	1,003	0	0	0	0	0	0	0	0	0	0
Andover	13,183	18	0	0	4	14	295	19	260	16	4
Anthony	2,164	7	0	2	0	5	46	12	31	3	9
Arkansas City	12,009	63	0	13	3	47	582	99	450	33	1
Atchison	10,628	37	1	4	1	31	368	47	294	27	3
Atwood	1,213	2	0	0	1	1	49	5	43	1	1
Auburn	1,209	0	0	0	0	0	0	0	0	0	0
Augusta	9,329	19	0	2	2	15	355	45	293	17	0
Basehor	5,835	4	0	0	1	3	103	27	61	15	0
Baxter Springs	3,921	9	0	0	2	7	87	13	68	6	1

Table 8. Offenses Known to Law Enforcement, by Selected State and City, 2017—Continued

(Number.)

State/city	Population	Violent crime	Murder and nonnegligent manslaughter	Rape (revised definition)[1]	Robbery	Aggravated assault	Property crime	Burglary	Larceny-theft	Motor vehicle theft	Arson[2]
Bel Aire	7,819	13	0	2	0	11	55	14	38	3	0
Belle Plaine	1,585	4	0	0	0	4	17	2	11	4	0
Beloit	3,761	5	0	0	0	5	42	10	31	1	0
Bucklin	777	0	0	0	0	0	0	0	0	0	0
Burlington	2,600	6	1	0	0	5	38	6	26	6	0
Burns	219	0	0	0	0	0	0	0	0	0	0
Caney	2,014	4	1	0	0	3	13	4	9	0	0
Cheney	2,176	3	0	2	0	1	54	17	36	1	0
Cherryvale	2,161	17	0	2	0	15	73	24	45	4	2
Claflin	620	2	0	0	0	2	8	4	4	0	0
Clay Center	4,025	8	0	0	0	8	70	9	58	3	2
Clearwater	2,524	3	0	1	0	2	57	10	45	2	0
Coffeyville	9,423	48	3	4	4	37	460	108	331	21	3
Colby	5,420	8	0	1	1	6	156	32	116	8	1
Colony	404	0	0	0	0	0	0	0	0	0	0
Columbus	3,072	8	0	1	2	5	60	13	42	5	1
Concordia	5,144	15	0	8	1	6	157	27	124	6	0
Council Grove	2,041	8	0	0	0	8	14	2	11	1	0
Derby	23,821	28	0	10	1	17	500	56	406	38	0
Dodge City	27,447	125	0	7	15	103	840	154	648	38	5
Edwardsville	4,395	23	0	6	1	16	134	19	95	20	7
El Dorado	13,125	28	0	8	5	15	313	59	218	36	0
Ellinwood	2,022	2	0	0	0	2	49	11	33	5	0
Ellsworth	3,034	12	0	0	1	11	33	5	27	1	0
Emporia	24,804	47	1	11	7	28	701	104	570	27	1
Eudora	6,417	16	1	3	0	12	52	5	39	8	0
Fairway	3,986	2	0	0	0	2	23	1	16	6	0
Fort Scott	7,725	35	0	5	0	30	301	63	222	16	1
Fredonia	2,261	10	1	1	0	8	70	16	51	3	0
Frontenac	3,410	2	0	1	0	1	65	20	39	6	0
Galena	2,855	11	1	0	0	10	77	13	57	7	2
Garden City	26,728	168	2	23	12	131	732	66	631	35	4
Gardner	21,449	41	1	5	5	30	305	39	248	18	1
Garnett	3,241	10	0	0	1	9	68	11	57	0	0
Girard	2,741	6	0	2	0	4	44	8	33	3	3
Goddard	4,761	8	0	2	0	6	110	7	96	7	0
Goodland[5]	4,433	13	0	2	0	11			49	3	0
Grandview Plaza	1,579	7	0	0	0	7	38	13	25	0	0
Great Bend	15,459	82	0	22	9	51	677	146	501	30	5
Halstead	2,080	2	0	0	1	1	26	11	15	0	0
Haven	1,207	5	0	1	0	4	20	4	15	1	0
Hays	21,110	65	0	4	6	55	517	56	439	22	0
Haysville	11,314	43	0	3	1	39	371	54	297	20	3
Herington	2,336	3	0	0	1	2	82	22	58	2	0
Hesston	3,817	1	0	0	0	1	46	12	34	0	0
Hiawatha	3,048	5	0	2	0	3	118	17	95	6	1
Hillsboro[5]	2,870	3	0	1	1	1			56	11	1
Holcomb	2,145	0	0	0	0	0	35	5	29	1	0
Holton	3,278	6	0	1	1	4	47	6	37	4	0
Horton	1,690	1	0	0	0	1	29	9	18	2	4
Hutchinson	41,160	240	2	36	37	165	1,941	427	1,376	138	17
Independence	8,692	60	1	5	7	47	577	111	440	26	14
Iola	5,413	33	1	8	1	23	281	57	214	10	2
Junction City	24,240	182	0	14	16	152	467	85	355	27	4
Kanopolis	467	0	0	0	0	0	0	0	0	0	0
Kingman	2,973	10	0	0	0	10	85	20	60	5	0
Lansing	11,941	28	0	6	4	18	135	31	93	11	0
Larned	3,875	13	0	2	1	10	128	26	96	6	1
Leavenworth	36,284	258	3	25	40	190	1,273	231	900	142	8
Leawood	35,029	31	0	4	2	25	439	44	369	26	2
Lenexa	53,717	90	1	17	9	63	938	145	696	97	1
Le Roy	552	0	0	0	0	0	0	0	0	0	0
Liberal	20,317	66	1	6	4	55	295	70	209	16	3
Lindsborg	3,319	3	0	0	0	3	38	7	29	2	0
Louisburg	4,391	5	0	0	1	4	69	6	60	3	1
Maize	4,621	8	0	0	1	7	69	18	48	3	2
Marysville	3,294	13	0	1	2	10	114	18	93	3	0
McLouth	842	1	0	0	0	1	31	3	27	1	0
McPherson	13,169	27	1	5	6	15	400	93	283	24	0
Meade	1,564	3	0	0	0	3	23	4	17	2	1
Merriam	11,278	42	1	6	3	32	676	36	529	111	1
Montezuma	967	0	0	0	0	0	0	0	0	0	0
Moran	511	0	0	0	0	0	0	0	0	0	0
Mulberry	519	3	0	0	0	3	14	4	10	0	1
Mulvane	6,343	7	0	5	1	1	215	18	184	13	0
Neodesha	2,293	3	0	0	0	3	40	7	32	1	0
Newton	19,095	121	2	22	8	89	683	95	564	24	8
North Newton	1,802	2	0	0	0	2	26	2	23	1	0
Norton	2,799	9	0	0	0	9	57	14	40	3	1
Nortonville	609	0	0	0	0	0	1	0	1	0	0
Oberlin	1,688	1	0	0	0	1	21	7	14	0	0
Olathe	137,070	255	2	71	33	149	1,958	165	1,641	152	9
Osage City	2,820	5	0	1	0	4	61	21	35	5	0

Table 8. Offenses Known to Law Enforcement, by Selected State and City, 2017—Continued

(Number.)

State/city	Population	Violent crime	Murder and nonnegligent manslaughter	Rape (revised definition)[1]	Robbery	Aggravated assault	Property crime	Burglary	Larceny-theft	Motor vehicle theft	Arson[2]
Osawatomie	4,284	7	0	1	0	6	69	11	57	1	1
Oswego	1,729	0	0	0	0	0	22	2	20	0	0
Overland Park	191,566	399	4	109	70	216	3,231	302	2,655	274	10
Paola	5,560	18	0	5	0	13	149	21	119	9	1
Park City	7,678	29	0	7	7	15	181	21	136	24	1
Parsons	9,815	77	1	11	5	60	442	115	305	22	4
Pittsburg	20,384	90	0	24	9	57	968	119	781	68	11
Pleasanton	1,170	2	0	0	1	1	5	2	2	1	0
Rose Hill	4,029	2	0	1	0	1	45	7	36	2	0
Russell	4,497	21	1	3	0	17	66	14	44	8	1
Sabetha	2,587	0	0	0	0	0	18	3	12	3	0
Salina	47,251	201	2	42	22	135	1,758	283	1,364	111	29
Scott City	3,901	8	0	2	0	6	29	6	23	0	0
Seneca	2,056	2	0	0	0	2	66	17	48	1	0
Shawnee	65,683	117	0	18	14	85	1,091	114	839	138	9
South Hutchinson	2,552	2	0	0	0	2	55	9	41	5	3
Sterling	2,253	3	0	1	1	1	24	4	18	2	0
Tonganoxie	5,379	12	0	2	1	9	57	5	44	8	0
Topeka	126,624	777	27	56	269	425	6,494	1,001	4,725	768	11
Troy	964	0	0	0	0	0	1	1	0	0	0
Ulysses	6,014	13	1	0	0	12	41	13	24	4	0
Valley Center	7,431	11	0	4	1	6	104	15	66	23	0
Valley Falls	1,142	3	0	0	1	2	20	5	10	5	0
Wellington	7,845	26	0	6	3	17	444	77	335	32	2
Wellsville	1,806	0	0	0	0	0	18	11	7	0	0
Westwood	2,285	1	0	0	1	0	45	4	36	5	0
Wichita	391,084	3,998	35	382	599	2,982	21,649	3,281	15,890	2,478	100
Winfield	12,274	23	1	2	3	17	419	63	335	21	1
KENTUCKY											
Adairville	873	2	0	0	0	2	3	1	2	0	0
Alexandria	9,486	2	0	2	0	0	159	19	126	14	0
Anchorage	2,438	1	0	0	0	1	7	1	6	0	0
Ashland	20,927	39	0	11	3	25	864	113	698	53	1
Audubon Park	1,511	1	0	0	1	0	38	7	21	10	0
Augusta	1,172	0	0	0	0	0	7	1	6	0	0
Barbourville	3,169	9	0	1	3	5	90	24	47	19	0
Bardstown	13,325	26	1	7	8	10	363	78	242	43	1
Beattyville	1,199	1	0	0	0	1	10	4	0	6	0
Beaver Dam	3,672	6	0	1	0	5	43	6	34	3	0
Bellevue	5,826	9	0	5	3	1	138	25	102	11	2
Benton	4,533	2	0	0	1	1	150	26	121	3	1
Berea	15,406	24	0	8	10	6	392	115	241	36	0
Bloomfield	1,071	0	0	0	0	0	7	2	4	1	0
Bowling Green	66,317	225	4	61	82	78	3,089	436	2,476	177	0
Brandenburg	2,904	2	0	2	0	0	32	5	18	9	0
Brownsville	831	0	0	0	0	0	4	1	2	1	0
Burnside	902	1	0	0	1	0	35	4	29	2	0
Cadiz	2,629	12	0	0	4	8	59	15	40	4	1
Calvert City	2,544	4	0	3	0	1	46	6	37	3	0
Campbellsville	11,486	23	0	7	3	13	431	114	290	27	3
Carlisle	1,992	0	0	0	0	0	9	2	6	1	0
Carrollton	3,864	3	0	0	0	3	55	11	38	6	0
Catlettsburg	1,794	4	0	0	3	1	64	14	44	6	0
Cave City	2,440	3	0	1	0	2	33	6	23	4	0
Central City	5,837	1	0	0	0	1	71	3	68	0	0
Clinton	1,312	4	0	0	0	4	17	6	11	0	0
Cloverport	1,156	2	0	1	0	1	7	3	3	1	0
Coal Run Village	1,538	1	0	0	1	0	30	5	25	0	0
Cold Spring	6,276	6	0	0	5	1	165	4	158	3	0
Columbia	4,940	4	0	0	0	4	17	3	7	7	0
Corbin	7,411	16	0	7	4	5	229	58	137	34	1
Covington	40,845	185	2	36	81	66	1,341	267	936	138	6
Cumberland	2,032	2	0	0	1	1	10	7	3	0	0
Cynthiana	6,375	6	0	3	0	3	150	30	111	9	0
Danville	16,891	25	0	6	2	17	251	70	164	17	1
Dawson Springs	2,712	3	0	1	2	0	73	16	51	6	0
Dayton	5,423	16	1	2	4	9	127	32	84	11	0
Dry Ridge	2,224	3	0	1	0	2	55	1	46	8	0
Eddyville	2,575	0	0	0	0	0	34	6	28	0	0
Edgewood	8,771	1	0	0	0	1	80	10	61	9	0
Edmonton	1,583	1	0	0	0	1	33	15	13	5	0
Elizabethtown	30,065	61	1	11	13	36	469	169	244	56	5
Elkton	2,134	3	0	0	1	2	43	16	26	1	0
Elsmere	8,541	7	0	0	2	5	126	17	96	13	0
Eminence	2,579	1	0	1	0	0	23	8	14	1	0
Erlanger	22,947	22	0	3	9	10	279	49	201	29	0
Eubank	326	0	0	0	0	0	0	0	0	0	0
Falmouth	2,127	1	0	0	0	1	25	6	17	2	0
Ferguson	942	0	0	0	0	0	8	3	4	1	0
Flatwoods	7,284	4	0	1	0	3	34	14	17	3	0
Flemingsburg	2,866	1	0	0	0	1	38	8	28	2	0
Florence	32,866	52	0	13	19	20	1,306	111	1,145	50	1

Table 8. Offenses Known to Law Enforcement, by Selected State and City, 2017—Continued

(Number.)

State/city	Population	Violent crime	Murder and nonnegligent manslaughter	Rape (revised definition)[1]	Robbery	Aggravated assault	Property crime	Burglary	Larceny-theft	Motor vehicle theft	Arson[2]
Fort Mitchell	8,306	6	0	1	3	2	90	23	64	3	0
Fort Thomas	16,485	8	0	2	4	2	116	17	88	11	1
Fort Wright	5,780	3	0	0	1	2	78	7	64	7	0
Frankfort	27,975	100	6	8	34	52	941	195	660	86	4
Franklin	8,884	24	1	6	7	10	224	46	155	23	0
Fulton	2,174	7	0	0	2	5	79	20	56	3	0
Georgetown	34,184	64	0	14	28	22	937	135	723	79	1
Glasgow	14,690	20	0	6	7	7	525	89	394	42	0
Graymoor-Devondale	2,974	1	0	0	1	0	35	11	17	7	0
Grayson	4,030	4	0	0	2	2	96	21	69	6	0
Greensburg	2,123	2	0	1	0	1	31	7	23	1	0
Greenville	4,347	2	0	0	0	2	29	8	16	5	0
Hardinsburg	2,324	1	0	0	0	1	17	6	10	1	0
Harlan	1,584	6	0	1	1	4	30	13	16	1	1
Harrodsburg	8,427	15	0	4	6	5	141	43	74	24	0
Hartford	2,787	0	0	0	0	0	8	0	5	3	0
Hazard	5,268	13	0	1	5	7	198	19	168	11	1
Henderson	28,846	69	2	14	23	30	673	125	479	69	0
Highland Heights	7,178	7	0	1	5	1	58	7	45	6	0
Hillview	8,942	5	0	1	3	1	118	27	76	15	0
Hodgenville	3,224	5	0	1	0	4	38	6	27	5	0
Hopkinsville	31,761	79	1	20	23	35	922	186	689	47	9
Horse Cave	2,373	0	0	0	0	0	2	1	1	0	0
Hurstbourne Acres	1,892	0	0	0	0	0	13	4	8	1	0
Hyden	348	0	0	0	0	0	0	0	0	0	0
Independence	27,400	25	0	11	8	6	149	33	102	14	0
Indian Hills	2,995	0	0	0	0	0	23	6	15	2	0
Irvine	2,385	4	0	0	2	2	18	9	5	4	1
Irvington	1,179	0	0	0	0	0	16	5	9	2	0
Jackson	2,100	1	0	0	0	1	88	11	67	10	0
Jamestown	1,807	0	0	0	0	0	13	3	8	2	0
Jeffersontown	27,400	31	0	4	18	9	662	87	491	84	0
Jenkins	2,043	0	0	0	0	0	0	0	0	0	0
Junction City	2,308	0	0	0	0	0	2	2	0	0	0
La Grange	8,831	8	0	1	5	2	148	23	117	8	2
Lakeside Park-Crestview Hills	6,133	0	0	0	0	0	95	10	83	2	0
Lancaster	3,874	8	0	0	1	7	55	16	35	4	0
Lawrenceburg	11,211	9	0	1	2	6	124	31	77	16	0
Lebanon	5,656	12	0	4	2	6	101	37	51	13	0
Lebanon Junction	1,946	0	0	0	0	0	3	0	1	2	0
Leitchfield	6,900	13	0	6	2	5	143	21	107	15	1
Lewisport	1,728	0	0	0	0	0	1	0	1	0	0
Lexington	322,332	1,131	29	200	547	355	12,191	2,087	8,831	1,273	41
London	8,184	18	0	3	8	7	363	77	244	42	0
Louisa	2,474	4	0	0	2	2	30	14	12	4	0
Louisville Metro[9]	684,362	4,428	109	175	1,326	2,818	28,211	5,623	18,724	3,864	5
Loyall	631	0	0	0	0	0	3	1	2	0	0
Ludlow	4,521	5	0	0	3	2	82	17	58	7	0
Madisonville	19,316	30	2	8	6	14	292	80	194	18	0
Manchester	1,382	1	0	0	0	1	23	4	13	6	0
Marion	2,972	4	0	1	1	2	72	28	40	4	0
Mayfield	9,991	39	1	4	11	23	538	129	388	21	1
Maysville	8,841	17	0	4	2	11	328	56	255	17	3
Middlesboro	9,534	21	0	5	6	10	551	55	472	24	0
Monticello	6,070	9	1	0	2	6	79	36	39	4	0
Morehead	7,915	4	0	4	0	0	150	18	126	6	0
Morganfield	3,541	2	2	0	0	0	15	6	7	2	0
Morgantown	2,454	4	0	1	1	2	29	6	18	5	1
Mount Sterling	7,298	14	1	3	5	5	254	30	210	14	3
Mount Vernon	2,482	1	0	0	1	0	26	14	6	6	0
Mount Washington	14,511	8	2	1	2	3	128	36	75	17	0
Muldraugh	995	0	0	0	0	0	16	2	13	1	1
Munfordville	1,660	0	0	0	0	0	16	4	9	3	0
Murray	19,205	26	0	8	9	9	583	110	452	21	0
Newport	15,202	42	1	9	22	10	618	96	471	51	1
Nicholasville	30,333	60	3	11	33	13	955	159	745	51	4
Oak Grove	7,347	34	0	7	15	12	415	80	316	19	0
Olive Hill	1,584	0	0	0	0	0	10	2	8	0	0
Owensboro	59,576	178	3	46	52	77	2,597	390	1,964	243	9
Owenton	1,539	0	0	0	0	0	5	1	4	0	0
Owingsville	1,605	1	0	0	0	1	12	4	5	3	0
Paducah	25,169	83	0	21	24	38	1,379	188	1,102	89	6
Paintsville	4,198	10	0	3	1	6	33	11	18	4	0
Paris	9,845	18	0	4	6	8	270	60	193	17	1
Park Hills	3,001	2	0	2	0	0	31	11	17	3	0
Pikeville	7,121	5	0	2	1	2	356	53	294	9	0
Pineville	1,739	3	0	1	1	1	43	14	26	3	0
Pioneer Village	2,931	1	0	0	1	0	22	6	11	5	0
Prestonsburg	3,517	11	0	0	1	10	44	17	19	8	0
Princeton	6,084	13	2	4	2	5	242	64	165	13	1
Prospect	4,905	0	0	0	0	0	48	6	40	2	0
Providence	3,088	0	0	0	0	0	27	8	17	2	0
Raceland	2,380	1	0	1	0	0	9	1	6	2	0

Table 8. Offenses Known to Law Enforcement, by Selected State and City, 2017—Continued

(Number.)

State/city	Population	Violent crime	Murder and nonnegligent manslaughter	Rape (revised definition)[1]	Robbery	Aggravated assault	Property crime	Burglary	Larceny-theft	Motor vehicle theft	Arson[2]
Radcliff	22,473	74	2	17	23	32	826	207	571	48	6
Ravenna	583	1	0	1	0	0	8	2	5	1	0
Richmond	35,161	92	2	24	30	36	1,226	216	899	111	3
Russell	3,229	5	0	1	3	1	45	3	41	1	0
Russell Springs	2,573	2	0	1	1	0	57	12	40	5	0
Russellville	7,006	24	0	2	9	13	249	45	194	10	1
Salyersville	1,787	2	0	0	0	2	1	0	1	0	1
Scottsville	4,446	9	0	2	1	6	211	59	139	13	1
Sebree	1,569	0	0	0	0	0	1	0	1	0	0
Shelbyville	15,758	28	0	2	18	8	297	59	212	26	1
Shepherdsville	12,204	25	0	6	10	9	348	65	245	38	1
Shively	15,830	65	2	10	36	17	653	115	410	128	0
Simpsonville	2,795	3	0	0	3	0	98	6	89	3	0
Smiths Grove	780	1	0	0	0	1	12	0	12	0	0
Somerset[5]	11,531	23	1	4	10	8			172	25	2
Southgate	3,856	3	0	0	2	1	25	3	15	7	0
South Shore	1,080	0	0	0	0	0	0	0	0	0	0
Springfield	3,167	6	0	3	2	1	12	3	7	2	0
Stanford	3,654	2	0	1	1	0	38	12	14	12	0
Stanton	2,658	3	0	0	0	3	52	18	31	3	0
St. Matthews	18,163	32	1	4	17	10	864	98	709	57	0
Sturgis	1,888	1	0	1	0	0	35	12	21	2	0
Taylor Mill	6,774	3	0	2	0	1	69	13	46	10	0
Taylorsville	1,264	1	0	0	0	1	43	35	8	0	1
Tompkinsville	2,261	1	0	0	0	1	1	1	0	0	0
Uniontown	943	4	0	1	0	3	20	6	11	3	0
Vanceburg	1,421	1	0	1	0	0	6	1	4	1	0
Versailles	26,320	27	0	13	5	9	506	124	357	25	0
Villa Hills	7,494	2	0	1	0	1	39	7	30	2	1
Vine Grove	6,055	0	0	0	0	0	67	15	45	7	1
Warsaw	1,689	1	0	0	0	1	11	5	5	1	0
West Buechel	1,280	7	0	0	6	1	81	2	67	12	0
West Liberty	3,388	1	0	0	0	1	11	4	4	3	0
West Point	860	3	0	0	0	3	17	4	11	2	2
Whitesburg	1,949	0	0	0	0	0	2	0	1	1	0
Wilder	3,077	3	0	1	1	1	36	2	32	2	0
Williamsburg	5,342	2	0	0	0	2	52	6	41	5	0
Williamstown	3,971	1	0	0	0	1	46	6	35	5	0
Wilmore	6,380	3	0	1	1	1	144	22	113	9	0
Winchester	18,478	41	2	6	17	16	1,125	186	858	81	7
LOUISIANA											
Abbeville[8]	12,491	98	0	4	8	86		131	0	6	0
Addis	5,117	9	0	0	0	9	0	0	0	0	0
Alexandria	47,860	690	17	9	129	535	4,197	987	2,953	257	0
Baker	13,584	51	2	4	8	37	366	51	303	12	4
Ball	4,011	8	0	0	1	7	12	7	3	2	0
Bastrop	10,458	158	1	4	31	122	986	357	597	32	6
Baton Rouge	227,403	2,335	87	100	868	1,280	12,721	3,226	8,504	991	166
Berwick	4,649	1	0	0	1	0	50	18	32	0	0
Blanchard	3,186	0	0	0	0	0	63	25	34	4	0
Bogalusa	11,865	154	1	12	24	117	619	198	385	36	1
Bossier City	69,632	535	4	48	79	404	3,283	451	2,549	283	2
Breaux Bridge	8,451	32	0	0	6	26	634	126	504	4	0
Broussard	12,125	27	0	1	7	19	271	94	165	12	0
Brusly	2,827	0	0	0	0	0	32	4	28	0	0
Carencro	8,944	20	2	1	4	13	211	24	173	14	0
Church Point	4,485	33	1	2	4	26	114	18	88	8	0
Clinton	1,571	5	0	0	1	4	5	2	3	0	0
Cottonport	1,945	0	0	0	0	0	24	10	13	1	0
Covington	10,571	29	1	1	1	26	241	27	205	9	0
Crowley	13,026	213	3	4	12	194	676	227	421	28	0
Cullen	1,107	2	0	0	0	2	4	4	0	0	0
Denham Springs	10,329	38	0	2	9	27	724	139	581	4	0
De Ridder	11,116	20	1	2	3	14	221	69	142	10	0
Epps	825	0	0	0	0	0	0	0	0	0	0
Erath	2,108	10	0	2	0	8	44	4	37	3	0
Eunice	10,258	49	1	1	12	35	543	91	431	21	2
Farmerville	3,841	21	0	0	3	18	230	33	196	1	0
Ferriday	3,300	14	0	0	5	9	90	28	62	0	0
Fisher	222	0	0	0	0	0	0	0	0	0	0
Florien	616	0	0	0	0	0	1	1	0	0	0
Folsom	826	3	0	0	1	2	9	0	8	1	0
Franklin	7,108	48	0	2	7	39	348	136	206	6	0
Franklinton	3,770	42	0	3	8	31	174	36	129	9	0
French Settlement	1,205	3	0	1	1	1	4	2	2	0	0
Georgetown	326	0	0	0	0	0	0	0	0	0	0
Golden Meadow	2,028	0	0	0	0	0	0	0	0	0	0
Gonzales	11,012	92	0	3	15	74	752	50	665	37	1
Gramercy[6]	3,425	9	0	0	0	9	124	41	75	8	0
Greenwood	3,145	3	0	0	0	3	87	24	56	7	0
Gretna	17,923	39	0	2	12	25	561	79	450	32	1
Hammond	20,712	308	2	24	64	218	2,006	655	1,272	79	2

Table 8. Offenses Known to Law Enforcement, by Selected State and City, 2017—Continued

(Number.)

State/city	Population	Violent crime	Murder and nonnegligent manslaughter	Rape (revised definition)[1]	Robbery	Aggravated assault	Property crime	Burglary	Larceny-theft	Motor vehicle theft	Arson[2]
Harahan	9,373	17	0	0	2	15	143	15	124	4	0
Haughton	3,301	0	0	0	0	0	15	3	8	4	0
Houma	34,083	123	2	20	18	83	1,245	168	1,027	50	4
Ida	211	0	0	0	0	0	0	0	0	0	0
Independence	1,910	17	0	0	2	15	92	30	54	8	0
Iowa	3,343	10	0	1	2	7	169	59	108	2	0
Jena	3,440	3	0	0	0	3	28	1	27	0	0
Jennings	10,074	21	0	0	0	21	384	63	320	1	1
Kaplan	4,621	17	0	1	6	10	53	11	41	1	0
Kenner	67,149	193	5	20	65	103	2,104	238	1,738	128	6
Kentwood	2,407	26	1	2	8	15	177	65	103	9	0
Kinder	2,430	6	0	1	1	4	78	9	67	2	1
Krotz Springs	1,205	2	0	0	0	2	44	10	31	3	1
Lafayette	128,691	721	22	21	175	503	5,863	1,011	4,555	297	26
Lake Charles	77,647	638	9	45	146	438	3,524	1,836	1,429	259	0
Lake Providence	3,648	36	0	0	2	34	9	6	3	0	0
Leesville	6,226	59	0	9	4	46	363	49	301	13	1
Lutcher	3,333	15	0	1	0	14	59	19	37	3	0
Mandeville	12,503	14	0	1	2	11	249	36	209	4	0
Mansfield	4,900	21	1	0	0	20	135	33	100	2	0
Many	2,780	20	0	1	0	19	156	16	135	5	0
Marion	752	5	0	0	0	5	10	3	5	2	0
Marksville	5,489	65	0	1	6	58	369	77	285	7	0
Minden	12,497	8	0	1	4	3	213	35	170	8	1
Monroe[6]	49,354	1,098	13	35	214	836	4,063	848	3,011	204	13
Montgomery	723	1	1	0	0	0	0	0	0	0	0
Moreauville	902	2	0	0	1	1	7	2	3	2	0
Morgan City	11,530	93	0	7	9	77	519	122	368	29	2
Natchitoches	18,284	217	1	0	20	196	1,182	249	908	25	6
New Orleans	397,447	4,457	157	575	1,308	2,417	16,867	2,229	12,107	2,531	41
Norwood	311	0	0	0	0	0	0	0	0	0	0
Oak Grove	1,620	9	0	0	2	7	99	23	73	3	3
Oil City	982	4	0	0	0	4	14	4	9	1	0
Olla	1,393	2	0	1	0	1	14	10	3	1	0
Opelousas	16,504	299	4	9	39	247	1,394	512	840	42	9
Patterson	6,053	32	0	0	0	32	166	0	165	1	0
Pearl River	2,575	16	0	2	1	13	52	6	40	6	0
Pineville	14,473	148	0	10	13	125	1,047	200	805	42	2
Plaquemine	6,727	30	3	1	0	26	198	39	154	5	0
Pollock	484	1	0	0	0	1	1	1	0	0	0
Ponchatoula	7,317	83	0	2	15	66	626	140	466	20	1
Port Allen	5,085	32	2	1	2	27	117	21	88	8	0
Port Vincent	773	0	0	0	0	0	28	14	10	4	0
Rayne	8,167	64	3	0	1	60	259	33	217	9	0
Ringgold	1,433	0	0	0	0	0	0	0	0	0	0
Ruston	22,438	123	1	3	7	112	720	152	555	13	0
Scott	8,780	6	1	0	1	4	201	49	135	17	0
Shreveport	193,937	1,850	52	152	498	1,148	10,813	2,256	7,673	884	91
Sibley	1,169	1	0	0	1	0	10	5	4	1	0
Slidell	28,163	97	3	9	22	63	995	111	841	43	1
Springhill	5,012	6	1	0	0	5	178	10	167	1	0
St. Gabriel	7,298	21	1	1	0	19	81	44	31	6	0
Sulphur	20,247	95	2	7	10	76	838	200	569	69	2
Tallulah	6,970	13	0	0	2	11	19	2	16	1	0
Thibodaux	14,617	61	1	3	14	43	578	89	468	21	1
Tickfaw	768	0	0	0	0	0	6	0	6	0	0
Vidalia	4,015	12	0	1	1	10	192	26	163	3	0
Ville Platte	7,244	40	0	0	5	35	489	91	379	19	0
Walker	6,447	52	0	5	4	43	368	48	306	14	0
Welsh	3,232	59	0	2	4	53	105	33	69	3	0
Westlake	4,676	11	0	2	2	7	123	35	88	0	0
West Monroe	12,891	84	0	4	13	67	1,041	255	737	49	0
Westwego	8,532	22	0	5	1	16	167	17	143	7	1
Wilson	571	0	0	0	0	0	0	0	0	0	0
Youngsville	13,679	16	0	4	1	11	169	32	135	2	0
Zachary	17,072	118	4	2	8	104	763	46	693	24	1
Zwolle	1,945	3	0	0	0	3	9	0	9	0	0
MAINE											
Ashland	1,217	0	0	0	0	0	12	5	4	3	0
Auburn	22,931	40	0	14	10	16	712	55	646	11	4
Augusta	18,394	55	0	18	8	29	557	70	478	9	0
Baileyville	1,433	3	0	1	0	2	13	4	7	2	0
Bangor	31,814	48	1	8	14	25	1,209	181	1,004	24	2
Bar Harbor	5,422	5	0	1	1	3	79	7	66	6	0
Bath	8,272	12	0	5	1	6	190	16	167	7	0
Belfast	6,644	3	0	0	0	3	97	30	64	3	0
Berwick	7,627	6	0	1	0	5	54	8	42	4	2
Biddeford	21,378	77	0	16	12	49	725	73	637	15	4
Boothbay Harbor	2,188	1	0	0	0	1	11	1	10	0	0
Brewer	9,048	8	0	0	2	6	262	7	248	7	0
Bridgton	5,414	4	0	3	1	0	105	34	67	4	0
Brunswick	20,711	29	0	11	4	14	314	50	254	10	2

Table 8. Offenses Known to Law Enforcement, by Selected State and City, 2017—Continued

(Number.)

State/city	Population	Violent crime	Murder and nonnegligent manslaughter	Rape (revised definition)[1]	Robbery	Aggravated assault	Property crime	Burglary	Larceny-theft	Motor vehicle theft	Arson[2]
Bucksport	4,924	3	1	0	0	2	55	9	44	2	0
Buxton	8,222	16	0	2	1	13	70	13	54	3	0
Calais	2,940	5	0	1	0	4	80	11	68	1	0
Camden	4,833	1	0	0	0	1	29	4	25	0	0
Cape Elizabeth	9,383	1	0	0	0	1	41	9	31	1	0
Caribou	7,666	7	1	0	3	3	105	16	84	5	0
Carrabassett Valley	781	0	0	0	0	0	33	2	27	4	0
Clinton	3,300	7	0	4	1	2	57	11	45	1	0
Cumberland	7,956	0	0	0	0	0	24	5	18	1	0
Damariscotta	2,166	1	0	0	0	1	64	5	59	0	0
Dexter	3,710	1	0	0	0	1	43	6	33	4	0
Dixfield	2,457	0	0	0	0	0	26	5	20	1	0
Dover-Foxcroft	4,045	2	0	1	0	1	96	10	81	5	0
East Millinocket	2,943	1	0	0	0	1	37	4	33	0	0
Eastport	1,243	0	0	0	0	0	5	2	2	1	0
Eliot	6,481	7	0	2	0	5	17	1	14	2	0
Ellsworth	7,940	5	0	0	0	5	271	28	241	2	0
Fairfield	6,560	5	0	1	1	3	152	25	120	7	0
Falmouth	12,260	4	0	2	0	2	122	23	97	2	0
Farmington	7,548	13	0	6	0	7	131	9	117	5	0
Fort Fairfield	3,294	6	0	1	1	4	26	9	17	0	1
Fort Kent	3,900	0	0	0	0	0	33	6	25	2	0
Freeport	8,520	9	0	2	2	5	150	12	137	1	0
Fryeburg	3,389	3	0	1	0	2	23	4	17	2	0
Gardiner	5,592	2	0	0	0	2	85	18	66	1	0
Gorham	17,554	11	0	0	1	10	110	13	93	4	0
Gouldsboro	1,750	0	0	0	0	0	10	3	7	0	0
Greenville	1,585	0	0	0	0	0	16	2	13	1	0
Hallowell	2,318	1	0	1	0	0	29	4	23	2	0
Hampden	7,363	0	0	0	0	0	54	24	27	3	0
Holden	3,049	2	0	0	0	2	22	8	14	0	0
Houlton	5,781	36	0	6	0	30	126	19	101	6	1
Islesboro	565	0	0	0	0	0	10	1	8	1	0
Jay	4,628	9	1	0	0	8	46	8	37	1	0
Kennebunk	11,406	7	0	4	0	3	46	6	38	2	0
Kennebunkport	3,604	1	0	0	1	0	20	4	16	0	0
Kittery[6]	9,669	13	0	5	4	4	157	5	149	3	0
Lewiston	36,067	98	0	24	31	43	788	164	582	42	5
Limestone	2,165	0	0	0	0	0	15	5	9	1	0
Lincoln	4,944	2	0	2	0	0	119	26	91	2	0
Lisbon	8,820	9	0	7	1	1	118	19	93	6	0
Livermore Falls	3,104	4	0	1	1	2	66	13	51	2	0
Machias	2,087	4	0	2	0	2	42	9	33	0	0
Madawaska	3,760	0	0	0	0	0	19	3	16	0	0
Mechanic Falls	2,986	1	0	1	0	0	31	7	20	4	0
Mexico	2,584	7	0	3	0	4	160	24	136	0	0
Milbridge	1,277	0	0	0	0	0	5	3	2	0	0
Millinocket	4,267	3	1	0	0	2	56	6	46	4	0
Milo	2,256	0	0	0	0	0	7	1	6	0	0
Monmouth	4,036	3	0	1	0	2	24	8	14	2	0
Newport	3,224	2	0	1	0	1	55	4	47	4	0
North Berwick	4,690	3	0	1	1	1	21	1	18	2	0
Norway	4,902	5	0	2	0	3	75	8	65	2	0
Oakland	6,145	9	0	4	1	4	69	16	47	6	0
Ogunquit	922	1	0	1	0	0	33	3	30	0	0
Old Orchard Beach	8,842	31	0	8	1	22	149	21	121	7	1
Old Town	7,466	9	0	3	2	4	71	9	61	1	0
Orono	11,400	9	0	5	2	2	79	13	59	7	0
Oxford	4,037	0	0	0	0	0	128	7	119	2	0
Paris	5,119	6	0	4	0	2	79	13	52	14	0
Phippsburg	2,246	0	0	0	0	0	23	5	16	2	0
Pittsfield	4,076	1	0	0	1	0	45	7	36	2	0
Portland	67,079	186	2	48	55	81	1,767	166	1,504	97	14
Presque Isle	9,016	34	0	13	0	21	192	21	167	4	0
Rangeley	1,159	0	0	0	0	0	14	1	12	1	0
Richmond	3,412	2	1	0	0	1	12	6	5	1	0
Rockland	7,161	8	0	1	0	7	165	14	146	5	0
Rockport	3,389	1	0	0	0	1	13	3	10	0	0
Rumford	5,692	8	0	3	2	3	208	32	171	5	0
Sabattus	5,038	5	0	2	0	3	35	14	21	0	0
Saco	19,332	27	1	14	3	9	334	58	253	23	0
Sanford	20,963	48	0	19	8	21	564	69	483	12	2
Scarborough	20,215	8	0	5	2	1	304	20	276	8	1
Searsport	2,638	0	0	0	0	0	38	9	20	9	0
Skowhegan	8,255	18	0	4	3	11	287	47	229	11	2
South Berwick	7,469	3	0	1	0	2	30	8	21	1	3
South Portland	25,679	56	0	4	13	39	578	78	481	19	1
Southwest Harbor	1,780	0	0	0	0	0	22	3	19	0	0
Thomaston	2,772	1	0	1	0	0	82	6	76	0	0
Topsham	8,790	2	0	0	0	2	130	21	104	5	0
Van Buren	2,068	0	0	0	0	0	15	1	13	1	0
Veazie	1,827	1	0	1	0	0	19	7	10	2	0
Waldoboro	5,023	6	0	0	1	5	52	17	32	3	0

Table 8. Offenses Known to Law Enforcement, by Selected State and City, 2017—Continued

(Number.)

State/city	Population	Violent crime	Murder and nonnegligent manslaughter	Rape (revised definition)[1]	Robbery	Aggravated assault	Property crime	Burglary	Larceny-theft	Motor vehicle theft	Arson[2]
Washburn	1,558	0	0	0	0	0	2	1	1	0	0
Waterville	16,522	32	0	9	10	13	694	64	618	12	2
Wells	10,287	4	0	1	0	3	85	19	63	3	0
Westbrook	18,560	34	0	15	4	15	395	41	344	10	0
Wilton	3,944	6	0	2	0	4	40	6	29	5	0
Windham	18,175	10	0	4	1	5	270	27	236	7	0
Winslow	7,534	10	0	5	1	4	92	12	76	4	1
Winter Harbor	515	0	0	0	0	0	0	0	0	0	0
Winthrop	5,950	5	0	0	1	4	64	21	39	4	0
Wiscasset	3,680	1	1	0	0	0	25	8	16	1	0
Yarmouth	8,594	6	0	2	0	4	61	6	52	3	0
York	13,018	9	0	2	0	7	143	40	98	5	2
MARYLAND											
Aberdeen	15,720	74	0	5	25	44	221	39	176	6	4
Annapolis	39,596	221	7	15	63	136	933	131	762	40	9
Baltimore	613,217	12,430	342	382	5,879	5,827	30,220	8,041	17,008	5,171	261
Baltimore City Sheriff		0	0	0	0	0	0	0	0	0	0
Bel Air	10,109	27	0	1	11	15	265	25	238	2	6
Berlin	4,628	2	0	0	2	0	85	5	80	0	0
Berwyn Heights	3,300	6	0	0	3	3	51	20	27	4	0
Bladensburg	9,683	76	1	3	30	42	315	38	211	66	0
Boonsboro	3,521	2	0	0	0	2	26	5	21	0	0
Bowie	58,891	81	4	3	35	39	759	76	606	77	0
Brentwood	3,205	6	0	0	4	2	19	6	9	4	0
Brunswick	6,219	24	0	0	1	23	115	30	78	7	1
Cambridge	12,471	162	0	4	27	131	853	199	628	26	14
Capitol Heights	4,582	12	0	0	8	4	43	12	25	6	0
Centreville	4,753	9	0	0	0	9	66	8	56	2	2
Chestertown	5,056	15	0	3	5	7	80	29	48	3	2
Cheverly	6,517	16	0	0	9	7	159	25	117	17	1
Chevy Chase Village	2,080	0	0	0	0	0	35	5	28	2	0
Colmar Manor	1,474	11	0	0	6	5	28	2	20	6	1
Cottage City	1,378	1	0	0	0	1	20	3	14	3	0
Crisfield	2,616	2	0	1	0	1	17	4	13	0	2
Cumberland	19,842	150	1	7	41	101	1,240	248	976	16	7
Delmar	3,216	18	0	1	5	12	89	20	67	2	2
Denton	4,385	5	0	0	2	3	188	19	161	8	1
District Heights	6,064	26	4	0	4	18	67	24	32	11	0
Easton	16,598	38	0	7	10	21	454	78	368	8	3
Edmonston	1,528	4	0	0	1	3	44	6	31	7	0
Elkton	15,794	184	1	7	46	130	977	187	741	49	20
Fairmount Heights	1,579	4	0	0	2	2	21	2	16	3	0
Federalsburg	2,664	17	0	2	0	15	92	17	67	8	1
Forest Heights	2,597	4	0	0	1	3	39	23	12	4	0
Frederick	70,860	468	1	28	87	352	1,298	148	1,107	43	
Frostburg	8,622	10	0	0	2	8	174	50	120	4	0
Fruitland	5,298	15	0	0	3	12	259	10	247	2	0
Glenarden	6,228	14	0	0	3	11	72	16	46	10	0
Greenbelt	24,099	144	4	9	79	52	775	98	610	67	0
Greensboro	1,876	3	0	0	1	2	30	9	21	0	3
Hagerstown	40,568	249	8	18	119	104	1,036	244	668	124	14
Hancock	1,552	3	0	0	0	3	19	3	16	0	1
Havre de Grace	13,610	40	2	7	4	27	192	33	156	3	3
Hurlock	2,019	4	0	0	0	4	118	17	89	12	1
Hyattsville	18,579	90	1	2	61	26	1,020	79	863	78	0
Landover Hills	1,821	6	0	0	3	3	56	19	33	4	0
La Plata	9,324	40	0	1	17	22	322	43	250	29	1
Laurel	25,997	159	1	9	55	94	930	84	788	58	1
Lonaconing	1,125	0	0	0	0	0	0	0	0	0	2
Luke	63	0	0	0	0	0	0	0	0	0	0
Manchester	4,820	0	0	0	0	0	17	3	13	1	0
New Carrollton	12,971	43	1	1	16	25	257	66	158	33	0
North East	3,661	4	0	0	2	2	82	7	71	4	7
Oakland	1,867	3	0	0	0	3	50	6	44	0	3
Ocean City	6,982	107	1	19	32	55	1,025	113	894	18	2
Ocean Pines	12,263	21	0	2	1	18	82	9	72	1	0
Oxford	612	0	0	0	0	0	26	0	1	25	0
Perryville	4,432	6	0	0	1	5	99	15	77	7	4
Pocomoke City	4,088	11	1	1	5	4	223	37	185	1	0
Princess Anne	3,639	33	0	5	9	19	136	42	93	1	2
Ridgely	1,622	1	0	0	0	1	34	9	24	1	0
Rising Sun	2,800	11	0	0	0	11	18	5	12	1	2
Riverdale Park	7,358	39	1	1	5	32	153	26	101	26	0
Rock Hall	1,297	4	0	0	0	4	14	4	10	0	0
Salisbury	33,558	326	7	21	94	204	1,784	273	1,443	68	16
Seat Pleasant	4,806	42	2	0	15	25	120	38	62	20	2
Smithsburg	3,002	2	0	1	1	0	22	5	17	0	2
Snow Hill	2,065	6	0	0	0	6	35	3	30	2	0
St. Michaels	1,039	3	0	1	1	1	30	1	29	0	0
Sykesville	3,940	31	0	0	0	31	33	20	11	2	3
Takoma Park	17,933	55	0	3	31	21	449	55	361	33	0
Taneytown	6,762	1	0	0	0	1	77	9	67	1	

Table 8. Offenses Known to Law Enforcement, by Selected State and City, 2017—Continued

(Number.)

State/city	Population	Violent crime	Murder and nonnegligent manslaughter	Rape (revised definition)[1]	Robbery	Aggravated assault	Property crime	Burglary	Larceny-theft	Motor vehicle theft	Arson[2]
Thurmont	6,584	8	0	0	0	8	53	4	48	1	0
Trappe	1,005	0	0	0	0	0	1	0	1	0	0
University Park	2,677	8	0	0	8	0	33	17	15	1	0
Upper Marlboro	672	1	0	0	0	1	4	1	2	1	0
Westminster	18,682	121	0	0	9	112	562	77	470	15	12
MASSACHUSETTS											
Abington	16,369	33	0	4	6	23	158	26	120	12	0
Acton	23,937	23	0	1	1	21	170	33	134	3	1
Acushnet	10,547	32	0	4	3	25	101	28	62	11	0
Adams	8,051	20	0	10	1	9	114	46	60	8	0
Agawam	28,839	66	0	3	9	54	519	178	313	28	3
Amesbury	17,636	50	0	6	0	44	120	12	105	3	0
Amherst	40,313	100	0	20	3	77	263	54	203	6	3
Andover	35,898	72	0	5	3	64	287	25	239	23	1
Arlington	45,449	38	0	7	7	24	257	80	162	15	0
Ashburnham	6,255	7	0	1	1	5	50	9	40	1	0
Ashland	17,878	18	0	4	1	13	92	11	73	8	1
Athol	11,630	58	0	6	3	49	202	47	150	5	2
Attleboro	44,607	120	1	17	18	84	593	118	457	18	1
Auburn	16,563	41	0	4	2	35	347	33	301	13	3
Avon	4,560	5	0	0	2	3	60	7	49	4	
Ayer	8,240	23	0	1	3	19	81	20	59	2	0
Barnstable	44,142	197	1	18	13	165	547	79	446	22	4
Bedford	14,607	9	0	1	4	4	59	9	47	3	0
Belchertown	15,097	25	0	5	2	18	91	23	65	3	0
Bellingham	17,121	28	0	4	3	21	263	17	238	8	0
Belmont	26,432	12	0	4	3	5	210	85	116	9	0
Berkley	6,745	12	0	5	2	5	40	9	26	5	0
Berlin	3,175	3	0	0	1	2	45	3	38	4	0
Bernardston	2,082	1	0	1	0	0	28	8	20	0	0
Beverly	41,678	48	0	6	6	36	235	25	202	8	0
Billerica	43,127	40	1	5	8	26	244	52	177	15	2
Blackstone	9,079	13	0	1	1	11	59	11	46	2	0
Bolton	5,272	5	0	0	1	4	36	5	29	2	0
Boston	682,903	4,570	57	290	1,404	2,819	14,266	2,109	10,952	1,205	
Bourne	19,867	41	0	4	5	32	262	103	149	10	1
Boxborough	5,972	18	0	3	0	15	24	3	18	3	0
Boxford	8,333	0	0	0	0	0	22	1	21	0	0
Boylston	4,610	2	0	0	0	2	16	1	14	1	0
Braintree	37,579	48	0	2	5	41	665	45	584	36	0
Brewster	9,895	22	0	14	0	8	98	22	76	0	0
Bridgewater	27,769	78	0	11	2	65	155	20	120	15	0
Brimfield	3,764	7	0	0	0	7	18	8	10	0	0
Brockton	96,016	917	7	93	172	645	1,961	327	1,250	384	16
Brookline	59,233	45	0	1	12	32	665	91	563	11	1
Burlington	26,678	53	0	7	5	41	485	26	447	12	1
Cambridge	111,707	313	2	17	101	193	2,031	252	1,685	94	3
Canton	23,551	90	0	8	8	74	149	22	122	5	0
Carver	11,671	25	0	5	1	19	114	26	86	2	1
Charlton	13,523	19	0	4	2	13	89	10	71	8	1
Chatham	6,158	5	0	2	0	3	90	8	81	1	0
Chelmsford	35,392	45	0	3	5	37	490	48	419	23	1
Chelsea	40,514	315	3	31	107	174	662	97	491	74	2
Chesterfield	1,266	0	0	0	0	0	6	3	3	0	0
Chicopee	56,255	289	3	35	60	191	1,381	325	928	128	0
Chilmark	925	2	0	0	0	2	14	1	13	0	0
Clinton	13,839	6	0	0	1	5	34	5	26	3	0
Cohasset	8,598	6	0	3	0	3	75	20	55	0	0
Concord	20,193	14	0	0	0	14	103	9	93	1	0
Dalton	6,602	15	0	0	0	15	42	17	24	1	0
Danvers	28,168	48	0	4	7	37	498	32	440	26	2
Dartmouth	34,802	73	0	8	11	54	707	87	581	39	5
Dedham	25,358	10	0	2	6	2	427	15	397	15	0
Deerfield	4,971	11	0	0	0	11	52	11	41	0	0
Dennis	13,976	58	0	7	2	49	291	86	191	14	0
Douglas	8,795	14	0	0	0	14	42	12	29	1	0
Dover	6,053	1	0	0	0	1	18	1	15	2	0
Dracut	31,685	41	0	3	5	33	320	63	237	20	0
Dudley	11,801	37	0	10	3	24	56	17	31	8	0
Dunstable	3,389	2	0	0	1	1	20	5	13	2	0
Duxbury	16,085	9	0	2	1	6	102	22	78	2	0
East Bridgewater	14,573	17	0	2	0	15	133	16	112	5	1
East Brookfield	2,180	4	0	2	0	2	14	5	9	0	0
Eastham	4,899	11	0	1	1	9	51	4	46	1	0
Easthampton	16,061	41	0	5	3	33	170	34	125	11	1
East Longmeadow	16,288	24	0	4	3	17	279	51	214	14	2
Easton	24,176	40	0	6	6	28	160	28	125	7	0
Edgartown	4,323	16	0	2	0	14	71	11	57	3	0
Erving	1,763	4	0	2	0	2	25	8	14	3	0
Everett	47,185	157	2	18	29	108	662	114	477	71	2
Fairhaven	16,188	40	1	8	1	30	338	44	276	18	0
Fall River	89,012	880	3	53	187	637	1,564	426	909	229	29

Table 8. Offenses Known to Law Enforcement, by Selected State and City, 2017—Continued

(Number.)

State/city	Population	Violent crime	Murder and nonnegligent manslaughter	Rape (revised definition)[1]	Robbery	Aggravated assault	Property crime	Burglary	Larceny-theft	Motor vehicle theft	Arson[2]
Falmouth	31,487	123	0	14	3	106	468	190	246	32	4
Fitchburg	40,445	299	0	45	47	207	741	169	516	56	7
Foxborough	17,636	45	1	4	0	40	192	45	138	9	1
Framingham	72,153	235	0	14	20	201	748	132	549	67	2
Franklin	33,397	9	0	0	1	8	74	20	51	3	0
Freetown	9,343	23	0	4	2	17	100	30	58	12	1
Gardner	20,491	99	1	18	7	73	336	82	234	20	5
Georgetown	8,715	4	0	1	0	3	51	7	42	2	0
Gloucester	29,980	82	0	5	7	70	207	19	181	7	1
Goshen	1,074	1	0	0	0	1	7	4	3	0	0
Grafton	18,763	22	0	6	1	15	60	11	43	6	0
Granby	6,379	10	0	1	0	9	34	9	22	3	0
Great Barrington	6,815	24	0	3	2	19	64	10	49	5	1
Greenfield	17,462	110	0	21	14	75	333	42	280	11	6
Groton	11,411	6	4	1	0	1	34	6	28	0	1
Hadley	5,382	17	0	2	2	13	134	11	117	6	2
Halifax	7,963	6	0	0	0	6	73	13	58	2	0
Hamilton	8,216	4	0	1	0	3	39	7	31	1	1
Hampden	5,217	6	0	0	0	6	39	4	28	7	0
Hanover	14,597	5	0	0	0	5	102	10	82	10	1
Hanson	10,860	31	0	5	1	25	49	15	32	2	1
Hardwick	4,031	24	0	3	0	21	35	9	25	1	0
Harvard	6,572	1	0	0	0	1	27	11	16	0	0
Harwich	12,150	23	0	1	0	22	151	58	88	5	0
Haverhill	63,244	391	3	15	40	333	917	201	597	119	4
Hingham	23,392	13	0	1	1	11	234	54	175	5	2
Holbrook	11,064	39	0	3	9	27	129	13	108	8	1
Holden	19,062	10	0	0	1	9	52	9	39	4	1
Holland	2,502	1	0	0	0	1	20	7	12	1	0
Holliston	14,736	8	0	1	2	5	30	2	28	0	0
Holyoke	40,451	438	4	32	96	306	1,946	297	1,538	111	9
Hopedale	5,959	7	0	1	0	6	26	5	19	2	1
Hopkinton	17,348	0	0	0	0	0	59	2	57	0	0
Hudson	19,963	7	0	2	1	4	150	21	127	2	1
Hull	10,553	29	1	10	2	16	79	11	61	7	0
Ipswich	13,951	9	0	1	0	8	80	15	62	3	1
Kingston	13,615	27	0	2	3	22	162	28	129	5	1
Lakeville	11,502	18	0	5	3	10	102	27	69	6	1
Lancaster	8,212	10	0	2	1	7	56	13	40	3	0
Lawrence	80,890	585	11	30	151	393	1,391	224	759	408	
Lee	5,749	8	0	1	0	7	105	16	85	4	0
Leicester	11,369	27	0	2	2	23	170	13	152	5	0
Lenox	4,947	11	0	3	1	7	83	16	64	3	0
Leominster	41,846	234	2	18	20	194	940	121	770	49	7
Leverett	1,835	0	0	0	0	0	7	3	4	0	0
Lincoln	6,860	2	0	0	0	2	40	5	35	0	0
Littleton	10,196	11	0	2	0	9	75	21	50	4	0
Longmeadow	15,848	6	0	2	2	2	147	33	109	5	0
Lowell	111,294	322	1	13	144	164	2,198	474	1,370	354	10
Ludlow	21,529	52	0	2	4	46	213	44	145	24	1
Lunenburg	11,477	25	0	5	0	20	158	35	115	8	1
Lynn	93,140	666	12	28	164	462	1,631	299	1,101	231	8
Lynnfield	13,042	7	0	0	2	5	104	5	93	6	0
Malden	61,098	207	1	7	35	164	780	119	588	73	0
Manchester-by-the-Sea	5,435	2	0	1	0	1	14	0	14	0	0
Mansfield	23,847	39	0	7	3	29	249	31	209	9	0
Marblehead	20,618	36	0	4	0	32	155	25	128	2	0
Marion	5,124	8	0	0	0	8	54	15	35	4	0
Marlborough	39,919	152	0	15	8	129	610	67	514	29	4
Marshfield	25,929	31	0	5	2	24	85	15	67	3	2
Mashpee	14,272	40	1	3	2	34	185	18	157	10	0
Mattapoisett	6,354	11	0	2	0	9	46	13	31	2	0
Maynard	10,756	21	0	3	0	18	54	8	43	3	0
Medford	57,418	88	0	5	14	69	663	115	485	63	1
Medway	13,407	6	0	2	0	4	53	12	38	3	0
Melrose	28,101	23	0	1	3	19	216	23	174	19	3
Mendon	6,069	9	0	1	0	8	43	11	27	5	0
Merrimac	6,948	2	0	2	0	0	26	8	16	2	0
Methuen	50,396	94	0	0	26	68	670	78	530	62	0
Middleboro	25,084	88	0	16	3	69	243	36	183	24	2
Middleton	9,788	15	1	0	0	14	67	4	56	7	0
Milford	28,772	58	2	13	2	41	308	38	251	19	1
Millbury	13,626	21	0	4	1	16	166	19	137	10	2
Millville	3,254	1	0	1	0	0	14	2	11	1	0
Milton	27,420	15	0	1	7	7	215	58	146	11	0
Monson	8,842	31	0	3	2	26	72	27	41	4	1
Montague	8,211	64	0	8	0	56	126	51	71	4	0
Nahant	3,500	12	0	1	1	10	27	5	20	2	1
Nantucket	11,165	47	0	7	0	40	264	34	213	17	5
Natick	36,705	39	0	4	2	33	455	46	396	13	1
Needham	31,054	9	1	2	0	6	194	6	187	1	0
New Bedford	95,107	633	8	37	241	347	2,717	570	1,971	176	35
Newbury	7,071	9	0	3	0	6	40	12	26	2	0

Table 8. Offenses Known to Law Enforcement, by Selected State and City, 2017—Continued

(Number.)

State/city	Population	Violent crime	Murder and nonnegligent manslaughter	Rape (revised definition)[1]	Robbery	Aggravated assault	Property crime	Burglary	Larceny-theft	Motor vehicle theft	Arson[2]
Newburyport	18,092	26	0	4	2	20	219	25	184	10	0
Newton	89,736	49	0	5	5	39	576	87	471	18	2
Norfolk	11,815	1	0	1	0	0	35	7	27	1	1
North Adams	12,948	193	0	15	11	167	399	115	280	4	2
Northampton	28,458	165	0	29	21	115	555	75	466	14	3
North Andover	31,035	27	0	3	2	22	164	19	136	9	0
North Attleboro	29,158	27	0	3	0	24	475	50	411	14	0
Northborough	15,109	3	0	3	0	0	155	4	148	3	1
Northbridge	16,711	39	0	9	1	29	202	28	161	13	0
Northfield	2,966	6	0	0	0	6	27	8	19	0	1
North Reading	15,780	24	0	6	5	13	65	6	52	7	0
Norton	19,654	1	0	0	0	1	18	12	5	1	0
Norwell	11,150	3	0	1	0	2	43	6	35	2	0
Norwood	29,194	42	0	4	2	36	293	25	245	23	0
Oakham	1,941	2	0	0	0	2	3	1	2	0	0
Orange	7,569	23	0	1	0	22	104	38	62	4	1
Orleans	5,837	8	0	3	1	4	69	21	48	0	0
Oxford	13,955	21	0	1	2	18	143	24	115	4	1
Palmer	12,136	50	0	7	3	40	129	34	86	9	0
Paxton	4,891	2	0	0	0	2	17	5	12	0	0
Peabody	52,721	153	2	12	17	122	624	83	496	45	0
Pembroke	18,454	12	0	2	0	10	105	9	91	5	1
Pepperell	12,267	15	0	2	1	12	79	20	52	7	1
Pittsfield	42,546	375	4	50	43	278	1,092	399	656	37	5
Plainville	9,334	12	0	1	1	10	126	16	105	5	0
Plymouth	59,803	151	1	21	10	119	591	81	486	24	0
Plympton	2,976	4	0	1	0	3	16	6	9	1	0
Princeton	3,472	1	0	0	0	1	17	4	12	1	0
Provincetown	2,993	23	0	3	0	20	127	12	111	4	0
Quincy	93,966	383	0	24	65	294	1,564	322	1,154	88	6
Randolph	33,837	121	1	10	20	90	483	93	351	39	0
Raynham	14,048	34	0	6	4	24	231	43	177	11	0
Reading	26,033	8	0	2	2	4	157	25	129	3	0
Rehoboth	12,153	10	0	1	0	9	63	15	41	7	1
Revere	53,425	248	2	16	42	188	1,010	134	770	106	1
Rochester	5,593	9	0	0	0	9	40	13	25	2	0
Rockport	7,255	7	0	3	0	4	12	0	12	0	1
Rowley	6,378	7	0	2	1	4	39	4	31	4	0
Rutland	8,687	18	0	3	0	15	70	19	47	4	1
Salem	43,385	116	0	19	28	69	951	113	787	51	3
Salisbury	9,517	33	0	2	2	29	121	18	84	19	1
Sandwich	20,362	34	0	5	0	29	155	30	117	8	0
Saugus	28,241	73	0	4	11	58	478	41	402	35	0
Seekonk	15,521	24	0	2	6	16	264	22	225	17	0
Sharon	18,419	15	0	3	4	8	45	4	39	2	0
Shelburne	1,829	0	0	0	0	0	16	5	9	2	0
Sherborn	4,318	6	0	1	0	5	7	0	7	0	0
Shirley	7,499	16	1	3	1	11	41	4	35	2	1
Shrewsbury	36,974	3	0	0	0	3	128	21	100	7	0
Somerset	18,239	35	0	15	2	18	169	18	138	13	1
Somerville	82,326	191	1	16	41	133	1,071	174	808	89	5
Southampton	6,263	11	0	3	0	8	41	13	25	3	1
Southborough	10,148	7	0	2	1	4	60	16	44	0	0
Southbridge	16,860	88	0	11	3	74	283	55	213	15	2
South Hadley	17,804	27	0	2	4	21	251	95	148	8	1
Southwick	9,778	11	0	3	0	8	75	23	51	1	0
Spencer	11,920	19	0	4	0	15	73	14	52	7	1
Springfield	154,562	1,351	14	73	380	884	4,594	1,183	2,902	509	37
Sterling	8,102	9	0	2	0	7	79	12	60	7	2
Stockbridge	1,919	5	0	3	0	2	38	12	25	1	0
Stoneham	22,077	27	0	1	1	25	199	72	118	9	0
Stoughton	28,678	104	0	8	9	87	389	29	333	27	4
Stow	7,196	5	0	0	0	5	31	7	19	5	0
Sturbridge	9,605	21	0	2	2	17	129	19	99	11	1
Sudbury	19,120	11	0	1	0	10	72	14	57	1	0
Sunderland	3,627	6	0	2	2	2	27	10	15	2	0
Sutton	9,401	9	0	1	0	8	84	29	48	7	1
Swampscott	15,016	14	0	2	1	11	181	17	159	5	0
Swansea	16,597	22	0	1	6	15	259	34	210	15	2
Taunton	57,047	220	0	15	28	177	492	133	299	60	3
Templeton	8,184	9	0	0	0	9	53	16	33	4	0
Tewksbury	31,245	85	0	23	10	52	331	52	258	21	2
Tisbury	4,114	26	0	0	0	26	75	14	56	5	0
Topsfield	6,604	7	0	0	0	7	24	6	18	0	0
Townsend	9,626	8	0	3	0	5	52	27	24	1	1
Truro	2,018	14	0	2	0	12	23	7	13	3	0
Tyngsboro	12,490	8	0	0	0	8	95	19	70	6	1
Upton	7,816	14	0	2	1	11	33	7	24	2	1
Wakefield	27,049	46	0	5	3	38	195	36	150	9	0
Wales	1,900	1	0	1	0	0	5	3	2	0	0
Walpole	25,312	59	0	10	2	47	249	29	209	11	0
Waltham	63,413	98	1	16	14	67	609	118	447	44	2
Ware	9,907	45	0	0	5	40	193	21	164	8	2

Table 8. Offenses Known to Law Enforcement, by Selected State and City, 2017—Continued

(Number.)

State/city	Population	Violent crime	Murder and nonnegligent manslaughter	Rape (revised definition)[1]	Robbery	Aggravated assault	Property crime	Burglary	Larceny-theft	Motor vehicle theft	Arson[2]
Wareham	22,743	129	0	9	6	114	425	75	326	24	2
Watertown	35,586	32	0	5	5	22	341	37	289	15	0
Wayland	13,976	2	0	0	0	2	9	5	1	3	0
Webster	16,883	123	0	6	11	106	252	51	186	15	4
Wellesley	29,434	12	0	1	3	8	131	15	111	5	0
Wellfleet	2,757	3	0	0	1	2	41	17	22	2	2
Wenham	5,242	2	0	0	1	1	8	0	8	0	0
Westborough	19,074	10	0	1	1	8	151	17	126	8	0
West Boylston	7,856	9	0	1	1	7	56	5	46	5	0
West Bridgewater	7,189	18	1	1	1	15	92	12	75	5	0
Westfield	41,735	105	0	21	14	70	559	96	432	31	3
Westford	24,639	9	0	1	2	6	76	14	57	5	1
Westminster	7,699	20	0	1	1	18	64	7	57	0	0
West Newbury	4,671	9	0	1	0	8	19	3	15	1	0
Weston	12,249	5	0	3	0	2	37	8	27	2	0
Westport	15,919	23	0	7	3	13	147	37	100	10	2
West Springfield	28,635	174	1	23	21	129	1,105	121	917	67	5
West Tisbury	2,920	9	0	2	0	7	26	5	19	2	0
Westwood	16,347	19	0	6	1	12	165	10	153	2	0
Weymouth	56,382	147	1	15	17	114	577	66	478	33	2
Whately	1,531	1	0	0	0	1	17	9	7	1	0
Whitman	15,000	25	0	3	0	22	96	15	76	5	1
Wilbraham	14,749	13	0	4	2	7	179	42	126	11	1
Williamstown	7,756	10	0	4	0	6	138	6	131	1	1
Wilmington	23,791	30	0	4	6	20	175	26	141	8	0
Winchendon	10,812	33	0	7	2	24	170	16	145	9	2
Winchester	23,059	9	0	1	1	7	119	18	99	2	1
Winthrop	18,319	36	0	1	4	31	111	25	78	8	0
Woburn	39,677	63	0	3	5	55	433	39	355	39	0
Worcester	185,107	1,345	5	42	324	974	4,047	866	2,784	397	7
Wrentham	11,838	8	0	0	0	8	198	14	175	9	0
Yarmouth	23,370	159	1	14	11	133	372	76	287	9	3
MICHIGAN											
Addison Township	6,542	2	0	0	0	2	26	12	9	5	0
Adrian Township	6,289	5	0	1	0	4	18	4	13	1	0
Akron	387	1	0	1	0	0	8	0	8	0	0
Albion	8,293	104	0	12	8	84	312	69	228	15	2
Allegan	5,085	12	0	3	0	9	82	3	77	2	1
Allen Park	27,062	45	0	8	10	27	626	50	516	60	2
Alma	9,113	30	0	12	3	15	113	15	96	2	2
Almont	2,780	14	0	0	0	14	40	10	27	3	0
Alpena	10,066	48	0	25	0	23	239	37	198	4	0
Ann Arbor	121,930	259	0	57	53	149	2,108	278	1,731	99	7
Argentine Township	6,544	4	0	0	0	4	60	20	38	2	0
Armada	1,742	0	0	0	0	0	2	0	1	1	0
Auburn Hills	23,034	63	0	11	8	44	656	45	585	26	0
Au Gres	848	0	0	0	0	0	2	0	2	0	0
Bad Axe	2,956	7	0	3	1	3	115	5	107	3	0
Bancroft	515	0	0	0	0	0	5	2	3	0	0
Bangor	1,839	10	0	3	0	7	62	15	45	2	1
Baroda-Lake Township	3,762	15	0	6	0	9	51	15	33	3	1
Barryton	360	0	0	0	0	0	4	1	3	0	0
Barry Township	3,431	7	0	4	0	3	13	5	6	2	0
Bath Township	12,759	19	0	7	5	7	123	41	78	4	2
Battle Creek	60,852	580	3	73	72	432	2,251	501	1,656	94	24
Bay City	33,286	242	1	57	35	149	998	223	716	59	10
Beaverton	1,044	2	0	0	0	2	9	2	7	0	0
Belding	5,772	16	0	4	2	10	85	17	65	3	1
Bellaire	1,061	0	0	0	0	0	8	0	8	0	0
Belleville	3,832	16	0	5	1	10	83	10	66	7	0
Bellevue	1,298	1	0	0	0	1	6	1	5	0	0
Benton Harbor	9,899	218	3	23	36	156	392	131	228	33	10
Benton Township	14,354	180	1	23	32	124	837	118	672	47	3
Berkley	15,322	7	0	1	1	5	104	12	84	8	0
Berrien Springs-Oronoko Township	9,039	8	0	6	0	2	73	11	60	2	0
Beverly Hills	10,504	1	0	1	0	0	69	5	64	0	0
Big Rapids	10,437	24	0	7	1	16	143	23	119	1	8
Birch Run	1,452	1	0	0	0	1	116	3	113	0	0
Birmingham	21,162	10	0	3	4	3	194	10	179	5	0
Blackman Township	36,908	127	0	33	9	85	1,140	150	947	43	5
Blissfield	3,229	6	0	0	0	6	27	5	21	1	0
Bloomfield Hills	4,021	1	0	1	0	0	42	9	30	3	0
Bloomfield Township	42,291	14	0	2	1	11	360	52	284	24	1
Boyne City	3,741	11	0	5	0	6	57	3	47	7	0
Brandon Township	15,752	13	1	4	0	8	60	15	41	4	1
Breckenridge	1,296	0	0	0	0	0	19	0	18	1	0
Bridgeport Township	9,909	41	0	3	4	34	109	45	59	5	3
Bridgman	2,247	9	1	5	0	3	21	3	14	4	0
Brighton	7,631	8	0	6	0	2	106	8	95	3	2
Bronson	2,315	4	0	2	0	2	43	7	34	2	0
Brown City	1,246	2	0	0	0	2	13	1	11	1	0

Table 8. Offenses Known to Law Enforcement, by Selected State and City, 2017—Continued

(Number.)

State/city	Population	Violent crime	Murder and nonnegligent manslaughter	Rape (revised definition)[1]	Robbery	Aggravated assault	Property crime	Burglary	Larceny-theft	Motor vehicle theft	Arson[2]
Brownstown Township	31,102	85	0	15	11	59	333	75	223	35	0
Buchanan	4,314	16	0	6	1	9	88	15	69	4	0
Buena Vista Township	8,084	88	2	8	5	73	174	85	75	14	2
Burton	28,439	133	2	22	21	88	655	111	493	51	2
Cadillac	10,473	85	0	35	1	49	228	24	194	10	14
Calumet	702	2	0	1	0	1	14	0	14	0	0
Cambridge Township	5,643	7	0	4	0	3	38	8	29	1	0
Canton Township	90,294	117	0	31	15	71	1,144	94	993	57	3
Capac	1,834	3	0	2	0	1	20	4	16	0	0
Carleton	2,342	6	0	1	0	5	36	2	32	2	0
Caro	4,037	10	0	2	0	8	118	11	103	4	1
Carrollton Township	5,728	12	0	1	1	10	64	25	37	2	1
Carson City	1,107	1	0	0	1	0	11	1	10	0	0
Caseville	732	1	0	0	0	1	13	1	12	0	0
Caspian-Gaastra	1,173	2	0	0	0	2	2	0	2	0	0
Cass City	2,322	3	0	2	0	1	38	3	33	2	1
Cassopolis	1,717	7	0	1	1	5	25	4	20	1	0
Center Line	8,304	28	0	7	7	14	225	36	159	30	1
Central Lake	929	0	0	0	0	0	6	1	5	0	0
Charlevoix	2,515	9	0	3	1	5	64	8	51	5	0
Charlotte	9,053	24	1	8	2	13	210	15	186	9	1
Cheboygan	4,705	14	0	7	1	6	101	8	92	1	0
Chelsea	5,225	2	0	1	0	1	49	2	46	1	0
Chesaning	2,253	3	0	0	0	3	7	0	7	0	0
Chesterfield Township	45,212	72	0	14	7	51	722	97	593	32	2
Chikaming Township	3,083	3	0	1	0	2	46	14	31	1	0
Chocolay Township	5,948	16	0	1	0	15	33	5	25	3	1
Clare	3,058	7	1	5	0	1	34	6	23	5	0
Clarkston	893	0	0	0	0	0	6	1	5	0	0
Clawson	11,994	18	0	4	1	13	64	8	53	3	0
Clayton Township	7,113	12	0	4	0	8	39	12	24	3	0
Clay Township	8,845	19	0	7	0	12	90	34	53	3	1
Clinton	2,253	1	0	0	0	1	6	1	3	2	1
Clinton Township	100,999	369	3	51	40	275	1,531	277	1,099	155	8
Clio	2,495	4	0	0	0	4	48	13	34	1	0
Coldwater	10,750	43	0	20	1	22	267	32	230	5	1
Coleman	1,191	1	0	0	0	1	14	1	12	1	0
Coloma Township	6,362	11	0	6	0	5	121	28	92	1	3
Colon	1,150	1	0	0	0	1	32	5	27	0	0
Columbia Township	7,379	17	0	4	2	11	81	17	61	3	1
Commerce Township	38,342	21	1	4	5	11	282	36	235	11	2
Constantine	2,042	7	0	3	0	4	37	7	26	4	0
Corunna	3,386	8	0	7	0	1	34	7	26	1	0
Covert Township	2,831	8	0	1	0	7	56	16	37	3	0
Croswell	2,278	10	0	1	0	9	35	4	28	3	0
Crystal Falls	1,380	1	0	1	0	0	12	2	10	0	0
Davison	4,891	12	0	8	0	4	64	9	51	4	0
Davison Township	19,029	29	0	6	3	20	160	35	121	4	0
Dearborn	93,889	256	0	38	51	167	2,272	218	1,776	278	11
Dearborn Heights	55,454	228	0	23	44	161	1,146	271	743	132	6
Decatur	1,755	15	1	6	1	7	60	14	46	0	0
Denton Township	5,324	1	0	0	0	1	55	5	49	1	0
Detroit	670,792	13,796	267	697	2,639	10,193	30,458	8,258	14,045	8,155	869
Dewitt	4,754	2	0	0	0	2	19	3	14	2	2
Dewitt Township	14,799	21	0	7	2	12	133	26	103	4	2
Dryden Township	4,767	3	0	1	0	2	28	6	20	2	1
Durand	3,312	8	0	3	0	5	42	5	35	2	0
East Grand Rapids	11,812	6	0	5	1	0	195	27	164	4	0
East Jordan	2,348	5	0	2	0	3	31	5	26	0	0
East Lansing	48,920	82	0	22	16	44	781	106	538	137	21
Eastpointe	32,712	262	0	37	59	166	1,088	232	675	181	10
Eaton Rapids	5,230	22	0	7	1	14	85	20	60	5	2
Eau Claire	613	1	0	1	0	0	9	2	6	1	0
Ecorse	9,132	140	0	11	23	106	327	71	210	46	5
Elk Rapids	1,610	1	0	1	0	0	20	2	18	0	0
Elkton	763	2	0	1	0	1	13	5	7	1	0
Elsie	974	0	0	0	0	0	1	1	0	0	0
Emmett Township	11,619	50	0	7	9	34	592	80	495	17	1
Erie Township	4,359	0	0	0	0	0	1	0	1	0	0
Escanaba	12,280	33	0	5	5	23	454	49	397	8	1
Essexville	3,340	7	0	2	2	3	40	10	30	0	1
Evart	1,858	6	0	2	0	4	28	2	25	1	0
Fair Haven Township	1,037	0	0	0	0	0	2	0	2	0	0
Farmington	10,537	4	0	1	1	2	89	12	71	6	0
Farmington Hills	81,359	93	1	15	16	61	915	119	719	77	8
Fennville	1,402	1	0	1	0	0	6	0	6	0	0
Fenton	11,306	17	0	4	1	12	236	22	203	11	1
Ferndale	20,131	44	0	0	17	27	417	48	312	57	4
Flat Rock	9,821	23	0	0	6	17	152	9	128	15	0
Flint	96,605	1,879	37	104	272	1,466	2,632	961	1,397	274	45
Flint Township	30,284	306	3	37	68	198	1,548	230	1,223	95	10
Flushing	7,972	10	0	3	2	5	75	6	69	0	0
Flushing Township	10,172	10	0	6	0	4	38	11	25	2	1

Table 8. Offenses Known to Law Enforcement, by Selected State and City, 2017—Continued

(Number.)

State/city	Population	Violent crime	Murder and nonnegligent manslaughter	Rape (revised definition)[1]	Robbery	Aggravated assault	Property crime	Burglary	Larceny- theft	Motor vehicle theft	Arson[2]
Forsyth Township	6,189	26	0	9	0	17	72	4	63	5	1
Fowlerville	2,922	6	0	2	0	4	56	7	47	2	0
Frankenmuth	5,159	3	0	1	0	2	62	10	50	2	0
Frankfort	1,291	2	0	2	0	0	37	4	32	1	2
Franklin	3,260	1	0	0	0	1	29	8	18	3	0
Fraser	14,645	28	0	9	5	14	303	35	241	27	1
Fremont	4,020	7	0	2	0	5	76	4	66	6	0
Fruitport Township	14,138	29	0	13	2	14	522	12	499	11	2
Gaines Township	6,139	5	0	4	0	1	28	6	19	3	1
Galesburg	2,055	3	0	1	0	2	13	1	12	0	0
Galien	528	0	0	0	0	0	0	0	0	0	0
Garden City	26,571	88	0	10	16	62	396	63	295	38	4
Garfield Township	812	0	0	0	0	0	0	0	0	0	0
Gaylord	3,697	14	0	2	0	12	321	23	292	6	1
Genesee Township	20,253	83	1	13	8	61	221	70	140	11	7
Gerrish Township	2,902	4	0	1	0	3	18	2	15	1	0
Gibraltar	4,472	8	0	5	0	3	48	3	36	9	0
Gladstone	4,767	3	0	2	0	1	94	5	87	2	0
Gladwin	2,865	7	0	3	0	4	65	14	50	1	1
Grand Beach	279	0	0	0	0	0	8	0	8	0	0
Grand Blanc	7,904	9	0	4	2	3	108	22	81	5	0
Grand Blanc Township	36,630	68	0	12	10	46	490	64	402	24	1
Grand Haven	11,004	17	0	14	0	3	195	17	167	11	0
Grand Ledge	7,809	8	0	6	0	2	122	12	106	4	1
Grand Rapids	197,868	1,408	12	141	351	904	4,102	763	2,976	363	54
Grandville	16,108	30	1	12	4	13	622	57	542	23	0
Grant	879	1	0	1	0	0	31	4	26	1	0
Grayling	1,830	12	0	3	0	9	57	12	44	1	0
Green Oak Township	18,839	22	0	6	2	14	150	19	124	7	2
Greenville	8,418	37	0	19	1	17	317	31	280	6	1
Grosse Ile Township	10,084	0	0	0	0	0	29	6	22	1	0
Grosse Pointe	5,151	10	0	0	2	8	103	11	87	5	2
Grosse Pointe Farms	9,106	5	0	0	2	3	113	15	95	3	0
Grosse Pointe Park	11,061	15	0	4	4	7	166	11	142	13	1
Grosse Pointe Shores	2,904	0	0	0	0	0	15	2	13	0	0
Grosse Pointe Woods	15,566	19	0	7	1	11	206	22	164	20	1
Hamburg Township	21,897	14	0	7	0	7	71	9	57	5	0
Hampton Township	9,522	16	0	8	1	7	167	15	143	9	0
Hamtramck	21,654	175	0	11	49	115	616	161	337	118	4
Hancock	4,576	2	0	1	1	0	25	5	18	2	0
Harbor Beach	1,602	7	0	4	0	3	38	12	25	1	0
Harbor Springs	1,208	1	0	1	0	0	24	4	20	0	0
Harper Woods	13,653	102	0	14	27	61	691	103	515	73	2
Hart	2,080	15	0	2	0	13	168	15	153	0	0
Hartford	2,602	8	0	1	1	6	38	2	30	6	0
Hastings	7,272	22	0	9	0	13	120	13	106	1	2
Hazel Park	16,551	67	0	7	12	48	374	57	257	60	4
Highland Park	10,757	183	5	8	39	131	391	83	204	104	5
Highland Township	19,912	8	0	1	2	5	136	26	96	14	0
Hillsdale	8,147	17	0	8	1	8	117	17	94	6	1
Holland	33,613	119	1	39	8	71	783	129	627	27	6
Holly	6,156	4	0	0	0	4	79	18	59	2	0
Hopkins	609	0	0	0	0	0	0	0	0	0	0
Houghton	8,031	1	0	0	0	1	166	4	158	4	0
Howell	9,538	22	0	7	0	15	115	17	92	6	1
Hudson	2,225	5	0	0	0	5	51	8	43	0	0
Huntington Woods	6,343	4	0	1	0	3	23	2	18	3	0
Huron Township	15,636	39	1	7	4	27	182	44	120	18	5
Imlay City	3,577	18	0	12	1	5	44	9	34	1	1
Independence Township	36,836	23	0	7	2	14	232	32	189	11	1
Inkster	24,324	354	9	37	48	260	662	230	343	89	8
Ionia	11,287	34	1	19	0	14	158	23	126	9	1
Iron Mountain	7,397	2	0	2	0	0	4	2	2	0	0
Iron River	2,838	13	1	0	0	12	65	14	51	0	0
Ironwood	4,887	6	0	0	0	6	68	4	59	5	0
Ishpeming	6,471	13	0	4	1	8	86	7	70	9	2
Jackson	32,822	371	7	58	55	251	1,371	211	1,052	108	16
Jonesville	2,208	3	0	2	1	0	87	2	82	3	0
Kalamazoo	76,263	913	10	130	152	621	3,174	710	2,132	332	46
Kalamazoo Township	24,590	83	0	13	9	61	579	160	362	57	0
Kalkaska	2,043	5	0	3	0	2	62	2	59	1	1
Keego Harbor	3,030	1	0	0	0	1	41	5	34	2	0
Kentwood	52,197	171	1	29	24	117	1,206	175	955	76	4
Kinde	422	0	0	0	0	0	0	0	0	0	0
Kingsford	5,003	3	0	2	0	1	30	0	30	0	0
Kinross Township	7,396	1	0	0	0	1	15	3	11	1	0
Laingsburg	1,284	0	0	0	0	0	10	4	6	0	0
Lake Angelus	297	0	0	0	0	0	1	0	1	0	0
Lake Linden	990	0	0	0	0	0	2	1	1	0	0
Lake Odessa	2,035	6	0	4	0	2	26	7	18	1	0
Lake Orion	3,058	3	0	2	0	1	34	1	31	2	0
Lakeview	1,011	3	0	3	0	0	46	8	38	0	0
Lansing	116,302	1,321	14	108	238	961	3,549	883	2,267	399	30

Table 8. Offenses Known to Law Enforcement, by Selected State and City, 2017—Continued

(Number.)

State/city	Population	Violent crime	Murder and nonnegligent manslaughter	Rape (revised definition)[1]	Robbery	Aggravated assault	Property crime	Burglary	Larceny-theft	Motor vehicle theft	Arson[2]
Lansing Township	8,150	54	1	3	21	29	364	63	281	20	3
Lapeer	8,735	26	0	11	1	14	336	66	255	15	0
Lapeer Township	5,058	0	0	0	0	0	20	4	16	0	0
Lathrup Village	4,126	6	0	1	0	5	33	5	26	2	1
Laurium	1,941	4	0	1	0	3	11	2	9	0	0
Lawton	1,860	9	0	3	0	6	37	3	33	1	0
Lennon	498	1	0	1	0	0	5	0	5	0	0
Leslie	1,875	5	0	0	0	5	17	3	14	0	0
Lexington	1,101	0	0	0	0	0	2	1	1	0	0
Lincoln Park	36,502	258	1	18	44	195	1,133	178	799	156	11
Lincoln Township	14,460	14	0	2	1	11	163	17	141	5	0
Linden	3,842	1	0	1	0	0	19	1	18	0	0
Litchfield	1,343	1	0	1	0	0	13	2	11	0	0
Livonia	93,603	108	0	16	16	76	1,431	165	1,137	129	6
Lowell	4,089	15	0	8	0	7	82	8	71	3	0
Ludington	8,068	31	0	17	1	13	171	19	149	3	0
Luna Pier	1,368	5	0	1	1	3	19	2	16	1	0
Lyon Township	19,890	12	0	1	1	10	124	26	94	4	0
Mackinac Island	475	2	0	0	1	1	167	0	167	0	0
Mackinaw City	801	1	0	0	0	1	35	3	32	0	0
Madison Heights	30,152	50	0	11	14	25	510	72	379	59	5
Madison Township	8,470	17	0	3	1	13	153	10	135	8	0
Mancelona	1,359	0	0	0	0	0	14	3	11	0	0
Manistee	6,030	16	2	5	1	8	134	42	92	0	0
Manistique	2,890	9	0	2	0	7	74	11	62	1	0
Marenisco Township	1,599	0	0	0	0	0	0	0	0	0	0
Marine City	4,108	13	0	1	0	12	30	9	19	2	1
Marlette	1,762	0	0	0	0	0	33	8	25	0	0
Marquette	20,442	40	1	27	0	12	257	19	225	13	0
Marshall	7,028	20	0	4	2	14	119	21	91	7	0
Marysville	9,702	21	1	1	1	18	131	11	117	3	0
Mason	8,418	23	0	6	1	16	169	12	146	11	1
Mattawan	1,936	8	0	1	0	7	26	11	12	3	0
Mayville	905	4	0	1	0	3	11	0	11	0	0
Melvindale	10,262	64	0	4	9	51	251	39	169	43	1
Mendon	854	0	0	0	0	0	14	2	12	0	0
Menominee	8,230	28	0	6	1	21	127	23	100	4	1
Meridian Township	42,878	85	2	16	17	50	1,054	211	813	30	3
Metamora Township	4,250	1	0	0	0	1	25	8	15	2	0
Metro Police Authority of Genesee County	20,001	28	0	6	1	21	210	33	170	7	0
Michiana	181	0	0	0	0	0	6	2	4	0	0
Midland	42,131	53	1	25	1	26	508	54	444	10	0
Milan	6,044	26	0	10	0	16	96	26	66	4	0
Milford	16,726	4	0	2	0	2	79	8	69	2	1
Millington	1,016	1	0	1	0	0	10	2	7	1	0
Monroe	19,868	107	1	25	9	72	389	54	303	32	1
Montague	2,358	3	0	0	0	3	34	3	30	1	0
Montrose Township	7,466	4	0	1	0	3	57	19	33	5	0
Morenci	2,174	6	0	2	0	4	17	9	8	0	0
Morrice	891	1	0	1	0	0	12	0	12	0	0
Mount Morris	2,918	10	0	2	0	8	93	15	72	6	0
Mount Morris Township	20,365	140	3	23	18	96	425	135	256	34	2
Mount Pleasant	26,366	62	0	22	3	37	370	59	293	18	1
Munising	2,232	3	0	1	0	2	44	8	35	1	0
Muskegon	38,375	229	3	29	55	142	2,059	395	1,467	197	20
Muskegon Heights	10,786	195	3	20	38	134	648	209	392	47	13
Muskegon Township	17,842	56	1	18	3	34	714	54	635	25	4
Napoleon Township	6,727	2	0	1	0	1	39	12	25	2	1
Nashville	1,644	15	0	2	0	13	27	7	19	1	0
Negaunee	4,576	7	0	3	0	4	49	3	44	2	0
Newaygo	2,045	6	0	5	0	1	85	14	66	5	0
New Baltimore	12,401	15	0	5	0	10	87	17	66	4	1
New Buffalo	1,870	1	0	0	0	1	20	2	17	1	0
New Era	443	0	0	0	0	0	5	1	4	0	0
New Lothrop	555	0	0	0	0	0	6	2	4	0	0
Niles	11,202	67	1	16	9	41	265	57	169	39	6
Northfield Township	8,634	10	0	1	0	9	44	14	29	1	1
North Muskegon	3,794	5	0	1	2	2	82	2	79	1	0
Northville	5,981	6	0	1	0	5	48	1	45	2	0
Northville Township	28,751	29	0	4	0	25	310	27	268	15	3
Norton Shores	24,402	43	1	10	8	24	673	82	564	27	4
Norway	2,757	0	0	0	0	0	0	0	0	0	0
Novi	59,895	43	0	11	6	26	617	42	543	32	0
Oakland Township	19,241	7	0	0	0	7	57	18	37	2	0
Oak Park	29,698	101	0	15	21	65	556	84	398	74	5
Olivet	1,707	2	0	1	0	1	7	1	6	0	1
Ontwa Township-Edwardsburg	6,487	19	0	1	1	17	120	32	80	8	2
Orchard Lake	2,431	5	0	2	0	3	22	2	20	0	1
Orion Township	35,857	10	0	0	2	8	246	34	201	11	3
Oscoda Township	6,831	28	0	7	0	21	118	19	97	2	0
Otisville	821	0	0	0	0	0	4	2	1	1	0
Otsego	4,005	6	0	4	1	1	57	12	42	3	0

Table 8. Offenses Known to Law Enforcement, by Selected State and City, 2017—Continued

(Number.)

State/city	Population	Violent crime	Murder and nonnegligent manslaughter	Rape (revised definition)[1]	Robbery	Aggravated assault	Property crime	Burglary	Larceny-theft	Motor vehicle theft	Arson[2]
Ovid	1,615	3	0	0	0	3	12	0	12	0	0
Owendale	227	0	0	0	0	0	0	0	0	0	0
Owosso	14,587	79	0	23	5	51	250	47	194	9	3
Oxford	3,548	1	0	1	0	0	17	1	14	2	0
Oxford Township	18,365	16	0	6	0	10	72	17	52	3	0
Paw Paw	3,435	16	0	4	1	11	133	11	119	3	0
Peck	598	0	0	0	0	0	0	0	0	0	0
Pentwater	839	0	0	0	0	0	9	2	7	0	0
Perry	2,094	12	0	2	0	10	10	1	7	2	0
Petoskey	5,764	5	0	2	0	3	51	6	45	0	0
Pigeon	1,143	0	0	0	0	0	0	0	0	0	0
Pinckney	2,463	2	0	1	0	1	18	6	11	1	0
Pinconning	1,249	0	0	0	0	0	9	3	6	0	0
Pittsfield Township	39,061	86	3	21	14	48	639	46	562	31	3
Plainwell	3,825	11	0	3	2	6	62	10	51	1	0
Pleasant Ridge	2,555	0	0	0	0	0	40	2	36	2	0
Plymouth	9,072	13	0	4	0	9	71	7	59	5	0
Plymouth Township	26,779	22	0	4	5	13	226	27	177	22	0
Pontiac	59,731	644	4	61	97	482	1,510	468	820	222	25
Portage	48,876	108	0	31	14	63	1,468	186	1,223	59	3
Port Austin	628	0	0	0	0	0	7	0	7	0	0
Port Huron	29,092	264	0	35	20	209	674	145	492	37	5
Portland	3,943	7	0	4	0	3	44	3	41	0	0
Port Sanilac	591	0	0	0	0	0	0	0	0	0	0
Potterville	2,634	2	0	1	0	1	8	3	5	0	0
Prairieville Township	3,452	1	0	0	0	1	12	6	6	0	0
Quincy	1,627	8	0	1	1	6	27	3	24	0	0
Raisin Township	7,619	13	0	3	0	10	19	7	12	0	0
Reading	1,046	3	0	2	0	1	9	0	8	1	0
Redford Township	46,867	320	1	42	64	213	1,278	359	707	212	7
Reed City	2,379	7	0	2	0	5	34	4	30	0	0
Reese	1,383	1	0	0	0	1	22	2	19	1	0
Richfield Township, Genesee County	8,270	8	0	4	1	3	64	14	46	4	0
Richfield Township, Roscommon County	3,607	5	0	2	0	3	22	5	16	1	0
Richland	809	1	0	1	0	0	14	2	10	2	0
Richland Township, Saginaw County	3,934	0	0	0	0	0	7	0	7	0	0
Richmond	5,893	19	0	1	0	18	60	11	47	2	0
River Rouge	7,417	76	1	5	10	60	212	55	130	27	3
Riverview	12,045	29	0	4	4	21	150	11	104	35	0
Rochester	13,068	21	0	1	0	20	72	12	58	2	0
Rochester Hills	73,827	39	0	13	3	23	471	50	403	18	1
Rockford	6,316	11	0	5	1	5	61	6	54	1	2
Rockwood	3,159	2	0	0	0	2	17	3	13	1	0
Rogers City	2,676	1	0	0	1	0	40	6	33	1	0
Romeo	3,616	5	0	2	0	3	34	5	27	2	0
Romulus	23,174	210	2	12	33	163	756	118	524	114	3
Roosevelt Park	3,826	10	0	3	3	4	263	3	251	9	0
Roseville	47,651	205	3	31	51	120	1,623	201	1,303	119	6
Rothbury	425	0	0	0	0	0	16	2	14	0	0
Royal Oak	59,303	54	0	7	7	40	543	46	446	51	4
Saginaw	48,589	762	15	50	75	622	913	383	455	75	19
Saginaw Township	39,319	101	0	16	25	60	878	113	739	26	4
Saline	9,207	13	0	3	0	10	54	3	48	3	0
Sand Lake	527	0	0	0	0	0	15	1	14	0	0
Sandusky	2,545	5	0	0	1	4	63	10	51	2	0
Saugatuck-Douglas	2,303	5	0	3	1	1	43	4	38	1	1
Sault Ste. Marie	13,630	47	1	13	4	29	247	20	218	9	2
Schoolcraft	1,571	1	0	0	0	1	23	3	19	1	0
Scottville	1,222	5	0	3	0	2	55	3	52	0	0
Sebewaing	1,655	2	0	1	0	1	12	1	11	0	0
Shelby Township	79,217	82	1	25	7	49	579	75	473	31	0
Shepherd	1,516	2	0	1	0	1	36	9	25	2	0
Somerset Township	4,556	2	0	1	0	1	17	3	14	0	0
Southfield	73,324	151	1	18	37	95	2,032	315	1,454	263	7
Southgate	28,939	81	0	13	18	50	774	67	629	78	3
South Haven	4,362	41	0	8	6	27	273	29	236	8	0
South Lyon	11,777	7	0	1	0	6	55	4	47	4	0
South Rockwood	1,638	0	0	0	0	0	9	2	6	1	1
Sparta	4,370	7	0	2	0	5	98	7	90	1	0
Spring Arbor Township	7,974	5	0	2	0	3	33	9	23	1	0
Springfield Township	14,341	17	1	1	1	14	66	8	50	8	1
Stanton	1,415	1	0	0	0	1	10	2	8	0	0
St. Charles	1,925	4	0	0	1	3	40	5	34	1	0
St. Clair	5,350	24	0	3	0	21	56	23	32	1	3
St. Clair Shores	59,782	113	0	29	14	70	695	92	558	45	5
Sterling Heights	132,882	245	4	42	19	180	1,504	164	1,233	107	6
St. Ignace	2,366	2	1	1	0	0	49	7	40	2	0
St. Johns	7,938	10	0	6	0	4	69	19	48	2	0
St. Joseph	8,276	17	0	7	0	10	113	9	100	4	1
St. Joseph Township	9,813	7	0	0	0	7	110	27	77	6	0

Table 8. Offenses Known to Law Enforcement, by Selected State and City, 2017—Continued

(Number.)

State/city	Population	Violent crime	Murder and nonnegligent manslaughter	Rape (revised definition)[1]	Robbery	Aggravated assault	Property crime	Burglary	Larceny-theft	Motor vehicle theft	Arson[2]
St. Louis	6,994	23	0	15	0	8	54	5	48	1	0
Stockbridge	1,237	1	0	0	0	1	6	0	6	0	0
Sturgis	10,858	27	0	5	1	21	344	42	286	16	0
Sumpter Township	9,215	10	0	0	0	10	103	34	61	8	0
Sylvan Lake	1,841	1	0	0	0	1	27	3	23	1	0
Tawas	4,522	6	0	2	0	4	93	5	87	1	0
Taylor	60,882	348	4	39	58	247	1,480	326	973	181	23
Tecumseh	8,345	14	1	7	1	5	86	11	71	4	0
Thetford Township	6,656	1	0	0	0	1	12	2	9	1	0
Thomas Township	11,450	10	0	3	0	7	105	15	88	2	1
Three Rivers	7,695	46	0	6	1	39	292	14	263	15	0
Tittabawassee Township	9,776	7	0	0	1	6	54	13	38	3	1
Traverse City	15,617	87	1	17	1	68	296	40	242	14	2
Trenton	18,161	20	0	3	3	14	129	17	94	18	0
Troy	84,086	55	0	14	6	35	1,275	94	1,114	67	1
Tuscarora Township	2,946	3	0	1	1	1	47	5	40	2	0
Ubly	811	1	0	0	0	1	5	2	3	0	0
Unadilla Township	3,435	10	0	2	0	8	20	6	11	3	0
Utica	4,960	13	0	5	2	6	198	7	185	6	0
Van Buren Township	27,911	82	3	25	10	44	646	64	513	69	4
Vassar	2,580	13	0	5	0	8	7	1	5	1	0
Vernon	752	1	0	0	0	1	3	1	2	0	0
Vicksburg	3,350	8	0	4	0	4	47	8	38	1	0
Walker	24,987	48	0	19	11	18	552	54	483	15	1
Walled Lake	7,104	11	0	2	1	8	62	12	48	2	0
Warren	135,303	681	7	125	97	452	2,900	659	1,804	437	26
Waterford Township	73,060	118	1	41	17	59	835	250	517	68	7
Watervliet	1,671	8	0	2	0	6	31	3	26	2	0
Wayland	4,228	11	0	1	0	10	65	17	46	2	0
Wayne	16,857	159	0	19	31	109	342	71	228	43	4
West Bloomfield Township	65,948	47	0	5	1	41	500	73	411	16	0
West Branch	2,052	5	0	3	1	1	28	3	25	0	0
Westland	81,158	258	5	64	48	141	1,388	269	980	139	11
White Cloud	1,372	6	0	4	0	2	22	4	18	0	2
Whitehall	2,726	5	0	3	0	2	60	5	55	0	0
White Lake Township	31,016	22	0	5	2	15	287	24	251	12	2
White Pigeon	1,509	3	0	0	0	3	28	8	19	1	0
Williamston	3,892	1	0	0	0	1	26	3	23	0	0
Wixom	13,801	34	0	5	4	25	233	31	185	17	0
Wolverine Lake	4,586	6	0	4	0	2	22	7	14	1	0
Wyandotte	24,817	56	0	17	6	33	418	54	316	48	1
Wyoming	76,153	356	3	74	83	196	1,666	235	1,221	210	11
Yale	1,889	12	0	0	0	12	22	8	12	2	0
Ypsilanti	21,267	184	2	32	37	113	606	135	428	43	5
Zeeland	5,594	14	0	3	1	10	98	27	68	3	1
Zilwaukee	1,546	1	0	0	0	1	9	2	6	1	0
MINNESOTA											
Aitkin	1,987	1	0	1	0	0	54	8	42	4	0
Akeley	430	0	0	0	0	0	14	1	12	1	0
Albany	2,682	6	0	1	1	4	35	3	25	7	0
Albert Lea[6]	17,608	15	0	1	2	12	416	72	324	20	0
Alexandria	13,756	41	0	8	1	32	400	46	326	28	0
Annandale	3,328	5	0	2	0	3	83	4	76	3	0
Anoka	17,439	41	0	8	11	22	505	52	433	20	1
Appleton	1,341	6	0	1	0	5	29	8	21	0	0
Apple Valley	52,439	65	0	21	19	25	1,166	107	1,028	31	5
Arlington	2,146	0	0	0	0	0	0	0	0	0	0
Atwater	1,118	0	0	0	0	0	2	0	2	0	0
Austin	24,692	52	0	10	7	35	639	118	495	26	2
Avon	1,550	3	0	0	1	2	26	5	17	4	0
Babbitt	1,513	1	0	0	0	1	13	0	11	2	0
Barnesville	2,578	2	0	0	0	2	2	1	1	0	0
Baxter	8,298	7	0	0	0	7	288	13	267	8	0
Bayport	3,420	0	0	0	0	0	17	3	13	1	0
Becker	4,825	6	0	0	0	6	28	4	22	2	0
Belgrade/Brooten	1,516	2	0	0	0	2	16	2	12	2	0
Belle Plaine	7,066	5	0	1	0	4	95	6	89	0	1
Bemidji	15,054	56	0	6	7	43	1,268	69	1,140	59	4
Benson	3,080	1	0	0	0	1	2	1	1	0	0
Big Lake	10,730	1	0	0	0	1	59	3	48	8	0
Blackduck	778	0	0	0	0	0	12	3	8	1	0
Blaine	63,857	56	0	16	18	22	1,941	158	1,705	78	7
Blooming Prairie	1,986	1	0	0	0	1	5	0	4	1	0
Bloomington	85,704	140	1	43	33	63	2,590	175	2,282	133	11
Blue Earth	3,191	1	0	0	0	1	22	4	15	3	0
Bovey	802	1	0	0	0	1	2	1	1	0	0
Braham	1,774	0	0	0	0	0	0	0	0	0	0
Brainerd	13,307	70	0	28	5	37	554	74	466	14	2
Breckenridge	3,250	3	0	0	0	3	68	5	57	6	0
Breezy Point	2,368	2	0	0	0	2	36	0	34	2	0
Breitung Township	607	1	0	1	0	0	5	1	3	1	0
Brooklyn Center	30,989	125	0	20	61	44	1,076	122	843	111	4

Table 8. Offenses Known to Law Enforcement, by Selected State and City, 2017—Continued

(Number.)

State/city	Population	Violent crime	Murder and nonnegligent manslaughter	Rape (revised definition)[1]	Robbery	Aggravated assault	Property crime	Burglary	Larceny-theft	Motor vehicle theft	Arson[2]
Brooklyn Park	80,347	281	1	49	63	168	2,167	293	1,716	158	7
Brownton	730	1	0	0	0	1	2	1	1	0	0
Buffalo	16,206	13	0	8	1	4	334	28	295	11	0
Buffalo Lake	687	1	0	0	0	1	7	1	5	1	0
Burnsville	61,442	101	0	11	28	62	1,753	184	1,465	104	6
Caledonia	2,773	1	0	0	0	1	3	2	1	0	0
Cambridge	8,770	5	0	0	0	5	372	28	327	17	1
Canby	1,708	1	0	1	0	0	3	0	3	0	0
Cannon Falls[6]	4,110	4	0	1	0	3	98	15	80	3	1
Centennial Lakes	10,956	10	0	5	1	4	150	25	114	11	1
Champlin	24,417	26	0	9	5	12	279	29	242	8	0
Chaska	26,383	22	0	9	2	11	255	23	224	8	1
Chisholm	4,935	2	0	0	0	2	42	6	34	2	0
Clara City	1,316	2	0	2	0	0	5	1	4	0	0
Clearbrook[6]	522	1	0	0	0	1	16	1	15	0	0
Cleveland	696	0	0	0	0	0	11	2	9	0	0
Cloquet	12,108	21	0	1	2	18	510	46	440	24	0
Cold Spring/Richmond	5,565	1	0	0	0	1	46	8	36	2	0
Coleraine	1,993	1	0	0	0	1	5	2	3	0	0
Columbia Heights	19,759	51	1	13	19	18	504	77	383	44	0
Coon Rapids	62,495	101	0	23	25	53	1,771	216	1,503	52	8
Corcoran	5,735	4	0	0	0	4	38	5	32	1	0
Cosmos	452	0	0	0	0	0	4	1	1	2	0
Cottage Grove	36,253	15	0	3	5	7	749	75	634	40	0
Crookston	7,789	22	1	12	0	9	164	19	143	2	1
Crosby	2,329	4	0	4	0	0	56	4	52	0	0
Crosslake	2,239	4	0	2	0	2	15	3	12	0	0
Crystal	23,173	50	3	12	15	20	465	54	389	22	3
Danube	454	0	0	0	0	0	8	0	6	2	0
Dawson/Boyd	1,564	0	0	0	0	0	21	7	13	1	0
Dayton	5,515	3	0	0	2	1	65	17	40	8	0
Deephaven	3,878	0	0	0	0	0	44	7	37	0	0
Deer River	932	1	0	0	0	1	21	1	19	1	0
Detroit Lakes[6]	9,242	14	0	2	2	10	323	37	262	24	1
Dilworth	4,462	3	0	0	0	3	145	9	128	8	0
Duluth	86,306	279	1	31	66	181	3,819	506	3,091	222	10
Dundas	1,513	0	0	0	0	0	2	1	1	0	0
Eagan	66,805	58	2	18	14	24	1,270	100	1,128	42	6
Eagle Lake	3,099	2	0	2	0	0	31	18	11	2	0
East Grand Forks	8,713	13	0	1	0	12	158	18	134	6	1
East Range	3,635	3	0	2	0	1	43	15	27	1	0
Eden Prairie	64,429	32	2	7	9	14	824	56	739	29	0
Eden Valley	1,034	0	0	0	0	0	2	0	2	0	0
Edina	51,923	23	0	13	5	5	1,061	166	865	30	0
Elko New Market	4,714	1	0	0	0	1	2	0	2	0	0
Elk River	24,593	24	0	9	2	13	429	70	342	17	3
Elmore	626	0	0	0	0	0	2	2	0	0	0
Ely	3,379	1	0	0	0	1	40	7	31	2	0
Eveleth	3,636	9	0	3	0	6	138	20	111	7	0
Fairfax	1,142	1	0	0	0	1	21	1	19	1	1
Fairmont	10,027	11	0	4	0	7	256	47	207	2	1
Falcon Heights	5,619	6	0	0	3	3	82	13	62	7	0
Faribault	23,713	69	0	17	7	45	541	94	415	32	9
Farmington	22,917	13	0	4	0	9	209	35	163	11	3
Fergus Falls[6]	13,468	21	1	1	2	17	533	66	451	16	1
Floodwood	515	0	0	0	0	0	14	0	13	1	0
Foley	2,656	4	0	2	0	2	12	1	11	0	
Forest Lake	19,804	30	0	13	5	12	736	90	597	49	1
Fridley	27,516	83	2	14	24	43	1,031	118	837	76	1
Fulda	1,218	0	0	0	0	0	7	4	3	0	0
Gaylord	2,221	5	0	1	0	4	11	3	8	0	0
Gilbert	1,789	2	0	0	0	2	97	12	82	3	0
Glencoe	5,478	8	0	2	0	6	73	5	65	3	0
Glenwood	2,563	1	0	0	0	1	39	8	31	0	0
Golden Valley	21,545	18	0	3	8	7	452	73	358	21	0
Goodhue[6]	1,186	0	0	0	0	0	0	0	0	0	0
Goodview	4,116	0	0	0	0	0	50	15	33	2	0
Grand Rapids	11,270	19	0	9	1	9	137	7	125	5	0
Granite Falls	2,735	9	0	1	0	8	54	3	48	3	0
Hallock	922	0	0	0	0	0	0	0	0	0	0
Hancock	743	0	0	0	0	0	1	0	1	0	0
Hastings	22,671	36	0	9	3	24	494	53	416	25	0
Hawley	2,215	2	0	0	0	2	0	0	0	0	0
Hector	1,047	3	0	1	0	2	33	5	27	1	0
Henning[6]	799	1	0	0	0	1	1	0	1	0	0
Hermantown	9,455	11	0	3	1	7	412	49	351	12	1
Hibbing	16,051	28	2	7	1	18	112	16	86	10	0
Hill City	581	0	0	0	0	0	22	3	13	6	0
Hilltop	733	6	0	3	2	1	71	5	57	9	0
Hokah	556	1	0	0	0	1	2	0	2	0	0
Hopkins	18,189	33	1	5	10	17	253	46	176	31	2
Houston	979	0	0	0	0	0	0	0	0	0	0
Howard Lake	2,057	0	0	0	0	0	4	0	4	0	0

Table 8. Offenses Known to Law Enforcement, by Selected State and City, 2017—Continued

(Number.)

State/city	Population	Violent crime	Murder and nonnegligent manslaughter	Rape (revised definition)[1]	Robbery	Aggravated assault	Property crime	Burglary	Larceny-theft	Motor vehicle theft	Arson[2]
Hutchinson	13,846	22	0	6	1	15	280	27	251	2	0
International Falls	6,009	12	0	3	1	8	82	9	67	6	0
Inver Grove Heights	35,254	74	0	19	12	43	677	137	462	78	4
Isanti	5,641	7	0	3	0	4	89	7	78	4	0
Isle	800	0	0	0	0	0	0	0	0	0	0
Janesville	2,274	1	0	1	0	0	26	9	16	1	0
Jordan	6,261	7	0	1	0	6	69	7	62	0	0
Kasson	6,308	7	0	1	1	5	79	5	70	4	1
Keewatin	1,029	2	0	2	0	0	11	1	9	1	0
Kimball	782	0	0	0	0	0	0	0	0	0	0
La Crescent	4,816	5	0	0	0	5	35	4	29	2	0
Lake City	5,039	3	0	2	0	1	45	7	36	2	0
Lake Crystal	2,489	1	0	0	0	1	34	16	14	4	0
Lakefield	1,618	1	0	0	0	1	5	2	3	0	0
Lakes Area	9,544	17	0	6	1	10	137	21	105	11	4
Lake Shore	1,044	0	0	0	0	0	2	0	2	0	0
Lakeville	62,958	44	0	11	6	27	598	84	494	20	2
Lamberton	773	0	0	0	0	0	0	0	0	0	0
Lauderdale	2,544	3	0	1	0	2	25	5	17	3	0
Le Center	2,436	0	0	0	0	0	7	0	7	0	0
Lester Prairie	1,680	4	0	0	0	4	17	5	10	2	0
Le Sueur	3,966	0	0	0	0	0	33	7	25	1	0
Lewiston	1,555	1	0	1	0	0	16	1	14	1	0
Lino Lakes	21,147	9	0	3	0	6	195	28	159	8	0
Litchfield	6,634	19	0	12	0	7	133	25	101	7	0
Little Falls	8,665	8	0	3	0	5	124	15	98	11	0
Long Prairie	3,313	5	1	1	0	3	55	5	47	3	0
Lonsdale	3,931	1	0	1	0	0	13	2	11	0	0
Madelia	2,229	7	0	1	0	6	49	23	26	0	0
Madison Lake	1,161	1	0	0	0	1	4	0	4	0	0
Mankato	42,047	107	0	24	17	66	1,301	183	1,067	51	4
Maple Grove	70,966	50	0	18	5	27	1,242	115	1,092	35	3
Mapleton	1,698	0	0	0	0	0	12	3	9	0	0
Maplewood	40,689	92	0	13	39	40	1,911	205	1,537	169	1
Marshall	13,660	32	0	12	4	16	259	49	203	7	0
McGregor	357	0	0	0	0	0	0	0	0	0	0
Medina	6,498	3	0	1	0	2	68	5	61	2	0
Melrose	3,614	2	0	0	0	2	19	7	12	0	0
Menahga	1,329	0	0	0	0	0	0	0	0	0	0
Mendota Heights	11,314	15	1	1	1	12	232	32	187	13	4
Milaca	2,891	2	0	1	0	1	39	2	35	2	0
Minneapolis	418,971	4,614	42	514	1,819	2,239	19,446	3,762	13,296	2,388	107
Minneota	1,357	1	0	1	0	0	7	5	2	0	0
Minnesota Lake	649	1	0	0	0	1	2	0	2	0	0
Minnetonka	52,811	35	2	13	4	16	899	110	755	34	2
Minnetrista	9,965	6	0	1	1	4	119	19	97	3	0
Montevideo	5,181	11	1	1	0	9	103	12	85	6	1
Montgomery	2,899	1	0	0	0	1	41	6	27	8	0
Moorhead	42,999	90	1	26	11	52	889	130	655	104	0
Moose Lake	2,834	12	0	2	0	10	69	4	64	1	0
Morris	5,297	4	0	3	0	1	53	6	44	3	0
Motley	641	0	0	0	0	0	1	0	1	0	0
Mounds View	13,146	11	0	3	3	5	391	37	325	29	0
Mountain Lake	2,101	3	0	1	0	2	9	2	5	2	0
Nashwauk	956	0	0	0	0	0	6	3	3	0	0
New Brighton	22,772	28	1	5	9	13	593	60	486	47	3
New Hope	20,967	29	0	6	9	14	406	43	341	22	0
New Prague	7,685	3	0	2	0	1	113	10	100	3	0
New Richland	1,198	1	0	1	0	0	20	2	18	0	0
New Ulm	13,316	23	0	10	2	11	174	43	121	10	1
North Branch	10,349	20	0	2	2	16	224	38	179	7	0
Northfield	20,512	28	0	15	1	12	197	25	166	6	2
North Mankato	13,664	16	0	2	1	13	162	32	119	11	2
North St. Paul	12,545	19	0	2	10	7	277	40	211	26	0
Oakdale	28,181	60	0	9	18	33	911	84	762	65	6
Oak Park Heights	4,915	2	0	0	0	2	218	14	195	9	3
Olivia	2,328	5	0	3	0	2	67	9	51	7	0
Onamia	862	0	0	0	0	0	0	0	0	0	0
Orono	19,923	11	1	5	1	4	122	18	99	5	0
Ortonville	1,815	1	0	0	0	1	19	4	15	0	0
Osakis	1,713	2	0	1	0	1	21	10	9	2	0
Osseo	2,810	1	0	0	1	0	16	1	15	0	0
Owatonna	25,810	32	0	8	6	18	463	64	372	27	1
Park Rapids	3,949	12	0	4	1	7	279	27	244	8	0
Paynesville	2,497	3	0	0	0	3	19	5	9	5	1
Pequot Lakes	2,278	3	0	0	0	3	82	1	78	3	0
Pierz	1,343	0	0	0	0	0	1	0	1	0	0
Pike Bay	1,651	1	0	1	0	0	3	0	3	0	0
Pillager	457	0	0	0	0	0	3	0	3	0	0
Pine River	926	0	0	0	0	0	9	0	8	1	0
Plainview	3,222	0	0	0	0	0	11	2	8	1	0
Plymouth	78,356	63	0	16	15	32	964	181	755	28	0
Preston	1,302	0	0	0	0	0	16	2	12	2	0

Table 8. Offenses Known to Law Enforcement, by Selected State and City, 2017—Continued

(Number.)

State/city	Population	Violent crime	Murder and nonnegligent manslaughter	Rape (revised definition)[1]	Robbery	Aggravated assault	Property crime	Burglary	Larceny-theft	Motor vehicle theft	Arson[2]
Princeton	4,701	1	0	1	0	0	184	12	163	9	0
Prior Lake	26,374	30	0	8	4	18	648	48	555	45	3
Proctor	3,059	2	0	0	0	2	95	17	74	4	0
Ramsey	26,643	14	0	6	2	6	418	41	360	17	1
Randall	615	0	0	0	0	0	0	0	0	0	0
Red Wing[6]	16,539	44	1	8	6	29	480	87	369	24	0
Redwood Falls	4,976	14	0	4	0	10	140	13	114	13	0
Renville	1,188	0	0	0	0	0	17	2	12	3	0
Rice	1,375	0	0	0	0	0	4	1	3	0	0
Richfield	36,087	93	1	26	30	36	922	143	712	67	0
Robbinsdale	14,545	37	1	4	13	19	368	66	274	28	1
Rochester	115,228	224	1	61	46	116	2,143	288	1,757	98	5
Rogers	13,021	14	0	3	1	10	344	23	307	14	0
Roseau	2,778	3	0	1	0	2	30	1	27	2	0
Rosemount	24,255	14	1	4	4	5	208	30	175	3	1
Roseville	36,196	89	1	11	31	46	1,948	215	1,633	100	4
Rushford	1,715	0	0	0	0	0	0	0	0	0	0
Sartell	17,353	20	0	7	1	12	285	41	238	6	0
Sauk Centre	4,376	9	0	3	2	4	70	14	52	4	0
Sauk Rapids	13,769	11	0	1	0	10	286	41	238	7	0
Savage	31,491	26	0	7	6	13	457	49	378	30	5
Sebeka	678	0	0	0	0	0	0	0	0	0	0
Shakopee	41,176	69	1	21	10	37	757	71	635	51	0
Sherburn	1,084	0	0	0	0	0	0	0	0	0	0
Silver Bay	1,791	0	0	0	0	0	0	0	0	0	0
Silver Lake	802	1	0	0	0	1	10	3	7	0	0
Slayton	2,017	0	0	0	0	0	16	1	15	0	0
Sleepy Eye	3,421	2	0	1	0	1	14	3	10	1	0
South Lake Minnetonka	12,343	11	0	4	1	6	114	19	88	7	0
South St. Paul	20,235	75	1	9	9	56	519	85	362	72	1
Springfield	2,040	2	0	0	0	2	3	1	2	0	0
Spring Grove	1,290	2	0	1	0	1	29	0	28	1	0
Spring Lake Park	6,482	13	0	1	5	7	250	26	197	27	1
St. Anthony	9,159	17	0	4	8	5	209	41	158	10	0
Staples	2,880	2	0	1	0	1	60	10	46	4	0
Starbuck	1,255	1	0	0	0	1	30	6	23	1	0
St. Charles	3,717	5	0	0	0	5	53	6	45	2	0
St. Cloud	67,911	256	3	62	49	142	2,789	330	2,278	181	16
St. Francis	7,507	9	0	2	2	5	118	5	107	6	1
Stillwater	19,394	21	0	7	6	8	395	54	320	21	5
St. James	4,422	9	0	6	0	3	75	22	52	1	1
St. Joseph	6,772	5	0	1	0	4	59	6	46	7	0
St. Louis Park	49,355	49	0	12	17	20	1,321	131	1,135	55	2
St. Paul	306,696	1,996	22	217	697	1,060	10,935	2,274	6,577	2,084	143
St. Paul Park	5,398	8	0	2	0	6	130	16	104	10	0
St. Peter	11,779	15	0	7	2	6	149	12	128	9	0
Thief River Falls	8,824	11	0	6	1	4	251	32	210	9	1
Tracy	2,052	3	0	0	0	3	22	8	11	3	1
Tri-City	1,403	0	0	0	0	0	13	2	10	1	0
Trimont	700	0	0	0	0	0	0	0	0	0	0
Truman	1,049	0	0	0	0	0	2	1	1	0	0
Twin Valley	778	0	0	0	0	0	2	0	2	0	0
Two Harbors	3,533	2	0	0	0	2	6	1	5	0	0
Virginia	8,493	45	0	10	4	31	354	58	277	19	0
Wabasha	2,442	3	0	1	0	2	48	7	37	4	1
Wadena	4,142	10	0	4	0	6	65	4	54	7	0
Waite Park	7,455	21	1	2	4	14	589	34	543	12	0
Walker	931	1	0	0	0	1	12	0	11	1	0
Warroad	1,794	0	0	0	0	0	0	0	0	0	0
Waseca	9,018	11	0	3	1	7	171	18	144	9	0
Waterville	1,841	2	0	0	0	2	5	1	4	0	0
Wayzata	6,517	8	0	2	3	3	101	11	85	5	0
Wells	2,208	0	0	0	0	0	10	2	8	0	0
West Concord	771	0	0	0	0	0	9	0	9	0	0
West Hennepin	5,591	4	0	2	0	2	46	6	37	3	0
West St. Paul	19,778	89	1	11	26	51	971	117	797	57	4
Wheaton	1,331	2	0	1	0	1	19	9	9	1	0
White Bear Lake	26,065	44	0	11	11	22	703	137	509	57	5
Willmar	19,553	68	0	11	7	50	490	71	379	40	2
Windom	4,499	8	0	2	0	6	82	21	60	1	0
Winnebago	1,356	3	0	0	0	3	26	8	17	1	0
Winona	27,071	49	1	25	1	22	618	38	564	16	1
Winsted	2,285	5	0	2	0	3	27	9	18	0	0
Woodbury	69,978	59	0	22	9	28	1,293	115	1,113	65	3
Worthington[6]	13,195	21	0	7	5	9	206	53	140	13	0
Wyoming	7,866	8	0	0	2	6	85	9	65	11	0
Zumbrota[6]	3,431	8	0	2	2	4	45	7	36	2	0
MISSISSIPPI											
Ackerman[7]	1,458		0		0	4	44	17	26	1	0
Batesville	7,380	30	1	0	20	9	305	53	241	11	0
Biloxi	46,263	178	1	39	74	64	2,963	871	1,933	159	7
Brandon	24,125	27	0	1	3	23	224	18	189	17	0

Table 8. Offenses Known to Law Enforcement, by Selected State and City, 2017—Continued

(Number.)

State/city	Population	Violent crime	Murder and nonnegligent manslaughter	Rape (revised definition)[1]	Robbery	Aggravated assault	Property crime	Burglary	Larceny-theft	Motor vehicle theft	Arson[2]
Brookhaven	12,334	67	1	2	10	54	342	147	170	25	2
Byram	11,549	18	0	4	7	7	238	25	203	10	0
Clinton[7]	25,202		0		15	63	493	71	406	16	0
D'Iberville	11,852	10	0	4	3	3	907	46	835	26	0
Edwards[7]	1,001		0		1	22	22	13	9	0	0
Florence[7]	4,438		0		0	1	20	6	13	1	0
Flowood	9,032	12	0	1	4	7	339	49	286	4	0
Fulton[7]	4,085		0		1	2	215	23	191	1	0
Gautier	18,451	64	2	6	8	48	721	193	458	70	4
Greenwood	14,146	84	0	5	23	56	830	197	614	19	2
Gulfport	72,792	299	10	26	82	181	3,662	562	2,897	203	16
Hattiesburg	47,116	130	3	9	43	75	2,113	347	1,645	121	3
Holly Springs[7]	7,682		5		17	78	259	63	176	20	0
Horn Lake	27,199	32	1	0	20	11	703	129	532	42	1
Iuka[7]	2,983		0		0	0	104	24	67	13	2
Jackson[7]	168,397		60		542	591	7,449	2,006	4,696	747	75
Laurel	18,790	84	2	10	30	42	915	297	562	56	0
Madison	26,339	11	0	1	1	9	251	13	231	7	0
McComb[7]	12,812		1		15	89	833	321	492	20	0
Meridian	38,778	194	9	18	89	78	1,502	435	975	92	10
Ocean Springs	17,698	32	2	3	10	17	671	83	542	46	0
Oxford	24,071	36	0	10	11	15	664	85	567	12	0
Pascagoula	21,928	72	0	25	22	25	1,450	246	1,135	69	4
Pass Christian	5,902	5	0	0	3	2	157	45	110	2	0
Petal[7]	10,743		0		2	1	90	37	41	12	0
Ridgeland	24,551	59	0	2	20	37	633	53	564	16	0
Southaven	53,928	75	5	8	26	36	1,479	196	1,219	64	5
Starkville	25,852	41	1	2	11	27	922	455	440	27	1
Summit[7]	1,642		0		0	0	33	14	17	2	0
Vicksburg[7]	22,772		5		18	97	1,362	231	1,079	52	8
Waveland[7]	6,426		0		1	0	348	33	302	13	0
West Point	10,817	49	0	3	15	31	276	108	167	1	5
Wiggins[7]	4,567		0		4	10	257	57	192	8	0
MISSOURI											
Adrian	1,609	5	0	0	1	4	34	8	23	3	0
Advance	1,368	2	0	1	0	1	9	2	7	0	0
Alma	393	0	0	0	0	0	1	0	1	0	0
Alton	861	0	0	0	0	0	6	1	5	0	0
Anderson	1,977	5	0	0	0	5	77	5	65	7	0
Annapolis	340	0	0	0	0	0	0	0	0	0	0
Arbyrd	474	2	0	0	0	2	1	1	0	0	0
Arcadia	559	0	0	0	0	0	2	0	2	0	0
Archie[6]	1,215	4	0	0	0	4	16	4	7	5	0
Arnold	21,399	38	0	5	7	26	818	32	744	42	0
Ash Grove	1,446	3	0	0	0	3	17	3	14	0	0
Ashland	3,902	6	1	0	0	5	45	9	35	1	0
Aurora	7,508	62	0	10	4	48	374	56	293	25	2
Ava	2,918	2	0	0	0	2	93	15	73	5	0
Ballwin	30,299	12	0	2	0	10	169	23	136	10	7
Bates City	219	0	0	0	0	0	9	2	5	2	0
Battlefield	6,127	2	0	0	2	0	124	31	82	11	0
Bella Villa	737	2	0	0	0	2	15	3	11	1	0
Belle	1,504	1	0	0	0	1	13	4	8	1	0
Bellefontaine Neighbors	10,678	85	3	0	21	61	302	77	167	58	1
Bellflower	358	0	0	0	0	0	5	2	2	1	0
Bel-Nor	1,461	3	0	0	0	3	21	2	17	2	1
Bel-Ridge	2,679	39	0	1	6	32	134	33	90	11	1
Belton	23,312	86	1	18	16	51	943	121	726	96	5
Berkeley	8,958	99	7	1	22	69	440	171	196	73	0
Bertrand	768	3	0	0	0	3	27	12	15	0	0
Bethany	3,095	1	0	0	0	1	44	8	35	1	0
Billings	1,101	2	0	0	1	1	12	3	8	1	0
Birch Tree	649	3	0	0	1	2	2	2	0	0	0
Bismarck	1,482	10	0	2	0	8	21	4	16	1	0
Blackburn	247	0	0	0	0	0	0	0	0	0	0
Bloomfield	1,872	4	0	2	0	2	15	6	7	2	0
Blue Springs	54,727	120	3	17	11	89	1,600	157	1,320	123	1
Bolivar	10,873	50	0	8	2	40	510	55	422	33	1
Bonne Terre	7,185	5	0	0	1	4	18	1	8	9	0
Boonville	8,482	22	0	1	4	17	195	25	162	8	3
Bourbon	1,610	8	0	4	0	4	65	6	53	6	1
Bowling Green	5,541	25	0	0	0	25	101	11	86	4	0
Branson	11,571	53	0	12	15	26	1,442	187	1,161	94	3
Branson West	433	1	0	1	0	0	160	5	151	4	0
Braymer	849	0	0	0	0	0	2	1	1	0	0
Breckenridge Hills	4,655	21	2	1	8	10	137	31	90	16	1
Brentwood	7,991	12	0	2	5	5	323	12	295	16	1
Bridgeton	11,703	87	1	10	24	52	961	74	835	52	4
Brookfield	4,266	10	0	0	0	10	89	21	66	2	0
Buckner	3,052	5	0	4	1	0	94	14	76	4	0
Buffalo	3,043	24	1	1	1	21	182	37	131	14	1
Butler	4,056	11	0	5	0	6	134	18	105	11	2

Table 8. Offenses Known to Law Enforcement, by Selected State and City, 2017—Continued

(Number.)

State/city	Population	Violent crime	Murder and nonnegligent manslaughter	Rape (revised definition)[1]	Robbery	Aggravated assault	Property crime	Burglary	Larceny-theft	Motor vehicle theft	Arson[2]
Butterfield Village	459	0	0	0	0	0	0	0	0	0	0
Byrnes Mill	2,955	1	0	0	0	1	15	3	10	2	0
Cabool	2,134	2	0	1	0	1	36	9	23	4	0
California	4,441	0	0	0	0	0	60	14	44	2	0
Calverton Park	1,283	10	0	0	0	10	21	9	11	1	0
Camden	184	0	0	0	0	0	0	0	0	0	0
Camdenton	3,980	14	0	4	0	10	204	21	173	10	0
Cameron	9,765	48	0	6	1	41	204	24	170	10	1
Canalou	304	0	0	0	0	0	4	4	0	0	0
Canton	2,377	12	0	1	0	11	50	11	34	5	0
Cape Girardeau	39,887	234	5	24	51	154	1,523	252	1,189	82	12
Cardwell	671	1	0	0	0	1	5	2	0	3	0
Carl Junction	7,822	12	0	0	0	12	180	26	147	7	0
Carrollton	3,574	14	0	3	0	11	90	27	60	3	0
Carterville	1,893	3	0	0	0	3	14	3	10	1	0
Carthage	14,292	61	0	10	2	49	593	60	510	23	1
Cassville	3,343	18	0	0	0	18	263	33	218	12	0
Center	504	0	0	0	0	0	1	0	1	0	0
Centralia	4,220	12	0	0	1	11	72	9	60	3	0
Charleston	5,698	40	3	1	5	31	124	25	95	4	0
Chesterfield	47,687	53	0	8	11	34	847	59	751	37	0
Chillicothe	9,760	41	0	7	3	31	173	40	118	15	3
Claycomo	1,477	2	0	0	1	1	49	4	37	8	1
Clayton	16,743	20	0	1	9	10	256	37	205	14	1
Cleveland	671	1	0	0	0	1	6	2	3	1	0
Clever	2,711	4	0	2	0	2	14	3	10	1	0
Clinton	8,817	46	1	4	4	37	341	71	249	21	0
Cole Camp	1,112	4	0	1	0	3	17	3	14	0	0
Columbia	122,585	610	9	115	117	369	3,597	505	2,826	266	10
Concordia	2,375	6	0	2	0	4	44	9	29	6	0
Conway	776	0	0	0	0	0	11	1	9	1	1
Corder	398	1	0	0	0	1	0	0	0	0	0
Cottleville	5,612	7	0	0	0	7	27	0	27	0	0
Country Club Hills	1,264	7	0	0	1	6	60	14	31	15	0
Country Club Village	2,471	2	0	0	0	2	34	7	22	5	0
Crane	1,338	5	0	0	1	4	13	4	8	1	0
Creighton	345	0	0	0	0	0	0	0	0	0	0
Crestwood	11,904	12	0	2	6	4	241	19	214	8	0
Creve Coeur	18,746	24	0	2	13	9	304	48	233	23	0
Crocker	1,042	2	0	0	0	2	34	8	25	1	0
Crystal City	4,817	9	0	0	4	5	135	12	117	6	0
Crystal Lakes	345	0	0	0	0	0	3	1	2	0	0
Cuba	3,339	4	0	0	0	4	98	8	86	4	0
Deepwater	406	0	0	0	0	0	0	0	0	0	0
Delta	440	0	0	0	0	0	1	1	0	0	0
Desloge	4,910	12	1	0	1	10	283	23	248	12	0
De Soto	6,488	13	0	1	0	12	140	14	123	3	0
Des Peres	8,567	12	0	1	7	4	470	16	447	7	0
Dexter	7,935	10	0	0	1	9	154	28	121	5	2
Diamond	941	0	0	0	0	0	7	2	5	0	0
Dixon	1,457	4	0	0	0	4	60	12	46	2	0
Doniphan	1,990	51	0	3	0	48	138	19	114	5	1
Doolittle	594	0	0	0	0	0	9	0	9	0	0
Drexel	958	3	0	1	0	2	9	5	3	1	0
Duenweg	1,295	2	0	0	0	2	29	3	19	7	0
Duquesne	1,725	4	0	1	0	3	67	5	60	2	0
East Lynne	306	0	0	0	0	0	4	3	0	1	0
East Prairie	3,094	7	0	1	0	6	84	19	65	0	1
Edmundson	832	7	0	1	4	2	47	3	25	19	1
Eldon	4,657	7	0	1	1	5	119	19	96	4	1
El Dorado Springs	3,575	12	1	0	0	11	180	25	151	4	2
Ellington	958	0	0	0	0	0	0	0	0	0	0
Ellisville	9,242	11	0	1	4	6	125	9	110	6	0
Elsberry	2,002	12	0	0	1	11	46	10	34	2	1
Eminence	579	0	0	0	0	0	2	1	1	0	0
Eureka	10,588	9	0	2	0	7	198	19	169	10	0
Everton	302	0	0	0	0	0	0	0	0	0	0
Excelsior Springs	11,592	21	0	7	4	10	307	54	236	17	0
Fair Grove	1,456	7	0	1	0	6	33	10	23	0	0
Fair Play	465	0	0	0	0	0	10	1	8	1	0
Fairview	386	0	0	0	0	0	0	0	0	0	0
Farmington	18,710	45	1	5	2	37	653	59	569	25	0
Fayette	2,697	1	0	0	0	1	39	9	28	2	0
Ferguson	20,789	150	11	5	65	69	939	276	547	116	0
Festus	12,187	41	0	3	3	35	210	36	147	27	2
Fleming	123	0	0	0	0	0	0	0	0	0	0
Flordell Hills	802	8	0	0	3	5	50	23	24	3	4
Florissant	51,693	108	2	9	46	51	1,035	146	764	125	4
Fordland	829	0	0	0	0	0	27	6	19	2	0
Foristell	559	2	0	0	0	2	32	3	28	1	0
Forsyth	2,426	6	0	0	0	6	99	7	87	5	0
Frankford	321	0	0	0	0	0	2	1	1	0	0
Fredericktown	4,108	24	0	2	0	22	100	19	78	3	0

Table 8. Offenses Known to Law Enforcement, by Selected State and City, 2017—Continued

(Number.)

State/city	Population	Violent crime	Murder and nonnegligent manslaughter	Rape (revised definition)[1]	Robbery	Aggravated assault	Property crime	Burglary	Larceny-theft	Motor vehicle theft	Arson[2]
Freeman	488	0	0	0	0	0	0	0	0	0	0
Frontenac	3,859	7	0	0	4	3	70	9	59	2	0
Fulton	13,160	35	0	2	4	29	461	83	357	21	5
Garden City	1,627	2	0	0	1	1	32	16	12	4	0
Gideon	1,011	5	0	0	0	5	8	1	5	2	1
Gladstone	27,390	120	1	14	26	79	703	116	504	83	5
Glasgow	1,089	0	0	0	0	0	6	1	5	0	0
Glendale	5,889	3	0	1	0	2	49	8	39	2	0
Goodman	1,226	0	0	0	0	0	9	1	3	5	0
Gower	1,494	0	0	0	0	0	42	11	28	3	0
Grain Valley	13,825	22	0	8	1	13	269	23	209	37	1
Granby	2,122	5	0	0	0	5	42	2	34	6	0
Grandview	25,308	168	1	11	54	102	1,073	168	743	162	2
Greenfield	1,312	5	0	0	0	5	8	4	4	0	0
Green Ridge	501	0	0	0	0	0	0	0	0	0	0
Greenwood	5,733	4	0	1	0	3	22	4	14	4	0
Hallsville	1,546	0	0	0	0	0	7	2	5	0	0
Hamilton	1,710	5	0	1	0	4	23	5	17	1	0
Hannibal	17,791	92	0	20	7	65	839	103	704	32	10
Hardin	534	0	0	0	0	0	8	3	5	0	1
Harrisonville	10,043	44	0	10	4	30	379	65	279	35	2
Hartville	592	1	0	0	1	0	3	1	2	0	0
Hawk Point	686	0	0	0	0	0	5	1	4	0	0
Hayti	2,684	19	0	3	6	10	157	35	112	10	2
Hazelwood	25,401	82	0	4	38	40	792	109	599	84	0
Henrietta	359	0	0	0	0	0	6	3	3	0	0
Herculaneum	4,050	7	0	1	0	6	53	4	41	8	1
Hermann	2,355	7	0	1	1	5	38	11	27	0	0
Higginsville	4,629	5	0	0	0	5	55	7	45	3	0
Highlandville	996	0	0	0	0	0	4	1	3	0	0
Hillsdale[4]	1,574		3	0	3		36	8	18	10	0
Holcomb	593	0	0	0	0	0	0	0	0	0	0
Holden	2,240	4	0	0	0	4	57	8	46	3	1
Hollister	4,499	19	0	2	1	16	105	16	83	6	0
Holts Summit[5]	3,784		0	4	0		62	2	54	6	0
Hornersville	621	3	0	0	0	3	5	2	2	1	0
Houston	2,094	6	0	0	1	5	117	13	102	2	1
Howardville	359	0	0	0	0	0	0	0	0	0	0
Humansville	1,033	1	0	0	0	1	7	3	4	0	0
Huntsville	1,508	2	0	0	0	2	12	3	9	0	0
Independence	117,055	646	11	33	156	446	6,702	785	4,655	1,262	12
Indian Point	512	0	0	0	0	0	0	0	0	0	0
Iron Mountain Lake	735	0	0	0	0	0	2	1	1	0	0
Ironton	1,364	1	0	0	0	1	27	4	23	0	0
Jackson	15,252	26	0	2	0	24	189	29	153	7	0
Jasper	938	1	0	0	0	1	17	3	11	3	1
Jefferson City	42,989	152	4	16	38	94	1,254	164	1,032	58	1
Jonesburg	716	2	0	1	0	1	13	2	11	0	0
Joplin	52,412	317	3	44	61	209	3,729	487	2,918	324	9
Kahoka	1,995	1	0	0	0	1	14	5	9	0	0
Kansas City	484,948	8,362	150	445	1,858	5,909	22,035	4,658	12,950	4,427	201
Kearney	10,032	11	0	4	0	7	153	19	122	12	0
Kennett	10,505	68	1	6	7	54	592	112	451	29	1
Kimberling City	2,293	5	0	0	0	5	30	4	25	1	0
Kimmswick	158	0	0	0	0	0	0	0	0	0	0
Kirksville	17,520	44	1	6	4	33	577	87	472	18	14
Kirkwood	27,621	28	0	4	6	18	354	42	289	23	2
Knob Noster	2,737	4	0	0	0	4	53	11	42	0	1
Laddonia	506	2	0	0	0	2	3	1	1	1	1
Ladue	8,593	4	1	0	1	2	109	18	81	10	0
La Grange	929	1	0	0	0	1	5	0	5	0	0
Lake Lafayette	321	0	0	0	0	0	2	1	1	0	0
Lake Lotawana	2,061	0	0	0	0	0	34	0	32	2	0
Lake Ozark	1,818	4	3	0	0	1	68	6	60	2	0
Lakeshire	1,412	5	0	1	1	3	13	5	6	2	0
Lake St. Louis	15,979	18	0	3	2	13	251	18	221	12	0
Lake Tapawingo	723	3	0	1	0	2	13	0	12	1	0
Lake Waukomis	916	0	0	0	0	0	13	2	8	3	0
Lake Winnebago	1,164	1	0	1	0	0	6	1	5	0	0
Lamar	4,338	12	0	5	0	7	121	34	82	5	0
Lanagan	408	3	0	0	0	3	8	2	5	1	0
La Plata	1,311	2	0	1	0	1	5	1	2	2	0
Lathrop	2,040	5	0	2	0	3	23	4	17	2	0
Laurie	932	2	0	0	0	2	40	15	22	3	0
Lawson	2,395	8	0	0	0	8	34	13	15	6	2
Leadington	510	1	0	1	0	0	25	7	14	4	0
Leadwood	1,176	2	1	0	0	1	23	4	19	0	1
Leasburg	332	0	0	0	0	0	11	1	9	1	0
Lebanon	14,739	44	0	5	2	37	727	102	562	63	2
Lee's Summit	96,855	133	1	26	37	69	1,869	178	1,572	119	2
Leeton	553	0	0	0	0	0	3	0	2	1	0
Lexington	4,560	7	0	2	0	5	62	7	48	7	0
Liberal	719	2	0	1	0	1	6	3	2	1	0

Table 8. Offenses Known to Law Enforcement, by Selected State and City, 2017—Continued

(Number.)

State/city	Population	Violent crime	Murder and nonnegligent manslaughter	Rape (revised definition)[1]	Robbery	Aggravated assault	Property crime	Burglary	Larceny-theft	Motor vehicle theft	Arson[2]
Liberty	30,850	72	0	13	11	48	543	61	408	74	2
Licking	3,115	4	0	0	0	4	58	14	40	4	0
Lilbourn	1,106	2	1	0	0	1	1	1	0	0	0
Lincoln	1,179	3	0	0	0	3	25	8	15	2	0
Linn Creek	245	0	0	0	0	0	2	2	0	0	0
Lone Jack	1,179	0	0	0	0	0	7	2	5	0	0
Louisiana	3,269	7	0	2	0	5	48	10	38	0	1
Macon	5,360	10	1	1	0	8	135	20	110	5	0
Malden	4,030	47	0	0	3	44	86	28	51	7	0
Manchester	18,154	9	0	1	2	6	218	11	202	5	1
Mansfield	1,255	4	0	0	2	2	94	6	84	4	0
Maplewood	7,843	37	0	0	14	23	649	23	605	21	0
Marble Hill	1,460	0	0	0	0	0	35	2	32	1	0
Marceline	2,112	4	0	0	0	4	44	16	23	5	1
Marionville	2,192	15	0	2	1	12	66	19	42	5	0
Marshall	12,867	25	0	3	2	20	411	66	335	10	3
Marshfield	7,341	17	1	1	0	15	235	35	196	4	0
Marston	461	0	0	0	0	0	12	7	1	4	0
Martinsburg	308	0	0	0	0	0	0	0	0	0	0
Maryland Heights	27,083	78	0	14	14	50	578	60	465	53	0
Maryville	11,820	24	0	2	2	20	151	26	111	14	0
Matthews	614	1	0	0	1	0	13	3	8	2	0
Maysville	1,083	0	0	0	0	0	4	1	3	0	0
Memphis	1,860	2	0	0	0	2	20	3	15	2	1
Merriam Woods	1,770	2	0	0	0	2	2	0	2	0	0
Mexico	11,709	15	0	2	5	8	298	29	252	17	0
Milan	1,802	5	0	3	0	2	12	4	8	0	0
Miller	686	2	0	1	1	0	6	3	3	0	0
Miner	945	10	0	1	2	7	47	7	36	4	1
Moberly	13,838	81	2	4	0	75	389	53	309	27	1
Moline Acres	2,399	27	0	0	5	22	135	28	90	17	0
Monett	9,048	16	0	3	1	12	330	82	234	14	2
Monroe City	2,428	9	0	4	0	5	54	15	39	0	0
Montgomery City	2,692	9	1	1	0	7	64	17	42	5	1
Morehouse	899	1	0	0	0	1	3	0	3	0	0
Moscow Mills	2,620	13	0	1	0	12	49	5	42	2	0
Mound City	1,032	2	0	0	0	2	24	4	16	4	0
Mountain Grove	4,674	24	0	1	1	22	133	20	103	10	0
Mountain View	2,669	8	0	2	0	6	51	14	34	3	1
Mount Vernon	4,551	2	0	1	0	1	119	12	104	3	0
Napoleon	217	0	0	0	0	0	0	0	0	0	0
Neosho	12,237	35	0	8	4	23	595	97	457	41	3
Nevada	8,198	60	0	5	7	48	591	98	458	35	8
New Bloomfield	677	0	0	0	0	0	0	0	0	0	0
Newburg	444	0	0	0	0	0	3	1	2	0	0
New Florence	717	0	0	0	0	0	6	6	0	0	0
New Franklin	1,065	0	0	0	0	0	1	0	1	0	0
New Haven	2,090	1	0	1	0	0	38	8	28	2	0
New London	969	0	0	0	0	0	15	4	11	0	0
Niangua	420	0	0	0	0	0	0	0	0	0	0
Nixa	21,575	21	0	8	4	9	311	40	244	27	0
Noel	1,814	2	0	1	0	1	34	6	27	1	0
Normandy	7,544	27	0	3	6	18	145	21	100	24	1
North Kansas City	4,407	33	1	7	9	16	426	25	283	118	1
Northmoor	328	2	0	0	0	2	20	3	11	6	0
Northwoods[8]	4,138		1	3	10		115	28	65	22	1
Oak Grove	8,019	8	0	2	1	5	179	15	146	18	1
Oakland	1,375	1	0	0	0	1	5	2	3	0	0
Oakview Village	396	1	0	1	0	0	9	3	4	2	0
O'Fallon	87,388	158	1	25	4	128	1,006	89	861	56	2
Olivette	7,859	9	0	0	6	3	138	24	107	7	0
Oregon	759	0	0	0	0	0	1	0	1	0	0
Oronogo	2,490	4	0	1	0	3	13	3	9	1	0
Orrick	802	0	0	0	0	0	0	0	0	0	0
Osage Beach	4,474	26	0	4	1	21	304	34	268	2	0
Osceola	892	2	0	0	1	1	5	2	3	0	0
Overland	15,760	43	1	6	2	34	562	58	466	38	0
Owensville	2,609	2	0	0	0	2	62	7	49	6	0
Ozark	19,688	47	0	10	3	34	584	67	483	34	0
Pacific	7,244	7	0	0	1	6	179	21	148	10	1
Pagedale	3,289	28	1	4	7	16	90	16	63	11	1
Palmyra	3,619	1	0	0	0	1	122	4	114	4	0
Park Hills	8,637	7	0	0	0	7	283	30	226	27	0
Parkville	6,685	12	0	1	0	11	116	12	96	8	0
Peculiar	5,039	7	0	1	2	4	100	23	69	8	1
Perry	697	0	0	0	0	0	2	2	0	0	0
Perryville	8,493	33	0	5	3	25	229	39	178	12	0
Pevely	5,748	21	0	9	0	12	179	23	142	14	1
Piedmont	1,931	6	0	1	0	5	33	6	26	1	0
Pierce City	1,298	5	0	0	0	5	35	9	22	4	0
Pilot Grove	762	2	0	0	0	2	6	1	4	1	0
Pilot Knob	699	0	0	0	0	0	5	2	3	0	0
Pineville	786	0	0	0	0	0	0	0	0	0	0

Table 8. Offenses Known to Law Enforcement, by Selected State and City, 2017—Continued

(Number.)

State/city	Population	Violent crime	Murder and nonnegligent manslaughter	Rape (revised definition)[1]	Robbery	Aggravated assault	Property crime	Burglary	Larceny-theft	Motor vehicle theft	Arson[2]
Platte City	4,900	1	0	0	0	1	77	8	66	3	0
Platte Woods	407	0	0	0	0	0	9	4	2	3	0
Plattsburg	2,280	7	0	0	0	7	18	5	8	5	0
Pleasant Hill	8,496	14	0	1	2	11	163	27	118	18	0
Pleasant Hope	613	1	0	1	0	0	1	1	0	0	1
Pleasant Valley	3,084	8	0	0	0	8	36	10	21	5	1
Polo[6]	534	3	0	0	0	3	6	1	5	0	0
Poplar Bluff	17,264	105	1	19	14	71	1,104	222	800	82	2
Portageville	3,090	0	0	0	0	0	12	11	0	1	0
Potosi	2,641	10	0	0	2	8	190	28	154	8	0
Purdy	1,102	3	0	1	1	1	36	8	26	2	0
Queen City	589	0	0	0	0	0	1	0	1	0	0
Qulin	448	2	0	0	0	2	5	1	4	0	0
Raymore	21,110	15	0	4	4	7	454	23	415	16	1
Raytown	29,224	165	2	20	47	96	1,410	384	827	199	2
Reeds Spring	857	0	0	0	0	0	2	1	0	1	0
Republic	16,316	49	1	4	2	42	376	49	298	29	0
Rich Hill	1,322	4	0	0	0	4	32	8	21	3	0
Richland	1,788	7	0	0	0	7	30	10	19	1	1
Richmond	5,540	37	0	4	1	32	238	48	179	11	4
Richmond Heights	8,362	43	1	3	18	21	479	24	420	35	1
Riverside	3,276	21	1	1	3	16	191	20	140	31	2
Riverview	2,795	46	2	0	10	34	109	43	51	15	2
Rockaway Beach	868	4	0	0	0	4	5	2	3	0	1
Rock Hill	4,616	1	0	0	0	1	42	9	31	2	0
Rock Port	1,214	5	0	0	0	5	7	0	7	0	0
Rogersville	3,598	5	1	0	0	4	90	10	69	11	0
Rolla	20,147	112	0	18	14	80	739	114	593	32	5
Rosebud	403	0	0	0	0	0	0	0	0	0	0
Rutledge	113	0	0	0	0	0	0	0	0	0	0
Salem	4,918	10	0	1	0	9	152	18	128	6	0
Sarcoxie	1,287	0	0	0	0	0	15	3	10	2	0
Savannah	5,136	4	0	0	0	4	59	12	41	6	0
Scott City	4,480	16	0	1	0	15	88	18	66	4	1
Sedalia	21,501	151	0	10	8	133	1,125	183	862	80	3
Seligman	831	1	0	0	0	1	43	7	32	4	5
Senath	1,679	12	0	0	0	12	14	6	6	2	0
Seneca	2,419	2	0	0	0	2	94	13	75	6	1
Seymour	1,997	4	0	1	0	3	3	0	1	2	0
Shelbina	1,610	8	0	2	0	6	24	2	20	2	0
Shrewsbury	6,135	10	1	1	1	7	212	12	199	1	0
Sikeston	16,324	61	1	2	15	43	816	141	645	30	7
Silex	307	0	0	0	0	0	1	0	1	0	1
Slater	1,797	2	0	0	0	2	29	4	24	1	0
Smithville	9,638	9	0	4	0	5	125	17	90	18	1
Southwest City	954	7	0	0	0	7	25	6	11	8	0
Sparta	1,883	2	0	0	0	2	34	8	22	4	0
Springfield	168,654	2,258	14	352	382	1,510	14,932	2,236	10,727	1,969	62
St. Ann	12,779	69	0	2	7	60	315	35	238	42	1
St. Charles	69,804	158	2	23	35	98	1,765	181	1,450	134	5
St. Clair	4,718	31	0	0	3	28	348	49	279	20	0
Steelville	1,692	1	0	1	0	0	93	30	57	6	1
Ste. Genevieve	4,508	3	0	0	0	3	55	6	47	2	0
St. James	4,102	16	0	1	1	14	178	25	146	7	1
St. John	6,378	19	1	2	9	7	195	24	140	31	0
St. Joseph	76,435	438	7	37	98	296	5,146	737	3,633	776	14
St. Louis	310,284	6,461	205	289	1,944	4,023	18,745	3,138	12,894	2,713	201
St. Marys	347	0	0	0	0	0	0	0	0	0	0
Stover	1,072	16	0	2	0	14	18	1	17	0	0
St. Peters	58,079	88	0	22	8	58	1,312	113	1,152	47	5
Strafford	2,341	3	0	0	1	2	69	8	52	9	0
St. Robert	6,020	27	0	5	4	18	331	42	281	8	1
Sturgeon	917	0	0	0	0	0	1	0	1	0	0
Sugar Creek	3,298	29	0	2	3	24	150	21	101	28	1
Sullivan	7,132	17	1	4	0	12	441	96	318	27	0
Summersville	502	4	0	0	0	4	6	5	0	1	0
Sunset Hills	8,498	16	0	4	4	8	153	21	118	14	0
Tarkio	1,457	1	0	0	0	1	8	0	7	1	0
Terre du Lac	2,371	9	0	0	3	6	18	1	17	0	0
Thayer	2,208	6	1	0	0	5	48	14	31	3	0
Tipton	3,397	1	0	0	0	1	15	2	11	2	0
Town and Country	11,157	5	0	2	0	3	130	12	113	5	1
Tracy	225	0	0	0	0	0	7	0	5	2	0
Trenton	5,920	13	0	2	1	10	93	37	48	8	1
Troy	12,079	43	0	2	4	37	249	28	207	14	1
Truesdale	747	1	0	0	0	1	9	0	8	1	0
Union	11,447	28	0	4	2	22	556	44	480	32	2
University City	34,601	209	2	4	60	143	1,210	226	876	108	9
Urbana	410	0	0	0	0	0	0	0	0	0	0
Van Buren	829	1	0	0	0	1	22	6	14	2	0
Vandalia	4,344	7	0	2	0	5	28	9	18	1	0
Velda City	1,382	7	0	0	1	6	24	7	13	4	0
Verona	602	4	0	0	0	4	6	3	3	0	1

Table 8. Offenses Known to Law Enforcement, by Selected State and City, 2017—Continued

(Number.)

State/city	Population	Violent crime	Murder and nonnegligent manslaughter	Rape (revised definition)[1]	Robbery	Aggravated assault	Property crime	Burglary	Larceny-theft	Motor vehicle theft	Arson[2]
Versailles[6]	2,452	7	0	0	1	6	52	2	47	3	1
Vienna	588	1	0	1	0	0	19	2	17	0	0
Vinita Park	11,061	141	9	7	36	89	409	97	255	57	4
Walnut Grove	812	6	0	0	0	6	2	1	0	1	0
Warrensburg	20,483	42	0	14	12	16	575	81	461	33	0
Warrenton	8,168	51	0	13	2	36	268	24	233	11	0
Warsaw	2,118	10	0	0	2	8	97	30	60	7	0
Warson Woods	1,936	0	0	0	0	0	17	2	15	0	0
Washburn	436	0	0	0	0	0	0	0	0	0	0
Washington	14,073	43	0	4	4	35	526	37	470	19	0
Waverly	829	5	0	0	0	5	13	9	3	1	1
Waynesville	5,381	16	0	6	1	9	103	14	79	10	1
Weatherby Lake	1,957	1	0	1	0	0	19	1	17	1	0
Webb City	11,259	13	0	0	4	9	321	24	279	18	2
Webster Groves	22,968	27	3	2	3	19	167	28	132	7	3
Wellington	796	0	0	0	0	0	7	1	6	0	0
Wellsville	1,154	2	0	0	0	2	18	5	13	0	0
Wentzville[6]	38,876	70	0	13	6	51	539	50	470	19	2
Weston	1,771	3	0	1	0	2	18	0	18	0	0
West Plains	12,367	37	1	9	5	22	491	96	361	34	0
Wheaton	693	0	0	0	0	0	0	0	0	0	0
Willard	5,452	7	0	0	0	7	61	9	47	5	0
Willow Springs	2,146	9	0	0	2	7	65	8	47	10	0
Winfield	1,442	4	0	1	0	3	24	2	21	1	0
Winona	1,289	6	0	0	0	6	11	1	7	3	0
Wood Heights	694	1	0	0	0	1	25	12	12	1	0
Woodson Terrace	4,043	17	0	1	1	15	147	18	72	57	3
Wright City	3,584	1	0	0	0	1	49	10	33	6	0
Wyatt	303	1	0	0	0	1	1	1	0	0	0
MONTANA											
Baker	2,029	2	0	0	0	2	2	0	2	0	0
Belgrade	8,393	24	0	7	5	12	181	11	160	10	0
Billings	111,317	549	2	76	87	384	6,076	783	4,451	842	25
Boulder	1,239	5	0	1	0	4	20	1	19	0	0
Bozeman	46,728	130	2	41	11	76	1,143	81	987	75	7
Bridger	736	3	0	2	0	1	10	2	8	0	0
Chinook	1,238	3	0	0	0	3	9	0	8	1	0
Colstrip	2,326	1	0	1	0	0	12	2	9	1	0
Columbia Falls	5,337	8	0	1	0	7	138	13	117	8	0
Columbus	2,050	1	0	0	0	1	22	2	18	2	0
Conrad	2,544	10	0	1	0	9	54	7	44	3	1
Cut Bank	3,031	17	0	2	0	15	72	4	59	9	0
Deer Lodge	2,968	9	0	0	0	9	77	4	68	5	2
Dillon	4,277	21	0	3	2	16	19	8	8	3	0
East Helena	2,084	5	0	0	0	5	42	8	27	7	0
Ennis	900	1	0	0	0	1	2	0	2	0	0
Eureka	1,092	1	0	0	0	1	7	0	6	1	0
Fort Benton	1,455	2	0	0	0	2	22	3	19	0	0
Fromberg	446	0	0	0	0	0	2	0	1	1	0
Glasgow	3,379	14	0	3	0	11	52	5	42	5	2
Glendive	5,402	8	0	1	0	7	96	18	72	6	0
Great Falls	59,167	246	3	20	30	193	3,023	284	2,539	200	11
Hamilton	4,739	22	0	7	0	15	158	5	148	5	1
Havre	9,900	95	0	18	8	69	401	52	325	24	2
Helena	31,668	217	1	56	23	137	1,346	167	1,082	97	14
Hot Springs	560	7	0	0	0	7	19	1	16	2	0
Kalispell	23,243	72	0	19	6	47	797	87	662	48	1
Laurel	6,887	15	0	1	1	13	181	12	148	21	0
Lewistown	5,860	23	0	3	0	20	83	16	59	8	4
Libby	2,684	8	0	0	0	8	69	3	65	1	0
Livingston	7,470	19	0	2	0	17	185	10	163	12	3
Manhattan	1,723	2	0	0	0	2	12	1	9	2	0
Miles City	8,690	9	0	1	0	8	159	12	142	5	0
Missoula	73,304	352	2	71	45	234	3,342	325	2,843	174	23
Plains	1,076	5	0	0	0	5	16	1	14	1	0
Polson	4,821	29	0	5	0	24	307	39	245	23	1
Red Lodge	2,256	6	0	0	0	6	41	2	35	4	0
Ronan City	2,036	4	0	0	0	4	77	11	56	10	0
Sidney	6,814	57	0	9	0	48	130	28	94	8	2
Stevensville	1,985	8	0	1	1	6	29	8	21	0	0
St. Ignatius	827	3	0	1	0	2	7	2	5	0	0
Thompson Falls	1,361	1	0	0	0	1	35	0	34	1	0
Troy	891	2	0	0	0	2	30	2	26	2	0
West Yellowstone	1,367	1	0	0	1	0	21	9	11	1	0
Whitefish	7,446	12	0	4	0	8	151	15	127	9	0
Wolf Point	2,840	14	0	1	1	12	85	7	74	4	0
NEBRASKA											
Bellevue	53,819	78	1	45	14	18	990	113	724	153	6
Bennington	1,518	1	0	0	1	0	13	1	9	3	
Cozad	3,775	7	0	0	2	5	19	4	15	0	0
Crete	7,071	46	0	13	1	32	126	18	96	12	0

Table 8. Offenses Known to Law Enforcement, by Selected State and City, 2017—Continued

(Number.)

State/city	Population	Violent crime	Murder and nonnegligent manslaughter	Rape (revised definition)[1]	Robbery	Aggravated assault	Property crime	Burglary	Larceny- theft	Motor vehicle theft	Arson[2]
Emerson	798	2	0	0	0	2	1	0	0	1	0
Fairbury	3,680	14	0	2	0	12	107	20	87	0	0
Madison	2,358	1	0	0	1	0	4	2	2	0	0
McCook	7,498	8	0	1	1	6	179	25	151	3	0
Milford	2,115	1	0	0	0	1	23	6	17	0	
Neligh	1,512	3	0	0	0	3	7	0	6	1	
Norfolk	24,364	36	1	14	9	12	466	60	381	25	2
Omaha	449,388	2,909	31	410	625	1,843	17,437	2,088	11,849	3,500	
O'Neill	3,618	5	0	5	0	0	17	3	13	1	
Plainview	1,197	7	0	1	0	6	6	0	6	0	
Scribner	841	1	0	0	0	1	0	0	0	0	
Superior	1,839	3	0	2	0	1	41	6	32	3	
Valley	2,225	2	0	0	0	2	45	6	37	2	
York	7,876	0	0	0	0	0	234	24	201	9	
NEVADA											
Boulder City	15,804	9	0	3	0	6	136	35	81	20	2
Carlin	2,299	23	0	0	0	23	21	5	11	5	0
Elko	20,807	81	2	21	11	47	665	192	414	59	0
Fallon	8,450	23	1	2	1	19	293	9	271	13	1
Henderson	299,285	554	10	86	240	218	5,486	1,089	3,756	641	21
Las Vegas Metropolitan Police Department	1,627,244	10,071	205	1,296	3,436	5,134	47,896	13,102	26,608	8,186	91
Lovelock	1,834	14	0	1	0	13	52	20	29	3	0
Mesquite	18,476	31	0	13	2	16	316	37	239	40	1
North Las Vegas	242,537	2,461	22	116	565	1,758	5,787	1,950	2,516	1,321	11
Reno	248,531	1,674	19	142	382	1,131	7,669	1,347	4,890	1,432	18
Sparks	99,732	474	2	54	105	313	2,692	591	1,684	417	11
West Wendover	4,236	27	1	8	2	16	141	39	88	14	0
Winnemucca	7,938	41	1	10	3	27	163	53	95	15	1
Yerington	3,147	4	0	2	0	2	16	4	9	3	0
NEW HAMPSHIRE											
Alexandria	1,620	0	0	0	0	0	13	6	7	0	0
Alstead	1,893	1	1	0	0	0	2	2	0	0	0
Alton	5,334	12	0	6	0	6	55	15	38	2	0
Amherst	11,250	5	0	4	0	1	101	12	85	4	0
Antrim	2,660	2	0	2	0	0	28	6	20	2	1
Ashland	2,056	5	0	2	2	1	60	12	44	4	0
Atkinson	6,876	1	0	0	0	1	28	5	22	1	0
Auburn	5,449	1	0	1	0	0	39	7	31	1	0
Barnstead	4,667	7	0	2	0	5	65	15	43	7	0
Barrington	8,981	6	0	0	0	6	45	15	29	1	0
Bartlett	2,755	3	0	0	1	2	23	6	16	1	0
Bedford	22,623	12	0	2	1	9	243	15	221	7	2
Belmont	7,293	14	0	3	1	10	139	22	107	10	4
Bennington	1,485	5	0	2	0	3	10	1	8	1	0
Berlin	10,489	25	0	7	1	17	140	20	118	2	4
Bethlehem	2,560	11	0	4	0	7	15	3	11	1	1
Boscawen	3,977	9	0	2	0	7	49	1	46	2	0
Bow	7,820	4	0	0	0	4	32	10	19	3	0
Bradford	1,678	2	0	1	1	0	3	1	2	0	0
Brentwood	4,743	2	0	1	0	1	23	3	17	3	0
Bristol	3,057	7	0	4	2	1	46	4	39	3	0
Brookline	5,304	3	0	0	0	3	15	4	11	0	0
Campton	3,286	11	0	6	1	4	52	8	41	3	0
Candia	3,903	1	0	0	1	0	26	3	19	4	1
Canterbury	2,416	0	0	0	0	0	31	2	27	2	0
Carroll	741	1	0	1	0	0	17	3	13	1	0
Center Harbor	1,098	0	0	0	0	0	18	9	9	0	0
Charlestown	4,971	17	0	0	2	15	26	4	21	1	0
Chester	5,068	3	0	0	0	3	35	10	24	1	0
Claremont	12,893	33	0	12	5	16	269	33	229	7	4
Colebrook	2,147	1	0	1	0	0	25	3	20	2	0
Concord	42,942	119	1	37	23	58	824	135	655	34	6
Conway	9,946	25	0	9	0	16	224	19	196	9	1
Cornish	1,612	0	0	0	0	0	5	1	2	2	0
Dalton	882	0	0	0	0	0	2	2	0	0	0
Danville	4,471	4	0	1	0	3	28	3	24	1	0
Deerfield	4,465	4	0	1	0	3	21	6	9	6	0
Deering	1,933	2	0	0	0	2	18	7	9	2	0
Derry	33,382	38	0	7	5	26	364	40	305	19	6
Dover	31,344	35	0	15	5	15	319	29	280	10	3
Dublin	1,522	4	0	3	0	1	14	7	7	0	0
Dunbarton	2,808	2	0	1	0	1	26	5	19	2	0
Durham	16,751	9	1	4	0	4	83	22	57	4	1
East Kingston	2,396	1	0	0	0	1	8	2	4	2	0
Effingham	1,439	3	0	0	0	3	14	4	9	1	0
Enfield	4,527	3	0	1	1	1	23	2	20	1	0
Epping	6,978	10	0	4	3	3	94	6	80	8	0
Epsom	4,701	12	0	4	0	8	30	9	18	3	0
Exeter	14,807	29	0	11	5	13	98	8	82	8	0
Farmington	6,858	17	4	1	0	12	128	34	87	7	2

Table 8. Offenses Known to Law Enforcement, by Selected State and City, 2017—Continued

(Number.)

State/city	Population	Violent crime	Murder and nonnegligent manslaughter	Rape (revised definition)[1]	Robbery	Aggravated assault	Property crime	Burglary	Larceny-theft	Motor vehicle theft	Arson[2]
Fitzwilliam	2,316	2	0	0	0	2	20	7	13	0	1
Franconia	1,102	1	0	1	0	0	22	1	21	0	0
Franklin	8,444	29	1	7	2	19	133	36	92	5	0
Freedom	1,488	0	0	0	0	0	3	1	1	1	0
Fremont	4,737	5	0	2	1	2	26	2	23	1	1
Gilford	7,191	10	0	0	1	9	169	17	147	5	1
Gilmanton	3,746	3	0	2	0	1	27	7	16	4	0
Goffstown	18,057	34	1	7	3	23	180	21	146	13	0
Gorham	2,592	4	0	0	0	4	51	6	44	1	0
Grantham	2,967	0	0	0	0	0	8	1	7	0	0
Greenland	3,966	0	0	0	0	0	19	3	16	0	0
Hampstead	8,625	10	0	2	0	8	58	15	39	4	0
Hampton	15,524	28	0	5	3	20	201	16	172	13	3
Hampton Falls	2,302	8	0	7	0	1	19	4	15	0	1
Hancock	1,628	0	0	0	0	0	11	5	6	0	0
Hanover	11,443	9	0	8	0	1	118	9	108	1	3
Haverhill	4,542	11	1	2	0	8	70	16	49	5	1
Henniker	4,947	10	0	6	1	3	60	15	42	3	0
Hillsborough	5,954	11	0	2	0	9	76	13	61	2	0
Hinsdale	3,835	12	0	4	1	7	68	10	55	3	1
Holderness	2,090	2	0	1	1	0	23	4	18	1	0
Hollis	7,838	6	0	2	1	3	39	6	30	3	0
Hooksett	14,274	19	0	3	3	13	200	14	177	9	1
Hopkinton	5,629	1	0	0	0	1	27	2	23	2	0
Hudson	25,212	26	0	8	1	17	250	28	209	13	2
Jackson	814	0	0	0	0	0	9	6	3	0	0
Jaffrey	5,211	8	0	2	0	6	35	10	24	1	1
Keene	23,386	55	0	10	19	26	680	83	577	20	3
Kensington	2,126	4	0	1	0	3	4	3	1	0	0
Kingston	6,185	3	0	2	0	1	18	5	6	7	0
Laconia	16,616	77	0	11	12	54	568	63	484	21	2
Lancaster	3,288	0	0	0	0	0	36	5	31	0	0
Lebanon	13,577	40	1	5	7	27	334	17	303	14	0
Lee	4,417	7	0	1	2	4	25	3	22	0	0
Lincoln	1,761	4	0	3	0	1	57	5	46	6	0
Lisbon	1,564	1	0	1	0	0	14	4	10	0	1
Litchfield	8,508	2	0	1	0	1	28	5	21	2	0
Littleton	5,871	17	0	6	1	10	120	10	106	4	1
Londonderry	26,254	29	0	7	3	19	214	30	173	11	1
Loudon	5,506	6	0	5	0	1	42	7	32	3	1
Lyndeborough	1,707	2	0	1	0	1	11	1	9	1	0
Madbury	1,828	1	0	0	0	1	7	1	6	0	0
Madison	2,523	5	0	1	0	4	23	10	11	2	0
Manchester	110,655	745	2	92	174	477	2,905	491	2,229	185	23
Marlborough	2,040	3	0	2	0	1	10	3	7	0	0
Meredith	6,404	9	0	5	1	3	79	5	68	6	0
Merrimack	25,675	6	0	0	2	4	184	14	166	4	1
Middleton	1,810	5	0	1	1	3	12	1	9	2	0
Milford	15,330	15	0	5	0	10	103	11	87	5	3
Milton	4,592	5	0	2	0	3	66	19	44	3	0
Mont Vernon	2,519	1	0	1	0	0	9	5	4	0	0
Moultonborough	4,038	2	0	1	1	0	41	3	30	8	0
Nashua	88,102	150	1	53	30	66	1,190	115	1,003	72	7
New Boston	5,618	3	0	1	0	2	20	3	15	2	0
Newbury	2,198	1	0	0	0	1	16	2	13	1	0
New Durham	2,671	2	0	1	0	1	18	3	15	0	0
Newfields	1,713	3	0	2	0	1	10	0	9	1	0
New Hampton	2,217	2	0	0	0	2	29	7	18	4	1
Newington	796	0	0	0	0	0	101	1	99	1	1
New Ipswich	5,248	2	0	1	0	1	37	14	20	3	2
New London	4,590	1	0	0	0	1	25	7	18	0	1
Newmarket	9,003	12	0	6	0	6	49	4	44	1	1
Newport	6,344	18	0	3	0	15	99	18	77	4	1
Newton	4,963	4	0	2	0	2	20	3	16	1	1
Northfield	4,814	8	0	2	1	5	49	1	38	10	1
North Hampton	4,447	2	0	1	0	1	43	8	33	2	0
Northumberland	2,122	3	0	2	0	1	22	3	19	0	1
Northwood	4,281	7	0	4	0	3	44	7	34	3	0
Nottingham	5,046	0	0	0	0	0	25	7	17	1	0
Ossipee	4,246	10	0	4	1	5	72	15	50	7	0
Pelham	13,513	12	0	1	1	10	86	14	67	5	2
Pembroke	7,115	11	0	7	0	4	94	17	69	8	1
Peterborough	6,568	11	0	3	1	7	58	12	43	3	0
Plaistow	7,695	9	0	0	8	1	145	8	129	8	0
Plymouth	6,303	21	0	6	1	14	216	10	197	9	2
Portsmouth	21,607	44	0	14	6	24	300	26	257	17	3
Raymond	10,347	12	0	3	0	9	104	12	83	9	1
Rindge	5,883	6	0	2	0	4	60	13	45	2	0
Rochester	30,441	145	0	37	25	83	1,003	107	873	23	3
Rollinsford	2,552	0	0	0	0	0	27	5	22	0	0
Rye	5,425	4	0	2	0	2	45	0	44	1	1
Salem	29,013	41	0	9	17	15	445	25	409	11	3
Sanbornton	2,996	2	0	2	0	0	27	3	19	5	0

Table 8. Offenses Known to Law Enforcement, by Selected State and City, 2017—Continued

(Number.)

State/city	Population	Violent crime	Murder and nonnegligent manslaughter	Rape (revised definition)[1]	Robbery	Aggravated assault	Property crime	Burglary	Larceny-theft	Motor vehicle theft	Arson[2]
Sandown	6,368	1	0	0	0	1	17	5	11	1	0
Sandwich	1,304	0	0	0	0	0	22	5	17	0	0
Seabrook	8,816	21	0	2	2	17	216	25	180	11	1
Somersworth	11,795	40	0	10	11	19	346	37	292	17	1
South Hampton	820	1	0	0	0	1	4	1	3	0	0
Springfield	1,319	0	0	0	0	0	6	2	2	2	0
Strafford	4,121	1	0	0	0	1	10	3	7	0	0
Stratham	7,452	3	0	1	0	2	40	7	33	0	1
Sugar Hill	571	0	0	0	0	0	0	0	0	0	0
Sunapee	3,449	3	0	1	0	2	19	3	15	1	0
Thornton	2,491	3	0	2	0	1	14	3	11	0	0
Tilton	3,556	13	0	6	2	5	213	13	193	7	0
Troy	2,054	3	0	1	0	2	13	6	7	0	0
Tuftonboro	2,327	2	0	0	0	2	21	3	16	2	0
Wakefield	5,613	6	0	1	0	5	57	18	35	4	1
Warner	2,879	0	0	0	0	0	14	2	12	0	1
Washington	1,108	0	0	0	0	0	12	5	6	1	0
Waterville Valley	245	2	0	2	0	0	9	1	8	0	0
Weare	8,935	14	0	5	0	9	53	17	34	2	0
Webster	1,906	0	0	0	0	0	9	4	5	0	0
Wilton	3,687	7	0	3	0	4	35	11	22	2	0
Winchester	4,146	3	0	0	0	3	55	9	44	2	0
Windham	14,686	6	0	1	0	5	74	10	59	5	0
Wolfeboro	6,189	12	0	7	0	5	70	15	52	3	1
Woodstock	1,367	2	0	1	0	1	33	8	24	1	0
NEW JERSEY											
Aberdeen Township	18,403	15	0	1	4	10	155	17	125	13	1
Absecon	8,261	11	1	2	5	3	229	27	194	8	0
Allendale	6,938	0	0	0	0	0	51	11	39	1	0
Allenhurst	486	0	0	0	0	0	25	1	24	0	0
Allentown	1,808	0	0	0	0	0	7	3	4	0	0
Alpha	2,285	1	0	0	0	1	27	10	17	0	0
Alpine	1,885	0	0	0	0	0	12	0	5	7	0
Andover Township	5,962	1	0	0	0	1	26	1	22	3	0
Asbury Park	15,656	213	2	15	82	114	746	138	589	19	5
Atlantic City	38,601	425	13	24	227	161	1,732	319	1,298	115	2
Atlantic Highlands	4,281	1	0	0	0	1	34	9	25	0	0
Audubon	8,748	8	0	0	5	3	291	15	272	4	0
Audubon Park	1,013	0	0	0	0	0	47	10	37	0	0
Avalon	1,270	1	0	0	0	1	190	22	167	1	0
Avon-by-the-Sea	1,775	0	0	0	0	0	34	6	28	0	0
Barnegat Light	591	1	0	0	0	1	0	0	0	0	0
Barnegat Township	22,652	8	0	1	2	5	143	33	102	8	1
Barrington	6,792	3	0	0	1	2	136	22	108	6	0
Bay Head	986	0	0	0	0	0	20	4	16	0	0
Bayonne	67,041	140	0	11	49	80	810	115	624	71	4
Beach Haven	1,181	2	0	1	0	1	110	5	104	1	0
Beachwood	11,296	6	0	3	2	1	134	20	114	0	0
Bedminster Township	8,285	1	0	0	0	1	24	1	21	2	0
Belleville	36,409	81	0	2	41	38	647	85	471	91	0
Bellmawr	11,505	10	0	0	7	3	231	59	150	22	0
Belmar	5,666	9	0	3	1	5	135	29	101	5	0
Belvidere	2,589	4	0	1	0	3	44	12	31	1	0
Bergenfield	27,891	2	1	0	1	0	103	22	78	3	0
Berkeley Heights Township	13,654	3	0	0	2	1	73	10	61	2	0
Berkeley Township	42,036	24	0	7	8	9	458	86	362	10	2
Berlin	7,619	10	0	0	1	9	139	22	107	10	1
Berlin Township	5,560	10	0	0	5	5	137	12	123	2	0
Bernards Township	27,219	1	0	0	0	1	117	16	88	13	0
Bernardsville	7,876	1	0	0	0	1	46	5	36	5	0
Beverly	2,506	17	0	1	4	12	37	10	26	1	1
Blairstown Township	5,767	0	0	0	0	0	35	15	20	0	0
Bloomfield	48,928	57	0	0	26	31	783	82	619	82	1
Bloomingdale	8,295	2	0	0	1	1	44	7	35	2	0
Bogota	8,595	1	0	0	1	0	51	3	45	3	0
Boonton	8,421	3	0	1	1	1	74	9	56	9	0
Boonton Township	4,395	3	0	1	1	1	7	4	3	0	0
Bordentown City	3,839	0	0	0	0	0	43	19	22	2	0
Bordentown Township	12,216	12	0	3	4	5	119	11	94	14	0
Bound Brook	10,537	17	1	0	9	7	165	23	133	9	0
Bradley Beach	4,236	3	0	0	0	3	75	9	65	1	0
Branchburg Township	14,822	3	0	1	1	1	59	13	46	0	0
Brick Township	75,566	107	0	24	25	58	1,051	142	898	11	5
Bridgeton	24,937	272	5	22	147	98	994	245	710	39	8
Bridgewater Township	45,417	19	1	0	4	14	387	61	313	13	0
Brielle	4,708	2	0	0	0	2	18	0	18	0	0
Brigantine	8,976	2	0	0	0	2	110	24	84	2	1
Brooklawn	1,937	20	0	1	10	9	197	14	178	5	0
Buena	4,432	14	2	2	3	7	111	19	90	2	1
Burlington City	9,854	45	2	0	20	23	250	42	190	18	0
Burlington Township	22,772	34	1	7	6	20	308	55	235	18	1
Butler	7,829	3	0	1	0	2	60	10	47	3	0

Table 8. Offenses Known to Law Enforcement, by Selected State and City, 2017—Continued

(Number.)

State/city	Population	Violent crime	Murder and nonnegligent manslaughter	Rape (revised definition)[1]	Robbery	Aggravated assault	Property crime	Burglary	Larceny-theft	Motor vehicle theft	Arson[2]
Byram Township	7,944	6	0	1	0	5	43	13	28	2	0
Caldwell	8,073	8	1	4	1	2	56	9	43	4	0
Califon	1,058	0	0	0	0	0	2	1	1	0	0
Camden County Police Department	74,299	1,462	23	75	410	954	2,526	583	1,393	550	55
Cape May	3,483	0	0	0	0	0	93	10	80	3	0
Cape May Point	279	0	0	0	0	0	7	1	5	1	0
Carlstadt	6,295	11	0	0	2	9	141	5	115	21	0
Carney's Point Township	7,729	21	0	7	6	8	153	36	110	7	5
Carteret	24,283	44	0	5	17	22	326	48	252	26	2
Cedar Grove Township	12,674	4	0	1	0	3	94	21	64	9	0
Chatham	9,011	2	0	0	1	1	46	5	37	4	0
Chatham Township	10,515	0	0	0	0	0	39	4	31	4	0
Cherry Hill Township	71,747	96	0	3	42	51	2,075	184	1,849	42	2
Chesilhurst	1,644	3	0	0	1	2	21	11	8	2	0
Chester	1,679	0	0	0	0	0	23	4	19	0	0
Chesterfield Township	7,451	0	0	0	0	0	21	0	21	0	0
Chester Township	7,961	0	0	0	0	0	45	9	32	4	0
Cinnaminson Township	16,696	8	0	2	4	2	336	47	278	11	1
Clark Township	16,084	5	0	0	4	1	213	7	192	14	0
Clayton	8,722	12	1	3	3	5	124	22	99	3	1
Clementon	4,937	17	0	0	9	8	170	54	105	11	0
Cliffside Park	25,166	23	0	2	9	12	180	27	147	6	1
Clifton	86,472	184	0	8	73	103	1,386	191	1,086	109	4
Clinton	2,694	2	0	1	0	1	11	2	9	0	0
Clinton Township	12,748	1	0	0	0	1	71	29	42	0	0
Closter	8,788	0	0	0	0	0	43	3	36	4	0
Collingswood	14,080	24	2	2	10	10	352	66	263	23	2
Colts Neck Township	9,936	6	0	0	1	5	50	10	29	11	1
Cranbury Township	3,966	0	0	0	0	0	27	1	25	1	0
Cranford Township	24,442	3	0	0	1	2	175	15	153	7	0
Cresskill	8,848	3	0	0	1	2	27	9	15	3	0
Deal	730	2	0	0	0	2	30	3	26	1	0
Delanco Township	4,528	4	0	2	1	1	92	22	59	11	0
Delaware Township	4,443	1	0	0	0	1	17	5	12	0	2
Delran Township	16,609	11	0	2	6	3	263	25	230	8	0
Demarest	5,034	1	0	0	0	1	14	4	6	4	0
Denville Township	16,811	1	0	0	0	1	87	21	62	4	1
Deptford Township	30,727	60	0	7	23	30	1,227	163	1,032	32	6
Dover	18,339	29	0	0	14	15	190	31	139	20	0
Dumont	18,018	4	0	0	1	3	88	8	71	9	0
Dunellen	7,428	10	0	0	6	4	139	33	92	14	3
Eastampton Township	5,962	3	0	2	1	0	77	14	60	3	0
East Brunswick Township	49,019	24	0	3	8	13	673	87	564	22	2
East Greenwich Township	10,573	7	0	0	1	6	59	11	40	8	0
East Hanover Township	11,284	4	0	0	1	3	196	16	174	6	0
East Newark	2,811	1	0	0	1	0	40	3	33	4	0
East Orange	65,160	473	9	20	199	245	1,059	271	552	236	13
East Rutherford	10,064	13	0	0	3	10	135	10	97	28	0
East Windsor Township	27,571	22	0	5	5	12	235	24	204	7	0
Eatontown	12,258	32	0	3	15	14	337	30	306	1	0
Edgewater	12,183	10	1	0	3	6	133	5	124	4	0
Edgewater Park Township	8,726	13	0	3	5	5	138	33	87	18	0
Edison Township	102,699	112	0	7	47	58	1,210	185	906	119	4
Egg Harbor City	4,182	15	0	1	7	7	136	20	107	9	0
Egg Harbor Township	43,515	55	1	0	14	40	812	106	681	25	6
Elizabeth	129,726	1,034	7	47	515	465	4,595	683	3,017	895	9
Elk Township	4,140	6	1	0	0	5	53	15	37	1	0
Elmer	1,317	0	0	0	0	0	10	8	2	0	0
Elmwood Park	20,515	20	0	0	14	6	348	50	273	25	1
Elsinboro Township	978	1	0	0	0	1	12	4	8	0	0
Emerson	7,747	2	0	0	0	2	25	4	20	1	0
Englewood	28,795	75	0	5	32	38	325	66	238	21	0
Englewood Cliffs	5,442	0	0	0	0	0	34	7	23	4	0
Englishtown	1,956	9	0	0	1	8	46	7	39	0	2
Essex Fells	2,135	0	0	0	0	0	13	2	7	4	0
Evesham Township	45,314	28	0	4	5	19	562	70	476	16	3
Ewing Township	36,161	76	1	2	29	44	743	150	544	49	2
Fairfield Township, Essex County	7,597	4	0	1	0	3	192	17	155	20	0
Fair Haven	5,953	0	0	0	0	0	25	3	22	0	0
Fair Lawn	33,759	23	0	4	5	14	356	56	293	7	3
Fairview	14,573	21	0	1	9	11	136	25	103	8	0
Fanwood	7,796	2	0	0	2	0	33	6	26	1	0
Far Hills	935	0	0	0	0	0	7	1	4	2	0
Fieldsboro	531	0	0	0	0	0	0	0	0	0	1
Flemington	4,627	9	0	0	0	3	79	7	72	0	0
Florence Township	12,755	19	0	2	8	9	82	18	56	8	0
Florham Park	11,818	6	0	4	0	2	81	6	69	6	1
Fort Lee	38,095	26	0	3	6	17	298	50	232	16	0
Franklin	4,773	2	0	0	0	2	47	4	42	1	0
Franklin Lakes	10,939	1	0	0	0	1	71	13	49	9	0

Table 8. Offenses Known to Law Enforcement, by Selected State and City, 2017—Continued

(Number.)

State/city	Population	Violent crime	Murder and nonnegligent manslaughter	Rape (revised definition)[1]	Robbery	Aggravated assault	Property crime	Burglary	Larceny-theft	Motor vehicle theft	Arson[2]
Franklin Township, Gloucester County	16,599	14	0	3	0	11	215	65	137	13	2
Franklin Township, Hunterdon County	3,223	0	0	0	0	0	17	0	17	0	0
Franklin Township, Somerset County	67,463	48	1	6	23	18	779	157	578	44	7
Freehold Borough	11,865	25	0	5	14	6	129	31	96	2	0
Freehold Township	35,531	45	0	3	10	32	585	41	523	21	0
Frenchtown	1,396	1	0	0	0	1	10	0	10	0	0
Galloway Township	36,672	73	0	6	9	58	665	143	497	25	1
Garfield	32,233	59	0	5	16	38	563	71	462	30	3
Garwood	4,384	0	0	0	0	0	45	6	38	1	0
Gibbsboro	2,253	1	0	0	0	1	38	11	27	0	0
Glassboro	20,134	17	1	0	12	4	395	80	307	8	1
Glen Ridge	7,694	7	0	0	3	4	157	35	114	8	0
Glen Rock	12,051	2	0	1	1	0	93	4	84	5	0
Gloucester City	11,366	21	0	1	7	13	280	49	215	16	0
Gloucester Township	64,094	101	1	9	32	59	1,130	171	922	37	3
Green Brook Township	7,273	2	0	1	0	1	83	19	53	11	0
Greenwich Township, Gloucester County	4,861	6	0	1	2	3	81	11	69	1	0
Greenwich Township, Warren County	5,501	2	0	0	1	1	161	9	150	2	1
Guttenberg	11,736	22	1	4	11	6	111	28	75	8	0
Hackensack	45,226	94	1	8	32	53	672	62	566	44	4
Hackettstown	9,520	3	0	0	1	2	47	4	42	1	0
Haddonfield	11,445	5	0	0	3	2	176	29	146	1	1
Haddon Heights	7,586	3	0	0	1	2	67	10	53	4	0
Haddon Township	14,731	15	0	2	6	7	321	51	258	12	1
Haledon	8,439	18	0	0	5	13	158	32	113	13	0
Hamburg	3,125	2	0	0	0	2	18	1	17	0	0
Hamilton Township, Atlantic County	26,482	37	2	3	10	22	880	160	690	30	3
Hamilton Township, Mercer County	88,723	126	1	7	61	57	1,922	363	1,401	158	3
Hammonton	14,370	17	0	0	3	14	177	37	134	6	0
Hanover Township	14,904	7	0	1	2	4	190	24	153	13	1
Harding Township	3,891	2	0	0	2	0	17	10	6	1	0
Hardyston Township	7,884	1	0	0	0	1	62	10	44	8	0
Harrington Park	4,848	1	0	1	0	0	8	1	6	1	0
Harrison	16,802	58	0	0	29	29	341	37	260	44	0
Harrison Township	13,128	6	0	3	0	3	102	19	79	4	0
Harvey Cedars	342	1	0	0	0	1	15	0	15	0	0
Hasbrouck Heights	12,286	2	0	0	1	1	61	6	55	0	0
Haworth	3,491	0	0	0	0	0	6	0	6	0	0
Hawthorne	19,041	2	0	0	0	2	227	27	192	8	0
Hazlet Township	19,938	13	0	3	3	7	223	34	181	8	1
Helmetta	2,228	1	0	0	0	1	10	1	7	2	0
High Bridge	3,524	0	0	0	0	0	31	14	16	1	2
Highland Park	14,287	5	0	1	1	3	186	23	152	11	0
Highlands	4,793	4	0	0	2	2	31	7	24	0	0
Hightstown	5,522	5	0	1	1	3	40	8	32	0	0
Hillsborough Township	40,369	9	0	5	2	2	255	45	205	5	2
Hillsdale	10,602	0	0	0	0	0	35	5	28	2	0
Hillside Township	22,125	47	1	2	26	18	588	83	415	90	0
Hi-Nella	869	4	0	0	1	3	16	5	10	3	0
Hoboken	55,348	131	1	10	32	88	1,064	121	911	32	0
Ho-Ho-Kus	4,169	2	0	0	0	2	30	18	9	3	0
Holland Township	5,113	3	0	2	0	1	12	2	7	3	0
Holmdel Township	16,576	12	1	5	1	5	150	15	122	13	1
Hopatcong	14,263	11	0	2	1	8	71	9	61	1	0
Hopewell Burough	1,932	2	0	1	0	1	13	4	9	0	0
Hopewell Township	18,633	7	1	4	0	2	99	25	68	6	0
Howell Township	52,432	35	0	6	8	21	407	89	312	6	3
Independence Township	5,482	3	0	0	0	3	26	8	13	5	0
Interlaken	798	0	0	0	0	0	14	2	12	0	0
Irvington	54,728	445	9	33	263	140	1,409	278	710	421	6
Island Heights	1,659	0	0	0	0	0	10	2	8	0	0
Jackson Township	57,400	24	0	3	7	14	483	112	355	16	6
Jamesburg	6,088	8	0	0	3	5	59	13	41	5	1
Jefferson Township	21,505	6	0	1	1	4	93	22	65	6	0
Jersey City	267,906	1,365	21	123	534	687	4,841	1,119	3,231	491	38
Keansburg	9,782	31	1	4	6	20	176	27	143	6	1
Kearny	42,527	51	1	1	20	29	632	55	503	74	0
Kenilworth	8,271	8	0	4	0	4	136	11	108	17	0
Keyport	7,062	16	0	0	7	9	98	23	67	8	0
Kinnelon	10,275	5	0	0	0	5	35	10	22	3	0
Lacey Township	28,915	27	2	8	3	14	312	33	279	0	0
Lake Como	1,709	4	0	0	0	4	37	6	30	1	0
Lakehurst	2,716	0	0	0	0	0	36	4	31	1	0
Lakewood Township	102,759	95	1	4	30	60	931	216	689	26	5
Lambertville	3,795	5	0	0	2	3	45	5	37	3	1
Laurel Springs	1,888	2	0	0	2	0	43	24	19	0	1

Table 8. Offenses Known to Law Enforcement, by Selected State and City, 2017—Continued

(Number.)

State/city	Population	Violent crime	Murder and nonnegligent manslaughter	Rape (revised definition)[1]	Robbery	Aggravated assault	Property crime	Burglary	Larceny-theft	Motor vehicle theft	Arson[2]
Lavallette	1,837	1	0	0	1	0	23	4	17	2	0
Lawnside	2,927	9	0	0	2	7	117	9	102	6	0
Lawrence Township, Mercer County	32,929	19	1	5	5	8	693	45	628	20	2
Lebanon Township	6,053	1	0	0	0	1	30	15	12	3	0
Leonia	9,273	3	0	0	3	0	42	12	27	3	0
Lincoln Park	10,466	4	0	1	0	3	72	21	47	4	0
Linden	42,948	131	1	13	39	78	1,050	166	839	45	1
Lindenwold	17,516	109	2	13	38	56	504	142	332	30	8
Linwood	6,859	1	0	0	0	1	100	19	81	0	0
Little Egg Harbor Township	21,076	12	0	9	1	2	286	67	213	6	6
Little Falls Township	14,479	19	0	0	2	17	115	12	93	10	0
Little Ferry	11,017	11	0	0	3	8	127	36	80	11	0
Little Silver	5,881	0	0	0	0	0	35	8	26	1	0
Livingston Township	29,987	9	0	1	5	3	339	23	299	17	0
Loch Arbour	181	0	0	0	0	0	7	2	5	0	0
Lodi	24,981	43	0	6	14	23	368	57	287	24	0
Logan Township	5,977	6	0	0	5	1	146	19	113	14	0
Long Beach Township	3,067	3	0	1	0	2	98	10	87	1	0
Long Branch	30,748	99	5	7	43	44	839	120	692	27	0
Long Hill Township	8,784	1	0	0	1	0	39	2	35	2	0
Longport	868	2	0	0	0	2	13	5	8	0	0
Lopatcong Township	8,298	3	0	0	2	1	84	11	67	6	0
Lower Alloways Creek Township	1,770	1	0	0	0	1	10	2	8	0	0
Lower Township	21,870	32	0	2	6	24	326	68	242	16	1
Lumberton Township	12,286	23	0	3	6	14	228	29	191	8	0
Lyndhurst Township	22,621	9	0	2	3	4	225	20	183	22	0
Madison	16,175	4	0	1	0	3	66	9	52	5	1
Magnolia	4,310	13	0	0	9	4	102	25	70	7	0
Mahwah Township	26,753	9	0	3	3	3	146	16	120	10	0
Manalapan Township	40,177	13	0	2	3	8	249	39	197	13	0
Manasquan	5,804	5	0	0	1	4	89	15	73	1	0
Manchester Township	43,916	11	0	0	2	9	224	31	186	7	5
Mansfield Township, Burlington County	8,593	5	0	1	1	3	72	12	49	11	0
Mansfield Township, Warren County	7,435	4	0	0	2	2	103	4	97	2	0
Mantoloking	247	0	0	0	0	0	9	1	8	0	0
Mantua Township	15,123	13	0	0	3	10	266	48	212	6	0
Manville	10,519	12	0	5	3	4	169	16	138	15	2
Maple Shade Township	18,797	31	3	6	4	18	456	102	326	28	0
Maplewood Township	24,863	35	4	0	17	14	414	45	332	37	0
Margate City	6,107	4	0	1	0	3	133	22	106	5	1
Marlboro Township	40,370	7	0	0	0	7	244	45	179	20	4
Matawan	8,838	0	0	0	0	0	28	2	24	2	0
Maywood	9,862	4	0	2	1	1	77	21	53	3	0
Medford Lakes	4,038	0	0	0	0	0	24	1	22	1	0
Medford Township	23,503	16	0	9	1	6	134	25	108	1	1
Mendham	5,006	1	0	0	0	1	17	7	7	3	0
Mendham Township	5,883	0	0	0	0	0	6	3	3	0	0
Merchantville	3,774	9	0	0	1	8	69	17	48	4	0
Metuchen	13,981	12	0	0	6	6	175	27	136	12	0
Middlesex Borough	13,897	8	0	2	3	3	132	17	107	8	2
Middle Township	18,542	36	1	4	7	24	469	121	326	22	0
Middletown Township	65,303	48	0	3	12	33	497	73	409	15	1
Midland Park	7,378	4	0	1	0	3	57	4	53	0	0
Millburn Township	20,421	7	0	0	7	0	438	31	391	16	0
Milltown	7,201	7	0	0	4	3	119	4	112	3	0
Millville	27,984	160	3	12	42	103	1,554	235	1,280	39	3
Mine Hill Township	3,606	3	0	0	0	3	24	6	18	0	0
Monmouth Beach	3,213	5	0	0	0	5	28	5	23	0	0
Monroe Township, Gloucester County	37,174	44	0	6	17	21	548	150	375	23	3
Monroe Township, Middlesex County	45,722	4	1	0	0	3	153	32	103	18	0
Montclair	39,029	60	0	13	18	29	650	170	450	30	4
Montgomery Township	23,706	6	0	0	0	6	103	12	81	10	0
Montvale	8,653	1	0	0	1	0	29	7	22	0	0
Montville Township	21,818	3	0	0	2	1	146	18	115	13	0
Moonachie	2,815	1	0	0	0	1	66	6	50	10	0
Moorestown Township	20,534	10	1	1	2	6	274	30	230	14	0
Morris Plains	5,626	4	1	0	2	1	50	3	47	0	0
Morristown	19,199	40	0	3	18	19	288	27	237	24	2
Morris Township	22,701	3	0	0	1	2	102	21	75	6	1
Mountain Lakes	4,377	0	0	0	0	0	50	15	25	10	0
Mountainside	6,943	1	0	0	0	1	51	27	18	6	0
Mount Arlington	5,551	1	0	0	0	1	49	5	42	2	0
Mount Ephraim	4,643	9	0	0	4	5	195	15	174	6	0
Mount Holly Township	9,522	42	1	7	16	18	340	23	303	14	0
Mount Laurel Township	41,712	38	0	10	12	16	570	44	507	19	3
Mount Olive Township	29,410	9	0	3	0	6	166	27	134	5	1
Mullica Township	6,024	3	0	0	0	3	98	32	65	1	1

Table 8. Offenses Known to Law Enforcement, by Selected State and City, 2017—Continued

(Number.)

State/city	Population	Violent crime	Murder and nonnegligent manslaughter	Rape (revised definition)[1]	Robbery	Aggravated assault	Property crime	Burglary	Larceny-theft	Motor vehicle theft	Arson[2]
National Park	3,002	4	0	0	0	4	43	9	33	1	0
Neptune City	4,725	13	0	1	4	8	144	15	124	5	0
Neptune Township	27,757	150	3	5	36	106	913	143	762	8	1
Netcong	3,247	5	0	0	4	1	55	14	36	5	0
Newark	283,673	2,543	77	116	1,070	1,280	6,794	1,202	3,200	2,392	72
New Brunswick	57,481	360	4	22	191	143	1,341	253	1,001	87	9
Newfield	1,569	0	0	0	0	0	16	8	8	0	0
New Hanover Township	8,264	0	0	0	0	0	4	1	3	0	0
New Milford	16,894	2	0	1	1	0	75	14	61	0	0
New Providence	12,904	0	0	0	0	0	58	4	53	1	0
Newton	7,874	10	0	5	0	5	87	10	77	0	0
North Arlington	16,009	16	0	1	5	10	143	11	117	15	0
North Bergen Township	63,490	96	0	9	35	52	485	55	364	66	1
North Brunswick Township	42,780	49	1	3	20	25	688	75	567	46	0
North Caldwell	6,782	2	0	0	0	2	15	7	5	3	0
Northfield	8,376	0	0	0	0	0	81	12	69	0	0
North Haledon	8,537	1	0	0	1	0	39	11	28	0	0
North Hanover Township	7,562	3	0	0	0	3	29	3	23	3	0
North Plainfield	22,255	63	0	6	41	16	508	77	404	27	3
Northvale	5,003	0	0	0	0	0	13	0	13	0	0
North Wildwood	3,856	13	0	0	6	7	169	18	147	4	0
Norwood	5,904	0	0	0	0	0	24	3	17	4	0
Nutley Township	28,833	22	0	0	10	12	224	36	174	14	1
Oakland	13,243	8	0	0	1	7	79	11	65	3	0
Oaklyn	4,002	2	0	0	2	0	145	22	121	2	0
Ocean City	11,281	12	1	3	2	6	385	34	350	1	0
Ocean Gate	2,023	0	0	0	0	0	42	7	34	1	0
Oceanport	5,705	4	0	2	1	1	32	7	23	2	0
Ocean Township, Monmouth County	26,637	30	1	3	13	13	668	99	551	18	1
Ocean Township, Ocean County	9,187	2	0	0	0	2	57	2	54	1	0
Ogdensburg	2,273	0	0	0	0	0	10	0	10	0	0
Old Bridge Township	67,162	44	2	0	11	31	581	77	460	44	1
Old Tappan	6,069	0	0	0	0	0	14	4	8	2	0
Oradell	8,291	2	0	1	0	1	26	10	16	0	0
Orange City	30,752	245	3	9	152	81	977	258	452	267	1
Oxford Township	2,447	0	0	0	0	0	15	4	10	1	0
Palisades Park	21,030	15	0	0	6	9	126	30	88	8	0
Palmyra	7,217	15	0	3	5	7	143	28	106	9	0
Paramus	27,075	14	1	0	7	6	1,154	29	1,095	30	0
Park Ridge	8,977	1	0	0	0	1	18	9	9	0	0
Parsippany-Troy Hills Township	53,478	36	0	7	14	15	413	70	314	29	0
Passaic	71,053	390	1	10	165	214	1,163	193	842	128	1
Paterson	147,690	1,028	21	45	488	474	3,399	992	1,776	631	10
Paulsboro	5,959	28	1	0	13	14	196	50	130	16	1
Peapack-Gladstone	2,624	3	0	0	0	3	17	7	10	0	0
Pemberton Borough	1,355	1	0	0	0	1	31	11	18	2	0
Pemberton Township	27,506	117	2	13	29	73	567	202	340	25	5
Pennington	2,576	0	0	0	0	0	8	0	8	0	0
Pennsauken Township	36,041	99	1	1	46	51	927	307	556	64	5
Penns Grove	4,844	37	1	7	9	20	237	43	185	9	3
Pennsville Township	12,564	14	1	0	4	9	208	31	175	2	0
Pequannock Township	15,472	1	0	0	0	1	96	13	82	1	0
Perth Amboy	52,978	171	2	5	56	108	843	151	598	94	2
Phillipsburg	14,379	24	0	6	7	11	367	76	282	9	3
Pine Beach	2,170	0	0	0	0	0	19	1	18	0	0
Pine Hill	10,616	32	1	0	9	22	249	68	170	11	4
Pine Valley	11	0	0	0	0	0	0	0	0	0	0
Piscataway Township	58,109	54	1	8	18	27	542	103	400	39	0
Pitman	8,886	2	0	0	2	0	67	10	53	4	0
Plainfield	50,983	321	4	14	174	129	1,055	232	726	97	4
Plainsboro Township	23,569	8	0	0	0	8	126	17	104	5	0
Pleasantville	20,530	116	2	5	48	61	312	106	189	17	1
Plumsted Township	8,604	0	0	0	0	0	17	5	10	2	0
Pohatcong Township	3,215	0	0	0	0	0	147	4	140	3	0
Point Pleasant	18,696	16	0	2	2	12	122	14	106	2	0
Point Pleasant Beach	4,552	1	0	0	1	0	82	9	73	0	0
Pompton Lakes	11,176	13	0	2	1	10	103	16	79	8	0
Princeton	31,845	7	0	0	2	5	229	43	180	6	3
Prospect Park	5,944	3	0	0	1	2	113	27	72	14	0
Rahway	29,930	38	0	3	15	20	295	51	209	35	1
Ramsey	15,273	5	0	0	2	3	139	5	129	5	0
Randolph Township	25,950	4	0	0	0	4	117	12	93	12	1
Raritan	8,273	4	0	0	1	3	90	10	76	4	0
Raritan Township	21,918	5	0	0	0	5	91	12	78	1	0
Readington Township	15,834	2	0	0	1	1	79	21	56	2	1
Red Bank	12,135	24	0	5	9	10	180	8	168	4	0
Ridgefield	11,457	2	0	0	1	1	73	10	55	8	0
Ridgefield Park	13,166	8	0	0	1	7	166	19	137	10	2
Ridgewood	25,729	6	0	1	1	4	175	16	152	7	0
Ringwood	12,470	3	1	0	0	2	37	14	19	4	0

Table 8. Offenses Known to Law Enforcement, by Selected State and City, 2017—Continued

(Number.)

State/city	Population	Violent crime	Murder and nonnegligent manslaughter	Rape (revised definition)[1]	Robbery	Aggravated assault	Property crime	Burglary	Larceny-theft	Motor vehicle theft	Arson[2]
Riverdale	4,398	1	0	0	1	0	109	5	100	4	0
River Edge	11,744	2	0	0	2	0	63	13	49	1	0
Riverside Township	7,897	9	0	0	0	9	16	12	3	1	0
Riverton	2,704	0	0	0	0	0	39	3	34	2	0
River Vale Township	10,270	1	0	0	1	0	15	2	12	1	0
Robbinsville Township	14,446	1	0	0	0	1	83	10	71	2	0
Rochelle Park Township	5,714	2	0	0	1	1	92	15	74	3	0
Rockaway	6,512	1	0	0	1	0	79	14	61	4	0
Rockaway Township	24,719	11	1	1	4	5	326	27	292	7	0
Rockleigh	535	2	0	0	0	2	1	0	0	1	0
Roseland	5,916	3	0	1	1	1	48	7	35	6	0
Roselle	21,796	32	2	0	12	18	327	69	223	35	2
Roselle Park	13,747	3	0	0	3	0	138	20	108	10	0
Roxbury Township	23,472	5	0	1	1	3	237	24	208	5	0
Rumson	6,783	0	0	0	0	0	40	9	29	2	0
Runnemede	8,402	7	0	1	2	4	265	56	198	11	0
Rutherford	18,804	11	0	3	4	4	206	23	166	17	0
Saddle Brook Township	14,190	9	0	0	3	6	247	34	190	23	0
Saddle River	3,263	0	0	0	0	0	19	3	13	3	0
Salem	4,776	54	1	2	12	39	206	74	120	12	0
Sayreville	45,460	29	0	3	8	18	392	41	311	40	1
Scotch Plains Township	24,375	10	0	1	3	6	203	63	116	24	0
Sea Bright	1,375	0	0	0	0	0	5	2	3	0	0
Sea Girt	1,777	1	0	0	0	1	14	3	11	0	0
Sea Isle City	2,079	1	0	0	0	1	175	43	130	2	0
Seaside Heights	2,918	34	0	0	10	24	133	31	101	1	0
Seaside Park	1,556	4	0	1	2	1	26	8	17	1	1
Secaucus	20,481	33	0	2	14	17	454	32	389	33	0
Ship Bottom	1,146	1	0	0	0	1	16	1	15	0	0
Shrewsbury	4,178	2	0	1	0	1	53	11	41	1	0
Somerdale	5,591	6	0	2	1	3	255	35	213	7	0
Somers Point	10,504	21	0	1	7	13	270	61	192	17	0
Somerville	12,263	10	0	0	3	7	135	20	99	16	0
South Amboy	8,839	1	0	1	0	0	84	16	54	14	1
South Bound Brook	4,652	3	0	1	0	2	29	4	23	2	0
South Brunswick Township	46,280	25	0	8	9	8	437	103	311	23	0
South Hackensack Township	2,479	10	0	1	3	6	65	13	48	4	0
South Harrison Township	3,193	0	0	0	0	0	13	7	6	0	0
South Orange Village	16,407	29	0	1	19	9	282	34	225	23	0
South Plainfield	24,458	28	0	0	6	22	454	22	413	19	1
South River	16,399	18	0	3	7	8	124	17	93	14	2
South Toms River	3,799	6	0	0	4	2	67	18	46	3	2
Sparta Township	18,807	9	0	4	0	5	66	12	49	5	0
Spotswood	8,492	1	0	0	0	1	64	9	54	1	0
Springfield Township, Burlington County	3,301	0	0	0	0	0	31	15	14	2	0
Springfield Township, Union County	17,805	11	0	5	1	5	142	24	108	10	0
Spring Lake	2,958	0	0	0	0	0	60	13	42	5	0
Spring Lake Heights	4,597	1	0	0	1	0	16	3	13	0	0
Stafford Township	27,433	25	0	1	3	21	201	13	179	9	0
Stanhope	3,327	3	0	2	0	1	20	2	17	1	1
Stone Harbor	827	1	0	0	1	0	98	8	88	2	0
Stratford	7,024	6	0	1	0	5	90	20	69	1	0
Summit	22,195	8	0	3	5	0	192	17	162	13	0
Surf City	1,186	1	0	0	0	1	26	3	23	0	0
Swedesboro	2,614	1	0	0	1	0	15	0	15	0	1
Tavistock	5	1	0	0	0	1	1	0	1	0	0
Teaneck Township	41,377	55	0	5	21	29	390	77	299	14	1
Tenafly	14,960	1	0	0	1	0	65	9	48	8	0
Teterboro	69	5	0	0	4	1	123	0	121	2	0
Tewksbury Township	5,809	0	0	0	0	0	19	8	10	1	0
Tinton Falls	17,761	3	0	0	1	2	270	19	245	6	0
Toms River Township	92,543	63	0	5	26	32	1,545	173	1,331	41	9
Totowa	10,964	10	0	0	5	5	288	29	243	16	1
Trenton	84,231	1,083	23	63	343	654	2,193	792	1,035	366	16
Tuckerton	3,406	3	0	0	0	3	49	8	41	0	0
Union Beach	5,479	4	0	1	1	2	26	10	16	0	0
Union City	70,053	164	1	1	58	104	1,235	114	1,028	93	1
Union Township	59,051	71	2	3	32	34	983	97	778	108	1
Upper Saddle River	8,385	2	0	0	1	1	18	4	14	0	0
Ventnor City	10,263	6	0	0	4	2	327	47	271	9	1
Vernon Township	22,193	8	0	0	0	8	191	51	131	9	0
Verona	13,584	4	0	0	1	3	76	16	57	3	1
Vineland	60,477	298	2	24	93	179	2,414	472	1,883	59	12
Voorhees Township	29,532	61	0	12	10	39	410	61	329	20	6
Waldwick	10,137	3	0	2	0	1	64	11	50	3	0
Wallington	11,794	6	0	0	3	3	141	14	120	7	0
Wall Township	25,956	19	0	0	5	14	254	38	207	9	0
Wanaque	11,925	6	0	2	0	4	80	9	69	2	0
Warren Township	16,264	3	0	1	1	1	42	7	31	4	0
Washington	6,499	3	0	0	0	3	82	17	63	2	0

Table 8. Offenses Known to Law Enforcement, by Selected State and City, 2017—Continued

(Number.)

State/city	Population	Violent crime	Murder and nonnegligent manslaughter	Rape (revised definition)[1]	Robbery	Aggravated assault	Property crime	Burglary	Larceny-theft	Motor vehicle theft	Arson[2]
Washington Township, Bergen County	9,432	3	0	0	0	3	15	6	8	1	0
Washington Township, Gloucester County	48,088	58	0	4	21	33	764	139	601	24	3
Washington Township, Morris County	18,793	3	0	2	1	0	42	4	38	0	0
Washington Township, Warren County	6,429	5	0	0	0	5	58	8	46	4	0
Watchung	6,010	1	0	1	0	0	366	26	334	6	0
Waterford Township	10,817	3	0	1	0	2	79	13	61	5	0
Wayne Township	54,903	29	1	1	8	19	979	85	851	43	0
Weehawken Township	15,683	15	0	1	4	10	300	30	253	17	0
Wenonah	2,252	0	0	0	0	0	20	4	16	0	0
Westampton Township	8,775	26	0	7	9	10	160	24	128	8	0
West Amwell Township	2,753	2	0	2	0	0	31	2	27	2	8
West Caldwell Township	11,013	8	0	0	2	6	66	8	54	4	0
West Cape May	1,016	0	0	0	0	0	6	2	4	0	1
West Deptford Township	21,386	12	0	1	6	5	349	97	246	6	0
Westfield	30,301	3	0	0	1	2	256	21	207	28	0
West Long Branch	7,944	7	0	2	2	3	121	9	107	5	0
West Milford Township	26,769	25	0	4	0	21	203	37	155	11	1
West New York	54,156	108	0	8	39	61	525	87	409	29	2
West Orange	47,615	93	0	9	32	52	839	138	616	85	4
Westville	4,214	14	0	1	7	6	138	27	105	6	0
West Wildwood	563	2	0	0	0	2	5	0	5	0	0
West Windsor Township	28,495	21	0	2	4	15	301	39	257	5	0
Westwood	11,328	9	0	1	2	6	49	12	35	2	0
Wharton	6,610	4	0	0	2	2	57	6	48	3	0
Wildwood	5,087	65	0	1	18	46	450	64	382	4	0
Wildwood Crest	3,147	9	0	1	1	7	87	20	66	1	0
Willingboro Township	31,726	92	3	10	20	59	552	167	354	31	6
Winfield Township	1,519	0	0	0	0	0	6	1	4	1	0
Winslow Township	39,406	32	2	3	8	19	171	74	82	15	1
Woodbridge Township	102,129	104	1	5	53	45	1,608	224	1,279	105	3
Woodbury	9,970	47	1	0	31	15	535	82	424	29	0
Woodbury Heights	3,011	2	0	0	2	0	73	10	63	0	0
Woodcliff Lake	5,942	1	0	0	1	0	24	4	18	2	0
Woodland Park	12,836	17	0	1	4	12	152	13	133	6	0
Woodlynne	2,951	8	1	0	2	5	51	6	36	9	0
Wood-Ridge	8,808	3	0	0	0	3	67	5	60	2	0
Woodstown	3,482	2	0	0	1	1	43	12	31	0	0
Woolwich Township	12,798	4	1	0	1	2	66	8	48	10	0
Wyckoff Township	17,373	8	0	4	0	4	107	26	76	5	0
NEW MEXICO											
Alamogordo	31,386	113	0	6	7	100	986	152	753	81	
Albuquerque	561,375	7,686	70	473	2,930	4,213	41,350	6,996	26,670	7,684	
Angel Fire	1,097	8	0	0	0	8	32	9	21	2	
Anthony	9,296	21	0	1	1	19	80	42	29	9	
Artesia	12,388	159	2	2	1	154	421	208	200	13	
Aztec	5,836	33	0	4	3	26	191	41	142	8	
Bayard	2,220	8	0	0	0	8	39	19	13	7	
Belen	7,095	144	0	2	12	130	576	126	370	80	
Bernalillo	9,355	79	0	3	11	65	426	166	210	50	
Bloomfield	6,932	89	0	8	1	80	172	36	127	9	
Bosque Farms	3,805	22	0	0	2	20	78	14	44	20	
Capitan	1,372	4	0	0	0	4	18	9	9	0	
Carlsbad	29,397	140	4	18	14	104	1,210	180	912	118	
Carrizozo	929	1	0	0	0	1	10	6	4	0	
Cimarron	881	6	0	0	0	6	11	4	7	0	
Clayton	2,729	5	0	0	0	5	8	2	6	0	
Cloudcroft	695	0	0	0	0	0	14	7	7	0	
Clovis	39,561	316	6	29	27	254	2,032	490	1,400	142	
Corrales	8,625	5	0	0	0	5	77	22	51	4	
Cuba	741	19	0	0	0	19	14	6	5	3	
Deming	14,428	83	2	6	10	65	596	177	365	54	
Dexter	1,263	1	0	0	0	1	0	0	0	0	
Edgewood	3,816	7	0	1	0	6	94	33	54	7	
Espanola	10,121	297	2	3	28	264	481	228	220	33	
Estancia	1,572	0	0	0	0	0	26	24	2	0	
Eunice	3,040	2	0	0	0	2	43	21	17	5	
Farmington	40,940	519	3	62	54	400	1,971	492	1,326	153	
Gallup	22,815	352	1	20	87	244	1,493	256	1,046	191	
Grants	9,313	39	1	0	5	33	158	93	44	21	
Hatch	1,585	7	0	0	0	7	36	5	30	1	
Hobbs	38,871	251	2	39	20	190	1,664	381	1,190	93	
Hope	107	0	0	0	0	0	6	6	0	0	
Hurley	1,232	3	0	0	0	3	6	4	2	0	
Jal	2,135	8	0	0	0	8	40	7	27	6	
Las Vegas	13,160	99	0	9	12	78	334	60	251	23	
Logan	940	0	0	0	0	0	22	7	12	3	
Lordsburg	2,415	2	0	0	1	1	28	11	14	3	
Los Alamos	18,204	30	0	4	2	24	93	11	80	2	

Table 8. Offenses Known to Law Enforcement, by Selected State and City, 2017—Continued

(Number.)

State/city	Population	Violent crime	Murder and nonnegligent manslaughter	Rape (revised definition)[1]	Robbery	Aggravated assault	Property crime	Burglary	Larceny-theft	Motor vehicle theft	Arson[2]
Los Lunas	15,527	185	0	7	17	161	788	152	508	128	
Magdalena	892	15	0	0	0	15	38	11	25	2	
Mesilla	1,848	0	0	0	0	0	4	2	1	1	
Moriarty	1,766	11	0	1	5	5	80	17	49	14	
Peralta	3,548	32	0	1	0	31	99	22	37	40	
Portales	11,928	24	0	4	3	17	442	213	194	35	
Questa	1,752	0	0	0	0	0	10	3	5	2	
Raton	5,983	8	0	0	1	7	234	83	128	23	
Red River	477	1	0	0	0	1	11	1	10	0	
Rio Rancho	97,444	167	1	16	33	117	1,990	302	1,464	224	
Roswell	48,134	306	5	42	19	240	1,992	426	1,468	98	
Ruidoso	7,729	26	0	5	2	19	221	71	137	13	
Ruidoso Downs	2,543	37	0	0	0	37	107	24	78	5	
Santa Clara	1,740	2	0	0	0	2	36	13	22	1	
Santa Fe	84,358	289	4	36	56	193	3,178	1,228	1,736	214	
Santa Rosa	2,652	15	0	0	1	14	68	13	50	5	
San Ysidro	198	0	0	0	0	0	4	3	1	0	
Socorro	8,547	85	0	2	4	79	425	92	312	21	
Springer	911	6	0	0	0	6	7	5	1	1	
Taos	5,771	36	1	1	5	29	513	139	334	40	
Taos Ski Valley	69	0	0	0	0	0	1	1	0	0	
Tatum	832	0	0	0	0	0	4	1	3	0	
Texico	1,104	1	0	0	0	1	10	7	2	1	
Truth or Consequences	5,949	20	0	0	0	20	163	37	117	9	
Tularosa	2,920	10	0	0	0	10	70	31	33	6	
NEW YORK											
Adams Village	1,766	1	0	0	0	1	3	1	1	1	0
Addison Town and Village	2,518	5	0	0	0	5	13	1	11	1	0
Afton Village	806	0	0	0	0	0	2	1	0	1	0
Akron Village	2,848	4	0	0	0	4	7	0	6	1	0
Albany	98,174	876	8	54	247	567	3,394	432	2,853	109	14
Albion Village	5,944	31	0	3	8	20	192	24	164	4	0
Alexandria Bay Village	1,061	1	0	0	0	1	5	1	4	0	0
Allegany Village	1,717	1	0	0	0	1	12	3	9	0	0
Amherst Town	121,150	124	0	13	51	60	1,868	195	1,632	41	3
Amity Town and Belmont Village	2,169	0	0	0	0	0	0	0	0	0	0
Amityville Village	9,492	11	0	0	5	6	126	15	109	2	0
Amsterdam	17,737	31	1	4	13	13	340	68	265	7	0
Andover Village	993	0	0	0	0	0	0	0	0	0	0
Angelica Village	825	0	0	0	0	0	1	0	1	0	0
Arcade Village	1,957	2	0	0	0	2	20	10	10	0	0
Ardsley Village	4,663	2	0	1	0	1	35	8	26	1	1
Asharoken Village	647	0	0	0	0	0	2	0	2	0	0
Avon Village	3,276	0	0	0	0	0	13	0	11	2	0
Bainbridge Village	1,326	0	0	0	0	0	4	0	4	0	0
Baldwinsville Village	7,656	6	0	2	0	4	67	9	55	3	1
Ballston Spa Village	5,302	1	0	0	0	1	48	3	43	2	0
Batavia	14,711	94	0	20	16	58	484	88	385	11	2
Bath Village	5,556	15	0	5	4	6	172	26	145	1	0
Beacon	14,212	44	0	5	5	34	240	50	184	6	0
Bedford Town	17,997	5	0	2	1	2	37	6	29	2	0
Bethlehem Town	35,607	19	0	5	3	11	487	43	437	7	0
Binghamton	45,399	362	4	42	90	226	1,983	370	1,557	56	11
Black River	1,273	0	0	0	0	0	6	1	5	0	0
Blooming Grove Town	11,863	11	0	0	1	10	62	19	39	4	3
Bolton Town	2,270	1	0	0	0	1	6	1	5	0	0
Brant Town	2,055	2	0	2	0	0	15	3	11	1	0
Brewster	2,334	1	0	0	1	0	16	1	14	1	0
Briarcliff Manor Village	8,064	2	0	0	1	1	20	1	19	0	0
Brighton Town	36,596	28	0	8	9	11	781	74	691	16	0
Brockport Village	8,310	20	1	3	5	11	86	25	57	4	1
Bronxville Village	6,420	0	0	0	0	0	29	4	23	2	0
Brownville Village	1,120	0	0	0	0	0	3	3	0	0	0
Buchanan Village	2,272	0	0	0	0	0	2	0	2	0	0
Buffalo	256,169	2,611	40	142	857	1,572	9,827	2,356	6,638	833	192
Cairo Town	6,422	4	0	0	0	4	35	9	26	0	0
Caledonia Village	2,115	2	0	0	0	2	1	0	1	0	0
Cambridge Village	1,810	1	0	1	0	0	16	8	8	0	0
Camden Village	2,181	1	0	1	0	0	24	4	20	0	0
Camillus Town and Village	24,696	16	0	2	1	13	297	15	272	10	0
Canajoharie Village	2,132	0	0	0	0	0	16	0	16	0	0
Canandaigua	10,337	33	1	11	1	20	206	36	165	5	1
Canastota Village	4,586	2	0	0	0	2	64	9	54	1	0
Canisteo Village	2,171	0	0	0	0	0	8	5	3	0	0
Canton Village	6,557	1	0	0	0	1	21	6	14	1	0
Cape Vincent Village	716	0	0	0	0	0	4	0	4	0	0
Carmel Town	34,243	9	1	0	3	5	125	23	99	3	1
Carroll Town	3,366	0	0	0	0	0	0	0	0	0	0
Carthage Village	3,425	7	0	2	3	2	57	8	47	2	0
Cattaraugus Village	927	0	0	0	0	0	1	0	1	0	0
Cayuga Heights Village	3,815	0	0	0	0	0	27	1	26	0	0

Table 8. Offenses Known to Law Enforcement, by Selected State and City, 2017—Continued

(Number.)

State/city	Population	Violent crime	Murder and nonnegligent manslaughter	Rape (revised definition)[1]	Robbery	Aggravated assault	Property crime	Burglary	Larceny-theft	Motor vehicle theft	Arson[2]
Cazenovia Village	2,849	5	0	2	2	1	37	5	32	0	0
Central Square Village	1,786	0	0	0	0	0	32	0	31	1	0
Centre Island Village	408	0	0	0	0	0	1	0	1	0	0
Chatham Village	1,650	0	0	0	0	0	3	0	3	0	0
Cheektowaga Town	77,576	187	1	14	82	90	2,296	300	1,908	88	3
Chester Town	7,970	7	0	0	0	7	7	0	6	1	0
Chester Village	3,960	6	0	0	0	6	53	5	47	1	0
Chittenango Village	4,888	5	0	0	1	4	25	4	19	2	0
Cicero Town	29,232	12	0	1	0	11	274	30	232	12	1
Clarkstown Town	81,810	89	0	20	24	45	1,125	59	1,046	20	2
Clayton Village	1,877	1	0	0	0	1	5	0	5	0	0
Clyde Village	1,971	1	0	1	0	0	41	8	33	0	0
Cobleskill Village	4,540	6	0	3	0	3	111	13	98	0	1
Coeymans Town	7,369	5	0	0	0	5	82	15	64	3	0
Cohoes	17,007	41	0	6	12	23	200	37	147	16	4
Colchester Town	1,988	0	0	0	0	0	10	4	6	0	0
Colonie Town	79,526	84	0	4	24	56	1,902	136	1,712	54	2
Corning	10,751	40	1	14	1	24	265	51	207	7	2
Cornwall-on-Hudson Village	2,915	3	0	0	1	2	22	1	21	0	0
Cornwall Town	9,544	2	0	0	0	2	21	4	17	0	0
Cortland	18,735	16	0	2	8	6	319	52	260	7	0
Crawford Town	9,183	9	0	0	2	7	98	25	68	5	0
Croton-on-Hudson Village	8,271	4	0	1	0	3	38	2	33	3	0
Cuba Town	3,061	6	0	0	0	6	46	7	39	0	0
Dansville Village	4,482	4	0	0	2	2	106	11	92	3	0
Deerpark Town	7,712	7	0	0	0	7	76	16	57	3	0
Delhi Village	3,147	5	0	4	0	1	24	4	20	0	0
Depew Village	15,150	17	0	4	6	7	246	41	197	8	0
Dewitt Town	25,405	48	1	4	17	26	715	78	617	20	4
Dobbs Ferry Village	11,127	4	0	0	1	3	89	4	85	0	0
Dolgeville Village	2,099	2	0	1	0	1	16	3	13	0	0
Dryden Village	2,115	3	0	3	0	0	67	11	56	0	0
Dunkirk	11,845	43	1	1	13	28	196	40	151	5	0
Durham Town	2,659	0	0	0	0	0	9	2	7	0	1
East Aurora-Aurora Town	13,806	3	0	1	1	1	91	13	75	3	1
Eastchester Town	20,052	5	0	0	4	1	171	6	157	8	0
East Fishkill Town	29,500	20	0	2	2	16	143	7	135	1	0
East Greenbush Town	16,461	7	0	2	1	4	335	22	307	6	0
East Hampton Town	19,937	17	0	3	3	11	226	33	184	9	0
East Hampton Village	1,121	1	0	0	0	1	49	4	45	0	0
East Rochester Village	6,613	4	0	0	2	2	88	14	70	4	0
Eden Town	7,644	5	1	2	0	2	37	12	24	1	0
Ellenville Village	4,032	18	0	3	3	12	136	24	110	2	0
Ellicott Town	5,093	9	0	1	3	5	185	20	162	3	3
Ellicottville	1,599	1	0	0	0	1	10	2	8	0	0
Elmira	27,740	80	2	2	29	47	863	126	717	20	6
Elmira Heights Village	3,909	3	0	0	1	2	56	3	51	2	0
Elmira Town	5,714	1	0	1	0	0	1	0	0	1	0
Elmsford Village	5,072	5	0	0	2	3	14	0	11	3	0
Endicott Village	12,932	74	0	13	22	39	428	89	326	13	3
Evans Town	16,162	18	0	2	2	14	215	25	184	6	4
Fairport Village	5,415	3	1	1	1	0	44	6	37	1	0
Fallsburg Town	12,042	13	0	2	2	9	107	47	56	4	0
Fishkill Town	21,532	7	0	0	5	2	121	10	107	4	0
Fishkill Village	2,107	2	0	0	1	1	27	3	23	1	0
Floral Park Village	15,959	9	0	1	7	1	42	7	29	6	1
Florida Village	2,866	1	0	0	0	1	4	1	3	0	0
Fort Edward Village	3,282	3	0	0	0	3	17	10	6	1	1
Fort Plain Village	2,212	5	0	2	0	3	64	9	54	1	0
Franklinville Village	1,661	1	0	0	0	1	20	4	16	0	0
Fredonia Village	10,543	13	0	3	6	4	157	20	136	1	0
Freeport Village	43,343	94	0	2	33	59	407	33	336	38	2
Friendship Town	1,897	2	0	0	0	2	3	0	3	0	0
Fulton City	11,321	18	0	2	5	11	329	77	245	7	1
Garden City Village	22,579	2	0	0	2	0	214	14	195	5	1
Gates Town	28,723	60	1	9	15	35	841	68	729	44	1
Geddes Town	10,245	7	0	0	3	4	215	20	194	1	0
Geneseo Village	8,179	2	0	2	0	0	163	13	149	1	1
Geneva	12,951	28	1	6	7	14	289	80	207	2	2
Germantown Town	1,845	0	0	0	0	0	1	0	1	0	0
Glen Cove	27,400	8	0	1	2	5	151	12	137	2	6
Glen Park Village	490	0	0	0	0	0	3	0	3	0	0
Glens Falls	14,268	29	2	1	3	23	190	28	156	6	1
Glenville Town	21,650	14	0	2	2	10	464	40	417	7	4
Gloversville	14,832	64	0	27	9	28	362	48	306	8	4
Goshen Town	8,661	4	0	1	1	2	89	14	70	5	1
Goshen Village	5,354	4	0	0	0	4	52	5	47	0	0
Granville Village	2,454	2	0	0	0	2	15	4	11	0	0
Greece Town	96,219	174	3	29	62	80	1,935	242	1,592	101	15
Greenburgh Town	45,923	50	1	10	18	21	613	31	558	24	1
Greene Village	1,463	0	0	0	0	0	13	4	7	2	0
Green Island Village	2,595	4	0	0	0	4	30	6	23	1	0
Greenport Town	4,278	0	0	0	0	0	116	0	116	0	0

Table 8. Offenses Known to Law Enforcement, by Selected State and City, 2017—Continued

(Number.)

State/city	Population	Violent crime	Murder and nonnegligent manslaughter	Rape (revised definition)[1]	Robbery	Aggravated assault	Property crime	Burglary	Larceny-theft	Motor vehicle theft	Arson[2]
Greenwich Village	1,725	3	0	2	0	1	22	5	17	0	0
Greenwood Lake Village	3,092	1	0	1	0	0	21	4	16	1	0
Groton Village	2,373	2	0	0	1	1	39	3	36	0	0
Guilderland Town	34,098	27	0	9	6	12	685	34	647	4	0
Hamburg Town	46,040	37	0	0	12	25	874	91	761	22	2
Hamilton Village	4,105	0	0	0	0	0	6	0	6	0	0
Hammondsport Village	634	3	0	0	1	2	6	3	3	0	0
Hancock Village	951	0	0	0	0	0	14	3	11	0	0
Harriman Village	2,469	1	0	0	1	0	19	0	16	3	0
Harrison Town	28,480	1	0	0	0	1	116	4	111	1	0
Hastings-on-Hudson Village	7,987	3	0	1	0	2	66	5	59	2	0
Haverstraw Town	37,535	42	0	1	16	25	298	48	239	11	3
Hempstead Village	55,807	332	6	6	109	211	593	92	393	108	3
Herkimer Village	7,410	50	0	1	2	47	324	29	295	0	0
Highland Falls Village	3,805	3	0	0	0	3	46	11	34	1	0
Highlands Town	8,275	2	0	0	0	2	8	0	8	0	0
Holley Village	1,709	3	0	1	0	2	28	4	21	3	0
Homer Village	3,120	0	0	0	0	0	8	1	7	0	0
Hoosick Falls Village	3,407	2	0	0	0	2	39	4	31	4	0
Hornell	8,213	4	0	0	0	4	100	8	91	1	0
Horseheads Village	6,559	0	0	0	0	0	43	5	38	0	0
Hudson	6,353	46	0	7	9	30	202	32	160	10	1
Hudson Falls Village	7,093	16	1	3	2	10	54	11	42	1	2
Huntington Bay Village	1,436	0	0	0	0	0	6	0	6	0	0
Hyde Park Town	20,960	10	0	1	1	8	106	20	84	2	0
Ilion Village	7,801	32	0	8	2	22	253	34	213	6	1
Independence Town	1,154	0	0	0	0	0	3	0	3	0	0
Inlet Town	309	0	0	0	0	0	3	1	2	0	0
Interlaken Village	621	0	0	0	0	0	2	0	2	0	0
Irondequoit Town	50,393	109	1	11	41	56	1,118	157	903	58	2
Irvington Village	6,614	3	0	0	1	2	16	2	13	1	0
Ithaca	30,875	56	1	6	21	28	898	75	805	18	
Jamestown	29,562	196	1	26	31	138	879	226	610	43	29
Johnson City Village	14,595	91	0	19	12	60	756	116	619	21	2
Johnstown	8,251	11	0	2	2	7	210	24	181	5	0
Jordan Village	1,309	0	0	0	0	0	1	1	0	0	0
Kenmore Village	15,085	13	0	0	6	7	231	38	188	5	0
Kensington Village	1,179	0	0	0	0	0	0	0	0	0	0
Kent Town	13,241	1	0	1	0	0	62	9	53	0	1
Kings Point Village	5,232	2	0	0	1	1	10	1	6	3	0
Kingston	23,110	73	1	5	22	45	449	53	392	4	3
Kirkland Town	8,204	0	0	0	0	0	20	0	20	0	0
Lackawanna	17,823	75	0	10	23	42	357	84	249	24	3
Lake Placid Village	2,424	2	0	0	1	1	32	5	25	2	0
Lake Success Village	3,127	1	0	0	0	1	19	4	12	3	0
Lakewood-Busti	7,326	3	0	1	1	1	334	23	305	6	1
Lancaster Town	37,458	23	0	4	5	14	406	48	350	8	0
Larchmont Village	6,161	3	0	0	2	1	103	9	88	6	0
Le Roy Village	4,227	6	0	2	0	4	48	6	40	2	0
Lewisboro Town	12,823	0	0	0	0	0	1	0	1	0	0
Liberty Village	4,050	26	1	6	1	18	138	22	115	1	2
Little Falls	4,709	16	0	5	2	9	123	21	99	3	0
Liverpool Village	2,246	0	0	0	0	0	31	5	22	4	0
Lloyd Harbor Village	3,696	2	0	0	0	2	9	0	9	0	0
Lloyd Town	10,465	6	0	1	1	4	100	12	88	0	0
Long Beach	33,771	21	0	0	9	12	199	11	180	8	0
Lowville Village	3,398	4	0	1	0	3	37	4	33	0	0
Lynbrook Village	19,577	18	0	1	7	10	102	13	79	10	0
Macedon Town and Village	8,977	9	0	5	1	3	119	22	92	5	0
Malone Village	5,650	27	0	12	1	14	135	31	99	5	1
Malverne Village	8,548	0	0	0	0	0	22	2	20	0	0
Mamaroneck Town	12,218	1	0	0	0	1	60	5	55	0	0
Mamaroneck Village	19,424	19	0	0	8	11	131	24	99	8	0
Manchester Village	1,643	0	0	0	0	0	1	1	0	0	0
Manlius Town	24,550	17	0	5	4	8	341	52	285	4	1
Marcellus Village	1,764	0	0	0	0	0	7	2	5	0	0
Marlborough Town	8,633	7	0	1	2	4	52	13	33	6	0
Maybrook Village	3,513	3	0	0	0	3	8	0	8	0	0
Mechanicville	5,081	13	1	4	2	6	54	6	46	2	0
Medina Village	5,739	24	0	5	3	16	149	18	128	3	2
Menands Village	3,960	10	0	1	5	4	151	4	143	4	0
Middleport Village	1,766	3	0	0	0	3	30	4	25	1	1
Middletown	27,607	103	2	11	37	53	658	75	572	11	7
Monroe Village	8,636	9	0	1	2	6	133	19	113	1	0
Montgomery Village	4,713	0	0	0	0	0	19	3	16	0	0
Monticello Village	6,373	36	1	2	9	24	182	40	136	6	1
Moriah Town	3,536	2	0	0	0	2	0	0	0	0	0
Mount Hope Town	6,904	0	0	0	0	0	5	0	5	0	0
Mount Morris Village	2,850	6	0	0	2	4	67	7	57	3	0
Mount Vernon	68,507	437	6	22	123	286	1,294	159	1,001	134	11
Nassau Village	1,117	3	0	1	0	2	3	0	3	0	0
New Berlin Town	1,522	0	0	0	0	0	17	4	13	0	0
Newburgh	28,080	347	6	23	101	217	747	160	546	41	8

Table 8. Offenses Known to Law Enforcement, by Selected State and City, 2017—Continued

(Number.)

State/city	Population	Violent crime	Murder and nonnegligent manslaughter	Rape (revised definition)[1]	Robbery	Aggravated assault	Property crime	Burglary	Larceny-theft	Motor vehicle theft	Arson[2]
Newburgh Town	30,862	24	0	1	11	12	1,059	61	984	14	8
New Hartford Town and Village	20,313	16	0	2	6	8	595	26	560	9	1
New Paltz Town and Village	14,125	22	0	4	1	17	165	16	149	0	0
New Rochelle	79,960	182	1	11	70	100	1,149	104	978	67	2
New Windsor Town	27,609	26	0	0	3	23	363	36	319	8	0
New York	8,616,333	46,433	292	2,375	13,995	29,771	124,815	11,104	107,976	5,735	
New York Mills Village	3,278	2	0	0	1	1	37	3	32	2	0
Niagara Falls	48,385	544	3	36	150	355	2,336	458	1,738	140	22
Niagara Town	8,030	9	0	0	5	4	358	36	304	18	0
Niskayuna Town	22,541	15	0	1	3	11	411	30	368	13	0
Nissequogue Village	1,747	0	0	0	0	0	7	1	6	0	0
Norfolk Town	4,447	0	0	0	0	0	1	1	0	0	0
North Greenbush Town	12,234	8	0	1	3	4	152	18	127	7	0
Northport Village	7,331	4	0	1	0	3	42	1	38	3	0
North Syracuse Village	6,796	9	0	2	1	6	99	13	81	5	0
North Tonawanda	30,452	37	0	5	8	24	507	84	400	23	2
Northville Village	1,052	0	0	0	0	0	5	0	5	0	0
Norwich	6,804	26	0	14	0	12	189	22	167	0	1
Norwood Village	1,582	2	0	0	0	2	6	2	4	0	0
Nunda Town and Village	2,951	1	0	1	0	0	12	2	10	0	0
Ocean Beach Village	82	0	0	0	0	0	8	0	8	0	0
Ogdensburg	10,685	29	1	1	5	22	381	70	306	5	2
Ogden Town	20,321	13	0	4	3	6	210	30	171	9	0
Old Brookville Village	2,219	1	0	0	1	0	34	6	23	5	0
Old Westbury Village	4,747	0	0	0	0	0	23	0	23	0	0
Olean	13,694	31	1	5	4	21	381	27	351	3	2
Olive Town	4,308	0	0	0	0	0	7	2	5	0	1
Oneida	11,027	25	1	6	6	12	380	54	322	4	0
Oneonta City	13,967	27	2	7	2	16	234	50	183	1	2
Orangetown Town	37,804	46	0	1	13	32	303	30	267	6	1
Orchard Park Town	29,725	29	0	2	4	23	255	33	208	14	0
Oriskany Village	1,355	1	0	0	0	1	11	5	6	0	0
Ossining Village	25,409	20	0	1	5	14	245	20	218	7	3
Oswego City	17,510	36	0	5	4	27	383	67	308	8	0
Owego Village	3,774	10	0	4	0	6	153	21	131	1	1
Oyster Bay Cove Village	4,337	0	0	0	0	0	14	4	8	2	0
Peekskill	24,127	34	0	3	12	19	179	17	156	6	0
Pelham Manor Village	5,577	4	0	1	0	3	162	14	141	7	0
Pelham Village	7,037	0	0	0	0	0	69	6	57	6	0
Penn Yan Village	4,961	3	0	2	0	1	58	14	44	0	1
Perry Village	3,467	4	0	4	0	0	58	6	50	2	1
Phoenix Village	2,265	2	0	0	1	1	22	5	16	1	0
Piermont Village	2,573	0	0	0	0	0	12	1	10	1	0
Pine Plains Town	2,414	0	0	0	0	0	0	0	0	0	0
Plattekill Town	10,174	7	0	0	2	5	55	10	42	3	0
Plattsburgh City	19,742	31	0	12	2	17	355	42	308	5	9
Pleasantville Village	7,172	1	0	0	0	1	50	5	44	1	0
Port Byron Village	1,221	0	0	0	0	0	1	0	1	0	0
Port Chester Village	29,616	49	0	2	23	24	322	29	280	13	1
Port Dickinson Village	1,573	0	0	0	0	0	16	1	15	0	0
Port Jervis	8,527	26	0	4	2	20	222	33	182	7	3
Portville Village	968	0	0	0	0	0	0	0	0	0	0
Port Washington	19,384	5	0	0	2	3	99	13	82	4	0
Potsdam Village	9,758	10	0	4	1	5	90	4	85	1	0
Poughkeepsie	30,159	213	2	28	55	128	603	111	467	25	4
Pound Ridge Town	5,253	5	2	1	0	2	33	4	27	2	0
Quogue Village	1,006	0	0	0	0	0	25	1	22	2	0
Ramapo Town	94,019	44	0	9	10	25	693	67	595	31	13
Rensselaer City	9,331	13	0	0	4	9	117	35	77	5	0
Rhinebeck Village	2,582	2	0	0	0	2	39	2	37	0	0
Rochester	208,591	1,872	27	141	707	997	7,934	1,337	5,981	616	105
Rockville Centre Village	24,654	24	0	0	2	22	186	3	176	7	0
Rome	32,200	71	1	10	13	47	563	109	440	14	3
Rosendale Town	5,875	1	0	0	0	1	29	7	22	0	1
Rotterdam Town	29,586	37	0	8	12	17	823	82	723	18	3
Rye	16,021	5	0	1	1	3	73	5	58	10	0
Rye Brook Village	9,608	0	0	0	0	0	92	12	78	2	0
Sackets Harbor Village	1,441	0	0	0	0	0	0	0	0	0	0
Sag Harbor Village	2,292	0	0	0	0	0	0	0	0	0	0
Salamanca	5,512	9	0	0	1	8	93	16	72	5	0
Sands Point Village	2,903	0	0	0	0	0	10	1	8	1	0
Saranac Lake Village	5,268	16	0	8	2	6	46	4	38	4	0
Saratoga Springs	27,962	56	0	7	9	40	459	52	395	12	3
Saugerties Town	19,033	24	0	3	2	19	212	30	171	11	2
Scarsdale Village	18,031	6	0	0	2	4	128	7	115	6	0
Schenectady	64,710	577	2	58	141	376	2,057	348	1,534	175	20
Schodack Town	11,685	3	0	0	1	2	43	5	37	1	1
Schoharie Village	825	0	0	0	0	0	0	0	0	0	0
Scotia Village	7,651	12	0	2	4	6	102	19	79	4	1
Seneca Falls Village	8,811	11	0	6	1	4	239	22	215	2	0
Shandaken Town	2,963	1	0	0	0	1	31	7	23	1	0
Shawangunk Town	14,018	2	0	0	0	2	78	9	69	0	1
Sherburne Village	1,325	1	0	1	0	0	8	0	8	0	0

Table 8. Offenses Known to Law Enforcement, by Selected State and City, 2017—Continued

(Number.)

State/city	Population	Violent crime	Murder and nonnegligent manslaughter	Rape (revised definition)[1]	Robbery	Aggravated assault	Property crime	Burglary	Larceny-theft	Motor vehicle theft	Arson[2]
Sherrill	3,045	0	0	0	0	0	21	0	21	0	0
Shortsville Village	1,434	0	0	0	0	0	0	0	0	0	0
Sidney Village	3,672	7	0	0	0	7	93	11	82	0	0
Skaneateles Village	2,493	1	0	0	0	1	18	1	17	0	0
Sodus Point Village	868	0	0	0	0	0	0	0	0	0	0
Sodus Village	1,725	0	0	0	0	0	5	1	4	0	0
Solvay Village	6,329	16	0	1	2	13	142	26	106	10	5
Southampton Town	50,987	62	0	11	11	40	611	81	494	36	0
Southampton Village	3,309	2	0	1	0	1	84	5	69	10	0
South Glens Falls Village	3,567	10	0	1	3	6	70	14	53	3	1
South Nyack Village	3,532	3	0	1	0	2	15	4	11	0	0
Southold Town	19,990	17	0	4	2	11	214	27	179	8	2
Spring Valley Village	32,795	133	0	28	30	75	390	35	340	15	2
Stillwater Town	6,875	1	0	0	1	0	32	6	25	1	0
St. Johnsville Village	1,669	4	0	1	0	3	20	2	17	1	0
Stony Point Town	15,540	9	0	1	2	6	76	13	61	2	0
Suffern Village	10,983	12	0	0	3	9	61	5	51	5	0
Syracuse	143,069	1,009	20	98	284	607	4,817	1,145	3,301	371	56
Tarrytown Village	11,577	9	0	2	3	4	49	3	45	1	0
Ticonderoga Town	4,890	10	1	4	0	5	38	11	25	2	0
Tonawanda	14,808	45	0	12	7	26	311	51	249	11	3
Tonawanda Town	57,223	100	1	3	29	67	912	190	697	25	2
Troy	49,644	351	6	31	114	200	1,732	370	1,272	90	11
Trumansburg Village	1,824	0	0	0	0	0	36	3	33	0	0
Tuckahoe Village	6,636	1	0	0	1	0	34	4	28	2	0
Tupper Lake Village	3,521	5	0	0	1	4	88	12	73	3	0
Tuxedo Town	2,927	0	0	0	0	0	3	1	2	0	0
Ulster Town	12,473	8	0	1	0	7	342	11	322	9	2
Utica	60,395	337	3	42	78	214	1,986	376	1,543	67	6
Vernon Village	1,163	1	0	0	0	1	21	0	21	0	0
Vestal Town	28,090	22	0	10	2	10	573	33	525	15	2
Walden Village	6,692	7	0	1	0	6	80	9	67	4	1
Wallkill Town	28,881	65	0	6	17	42	632	30	581	21	1
Warsaw Village	3,327	4	0	1	0	3	36	3	32	1	0
Warwick Town	18,375	13	0	1	2	10	104	13	77	14	0
Washingtonville Village	5,752	3	0	0	1	2	33	4	28	1	1
Waterford Town and Village	8,506	5	0	0	2	3	41	9	28	4	0
Waterloo Village	4,996	5	0	0	2	3	76	19	56	1	1
Watertown	25,746	139	1	39	16	83	1,054	153	880	21	5
Watervliet	10,100	42	0	6	10	26	205	49	144	12	0
Watkins Glen Village	1,896	1	0	0	0	1	19	1	18	0	0
Waverly Village	4,151	6	0	1	0	5	17	2	13	2	0
Webb Town	1,811	0	0	0	0	0	5	0	4	1	0
Webster Town and Village	45,096	32	0	15	7	10	411	47	355	9	3
Weedsport Village	1,736	0	0	0	0	0	15	0	15	0	0
Wellsville Village	4,454	11	0	0	1	10	69	9	59	1	0
West Carthage Village	1,997	1	0	1	0	0	20	2	17	1	0
Westfield Village	3,029	3	0	0	0	3	10	3	7	0	0
Westhampton Beach Village	1,774	0	0	0	0	0	38	6	30	2	0
West Seneca Town	45,597	44	1	9	9	25	563	82	465	16	1
White Plains	58,461	103	0	9	26	68	982	34	916	32	0
Whitesboro Village	3,651	0	0	0	0	0	36	4	31	1	0
Whitestown Town	9,207	1	0	0	1	0	30	7	22	1	0
Windham Town	1,679	0	0	0	0	0	13	5	8	0	0
Wolcott Village	1,615	0	0	0	0	0	5	0	5	0	0
Woodbury Town	11,017	4	0	0	1	3	505	4	497	4	0
Woodridge Village	793	0	0	0	0	0	16	6	9	1	0
Woodstock Town	5,812	2	0	1	1	0	61	16	45	0	0
Yonkers	201,554	810	8	36	271	495	2,023	360	1,481	182	15
Yorktown Town	37,142	12	0	3	2	7	217	31	180	6	1
Yorkville Village	2,605	5	0	0	2	3	24	9	14	1	1
Youngstown Village	1,901	1	0	0	0	1	1	0	1	0	0
NORTH CAROLINA[7]											
Aberdeen	7,707		1		9	8	275	37	232	6	2
Albemarle	16,022		1		21	67	738	221	486	31	5
Angier	5,227		0		2	4	120	47	69	4	0
Apex	49,159		1		7	16	643	81	548	14	4
Archdale	11,664		1		3	8	192	57	126	9	0
Asheboro	26,253		2		43	82	1,527	243	1,207	77	6
Asheville	90,103		7		181	363	4,248	733	3,191	324	7
Atlantic Beach	1,491		0		0	7	108	31	75	2	1
Ayden	5,215		0		2	14	167	35	125	7	0
Bailey	568		0		0	0	14	8	5	1	1
Banner Elk	1,166		0		0	0	12	3	9	0	0
Beaufort	4,223		0		2	3	141	30	109	2	1
Beech Mountain	321		0		0	2	19	2	17	0	0
Belhaven	1,572		0		0	5	26	7	17	2	0
Belmont	10,880		0		9	33	634	38	575	21	2
Benson	3,764		1		8	13	187	60	118	9	0
Bessemer City	5,586		0		2	11	92	26	60	6	1
Beulaville	1,326		0		0	7	26	5	21	0	0
Biltmore Forest	1,482		0		0	0	15	1	13	1	0

Table 8. Offenses Known to Law Enforcement, by Selected State and City, 2017—Continued

(Number.)

State/city	Population	Violent crime	Murder and nonnegligent manslaughter	Rape (revised definition)[1]	Robbery	Aggravated assault	Property crime	Burglary	Larceny-theft	Motor vehicle theft	Arson[2]
Biscoe	1,676		0		2	2	119	3	114	2	0
Black Mountain	8,477		2		0	5	111	27	75	9	0
Blowing Rock	1,297		0		0	1	22	4	16	2	0
Boone	19,138		1		6	18	382	52	318	12	1
Brevard	7,846		1		2	9	174	23	142	9	1
Bunn	362		0		0	0	21	5	16	0	0
Burgaw	4,135		0		4	3	211	33	172	6	0
Burlington	52,986		4		114	381	2,016	502	1,402	112	7
Burnsville	1,650		0		0	3	39	3	33	3	0
Butner	7,718		0		3	13	157	41	111	5	2
Carrboro	21,553		0		9	29	430	91	324	15	0
Carthage	2,463		0		0	2	82	18	60	4	0
Cary	166,986		0		44	63	1,795	285	1,438	72	10
Chapel Hill	59,553		1		40	38	1,284	251	980	53	5
Charlotte-Mecklenburg	914,609		86		2,017	3,965	34,894	6,416	25,856	2,622	194
Clayton	21,012		0		9	14	367	71	277	19	0
Cleveland	879		0		0	0	29	10	16	3	0
Clinton	8,666		0		19	57	477	101	357	19	2
Columbus	979		0		0	0	27	2	22	3	0
Concord	91,756		1		31	62	1,791	293	1,433	65	4
Conover	8,354		0		6	19	452	86	353	13	1
Cramerton	4,461		0		1	2	106	23	80	3	0
Creedmoor	4,563		0		4	4	139	32	103	4	1
Davidson	12,723		0		0	4	157	22	130	5	0
Dobson	1,591		0		1	1	62	12	46	4	0
Drexel	1,872		0		0	1	22	4	15	3	0
Duck	386		0		0	1	46	27	19	0	0
Durham	269,088		23		852	1,257	10,296	2,334	7,200	762	31
Eden	15,321		0		21	70	572	133	412	27	5
Edenton	4,823		1		1	54	118	34	81	3	0
Elizabeth City	17,802		1		23	101	821	188	608	25	2
Elkin	4,120		1		3	19	337	43	281	13	1
Elon	10,283		0		2	4	52	19	32	1	0
Emerald Isle	3,710		0		1	11	179	89	82	8	0
Erwin	5,017		1		6	23	212	64	144	4	0
Fairmont	2,680		0		7	10	137	62	68	7	2
Farmville	4,759		0		8	33	217	55	157	5	1
Fayetteville	205,432		24		292	1,105	8,811	1,818	6,578	415	39
Fletcher	8,237		0		1	1	119	43	66	10	1
Fuquay-Varina	27,429		0		7	26	376	63	292	21	1
Garner	29,287		1		32	63	1,082	217	822	43	1
Gastonia	76,191		4		158	405	3,714	587	2,865	262	22
Gibsonville	7,131		1		1	13	99	53	39	7	0
Goldsboro	35,824		10		75	184	1,796	337	1,399	60	2
Granite Falls	4,680		0		1	1	220	9	194	17	0
Greensboro	290,051		46		664	1,394	10,332	2,062	7,424	846	115
Greenville	92,630		4		154	420	3,394	724	2,566	104	13
Havelock	20,157		0		3	18	486	160	316	10	3
Haw River	2,467		0		4	9	78	30	44	4	0
Henderson	15,131		6		45	131	673	203	429	41	5
Hendersonville	13,967		0		21	26	691	126	530	35	0
Hertford	2,122		0		5	15	50	13	34	3	0
Hickory	40,653		8		54	152	2,093	325	1,590	178	9
Highlands	944		0		0	2	34	9	25	0	0
High Point	112,368		20		206	530	4,161	754	3,127	280	14
Hillsborough	6,640		0		7	21	345	38	300	7	0
Holly Ridge	2,466		0		0	10	48	12	32	4	0
Holly Springs	34,897		0		6	10	317	36	273	8	0
Hope Mills	16,325		1		32	74	809	124	674	11	3
Hudson	3,717		0		0	10	96	10	80	6	1
Huntersville	56,279		2		17	42	993	100	857	36	5
Indian Beach	114		0		0	1	7	0	7	0	0
Jacksonville	67,293		5		71	142	1,961	380	1,529	52	9
Jefferson	1,542		0		0	0	17	6	10	1	0
Jonesville	2,240		0		1	12	109	24	79	6	1
Kannapolis	48,754		0		40	44	980	222	688	70	4
Kernersville	24,222		2		24	52	1,249	147	1,052	50	5
Kill Devil Hills	7,194		0		1	20	444	219	214	11	0
King	7,046		0		0	17	269	19	245	5	1
Kings Mountain	10,824		2		7	17	362	95	266	1	2
Kinston	20,791		6		40	220	1,219	293	892	34	3
Kitty Hawk	3,507		0		0	2	184	35	146	3	0
Knightdale	15,423		0		4	6	269	40	213	16	1
Lake Lure	1,178		0		0	1	35	7	27	1	0
Laurel Park	2,344		0		1	1	11	1	9	1	0
Leland	19,786		0		4	13	349	56	287	6	3
Lenoir	17,932		0		13	36	791	150	592	49	1
Lincolnton	10,823		0		9	37	369	48	304	17	4
Long View	4,900		3		6	24	224	81	111	32	6
Louisburg	3,576		0		4	12	110	31	75	4	1
Maiden	3,403		0		0	2	117	21	93	3	3
Manteo	1,421		0		1	7	68	11	55	2	1
Marion	7,819		0		3	31	630	220	375	35	2

Table 8. Offenses Known to Law Enforcement, by Selected State and City, 2017—Continued

(Number.)

State/city	Population	Violent crime	Murder and nonnegligent manslaughter	Rape (revised definition)[1]	Robbery	Aggravated assault	Property crime	Burglary	Larceny-theft	Motor vehicle theft	Arson[2]
Mars Hill	2,239		0		0	2	10	2	8	0	0
Marshville	2,692		0		9	19	137	59	75	3	0
Matthews	32,255		0		14	39	1,005	127	827	51	9
Maxton	2,434		1		8	2	168	96	65	7	2
Mayodan	2,445		0		1	1	163	20	141	2	0
Maysville	973		0		0	0	16	3	13	0	0
Mebane	14,619		0		9	49	579	46	514	19	0
Mint Hill	26,868		2		22	19	467	105	332	30	3
Mocksville	5,302		0		6	19	219	55	152	12	1
Mooresville	37,049		0		16	43	998	80	885	33	3
Morehead City	9,520		0		6	17	462	45	408	9	2
Morrisville	25,904		0		10	9	411	59	344	8	4
Mount Airy	10,338		0		7	25	448	59	342	47	1
Mount Holly	14,640		2		7	18	261	53	197	11	5
Mount Olive	4,760		0		5	7	109	24	82	3	0
Murfreesboro	3,057		0		2	4	84	23	59	2	0
Murphy	1,648		0		5	14	133	48	77	8	0
Nags Head	2,943		0		1	17	207	100	105	2	0
New Bern	30,191		1		47	92	1,005	198	792	15	2
Newport	4,776		0		0	5	77	14	62	1	0
Newton	13,059		0		4	42	451	126	304	21	4
North Wilkesboro	4,228		0		2	6	151	1	145	5	3
Oak Island	7,883		1		0	20	233	82	144	7	0
Oxford	8,887		1		12	36	427	95	314	18	2
Pinebluff	1,491		0		0	0	22	12	8	2	0
Pinehurst	16,145		0		1	4	130	7	121	2	0
Pine Knoll Shores	1,359		0		0	1	17	1	16	0	1
Pine Level	1,922		0		1	3	34	2	32	0	0
Pineville	8,788		0		27	23	1,236	68	1,127	41	0
Pittsboro	4,355		1		2	6	88	12	72	4	0
Plymouth	3,551		1		5	43	184	57	122	5	0
Raeford	5,057		0		7	8	191	44	142	5	0
Ramseur	1,713		2		5	4	90	21	65	4	0
Reidsville	13,900		1		24	93	749	152	561	36	6
Richlands	1,702		0		0	0	28	3	23	2	0
Roanoke Rapids	15,083		2		28	77	850	208	617	25	3
Robbins	1,189		0		0	2	45	6	39	0	0
Robersonville	1,402		0		0	13	35	11	23	1	0
Rockingham	9,005		0		20	40	754	137	592	25	4
Rockwell	2,148		0		0	2	53	14	35	4	0
Rocky Mount	55,098		15		95	270	1,984	554	1,310	120	16
Rolesville	7,709		0		1	1	107	15	85	7	0
Rowland	1,043		0		6	8	81	40	39	2	0
Rutherfordton	4,134		0		0	0	146	1	142	3	0
Selma	6,678		0		13	26	287	113	163	11	1
Shallotte	4,050		0		2	3	171	17	149	5	0
Siler City	8,531		0		11	46	369	72	287	10	0
Smithfield	12,489		0		21	49	568	100	454	14	0
Snow Hill	1,551		0		2	4	56	14	42	0	0
Southern Pines	14,025		1		16	25	471	85	380	6	8
Spencer	3,315		0		4	15	123	19	98	6	0
Spruce Pine	2,095		0		0	1	39	1	36	2	0
Stallings	15,656		0		4	8	181	52	120	9	0
Surf City	2,342		0		0	6	143	12	130	1	0
Swansboro	3,261		0		0	12	107	18	88	1	0
Sylva	2,653		0		1	10	268	53	206	9	0
Tabor City	4,225		1		1	12	144	48	87	9	3
Tarboro	10,924		0		11	28	359	73	276	10	2
Thomasville	27,071		2		45	69	1,270	320	882	68	3
Trent Woods	4,162		0		0	0	29	13	15	1	0
Troutman	2,610		0		0	3	83	9	70	4	1
Troy	3,399		0		1	5	102	25	72	5	0
Tryon	1,618		0		0	1	34	13	20	1	0
Valdese	4,477		0		0	2	44	10	30	4	0
Wadesboro	5,413		6		11	66	319	107	197	15	3
Wake Forest	42,019		0		7	34	741	84	642	15	2
Warsaw	3,160		0		1	7	116	36	77	3	1
Washington	9,793		0		16	56	515	95	402	18	2
Waxhaw	15,089		0		2	12	170	26	142	2	0
Waynesville	9,977		2		5	11	516	155	327	34	2
Weaverville	4,034		0		4	3	131	2	128	1	0
Weldon	1,563		1		4	11	59	22	34	3	0
Wendell	6,901		0		0	4	94	33	57	4	0
West Jefferson	1,305		0		0	2	80	2	77	1	1
Whispering Pines	3,342		0		0	0	18	5	13	0	0
Whiteville	5,534		4		20	45	440	80	344	16	0
Wilkesboro	3,554		0		2	14	293	10	276	7	1
Williamston	5,438		4		11	25	334	80	240	14	0
Wilmington	119,422		18		195	535	4,318	998	3,039	281	6
Windsor	3,795		1		3	6	38	8	30	0	0
Winterville	9,476		0		5	3	114	48	64	2	0
Woodfin	6,444		0		0	4	121	49	66	6	0
Wrightsville Beach	2,574		0		3	10	115	23	91	1	0

Table 8. Offenses Known to Law Enforcement, by Selected State and City, 2017—Continued

(Number.)

State/city	Population	Violent crime	Murder and nonnegligent manslaughter	Rape (revised definition)[1]	Robbery	Aggravated assault	Property crime	Burglary	Larceny-theft	Motor vehicle theft	Arson[2]
Yadkinville	2,918		1		2	7	100	19	76	5	1
Youngsville	1,317		0		0	1	39	6	31	2	0
Zebulon	5,288		0		4	23	222	41	176	5	0
NORTH DAKOTA											
Arnegard	161	0	0	0	0	0	1	0	1	0	0
Belfield	1,055	2	0	0	0	2	6	0	5	1	0
Berthold	502	0	0	0	0	0	4	2	0	2	0
Beulah	3,420	4	0	0	0	4	14	1	13	0	0
Bismarck	74,397	256	0	45	33	178	2,438	322	1,884	232	5
Bowman	1,724	1	0	0	0	1	18	4	13	1	0
Burlington	1,215	2	0	1	0	1	6	0	4	2	0
Carrington	2,039	1	0	0	0	1	20	3	16	1	0
Cavalier	1,231	1	0	0	0	1	19	2	15	2	0
Devils Lake	7,344	23	0	4	2	17	351	51	261	39	2
Dickinson	23,967	39	0	6	2	31	466	47	390	29	0
Ellendale	1,269	2	0	0	0	2	8	3	4	1	0
Emerado	430	1	0	1	0	0	26	1	23	2	0
Fargo	123,430	497	3	83	68	343	3,870	593	2,975	302	10
Fessenden	462	0	0	0	0	0	2	1	1	0	0
Grafton	4,240	8	0	2	0	6	99	20	70	9	0
Grand Forks	58,090	183	0	29	32	122	1,720	265	1,331	124	3
Harvey	1,737	3	0	2	0	1	26	8	16	2	0
Hillsboro	1,584	0	0	0	0	0	5	1	4	0	0
Jamestown	15,439	57	1	17	3	36	400	73	297	30	2
Kenmare	1,053	3	0	0	0	3	8	1	7	0	0
Killdeer	1,268	9	0	2	1	6	16	3	12	1	0
Lamoure	913	0	0	0	0	0	1	1	0	0	0
Lincoln	3,935	1	0	0	0	1	9	2	5	2	0
Lisbon	2,121	6	0	2	0	4	57	8	45	4	0
Mandan	22,369	41	0	9	1	31	720	101	526	93	4
Medora	136	1	0	0	0	1	0	0	0	0	0
Minot	50,118	134	2	32	17	83	1,120	243	662	215	2
New Town	2,642	1	0	0	0	1	18	5	10	3	0
Northwood	913	1	0	0	0	1	6	2	4	0	0
Oakes	1,769	1	0	0	0	1	9	4	5	0	0
Powers Lake	296	0	0	0	0	0	4	2	2	0	0
Ray	838	1	0	0	0	1	4	0	2	2	0
Rolla	1,331	0	0	0	0	0	21	2	17	2	0
Rugby	2,806	2	0	0	0	2	53	3	38	12	1
Sherwood	250	0	0	0	0	0	8	6	2	0	0
Stanley	2,974	1	0	0	1	0	2	0	2	0	0
Steele	707	0	0	0	0	0	7	2	5	0	0
Surrey	1,453	1	0	0	1	0	5	1	1	3	0
Thompson	1,016	1	0	0	0	1	2	1	1	0	0
Tioga	1,607	4	0	1	0	3	29	4	24	1	0
Valley City	6,558	11	0	1	0	10	151	18	122	11	1
Wahpeton	7,841	13	0	2	0	11	177	27	146	4	0
Watford City	8,015	27	0	3	0	24	126	21	86	19	0
West Fargo	36,624	53	0	14	6	33	494	84	369	41	1
Williston	28,748	100	1	17	7	75	671	120	490	61	8
Wishek	945	1	0	0	0	1	2	1	1	0	0
OHIO											
Ada	5,551	2	0	2	0	0	30	5	24	1	0
Addyston	936	3	0	1	0	2	21	5	15	1	0
Akron	197,412	1,377	42	209	395	731	8,360	2,301	5,304	755	103
Albany	899	0	0	0	0	0	11	1	10	0	0
Alliance	21,838	75	0	14	11	50	800	109	650	41	6
Amberley Village	3,607	0	0	0	0	0	29	1	28	0	0
Amelia	4,982	3	0	0	0	3	63	2	58	3	0
American Township	12,208	1	0	0	0	1	209	15	183	11	0
Amherst	12,090	5	0	0	2	3	157	14	140	3	1
Archbold	4,338	2	0	1	0	1	41	6	34	1	0
Ashland	20,485	25	0	7	4	14	375	44	326	5	0
Ashville	4,211	3	1	0	1	1	53	9	40	4	0
Athens	25,526	34	0	4	6	24	433	44	370	19	5
Aurora	15,932	3	0	0	1	2	187	17	168	2	0
Austintown	35,303	62	0	9	14	39	789	109	659	21	1
Avon Lake	23,839	8	0	0	1	7	124	21	97	6	1
Bainbridge Township	11,528	1	0	0	0	1	243	5	238	0	0
Baltimore	2,973	0	0	0	0	0	15	3	11	1	1
Barberton	26,050	103	1	19	14	69	881	158	682	41	8
Barnesville	4,096	0	0	0	0	0	16	4	11	1	0
Batavia	1,656	0	0	0	0	0	57	7	46	4	0
Bath Township, Summit County	9,678	9	0	2	3	4	116	14	100	2	0
Bazetta Township	5,614	6	0	1	0	5	127	18	109	0	0
Beavercreek	46,572	38	0	13	9	16	1,111	49	1,013	49	2
Beaver Township	6,427	2	0	1	0	1	102	23	74	5	1
Bedford	12,641	25	1	1	16	7	228	50	146	32	0
Bedford Heights[7]	10,558		1		9	11	255	32	173	50	0
Bellaire	4,153	8	1	2	1	4	39	6	33	0	0

Table 8. Offenses Known to Law Enforcement, by Selected State and City, 2017—Continued

(Number.)

State/city	Population	Violent crime	Murder and nonnegligent manslaughter	Rape (revised definition)[1]	Robbery	Aggravated assault	Property crime	Burglary	Larceny-theft	Motor vehicle theft	Arson[2]
Bellbrook	7,159	5	0	1	0	4	39	0	39	0	0
Bellefontaine	13,144	14	0	6	2	6	331	46	280	5	2
Bellville	1,864	0	0	0	0	0	18	2	15	1	0
Belpre	6,466	2	0	0	0	2	76	15	56	5	0
Berea	18,871	8	0	1	1	6	140	27	105	8	2
Bethel	2,791	3	0	0	0	3	87	14	71	2	0
Bexley	13,773	20	1	4	10	5	420	104	301	15	0
Blanchester	4,261	12	0	6	2	4	99	23	71	5	0
Blue Ash	12,248	16	2	2	4	8	278	42	229	7	0
Bluffton	4,157	1	0	1	0	0	48	9	38	1	0
Bowling Green	31,779	41	0	20	6	15	587	86	486	15	3
Brecksville	13,432	2	0	1	0	1	52	4	47	1	0
Bridgeport	1,783	3	0	1	0	2	22	2	15	5	0
Brimfield Township	10,348	7	0	1	2	4	291	28	254	9	0
Broadview Heights	19,228	1	0	0	0	1	21	5	11	5	0
Brooklyn[7]	10,809		1		11	6	677	31	612	34	0
Brookville[7]	5,896		0		3	0	67	15	47	5	0
Brunswick	34,838	21	1	2	4	14	194	22	161	11	0
Brunswick Hills Township	10,309	2	0	1	0	1	40	11	27	2	0
Bucyrus	11,828	26	0	6	4	16	436	82	348	6	0
Butler Township	7,799	24	0	5	9	10	425	29	372	24	2
Byesville	2,372	0	0	0	0	0	16	4	9	3	0
Cambridge[7]	10,391		1		3	3	456	75	375	6	1
Campbell	7,875	9	0	0	2	7	50	19	25	6	0
Canal Fulton	5,428	2	0	1	0	1	75	26	47	2	0
Canfield	7,246	3	0	1	0	2	46	10	36	0	2
Canton	71,031	836	16	97	188	535	3,766	1,008	2,512	246	12
Cardington	2,064	4	0	2	0	2	23	9	14	0	0
Carey	3,566	1	0	0	0	1	8	2	6	0	0
Carlisle	5,395	3	0	1	0	2	44	11	33	0	0
Carroll Township	2,085	2	1	0	0	1	17	3	14	0	0
Centerville	23,782	14	0	2	4	8	373	30	327	16	0
Chagrin Falls	3,991	2	0	1	0	1	39	3	36	0	0
Chardon[7]	5,199		0		0	9	96	4	91	1	0
Chester Township	10,355	0	0	0	0	0	8	1	7	0	0
Cheviot	8,269	15	0	1	9	5	231	33	177	21	0
Chillicothe	21,695	93	0	14	28	51	1,496	284	1,160	52	6
Cincinnati	299,116	2,833	70	292	1,196	1,275	15,105	3,448	10,172	1,485	
Circleville	13,972	57	0	13	21	23	714	136	550	28	4
Clayton	13,149	5	0	0	4	1	118	17	92	9	
Clay Township, Montgomery County	4,193	8	0	3	0	5	22	7	14	1	0
Clearcreek Township	15,531	11	1	2	0	8	74	8	63	3	0
Cleveland	385,351	5,999	107	497	2,697	2,698	18,944	5,853	9,696	3,395	253
Cleveland Heights	44,525	131	2	16	79	34	879	125	655	99	1
Clyde	6,191	4	0	0	0	4	116	21	92	3	1
Coitsville Township	1,326	3	0	1	0	2	44	16	24	4	0
Coldwater	4,519	3	0	3	0	0	53	6	47	0	0
Colerain Township	58,996	100	1	14	41	44	1,708	223	1,400	85	7
Columbiana	6,233	3	0	1	1	1	37	3	34	0	0
Columbus	872,205	4,478	142	919	1,963	1,454	34,408	7,111	23,121	4,176	379
Commercial Point	1,617	0	0	0	0	0	21	6	14	1	0
Copley Township	17,280	15	1	1	2	11	163	24	133	6	0
Cortland	6,844	1	0	0	1	0	46	6	39	1	0
Covington	2,637	3	0	0	0	3	16	2	14	0	0
Crestline	4,408	11	0	6	3	2	69	24	40	5	0
Creston	2,188	1	0	0	0	1	21	6	13	2	1
Cuyahoga Falls	49,145	49	2	18	8	21	1,209	143	1,027	39	1
Dayton	140,171	1,232	30	122	393	687	6,083	1,779	3,688	616	26
Deer Park	5,665	6	0	1	0	5	51	4	44	3	0
Defiance	16,594	26	0	14	3	9	464	54	390	20	1
Delaware	39,315	64	0	35	8	21	697	119	556	22	11
Delhi Township	29,619	15	0	5	3	7	416	71	319	26	1
Delphos[7]	6,979		0		0	0	159	30	128	1	0
Dennison	2,625	2	0	0	0	2	7	0	6	1	1
Dover	12,839	9	0	2	1	6	122	27	90	5	0
Dublin	46,286	31	1	12	9	9	538	60	458	20	1
East Cleveland	17,178	136	5	8	83	40	339	100	89	150	3
Eastlake	18,056	14	1	2	5	6	330	38	282	10	1
East Palestine	4,503	11	0	2	1	8	82	22	58	2	1
Elyria	53,586	191	3	39	64	85	1,146	248	842	56	12
Englewood	13,504	19	0	1	7	11	443	8	423	12	5
Euclid	47,270	303	4	26	118	155	1,267	226	910	131	6
Evendale	2,767	9	0	0	1	8	233	8	218	7	0
Fairborn	33,936	82	0	30	13	39	723	165	505	53	4
Fairfax	1,702	3	1	0	2	0	253	2	249	2	0
Fairfield	42,627	90	1	11	12	66	932	99	782	51	2
Fairfield Township	22,524	26	1	2	7	16	758	55	695	8	1
Fairview Park	16,307	18	1	1	4	12	176	14	155	7	1
Felicity	825	3	0	1	0	2	31	4	26	1	0
Findlay	41,474	128	3	25	24	76	1,304	216	1,050	38	3
Forest Park	18,665	50	1	7	20	22	435	70	345	20	1
Frazeysburg	1,294	1	0	0	0	1	9	4	5	0	0

Table 8. Offenses Known to Law Enforcement, by Selected State and City, 2017—Continued

(Number.)

State/city	Population	Violent crime	Murder and nonnegligent manslaughter	Rape (revised definition)[1]	Robbery	Aggravated assault	Property crime	Burglary	Larceny-theft	Motor vehicle theft	Arson[2]
Fredericktown	2,461	4	0	0	0	4	55	12	43	0	0
Fremont[7]	16,241		1		12	16	866	151	699	16	0
Gahanna	35,243	25	1	13	5	6	791	87	677	27	6
Galion	10,073	12	0	7	0	5	285	51	229	5	2
Gallipolis	3,431	15	1	4	2	8	291	62	220	9	1
Gates Mills	2,232	2	0	0	1	1	24	2	20	2	0
Georgetown	4,356	10	0	6	3	1	104	23	78	3	0
Germantown	5,477	4	0	2	1	1	68	15	49	4	0
German Township, Montgomery County	2,876	2	0	0	0	2	20	7	11	2	0
Glouster	1,793	3	0	1	0	2	33	9	23	1	0
Goshen Township, Clermont County	15,860	7	0	5	1	1	165	32	118	15	1
Goshen Township, Mahoning County	3,072	3	0	2	0	1	55	6	44	5	1
Grafton[6]	6,182	1	0	1	0	0	40	16	24	0	0
Granville	5,787	0	0	0	0	0	39	5	32	2	0
Greenfield	4,582	13	3	3	2	5	99	28	50	21	2
Greenhills	3,584	1	0	0	0	1	43	4	38	1	0
Green Township	58,853	52	0	14	19	19	1,237	218	963	56	0
Greenville	12,772	40	0	13	7	20	274	36	217	21	7
Grove City	40,421	47	4	14	24	5	1,365	112	1,197	56	0
Groveport	5,583	12	0	3	6	3	185	29	144	12	1
Hamilton	62,094	312	3	75	111	123	2,608	716	1,890	2	33
Harrison	11,246	6	1	0	5	0	182	16	157	9	0
Hartville	3,030	2	0	0	0	2	78	1	77	0	1
Heath	10,681	23	0	7	2	14	598	77	493	28	0
Highland Heights[7]	8,434		0		2	4	132	9	119	4	0
Hilliard	36,144	17	0	6	2	9	404	75	293	36	2
Hillsboro	6,576	9	0	7	1	1	168	23	134	11	1
Hinckley Township	7,970	1	0	0	0	1	17	3	13	1	0
Holland	1,662	7	0	1	4	2	349	10	335	4	3
Howland Township	16,608	14	0	1	7	6	383	44	319	20	0
Hubbard	7,533	8	0	3	0	5	110	10	99	1	2
Hubbard Township	5,372	7	0	3	1	3	93	21	65	7	0
Huber Heights	37,996	77	0	15	21	41	951	117	782	52	5
Hudson	22,248	12	0	2	1	9	114	36	76	2	4
Huron	6,950	4	0	1	1	2	116	24	92	0	0
Independence	7,135	3	0	1	1	1	129	4	123	2	0
Indian Hill	5,830	2	0	2	0	0	43	5	35	3	0
Ironton	10,853	15	0	2	5	8	249	65	169	15	1
Jackson	6,305	9	0	2	2	5	141	12	126	3	0
Jackson Township, Mahoning County	2,018	2	0	0	0	2	32	14	18	0	0
Jackson Township, Stark County	40,624	58	1	14	24	19	1,101	120	963	18	7
Jamestown	2,036	3	0	1	2	0	84	27	53	4	1
Johnstown	5,025	2	0	1	0	1	63	4	56	3	0
Kent	30,270	44	0	1	11	32	451	75	359	17	1
Kenton	8,190	9	0	5	0	4	382	84	285	13	3
Kettering	55,152	70	0	23	26	21	860	192	616	52	3
Kirtland	6,759	1	0	0	0	1	18	5	13	0	0
Kirtland Hills[7]	638		0		0	0	0	0	0	0	0
Lakewood	50,151	74	2	6	40	26	1,199	469	652	78	5
Lancaster	40,026	127	0	24	33	70	1,706	236	1,382	88	12
Lawrence Township	8,273	9	2	2	0	5	85	31	48	6	0
Lexington	4,686	0	0	0	0	0	9	1	8	0	1
Liberty Township	11,556	30	0	2	5	23	148	32	102	14	0
Lima	37,220	275	5	52	81	137	1,982	569	1,334	79	
Lisbon	2,680	1	0	1	0	0	26	6	19	1	0
Lithopolis	1,490	0	0	0	0	0	13	4	9	0	0
Lockland	3,427	16	1	1	3	11	131	27	85	19	1
Logan	7,077	18	0	5	3	10	289	21	254	14	2
London	10,202	14	0	2	2	10	254	52	189	13	1
Lorain	63,672	373	2	30	87	254	2,019	590	1,335	94	11
Lordstown	3,242	3	0	1	0	2	44	10	31	3	1
Loudonville	2,642	3	1	1	1	0	67	6	60	1	1
Louisville	9,373	2	0	0	0	2	123	22	98	3	1
Loveland	12,846	12	0	6	1	5	111	25	79	7	1
Lyndhurst	13,586	18	0	0	7	11	180	21	148	11	0
Macedonia	12,027	5	0	1	1	3	206	14	189	3	1
Madison Township, Franklin County	18,661	19	0	2	5	12	187	51	129	7	0
Madison Township, Lake County	15,380	4	0	0	0	4	67	8	57	2	1
Magnolia	972	1	0	1	0	0	17	3	13	1	0
Mansfield	46,507	248	7	45	75	121	2,392	569	1,745	78	19
Mariemont[7]	3,435		0		0	0	41	5	34	2	0
Marietta	13,582	23	0	11	2	10	250	37	197	16	2
Marion	36,230	100	3	40	28	29	995	316	649	30	11
Martins Ferry	6,731	13	0	6	0	7	70	12	52	6	0
Mason	33,406	12	0	5	3	4	357	31	321	5	0
Maumee	13,809	5	0	0	3	2	305	31	265	9	0

Table 8. Offenses Known to Law Enforcement, by Selected State and City, 2017—Continued

(Number.)

State/city	Population	Violent crime	Murder and nonnegligent manslaughter	Rape (revised definition)[1]	Robbery	Aggravated assault	Property crime	Burglary	Larceny-theft	Motor vehicle theft	Arson[2]
Mayfield Heights	18,724	13	1	1	5	6	188	12	170	6	0
McArthur	1,636	1	0	0	1	0	43	8	32	3	2
McConnelsville	1,804	5	0	1	0	4	22	3	17	2	0
Mechanicsburg	1,585	3	0	1	0	2	28	5	22	1	1
Medina	26,199	17	1	5	5	6	324	55	269	0	0
Medina Township	8,940	5	0	1	0	4	109	3	101	5	0
Mentor	46,663	72	0	11	17	44	908	105	780	23	6
Mentor-on-the-Lake	7,359	9	0	0	1	8	81	14	61	6	0
Miamisburg	19,928	14	0	4	2	8	257	46	204	7	3
Miami Township, Clermont County	42,352	34	0	12	3	19	625	77	529	19	0
Miami Township, Montgomery County	28,996	28	0	5	6	17	953	71	839	43	2
Middlefield[7]	2,715		0		0	1	86	2	84	0	0
Middleport	2,455	0	0	0	0	0	13	5	7	1	0
Middletown	48,828	249	5	41	87	116	2,956	684	2,092	180	0
Milford	6,939	14	0	4	1	9	192	22	159	11	0
Millersburg	3,186	1	0	1	0	0	104	3	100	1	0
Milton Township	2,445	2	0	1	1	0	36	7	27	2	1
Minerva	3,662	2	0	0	0	2	36	7	26	3	0
Mogadore[7]	3,829		0		0	0	49	12	36	1	0
Monroe	16,002	19	0	2	5	12	406	35	364	7	0
Montgomery	10,638	4	0	2	1	1	152	8	139	5	0
Montpelier	3,976	27	0	5	1	21	139	28	105	6	0
Montville Township	11,718	0	0	0	0	0	61	15	46	0	0
Moreland Hills	3,315	0	0	0	0	0	14	2	12	0	0
Mount Healthy	6,020	29	0	6	10	13	249	56	170	23	1
Mount Orab	3,525	4	1	2	0	1	96	4	84	8	0
Mount Vernon	16,553	22	1	6	0	15	621	89	525	7	3
Munroe Falls	5,051	1	0	0	0	1	39	7	32	0	0
Napoleon	8,410	13	0	2	4	7	177	27	147	3	0
Navarre	1,901	1	0	0	0	1	22	3	18	1	0
Nelsonville	5,284	13	0	2	4	7	152	32	114	6	0
New Albany	10,838	4	0	2	0	2	92	6	82	4	0
New Boston	2,134	7	0	0	3	4	216	29	176	11	1
Newcomerstown[7]	3,767		1		1	1	69	13	50	6	0
New Concord	2,337	0	0	0	0	0	7	0	7	0	0
New Franklin	14,137	15	0	3	2	10	117	29	84	4	0
New Lebanon	3,966	10	0	2	4	4	95	22	70	3	1
New Lexington	4,716	11	0	6	1	4	134	14	112	8	1
New Middletown	1,553	0	0	0	0	0	15	4	9	2	0
New Philadelphia	17,492	9	0	0	2	7	139	15	120	4	0
New Richmond	2,663	6	0	0	0	6	61	13	45	3	0
Newton Falls	4,567	10	0	4	0	6	100	18	76	6	0
Newtown	2,679	1	0	0	0	1	21	5	16	0	0
New Vienna	1,201	0	0	0	0	0	13	3	7	3	0
North Baltimore	3,546	10	0	2	0	8	46	9	36	1	0
North Canton	17,348	12	0	4	3	5	281	41	232	8	0
North College Hill	9,311	44	1	8	17	18	310	48	236	26	3
Northfield	3,669	5	0	0	1	4	39	4	32	3	0
North Olmsted	31,779	26	0	6	11	9	470	40	398	32	0
North Ridgeville	33,586	17	1	7	2	7	140	47	89	4	0
Norton	11,998	9	0	4	0	5	186	38	137	11	1
Norwood	19,994	68	0	15	28	25	895	132	707	56	2
Oak Harbor	2,731	1	0	1	0	0	36	8	28	0	0
Oak Hill	1,504	3	0	0	1	2	41	7	34	0	0
Oberlin	8,321	13	0	6	0	7	171	33	136	2	1
Olmsted Falls	8,898	3	0	1	1	1	31	9	19	3	0
Olmsted Township	13,157	1	0	1	0	0	50	16	32	2	0
Ontario	6,058	8	0	0	7	1	328	7	320	1	0
Oregon	19,991	36	1	10	8	17	779	75	682	22	1
Orrville	8,527	15	0	6	0	9	107	17	84	6	0
Ottawa	4,394	6	0	2	0	4	14	0	13	1	0
Ottawa Hills	4,488	0	0	0	0	0	50	11	35	4	0
Owensville	823	2	0	0	0	2	6	0	5	1	0
Oxford[6]	22,459	18	0	5	7	6	488	82	400	6	2
Oxford Township	2,181	2	0	0	0	2	25	4	16	5	0
Parma	79,340	141	0	39	37	65	906	199	633	74	2
Peninsula	563	0	0	0	0	0	22	2	19	1	0
Pepper Pike	6,256	3	1	1	0	1	42	10	32	0	0
Perrysburg	21,732	7	0	3	4	0	232	10	221	1	0
Perrysburg Township	12,784	5	0	1	0	4	167	21	139	7	0
Perry Township, Columbiana County	4,381	0	0	0	0	0	3	2	1	0	0
Perry Township, Franklin County	3,758	2	0	0	1	1	53	4	47	2	0
Pickerington	20,373	38	0	6	12	20	352	20	316	16	0
Pierce Township	11,623	5	0	2	1	2	151	28	118	5	3
Pioneer	1,412	3	0	2	0	1	31	5	24	2	0
Piqua	20,973	54	1	33	11	9	819	120	681	18	2
Poland Township	11,921	3	0	1	1	1	53	14	39	0	0
Poland Village	2,444	0	0	0	0	0	8	0	6	2	1
Port Clinton	5,928	21	0	12	3	6	170	31	126	13	0

Table 8. Offenses Known to Law Enforcement, by Selected State and City, 2017—Continued

(Number.)

State/city	Population	Violent crime	Murder and nonnegligent manslaughter	Rape (revised definition)[1]	Robbery	Aggravated assault	Property crime	Burglary	Larceny-theft	Motor vehicle theft	Arson[2]
Portsmouth	20,451	118	4	22	34	58	1,235	275	891	69	2
Powell	13,029	6	0	2	2	2	103	12	90	1	0
Reading	10,307	28	1	4	7	16	291	52	232	7	0
Reminderville	4,235	2	0	1	1	0	30	3	26	1	0
Reynoldsburg	37,704	99	1	23	48	27	1,062	133	894	35	4
Richmond Heights	10,432	19	0	0	12	7	206	37	146	23	0
Ripley	1,707	2	0	1	0	1	19	3	13	3	0
Rittman	6,610	9	0	3	2	4	109	36	65	8	1
Roseville	1,846	4	0	2	1	1	22	4	14	4	0
Ross Township	8,755	16	0	3	1	12	82	27	52	3	0
Russells Point	1,367	4	1	2	0	1	22	3	19	0	0
Russell Township	5,243	4	0	0	0	4	10	1	9	0	0
Sabina	2,534	3	0	2	0	1	52	15	37	0	1
Sagamore Hills	10,951	0	0	0	0	0	35	7	27	1	0
Salem	11,887	21	0	4	1	16	348	20	324	4	1
Salineville	1,240	0	0	0	0	0	18	4	14	0	2
Sandusky	24,861	70	1	13	31	25	995	187	769	39	2
Sebring	4,232	11	0	4	0	7	111	14	92	5	0
Seven Hills	11,668	3	0	0	1	2	50	14	33	3	0
Sharon Township	2,390	0	0	0	0	0	41	3	37	1	0
Shawnee Township	12,096	14	1	4	3	6	135	24	108	3	0
Sheffield Lake	8,983	7	0	5	2	0	115	23	84	8	0
Shelby	8,987	11	0	9	0	2	262	54	205	3	1
Sidney	20,466	42	3	24	9	6	822	162	641	19	6
Solon	23,023	13	0	2	4	7	182	25	146	11	0
South Bloomfield	1,884	0	0	0	0	0	39	2	34	3	0
South Charleston	1,640	2	0	0	0	2	37	5	28	4	0
South Euclid	21,628	33	0	5	14	14	645	74	536	35	0
South Point[7]	3,935		0		0	1	42	8	31	3	0
South Russell	3,819	0	0	0	0	0	7	0	7	0	0
South Zanesville	1,970	1	0	0	0	1	34	4	29	1	0
Springboro	18,632	10	0	5	0	5	122	15	105	2	0
Springfield	58,843	370	9	25	177	159	4,024	1,040	2,691	293	76
Springfield Township, Hamilton County	36,571	73	1	6	31	35	674	131	495	48	7
Springfield Township, Mahoning County	6,374	7	0	2	0	5	55	17	34	4	1
Springfield Township, Summit County	14,434	32	0	8	11	13	781	108	645	28	4
St. Clairsville	5,096	1	0	0	0	1	9	1	8	0	0
St. Clair Township	7,583	0	0	0	0	0	26	0	26	0	0
Steubenville	17,979	49	3	4	11	31	1,132	89	1,021	22	6
St. Marys	8,215	3	0	0	1	2	129	34	89	6	2
Stow	34,692	32	1	19	6	6	690	102	584	4	0
Strasburg	2,689	1	0	0	1	0	23	5	18	0	0
Streetsboro	16,308	11	0	2	5	4	343	24	309	10	0
Strongsville	44,758	18	2	1	9	6	852	67	760	25	
Struthers	10,228	15	0	1	4	10	216	58	148	10	0
Sugarcreek Township	8,300	4	0	3	0	1	181	14	162	5	0
Swanton	3,913	5	0	4	0	1	52	8	40	4	0
Sylvania	18,908	6	0	3	0	3	86	12	67	7	0
Sylvania Township	29,536	39	0	4	12	23	688	73	577	38	0
Tallmadge[7]	17,529		0		8	4	334	55	267	12	5
Tiffin[7]	17,481		0		4	12	390	55	331	4	1
Tipp City	9,957	4	0	4	0	0	140	11	119	10	4
Toledo[6,8,10]	277,116		35		780	1,834	11,095	3,103	7,247	745	
Toronto	4,814	14	0	1	0	13	20	4	15	1	0
Trotwood	24,308	69	3	15	35	16	891	257	489	145	6
Troy	25,865	38	1	20	6	11	502	60	434	8	0
Twinsburg	18,891	18	2	0	4	12	111	9	99	3	
Uhrichsville	5,372	5	0	3	1	1	48	7	30	11	0
Uniontown	3,340	3	0	2	0	1	80	16	58	6	0
Union Township, Clermont County	48,214	39	0	25	4	10	891	123	752	16	3
University Heights	13,104	30	0	4	19	7	288	16	257	15	0
Upper Arlington	35,214	12	0	3	6	3	512	88	417	7	2
Upper Sandusky	6,529	15	0	4	0	11	159	30	126	3	1
Urbana	11,351	25	1	3	5	16	404	62	329	13	3
Utica	2,199	3	0	0	0	3	28	7	20	1	0
Valley View, Cuyahoga County[7]	2,007		0		0	1	47	7	34	6	1
Vandalia	15,022	26	0	10	11	5	310	66	219	25	2
Van Wert	10,713	22	1	7	3	11	330	56	268	6	0
Vermilion	10,381	3	0	1	0	2	95	14	80	1	0
Village of Leesburg	1,295	1	0	0	0	1	54	5	47	2	0
Wadsworth	23,388	24	0	4	1	19	333	28	301	4	1
Waite Hill	449	1	0	0	0	1	0	0	0	0	0
Walton Hills[7]	2,308		0		0	0	19	7	11	1	0
Wapakoneta	9,809	14	0	6	3	5	164	25	137	2	1
Warren	39,643	227	11	32	101	83	1,608	494	1,008	106	2
Warren Township	5,255	21	0	1	3	17	172	52	106	14	0
Washington Court House	14,136	41	0	16	14	11	548	79	459	10	4
Waterville	5,518	1	0	0	0	1	25	3	22	0	0
Wauseon	7,407	10	0	1	1	8	169	14	151	4	0

Table 8. Offenses Known to Law Enforcement, by Selected State and City, 2017—Continued

(Number.)

State/city	Population	Violent crime	Murder and nonnegligent manslaughter	Rape (revised definition)[1]	Robbery	Aggravated assault	Property crime	Burglary	Larceny-theft	Motor vehicle theft	Arson[2]
Waverly	4,357	4	1	0	0	3	59	0	58	1	0
Wellston	5,534	11	0	2	1	8	89	21	63	5	0
West Carrollton	12,898	23	1	5	11	6	285	66	198	21	4
West Chester Township	61,386	64	0	21	15	28	1,300	170	1,086	44	5
Westerville	39,418	44	0	12	16	16	945	77	851	17	2
West Jefferson	4,347	2	0	0	0	2	58	5	51	2	0
West Lafayette	2,287	3	0	2	0	1	6	1	5	0	0
Westlake	32,330	13	0	1	9	3	366	25	326	15	
West Union	3,168	6	0	0	0	6	19	1	13	5	0
Whitehall	18,835	125	0	11	69	45	1,269	187	1,001	81	12
Wickliffe	12,679	9	0	0	4	5	152	26	118	8	0
Willard	6,032	7	0	0	4	3	288	59	218	11	0
Williamsburg	2,565	4	0	1	0	3	58	11	45	2	1
Willoughby	22,857	34	0	1	17	16	440	37	385	18	1
Wilmington	12,416	23	0	3	8	12	645	72	562	11	0
Windham	2,199	4	0	0	0	4	36	10	24	2	0
Wintersville	3,750	2	0	1	1	0	68	8	58	2	0
Woodlawn	3,292	12	0	0	4	8	129	4	120	5	0
Woodmere Village	859	1	0	0	1	0	41	0	36	5	0
Wooster	27,172	102	0	30	24	48	916	157	722	37	6
Worthington	14,692	11	2	2	3	4	267	27	227	13	1
Wyoming	8,531	3	0	0	3	0	85	15	68	2	0
Xenia	26,331	55	1	16	8	30	811	141	636	34	6
Yellow Springs	3,713	11	0	4	4	3	72	20	47	5	0
Youngstown	63,889	447	23	32	151	241	2,362	847	1,283	232	82
Zanesville	25,457	100	0	19	21	60	1,157	203	897	57	16
OKLAHOMA											
Achille	521	0	0	0	0	0	0	0	0	0	0
Ada	17,455	57	0	7	4	46	605	170	394	41	6
Allen	935	0	0	0	0	0	7	0	5	2	0
Altus	19,054	53	1	10	2	40	509	155	313	41	2
Alva	5,149	6	0	1	0	5	69	12	51	6	1
Amber	460	0	0	0	0	0	3	1	1	1	0
Anadarko	6,756	33	0	5	5	23	257	59	183	15	5
Antlers	2,306	3	0	0	0	3	38	13	22	3	1
Apache	1,439	4	0	1	1	2	33	12	17	4	0
Ardmore	25,211	131	2	11	17	101	1,112	282	767	63	3
Arkoma	1,914	3	0	0	1	2	19	2	10	7	0
Atoka	3,056	11	0	3	2	6	101	35	58	8	0
Barnsdall	1,197	5	0	0	0	5	16	2	12	2	2
Bartlesville	36,788	82	1	6	10	65	1,147	275	771	101	11
Beaver	1,429	0	0	0	0	0	3	1	2	0	0
Beggs	1,244	0	0	0	0	0	7	4	3	0	1
Bethany	19,620	56	0	11	20	25	557	151	334	72	1
Big Cabin	257	0	0	0	0	0	18	4	13	1	0
Bixby	26,131	34	0	6	4	24	519	80	373	66	5
Blackwell	6,765	15	0	6	1	8	117	39	70	8	5
Blanchard	8,649	7	0	0	0	7	113	30	71	12	1
Boise City	1,074	0	0	0	0	0	4	2	2	0	0
Bokoshe	493	6	0	0	0	6	6	5	1	0	0
Boley	1,183	0	0	0	0	0	0	0	0	0	0
Bristow	4,251	6	0	1	0	5	253	88	147	18	0
Broken Arrow	108,823	135	1	31	27	76	2,374	380	1,765	229	1
Broken Bow	4,100	20	0	3	1	16	232	55	155	22	4
Cache	2,857	3	0	2	1	0	38	7	28	3	0
Caddo	1,070	0	0	0	0	0	19	9	6	4	0
Calera	2,295	19	0	1	1	17	22	3	15	4	0
Caney	197	2	0	0	0	2	7	0	6	1	0
Carnegie	1,711	3	0	1	0	2	17	5	10	2	0
Carney	664	0	0	0	0	0	13	3	8	2	0
Cashion	860	0	0	0	0	0	1	0	1	0	0
Catoosa	7,129	75	1	4	6	64	373	38	267	68	0
Cement	499	0	0	0	0	0	1	1	0	0	0
Chandler	3,194	12	0	1	2	9	45	13	29	3	0
Chattanooga	441	0	0	0	0	0	2	1	1	0	0
Checotah	3,207	10	0	0	1	9	108	14	79	15	2
Chelsea	1,972	3	0	1	1	1	26	5	20	1	0
Cherokee	1,553	5	0	0	1	4	21	11	9	1	0
Chickasha	16,489	90	1	6	10	73	492	157	302	33	1
Choctaw	12,556	18	0	2	1	15	217	73	132	12	2
Chouteau	2,088	3	0	1	0	2	23	9	12	2	0
Claremore	19,147	31	2	9	4	16	511	80	401	30	5
Clayton	780	1	0	0	0	1	12	2	4	6	0
Cleveland	3,217	6	0	1	1	4	23	0	20	3	0
Clinton	9,455	21	0	5	3	13	173	49	105	19	0
Coalgate	1,850	0	0	0	0	0	4	0	3	1	0
Colbert	1,207	0	0	0	0	0	2	0	1	1	0
Colcord	814	3	0	1	0	2	28	8	18	2	1
Collinsville	6,836	6	1	3	0	2	110	34	72	4	0
Comanche	1,595	4	0	2	0	2	39	14	22	3	0
Cordell	2,852	6	1	1	1	3	38	9	25	4	0
Covington	547	0	0	0	0	0	0	0	0	0	0

Table 8. Offenses Known to Law Enforcement, by Selected State and City, 2017—Continued

(Number.)

State/city	Population	Violent crime	Murder and nonnegligent manslaughter	Rape (revised definition)[1]	Robbery	Aggravated assault	Property crime	Burglary	Larceny-theft	Motor vehicle theft	Arson[2]
Coweta	9,718	23	0	5	0	18	283	40	206	37	2
Crescent	1,564	2	0	0	0	2	19	4	14	1	0
Cushing	7,790	34	0	8	3	23	287	63	209	15	3
Cyril	1,053	0	0	0	0	0	0	0	0	0	0
Davenport	826	0	0	0	0	0	4	0	3	1	0
Davis	2,822	16	0	3	3	10	103	36	62	5	1
Del City	22,046	165	3	20	41	101	875	220	550	105	2
Depew	482	0	0	0	0	0	3	2	1	0	0
Dewar	865	2	0	0	1	1	4	3	0	1	0
Dewey	3,513	5	0	1	0	4	91	31	54	6	0
Dibble	846	1	0	0	0	1	15	9	6	0	0
Dickson	1,253	0	0	0	0	0	3	2	1	0	0
Drumright	2,870	11	2	0	0	9	92	28	59	5	0
Duncan	22,909	34	3	3	5	23	808	250	511	47	5
Durant	17,871	61	0	7	6	48	944	225	667	52	0
Earlsboro	644	3	0	0	0	3	14	4	5	5	0
Edmond	92,876	154	2	28	27	97	1,234	198	970	66	2
Elgin	3,164	1	0	0	0	1	9	3	5	1	0
Elk City	12,057	9	0	1	0	8	264	49	198	17	0
Elmore City	708	0	0	0	0	0	5	3	2	0	0
El Reno	19,133	53	0	12	5	36	329	68	236	25	9
Enid	51,257	174	0	34	21	119	1,751	417	1,242	92	4
Erick	1,034	3	0	0	0	3	5	2	2	1	0
Eufaula	2,971	13	1	2	0	10	124	28	79	17	0
Fairfax	1,335	8	0	2	0	6	9	4	3	2	0
Fairview	2,672	5	0	1	0	4	24	9	11	4	0
Fletcher	1,138	0	0	0	0	0	0	0	0	0	0
Forest Park	1,082	0	0	0	0	0	6	1	4	1	0
Fort Gibson	4,045	13	0	2	1	10	77	38	34	5	2
Frederick	3,621	10	0	3	0	7	119	40	75	4	1
Geary	1,286	2	0	1	0	1	37	11	19	7	0
Glenpool	13,954	51	0	5	4	42	219	58	143	18	1
Goodwell	1,311	0	0	0	0	0	7	4	3	0	0
Gore	939	2	0	0	0	2	14	2	11	1	0
Grandfield	955	2	0	0	0	2	12	5	7	0	0
Granite	2,008	0	0	0	0	0	11	5	6	0	0
Grove	6,868	26	0	3	2	21	290	52	215	23	2
Guthrie	11,713	38	1	3	3	31	267	72	174	21	1
Guymon	11,733	22	0	7	3	12	165	33	122	10	0
Haileyville	762	0	0	0	0	0	0	0	0	0	0
Harrah	6,215	12	0	1	0	11	125	36	83	6	1
Hartshorne	1,966	11	0	1	1	9	30	9	15	6	0
Haskell	1,960	2	0	0	0	2	5	3	2	0	0
Healdton	2,757	12	0	1	0	11	44	25	17	2	0
Heavener	3,328	12	0	1	1	10	33	10	20	3	0
Hennessey	2,219	3	0	1	0	2	26	9	15	2	0
Henryetta	5,737	11	0	5	0	6	178	29	131	18	2
Hinton	3,273	2	0	0	0	2	31	0	25	6	0
Hobart	3,567	9	0	0	0	9	60	16	44	0	0
Holdenville	5,663	9	0	0	1	8	82	29	43	10	2
Hollis	1,886	13	0	2	0	11	42	21	19	2	2
Hominy	3,485	5	0	0	0	5	47	18	22	7	0
Hooker	1,959	2	0	0	1	1	18	7	10	1	0
Howe	789	1	0	0	0	1	4	3	1	0	0
Hulbert	607	0	0	0	0	0	0	0	0	0	0
Hydro	959	0	0	0	0	0	6	2	3	1	0
Idabel	6,940	23	2	3	4	14	373	94	265	14	5
Jay	2,520	4	0	1	0	3	93	24	65	4	1
Jenks	22,693	44	0	6	3	35	287	47	208	32	2
Jennings	359	0	0	0	0	0	10	2	6	2	1
Jones	3,067	6	0	1	0	5	40	12	21	7	1
Kellyville	1,147	2	0	0	0	2	16	3	11	2	0
Kiefer	1,968	2	0	0	1	1	48	10	34	4	1
Kingfisher	4,931	5	0	3	0	2	111	19	86	6	0
Kingston	1,634	2	0	2	0	0	18	12	5	1	1
Konawa	1,267	11	0	0	0	11	21	7	10	4	0
Krebs	1,928	7	0	0	2	5	74	15	50	9	1
Lahoma	645	0	0	0	0	0	4	1	3	0	0
Lamont	402	1	0	1	0	0	2	0	2	0	0
Langley	819	2	0	0	1	1	37	5	25	7	0
Langston	1,857	3	0	0	0	3	3	1	2	0	1
Lawton	94,134	831	8	83	131	609	3,618	1,207	2,097	314	5
Lexington	2,169	4	0	0	0	4	45	6	32	7	0
Lindsay	2,827	9	1	2	0	6	126	63	57	6	0
Locust Grove	1,401	7	0	0	0	7	35	9	23	3	2
Lone Grove	5,252	11	0	3	3	5	58	23	32	3	1
Luther	1,675	1	0	0	0	1	18	5	12	1	0
Madill	3,937	8	0	2	3	3	103	10	86	7	0
Mangum	2,848	12	0	1	1	10	42	15	21	6	1
Mannford	3,150	4	0	0	0	4	30	11	16	3	0
Marietta	2,782	3	0	1	0	2	79	19	54	6	2
Marlow	4,520	11	0	4	0	7	112	40	65	7	1
Maud	1,077	5	0	1	0	4	29	8	19	2	0

Table 8. Offenses Known to Law Enforcement, by Selected State and City, 2017—Continued

(Number.)

State/city	Population	Violent crime	Murder and nonnegligent manslaughter	Rape (revised definition)[1]	Robbery	Aggravated assault	Property crime	Burglary	Larceny-theft	Motor vehicle theft	Arson[2]
Maysville	1,233	0	0	0	0	0	6	2	4	0	0
McAlester	18,181	105	2	18	6	79	841	173	620	48	7
McCurtain	510	4	0	0	0	4	8	2	5	1	0
McLoud	4,656	20	1	2	2	15	79	26	43	10	2
Medicine Park	447	0	0	0	0	0	11	1	10	0	0
Meeker	1,179	2	0	0	0	2	17	4	13	0	1
Miami	13,470	34	0	9	1	24	296	111	172	13	0
Midwest City	57,772	153	6	33	50	64	1,841	358	1,340	143	11
Minco	1,649	1	0	0	0	1	6	2	4	0	0
Moffett	121	0	0	0	0	0	0	0	0	0	0
Moore	62,476	110	0	20	32	58	1,184	262	821	101	6
Mooreland	1,240	0	0	0	0	0	7	4	3	0	1
Morris	1,464	3	0	0	0	3	7	2	5	0	0
Mounds	1,200	1	0	0	0	1	10	4	6	0	1
Mountain View	759	0	0	0	0	0	7	3	3	1	0
Muldrow	3,250	23	0	2	0	21	66	15	44	7	1
Muskogee	38,199	461	1	32	49	379	1,711	543	1,058	110	12
Mustang	21,392	34	0	3	2	29	218	43	162	13	0
Nash	202	0	0	0	0	0	1	1	0	0	0
Newcastle	10,011	7	0	2	1	4	212	57	131	24	0
Newkirk	2,217	8	0	0	1	7	26	7	17	2	0
Nichols Hills	3,940	2	0	1	0	1	56	12	38	6	0
Nicoma Park	2,473	6	0	1	3	2	76	34	35	7	0
Ninnekah	1,033	0	0	0	0	0	4	2	2	0	0
Noble	6,799	15	0	5	3	7	106	29	67	10	2
Norman	124,074	350	6	90	55	199	3,365	553	2,535	277	2
North Enid	922	0	0	0	0	0	4	1	3	0	0
Nowata	3,709	11	0	1	1	9	87	33	52	2	0
Oilton	1,015	0	0	0	0	0	13	8	4	1	0
Okemah	3,239	18	0	5	3	10	115	39	66	10	1
Oklahoma City	648,260	5,104	81	474	1,120	3,429	24,326	6,105	15,421	2,800	82
Okmulgee	12,183	89	1	22	5	61	498	89	384	25	6
Olustee	576	2	0	0	0	2	0	0	0	0	0
Owasso	36,869	69	0	17	9	43	729	102	550	77	1
Paoli	616	0	0	0	0	0	0	0	0	0	0
Pauls Valley	6,225	25	0	8	1	16	300	73	211	16	0
Pawhuska	3,461	19	0	5	0	14	98	37	56	5	1
Pawnee	2,160	11	0	2	1	8	50	13	30	7	1
Perkins	2,841	4	0	1	1	2	60	13	41	6	0
Perry	5,000	15	0	4	3	8	97	22	69	6	2
Piedmont	7,738	5	0	0	0	5	32	9	22	1	0
Pocola	4,073	10	0	2	0	8	30	7	19	4	0
Ponca City	24,397	202	0	35	22	145	957	208	701	48	11
Pond Creek	854	0	0	0	0	0	11	7	4	0	0
Porum	707	0	0	0	0	0	1	1	0	0	0
Poteau	8,913	52	0	8	1	43	544	139	384	21	3
Prague	2,464	9	0	1	3	5	59	18	37	4	0
Pryor Creek	9,517	81	0	4	6	71	277	67	170	40	1
Purcell	6,483	25	0	4	5	16	307	85	200	22	1
Quinton	987	6	0	0	1	5	9	2	4	3	0
Ringling	989	3	0	0	2	1	10	4	5	1	0
Roland	3,720	13	0	3	1	9	83	17	60	6	0
Rush Springs	1,271	2	0	0	0	2	26	9	14	3	0
Salina	1,381	9	0	2	1	6	22	5	14	3	1
Sallisaw	8,548	17	1	8	1	7	337	50	279	8	0
Sand Springs	19,977	25	0	4	15	6	579	88	416	75	3
Sapulpa	21,062	54	2	8	10	34	556	106	367	83	1
Savanna	642	1	0	0	0	1	25	6	17	2	0
Sawyer	312	1	0	1	0	0	1	0	1	0	0
Sayre	4,644	5	0	1	0	4	45	13	26	6	0
Seiling	850	0	0	0	0	0	6	2	4	0	1
Seminole	7,415	25	0	3	2	20	151	40	93	18	1
Shady Point	995	1	0	0	0	1	5	3	1	1	0
Shattuck	1,333	0	0	0	0	0	10	5	4	1	0
Shawnee	31,725	388	2	24	23	339	1,435	354	926	155	6
Skiatook	8,018	14	0	1	3	10	193	44	128	21	0
Snyder	1,326	0	0	0	0	0	8	2	5	1	0
South Coffeyville	758	2	0	0	1	1	13	5	6	2	0
Sparks	174	0	0	0	0	0	3	2	1	0	0
Spencer	4,031	11	0	1	2	8	63	24	26	13	0
Sperry	1,292	7	0	0	1	6	45	8	27	10	0
Spiro	2,184	2	0	0	0	2	15	4	9	2	0
Sportsmen Acres	312	0	0	0	0	0	1	1	0	0	0
Stigler	2,760	8	0	1	1	6	80	21	54	5	0
Stillwater	50,159	137	3	27	7	100	1,123	207	856	60	14
Stilwell	4,062	16	1	1	4	10	271	42	209	20	0
Stratford	1,539	6	0	0	0	6	30	10	16	4	0
Stringtown	401	0	0	0	0	0	0	0	0	0	0
Stroud	2,792	7	0	0	1	6	76	22	45	9	1
Sulphur	5,105	13	0	0	2	11	153	35	112	6	4
Tahlequah	16,905	26	0	2	8	16	920	119	758	43	2
Talala	278	0	0	0	0	0	3	0	2	1	0
Talihina	1,094	3	0	0	0	3	14	4	9	1	1

Table 8. Offenses Known to Law Enforcement, by Selected State and City, 2017—Continued

(Number.)

State/city	Population	Violent crime	Murder and nonnegligent manslaughter	Rape (revised definition)[1]	Robbery	Aggravated assault	Property crime	Burglary	Larceny-theft	Motor vehicle theft	Arson[2]
Tecumseh	6,699	14	1	3	2	8	203	56	133	14	0
Texhoma	955	2	0	0	0	2	3	1	1	1	0
Thackerville	478	0	0	0	0	0	6	3	3	0	0
The Village	9,512	25	0	7	3	15	223	42	170	11	0
Thomas	1,235	0	0	0	0	0	1	0	0	1	0
Tipton	779	0	0	0	0	0	5	1	4	0	2
Tishomingo	3,119	4	0	1	0	3	33	12	15	6	0
Tonkawa	3,077	4	0	3	0	1	50	17	30	3	0
Tryon	505	0	0	0	0	0	1	0	0	1	0
Tulsa	404,868	4,214	70	423	964	2,757	22,088	5,574	13,054	3,460	144
Tupelo	313	0	0	0	0	0	17	12	4	1	0
Tushka	301	0	0	0	0	0	2	0	2	0	0
Tuttle	7,140	21	0	3	0	18	148	31	93	24	0
Tyrone	769	2	0	0	1	1	5	2	3	0	0
Union City	2,053	2	0	1	0	1	21	6	13	2	0
Valley Brook	779	6	0	0	0	6	37	11	17	9	0
Valliant	737	5	2	0	0	3	13	7	6	0	0
Velma	602	1	0	0	0	1	9	5	4	0	0
Verden	527	0	0	0	0	0	2	2	0	0	0
Verdigris	4,488	3	0	0	0	3	59	7	48	4	0
Vian	1,383	7	0	2	0	5	24	6	14	4	1
Vici	702	2	0	0	0	2	3	0	3	0	0
Vinita	5,532	11	0	3	1	7	136	31	96	9	0
Wagoner	8,931	36	2	13	2	19	302	73	219	10	1
Wakita	339	1	0	1	0	0	5	0	4	1	0
Walters	2,464	4	0	2	0	2	55	16	37	2	1
Warner	1,614	1	0	0	0	1	3	1	1	1	0
Warr Acres	10,480	55	1	4	18	32	455	189	220	46	1
Washington	655	1	0	1	0	0	1	0	1	0	0
Watonga	2,931	6	0	0	0	6	41	11	28	2	1
Watts	310	0	0	0	0	0	5	2	1	2	0
Waukomis	1,349	2	0	0	0	2	9	0	9	0	0
Waynoka	960	0	0	0	0	0	7	2	3	2	0
Weatherford	12,178	20	0	7	4	9	231	53	164	14	2
Webbers Falls	593	2	0	2	0	0	3	1	2	0	0
Weleetka	981	4	0	1	1	2	20	8	10	2	0
West Siloam Springs	839	11	1	2	0	8	66	12	40	14	0
Westville	1,561	1	0	0	0	1	48	11	29	8	1
Wewoka	3,390	14	0	0	0	14	59	9	47	3	1
Wilburton	2,633	10	0	0	0	10	59	18	37	4	0
Wilson	1,721	4	0	2	0	2	14	11	3	0	1
Wister	1,067	7	0	0	0	7	20	3	16	1	0
Woodward	12,655	38	0	12	0	26	347	108	221	18	2
Wright City	733	0	0	0	0	0	5	1	4	0	0
Wyandotte	330	2	0	0	0	2	4	0	4	0	0
Wynnewood	2,227	2	0	0	0	2	29	11	16	2	0
Wynona	440	0	0	0	0	0	0	0	0	0	0
Yale	1,207	5	0	1	0	4	45	4	36	5	1
Yukon	26,971	37	0	2	4	31	424	56	351	17	4
OREGON											
Albany[6]	53,701	56	0	8	20	28	1,406	158	1,137	111	10
Ashland	21,908	41	1	3	11	26	783	82	672	29	8
Astoria[6]	9,857	36	0	7	7	22	447	67	343	37	5
Aumsville	4,141	4	0	0	1	3	35	3	26	6	1
Baker City	9,764	19	0	8	1	10	250	33	202	15	3
Bandon	3,146	0	0	0	0	0	57	11	38	8	1
Banks	2,019	2	0	0	2	0	19	1	16	2	0
Beaverton	98,897	172	1	60	32	79	1,760	157	1,396	207	14
Bend	93,786	154	0	33	24	97	1,960	177	1,680	103	12
Boardman	3,408	8	0	1	0	7	41	5	29	7	0
Brookings[6]	6,560	22	0	6	3	13	99	15	62	22	1
Canby	17,823	28	0	10	8	10	226	43	167	16	4
Cannon Beach	1,710	7	0	1	1	5	36	10	24	2	0
Central Point	18,525	49	1	5	8	35	477	48	407	22	1
Coos Bay	16,347	60	1	19	15	25	1,244	198	871	175	16
Coquille	3,912	13	0	0	0	13	86	12	63	11	1
Cornelius	12,515	37	0	5	6	26	233	25	198	10	2
Corvallis	57,576	75	2	20	13	40	1,440	153	1,229	58	26
Cottage Grove	10,182	30	0	6	4	20	520	68	415	37	5
Dallas	16,152	47	0	9	4	34	335	34	281	20	3
Eagle Point	9,143	24	0	2	4	18	281	29	237	15	0
Eugene	168,310	651	3	101	177	370	6,276	1,129	4,602	545	55
Florence	8,857	21	1	5	3	12	440	32	378	30	2
Forest Grove	24,520	62	1	25	8	28	432	52	342	38	4
Gearhart	1,580	1	0	0	0	1	17	5	11	1	0
Gervais	2,710	4	0	2	0	2	48	7	31	10	0
Grants Pass	38,082	103	0	17	15	71	1,627	156	1,264	207	12
Gresham	112,466	386	9	76	86	215	3,713	424	2,034	1,255	23
Hermiston	17,377	47	0	3	4	40	482	49	390	43	2
Hillsboro	107,433	268	1	80	60	127	2,144	209	1,714	221	26
Hubbard	3,421	3	0	1	0	2	20	9	11	0	1
Independence	9,854	28	0	4	5	19	145	23	118	4	2

Table 8. Offenses Known to Law Enforcement, by Selected State and City, 2017—Continued

(Number.)

State/city	Population	Violent crime	Murder and nonnegligent manslaughter	Rape (revised definition)[1]	Robbery	Aggravated assault	Property crime	Burglary	Larceny-theft	Motor vehicle theft	Arson[2]
Jacksonville	2,917	1	0	1	0	0	40	6	29	5	0
Junction City[6]	6,174	2	0	0	1	1	12	4	5	3	1
Keizer	39,397	79	1	10	13	55	826	93	640	93	10
King City[6]	3,945	5	0	1	2	2	43	9	30	4	0
Klamath Falls	22,436	106	0	10	16	80	695	126	490	79	4
La Grande[6]	13,252	18	0	7	4	7	284	50	221	13	0
Lake Oswego	39,318	15	0	7	1	7	452	65	358	29	3
Lebanon	16,826	45	1	9	4	31	621	43	528	50	6
Lincoln City	8,798	48	0	7	4	37	412	105	290	17	3
Madras	6,800	26	0	5	5	16	232	24	194	14	3
McMinnville	35,125	50	1	14	6	29	904	90	755	59	8
Medford	82,792	376	4	33	98	241	4,936	489	4,145	302	36
Milton-Freewater[6]	7,011	30	0	8	1	21	191	38	140	13	3
Milwaukie	21,033	32	0	7	7	18	475	82	298	95	2
Molalla	9,245	18	1	3	1	13	203	18	162	23	0
Monmouth	10,282	13	0	1	1	11	133	15	108	10	0
Mount Angel	3,569	5	0	1	0	4	52	8	35	9	0
Myrtle Creek	3,494	4	0	0	0	4	69	7	51	11	0
Newberg-Dundee[8]	26,769	38	0	16	4	18			310	33	2
North Bend	9,806	9	0	2	1	6	503	60	385	58	2
North Plains	2,158	5	0	0	0	5	35	7	27	1	1
Nyssa[7]	3,174		0		0	2	76	31	36	9	
Philomath	4,691	18	0	2	0	16	42	7	34	1	0
Phoenix	4,614	11	0	5	4	2	195	16	157	22	0
Portland	649,408	3,349	24	438	1,045	1,842	36,867	4,735	24,837	7,295	307
Prineville[6]	10,053	32	1	9	5	17	362	120	227	15	2
Rainier	1,968	2	0	0	0	2	33	5	27	1	0
Redmond	29,870	82	0	16	11	55	933	114	740	79	3
Reedsport	4,106	12	0	1	2	9	126	18	100	8	2
Rockaway Beach	1,387	7	0	0	0	7	53	21	28	4	0
Rogue River	2,289	4	0	2	1	1	78	7	64	7	0
Roseburg	22,505	53	0	9	18	26	1,278	151	1,027	100	12
Salem	169,565	641	6	44	167	424	7,195	897	5,437	861	34
Scappoose[6]	7,236	10	0	6	0	4	83	22	51	10	3
Seaside[6]	6,726	71	0	1	5	65	354	32	303	19	2
Sherwood	19,473	16	0	10	2	4	228	15	198	15	1
Silverton	10,136	18	0	5	3	10	218	39	149	30	3
Springfield	62,318	169	1	25	41	102	2,466	238	2,063	165	17
Stanfield	2,083	9	0	2	1	6	43	10	28	5	2
Stayton	8,148	27	0	1	5	21	254	25	216	13	0
St. Helens[6]	13,611	22	1	9	1	11	246	26	199	21	6
Sunriver		4	0	0	0	4	67	7	59	1	1
Sutherlin	8,027	19	0	2	3	14	206	24	152	30	2
Sweet Home	9,500	21	0	5	2	14	383	43	302	38	3
Talent	6,558	11	0	1	1	9	120	18	93	9	0
Tigard	52,524	101	0	22	40	39	1,429	164	1,179	86	4
Tillamook	5,214	11	1	0	1	9	159	19	131	9	1
Tualatin	27,781	40	0	11	15	14	852	109	695	48	4
Umatilla	7,009	8	0	0	1	7	36	6	25	5	1
Woodburn	25,848	86	0	13	24	49	857	115	609	133	10
PENNSYLVANIA											
Abington Township, Montgomery County	55,578	54	0	8	30	16	1,244	107	1,112	25	1
Adamstown	1,844	0	0	0	0	0	13	4	8	1	0
Adams Township, Butler County	13,876	5	0	0	0	5	49	8	39	2	0
Adams Township, Cambria County	5,651	0	0	0	0	0	19	1	17	1	0
Akron	3,999	3	0	0	0	3	16	3	13	0	0
Albion	1,457	4	0	0	0	4	26	8	18	0	1
Alburtis	2,598	2	0	0	1	1	16	2	14	0	0
Aldan	4,154	10	0	1	1	8	141	13	125	3	0
Aleppo Township	1,887	0	0	0	0	0	8	0	8	0	0
Aliquippa	9,048	57	2	1	8	46	164	54	97	13	0
Allegheny Township, Blair County	6,602	46	0	4	1	41	169	4	162	3	2
Allentown	120,823	557	16	70	269	202	3,302	634	2,362	306	13
Altoona	44,366	120	0	33	31	56	918	167	708	43	7
Ambler	6,509	10	0	9	1	0	50	4	41	5	0
Ambridge	6,744	105	0	3	17	85	291	44	235	12	2
Amity Township	12,921	8	0	2	2	4	113	20	86	7	0
Annville Township	4,940	29	0	0	3	26	47	6	41	0	1
Apollo	1,560	7	0	0	1	6	4	2	2	0	0
Archbald	6,975	6	1	0	2	3	69	13	54	2	0
Armagh Township	3,799	0	0	0	0	0	16	2	14	0	0
Arnold	4,904	68	0	2	8	58	238	60	166	12	0
Ashland	2,694	17	0	3	2	12	87	16	67	4	2
Ashley	2,691	10	0	0	2	8	25	5	19	1	0
Ashville	215	0	0	0	0	0	0	0	0	0	0
Aspinwall	2,726	0	0	0	0	0	60	2	58	0	0
Aston Township	16,714	5	0	1	2	2	134	18	110	6	0
Athens	3,195	1	0	0	0	1	39	7	32	0	0

Table 8. Offenses Known to Law Enforcement, by Selected State and City, 2017—Continued

(Number.)

State/city	Population	Violent crime	Murder and nonnegligent manslaughter	Rape (revised definition)[1]	Robbery	Aggravated assault	Property crime	Burglary	Larceny-theft	Motor vehicle theft	Arson[2]
Athens Township	5,009	3	0	1	1	1	202	8	192	2	0
Avalon	4,582	19	0	0	1	18	67	13	48	6	1
Avis	1,498	3	0	0	1	2	2	1	1	0	0
Avoca	2,606	3	0	0	1	2	24	5	18	1	0
Avondale	1,416	0	0	0	0	0	0	0	0	0	0
Avonmore Boro	967	0	0	0	0	0	0	0	0	0	0
Baden	3,976	9	0	2	0	7	35	4	31	0	1
Baldwin Borough	19,727	19	1	0	6	12	137	23	104	10	0
Baldwin Township	1,942	0	0	0	0	0	12	0	11	1	0
Bally	1,103	0	0	0	0	0	0	0	0	0	0
Bangor	5,179	28	0	0	3	25	87	19	66	2	0
Beallsville	442	0	0	0	0	0	0	0	0	0	0
Beaver	4,353	3	0	0	0	3	79	10	65	4	0
Beaver Falls	8,516	34	0	0	10	24	316	23	279	14	1
Beaver Meadows	831	0	0	0	0	0	0	0	0	0	0
Bedford	2,702	5	0	0	0	5	27	9	17	1	0
Bedminster Township	7,117	2	0	0	0	2	31	0	30	1	0
Bell Acres	1,392	0	0	0	0	0	5	3	2	0	0
Bellefonte	6,321	2	1	0	0	1	57	5	52	0	1
Bellevue	8,140	26	0	0	16	10	243	36	196	11	0
Bellwood	1,759	0	0	0	0	0	16	2	13	1	0
Ben Avon	1,754	2	1	0	0	1	19	0	19	0	0
Ben Avon Heights	375	0	0	0	0	0	3	0	3	0	0
Bensalem Township	60,310	82	1	9	40	32	1,534	151	1,313	70	7
Bentleyville	2,492	5	0	0	0	5	10	1	8	1	0
Benton Area	1,932	0	0	0	0	0	9	1	8	0	0
Berlin	1,990	2	0	0	0	2	2	0	2	0	0
Bern Township	6,975	4	0	0	0	4	69	3	60	6	0
Bernville	946	0	0	0	0	0	0	0	0	0	0
Berwick	10,080	22	1	2	2	17	195	23	167	5	1
Bessemer	1,064	0	0	0	0	0	2	0	2	0	0
Bethel Park	31,842	23	0	3	5	15	292	27	259	6	1
Bethel Township, Berks County	4,122	0	0	0	0	0	21	4	15	2	0
Bethel Township, Delaware County	9,263	17	0	1	0	16	77	3	74	0	0
Bethlehem	75,336	594	0	29	61	504	1,359	187	1,124	48	7
Bethlehem Township	23,973	24	2	2	6	14	336	27	290	19	2
Biglerville	1,207	0	0	0	0	0	14	0	14	0	0
Birdsboro	5,138	1	0	0	0	1	40	10	28	2	0
Birmingham Township	4,255	2	0	0	0	2	5	0	5	0	0
Blacklick Township	1,896	0	0	0	0	0	0	0	0	0	0
Blairsville	3,275	17	0	0	0	17	89	11	76	2	0
Blair Township	4,559	1	0	1	0	0	29	5	24	0	0
Blakely	6,244	5	0	1	0	4	71	8	62	1	0
Blawnox	1,398	4	0	0	0	4	6	2	4	0	0
Bloomsburg Town	14,542	35	0	6	2	27	175	35	138	2	0
Blossburg	1,504	4	0	0	0	4	1	1	0	0	0
Bonneauville	1,828	0	0	0	0	0	9	1	6	2	0
Boyertown	4,026	9	0	1	5	3	81	15	64	2	1
Brackenridge	3,167	4	0	0	2	2	47	3	41	3	0
Braddock	2,111	21	0	0	3	18	47	12	28	7	0
Braddock Hills	1,838	8	0	0	1	7	5	0	5	0	0
Bradford	8,307	65	0	2	1	62	285	31	249	5	0
Bradford Township	4,761	6	0	0	1	5	28	4	24	0	1
Branch Township	1,766	0	0	0	0	0	2	0	1	1	0
Brecknock Township, Berks County	4,626	1	0	0	0	1	29	10	19	0	0
Brentwood	9,386	24	0	0	9	15	120	29	87	4	0
Briar Creek Township	2,989	2	0	0	0	2	45	12	32	1	0
Bridgeport	4,562	8	0	0	2	6	67	5	60	2	0
Bridgeville	5,029	8	0	2	2	4	108	4	104	0	0
Bridgewater	682	1	0	0	0	1	15	2	13	0	0
Brighton Township	8,392	3	0	0	0	3	19	1	18	0	0
Bristol	9,503	12	0	2	7	3	222	17	197	8	0
Bristol Township	53,628	87	0	14	51	22	1,081	124	872	85	4
Brockway	2,016	10	0	1	0	9	25	4	21	0	1
Brookhaven	8,074	13	0	1	9	3	106	9	92	5	0
Brookville	3,820	1	0	1	0	0	25	4	21	0	0
Brownsville	2,260	0	0	0	0	0	22	6	14	2	0
Bryn Athyn	1,394	0	0	0	0	0	9	0	9	0	0
Buckingham Township	20,339	1	0	0	1	0	89	19	67	3	0
Buffalo Township	7,276	8	0	0	0	8	81	16	65	0	0
Buffalo Valley Regional	12,590	3	1	0	0	2	128	17	111	0	1
Burgettstown	1,325	3	0	0	0	3	16	4	12	0	1
Bushkill Township	8,494	14	0	0	1	13	35	2	33	0	1
Butler	13,057	66	2	0	25	39	475	99	359	17	1
Butler Township, Butler County	16,690	26	1	3	3	19	382	18	359	5	1
Butler Township, Luzerne County	9,709	14	0	0	1	13	50	9	37	4	0
Butler Township, Schuylkill County	5,389	1	0	0	0	1	21	6	13	2	0
Caernarvon Township, Berks County	4,079	10	0	3	0	7	113	27	83	3	0

Table 8. Offenses Known to Law Enforcement, by Selected State and City, 2017—Continued

(Number.)

State/city	Population	Violent crime	Murder and nonnegligent manslaughter	Rape (revised definition)[1]	Robbery	Aggravated assault	Property crime	Burglary	Larceny-theft	Motor vehicle theft	Arson[2]
California	6,840	26	0	4	0	22	91	3	86	2	0
Callery	386	0	0	0	0	0	0	0	0	0	0
Caln Township	14,137	36	0	2	12	22	309	20	272	17	1
Cambria Township	5,823	5	0	1	0	4	79	2	75	2	0
Cambridge Springs	2,556	5	0	0	0	5	2	1	1	0	0
Camp Hill	7,941	1	0	0	1	0	65	3	60	2	0
Canonsburg	8,859	16	0	0	1	15	33	3	30	0	0
Canton	1,883	0	0	0	0	0	10	3	7	0	1
Carbondale	8,435	7	1	1	3	2	107	20	85	2	0
Carlisle	19,233	35	1	5	12	17	370	33	332	5	2
Carnegie	7,904	17	0	0	8	9	145	17	128	0	0
Carrolltown	804	1	0	0	0	1	5	0	5	0	0
Carroll Township, Washington County	5,503	18	0	0	0	18	55	10	42	3	0
Carroll Township, York County	6,359	3	0	1	1	1	92	6	81	5	0
Carroll Valley	3,949	1	0	0	0	1	22	1	21	0	0
Cass Township	1,893	2	0	0	0	2	11	3	7	1	0
Castle Shannon	8,213	4	0	1	1	2	43	8	33	2	0
Catasauqua	6,562	16	0	0	8	8	158	27	124	7	2
Catawissa	1,490	1	0	0	0	1	15	4	11	0	0
Cecil Township	12,605	2	0	0	0	2	56	7	48	1	0
Center Township	11,628	31	0	1	5	25	293	28	265	0	0
Centerville	3,156	8	0	0	1	7	24	4	20	0	0
Central Berks Regional	9,416	15	1	2	4	8	163	10	148	5	0
Central Bucks Regional	15,330	9	0	2	2	5	106	7	95	4	1
Chambersburg	20,757	56	2	4	19	31	601	72	512	17	3
Charleroi Regional	6,556	39	0	2	10	27	213	28	185	0	0
Chartiers Township	7,985	5	0	0	1	4	61	4	56	1	0
Cherry Tree	349	0	0	0	0	0	0	0	0	0	0
Chester	33,984	547	29	21	178	319	1,121	327	653	141	14
Chester Township	4,115	40	2	1	3	34	92	9	68	15	0
Cheswick	1,709	0	0	0	0	0	8	0	8	0	0
Chippewa Township	8,116	3	0	0	1	2	164	4	159	1	0
Christiana	1,168	5	0	0	0	5	21	3	16	2	0
Churchill	2,946	12	0	0	0	12	12	3	7	2	1
Clairton	6,588	44	0	1	23	20	115	34	62	19	0
Clarion	5,361	4	0	0	1	3	38	5	33	0	0
Clarks Summit	6,294	3	0	1	0	2	31	6	24	1	0
Clearfield	5,940	43	0	1	0	42	204	29	172	3	1
Cleona	2,183	0	0	0	0	0	7	2	5	0	0
Clifton Heights	6,695	30	0	0	5	25	146	10	126	10	0
Clymer	1,283	0	0	0	0	0	0	0	0	0	0
Coaldale	2,172	1	0	0	0	1	6	2	4	0	1
Coal Township	10,349	14	0	1	1	12	153	23	125	5	1
Coatesville	13,057	75	1	2	24	48	279	65	193	21	3
Cochranton	1,101	0	0	0	0	0	1	0	1	0	0
Colebrookdale District	5,985	3	0	1	0	2	103	10	93	0	0
Collegeville	5,282	4	0	0	0	4	47	7	37	3	2
Collier Township	8,164	2	0	0	1	1	132	14	115	3	0
Collingdale	8,762	94	0	3	11	80	220	37	159	24	1
Colonial Regional	20,540	14	0	6	5	3	456	34	415	7	2
Columbia	10,352	24	0	5	9	10	161	18	138	5	0
Colwyn	2,546	13	4	0	2	7	46	6	31	9	0
Conemaugh Township, Cambria County	1,886	2	0	0	0	2	7	5	2	0	0
Conemaugh Township, Somerset County	6,900	12	0	0	2	10	28	10	18	0	0
Conewago Township, Adams County	7,184	5	0	1	0	4	30	5	23	2	3
Conewango Township	3,392	23	0	3	0	20	85	6	79	0	0
Conneaut Lake Regional	3,506	0	0	0	0	0	34	15	17	2	0
Connellsville	7,405	35	0	7	18	10	264	53	200	11	0
Conoy Township	3,483	3	0	0	0	3	19	6	11	2	0
Conshohocken	8,006	4	0	1	0	3	70	6	60	4	0
Conway	2,121	4	0	0	2	2	25	3	17	5	0
Conyngham	1,863	0	0	0	0	0	4	1	3	0	0
Coopersburg	2,494	6	0	0	0	6	21	5	13	3	0
Coplay	3,239	2	0	1	0	1	44	2	42	0	0
Coraopolis	5,513	17	0	0	5	12	157	25	129	3	0
Cornwall	4,318	1	0	1	0	0	0	0	0	0	0
Corry	6,321	26	0	0	0	26	168	12	154	2	2
Coudersport	2,433	1	0	1	0	0	8	1	7	0	0
Courtdale	722	0	0	0	0	0	3	1	2	0	0
Covington Township	2,250	6	0	0	0	6	41	6	33	2	0
Crafton	6,251	11	0	0	2	9	214	12	197	5	0
Cranberry Township	31,191	7	1	1	2	3	290	19	264	7	0
Crescent Township	2,574	6	0	0	0	6	23	7	16	0	0
Cresson	1,598	4	0	0	2	2	24	4	20	0	0
Cresson Township	2,574	2	0	1	0	1	14	0	14	0	0
Croyle Township	2,249	1	0	0	0	1	5	0	5	0	0
Cumberland Township, Adams County	6,225	5	0	1	0	4	41	6	29	6	0

Table 8. Offenses Known to Law Enforcement, by Selected State and City, 2017—Continued

(Number.)

State/city	Population	Violent crime	Murder and nonnegligent manslaughter	Rape (revised definition)[1]	Robbery	Aggravated assault	Property crime	Burglary	Larceny-theft	Motor vehicle theft	Arson[2]
Cumberland Township, Greene County	6,333	11	1	0	1	9	102	9	84	9	0
Cumru Township	15,341	22	0	1	11	10	199	36	156	7	0
Curwensville	2,443	16	1	0	0	15	24	3	20	1	0
Dallas	2,762	11	0	0	0	11	39	2	37	0	0
Dallas Township	9,252	1	0	0	0	1	57	10	47	0	0
Dalton	1,204	3	0	0	0	3	33	4	29	0	1
Danville	4,604	22	0	8	0	14	74	7	63	4	0
Darby	10,648	172	4	8	50	110	401	86	278	37	3
Darby Township	9,302	49	0	1	10	38	174	20	138	16	1
Darlington Township	1,897	2	0	0	0	2	27	7	19	1	0
Decatur Township	4,804	2	0	0	0	2	9	5	4	0	0
Delano Township	421	0	0	0	0	0	0	0	0	0	0
Delaware Water Gap	703	0	0	0	0	0	0	0	0	0	0
Delmont	2,612	2	0	0	1	1	14	1	13	0	0
Denver	3,867	2	0	1	1	0	25	3	21	1	0
Derry	2,551	0	0	0	0	0	1	0	1	0	0
Derry Township, Dauphin County	25,082	26	0	1	3	22	422	61	357	4	3
Dickson City	5,794	24	0	1	2	21	266	15	246	5	2
Donegal Township	2,418	3	0	1	1	1	22	0	20	2	0
Donora	4,597	7	0	2	1	4	35	8	27	0	0
Dormont	8,347	12	0	0	2	10	72	13	53	6	0
Douglass Township, Berks County	3,584	2	0	0	1	1	35	9	24	2	1
Douglass Township, Montgomery County	10,534	12	0	1	1	10	76	8	67	1	0
Downingtown	7,907	18	0	0	7	11	189	8	175	6	0
Doylestown Township	17,538	10	0	1	1	8	141	12	127	2	0
Dublin Borough	2,157	3	0	0	0	3	7	0	6	1	0
Du Bois	7,504	24	0	1	1	22	159	20	138	1	0
Duboistown	1,200	0	0	0	0	0	0	0	0	0	0
Dunbar	1,003	0	0	0	0	0	0	0	0	0	0
Duncansville	1,186	2	0	1	1	0	2	0	2	0	0
Dunnstable Township	1,015	0	0	0	0	0	0	0	0	0	0
Dupont	2,665	2	0	0	1	1	33	8	25	0	0
Duquesne	5,507	86	1	6	20	59	218	74	118	26	4
Duryea	4,840	10	0	0	0	10	59	16	39	4	1
Earl Township	7,174	3	0	0	0	3	69	18	39	12	0
East Bangor	1,705	0	0	0	0	0	6	1	5	0	0
East Berlin	1,530	0	0	0	0	0	2	0	2	0	0
East Brandywine Township	8,721	6	0	1	1	4	43	5	37	1	1
East Cocalico Township	10,525	7	0	3	3	1	87	18	68	1	0
East Conemaugh	1,427	5	0	1	0	4	17	7	9	1	0
East Coventry Township	6,738	2	1	0	0	1	23	3	18	2	0
East Deer Township	1,455	2	0	0	2	0	18	4	14	0	0
East Earl Township	6,838	1	0	1	0	0	65	9	54	2	2
Eastern Adams Regional	7,388	7	0	1	1	5	41	6	32	3	0
Eastern Pike Regional	4,607	15	0	4	0	11	111	4	105	2	1
East Fallowfield Township	7,539	0	0	0	0	0	77	9	66	2	0
East Franklin Township	3,917	0	0	0	0	0	28	0	28	0	0
East Hempfield Township	24,504	25	0	5	9	11	344	50	293	1	1
East Lampeter Township	17,084	17	0	3	7	7	599	33	552	14	0
East Lansdowne	2,654	18	0	0	4	14	68	10	57	1	4
East Marlborough Township	7,310	0	0	0	0	0	16	0	16	0	0
East McKeesport	2,644	4	0	0	1	3	10	1	8	1	0
East Norriton Township	14,154	40	0	0	5	35	291	15	273	3	0
Easton	27,013	69	0	11	30	28	477	48	404	25	1
East Pennsboro Township	21,800	15	1	5	4	5	202	22	173	7	0
East Petersburg	4,522	6	0	0	0	6	48	9	35	4	1
East Pikeland Township	7,360	1	0	0	0	1	51	4	44	3	0
East Pittsburgh	1,769	47	0	4	8	35	60	19	27	14	1
East Rochester	540	1	0	1	0	0	37	1	36	0	0
East Taylor Township	2,547	2	0	0	0	2	5	2	3	0	0
Easttown Township	10,609	3	0	0	0	3	67	4	59	4	0
East Union Township	1,593	6	0	0	0	6	2	0	1	1	0
East Vincent Township	7,065	1	0	0	1	0	23	7	15	1	0
East Washington	1,833	3	0	0	0	3	39	6	33	0	0
East Whiteland Township	11,672	6	0	0	0	6	145	11	129	5	0
Ebensburg	3,137	1	0	0	0	1	17	2	14	1	0
Economy	9,338	3	0	1	1	1	119	5	113	1	0
Eddystone	2,397	20	0	0	3	17	301	11	287	3	0
Edgewood	3,026	5	0	0	3	2	82	6	74	2	0
Edgeworth	1,644	0	0	0	0	0	2	2	0	0	0
Edinboro	6,204	9	0	1	1	7	65	9	54	2	0
Edwardsville	4,684	21	0	3	0	18	107	5	101	1	0
Elderton	347	0	0	0	0	0	0	0	0	0	0
Elizabeth	1,983	3	0	0	0	3	7	2	1	4	0
Elizabethtown	11,641	29	2	12	4	11	123	21	100	2	0
Elizabeth Township	13,079	8	0	5	0	3	88	19	69	0	1
Elkland	1,758	0	0	0	0	0	37	3	31	3	0
Elk Lick Township	2,133	0	0	0	0	0	0	0	0	0	0
Ellwood City	7,476	9	1	0	4	4	126	15	106	5	0

Table 8. Offenses Known to Law Enforcement, by Selected State and City, 2017—Continued

(Number.)

State/city	Population	Violent crime	Murder and nonnegligent manslaughter	Rape (revised definition)[1]	Robbery	Aggravated assault	Property crime	Burglary	Larceny-theft	Motor vehicle theft	Arson[2]
Emlenton Borough	587	2	0	0	0	2	13	2	10	1	0
Emmaus	11,424	8	0	1	6	1	164	26	114	24	1
Emporium	1,887	3	0	0	0	3	36	4	32	0	0
Emsworth	2,387	0	0	0	0	0	30	2	28	0	0
Ephrata	13,907	37	0	4	5	28	168	24	139	5	0
Ephrata Township	10,348	10	0	2	3	5	150	16	130	4	1
Erie	98,071	306	6	32	98	170	2,258	531	1,619	108	43
Etna	3,354	8	0	0	1	7	56	5	47	4	0
Evans City-Seven Fields Regional	4,554	2	0	0	0	2	30	2	28	0	0
Everett	1,731	1	0	0	0	1	22	0	22	0	0
Everson	765	0	0	0	0	0	0	0	0	0	0
Exeter	5,542	15	0	1	1	13	87	23	61	3	0
Exeter Township, Berks County	25,830	23	0	6	6	11	304	29	267	8	0
Fairfield	508	0	0	0	0	0	2	0	2	0	0
Fairview Township, Luzerne County	4,479	2	1	0	0	1	26	0	26	0	0
Fairview Township, York County	17,393	42	0	3	3	36	178	20	157	1	0
Falls Township, Bucks County	33,618	70	0	16	19	35	578	53	486	39	2
Farrell	4,702	54	1	1	8	44	134	30	98	6	3
Fawn Township	2,330	3	0	0	0	3	15	6	7	2	0
Fayette City	575	0	0	0	0	0	0	0	0	0	0
Ferguson Township	19,630	6	0	0	3	3	96	9	83	4	0
Ferndale	1,524	0	0	0	0	0	1	0	1	0	0
Findlay Township	5,739	4	0	0	0	4	30	2	26	2	0
Fleetwood	4,070	8	0	0	3	5	74	10	58	6	0
Folcroft	6,623	40	0	3	6	31	130	20	93	17	0
Ford City	2,825	0	0	0	0	0	4	0	4	0	0
Forest City	1,742	3	0	0	0	3	10	2	8	0	0
Forest Hills	6,357	8	0	0	5	3	66	5	52	9	0
Forks Township	15,518	5	0	4	1	0	110	15	93	2	0
Forty Fort	4,079	8	0	2	1	5	34	4	29	1	0
Forward Township	3,300	2	0	0	0	2	19	1	16	2	1
Foster Township, McKean County	4,116	5	0	1	0	4	74	2	72	0	0
Foster Township, Schuykill County	253	1	1	0	0	0	7	2	5	0	0
Fountain Hill	4,638	9	1	2	1	5	129	16	109	4	2
Fox Chapel	5,329	1	0	0	0	1	14	4	10	0	0
Frackville	3,651	8	1	0	0	7	18	1	16	1	0
Franconia Township	13,293	5	0	0	0	5	62	4	55	3	0
Franklin	6,181	14	1	5	0	8	117	16	95	6	1
Franklin Park	14,690	2	0	0	1	1	51	10	41	0	0
Franklin Township, Beaver County	3,934	5	1	0	0	4	27	7	19	1	0
Franklin Township, Carbon County	4,104	11	0	0	1	10	32	7	24	1	0
Franklin Township, Columbia County	581	0	0	0	0	0	0	0	0	0	0
Frazer Township	1,143	6	1	0	0	5	146	2	144	0	0
Freedom	1,503	1	0	1	0	0	26	3	20	3	2
Freedom Township	3,385	3	0	0	0	3	92	2	90	0	1
Freemansburg	2,619	4	0	3	0	1	22	1	19	2	0
Freeport	1,710	4	1	0	0	3	9	5	4	0	0
Gaines Township	544	0	0	0	0	0	0	0	0	0	0
Galeton	1,102	7	0	1	0	6	16	4	12	0	0
Gallitzin	1,807	0	0	0	0	0	13	2	11	0	0
Gallitzin Township	1,271	1	0	0	0	1	0	0	0	0	0
Garrett	427	0	0	0	0	0	0	0	0	0	0
Geistown	2,326	0	0	0	0	0	4	0	2	2	0
Gettysburg	7,716	37	0	4	7	26	136	15	120	1	0
Gilpin Township	2,403	2	0	0	0	2	1	1	0	0	0
Girard	2,978	8	0	0	0	8	49	6	39	4	0
Girardville	1,453	3	0	0	0	3	5	1	4	0	0
Glassport	4,360	17	0	0	4	13	122	18	97	7	0
Glenolden	7,153	16	0	0	8	8	148	15	116	17	0
Granville Township	5,022	2	0	2	0	0	90	6	84	0	1
Great Bend	669	0	0	0	0	0	0	0	0	0	0
Greencastle	4,041	1	0	0	0	1	23	3	19	1	1
Greenfield Township, Blair County	4,035	0	0	0	0	0	22	1	20	1	0
Greensburg	14,356	43	0	4	13	26	297	23	270	4	0
Green Tree	5,020	6	0	0	1	5	49	9	39	1	1
Greenville	5,547	13	0	3	2	8	53	17	32	4	0
Greenwood Township	1,898	0	0	0	0	0	0	0	0	0	0
Grove City	8,029	3	0	0	0	3	51	5	44	2	0
Halifax	828	0	0	0	0	0	5	2	3	0	1
Hamburg	4,394	17	0	0	3	14	42	10	29	3	0
Hampden Township	29,905	11	0	5	3	3	258	32	222	4	1
Hampton Township	18,451	11	0	4	2	5	73	6	66	1	0
Hanover	15,606	36	0	2	10	24	378	32	340	6	1

Table 8. Offenses Known to Law Enforcement, by Selected State and City, 2017—Continued

(Number.)

State/city	Population	Violent crime	Murder and nonnegligent manslaughter	Rape (revised definition)[1]	Robbery	Aggravated assault	Property crime	Burglary	Larceny-theft	Motor vehicle theft	Arson[2]
Hanover Township, Luzerne County	10,822	27	1	2	4	20	249	56	189	4	0
Harmar Township	3,064	5	0	0	1	4	87	5	78	4	0
Harmony Township	3,066	3	0	0	2	1	39	1	36	2	0
Harrisburg	48,804	564	13	50	178	323	1,494	348	963	183	15
Harrison Township	10,358	12	0	0	4	8	240	46	190	4	0
Harrisville	870	0	0	0	0	0	2	0	2	0	0
Hartleton	286	0	0	0	0	0	0	0	0	0	0
Harveys Lake	2,770	1	0	0	0	1	23	0	21	2	0
Hastings	2,178	3	0	0	0	3	19	5	13	1	0
Hatboro	7,445	4	0	1	2	1	63	8	49	6	2
Hatfield Township	20,927	23	1	4	6	12	193	14	171	8	1
Haverford Township	49,116	29	3	3	15	8	655	51	588	16	0
Hawley	1,126	0	0	0	0	0	0	0	0	0	0
Hazleton	24,549	91	1	7	26	57	304	82	191	31	0
Hegins Township	3,440	5	0	1	0	4	50	16	33	1	0
Heidelberg	1,215	2	0	0	0	2	3	0	3	0	0
Heidelberg Township, Berks County	1,739	1	0	0	0	1	16	5	11	0	0
Hellam Township	8,646	16	0	10	0	6	54	8	43	3	0
Hellertown	5,819	7	0	0	1	6	43	4	38	1	0
Hemlock Township	2,260	7	0	0	0	7	90	2	87	1	1
Hempfield Township, Mercer County	3,655	23	0	1	3	19	126	16	109	1	0
Hermitage	15,782	31	1	4	10	16	461	56	397	8	1
Hickory Township	2,393	2	0	0	0	2	5	2	3	0	0
Highland Township	1,284	0	0	0	0	0	1	0	1	0	0
Highspire	2,366	17	0	0	5	12	64	8	56	0	0
Hilltown Township	15,278	14	1	3	5	5	205	17	181	7	0
Hollidaysburg	5,751	9	0	0	0	9	30	2	26	2	1
Homer City	1,614	0	0	0	0	0	5	0	5	0	0
Homestead	3,160	47	0	2	16	29	303	28	257	18	0
Honesdale	4,132	9	0	4	1	4	61	8	51	2	0
Honey Brook	1,751	2	0	0	1	1	3	0	1	2	0
Hooversville	607	0	0	0	0	0	2	0	2	0	0
Hopewell Township	12,346	21	0	2	2	17	185	31	150	4	2
Horsham Township	26,723	7	0	0	3	4	141	13	114	14	0
Houston	1,240	3	0	0	0	3	4	1	3	0	0
Hughestown	1,370	2	0	0	0	2	13	2	10	1	0
Hughesville	2,076	1	0	0	0	1	28	1	27	0	0
Hulmeville	987	0	0	0	0	0	8	1	6	1	0
Hummelstown	4,621	6	0	0	1	5	55	2	53	0	1
Huntingdon	6,974	35	0	0	1	34	75	8	67	0	0
Independence Township, Beaver County	2,419	1	0	0	0	1	15	5	6	4	0
Independence Township, Washington County	1,514	0	0	0	0	0	3	1	2	0	0
Indiana	13,984	121	2	8	4	107	243	43	196	4	0
Indiana Township	7,225	2	0	1	1	0	25	5	19	1	0
Indian Lake	386	0	0	0	0	0	1	0	1	0	0
Ingram	3,235	6	0	0	1	5	34	2	30	2	0
Irwin	3,801	12	0	0	0	12	39	1	38	0	0
Ivyland	1,047	1	0	0	0	1	4	1	3	0	0
Jackson Township, Cambria County	4,130	2	0	0	1	1	4	0	4	0	0
Jackson Township, Luzerne County	4,631	0	0	0	0	0	15	2	13	0	0
Jamestown	582	1	0	0	0	1	5	1	4	0	0
Jeannette	9,180	9	1	0	3	5	60	14	46	0	0
Jefferson Hills Borough	11,418	8	0	0	0	8	42	8	33	1	3
Jefferson Township, Lackawanna County	3,659	0	0	0	0	0	3	0	3	0	0
Jefferson Township, Mercer County	1,846	0	0	0	0	0	2	1	1	0	0
Jefferson Township, Washington County	1,148	0	0	0	0	0	0	0	0	0	0
Jenkins Township	4,447	3	0	1	1	1	53	5	47	1	0
Jenkintown	4,421	8	0	0	2	6	81	7	73	1	0
Jennerstown	657	0	0	0	0	0	1	1	0	0	0
Jermyn	2,065	9	0	0	0	9	43	13	26	4	0
Jessup	4,423	8	0	5	0	3	29	3	23	3	0
Jim Thorpe	4,579	16	0	4	1	11	80	6	69	5	1
Johnsonburg	2,313	8	0	1	0	7	63	18	43	2	2
Johnstown	20,946	157	9	10	27	111	634	190	419	25	7
Kane	3,520	4	0	1	0	3	63	14	48	1	0
Kenhorst	2,852	2	0	1	0	1	54	16	35	3	0
Kennedy Township	8,213	13	1	1	4	7	178	19	157	2	0
Kennett Square	6,176	8	0	1	3	4	108	6	92	10	1
Kennett Township	8,312	4	0	1	0	3	39	13	24	2	0
Kidder Township	1,929	3	0	0	0	3	42	9	33	0	0
Kilbuck Township	710	0	0	0	0	0	7	0	7	0	0
Kingston	12,809	28	0	1	10	17	214	24	183	7	0
Kingston Township	6,924	14	0	0	1	13	35	3	31	1	0

Table 8. Offenses Known to Law Enforcement, by Selected State and City, 2017—Continued

(Number.)

State/city	Population	Violent crime	Murder and nonnegligent manslaughter	Rape (revised definition)[1]	Robbery	Aggravated assault	Property crime	Burglary	Larceny-theft	Motor vehicle theft	Arson[2]
Kiskiminetas Township	4,565	3	0	0	0	3	7	4	3	0	0
Kittanning	3,818	22	0	0	2	20	134	38	87	9	0
Kline Township	1,380	3	0	3	0	0	23	1	21	1	0
Knox	1,076	2	0	0	0	2	8	3	5	0	1
Koppel	732	3	0	0	0	3	9	0	8	1	0
Kulpmont	2,812	2	0	0	1	1	15	2	12	1	0
Kutztown	5,019	17	1	5	1	10	52	18	33	1	0
Lake City	2,923	2	0	0	0	2	43	5	38	0	0
Lamar Township	2,562	0	0	0	0	0	6	2	3	1	0
Lancaster	59,199	530	5	97	141	287	1,999	205	1,689	105	20
Lancaster Township, Butler County	2,513	0	0	0	0	0	21	3	18	0	0
Lancaster Township, Lancaster County	17,229	33	1	6	6	20	426	30	371	25	1
Lanesboro	462	0	0	0	0	0	0	0	0	0	0
Langhorne Manor	1,423	0	0	0	0	0	4	0	4	0	0
Lansdale	16,561	16	0	6	2	8	246	21	219	6	4
Lansdowne	10,604	31	0	1	11	19	239	55	166	18	2
Lansford	3,740	33	0	0	2	31	125	20	98	7	1
Larksville	4,389	2	0	0	0	2	22	3	18	1	0
Latimore Township	2,604	2	0	2	0	0	15	1	14	0	0
Latrobe	7,950	28	1	2	3	22	180	31	145	4	0
Laureldale	3,868	7	0	3	1	3	37	12	22	3	0
Lawrence Park Township	3,793	17	0	0	1	16	9	0	9	0	0
Lawrence Township, Clearfield County	7,694	79	0	0	1	78	218	8	204	6	0
Lawrence Township, Tioga County	1,686	3	0	0	0	3	0	0	0	0	0
Lawrenceville	616	0	0	0	0	0	0	0	0	0	0
Lebanon	25,771	89	2	6	34	47	538	126	389	23	3
Leechburg	2,033	4	0	1	0	3	25	4	16	5	0
Leetsdale	1,182	1	0	0	1	0	24	6	18	0	0
Leet Township	1,600	1	0	0	0	1	16	3	12	1	0
Lehighton	5,241	13	0	4	1	8	110	14	91	5	1
Lehigh Township, Northampton County	10,400	21	0	1	1	19	77	16	58	3	1
Lehigh Township, Wayne County	1,753	3	1	0	0	2	8	5	3	0	0
Lehman Township	3,448	5	0	0	0	5	19	3	15	1	0
Lewistown	8,196	31	0	6	2	23	243	36	202	5	2
Liberty	2,489	2	0	0	0	2	8	3	5	0	0
Liberty Township, Adams County	1,246	0	0	0	0	0	11	0	11	0	0
Ligonier	1,523	0	0	0	0	0	8	0	8	0	0
Ligonier Township	6,463	8	0	0	0	8	18	1	14	3	0
Limerick Township	19,145	9	0	6	1	2	353	18	328	7	0
Lincoln	1,047	0	0	0	0	0	0	0	0	0	0
Linesville	988	0	0	0	0	0	13	1	12	0	0
Lititz	9,214	4	0	1	0	3	43	3	39	1	0
Little Beaver Township	1,340	0	0	0	0	0	0	0	0	0	0
Littlestown	4,473	4	0	1	1	2	36	4	32	0	1
Lock Haven	9,514	24	0	5	4	15	123	24	97	2	3
Locust Township	1,400	2	0	1	0	1	5	3	2	0	0
Logan Township	12,547	14	0	3	2	9	175	15	155	5	1
Loretto	1,399	0	0	0	0	0	0	0	0	0	0
Lower Allen Township	19,604	27	0	4	7	16	353	33	316	4	1
Lower Burrell	11,303	9	0	2	0	7	135	19	112	4	0
Lower Chichester Township	3,468	25	0	1	3	21	66	7	49	10	0
Lower Frederick Township	4,901	3	0	0	0	3	18	3	15	0	1
Lower Gwynedd Township	11,581	11	0	0	2	9	150	15	126	9	0
Lower Heidelberg Township	6,143	3	0	0	0	3	22	1	19	2	0
Lower Mahanoy Township	1,663	0	0	0	0	0	0	0	0	0	0
Lower Makefield Township	32,779	18	0	2	1	15	291	42	243	6	0
Lower Merion Township	58,354	39	0	4	20	15	1,034	94	894	46	0
Lower Moreland Township	13,246	6	0	0	2	4	163	20	134	9	2
Lower Paxton Township	48,971	99	1	23	17	58	741	73	647	21	4
Lower Pottsgrove Township	12,179	22	0	1	3	18	192	28	160	4	1
Lower Providence Township	26,813	50	0	0	2	48	309	32	266	11	0
Lower Salford Township	15,487	8	0	1	0	7	85	7	74	4	0
Lower Saucon Township	10,818	18	0	0	1	17	76	13	61	2	0
Lower Southampton Township	19,120	83	0	1	8	74	353	23	311	19	3
Lower Swatara Township	8,855	7	0	0	1	6	94	18	76	0	0
Lower Windsor Township	7,500	6	0	0	0	6	70	12	56	2	0
Luzerne Township	5,868	0	0	0	0	0	0	0	0	0	0
Lykens	1,746	0	0	0	0	0	0	0	0	0	0
Macungie	3,162	2	0	0	0	2	10	2	8	0	0
Madison Township	1,594	1	0	0	0	1	1	1	0	0	0
Mahanoy City	3,981	0	0	0	0	0	4	1	3	0	0
Mahanoy Township	3,322	1	0	0	1	0	4	1	3	0	0
Mahoning Township, Carbon County	4,188	21	0	1	0	20	175	11	158	6	0
Mahoning Township, Lawrence County	2,910	2	0	0	0	2	0	0	0	0	0

Table 8. Offenses Known to Law Enforcement, by Selected State and City, 2017—Continued

(Number.)

State/city	Population	Violent crime	Murder and nonnegligent manslaughter	Rape (revised definition)[1]	Robbery	Aggravated assault	Property crime	Burglary	Larceny-theft	Motor vehicle theft	Arson[2]
Mahoning Township, Montour County	4,207	13	0	1	1	11	40	1	39	0	0
Main Township	1,292	0	0	0	0	0	0	0	0	0	0
Malvern	3,487	7	0	0	2	5	23	1	20	2	0
Manheim	4,855	30	0	2	7	21	117	13	101	3	0
Manheim Township	40,170	59	0	10	15	34	678	34	619	25	1
Manor	3,334	0	0	0	0	0	6	0	5	1	0
Manor Township, Armstrong County	4,164	3	1	0	0	2	66	8	57	1	0
Manor Township, Lancaster County	20,949	42	0	1	1	40	141	22	109	10	0
Mansfield	3,147	1	0	0	0	1	8	1	7	0	0
Marcus Hook	2,388	49	0	2	1	46	64	9	50	5	1
Marietta	2,603	12	0	2	2	8	27	8	16	3	1
Marion Township, Beaver County	889	0	0	0	0	0	0	0	0	0	0
Marion Township, Berks County	1,874	0	0	0	0	0	4	1	2	1	0
Marlborough Township	3,347	4	0	1	0	3	18	6	12	0	0
Marple Township	23,838	11	0	2	2	7	340	10	321	9	0
Mars	1,636	0	0	0	0	0	2	0	2	0	0
Martinsburg	1,884	3	0	1	0	2	12	1	10	1	0
Marysville	2,531	1	0	0	1	0	23	2	21	0	0
Masontown	3,351	7	0	0	1	6	79	15	59	5	0
Mayfield	1,709	0	0	0	0	0	0	0	0	0	0
McAdoo	2,176	6	0	0	0	6	47	3	43	1	1
McCandless	28,788	13	1	0	0	12	178	11	165	2	0
McDonald Borough	2,060	8	0	0	0	8	43	5	36	2	0
McKeesport	20,937	445	13	7	48	377	579	152	366	61	11
McKees Rocks	5,926	79	3	5	28	43	324	98	217	9	5
McSherrystown	3,062	5	0	0	0	5	9	0	8	1	0
Meadville	12,896	14	1	0	6	7	231	27	197	7	0
Media	5,354	22	0	1	6	15	71	15	55	1	0
Mercer	1,896	2	0	0	1	1	8	4	4	0	0
Mercersburg	1,553	1	0	0	1	0	17	2	15	0	0
Meshoppen	1,444	3	0	0	0	3	36	3	31	2	0
Meyersdale	2,046	0	0	0	0	0	5	0	5	0	0
Middleburg	1,305	3	0	1	1	1	22	1	21	0	1
Middlesex Township, Butler County	5,673	1	0	0	0	1	18	1	14	3	0
Middlesex Township, Cumberland County	7,422	11	1	4	0	6	105	8	94	3	0
Middletown	9,279	27	0	1	4	22	81	19	62	0	3
Middletown Township	45,282	39	0	7	11	21	831	85	719	27	4
Midland	2,523	9	0	1	0	8	68	3	65	0	0
Midway	883	1	0	1	0	0	11	3	8	0	0
Mifflinburg	3,518	6	0	0	1	5	27	1	26	0	0
Mifflin County Regional	16,872	16	0	3	4	9	154	21	131	2	0
Milford	966	3	0	1	0	2	16	1	14	1	0
Millbourne	1,159	16	0	0	8	8	26	5	19	2	0
Millcreek Township, Erie County	53,806	111	0	8	3	100	734	118	594	22	3
Millcreek Township, Lebanon County	5,670	0	0	0	0	0	18	1	17	0	0
Millersburg	2,528	4	0	2	0	2	29	6	22	1	1
Millersville	8,419	5	0	0	2	3	75	9	63	3	0
Mill Hall	1,613	0	0	0	0	0	0	0	0	0	0
Millvale	3,638	3	0	0	2	1	106	2	100	4	0
Millville	946	0	0	0	0	0	1	1	0	0	0
Milton	6,879	63	0	2	4	57	96	27	66	3	1
Minersville	4,185	4	0	0	1	3	24	2	22	0	0
Mohnton	3,044	1	0	1	0	0	24	12	12	0	0
Monaca	5,567	10	0	1	2	7	89	15	62	12	0
Monessen	7,364	61	0	2	3	56	188	41	146	1	3
Monongahela	4,129	21	0	2	4	15	133	25	100	8	2
Monroeville	27,888	64	0	4	12	48	478	36	420	22	0
Montgomery	1,537	0	0	0	0	0	0	0	0	0	0
Montgomery Township	26,369	9	0	0	5	4	375	22	350	3	0
Montoursville	4,497	4	0	1	0	3	116	1	114	1	0
Montour Township	1,302	3	0	0	0	3	5	0	5	0	0
Montrose	1,471	2	0	0	0	2	0	0	0	0	0
Moon Township	25,818	15	0	3	4	8	293	32	259	2	2
Moore Township	9,294	8	0	1	0	7	45	5	39	1	0
Moosic	5,759	32	0	3	2	27	156	21	126	9	0
Morrisville	8,523	17	1	1	8	7	259	44	188	27	0
Morton	2,693	2	0	0	1	1	60	1	58	1	0
Moscow	1,934	7	0	0	0	7	12	1	11	0	0
Mount Carmel	5,644	40	1	3	0	36	112	23	80	9	0
Mount Carmel Township	3,030	19	1	0	0	18	23	1	20	2	0
Mount Gretna Borough	203	0	0	0	0	0	0	0	0	0	0
Mount Holly Springs	2,042	0	0	0	0	0	32	6	26	0	0
Mount Joy	8,221	19	0	1	2	16	78	18	58	2	0
Mount Lebanon	32,367	23	0	2	5	16	224	38	179	7	1

Table 8. Offenses Known to Law Enforcement, by Selected State and City, 2017—Continued

(Number.)

State/city	Population	Violent crime	Murder and nonnegligent manslaughter	Rape (revised definition)[1]	Robbery	Aggravated assault	Property crime	Burglary	Larceny-theft	Motor vehicle theft	Arson[2]
Mount Oliver	3,308	64	0	0	16	48	104	34	68	2	4
Mount Pleasant	4,304	13	1	0	0	12	27	3	24	0	0
Mount Pleasant Township	3,497	1	0	0	0	1	24	2	22	0	0
Mount Union	2,385	3	0	0	2	1	12	0	12	0	0
Mountville	2,855	3	0	0	0	3	26	2	24	0	1
Muhlenberg Township	20,150	24	1	1	7	15	532	36	472	24	1
Muncy	2,441	2	0	2	0	0	11	2	8	1	0
Muncy Township	1,081	0	0	0	0	0	46	1	45	0	0
Munhall	11,140	6	0	0	0	6	67	0	66	1	0
Murrysville	20,034	12	0	1	1	10	112	12	98	2	1
Nanticoke	10,144	28	1	1	11	15	168	18	145	5	10
Nanty Glo	2,540	1	0	1	0	0	10	5	5	0	0
Narberth	4,338	1	0	0	0	1	27	0	26	1	0
Nazareth	5,675	6	0	1	0	5	74	7	62	5	0
Nescopeck	1,534	2	0	0	0	2	2	2	0	0	0
Neshannock Township	9,241	6	0	0	2	4	54	12	41	1	0
Nether Providence Township	13,790	10	1	0	1	8	135	18	116	1	0
Neville Township	1,052	0	0	0	0	0	52	2	50	0	0
New Beaver	1,427	0	0	0	0	0	2	0	2	0	0
New Berlin	866	0	0	0	0	0	2	1	1	0	0
Newberry Township	15,530	22	0	3	1	18	217	15	195	7	0
New Brighton	8,907	28	0	0	5	23	300	63	229	8	0
New Britain Township	11,220	4	0	0	0	4	63	10	52	1	0
New Castle	21,968	94	0	5	48	41	724	243	457	24	7
New Castle Township	387	0	0	0	0	0	0	0	0	0	0
New Cumberland	7,302	2	0	2	0	0	73	12	59	2	0
New Florence	654	0	0	0	0	0	1	1	0	0	0
New Hanover Township	13,095	6	0	0	0	6	50	7	38	5	0
New Holland	5,443	10	0	0	1	9	74	10	62	2	1
New Hope	2,492	4	0	0	0	4	50	1	49	0	0
New Kensington	12,508	50	1	8	21	20	486	105	349	32	2
New Philadelphia	1,041	0	0	0	0	0	1	0	1	0	0
Newport Township	5,257	8	0	0	1	7	31	8	22	1	0
New Sewickley Township	7,367	12	0	1	0	11	91	21	62	8	0
Newtown	2,226	1	0	0	0	1	20	3	16	1	0
Newtown Township, Bucks County	22,903	15	0	0	5	10	119	12	104	3	0
Newtown Township, Delaware County	13,190	8	0	1	2	5	102	7	87	8	0
New Wilmington	2,183	2	0	1	0	1	21	2	19	0	0
Norristown	34,374	187	4	6	103	74	574	67	463	44	2
Northampton	9,854	11	0	2	1	8	102	9	85	8	0
Northampton Township	39,395	18	0	2	5	11	147	18	117	12	0
North Beaver	3,957	0	0	0	0	0	5	0	4	1	0
North Belle Vernon	1,871	9	0	0	1	8	41	5	36	0	0
North Braddock	4,721	3	0	0	1	2	5	3	2	0	1
North Buffalo	2,936	0	0	0	0	0	0	0	0	0	0
North Catasauqua	2,828	4	0	1	0	3	66	5	55	6	0
North Cornwall Township	7,909	12	0	1	3	8	144	13	128	3	0
North Coventry Township	8,001	8	1	1	1	5	145	12	133	0	0
Northeast, Bradford County	407	1	0	0	1	0	1	0	0	1	0
North East, Erie County	4,109	6	0	1	0	5	106	9	95	2	0
Northeastern Regional	11,728	15	1	4	0	10	132	7	125	0	0
Northern Berks Regional	13,282	4	0	2	1	1	100	16	78	6	0
Northern Cambria Borough	3,582	4	0	0	0	4	46	9	36	1	0
Northern Lancaster County Regional	35,500	31	0	7	3	21	169	25	137	7	0
Northern Regional	35,113	8	0	0	0	8	185	1	176	8	0
Northern York Regional	69,203	45	3	1	10	31	747	104	607	36	6
North Fayette Township	14,656	17	0	0	2	15	181	16	163	2	0
North Franklin Township	4,571	10	0	0	0	10	79	3	75	1	1
North Hopewell Township	2,803	2	0	0	0	2	8	1	6	1	0
North Huntingdon Township	30,687	17	0	4	3	10	340	26	296	18	0
North Lebanon Township	11,975	28	0	1	4	23	225	28	193	4	7
North Londonderry Township	8,525	0	0	0	0	0	132	3	129	0	0
North Middleton Township	11,625	16	0	3	0	13	56	4	47	5	0
North Sewickley Township	5,474	9	0	0	0	9	42	5	36	1	1
North Strabane Township	14,778	18	0	1	1	16	116	6	108	2	0
Northumberland	3,687	4	0	1	0	3	26	8	18	0	0
North Union Township	1,420	0	0	0	0	0	0	0	0	0	0
North Versailles Township	12,193	26	0	0	11	15	175	15	151	9	1
North Wales	3,244	2	0	0	0	2	25	0	24	1	0
Northwest Lancaster County Regional	19,758	9	1	3	2	3	90	0	87	3	0
North Woodbury	2,654	0	0	0	0	0	18	1	16	1	0
Norwood	5,878	19	0	3	3	13	57	2	51	4	0
Oakdale	1,455	1	0	0	0	1	0	0	0	0	0
Oakland	559	0	0	0	0	0	8	2	6	0	0
Oakmont	6,449	10	0	2	0	8	78	5	69	4	0
O'Hara Township	8,514	0	0	0	0	0	19	7	11	1	0
Ohio Township	6,665	1	0	0	0	1	97	0	96	1	0
Ohioville	3,422	5	0	0	1	4	27	3	19	5	0
Oil City	9,931	14	0	5	2	7	153	12	140	1	0

Table 8. Offenses Known to Law Enforcement, by Selected State and City, 2017—Continued

(Number.)

State/city	Population	Violent crime	Murder and nonnegligent manslaughter	Rape (revised definition)[1]	Robbery	Aggravated assault	Property crime	Burglary	Larceny-theft	Motor vehicle theft	Arson[2]
Old Forge	7,949	10	0	1	3	6	78	14	59	5	0
Old Lycoming Township	5,014	5	0	0	2	3	160	16	140	4	1
Oley Township	3,760	2	0	0	0	2	17	7	10	0	0
Olyphant	5,075	1	0	0	1	0	17	2	15	0	0
Orwigsburg	2,979	3	0	0	0	3	29	1	27	1	0
Osceola Township	643	0	0	0	0	0	0	0	0	0	0
Otto Eldred Regional	2,286	1	0	0	1	0	2	0	2	0	0
Overfield Township	2,785	0	0	0	0	0	0	0	0	0	0
Oxford	5,447	25	0	1	3	21	75	7	62	6	0
Palmerton	5,253	5	0	0	0	5	136	14	114	8	0
Palmer Township	21,598	14	0	2	1	11	342	18	313	11	0
Palmyra	7,541	21	0	1	2	18	102	19	74	9	0
Parker	817	0	0	0	0	0	0	0	0	0	0
Parkesburg	3,772	9	0	0	3	6	32	7	19	6	1
Parkside	2,328	9	0	0	0	9	46	5	35	6	0
Parks Township	2,603	1	0	0	0	1	2	2	0	0	0
Patterson Township	2,930	3	0	0	3	0	51	9	39	3	0
Patton	1,641	4	0	0	1	3	4	1	3	0	1
Patton Township	16,100	4	0	3	1	0	154	11	140	3	0
Penbrook	2,955	17	0	2	7	8	59	8	48	3	1
Penn	468	2	0	0	0	2	0	0	0	0	0
Penndel	2,179	4	0	0	1	3	16	3	11	2	0
Penn Hills	41,425	181	5	6	51	119	759	161	540	58	10
Pennridge Regional	10,979	11	0	1	0	10	82	6	72	4	0
Penn Township, Butler County	4,910	2	0	1	0	1	44	7	34	3	0
Penn Township, Westmoreland County	19,510	18	0	0	2	16	30	8	21	1	0
Penn Township, York County	16,394	20	0	0	4	16	147	29	114	4	0
Pequea Township	4,827	13	0	1	1	11	37	8	27	2	0
Perkasie	8,474	10	0	0	1	9	121	11	104	6	0
Perryopolis	1,709	2	0	0	0	2	8	1	7	0	0
Peters Township	22,297	4	0	0	0	4	137	26	111	0	0
Philadelphia	1,575,595	14,930	316	1,182	6,026	7,406	48,268	6,590	36,195	5,483	413
Phoenixville	16,955	29	2	0	2	25	193	7	180	6	1
Pine Creek Township	3,273	1	0	0	0	1	4	1	3	0	0
Pine Grove	2,095	0	0	0	0	0	0	0	0	0	0
Pitcairn	3,202	34	1	0	3	30	94	21	71	2	0
Pittsburgh	305,932	2,008	55	90	802	1,061	9,528	1,610	7,238	680	136
Pittston	7,581	13	1	0	3	9	147	11	130	6	1
Pittston Township	3,387	9	0	0	3	6	89	8	80	1	0
Plains Township	9,690	20	0	3	3	14	178	21	151	6	0
Pleasant Hills	8,175	0	0	0	0	0	99	6	91	2	0
Plum	27,440	71	1	2	5	63	114	30	76	8	1
Plumstead Township	13,906	13	0	1	0	12	87	12	70	5	1
Plymouth	5,766	78	1	1	16	60	117	30	79	8	2
Plymouth Township, Montgomery County	17,835	35	1	4	18	12	479	23	438	18	4
Pocono Mountain Regional	42,213	93	3	27	9	54	763	169	575	19	4
Pocono Township	10,706	25	0	0	5	20	249	27	215	7	0
Point Township	3,670	4	0	0	0	4	30	6	23	1	0
Polk	782	0	0	0	0	0	0	0	0	0	0
Portage	2,451	3	0	0	0	3	28	1	27	0	1
Port Allegany	2,037	1	0	0	0	1	8	1	7	0	0
Port Carbon	1,794	0	0	0	0	0	1	0	1	0	0
Portersville	234	0	0	0	0	0	0	0	0	0	0
Portland	509	1	0	0	0	1	13	1	11	1	0
Port Vue	3,693	5	0	0	1	4	28	12	15	1	0
Pottstown	22,706	165	1	21	59	84	817	110	661	46	5
Pottsville	13,645	63	0	12	6	45	259	38	215	6	1
Pringle	956	1	0	0	1	0	36	6	28	2	0
Prospect	1,118	0	0	0	0	0	0	0	0	0	0
Prospect Park	6,475	14	0	0	3	11	70	5	63	2	0
Pulaski Township, Lawrence County	3,291	4	0	0	0	4	23	6	13	4	2
Punxsutawney	5,790	8	4	1	1	2	52	3	49	0	1
Pymatuning Township	3,120	25	0	1	1	23	48	13	34	1	0
Quakertown	8,768	37	0	1	0	36	174	15	154	5	2
Quarryville	2,771	18	0	0	0	18	40	2	38	0	0
Raccoon Township	2,967	2	0	1	1	0	16	4	12	0	0
Radnor Township	31,859	25	0	1	4	20	294	21	255	18	0
Ralpho Township	4,279	2	0	1	1	0	9	1	8	0	0
Rankin	2,060	5	0	0	1	4	30	9	19	2	1
Reading	87,487	624	9	60	219	336	2,106	631	1,278	197	11
Reading Township	5,840	3	0	1	0	2	12	0	12	0	0
Redstone Township	4,284	1	0	0	0	1	11	1	9	1	1
Reilly Township	692	1	0	0	0	1	3	0	3	0	0
Renovo	1,216	4	0	0	0	4	27	7	20	0	0
Resa Regional	2,495	2	0	0	0	2	17	5	11	1	0
Reserve Township	3,260	2	0	0	1	1	41	7	33	1	0
Reynoldsville	2,676	1	0	0	0	1	8	3	5	0	1
Rice Township	3,545	3	0	1	0	2	11	2	9	0	0
Richland Township, Bucks County	13,225	15	1	8	4	2	211	10	194	7	0

Table 8. Offenses Known to Law Enforcement, by Selected State and City, 2017—Continued

(Number.)

State/city	Population	Violent crime	Murder and nonnegligent manslaughter	Rape (revised definition)[1]	Robbery	Aggravated assault	Property crime	Burglary	Larceny-theft	Motor vehicle theft	Arson[2]
Richland Township, Cambria County	12,153	12	1	3	3	5	515	28	485	2	1
Ridgway	3,799	14	0	0	1	13	99	12	84	3	0
Ridley Park	7,026	7	0	0	2	5	65	5	55	5	0
Ridley Township	31,082	31	0	1	11	19	344	23	305	16	0
Ringtown	787	0	0	0	0	0	0	0	0	0	0
Riverside	1,894	0	0	0	0	0	6	0	6	0	0
Roaring Brook Township	1,957	0	0	0	0	0	8	1	7	0	0
Roaring Creek Township	536	0	0	0	0	0	0	0	0	0	0
Roaring Spring	2,502	0	0	0	0	0	16	1	15	0	0
Robeson Township	7,379	5	0	0	0	5	51	15	32	4	2
Robinson Township, Allegheny County	13,777	21	0	4	6	11	302	11	288	3	0
Robinson Township, Washington County	1,891	2	0	0	0	2	17	4	12	1	0
Rochester	3,514	14	0	5	1	8	163	29	131	3	1
Rochester Township	2,699	2	0	0	0	2	27	4	22	1	0
Rockledge	2,535	2	0	0	0	2	28	5	22	1	0
Rockwood	839	0	0	0	0	0	0	0	0	0	0
Roseto	1,545	0	0	0	0	0	13	2	10	1	0
Rosslyn Farms	424	0	0	0	0	0	0	0	0	0	0
Ross Township	30,684	27	0	3	10	14	606	24	566	16	0
Rostraver Township	11,046	13	0	0	3	10	271	12	253	6	0
Royalton	1,039	0	0	0	0	0	3	1	2	0	0
Royersford	4,761	20	0	8	0	12	84	4	78	2	0
Rural Valley	836	1	0	0	0	1	1	0	1	0	0
Rush Township	3,305	12	0	2	0	10	101	10	90	1	0
Ryan Township	2,528	0	0	0	0	0	4	1	3	0	0
Sadsbury Township, Chester County	3,934	5	0	0	0	5	17	2	14	1	0
Salem Township, Luzerne County	4,178	2	0	0	0	2	34	5	29	0	0
Salisbury Township	13,807	8	0	0	2	6	211	39	163	9	0
Saltsburg	815	0	0	0	0	0	6	1	5	0	0
Sandy Lake	642	0	0	0	0	0	1	1	0	0	0
Sandy Township	10,661	20	0	2	0	18	163	34	122	7	0
Sankertown	636	0	0	0	0	0	0	0	0	0	0
Saxonburg	1,473	0	0	0	0	0	0	0	0	0	0
Sayre	6,335	23	0	2	0	21	91	9	82	0	0
Schuylkill Haven	5,166	7	1	0	0	6	65	2	61	2	0
Schuylkill Township, Chester County	8,580	5	0	0	0	5	74	8	65	1	0
Scottdale	4,184	15	0	0	1	14	81	7	72	2	0
Scott Township, Allegheny County	16,684	32	0	5	5	22	218	37	179	2	0
Scott Township, Columbia County	5,035	2	0	1	0	1	90	14	74	2	0
Scott Township, Lackawanna County	4,789	0	0	0	0	0	0	0	0	0	0
Scranton	77,499	198	1	22	90	85	1,698	351	1,215	132	13
Selinsgrove	5,930	42	0	4	2	36	123	27	95	1	0
Seward	468	0	0	0	0	0	0	0	0	0	0
Sewickley	4,370	3	0	0	1	2	53	5	47	1	0
Sewickley Heights	811	0	0	0	0	0	3	3	0	0	0
Shade Township	2,611	0	0	0	0	0	1	0	1	0	0
Shaler Township	28,207	19	0	0	3	16	218	30	183	5	0
Shamokin	7,056	16	0	1	2	13	132	20	105	7	0
Shamokin Dam	1,726	2	0	0	0	2	18	0	16	2	0
Sharon	13,305	69	2	12	19	36	413	90	305	18	8
Sharon Hill	5,683	48	0	5	8	35	163	13	143	7	0
Sharpsburg	3,352	28	0	0	2	26	25	10	12	3	0
Sharpsville	4,187	3	0	0	0	3	76	8	66	2	0
Shenango Township, Lawrence County	7,251	4	0	0	1	3	81	20	59	2	0
Shenango Township, Mercer County	3,761	6	0	0	1	5	41	15	26	0	0
Shillington	5,241	7	0	0	2	5	59	4	49	6	0
Shinglehouse	1,074	4	0	0	0	4	0	0	0	0	0
Shippensburg	5,567	2	0	2	0	0	76	17	56	3	0
Shippingport	209	0	0	0	0	0	0	0	0	0	0
Shiremanstown	1,584	0	0	0	0	0	5	0	5	0	0
Shohola Township	2,308	0	0	0	0	0	11	3	6	2	0
Silver Lake Township	1,604	0	0	0	0	0	7	1	5	1	0
Silver Spring Township	17,558	1	0	1	0	0	92	10	82	0	0
Sinking Spring	4,100	2	0	1	0	1	50	7	41	2	0
Slate Belt Regional	12,398	32	0	3	3	26	144	15	124	5	1
Slatington	4,289	1	0	0	1	0	81	7	71	3	0
Slippery Rock	3,572	12	0	2	1	9	34	2	32	0	0
Smethport	1,552	3	0	0	0	3	0	0	0	0	0
Smithton Borough	375	0	0	0	0	0	4	1	3	0	0
Smith Township	4,391	21	0	0	1	20	10	7	2	1	1
Solebury Township	8,583	15	4	3	0	8	58	10	45	3	0
Somerset	5,945	9	1	1	2	5	80	7	70	3	1

Table 8. Offenses Known to Law Enforcement, by Selected State and City, 2017—Continued

(Number.)

State/city	Population	Violent crime	Murder and nonnegligent manslaughter	Rape (revised definition)[1]	Robbery	Aggravated assault	Property crime	Burglary	Larceny-theft	Motor vehicle theft	Arson[2]
Souderton	6,927	22	0	4	2	16	47	9	35	3	0
South Abington Township	8,995	7	0	0	1	6	78	9	63	6	0
South Annville Township	2,972	2	0	0	0	2	34	3	31	0	0
South Beaver Township	2,632	2	0	0	0	2	23	7	16	0	0
South Buffalo Township	2,583	0	0	0	0	0	10	2	7	1	0
South Centre Township	4,197	2	0	0	0	2	6	0	6	0	1
South Coatesville	1,447	11	1	1	0	9	34	8	19	7	0
South Connellsville Borough	1,905	3	0	0	0	3	0	0	0	0	0
Southern Regional Lancaster County	3,867	10	0	1	1	8	15	2	13	0	0
Southern Regional York County	11,488	19	0	6	2	11	155	28	122	5	1
South Fayette Township	15,772	4	0	1	3	0	63	6	56	1	0
South Fork	854	1	0	0	0	1	0	0	0	0	0
South Greensburg	2,020	4	0	0	1	3	33	1	32	0	0
South Heidelberg Township	7,359	2	0	0	0	2	84	7	73	4	0
South Heights	451	0	0	0	0	0	0	0	0	0	0
South Lebanon Township	9,903	5	0	0	0	5	79	6	73	0	0
South Londonderry Township	8,110	5	0	1	1	3	41	5	36	0	2
South Park Township	13,371	6	0	0	2	4	27	8	17	2	0
South Pymatuning Township	2,587	0	0	0	0	0	3	2	1	0	0
South Strabane Township	9,526	7	0	1	2	4	442	13	425	4	0
Southwestern Regional	17,764	18	1	8	2	7	74	9	58	7	1
Southwest Greensburg	2,052	13	0	0	0	13	29	5	23	1	0
South Whitehall Township	19,893	16	0	0	11	5	573	27	523	23	0
South Williamsport	6,206	11	0	0	0	11	138	5	131	2	0
Spring City	3,297	7	0	2	0	5	41	11	28	2	0
Springdale	3,334	12	0	0	0	12	52	12	37	3	0
Springdale Township	1,598	2	0	0	1	1	12	0	12	0	0
Springettsbury Township	26,895	30	0	7	12	11	860	46	788	26	1
Springfield Township, Bucks County	5,030	5	0	0	0	5	26	6	19	1	0
Springfield Township, Delaware County	24,363	14	0	0	6	8	588	29	554	5	1
Springfield Township, Montgomery County	19,728	19	0	0	6	13	234	17	199	18	1
Spring Garden Township	13,044	33	0	3	13	17	302	38	244	20	0
Spring Township, Berks County	27,446	10	0	0	7	3	328	31	289	8	2
Spring Township, Centre County	7,712	4	1	0	0	3	23	0	23	0	0
State College	58,169	44	0	7	9	28	616	45	566	5	4
St. Clair Boro	2,855	2	0	0	0	2	137	0	137	0	0
St. Clair Township	1,449	0	0	0	0	0	4	1	3	0	0
Steelton	5,897	59	2	0	15	42	186	25	146	15	2
St. Marys City	12,413	9	0	3	2	4	107	14	91	2	0
Stockertown	914	1	0	0	0	1	3	0	3	0	0
Stoneboro	993	0	0	0	0	0	5	1	4	0	0
Stowe Township	6,181	27	0	0	11	16	173	37	126	10	0
Strasburg	2,960	3	0	0	0	3	16	2	14	0	0
Stroud Area Regional	34,259	86	3	16	30	37	1,056	91	940	25	1
Sugarcreek	5,034	5	0	0	0	5	54	8	46	0	0
Sugarloaf Township, Luzerne County	4,029	5	0	0	2	3	38	8	29	1	0
Sugar Notch	963	1	0	0	0	1	11	2	9	0	0
Summerhill Township	2,321	2	0	1	1	0	23	5	18	0	0
Summit Township	2,165	0	0	0	0	0	0	0	0	0	0
Sunbury	9,520	59	0	2	3	54	169	26	137	6	5
Susquehanna	1,506	4	0	0	0	4	29	1	26	2	0
Susquehanna Regional	8,405	13	1	1	0	11	71	14	55	2	0
Susquehanna Township, Dauphin County	25,055	75	0	8	19	48	359	64	278	17	6
Swarthmore	6,246	8	0	0	0	8	49	6	42	1	0
Swatara Township	24,867	88	6	13	35	34	1,049	62	975	12	4
Sweden Township	840	0	0	0	0	0	0	0	0	0	0
Swissvale	8,734	32	5	0	11	16	150	34	103	13	0
Swoyersville	4,941	2	0	0	0	2	47	12	34	1	0
Sykesville	1,122	0	0	0	0	0	0	0	0	0	0
Tamaqua	6,748	23	1	0	3	19	156	17	128	11	0
Tarentum	4,401	10	0	1	3	6	69	15	50	4	0
Tatamy	1,131	2	0	0	0	2	15	4	11	0	0
Taylor	5,929	59	0	0	3	56	203	31	162	10	0
Telford	4,844	16	0	4	1	11	44	2	39	3	0
Terre Hill	1,414	0	0	0	0	0	3	0	3	0	0
Throop	3,902	12	0	0	1	11	41	8	31	2	0
Tiadaghton Valley Regional	7,666	12	0	0	2	10	82	7	74	1	1
Tidioute	652	0	0	0	0	0	0	0	0	0	0
Tilden Township	3,575	0	0	0	0	0	39	0	34	5	0
Tinicum Township, Bucks County	3,936	3	0	1	0	2	17	5	12	0	0
Tinicum Township, Delaware County	4,105	17	0	2	4	11	115	6	96	13	0
Tioga	657	0	0	0	0	0	1	0	1	0	0
Titusville	5,345	13	0	1	0	12	86	13	72	1	0

Table 8. Offenses Known to Law Enforcement, by Selected State and City, 2017—Continued

(Number.)

State/city	Population	Violent crime	Murder and nonnegligent manslaughter	Rape (revised definition)[1]	Robbery	Aggravated assault	Property crime	Burglary	Larceny-theft	Motor vehicle theft	Arson[2]
Towamencin Township	18,484	8	0	2	2	4	97	6	87	4	0
Towanda	2,839	5	0	1	0	4	61	4	53	4	1
Trainer	1,840	8	0	2	1	5	77	12	56	9	0
Tredyffrin Township	29,435	13	0	1	3	9	226	16	204	6	1
Troy	1,247	2	0	2	0	0	21	1	19	1	0
Tullytown	1,844	5	1	0	2	2	57	2	55	0	0
Tulpehocken Township	3,313	1	0	0	0	1	19	2	17	0	0
Tunkhannock	1,749	2	0	0	1	1	11	2	7	2	0
Tunkhannock Township, Wyoming County	6,212	4	0	0	1	3	51	12	38	1	0
Turtle Creek	5,200	9	0	0	1	8	10	1	9	0	1
Tyrone	5,273	19	0	3	3	13	93	10	82	1	0
Union City	3,167	3	0	2	1	0	55	6	49	0	0
Uniontown	9,875	28	3	0	14	11	255	47	202	6	0
Union Township, Lawrence County	4,937	3	0	0	0	3	94	3	90	1	0
Union Township, Schuylkill County	1,223	0	0	0	0	0	0	0	0	0	0
Upland	3,243	33	1	0	3	29	102	13	82	7	0
Upper Allen Township	20,119	0	0	0	0	0	164	30	132	2	1
Upper Burrell Township	2,244	2	0	2	0	0	12	2	10	0	0
Upper Chichester Township	17,033	30	0	1	15	14	352	35	301	16	1
Upper Darby Township	82,601	388	1	9	177	201	1,297	152	997	148	4
Upper Dublin Township	26,329	18	0	1	5	12	237	13	217	7	3
Upper Gwynedd Township	16,042	11	0	0	3	8	124	17	103	4	0
Upper Leacock Township	8,904	5	0	0	2	3	82	21	54	7	0
Upper Macungie Township	24,535	4	0	1	2	1	255	22	224	9	0
Upper Makefield Township	8,425	3	1	0	0	2	59	12	47	0	0
Upper Merion Township	28,677	18	0	3	12	3	1,074	29	1,025	20	2
Upper Moreland Township	24,238	21	0	4	10	7	381	36	332	13	1
Upper Nazareth Township	6,891	11	0	0	1	10	18	1	17	0	0
Upper Perkiomen	3,870	6	0	4	1	1	50	10	39	1	1
Upper Pottsgrove Township	5,605	12	0	1	0	11	51	18	33	0	0
Upper Providence Township, Delaware County	10,497	1	0	0	0	1	29	6	23	0	0
Upper Providence Township, Montgomery County	24,315	10	0	2	1	7	283	9	272	2	0
Upper Saucon Township	16,746	7	1	0	1	5	93	13	69	11	0
Upper Southampton Township	15,022	8	0	2	4	2	118	14	98	6	1
Upper St. Clair Township	19,911	6	0	0	1	5	105	9	96	0	0
Upper Uwchlan Township	11,540	2	0	0	0	2	52	8	44	0	0
Upper Yoder Township	5,158	2	0	0	0	2	5	2	3	0	0
Uwchlan Township	19,128	20	0	5	6	9	98	15	83	0	2
Valley Township	7,800	9	0	1	0	8	97	14	80	3	0
Vandergrift	4,945	12	0	1	1	10	5	4	0	1	0
Vandling	713	2	0	0	0	2	3	0	3	0	0
Vernon Township	5,438	3	0	0	1	2	49	0	49	0	0
Verona	2,410	10	0	1	5	4	83	18	64	1	0
Versailles	1,477	10	1	0	0	9	19	5	14	0	0
Vintondale	381	0	0	0	0	0	0	0	0	0	0
Walker Township	1,013	0	0	0	0	0	2	0	2	0	0
Walnutport	2,084	0	0	0	0	0	0	0	0	0	0
Wampum	674	2	0	0	0	2	2	0	2	0	1
Warminster Township	32,423	48	0	8	21	19	385	17	347	21	0
Warren	9,171	28	0	1	1	26	155	10	144	1	1
Warrington Township	24,360	15	0	5	4	6	240	13	218	9	1
Warwick Township, Bucks County	14,661	9	0	1	2	6	51	9	39	3	0
Washington, Washington County	13,435	63	1	7	18	37	419	81	310	28	3
Washington Township, Fayette County	3,714	13	0	0	0	13	32	2	30	0	0
Washington Township, Franklin County	14,678	3	0	2	1	0	320	36	281	3	3
Washington Township, Northampton County	5,232	3	0	1	0	2	33	6	25	2	0
Washington Township, Westmoreland County	7,170	5	0	0	0	5	36	4	32	0	0
Watsontown	2,293	3	0	2	1	0	26	7	18	1	1
Waverly Township	1,699	0	0	0	0	0	9	6	3	0	0
Waymart	1,251	1	0	0	0	1	10	0	9	1	0
Waynesboro	10,889	15	0	2	5	8	236	37	193	6	3
Waynesburg	3,965	16	0	5	2	9	83	19	61	3	0
Wayne Township, Lawrence County	2,495	0	0	0	0	0	4	0	4	0	0
Weatherly	2,431	23	0	2	0	21	87	35	52	0	0
Weissport	385	0	0	0	0	0	0	0	0	0	0
Wellsboro	3,277	3	0	0	0	3	27	3	24	0	0
Wesleyville	3,170	3	0	0	0	3	103	15	86	2	0
West Brandywine Township	7,451	27	3	4	0	20	55	20	29	6	1
West Brownsville	960	2	0	0	2	0	68	2	66	0	0
West Caln Township	9,067	24	0	0	2	22	64	18	41	5	0
West Carroll Township	1,222	5	0	1	0	4	2	0	2	0	1

Table 8. Offenses Known to Law Enforcement, by Selected State and City, 2017—Continued

(Number.)

State/city	Population	Violent crime	Murder and nonnegligent manslaughter	Rape (revised definition)[1]	Robbery	Aggravated assault	Property crime	Burglary	Larceny-theft	Motor vehicle theft	Arson[2]
West Chester	20,183	50	0	11	18	21	304	36	260	8	0
West Cocalico Township	7,431	7	0	1	0	6	30	6	22	2	1
West Conshohocken	1,402	2	0	0	0	2	22	3	16	3	0
West Cornwall Township	2,017	2	0	0	0	2	1	0	1	0	0
West Deer Township	11,921	6	0	0	1	5	77	16	58	3	0
West Earl Township	8,368	10	0	7	1	2	54	18	31	5	1
Western Berks Regional	4,591	7	0	0	2	5	24	10	11	3	0
West Fallowfield Township	2,591	2	0	0	0	2	16	2	10	4	0
Westfield	1,039	1	0	0	0	1	4	0	4	0	1
West Goshen Township	23,237	26	2	3	2	19	249	17	226	6	0
West Hazleton	4,452	29	0	1	7	21	97	19	74	4	0
West Hempfield Township	16,540	12	1	0	2	9	166	16	147	3	0
West Hills Regional	10,167	6	1	0	2	3	99	9	90	0	0
West Homestead	1,902	2	0	0	2	0	19	0	19	0	0
West Kittanning	1,114	1	0	1	0	0	5	0	5	0	0
West Lampeter Township	16,080	10	0	2	1	7	87	9	75	3	0
West Lebanon Township	814	1	0	0	0	1	59	0	58	1	0
West Leechburg	1,251	2	0	0	0	2	4	2	2	0	0
West Mahanoy Township	2,749	2	0	0	0	2	5	0	3	2	0
West Manchester Township	18,865	41	2	6	10	23	539	32	498	9	1
West Manheim Township	8,438	2	0	0	0	2	79	4	73	2	0
West Mead Township	5,125	4	0	0	1	3	51	4	46	1	0
West Mifflin	19,856	24	0	2	8	14	115	9	106	0	1
West Newton	2,501	11	0	1	1	9	28	7	20	1	0
West Norriton Township	15,780	22	0	3	5	14	273	22	246	5	0
West Nottingham Township	2,679	0	0	0	0	0	0	0	0	0	0
West Penn Township	4,331	1	0	0	0	1	11	4	7	0	0
West Pikeland Township	4,092	2	0	0	0	2	15	3	11	1	0
West Pike Run	1,547	0	0	0	0	0	1	0	0	1	0
West Pittston	4,720	10	0	0	2	8	60	7	52	1	0
West Pottsgrove Township	3,883	9	0	1	4	4	122	23	95	4	0
West Reading	4,169	28	0	0	2	26	177	11	160	6	0
West Sadsbury Township	2,469	4	0	1	1	2	85	5	79	1	0
West Salem Township	3,447	12	0	2	2	8	50	17	29	4	0
West Shore Regional	7,736	5	0	0	4	1	60	8	46	6	0
Westtown-East Goshen Regional	32,299	34	0	3	7	24	242	15	220	7	0
West View	6,598	11	0	0	2	9	113	0	110	3	1
West Vincent Township	5,172	1	0	1	0	0	21	4	17	0	0
West Whiteland Township	18,430	17	0	5	8	4	438	9	426	3	5
West Wyoming	2,667	6	0	0	1	5	36	8	27	1	0
West York	4,550	18	1	2	4	11	104	25	63	16	2
Whitaker Borough	1,236	2	0	0	1	1	21	5	16	0	0
Whitehall	13,717	4	0	0	0	4	39	6	30	3	1
Whitehall Township	27,536	40	1	0	20	19	1,015	64	930	21	0
White Haven Borough	1,090	1	0	0	0	1	10	2	7	1	0
Whitemarsh Township	17,866	10	0	2	1	7	145	4	132	9	0
White Oak	7,682	3	0	0	2	1	76	9	61	6	0
Whitpain Township	19,377	32	1	1	5	25	256	35	215	6	2
Wiconisco Township	1,184	1	0	1	0	0	0	0	0	0	0
Wilkes-Barre	40,418	251	2	12	104	133	1,101	225	816	60	8
Wilkes-Barre Township	2,891	13	0	0	4	9	524	16	506	2	0
Wilkinsburg	15,530	115	0	7	53	55	512	134	316	62	7
Wilkins Township	6,222	9	2	2	4	1	92	18	69	5	2
Williamsburg	1,202	0	0	0	0	0	8	1	7	0	0
Williamsport	28,743	107	2	12	27	66	880	119	741	20	8
Willistown Township	10,965	0	0	0	0	0	45	4	38	3	1
Wilson	7,768	72	0	1	12	59	247	29	207	11	0
Windber	3,901	31	0	0	1	30	21	3	16	2	1
Womelsdorf	2,854	2	0	2	0	0	12	1	10	1	0
Woodward Township	2,389	0	0	0	0	0	0	0	0	0	0
Worthington	602	0	0	0	0	0	0	0	0	0	0
Wrightsville	2,280	0	0	0	0	0	39	2	37	0	0
Wright Township	5,636	2	0	0	0	2	46	5	37	4	0
Wyoming	3,001	17	0	0	3	14	56	7	48	1	0
Wyomissing	10,415	12	0	0	8	4	314	27	285	2	0
Yardley	2,455	2	0	0	0	2	22	2	20	0	0
Yeadon	11,499	84	0	3	22	59	362	69	257	36	1
York	43,857	472	14	10	191	257	1,288	251	885	152	6
York Area Regional	55,256	87	0	15	20	52	439	73	350	16	2
Youngsville	1,638	13	0	0	0	13	4	1	3	0	0
Zelienople	3,670	0	0	0	0	0	35	3	32	0	0
Zerbe Township	1,805	1	0	0	0	1	4	0	4	0	0
RHODE ISLAND											
Barrington	16,307	10	0	6	0	4	127	26	101	0	2
Bristol	22,255	15	1	2	1	11	97	8	83	6	0
Burrillville	16,441	16	0	4	1	11	93	18	73	2	4
Central Falls	19,389	97	0	12	13	72	391	58	271	62	8
Charlestown	7,764	9	0	4	3	2	62	18	40	4	1
Coventry	35,083	35	0	14	3	18	509	84	405	20	4
Cranston	81,337	111	2	26	22	61	1,248	214	943	91	10
Cumberland	34,973	15	0	5	0	10	269	43	205	21	3

Table 8. Offenses Known to Law Enforcement, by Selected State and City, 2017—Continued

(Number.)

State/city	Population	Violent crime	Murder and nonnegligent manslaughter	Rape (revised definition)[1]	Robbery	Aggravated assault	Property crime	Burglary	Larceny-theft	Motor vehicle theft	Arson[2]
East Greenwich	13,139	6	0	1	0	5	136	21	113	2	1
East Providence	47,502	69	1	14	9	45	578	67	465	46	8
Foster	4,736	7	0	0	1	6	32	13	18	1	0
Glocester	10,108	3	0	0	0	3	33	6	20	7	0
Hopkinton	8,104	4	0	2	0	2	101	42	52	7	0
Jamestown	5,483	8	0	1	0	7	25	5	19	1	0
Johnston	29,375	45	0	7	6	32	361	73	252	36	1
Lincoln	21,863	28	1	3	4	20	406	44	337	25	2
Little Compton	3,498	0	0	0	0	0	35	6	29	0	0
Middletown	15,993	16	0	6	0	10	178	22	142	14	1
Narragansett	15,556	10	0	2	2	6	108	20	84	4	0
Newport	24,812	60	0	20	7	33	785	90	668	27	9
New Shoreham	1,044	0	0	0	0	0	18	4	13	1	0
North Kingstown	26,069	18	0	7	1	10	273	37	228	8	1
North Providence	32,641	43	0	12	6	25	299	68	198	33	1
North Smithfield	12,447	8	0	6	0	2	204	16	177	11	0
Pawtucket	71,648	311	1	45	45	220	1,788	373	1,224	191	16
Portsmouth	17,381	11	0	4	0	7	102	17	79	6	0
Providence	179,854	960	12	104	255	589	5,925	1,013	4,332	580	16
Richmond	7,598	3	0	2	0	1	50	11	39	0	0
Scituate	10,631	5	0	1	0	4	43	13	27	3	1
Smithfield	21,884	10	0	4	2	4	238	23	210	5	2
South Kingstown	30,823	14	0	4	2	8	197	46	146	5	2
Tiverton	15,767	21	0	4	4	13	189	35	137	17	1
Warren	10,498	15	0	4	1	10	137	29	101	7	4
Warwick	81,617	97	1	27	12	57	1,383	173	1,149	61	9
Westerly	22,629	17	0	2	7	8	384	79	292	13	2
West Greenwich	6,167	2	0	0	0	2	64	16	46	2	1
West Warwick	28,790	66	0	17	9	40	319	94	197	28	6
Woonsocket	41,543	221	0	39	55	127	947	262	607	78	12
SOUTH CAROLINA											
Abbeville[5]	5,153	33	0	6	2	25			125	7	1
Aiken[8]	31,158	165	4	28	23	110				84	13
Allendale	2,983	37	1	1	3	32	119	60	54	5	3
Anderson	27,728	181	2	14	20	145	1,666	229	1,310	127	5
Andrews	2,903	22	0	1	7	14	120	32	83	5	0
Aynor	803	2	0	1	0	1	24	10	13	1	0
Bamberg	3,300	21	0	1	3	17	117	27	82	8	3
Barnwell	4,508	29	0	2	6	21	207	59	142	6	1
Batesburg-Leesville	5,462	43	0	4	3	36	266	46	203	17	0
Beaufort	13,612	92	1	3	21	67	667	98	536	33	5
Belton	4,426	17	0	2	4	11	242	29	188	25	0
Bennettsville	8,127	67	1	4	6	56	323	55	259	9	1
Bishopville	3,201	28	0	4	6	18	154	33	109	12	3
Blacksburg	1,894	22	0	5	4	13	127	22	93	12	0
Blackville	2,242	19	0	3	5	11	124	55	63	6	1
Bluffton	20,024	41	0	6	5	30	330	33	275	22	1
Branchville	968	4	1	0	0	3	27	4	21	2	0
Burnettown	2,819	2	0	1	0	1	47	8	36	3	0
Camden	7,173	112	0	1	17	94	515	71	424	20	0
Cameron	415	2	0	0	0	2	9	2	3	4	0
Cayce	14,434	114	1	9	17	87	739	72	573	94	1
Central	5,238	6	0	3	0	3	181	12	163	6	0
Chapin	1,599	2	0	0	1	1	36	2	33	1	0
Charleston	136,845	388	6	50	100	232	3,144	399	2,442	303	12
Cheraw	5,770	70	0	3	7	60	416	60	336	20	0
Chesnee	922	2	0	0	1	1	47	5	37	5	0
Chester	5,452	43	1	1	6	35	234	39	186	9	3
Clemson	16,442	8	0	2	4	2	315	25	254	36	0
Clinton	8,473	88	0	11	9	68	319	83	224	12	0
Clover	6,098	25	0	2	2	21	176	31	135	10	0
Columbia	134,957	991	10	66	273	642	7,134	954	5,389	791	17
Conway	23,806	142	2	21	18	101	936	100	769	67	1
Coward	760	0	0	0	0	0	13	1	11	1	0
Cowpens	2,326	5	0	1	0	4	51	14	31	6	0
Darlington	6,090	66	2	3	7	54	501	66	414	21	2
Denmark	2,942	11	1	0	2	8	85	30	50	5	0
Dillon	6,568	155	2	3	14	136	632	153	458	21	3
Due West	1,300	1	0	0	0	1	21	6	13	2	0
Duncan	3,405	5	0	1	1	3	65	9	53	3	0
Easley	21,107	125	0	8	15	102	1,308	127	1,117	64	3
Edgefield	4,752	4	0	0	0	4	49	11	34	4	0
Edisto Beach	419	1	0	0	0	1	20	0	17	3	0
Elgin	1,582	9	0	0	4	5	100	10	88	2	1
Elloree	666	3	1	1	1	0	10	1	9	0	0
Estill	1,915	60	3	1	11	45	88	29	56	3	2
Eutawville	300	1	0	0	0	1	5	1	4	0	0
Florence	38,449	487	5	27	61	394	2,728	353	2,242	133	10
Forest Acres	10,563	59	0	4	13	42	635	100	500	35	0
Fort Lawn	859	4	0	0	0	4	16	2	12	2	0
Fort Mill	15,737	42	0	6	12	24	290	35	246	9	4
Fountain Inn	8,666	30	0	4	3	23	206	35	148	23	1

Table 8. Offenses Known to Law Enforcement, by Selected State and City, 2017—Continued

(Number.)

State/city	Population	Violent crime	Murder and nonnegligent manslaughter	Rape (revised definition)[1]	Robbery	Aggravated assault	Property crime	Burglary	Larceny-theft	Motor vehicle theft	Arson[2]
Gaffney	12,982	93	3	7	14	69	450	69	356	25	1
Gaston	1,660	1	0	0	1	0	38	2	27	9	0
Georgetown	9,003	128	1	10	8	109	524	65	435	24	0
Gifford	269	0	0	0	0	0	0	0	0	0	0
Goose Creek	43,006	162	3	26	24	109	986	152	777	57	1
Great Falls	1,920	4	0	1	0	3	77	6	63	8	1
Greeleyville	400	0	0	0	0	0	7	4	3	0	0
Greenville	68,922	415	4	28	91	292	2,831	393	2,281	157	6
Greenwood	23,329	316	3	25	43	245	1,702	274	1,380	48	6
Greer	29,585	123	0	9	25	89	1,058	147	811	100	5
Hampton	2,613	34	0	1	6	27	161	34	110	17	1
Hanahan	24,487	74	0	12	16	46	396	80	274	42	1
Hardeeville	6,328	37	2	1	14	20	198	20	164	14	1
Harleyville	693	2	0	0	0	2	13	2	10	1	0
Hartsville	7,769	134	1	5	16	112	865	127	711	27	3
Hemingway	421	1	0	0	1	0	46	16	27	3	0
Holly Hill	1,211	11	0	0	4	7	62	13	45	4	1
Honea Path	3,779	17	0	6	2	9	242	50	172	20	3
Irmo	12,353	55	0	6	6	43	447	103	329	15	1
Isle of Palms	4,439	0	0	0	0	0	69	18	44	7	0
Iva	1,296	6	0	0	0	6	53	13	35	5	0
Jackson	1,794	1	0	0	0	1	29	7	21	1	0
Johnsonville	1,508	2	0	0	0	2	23	7	16	0	0
Johnston	2,342	7	0	3	0	4	30	11	14	5	0
Jonesville	852	1	0	0	1	0	9	3	6	0	1
Kingstree	3,204	25	0	2	11	12	223	55	157	11	1
Lake City	6,774	109	0	7	15	87	437	108	302	27	0
Landrum	2,558	10	0	1	1	8	63	16	43	4	0
Lane	464	0	0	0	0	0	1	0	1	0	0
Latta	1,326	26	0	1	8	17	87	10	71	6	2
Laurens	9,089	109	0	3	6	100	451	74	357	20	3
Lexington	21,434	66	0	3	7	56	643	39	570	34	2
Liberty	3,250	17	1	1	0	15	191	61	119	11	0
Loris	2,695	24	0	6	3	15	123	15	99	9	0
Lyman	3,513	21	0	0	2	19	95	22	66	7	0
Manning	4,031	39	0	3	4	32	371	61	293	17	0
Marion	6,677	47	2	5	22	18	604	145	422	37	2
Mauldin	25,535	65	1	5	12	47	409	45	332	32	0
McColl	2,019	23	0	2	3	18	70	31	39	0	1
McCormick	2,493	6	0	0	1	5	66	20	45	1	1
Moncks Corner	10,818	48	0	5	4	39	546	59	455	32	2
Mount Pleasant	87,216	165	2	20	24	119	1,332	169	1,076	87	2
Mullins	4,502	62	1	4	12	45	237	77	138	22	6
Myrtle Beach	33,167	523	5	60	146	312	4,331	378	3,608	345	8
Newberry	10,373	68	2	12	8	46	435	57	371	7	0
New Ellenton	2,160	12	0	1	3	8	26	10	15	1	0
Ninety Six	2,060	7	0	0	0	7	46	12	31	3	0
North	726	7	0	0	2	5	61	9	49	3	0
North Augusta	23,198	59	0	18	22	19	950	97	816	37	0
North Charleston	111,305	1,026	35	74	305	612	6,291	919	4,687	685	18
North Myrtle Beach	16,422	72	0	22	13	37	1,278	197	976	105	3
Orangeburg	13,076	124	1	8	26	89	871	152	670	49	2
Pacolet	2,411	2	0	0	0	2	47	9	33	5	0
Pageland	2,704	52	0	3	4	45	160	56	95	9	0
Pendleton	3,213	9	0	1	1	7	50	5	42	3	0
Pickens	3,201	27	0	4	1	22	209	23	176	10	0
Port Royal	13,161	48	0	5	7	36	303	45	236	22	0
Prosperity	1,209	3	1	0	0	2	27	3	23	1	0
Quinby	945	0	0	0	0	0	0	0	0	0	0
Ridgeland	4,158	3	0	0	1	2	113	15	91	7	0
Ridge Spring	754	0	0	0	0	0	4	1	2	1	0
Rock Hill	74,053	469	9	51	95	314	3,007	365	2,506	136	4
Salem	149	0	0	0	0	0	0	0	0	0	0
Salley	424	0	0	0	0	0	2	1	1	0	0
Saluda	3,626	16	1	1	4	10	59	10	45	4	0
Santee	917	9	0	0	1	8	86	10	70	6	0
Scranton	861	0	0	0	0	0	7	1	6	0	1
Seneca	8,389	34	1	6	2	25	194	33	148	13	1
Simpsonville	21,829	68	0	14	12	42	761	87	616	58	0
Society Hill	539	1	0	0	1	0	6	2	4	0	0
South Congaree	2,427	5	0	0	3	2	59	4	48	7	0
Springdale	2,817	19	0	3	5	11	109	11	83	15	0
St. George	2,181	12	0	1	3	8	122	25	90	7	0
St. Matthews	1,994	12	0	0	0	12	63	20	40	3	1
St. Stephen	1,824	3	0	0	0	3	71	19	47	5	0
Sullivans Island	1,961	1	0	0	0	1	49	12	33	4	0
Summerton	961	4	0	0	1	3	69	19	47	3	0
Summerville	50,498	147	4	22	31	90	1,745	173	1,457	115	5
Sumter	40,747	333	5	13	63	252	1,839	354	1,411	74	5
Surfside Beach	4,488	10	0	1	3	6	232	64	145	23	3
Swansea	916	7	0	2	1	4	40	2	32	6	0
Tega Cay	10,367	5	0	1	1	3	219	8	210	1	2
Travelers Rest	5,130	8	0	0	2	6	250	4	232	14	0

Table 8. Offenses Known to Law Enforcement, by Selected State and City, 2017—Continued

(Number.)

State/city	Population	Violent crime	Murder and nonnegligent manslaughter	Rape (revised definition)[1]	Robbery	Aggravated assault	Property crime	Burglary	Larceny-theft	Motor vehicle theft	Arson[2]
Turbeville	798	9	0	1	1	7	39	16	20	3	0
Union	7,940	83	0	7	16	60	488	106	374	8	2
Walhalla	4,332	7	0	1	0	6	78	26	43	9	1
Walterboro	5,275	54	0	0	5	49	400	39	350	11	0
Ware Shoals	2,184	24	0	2	0	22	117	20	92	5	0
Wellford	2,588	10	0	0	1	9	26	7	17	2	1
West Columbia	16,426	177	0	30	40	107	1,112	143	817	152	2
Westminster	2,514	10	0	0	1	9	65	11	49	5	1
West Pelzer	934	5	0	0	0	5	17	1	15	1	0
Whitmire	1,480	3	0	0	2	1	56	14	41	1	0
Williamston	4,229	26	0	2	0	24	126	17	102	7	0
Williston	2,975	8	0	1	0	7	98	25	67	6	0
Winnsboro	3,276	27	0	3	2	22	112	19	88	5	1
Woodruff	4,209	20	0	1	3	16	92	13	68	11	1
Yemassee	964	12	0	1	1	10	43	10	31	2	0
York	8,108	71	0	7	9	55	387	47	318	22	3
SOUTH DAKOTA											
Aberdeen	28,800	99	0	16	8	75	681	117	524	40	0
Belle Fourche	5,662	9	0	2	1	6	94	18	73	3	0
Box Elder	9,623	32	0	10	1	21	194	39	135	20	0
Brandon	10,090	0	0	0	0	0	26	2	24	0	0
Brookings	24,198	36	0	8	0	28	315	40	248	27	1
Canton	3,437	6	0	1	0	5	33	9	17	7	0
Chamberlain	2,364	10	0	1	0	9	54	7	47	0	0
Deadwood	1,262	5	0	1	1	3	4	0	4	0	0
Flandreau	2,331	19	0	4	1	14	57	7	47	3	0
Hot Springs	3,540	2	0	0	0	2	84	12	66	6	0
Huron	13,204	49	0	11	1	37	211	26	171	14	0
Lead	2,990	2	0	0	0	2	17	3	11	3	0
Lennox	2,364	3	0	0	0	3	4	1	3	0	0
Madison	7,584	11	0	3	0	8	87	18	68	1	0
Martin	1,071	28	0	2	4	22	94	23	68	3	0
Mitchell	15,806	88	2	21	6	59	570	86	447	37	1
Mobridge	3,587	14	0	3	0	11	49	2	42	5	0
North Sioux City	2,766	1	0	1	0	0	45	4	37	4	0
Pierre	14,064	55	0	14	1	40	521	65	433	23	0
Rapid City	74,986	480	6	101	68	305	2,872	466	2,102	304	8
Sioux Falls	177,888	801	4	121	100	576	5,083	655	3,959	469	47
Sisseton	2,426	8	0	1	0	7	16	3	12	1	1
Spearfish	11,697	41	0	16	4	21	379	76	294	9	0
Sturgis	6,868	18	0	1	2	15	193	34	149	10	0
Summerset	2,499	1	0	0	0	1	49	8	41	0	0
Tea	5,261	9	0	2	0	7	72	13	54	5	0
Vermillion	10,892	43	0	12	2	29	233	24	197	12	0
Wagner	1,589	6	0	4	0	2	16	1	14	1	0
Watertown	22,283	81	1	20	4	56	444	86	342	16	0
Whitewood	931	1	0	0	0	1	5	1	4	0	0
Winner	2,850	8	0	0	0	8	29	5	23	1	0
Yankton	14,579	57	0	10	0	47	364	40	314	10	2
TENNESSEE											
Adamsville	2,207	19	0	2	0	17	64	7	52	5	0
Alamo	2,452	5	0	1	0	4	28	6	20	2	0
Alcoa	10,128	87	2	7	14	64	584	58	477	49	4
Alexandria	974	0	0	0	0	0	21	5	13	3	0
Algood	4,323	8	0	1	1	6	129	9	118	2	0
Ardmore	1,218	3	0	0	2	1	24	3	21	0	0
Ashland City	4,642	17	0	1	0	16	205	21	171	13	0
Athens	13,783	123	0	12	15	96	937	141	719	77	3
Atoka	9,197	14	0	0	0	14	104	19	82	3	0
Baileyton	434	0	0	0	0	0	25	5	18	2	0
Bartlett	58,895	233	0	18	15	200	1,177	162	958	57	3
Baxter	1,413	5	0	0	0	5	44	4	38	2	0
Bean Station	3,090	4	0	0	0	4	35	8	21	6	0
Belle Meade	2,975	0	0	0	0	0	30	4	24	2	0
Bells	2,423	13	0	0	1	12	34	3	28	3	1
Benton	1,307	1	0	0	0	1	26	4	21	1	0
Berry Hill	536	3	0	0	1	2	107	11	94	2	0
Big Sandy	533	6	0	0	0	6	28	8	19	1	0
Blaine	1,879	1	0	0	1	0	13	2	9	2	0
Bluff City	1,651	7	1	1	0	5	43	14	21	8	0
Bolivar	5,066	69	0	3	10	56	139	33	88	18	0
Bradford	989	2	0	0	0	2	15	5	10	0	0
Brentwood	43,468	31	0	10	5	16	409	56	336	17	2
Brighton	2,949	14	0	1	0	13	48	9	34	5	0
Bristol	27,176	110	2	14	8	86	915	137	704	74	3
Brownsville	9,698	121	2	10	10	99	422	90	309	23	1
Bruceton	1,427	2	0	0	0	2	20	4	15	1	0
Burns	1,475	2	1	1	0	0	5	0	5	0	0
Calhoun	498	0	0	0	0	0	2	0	2	0	0
Camden	3,546	9	0	0	1	8	125	9	110	6	0
Carthage	2,283	7	0	0	1	6	67	10	56	1	0

Table 8. Offenses Known to Law Enforcement, by Selected State and City, 2017—Continued

(Number.)

State/city	Population	Violent crime	Murder and nonnegligent manslaughter	Rape (revised definition)[1]	Robbery	Aggravated assault	Property crime	Burglary	Larceny-theft	Motor vehicle theft	Arson[2]
Caryville	2,161	4	0	0	1	3	63	8	40	15	0
Celina	1,487	0	0	0	0	0	32	4	26	2	0
Centerville	3,564	14	0	2	1	11	80	28	50	2	0
Chapel Hill	1,481	7	0	0	0	7	6	2	4	0	0
Charleston	678	0	0	0	0	0	3	1	2	0	0
Chattanooga	178,753	1,905	31	120	330	1,424	10,700	1,540	7,818	1,342	17
Church Hill	6,739	5	1	0	0	4	27	9	14	4	0
Clarksburg	384	1	0	0	0	1	1	1	0	0	0
Clarksville	153,294	956	14	80	127	735	4,411	743	3,427	241	17
Cleveland	44,778	390	1	27	53	309	2,515	369	1,921	225	3
Clifton	2,653	3	0	0	0	3	7	2	3	2	0
Clinton	10,146	69	1	2	7	59	439	68	323	48	3
Collegedale	12,005	6	0	1	2	3	199	19	165	15	1
Collierville	49,790	75	0	11	10	54	911	67	813	31	1
Collinwood	963	0	0	0	0	0	10	2	5	3	0
Columbia	38,031	281	1	27	42	211	1,298	300	919	79	7
Cookeville	32,860	129	3	18	14	94	1,654	301	1,218	135	3
Coopertown	4,455	4	0	0	0	4	18	9	8	1	0
Cornersville	1,252	2	0	0	0	2	8	1	6	1	0
Covington	8,909	150	0	13	11	126	486	106	356	24	2
Cowan	1,678	6	0	0	0	6	23	7	15	1	0
Cross Plains	1,736	2	0	1	0	1	3	1	1	1	0
Crossville	11,555	100	1	15	4	80	580	80	445	55	2
Crump	1,390	4	0	0	0	4	24	5	16	3	0
Cumberland City	298	1	0	1	0	0	6	1	5	0	0
Dandridge	2,983	8	0	2	1	5	92	17	71	4	0
Dayton	7,262	15	0	2	2	11	197	39	146	12	1
Decatur	1,571	11	0	0	1	10	55	13	33	9	0
Decaturville	876	3	0	0	0	3	13	5	5	3	0
Decherd	2,426	17	0	0	1	16	54	5	49	0	0
Dickson	15,637	175	1	12	12	150	936	108	773	55	1
Dover	1,450	4	0	0	0	4	18	2	16	0	0
Dresden	2,825	6	0	1	0	5	45	7	36	2	1
Dunlap	5,185	37	0	4	3	30	228	45	152	31	2
Dyer	2,225	7	0	1	2	4	48	2	42	4	0
Dyersburg	16,612	187	0	17	24	146	995	206	745	44	3
Eagleville	674	1	0	0	0	1	1	0	1	0	0
East Ridge	21,351	150	1	13	17	119	902	154	657	91	0
Elizabethton	13,771	58	0	3	8	47	814	159	618	37	2
Elkton	541	4	0	0	0	4	6	1	5	0	0
Englewood	1,530	10	0	1	0	9	33	7	17	9	0
Erin	1,277	2	0	0	0	2	15	5	10	0	0
Erwin	5,894	18	0	0	0	18	94	9	76	9	0
Estill Springs	2,031	16	0	0	0	16	23	2	18	3	0
Ethridge	482	0	0	0	0	0	9	4	5	0	0
Etowah	3,512	19	1	1	1	16	97	36	50	11	0
Fairview	8,648	19	0	4	0	15	148	16	126	6	1
Fayetteville	7,099	89	0	4	10	75	315	40	252	23	0
Franklin	76,995	146	1	18	14	113	1,048	78	940	30	3
Friendship	658	0	0	0	0	0	10	1	9	0	2
Gadsden	461	1	0	0	0	1	5	3	2	0	0
Gainesboro	944	0	0	0	0	0	16	1	14	1	0
Gallatin	36,689	126	0	7	9	110	480	55	403	22	1
Gallaway	653	3	0	0	0	3	11	1	8	2	0
Gates	611	0	0	0	0	0	15	3	12	0	0
Gatlinburg	4,247	31	1	6	5	19	241	45	179	17	1
Germantown	39,086	31	0	1	10	20	491	59	405	27	4
Gibson	376	2	0	0	0	2	3	1	2	0	0
Gleason	1,381	2	0	0	0	2	30	9	19	2	0
Goodlettsville	17,119	72	0	9	20	43	585	83	471	31	0
Gordonsville	1,209	1	0	0	0	1	22	4	11	7	0
Grand Junction	275	0	0	0	0	0	8	1	7	0	0
Graysville	1,525	6	0	0	0	6	10	6	4	0	0
Greenbrier	6,853	13	0	3	0	10	84	22	55	7	0
Greeneville	15,065	78	0	1	5	72	546	64	416	66	0
Greenfield	2,077	4	0	0	0	4	39	11	28	0	0
Harriman	6,196	37	2	1	2	32	221	50	152	19	2
Henderson	6,589	39	1	3	1	34	138	37	98	3	0
Hendersonville	58,034	102	0	6	11	85	1,017	71	902	44	3
Henry	462	1	0	0	0	1	14	1	11	2	0
Hohenwald	3,666	39	1	2	0	36	182	19	141	22	2
Hollow Rock	685	0	0	0	0	0	9	4	5	0	0
Hornbeak	386	0	0	0	0	0	0	0	0	0	0
Humboldt	8,210	95	1	10	6	78	335	78	245	12	4
Huntingdon	3,899	8	0	0	1	7	123	7	112	4	1
Jacksboro	1,929	5	0	0	0	5	87	1	86	0	0
Jackson	67,031	655	7	28	91	529	2,917	497	2,271	149	16
Jamestown	1,964	10	0	0	0	10	60	3	57	0	0
Jasper	3,371	11	0	0	0	11	97	10	78	9	0
Jefferson City	8,351	32	0	0	2	30	373	38	325	10	1
Jellico	2,219	8	0	0	1	7	57	8	43	6	0
Johnson City	67,193	267	2	26	42	197	2,831	377	2,296	158	5
Jonesborough	5,378	9	0	1	2	6	116	20	89	7	0

Table 8. Offenses Known to Law Enforcement, by Selected State and City, 2017—Continued

(Number.)

State/city	Population	Violent crime	Murder and nonnegligent manslaughter	Rape (revised definition)[1]	Robbery	Aggravated assault	Property crime	Burglary	Larceny-theft	Motor vehicle theft	Arson[2]
Kenton	1,208	5	0	1	0	4	31	5	26	0	0
Kimball	1,387	6	0	0	4	2	159	10	143	6	0
Kingsport	52,810	381	3	17	58	303	2,884	377	2,303	204	4
Kingston	5,823	13	0	2	4	7	87	18	59	10	1
Kingston Springs	2,765	0	0	0	0	0	5	0	5	0	0
Knoxville	187,539	1,676	33	145	371	1,127	10,211	1,665	7,510	1,036	12
Lafayette	5,251	12	0	0	0	12	192	36	141	15	0
La Follette	6,897	55	0	3	3	49	308	73	209	26	1
Lawrenceburg	10,780	74	0	11	3	60	555	113	415	27	1
Lebanon	32,248	228	3	22	16	187	939	126	729	84	3
Lenoir City	9,187	27	0	8	5	14	295	43	230	22	2
Lewisburg	11,684	79	1	2	6	70	266	57	197	12	1
Lexington	7,792	71	0	3	3	65	291	35	229	27	0
Livingston	4,061	29	0	4	0	25	95	16	73	6	1
Lookout Mountain	1,892	0	0	0	0	0	24	0	24	0	0
Loretto	1,760	6	0	0	1	5	30	9	15	6	0
Loudon	5,811	5	1	0	0	4	79	4	70	5	0
Madisonville	4,805	21	0	0	3	18	267	61	181	25	0
Manchester	10,702	99	0	1	4	94	408	72	317	19	0
Martin	10,656	35	2	2	6	25	276	37	234	5	1
Maryville	28,918	49	0	6	5	38	639	94	501	44	3
Mason	1,574	21	0	0	0	21	23	8	13	2	0
Maury City	664	1	0	0	0	1	9	2	5	2	0
Maynardville	2,348	3	0	0	0	3	63	16	41	6	0
McEwen	1,712	7	0	0	0	7	47	12	33	2	0
McKenzie	5,610	13	0	2	1	10	102	31	66	5	1
McMinnville	13,786	71	1	5	5	60	589	107	440	42	2
Medina	4,290	8	0	1	0	7	37	7	28	2	1
Memphis	652,765	13,077	181	590	3,457	8,849	41,110	9,532	27,576	4,002	365
Middleton	641	3	0	0	0	3	11	2	8	1	0
Milan	7,780	67	2	7	3	55	242	58	176	8	2
Millersville	6,792	13	0	1	0	12	68	20	41	7	1
Millington	10,944	119	0	4	22	93	536	60	436	40	7
Minor Hill	519	0	0	0	0	0	0	0	0	0	0
Monteagle	1,169	9	0	0	1	8	27	12	14	1	1
Monterey	2,867	17	0	0	1	16	57	15	30	12	0
Morristown	29,774	222	2	12	23	185	1,387	210	1,066	111	6
Moscow	524	6	0	0	0	6	9	4	5	0	0
Mountain City	2,431	3	0	0	0	3	4	0	3	1	0
Mount Carmel	5,427	13	0	1	1	11	44	11	30	3	0
Mount Juliet	34,888	61	0	14	11	36	613	34	527	52	2
Mount Pleasant	4,902	20	0	3	2	15	82	6	65	11	0
Munford	6,079	16	0	3	1	12	107	11	88	8	1
Murfreesboro	136,102	735	3	89	144	499	4,339	522	3,548	269	7
Nashville Metropolitan	674,942	7,682	110	492	2,046	5,034	25,769	4,261	18,943	2,565	70
Newbern	3,288	28	0	0	1	27	75	28	46	1	1
New Johnsonville	1,909	4	0	1	0	3	36	16	19	1	0
New Market	1,366	3	0	1	0	2	16	4	10	2	0
Newport	6,816	100	0	5	1	94	615	77	506	32	3
New Tazewell	2,754	15	0	2	0	13	129	15	105	9	0
Niota	724	1	0	0	0	1	33	10	20	3	0
Nolensville	7,889	10	1	2	1	6	100	26	71	3	0
Norris	1,645	0	0	0	0	0	21	3	15	3	0
Oakland	7,884	9	0	2	0	7	60	5	55	0	0
Oak Ridge	29,355	155	3	14	13	125	769	144	560	65	4
Obion	1,064	0	0	0	0	0	6	2	3	1	0
Oliver Springs	3,255	7	0	0	0	7	105	13	74	18	0
Oneida	3,716	11	0	0	0	11	155	11	136	8	0
Paris	10,194	51	2	2	8	39	390	78	287	25	0
Parsons	2,355	14	0	2	0	12	35	9	23	3	0
Petersburg	544	1	0	0	0	1	8	1	7	0	0
Pigeon Forge	6,254	48	0	9	3	36	438	83	293	62	1
Pikeville	1,656	6	0	0	0	6	52	10	37	5	1
Piperton	1,725	0	0	0	0	0	25	9	13	3	0
Pittman Center	582	0	0	0	0	0	5	1	3	1	0
Plainview	2,035	7	0	1	0	6	15	6	7	2	0
Pleasant View	4,382	1	0	0	0	1	66	17	43	6	0
Portland	12,710	37	2	2	4	29	234	50	173	11	0
Pulaski	7,742	57	1	6	6	44	346	55	278	13	4
Puryear	672	1	1	0	0	0	12	2	9	1	0
Red Bank	11,838	71	0	3	8	60	382	78	268	36	0
Red Boiling Springs	1,142	1	0	1	0	0	17	11	3	3	0
Ridgely	1,693	6	0	0	1	5	30	8	19	3	0
Ridgetop	2,061	0	0	0	0	0	10	1	9	0	0
Ripley	8,067	102	0	9	8	85	308	115	185	8	1
Rockwood	5,424	29	0	1	3	25	284	39	221	24	0
Rocky Top	1,779	7	0	1	0	6	127	18	86	23	1
Rogersville	4,367	24	0	0	0	24	228	46	174	8	2
Rossville	848	2	0	1	0	1	4	0	3	1	0
Rutherford	1,101	1	0	0	0	1	9	3	5	1	0
Rutledge	1,201	2	0	0	0	2	17	6	9	2	0
Saltillo	500	1	0	1	0	0	17	5	6	6	0
Savannah	7,023	76	0	4	10	62	518	100	390	28	1

Table 8. Offenses Known to Law Enforcement, by Selected State and City, 2017—Continued

(Number.)

State/city	Population	Violent crime	Murder and nonnegligent manslaughter	Rape (revised definition)[1]	Robbery	Aggravated assault	Property crime	Burglary	Larceny-theft	Motor vehicle theft	Arson[2]
Scotts Hill	986	5	0	2	0	3	8	2	3	3	0
Selmer	4,476	25	0	2	1	22	151	31	112	8	2
Sevierville	16,991	71	0	6	7	58	823	58	698	67	0
Sharon	897	3	0	0	2	1	12	3	8	1	0
Shelbyville	21,618	173	0	12	13	148	667	125	495	47	3
Signal Mountain	8,624	9	0	0	1	8	51	11	40	0	0
Smithville	4,717	22	0	3	1	18	167	34	118	15	0
Smyrna	50,091	174	2	21	32	119	1,447	168	1,173	106	5
Sneedville	1,340	1	0	1	0	0	37	1	34	2	0
Soddy-Daisy	13,264	27	0	3	2	22	307	70	211	26	2
Somerville	3,139	19	1	1	3	14	86	19	62	5	0
South Carthage	1,348	4	0	0	0	4	32	3	28	1	0
South Fulton	2,238	17	0	1	2	14	49	23	25	1	0
South Pittsburg	3,097	13	0	0	1	12	50	9	35	6	1
Sparta	5,101	8	0	3	0	5	307	43	251	13	1
Spencer	1,634	1	0	0	0	1	6	0	5	1	0
Spring City	1,990	11	0	0	0	11	35	7	28	0	0
Springfield	16,869	156	2	6	17	131	537	56	450	31	1
Spring Hill	39,366	68	1	6	3	58	395	54	330	11	0
St. Joseph	790	0	0	0	0	0	2	2	0	0	0
Sunbright	544	0	0	0	0	0	0	0	0	0	0
Surgoinsville	1,785	0	0	0	0	0	20	6	13	1	0
Sweetwater	5,957	75	0	1	4	70	377	83	270	24	0
Tazewell	2,291	11	0	1	3	7	60	7	45	8	0
Tellico Plains	952	10	0	1	0	9	24	8	10	6	0
Tiptonville	4,331	12	0	5	2	5	34	7	25	2	0
Toone	335	4	0	0	0	4	1	1	0	0	0
Townsend	445	0	0	0	0	0	28	5	22	1	1
Tracy City	1,418	10	0	0	0	10	41	8	25	8	1
Trenton	4,116	16	0	1	0	15	61	6	55	0	0
Trezevant	831	1	0	0	0	1	15	5	10	0	0
Trimble	621	0	0	0	0	0	1	1	0	0	1
Troy	1,275	1	0	0	0	1	21	5	16	0	0
Tullahoma	19,386	118	1	6	8	103	610	120	461	29	6
Tusculum	2,672	0	0	0	0	0	8	0	7	1	0
Union City	10,544	91	2	8	8	73	649	128	494	27	3
Vonore	1,506	7	0	0	0	7	55	9	39	7	0
Wartburg	903	2	0	0	2	0	2	0	1	1	0
Wartrace	658	0	0	0	0	0	4	1	3	0	0
Watertown	1,537	7	0	0	2	5	21	10	11	0	0
Waverly	4,139	10	1	0	0	9	125	21	96	8	0
Waynesboro	2,347	8	0	0	0	8	27	2	19	6	0
Westmoreland	2,328	9	0	0	0	9	40	2	37	1	0
White Bluff	3,483	18	1	1	1	15	58	16	40	2	0
White House	11,591	34	0	5	3	26	220	14	196	10	0
White Pine	2,270	1	0	1	0	0	63	8	52	3	0
Whiteville	4,481	8	0	0	2	6	23	7	15	1	0
Whitwell	1,720	6	0	0	0	6	59	15	35	9	1
Winchester	8,573	64	1	6	3	54	326	58	254	14	2
Winfield	957	3	0	0	0	3	16	8	8	0	0
Woodbury	2,799	5	0	0	0	5	35	7	23	5	0
TEXAS											
Abernathy	2,756	8	0	0	0	8	27	3	16	8	0
Abilene[5, 6]	122,981	636	4	100	138	394			2,605	260	20
Addison	15,795	95	0	22	16	57	773	111	565	97	5
Alamo	19,351	178	0	15	20	143	946	124	771	51	2
Alamo Heights	8,507	14	0	0	1	13	182	25	152	5	0
Alice	19,311	90	0	8	3	79	1,031	308	685	38	12
Allen	101,779	100	2	24	30	44	1,268	155	1,061	52	0
Alpine	5,983	12	0	1	0	11	64	33	24	7	3
Alton	17,432	16	0	0	7	9	286	40	234	12	1
Alvarado	4,033	18	0	4	1	13	94	26	55	13	0
Alvin	26,488	49	1	21	13	14	485	83	342	60	1
Amarillo	200,993	1,518	16	183	237	1,082	8,787	1,684	6,113	990	46
Andrews	14,032	50	0	8	1	41	175	27	132	16	2
Anna	12,716	5	1	0	1	3	144	21	112	11	1
Anson	2,313	18	0	0	0	18	15	8	4	3	0
Anthony	5,681	11	0	2	2	7	133	10	112	11	1
Aransas Pass	8,431	53	0	1	4	48	428	115	290	23	3
Arcola	2,315	1	0	0	0	1	2	2	0	0	0
Argyle	4,145	3	1	0	1	1	28	3	23	2	0
Arlington[6]	397,377	2,054	19	254	576	1,205	12,707	1,801	9,546	1,360	29
Arp	1,008	2	0	2	0	0	5	3	2	0	0
Athens	12,826	41	0	9	7	25	339	78	234	27	1
Atlanta	5,634	32	0	5	2	25	183	54	124	5	0
Aubrey	3,535	4	0	0	3	1	13	7	3	3	0
Austin	971,949	4,032	25	834	987	2,186	31,001	4,380	24,542	2,079	76
Azle	12,266	21	0	0	3	18	298	42	249	7	6
Baird	1,516	8	0	2	0	6	19	3	12	4	0
Balch Springs[6]	25,199	193	2	17	54	120	857	139	572	146	0
Balcones Heights	3,386	41	0	2	12	27	459	36	381	42	0
Ballinger	3,725	6	0	0	0	6	44	11	32	1	1

Table 8. Offenses Known to Law Enforcement, by Selected State and City, 2017—Continued

(Number.)

State/city	Population	Violent crime	Murder and nonnegligent manslaughter	Rape (revised definition)[1]	Robbery	Aggravated assault	Property crime	Burglary	Larceny-theft	Motor vehicle theft	Arson[2]
Bangs	1,579	9	0	0	0	9	9	3	6	0	0
Bartonville	1,715	2	0	2	0	0	12	1	9	2	0
Bastrop	8,755	51	0	4	9	38	419	38	358	23	1
Bay City[6]	17,842	93	3	9	23	58	576	149	416	11	7
Bayou Vista	1,625	0	0	0	0	0	5	1	4	0	0
Baytown	76,704	288	6	38	108	136	2,678	506	1,846	326	1
Beaumont	118,456	1,259	16	86	304	853	5,136	1,259	3,472	405	42
Bedford	49,947	112	1	23	34	54	1,028	151	775	102	0
Bee Cave	7,087	9	0	1	1	7	158	15	138	5	1
Beeville	13,317	33	1	1	0	31	301	90	203	8	1
Bellaire	18,892	26	0	4	20	2	301	45	244	12	0
Bellmead[6]	10,371	239	0	21	16	202	675	66	581	28	3
Bellville[6]	4,304	12	0	8	0	4	57	15	42	0	1
Belton	21,310	35	1	5	11	18	553	102	447	4	1
Benbrook	23,236	37	1	9	10	17	441	61	359	21	2
Beverly Hills	2,021	11	0	0	1	10	68	16	43	9	0
Big Sandy	1,388	0	0	0	0	0	2	1	0	1	0
Big Spring	28,747	166	2	8	22	134	1,029	221	723	85	7
Bishop	3,135	8	0	0	1	7	43	14	25	4	0
Blanco	1,989	3	0	0	0	3	32	11	20	1	0
Blue Mound	2,514	3	0	0	1	2	21	2	15	4	0
Boerne	15,521	23	1	12	0	10	352	21	302	29	0
Bogata	1,074	3	0	0	0	3	25	7	17	1	0
Bonham	10,123	26	0	8	1	17	198	54	140	4	4
Borger[6]	12,791	51	2	27	3	19	514	158	320	36	2
Bovina	1,762	8	0	0	0	8	15	5	9	1	0
Bowie	5,131	9	0	1	3	5	205	51	145	9	0
Boyd	1,399	2	0	0	0	2	22	5	16	1	0
Brady	5,414	6	0	0	0	6	152	52	94	6	0
Brazoria	3,080	6	0	0	2	4	58	11	42	5	0
Breckenridge	5,530	15	0	2	0	13	105	24	78	3	2
Bridge City	8,219	25	0	3	1	21	120	20	87	13	0
Bridgeport[6]	6,601	28	0	6	1	21	68	11	53	4	0
Brookshire	5,323	19	0	2	3	14	62	17	33	12	1
Brownfield	9,798	28	0	1	4	23	127	30	89	8	1
Brownsville	185,216	476	5	79	133	259	5,176	661	4,374	141	6
Brownwood	19,133	81	1	20	9	51	672	96	554	22	0
Bryan	84,438	363	4	53	69	237	2,028	348	1,557	123	16
Buda	16,857	9	0	0	3	6	245	19	215	11	0
Bullard	3,157	2	0	1	0	1	30	6	23	1	0
Bulverde	5,101	3	0	1	0	2	139	17	122	0	0
Burkburnett	11,142	46	0	8	1	37	301	60	220	21	1
Burleson	46,531	94	4	25	10	55	919	105	747	67	0
Burnet[6]	6,422	24	0	6	2	16	95	26	60	9	1
Cactus	3,176	3	0	0	0	3	20	9	8	3	0
Caddo Mills	1,587	7	0	2	1	4	9	7	2	0	0
Caldwell	4,362	14	0	1	1	12	21	2	19	0	1
Calvert	1,135	3	0	0	1	2	26	14	10	2	0
Cameron	5,571	22	1	0	2	19	96	36	59	1	2
Canton	3,882	14	0	2	0	12	73	10	60	3	0
Canyon	15,458	23	0	3	0	20	95	10	75	10	0
Carrollton	135,823	166	2	36	61	67	2,380	463	1,690	227	0
Carthage	6,753	28	0	1	2	25	248	39	199	10	0
Castle Hills[6]	4,533	10	1	1	5	3	276	76	179	21	0
Castroville	3,058	0	0	0	0	0	84	3	68	13	0
Cedar Hill	48,904	115	1	23	42	49	1,503	154	1,251	98	2
Cedar Park	72,143	125	0	51	14	60	1,006	109	846	51	3
Celina	8,388	6	0	0	1	5	109	34	71	4	0
Center	5,412	48	2	5	3	38	166	18	141	7	1
Chandler	3,031	5	0	0	0	5	35	9	24	2	0
Cibolo	29,323	31	1	11	6	13	283	34	235	14	1
Cisco	3,788	10	0	1	0	9	47	10	26	11	0
Clarksville	3,179	10	0	4	1	5	55	30	25	0	0
Cleburne	30,320	69	0	24	6	39	700	142	507	51	1
Cleveland	8,183	54	0	4	9	41	265	27	208	30	3
Clifton	3,383	4	0	0	0	4	41	13	24	4	0
Clint	1,175	1	0	0	0	1	7	1	6	0	0
Clute	11,649	20	1	1	2	16	251	43	190	18	0
Clyde	3,865	5	0	2	0	3	71	33	36	2	0
Cockrell Hill	4,294	13	0	2	6	5	127	17	95	15	0
Coleman	4,388	21	0	0	0	21	40	20	19	1	0
College Station	115,357	230	1	53	49	127	2,304	300	1,887	117	0
Colleyville	26,737	5	0	0	2	3	154	37	110	7	0
Collinsville	1,748	1	0	0	0	1	14	4	10	0	0
Colorado City	3,977	9	0	2	0	7	154	50	97	7	1
Comanche	4,186	29	0	5	2	22	113	22	90	1	1
Combes	3,079	7	0	0	0	7	27	7	20	0	0
Commerce	9,269	42	0	2	12	28	169	44	123	2	1
Conroe	85,534	249	4	54	65	126	1,931	276	1,479	176	3
Converse	23,510	173	3	5	21	144	462	88	327	47	1
Coppell	41,809	28	1	5	6	16	533	89	421	23	2
Copperas Cove	32,895	229	1	4	22	202	846	181	631	34	4
Corinth	21,297	27	1	0	4	22	260	31	208	21	1

Table 8. Offenses Known to Law Enforcement, by Selected State and City, 2017—Continued

(Number.)

State/city	Population	Violent crime	Murder and nonnegligent manslaughter	Rape (revised definition)[1]	Robbery	Aggravated assault	Property crime	Burglary	Larceny-theft	Motor vehicle theft	Arson[2]
Corpus Christi	329,256	2,313	21	232	470	1,590	11,739	2,232	8,776	731	57
Corrigan[6]	1,586	11	0	0	1	10	27	8	15	4	0
Corsicana	24,011	157	0	28	21	108	749	158	554	37	2
Crandall	3,415	6	0	2	0	4	48	15	23	10	0
Crane	3,790	3	0	0	0	3	5	1	3	1	0
Crockett	6,481	43	0	0	3	40	181	42	132	7	0
Crosbyton	1,688	0	0	0	0	0	5	5	0	0	0
Crowell	823	0	0	0	0	0	0	0	0	0	0
Crowley	15,340	27	2	3	6	16	310	26	272	12	0
Crystal City	7,394	20	0	0	1	19	60	30	30	0	0
Cuero[5]	8,572	109	0	10	0	99			138	9	1
Cumby	796	0	0	0	0	0	0	0	0	0	0
Daingerfield	2,445	6	0	0	1	5	95	24	68	3	0
Dalhart	8,366	76	0	11	5	60	275	112	147	16	0
Dallas	1,338,551	10,369	167	831	4,377	4,994	42,634	9,874	24,847	7,913	351
Dalworthington Gardens	2,403	4	0	0	2	2	43	8	31	4	0
Danbury	1,791	1	0	0	0	1	1	1	0	0	0
Dayton[6]	7,815	29	0	2	8	19	196	33	143	20	1
Decatur	6,755	10	0	1	1	8	178	14	153	11	0
Deer Park	34,069	38	0	12	3	23	500	70	396	34	2
De Kalb	1,652	3	0	0	2	1	30	11	15	4	0
De Leon	2,166	6	0	2	0	4	27	10	15	2	0
Del Rio	35,994	28	0	4	10	14	693	145	529	19	2
Denison	23,814	107	4	18	15	70	525	115	340	70	0
Denton	136,836	416	1	120	94	201	3,091	426	2,367	298	0
Denver City	4,909	3	0	0	0	3	44	8	34	2	0
DeSoto	53,163	216	3	28	73	112	1,424	257	1,009	158	1
Devine[6]	4,847	8	0	3	2	3	154	14	125	15	1
Diboll	5,363	0	0	0	0	0	61	8	50	3	0
Dickinson	20,303	48	0	16	10	22	483	131	305	47	1
Dilley	4,309	15	0	0	0	15	73	21	47	5	0
Dimmitt	4,164	2	0	0	0	2	97	34	54	9	0
Donna[6]	16,641	236	0	33	9	194	920	195	678	47	0
Double Oak[6]	3,116	2	0	0	0	2	29	8	21	0	0
Driscoll	744	8	0	0	1	7	18	2	15	1	0
Dublin	3,628	1	0	1	0	0	16	5	10	1	0
Dumas	14,943	36	1	8	2	25	303	51	224	28	0
Duncanville	39,603	185	1	19	87	78	1,085	200	716	169	3
Eagle Lake	3,722	11	0	0	1	10	3	0	3	0	0
Eagle Pass	29,257	35	0	0	4	31	548	131	384	33	2
Early	3,026	14	0	5	0	9	66	13	51	2	1
Eastland[6]	3,878	8	0	5	0	3	95	19	75	1	0
Edcouch	3,397	5	0	1	0	4	19	5	11	3	0
Edinburg	89,595	299	2	51	44	202	3,373	472	2,793	108	8
Edna	5,874	11	1	2	2	6	109	23	79	7	0
El Campo[6]	11,782	40	1	3	2	34	343	69	255	19	2
Electra[6]	2,711	10	0	1	0	9	45	12	28	5	0
El Paso	688,667	2,609	19	371	400	1,819	12,526	1,297	10,429	800	38
Elsa	6,798	85	1	0	1	83	276	30	246	0	0
Encinal	591	1	0	0	0	1	3	0	2	1	0
Ennis	19,331	66	0	18	9	39	437	62	340	35	0
Estelline	136	0	0	0	0	0	0	0	0	0	0
Euless	55,345	84	1	1	29	53	1,263	214	909	140	2
Fairfield	2,922	12	0	0	4	8	45	15	27	3	1
Fair Oaks Ranch	9,042	3	0	0	0	3	42	12	28	2	0
Fairview	8,547	1	0	0	0	1	55	11	43	1	0
Falfurrias	4,928	16	0	0	2	14	186	70	116	0	0
Farmers Branch	36,186	57	0	10	27	20	790	159	539	92	2
Farmersville	3,425	8	0	2	0	6	54	18	34	2	0
Farwell	1,309	6	0	1	0	5	9	4	5	0	0
Fate[6]	11,505	10	1	3	0	6	40	6	31	3	0
Ferris	2,595	7	0	1	3	3	49	14	34	1	0
Flatonia	1,412	0	0	0	0	0	13	8	4	1	0
Floresville	7,677	16	0	1	1	14	160	31	117	12	0
Flower Mound	75,101	44	0	9	4	31	694	79	596	19	4
Floydada	2,749	26	0	4	1	21	50	23	23	4	0
Forest Hill	13,044	62	1	2	30	29	375	43	296	36	0
Forney	20,155	24	0	4	8	12	301	45	233	23	0
Fort Stockton	8,551	38	1	7	3	27	157	38	112	7	1
Fort Worth	873,069	4,891	70	569	1,286	2,966	28,072	5,116	20,250	2,706	151
Frankston[6]	1,199	6	0	2	0	4	39	5	32	2	0
Fredericksburg	11,526	9	0	0	3	6	147	20	124	3	0
Freeport	12,170	37	0	4	6	27	241	43	186	12	0
Freer	2,739	12	0	3	0	9	41	18	20	3	0
Friendswood	39,990	36	0	16	11	9	321	57	247	17	1
Friona	3,862	5	0	3	0	2	22	13	8	1	0
Frisco	172,804	176	2	39	36	99	2,571	309	2,178	84	2
Fulshear	8,350	6	0	0	1	5	55	5	48	2	0
Fulton	1,616	0	0	0	0	0	30	18	9	3	0
Gainesville	16,372	85	0	18	13	54	528	109	396	23	7
Galveston	51,021	257	2	63	82	110	1,790	275	1,231	284	3
Ganado	2,121	0	0	0	0	0	16	5	10	1	0
Garden Ridge	4,079	3	0	1	0	2	47	8	39	0	0

Table 8. Offenses Known to Law Enforcement, by Selected State and City, 2017—Continued

(Number.)

State/city	Population	Violent crime	Murder and nonnegligent manslaughter	Rape (revised definition)[1]	Robbery	Aggravated assault	Property crime	Burglary	Larceny-theft	Motor vehicle theft	Arson[2]
Garland	236,243	748	8	129	319	292	7,164	1,214	5,140	810	15
Gatesville	12,504	19	0	8	1	10	204	41	148	15	0
Georgetown	71,007	83	0	31	14	38	696	97	564	35	4
George West	2,602	11	0	1	0	10	9	3	1	5	0
Giddings	5,154	15	0	2	1	12	109	0	107	2	0
Gilmer	5,270	52	0	4	5	43	150	29	114	7	0
Gladewater	6,422	27	0	3	6	18	179	53	117	9	1
Glenn Heights	12,509	68	0	9	17	42	220	59	149	12	0
Godley	1,130	5	0	0	0	5	9	4	2	3	0
Gonzales	7,734	58	0	6	1	51	119	20	91	8	0
Gorman	1,024	0	0	0	0	0	5	0	4	1	0
Graham	8,774	21	1	6	1	13	108	25	73	10	0
Granbury	10,076	15	1	5	2	7	493	35	445	13	0
Grand Prairie	193,249	573	2	136	174	261	4,706	582	3,629	495	5
Grand Saline	3,151	3	0	1	0	2	72	29	41	2	0
Granger	1,530	4	0	0	0	4	14	3	10	1	0
Granite Shoals	5,153	7	0	0	0	7	35	4	25	6	0
Grapeland	1,408	4	0	0	0	4	21	8	13	0	0
Grapevine	52,925	107	1	14	19	73	1,265	114	1,066	85	4
Greenville	27,434	110	4	31	19	56	687	111	511	65	12
Gregory	1,990	7	0	2	0	5	20	7	12	1	0
Groesbeck	4,320	8	0	4	1	3	117	28	86	3	0
Groves	15,701	79	0	13	10	56	380	85	266	29	0
Gun Barrel City	6,062	13	1	1	2	9	117	33	72	12	0
Hallettsville[6]	2,591	10	0	1	0	9	63	7	55	1	0
Hallsville	4,254	3	0	1	0	2	55	18	34	3	0
Haltom City	44,685	151	0	37	45	69	1,181	231	800	150	8
Hamilton	2,951	15	0	2	0	13	80	12	64	4	1
Hamlin	2,024	8	1	1	1	5	34	23	11	0	0
Happy	646	0	0	0	0	0	0	0	0	0	0
Harker Heights	30,252	78	5	23	24	26	1,034	130	852	52	4
Harlingen	65,617	233	0	18	32	183	2,693	523	2,079	91	15
Haskell	3,173	5	0	2	0	3	13	7	5	1	0
Hawkins	1,305	5	0	0	2	3	15	4	11	0	1
Hawley	611	0	0	0	0	0	10	5	4	1	0
Hearne	4,490	32	2	8	1	21	171	60	107	4	0
Heath	8,638	4	0	0	1	3	62	17	43	2	1
Hedwig Village	2,681	6	1	0	4	1	192	9	177	6	0
Helotes	9,011	8	0	1	2	5	143	24	116	3	0
Hemphill	1,224	2	0	0	0	2	10	2	8	0	0
Henderson	13,366	94	0	6	6	82	489	52	421	16	2
Hereford	14,832	58	0	3	5	50	356	69	263	24	4
Hewitt	14,443	18	0	4	4	10	172	32	132	8	1
Hickory Creek	4,413	6	0	2	1	3	78	6	66	6	2
Hidalgo	14,048	39	0	5	3	31	216	21	185	10	0
Highland Park	9,248	4	0	0	1	3	196	28	163	5	0
Highland Village	16,884	11	0	0	0	11	167	11	151	5	0
Hill Country Village	1,098	0	0	0	0	0	45	9	34	2	0
Hillsboro	8,348	23	1	3	4	15	365	34	307	24	2
Hitchcock	7,949	14	0	2	0	12	188	39	128	21	0
Hollywood Park[6]	3,371	1	0	0	1	0	83	16	61	6	0
Hondo	9,353	40	0	5	1	34	306	52	238	16	0
Hooks	2,734	4	0	1	0	3	40	11	27	2	1
Horizon City	19,695	16	0	0	3	13	118	17	94	7	1
Horseshoe Bay	3,732	14	0	1	0	13	48	8	38	2	0
Houston	2,338,235	25,609	269	1,366	9,773	14,201	96,532	17,108	67,828	11,596	665
Hughes Springs	1,777	6	0	0	0	6	7	2	5	0	1
Humble	15,631	147	1	36	61	49	1,521	136	1,209	176	0
Huntington	2,105	6	0	3	0	3	51	21	27	3	0
Huntsville	41,634	160	1	23	24	112	675	102	485	88	2
Hurst	39,459	87	0	28	41	18	1,543	148	1,327	68	4
Hutchins	5,693	16	0	0	8	8	220	67	153	0	0
Hutto	25,283	22	0	6	4	12	138	16	118	4	0
Idalou	2,348	3	0	1	0	2	11	2	8	1	0
Indian Lake[6]	657	0	0	0	0	0	5	2	3	0	0
Ingleside	10,698	21	1	6	4	10	206	54	135	17	0
Ingram	1,843	2	0	0	0	2	18	6	9	3	1
Iowa Park	6,361	7	0	3	0	4	49	8	34	7	0
Irving	242,062	549	8	54	228	259	6,147	969	4,467	711	23
Itasca	1,650	2	0	0	0	2	30	7	22	1	0
Jacinto City	10,718	18	0	0	11	7	254	30	189	35	0
Jacksboro	4,323	9	0	3	0	6	65	9	52	4	3
Jacksonville[6]	14,955	107	1	8	9	89	386	100	270	16	0
Jamaica Beach	1,078	1	0	1	0	0	19	7	11	1	0
Jarrell	1,416	3	0	0	0	3	23	10	12	1	0
Jasper	7,663	37	0	0	5	32	349	93	242	14	2
Jersey Village	7,938	14	0	1	6	7	176	41	103	32	0
Jones Creek	2,070	1	0	0	0	1	14	4	9	1	0
Jonestown	2,065	5	0	1	2	2	38	13	19	6	0
Josephine	1,328	1	0	0	0	1	5	3	2	0	1
Joshua	6,983	12	0	3	1	8	105	31	67	7	0
Jourdanton	4,404	3	0	0	1	2	3	0	3	0	0
Junction	2,445	2	0	0	0	2	14	6	7	1	0

Table 8. Offenses Known to Law Enforcement, by Selected State and City, 2017—Continued

(Number.)

State/city	Population	Violent crime	Murder and nonnegligent manslaughter	Rape (revised definition)[1]	Robbery	Aggravated assault	Property crime	Burglary	Larceny-theft	Motor vehicle theft	Arson[2]
Karnes City	3,400	15	0	5	0	10	61	18	40	3	0
Katy	17,669	57	0	13	15	29	668	60	572	36	0
Kaufman5, 6	7,276	28	0	5	4	19			135	17	0
Keene	6,334	31	0	3	1	27	66	18	44	4	0
Keller	47,892	25	0	7	7	11	300	56	233	11	1
Kemah	2,037	7	0	0	6	1	157	8	143	6	0
Kenedy	3,401	11	0	0	1	10	141	28	108	5	1
Kennedale	8,032	21	0	6	8	7	139	27	102	10	0
Kermit	6,459	0	0	0	0	0	14	6	8	0	0
Kerrville	23,610	53	0	4	6	43	561	49	489	23	3
Kilgore	15,074	53	2	10	0	41	422	80	313	29	3
Killeen	145,912	1,118	18	151	313	636	4,109	1,140	2,403	566	29
Kingsville	26,048	109	1	3	24	81	925	221	679	25	6
Kirby	8,746	37	1	3	16	17	275	55	178	42	0
Knox City	1,167	7	0	1	0	6	17	11	6	0	0
Kountze	2,094	7	0	0	1	6	40	7	26	7	0
Kress	675	0	0	0	0	0	2	1	1	0	0
Kyle	41,189	86	0	16	18	52	649	64	524	61	2
Lacy-Lakeview	6,633	42	0	9	6	27	222	44	167	11	0
La Feria	7,279	42	0	0	2	40	164	27	131	6	0
Lago Vista	6,718	13	0	3	0	10	66	15	48	3	0
La Grange	4,699	29	0	8	2	19	115	16	95	4	2
La Grulla	1,720	6	0	0	1	5	15	8	7	0	0
Laguna Vista	3,207	2	0	0	0	2	26	2	22	2	0
La Joya	4,343	10	0	1	0	9	69	11	57	1	0
Lake City	527	0	0	0	0	0	0	0	0	0	0
Lake Dallas	8,013	23	0	3	1	19	109	30	75	4	0
Lake Jackson	27,647	45	1	14	8	22	575	67	484	24	2
Lakeside	1,411	2	0	0	0	2	26	2	18	6	0
Lakeview, Harrison County	6,410	5	0	1	0	4	53	9	38	6	0
Lakeway	15,195	20	0	3	2	15	169	13	148	8	0
Lake Worth	4,921	13	0	1	8	4	444	88	341	15	0
La Marque	16,796	90	6	19	14	51	752	112	576	64	3
Lampasas	7,910	18	1	2	2	13	213	28	177	8	0
Lancaster	39,225	222	0	14	94	114	1,247	193	814	240	5
La Porte	35,293	103	0	20	16	67	527	77	401	49	3
Laredo	260,669	839	10	114	154	561	6,474	874	5,430	170	71
La Vernia	1,484	8	0	3	0	5	46	20	21	5	0
La Villa	2,702	3	0	0	0	3	16	5	11	0	0
Lavon	3,247	2	0	1	0	1	18	1	17	0	0
League City	105,351	97	3	34	18	42	1,718	218	1,407	93	3
Leander	46,219	58	0	22	5	31	523	73	426	24	4
Leon Valley	11,508	67	0	8	22	37	670	78	530	62	1
Levelland	13,901	121	0	19	3	99	514	117	366	31	4
Lewisville	106,199	280	3	51	71	155	2,134	340	1,565	229	6
Liberty	9,308	52	0	11	5	36	228	35	181	12	0
Lindale	6,044	24	0	10	1	13	213	42	158	13	1
Linden	1,971	5	0	0	0	5	47	13	30	4	0
Little Elm	46,097	36	1	8	8	19	267	43	198	26	0
Littlefield6	5,983	39	0	6	0	33	86	21	58	7	3
Live Oak	16,214	31	0	9	12	10	628	35	554	39	1
Livingston6	5,107	24	0	3	1	20	218	34	177	7	1
Lockhart	13,662	35	0	3	5	27	278	34	226	18	2
Log Cabin	721	0	0	0	0	0	29	13	13	3	0
Lone Star	1,524	19	0	0	1	18	21	3	18	0	0
Longview	82,303	396	6	62	99	229	2,803	614	1,947	242	6
Lorena	1,752	3	0	1	0	2	40	3	33	4	0
Los Indios	1,068	4	0	0	0	4	8	3	5	0	2
Lufkin	36,329	142	4	0	33	105	1,553	264	1,206	83	2
Luling	5,962	35	2	6	3	24	106	13	81	12	1
Lumberton5	12,690	17	0	2	2	13			121	10	1
Lyford	2,592	10	0	3	0	7	43	9	31	3	0
Lytle	2,967	18	0	4	3	11	88	8	74	6	0
Madisonville	4,672	50	0	2	2	46	146	50	96	0	0
Magnolia	2,107	1	0	0	1	0	26	9	15	2	1
Manor	9,102	45	0	12	5	28	317	37	265	15	1
Mansfield	67,233	78	0	21	20	37	808	154	612	42	0
Manvel	9,756	9	1	0	2	6	108	40	59	9	1
Marble Falls	6,358	24	0	11	0	13	234	55	172	7	0
Marshall	23,564	157	0	6	28	123	908	264	579	65	3
Martindale	1,255	2	0	0	1	1	1	1	0	0	0
Mathis	4,939	62	3	0	3	56	173	58	112	3	4
McAllen	144,162	208	7	27	49	125	4,007	185	3,776	46	8
McGregor	5,082	15	0	0	2	13	28	11	16	1	0
McKinney	179,934	267	2	46	68	151	2,417	297	1,965	155	12
Meadows Place	4,745	4	0	0	1	3	136	18	106	12	0
Melissa	9,270	4	0	2	1	1	34	7	22	5	1
Memorial Villages	12,319	1	0	0	1	0	85	10	75	0	0
Memphis	2,113	15	0	0	0	15	6	1	4	1	0
Mercedes	16,762	98	0	14	9	75	713	123	557	33	10
Merkel	2,613	3	0	1	0	2	29	9	18	2	0
Mesquite	144,406	616	6	74	244	292	5,264	773	3,642	849	6
Mexia	7,441	41	0	4	9	28	243	30	210	3	0

Table 8. Offenses Known to Law Enforcement, by Selected State and City, 2017—Continued

(Number.)

State/city	Population	Violent crime	Murder and nonnegligent manslaughter	Rape (revised definition)[1]	Robbery	Aggravated assault	Property crime	Burglary	Larceny-theft	Motor vehicle theft	Arson[2]
Midland	138,954	377	2	37	59	279	2,677	431	2,026	220	5
Midlothian	24,617	22	0	5	0	17	415	34	359	22	4
Milford	750	6	1	2	0	3	12	4	7	1	0
Mineola	4,756	20	0	1	0	19	92	6	81	5	0
Mission	84,511	98	0	27	30	41	2,005	231	1,700	74	19
Missouri City	75,863	149	2	23	46	78	969	133	767	69	0
Monahans	7,765	11	0	0	2	9	83	19	58	6	0
Mont Belvieu[6]	5,913	10	0	6	0	4	141	17	107	17	0
Montgomery	985	1	0	1	0	0	8	1	7	0	1
Moulton	911	1	0	1	0	0	1	1	0	0	0
Mount Pleasant	16,316	75	1	23	4	47	580	84	478	18	1
Muleshoe	5,160	6	0	0	0	6	50	12	34	4	0
Munday	1,328	0	0	0	0	0	4	3	1	0	0
Murphy	20,926	6	0	4	0	2	127	11	113	3	1
Nacogdoches	34,093	94	1	19	25	49	946	146	773	27	1
Naples	1,344	13	1	0	0	12	13	6	7	0	2
Nash	3,393	8	0	3	2	3	75	32	37	6	0
Nassau Bay	4,073	6	1	1	4	0	115	23	84	8	1
Natalia	1,537	3	0	0	0	3	18	11	7	0	0
Navasota	7,604	30	2	7	4	17	160	51	95	14	1
Nederland	17,344	59	0	7	8	44	462	79	347	36	1
Needville	3,101	5	0	1	0	4	20	3	15	2	0
New Boston	4,667	10	0	0	3	7	156	15	132	9	0
New Braunfels	76,993	193	1	33	29	130	1,321	221	952	148	8
Newton	2,391	2	0	0	0	2	18	8	8	2	0
Nixon	2,514	6	0	0	0	6	26	10	13	3	0
Nocona	2,952	3	0	1	0	2	20	12	7	1	0
Nolanville	5,072	9	1	2	1	5	60	17	40	3	0
Normangee	704	0	0	0	0	0	0	0	0	0	0
Northeast	2,981	2	0	0	0	2	59	7	49	3	0
Northlake	2,507	4	0	0	2	2	66	8	51	7	1
North Richland Hills	70,910	147	2	31	34	80	1,373	208	1,064	101	2
Oak Ridge	194	0	0	0	0	0	0	0	0	0	0
Odessa	121,194	912	7	78	101	726	3,219	560	2,386	273	10
Olmos Park	2,448	0	0	0	0	0	38	2	34	2	0
Olney	3,147	3	0	0	2	1	51	23	25	3	0
Olton	2,097	3	0	0	0	3	15	7	7	1	0
Omaha	993	0	0	0	0	0	7	3	3	1	0
Onalaska	2,529	9	0	1	0	8	13	5	5	3	0
Orange	19,552	132	2	1	43	86	420	147	226	47	10
Ovilla	4,060	3	0	1	0	2	30	4	24	2	0
Oyster Creek	1,129	15	0	0	1	14	43	13	27	3	0
Paducah	1,089	3	0	0	0	3	2	1	1	0	0
Palacios	4,676	7	0	0	2	5	121	40	78	3	0
Palestine[6]	18,316	130	2	16	12	100	364	88	248	28	1
Palmer	2,081	3	0	0	0	3	31	4	22	5	0
Palmhurst	2,746	8	0	0	0	8	150	1	149	0	0
Palm Valley	1,288	0	0	0	0	0	0	0	0	0	0
Palmview	5,791	52	1	3	5	43	255	50	202	3	2
Panhandle	2,358	10	0	1	0	9	11	2	8	1	0
Pantego[6]	2,569	18	0	1	3	14	119	21	89	9	0
Paris	24,978	218	1	4	31	182	852	191	613	48	0
Parker	4,541	3	0	1	0	2	22	10	8	4	0
Pasadena	154,000	711	5	93	195	418	3,773	636	2,758	379	23
Patton Village	1,953	3	1	0	0	2	37	7	23	7	2
Pearsall	10,222	7	0	0	1	6	215	65	139	11	1
Pecos	9,820	116	0	7	5	104	153	31	121	1	0
Pelican Bay	1,664	3	0	0	0	3	22	15	7	0	1
Penitas	4,935	6	0	0	0	6	11	1	8	2	0
Perryton[6]	8,890	41	0	0	0	41	117	31	74	12	0
Pflugerville[6]	61,212	102	1	31	15	55	968	127	796	45	2
Pharr	78,467	204	4	44	33	123	1,673	268	1,343	62	2
Pilot Point	4,313	5	0	3	0	2	37	11	25	1	0
Pinehurst	2,085	10	0	0	3	7	49	8	38	3	0
Pittsburg	4,736	19	0	3	3	13	137	38	94	5	0
Plainview	20,641	66	0	21	10	35	603	112	442	49	1
Plano	290,413	435	15	81	119	220	5,035	728	3,968	339	25
Pleasanton	10,563	39	0	13	5	21	411	71	311	29	0
Ponder[6]	1,602	3	0	2	0	1	20	8	11	1	0
Port Aransas	4,156	10	0	5	0	5	359	60	272	27	1
Port Arthur	55,583	378	6	15	110	247	2,031	767	1,111	153	5
Port Isabel	5,017	33	0	0	0	33	219	15	192	12	1
Portland	16,849	26	1	7	8	10	415	41	365	9	1
Port Lavaca	12,432	85	1	17	3	64	235	72	140	23	1
Port Mansfield	233	0	0	0	0	0	15	0	15	0	0
Port Neches	12,775	50	1	8	2	39	208	41	141	26	0
Poteet	3,476	9	0	1	1	7	112	28	71	13	2
Poth	2,266	0	0	0	0	0	14	4	8	2	0
Pottsboro	2,330	3	0	0	0	3	6	0	6	0	0
Prairie View	6,597	12	1	0	1	10	25	11	13	1	0
Premont	2,622	5	0	0	0	5	47	21	24	2	3
Presidio	3,882	2	0	1	0	1	9	1	7	1	0
Primera	4,860	2	0	0	0	2	33	3	29	1	0

Table 8. Offenses Known to Law Enforcement, by Selected State and City, 2017—Continued

(Number.)

State/city	Population	Violent crime	Murder and nonnegligent manslaughter	Rape (revised definition)[1]	Robbery	Aggravated assault	Property crime	Burglary	Larceny-theft	Motor vehicle theft	Arson[2]
Princeton[6]	9,934	34	1	8	1	24	199	16	178	5	4
Prosper	20,442	14	1	3	3	7	229	67	155	7	0
Queen City	1,464	8	0	1	2	5	17	3	12	2	0
Quitman	1,849	1	0	0	0	1	31	6	24	1	0
Ralls	1,898	0	0	0	0	0	3	1	2	0	0
Rancho Viejo	2,504	1	0	0	0	1	17	5	12	0	0
Ranger	2,454	24	0	2	0	22	35	14	18	3	2
Raymondville	11,151	76	0	6	4	66	389	124	259	6	3
Red Oak	12,833	17	0	0	9	8	364	78	262	24	0
Refugio	2,875	3	0	0	0	3	5	4	1	0	0
Reno	3,324	4	0	0	1	3	36	1	31	4	0
Richardson	115,824	193	3	25	97	68	2,295	389	1,717	189	5
Richland Hills	8,176	24	0	5	3	16	268	42	198	28	0
Richmond	12,174	42	0	6	13	23	211	45	157	9	0
Richwood	3,965	7	0	1	0	6	39	9	27	3	0
Riesel	1,019	2	0	0	0	2	8	1	7	0	0
Rio Bravo	4,738	0	0	0	0	0	0	0	0	0	0
Rio Grande City	14,592	25	0	1	4	20	191	37	115	39	3
Rio Hondo	2,650	2	0	0	0	2	34	9	23	2	0
River Oaks	7,793	6	1	0	2	3	134	26	91	17	0
Roanoke	8,145	10	0	0	3	7	144	14	119	11	0
Robinson	11,653	33	0	0	1	32	127	22	100	5	1
Robstown	11,524	103	2	2	7	92	442	149	281	12	2
Rockdale[6]	5,647	20	1	3	0	16	167	41	118	8	0
Rockport	10,870	21	0	5	0	16	430	115	291	24	0
Rockwall	44,599	48	0	15	5	28	796	70	675	51	0
Rollingwood	1,588	0	0	0	0	0	12	2	10	0	0
Roma	10,345	19	0	2	0	17	128	26	80	22	0
Roman Forest	1,927	0	0	0	0	0	12	4	6	2	0
Rosenberg	37,822	126	1	29	36	60	556	119	378	59	0
Round Rock	124,617	169	2	33	44	90	2,701	232	2,405	64	4
Rowlett	62,998	141	1	20	23	97	1,081	133	877	71	1
Royse City	12,599	19	1	3	0	15	125	14	100	11	0
Runaway Bay	1,499	0	0	0	0	0	3	2	0	1	0
Rusk	5,576	11	0	1	1	9	82	19	61	2	1
Sabinal	1,711	2	0	0	0	2	24	1	23	0	1
Sachse	25,907	13	0	10	1	2	290	45	223	22	0
Saginaw	22,994	31	0	2	8	21	524	61	404	59	1
Salado	2,160	2	0	0	0	2	23	6	13	4	0
San Angelo	101,931	282	3	74	40	165	4,499	802	3,425	272	10
San Antonio	1,520,712	10,759	124	1,270	2,298	7,067	73,676	11,722	55,090	6,864	207
San Augustine	1,895	4	0	0	0	4	2	1	0	1	0
San Benito	24,503	76	0	52	4	20	910	156	729	25	1
San Diego	4,369	6	0	0	2	4	6	5	1	0	0
Sanger	8,175	18	2	4	0	12	84	22	57	5	0
San Juan	37,114	157	1	24	21	111	873	110	712	51	1
San Marcos	65,327	222	5	50	47	120	1,511	278	1,064	169	8
San Saba	3,071	5	0	0	0	5	23	10	10	3	0
Sansom Park Village	4,904	3	0	0	0	3	126	45	71	10	0
Santa Anna	1,037	2	0	0	1	1	5	4	1	0	0
Santa Fe	13,347	12	0	3	3	6	179	42	119	18	1
Santa Rosa	2,848	0	0	0	0	0	16	4	10	2	0
Schertz	40,830	99	0	20	15	64	695	115	523	57	0
Schulenburg	2,943	34	0	2	1	31	42	4	33	5	0
Seabrook	13,958	23	0	4	8	11	142	34	94	14	0
Seagoville	16,290	20	1	0	8	11	393	69	245	79	2
Seagraves	2,892	6	0	0	0	6	30	15	14	1	0
Sealy	6,555	22	0	0	4	18	119	35	69	15	0
Seguin	29,132	112	1	33	17	61	990	174	789	27	1
Selma	11,117	21	0	2	10	9	328	35	266	27	0
Seminole[6]	7,795	41	1	4	1	35	109	13	88	8	0
Seven Points	1,462	9	0	1	2	6	60	11	43	6	0
Seymour[6]	2,717	8	0	0	1	7	18	6	10	2	0
Shallowater	2,560	0	0	0	0	0	36	24	5	7	0
Shamrock	1,953	0	0	0	0	0	8	3	5	0	0
Shavano Park	3,801	1	0	0	1	0	36	6	28	2	0
Shenandoah[6]	3,019	11	0	2	5	4	203	11	167	25	0
Sherman	42,122	158	2	20	35	101	1,306	287	942	77	3
Shiner	2,148	6	0	0	0	6	7	4	3	0	0
Shoreacres	1,617	0	0	0	0	0	9	2	7	0	0
Sinton	5,614	45	0	5	4	36	231	47	170	14	0
Slaton	6,051	16	0	1	1	14	127	44	70	13	0
Smithville	4,288	9	0	0	2	7	73	16	55	2	0
Socorro	33,473	48	0	6	7	35	293	38	233	22	1
Somerset	1,836	2	0	0	1	1	21	6	13	2	0
Sonora	2,812	4	0	4	0	0	28	5	23	0	0
Sour Lake	1,835	4	0	0	0	4	27	5	19	3	0
South Houston[6]	17,537	57	0	3	25	29	460	71	283	106	1
Southlake	31,778	21	0	2	4	15	372	56	311	5	0
South Padre Island	2,881	52	0	16	8	28	416	33	369	14	0
Southside Place	1,857	2	0	0	1	1	23	3	20	0	0
Spearman	3,332	2	0	0	0	2	6	5	1	0	0
Splendora	2,026	2	0	0	0	2	16	7	5	4	0

Table 8. Offenses Known to Law Enforcement, by Selected State and City, 2017—Continued

(Number.)

State/city	Population	Violent crime	Murder and nonnegligent manslaughter	Rape (revised definition)[1]	Robbery	Aggravated assault	Property crime	Burglary	Larceny-theft	Motor vehicle theft	Arson[2]
Springtown	2,907	8	0	1	0	7	52	10	42	0	1
Spring Valley	4,312	4	0	0	2	2	72	4	64	4	0
Spur	1,177	6	0	0	0	6	7	7	0	0	0
Stafford	18,530	121	1	7	41	72	828	118	656	54	1
Stagecoach	612	0	0	0	0	0	0	0	0	0	0
Stamford	2,961	13	0	0	1	12	55	17	35	3	1
Stephenville	21,274	38	0	22	5	11	374	43	316	15	0
Sugar Land	89,790	71	0	15	36	20	1,289	158	1,075	56	0
Sullivan City	4,223	36	0	2	0	34	75	17	54	4	0
Sulphur Springs	16,281	29	0	6	4	19	166	27	126	13	2
Sunrise Beach Village	767	0	0	0	0	0	8	4	4	0	0
Sunset Valley	704	8	0	0	2	6	163	10	152	1	0
Surfside Beach	575	1	0	0	0	1	21	4	17	0	0
Sweeny	3,773	15	0	2	0	13	92	13	77	2	0
Sweetwater[6]	10,726	46	0	3	1	42	361	156	179	26	0
Taft	3,022	4	0	0	0	4	36	8	25	3	0
Tahoka	2,544	0	0	0	0	0	32	11	19	2	0
Tatum	1,366	2	0	1	0	1	22	5	16	1	0
Taylor	17,116	42	0	2	7	33	521	78	410	33	2
Teague	3,538	8	0	4	1	3	41	15	19	7	0
Temple	74,794	238	5	63	65	105	2,130	409	1,483	238	6
Terrell	17,579	114	1	13	29	71	793	167	559	67	0
Terrell Hills	5,457	1	0	0	0	1	72	16	56	0	1
Texarkana	37,882	478	3	31	86	358	1,889	311	1,457	121	21
Texas City	48,774	237	2	47	46	142	1,704	336	1,245	123	1
The Colony	43,484	114	1	60	9	44	501	86	373	42	6
Thorndale	1,293	4	0	0	0	4	20	4	16	0	0
Thrall	943	0	0	0	0	0	2	0	2	0	0
Three Rivers	1,956	12	0	0	0	12	18	9	9	0	0
Tioga	958	1	0	0	0	1	4	1	1	2	0
Tomball	11,807	31	1	7	7	16	329	37	252	40	1
Tool	2,284	2	0	1	0	1	19	5	10	4	0
Trophy Club	12,999	2	0	0	1	1	88	8	72	8	0
Troup	2,001	15	0	2	1	12	55	19	34	2	0
Tulia	4,673	21	0	2	3	16	110	18	87	5	0
Tye	1,260	4	0	0	0	4	25	4	19	2	0
Tyler	106,115	464	6	65	60	333	3,337	446	2,745	146	4
Universal City	20,668	77	2	9	19	47	584	123	416	45	7
University Park	25,218	11	0	5	4	2	314	38	257	19	1
Uvalde	16,671	39	1	4	11	23	616	81	525	10	0
Van	2,745	6	0	2	1	3	45	7	31	7	0
Van Alstyne	3,700	3	0	0	0	3	47	8	36	3	2
Venus	3,535	4	1	0	1	2	27	5	18	4	0
Vernon	10,378	38	1	7	4	26	338	56	268	14	3
Victoria	68,544	217	4	48	49	116	2,436	646	1,680	110	4
Vidor	11,000	30	2	3	5	20	313	60	219	34	1
Waco	135,997	690	5	117	108	460	4,889	957	3,741	191	15
Waelder	1,133	3	0	1	0	2	2	2	0	0	0
Wake Village	5,448	8	1	1	3	3	139	25	104	10	0
Waller	2,847	7	0	1	1	5	60	13	42	5	0
Wallis	1,306	2	0	0	0	2	5	1	4	0	0
Watauga	24,814	38	0	14	5	19	410	68	328	14	2
Waxahachie	35,169	51	3	3	19	26	749	80	599	70	0
Weatherford	30,712	33	0	3	5	25	707	113	555	39	2
Webster	11,149	57	0	18	23	16	844	123	640	81	0
Weimar	2,173	6	0	3	0	3	20	6	10	4	0
Weslaco	40,554	147	0	24	26	97	1,630	146	1,434	50	2
West	2,892	8	0	5	1	2	51	10	40	1	0
West Lake Hills[6]	3,438	2	0	0	1	1	70	12	53	5	0
West Orange	3,457	5	0	0	0	5	112	12	94	6	0
Westover Hills	714	2	0	0	1	1	32	14	17	1	0
West University Place	15,676	10	0	0	9	1	137	44	89	4	0
Westworth	2,765	8	0	1	5	2	270	9	256	5	0
Wharton	8,769	51	0	1	14	36	286	54	226	6	4
Whitehouse	8,366	35	0	4	0	31	78	19	57	2	0
White Oak	6,343	6	0	3	0	3	100	11	70	19	0
Whitesboro	4,002	7	0	0	0	7	35	2	30	3	0
White Settlement	17,385	32	1	0	17	14	432	101	282	49	0
Wichita Falls	104,706	374	4	78	127	165	3,257	725	2,294	238	0
Willis	6,450	42	0	8	9	25	161	27	123	11	2
Willow Park[6]	5,371	6	2	2	0	2	56	11	42	3	0
Wills Point	3,622	12	0	3	1	8	80	21	57	2	0
Wilmer	4,069	4	0	0	2	2	83	21	54	8	0
Windcrest	5,939	19	1	4	8	6	394	19	345	30	0
Wink	1,066	1	0	1	0	0	3	0	2	1	0
Winnsboro	3,356	9	0	1	0	8	94	20	68	6	0
Winters	2,529	28	0	2	0	26	33	15	15	3	1
Wolfforth	4,552	0	0	0	0	0	22	11	11	0	0
Woodbranch	1,396	0	0	0	0	0	7	3	4	0	0
Woodville	2,458	1	0	0	0	1	9	5	4	0	0
Woodway	8,894	14	0	3	1	10	91	8	83	0	0
Wortham	1,009	0	0	0	0	0	13	6	6	1	0
Wylie	48,772	46	0	14	4	28	425	50	347	28	2

Table 8. Offenses Known to Law Enforcement, by Selected State and City, 2017—Continued

(Number.)

State/city	Population	Violent crime	Murder and nonnegligent manslaughter	Rape (revised definition)[1]	Robbery	Aggravated assault	Property crime	Burglary	Larceny-theft	Motor vehicle theft	Arson[2]
Yoakum	6,055	11	0	7	0	4	91	45	43	3	1
Yorktown	2,177	5	0	3	1	1	26	10	14	2	0
UTAH											
American Fork/Cedar Hills	39,603	27	1	9	7	10	922	81	801	40	2
Big Water	480	0	0	0	0	0	3	2	1	0	0
Blanding	4,161	5	0	3	0	2	42	8	31	3	0
Bluffdale	12,718	18	0	6	0	12	125	27	81	17	0
Bountiful	44,312	47	0	24	5	18	706	86	560	60	0
Brian Head	90	0	0	0	0	0	16	1	15	0	0
Brigham City	19,150	28	0	8	5	15	371	62	291	18	2
Cedar City	31,624	70	0	9	5	56	639	110	492	37	11
Centerville	17,635	11	0	4	2	5	452	32	385	35	2
Clearfield	30,994	41	1	7	9	24	615	73	492	50	5
Clinton	21,860	17	0	2	2	13	363	32	315	16	0
Cottonwood Heights	34,400	63	0	12	23	28	1,007	144	815	48	2
Draper	48,197	75	0	23	13	39	1,588	229	1,099	260	6
Enoch	6,691	28	0	0	0	28	60	15	39	6	1
Fairview	1,296	2	0	0	0	2	9	1	6	2	0
Farmington	24,040	14	0	4	2	8	324	36	260	28	0
Fountain Green	1,110	0	0	0	0	0	24	0	23	1	0
Garland	2,500	5	0	2	0	3	39	9	28	2	0
Grantsville	10,731	30	0	18	0	12	248	27	187	34	0
Harrisville	6,512	4	1	1	0	2	286	37	227	22	0
Heber	15,653	12	0	2	0	10	196	24	157	15	0
Helper	2,077	5	0	0	0	5	30	9	21	0	0
Hurricane	16,592	18	0	5	0	13	263	40	201	22	0
Kanab	4,562	6	0	1	0	5	37	3	32	2	0
Kaysville	31,873	16	0	7	3	6	307	76	207	24	0
La Verkin	4,277	9	0	1	0	8	70	7	53	10	0
Layton	77,048	106	1	42	11	52	1,730	250	1,397	83	11
Lehi	63,605	49	0	23	8	18	895	142	697	56	1
Lindon	11,085	11	0	1	1	9	296	22	255	19	0
Logan	51,059	48	1	23	1	23	678	94	547	37	0
Lone Peak	29,691	5	0	5	0	0	258	52	189	17	1
Mapleton	9,772	7	3	2	1	1	95	23	69	3	1
Moab	5,266	33	0	8	0	25	67	6	54	7	1
Monticello	2,257	2	0	1	0	1	26	3	22	1	0
Mount Pleasant[6]	3,380	3	0	0	1	2	38	6	28	4	0
Murray	49,650	241	2	69	50	120	3,408	467	2,469	472	0
Naples	2,203	0	0	0	0	0	18	6	11	1	1
Nephi	5,859	6	0	2	2	2	135	30	98	7	0
North Ogden	19,021	12	0	1	1	10	260	26	210	24	0
North Park	15,658	12	0	12	0	0	187	19	155	13	0
North Salt Lake	21,053	16	0	8	3	5	403	64	289	50	2
Ogden	87,323	463	6	49	91	317	3,794	546	2,780	468	23
Orem	99,045	69	0	14	22	33	2,016	191	1,696	129	2
Park City	8,415	33	1	9	2	21	264	23	235	6	1
Payson	20,010	9	0	0	4	5	370	40	312	18	0
Perry	4,902	2	0	0	1	1	111	12	97	2	2
Pleasant Grove	39,666	29	0	3	1	25	131	22	105	4	0
Pleasant View	10,036	3	0	3	0	0	101	27	61	13	0
Price	8,313	17	0	7	0	10	419	86	329	4	1
Provo	117,540	148	1	52	29	66	2,036	155	1,764	117	5
Richfield	7,755	10	0	5	0	5	242	31	193	18	0
Riverdale	8,745	24	0	1	8	15	596	27	541	28	2
Roosevelt	7,057	29	0	25	0	4	309	24	228	57	1
Roy	38,410	49	1	20	3	25	519	84	397	38	2
Salem	8,086	2	0	1	0	1	37	2	33	2	0
Salina	2,561	7	0	0	0	7	81	13	62	6	0
Salt Lake City	194,968	1,713	10	334	508	861	15,694	1,884	11,924	1,886	27
Sandy	96,957	217	3	53	60	101	3,195	541	2,384	270	4
Santa Clara/Ivins	15,615	2	0	1	0	1	102	27	62	13	0
Santaquin/Genola	12,900	5	0	2	1	2	118	17	93	8	0
Saratoga Springs	28,739	14	0	10	0	4	224	45	168	11	1
Smithfield	11,409	7	0	5	1	1	35	7	22	6	0
South Jordan	72,533	45	0	10	5	30	1,721	226	1,339	156	3
South Ogden	17,177	18	0	5	4	9	322	52	234	36	1
South Salt Lake	24,811	235	3	44	54	134	1,971	353	1,221	397	6
Spanish Fork	39,512	22	1	6	7	8	398	50	333	15	2
Spring City	1,028	0	0	0	0	0	15	1	13	1	0
Springdale	577	0	0	0	0	0	19	5	14	0	0
Springville	33,617	15	0	7	3	5	707	62	615	30	0
Stockton	649	4	0	0	0	4	10	4	6	0	0
Sunset	5,246	9	1	7	0	1	94	10	81	3	0
Syracuse	29,114	25	0	9	0	16	338	35	289	14	3
Tooele[6]	34,112	111	0	40	20	51	1,185	180	931	74	5
Tremonton	8,551	14	0	6	0	8	143	35	99	9	0
Vernal	10,985	18	0	5	1	12	256	27	220	9	0
Washington	26,618	31	0	9	0	22	468	67	380	21	2
West Bountiful	5,625	10	0	9	0	1	143	8	108	27	0
West Jordan	115,390	295	3	36	53	203	3,539	388	2,767	384	3
West Valley	137,762	802	8	164	150	480	5,837	861	3,830	1,146	14

Table 8. Offenses Known to Law Enforcement, by Selected State and City, 2017—Continued

(Number.)

State/city	Population	Violent crime	Murder and nonnegligent manslaughter	Rape (revised definition)[1]	Robbery	Aggravated assault	Property crime	Burglary	Larceny-theft	Motor vehicle theft	Arson[2]
Willard	1,818	1	1	0	0	0	35	24	10	1	0
Woods Cross	11,627	15	0	3	2	10	117	11	96	10	0
VERMONT											
Barre	8,655	31	0	11	3	17	404	55	349	0	4
Barre Town	7,768	10	0	0	0	10	92	20	72	0	0
Bellows Falls	2,996	10	0	3	0	7	62	2	60	0	0
Bennington	15,215	25	0	2	1	22	340	63	259	18	0
Berlin	2,789	7	0	1	0	6	98	4	93	1	0
Bradford	2,711	0	0	0	0	0	16	1	15	0	0
Brandon	3,778	5	0	0	0	5	35	6	29	0	0
Brattleboro	11,536	27	0	3	6	18	409	95	299	15	0
Bristol	3,908	5	0	1	0	4	13	3	10	0	0
Burlington	42,230	132	1	21	11	99	1,164	223	941	0	3
Chester	3,039	8	0	2	0	6	14	6	6	2	0
Colchester	17,353	25	0	9	5	11	298	31	267	0	0
Dover	1,076	5	0	0	0	5	104	7	96	1	0
Essex	21,470	17	0	0	5	12	257	47	198	12	1
Hardwick	2,862	3	0	1	0	2	65	22	43	0	2
Hartford	9,628	22	0	7	5	10	118	21	90	7	1
Hinesburg	4,561	1	0	0	0	1	14	6	7	1	0
Ludlow	1,894	5	0	1	3	1	17	2	15	0	0
Lyndonville	1,166	3	0	0	0	3	20	2	18	0	1
Manchester	4,299	2	0	0	0	2	58	8	50	0	0
Middlebury	8,681	4	0	1	0	3	88	9	79	0	1
Milton	10,825	8	0	1	0	7	97	11	86	0	0
Montpelier	7,484	16	0	4	2	10	174	18	156	0	1
Morristown	5,475	6	0	1	1	4	71	2	69	0	0
Newport	4,287	38	0	17	0	21	81	18	63	0	0
Northfield	6,014	9	0	2	2	5	50	18	30	2	0
Randolph	4,712	4	0	0	0	4	18	5	13	0	0
Richmond	4,120	1	0	0	0	1	20	3	17	0	1
Rutland	15,462	85	1	9	8	67	510	99	402	9	1
Rutland Town	4,061	4	0	4	0	0	27	0	26	1	0
Shelburne	7,827	1	0	0	1	0	45	8	35	2	0
South Burlington	19,146	37	0	16	5	16	510	47	463	0	1
Springfield	8,993	20	1	4	0	15	171	31	140	0	2
St. Albans	6,772	46	1	10	7	28	504	30	474	0	1
St. Johnsbury	7,196	16	0	3	1	12	135	19	116	0	0
Stowe	4,440	4	0	2	1	1	88	15	73	0	0
Swanton	6,529	6	0	0	0	6	18	0	18	0	0
Thetford	2,576	1	0	1	0	0	8	4	4	0	0
Vergennes	2,593	4	0	0	0	4	29	3	26	0	0
Weathersfield	2,767	0	0	0	0	0	15	9	5	1	0
Williston	9,731	7	0	0	1	6	139	14	125	0	0
Wilmington	1,807	2	0	0	0	2	14	2	11	1	0
Windsor	3,398	5	0	2	0	3	17	3	14	0	0
Winooski	7,105	25	0	4	4	17	188	40	148	0	0
Woodstock	2,938	0	0	0	0	0	27	11	16	0	0
VIRGINIA											
Abingdon	8,066	14	0	2	2	10	141	16	116	9	1
Alexandria	158,256	262	6	16	102	138	2,482	163	2,046	273	8
Altavista	3,470	4	0	0	0	4	110	12	94	4	0
Amherst	2,201	1	0	0	1	0	12	1	10	1	0
Appalachia	1,638	4	0	0	1	3	20	8	12	0	1
Ashland	7,722	31	1	1	4	25	160	13	141	6	0
Bedford	6,622	15	1	4	4	6	234	10	217	7	1
Berryville	4,324	1	0	1	0	0	38	7	30	1	0
Big Stone Gap	5,334	6	0	3	1	2	173	16	154	3	5
Blacksburg	45,443	24	0	10	1	13	339	40	289	10	1
Blackstone	3,427	14	0	2	3	9	139	17	114	8	1
Bluefield	4,894	16	3	7	3	3	248	19	228	1	0
Bridgewater	6,119	1	0	0	0	1	12	0	12	0	0
Bristol	16,795	54	0	15	3	36	562	86	428	48	1
Broadway	3,889	4	0	2	0	2	12	2	10	0	0
Brookneal	1,117	4	0	0	1	3	18	3	14	1	0
Burkeville	402	0	0	0	0	0	19	2	16	1	0
Cape Charles	1,044	1	0	0	0	1	10	0	10	0	0
Cedar Bluff	1,049	0	0	0	0	0	3	1	1	1	0
Charlottesville	47,446	185	3	31	22	129	1,036	145	820	71	6
Chase City	2,268	11	1	0	2	8	38	15	17	6	1
Chatham	1,473	0	0	0	0	0	8	0	8	0	0
Chesapeake	240,119	1,006	11	87	198	710	5,456	663	4,543	250	20
Chilhowie	1,712	0	0	0	0	0	17	4	13	0	0
Chincoteague	2,916	4	0	2	1	1	37	7	28	2	1
Clarksville	1,181	1	0	0	0	1	24	3	21	0	0
Clifton Forge	3,689	9	0	0	1	8	48	3	42	3	1
Clintwood	1,285	1	0	0	0	1	24	5	19	0	0
Coeburn	1,970	10	0	4	0	6	44	4	36	4	1
Colonial Beach	3,577	11	1	2	0	8	47	11	32	4	0
Colonial Heights	17,820	67	3	25	20	19	728	25	688	15	8
Covington	5,442	17	0	1	0	16	88	9	76	3	1

Table 8. Offenses Known to Law Enforcement, by Selected State and City, 2017—Continued

(Number.)

State/city	Population	Violent crime	Murder and nonnegligent manslaughter	Rape (revised definition)[1]	Robbery	Aggravated assault	Property crime	Burglary	Larceny-theft	Motor vehicle theft	Arson[2]
Crewe	2,199	8	0	0	5	3	58	9	45	4	0
Culpeper	18,232	45	0	5	13	27	320	22	279	19	3
Damascus	796	2	0	0	0	2	38	4	33	1	0
Danville	41,680	250	13	14	68	155	1,808	288	1,422	98	13
Dayton	1,621	0	0	0	0	0	3	0	3	0	0
Dublin	2,710	5	0	2	0	3	17	3	12	2	0
Dumfries	5,219	4	0	0	1	3	47	7	34	6	0
Elkton	2,871	2	0	0	1	1	31	3	25	3	0
Emporia	5,201	22	2	1	9	10	223	29	189	5	0
Exmore	1,438	2	0	1	0	1	26	2	24	0	0
Fairfax City	24,406	33	0	7	23	3	366	10	339	17	1
Falls Church	14,278	10	0	4	2	4	213	10	194	9	1
Farmville	8,127	18	0	5	4	9	226	21	195	10	1
Franklin	8,250	30	1	4	14	11	465	62	386	17	2
Fredericksburg	29,016	108	2	9	17	80	1,026	53	922	51	6
Galax	6,728	19	1	2	3	13	260	35	208	17	0
Gate City	1,911	4	0	2	0	2	29	5	21	3	2
Glade Spring	1,446	0	0	0	0	0	4	0	3	1	0
Glasgow	1,117	0	0	0	0	0	0	0	0	0	0
Glen Lyn	118	0	0	0	0	0	3	1	2	0	0
Gordonsville	1,599	3	0	1	0	2	14	3	10	1	0
Gretna	1,231	0	0	0	0	0	11	5	5	1	0
Grottoes	2,821	3	0	1	0	2	20	0	20	0	0
Grundy	949	0	0	0	0	0	23	0	22	1	0
Halifax	1,240	1	0	0	1	0	15	2	11	2	0
Hampton	134,929	407	17	26	185	179	4,364	551	3,481	332	18
Harrisonburg	53,717	128	3	24	12	89	897	115	739	43	3
Haymarket	2,001	1	0	0	0	1	16	1	14	1	0
Haysi	473	1	0	0	1	0	5	3	2	0	0
Herndon	24,561	38	0	4	12	22	287	10	268	9	0
Hillsville	2,643	1	0	1	0	0	65	12	48	5	0
Honaker	1,352	3	0	0	0	3	31	4	26	1	0
Hopewell	22,723	79	2	2	28	47	596	147	392	57	3
Hurt	1,260	0	0	0	0	0	2	0	2	0	0
Independence	919	2	0	1	0	1	11	1	8	2	1
Jonesville	948	1	0	0	0	1	8	1	7	0	0
Kenbridge	1,214	0	0	0	0	0	0	0	0	0	0
Kilmarnock	1,431	1	0	0	0	1	34	5	24	5	0
La Crosse	581	0	0	0	0	0	5	1	4	0	0
Lebanon	3,260	2	0	1	0	1	110	4	101	5	1
Lexington	7,034	9	0	2	1	6	40	6	33	1	0
Louisa	1,665	1	0	0	0	1	34	0	34	0	0
Luray	4,804	8	0	3	2	3	122	11	107	4	0
Lynchburg	80,890	287	4	33	42	208	1,886	224	1,522	140	7
Manassas	41,995	95	3	15	36	41	788	100	649	39	9
Manassas Park	16,158	20	0	9	4	7	147	12	124	11	3
Marion	5,837	20	0	2	2	16	247	43	188	16	1
Martinsville	13,383	40	2	4	4	30	395	68	306	21	0
Middleburg	856	0	0	0	0	0	7	0	6	1	0
Middletown	1,345	1	0	1	0	0	4	1	2	1	0
Mount Jackson	2,048	2	0	0	0	2	50	3	47	0	0
Narrows	1,963	1	0	0	0	1	3	0	3	0	0
New Market	2,217	1	0	0	0	1	17	0	17	0	0
Newport News	181,738	907	24	93	239	551	5,528	829	4,211	488	46
Norfolk	245,190	1,363	36	135	371	821	9,192	1,156	7,318	718	8
Norton	3,842	5	0	2	1	2	132	9	117	6	1
Occoquan	1,082	0	0	0	0	0	2	0	2	0	0
Onancock	1,266	8	0	1	0	7	14	0	12	2	0
Onley	513	2	0	0	1	1	17	1	16	0	0
Orange	5,033	7	0	0	1	6	65	5	53	7	1
Parksley	841	0	0	0	0	0	3	1	2	0	0
Pearisburg	2,683	5	0	2	0	3	58	6	49	3	0
Pembroke	1,086	0	0	0	0	0	19	1	16	2	0
Pennington Gap	1,759	2	0	0	0	2	15	1	14	0	0
Petersburg	31,739	252	12	13	75	152	1,080	177	790	113	5
Pocahontas	372	0	0	0	0	0	0	0	0	0	0
Poquoson	11,981	19	0	3	2	14	183	34	149	0	1
Portsmouth	95,100	677	17	36	224	400	5,447	1,160	3,903	384	6
Pound	945	0	0	0	0	0	4	0	1	3	0
Pulaski	8,799	22	1	12	1	8	262	52	196	14	2
Purcellville	9,779	10	0	1	0	9	49	3	43	3	0
Quantico	550	0	0	0	0	0	1	0	1	0	0
Radford	17,641	68	0	16	7	45	237	59	172	6	2
Rich Creek	752	4	0	3	1	0	10	1	8	1	0
Richlands	5,365	10	0	4	0	6	94	20	71	3	0
Roanoke	100,027	402	16	41	79	266	4,493	487	3,719	287	26
Rocky Mount	4,801	16	0	5	3	8	170	16	150	4	3
Rural Retreat	1,480	0	0	0	0	0	9	3	6	0	0
Salem	25,624	18	0	3	8	7	555	41	470	44	1
Saltville	1,998	3	1	2	0	0	16	4	9	3	1
Shenandoah	2,328	1	0	0	0	1	34	4	28	2	0
Smithfield	8,492	23	1	0	4	18	92	13	72	7	0
South Boston	7,919	37	0	1	16	20	298	56	234	8	1

Table 8. Offenses Known to Law Enforcement, by Selected State and City, 2017—Continued

(Number.)

State/city	Population	Violent crime	Murder and nonnegligent manslaughter	Rape (revised definition)[1]	Robbery	Aggravated assault	Property crime	Burglary	Larceny-theft	Motor vehicle theft	Arson[2]
South Hill	4,449	11	0	1	5	5	123	13	105	5	0
Stanley	1,643	1	0	0	0	1	24	1	21	2	0
Staunton	24,423	35	0	7	8	20	551	77	456	18	13
Stephens City	1,990	1	0	0	0	1	25	3	21	1	0
St. Paul	899	2	0	1	0	1	25	5	18	2	0
Strasburg	6,613	7	0	2	1	4	59	11	47	1	0
Suffolk	89,922	274	3	26	69	176	2,231	343	1,791	97	13
Tappahannock	2,386	11	0	1	0	10	79	4	73	2	0
Tazewell	4,320	3	0	1	0	2	48	8	38	2	0
Timberville	2,659	0	0	0	0	0	6	0	6	0	0
Victoria	1,663	3	0	0	0	3	28	10	17	1	1
Vienna	16,590	4	1	2	1	0	132	10	119	3	1
Vinton	8,207	13	0	2	4	7	220	14	193	13	0
Virginia Beach	454,353	625	14	102	272	237	8,790	754	7,577	459	51
Warrenton	9,901	13	1	4	4	4	186	7	174	5	0
Warsaw	1,483	0	0	0	0	0	14	2	11	1	0
Waverly	2,033	4	1	1	0	2	37	9	25	3	0
Waynesboro	22,004	40	0	13	10	17	528	46	459	23	1
Weber City	1,234	1	0	1	0	0	14	2	12	0	0
West Point	3,313	3	0	0	0	3	28	2	24	2	0
White Stone	340	0	0	0	0	0	2	0	2	0	0
Williamsburg	15,464	24	1	3	9	11	181	12	156	13	2
Winchester	27,715	115	0	36	25	54	688	81	584	23	2
Windsor	2,694	4	0	1	1	2	29	3	26	0	0
Wise	3,056	4	0	3	0	1	26	8	15	3	0
Woodstock	5,272	12	1	1	3	7	113	5	102	6	1
Wytheville	8,084	11	0	3	2	6	170	7	153	10	2
WASHINGTON											
Aberdeen	16,243	85	0	15	22	48	753	138	554	61	6
Airway Heights	8,460	11	1	1	2	7	268	31	209	28	0
Algona	3,177	2	0	0	1	1	52	14	36	2	0
Anacortes	16,838	19	0	4	0	15	470	64	386	20	2
Arlington	19,302	66	0	9	14	43	764	117	540	107	3
Auburn[5]	78,718	376	3	64	117	192			2,124	653	19
Bainbridge Island	24,635	16	0	8	1	7	265	48	210	7	2
Battle Ground	20,516	37	0	12	5	20	287	31	233	23	4
Bellevue	143,703	144	0	24	55	65	4,175	592	3,274	309	20
Bellingham	88,652	258	2	56	73	127	4,151	552	3,435	164	10
Bingen	723	3	0	0	1	2	18	3	14	1	0
Black Diamond	4,422	1	0	1	0	0	30	10	20	0	0
Blaine	5,245	11	0	4	2	5	174	46	119	9	1
Bonney Lake	20,844	38	0	4	5	29	556	111	387	58	2
Bothell	45,357	49	0	13	18	18	1,260	209	945	106	5
Bremerton	41,173	216	3	26	29	158	1,670	264	1,206	200	7
Brier	6,840	4	0	0	0	4	69	25	43	1	0
Buckley	5,234	6	0	2	0	4	17	8	9	0	0
Burien[7]	51,479		4		74	115	2,089	449	1,097	543	9
Camas	22,973	13	0	4	3	6	374	70	268	36	4
Carnation[7]	2,032		0		1	2	31	8	17	6	0
Castle Rock	2,228	2	0	0	1	1	40	5	33	2	0
Centralia	17,048	80	0	17	21	42	1,041	180	746	115	4
Chehalis	7,538	17	0	1	5	11	540	66	442	32	1
Cheney	12,510	29	0	14	3	12	215	37	155	23	0
Chewelah	2,641	7	0	0	0	7	52	14	35	3	0
Cle Elum	2,895	8	0	1	2	5	92	17	72	3	0
Clyde Hill	3,316	0	0	0	0	0	19	5	12	2	0
College Place	9,198	12	0	1	0	11	253	31	202	20	3
Colville	4,805	3	0	0	0	3	130	7	118	5	0
Connell	5,656	11	0	3	1	7	24	8	15	1	0
Cosmopolis	1,593	0	0	0	0	0	23	4	18	1	0
Covington[7]	21,001		1		16	13	716	104	552	60	1
Darrington	1,391	11	0	4	0	7	40	16	20	4	0
Des Moines	31,415	125	2	12	58	53	1,151	165	744	242	8
Dupont	9,721	16	0	2	2	12	114	16	93	5	2
Duvall	7,875	4	0	2	0	2	31	4	24	3	0
East Wenatchee	14,097	17	0	4	1	12	390	40	336	14	0
Eatonville	2,994	4	0	0	2	2	60	18	36	6	0
Edgewood	10,984	13	0	0	3	10	269	95	136	38	2
Edmonds	42,197	72	0	8	24	40	927	198	658	71	7
Ellensburg	20,026	32	1	11	4	16	564	62	453	49	3
Elma	3,044	10	0	0	4	6	103	21	70	12	0
Enumclaw	11,745	10	0	4	1	5	220	19	177	24	0
Ephrata	8,086	15	0	2	4	9	418	95	301	22	0
Everett	110,040	497	5	52	131	309	5,099	869	3,292	938	13
Everson	4,217	1	0	0	0	1	40	2	37	1	0
Federal Way	98,014	440	7	39	170	224	5,339	679	3,716	944	10
Ferndale	13,757	20	1	5	4	10	289	55	210	24	0
Fife	10,264	99	1	18	32	48	740	108	471	161	1
Fircrest	6,830	13	0	1	2	10	138	36	95	7	0
Forks	3,822	10	0	3	1	6	95	16	77	2	2
Gig Harbor	9,494	19	0	5	2	12	507	50	434	23	2
Gold Bar	2,140	7	0	1	1	5	46	20	22	4	0

Table 8. Offenses Known to Law Enforcement, by Selected State and City, 2017—Continued

(Number.)

State/city	Population	Violent crime	Murder and nonnegligent manslaughter	Rape (revised definition)[1]	Robbery	Aggravated assault	Property crime	Burglary	Larceny-theft	Motor vehicle theft	Arson[2]
Goldendale	3,455	8	0	0	1	7	127	21	99	7	0
Grand Coulee	2,051	0	0	0	0	0	98	31	54	13	0
Grandview	11,203	21	0	0	0	21	173	35	110	28	1
Granite Falls	3,550	7	0	0	2	5	85	26	41	18	0
Hoquiam	8,386	13	2	2	2	7	314	52	241	21	1
Ilwaco	928	1	0	1	0	0	12	2	5	5	1
Issaquah	38,592	25	1	6	8	10	1,163	115	945	103	3
Kalama	2,509	1	0	1	0	0	33	6	23	4	0
Kelso	12,070	45	1	7	5	32	570	90	435	45	3
Kenmore[7]	22,673		0		4	8	312	88	180	44	0
Kennewick	81,499	213	1	30	59	123	2,228	307	1,732	189	25
Kent	128,990	465	7	70	203	185	6,928	948	4,666	1,314	17
Kettle Falls	1,609	2	0	2	0	0	24	12	11	1	0
Kirkland	88,898	75	1	24	16	34	2,181	231	1,724	226	6
Kittitas	1,452	1	0	1	0	0	11	1	10	0	0
La Center	3,177	2	0	0	0	2	38	9	22	7	0
Lacey	48,597	139	2	31	28	78	1,489	198	1,165	126	6
Lake Forest Park	13,375	11	0	1	4	6	252	50	179	23	0
Lake Stevens	32,288	49	0	8	8	33	418	68	270	80	10
Lakewood	61,080	425	4	54	89	278	2,793	488	1,927	378	11
Liberty Lake	9,505	6	0	1	2	3	156	23	116	17	0
Long Beach	1,389	0	0	0	0	0	43	9	23	11	0
Longview	37,424	112	2	46	21	43	1,360	262	956	142	12
Lynden	14,302	9	0	3	1	5	189	28	157	4	1
Lynnwood	38,469	139	1	33	48	57	2,292	236	1,876	180	6
Mabton	2,292	5	0	0	1	4	70	27	37	6	0
Maple Valley[7]	26,214		0		3	6	289	56	196	37	7
Marysville	68,950	151	3	32	30	86	1,799	292	1,206	301	5
Mattawa	4,423	4	0	2	1	1	59	16	32	11	0
Medina	3,293	0	0	0	0	0	69	7	62	0	0
Mercer Island	25,553	7	0	0	2	5	462	61	379	22	0
Mill Creek	20,664	44	1	5	7	31	447	66	336	45	2
Milton	8,121	22	2	0	3	17	265	41	178	46	1
Monroe	18,596	69	0	16	6	47	421	33	339	49	2
Montesano	3,902	2	0	0	1	1	59	12	45	2	0
Morton	1,149	1	0	0	1	0	15	2	12	1	0
Moses Lake	22,985	131	0	16	19	96	1,087	164	838	85	2
Mossyrock	764	0	0	0	0	0	8	1	6	1	0
Mountlake Terrace	21,402	42	0	6	12	24	541	127	328	86	4
Mount Vernon	35,085	82	3	15	23	41	1,302	234	947	121	3
Moxee	4,120	5	0	2	0	3	25	11	13	1	0
Mukilteo	21,662	29	0	13	6	10	457	93	315	49	3
Napavine	1,881	2	0	1	0	1	34	7	21	6	0
Newcastle[7]	11,775		0		1	4	241	58	158	25	2
Normandy Park	6,702	6	0	1	3	2	166	25	124	17	0
North Bend	6,898	6	0	2	2	2	266	21	236	9	1
Oak Harbor	23,371	33	0	7	1	25	186	18	141	27	1
Oakville	662	1	0	0	0	1	16	5	11	0	0
Ocean Shores	5,872	12	0	5	3	4	196	89	105	2	2
Odessa	863	0	0	0	0	0	14	3	10	1	0
Olympia	51,923	256	1	42	67	146	2,171	371	1,596	204	6
Oroville	1,673	1	0	0	0	1	49	5	44	0	0
Orting	7,863	9	0	3	3	3	106	6	85	15	0
Othello	8,225	13	0	2	1	10	181	36	115	30	3
Pacific	7,210	6	0	2	0	4	141	14	89	38	0
Pasco	72,146	154	1	21	43	89	1,431	255	1,009	167	16
Port Angeles	19,964	114	1	30	17	66	787	122	610	55	2
Port Orchard	14,253	52	0	7	6	39	708	81	561	66	0
Port Townsend	9,596	30	0	4	5	21	176	35	130	11	1
Poulsbo	10,600	18	0	6	2	10	359	48	284	27	0
Prosser	6,091	20	0	1	1	18	148	43	89	16	0
Pullman	33,897	23	0	14	1	8	516	87	419	10	3
Puyallup	41,242	145	0	25	47	73	2,344	268	1,850	226	16
Quincy	7,488	27	2	2	3	20	256	43	198	15	0
Raymond	2,872	5	0	0	0	5	31	13	18	0	0
Reardan	567	0	0	0	0	0	4	2	1	1	0
Redmond	63,889	96	2	11	33	50	2,077	271	1,695	111	2
Renton	102,470	328	3	45	113	167	5,128	607	3,640	881	14
Richland	56,151	102	0	19	14	69	1,321	184	1,086	51	5
Ridgefield	7,532	7	0	2	0	5	75	13	50	12	1
Ritzville	1,617	2	0	1	0	1	106	41	60	5	1
Roy	827	5	0	2	0	3	19	6	10	3	0
Royal City	2,203	1	0	0	0	1	33	10	16	7	0
Ruston	828	1	0	0	1	0	48	6	31	11	0
Sammamish[7]	64,857		3		1	11	442	91	312	39	7
SeaTac[7]	29,200		4		58	56	1,504	221	812	471	7
Seattle	721,365	4,564	27	266	1,515	2,756	37,934	7,805	26,499	3,630	149
Sedro Woolley	11,545	15	1	4	1	9	357	50	283	24	0
Selah	7,839	6	0	0	2	4	171	32	129	10	1
Sequim	7,025	26	0	6	1	19	300	40	249	11	0
Shelton	10,000	31	0	7	8	16	530	96	388	46	0
Shoreline[7]	55,703		0		42	30	1,424	329	919	176	11
Snohomish	10,045	23	0	2	6	15	332	56	226	50	1

Table 8. Offenses Known to Law Enforcement, by Selected State and City, 2017—Continued

(Number.)

State/city	Population	Violent crime	Murder and nonnegligent manslaughter	Rape (revised definition)[1]	Robbery	Aggravated assault	Property crime	Burglary	Larceny-theft	Motor vehicle theft	Arson[2]
Snoqualmie	13,648	2	0	1	1	0	147	12	126	9	1
Soap Lake	1,574	8	0	1	1	6	39	8	29	2	0
South Bend	1,637	2	0	2	0	0	3	2	0	1	0
Spokane	217,066	1,360	6	238	229	887	15,697	2,221	11,739	1,737	50
Spokane Valley	97,430	200	2	48	29	121	4,417	606	3,376	435	5
Stanwood	7,142	16	0	5	5	6	189	31	136	22	1
Steilacoom	6,364	6	0	1	0	5	88	14	65	9	0
Sultan	5,129	13	0	2	1	10	78	15	48	15	0
Sumas	1,426	1	0	0	0	1	12	3	7	2	0
Sumner	10,060	32	0	3	9	20	535	96	374	65	5
Sunnyside	16,480	49	1	8	14	26	353	48	253	52	2
Tacoma	213,504	1,737	10	171	403	1,153	11,901	2,073	7,742	2,086	63
Tenino	1,842	1	0	0	0	1	39	12	24	3	0
Toledo	740	1	0	0	1	0	13	2	11	0	0
Toppenish	8,974	29	3	2	10	14	373	87	216	70	3
Tumwater	22,961	71	1	13	10	47	691	142	453	96	3
Twisp	957	1	0	0	0	1	18	9	7	2	0
Union Gap	6,104	22	0	1	12	9	670	54	577	39	0
University Place	33,662	74	0	13	19	42	866	164	614	88	4
Vancouver	176,884	652	9	154	122	367	5,469	749	3,657	1,063	52
Walla Walla	32,189	140	1	31	24	84	1,131	148	917	66	11
Wapato	5,073	5	0	0	2	3	145	37	54	54	0
Warden	2,722	2	0	0	1	1	68	10	41	17	0
Washougal	15,698	38	1	20	3	14	196	27	151	18	1
Wenatchee	34,191	73	1	18	16	38	818	123	647	48	7
West Richland	14,603	13	0	4	1	8	171	54	111	6	0
White Salmon	2,495	2	0	0	1	1	29	4	21	4	0
Winlock	1,337	2	0	1	0	1	27	4	20	3	1
Winthrop	436	0	0	0	0	0	3	2	1	0	0
Woodinville[7]	12,181		0		6	6	364	62	249	53	3
Woodland	6,022	7	0	4	0	3	292	32	238	22	0
Woodway	1,389	0	0	0	0	0	10	3	7	0	0
Yakima	94,375	593	13	70	150	360	4,306	901	2,841	564	15
Yelm	9,304	24	0	2	7	15	535	45	460	30	1
Zillah	3,162	2	0	2	0	0	55	6	46	3	0
WEST VIRGINIA											
Alderson	1,171	2	0	0	0	2	25	6	19	0	0
Barboursville	4,315	3	0	0	3	0	298	38	253	7	0
Beckley	16,862	117	1	22	19	75	1,006	172	791	43	6
Bluefield	10,148	121	2	13	9	97	212	65	132	15	4
Bridgeport	8,401	24	0	3	1	20	268	22	237	9	0
Buckhannon	5,610	3	0	3	0	0	237	20	201	16	0
Ceredo	1,365	0	0	0	0	0	26	4	21	1	0
Charleston	48,788	572	10	57	84	421	3,516	736	2,427	353	26
Charles Town	6,062	4	0	0	0	4	78	36	41	1	1
Dunbar	7,486	35	1	2	3	29	213	43	132	38	0
Fairmont	18,604	56	3	4	11	38	370	100	220	50	6
Fayetteville	2,839	3	0	0	1	2	68	6	59	3	0
Glen Dale	1,433	2	0	0	0	2	15	2	12	1	0
Grafton	5,121	0	0	0	0	0	8	1	7	0	0
Huntington	47,933	428	16	54	120	238	2,082	599	1,303	180	17
Kenova	3,029	6	0	0	2	4	83	4	73	6	2
Lewisburg	3,935	4	0	0	0	4	147	4	143	0	0
Madison	2,831	1	0	0	0	1	46	7	34	5	4
Martinsburg	17,761	84	1	12	20	51	804	93	690	21	5
Mason	927	2	0	1	1	0	59	3	56	0	1
Moorefield	2,460	38	0	2	0	36	80	5	73	2	1
Morgantown	31,215	83	0	10	16	57	480	88	369	23	0
Moundsville	8,691	26	0	3	4	19	254	41	204	9	1
Mount Hope	1,341	2	0	0	0	2	19	4	15	0	0
Nitro	6,645	14	0	1	2	11	173	22	135	16	0
Oak Hill	8,490	15	0	5	0	10	211	43	158	10	3
Parkersburg	30,475	221	4	26	11	180	1,431	413	905	113	14
Point Pleasant	4,219	5	0	2	0	3	83	14	65	4	2
Princeton	5,935	26	0	3	4	19	209	66	133	10	0
Ridgeley	638	0	0	0	0	0	13	1	12	0	0
Ripley	3,243	3	0	0	0	3	24	2	22	0	0
Ronceverte	1,731	3	0	2	0	1	14	1	12	1	0
South Charleston	12,756	73	0	8	5	60	690	64	547	79	1
St. Albans[8]	10,476	16	0	4	2	10				32	0
Summersville	3,411	6	0	1	0	5	118	2	111	5	0
Vienna	10,409	22	0	3	0	19	352	25	318	9	0
Weirton	18,870	21	0	3	5	13	188	39	134	15	2
Wellsburg	2,634	1	0	0	0	1	33	6	25	2	2
Weston	4,035	3	0	0	0	3	12	0	10	2	0
Wheeling	27,196	332	2	15	31	284	584	153	407	24	1
Williamson	2,883	7	0	3	1	3	31	7	24	0	1
WISCONSIN											
Adams	1,878	15	0	4	0	11	115	15	97	3	0
Albany	1,010	0	0	0	0	0	19	3	15	1	0
Algoma	3,086	4	0	2	1	1	30	6	23	1	0

Table 8. Offenses Known to Law Enforcement, by Selected State and City, 2017—Continued

(Number.)

State/city	Population	Violent crime	Murder and nonnegligent manslaughter	Rape (revised definition)[1]	Robbery	Aggravated assault	Property crime	Burglary	Larceny-theft	Motor vehicle theft	Arson[2]
Alma	712	0	0	0	0	0	0	0	0	0	0
Altoona	7,624	3	0	0	1	2	83	14	63	6	0
Amery	2,825	12	0	1	0	11	50	11	33	6	0
Antigo	7,807	18	0	0	1	17	496	36	450	10	0
Appleton	74,660	203	1	39	17	146	1,155	136	996	23	15
Arcadia	3,077	3	0	0	1	2	9	0	7	2	0
Ashland	7,915	34	0	6	2	26	359	106	243	10	1
Ashwaubenon	17,326	18	0	4	1	13	621	27	581	13	0
Athens	1,090	0	0	0	0	0	3	0	2	1	0
Avoca	616	0	0	0	0	0	0	0	0	0	0
Balsam Lake	975	10	0	5	0	5	15	4	10	1	0
Bangor	1,487	1	0	0	0	1	9	1	8	0	0
Baraboo	12,191	32	1	15	4	12	373	39	323	11	1
Barneveld	1,226	0	0	0	0	0	6	0	6	0	0
Barron	3,294	1	0	0	0	1	4	4	0	0	0
Bayfield	473	1	0	0	1	0	22	5	17	0	0
Bayside	4,398	0	0	0	0	0	46	6	37	3	0
Beaver Dam	16,525	31	0	2	3	26	306	41	264	1	0
Beaver Dam Township	3,864	1	0	0	1	0	3	0	3	0	0
Belleville	2,438	1	0	1	0	0	21	2	17	2	0
Beloit	36,724	156	1	32	34	89	1,114	211	863	40	5
Beloit Town	7,648	5	0	2	1	2	107	27	76	4	0
Berlin	5,371	2	0	1	0	1	92	9	78	5	0
Big Bend	1,324	3	0	0	0	3	18	4	12	2	0
Birchwood	425	0	0	0	0	0	2	2	0	0	0
Black River Falls	3,541	1	0	0	0	1	112	5	107	0	0
Blair	1,384	0	0	0	0	0	8	3	5	0	0
Blanchardville	803	0	0	0	0	0	5	2	3	0	0
Bloomer	3,503	2	0	1	0	1	31	5	25	1	0
Bloomfield	6,295	8	0	3	0	5	79	11	63	5	1
Blue Mounds	967	0	0	0	0	0	8	1	6	1	0
Boscobel	3,137	16	0	0	0	16	22	4	14	4	1
Boyceville	1,099	4	0	3	0	1	27	11	14	2	0
Brandon-Fairwater	1,217	1	0	0	0	1	0	0	0	0	0
Brillion	3,121	1	0	0	0	1	25	1	24	0	0
Brodhead	3,274	0	0	0	0	0	35	1	34	0	0
Brookfield	38,033	47	0	13	17	17	938	91	814	33	0
Brookfield Township	6,108	6	0	1	1	4	126	19	101	6	0
Brooklyn	1,458	0	0	0	0	0	0	0	0	0	0
Brown Deer	12,015	41	0	5	15	21	514	39	433	42	2
Brownsville	584	0	0	0	0	0	2	1	1	0	0
Burlington	10,686	9	0	1	1	7	154	12	140	2	0
Butler	1,817	4	0	0	0	4	58	7	45	6	0
Caledonia	24,945	36	0	11	2	23	203	44	154	5	0
Campbellsport	1,971	0	0	0	0	0	5	2	3	0	0
Campbell Township	4,380	4	1	0	0	3	55	7	45	3	0
Cascade	695	0	0	0	0	0	1	0	1	0	0
Cashton	1,100	2	0	0	0	2	3	0	2	1	0
Cedarburg	11,529	1	0	0	0	1	71	5	65	1	0
Chenequa	588	0	0	0	0	0	3	1	2	0	0
Chetek	2,155	4	0	1	1	2	16	4	12	0	0
Chilton	3,809	8	0	1	0	7	12	0	11	1	0
Chippewa Falls	14,141	31	0	3	4	24	238	15	209	14	1
Cleveland	1,455	0	0	0	0	0	3	0	3	0	0
Clinton	2,122	0	0	0	0	0	18	4	14	0	2
Clintonville	4,379	6	0	1	0	5	220	33	181	6	1
Colby-Abbotsford	4,079	0	0	0	0	0	29	1	25	3	0
Colfax	1,161	5	0	2	0	3	15	3	12	0	0
Columbus	5,035	15	0	2	0	13	31	0	30	1	0
Cornell	1,419	1	0	0	0	1	30	6	23	1	0
Cottage Grove	7,105	7	0	1	0	6	37	4	31	2	0
Crandon	1,850	1	0	0	0	1	26	2	23	1	0
Cross Plains	4,236	1	0	0	0	1	53	16	35	2	0
Cuba City	2,050	1	0	0	0	1	3	1	1	1	0
Cudahy	18,191	22	0	2	8	12	308	44	250	14	1
Cumberland	2,130	2	0	0	0	2	0	0	0	0	0
Darlington	2,365	7	0	1	0	6	26	2	24	0	0
Deforest	9,818	9	0	1	0	8	62	10	50	2	0
Delafield	7,563	4	0	0	1	3	126	8	115	3	0
Delavan	9,986	18	0	3	1	14	221	18	197	6	6
Delavan Town	5,333	7	0	0	1	6	47	10	34	3	0
De Pere	25,066	46	0	5	2	39	204	22	178	4	2
Dodgeville	4,737	9	0	6	0	3	50	15	34	1	0
Durand	1,833	1	0	0	0	1	5	1	4	0	0
Eagle River	1,423	3	1	0	0	2	62	7	52	3	0
Eagle Village	2,006	0	0	0	0	0	5	1	4	0	0
East Troy	4,283	7	0	1	0	6	59	1	58	0	0
Eau Claire	68,687	162	1	32	44	85	2,000	385	1,531	84	10
Edgar	1,450	3	0	1	0	2	2	0	2	0	0
Edgerton	5,574	6	0	1	2	3	113	8	103	2	1
Elkhart Lake	965	0	0	0	0	0	10	0	10	0	0
Elkhorn	9,817	11	0	4	0	7	111	19	85	7	7
Elk Mound	871	0	0	0	0	0	2	0	2	0	0

Table 8. Offenses Known to Law Enforcement, by Selected State and City, 2017—Continued

(Number.)

State/city	Population	Violent crime	Murder and nonnegligent manslaughter	Rape (revised definition)[1]	Robbery	Aggravated assault	Property crime	Burglary	Larceny- theft	Motor vehicle theft	Arson[2]
Ellsworth	3,220	7	0	4	0	3	38	6	29	3	0
Elm Grove	6,216	4	0	1	3	0	57	4	49	4	0
Elroy	1,354	0	0	0	0	0	11	0	11	0	0
Endeavor	460	0	0	0	0	0	3	2	1	0	0
Evansville	5,305	1	0	0	0	1	43	9	33	1	0
Everest Metropolitan	17,321	43	2	7	2	32	239	29	210	0	1
Fall Creek	1,304	1	0	1	0	0	3	1	2	0	0
Fall River	1,681	1	0	0	0	1	13	2	11	0	0
Fennimore	2,485	8	0	2	0	6	15	0	15	0	0
Fitchburg	29,535	98	0	10	32	56	605	97	440	68	1
Fond du Lac	42,929	110	1	28	19	62	901	82	788	31	0
Fontana	1,718	0	0	0	0	0	11	1	8	2	0
Fort Atkinson	12,566	21	0	1	3	17	180	12	164	4	0
Fox Lake	1,461	0	0	0	0	0	6	1	5	0	0
Fox Point	6,694	8	0	0	3	5	52	7	40	5	0
Fox Valley Metro	21,789	13	0	0	3	10	124	17	100	7	1
Franklin	36,248	28	0	4	12	12	619	69	504	46	2
Freedom	6,132	1	0	0	0	1	9	7	1	1	0
Fulton	3,348	0	0	0	0	0	3	0	3	0	0
Galesville	1,546	0	0	0	0	0	9	1	8	0	0
Geneva Town	5,049	1	0	0	1	0	28	5	23	0	0
Genoa City	3,019	1	0	0	0	1	27	5	22	0	0
Gillett	1,328	4	0	0	1	3	31	9	21	1	0
Gilman	393	0	0	0	0	0	3	0	3	0	0
Glendale	12,763	20	1	2	8	9	770	49	679	42	0
Grafton	11,579	4	0	1	2	1	164	6	155	3	0
Grand Chute	22,667	38	1	6	6	25	912	70	823	19	0
Grand Rapids	7,392	0	0	0	0	0	42	20	20	2	1
Grantsburg	1,279	3	0	2	0	1	48	7	38	3	0
Green Bay	105,331	498	0	76	65	357	2,147	321	1,738	88	19
Greendale	14,242	11	1	1	1	8	377	9	359	9	0
Greenfield	36,882	77	0	10	27	40	957	124	772	61	3
Green Lake	933	2	0	0	0	2	13	1	12	0	0
Hales Corners	7,675	10	0	1	4	5	163	27	128	8	2
Hammond	1,886	1	0	0	0	1	7	0	7	0	0
Hancock	400	0	0	0	0	0	0	0	0	0	0
Hartford	14,664	15	0	8	1	6	269	23	241	5	0
Hartford Township	3,568	0	0	0	0	0	0	0	0	0	0
Hartland	9,229	6	0	4	0	2	96	9	86	1	0
Hayward	2,313	5	0	1	0	4	110	8	99	3	0
Hazel Green	1,241	2	0	1	0	1	8	1	7	0	0
Highland	836	0	0	0	0	0	11	2	9	0	0
Hobart-Lawrence	14,231	7	0	2	1	4	53	7	43	3	0
Holmen	9,714	5	0	0	0	5	114	26	84	4	0
Horicon	3,657	0	0	0	0	0	23	1	22	0	0
Hortonville	2,739	0	0	0	0	0	55	0	55	0	0
Hudson	13,788	16	0	2	1	13	352	32	308	12	0
Hurley	1,448	1	0	0	0	1	15	1	14	0	0
Independence	1,336	2	0	0	1	1	29	2	27	0	0
Iron Ridge	893	0	0	0	0	0	15	2	13	0	0
Iron River	1,121	2	0	1	0	1	7	0	6	1	0
Jackson	6,960	1	0	1	0	0	73	3	67	3	0
Janesville	64,257	170	2	45	30	93	1,948	308	1,572	68	4
Jefferson	8,033	9	0	4	0	5	150	7	135	8	0
Juneau	2,703	5	0	0	0	5	42	16	21	5	0
Kaukauna	15,969	12	0	3	2	7	165	14	141	10	0
Kendall	472	0	0	0	0	0	0	0	0	0	0
Kenosha	99,671	401	5	61	116	219	1,805	337	1,392	76	5
Kewaskum	4,122	1	0	0	1	0	51	6	43	2	0
Kewaunee	2,857	0	0	0	0	0	21	1	20	0	0
Kiel	3,697	11	0	0	0	11	29	5	20	4	0
Kohler	2,102	0	0	0	0	0	73	2	71	0	0
Kronenwetter	7,687	7	0	2	0	5	26	6	20	0	0
La Crosse	52,234	140	0	29	35	76	2,167	365	1,746	56	5
Ladysmith	3,149	6	0	0	0	6	44	2	41	1	0
La Farge	775	3	0	0	0	3	9	2	7	0	0
Lake Delton	2,982	22	0	6	2	14	486	30	448	8	0
Lake Geneva	7,850	10	0	4	2	4	212	17	188	7	0
Lake Hallie	6,678	5	0	1	1	3	195	12	174	9	0
Lake Mills	5,857	6	0	2	1	3	41	1	37	3	0
Lancaster	3,742	21	0	5	0	16	34	2	32	0	0
Lena	542	1	0	0	0	1	7	0	7	0	0
Linden	527	0	0	0	0	0	1	0	1	0	0
Linn Township	2,401	1	0	0	0	1	7	2	4	1	0
Lodi	3,060	3	0	0	0	3	8	1	7	0	0
Lomira	2,356	1	0	1	0	0	20	4	16	0	1
Luxemburg	2,562	0	0	0	0	0	13	1	11	1	0
Lyndon Station	476	0	0	0	0	0	0	0	0	0	0
Madison	255,850	958	11	95	212	640	6,811	927	5,452	432	10
Manawa	1,290	1	0	0	0	1	16	1	13	2	0
Manitowoc	32,813	100	0	8	14	78	913	164	719	30	0
Maple Bluff	1,342	1	0	0	0	1	23	4	16	3	0
Marathon City	1,505	4	0	1	0	3	12	2	10	0	0

Table 8. Offenses Known to Law Enforcement, by Selected State and City, 2017—Continued

(Number.)

State/city	Population	Violent crime	Murder and nonnegligent manslaughter	Rape (revised definition)[1]	Robbery	Aggravated assault	Property crime	Burglary	Larceny-theft	Motor vehicle theft	Arson[2]
Marinette	10,655	8	0	3	1	4	251	29	216	6	0
Marion	1,199	0	0	0	0	0	7	1	5	1	0
Markesan	1,400	1	0	1	0	0	17	1	15	1	0
Marshall Village	3,950	5	0	0	0	5	16	3	11	2	0
Marshfield	18,366	12	0	5	2	5	386	47	330	9	1
Mauston	4,368	13	0	0	0	13	79	5	72	2	0
Mayville	4,907	10	0	3	1	6	75	3	67	5	0
McFarland	8,407	10	0	0	1	9	92	17	68	7	1
Medford	4,336	9	0	1	0	8	99	1	93	5	0
Menasha	17,899	46	0	17	1	28	375	23	342	10	1
Menomonee Falls	36,963	11	0	2	5	4	448	34	374	40	0
Menomonie[6]	16,493	45	0	19	2	24	359	29	318	12	0
Mequon	24,250	11	0	2	7	2	198	50	133	15	0
Merrill	9,154	31	0	4	0	27	194	31	159	4	0
Middleton	19,369	16	1	5	5	5	282	37	236	9	0
Milton	5,585	4	1	0	0	3	77	10	63	4	0
Milton Town	3,080	0	0	0	0	0	3	0	3	0	0
Milwaukee	595,168	9,507	118	434	2,919	6,036	22,569	5,518	11,548	5,503	313
Mineral Point	2,489	1	0	0	0	1	26	2	23	1	0
Minocqua	4,447	7	0	0	0	7	86	2	82	2	0
Mishicot	1,402	0	0	0	0	0	4	1	3	0	0
Mondovi	2,612	6	0	0	0	6	17	5	12	0	0
Monona	8,285	9	0	1	4	4	534	14	498	22	0
Monroe	10,709	16	0	3	2	11	143	19	120	4	3
Montello	1,429	1	0	0	0	1	27	0	27	0	0
Mosinee	4,016	1	0	0	0	1	43	3	35	5	0
Mount Horeb	7,518	4	0	1	0	3	53	6	47	0	0
Mount Pleasant	26,387	40	0	5	7	28	535	45	466	24	3
Mukwonago	7,898	5	0	1	3	1	138	11	120	7	0
Mukwonago Town	8,141	5	0	1	0	4	12	5	7	0	0
Muscoda	1,241	2	0	0	0	2	22	1	20	1	0
Muskego	25,004	6	0	2	1	3	192	16	171	5	1
Neenah	25,983	50	0	7	2	41	496	40	444	12	1
Neillsville	2,425	1	0	1	0	0	40	3	35	2	0
Nekoosa	2,421	0	0	0	0	0	52	11	36	5	1
Neshkoro	420	0	0	0	0	0	7	1	6	0	0
New Berlin	39,839	13	0	5	4	4	328	37	287	4	2
New Glarus	2,159	1	0	0	0	1	31	7	22	2	0
New Holstein	3,112	8	0	1	1	6	17	0	17	0	0
New Lisbon	2,490	2	0	0	0	2	12	0	12	0	0
New London	7,150	14	0	1	0	13	85	5	80	0	1
New Richmond	8,987	18	0	0	3	15	122	9	108	5	2
Niagara	1,564	2	0	1	0	1	7	4	3	0	0
North Fond du Lac	5,038	9	0	4	0	5	70	9	57	4	1
North Hudson	3,825	3	0	2	0	1	24	4	18	2	0
North Prairie	2,210	0	0	0	0	0	14	4	10	0	0
Norwalk	631	0	0	0	0	0	1	1	0	0	0
Oak Creek	36,126	42	1	6	15	20	862	62	745	55	0
Oconomowoc	16,650	5	0	2	1	2	173	21	149	3	0
Oconomowoc Lake	589	0	0	0	0	0	4	1	3	0	0
Oconomowoc Town	8,670	3	0	0	0	3	13	8	5	0	0
Oconto[6]	4,455	2	0	1	0	1	78	11	64	3	0
Oconto Falls	2,825	3	0	0	0	3	32	0	30	2	0
Omro	3,562	1	0	0	0	1	50	8	40	2	0
Onalaska	18,847	15	0	4	0	11	532	26	495	11	0
Oregon	10,426	14	0	1	0	13	42	4	37	1	1
Osceola	2,510	13	0	0	0	13	25	2	22	1	0
Oshkosh	66,652	157	0	4	28	125	1,363	177	1,116	70	4
Osseo	1,695	3	0	0	1	2	30	2	26	2	0
Owen	930	0	0	0	0	0	4	1	3	0	0
Oxford	589	0	0	0	0	0	14	2	12	0	0
Palmyra	1,768	1	0	1	0	0	30	3	27	0	0
Park Falls	2,266	1	0	0	0	1	4	3	1	0	0
Pepin	786	2	0	2	0	0	38	1	35	2	0
Peshtigo	3,391	2	0	1	0	1	51	2	47	2	2
Pewaukee Village	8,171	3	0	3	0	0	97	8	87	2	1
Phillips	1,359	4	0	1	0	3	20	4	16	0	0
Pittsville	833	0	0	0	0	0	18	2	16	0	0
Platteville	12,769	32	0	7	2	23	262	16	239	7	1
Pleasant Prairie	20,904	25	1	8	6	10	457	37	407	13	0
Plover	12,627	20	0	6	2	12	157	17	135	5	9
Plymouth	8,544	13	0	6	1	6	117	20	97	0	0
Portage	10,372	34	0	9	2	23	193	27	162	4	0
Port Edwards	1,739	4	0	2	0	2	16	6	10	0	0
Port Washington	11,702	23	0	4	1	18	102	7	94	1	0
Poynette	2,492	5	0	4	0	1	8	4	4	0	0
Prairie du Chien	5,690	7	0	2	0	5	110	2	106	2	0
Prescott	4,223	4	0	1	0	3	35	9	21	5	0
Princeton	1,169	1	1	0	0	0	20	0	20	0	1
Pulaski	3,544	5	0	0	0	5	27	2	24	1	0
Racine[6]	77,371	520	1	61	122	336	1,762	417	1,216	129	13
Reedsburg	9,583	7	0	5	0	2	110	5	102	3	0
Rhinelander	7,560	8	0	0	0	8	179	34	143	2	1

Table 8. Offenses Known to Law Enforcement, by Selected State and City, 2017—Continued

(Number.)

State/city	Population	Violent crime	Murder and nonnegligent manslaughter	Rape (revised definition)[1]	Robbery	Aggravated assault	Property crime	Burglary	Larceny-theft	Motor vehicle theft	Arson[2]
Rib Lake	888	0	0	0	0	0	4	0	4	0	0
Rice Lake	8,406	32	0	17	1	14	214	16	184	14	1
Richland Center	4,986	6	0	1	0	5	95	8	84	3	0
Rio	1,043	0	0	0	0	0	9	1	7	1	0
Ripon	7,770	2	0	0	0	2	80	6	73	1	0
Ripon Town	1,391	0	0	0	0	0	2	0	0	2	0
River Falls	15,389	30	0	8	0	22	262	29	214	19	0
River Hills	1,591	0	0	0	0	0	6	1	5	0	0
Rome Town	2,710	4	0	2	0	2	20	5	15	0	0
Rosendale	1,035	0	0	0	0	0	0	0	0	0	0
Rothschild	5,361	5	2	1	0	2	73	6	66	1	0
Sauk Prairie	4,652	10	0	5	1	4	47	8	38	1	1
Saukville	4,473	1	0	0	1	0	75	3	70	2	0
Seymour	3,441	4	0	1	0	3	24	0	24	0	0
Sharon	1,576	1	0	0	1	0	6	2	4	0	0
Shawano	9,014	24	0	6	1	17	457	45	392	20	1
Sheboygan	48,595	161	0	40	12	109	821	90	698	33	12
Sheboygan Falls	7,829	1	0	1	0	0	49	6	43	0	0
Shiocton	918	0	0	0	0	0	15	1	13	1	0
Shorewood	13,405	17	0	1	9	7	320	26	261	33	0
Shorewood Hills	2,131	2	0	0	0	2	46	7	34	5	0
Shullsburg	1,205	1	0	0	0	1	10	3	7	0	0
Siren	774	1	0	0	0	1	43	13	29	1	0
Slinger	5,320	1	0	0	0	1	74	7	65	2	0
South Milwaukee	21,039	34	0	7	11	16	441	44	376	21	2
Sparta	9,721	6	0	6	0	0	116	15	96	5	0
Spencer	1,909	9	0	4	0	5	11	3	7	1	2
Spooner	2,581	11	0	0	0	11	38	3	35	0	0
Spring Green	1,658	0	0	0	0	0	11	4	7	0	0
Spring Valley	1,347	0	0	0	0	0	2	0	1	1	0
Stanley	3,668	5	0	0	0	5	28	4	23	1	0
St. Croix Falls	2,050	4	0	1	0	3	119	3	114	2	0
Stevens Point	26,379	41	0	3	3	35	454	40	409	5	2
St. Francis	9,487	9	0	1	3	5	166	31	129	6	2
Stoughton	13,213	31	1	2	2	26	256	23	228	5	0
Strum	1,114	0	0	0	0	0	2	0	1	1	0
Sturgeon Bay	8,876	6	0	0	0	6	94	7	84	3	0
Sturtevant	6,931	2	0	0	1	1	40	10	29	1	0
Summit	4,871	9	0	2	0	7	33	4	29	0	0
Sun Prairie	33,385	40	1	3	10	26	535	58	456	21	3
Superior	26,352	44	1	8	8	27	1,148	133	944	71	2
Theresa	1,198	0	0	0	0	0	12	1	11	0	0
Thiensville	3,174	1	0	0	0	1	16	0	14	2	0
Thorp	1,631	0	0	0	0	0	0	0	0	0	0
Three Lakes	2,120	2	0	0	0	2	22	4	17	1	0
Tomah	9,441	23	0	5	0	18	243	30	206	7	0
Tomahawk	3,169	3	1	0	0	2	80	20	59	1	0
Town of East Troy	4,113	1	0	0	0	1	10	1	9	0	0
Town of Madison	6,953	46	0	4	13	29	155	33	96	26	0
Town of Menasha	18,872	16	0	1	1	14	198	26	158	14	0
Trempealeau	1,633	1	0	0	0	1	9	5	4	0	0
Twin Lakes	6,100	6	2	0	2	2	63	9	51	3	0
Two Rivers	11,190	37	0	2	2	33	180	22	152	6	0
Verona	13,390	13	0	3	0	10	229	30	188	11	2
Viroqua	4,402	7	0	2	0	5	66	7	56	3	0
Walworth	2,842	2	0	0	0	2	31	3	28	0	0
Washburn	2,034	6	0	0	0	6	13	0	10	3	0
Waterloo	3,333	5	0	1	0	4	27	0	27	0	0
Watertown	23,814	56	0	12	8	36	292	43	247	2	2
Waukesha	72,565	119	0	43	25	51	1,007	126	845	36	2
Waunakee	13,866	14	0	3	1	10	79	28	49	2	0
Waupaca	5,924	10	0	2	0	8	198	13	181	4	0
Waupun	11,332	9	0	8	0	1	81	8	69	4	0
Wausau	38,832	123	0	32	14	77	736	90	620	26	2
Wautoma	2,120	6	0	0	0	6	136	0	132	4	0
Wauwatosa	48,208	64	0	0	42	22	1,727	173	1,417	137	1
Webster	622	2	0	0	0	2	17	1	15	1	0
West Allis	60,043	205	2	26	82	95	2,044	324	1,536	184	7
West Bend	31,783	51	0	19	10	22	763	42	704	17	1
Westby	2,283	2	0	0	0	2	62	9	52	1	0
Westfield	1,226	1	0	0	0	1	22	2	18	2	0
West Milwaukee	4,169	54	0	1	26	27	457	36	378	43	1
West Salem	4,993	8	0	0	0	8	29	4	24	1	0
Whitefish Bay	13,952	5	0	1	2	2	195	27	150	18	0
Whitehall	1,609	0	0	0	0	0	18	0	15	3	0
Whitewater	14,538	30	0	11	2	17	200	31	164	5	0
Wild Rose	699	0	0	0	0	0	1	0	1	0	0
Williams Bay	2,598	1	0	1	0	0	19	2	17	0	0
Wilton	501	0	0	0	0	0	1	0	1	0	0
Winneconne	2,444	2	0	0	0	2	17	0	16	1	0
Wisconsin Dells	2,823	12	0	1	4	7	168	10	147	11	0
Wisconsin Rapids	17,807	30	1	18	4	7	708	83	595	30	1
Woodruff	1,977	2	0	0	1	1	13	8	5	0	0

Table 8. Offenses Known to Law Enforcement, by Selected State and City, 2017—Continued

(Number.)

State/city	Population	Violent crime	Murder and nonnegligent manslaughter	Rape (revised definition)[1]	Robbery	Aggravated assault	Property crime	Burglary	Larceny-theft	Motor vehicle theft	Arson[2]
WYOMING											
Afton	2,008	0	0	0	0	0	22	6	16	0	0
Buffalo	4,590	2	0	0	0	2	54	6	45	3	0
Casper	60,034	91	1	29	14	47	1,727	318	1,281	128	6
Cheyenne	64,730	209	2	29	34	144	2,265	264	1,817	184	6
Cody	9,885	11	0	1	1	9	149	26	120	3	0
Diamondville	744	0	0	0	0	0	0	0	0	0	0
Douglas	6,615	18	0	3	0	15	99	12	85	2	1
Evanston	12,044	16	0	3	0	13	243	29	200	14	0
Evansville	3,014	33	0	4	0	29	67	11	49	7	0
Gillette	32,826	41	0	4	4	33	569	67	475	27	3
Glenrock	2,599	3	0	1	0	2	24	1	21	2	0
Green River	12,289	20	0	0	0	20	122	22	93	7	0
Greybull	1,876	11	0	1	0	10	10	2	5	3	0
Hanna	808	1	0	0	0	1	0	0	0	0	0
Jackson	10,692	28	0	6	2	20	170	9	149	12	0
Kemmerer	2,792	3	0	1	0	2	18	6	12	0	1
Lander	7,672	0	0	0	0	0	215	8	199	8	0
Laramie	32,632	30	0	12	3	15	449	64	365	20	4
Mills	3,875	5	0	1	0	4	84	34	39	11	0
Moorcroft	1,072	3	0	0	0	3	9	0	8	1	0
Newcastle	3,537	11	0	5	0	6	56	10	43	3	1
Pine Bluffs	1,155	1	0	1	0	0	17	1	14	2	0
Powell	6,422	22	0	15	0	7	132	20	108	4	0
Rawlins	9,050	27	0	3	0	24	183	28	142	13	0
Riverton	11,028	35	1	4	5	25	536	41	467	28	1
Rock Springs	23,886	111	0	31	2	78	476	62	389	25	3
Saratoga	1,686	1	0	0	0	1	7	0	7	0	0
Sheridan	18,036	8	0	0	0	8	357	52	285	20	2
Sundance	1,294	1	0	0	0	1	2	2	0	0	0
Thermopolis	2,925	15	0	1	0	14	46	8	38	0	0
Torrington	6,729	14	0	0	0	14	72	12	57	3	0
Wheatland	3,602	2	0	0	1	1	71	20	44	7	0
Worland	5,287	9	0	2	0	7	68	14	51	3	0

1 The figures shown in this column for the offense of rape were reported using only the revised Uniform Crime Reporting (UCR) definition of rape. See the chapter notes for further explanation.   2 The FBI does not publish arson data unless it receives data from either the agency or the state for all 12 months of the calendar year.   3 The population for the city of Mobile, Alabama, includes 55,819 inhabitants from the jurisdiction of the Mobile County Sheriff's Department.   4 The FBI determined that the agency did not follow national UCR Program guidelines for reporting an offense. Consequently, this figure is not included in this table.   5 The FBI determined that the agency's data were overreported. Consequently, those data are not included in this table.   6 Because of changes in the state/local agency's reporting practices, figures are not comparable to previous years' data.   7 This agency/state submits rape data classified according to the legacy UCR definition; therefore the rape offense and violent crime total, which rape is a part of, is not included in this table. See the chapter notes for further explanation.   8 The FBI determined that the agency's data were underreported. Consequently, those data are not included in this table.   9 Arson offenses are also reported by the Louisville Fire Department. Those figures are not included in this table.   10 Arson offenses are reported by the Toledo Fire Department; therefore, those figures are not included in this report.

Table 9. Offenses Known to Law Enforcement, by Selected State and University and College, 2017

(Number.)

State and university/college	Student enrollment[1]	Violent crime	Murder and nonnegligent manslaughter	Rape[2]	Robbery	Aggravated assault	Property crime	Burglary	Larceny-theft	Motor vehicle theft	Arson[3]
ALABAMA											
Jacksonville State University	8,514	13	0	3	0	10	57	13	43	1	
Samford University	5,471	3	0	1	0	2	105	21	84	0	
Troy University	17,855	1	0	1	0	0	76	14	58	4	
University of Alabama											
Birmingham	19,535	28	0	1	5	22	456	8	429	19	
Tuscaloosa	37,663	34	1	6	4	23	291	42	245	4	
University of North Alabama	7,333	7	0	0	2	5	40	6	34	0	
University of South Alabama	16,443	22	0	0	0	22	168	14	148	6	
ALASKA											
University of Alaska											
Anchorage	16,318	2	0	0	1	1	76	3	65	8	0
Fairbanks	8,283	4	0	1	0	3	66	0	62	4	0
ARIZONA											
Arizona State University, Main Campus	97,849	32	0	15	2	15	866	81	764	21	2
Central Arizona College	5,585	0	0	0	0	0	12	2	9	1	0
Northern Arizona University	30,361	24	0	12	1	11	267	18	249	0	0
Pima Community College	24,956	3	0	2	1	0	76	8	66	2	0
University of Arizona	43,161	22	0	9	4	9	617	64	536	17	1
ARKANSAS											
Arkansas State University											
Beebe	3,989	0	0	0	0	0	6	2	4	0	0
Jonesboro	14,085	5	0	2	0	3	62	10	52	0	1
Newport	2,735	0	0	0	0	0	0	0	0	0	0
Arkansas Tech University	11,894	1	0	1	0	0	101	10	90	1	0
Henderson State University	3,551	5	0	2	2	1	30	2	27	1	2
Southern Arkansas University	4,771	3	0	2	1	0	18	3	14	1	0
University of Arkansas Community College,											
Morrilton	2,029	0	0	0	0	0	7	0	7	0	1
University of Arkansas											
Fayetteville	27,194	9	0	2	2	5	226	13	170	43	2
Little Rock	11,746	3	0	0	1	2	80	5	74	1	0
Medical Sciences	2,869	9	0	0	1	8	95	0	88	7	0
Pine Bluff	2,821	3	0	0	1	2	57	12	44	1	0
CALIFORNIA											
Allan Hancock College	12,012	0	0	0	0	0	6	1	5	0	0
California State Polytechnic University											
Pomona	25,326	4	0	2	2	0	213	23	159	31	1
San Luis Obispo	21,306	9	0	4	1	4	147	23	116	8	0
California State University											
Bakersfield	9,341	3	0	2	0	1	75	10	65	0	0
Channel Islands	6,611	1	0	0	0	1	44	0	42	2	0
Chico	17,557	13	0	8	1	4	207	13	184	10	0
Dominguez Hills	14,731	7	0	1	3	3	40	5	34	1	0
East Bay	15,855	6	0	3	2	1	122	49	73	0	0
Fresno	24,405	14	0	3	2	9	255	48	195	12	2
Fullerton	40,235	5	0	3	1	1	187	13	167	7	1
Long Beach	37,776	9	0	5	2	2	169	7	141	21	0
Los Angeles	27,827	3	0	1	1	1	120	6	102	12	0
Monterey Bay	7,274	12	0	4	0	8	39	6	32	1	0
Northridge	39,916	9	0	4	0	5	297	13	258	26	4
Sacramento	30,510	2	0	1	1	0	200	26	171	3	2
San Bernardino	20,767	6	0	1	3	2	120	15	81	24	1
San Jose	32,154	33	0	11	7	15	307	28	269	10	7
San Marcos	13,144	6	0	5	0	1	20	0	19	1	1
Stanislaus	9,762	5	0	4	0	1	47	0	39	8	1
College of the Sequoias	11,959	1	0	0	1	0	75	5	62	8	1
Contra Costa Community College	34,487	11	0	0	4	7	176	20	145	11	1
Cuesta College	10,232	0	0	0	0	0	9	0	8	1	0
El Camino College	24,033	4	0	0	0	4	73	7	61	5	0
Foothill-De Anza College	37,085	1	0	0	0	1	21	1	18	2	0
Humboldt State University	8,503	4	0	3	0	1	73	7	65	1	1
Irvine Valley College	14,147	0	0	0	0	0	21	1	20	0	0
Marin Community College	5,621	2	1	0	0	1	23	1	22	0	0
Mt. San Jacinto College	15,497	1	0	0	0	1	31	4	24	3	0
Pasadena Community College	27,165	1	0	0	1	0	93	3	86	4	1
Riverside Community College	38,677	2	0	1	1	0	73	7	56	10	1
San Bernardino Community College	5,937	11	0	0	4	7	74	12	54	8	1
San Diego State University	34,688	15	0	2	11	2	547	73	460	14	1
San Francisco State University	29,045	9	0	2	5	2	189	27	153	9	0
San Jose/Evergreen Community College	17,213	0	0	0	0	0	37	8	22	7	0
Santa Rosa Junior College	21,217	0	0	0	0	0	52	4	47	1	0
Sonoma State University	9,323	4	0	4	0	0	71	8	47	16	0
State Center Community College District	39,661	4	0	1	1	2	162	33	119	10	2
University of California											
Berkeley	40,154	71	0	16	29	26	780	46	704	30	17
Davis	36,460	17	0	4	2	11	566	25	535	6	4
Irvine	32,754	15	0	6	0	9	503	21	473	9	1

Table 9. Offenses Known to Law Enforcement, by Selected State and University and College, 2017—Continued

(Number.)

State and university/college	Student enrollment[1]	Violent crime	Murder and nonnegligent manslaughter	Rape[2]	Robbery	Aggravated assault	Property crime	Burglary	Larceny-theft	Motor vehicle theft	Arson[3]
Los Angeles	43,548	108	0	20	18	70	831	169	635	27	2
Medical Center, Sacramento[4]		5	0	1	0	4	168	6	159	3	4
Merced	7,336	0	0	0	0	0	51	8	42	1	2
Riverside	22,715	13	0	6	6	1	296	27	262	7	0
San Diego	34,979	8	0	2	2	4	608	25	566	17	9
San Francisco	3,145	22	0	2	4	16	419	25	389	5	0
Santa Barbara	24,346	56	0	44	0	12	300	35	263	2	1
Santa Cruz	18,783	13	0	6	0	7	219	24	189	6	6
Ventura County Community College District	33,976	1	0	1	0	0	64	15	46	3	0
West Valley-Mission College	16,131	3	0	0	0	3	22	8	10	4	0
COLORADO											
Adams State University	3,370	0	0	0	0	0	21	2	17	2	0
Aims Community College	5,652	0	0	0	0	0	1	0	1	0	0
Arapahoe Community College	10,261	1	0	0	0	1	6	0	6	0	0
Auraria Higher Education Center[4]		5	0	0	2	3	130	22	99	9	4
Colorado School of Mines	6,069	0	0	0	0	0	42	2	38	2	0
Colorado State University, Fort Collins	31,856	11	0	5	0	6	395	23	365	7	6
Fort Lewis College	3,600	4	0	3	1	0	35	4	31	0	0
Pikes Peak Community College	13,154	2	0	1	0	1	26	2	24	0	0
Red Rocks Community College	7,738	0	0	0	0	0	17	1	15	1	0
University of Colorado											
Boulder	33,977	18	0	11	2	5	510	17	485	8	5
Colorado Springs	12,559	2	0	1	1	0	69	2	62	5	0
Denver	23,960	4	0	0	0	4	93	1	83	9	0
University of Northern Colorado	13,087	3	0	2	0	1	130	3	125	2	1
CONNECTICUT											
Central Connecticut State University	11,784	0	0	0	0	0	38	4	32	2	0
Eastern Connecticut State University	5,362	0	0	0	0	0	34	0	33	1	0
Southern Connecticut State University	10,320	1	0	1	0	0	39	3	35	1	0
University of Connecticut											
Health Center[4]		0	0	0	0	0	2	0	2	0	0
Storrs, Avery Point, and Hartford[4]		15	0	11	3	1	194	11	178	5	1
Western Connecticut State University	5,721	0	0	0	0	0	35	3	32	0	0
Yale University	12,458	3	0	0	2	1	253	33	217	3	0
DELAWARE											
Delaware State University	4,328	12	0	5	3	4	99	9	89	1	0
University of Delaware	23,009	3	0	1	0	2	163	8	154	1	4
FLORIDA											
Florida A&M University	9,619	1	0	1	0	0	61	22	36	3	0
Florida Atlantic University	30,541	13	0	7	0	6	180	19	141	20	0
Florida Gulf Coast University	14,821	6	0	4	0	2	69	2	65	2	0
Florida International University	55,003	11	0	3	3	5	303	23	265	15	0
Florida Polytechnic University[4]		0	0	0	0	0	7	1	6	0	0
Florida SouthWestern State College	16,627	0	0	0	0	0	11	0	11	0	0
Florida State University											
Panama City[4]		0	0	0	0	0	5	0	5	0	0
Tallahassee	41,173	25	0	13	8	4	441	32	385	24	0
New College of Florida	875	0	0	0	0	0	28	1	27	0	0
Pensacola State College	9,643	2	0	1	1	0	38	7	30	1	1
Santa Fe College	15,404	0	0	0	0	0	19	0	19	0	0
Tallahassee Community College	12,200	2	0	2	0	0	63	1	60	2	0
University of Central Florida	64,088	19	0	7	0	12	268	24	236	8	0
University of Florida	52,367	13	0	5	1	7	323	25	282	16	0
University of North Florida	15,762	9	0	4	2	3	64	0	61	3	0
University of South Florida											
St. Petersburg	4,702	0	0	0	0	0	28	1	27	0	0
Tampa	42,861	14	0	3	1	10	267	25	221	21	1
University of West Florida	12,966	4	0	3	1	0	39	3	36	0	0
GEORGIA											
Abraham Baldwin Agricultural College	3,475	0	0	0	0	0	32	0	32	0	0
Agnes Scott College	927	1	0	1	0	0	18	4	14	0	0
Albany State University	3,041	0	0	0	0	0	12	0	11	1	0
Andrew College	276	0	0	0	0	0	16	4	12	0	0
Armstrong State University	7,157	2	0	2	0	0	39	13	24	2	0
Athens Technical College	4,210	0	0	0	0	0	0	0	0	0	0
Atlanta Metropolitan State College	2,783	3	0	0	1	2	9	0	9	0	0
Augusta Technical College	4,370	0	0	0	0	0	8	0	7	1	0
Augusta University	7,938	1	0	1	0	0	174	4	155	15	0
Bainbridge State College	2,468	0	0	0	0	0	0	0	0	0	0
Berry College	2,174	0	0	0	0	0	57	16	41	0	0
Chattahoochee Technical College	9,999	0	0	0	0	0	8	0	8	0	0
Clark Atlanta University	3,884	11	0	0	11	0	84	7	75	2	0
Clayton State University	6,996	0	0	0	0	0	25	0	24	1	0
College of Coastal Georgia	3,529	2	0	0	0	2	4	0	4	0	0
Columbus State University	8,407	7	0	3	1	3	67	5	62	0	0
Dalton State College	5,188	1	0	0	0	1	5	0	5	0	0
East Georgia College	3,152	0	0	0	0	0	18	4	14	0	0
Emory University	14,067	15	0	9	1	5	415	38	373	4	0

Table 9. Offenses Known to Law Enforcement, by Selected State and University and College, 2017—Continued

(Number.)

State and university/college	Student enrollment[1]	Violent crime	Murder and nonnegligent manslaughter	Rape[2]	Robbery	Aggravated assault	Property crime	Burglary	Larceny-theft	Motor vehicle theft	Arson[3]
Fort Valley State University	2,679	0	0	0	0	0	26	5	19	2	0
Georgia College and State University	6,915	4	0	4	0	0	34	1	26	7	0
Georgia Gwinnett College	12,052	4	0	1	0	3	61	2	59	0	0
Georgia Institute of Technology	26,839	16	0	5	2	9	298	26	262	10	1
Georgia Military College	8,234	0	0	0	0	0	0	0	0	0	0
Georgia Southern University	20,673	10	0	6	3	1	119	3	116	0	0
Georgia Southwestern State University	2,954	4	0	0	0	4	27	0	27	0	0
Georgia State University	32,237	21	0	2	14	5	259	4	245	10	0
Gordon State College	3,901	1	0	0	1	0	23	3	20	0	0
Gwinnett Technical College	7,479	0	0	0	0	0	6	0	6	0	0
Kennesaw State University	35,018	12	0	8	3	1	136	17	117	2	1
Mercer University	8,615	3	0	2	0	1	68	1	63	4	0
Middle Georgia State University	7,714	2	0	1	0	1	16	1	14	1	0
Morehouse College	2,108	2	0	0	2	0	130	56	70	4	0
Piedmont College	2,266	0	0	0	0	0	0	0	0	0	0
Southern Crescent Technical College	4,703	0	0	0	0	0	5	1	4	0	0
South Georgia State College	2,542	0	0	0	0	0	1	1	0	0	0
Spelman College	2,125	0	0	0	0	0	21	3	18	0	0
University of Georgia	36,574	15	0	12	1	2	316	31	281	4	1
University of North Georgia	18,219	0	0	0	0	0	26	0	26	0	0
University of West Georgia	13,308	3	0	2	0	1	103	20	83	0	0
Valdosta State University	11,375	4	0	1	1	2	139	11	122	6	1
Wesleyan College	676	2	0	2	0	0	2	0	2	0	
West Georgia Technical College	6,743	0	0	0	0	0	20	0	20	0	0
Young Harris College	1,200	3	0	2	0	1	3	0	3	0	0
ILLINOIS											
Black Hawk College											
Kewanee[4]		0	0	0	0	0	1	0	1	0	0
Moline	5,613	0	0	0	0	0	3	1	2	0	0
Chicago State University	3,578	0	0	0	0	0	36	4	32	0	0
College of DuPage	26,901	1	0	0	1	0	23	0	21	2	0
College of Lake County	14,768	0	0	0	0	0	37	2	35	0	0
Eastern Illinois University	7,415	5	0	3	0	2	33	0	33	0	0
Elgin Community College	9,918	0	0	0	0	0	5	0	5	0	0
Illinois Central College	9,290	0	0	0	0	0	26	4	22	0	0
Illinois State University	21,039	13	0	8	0	5	97	11	84	2	1
John Wood Community College	1,968	0	0	0	0	0	1	0	1	0	0
Joliet Junior College	15,383	0	0	0	0	0	13	0	13	0	0
Kankakee Community College	3,078	0	0	0	0	0	0	0	0	0	0
Lake Land College	5,107	0	0	0	0	0	3	0	3	0	0
Lewis University	6,544	4	0	2	2	0	12	2	10	0	0
Lincoln Land Community College	5,744	0	0	0	0	0	12	0	11	1	0
Loyola University of Chicago	16,422	20	0	2	13	5	127	1	123	3	0
McHenry County College	6,371	1	0	0	0	1	5	2	3	0	0
Millikin University	2,055	0	0	0	0	0	33	1	32	0	0
Moraine Valley Community College	15,021	1	0	0	0	1	22	0	22	0	0
Morton College	4,397	0	0	0	0	0	4	1	3	0	0
Northeastern Illinois University	9,538	2	0	0	0	2	14	0	13	1	0
Northern Illinois University	19,015	11	0	5	0	6	147	26	121	0	0
Northwestern University, Evanston	21,823	12	0	6	5	1	193	26	165	2	1
Oakton Community College	9,443	0	0	0	0	0	5	0	5	0	0
Parkland College	7,569	2	0	0	0	2	23	0	23	0	0
Prairie State College	4,484	1	0	0	0	1	6	0	6	0	0
Rend Lake College	2,489	0	0	0	0	0	0	0	0	0	0
Southern Illinois University											
Carbondale	15,987	5	0	1	2	2	117	6	109	2	0
Edwardsville	14,142	5	0	3	0	2	53	3	50	0	0
School of Medicine[4]		0	0	0	0	0	0	0	0	0	0
South Suburban College	3,703	0	0	0	0	0	6	1	5	0	0
Southwestern Illinois College	9,515	0	0	0	0	0	25	1	23	1	0
Triton College	11,386	2	0	0	1	1	20	0	20	0	0
University of Chicago, Cook County	15,775	19	0	0	8	11	214	21	189	4	0
University of Illinois											
Springfield	5,428	2	0	0	0	2	30	5	25	0	0
Urbana	46,951	22	0	12	4	6	316	10	305	1	1
Waubonsee Community College	10,081	0	0	0	0	0	22	0	22	0	0
Western Illinois University	10,373	11	0	9	0	2	83	6	77	0	1
INDIANA											
Ball State University	21,998	11	0	9	1	1	204	22	177	5	0
Indiana State University	13,565	15	0	1	0	14	53	0	51	2	
Indiana University											
Bloomington	49,695	18	0	7	2	9	433	55	371	7	
Indianapolis	29,804	14	0	6	5	3	252	18	223	11	2
Northwest	5,591	0	0	0	0	0	20	0	20	0	
Southeast	5,874	2	0	2	0	0	6	0	6	0	0
Marian University	3,165	1	0	1	0	0	20	1	17	2	0
Purdue University	41,513	18	0	6	1	11	308	18	284	6	0
IOWA											
Iowa State University	36,350	19	0	9	1	9	225	9	211	5	0
University of Iowa	32,011	25	0	16	1	8	312	24	277	11	1
University of Northern Iowa	11,905	9	0	6	0	3	85	6	78	1	0

Table 9. Offenses Known to Law Enforcement, by Selected State and University and College, 2017—Continued

(Number.)

State and university/college	Student enrollment[1]	Violent crime	Murder and nonnegligent manslaughter	Rape[2]	Robbery	Aggravated assault	Property crime	Burglary	Larceny-theft	Motor vehicle theft	Arson[3]
KANSAS											
Emporia State University	5,887	0	0	0	0	0	19	3	16	0	0
Garden City Community College	2,053	0	0	0	0	0	8	8	0	0	0
Kansas City Kansas Community College	5,726	0	0	0	0	0	19	2	15	2	0
Kansas State University	23,779	1	0	1	0	0	116	13	101	2	0
University of Kansas											
Main Campus	27,565	5	0	2	2	1	152	13	138	1	0
Medical Center[4]		17	0	1	2	14	119	0	116	3	0
Washburn University	6,636	3	0	2	1	0	69	2	66	1	1
Wichita State University	14,166	4	0	1	1	2	74	5	67	2	0
KENTUCKY											
Eastern Kentucky University	16,881	7	0	5	0	2	185	27	147	11	0
Morehead State University	10,746	3	0	3	0	0	44	3	41	0	0
Murray State University	10,486	2	0	2	0	0	72	6	66	0	1
Northern Kentucky University	14,542	4	0	3	0	1	60	0	59	1	0
University of Kentucky[5]	29,781	12	0	4	1	7		30		22	3
University of Louisville	21,578	10	0	0	10	0	316	26	278	12	0
Western Kentucky University	20,271	5	0	4	0	1	96	6	88	2	0
LOUISIANA											
Delgado Community College	15,110	3	0	0	0	3	22	2	20	0	0
Dillard University	1,261	1	0	1	0	0	25	9	16	0	0
Grambling State University	4,863	13	2	4	2	5	99	34	62	3	0
Louisiana State University											
Baton Rouge	31,409	15	1	4	2	8	287	40	238	9	0
Health Sciences Center, New Orleans	2,758	0	0	0	0	0	0	0	0	0	0
Health Sciences Center, Shreveport	874	2	0	0	0	2	26	2	24	0	0
Shreveport	4,746	2	0	0	1	1	21	15	6	0	0
Louisiana Tech University	12,672	3	0	2	0	1	73	7	66	0	0
McNeese State University[5]	7,621	0	0	0	0	0	20	2	18	0	0
Nicholls State University	6,255	3	0	0	0	3	24	3	21	0	0
Southern University and A&M College											
Baton Rouge	5,877	6	0	0	2	4	113	4	108	1	0
New Orleans	2,430	0	0	0	0	0	0	0	0	0	0
Shreveport	3,240	1	0	0	0	1	1	1	0	0	0
Tulane University	12,581	1	0	0	1	0	214	31	182	1	0
University of Louisiana											
Lafayette	17,519	19	0	3	2	14	202	40	159	3	1
Monroe	9,038	4	0	1	1	2	53	4	49	0	1
University of New Orleans	8,037	4	0	2	0	2	95	6	89	0	0
MAINE											
University of Maine											
Farmington	2,000	5	0	5	0	0	22	0	22	0	0
Orono	11,219	10	0	9	0	1	104	7	96	1	1
University of Southern Maine	7,855	2	0	1	0	1	21	0	21	0	0
MARYLAND											
Bowie State University	5,669	8	0	0	0	8	39	13	26	0	0
Coppin State University	2,939	3	0	0	1	2	38	9	26	3	0
Frostburg State University	5,676	0	0	0	0	0	26	3	23	0	0
Hagerstown Community College	4,061	0	0	0	0	0	4	1	3	0	0
Morgan State University	7,689	9	0	3	4	2	115	4	111	0	0
Prince George's County Community College	12,417	2	0	0	0	2	26	0	26	0	0
Salisbury University	8,748	2	0	0	1	1	65	2	63	0	1
Towson University	22,343	5	0	2	1	2	78	1	73	4	1
University of Baltimore	5,983	3	0	0	2	1	25	1	24	0	0
University of Maryland											
Baltimore City	6,482	11	0	0	5	6	64	1	59	4	0
Baltimore County	13,640	1	0	1	0	0	66	9	55	2	0
College Park	39,083	14	1	3	3	7	316	20	291	5	0
Eastern Shore	3,904	3	0	1	2	0	50	14	36	0	0
MASSACHUSETTS											
Amherst College	1,849	16	0	16	0	0	45	13	32	0	
Assumption College	2,607	6	0	3	0	3	16	1	15	0	0
Babson College	3,165	7	0	6	0	1	39	3	36	0	
Becker College	2,189	4	0	1	1	2	12	3	8	1	0
Bentley University	5,506	4	0	3	0	1	52	6	45	1	2
Boston University	32,695	17	0	9	3	5	383	23	358	2	0
Brandeis University	5,729	3	0	1	1	1	35	5	30	0	
Bridgewater State University	10,998	17	0	8	1	8	35	4	31	0	0
Bunker Hill Community College	13,253	0	0	0	0	0	43	0	43	0	
Clark University	3,298	3	0	1	1	1	27	2	24	1	
College of the Holy Cross	2,720	2	0	0	0	2	20	5	15	0	
Dean College	1,339	1	0	0	1	0	26	13	13	0	0
Emerson College	4,442	7	0	4	2	1	38	3	35	0	
Endicott College	4,835	5	0	5	0	0	18	0	18	0	
Fitchburg State University	6,763	13	0	6	7	0	15	2	13	0	
Gordon College	2,004	2	0	2	0	0	66	3	63	0	
Hampshire College	1,321	3	0	2	0	1	36	6	30	0	1
Harvard University	29,908	10	0	3	2	5	405	50	348	7	

Table 9. Offenses Known to Law Enforcement, by Selected State and University and College, 2017—Continued

(Number.)

State and university/college	Student enrollment[1]	Violent crime	Murder and nonnegligent manslaughter	Rape[2]	Robbery	Aggravated assault	Property crime	Burglary	Larceny-theft	Motor vehicle theft	Arson[3]
Massachusetts College of Art	1,982	0	0	0	0	0	46	0	46	0	
Massachusetts College of Liberal Arts	1,644	1	0	0	0	1	8	1	7	0	0
Massachusetts Institute of Technology	11,376	9	0	3	1	5	252	15	236	1	0
Massasoit Community College	7,471	4	0	0	0	4	17	0	17	0	0
MCPHS University	7,095	0	0	0	0	0	8	1	7	0	
Merrimack College	4,014	12	0	3	0	9	36	8	27	1	
Mount Holyoke College	2,327	1	0	1	0	0	18	0	18	0	0
Mount Wachusett Community College	3,961	0	0	0	0	0	9	0	9	0	
Northeastern University	20,381	15	0	9	0	6	229	10	216	3	
Salem State University	9,001	1	0	0	0	1	49	7	41	1	0
Smith College	2,896	1	0	1	0	0	47	8	39	0	0
Springfield College	3,144	5	0	4	1	0	44	3	38	3	
Springfield Technical Community College	5,622	0	0	0	0	0	26	1	24	1	0
Stonehill College	2,481	8	0	5	0	3	12	1	11	0	
Tufts University											
Medford	11,489	5	0	1	1	3	49	4	45	0	0
Worcester[4]		0	0	0	0	0	1	0	1	0	0
University of Massachusetts											
Harbor Campus, Boston	16,847	4	0	1	0	3	27	0	27	0	0
Medical Center, Worcester	1,108	18	0	1	0	17	59	1	56	2	0
Wellesley College	2,482	2	0	2	0	0	25	2	23	0	
Wentworth Institute of Technology	4,526	1	0	1	0	0	51	3	48	0	
Western New England University	3,810	1	0	1	0	0	36	3	33	0	
Westfield State University	6,335	8	0	3	0	5	33	2	30	1	0
Worcester Polytechnic Institute	6,642	4	0	1	2	1	57	1	56	0	0
MICHIGAN											
Central Michigan University	25,986	4	0	1	0	3	74	5	68	1	0
Delta College	9,132	0	0	0	0	0	13	3	10	0	0
Eastern Michigan University	21,246	16	0	10	0	6	170	25	140	5	2
Ferris State University	14,187	4	0	2	0	2	45	3	39	3	0
Grand Rapids Community College	14,464	0	0	0	0	0	69	4	63	2	0
Grand Valley State University	25,460	2	0	2	0	0	140	10	130	0	0
Kalamazoo Valley Community College	8,549	0	0	0	0	0	23	1	22	0	0
Kellogg Community College	4,815	0	0	0	0	0	4	0	4	0	0
Kirtland Community College	1,529	0	0	0	0	0	1	0	1	0	0
Lansing Community College	13,583	3	0	1	0	2	45	0	45	0	0
Macomb Community College	21,734	2	0	0	0	2	26	3	21	2	0
Michigan State University	50,340	24	0	12	1	11	603	56	519	28	1
Michigan Technological University	7,252	0	0	0	0	0	36	0	36	0	1
Mott Community College	8,013	1	0	0	0	1	27	0	27	0	0
Northern Michigan University	7,865	13	0	13	0	0	58	1	56	1	0
Oakland Community College	18,923	1	0	0	0	1	19	0	17	2	0
Oakland University	20,012	1	0	0	0	1	46	3	43	0	0
Saginaw Valley State University	9,105	3	0	1	0	2	52	0	52	0	0
Schoolcraft College	11,339	2	0	1	1	0	18	1	17	0	0
University of Michigan											
Ann Arbor	44,718	18	0	4	2	12	529	28	493	8	1
Dearborn	9,131	0	0	0	0	0	29	0	25	4	0
Flint	8,044	1	0	0	0	1	49	1	48	0	1
Western Michigan University	23,227	9	0	3	0	6	168	3	162	3	2
MINNESOTA											
University of Minnesota											
Duluth	11,018	2	0	0	2	0	48	6	41	1	0
Morris	1,771	1	0	1	0	0	6	1	5	0	0
Twin Cities	51,579	16	0	2	9	5	546	27	494	25	0
MISSISSIPPI											
Coahoma Community College	2,064	1	0	0	1	0	17	17	0	0	0
Jackson State University	9,811	21	0	0	2	19	164	34	129	1	0
Mississippi State University	21,622	4	0	3	0	1	200	14	181	5	0
Northeast Mississippi Community College	3,521	0	0	0	0	0	28	3	25	0	0
University of Mississippi											
Medical Center[4,5]			0			3	106	0	104	2	0
Oxford[6]	23,610		0			6	92	6	83	3	0
MISSOURI											
Jefferson College	4,692	0	0	0	0	0	3	2	1	0	0
Lincoln University	2,738	7	0	3	0	4	62	14	47	1	0
Metropolitan Community College	15,790	1	0	0	0	1	30	0	30	0	0
Mineral Area College	4,173	0	0	0	0	0	2	2	0	0	0
Missouri Southern State University	6,231	4	0	3	0	1	44	17	25	2	0
Missouri University of Science and Technology	8,835	1	0	1	0	0	58	0	55	3	0
Missouri Western State University	5,363	0	0	0	0	0	29	2	26	1	0
Northwest Missouri State University	6,530	6	0	4	0	2	39	3	36	0	0
Southeast Missouri State University	11,978	2	0	2	0	0	70	30	36	4	0
St. Charles Community College	6,755	0	0	0	0	0	12	0	12	0	0
St. Louis Community College, Meramec	19,052	0	0	0	0	0	58	0	58	0	0
Truman State University	6,379	1	0	1	0	0	41	3	37	1	0
University of Central Missouri	13,988	7	0	4	1	2	86	11	73	2	0
University of Missouri											

Table 9. Offenses Known to Law Enforcement, by Selected State and University and College, 2017—Continued

(Number.)

State and university/college	Student enrollment[1]	Violent crime	Murder and nonnegligent manslaughter	Rape[2]	Robbery	Aggravated assault	Property crime	Burglary	Larceny-theft	Motor vehicle theft	Arson[3]
Columbia	33,239	6	0	2	2	2	252	2	239	11	5
Kansas City	16,936	7	0	6	1	0	59	16	41	2	0
St. Louis	16,989	0	0	0	0	0	55	8	46	1	0
Washington University	15,047	1	0	0	1	0	86	0	86	0	0
					1						
MONTANA											
Montana State University	16,359	11	0	3	1	7	149	1	148	0	1
NEVADA											
College of Southern Nevada	33,556	0	0	0	0	0	34	3	29	2	0
University of Nevada											
Las Vegas	29,702	16	1	2	5	8	399	59	319	21	1
Reno	21,353	9	0	4	1	4	165	26	134	5	0
NEW HAMPSHIRE											
University of New Hampshire	15,188	8	0	5	0	3	148	8	140	0	0
NEW JERSEY											
Brookdale Community College	13,165	1	0	1	0	0	12	0	12	0	0
Essex County College	9,596	3	0	1	0	2	60	1	59	0	0
Kean University	14,070	0	0	0	0	0	83	7	68	8	0
Middlesex County College	11,371	1	0	1	0	0	13	0	13	0	0
Monmouth University	6,371	3	0	3	0	0	27	1	25	1	0
Montclair State University	20,987	5	0	2	1	2	72	0	70	2	0
New Jersey Institute of Technology	11,317	5	0	2	2	1	82	4	76	2	0
Princeton University	8,181	3	0	1	1	1	269	18	242	9	0
Rowan University	17,372	10	0	3	4	3	151	18	131	2	1
Rutgers University											
Camden	6,475	5	0	0	3	2	72	2	70	0	0
Newark	12,321	20	0	2	13	5	250	14	234	2	0
New Brunswick	50,146	28	0	14	4	10	390	42	347	1	1
Stevens Institute of Technology	6,617	0	0	0	0	0	33	10	23	0	0
Stockton University	8,728	4	0	4	0	0	23	1	22	0	0
The College of New Jersey	7,396	2	0	1	0	1	78	7	69	2	5
William Paterson University	10,583	1	0	0	1	0	53	0	53	0	0
NEW MEXICO											
Eastern New Mexico University	6,010	1	0	0	1	0	48	7	41	0	
New Mexico Military Institute	422	1	0	0	0	1	11	2	9	0	
New Mexico State University	14,852	6	0	1	0	5	186	17	161	8	
University of New Mexico	26,999	51	0	7	6	38	833	52	641	140	
Western New Mexico University	3,427	1	0	0	0	1	31	6	25	0	
NEW YORK											
Cornell University	22,319	3	0	1	1	1	282	20	262	0	0
Ithaca College	6,678	11	0	11	0	0	75	7	68	0	0
Rensselaer Polytechnic Institute	7,363	0	0	0	0	0	53	1	52	0	1
State University of New York Police											
Alfred	3,735	3	0	0	0	3	61	6	53	2	3
Binghamton	17,292	8	0	5	2	1	184	13	171	0	5
Brockport	8,243	3	0	1	1	1	53	8	45	0	0
Buffalo	30,184	6	0	2	0	4	238	32	203	3	0
Buffalo State College	9,475	15	0	7	0	8	150	23	125	2	2
Canton	3,205	5	0	2	0	3	22	0	22	0	0
Cobleskill	2,287	8	0	8	0	0	19	6	13	0	1
Cortland	6,900	3	0	3	0	0	47	10	37	0	0
Delhi	3,511	2	0	2	0	0	27	1	26	0	0
Downstate Medical	1,839	0	0	0	0	0	45	0	45	0	0
Environmental Science	2,186	0	0	0	0	0	17	0	17	0	0
Farmingdale	9,235	1	0	0	1	0	36	0	33	3	0
Fredonia	4,603	3	0	3	0	0	46	6	40	0	0
Geneseo	5,602	4	0	3	0	1	54	4	50	0	0
Maritime	1,832	0	0	0	0	0	22	7	15	0	0
Morrisville	3,003	3	0	3	0	0	26	5	21	0	0
New Paltz	7,628	2	0	1	0	1	27	4	23	0	1
Oneonta	6,055	5	0	4	0	1	53	5	48	0	3
Optometry	401	0	0	0	0	0	2	0	2	0	0
Oswego	8,004	1	0	0	1	0	84	16	66	2	0
Plattsburgh	5,520	3	0	1	1	1	37	2	35	0	0
Polytechnic Institute	2,697	0	0	0	0	0	11	1	10	0	0
Potsdam	3,696	1	0	0	0	1	52	6	45	1	0
Purchase	4,156	3	0	3	0	0	35	4	31	0	0
Stony Brook	25,734	12	0	5	3	4	236	23	211	2	0
Upstate Medical	1,491	5	0	0	1	4	105	7	93	5	0
NORTH CAROLINA[6]											
Appalachian State University	18,295		0		0	0	77	8	69	0	0
Duke University	15,735		0		1	8	411	36	351	24	0
East Carolina University	28,962		0		1	3	133	9	124	0	0
Elizabeth City State University	1,357		0		1	2	32	13	19	0	0
Elon University	6,739		0		0	0	7	0	7	0	0
Fayetteville State University	6,223		0		2	1	49	9	40	0	0
Meredith College	1,981		0		0	0	14	1	13	0	0

Table 9. Offenses Known to Law Enforcement, by Selected State and University and College, 2017—Continued

(Number.)

State and university/college	Student enrollment[1]	Violent crime	Murder and nonnegligent manslaughter	Rape[2]	Robbery	Aggravated assault	Property crime	Burglary	Larceny-theft	Motor vehicle theft	Arson[3]
Methodist University	2,446		0		0	0	51	4	46	1	0
North Carolina Central University	8,094		0		2	6	150	49	101	0	0
North Carolina State University, Raleigh	33,755		0		3	13	249	25	218	6	0
University of North Carolina											
Asheville	3,821		0		0	1	24	4	20	0	1
Chapel Hill	29,468		1		3	1	234	25	204	5	1
Charlotte	28,721		0		0	3	149	17	129	3	1
Greensboro	19,647		0		0	0	142	22	119	1	1
Wilmington	15,740		0		0	1	229	3	224	2	2
Winston-Salem State University	5,151		0		1	0	70	17	52	1	0
NORTH DAKOTA											
North Dakota State College of Science	3,003	0	0	0	0	0	12	1	10	1	0
North Dakota State University	14,432	2	0	2	0	0	116	7	108	1	0
University of North Dakota	14,648	9	0	5	1	3	127	15	112	0	0
OHIO											
Capital University	3,367	0	0	0	0	0	53	10	41	2	0
Cleveland State University	16,864	13	0	3	10	0	146	6	124	16	0
Columbus State Community College	27,109	1	0	0	1	0	43	1	41	1	0
Cuyahoga Community College	23,987	0	0	0	0	0	32	2	29	1	0
Kent State University[7]	30,167		0	0	0	3	167	2	164	1	0
Lakeland Community College	7,997	0	0	0	0	0	14	0	14	0	0
Miami University	19,697	26	0	19	1	6	140	9	131	0	9
Ohio State University, Columbus	59,482	41	0	30	5	6	798	24	763	11	1
Otterbein University	2,928	0	0	0	0	0	24	1	23	0	0
Shawnee State University	3,772	2	0	0	1	1	19	4	15	0	0
Sinclair Community College	18,610	1	0	0	1	0	39	11	28	0	0
University of Akron	21,100	6	0	5	0	1	183	5	171	7	0
University of Cincinnati	36,596	39	0	31	1	7	283	15	261	7	0
University of Toledo	20,615	7	0	0	5	2	185	5	177	3	0
Wright State University	16,655	7	0	4	3	0	55	2	53	0	0
OKLAHOMA											
Cameron University	4,846	0	0	0	0	0	11	2	9	0	0
East Central University	4,160	0	0	0	0	0	18	2	16	0	0
Langston University	2,420	16	0	3	2	11	58	25	32	1	1
Mid-America Christian University	2,405	0	0	0	0	0	2	1	0	1	0
Northeastern Oklahoma A&M College	2,077	1	0	0	1	0	48	25	21	2	0
Northeastern State University, Tahlequah	8,109	1	0	1	0	0	12	2	9	1	0
Northwestern Oklahoma State University	2,218	0	0	0	0	0	7	1	6	0	0
Oklahoma City Community College	12,557	0	0	0	0	0	40	1	39	0	0
Oklahoma City University	2,968	1	0	0	0	1	34	6	28	0	0
Oklahoma State University											
Main Campus	25,622	7	0	6	0	1	195	61	132	2	1
Okmulgee	2,396	1	0	0	0	1	14	0	13	1	0
Tulsa	926	0	0	0	0	0	12	2	9	1	0
Rogers State University	3,903	0	0	0	0	0	3	1	1	1	0
Seminole State College	1,729	0	0	0	0	0	3	0	3	0	0
Southeastern Oklahoma State University	3,725	1	0	1	0	0	13	1	10	2	1
Southwestern Oklahoma State University	5,320	2	0	1	0	1	10	3	7	0	0
Tulsa Community College	17,135	5	0	0	0	5	27	3	21	3	0
University of Central Oklahoma	16,428	4	0	1	1	2	45	5	39	1	0
University of Oklahoma											
Health Sciences Center	3,322	4	0	0	2	2	138	9	126	3	0
Norman	27,918	13	0	10	2	1	280	9	260	11	0
OREGON											
Portland State University	26,627	10	0	2	4	4	328	35	291	2	4
PENNSYLVANIA											
Bloomsburg University	9,637	1	0	1	0	0	29	2	26	1	0
California University	7,553	2	0	1	0	1	35	2	32	1	0
Cheyney University	746	2	0	0	0	2	20	6	14	0	0
Clarion University	5,224	7	0	4	0	3	15	1	14	0	0
Dickinson College	2,420	3	0	3	0	0	63	11	52	0	1
East Stroudsburg University	6,822	7	0	2	3	2	52	2	50	0	0
Edinboro University	6,181	2	0	0	0	2	42	11	31	0	0
Elizabethtown College	1,784	3	0	2	0	1	15	1	14	0	0
Indiana University	12,971	19	0	9	1	9	49	0	49	0	0
Kutztown University	8,513	12	0	10	2	0	45	2	43	0	0
Lehigh University	7,059	2	0	2	0	0	30	0	30	0	0
Lock Haven University	4,220	3	0	2	0	1	23	2	21	0	0
Mansfield University	2,180	0	0	0	0	0	7	0	7	0	0
Millersville University	7,914	0	0	0	0	0	22	1	21	0	0
Moravian College	2,426	0	0	0	0	0	34	7	27	0	0
Pennsylvania State University											
Altoona	3,491	1	0	1	0	0	28	5	22	1	1
Beaver	726	2	0	1	1	0	8	0	8	0	6
Behrend	4,566	1	0	1	0	0	15	2	13	0	0
Berks	2,888	1	0	0	0	1	6	0	6	0	0
Brandywine	1,379	1	0	1	0	0	5	0	4	1	0
Fayette	643	0	0	0	0	0	0	0	0	0	0

Table 9. Offenses Known to Law Enforcement, by Selected State and University and College, 2017—Continued

(Number.)

State and university/college	Student enrollment[1]	Violent crime	Murder and nonnegligent manslaughter	Rape[2]	Robbery	Aggravated assault	Property crime	Burglary	Larceny-theft	Motor vehicle theft	Arson[3]
Greater Allegheny	550	1	0	1	0	0	1	0	1	0	0
Harrisburg	5,046	2	0	2	0	0	6	0	6	0	0
Hazleton	863	1	0	1	0	0	4	0	4	0	0
Mont Alto	903	0	0	0	0	0	2	0	2	0	0
Schuylkill	759	2	0	1	0	1	4	1	3	0	0
University Park	47,789	42	0	25	2	15	411	35	373	3	7
Worthington Scranton	1,019	0	0	0	0	0	3	0	3	0	0
Shippensburg University	6,972	0	0	0	0	0	31	9	22	0	0
Slippery Rock University	8,854	0	0	0	0	0	34	1	33	0	0
University of Pittsburgh											
Bradford	1,465	1	0	1	0	0	8	1	7	0	0
Greensburg	1,520	1	0	1	0	0	7	0	7	0	0
Johnstown	2,769	0	0	0	0	0	30	3	27	0	0
Pittsburgh	28,664	3	0	1	0	2	170	3	165	2	1
Titusville	332	0	0	0	0	0	4	1	3	0	1
West Chester University	17,005	3	0	3	0	0	64	4	59	1	0
RHODE ISLAND											
Brown University	9,781	0	0	0	0	0	118	14	104	0	0
University of Rhode Island	17,822	7	0	4	0	3	75	2	72	1	0
SOUTH CAROLINA											
Benedict College	2,281	23	0	4	4	15	98	12	83	3	0
Bob Jones University	2,901	0	0	0	0	0	16	9	7	0	0
Clemson University	23,406	9	0	5	0	4	216	20	163	33	1
Coastal Carolina University	10,479	17	0	7	2	8	172	4	168	0	0
College of Charleston	11,294	1	0	0	0	1	71	1	69	1	0
Erskine College	822	0	0	0	0	0	1	1	0	0	0
Francis Marion University	3,874	2	0	2	0	0	21	0	21	0	0
Greenville Technical College	11,932	8	0	2	0	6	27	2	23	2	0
Medical University of South Carolina	2,986	8	0	3	1	4	107	2	103	2	0
Midlands Technical College	10,749	0	0	0	0	0	13	0	12	1	0
Orangeburg-Calhoun Technical College	2,640	0	0	0	0	0	0	0	0	0	0
Presbyterian College	1,352	2	0	2	0	0	35	16	18	1	1
South Carolina State University	2,905	3	0	1	1	1	74	32	41	1	0
Spartanburg Methodist College	737	2	0	2	0	0	4	2	2	0	0
The Citadel	3,602	3	0	0	0	3	24	5	18	1	0
University of South Carolina											
Aiken	3,548	1	0	0	0	1	11	2	9	0	0
Beaufort	2,005	5	0	3	1	1	6	0	6	0	0
Columbia	34,099	16	0	10	2	4	329	17	251	61	0
Upstate	5,821	0	0	0	0	0	38	1	36	1	0
Winthrop University	6,109	6	0	1	1	4	38	2	35	1	0
SOUTH DAKOTA											
South Dakota State University	12,600	2	0	1	0	1	57	3	54	0	0
TENNESSEE											
Austin Peay State University	10,344	1	0	0	1	0	54	9	43	2	0
Chattanooga State Community College	8,628	0	0	0	0	0	6	0	6	0	0
Christian Brothers University	2,138	0	0	0	0	0	19	1	15	3	0
Cleveland State Community College	3,315	0	0	0	0	0	4	0	4	0	0
East Tennessee State University	14,022	5	0	4	0	1	78	4	71	3	1
Jackson State Community College	4,689	0	0	0	0	0	1	1	0	0	0
Lincoln Memorial University	4,254	0	0	0	0	0	1	0	1	0	0
Middle Tennessee State University	22,050	12	0	5	1	6	153	20	128	5	0
Motlow State Community College	5,838	0	0	0	0	0	0	0	0	0	0
Northeast State Community College	6,124	0	0	0	0	0	5	0	5	0	0
Pellissippi State Community College	10,244	0	0	0	0	0	22	0	22	0	0
Roane State Community College	5,756	0	0	0	0	0	2	0	2	0	0
Southwest Tennessee Community College	8,327	1	0	1	0	0	15	0	15	0	0
Tennessee State University	8,760	5	0	1	1	3	66	6	59	1	0
Tennessee Technological University	10,493	0	0	0	0	0	85	7	76	2	0
University of Memphis	21,301	12	0	6	2	4	129	15	113	1	0
University of Tennessee											
Chattanooga	11,533	7	0	2	1	4	102	13	84	5	0
Health Science Center	3,097	0	0	0	0	0	16	2	13	1	0
Knoxville	28,052	10	0	2	0	8	229	20	197	12	0
Martin	6,705	1	0	0	0	1	57	4	53	0	0
University of the South	1,815	12	0	8	0	4	91	40	50	1	0
Vanderbilt University	12,587	24	0	7	0	17	383	5	371	7	0
Volunteer State Community College	8,684	2	0	0	0	2	13	0	13	0	0
TEXAS											
Abilene Christian University	4,910	8	0	7	0	1	63	6	56	1	0
Alamo Colleges District	56,533	8	0	1	2	5	126	17	101	8	0
Alvin Community College	5,677	0	0	0	0	0	5	0	5	0	0
Amarillo College	10,195	1	0	0	0	1	13	0	13	0	0
Angelo State University	9,581	1	0	1	0	0	35	2	31	2	0
Austin College	1,278	1	0	1	0	0	39	8	30	1	1
Baylor Health Care System[4]		2	0	0	2	0	325	15	297	13	0
Baylor University, Waco	16,959	7	0	4	2	1	219	15	193	11	0
Brookhaven College	12,775	0	0	0	0	0	6	1	5	0	0

Table 9. Offenses Known to Law Enforcement, by Selected State and University and College, 2017—Continued

(Number.)

State and university/college	Student enrollment[1]	Violent crime	Murder and nonnegligent manslaughter	Rape[2]	Robbery	Aggravated assault	Property crime	Burglary	Larceny-theft	Motor vehicle theft	Arson[3]
Central Texas College	18,117	1	0	0	0	1	14	1	13	0	0
Cisco College	3,244	1	0	1	0	0	8	0	8	0	0
College of the Mainland	3,995	0	0	0	0	0	13	1	12	0	0
El Paso Community College	29,460	1	0	0	0	1	28	3	23	2	0
Grayson College	4,600	1	0	0	0	1	15	2	13	0	0
Hardin-Simmons University	2,205	2	0	0	0	2	19	2	17	0	0
Houston Baptist University	3,270	2	0	0	2	0	40	11	28	1	0
Houston Community College	57,032	10	0	1	8	1	176	11	149	16	0
Lamar University, Beaumont	15,001	7	0	2	0	5	53	3	47	3	0
Laredo Community College	9,176	2	0	0	0	2	7	0	7	0	0
Midwestern State University	6,064	9	0	8	0	1	64	11	53	0	0
Paris Junior College	4,806	1	0	0	0	1	4	0	4	0	0
Prairie View A&M University	8,782	12	0	7	2	3	57	27	30	0	0
Rice University	6,855	5	0	0	2	3	187	3	183	1	0
Southern Methodist University	11,739	7	0	4	0	3	119	5	110	4	0
South Plains College	9,478	0	0	0	0	0	13	3	9	1	0
Southwestern University	1,489	0	0	0	0	0	20	4	16	0	0
Stephen F. Austin State University	12,742	4	0	4	0	0	45	3	42	0	0
St. Mary's University	3,567	7	0	2	1	4	34	4	30	0	0
St. Thomas University	3,247	0	0	0	0	0	25	0	25	0	0
Sul Ross State University	2,944	0	0	0	0	0	24	7	17	0	0
Tarleton State University	13,049	5	0	3	0	2	66	9	56	1	0
Texas A&M International University	7,390	4	0	2	1	1	26	5	21	0	0
Texas A&M University											
Central Texas	2,619	0	0	0	0	0	2	0	2	0	0
College Station	65,632	19	0	10	1	8	390	31	347	12	0
Commerce	13,514	7	0	4	1	2	77	32	45	0	0
Galveston[4]		0	0	0	0	0	16	2	14	0	0
Kingsville	9,278	6	0	5	0	1	64	7	57	0	0
San Antonio	5,474	0	0	0	0	0	9	0	9	0	0
Texas Christian University	10,394	5	0	3	1	1	93	13	70	10	0
Texas State Technical College											
Harlingen[4]		1	0	1	0	0	15	0	15	0	0
Waco[4]		12	0	7	1	4	59	16	43	0	1
West Texas[4]		0	0	0	0	0	1	0	1	0	0
Texas Tech University, Lubbock[7]	36,551	15	1	5	1	8	436	15	412	9	0
Texas Woman's University	15,655	3	0	3	0	0	40	2	38	0	0
Tyler Junior College	11,493	3	0	2	0	1	31	5	25	1	0
University of Houston										23	0
Central Campus	43,774	25	0	10	10	5	440	32	383	25	2
Clearlake	8,669	2	0	2	0	0	24	0	23	1	0
Downtown Campus	14,251	0	0	0	0	0	40	1	35	4	0
University of North Texas, Denton	38,145	9	0	5	0	4	169	14	149	6	1
University of Texas											
Arlington	45,282	13	0	4	3	6	125	14	109	2	0
Austin	51,331	15	1	6	3	5	380	17	355	8	2
Dallas	26,793	3	0	2	0	1	194	7	185	2	0
El Paso	23,922	6	0	5	0	1	132	13	118	1	0
Health Science Center, San Antonio[7]	3,250	0	0	0	0	0	42	0	41	1	0
Health Science Center, Tyler	12	3	0	0	0	3	11	0	11	0	0
Houston	5,411	2	0	1	0	1	275	20	250	5	0
Medical Branch	3,277	0	0	0	0	0	82	0	81	1	1
Permian Basin	6,673	1	0	0	0	1	15	6	8	1	0
Rio Grande Valley	27,560	4	0	1	0	3	91	16	75	0	0
San Antonio	28,959	9	0	6	2	1	126	5	117	4	0
Southwestern Medical School	2,316	6	0	1	0	5	175	7	163	5	0
Tyler	9,835	2	0	1	0	1	31	4	26	1	0
West Texas A&M University	9,901	2	0	1	0	1	56	4	52	0	0
UTAH											
Brigham Young University	34,240	5	0	1	0	4	158	2	151	5	1
Southern Utah University	9,299	1	0	1	0	0	19	3	16	0	0
University of Utah	31,860	12	1	6	0	5	395	32	326	37	0
Utah State University		0	0	0	0	0	47	2	45	0	0
Eastern[4]		1	0	1	0	0	10	3	7	0	0
Logan	28,118	4	0	4	0	0	20	2	17	1	0
Utah Valley University	34,978	1	0	0	0	1	65	3	62	0	0
Weber State University	26,809	3	0	2	1	0	28	6	20	2	0
VERMONT											
University of Vermont	13,105	5	0	4	0	1	103	5	98	0	2
VIRGINIA											
Bridgewater College	1,882	0	0	0	0	0	14	0	13	1	0
Christopher Newport University	5,042	1	0	0	0	1	84	1	79	4	0
Eastern Virginia Medical School	1,130	1	0	1	0	0	35	0	35	0	0
Emory and Henry College	1,167	0	0	0	0	0	3	0	3	0	0
Ferrum College	1,294	2	0	0	2	0	21	0	21	0	0
George Mason University	34,909	2	0	2	0	0	125	5	119	1	0
Hampton University	4,646	6	0	4	0	2	27	6	21	0	0
James Madison University	21,270	4	0	1	0	3	109	7	97	5	2
J. Sargeant Reynolds Community College	10,375	1	0	0	0	1	13	0	13	0	0
Longwood University	4,884	1	0	1	0	0	23	0	22	1	0

Table 9. Offenses Known to Law Enforcement, by Selected State and University and College, 2017—Continued

(Number.)

State and university/college	Student enrollment[1]	Violent crime	Murder and nonnegligent manslaughter	Rape[2]	Robbery	Aggravated assault	Property crime	Burglary	Larceny-theft	Motor vehicle theft	Arson[3]
Norfolk State University	5,421	7	0	4	3	0	92	6	86	0	2
Northern Virginia Community College	50,835	1	0	0	1	0	52	0	51	1	0
Old Dominion University	24,322	32	0	7	3	22	255	18	231	6	0
Radford University	9,401	4	0	3	0	1	66	6	56	4	3
Richard Bland College	2,409	0	0	0	0	0	9	0	9	0	0
University of Mary Washington	4,726	5	0	4	1	0	48	1	47	0	0
University of Richmond	4,131	4	0	3	0	1	90	13	75	2	0
University of Virginia's College at Wise	2,212	0	0	0	0	0	9	5	4	0	0
Virginia Commonwealth University	30,872	22	0	7	2	13	492	8	478	6	2
Virginia Military Institute	1,713	0	0	0	0	0	21	9	12	0	0
Virginia Polytechnic Institute and State University	33,170	8	0	4	0	4	204	34	170	0	0
Virginia State University	4,584	14	0	3	7	4	48	4	43	1	0
Virginia Western Community College	7,719	0	0	0	0	0	2	0	2	0	0
WASHINGTON											
Central Washington University	11,971	5	0	5	0	0	129	8	118	3	0
Eastern Washington University	12,279	6	0	6	0	0	31	4	27	0	0
Evergreen State College	4,089	1	0	1	0	0	40	0	39	1	0
University of Washington	45,591	18	0	7	7	4	536	52	476	8	1
Washington State University											
Pullman	30,142	9	0	7	0	2	88	17	70	1	0
Vancouver[4]		1	0	1	0	0	3	0	2	1	0
Western Washington University	15,574	0	0	0	0	0	142	9	133	0	0
WEST VIRGINIA											
Marshall University	13,647	12	0	3	2	7	72	6	66	0	0
Shepherd University	3,779	1	0	1	0	0	9	2	7	0	0
West Virginia University	28,488	30	0	11	4	15	255	9	243	3	1
WISCONSIN											
Marquette University	11,294	33	0	5	15	13	355	42	280	33	1
University of Wisconsin											
Eau Claire	10,747	3	0	2	0	1	79	8	71	0	1
Green Bay	7,029	1	0	1	0	0	19	2	17	0	0
La Crosse	10,637	1	0	1	0	0	72	0	72	0	0
Madison	42,582	6	0	6	0	0	259	46	210	3	0
Milwaukee	25,601	5	0	5	0	0	121	20	99	2	1
Oshkosh	13,958	5	0	3	0	2	45	14	31	0	1
Parkside	4,371	4	0	2	0	2	29	3	26	0	0
Platteville	8,779	1	0	1	0	0	35	4	30	1	0
River Falls	5,938	2	0	1	0	1	56	5	51	0	0
Stevens Point	8,627	0	0	0	0	0	43	2	41	0	0
Stout	9,633	3	0	1	0	2	99	4	95	0	0
Superior	2,489	3	0	3	0	0	24	1	23	0	0
Whitewater[7]	12,657	5	0	3	2	0	55	5	49	1	0
WYOMING											
University of Wyoming	12,366	0	0	0	0	0	103	7	95	1	0

Note: Caution should be exercised in making any intercampus comparisons or ranking schools because university/college crime statistics are affected by a variety of factors. These include demographic characteristics of the surrounding community, ratio of male to female students, number of on-campus residents, accessibility of the campus to outside visitors, size of enrollment, etc.
1 The student enrollment figures provided by the United States Department of Education are for the 2016 school year, the most recent available. The enrollment figures include full-time and part-time students.   2 The figures shown in this column for the offense of rape were reported using only the revised Uniform Crime Reporting (UCR) definition of rape. See chapter notes for more detail.   3 The FBI does not publish arson data unless it receives data from either the agency or the state for all 12 months of the calendar year.   4 Student enrollment figures were not available.   5 The FBI determined that the agency's data were overreported. Consequently, those data are not included in this report.   6 This agency/state submits rape data classified according to the legacy UCR definition; therefore the rape offense and violent crime total, which rape is a part of, is not included in this table. See chapter notes for more detail.   7 Because of changes in the local agency's reporting practices, figures are not comparable to previous years' data.

Table 10. Offenses Known to Law Enforcement, by Selected State Metropolitan and Nonmetropolitan Counties, 2017

(Number.)

State/county	Violent crime	Murder and nonnegligent manslaughter	Rape[1]	Robbery	Aggravated assault	Property crime	Burglary	Larceny-theft	Motor vehicle theft	Arson[2]
ALABAMA										
Metropolitan Counties										
Autauga	55	2	5	5	43	384	131	206	47	
Baldwin	163	1	9	18	135	737	226	442	69	
Bibb	3	0	1	1	1	69	41	24	4	
Blount	313	1	14	5	293	812	198	502	112	
Calhoun	18	0	7	7	4	211	93	117	1	
Chilton	168	2	15	7	144	715	268	368	79	
Colbert	58	0	13	3	42	267	84	151	32	
Elmore	60	1	13	9	37	757	228	467	62	
Etowah	104	2	13	3	86	526	186	276	64	
Geneva	58	0	7	3	48	227	73	124	30	
Hale	17	0	1	0	16	39	9	21	9	
Henry	14	0	2	0	12	48	17	26	5	
Houston	103	2	12	10	79	580	144	396	40	
Jefferson	700	5	34	163	498	2,311	1,203	974	134	
Lauderdale	37	0	4	1	32	165	41	87	37	
Lawrence	71	2	9	3	57	356	101	206	49	
Lee	420	2	20	12	386	1,072	253	704	115	
Limestone	154	2	28	10	114	1,015	284	649	82	
Lowndes	68	1	12	11	44	236	95	111	30	
Madison	380	6	31	32	311	2,074	549	1,299	226	
Mobile	136	5	11	21	99	2,375	728	1,310	337	
Montgomery	115	0	2	14	99	389	122	222	45	
Morgan	143	0	11	1	131	284	157	109	18	
Russell	45	1	9	6	29	351	98	214	39	
Shelby	98	0	30	6	62	690	232	401	57	
Tuscaloosa	215	5	10	22	178	1,363	414	781	168	
Walker	84	0	9	10	65	587	144	330	113	
Nonmetropolitan Counties										
Barbour	34	0	3	3	28	100	33	57	10	
Bullock	6	0	1	1	4	46	19	21	6	
Butler	33	2	2	5	24	190	69	111	10	
Chambers	3	0	0	1	2	89	33	52	4	
Cherokee	48	3	8	2	35	357	131	196	30	
Choctaw	13	1	0	0	12	21	4	13	4	
Clarke	40	1	3	2	34	91	36	47	8	
Cleburne	6	0	0	1	5	136	41	82	13	
Coffee	23	2	5	2	14	138	46	77	15	
Coosa	25	2	2	2	19	157	54	92	11	
Covington	4	0	1	0	3	46	13	29	4	
Cullman	73	0	34	10	29	954	224	608	122	
Dale	44	2	15	4	23	194	53	114	27	
Dallas	109	1	8	13	87	501	187	282	32	
DeKalb	147	0	32	9	106	755	248	382	125	
Franklin	30	0	9	1	20	291	101	155	35	
Greene	32	0	0	3	29	99	39	44	16	
Lamar	9	0	3	0	6	67	25	37	5	
Macon	23	0	3	0	20	152	70	61	21	
Marengo	52	2	6	4	40	211	99	90	22	
Marion	19	0	2	0	17	153	63	75	15	
Marshall	102	1	13	3	85	511	168	280	63	
Monroe	39	0	0	4	35	108	40	61	7	
Pike	19	0	3	1	15	88	33	51	4	
Randolph	6	0	1	0	5	182	68	97	17	
Sumter	15	1	0	1	13	60	23	26	11	
Talladega	96	2	13	7	74	720	192	460	68	
Tallapoosa	21	0	8	3	10	118	34	81	3	
Wilcox	46	2	2	4	38	123	74	45	4	
Winston	19	0	6	1	12	83	30	47	6	
ARIZONA										
Metropolitan Counties										
Cochise	189	0	14	8	167	616	64	492	60	0
Coconino	105	3	18	3	81	422	108	287	27	12
Maricopa	1,389	18	151	133	1,087	5,411	1,004	3,733	674	66
Mohave	172	4	21	24	123	2,425	800	1,394	231	13
Pima	650	15	82	189	364	8,851	1,776	6,411	664	57
Pinal	219	7	27	16	169	2,195	555	1,411	229	15
Yavapai	249	3	30	12	204	1,153	301	743	109	16
Yuma	149	11	22	8	108	1,001	378	521	102	11
Nonmetropolitan Counties										
Graham	8	0	0	1	7	130	29	83	18	14
Greenlee	1	0	0	0	1	51	30	15	6	0
Navajo	85	1	3	4	77	441	182	211	48	1
ARKANSAS										
Metropolitan Counties										
Benton	125	1	38	0	86	712	408	255	49	1

Table 10. Offenses Known to Law Enforcement, by Selected State Metropolitan and Nonmetropolitan Counties, 2017—Continued

(Number.)

State/county	Violent crime	Murder and nonnegligent manslaughter	Rape[1]	Robbery	Aggravated assault	Property crime	Burglary	Larceny-theft	Motor vehicle theft	Arson[2]
Cleveland	11	0	1	1	9	94	47	41	6	0
Craighead	51	2	8	2	39	296	5	244	47	4
Crawford	30	0	1	1	28	299	61	204	34	1
Crittenden	143	1	15	9	118	275	83	162	30	3
Faulkner	116	2	28	6	80	941	259	576	106	10
Garland	296	0	28	10	258	1,612	676	804	132	0
Grant	46	0	7	0	39	185	55	115	15	4
Jefferson	71	4	14	3	50	428	165	208	55	8
Lincoln	5	0	1	1	3	66	18	36	12	1
Little River	27	0	2	0	25	122	45	70	7	2
Lonoke	85	3	4	3	75	426	83	233	110	4
Madison	39	0	8	4	27	137	56	77	4	1
Miller	24	1	3	2	18	319	112	180	27	2
Perry	41	0	7	1	33	151	28	123	0	0
Pulaski	412	3	20	40	349	1,805	460	1,093	252	21
Saline	167	2	30	14	121	838	321	407	110	10
Sebastian	62	0	10	1	51	222	77	126	19	3
Washington	198	0	19	1	178	583	186	339	58	10
Nonmetropolitan Counties										
Arkansas	13	0	1	0	12	108	31	62	15	1
Ashley	23	1	1	1	20	235	65	158	12	0
Baxter	73	2	12	1	58	632	80	495	57	10
Boone	199	0	52	1	146	320	81	199	40	6
Bradley	8	1	1	0	6	32	18	11	3	0
Calhoun	15	0	4	0	11	40	16	21	3	0
Carroll	44	8	3	0	33	191	42	119	30	1
Chicot	3	0	0	0	3	59	21	38	0	1
Clark	12	0	1	0	11	76	28	41	7	0
Clay	9	0	1	0	8	67	19	45	3	1
Cleburne	88	1	18	0	69	336	100	219	17	9
Columbia	12	0	0	0	12	51	17	25	9	2
Conway	50	0	11	2	37	252	69	159	24	3
Cross	25	0	6	0	19	143	36	98	9	0
Dallas	2	0	1	0	1	31	16	12	3	0
Drew	21	1	4	1	15	114	35	71	8	3
Franklin	68	1	11	1	55	203	81	100	22	5
Fulton	35	0	3	0	32	69	0	65	4	0
Greene	33	0	6	1	26	189	52	115	22	0
Hempstead	35	0	2	1	32	189	56	104	29	0
Hot Spring	38	3	2	3	30	205	52	122	31	5
Howard	8	0	3	0	5	42	30	11	1	0
Independence	176	1	29	3	143	477	181	242	54	17
Izard	35	0	9	1	25	260	60	182	18	8
Jackson	24	1	3	1	19	128	36	74	18	1
Johnson	37	1	6	2	28	217	56	134	27	6
Lawrence	12	0	5	0	7	61	16	42	3	2
Lee	1	0	1	0	0	68	14	42	12	0
Logan	20	0	9	1	10	183	30	128	25	0
Marion	48	0	8	0	40	325	86	223	16	1
Mississippi	16	0	4	2	10	254	75	147	32	1
Monroe	2	0	0	0	2	48	5	36	7	0
Montgomery	10	0	4	2	4	85	32	42	11	1
Pike	2	0	1	1	0	53	17	33	3	0
Polk	30	5	6	1	18	96	27	61	8	5
Pope	79	1	8	1	69	379	136	188	55	1
Prairie	4	0	1	0	3	67	28	35	4	0
Randolph	33	0	15	0	18	173	43	118	12	1
Scott	22	0	2	0	20	91	41	41	9	2
Searcy	6	0	2	0	4	52	20	29	3	0
Sevier	24	0	6	0	18	69	34	33	2	1
St. Francis	25	0	7	2	16	272	68	204	0	2
Union	49	1	4	5	39	317	108	171	38	0
Van Buren	28	0	1	0	27	177	19	121	37	2
White	146	3	20	1	122	779	218	472	89	3
Woodruff	4	0	0	0	4	33	8	21	4	0
Yell	63	3	15	1	44	190	63	100	27	4
CALIFORNIA										
Metropolitan Counties										
Alameda	675	8	28	227	412	2,202	377	1,156	669	30
Butte	161	5	49	27	80	1,229	616	589	24	0
Contra Costa	318	3	28	110	177	1,525	500	993	32	12
El Dorado	206	5	37	19	145	2,003	525	1,446	32	3
Fresno	1,213	15	38	86	1,074	3,334	1,469	1,249	616	210
Imperial	137	1	11	6	119	641	218	358	65	14
Kern	2,187	32	138	429	1,588	9,086	2,815	4,316	1,955	341
Kings	165	2	22	13	128	473	165	283	25	2
Los Angeles	6,118	71	327	1,566	4,154	17,336	3,789	9,155	4,392	253
Madera	451	3	23	27	398	1,102	452	606	44	10
Marin	91	1	12	10	68	776	153	615	8	3
Merced	521	7	16	38	460	1,504	554	908	42	13

Table 10. Offenses Known to Law Enforcement, by Selected State Metropolitan and Nonmetropolitan Counties, 2017—Continued

(Number.)

State/county	Violent crime	Murder and nonnegligent manslaughter	Rape[1]	Robbery	Aggravated assault	Property crime	Burglary	Larceny-theft	Motor vehicle theft	Arson[2]
Monterey	243	7	31	48	157	1,311	338	927	46	7
Napa	56	0	6	3	47	217	71	143	3	1
Orange	271	0	16	34	221	1,178	203	751	224	3
Placer	302	3	42	33	224	1,447	380	1,026	41	4
Riverside	775	16	48	161	550	7,700	1,711	4,579	1,410	28
Sacramento	2,612	32	154	772	1,654	9,224	2,492	6,545	187	58
San Benito	51	1	10	6	34	144	50	80	14	1
San Bernardino	862	27	76	160	599	5,076	1,358	2,556	1,162	70
San Diego	1,486	18	119	232	1,117	4,548	1,075	2,645	828	32
San Joaquin	746	5	25	141	575	2,961	751	2,068	142	27
San Luis Obispo[3]		1	21	16		1,116	400	691	25	5
San Mateo	311	2	65	70	174	3,109	337	2,411	361	14
Santa Barbara	272	2	43	24	203	1,499	421	1,054	24	6
Santa Clara	383	2	43	33	305	1,271	229	834	208	1
Santa Cruz	288	0	41	42	205	1,794	427	1,349	18	9
Shasta	527	4	48	24	451	944	431	468	45	48
Solano	105	1	9	15	80	368	164	139	65	8
Sonoma	636	6	81	60	489	1,149	388	753	8	15
Stanislaus	398	16	26	126	230	1,647	570	1,013	64	11
Sutter	87	1	9	5	72	600	230	303	67	2
Tulare[4]	362	13	35	68	246	1,883	634	1,246	3	0
Ventura	176	2	30	26	118	817	194	531	92	8
Yolo	56	2	4	10	40	282	99	166	17	3
Yuba	224	2	17	37	168	1,156	433	718	5	16
Nonmetropolitan Counties										
Alpine	13	0	0	0	13	29	8	21	0	0
Amador	87	0	7	5	75	356	98	248	10	0
Calaveras	200	2	29	17	152	588	214	359	15	0
Colusa	60	1	9	1	49	151	57	91	3	2
Del Norte	113	4	29	12	68	348	189	148	11	18
Glenn	81	0	5	6	70	235	100	123	12	2
Humboldt	273	4	25	51	193	949	362	546	41	15
Inyo	84	0	6	6	72	170	63	102	5	3
Lake	221	6	26	9	180	558	284	266	8	14
Lassen	60	1	6	2	51	233	106	124	3	3
Mariposa	107	0	9	3	95	269	83	184	2	0
Mendocino	254	3	26	21	204	381	185	189	7	11
Modoc	19	0	0	0	19	43	9	34	0	0
Mono	16	0	1	0	15	58	15	38	5	0
Nevada	174	3	13	12	146	620	294	304	22	3
Plumas	146	0	23	7	116	293	140	152	1	6
Sierra	5	0	0	1	4	24	12	11	1	0
Siskiyou	54	3	4	3	44	241	146	85	10	1
Tehama	89	8	22	10	49	432	212	206	14	0
Trinity	75	1	5	8	61	179	84	94	1	1
Tuolumne	173	2	39	13	119	622	322	294	6	6
COLORADO										
Metropolitan Counties										
Adams	549	7	112	80	350	2,895	411	1,587	897	36
Arapahoe	305	2	76	53	174	2,023	360	1,317	346	20
Boulder	94	3	25	9	57	575	128	395	52	6
Clear Creek	15	0	2	0	13	79	12	58	9	9
Douglas	292	3	117	16	156	2,410	487	1,695	228	23
Elbert	22	0	0	0	22	3	0	2	1	0
El Paso	411	4	90	33	284	2,096	374	1,461	261	25
Gilpin	15	1	5	1	8	91	17	65	9	0
Jefferson	218	2	45	17	154	2,695	411	2,051	233	13
Larimer	180	0	27	8	145	939	210	639	90	19
Mesa	216	2	57	12	145	1,326	274	911	141	23
Pueblo	34	1	1	7	25	1,162	186	834	142	3
Teller	25	0	5	1	19	91	23	59	9	2
Weld	150	2	16	5	127	745	182	455	108	9
Nonmetropolitan Counties										
Alamosa	2	0	2	0	0	34	4	27	3	0
Archuleta	26	1	0	0	25	113	44	64	5	0
Baca	3	0	0	0	3	3	1	1	1	0
Bent	11	0	1	3	7	111	33	68	10	0
Chaffee	6	0	0	0	6	74	13	58	3	0
Cheyenne	2	0	0	0	2	4	2	1	1	0
Conejos	4	0	0	0	4	62	62	0	0	1
Crowley	6	0	1	0	5	60	37	22	1	2
Custer	9	0	0	0	9	101	23	73	5	0
Delta	20	0	15	0	5	221	99	101	21	2
Dolores	7	0	0	0	7	26	9	15	2	0
Fremont	42	1	13	0	28	222	60	134	28	3
Garfield	41	0	20	2	19	199	46	142	11	4
Grand	4	0	0	0	4	42	13	28	1	0
Gunnison	5	0	2	0	3	33	4	21	8	0

Table 10. Offenses Known to Law Enforcement, by Selected State Metropolitan and Nonmetropolitan Counties, 2017—Continued

(Number.)

State/county	Violent crime	Murder and nonnegligent manslaughter	Rape[1]	Robbery	Aggravated assault	Property crime	Burglary	Larceny-theft	Motor vehicle theft	Arson[2]
Hinsdale	1	0	1	0	0	7	0	7	0	0
Huerfano	15	0	0	2	13	102	21	66	15	3
Jackson	0	0	0	0	0	7	0	7	0	0
Kit Carson	2	0	0	0	2	34	10	15	9	0
Lake	8	0	0	1	7	56	17	34	5	2
La Plata	45	2	12	0	31	190	55	114	21	1
Lincoln	2	1	1	0	0	22	7	12	3	0
Logan	6	0	3	0	3	119	36	70	13	4
Mineral	1	0	0	0	1	0	0	0	0	0
Moffat	8	0	0	0	8	51	7	36	8	5
Montezuma	17	0	1	0	16	161	42	101	18	3
Montrose	8	0	1	0	7	287	114	141	32	1
Morgan	21	2	8	0	11	92	25	57	10	1
Otero	6	0	0	0	6	63	18	34	11	1
Phillips	0	0	0	0	0	8	4	4	0	0
Pitkin	5	0	2	1	2	39	2	34	3	0
Prowers	12	0	1	0	11	10	4	6	0	0
Rio Blanco	0	0	0	0	0	18	2	15	1	0
Rio Grande	1	0	0	0	1	4	3	0	1	0
Routt	1	0	1	0	0	43	8	32	3	0
Saguache	0	0	0	0	0	21	8	10	3	0
San Juan	0	0	0	0	0	5	3	2	0	0
Summit	45	0	16	1	28	261	32	218	11	3
Washington	9	0	4	0	5	99	6	84	9	0
DELAWARE										
Metropolitan Counties										
New Castle County Police Department	933	5	50	161	717	4,308	951	2,968	389	4
FLORIDA										
Metropolitan Counties										
Alachua	617	5	74	104	434	1,939	533	1,278	128	14
Baker	88	2	5	5	76	331	101	208	22	1
Bay	357	4	45	31	277	2,416	492	1,724	200	4
Brevard	729	10	67	86	566	4,216	844	3,023	349	14
Broward	313	8	27	85	193	813	128	610	75	5
Charlotte	360	1	33	23	303	2,051	368	1,573	110	1
Citrus	399	3	42	40	314	2,037	431	1,472	134	12
Clay	514	4	78	81	351	2,993	543	2,290	160	20
Collier	957	6	77	152	722	3,873	639	3,025	209	15
Escambia	1,400	19	176	236	969	8,035	1,692	5,879	464	0
Flagler	228	3	21	28	176	1,616	252	1,272	92	5
Gadsden	114	0	19	4	91	407	193	195	19	4
Gilchrist	25	0	0	6	19	70	38	28	4	0
Gulf	27	0	1	1	25	175	79	90	6	2
Hernando	457	8	72	61	316	2,939	553	2,190	196	13
Highlands	250	5	31	29	185	2,040	550	1,397	93	14
Hillsborough	2,037	24	212	351	1,450	13,751	2,496	10,091	1,164	49
Indian River	355	3	26	34	292	1,902	361	1,422	119	4
Jefferson	107	0	5	2	100	180	58	110	12	2
Lake	489	9	74	37	369	2,644	620	1,764	260	17
Lee	1,299	32	174	313	780	6,002	1,339	4,108	555	41
Leon	362	5	36	26	295	1,914	382	1,431	101	6
Manatee	1,484	16	148	195	1,125	4,850	941	3,594	315	12
Marion	881	12	86	125	658	4,517	1,348	2,643	526	2
Martin	323	1	61	45	216	2,288	480	1,724	84	1
Miami-Dade	5,957	90	474	1,383	4,010	35,112	4,387	27,223	3,502	44
Nassau	179	1	16	14	148	904	367	473	64	5
Okaloosa	512	5	68	47	392	2,957	554	2,225	178	2
Orange	4,367	42	429	999	2,897	23,807	4,692	17,036	2,079	0
Osceola	836	11	91	86	648	4,672	1,067	3,305	300	3
Palm Beach	1,893	21	212	400	1,260	12,337	2,098	9,131	1,108	51
Pasco	1,377	6	182	196	993	7,375	1,532	5,235	608	44
Pinellas	647	5	97	108	437	4,940	766	3,877	297	15
Polk	1,206	11	81	133	981	5,851	1,475	3,790	586	8
Santa Rosa	234	4	32	20	178	1,562	323	1,158	81	2
Sarasota	502	6	26	70	400	4,440	753	3,518	169	5
Seminole	580	4	89	53	434	3,079	620	2,286	173	7
St. Johns	318	3	17	39	259	2,717	524	2,038	155	6
St. Lucie	223	2	40	33	148	1,469	311	1,070	88	6
Sumter	259	5	22	18	214	966	242	670	54	0
Volusia	589	7	63	109	410	3,073	657	2,162	254	27
Wakulla	88	0	12	2	74	507	174	307	26	3
Walton	151	0	15	8	128	1,111	304	727	80	6
Nonmetropolitan Counties										
Bradford	55	0	3	1	51	207	90	106	11	1
Calhoun	22	0	4	0	18	56	22	30	4	0
Columbia	199	1	21	18	159	1,012	451	511	50	9
DeSoto	85	1	5	7	72	639	214	371	54	3
Dixie	84	1	4	2	77	246	107	116	23	2

Table 10. Offenses Known to Law Enforcement, by Selected State Metropolitan and Nonmetropolitan Counties, 2017—Continued

(Number.)

State/county	Violent crime	Murder and nonnegligent manslaughter	Rape[1]	Robbery	Aggravated assault	Property crime	Burglary	Larceny-theft	Motor vehicle theft	Arson[2]
Franklin	22	0	3	1	18	121	37	78	6	1
Glades	31	0	1	0	30	178	45	116	17	0
Hamilton	58	2	6	6	44	223	77	126	20	4
Hardee	49	0	6	2	41	294	94	177	23	1
Hendry	134	4	13	30	87	790	354	392	44	7
Holmes	64	0	10	0	54	257	74	161	22	1
Jackson	147	6	30	3	108	707	117	565	25	3
Lafayette	35	1	3	0	31	35	12	21	2	0
Levy	447	2	21	5	419	527	217	265	45	1
Liberty	12	0	0	0	12	69	19	41	9	0
Madison	158	0	11	5	142	237	96	141	0	1
Monroe	191	6	11	14	160	1,015	162	817	36	2
Okeechobee	132	0	27	15	90	948	209	678	61	0
Putnam	169	4	17	15	133	1,011	275	690	46	4
Suwannee	144	0	15	3	126	390	119	247	24	0
Taylor	180	0	8	2	170	262	120	124	18	2
Union	31	1	0	3	27	112	60	48	4	3
Washington	44	2	1	3	38	175	44	114	17	0
GEORGIA										
Metropolitan Counties										
Augusta-Richmond	872	23	46	281	522	8,745	1,582	6,508	655	46
Barrow	238	0	14	10	214	1,153	228	864	61	4
Bibb	924	29	66	309	520	7,607	1,761	5,298	548	61
Brantley	27	1	4	2	20	421	90	314	17	0
Brooks	40	1	4	1	34	173	44	114	15	0
Bryan	87	0	5	5	77	281	75	197	9	3
Burke	40	3	2	6	29	237	71	133	33	0
Butts	69	0	3	7	59	376	58	288	30	0
Carroll	159	3	14	16	126	1,315	426	735	154	6
Catoosa	76	0	9	7	60	843	189	530	124	4
Cherokee	119	0	19	20	80	1,449	282	1,087	80	0
Clarke	0	0	0	0	0	0	0	0	0	0
Clayton	6	0	0	0	6	10	0	8	2	0
Clayton County Police Department	1,543	35	183	506	819	8,711	2,078	5,210	1,423	12
Cobb	7	0	2	4	1	26	2	24	0	0
Cobb County Police Department	1,221	19	116	408	678	11,899	1,846	9,004	1,049	30
Columbia	67	0	11	19	37	1,963	166	1,717	80	3
Coweta	109	6	18	24	61	1,256	243	908	105	2
Crawford	15	1	0	2	12	261	83	161	17	2
Dawson	36	0	7	3	26	454	69	356	29	0
DeKalb	0	0	0	0	0	0	0	0	0	0
DeKalb County Police Department	3,184	89	112	1,249	1,734	23,246	4,994	15,029	3,223	122
Dougherty	1	0	0	0	1	98	0	97	1	0
Dougherty County Police Department	35	0	5	7	23	322	95	202	25	1
Douglas	189	4	10	47	128	2,025	279	1,652	94	6
Echols	2	0	0	0	2	45	13	32	0	1
Effingham	49	0	3	5	41	450	208	195	47	0
Fayette	51	2	7	12	30	365	98	243	24	2
Floyd	33	0	2	1	30	122	19	95	8	0
Forsyth	125	4	21	15	85	1,758	272	1,391	95	2
Fulton	11	0	0	1	10	7	0	7	0	0
Fulton County Police Department	981	17	32	276	656	5,339	686	3,690	963	8
Glynn	0	0	0	0	0	0	0	0	0	0
Glynn County Police Department	182	7	12	40	123	1,822	469	1,236	117	3
Gwinnett County Police Department	1,604	26	166	677	735	15,079	2,793	10,876	1,410	44
Hall	267	3	51	32	181	1,805	371	1,181	253	19
Heard	13	0	1	0	12	111	35	57	19	2
Henry	0	0	0	0	0	87	0	87	0	2
Henry County Police Department	351	3	34	99	215	3,949	811	2,735	403	13
Houston	98	3	4	17	74	1,264	181	998	85	1
Jasper	61	0	0	3	58	226	55	159	12	0
Jones	27	0	0	5	22	329	101	203	25	3
Lamar	8	0	0	0	8	146	34	91	21	0
Lanier	24	0	0	0	24	119	24	87	8	0
Lee	51	1	6	14	30	561	87	460	14	0
Liberty	105	1	1	3	100	288	85	172	31	0
Lincoln	24	0	0	0	24	129	20	105	4	0
Long	20	0	8	2	10	190	86	91	13	0
Lowndes	62	0	1	4	57	775	255	440	80	0
Madison	41	0	3	4	34	402	96	285	21	0
Marion	2	0	0	0	2	31	25	6	0	0
McDuffie	37	0	1	5	31	224	117	92	15	0
McIntosh	29	1	1	4	23	327	135	176	16	0
Meriwether	52	1	2	3	46	244	58	172	14	2
Monroe	28	1	1	4	22	416	81	298	37	2
Muscogee	0	0	0	0	0	0	0	0	0	
Newton	357	6	13	53	285	1,669	416	1,004	249	6
Oconee	27	1	0	2	24	419	58	344	17	0
Oglethorpe	32	0	0	2	30	216	47	153	16	0
Paulding	180	2	13	20	145	2,450	464	1,670	316	6

Table 10. Offenses Known to Law Enforcement, by Selected State Metropolitan and Nonmetropolitan Counties, 2017—Continued

(Number.)

State/county	Violent crime	Murder and nonnegligent manslaughter	Rape[1]	Robbery	Aggravated assault	Property crime	Burglary	Larceny-theft	Motor vehicle theft	Arson[2]
Peach	23	2	1	1	19	273	59	194	20	0
Pickens	74	0	6	2	66	322	79	215	28	0
Pike	13	0	3	1	9	181	37	135	9	0
Pulaski	57	2	2	5	48	235	52	178	5	0
Rockdale	171	2	15	31	123	1,683	275	1,283	125	9
Spalding	148	3	14	16	115	1,094	337	647	110	
Terrell	7	0	0	1	6	58	15	41	2	
Twiggs	16	1	1	1	13	124	48	62	14	1
Walker	237	2	4	13	218	965	303	549	113	2
Walton	79	7	10	9	53	635	120	443	72	0
Whitfield	138	2	18	6	112	1,263	342	815	106	4
Worth	44	0	9	2	33	207	69	130	8	0
Nonmetropolitan Counties										
Appling	20	0	0	2	18	304	109	175	20	0
Bacon	15	0	0	1	14	126	49	70	7	0
Baldwin	200	6	4	6	184	649	148	478	23	0
Banks	43	0	6	5	32	471	122	328	21	1
Ben Hill	17	0	5	0	12	192	72	110	10	0
Berrien	20	0	2	1	17	173	47	112	14	0
Bleckley	21	0	9	1	11	111	31	72	8	0
Bulloch	33	0	3	3	27	553	164	358	31	0
Calhoun	1	0	0	0	1	4	2	0	2	0
Candler	7	0	0	1	6	117	26	87	4	0
Charlton	18	0	1	1	16	108	33	57	18	0
Chattooga	37	0	1	0	36	287	64	212	11	0
Clay	8	0	0	2	6	25	8	15	2	0
Clinch	10	0	0	0	10	46	23	22	1	2
Coffee	107	3	8	5	91	653	184	407	62	1
Cook	33	0	2	1	30	121	35	73	13	0
Crisp	12	0	0	1	11	336	39	288	9	0
Decatur	46	1	4	2	39	293	80	207	6	1
Dodge	20	0	2	1	17	213	67	132	14	0
Dooly	9	0	0	1	8	86	10	64	12	1
Early	31	0	12	0	19	87	28	53	6	0
Elbert	22	1	5	2	14	269	80	177	12	0
Emanuel	4	0	1	2	1	240	89	125	26	0
Evans	6	0	0	4	2	19	16	2	1	0
Fannin	12	0	1	0	11	212	58	142	12	3
Franklin	12	3	2	2	5	241	73	152	16	0
Gilmer	59	3	7	1	48	414	131	254	29	0
Glascock	1	0	0	0	1	15	4	9	2	0
Gordon	104	0	9	1	94	537	142	360	35	0
Grady	30	0	0	2	28	182	53	117	12	0
Greene	10	0	1	0	9	152	30	115	7	0
Habersham	44	0	13	2	29	254	114	123	17	0
Hancock	16	0	1	0	15	91	18	61	12	2
Hart	46	0	1	1	44	248	67	171	10	1
Irwin	6	0	0	0	6	108	29	68	11	0
Jackson	72	1	5	8	58	745	148	559	38	0
Jeff Davis	13	0	0	1	12	170	40	125	5	0
Jefferson	36	0	2	3	31	128	68	53	7	0
Laurens	73	1	8	6	58	559	166	340	53	3
Lumpkin	13	2	8	2	1	396	78	302	16	1
Macon	0	0	0	0	0	35	13	17	5	0
Miller	1	0	0	0	1	44	9	34	1	1
Mitchell	33	0	0	0	33	265	70	169	26	0
Pierce	54	2	4	1	47	239	64	170	5	0
Polk	0	0	0	0	0	0	0	0	0	0
Polk County Police Department	40	2	4	2	32	527	136	319	72	5
Putnam	41	2	4	1	34	327	71	253	3	
Quitman	5	0	1	2	2	8	4	2	2	0
Rabun	15	0	6	1	8	234	57	166	11	0
Randolph	9	0	0	3	6	41	12	24	5	0
Schley	5	0	1	0	4	18	3	14	1	0
Screven	39	1	1	5	32	180	66	87	27	7
Seminole	30	0	0	0	30	64	24	37	3	0
Stephens	17	0	6	1	10	330	78	243	9	
Sumter	18	1	2	2	13	141	41	84	16	
Talbot	15	0	0	2	13	90	26	55	9	0
Taliaferro	5	0	0	0	5	20	9	10	1	0
Tattnall	23	0	0	0	23	270	106	152	12	0
Taylor	12	1	2	0	9	76	38	32	6	
Thomas	53	0	9	10	34	471	150	278	43	4
Tift	72	0	1	16	55	587	125	428	34	
Towns	31	0	0	0	31	131	31	91	9	0
Treutlen	3	0	0	1	2	63	27	35	1	0
Troup	51	0	5	11	35	594	139	421	34	0
Union	14	0	3	4	7	211	69	125	17	
Upson	23	0	2	3	18	254	44	190	20	
Ware	92	2	4	8	78	623	99	500	24	5

Table 10. Offenses Known to Law Enforcement, by Selected State Metropolitan and Nonmetropolitan Counties, 2017—Continued

(Number.)

State/county	Violent crime	Murder and nonnegligent manslaughter	Rape[1]	Robbery	Aggravated assault	Property crime	Burglary	Larceny-theft	Motor vehicle theft	Arson[2]
Warren	15	0	2	0	13	47	19	27	1	0
Washington	12	0	2	4	6	119	39	75	5	0
Wayne	156	0	15	7	134	802	210	569	23	0
Webster	0	0	0	0	0	3	2	1	0	0
Wheeler	6	0	1	0	5	42	9	33	0	0
White	34	1	3	2	28	162	45	103	14	0
Wilkes	19	2	1	0	16	30	13	14	3	1
Wilkinson	19	0	1	1	17	43	18	17	8	
HAWAII										
Metropolitan Counties										
Maui Police Department	446	2	95	67	282	5,729	906	4,016	807	109
Nonmetropolitan Counties										
Hawaii Police Department	508	5	142	77	284	5,373	872	3,770	731	32
Kauai Police Department	183	0	45	25	113	1,813	440	1,248	125	39
IDAHO										
Metropolitan Counties										
Ada	241	1	39	6	195	713	153	512	48	6
Bannock	1	0	0	0	1	13	3	7	3	0
Boise	10	0	3	0	7	56	17	30	9	2
Bonneville	112	0	19	1	92	546	187	319	40	3
Canyon	94	0	15	1	78	507	193	241	73	6
Franklin	1	0	0	0	1	56	6	46	4	0
Gem	9	0	0	0	9	23	3	18	2	1
Jefferson	13	0	0	0	13	126	41	70	15	0
Jerome	28	0	5	2	21	112	29	60	23	1
Kootenai[5]	100	1	25	6	68			755	47	6
Nez Perce	6	0	0	0	6	81	46	34	1	0
Owyhee	24	0	2	0	22	76	16	50	10	0
Twin Falls	57	0	6	2	49	210	108	75	27	2
Nonmetropolitan Counties										
Adams	13	0	0	0	13	39	4	29	6	0
Bear Lake	0	0	0	0	0	44	16	24	4	0
Benewah	24	0	5	1	18	89	24	50	15	0
Bingham	28	1	7	0	20	189	60	114	15	2
Blaine	5	0	0	0	5	23	9	12	2	0
Caribou	0	0	0	0	0	21	8	12	1	0
Cassia	45	0	6	2	37	367	62	250	55	0
Clearwater	29	0	2	0	27	48	15	32	1	0
Custer	1	0	0	0	1	23	5	17	1	0
Elmore	17	1	4	0	12	85	24	48	13	0
Fremont	8	0	3	0	5	71	7	57	7	0
Gooding	14	0	1	1	12	56	17	25	14	0
Idaho	18	0	3	0	15	79	25	51	3	0
Latah	16	0	5	0	11	155	59	88	8	0
Lewis	2	0	0	0	2	18	3	15	0	0
Madison	20	0	15	0	5	80	18	49	13	0
Minidoka	19	0	3	1	15	112	12	85	15	1
Oneida	6	0	1	0	5	68	15	51	2	0
Payette	14	0	1	0	13	77	14	50	13	0
Power	2	0	1	0	1	33	6	19	8	0
Teton	13	0	1	0	12	55	8	40	7	0
Valley	8	1	2	0	5	57	21	33	3	0
Washington	14	0	4	0	10	12	3	9	0	0
ILLINOIS										
Metropolitan Counties										
Alexander	7	0	0	0	7	50	16	33	1	0
Bond	2	0	1	0	1	61	23	37	1	0
Boone	32	1	18	0	13	152	39	104	9	0
Champaign	91	1	17	11	62	466	145	305	16	5
Clinton	15	0	1	2	12	43	7	31	5	0
Cook	182	8	23	42	109	467	106	311	50	12
De Kalb	43	0	12	0	31	120	33	86	1	0
DuPage	80	0	18	16	46	702	134	521	47	2
Ford	24	0	1	1	22	79	22	54	3	1
Grundy	18	0	7	0	11	137	33	96	8	1
Henry	6	0	1	0	5	58	13	45	0	1
Jackson	31	2	7	0	22	266	92	165	9	1
Jersey	14	0	5	0	9	112	44	65	3	2
Kane	67	0	15	10	42	318	87	194	37	4
Kankakee	49	1	10	5	33	302	102	174	26	4
Kendall	78	0	19	6	53	152	69	71	12	3
Lake	101	1	24	12	64	1,048	264	710	74	2
Macon	27	0	7	1	19	270	57	202	11	2
Macoupin	11	0	1	0	10	180	38	124	18	0
Madison	150	1	24	23	102	1,025	239	718	68	5
Marshall	5	0	1	0	4	27	17	9	1	1

Table 10. Offenses Known to Law Enforcement, by Selected State Metropolitan and Nonmetropolitan Counties, 2017—Continued

(Number.)

State/county	Violent crime	Murder and nonnegligent manslaughter	Rape[1]	Robbery	Aggravated assault	Property crime	Burglary	Larceny-theft	Motor vehicle theft	Arson[2]
McHenry	68	1	20	1	46	372	117	242	13	2
McLean	24	1	9	0	14	118	40	66	12	0
Menard	7	0	4	0	3	28	8	19	1	0
Peoria	114	0	33	9	72	866	206	601	59	6
Piatt	7	0	5	0	2	39	25	10	4	1
Rock Island	61	0	17	3	41	285	61	219	5	1
Sangamon	149	0	24	9	116	624	186	364	74	5
Stark	6	0	0	0	6	49	16	30	3	0
St. Clair	98	1	21	22	54	730	209	464	57	4
Vermilion	70	0	29	4	37	398	138	243	17	0
Will	144	5	24	27	88	865	234	543	88	20
Williamson	8	0	5	3	0	321	105	196	20	1
Winnebago	118	0	23	12	83	758	248	453	57	10
Woodford	11	0	4	0	7	89	23	60	6	0
Nonmetropolitan Counties										
Adams	37	0	18	1	18	186	46	136	4	0
Brown	3	0	0	0	3	15	4	10	1	2
Bureau	17	0	6	0	11	156	56	100	0	2
Carroll	2	0	0	0	2	70	19	50	1	0
Cass	6	0	0	0	6	9	3	5	1	0
Clark	5	0	1	0	4	42	20	17	5	3
Clay	3	0	1	0	2	55	16	30	9	1
Coles	22	0	5	0	17	104	34	63	7	4
Crawford	1	0	1	0	0	40	8	31	1	5
Cumberland	2	0	0	1	1	30	16	12	2	0
Douglas	4	0	2	0	2	46	13	29	4	0
Edgar	4	0	0	0	4	59	31	27	1	0
Effingham	11	0	0	0	11	131	48	71	12	1
Fayette	2	0	0	0	2	93	19	66	8	1
Franklin	26	0	0	0	26	228	71	153	4	2
Fulton	12	0	4	1	7	106	33	68	5	1
Gallatin	2	0	0	0	2	40	10	27	3	1
Greene	2	0	0	0	2	31	13	16	2	0
Hancock	7	0	1	0	6	86	31	55	0	1
Hardin	19	1	1	1	16	31	13	14	4	1
Iroquois	21	0	5	3	13	156	59	91	6	1
Jasper	0	0	0	0	0	6	3	3	0	0
Jefferson	48	0	7	1	40	234	96	115	23	4
Jo Daviess	2	0	1	0	1	77	25	51	1	2
Knox	30	0	4	1	25	128	54	69	5	1
La Salle	50	1	29	0	20	297	93	197	7	5
Lee	34	0	0	1	33	147	52	87	8	2
Livingston	20	0	5	3	12	169	37	121	11	3
Logan	20	0	2	0	18	43	23	17	3	0
Marion	39	0	4	3	32	141	71	54	16	0
Mason	13	0	6	0	7	65	18	42	5	1
Massac	13	0	2	1	10	95	35	51	9	1
McDonough	3	0	0	0	3	36	8	27	1	0
Montgomery	1	0	0	1	0	107	37	70	0	1
Morgan	24	1	12	0	11	110	31	73	6	1
Ogle	15	0	1	0	14	142	36	99	7	0
Perry	6	0	0	0	6	37	14	22	1	1
Pike	5	0	4	0	1	60	16	44	0	0
Putnam	2	0	0	0	2	18	4	14	0	0
Randolph	1	0	1	0	0	13	4	9	0	0
Richland	20	0	3	0	17	76	22	44	10	1
Saline	20	0	0	1	19	175	62	104	9	0
Schuyler	1	0	0	0	1	0	0	0	0	0
Scott	0	0	0	0	0	17	8	8	1	0
Shelby	4	0	4	0	0	23	3	19	1	0
Stephenson	9	0	7	0	2	157	34	115	8	0
Union	22	0	6	1	15	99	31	58	10	1
Wabash	0	0	0	0	0	11	3	8	0	0
Washington	27	0	0	0	27	42	20	18	4	2
White	27	0	1	0	26	114	26	81	7	3
Whiteside	24	0	7	0	17	106	44	50	12	1
INDIANA										
Metropolitan Counties										
Allen	167	1	25	25	116	731	169	503	59	1
Bartholomew	62	1	9	23	29	579	152	335	92	0
Clark	114	0	12	7	95	524	178	267	79	2
Delaware	59	2	3	9	45	377	91	228	58	2
Johnson	63	0	0	9	54	536	70	454	12	0
Lake	61	2	4	29	26	654	75	505	74	1
La Porte[6]	68	0	7	4	57	457	158	251	48	0
Madison	32	0	19	6	7	428	115	281	32	1
Monroe	42	0	11	7	24	682	84	529	69	6
Shelby	50	0	9	1	40	213	71	110	32	0
St. Joseph	119	1	24	28	66	1,239	385	745	109	3

Table 10. Offenses Known to Law Enforcement, by Selected State Metropolitan and Nonmetropolitan Counties, 2017—Continued

(Number.)

State/county	Violent crime	Murder and nonnegligent manslaughter	Rape[1]	Robbery	Aggravated assault	Property crime	Burglary	Larceny-theft	Motor vehicle theft	Arson[2]
Tippecanoe	45	1	7	7	30	515	146	335	34	10
Vanderburgh	89	1	12	12	64	688	131	524	33	6
Vigo[6]	61	1	8	6	46	879	279	486	114	3
Nonmetropolitan Counties										
Clinton	13	0	9	1	3	194	71	100	23	1
Crawford	28	0	1	0	27	90	76	0	14	0
Daviess	1	1	0	0	0	92	24	57	11	
De Kalb	10	0	7	2	1	175	42	113	20	
Franklin	3	0	0	3	0	137	49	70	18	
Grant	28	0	3	0	25	223	63	153	7	0
Greene	2	1	1	0	0	213	37	154	22	0
Huntington	5	0	1	0	4	94	11	70	13	
Jackson	17	0	5	0	12	349	109	227	13	
Jennings	22	1	6	0	15	229	127	93	9	0
LaGrange	38	0	5	3	30	172	42	92	38	0
Lawrence	69	0	3	1	65	251	114	97	40	2
Miami	11	0	1	0	10	246	75	164	7	0
Noble	12	0	4	0	8	243	113	105	25	0
Starke	18	2	3	0	13	403	46	351	6	
Wayne	14	1	3	2	8	198	60	123	15	
IOWA										
Metropolitan Counties										
Benton	24	0	1	1	22	98	35	55	8	0
Black Hawk	26	0	3	1	22	146	66	60	20	1
Dallas	34	1	5	3	25	103	37	56	10	2
Dubuque	16	0	10	0	6	166	57	95	14	1
Grundy	10	0	0	0	10	60	22	36	2	0
Guthrie	6	0	0	2	4	54	27	18	9	0
Harrison	17	0	4	0	13	68	14	43	11	1
Johnson	70	0	17	2	51	234	42	177	15	0
Linn	33	0	17	1	15	311	125	147	39	1
Madison	1	0	0	0	1	41	17	19	5	2
Mills	21	0	1	0	20	97	26	50	21	1
Plymouth	14	0	3	0	11	32	11	15	6	0
Polk	113	6	24	11	72	677	204	355	118	5
Pottawattamie	64	0	8	3	53	311	95	173	43	5
Scott	50	0	6	3	41	207	76	99	32	1
Story	14	0	3	1	10	131	56	65	10	5
Warren	52	1	8	0	43	191	56	106	29	5
Washington	31	0	3	0	28	84	37	40	7	0
Woodbury	27	0	2	0	25	166	62	78	26	1
Nonmetropolitan Counties										
Adair	4	0	0	0	4	39	15	18	6	0
Appanoose	17	1	1	0	15	126	63	50	13	1
Audubon	3	0	0	0	3	19	0	18	1	1
Boone	20	0	1	0	19	57	21	25	11	2
Buchanan	5	2	1	0	2	122	42	68	12	2
Buena Vista	11	0	1	0	10	29	9	18	2	1
Butler	2	0	1	0	1	9	5	3	1	1
Calhoun	7	0	1	0	6	36	10	23	3	2
Carroll	3	0	2	0	1	3	1	0	2	0
Cass	16	0	5	0	11	50	15	30	5	0
Cedar	7	0	4	0	3	64	15	42	7	0
Cerro Gordo	11	0	0	0	11	98	31	57	10	0
Cherokee	4	0	1	0	3	21	8	10	3	0
Chickasaw	11	1	1	0	9	32	5	22	5	0
Clarke	4	0	1	0	3	36	15	13	8	0
Clay	9	0	0	0	9	40	9	25	6	0
Clayton	9	0	4	1	4	46	16	24	6	0
Clinton	38	2	0	0	36	126	38	78	10	0
Crawford	4	0	0	0	4	14	5	7	2	2
Davis	2	0	0	0	2	8	4	4	0	0
Decatur	7	0	0	0	7	17	6	9	2	0
Delaware	14	0	7	0	7	86	43	39	4	2
Des Moines	7	0	1	1	5	157	98	49	10	0
Dickinson	10	1	2	0	7	27	8	11	8	0
Emmet	10	0	0	0	10	37	7	25	5	0
Fayette	11	0	1	1	9	39	12	21	6	0
Floyd	2	0	0	0	2	23	12	8	3	0
Franklin	1	0	0	0	1	0	0	0	0	0
Fremont	21	0	7	0	14	59	23	26	10	0
Hamilton	5	0	0	0	5	40	13	24	3	3
Henry	16	0	1	0	15	89	34	50	5	3
Howard	1	0	0	0	1	63	38	20	5	0
Humboldt	3	0	0	0	3	41	9	29	3	0
Ida	9	0	0	0	9	23	8	12	3	0
Iowa	17	1	0	0	16	69	20	36	13	0
Jackson	3	0	0	0	3	21	14	2	5	0

Table 10. Offenses Known to Law Enforcement, by Selected State Metropolitan and Nonmetropolitan Counties, 2017—Continued

(Number.)

State/county	Violent crime	Murder and nonnegligent manslaughter	Rape[1]	Robbery	Aggravated assault	Property crime	Burglary	Larceny-theft	Motor vehicle theft	Arson[2]
Jasper	32	1	5	0	26	121	49	60	12	2
Jefferson	0	0	0	0	0	45	22	18	5	0
Keokuk	6	0	3	0	3	48	22	20	6	0
Kossuth	14	0	1	0	13	15	5	9	1	0
Lee	27	1	0	1	25	99	38	46	15	0
Louisa	30	0	5	1	24	100	48	45	7	2
Lucas	13	0	3	0	10	86	47	34	5	2
Lyon	11	0	1	0	10	62	19	39	4	1
Mahaska	15	0	1	0	14	130	79	39	12	1
Marion	42	0	20	0	22	67	34	24	9	1
Marshall	26	0	0	1	25	91	32	54	5	1
Monona	11	0	1	0	10	34	5	24	5	0
Monroe	7	0	2	0	5	23	6	13	4	0
Muscatine	29	0	4	1	24	67	34	22	11	2
O'Brien	25	0	3	0	22	73	20	52	1	0
Osceola	5	0	1	0	4	81	22	59	0	0
Page	7	0	1	0	6	42	16	17	9	0
Palo Alto	18	0	2	0	16	67	31	30	6	0
Sac	8	0	4	0	4	50	14	31	5	0
Shelby	6	0	0	0	6	24	11	13	0	1
Sioux	2	0	1	0	1	51	17	31	3	1
Tama	36	0	5	0	31	83	42	35	6	1
Taylor	3	0	0	0	3	17	4	11	2	0
Union	6	0	0	0	6	44	16	21	7	1
Van Buren	4	0	0	0	4	53	27	23	3	1
Wapello	22	0	2	0	20	186	80	89	17	2
Wayne	13	0	2	0	11	54	22	28	4	0
Webster	46	1	2	1	42	127	54	56	17	5
Winneshiek	8	0	1	0	7	32	5	23	4	0
Worth	10	0	1	0	9	50	13	28	9	0
Wright	2	0	2	0	0	19	11	8	0	0
KANSAS										
Metropolitan Counties										
Butler	49	1	7	1	40	442	134	271	37	4
Doniphan	4	1	0	0	3	31	13	12	6	0
Harvey	23	3	1	0	19	72	28	36	8	0
Jackson	21	0	3	0	18	90	19	62	9	2
Johnson	46	0	8	3	35	317	76	209	32	3
Kingman	7	0	0	0	7	55	24	30	1	0
Leavenworth	32	0	5	1	26	186	68	89	29	6
Miami	31	1	4	1	25	196	77	95	24	7
Osage	13	0	3	0	10	52	16	29	7	0
Pottawatomie	45	0	2	1	42	214	45	158	11	6
Riley County Police Department	221	2	55	23	141	1,355	226	1,051	78	13
Sedgwick[5]	158	3	15	6	134			259	60	6
Shawnee	79	0	4	9	66	899	186	626	87	2
Sumner	33	0	2	3	28	170	60	92	18	1
Wabaunsee	7	0	3	0	4	70	23	39	8	2
Wyandotte	59	2	7	6	44	77	6	62	9	1
Nonmetropolitan Counties										
Allen	12	0	1	1	10	71	25	39	7	2
Anderson	6	0	2	0	4	52	17	29	6	0
Atchison	6	0	0	1	5	26	3	21	2	0
Barber	2	0	0	0	2	12	6	5	1	0
Barton	12	0	2	0	10	51	2	41	8	2
Bourbon	16	0	2	0	14	102	47	50	5	0
Brown	10	0	1	0	9	15	8	5	2	0
Chautauqua	1	0	0	0	1	18	6	8	4	0
Cherokee	30	2	1	2	25	180	82	82	16	4
Cheyenne	5	0	0	1	4	16	2	13	1	0
Cloud	14	0	2	0	12	54	26	25	3	3
Cowley	23	0	2	0	21	123	41	74	8	2
Crawford	35	0	2	0	33	161	2	135	24	10
Dickinson	16	0	2	0	14	139	39	84	16	1
Edwards	2	1	0	0	1	19	3	15	1	0
Ellis	21	0	2	1	18	62	28	28	6	2
Ellsworth	8	0	2	0	6	46	16	24	6	2
Finney	30	0	2	3	25	162	46	96	20	0
Ford	23	0	0	1	22	99	44	45	10	3
Franklin	48	0	4	0	44	161	56	87	18	0
Geary	15	0	1	0	14	32	11	20	1	2
Gove	2	1	0	0	1	13	2	10	1	2
Grant	5	1	1	0	3	10	1	9	0	0
Gray	15	0	1	0	14	79	26	41	12	1
Greeley	2	0	0	1	1	13	3	9	1	0
Greenwood	17	1	1	0	15	58	15	38	5	0
Harper	1	0	0	0	1	14	6	8	0	0
Haskell	0	0	0	0	0	32	8	22	2	0
Hodgeman	1	0	0	0	1	10	2	6	2	0

Table 10. Offenses Known to Law Enforcement, by Selected State Metropolitan and Nonmetropolitan Counties, 2017—Continued

(Number.)

State/county	Violent crime	Murder and nonnegligent manslaughter	Rape[1]	Robbery	Aggravated assault	Property crime	Burglary	Larceny-theft	Motor vehicle theft	Arson[2]
Kearny	7	0	2	0	5	52	8	42	2	0
Kiowa	0	0	0	0	0	28	9	18	1	0
Lane	4	0	1	0	3	3	0	3	0	0
Logan	0	0	0	0	0	19	4	13	2	1
Lyon	16	0	3	1	12	78	25	50	3	4
Marion	4	0	0	1	3	69	31	33	5	0
McPherson	5	0	0	0	5	53	20	29	4	1
Mitchell	0	0	0	0	0	10	4	4	2	0
Montgomery	11	0	3	0	8	113	53	52	8	0
Morris	5	0	0	0	5	42	11	27	4	3
Morton	1	0	0	0	1	25	7	18	0	1
Nemaha	2	0	0	0	2	52	20	25	7	1
Neosho	9	0	0	0	9	74	30	37	7	7
Ness	8	0	1	0	7	28	7	16	5	0
Norton	5	0	0	0	5	20	5	11	4	0
Ottawa	3	0	1	0	2	71	17	49	5	2
Pawnee	0	0	0	0	0	19	9	8	2	0
Phillips	3	0	0	0	3	29	10	18	1	1
Pratt	5	0	0	0	5	24	9	13	2	0
Reno	30	0	5	0	25	257	90	141	26	12
Republic	3	0	0	0	3	27	6	17	4	1
Rice	9	0	0	2	7	70	31	36	3	1
Rooks	3	0	1	0	2	32	12	19	1	0
Rush	6	0	1	0	5	73	28	38	7	2
Russell	10	0	2	0	8	28	7	18	3	0
Saline	20	1	5	0	14	104	31	59	14	1
Seward	13	0	0	1	12	15	2	12	1	1
Sherman	2	0	0	0	2	4	1	2	1	0
Stafford	4	0	0	0	4	17	6	7	4	0
Thomas	7	0	1	0	6	43	14	27	2	0
Trego	0	0	0	0	0	12	4	5	3	0
Washington	1	0	1	0	0	22	10	9	3	0
Wichita	5	0	0	0	5	23	3	18	2	0
Wilson	5	0	0	0	5	42	13	25	4	2
Woodson	4	0	0	0	4	26	6	18	2	0
KENTUCKY										
Metropolitan Counties										
Allen	9	0	5	0	4	145	69	60	16	1
Boone	65	2	29	13	21	911	164	669	78	2
Bourbon	2	0	0	1	1	77	30	44	3	0
Boyd	14	0	2	2	10	171	47	94	30	1
Bracken	2	0	0	1	1	22	6	13	3	0
Bullitt	33	0	11	5	17	500	122	288	90	0
Butler	2	0	0	2	0	71	26	33	12	0
Campbell	0	0	0	0	0	0	0	0	0	0
Campbell County Police Department	20	1	14	2	3	197	44	131	22	0
Christian	22	0	5	1	16	322	123	169	30	5
Clark	13	0	2	7	4	220	90	104	26	2
Daviess	10	1	3	0	6	405	115	245	45	2
Edmonson	3	0	0	1	2	28	14	12	2	0
Fayette	0	0	0	0	0	0	0	0	0	0
Gallatin	0	0	0	0	0	34	11	18	5	0
Grant	5	0	3	0	2	128	36	74	18	0
Greenup	2	0	0	1	1	27	8	9	10	0
Hardin	12	1	0	1	10	157	36	99	22	2
Henderson	14	2	2	3	7	162	53	83	26	0
Henry	2	0	0	0	2	3	2	1	0	2
Jefferson	0	0	0	0	0	0	0	0	0	0
Jessamine	15	0	3	8	4	280	105	149	26	0
Kenton	1	0	0	1	0	6	0	6	0	0
Kenton County Police Department	18	1	11	0	6	125	44	67	14	1
Larue	1	0	0	0	1	32	14	12	6	0
McLean	6	0	3	1	2	52	24	21	7	1
Meade	11	1	0	0	10	154	61	56	37	2
Oldham	0	0	0	0	0	4	2	2	0	0
Oldham County Police Department	27	0	9	5	13	450	139	285	26	2
Pendleton	4	0	1	0	3	71	26	35	10	0
Scott	9	0	2	2	5	220	62	142	16	0
Shelby	21	0	3	4	14	312	66	215	31	0
Spencer	1	0	0	0	1	56	17	36	3	0
Trigg	12	0	1	1	10	47	20	21	6	0
Trimble	1	0	0	0	1	14	7	5	2	0
Warren	37	1	13	6	17	516	182	289	45	2
Nonmetropolitan Counties										
Adair	0	0	0	0	0	17	4	8	5	1
Anderson	3	0	0	0	3	44	15	23	6	0
Ballard	5	0	2	0	3	65	23	35	7	0
Barren	13	0	1	2	10	124	70	42	12	0
Bath	0	0	0	0	0	21	3	17	1	0

Table 10. Offenses Known to Law Enforcement, by Selected State Metropolitan and Nonmetropolitan Counties, 2017—Continued

(Number.)

State/county	Violent crime	Murder and nonnegligent manslaughter	Rape[1]	Robbery	Aggravated assault	Property crime	Burglary	Larceny-theft	Motor vehicle theft	Arson[2]
Bell	15	0	3	3	9	113	32	62	19	4
Boyle	4	0	2	0	2	44	19	24	1	0
Breckinridge	5	1	0	0	4	51	25	16	10	0
Caldwell	1	0	0	0	1	48	23	19	6	2
Calloway	19	0	8	2	9	328	158	143	27	3
Carlisle	0	0	0	0	0	9	3	5	1	0
Carroll	1	0	0	0	1	5	0	4	1	0
Carter	7	0	1	2	4	66	31	28	7	0
Casey	1	0	0	0	1	29	13	8	8	0
Clay	1	0	0	0	1	108	25	42	41	0
Clinton	2	0	0	0	2	27	12	6	9	0
Crittenden	1	0	0	0	1	17	7	8	2	1
Cumberland	0	0	0	0	0	6	0	5	1	0
Fleming	4	0	0	0	4	11	9	1	1	0
Floyd	3	0	0	0	3	59	18	29	12	0
Franklin	28	0	7	2	19	265	62	168	35	0
Fulton	1	0	0	0	1	6	1	5	0	0
Graves	31	1	10	5	15	284	90	162	32	1
Grayson	7	0	2	0	5	53	23	16	14	0
Harlan	3	0	0	1	2	23	6	13	4	1
Harrison	1	0	0	0	1	107	50	50	7	0
Hart	7	0	0	1	6	57	24	29	4	0
Hickman	2	0	1	0	1	16	7	5	4	0
Hopkins	8	0	1	1	6	236	74	127	35	1
Jackson	5	0	0	1	4	70	33	26	11	0
Johnson	3	0	1	0	2	45	13	17	15	1
Knott	0	0	0	0	0	20	3	10	7	0
Knox	14	0	0	3	11	150	57	49	44	1
Laurel	49	3	1	10	35	599	190	295	114	0
Lawrence	0	0	0	0	0	44	17	16	11	0
Lee	0	0	0	0	0	2	1	1	0	0
Leslie	3	0	0	0	3	2	0	2	0	0
Letcher	0	0	0	0	0	19	8	8	3	0
Lewis	2	0	0	0	2	16	4	7	5	0
Lincoln	4	0	1	3	0	77	24	30	23	0
Livingston	5	0	0	1	4	66	24	34	8	2
Logan	15	0	5	1	9	151	71	68	12	0
Lyon	0	0	0	0	0	32	14	15	3	0
Madison	10	0	3	1	6	341	123	193	25	2
Magoffin	1	0	0	0	1	6	3	1	2	1
Marion	2	0	0	0	2	68	22	35	11	0
Marshall	28	1	8	5	14	181	72	90	19	4
Martin	3	0	0	0	3	15	5	8	2	0
Mason	11	0	3	4	4	85	31	48	6	0
McCracken	43	1	19	4	19	499	155	286	58	0
McCreary	4	0	0	1	3	37	7	22	8	0
Menifee	4	1	2	0	1	28	15	9	4	0
Mercer	3	0	1	0	2	26	8	12	6	0
Metcalfe	4	0	0	1	3	58	30	19	9	1
Monroe	0	0	0	0	0	9	5	3	1	0
Montgomery	14	0	2	2	10	273	98	155	20	0
Morgan	0	0	0	0	0	19	5	8	6	0
Muhlenberg	11	0	3	0	8	95	56	23	16	1
Nelson	18	1	4	1	12	217	66	130	21	0
Nicholas	0	0	0	0	0	5	3	2	0	0
Ohio	10	0	1	3	6	94	35	46	13	0
Owen	3	0	1	0	2	50	26	21	3	0
Owsley	0	0	0	0	0	5	5	0	0	0
Perry	3	0	0	0	3	21	4	11	6	0
Pike	3	0	0	1	2	91	17	72	2	0
Powell	0	0	0	0	0	24	9	11	4	0
Pulaski	34	1	9	4	20	373	163	158	52	1
Robertson	0	0	0	0	0	1	0	1	0	0
Rockcastle	4	0	0	1	3	45	20	16	9	1
Rowan	3	0	0	0	3	120	30	80	10	0
Russell	3	0	2	0	1	28	12	9	7	0
Simpson	12	0	0	1	11	39	20	14	5	0
Taylor	7	0	2	1	4	162	68	81	13	1
Todd	2	0	0	0	2	46	20	20	6	0
Union	4	0	1	1	2	55	29	17	9	1
Washington	4	0	1	0	3	31	15	13	3	0
Wayne	1	0	1	0	0	32	14	14	4	1
Webster	1	0	0	0	1	27	10	8	9	0
Whitley	12	3	0	1	8	115	55	46	14	0
Wolfe	0	0	0	0	0	13	4	8	1	0
LOUISIANA										
Metropolitan Counties										
Acadia[5]	101	0	4	22	75		415	327		0
Ascension	311	5	11	38	257	3,014	615	2,208	191	11

Table 10. Offenses Known to Law Enforcement, by Selected State Metropolitan and Nonmetropolitan Counties, 2017—Continued

(Number.)

State/county	Violent crime	Murder and nonnegligent manslaughter	Rape[1]	Robbery	Aggravated assault	Property crime	Burglary	Larceny-theft	Motor vehicle theft	Arson[2]
Bossier	67	1	5	4	57	646	167	434	45	2
Caddo	67	1	3	5	58	810	225	527	58	1
Calcasieu	465	8	45	43	369	4,387	1,254	2,892	241	11
Cameron	20	2	1	0	17	148	17	126	5	0
De Soto	53	1	5	4	43	340	82	237	21	0
East Baton Rouge	493	14	45	209	225	8,113	1,175	6,557	381	10
East Feliciana	97	0	8	2	87	171	39	107	25	0
Iberville	257	1	4	13	239	534	109	419	6	0
Jefferson	1,535	31	92	380	1,032	9,937	1,358	7,908	671	64
Lafayette	304	4	31	28	241	1,441	345	967	129	9
Lafourche	200	5	31	9	155	1,720	391	1,247	82	7
Livingston	332	13	28	11	280	3,443	975	2,441	27	1
Ouachita	393	4	24	41	324	2,803	1,061	1,564	178	13
Plaquemines	45	0	5	3	37	279	62	203	14	1
Pointe Coupee	85	0	5	6	74	285	96	173	16	0
Rapides	199	2	9	11	177	1,517	457	970	90	5
St. Bernard	146	2	9	43	92	1,409	246	1,068	95	10
St. Charles	181	4	3	38	136	961	217	684	60	5
St. Helena	66	4	3	4	55	135	38	83	14	0
St. James	33	1	3	2	27	334	103	195	36	0
St. John the Baptist	90	2	2	21	65	978	219	708	51	3
St. Martin	154	3	23	24	104	677	106	553	18	0
St. Tammany	247	12	29	17	189	1,795	412	1,264	119	9
Tangipahoa	739	9	51	136	543	2,758	819	1,676	263	11
Terrebonne	298	2	13	27	256	2,164	346	1,725	93	6
Union	34	0	2	0	32	31	13	18	0	0
Vermilion	77	0	0	18	59	815	287	292	236	0
Webster	48	1	4	2	41	200	96	84	20	0
West Baton Rouge	60	1	5	5	49	483	49	393	41	0
West Feliciana	41	2	7	3	29	78	12	57	9	0
Nonmetropolitan Counties										
Allen	15	0	7	0	8	84	7	65	12	0
Assumption	60	1	5	2	52	246	49	191	6	0
Avoyelles	206	0	8	3	195	440	137	276	27	3
Beauregard	17	0	4	0	13	100	8	63	29	4
Bienville	49	1	1	5	42	213	72	129	12	0
Caldwell	24	1	0	0	23	226	56	159	11	0
Catahoula	36	0	3	0	33	96	30	63	3	0
Claiborne	14	0	0	0	14	106	31	69	6	0
Concordia	56	0	2	3	51	241	80	148	13	0
Evangeline	54	0	3	2	49	480	112	326	42	0
Franklin	63	0	0	5	58	142	35	96	11	0
Jackson	2	1	0	1	0	50	16	33	1	0
La Salle	37	1	0	3	33	61	14	35	12	1
Lincoln	59	5	4	2	48	268	58	204	6	0
Madison	28	1	2	0	25	45	18	21	6	0
Morehouse	43	0	3	3	37	255	40	207	8	1
Natchitoches	48	0	0	1	47	391	95	262	34	0
Red River	15	0	2	2	11	153	47	97	9	0
Richland[3]	42	2	1	0	39				7	0
Sabine	13	1	1	1	10	168	4	164	0	0
St. Landry	170	0	8	21	141	942	431	408	103	0
St. Mary	128	2	10	12	104	763	216	493	54	4
Tensas	13	0	2	0	11	30	6	23	1	0
Vernon	58	2	8	3	45	526	89	380	57	3
Washington	184	0	15	8	161	582	160	362	60	0
West Carroll	24	0	0	0	24	100	39	49	12	1
Winn	42	0	1	0	41	56	19	24	13	0
MAINE										
Metropolitan Counties										
Androscoggin	12	0	8	2	2	135	32	95	8	1
Cumberland	23	0	3	3	17	457	145	289	23	0
Penobscot	4	0	0	1	3	283	84	181	18	0
Sagadahoc	5	0	1	0	4	97	41	50	6	0
York	23	0	4	5	14	265	78	180	7	0
Nonmetropolitan Counties										
Aroostook	6	0	0	1	5	55	17	36	2	0
Franklin	8	0	5	1	2	49	9	34	6	0
Hancock	4	0	0	0	4	127	32	92	3	0
Kennebec	24	0	5	1	18	159	41	103	15	0
Knox	16	0	0	2	14	168	23	134	11	0
Lincoln	26	0	16	2	8	189	33	147	9	0
Oxford	28	0	15	2	11	279	73	186	20	0
Piscataquis	3	0	1	0	2	53	14	35	4	0
Somerset	31	3	14	1	13	366	95	247	24	1
Waldo	13	0	4	1	8	157	39	113	5	0
Washington	7	0	1	4	2	113	42	65	6	0

Table 10. Offenses Known to Law Enforcement, by Selected State Metropolitan and Nonmetropolitan Counties, 2017—Continued

(Number.)

State/county	Violent crime	Murder and nonnegligent manslaughter	Rape[1]	Robbery	Aggravated assault	Property crime	Burglary	Larceny-theft	Motor vehicle theft	Arson[2]
MARYLAND										
Metropolitan Counties										
Allegany	41	0	2	10	29	309	62	236	11	0
Anne Arundel	2	0	0	0	2	0	0	0	0	0
Anne Arundel County Police Department	2,021	13	156	566	1,286	10,813	1,593	8,598	622	0
Baltimore County	0	0	0	0	0	0	0	0	0	0
Baltimore County Police Department	5,037	35	323	1,533	3,146	23,155	3,114	18,023	2,018	206
Carroll	126	0	38	7	81	774	149	592	33	0
Cecil	59	2	5	17	35	485	155	297	33	3
Charles	497	8	38	109	342	2,352	365	1,836	151	35
Frederick	156	2	20	30	104	1,328	215	1,068	45	
Harford	350	8	39	83	220	1,974	358	1,553	63	0
Howard	0	0	0	0	0	0	0	0	0	0
Howard County Police Department	769	5	70	202	492	5,499	810	4,336	353	
Montgomery	0	0	0	0	0	0	0	0	0	0
Montgomery County Police Department[6]	1,394	13	230	613	538	13,551	1,376	11,387	788	14
Prince George's County Police Department	2,031	54	97	854	1,026	13,802	1,951	9,276	2,575	48
Queen Anne's	38	1	3	3	31	453	104	338	11	1
Washington	285	2	16	36	231	1,346	312	946	88	0
Wicomico	90	2	6	10	72	625	176	419	30	2
Worcester	18	0	2	1	15	208	39	155	14	0
Nonmetropolitan Counties										
Caroline	20	0	4	6	10	237	84	142	11	0
Dorchester	15	0	0	6	9	215	49	138	28	0
Garrett	41	0	2	1	38	297	94	194	9	0
Kent	7	1	1	3	2	86	30	55	1	0
Talbot	8	0	0	0	8	169	67	100	2	0
MICHIGAN										
Metropolitan Counties										
Barry	42	2	21	1	18	296	76	204	16	4
Bay	72	1	27	6	38	548	91	437	20	2
Berrien	137	1	31	12	93	569	140	391	38	2
Calhoun	115	1	35	6	73	491	109	359	23	4
Cass	52	3	31	4	14	295	126	145	24	5
Clinton	37	0	18	1	18	164	41	110	13	2
Eaton	118	1	45	22	50	1,032	179	803	50	9
Genesee	66	1	10	2	53	276	53	211	12	2
Ingham	144	2	44	8	90	563	146	375	42	3
Jackson	205	0	30	12	163	631	120	472	39	5
Kalamazoo	255	3	51	44	157	2,220	498	1,541	181	11
Kent	364	4	116	38	206	2,465	441	1,913	111	19
Lapeer	60	0	21	0	39	277	70	190	17	1
Livingston	72	0	25	2	45	508	78	396	34	7
Macomb	323	2	70	27	224	1,385	248	1,022	115	4
Midland	51	0	12	0	39	296	65	220	11	2
Monroe	177	2	59	19	97	1,478	363	1,004	111	14
Montcalm	40	0	22	0	18	127	35	84	8	0
Muskegon	64	0	23	6	35	514	74	412	28	0
Oakland	25	0	10	1	14	39	3	29	7	3
Ottawa	533	2	215	26	290	2,405	470	1,840	95	10
Saginaw	85	0	18	11	56	468	77	372	19	1
St. Clair	222	0	30	10	182	855	228	574	53	8
Washtenaw	558	6	82	70	400	1,643	273	1,173	197	13
Wayne	1	0	0	0	1	1	0	0	1	0
Nonmetropolitan Counties										
Alcona	13	0	6	1	6	108	27	77	4	2
Alger	0	0	0	0	0	2	2	0	0	0
Allegan	92	0	28	3	61	572	138	399	35	7
Alpena	7	0	5	0	2	61	12	49	0	0
Antrim	20	0	10	0	10	147	35	108	4	1
Arenac	25	0	12	1	12	81	26	43	12	0
Baraga	2	0	1	0	1	14	6	7	1	0
Benzie	20	0	5	0	15	86	36	48	2	1
Branch	9	0	5	0	4	68	18	43	7	0
Charlevoix	20	0	14	0	6	94	16	73	5	0
Cheboygan	23	0	17	0	6	66	20	45	1	0
Clare	79	2	23	4	50	383	125	235	23	3
Crawford	8	0	6	0	2	87	32	51	4	1
Delta	5	0	0	0	5	58	9	47	2	0
Dickinson	2	0	1	0	1	0	0	0	0	0
Emmet	20	0	7	0	13	131	16	109	6	1
Gladwin	57	1	9	1	46	144	49	87	8	0
Gogebic	8	0	2	0	6	54	17	37	0	0
Grand Traverse	143	2	40	4	97	596	102	465	29	7
Gratiot	36	0	16	0	20	323	43	267	13	1
Hillsdale	33	0	21	0	12	170	46	114	10	0
Houghton	6	0	4	0	2	63	26	34	3	1

Table 10. Offenses Known to Law Enforcement, by Selected State Metropolitan and Nonmetropolitan Counties, 2017—Continued

(Number.)

State/county	Violent crime	Murder and nonnegligent manslaughter	Rape[1]	Robbery	Aggravated assault	Property crime	Burglary	Larceny-theft	Motor vehicle theft	Arson[2]
Huron	18	0	4	0	14	79	32	47	0	1
Ionia	77	0	31	1	45	293	80	191	22	4
Iosco	2	0	0	0	2	4	2	2	0	0
Iron	5	0	0	0	5	19	1	18	0	2
Isabella	64	0	28	1	35	317	97	206	14	4
Kalkaska	55	1	5	0	49	159	25	126	8	0
Keweenaw	1	0	0	0	1	9	0	9	0	0
Lake	33	0	9	2	22	207	78	120	9	1
Lenawee	45	1	16	4	24	223	61	149	13	2
Luce	14	0	3	1	10	73	26	39	8	0
Mackinac	5	0	3	0	2	75	18	54	3	1
Manistee	27	0	15	0	12	190	18	165	7	0
Marquette	15	0	4	1	10	158	19	132	7	0
Mason	36	0	11	1	24	159	36	116	7	0
Mecosta	195	2	9	1	183	350	56	285	9	2
Menominee	19	1	5	0	13	87	53	34	0	0
Missaukee	30	0	10	0	20	136	28	99	9	0
Montmorency	2	0	1	0	1	43	13	18	12	2
Newaygo	81	1	40	2	38	255	74	171	10	2
Oceana	28	0	4	1	23	229	49	174	6	2
Ogemaw	15	2	1	0	12	119	37	75	7	0
Ontonagon	22	0	0	0	22	25	13	12	0	0
Osceola	26	0	8	0	18	131	30	93	8	0
Oscoda	11	0	1	0	10	107	39	65	3	0
Otsego	20	0	11	0	9	58	13	43	2	1
Presque Isle	17	0	4	1	12	23	9	14	0	2
Roscommon	26	0	12	0	14	123	30	86	7	1
Sanilac	48	0	6	3	39	115	36	71	8	3
Shiawassee	16	1	3	0	12	138	31	100	7	0
St. Joseph	57	1	11	0	45	183	26	141	16	1
Tuscola	47	0	16	1	30	215	70	131	14	2
Wexford	43	0	16	0	27	215	60	145	10	1
MINNESOTA										
Metropolitan Counties										
Anoka	48	3	9	6	30	1,021	118	833	70	4
Benton	14	0	11	0	3	178	33	118	27	2
Blue Earth	17	0	12	0	5	99	34	54	11	1
Carlton	17	0	6	1	10	204	41	141	22	0
Carver	34	0	8	3	23	583	91	462	30	6
Chisago	6	1	1	0	4	102	14	79	9	0
Clay	7	0	1	0	6	98	35	50	13	0
Dakota	27	0	3	1	23	136	37	93	6	0
Dodge	6	0	0	0	6	89	3	82	4	0
Fillmore	16	0	2	1	13	67	20	45	2	0
Hennepin	14	0	0	0	14	63	3	58	2	2
Houston	8	0	1	1	6	40	13	26	1	0
Isanti	17	0	9	0	8	294	70	182	42	0
Le Sueur	5	0	4	0	1	98	30	60	8	0
Mille Lacs	35	0	1	2	32	632	153	433	46	0
Nicollet	7	0	2	0	5	51	12	35	4	0
Olmsted	50	0	19	3	28	307	86	193	28	0
Ramsey	79	0	24	11	44	1,258	180	974	104	3
Scott	6	0	1	0	5	7	1	3	3	0
Sherburne	27	0	6	3	18	452	62	362	28	0
Stearns	31	0	10	0	21	374	83	262	29	1
St. Louis	44	0	14	1	29	689	231	382	76	5
Wabasha	9	0	0	0	9	48	4	35	9	0
Washington	48	2	8	3	35	821	166	583	72	4
Wright	126	0	47	7	72	1,483	163	1,267	53	0
Nonmetropolitan Counties										
Aitkin	13	0	4	0	9	268	117	138	13	1
Becker[6]	26	0	9	0	17	212	81	111	20	3
Beltrami	46	0	10	7	29	371	105	228	38	1
Big Stone	2	0	1	0	1	32	5	24	3	0
Brown	0	0	0	0	0	18	1	15	2	0
Cass	44	0	28	1	15	333	133	154	46	1
Chippewa	2	0	1	0	1	24	10	14	0	0
Clearwater[6]	15	0	1	0	14	93	21	57	15	1
Cook	11	0	3	0	8	84	10	67	7	1
Cottonwood	4	0	1	0	3	40	8	32	0	0
Crow Wing	33	0	13	2	18	330	151	158	21	0
Douglas	21	0	3	0	18	181	54	111	16	0
Faribault	8	0	5	0	3	83	34	38	11	1
Freeborn[6]	12	0	1	1	10	118	37	68	13	2
Goodhue[6]	9	0	3	1	5	190	36	123	31	0
Grant	1	0	0	0	1	19	4	13	2	0
Hubbard	13	0	3	0	10	226	84	126	16	0
Itasca	29	0	10	0	19	162	37	117	8	2
Jackson	7	0	4	0	3	51	19	30	2	0

Table 10. Offenses Known to Law Enforcement, by Selected State Metropolitan and Nonmetropolitan Counties, 2017—Continued

(Number.)

State/county	Violent crime	Murder and nonnegligent manslaughter	Rape[1]	Robbery	Aggravated assault	Property crime	Burglary	Larceny-theft	Motor vehicle theft	Arson[2]
Kanabec	23	0	0	2	21	165	43	93	29	0
Kandiyohi	32	0	6	2	24	217	56	143	18	2
Kittson	0	0	0	0	0	5	0	5	0	0
Koochiching	4	0	0	0	4	73	16	50	7	0
Lac qui Parle	2	0	0	0	2	20	12	5	3	0
Lake	5	0	2	0	3	17	4	9	4	1
Lake of the Woods	1	0	0	0	1	5	0	4	1	1
Lincoln[6]	12	0	0	0	12	4	0	4	0	1
Lyon	5	0	1	0	4	46	18	24	4	1
Mahnomen[6]	11	2	1	0	8	159	37	95	27	1
Marshall	4	0	0	0	4	14	5	9	0	0
Martin	3	0	0	0	3	17	4	11	2	1
McLeod	11	0	6	1	4	83	30	50	3	0
Meeker	18	0	10	1	7	126	45	67	14	0
Morrison	6	0	2	0	4	193	28	138	27	0
Mower	9	0	6	1	2	83	31	41	11	2
Murray	1	0	1	0	0	41	4	34	3	1
Nobles[6]	3	0	3	0	0	34	14	17	3	1
Norman	0	0	0	0	0	3	1	2	0	0
Otter Tail[6]	21	0	7	1	13	333	110	195	28	2
Pennington	4	0	0	0	4	79	24	48	7	0
Pine	65	1	17	4	43	1,086	198	795	93	4
Pipestone	1	0	0	0	1	70	16	54	0	0
Pope	3	0	0	0	3	34	15	15	4	0
Red Lake	0	0	0	0	0	16	5	11	0	0
Redwood	8	0	3	0	5	61	16	37	8	0
Renville	6	0	1	0	5	84	24	48	12	0
Rice	14	0	5	1	8	120	32	81	7	0
Rock	4	0	2	0	2	83	17	65	1	0
Roseau	7	0	1	0	6	69	11	46	12	0
Steele	10	0	3	0	7	65	27	32	6	0
Stevens	3	0	1	0	2	29	17	11	1	0
Swift	1	0	1	0	0	0	0	0	0	0
Todd	9	0	6	0	3	180	56	113	11	4
Traverse	2	0	0	1	1	24	6	16	2	0
Wadena	3	0	0	0	3	3	1	2	0	0
Waseca	6	0	2	0	4	59	23	34	2	0
Watonwan	2	0	1	0	1	45	21	22	2	0
Wilkin	4	0	1	1	2	40	11	26	3	0
Winona	11	0	4	0	7	72	16	43	13	0
Yellow Medicine	5	0	1	0	4	42	15	26	1	0
MISSISSIPPI										
Metropolitan Counties										
DeSoto	28	5	6	4	13	402	201	172	29	0
Hancock	32	2	0	5	25	581	115	408	58	1
Harrison	41	2	5	10	24	901	237	547	117	6
Hinds	83	2	5	11	65	389	155	175	59	0
Jackson	138	2	32	18	86	1,642	427	1,042	173	10
Lamar	70	0	7	0	63	712	238	464	10	0
Madison[7]		4			3	254	83	142	29	1
Marshall	0	0	0	0	0	140	2	121	17	2
Rankin	48	2	5	7	34	457	97	341	19	5
Tunica[7]		4			14	25	420	61	320	39	1
Nonmetropolitan Counties										
Choctaw[7]		0			0	8	58	29	27	2	0
Claiborne	21	0	2		2	17	101	63	24	14	0
Grenada[7]		1			0	25	133	36	84	13	1
Kemper[7]		0			1	6	38	25	11	2	0
Lauderdale	45	5	8	8	24	495	277	191	27	15
Lincoln	14	1	0	2	11	248	92	131	25	1
Oktibbeha[7]		0			7	33	585	415	145	25	1
Panola[7]		3			8	98	825	424	380	21	2
Scott	25	3	0	2	20	205	85	89	31	7
Stone	37	0	7	2	28	211	82	97	32	2
Warren	12	2	2	3	5	275	76	171	28	1
Washington	23	3	1	2	17	389	108	236	45	0
MISSOURI										
Metropolitan Counties										
Andrew	13	0	0	0	13	82	34	39	9	1
Bates	36	0	2	1	33	112	47	61	4	0
Bollinger	17	0	5	1	11	82	31	51	0	2
Boone	101	0	11	9	81	698	114	507	77	8
Buchanan	26	0	1	5	20	256	64	159	33	9
Caldwell	24	0	3	0	21	76	22	43	11	1
Callaway	129	0	32	5	92	431	138	257	36	1
Cape Girardeau	38	0	3	3	32	213	64	136	13	0
Cass	54	0	3	3	48	345	107	193	45	0
Christian	53	0	8	0	45	293	77	199	17	0

Table 10. Offenses Known to Law Enforcement, by Selected State Metropolitan and Nonmetropolitan Counties, 2017—Continued

(Number.)

State/county	Violent crime	Murder and nonnegligent manslaughter	Rape[1]	Robbery	Aggravated assault	Property crime	Burglary	Larceny-theft	Motor vehicle theft	Arson[2]
Clay	42	0	5	4	33	236	68	142	26	0
Clinton	18	1	4	2	11	95	38	44	13	0
Cole	70	1	0	0	69	233	44	165	24	2
Dallas	6	1	0	0	5	58	11	45	2	0
DeKalb	7	0	0	1	6	34	10	19	5	0
Franklin	79	1	5	0	73	591	220	320	51	2
Greene	47	3	22	11	11	1,303	360	775	168	8
Jackson[6]	61	1	9	1	50	367	109	194	64	10
Jasper	139	1	11	8	119	543	143	331	69	0
Jefferson	380	6	15	15	344	2,380	484	1,538	358	8
Lafayette	10	0	1	0	9	181	41	123	17	2
Lincoln	89	0	13	3	73	153	39	113	1	3
McDonald	80	1	9	0	70	298	56	239	3	0
Moniteau	2	1	0	0	1	31	14	13	4	0
Newton	111	1	14	2	94	668	129	470	69	5
Osage	2	0	0	0	2	75	25	40	10	0
Platte	44	0	14	4	26	277	51	189	37	0
Polk	43	0	8	2	33	282	106	143	33	2
Ray	76	0	0	0	76	116	34	67	15	1
St. Charles	0	0	0	0	0	1	0	1	0	0
St. Charles County Police Department	95	3	11	15	66	844	174	588	82	3
St. Louis County Police Department	1,917	32	158	401	1,326	7,973	1,502	5,671	800	55
Warren	77	1	12	2	62	182	53	114	15	1
Webster	9	1	3	1	4	232	65	136	31	0
Nonmetropolitan Counties										
Adair	10	0	0	0	10	87	22	61	4	1
Atchison	5	0	0	0	5	10	0	8	2	0
Audrain	17	2	0	1	14	112	57	47	8	0
Barry	38	1	2	3	32	398	146	194	58	1
Barton	26	0	0	1	25	82	34	41	7	3
Benton	44	1	1	0	42	149	63	70	16	2
Butler	98	1	1	2	94	499	134	327	38	0
Camden	124	0	24	3	97	448	197	231	20	0
Carroll	5	0	4	0	1	42	17	22	3	0
Carter	27	0	6	0	21	73	32	33	8	0
Cedar	29	0	5	0	24	71	22	48	1	1
Clark	24	0	0	0	24	34	7	25	2	0
Cooper	5	0	0	3	2	74	18	44	12	0
Crawford	23	3	2	0	18	176	45	105	26	0
Dade	29	0	3	1	25	74	37	34	3	0
Daviess	6	0	0	1	5	44	22	17	5	0
Dent	4	0	1	0	3	77	35	34	8	0
Douglas	20	2	2	0	16	36	17	14	5	0
Dunklin	12	0	0	0	12	135	30	86	19	2
Gasconade	20	0	0	0	20	99	38	49	12	0
Gentry	1	0	0	0	1	48	11	25	12	0
Grundy	0	0	0	0	0	23	13	10	0	0
Harrison	5	0	0	0	5	33	19	9	5	0
Henry	74	0	7	1	66	196	88	106	2	2
Hickory	3	0	0	0	3	126	46	71	9	0
Holt	6	0	0	0	6	35	15	15	5	0
Howard	10	0	1	0	9	77	18	55	4	0
Howell	68	1	4	1	62	323	99	177	47	0
Iron	4	1	0	0	3	32	12	15	5	0
Johnson	18	1	6	2	9	245	79	138	28	0
Knox	1	0	0	0	1	13	2	9	2	0
Laclede	27	0	2	3	22	275	94	147	34	3
Lawrence	15	1	0	3	11	200	91	92	17	2
Lewis	1	1	0	0	0	51	11	36	4	0
Linn	5	0	0	0	5	41	16	21	4	0
Livingston	1	0	0	0	1	36	8	22	6	0
Macon	12	0	2	0	10	92	38	53	1	0
Madison	11	0	1	1	9	61	18	38	5	1
Maries	12	2	0	0	10	53	22	21	10	1
Marion	8	0	0	0	8	157	13	140	4	0
Mercer	3	0	0	0	3	12	4	5	3	1
Miller	28	0	0	0	28	198	82	108	8	0
Mississippi	7	1	2	0	4	39	20	15	4	0
Monroe	28	0	16	0	12	45	24	15	6	0
Montgomery	1	0	0	0	1	65	28	37	0	0
Morgan	45	0	11	1	33	131	60	64	7	1
Nodaway	3	0	0	0	3	64	18	38	8	1
Oregon	33	1	4	0	28	84	27	43	14	0
Ozark	18	1	2	0	15	81	39	30	12	3
Pemiscot	25	0	1	1	23	99	30	58	11	1
Perry	14	0	0	0	14	70	29	38	3	0
Pettis	27	1	2	3	21	250	69	155	26	1
Phelps	33	0	1	1	31	215	44	151	20	0
Pike	9	1	0	1	7	58	27	22	9	0
Pulaski	87	0	7	2	78	281	83	164	34	0

Table 10. Offenses Known to Law Enforcement, by Selected State Metropolitan and Nonmetropolitan Counties, 2017—Continued

(Number.)

State/county	Violent crime	Murder and nonnegligent manslaughter	Rape[1]	Robbery	Aggravated assault	Property crime	Burglary	Larceny-theft	Motor vehicle theft	Arson[2]
Ralls	9	0	0	0	9	77	16	56	5	2
Randolph	14	0	1	0	13	68	17	40	11	0
Reynolds	7	2	0	0	5	47	17	26	4	2
Ripley	32	4	0	0	28	116	42	64	10	2
Saline	8	0	1	0	7	56	21	33	2	1
Schuyler	3	0	0	0	3	32	6	24	2	1
Scotland	3	0	2	0	1	25	1	24	0	1
Shannon	13	0	1	1	11	32	7	20	5	0
Shelby	0	0	0	0	0	18	0	17	1	0
St. Clair	11	0	1	1	9	132	47	67	18	3
Ste. Genevieve	19	0	5	1	13	86	10	66	10	0
St. Francois	45	0	1	1	43	376	85	194	97	3
Stoddard	17	0	0	0	17	124	39	76	9	0
Stone	78	1	3	2	72	239	98	132	9	1
Sullivan	7	0	1	0	6	48	21	19	8	1
Taney	101	3	3	2	93	328	80	202	46	1
Texas	28	2	1	0	25	166	54	93	19	2
Vernon	95	0	3	5	87	291	94	149	48	0
Washington	72	0	13	1	58	280	80	169	31	1
Wayne	28	1	1	0	26	252	81	144	27	0
Worth	0	0	0	0	0	7	0	7	0	0
Wright	16	0	1	0	15	91	43	41	7	6
MONTANA										
Metropolitan Counties										
Carbon	11	0	1	0	10	69	20	45	4	1
Cascade	29	2	3	0	24	143	31	97	15	2
Golden Valley	4	0	1	0	3	9	2	7	0	0
Missoula	115	2	18	4	91	345	97	212	36	1
Yellowstone	92	2	15	4	71	768	130	534	104	3
Nonmetropolitan Counties										
Beaverhead	6	0	2	0	4	9	2	5	2	0
Big Horn	52	0	2	0	50	241	15	191	35	2
Blaine	6	0	1	0	5	10	0	5	5	0
Broadwater	22	1	1	0	20	40	6	29	5	0
Carter	1	1	0	0	0	0	0	0	0	0
Chouteau	0	0	0	0	0	6	4	2	0	0
Custer	5	0	2	0	3	60	22	34	4	0
Daniels	1	0	1	0	0	0	0	0	0	0
Dawson	8	1	0	0	7	60	17	38	5	0
Deer Lodge	50	1	7	0	42	216	57	136	23	5
Fallon	2	0	0	0	2	3	1	1	1	0
Fergus	9	0	7	0	2	39	19	16	4	2
Flathead	189	2	22	3	162	1,048	168	775	105	3
Gallatin	103	1	27	2	73	467	53	367	47	5
Garfield	1	0	0	0	1	2	0	2	0	0
Glacier	12	1	0	0	11	37	11	16	10	0
Granite	3	0	0	0	3	25	3	21	1	0
Hill	37	0	7	2	28	159	32	115	12	0
Jefferson	26	1	1	0	24	102	36	62	4	0
Judith Basin	2	0	0	0	2	3	0	2	1	0
Lake	109	1	18	5	85	299	93	161	45	9
Lewis and Clark	99	1	28	3	67	416	124	252	40	5
Liberty	2	0	0	0	2	0	0	0	0	0
Lincoln	20	1	1	0	18	119	15	94	10	3
Madison	4	0	1	0	3	69	19	39	11	0
McCone	2	0	0	0	2	6	0	4	2	1
Meagher	3	0	0	0	3	17	3	10	4	1
Mineral	3	0	0	0	3	0	0	0	0	0
Musselshell	20	1	0	0	19	111	12	85	14	2
Park	21	0	2	0	19	55	6	42	7	1
Phillips	12	0	1	0	11	48	10	36	2	0
Pondera	1	0	0	0	1	7	2	5	0	0
Powder River	1	0	0	0	1	6	1	3	2	0
Powell	6	0	5	0	1	13	4	8	1	0
Prairie	4	0	1	0	3	4	2	1	1	0
Ravalli	53	1	4	0	48	244	31	202	11	0
Richland	8	0	3	0	5	54	6	44	4	0
Roosevelt	108	1	0	0	107	62	36	10	16	2
Rosebud	10	0	2	1	7	26	8	13	5	2
Sanders	29	1	3	0	25	51	5	39	7	1
Sheridan	2	0	0	0	2	25	2	20	3	1
Silver Bow	169	0	10	6	153	1,864	246	1,437	181	5
Stillwater	16	0	1	0	15	51	14	32	5	0
Sweet Grass	8	0	0	1	7	36	6	25	5	1
Teton	13	0	5	0	8	39	7	28	4	0
Toole	22	0	3	0	19	92	6	80	6	1
Valley	9	0	2	0	7	18	6	11	1	1
Wheatland	2	0	0	0	2	6	3	3	0	0
Wibaux	0	0	0	0	0	4	0	3	1	0

Table 10. Offenses Known to Law Enforcement, by Selected State Metropolitan and Nonmetropolitan Counties, 2017—Continued

(Number.)

State/county	Violent crime	Murder and nonnegligent manslaughter	Rape[1]	Robbery	Aggravated assault	Property crime	Burglary	Larceny-theft	Motor vehicle theft	Arson[2]
NEBRASKA										
Metropolitan Counties										
Dakota	19	0	1	2	16	74	15	43	16	
Hall	23	0	5	0	18	137	64	61	12	2
Hamilton	2	0	0	0	2	43	15	21	7	0
Merrick	2	0	0	0	2	13	2	8	3	0
Nonmetropolitan Counties										
Antelope	7	0	1	0	6	34	4	25	5	
Boone	4	0	0	0	4	2	0	1	1	0
Box Butte	1	0	0	0	1	15	2	7	6	
Burt	7	0	2	1	4	24	9	14	1	
Cedar	1	0	0	0	1	18	0	17	1	
Chase	1	0	0	0	1	5	3	2	0	
Cherry	2	0	0	0	2	16	7	7	2	
Clay	2	0	0	0	2	16	8	6	2	1
Dawes	0	0	0	0	0	11	1	9	1	
Dawson	14	0	2	0	12	39	18	17	4	0
Deuel	0	0	0	0	0	1	0	1	0	0
Dodge	9	0	1	1	7	89	12	64	13	
Franklin	0	0	0	0	0	21	5	13	3	
Harlan	0	0	0	0	0	1	0	0	1	1
Hitchcock	3	0	0	0	3	20	6	10	4	
Johnson	4	0	0	0	4	12	3	8	1	1
Kearney	5	0	1	0	4	50	15	32	3	1
Kimball	0	0	0	0	0	8	2	1	5	
Knox	6	0	2	0	4	31	8	19	4	
Madison	12	0	4	0	8	67	24	35	8	0
Morrill	1	0	0	0	1	44	5	37	2	
Pawnee	3	0	0	0	3	32	10	20	2	
Perkins	2	0	1	0	1	13	1	12	0	0
Pierce	7	0	3	2	2	22	9	12	1	
Stanton	2	0	2	0	0	28	3	23	2	
Thurston	0	0	0	0	0	11	5	3	3	1
Webster	0	0	0	0	0	39	18	16	5	
Wheeler	0	0	0	0	0	2	0	2	0	
NEVADA										
Metropolitan Counties										
Carson City	191	1	0	18	172	879	166	632	81	7
Storey	34	0	0	0	34	93	27	55	11	0
Washoe	175	0	26	12	137	750	173	461	116	5
Nonmetropolitan Counties										
Churchill	26	0	6	0	20	191	55	117	19	2
Douglas	65	1	13	4	47	769	113	604	52	4
Elko	38	0	6	1	31	174	46	102	26	3
Esmeralda	0	0	0	0	0	5	2	2	1	0
Eureka	6	0	1	0	5	24	6	14	4	1
Humboldt	15	0	1	0	14	69	37	22	10	2
Lander	49	0	5	0	44	99	54	33	12	3
Lincoln	5	0	0	0	5	56	7	43	6	0
Lyon	129	4	21	3	101	570	152	370	48	11
Mineral	0	0	0	0	0	32	13	12	7	0
Nye	61	3	9	8	41	788	299	367	122	18
Pershing	25	0	5	0	20	52	19	29	4	0
White Pine	18	0	6	2	10	83	39	31	13	1
NEW HAMPSHIRE										
Metropolitan Counties										
Rockingham	5	0	0	0	5	1	0	1	0	0
Strafford	3	0	0	0	3	0	0	0	0	0
Nonmetropolitan Counties										
Carroll	9	0	2	1	6	52	10	40	2	0
Cheshire	0	0	0	0	0	5	3	2	0	0
Grafton	1	0	1	0	0	2	0	2	0	0
Merrimack	1	0	1	0	0	1	0	1	0	0
NEW JERSEY										
Metropolitan Counties										
Atlantic	1	0	0	0	1	0	0	0	0	0
Bergen	7	0	4	0	3	51	1	48	2	0
Burlington	0	0	0	0	0	0	0	0	0	0
Camden	2	0	0	1	1	21	0	19	2	0
Cape May	0	0	0	0	0	0	0	0	0	0
Cumberland	0	0	0	0	0	1	0	1	0	0
Essex	65	0	0	22	43	58	22	36	0	0
Gloucester	1	0	0	0	1	3	0	3	0	0
Hudson	0	0	0	0	0	0	0	0	0	0

Table 10. Offenses Known to Law Enforcement, by Selected State Metropolitan and Nonmetropolitan Counties, 2017—Continued

(Number.)

State/county	Violent crime	Murder and nonnegligent manslaughter	Rape[1]	Robbery	Aggravated assault	Property crime	Burglary	Larceny-theft	Motor vehicle theft	Arson[2]
Hunterdon	0	0	0	0	0	0	0	0	0	0
Mercer	6	0	0	0	6	19	9	10	0	0
Middlesex	0	0	0	0	0	0	0	0	0	0
Monmouth	4	0	1	0	3	1	0	1	0	0
Morris	0	0	0	0	0	0	0	0	0	0
Ocean	0	0	0	0	0	4	0	4	0	0
Passaic	0	0	0	0	0	0	0	0	0	0
Salem	1	0	0	0	1	0	0	0	0	0
Somerset	1	0	0	0	1	1	0	1	0	0
Sussex	0	0	0	0	0	0	0	0	0	0
Union	0	0	0	0	0	0	0	0	0	0
Warren	0	0	0	0	0	0	0	0	0	0
NEW MEXICO										
Metropolitan Counties										
Bernalillo	916	6	72	152	686	2,640	735	1,416	489	
Sandoval	122	2	2	0	118	133	43	82	8	
San Juan	609	2	59	8	540	810	223	515	72	
Santa Fe	74	0	3	5	66	494	272	222	0	
Torrance	69	1	4	1	63	163	73	60	30	
Valencia	381	1	19	8	353	975	292	469	214	
Nonmetropolitan Counties										
Catron	3	0	0	0	3	31	13	8	10	
Chaves	47	1	13	3	30	167	79	70	18	
Cibola	27	1	5	1	20	84	39	32	13	
Colfax	17	0	0	0	17	28	18	8	2	
Curry	11	0	2	1	8	109	60	36	13	
De Baca	6	0	0	1	5	43	23	11	9	
Eddy	67	0	3	1	63	246	68	147	31	
Grant	18	0	5	1	12	195	107	88	0	
Guadalupe	1	0	0	0	1	5	5	0	0	
Hidalgo	8	0	0	0	8	31	13	13	5	
Lea	31	0	3	1	27	291	107	155	29	
Lincoln	26	1	1	0	24	81	43	33	5	
Luna	59	0	1	1	57	237	76	108	53	
McKinley	123	1	7	6	109	231	60	133	38	
Mora	5	0	0	0	5	31	10	15	6	
Otero	165	0	14	3	148	318	139	152	27	
Quay	5	0	0	0	5	24	10	9	5	
Rio Arriba	77	3	6	10	58	325	158	134	33	
San Miguel	0	0	0	0	0	0	0	0	0	
Sierra	13	0	2	0	11	76	24	46	6	
Socorro	24	0	2	0	22	81	26	46	9	
Taos	66	0	1	5	60	101	41	24	36	
Union	8	0	0	0	8	19	11	7	1	
NEW YORK										
Metropolitan Counties										
Albany	18	0	8	0	10	140	15	117	8	2
Broome	58	0	16	6	36	495	80	397	18	0
Chemung	9	2	0	1	6	258	32	221	5	0
Erie	49	2	0	12	35	646	92	542	12	4
Herkimer	6	0	0	0	6	0	0	0	0	0
Jefferson	20	0	3	1	16	302	37	257	8	0
Livingston	18	0	9	1	8	307	36	254	17	3
Madison	21	0	5	1	15	144	28	106	10	3
Monroe	229	1	40	49	139	2,786	327	2,372	87	7
Nassau	1,113	10	28	416	659	10,103	888	8,768	447	65
Niagara	59	0	11	7	41	698	128	527	43	3
Oneida	133	0	99	4	30	269	40	216	13	1
Onondaga	210	3	56	39	112	1,720	272	1,349	99	2
Ontario	37	0	13	7	17	755	115	623	17	
Orleans	18	0	5	0	13	246	34	203	9	0
Oswego	51	0	21	3	27	296	66	212	18	1
Putnam	19	0	4	3	12	264	51	211	2	0
Rensselaer	13	0	1	1	11	206	22	178	6	1
Saratoga	95	1	16	9	69	1,111	182	897	32	7
Schenectady	0	0	0	0	0	16	4	11	1	0
Schoharie	6	0	4	0	2	24	5	18	1	0
Suffolk	41	0	0	0	41	0	0	0	0	0
Suffolk County Police Department	1,427	22	64	473	868	16,996	1,423	14,565	1,008	87
Tioga	18	0	10	0	8	151	34	100	17	0
Ulster	34	1	4	3	26	186	34	139	13	0
Warren	48	1	23	6	18	528	68	447	13	4
Washington	23	1	14	0	8	157	17	133	7	0
Wayne	63	2	20	8	33	453	103	333	17	0
Westchester Public Safety	56	0	1	6	49	237	14	212	11	3
Yates	17	0	7	0	10	157	27	127	3	0
Nonmetropolitan Counties										
Allegany	0	0	0	0	0	0	0	0	0	0

Table 10. Offenses Known to Law Enforcement, by Selected State Metropolitan and Nonmetropolitan Counties, 2017—Continued

(Number.)

State/county	Violent crime	Murder and nonnegligent manslaughter	Rape[1]	Robbery	Aggravated assault	Property crime	Burglary	Larceny-theft	Motor vehicle theft	Arson[2]
Cattaraugus	39	1	15	4	19	278	78	183	17	2
Cayuga	40	0	15	1	24	163	39	121	3	0
Chautauqua	49	1	14	3	31	453	135	302	16	5
Clinton	6	0	0	0	6	27	5	22	0	0
Columbia	30	0	5	1	24	330	70	252	8	1
Cortland	18	0	13	2	3	407	73	332	2	1
Delaware	23	0	11	1	11	150	42	101	7	0
Franklin	0	0	0	0	0	0	0	0	0	0
Fulton	22	0	8	1	13	310	42	260	8	2
Genesee	57	0	16	4	37	345	51	280	14	3
Greene	6	0	0	0	6	19	1	15	3	0
Hamilton	1	0	0	0	1	7	1	3	3	0
Lewis	6	0	1	0	5	99	33	64	2	0
Montgomery	16	0	6	1	9	329	28	292	9	1
Otsego	17	3	4	0	10	64	17	41	6	0
Schuyler	5	0	2	0	3	15	2	11	2	0
Steuben	21	0	7	0	14	91	24	64	3	0
St. Lawrence	10	0	0	1	9	36	4	30	2	0
Sullivan	23	0	4	0	19	293	45	242	6	2
Wyoming	21	0	8	3	10	143	39	94	10	1
NORTH CAROLINA[7]										
Metropolitan Counties										
Alexander		1		2	56	556	193	328	35	6
Buncombe		3		24	106	1,570	561	863	146	15
Cabarrus		0		14	20	657	213	404	40	2
Caldwell		0		16	54	1,306	448	729	129	6
Catawba		8		16	108	1,227	443	691	93	14
Chatham		1		9	65	602	242	336	24	2
Currituck		0		3	36	347	97	237	13	2
Davidson		3		29	85	1,608	949	507	152	10
Davie		0		4	47	542	175	334	33	0
Durham		1		35	26	672	285	339	48	1
Edgecombe		3		9	28	479	212	249	18	5
Forsyth		0		42	217	2,105	459	1,494	152	12
Franklin		5		9	65	790	309	421	60	6
Gaston County Police Department		2		14	161	1,070	374	586	110	20
Guilford		2		24	135	1,166	381	722	63	9
Haywood		2		6	119	951	434	452	65	3
Hoke		6		14	55	1,045	445	558	42	1
Iredell		3		18	181	1,439	589	746	104	6
Johnston		2		18	105	1,670	667	885	118	4
Lincoln		1		4	84	1,010	315	644	51	5
Madison		0		1	7	138	53	72	13	4
New Hanover		5		41	81	1,709	419	1,239	51	6
Orange		1		15	52	591	267	299	25	3
Pender		2		10	62	1,017	256	721	40	5
Person		1		6	51	346	163	165	18	2
Pitt		1		25	138	1,065	347	655	63	5
Rockingham		4		7	26	721	296	380	45	0
Rowan		1		20	66	990	306	604	80	7
Stokes		2		2	71	763	216	488	59	2
Union		1		26	131	2,168	536	1,533	99	11
Wake		0		25	135	1,649	607	910	132	12
Wayne		1		33	148	1,610	636	829	145	3
Yadkin		1		3	48	584	192	370	22	4
Nonmetropolitan Counties										
Alleghany		0		0	9	88	25	53	10	3
Anson		1		4	29	260	187	69	4	2
Beaufort		1		7	57	464	191	252	21	4
Camden		0		0	0	59	24	35	0	0
Chowan		3		1	5	114	51	56	7	0
Clay		0		1	18	308	140	142	26	1
Cleveland		0		8	8	732	276	402	54	0
Columbus		3		15	91	1,014	547	398	69	5
Dare		1		1	18	384	101	279	4	2
Graham		0		1	15	176	39	121	16	1
Granville		0		10	46	616	275	306	35	6
Halifax		7		18	70	553	274	275	4	4
Harnett		8		39	205	1,702	616	996	90	19
Hertford		1		2	23	211	104	91	16	1
Jackson		0		0	63	772	477	249	46	4
Lee		2		13	33	391	107	263	21	3
Macon		0		2	35	491	155	298	38	3
Martin		1		1	33	239	101	121	17	2
McDowell		2		4	25	802	278	425	99	13
Montgomery		1		3	22	236	105	126	5	3
Moore		2		10	49	567	236	325	6	2
Northampton		4		7	27	344	175	144	25	1
Pasquotank		0		7	55	289	104	174	11	2

Table 10. Offenses Known to Law Enforcement, by Selected State Metropolitan and Nonmetropolitan Counties, 2017—Continued

(Number.)

State/county	Violent crime	Murder and nonnegligent manslaughter	Rape[1]	Robbery	Aggravated assault	Property crime	Burglary	Larceny-theft	Motor vehicle theft	Arson[2]
Perquimans		1		1	2	82	43	35	4	1
Polk		0		0	6	187	70	102	15	2
Richmond		4		33	125	1,079	471	537	71	6
Rutherford		0		7	139	848	461	318	69	7
Scotland		2		11	36	404	219	160	25	12
Stanly		0		6	23	476	214	245	17	1
Surry		2		8	46	1,120	436	572	112	7
Swain		0		1	23	197	89	80	28	0
Transylvania		0		6	28	317	101	197	19	3
Tyrrell		0		2	9	30	8	21	1	0
Watauga		0		1	19	299	32	253	14	1
Wilkes		1		11	114	738	298	363	77	14
Wilson		3		4	46	535	184	316	35	8
Yancey		1		1	4	79	47	28	4	2
NORTH DAKOTA										
Metropolitan Counties										
Burleigh	29	0	13	0	16	200	53	131	16	1
Cass	14	0	7	0	7	141	43	84	14	1
Grand Forks	9	0	0	2	7	108	34	67	7	2
Morton	12	0	8	0	4	108	22	72	14	3
Oliver	1	0	0	0	1	10	4	5	1	0
Sioux	0	0	0	0	0	1	1	0	0	0
Nonmetropolitan Counties										
Adams	1	0	0	0	1	11	2	9	0	0
Barnes	1	0	0	1	0	37	12	20	5	2
Benson	3	0	1	0	2	22	6	12	4	1
Billings	0	0	0	0	0	4	0	3	1	0
Bottineau	3	0	2	0	1	62	11	35	16	1
Burke	3	0	1	0	2	5	0	2	3	0
Cavalier	1	0	0	0	1	12	6	6	0	0
Dickey	1	0	0	0	1	7	1	5	1	0
Divide	1	0	0	0	1	0	0	0	0	0
Dunn	9	0	0	0	9	18	3	10	5	1
Eddy	0	0	0	0	0	25	9	13	3	0
Emmons	4	0	0	0	4	27	1	25	1	0
Foster	0	0	0	0	0	15	4	11	0	1
Golden Valley	2	0	1	0	1	0	0	0	0	1
Grant	2	0	0	0	2	8	3	5	0	0
Griggs	1	0	1	0	0	5	1	1	3	0
Hettinger	4	0	0	0	4	19	3	13	3	0
Kidder	0	0	0	0	0	11	3	6	2	0
Lamoure	2	0	0	0	2	6	2	2	2	0
Logan	2	0	0	1	1	10	4	6	0	0
McHenry	1	0	0	0	1	85	23	51	11	0
McIntosh	0	0	0	0	0	3	3	0	0	0
McKenzie	19	1	2	0	16	139	20	93	26	1
McLean	6	0	2	0	4	101	18	74	9	1
Mercer	5	0	0	1	4	35	4	29	2	0
Mountrail	5	0	0	0	5	53	7	38	8	0
Nelson	1	0	1	0	0	19	5	13	1	0
Pembina	5	0	1	0	4	53	14	27	12	1
Pierce	0	0	0	0	0	27	11	10	6	0
Ramsey	4	0	1	0	3	39	6	24	9	0
Ransom	1	0	1	0	0	32	13	10	9	0
Renville	1	0	1	0	0	8	2	6	0	1
Richland	4	0	0	0	4	115	31	76	8	0
Rolette	8	1	1	1	5	68	22	39	7	1
Sargent	1	0	0	0	1	12	4	6	2	0
Sheridan	1	0	0	0	1	10	2	8	0	0
Slope	0	0	0	0	0	1	0	1	0	0
Stark	4	0	1	0	3	38	10	27	1	0
Steele	0	0	0	0	0	4	2	0	2	0
Stutsman	4	0	1	0	3	38	12	20	6	0
Towner	1	0	0	0	1	11	2	6	3	0
Traill	5	0	4	0	1	57	18	31	8	0
Walsh	13	0	5	0	8	81	21	51	9	2
Ward	37	0	11	1	25	165	58	62	45	1
Wells	0	0	0	0	0	10	4	2	4	0
Williams	15	0	4	0	11	189	41	124	24	1
OHIO										
Metropolitan Counties										
Allen	30	0	12	12	6	659	162	481	16	3
Belmont	34	2	10	2	20	314	52	232	30	4
Butler	37	1	11	12	13	989	220	761	8	1
Clark	21	0	7	3	11	798	221	548	29	5
Clermont	141	0	39	10	92	1,166	358	744	64	5
Delaware	60	0	23	9	28	1,139	211	908	20	6
Fairfield	38	0	15	6	17	962	153	793	16	2

Table 10. Offenses Known to Law Enforcement, by Selected State Metropolitan and Nonmetropolitan Counties, 2017—Continued

(Number.)

State/county	Violent crime	Murder and nonnegligent manslaughter	Rape[1]	Robbery	Aggravated assault	Property crime	Burglary	Larceny-theft	Motor vehicle theft	Arson[2]
Fulton	24	0	7	1	16	191	58	131	2	0
Geauga	19	0	8	4	7	185	43	127	15	0
Greene	36	3	16	2	15	421	97	298	26	2
Hamilton	183	4	44	54	81	2,507	399	1,918	190	6
Hocking	25	0	4	1	20	351	85	245	21	2
Jefferson	3	0	0	0	3	17	5	11	1	0
Lake[5,7]		0		45		334	61	269	4	1
Lawrence	62	7	11	5	39	662	173	436	53	6
Licking	60	4	19	12	25	983	291	613	79	1
Lorain	55	0	14	9	32	563	203	344	16	9
Lucas	90	0	19	25	46	991	224	706	61	4
Madison	14	0	4	2	8	347	102	224	21	3
Mahoning	4	0	0	0	4	67	19	40	8	0
Miami	25	0	14	1	10	390	101	262	27	1
Montgomery	237	2	36	96	103	1,278	360	693	225	19
Perry	12	0	5	3	4	72	24	47	1	1
Pickaway	24	0	6	5	13	656	182	449	25	5
Portage[7]		0		6		1,029	255	730	44	8
Richland	57	0	15	15	27	958	264	649	45	3
Stark	122	4	34	27	57	1,795	449	1,233	113	7
Summit	59	2	22	11	24	1,105	195	852	58	7
Trumbull	24	1	6	3	14	318	136	153	29	2
Union	24	0	5	0	19	221	44	158	19	1
Warren	60	1	15	10	34	888	129	679	80	3
Wood	26	2	12	1	11	343	99	228	16	3
Nonmetropolitan Counties										
Adams	13	2	4	1	6	178	71	94	13	0
Ashland	35	0	20	0	15	204	50	137	17	1
Ashtabula	42	0	8	4	30	580	170	366	44	1
Athens	20	1	9	4	6	391	118	255	18	1
Auglaize	6	0	2	2	2	123	32	89	2	1
Champaign	15	1	1	1	12	227	82	128	17	2
Clinton	4	0	0	1	3	37	7	25	5	1
Coshocton	37	0	8	5	24	457	123	319	15	5
Crawford	0	0	0	0	0	110	37	64	9	0
Defiance	13	0	9	0	4	135	31	100	4	1
Erie	3	0	0	0	3	292	53	234	5	0
Fayette	37	1	5	3	28	432	109	308	15	1
Gallia	21	1	2	1	17	370	104	251	15	2
Hancock	8	0	2	0	6	185	38	146	1	1
Hardin	5	0	3	0	2	124	41	79	4	4
Henry	14	0	4	2	8	159	63	93	3	0
Highland	28	2	9	7	10	348	95	227	26	2
Jackson	22	1	11	1	9	222	54	148	20	2
Knox	56	2	26	1	27	384	108	276	0	0
Logan	20	1	11	0	8	255	68	177	10	3
Marion	22	1	9	2	10	821	113	693	15	4
Meigs	25	0	7	3	15	194	45	126	23	1
Mercer	5	0	3	0	2	106	15	87	4	0
Monroe	7	0	1	1	5	51	17	26	8	0
Morgan	29	0	5	0	24	128	42	64	22	1
Muskingum	59	0	38	10	11	903	233	610	60	4
Noble	1	0	1	0	0	107	37	62	8	0
Ottawa	4	0	4	0	0	217	43	166	8	0
Pike	33	2	12	2	17	319	84	211	24	14
Preble	24	2	6	0	16	243	69	149	25	0
Ross	104	0	39	8	57	1,290	358	824	108	16
Scioto	49	0	20	7	22	803	246	506	51	7
Shelby	22	1	4	1	16	131	31	95	5	1
Van Wert	17	0	5	0	12	109	35	70	4	0
Vinton	13	0	6	0	7	107	36	62	9	1
Wayne	66	2	13	4	47	541	214	297	30	6
Wyandot	2	0	0	0	2	15	6	8	1	0
OKLAHOMA										
Metropolitan Counties										
Canadian	10	0	3	1	6	143	29	101	13	2
Cleveland	61	0	18	2	41	312	108	167	37	2
Comanche	13	0	5	0	8	241	76	139	26	3
Cotton	2	0	1	0	1	18	7	11	0	0
Creek	54	0	10	3	41	432	144	194	94	1
Garfield	13	0	2	0	11	122	39	71	12	17
Grady	47	0	7	0	40	347	123	184	40	8
Le Flore	59	0	7	1	51	325	127	168	30	1
Lincoln	21	1	4	1	15	291	98	145	48	4
Logan	57	1	12	5	39	304	82	181	41	1
McClain	35	1	7	7	20	244	76	133	35	1
Oklahoma	23	1	3	4	15	197	51	108	38	0
Okmulgee	31	0	7	1	23	263	117	119	27	12
Osage	57	2	8	2	45	368	128	185	55	3

Table 10. Offenses Known to Law Enforcement, by Selected State Metropolitan and Nonmetropolitan Counties, 2017—Continued

(Number.)

State/county	Violent crime	Murder and nonnegligent manslaughter	Rape[1]	Robbery	Aggravated assault	Property crime	Burglary	Larceny-theft	Motor vehicle theft	Arson[2]
Pawnee	22	0	0	1	21	124	43	52	29	3
Rogers	75	3	22	8	42	545	206	291	48	6
Sequoyah	101	2	5	1	93	379	141	205	33	5
Tulsa	304	1	29	17	257	913	343	379	191	6
Wagoner	42	2	5	4	31	543	208	259	76	10
Nonmetropolitan Counties										
Adair	47	0	3	0	44	178	63	79	36	1
Alfalfa	4	1	2	0	1	23	7	14	2	1
Atoka	3	0	2	1	0	108	46	43	19	2
Beaver	3	0	0	0	3	30	11	15	4	1
Beckham	5	0	2	0	3	72	25	40	7	1
Blaine	8	0	1	0	7	66	16	43	7	1
Caddo	21	0	2	1	18	143	47	82	14	2
Carter	15	0	2	0	13	165	47	105	13	1
Cherokee	102	2	5	4	91	537	203	242	92	9
Choctaw	62	0	1	5	56	115	45	63	7	4
Coal	3	0	0	1	2	72	11	56	5	0
Craig	14	0	5	0	9	113	50	50	13	3
Custer	22	0	1	0	21	73	29	36	8	1
Delaware	53	0	7	2	44	327	121	158	48	7
Dewey	4	0	1	1	2	32	8	18	6	1
Ellis	3	0	1	0	2	22	6	10	6	0
Garvin	29	1	4	0	24	283	80	176	27	6
Grant	4	0	1	0	3	39	17	18	4	1
Harmon	3	0	1	0	2	14	5	7	2	0
Harper	1	0	0	0	1	3	1	2	0	0
Haskell	9	0	1	0	8	60	25	31	4	0
Hughes	11	0	1	1	9	71	19	40	12	2
Jackson	7	0	1	0	6	68	14	49	5	0
Jefferson	9	1	2	0	6	41	13	26	2	0
Johnston	6	0	0	0	6	92	37	51	4	0
Kay	24	0	1	1	22	71	44	25	2	1
Kingfisher	8	0	2	1	5	74	14	49	11	0
Kiowa	6	0	0	1	5	33	17	12	4	0
Latimer	14	0	0	0	14	118	37	74	7	3
Love	14	0	1	1	12	100	17	62	21	2
Major	4	0	0	0	4	46	15	25	6	2
Marshall	25	0	3	1	21	207	85	98	24	3
Mayes	42	0	4	1	37	339	136	162	41	16
McCurtain	12	0	1	0	11	203	75	120	8	8
McIntosh	24	0	1	2	21	201	67	91	43	2
Murray	3	0	1	0	2	17	9	5	3	0
Muskogee	84	0	7	3	74	354	115	202	37	14
Noble	8	1	3	0	4	87	35	45	7	0
Nowata	7	0	0	0	7	44	15	27	2	1
Okfuskee	9	0	0	0	9	76	26	36	14	3
Ottawa	23	0	6	2	15	176	62	99	15	6
Payne	34	0	6	0	28	296	73	186	37	6
Pittsburg	58	0	10	2	46	417	169	203	45	3
Pontotoc	27	0	3	0	24	155	64	75	16	4
Pottawatomie	44	0	6	3	35	552	198	289	65	3
Pushmataha	4	0	0	0	4	42	14	23	5	1
Roger Mills	4	1	1	0	2	32	9	20	3	1
Seminole	26	0	3	2	21	267	105	129	33	9
Stephens	16	0	0	1	15	177	51	103	23	2
Texas	2	0	0	0	2	36	16	16	4	2
Tillman	1	0	0	0	1	38	10	25	3	1
Washita	25	1	8	0	16	75	27	36	12	3
Woods	0	0	0	0	0	29	8	20	1	0
Woodward	11	0	3	0	8	69	29	34	6	1
OREGON										
Metropolitan Counties										
Benton	21	1	9	2	9	155	39	106	10	0
Clackamas	401	6	107	84	204	5,200	725	3,792	683	27
Columbia[6]	30	0	7	0	23	68	22	36	10	0
Deschutes	71	0	20	4	47	721	160	505	56	7
Jackson	176	1	27	10	138	1,587	464	960	163	14
Josephine[6]	28	2	2	3	21	390	106	139	145	4
Lane	331	3	30	22	276	1,378	431	767	180	21
Linn[6]	72	1	20	3	48	926	266	545	115	17
Marion[7]		7		38	37	2,459	376	1,636	447	
Multnomah	124	1	22	15	86	1,527	155	1,034	338	3
Polk	71	0	5	3	63	270	84	161	25	1
Washington	338	3	116	32	187	2,210	414	1,567	229	33
Yamhill	53	0	17	2	34	477	129	306	42	3
Nonmetropolitan Counties										
Baker	6	0	3	0	3	67	24	39	4	0
Crook	43	1	9	1	32	189	59	118	12	2

Table 10. Offenses Known to Law Enforcement, by Selected State Metropolitan and Nonmetropolitan Counties, 2017—Continued

(Number.)

State/county	Violent crime	Murder and nonnegligent manslaughter	Rape[1]	Robbery	Aggravated assault	Property crime	Burglary	Larceny-theft	Motor vehicle theft	Arson[2]
Douglas	164	3	21	9	131	994	283	490	221	14
Harney[6]	6	1	0	1	4	20	8	11	1	0
Hood River	10	0	2	1	7	116	22	83	11	0
Jefferson	13	0	5	0	8	175	46	85	44	6
Lincoln	79	0	14	3	62	362	129	211	22	3
Morrow	28	0	3	2	23	159	42	96	21	1
Tillamook	16	0	5	0	11	204	63	114	27	1
Umatilla	61	0	9	2	50	401	120	224	57	8
Union	6	0	3	1	2	211	36	162	13	2
Wasco	25	0	1	0	24	90	22	60	8	3
PENNSYLVANIA										
Metropolitan Counties										
Adams	0	0	0	0	0	0	0	0	0	0
Allegheny	2	0	0	0	2	1	0	1	0	0
Allegheny County Police Department	176	3	33	13	127	180	24	143	13	10
Beaver	3	0	0	0	3	1	0	1	0	0
Berks	0	0	0	0	0	0	0	0	0	0
Blair	1	0	0	0	1	1	0	1	0	0
Bucks	0	0	0	0	0	1	0	1	0	0
Butler	0	0	0	0	0	0	0	0	0	0
Centre	0	0	0	0	0	0	0	0	0	0
Cumberland	0	0	0	0	0	0	0	0	0	0
Erie	0	0	0	0	0	1	0	1	0	0
Lancaster	0	0	0	0	0	0	0	0	0	0
Lycoming	0	0	0	0	0	0	0	0	0	0
Mercer	1	0	0	0	1	0	0	0	0	0
Monroe	0	0	0	0	0	0	0	0	0	0
Montgomery	0	0	0	0	0	0	0	0	0	0
Northampton	0	0	0	0	0	0	0	0	0	0
Pike	0	0	0	0	0	0	0	0	0	0
Washington	1	0	0	0	1	3	0	3	0	0
Westmoreland	0	0	0	0	0	0	0	0	0	0
Wyoming	0	0	0	0	0	0	0	0	0	0
York	3	0	0	0	3	0	0	0	0	0
Nonmetropolitan Counties										
Bedford	0	0	0	0	0	0	0	0	0	0
Bradford	0	0	0	0	0	1	0	1	0	0
Clarion	0	0	0	0	0	0	0	0	0	0
Elk	0	0	0	0	0	1	0	1	0	0
Greene	0	0	0	0	0	0	0	0	0	0
Indiana	2	0	0	0	2	0	0	0	0	0
Jefferson	1	0	0	0	1	0	0	0	0	0
Lawrence	0	0	0	0	0	0	0	0	0	0
Northumberland	0	0	0	0	0	0	0	0	0	0
Schuylkill	0	0	0	0	0	0	0	0	0	0
Snyder	2	0	0	0	2	0	0	0	0	0
Tioga	0	0	0	0	0	0	0	0	0	0
Union	0	0	0	0	0	0	0	0	0	0
Warren	0	0	0	0	0	0	0	0	0	0
Wayne	0	0	0	0	0	0	0	0	0	0
SOUTH CAROLINA										
Metropolitan Counties										
Anderson	738	8	53	100	577	5,257	1,055	3,564	638	27
Beaufort[3]	538	6	81	45	406				166	10
Berkeley[3]	433	8	57	68	300				326	11
Calhoun	35	0	2	6	27	257	70	145	42	2
Chester	112	2	11	5	94	523	93	395	35	2
Darlington	425	28	17	46	334	1,937	690	1,100	147	18
Fairfield	180	4	5	11	160	471	106	321	44	11
Florence	470	12	50	60	348	2,423	615	1,606	202	7
Greenville	1,679	26	212	264	1,177	8,604	1,907	5,827	870	48
Horry	2	0	0	0	2	3	0	3	0	0
Horry County Police Department	916	20	212	115	569	7,332	1,470	5,146	716	45
Kershaw	104	5	15	12	72	792	163	571	58	3
Lancaster	219	3	15	28	173	1,709	451	1,181	77	12
Laurens	301	3	23	12	263	1,176	375	645	156	5
Lexington[3]	525	15	79	56	375		789		650	8
Pickens	297	2	53	13	229	1,721	506	1,005	210	10
Richland	1,977	23	122	319	1,513	10,546	1,995	7,238	1,313	48
Saluda	38	0	3	1	34	185	56	105	24	2
Spartanburg	1,031	10	79	125	817	5,756	1,465	3,618	673	25
Sumter	403	3	23	36	341	1,973	636	1,164	173	16
Union	71	0	6	6	59	615	205	388	22	2
York	356	2	33	50	271	2,322	532	1,605	185	5
Nonmetropolitan Counties										
Abbeville	25	1	1	2	21	221	73	132	16	0
Bamberg	10	0	1	0	9	155	49	82	24	1

Table 10. Offenses Known to Law Enforcement, by Selected State Metropolitan and Nonmetropolitan Counties, 2017—Continued

(Number.)

State/county	Violent crime	Murder and nonnegligent manslaughter	Rape[1]	Robbery	Aggravated assault	Property crime	Burglary	Larceny-theft	Motor vehicle theft	Arson[2]
Barnwell	87	1	6	7	73	291	78	165	48	3
Cherokee	101	1	11	15	74	1,243	365	749	129	6
Chesterfield	146	7	19	11	109	858	347	472	39	3
Clarendon	105	0	8	13	84	744	234	467	43	3
Dillon	175	4	7	21	143	675	264	373	38	12
Georgetown	178	5	24	17	132	1,216	414	703	99	9
Greenwood	211	1	32	17	161	1,166	216	862	88	4
Hampton	47	0	5	3	39	265	102	152	11	4
Lee	60	1	4	6	49	299	102	178	19	2
Marion	91	4	9	12	66	608	242	323	43	1
Marlboro	92	3	7	8	74	437	161	249	27	4
McCormick	23	3	5	0	15	105	32	60	13	1
Newberry	47	0	6	4	37	224	39	163	22	0
Oconee	153	3	31	15	104	1,670	378	1,153	139	9
Orangeburg	335	8	19	41	267	2,535	711	1,567	257	15
Williamsburg	126	1	10	17	98	618	206	334	78	11
SOUTH DAKOTA										
Metropolitan Counties										
Custer	14	0	3	0	11	61	13	44	4	1
Lincoln	24	2	5	1	16	256	61	187	8	0
McCook	3	0	1	0	2	34	10	21	3	0
Meade	41	1	5	0	35	102	29	61	12	0
Minnehaha	60	0	13	0	47	292	62	208	22	3
Pennington	119	0	53	1	65	389	96	263	30	1
Turner	10	0	3	1	6	47	16	27	4	0
Union	4	0	2	0	2	56	9	42	5	0
Nonmetropolitan Counties										
Bennett	4	0	0	0	4	4	2	0	2	0
Bon Homme	2	0	1	0	1	1	0	1	0	0
Brookings	12	0	4	0	8	47	16	31	0	0
Brown	4	0	1	0	3	29	10	17	2	0
Butte	7	0	1	0	6	60	10	50	0	0
Charles Mix	8	0	0	0	8	63	26	29	8	1
Clay	3	0	0	0	3	51	11	27	13	0
Codington	6	0	1	0	5	29	3	23	3	0
Corson	2	0	0	0	2	9	4	5	0	1
Davison	3	0	0	0	3	25	8	14	3	1
Deuel	5	0	2	0	3	4	0	4	0	0
Edmunds	1	0	0	0	1	0	0	0	0	0
Hamlin	6	0	0	0	6	11	2	9	0	0
Hughes	1	0	0	1	0	7	0	7	0	0
Lake	12	0	5	0	7	37	10	27	0	1
Lawrence	3	0	0	1	2	124	10	113	1	0
Marshall	9	0	3	0	6	29	7	19	3	1
McPherson	1	0	1	0	0	31	25	5	1	0
Moody	2	0	1	0	1	9	2	4	3	0
Perkins	5	0	4	0	1	16	4	12	0	0
Roberts	3	0	0	0	3	6	3	1	2	0
Sanborn	1	0	1	0	0	12	7	5	0	1
Spink	5	0	0	0	5	47	15	30	2	0
Tripp	1	0	1	0	0	5	0	5	0	0
Walworth	0	0	0	0	0	3	0	0	3	0
Yankton	11	0	6	0	5	41	12	19	10	0
TENNESSEE										
Metropolitan Counties										
Anderson	109	1	6	5	97	607	223	320	64	3
Blount	402	2	32	16	352	1,167	312	740	115	5
Bradley	217	1	14	5	197	954	247	552	155	1
Campbell	61	1	15	5	40	584	203	312	69	0
Cannon	29	2	0	2	25	77	36	24	17	2
Carter	73	1	4	2	66	612	140	420	52	1
Cheatham	110	2	5	7	96	556	147	339	70	7
Chester	23	0	1	1	21	56	21	30	5	1
Crockett	36	0	0	2	34	100	30	61	9	1
Dickson	111	1	19	4	87	455	144	255	56	1
Grainger	42	1	7	1	33	209	53	130	26	0
Hamblen	111	1	9	6	95	485	143	282	60	14
Hamilton	282	0	31	13	238	1,606	379	1,033	194	4
Hartsville/Trousdale	50	0	2	2	46	169	26	133	10	0
Hawkins	74	1	11	7	55	594	187	341	66	7
Hickman	112	1	8	2	101	416	112	235	69	3
Jefferson	100	0	9	7	84	602	179	358	65	3
Knox	722	6	49	63	604	4,010	828	2,680	502	16
Loudon	76	3	0	3	70	396	101	258	37	2
Macon	51	2	1	0	48	162	57	86	19	1
Madison	125	0	8	8	109	426	142	244	40	0
Marion	66	0	3	2	61	256	85	131	40	1
Maury	171	1	16	4	150	458	83	310	65	0

Table 10. Offenses Known to Law Enforcement, by Selected State Metropolitan and Nonmetropolitan Counties, 2017—Continued

(Number.)

State/county	Violent crime	Murder and nonnegligent manslaughter	Rape[1]	Robbery	Aggravated assault	Property crime	Burglary	Larceny-theft	Motor vehicle theft	Arson[2]
Montgomery	81	0	8	4	69	801	216	515	70	1
Morgan	54	0	1	1	52	307	99	155	53	0
Polk	32	2	0	4	26	373	80	213	80	2
Roane	78	1	6	0	71	372	124	202	46	0
Robertson	55	2	6	1	46	271	100	150	21	0
Rutherford	263	2	18	15	228	771	193	495	83	6
Sequatchie	24	1	3	0	20	126	32	64	30	2
Shelby	579	4	36	75	464	2,675	590	1,855	230	20
Smith	26	0	3	3	20	196	79	100	17	0
Sullivan	315	3	42	6	264	1,185	266	764	155	15
Sumner	127	1	20	8	98	470	123	300	47	4
Tipton	140	2	22	4	112	580	154	357	69	4
Unicoi	50	3	2	2	43	218	47	155	16	1
Union	46	3	2	2	39	236	74	137	25	1
Washington	184	2	14	9	159	907	204	631	72	8
Williamson	75	1	5	3	66	367	98	242	27	3
Wilson	94	1	0	5	88	791	236	457	98	4
Nonmetropolitan Counties										
Bedford	81	0	14	1	66	230	57	148	25	3
Benton	24	1	2	1	20	162	55	84	23	1
Bledsoe	1	0	0	0	1	50	11	24	15	0
Carroll	47	0	2	1	44	161	87	58	16	0
Claiborne	71	2	2	5	62	391	161	183	47	5
Clay	19	0	2	0	17	50	4	37	9	0
Cocke	146	0	6	8	132	565	219	268	78	8
Coffee	77	0	6	2	69	371	131	210	30	1
Cumberland	26	0	1	0	25	719	213	413	93	2
Decatur	15	0	4	0	11	120	48	58	14	1
Dyer	41	0	5	4	32	290	59	209	22	0
Fentress	24	1	9	0	14	164	37	112	15	2
Franklin	97	0	6	1	90	245	40	173	32	2
Gibson	75	0	10	11	54	224	60	136	28	1
Giles	54	1	6	2	45	241	71	149	21	0
Greene	174	1	13	12	148	980	321	511	148	7
Grundy	95	2	5	2	86	176	57	82	37	3
Hancock	5	0	0	0	5	61	3	51	7	0
Hardeman	72	0	3	1	68	177	71	81	25	5
Hardin	57	0	7	6	44	369	138	178	53	6
Haywood	24	2	3	2	17	125	38	66	21	1
Henderson	76	2	7	2	65	297	98	164	35	3
Henry	53	0	2	1	50	405	160	201	44	0
Houston	12	0	0	0	12	42	12	26	4	1
Humphreys	35	0	4	2	29	205	91	98	16	1
Jackson	23	0	5	0	18	98	28	63	7	0
Johnson	40	0	0	1	39	210	64	126	20	2
Lake	4	0	1	1	2	23	1	20	2	0
Lauderdale	61	1	4	3	53	264	107	131	26	5
Lewis	30	1	1	1	27	151	32	90	29	2
Lincoln	139	0	2	7	130	348	103	201	44	6
Marshall	26	0	0	0	26	99	24	59	16	0
McMinn	95	0	1	3	91	650	182	342	126	0
McNairy	100	1	10	3	86	338	99	186	53	4
Meigs	49	0	6	0	43	295	97	160	38	2
Monroe	174	1	10	7	156	986	282	559	145	1
Moore	13	0	0	0	13	80	8	58	14	0
Obion	19	0	0	0	19	149	43	96	10	1
Overton	8	0	0	0	8	155	28	113	14	0
Perry	10	0	1	0	9	74	15	53	6	1
Pickett	9	1	0	0	8	64	17	38	9	0
Putnam	98	1	15	4	78	664	143	420	101	3
Rhea	63	1	11	5	46	306	88	178	40	0
Scott	32	0	0	0	32	151	67	63	21	0
Sevier	194	0	14	8	172	1,017	278	570	169	2
Stewart	28	0	3	0	25	120	47	57	16	1
Van Buren	7	0	1	0	6	69	7	56	6	1
Warren	65	1	8	3	53	327	96	181	50	3
Wayne	22	0	0	1	21	92	27	52	13	4
Weakley	30	0	1	0	29	146	64	69	13	0
White	60	0	3	1	56	312	32	245	35	0
TEXAS										
Metropolitan Counties										
Aransas	68	1	13	2	52	306	105	189	12	0
Armstrong	5	0	0	1	4	24	9	10	5	0
Atascosa	77	0	1	6	70	441	150	235	56	0
Austin	13	0	3	1	9	138	45	64	29	1
Bandera	31	0	16	1	14	279	117	136	26	0
Bastrop	178	2	33	22	121	726	235	421	70	8
Bell	70	0	35	2	33	777	243	472	62	28
Bexar	620	11	153	121	335	5,985	1,254	4,211	520	48

Table 10. Offenses Known to Law Enforcement, by Selected State Metropolitan and Nonmetropolitan Counties, 2017—Continued

(Number.)

State/county	Violent crime	Murder and nonnegligent manslaughter	Rape[1]	Robbery	Aggravated assault	Property crime	Burglary	Larceny-theft	Motor vehicle theft	Arson[2]
Bowie	121	2	31	7	81	438	142	246	50	12
Brazoria	167	4	15	27	121	1,096	303	684	109	5
Brazos	38	1	9	1	27	308	73	220	15	0
Burleson	22	0	1	5	16	141	44	88	9	0
Caldwell	26	0	0	4	22	183	55	108	20	2
Callahan	9	0	0	1	8	42	12	23	7	0
Cameron	181	3	53	12	113	946	307	589	50	7
Carson	9	0	1	0	8	25	8	16	1	0
Chambers	93	0	19	16	58	567	130	437	0	5
Clay	16	0	5	2	9	137	43	75	19	8
Collin	89	1	24	2	62	375	109	242	24	1
Comal	178	4	47	7	120	668	199	420	49	0
Coryell	21	1	1	0	19	104	22	81	1	0
Crosby	1	0	0	0	1	0	0	0	0	0
Dallas	43	1	15	1	26	288	61	188	39	0
Denton	72	0	26	3	43	551	142	351	58	2
Ector	91	5	8	22	56	1,505	289	1,022	194	2
Ellis	182	4	23	5	150	485	155	293	37	0
El Paso	281	2	46	17	216	723	192	477	54	8
Fort Bend	819	9	105	146	559	4,018	723	3,049	246	32
Galveston	133	2	19	16	96	901	281	536	84	18
Goliad	16	1	2	0	13	92	28	60	4	0
Grayson	76	0	25	2	49	504	177	248	79	3
Gregg	88	0	13	9	66	470	135	266	69	1
Guadalupe	67	4	34	3	26	502	133	320	49	13
Hardin	52	0	2	3	47	305	105	156	44	4
Harris	8,994	92	533	2,906	5,463	42,894	8,057	29,396	5,441	272
Hays	145	2	37	13	93	770	192	503	75	0
Hidalgo	616	22	139	103	352	3,820	1,173	2,423	224	27
Hood[6]	104	0	19	2	83	393	117	238	38	2
Hudspeth	1	0	0	0	1	2	0	1	1	0
Hunt	148	3	19	7	119	592	226	279	87	0
Irion	1	0	0	0	1	24	11	9	4	0
Jefferson	39	0	2	6	31	419	125	248	46	4
Johnson	189	2	22	5	160	771	248	424	99	8
Jones	5	1	3	1	0	68	17	43	8	0
Kaufman	116	2	28	7	79	668	203	372	93	1
Kendall[5]	18	0	6	1	11			91	26	0
Lampasas	13	0	0	0	13	94	51	40	3	0
Lubbock	32	1	7	0	24	522	148	328	46	1
Medina	52	2	18	1	31	364	121	206	37	2
Midland	54	0	0	5	49	552	96	365	91	2
Montgomery[3]	534	17	72	88	357			3,014		29
Newton	10	0	0	0	10	79	34	35	10	0
Nueces	49	1	11	6	31	168	55	110	3	0
Oldham	2	0	0	0	2	23	7	14	2	0
Orange	90	0	7	9	74	460	149	232	79	0
Potter	39	0	4	1	34	196	49	125	22	0
Randall	71	1	27	4	39	277	67	158	52	2
Robertson[6]	13	0	1	0	12	85	31	48	6	1
Rockwall	22	0	8	1	13	83	21	50	12	1
Rusk	98	1	11	2	84	476	197	237	42	0
San Patricio	45	0	0	4	41	305	100	173	32	0
Smith	252	3	29	23	197	1,829	609	996	224	3
Somervell	7	0	0	0	7	74	23	50	1	1
Tarrant	98	4	30	13	51	897	300	531	66	6
Taylor	34	1	4	1	28	138	75	55	8	0
Tom Green	19	1	17	1	0	354	162	166	26	3
Travis	692	12	115	61	504	3,316	792	2,294	230	27
Upshur	101	3	3	3	92	320	167	124	29	0
Victoria	106	1	35	8	62	598	267	286	45	0
Waller	33	1	17	4	11	295	93	174	28	1
Webb	39	0	8	1	30	195	51	140	4	2
Wichita	12	2	0	2	8	135	62	56	17	0
Williamson	184	0	43	9	132	1,492	307	1,066	119	4
Wilson	26	2	2	4	18	233	87	113	33	0
Wise	93	2	28	2	61	353	110	211	32	3
Nonmetropolitan Counties										
Anderson	48	0	7	4	37	399	167	202	30	1
Andrews	13	0	0	0	13	92	30	53	9	1
Angelina	93	2	21	5	65	619	171	377	71	2
Bailey	2	0	0	1	1	40	19	19	2	0
Baylor	0	0	0	0	0	10	4	4	2	0
Bee	42	0	1	3	38	232	75	139	18	1
Blanco	12	0	2	1	9	68	28	29	11	0
Borden	2	0	0	0	2	18	2	14	2	0
Bosque	4	0	0	0	4	77	28	48	1	0
Brewster	11	1	2	0	8	14	3	8	3	1
Briscoe	1	0	1	0	0	8	4	2	2	0
Brooks	1	0	0	0	1	0	0	0	0	0

Table 10. Offenses Known to Law Enforcement, by Selected State Metropolitan and Nonmetropolitan Counties, 2017—Continued

(Number.)

State/county	Violent crime	Murder and nonnegligent manslaughter	Rape[1]	Robbery	Aggravated assault	Property crime	Burglary	Larceny-theft	Motor vehicle theft	Arson[2]
Brown	20	0	0	2	18	149	49	90	10	2
Burnet	46	0	19	3	24	213	72	117	24	0
Calhoun[6]	22	0	3	0	19	105	31	64	10	0
Camp	4	2	0	1	1	112	41	58	13	1
Cass	20	0	2	4	14	265	125	117	23	2
Castro	3	0	0	0	3	42	12	26	4	0
Cherokee	89	0	16	3	70	469	141	273	55	0
Childress	3	0	0	0	3	12	4	8	0	0
Cochran	5	0	0	0	5	3	0	1	2	0
Colorado	36	0	0	0	36	130	36	72	22	0
Comanche	2	0	0	0	2	66	17	48	1	0
Cooke	48	0	3	0	45	151	67	69	15	3
Cottle	0	0	0	0	0	0	0	0	0	0
Crane	0	0	0	0	0	21	0	19	2	0
Crockett	5	0	0	0	5	33	16	16	1	0
Culberson	0	0	0	0	0	0	0	0	0	0
Dallam	0	0	0	0	0	4	1	1	2	0
Dawson	2	0	0	0	2	41	14	24	3	0
Deaf Smith	6	0	4	0	2	55	10	37	8	0
Delta[6]	2	0	0	0	2	24	13	10	1	0
DeWitt	19	0	11	0	8	88	27	51	10	0
Dickens	1	0	0	0	1	2	1	1	0	0
Dimmit	17	0	0	1	16	125	21	98	6	2
Donley	2	0	0	0	2	42	15	25	2	0
Edwards	0	0	0	0	0	26	9	16	1	1
Erath	51	1	13	0	37	118	46	62	10	0
Fannin	53	0	14	4	35	164	95	65	4	0
Fayette	9	2	1	2	4	122	37	76	9	2
Floyd	11	0	0	0	11	38	13	22	3	0
Foard	0	0	0	0	0	0	0	0	0	0
Franklin	25	0	6	0	19	86	45	34	7	0
Freestone	10	0	1	0	9	110	33	69	8	0
Frio	11	0	0	0	11	146	46	86	14	2
Gaines	6	1	1	0	4	84	24	45	15	0
Garza	13	0	2	0	11	61	14	44	3	0
Gillespie	5	0	0	0	5	68	15	53	0	0
Glasscock	4	0	0	0	4	27	16	9	2	0
Gonzales	17	0	8	2	7	117	42	65	10	1
Gray	11	0	0	1	10	94	32	56	6	0
Grimes	27	3	0	5	19	149	56	85	8	1
Hale	17	0	0	1	16	87	39	42	6	0
Hall	5	0	0	0	5	6	2	3	1	0
Hansford	0	0	0	0	0	11	1	8	2	0
Harrison	61	0	29	3	29	620	222	324	74	0
Hartley	1	1	0	0	0	12	4	6	2	4
Haskell	4	0	0	2	2	19	9	7	3	1
Hemphill	0	0	0	0	0	13	2	10	1	0
Henderson	201	5	46	9	141	831	377	393	61	0
Hill	31	1	9	2	19	247	105	122	20	1
Hockley	11	1	0	0	10	54	24	24	6	1
Hopkins	36	2	4	1	29	82	24	47	11	0
Houston	5	0	0	2	3	131	57	62	12	0
Howard	31	1	1	1	28	147	39	93	15	1
Hutchinson	16	0	5	0	11	85	23	52	10	0
Jack	6	0	0	1	5	47	5	33	9	0
Jackson	7	0	3	2	2	50	18	27	5	0
Jasper	100	1	35	6	58	312	132	149	31	3
Jeff Davis	4	1	0	0	3	9	5	3	1	0
Jim Hogg	7	0	1	0	6	15	4	8	3	0
Jim Wells	112	0	21	2	89	268	130	117	21	7
Karnes	13	0	0	0	13	99	33	57	9	1
Kenedy	3	0	0	0	3	3	0	3	0	0
Kent	0	0	0	0	0	4	1	3	0	0
Kerr	34	1	13	1	19	251	84	153	14	1
Kimble	3	0	0	0	3	15	5	7	3	0
Kinney	5	0	0	1	4	6	5	0	1	1
Kleberg	48	0	6	0	42	65	16	38	11	1
Knox	1	0	1	0	0	14	3	9	2	0
Lamar	29	0	9	0	20	221	77	129	15	0
Lamb	6	0	2	1	3	70	24	37	9	0
La Salle	11	0	0	3	8	54	7	47	0	0
Lavaca	13	0	3	1	9	67	32	31	4	0
Lee	25	1	8	1	15	93	31	58	4	0
Leon	19	0	1	1	17	155	45	101	9	1
Limestone	28	1	2	2	23	157	59	85	13	1
Lipscomb	6	0	0	0	6	14	4	6	4	0
Live Oak	9	0	1	2	6	134	66	59	9	0
Llano	9	0	2	1	6	133	49	77	7	0
Loving	0	0	0	0	0	1	0	1	0	0
Madison	4	0	0	0	4	64	37	22	5	0
Marion	59	4	6	2	47	171	72	82	17	2

Table 10. Offenses Known to Law Enforcement, by Selected State Metropolitan and Nonmetropolitan Counties, 2017—Continued

(Number.)

State/county	Violent crime	Murder and nonnegligent manslaughter	Rape[1]	Robbery	Aggravated assault	Property crime	Burglary	Larceny-theft	Motor vehicle theft	Arson[2]
Mason	6	0	0	0	6	15	2	11	2	0
Matagorda	71	0	6	6	59	306	73	220	13	0
Maverick	48	0	11	5	32	423	120	277	26	0
McCulloch	1	0	0	0	1	8	2	5	1	2
McMullen	0	0	0	0	0	24	9	15	0	1
Menard	1	0	0	0	1	5	3	2	0	1
Milam	12	0	1	1	10	94	27	61	6	2
Mills	2	0	0	0	2	22	12	8	2	0
Mitchell	1	0	0	0	1	33	12	20	1	0
Montague	49	0	2	0	47	126	52	58	16	0
Moore	9	0	0	0	9	39	13	20	6	0
Morris	10	1	3	0	6	64	27	31	6	0
Nacogdoches	63	1	11	1	50	248	92	139	17	3
Navarro[6]	55	2	16	2	35	326	162	143	21	3
Nolan	6	0	0	0	6	50	22	22	6	1
Ochiltree	0	0	0	0	0	25	8	12	5	0
Palo Pinto	7	0	0	0	7	108	50	50	8	0
Panola	43	2	2	3	36	284	68	184	32	2
Parmer	1	0	0	0	1	28	11	13	4	0
Pecos	6	0	0	0	6	72	16	52	4	0
Polk	82	5	40	3	34	579	177	350	52	2
Presidio	1	0	0	0	1	11	5	6	0	0
Rains	19	0	3	0	16	94	35	46	13	0
Reagan	6	0	0	0	6	58	10	45	3	0
Real	2	0	0	0	2	50	13	35	2	0
Red River	10	0	0	0	10	69	30	32	7	3
Reeves	3	0	0	0	3	100	1	98	1	0
Refugio	5	0	1	0	4	20	3	17	0	1
Roberts	1	0	0	0	1	6	4	2	0	0
Runnels	5	0	0	0	5	19	8	10	1	0
Sabine	36	0	4	2	30	123	35	74	14	1
San Augustine	27	1	4	0	22	61	26	20	15	0
San Jacinto	56	0	27	3	26	466	195	198	73	0
Schleicher	2	0	1	0	1	31	8	22	1	0
Scurry	4	0	3	0	1	51	19	28	4	0
Shelby	42	2	4	1	35	219	74	130	15	2
Sherman	0	0	0	0	0	6	1	2	3	0
Starr	94	1	24	7	62	292	117	140	35	6
Stephens	4	0	1	0	3	22	9	8	5	0
Sterling	0	0	0	0	0	0	0	0	0	0
Stonewall	0	0	0	0	0	8	3	5	0	0
Sutton	1	0	0	0	1	13	5	6	2	1
Swisher	1	0	0	0	1	10	3	4	3	0
Terry	0	0	0	0	0	45	9	27	9	0
Throckmorton	2	0	0	0	2	6	5	0	1	0
Titus	61	2	12	4	43	183	74	101	8	1
Trinity	23	0	3	1	19	184	52	108	24	3
Tyler	90	2	8	2	78	317	163	114	40	5
Upton	8	0	1	0	7	20	2	18	0	0
Uvalde	6	0	0	0	6	78	26	48	4	1
Val Verde	33	1	8	1	23	103	36	65	2	0
Van Zandt	0	0	0	0	0	251	130	114	7	0
Walker	73	3	24	7	39	208	91	85	32	0
Ward	61	0	14	1	46	113	36	69	8	1
Washington	26	1	3	1	21	155	67	75	13	1
Wharton	78	1	12	7	58	286	87	162	37	0
Wheeler	5	0	0	0	5	30	6	21	3	1
Wilbarger	3	0	0	0	3	13	10	2	1	0
Willacy	53	1	10	1	41	171	57	108	6	2
Winkler	2	1	1	0	0	40	4	33	3	0
Wood	41	0	19	1	21	260	124	114	22	0
Yoakum	5	0	4	0	1	28	8	15	5	1
Young	3	0	0	0	3	22	6	14	2	1
Zapata	25	0	0	4	21	258	113	135	10	0
Zavala	15	0	3	0	12	64	19	37	8	0
UTAH										
Metropolitan Counties										
Box Elder	13	0	3	4	6	191	38	136	17	0
Cache	28	0	10	1	17	217	50	131	36	1
Davis	36	1	9	0	26	209	34	158	17	0
Juab	6	0	2	0	4	63	22	32	9	0
Salt Lake County Unified Police Department	887	13	177	216	481	11,776	1,724	8,304	1,748	33
Tooele[6]	29	1	7	1	20	265	39	217	9	0
Utah	56	1	22	4	29	429	79	325	25	2
Washington	26	0	7	1	18	110	25	75	10	0
Weber	51	2	17	10	22	1,020	238	692	90	5
Nonmetropolitan Counties										
Beaver	5	1	0	1	3	103	21	75	7	0
Carbon	13	0	2	0	11	102	21	76	5	0

Table 10. Offenses Known to Law Enforcement, by Selected State Metropolitan and Nonmetropolitan Counties, 2017—Continued

(Number.)

State/county	Violent crime	Murder and nonnegligent manslaughter	Rape[1]	Robbery	Aggravated assault	Property crime	Burglary	Larceny-theft	Motor vehicle theft	Arson[2]
Daggett[6]	0	0	0	0	0	7	4	3	0	0
Duchesne	34	2	9	0	23	305	69	170	66	3
Iron	26	0	7	0	19	110	42	54	14	2
Kane	8	0	1	1	6	8	4	4	0	0
Millard	25	0	7	0	18	191	30	143	18	1
Rich	3	0	0	0	3	29	13	16	0	0
San Juan	5	0	3	0	2	73	22	47	4	0
Sanpete	2	0	0	0	2	108	24	78	6	1
Sevier	7	0	2	0	5	137	17	110	10	0
Summit	34	0	4	1	29	498	45	430	23	0
Uintah	40	0	15	0	25	214	52	144	18	0
Wasatch	16	0	1	0	15	79	24	50	5	0
VERMONT										
Metropolitan Counties										
Franklin	26	0	14	3	9	55	14	41	0	0
Grand Isle	1	0	0	0	1	38	8	29	1	0
Nonmetropolitan Counties										
Bennington	1	0	0	0	1	7	4	3	0	0
Essex	0	0	0	0	0	19	13	5	1	0
Lamoille	13	0	3	0	10	51	4	47	0	0
Orange	3	0	2	0	1	10	1	9	0	1
Orleans	0	0	0	0	0	22	4	18	0	0
Rutland	3	0	1	0	2	20	3	17	0	0
Washington	0	0	0	0	0	1	0	1	0	0
Windham	1	0	0	0	1	41	4	37	0	0
Windsor	0	0	0	0	0	7	3	4	0	0
VIRGINIA										
Metropolitan Counties										
Albemarle County Police Department	100	5	44	11	40	1,261	144	1,038	79	4
Amelia	22	1	3	6	12	159	35	109	15	0
Amherst	40	0	4	5	31	334	31	276	27	0
Appomattox	3	0	0	2	1	79	15	58	6	0
Arlington County Police Department	359	5	71	73	210	2,913	157	2,610	146	3
Augusta	79	1	26	5	47	876	209	581	86	2
Bedford	64	1	11	4	48	560	122	395	43	2
Botetourt	34	1	9	1	23	210	31	161	18	1
Buckingham	16	1	1	0	14	128	22	84	22	2
Campbell	76	1	24	7	44	744	125	555	64	4
Caroline	39	0	16	3	20	259	55	204	0	1
Charles City	17	0	3	2	12	54	6	41	7	0
Chesterfield County Police Department	437	10	97	160	170	6,208	837	5,005	366	42
Clarke	4	1	1	1	1	75	13	57	5	1
Craig	0	0	0	0	0	4	0	4	0	0
Culpeper	26	0	3	4	19	171	36	121	14	2
Dinwiddie	59	0	6	4	49	270	53	202	15	3
Fairfax County Police Department	1,048	19	183	430	416	13,925	761	12,444	720	26
Fauquier	43	1	16	1	25	369	63	299	7	12
Floyd	29	0	10	0	19	103	30	63	10	2
Fluvanna	38	0	6	5	27	135	17	105	13	0
Franklin	61	7	20	4	30	560	104	388	68	8
Frederick	90	0	38	18	34	1,143	148	934	61	1
Giles	24	0	8	0	16	81	18	60	3	0
Gloucester	29	2	7	4	16	418	30	355	33	2
Greene	15	0	2	3	10	221	24	183	14	2
Hanover	101	2	29	8	62	1,007	45	918	44	2
Henrico County Police Department	556	25	60	160	311	7,677	799	6,355	523	27
Isle of Wight	28	2	0	3	23	259	56	189	14	1
James City County Police Department	100	4	18	22	56	1,068	86	956	26	4
King William	8	0	0	0	8	89	11	77	1	0
Loudoun	319	2	153	45	119	2,754	144	2,469	141	38
Mathews	2	1	1	0	0	56	10	44	2	0
Montgomery	43	2	15	1	25	254	56	175	23	2
Nelson	25	1	8	1	15	156	32	114	10	0
New Kent	25	0	9	4	12	205	28	167	10	3
Powhatan	13	0	4	0	9	225	31	181	13	2
Prince George County Police Department	60	1	17	13	29	398	65	299	34	0
Prince William County Police Department	950	4	148	243	555	5,343	499	4,438	406	29
Pulaski	50	1	9	1	39	586	77	495	14	1
Rappahannock	2	0	1	0	1	18	3	14	1	0
Roanoke County Police Department	153	0	30	18	105	1,253	170	1,028	55	4
Rockingham	40	1	19	0	20	367	95	255	17	5
Scott	15	0	6	1	8	195	65	116	14	5
Spotsylvania	226	4	50	26	146	1,860	201	1,530	129	4
Stafford	286	4	84	29	169	1,829	195	1,541	93	8
Sussex	16	2	3	4	7	89	17	67	5	1
Warren	30	1	17	1	11	225	26	191	8	2

Table 10. Offenses Known to Law Enforcement, by Selected State Metropolitan and Nonmetropolitan Counties, 2017—Continued

(Number.)

State/county	Violent crime	Murder and nonnegligent manslaughter	Rape[1]	Robbery	Aggravated assault	Property crime	Burglary	Larceny-theft	Motor vehicle theft	Arson[2]
Washington	57	5	10	2	40	647	105	494	48	4
York	106	4	39	21	42	1,093	122	932	39	3
Nonmetropolitan Counties										
Accomack	37	1	11	8	17	312	102	193	17	1
Alleghany	9	0	2	0	7	59	18	33	8	0
Bath	3	1	0	0	2	17	2	15	0	0
Bland	3	0	1	0	2	25	5	18	2	0
Brunswick	18	0	1	3	14	82	30	45	7	3
Buchanan	54	1	15	2	36	300	90	190	20	3
Carroll	20	0	3	4	13	317	89	178	50	2
Charlotte	16	0	6	1	9	105	32	61	12	0
Cumberland	12	0	4	0	8	54	18	30	6	0
Dickenson	17	1	11	0	5	78	16	52	10	6
Essex	5	0	1	0	4	71	47	19	5	0
Grayson	13	0	5	0	8	172	39	114	19	4
Greensville	12	1	4	2	5	84	26	52	6	0
Halifax	34	2	6	4	22	274	86	167	21	2
Henry	128	0	16	13	99	1,316	287	922	107	6
Highland	1	0	0	0	1	27	9	18	0	1
King and Queen	11	0	3	2	6	38	9	20	9	0
King George	32	0	5	0	27	292	42	230	20	4
Lancaster	29	0	6	0	23	87	21	61	5	0
Lee	24	0	6	2	16	256	19	235	2	1
Louisa	55	4	12	0	39	434	39	358	37	0
Lunenburg	13	0	0	0	13	53	21	30	2	0
Madison	10	1	5	1	3	89	12	74	3	1
Mecklenburg	53	0	21	4	28	280	110	154	16	3
Middlesex	14	1	8	0	5	150	20	114	16	5
Northampton	7	0	1	1	5	53	17	34	2	0
Northumberland	7	0	4	0	3	88	26	57	5	1
Nottoway	11	1	4	0	6	80	19	55	6	1
Orange	11	0	2	1	8	144	23	110	11	2
Page	24	1	12	1	10	193	41	134	18	4
Patrick	35	0	14	4	17	248	67	162	19	2
Pittsylvania	61	2	22	6	31	406	113	277	16	2
Prince Edward	26	1	6	0	19	87	32	53	2	0
Richmond	6	0	2	0	4	31	7	19	5	0
Rockbridge	28	2	10	2	14	228	38	180	10	1
Russell	35	3	7	0	25	171	40	120	11	2
Shenandoah	32	0	12	2	18	240	57	168	15	1
Smyth	18	3	5	3	7	306	69	214	23	6
Southampton	18	0	9	3	6	179	41	126	12	2
Surry	4	0	1	1	2	33	5	24	4	0
Tazewell	41	1	16	2	22	337	87	228	22	3
Westmoreland	9	0	4	0	5	128	36	90	2	0
Wise	42	1	22	3	16	281	47	209	25	2
Wythe	22	2	7	2	11	141	19	99	23	0
WASHINGTON										
Metropolitan Counties										
Asotin	16	0	2	2	12	147	34	102	11	0
Benton	60	0	7	3	50	468	147	269	52	3
Chelan	32	1	9	4	18	521	171	312	38	1
Clark	331	3	91	51	186	2,021	421	1,073	527	18
Columbia	18	0	3	1	14	60	21	34	5	1
Cowlitz	92	0	38	4	50	407	169	186	52	8
Douglas	18	0	4	4	10	334	80	216	38	0
Franklin	21	0	0	1	20	135	42	72	21	6
King[7]		8		100	234	3,704	1,105	1,822	777	70
Kitsap	380	8	85	29	258	3,163	755	2,134	274	9
Pend Oreille	16	0	3	0	13	271	83	167	21	3
Pierce	1,255	7	124	211	913	8,567	2,230	5,119	1,218	55
Skagit	119	5	19	15	80	1,083	359	647	77	14
Skamania	6	2	2	0	2	40	6	26	8	0
Snohomish	562	8	72	91	391	6,021	1,411	3,499	1,111	38
Spokane	148	4	47	18	79	3,348	856	2,199	293	7
Stevens	22	0	5	2	15	418	170	215	33	2
Thurston	264	5	32	25	202	2,178	773	1,152	253	10
Walla Walla	47	0	13	1	33	263	59	170	34	3
Whatcom	150	0	34	13	103	1,189	309	768	112	13
Yakima	148	5	20	16	107	1,719	505	928	286	7
Nonmetropolitan Counties										
Adams	15	1	2	3	9	150	50	72	28	1
Clallam	60	1	20	3	36	581	177	373	31	4
Ferry	2	0	2	0	0	18	6	11	1	0
Garfield	3	0	2	0	1	36	16	19	1	1
Grant	99	2	13	12	72	999	281	586	132	4
Grays Harbor	43	1	10	3	29	451	215	197	39	3

Table 10. Offenses Known to Law Enforcement, by Selected State Metropolitan and Nonmetropolitan Counties, 2017—Continued

(Number.)

State/county	Violent crime	Murder and nonnegligent manslaughter	Rape[1]	Robbery	Aggravated assault	Property crime	Burglary	Larceny-theft	Motor vehicle theft	Arson[2]
Jefferson	28	0	4	3	21	170	60	99	11	0
Kittitas	5	0	1	0	4	213	56	139	18	2
Klickitat	4	0	0	1	3	64	42	14	8	0
Lewis	56	0	9	2	45	631	215	370	46	5
Lincoln	1	0	1	0	0	113	41	62	10	0
Mason	74	6	7	7	54	1,084	491	480	113	2
Okanogan	33	1	4	1	27	166	70	79	17	2
Pacific	26	0	1	0	25	168	78	81	9	0
San Juan	9	0	4	0	5	168	29	125	14	1
Wahkiakum	4	0	1	0	3	54	12	37	5	0
Whitman	15	0	5	0	10	53	10	34	9	0
WEST VIRGINIA										
Metropolitan Counties										
Berkeley	80	0	16	9	55	668	152	474	42	4
Brooke	3	0	1	1	1	74	23	41	10	3
Fayette	72	3	10	7	52	249	86	121	42	7
Hancock	9	1	2	0	6	47	17	24	6	1
Jefferson	41	1	12	5	23	300	76	199	25	1
Kanawha	338	2	30	8	298	1,551	491	720	340	15
Marshall	33	0	1	0	32	93	30	51	12	0
Monongalia	145	0	16	9	120	357	93	243	21	0
Preston	54	0	2	4	48	62	25	30	7	2
Putnam	161	0	4	4	153	375	75	222	78	2
Raleigh	104	0	4	7	93	535	173	324	38	6
Wirt	4	0	0	0	4	21	9	11	1	1
Nonmetropolitan Counties										
Barbour	25	0	1	0	24	19	3	14	2	0
Calhoun	1	0	0	1	0	49	14	31	4	0
Doddridge	1	0	0	0	1	25	12	12	1	1
Greenbrier	2	0	0	2	0	60	31	23	6	1
Hardy	13	0	0	0	13	7	1	4	2	0
Harrison	37	0	5	3	29	198	54	117	27	4
Jackson	88	2	2	0	84	42	12	24	6	1
Lewis	4	0	0	0	4	61	11	43	7	2
Logan	133	0	4	1	128	52	12	34	6	0
Marion	103	0	8	3	92	108	28	69	11	1
Mason	18	1	5	0	12	161	51	85	25	3
McDowell	4	1	0	1	2	16	6	9	1	1
Mercer	88	3	7	6	72	358	155	175	28	4
Mingo	2	0	0	0	2	2	0	2	0	0
Monroe	2	1	0	0	1	60	10	48	2	0
Morgan	47	0	5	1	41	56	21	34	1	2
Nicholas	154	0	5	1	148	148	39	109	0	1
Randolph	75	0	1	0	74	129	45	83	1	0
Roane	17	0	0	0	17	67	0	63	4	0
Summers	18	0	2	0	16	38	20	9	9	0
Tyler	7	0	1	0	6	15	3	11	1	2
Upshur	4	0	1	0	3	74	14	43	17	1
Wetzel	6	0	1	0	5	24	6	17	1	0
Wyoming	50	0	2	1	47	80	31	45	4	2
WISCONSIN										
Metropolitan Counties										
Brown	76	0	18	2	56	857	115	723	19	3
Calumet	18	0	2	1	15	104	24	77	3	0
Chippewa	30	0	12	0	18	272	48	204	20	1
Columbia	30	0	7	1	22	217	65	142	10	0
Dane	65	1	19	12	33	715	153	503	59	0
Douglas	11	0	5	0	6	182	64	104	14	1
Eau Claire[5]		2	3	2		199	78	108	13	0
Fond du Lac	24	1	8	0	15	143	49	85	9	3
Green	3	0	0	0	3	60	16	43	1	1
Iowa	22	0	5	0	17	36	17	16	3	0
Kenosha	89	3	27	10	49	346	79	247	20	3
Kewaunee	22	0	18	0	4	41	6	30	5	0
La Crosse	22	0	2	0	20	155	47	105	3	0
Marathon	22	0	10	2	10	271	54	211	6	0
Milwaukee	63	1	2	9	51	138	2	73	63	0
Outagamie	20	0	1	0	19	244	69	155	20	0
Ozaukee	9	0	4	0	5	110	25	81	4	0
Pierce	11	0	0	0	11	120	30	87	3	1
Racine	66	1	1	10	54	267	51	192	24	0
Rock	49	0	25	3	21	348	87	236	25	6
Sheboygan	36	2	19	1	14	345	52	282	11	0
St. Croix	36	0	1	0	35	294	75	199	20	0
Washington	10	0	7	1	2	310	56	241	13	0
Waukesha	70	0	3	1	66	382	72	286	24	3
Winnebago	16	0	1	0	15	216	63	139	14	1

Table 10. Offenses Known to Law Enforcement, by Selected State Metropolitan and Nonmetropolitan Counties, 2017—Continued

(Number.)

State/county	Violent crime	Murder and nonnegligent manslaughter	Rape[1]	Robbery	Aggravated assault	Property crime	Burglary	Larceny-theft	Motor vehicle theft	Arson[2]
Nonmetropolitan Counties										
Adams	20	0	0	1	19	236	115	116	5	1
Ashland	21	0	0	0	21	26	9	17	0	0
Barron	4	3	0	0	1	137	40	86	11	0
Bayfield	15	0	2	0	13	125	46	73	6	0
Buffalo	11	0	6	0	5	25	2	17	6	0
Burnett	27	0	2	1	24	313	139	162	12	4
Clark	12	0	0	0	12	83	15	62	6	1
Crawford	15	0	7	0	8	107	16	89	2	0
Dodge	41	0	10	4	27	162	52	102	8	1
Door	8	0	1	0	7	106	29	73	4	1
Dunn	18	0	5	0	13	84	28	46	10	0
Florence	1	0	0	0	1	71	19	49	3	0
Forest	22	2	9	0	11	100	23	72	5	1
Grant	41	0	15	0	26	145	31	106	8	0
Green Lake	5	0	2	0	3	56	18	36	2	0
Iron	3	1	0	1	1	72	22	45	5	0
Jackson	9	0	2	0	7	190	79	92	19	0
Jefferson	42	0	1	2	39	179	38	131	10	3
Juneau	37	0	9	0	28	219	70	135	14	0
Lafayette	14	0	5	0	9	81	16	61	4	1
Langlade	6	0	0	0	6	183	59	118	6	0
Lincoln	33	0	12	0	21	90	28	59	3	2
Manitowoc	35	0	2	2	31	159	49	104	6	1
Marinette	13	0	7	0	6	224	96	112	16	1
Marquette	11	0	3	1	7	84	27	53	4	0
Menominee	0	0	0	0	0	31	16	12	3	0
Monroe	6	0	3	0	3	120	54	55	11	2
Oneida	41	1	11	1	28	163	41	110	12	2
Pepin	6	0	2	0	4	30	12	18	0	0
Polk	28	0	8	1	19	245	81	137	27	1
Portage	39	0	5	1	33	183	46	127	10	1
Price	6	0	0	0	6	89	19	66	4	1
Richland	1	0	0	0	1	15	14	0	1	0
Rusk	19	1	2	0	16	38	10	25	3	2
Sauk	33	0	18	3	12	365	91	262	12	0
Sawyer	14	0	1	0	13	195	56	124	15	0
Shawano	36	0	13	0	23	313	112	183	18	1
Taylor	15	0	0	0	15	87	6	80	1	2
Trempealeau	15	0	4	0	11	133	17	108	8	0
Vernon	5	0	1	0	4	70	19	46	5	0
Vilas	0	0	0	0	0	154	39	106	9	0
Walworth	18	0	13	0	5	174	38	120	16	0
Washburn	40	0	9	0	31	125	35	80	10	0
Waupaca	49	0	16	0	33	444	70	347	27	0
Waushara	22	0	9	0	13	203	35	157	11	0
Wood	12	0	7	3	2	160	44	103	13	1
WYOMING										
Metropolitan Counties										
Laramie	78	3	10	1	64	490	112	323	55	6
Natrona	48	0	20	6	22	231	44	155	32	2
Nonmetropolitan Counties										
Albany	10	1	1	0	8	41	15	23	3	0
Big Horn	7	0	2	0	5	25	4	19	2	0
Campbell	105	1	21	1	82	134	30	86	18	4
Carbon	8	0	2	0	6	12	1	8	3	0
Crook	3	0	0	0	3	20	4	16	0	0
Fremont	16	0	4	0	12	191	25	153	13	0
Goshen	31	0	2	0	29	46	17	23	6	0
Hot Springs	2	0	0	0	2	27	3	21	3	0
Johnson	12	0	4	0	8	24	8	13	3	0
Lincoln	13	0	7	0	6	57	16	34	7	0
Park	26	2	0	0	24	64	18	43	3	0
Platte	2	0	0	0	2	20	6	10	4	0
Sheridan	6	0	0	1	5	58	8	47	3	0
Sublette	10	0	0	0	10	81	9	68	4	2
Sweetwater	23	1	3	0	19	99	24	63	12	1
Uinta	2	0	0	0	2	78	7	64	7	0
Washakie	4	0	2	0	2	11	3	8	0	0
Weston	2	0	0	0	2	2	0	2	0	0

Note: The data shown in this table do not reflect county totals but are the number of offenses reported by the sheriff's office or county police department.
1 The figures shown in this column for the offense of rape were reported using only the revised Uniform Crime Reporting (UCR) definition of rape. See chapter notes for more detail.   2 The FBI does not publish arson data unless it receives data from either the agency or the state for all 12 months of the calendar year.   3 The FBI determined that the agency's data were underreported. Consequently, those data are not included in this table.   4 The Tulare County Highway Patrol collects the motor vehicle thefts for this county. These data can be found in Table 11.   5 The FBI determined that the agency's data were overreported. Consequently, those data are not included in this table.   6 Because of changes in the state/local agency's reporting practices, figures are not comparable to previous years' data.   7 This agency/state submits rape data classified according to the legacy UCR definition; therefore the rape offense and violent crime total, which rape is a part of, is not included in this table. See the chapter notes for more detail.

Table 11. Offenses Known to Law Enforcement, by Selected State, Tribal, and Other Agencies, 2017

(Number.)

State/other agency unit/office	Violent crime	Murder and nonnegligent manslaughter	Rape[1]	Robbery	Aggravated assault	Property crime	Burglary	Larceny-theft	Motor vehicle theft	Arson[2]
ALABAMA										
Tribal Agencies										
Poarch Creek Tribal	9	0	0	6	385	9	363	13	0	0
ALASKA										
State Agencies										
Alaska State Troopers	1,210	18	227	38	927	3,309	1,065	1,763	481	49
Other Agencies										
Fairbanks International Airport	0	0	0	0	0	16	0	14	2	1
Ted Stevens Anchorage International Airport	5	0	0	1	4	232	5	124	103	0
ARIZONA										
State Agencies										
Arizona Department of Public Safety	77	2	1	7	67	23	4	19	0	1
Tribal Agencies										
Ak-Chin Tribal	2	0	1	0	1	1	0	1	0	0
Cocopah Tribal	12	0	0	0	12	9	1	7	1	0
Colorado River Tribal	26	0	6	0	20	91	7	81	3	
Fort Apache Agency	47	0	25	1	21	3	3	0	0	
Fort McDowell Tribal	16	0	0	1	15	29	4	23	2	0
Fort Mojave Tribal	16	0	0	0	16	24	4	18	2	
Gila River Indian Community	337	9	38	13	277	512	60	376	76	57
Hopi Tribal	31	0	2	1	28	155	62	87	6	0
Hualapai Tribal	26	1	2	0	23	115	39	70	6	0
Kaibab Paiute Tribal	0	0	0	0	0	0	0	0	0	0
Navajo Nation	2,524	26	160	27	2,311	937	307	352	278	34
Pascua Yaqui Tribal	48	1	2	10	35	268	35	219	14	1
Salt River Tribal	604	0	1	4	599	736	63	582	91	3
San Carlos Agency	0	0	0	0	0	0	0	0	0	3
Tohono O'odham Nation	201	3	5	15	178	306	89	161	56	14
Tonto Apache Tribal	1	0	0	0	1	18	4	12	2	0
White Mountain Apache Tribal	275	0	28	2	245	285	80	200	5	
Yavapai-Apache Nation	5	0	0	0	5	7	0	4	3	0
Yavapai-Prescott Tribal	1	0	0	0	1	75	4	70	1	
Other Agencies										
Tucson Airport Authority	2	0	0	0	2	50	3	25	22	0
ARKANSAS										
State Agencies										
Camp Robinson	2	0	1	0	1	7	1	4	2	0
State Capitol Police	0	0	0	0	0	45	0	44	1	0
CALIFORNIA										
State Agencies										
Atascadero State Hospital	217	0	0	0	217	1	0	1	0	0
California State Fair	7	0	0	2	5	61	10	49	2	3
Coalinga State Hospital	231	0	1	1	229	3	1	2	0	0
Department of Parks and Recreation										
Angeles	2	0	0	0	2	33	2	31	0	0
Bay Area	0	0	0	0	0	3	1	2	0	0
Calaveras County	1	0	0	0	1	0	0	0	0	0
Capital	1	0	0	1	0	3	1	2	0	0
Channel Coast	3	0	0	1	2	75	7	67	1	0
Colorado	0	0	0	0	0	0	0	0	0	0
Four Rivers District	1	0	0	0	1	0	0	0	0	0
Gold Fields District	0	0	0	0	0	49	0	48	1	0
Hollister Hills	0	0	0	0	0	0	0	0	0	0
Hungry Valley	0	0	0	0	0	0	0	0	0	0
Inland Empire	1	0	0	0	1	2	0	2	0	1
Marin County	2	0	0	0	2	11	7	4	0	0
Monterey County	0	0	0	0	0	56	11	45	0	0
North Coast Redwoods	2	0	1	0	1	26	2	21	3	0
Northern Buttes	1	0	0	0	1	14	0	14	0	1
Oceano Dunes	8	0	0	1	7	30	0	29	1	6
Ocotillo Wells	0	0	0	0	0	4	0	0	4	0
Orange Coast	0	0	0	0	0	113	49	64	0	0
San Diego Coast	5	0	0	0	5	64	7	51	6	1
San Joaquin	1	0	0	0	1	1	0	1	0	0
San Luis Obispo Coast	0	0	0	0	0	23	1	22	0	0
Santa Cruz Mountains	0	0	0	0	0	133	31	101	1	4
Sierra	0	0	0	0	0	8	0	8	0	0
Silverado	0	0	0	0	0	0	0	0	0	0
Sonoma-Mendocino Coast	2	0	1	0	1	43	0	42	1	2
Tehachapi District	0	0	0	0	0	12	12	0	0	1
Twin Cities	0	0	0	0	0	0	0	0	0	0
Fairview Developmental Center	3	0	0	0	3	1	1	0	0	0
Highway Patrol										
Alameda County	13	0	0	2	11	253	2	64	187	0
Alpine County	0	0	0	0	0	3	0	1	2	0
Amador County	0	0	0	0	0	42	0	15	27	0
Butte County	0	0	0	0	0	290	1	88	201	0
Calaveras County	0	0	0	0	0	145	1	68	76	0

Table 11. Offenses Known to Law Enforcement, by Selected State, Tribal, and Other Agencies, 2017—Continued

(Number.)

State/other agency unit/office	Violent crime	Murder and nonnegligent manslaughter	Rape[1]	Robbery	Aggravated assault	Property crime	Burglary	Larceny-theft	Motor vehicle theft	Arson[2]
Colusa County	2	0	0	0	2	22	4	4	14	0
Contra Costa County	11	2	0	0	9	609	0	29	580	0
Del Norte County	0	0	0	0	0	116	2	35	79	0
El Dorado County	1	0	0	0	1	170	0	83	87	0
Fresno County	2	0	0	0	2	213	5	35	173	2
Glenn County	0	0	0	0	0	52	0	9	43	0
Humboldt County	2	1	0	1	0	465	1	78	386	0
Imperial County	0	0	0	0	0	47	0	10	37	0
Inyo County	0	0	0	0	0	48	0	8	40	0
Kern County	1	0	0	0	1	260	1	26	233	0
Kings County	0	0	0	0	0	131	1	28	102	0
Lake County	3	0	0	1	2	207	1	42	164	0
Lassen County	1	0	0	0	1	50	1	4	45	0
Los Angeles County	46	1	0	3	42	837	20	153	664	0
Madera County	0	0	0	0	0	227	3	49	175	0
Marin County	4	0	0	0	4	80	5	32	43	0
Mariposa County	1	0	0	0	1	21	0	9	12	0
Mendocino County	1	0	0	1	0	156	1	39	116	0
Merced County	0	0	0	0	0	360	0	83	277	0
Modoc County	0	0	0	0	0	7	0	2	5	0
Mono County	0	0	0	0	0	6	0	1	5	0
Monterey County	3	0	0	0	3	441	0	70	371	0
Napa County	1	0	0	0	1	24	0	9	15	0
Nevada County	3	0	0	0	3	111	0	6	105	0
Orange County	12	0	0	0	12	51	1	21	29	0
Placer County	0	0	0	0	0	175	0	79	96	0
Plumas County	0	0	0	0	0	10	0	5	5	0
Riverside County	17	0	0	0	17	124	8	35	81	0
Sacramento County	14	0	0	1	13	3,826	12	1,517	2,297	0
San Benito County	0	0	0	0	0	16	0	2	14	0
San Bernardino County	31	0	1	0	30	163	15	78	70	0
San Diego County	33	0	1	1	31	114	8	44	62	1
San Francisco County	9	0	2	2	5	34	0	9	25	0
San Joaquin County	0	0	0	0	0	745	0	147	598	0
San Luis Obispo County	3	0	1	0	2	117	1	12	104	0
San Mateo County	6	0	0	0	6	18	0	2	16	0
Santa Barbara County	6	0	1	0	5	158	1	45	112	0
Santa Clara County	9	0	1	0	8	111	0	24	87	0
Santa Cruz County	0	0	0	0	0	557	0	193	364	0
Shasta County	0	0	0	0	0	360	3	73	284	0
Sierra County	0	0	0	0	0	4	0	1	3	0
Siskiyou County	4	0	0	1	3	66	5	16	45	1
Solano County	6	0	0	0	6	50	2	12	36	0
Sonoma County	2	0	0	1	1	195	0	64	131	0
Stanislaus County	1	0	0	0	1	707	6	155	546	0
Sutter County	0	0	0	0	0	40	0	2	38	0
Tehama County	0	0	0	0	0	145	0	44	101	0
Trinity County	2	0	0	0	2	75	0	12	63	0
Tulare County	0	0	0	0	0	757	1	77	679	14
Tuolumne County	0	0	0	0	0	178	1	90	87	0
Ventura County	1	0	0	0	1	60	1	25	34	0
Yolo County	1	0	0	1	0	59	2	12	45	0
Yuba County	0	0	0	0	0	368	0	24	344	0
Napa State Hospital	198	0	5	0	193	4	1	1	2	0
Patton State Hospital	547	0	5	1	541	7	3	4	0	0
Porterville Developmental Center	20	0	1	1	18	6	1	5	0	0
Sonoma Developmental Center	1	0	0	0	1	1	0	1	0	0
Tribal Agencies										
La Jolla Tribal	5	1	0	0	4	5	4	1	0	0
Los Coyotes Tribal	3	0	0	0	3	14	10	4	0	0
Sycuan Tribal	5	0	0	1	4	72	11	27	34	0
Table Mountain Rancheria	2	0	0	0	2	116	0	110	6	0
Other Agencies										
East Bay Regional Park District, Alameda County	42	0	6	16	20	343	53	277	13	11
Fontana Unified School District	21	0	0	2	19	61	23	32	6	3
Los Angeles County Metropolitan Transportation Authority	1	0	0	0	1	9	0	9	0	0
Los Angeles Transportation Services Bureau[3]	411	2	4	235	170	547	10	469	68	1
Monterey Peninsula Airport	0	0	0	0	0	9	5	0	4	0
Port of San Diego Harbor	62	0	4	11	47	461	41	416	4	0
San Bernardino Unified School District	51	0	1	43	7	233	97	121	15	11
San Francisco Bay Area Rapid Transit										
Alameda County	264	0	4	192	68	1,738	16	1,464	258	3
Contra Costa County	67	0	1	36	30	819	3	681	135	0
San Francisco County	69	0	0	50	19	255	6	247	2	0
San Mateo County	28	0	0	15	13	224	9	196	19	0
Santa Clara Transit District	110	0	1	38	71	124	0	86	38	0
Shasta County Marshal	1	0	0	0	1	0	0	0	0	0
Stockton Unified School District	47	0	0	24	23	208	83	121	4	2
Twin Rivers Unified School District	19	0	1	7	11	100	58	38	4	0
Union Pacific Railroad										

Table 11. Offenses Known to Law Enforcement, by Selected State, Tribal, and Other Agencies, 2017—Continued

(Number.)

State/other agency unit/office	Violent crime	Murder and nonnegligent manslaughter	Rape[1]	Robbery	Aggravated assault	Property crime	Burglary	Larceny-theft	Motor vehicle theft	Arson[2]
Alameda County	0	0	0	0	0	15	8	7	0	0
Amador County	0	0	0	0	0	0	0	0	0	0
Butte County	0	0	0	0	0	11	7	4	0	0
Calaveras County	0	0	0	0	0	0	0	0	0	0
Colusa County	0	0	0	0	0	0	0	0	0	0
Contra Costa County	0	0	0	0	0	1	0	1	0	0
El Dorado County	0	0	0	0	0	0	0	0	0	0
Fresno County	0	0	0	0	0	5	3	2	0	0
Glenn County	0	0	0	0	0	0	0	0	0	0
Humboldt County	0	0	0	0	0	0	0	0	0	0
Imperial County	0	0	0	0	0	9	1	8	0	0
Inyo County	0	0	0	0	0	0	0	0	0	0
Kern County	0	0	0	0	0	30	13	17	0	0
Kings County	0	0	0	0	0	0	0	0	0	0
Lassen County	0	0	0	0	0	1	0	1	0	0
Los Angeles County	2	0	0	0	2	356	293	63	0	3
Madera County	0	0	0	0	0	0	0	0	0	0
Marin County	0	0	0	0	0	0	0	0	0	0
Mendocino County	0	0	0	0	0	0	0	0	0	0
Merced County	0	0	0	0	0	0	0	0	0	0
Modoc County	0	0	0	0	0	0	0	0	0	0
Monterey County	0	0	0	0	0	0	0	0	0	0
Napa County	0	0	0	0	0	0	0	0	0	0
Nevada County	0	0	0	0	0	2	1	1	0	0
Orange County	0	0	0	0	0	2	1	1	0	0
Placer County	0	0	0	0	0	6	0	6	0	0
Plumas County	0	0	0	0	0	1	0	1	0	0
Riverside County	1	0	0	0	1	11	4	7	0	0
Sacramento County	0	0	0	0	0	7	2	5	0	0
San Benito County	0	0	0	0	0	0	0	0	0	0
San Bernardino County	0	0	0	0	0	14	10	4	0	0
San Francisco County	0	0	0	0	0	0	0	0	0	0
San Joaquin County	0	0	0	0	0	50	28	22	0	0
San Luis Obispo County	0	0	0	0	0	2	0	2	0	0
San Mateo County	0	0	0	0	0	0	0	0	0	0
Santa Barbara County	0	0	0	0	0	3	1	2	0	0
Santa Clara County	0	0	0	0	0	1	0	1	0	0
Santa Cruz County	0	0	0	0	0	0	0	0	0	0
Shasta County	0	0	0	0	0	8	1	7	0	0
Sierra County	0	0	0	0	0	0	0	0	0	0
Siskiyou County	1	0	0	0	1	3	0	3	0	0
Solano County	0	0	0	0	0	1	1	0	0	0
Sonoma County	0	0	0	0	0	0	0	0	0	0
Stanislaus County	0	0	0	0	0	2	0	2	0	0
Sutter County	0	0	0	0	0	0	0	0	0	0
Tehama County	0	0	0	0	0	0	0	0	0	0
Trinity County	0	0	0	0	0	0	0	0	0	0
Tulare County	0	0	0	0	0	4	0	4	0	0
Ventura County	0	0	0	0	0	3	0	3	0	0
Yolo County	0	0	0	0	0	0	0	0	0	0
Yuba County	0	0	0	0	0	3	0	3	0	0
COLORADO										
State Agencies										
Colorado Bureau of Investigation	0	0	0	0	0	0	0	0	0	0
Colorado Mental Health Institute	0	0	0	0	0	4	0	4	0	0
Colorado State Patrol	3	0	0	0	3	20	0	5	15	0
Tribal Agencies										
Southern Ute Tribal	19	0	1	0	18	78	6	63	9	0
Ute Mountain Tribal	28	0	8	0	20	4	3	0	1	4
Other Agencies										
All Crimes Enforcement Team	0	0	0	0	0	0	0	0	0	0
Delta Montrose Drug Task Force	0	0	0	0	0	0	0	0	0	0
Southwest Drug Task Force	0	0	0	0	0	0	0	0	0	0
CONNECTICUT										
State Agencies										
Connecticut State Police	316	6	81	46	183	2,557	670	1,528	359	11
Department of Motor Vehicles	0	0	0	0	0	1	0	0	1	0
State Capitol Police	1	0	0	1	0	2	0	2	0	0
Tribal Agencies										
Mashantucket Pequot Tribal	19	0	10	0	9	147	4	141	2	1
Mohegan Tribal	11	0	0	2	9	287	3	279	5	0
Other Agencies										
Metropolitan Transportation Authority	2	0	0	2	0	55	2	53	0	0
DELAWARE										
State Agencies										
Alcohol and Tobacco Enforcement	0	0	0	0	0	0	0	0	0	0
Animal Welfare										
Kent County	0	0	0	0	0	0	0	0	0	0
New Castle County	0	0	0	0	0	0	0	0	0	0
Sussex County	0	0	0	0	0	1	0	1	0	0

Table 11. Offenses Known to Law Enforcement, by Selected State, Tribal, and Other Agencies, 2017—Continued

(Number.)

State/other agency unit/office	Violent crime	Murder and nonnegligent manslaughter	Rape[1]	Robbery	Aggravated assault	Property crime	Burglary	Larceny-theft	Motor vehicle theft	Arson[2]
Attorney General										
Kent County	0	0	0	0	0	2	0	2	0	0
New Castle County	1	0	0	0	1	1	0	1	0	0
Sussex County	0	0	0	0	0	1	0	1	0	0
Environmental Control	0	0	0	0	0	4	0	4	0	0
Fish and Wildlife	1	0	0	0	1	23	3	19	1	0
Park Rangers	8	0	0	1	7	118	31	87	0	0
River and Bay Authority	3	0	0	0	3	9	0	8	1	0
State Capitol Police	3	0	0	0	3	11	1	8	2	0
State Fire Marshal	4	0	0	0	4	12	8	3	1	102
State Police	0	0	0	0	0	1	1	0	0	0
Kent County	292	2	48	32	210	1,166	312	795	59	0
New Castle County	512	4	27	217	264	4,693	467	4,067	159	0
Sussex County	473	3	83	56	331	2,837	774	1,945	118	1
Other Agencies										
Amtrak Police	4	0	0	1	3	9	0	9	0	0
Wilmington Fire Department	0	0	0	0	0	0	0	0	0	3
DISTRICT OF COLUMBIA										
Other Agencies										
District of Columbia Fire and Emergency Medical Services, Arson Investigation Unit	0	0	0	0	0	0	0	0	0	224
Metro Transit Police	390	0	1	272	117	886	1	843	42	0
FLORIDA										
State Agencies										
Capitol Police	0	0	0	0	0	16	0	15	1	0
Department of Corrections, Office of the Inspector General										
Alachua County	0	0	0	0	0	0	0	0	0	0
Baker County	0	0	0	0	0	0	0	0	0	0
Bay County	0	0	0	0	0	0	0	0	0	0
Bradford County	0	0	0	0	0	0	0	0	0	0
Brevard County	0	0	0	0	0	0	0	0	0	0
Broward County	0	0	0	0	0	0	0	0	0	0
Calhoun County	0	0	0	0	0	0	0	0	0	0
Charlotte County	0	0	0	0	0	0	0	0	0	0
Citrus County	0	0	0	0	0	0	0	0	0	0
Clay County	0	0	0	0	0	0	0	0	0	0
Collier County	0	0	0	0	0	0	0	0	0	0
Columbia County	0	0	0	0	0	0	0	0	0	0
DeSoto County	0	0	0	0	0	0	0	0	0	0
Dixie County	0	0	0	0	0	0	0	0	0	0
Duval County	0	0	0	0	0	0	0	0	0	0
Escambia County	0	0	0	0	0	0	0	0	0	0
Flagler County	0	0	0	0	0	0	0	0	0	0
Franklin County	0	0	0	0	0	0	0	0	0	0
Gadsden County	0	0	0	0	0	0	0	0	0	0
Gilchrist County	0	0	0	0	0	0	0	0	0	0
Glades County	0	0	0	0	0	0	0	0	0	0
Gulf County	0	0	0	0	0	0	0	0	0	0
Hamilton County	0	0	0	0	0	0	0	0	0	0
Hardee County	0	0	0	0	0	0	0	0	0	0
Hendry County	0	0	0	0	0	0	0	0	0	0
Hernando County	0	0	0	0	0	0	0	0	0	0
Highlands County	0	0	0	0	0	0	0	0	0	0
Hillsborough County	0	0	0	0	0	0	0	0	0	0
Holmes County	0	0	0	0	0	0	0	0	0	0
Indian River County	0	0	0	0	0	0	0	0	0	0
Jackson County	0	0	0	0	0	0	0	0	0	0
Jefferson County	0	0	0	0	0	0	0	0	0	0
Lafayette County	0	0	0	0	0	0	0	0	0	0
Lake County	0	0	0	0	0	0	0	0	0	0
Lee County	0	0	0	0	0	0	0	0	0	0
Leon County	0	0	0	0	0	0	0	0	0	0
Levy County	0	0	0	0	0	0	0	0	0	0
Liberty County	0	0	0	0	0	0	0	0	0	0
Madison County	0	0	0	0	0	0	0	0	0	0
Manatee County	0	0	0	0	0	0	0	0	0	0
Marion County	0	0	0	0	0	0	0	0	0	0
Martin County	0	0	0	0	0	0	0	0	0	0
Miami-Dade County	0	0	0	0	0	0	0	0	0	0
Monroe County	0	0	0	0	0	0	0	0	0	0
Nassau County	0	0	0	0	0	0	0	0	0	0
Okaloosa County	0	0	0	0	0	0	0	0	0	0
Okeechobee County	0	0	0	0	0	0	0	0	0	0
Orange County	0	0	0	0	0	0	0	0	0	0
Osceola County	0	0	0	0	0	0	0	0	0	0
Palm Beach County	0	0	0	0	0	0	0	0	0	0
Pasco County	0	0	0	0	0	0	0	0	0	0
Pinellas County	0	0	0	0	0	0	0	0	0	0
Polk County	0	0	0	0	0	0	0	0	0	0

Table 11. Offenses Known to Law Enforcement, by Selected State, Tribal, and Other Agencies, 2017—Continued

(Number.)

State/other agency unit/office	Violent crime	Murder and nonnegligent manslaughter	Rape[1]	Robbery	Aggravated assault	Property crime	Burglary	Larceny-theft	Motor vehicle theft	Arson[2]
Putnam County	0	0	0	0	0	0	0	0	0	0
Santa Rosa County	0	0	0	0	0	0	0	0	0	0
Sarasota County	0	0	0	0	0	0	0	0	0	0
Seminole County	0	0	0	0	0	0	0	0	0	0
St. Johns County	0	0	0	0	0	0	0	0	0	0
St. Lucie County	0	0	0	0	0	0	0	0	0	0
Sumter County	0	0	0	0	0	0	0	0	0	0
Suwannee County	0	0	0	0	0	0	0	0	0	0
Taylor County	0	0	0	0	0	0	0	0	0	0
Union County	0	0	0	0	0	0	0	0	0	0
Volusia County	0	0	0	0	0	0	0	0	0	0
Wakulla County	0	0	0	0	0	0	0	0	0	0
Walton County	0	0	0	0	0	0	0	0	0	0
Washington County	0	0	0	0	0	0	0	0	0	0
Department of Law Enforcement										
Duval County, Jacksonville	0	0	0	0	0	0	0	0	0	0
Escambia County, Pensacola	0	0	0	0	0	0	0	0	0	0
Hillsborough County, Tampa	0	0	0	0	0	1	0	1	0	0
Lee County, Fort Myers	0	0	0	0	0	0	0	0	0	0
Leon County, Tallahassee	0	0	0	0	0	2	0	2	0	0
Miami-Dade County, Miami	0	0	0	0	0	0	0	0	0	0
Orange County, Orlando	3	1	0	0	2	5	0	5	0	0
Division of Investigative and Forensic Services										
Broward County	0	0	0	0	0	0	0	0	0	0
Duval County	0	0	0	0	0	0	0	0	0	0
Escambia County	0	0	0	0	0	0	0	0	0	0
Hillsborough County	0	0	0	0	0	0	0	0	0	0
Lee County	0	0	0	0	0	0	0	0	0	0
Leon County	0	0	0	0	0	0	0	0	0	0
Miami-Dade County	0	0	0	0	0	0	0	0	0	0
Orange County	0	0	0	0	0	0	0	0	0	0
Palm Beach County	0	0	0	0	0	0	0	0	0	0
Pinellas County	0	0	0	0	0	0	0	0	0	0
Fish and Wildlife Conservation Commission										
Alachua County	0	0	0	0	0	0	0	0	0	0
Baker County	0	0	0	0	0	0	0	0	0	0
Bay County	0	0	0	0	0	0	0	0	0	0
Bradford County	0	0	0	0	0	0	0	0	0	0
Brevard County	0	0	0	0	0	0	0	0	0	0
Broward County	0	0	0	0	0	0	0	0	0	0
Calhoun County	0	0	0	0	0	0	0	0	0	0
Charlotte County	0	0	0	0	0	0	0	0	0	0
Citrus County	0	0	0	0	0	0	0	0	0	0
Clay County	0	0	0	0	0	0	0	0	0	0
Collier County	0	0	0	0	0	0	0	0	0	0
Columbia County	0	0	0	0	0	0	0	0	0	0
DeSoto County	0	0	0	0	0	0	0	0	0	0
Dixie County	0	0	0	0	0	0	0	0	0	0
Duval County	0	0	0	0	0	0	0	0	0	0
Escambia County	0	0	0	0	0	0	0	0	0	0
Flagler County	0	0	0	0	0	0	0	0	0	0
Franklin County	0	0	0	0	0	0	0	0	0	0
Gadsden County	0	0	0	0	0	0	0	0	0	0
Gilchrist County	0	0	0	0	0	0	0	0	0	0
Glades County	0	0	0	0	0	0	0	0	0	0
Gulf County	0	0	0	0	0	0	0	0	0	0
Hamilton County	0	0	0	0	0	0	0	0	0	0
Hardee County	0	0	0	0	0	0	0	0	0	0
Hendry County	0	0	0	0	0	0	0	0	0	0
Hernando County	0	0	0	0	0	0	0	0	0	0
Highlands County	0	0	0	0	0	0	0	0	0	0
Hillsborough County	0	0	0	0	0	0	0	0	0	0
Holmes County	0	0	0	0	0	0	0	0	0	0
Indian River County	0	0	0	0	0	0	0	0	0	0
Jackson County	0	0	0	0	0	0	0	0	0	0
Jefferson County	0	0	0	0	0	0	0	0	0	0
Lafayette County	0	0	0	0	0	0	0	0	0	0
Lake County	0	0	0	0	0	0	0	0	0	0
Lee County	0	0	0	0	0	0	0	0	0	0
Leon County	0	0	0	0	0	0	0	0	0	0
Levy County	0	0	0	0	0	0	0	0	0	0
Liberty County	0	0	0	0	0	0	0	0	0	0
Madison County	0	0	0	0	0	0	0	0	0	0
Manatee County	0	0	0	0	0	0	0	0	0	0
Marion County	0	0	0	0	0	0	0	0	0	0
Martin County	0	0	0	0	0	0	0	0	0	0
Miami-Dade County	0	0	0	0	0	0	0	0	0	0
Monroe County	0	0	0	0	0	0	0	0	0	0
Nassau County	0	0	0	0	0	0	0	0	0	0
Okaloosa County	0	0	0	0	0	0	0	0	0	0
Okeechobee County	0	0	0	0	0	0	0	0	0	0

Table 11. Offenses Known to Law Enforcement, by Selected State, Tribal, and Other Agencies, 2017—Continued

(Number.)

State/other agency unit/office	Violent crime	Murder and nonnegligent manslaughter	Rape[1]	Robbery	Aggravated assault	Property crime	Burglary	Larceny-theft	Motor vehicle theft	Arson[2]
Orange County	0	0	0	0	0	0	0	0	0	0
Osceola County	0	0	0	0	0	0	0	0	0	0
Palm Beach County	0	0	0	0	0	0	0	0	0	0
Pasco County	0	0	0	0	0	0	0	0	0	0
Pinellas County	0	0	0	0	0	0	0	0	0	0
Polk County	0	0	0	0	0	0	0	0	0	0
Putnam County	0	0	0	0	0	0	0	0	0	0
Santa Rosa County	0	0	0	0	0	0	0	0	0	0
Sarasota County	0	0	0	0	0	0	0	0	0	0
Seminole County	0	0	0	0	0	0	0	0	0	0
St. Johns County	0	0	0	0	0	0	0	0	0	0
St. Lucie County	0	0	0	0	0	0	0	0	0	0
Sumter County	0	0	0	0	0	0	0	0	0	0
Suwannee County	0	0	0	0	0	0	0	0	0	0
Taylor County	0	0	0	0	0	0	0	0	0	0
Union County	0	0	0	0	0	0	0	0	0	0
Volusia County	0	0	0	0	0	0	0	0	0	0
Wakulla County	0	0	0	0	0	0	0	0	0	0
Walton County	0	0	0	0	0	0	0	0	0	0
Washington County	0	0	0	0	0	0	0	0	0	0
Highway Patrol										
Alachua County	9	0	0	0	9	3	0	0	3	0
Baker County	3	0	0	0	3	0	0	0	0	0
Bay County	0	0	0	0	0	0	0	0	0	0
Bradford County	0	0	0	0	0	0	0	0	0	0
Brevard County	7	0	0	0	7	0	0	0	0	0
Broward County	12	0	0	0	12	6	0	0	6	0
Calhoun County	2	0	0	0	2	0	0	0	2	0
Charlotte County	0	0	0	0	0	2	0	0	0	0
Citrus County	0	0	0	0	0	0	0	0	0	0
Clay County	0	0	0	0	0	0	0	0	0	0
Collier County	5	0	0	0	5	8	0	2	6	0
Columbia County	0	0	0	0	0	0	0	0	0	0
DeSoto County	0	0	0	0	0	0	0	0	0	0
Dixie County	0	0	0	0	0	0	0	0	0	0
Duval County	2	0	0	0	2	9	0	2	7	0
Escambia County	8	0	0	0	8	3	0	3	0	0
Flagler County	0	0	0	0	0	0	0	0	0	0
Franklin County	0	0	0	0	0	0	0	0	0	0
Gadsden County	1	0	0	0	1	3	0	0	3	0
Gilchrist County	0	0	0	0	0	0	0	0	0	0
Glades County	0	0	0	0	0	0	0	0	0	0
Gulf County	0	0	0	0	0	1	0	0	1	0
Hamilton County	0	0	0	0	0	0	0	0	0	0
Hardee County	0	0	0	0	0	0	0	0	0	0
Hendry County	0	0	0	0	0	0	0	0	0	0
Hernando County	0	0	0	0	0	4	0	4	0	0
Highlands County	0	0	0	0	0	0	0	0	0	0
Hillsborough County	0	0	0	0	0	7	0	5	2	0
Holmes County	0	0	0	0	0	3	0	0	3	0
Indian River County	0	0	0	0	0	2	0	0	2	0
Jackson County	7	0	0	0	7	0	0	0	0	0
Jefferson County	0	0	0	0	0	1	0	0	1	0
Lafayette County	0	0	0	0	0	0	0	0	0	0
Lake County	0	0	0	0	0	0	0	0	0	0
Lee County	0	0	0	0	0	3	0	0	3	0
Leon County	4	0	0	0	4	4	0	2	2	0
Levy County	0	0	0	0	0	0	0	0	0	0
Liberty County	0	0	0	0	0	0	0	0	0	0
Madison County	0	0	0	0	0	3	0	0	3	0
Manatee County	0	0	0	0	0	0	0	0	0	0
Marion County	2	0	0	0	2	1	0	1	0	0
Martin County	3	0	0	0	3	1	0	0	1	0
Miami-Dade County	9	0	0	0	9	12	0	8	4	0
Monroe County	0	0	0	0	0	0	0	0	0	0
Nassau County	0	0	0	0	0	0	0	0	0	0
Okaloosa County	2	0	0	0	2	0	0	0	0	0
Okeechobee County	1	0	0	0	1	1	0	0	1	0
Orange County	5	0	0	0	5	3	0	3	0	0
Osceola County	5	0	0	0	5	1	0	1	0	0
Palm Beach County	11	0	0	0	11	6	0	0	6	0
Pasco County	4	0	0	0	4	2	0	0	2	0
Pinellas County	0	0	0	0	0	1	0	0	1	0
Polk County	3	0	0	0	3	2	0	0	2	0
Putnam County	0	0	0	0	0	2	0	0	2	0
Santa Rosa County	0	0	0	0	0	0	0	0	0	0
Sarasota County	8	0	0	0	8	0	0	0	0	0
Seminole County	0	0	0	0	0	0	0	0	0	0
St. Johns County	0	0	0	0	0	1	0	0	1	0
St. Lucie County	0	0	0	0	0	10	0	6	4	0
Sumter County	2	0	0	0	2	3	0	2	1	0
Suwannee County	0	0	0	0	0	0	0	0	0	0
Taylor County	0	0	0	0	0	1	0	1	0	0

Table 11. Offenses Known to Law Enforcement, by Selected State, Tribal, and Other Agencies, 2017—Continued

(Number.)

State/other agency unit/office	Violent crime	Murder and nonnegligent manslaughter	Rape[1]	Robbery	Aggravated assault	Property crime	Burglary	Larceny-theft	Motor vehicle theft	Arson[2]
Union County	0	0	0	0	0	0	0	0	0	0
Volusia County	1	0	0	0	1	0	0	0	0	0
Wakulla County	0	0	0	0	0	1	0	1	0	0
Walton County	2	0	0	0	2	4	0	2	2	0
Washington County	0	0	0	0	0	0	0	0	0	0
Tribal Agencies										
Miccosukee Tribal	12	0	2	1	9	113	4	102	7	0
Seminole Tribal	61	0	10	21	30	541	39	455	47	0
Other Agencies										
Duval County Schools	64	0	7	7	50	417	104	306	7	1
Florida School for the Deaf and Blind	0	0	0	0	0	0	0	0	0	0
Fort Lauderdale Airport	7	5	0	1	1	331	12	272	47	0
Jacksonville Aviation Authority	0	0	0	0	0	107	1	28	78	0
Lee County Port Authority	0	0	0	0	0	32	0	32	0	0
Melbourne International Airport	0	0	0	0	0	2	0	1	1	0
Miami-Dade County Public Schools	110	0	8	34	68	850	322	509	19	8
Northwest Florida Beaches International Airport	0	0	0	0	0	3	0	1	2	0
Palm Beach County School District	87	0	6	30	51	595	42	546	7	1
Port Everglades	23	0	9	1	13	56	2	53	1	0
Sarasota-Manatee Airport Authority	0	0	0	0	0	17	0	4	13	0
St. Petersburg-Clearwater International Airport	0	0	0	0	0	7	0	7	0	0
Tampa International Airport	8	0	0	0	8	247	10	122	115	0
Volusia County Beach Safety	7	0	0	2	5	108	3	103	2	0
GEORGIA										
State Agencies										
Georgia Department of Public Safety	3	0	0	0	3	23	1	21	1	
Georgia Department of Transportation, Office of Investigations	0	0	0	0	0	0	0	0	0	0
Georgia Forestry Commission	0	0	0	0	0	0	0	0	0	50
Georgia Public Safety Training Center	0	0	0	0	0	0	0	0	0	0
Georgia World Congress	5	0	0	4	1	233	0	229	4	0
Ports Authority, Savannah	0	0	0	0	0	9	0	9	0	0
State Board of Workers Compensation, Fraud Investigation Division	0	0	0	0	0	0	0	0	0	0
State Patrol, Jekyll Island	1	0	1	0	0	42	1	38	3	
Other Agencies										
Appling County Board of Education	0	0	0	0	0	3	1	2	0	0
Atlanta Public Schools	29	0	2	17	10	375	50	308	17	3
Augusta Board of Education	1	0	0	1	0	113	7	106	0	
Chatham County Board of Education	4	0	0	1	3	72	4	66	2	0
Cherokee County Board of Education	1	0	1	0	0	68	3	65	0	0
Cherokee County Marshal	0	0	0	0	0	0	0	0	0	0
Cobb County Board of Education	61	0	0	7	54	355	20	332	3	1
Decatur County Schools	0	0	0	0	0	2	0	2	0	0
Dougherty County Board of Education	13	0	1	0	12	34	2	32	0	0
Fayette County Marshal	0	0	0	0	0	0	0	0	0	0
Forsyth County Fire Investigation Unit	0	0	0	0	0	0	0	0	0	5
Fulton County Marshal	2	0	0	0	2	21	1	20	0	0
Fulton County School System	12	0	3	2	7	190	21	157	12	3
Glynn County School System	3	0	0	0	3	52	2	50	0	0
Hall County Marshal	0	0	0	0	0	0	0	0	0	0
Hartsfield-Jackson Atlanta International Airport	9	0	2	1	6	493	1	341	151	0
Metropolitan Atlanta Rapid Transit Authority	208	3	1	47	157	294	5	260	29	5
Stone Mountain Park	2	0	0	1	1	12	1	10	1	0
Twiggs County Board of Education	1	0	0	0	1	5	0	5	0	0
Washington County Board of Education	0	0	0	0	0	0	0	0	0	0
IDAHO										
Tribal Agencies										
Coeur d'Alene Tribal	27	1	5	0	21	64	31	32	1	0
Fort Hall Tribal	72	2	10	4	56	101	8	69	24	1
ILLINOIS										
State Agencies										
Illinois Department of Natural Resources	1	0	0	0	1	6	1	5	0	0
Illinois State Police	220	16	53	10	141	95	15	66	14	4
Secretary of State Police	1	0	0	0	1	16	0	7	9	0
Other Agencies	0	0	0	0	0	0	0	0	0	340
Alton & Southern Railway	0	0	0	0	0	6	3	3	0	0
Belt Railway	0	0	0	0	0	6	0	6	0	0
Canadian National Railway	0	0	0	0	0	26	0	26	0	0
Canton Park District	0	0	0	0	0	0	0	0	0	0
Capitol Airport Authority	0	0	0	0	0	0	0	0	0	0
Cook County Forest Preserve	13	0	3	3	7	101	2	98	1	0
Crystal Lake Park District	2	0	1	1	0	8	0	8	0	0
Decatur Park District	16	0	4	4	8	19	6	12	1	4
DuPage County Forest Preserve	7	0	3	4	0	15	0	15	0	0
Fon du Lac Park District	1	0	0	0	1	3	0	3	0	0

Table 11. Offenses Known to Law Enforcement, by Selected State, Tribal, and Other Agencies, 2017—Continued

(Number.)

State/other agency unit/office	Violent crime	Murder and nonnegligent manslaughter	Rape[1]	Robbery	Aggravated assault	Property crime	Burglary	Larceny-theft	Motor vehicle theft	Arson[2]
Fox Valley Park District	3	0	1	2	0	46	2	44	0	0
Indiana Harbor Belt Railroad	0	0	0	0	0	8	7	1	0	0
Kane County Forest Preserve	0	0	0	0	0	8	1	7	0	0
Lake County Forest Preserve	0	0	0	0	0	15	1	14	0	1
McHenry County Conservation District	3	0	2	1	0	7	0	6	1	0
Naperville Park District	0	0	0	0	0	17	1	16	0	3
Norfolk Southern Railway										
Cook County	0	0	0	0	0	470	347	123	0	0
Macon County	0	0	0	0	0	7	0	7	0	0
Madison County	0	0	0	0	0	4	2	2	0	0
Pekin Park District	0	0	0	0	0	2	0	2	0	0
Rockford Metro Centre	2	0	0	0	2	1	0	1	0	0
Rockford Park District	49	0	2	8	39	50	22	26	2	4
Springfield Park District	22	2	3	2	15	25	9	13	3	2
Terminal Railroad Association	0	0	0	0	0	1	1	0	0	0
Tri-County Drug Enforcement Narcotics Team	0	0	0	0	0	0	0	0	0	0
Union Pacific Railroad, Cook County	0	0	0	0	0	332	83	249	0	1
INDIANA										
State Agencies										
Indiana State Excise Police	2	0	0	1	1	8	0	8	0	0
Northern Indiana Commuter Transportation District	0	0	0	0	0	30	0	26	4	0
State Police										
Adams County	2	0	1	0	1	1	1	0	0	0
Allen County	3	0	1	0	2	25	1	22	2	0
Bartholomew County	6	0	1	1	4	20	1	13	6	0
Benton County	4	0	2	0	2	2	1	1	0	0
Boone County	3	0	0	0	3	2	0	2	0	0
Brown County	1	0	1	0	0	1	0	0	1	0
Clark County	7	0	3	0	4	49	5	33	11	0
Clay County	6	0	0	0	6	6	0	5	1	0
Crawford County	6	0	0	1	5	16	4	9	3	0
Daviess County	0	0	0	0	0	10	3	7	0	0
Dearborn County	6	1	2	0	3	5	1	2	2	0
Decatur County	1	0	0	0	1	6	0	6	0	0
Delaware County	8	0	0	0	8	8	1	5	2	0
Dubois County	5	0	3	0	2	32	5	25	2	0
Elkhart County	4	0	1	0	3	17	1	11	5	0
Floyd County	3	0	0	0	3	15	2	4	9	0
Fountain County	2	0	0	0	2	1	0	1	0	0
Franklin County	2	0	0	0	2	5	1	3	1	0
Fulton County	4	0	1	0	3	5	0	4	1	0
Gibson County	6	0	2	0	4	10	2	6	2	0
Grant County	0	0	0	0	0	3	0	3	0	0
Greene County	9	0	1	0	8	8	2	4	2	0
Hancock County	1	0	0	0	1	5	0	3	2	0
Harrison County	0	0	0	0	0	14	1	12	1	0
Henry County	1	0	0	0	1	9	1	8	0	0
Howard County	0	0	0	0	0	7	2	4	1	0
Huntington County	6	0	2	1	3	10	1	8	1	0
Jackson County	4	0	1	0	3	16	5	6	5	0
Jasper County	2	0	0	0	2	4	0	0	4	0
Jefferson County	8	0	5	0	3	11	4	5	2	1
Jennings County	10	0	1	0	9	8	2	4	2	1
Johnson County	0	0	0	0	0	7	0	3	4	0
Knox County	1	0	0	0	1	13	3	7	3	0
Kosciusko County	1	0	1	0	0	10	1	7	2	0
LaGrange County	3	0	1	1	1	10	1	7	2	0
Lake County	6	1	1	0	4	64	0	34	30	0
Lawrence County	6	0	3	0	3	26	7	13	6	0
Madison County	1	1	0	0	0	18	2	13	3	0
Marion County	36	0	8	5	23	299	1	118	180	0
Marshall County	11	0	1	0	10	12	0	10	2	1
Martin County	7	0	2	0	5	8	3	4	1	0
Miami County	15	0	3	0	12	17	5	10	2	0
Monroe County	9	0	5	0	4	43	5	32	6	0
Morgan County	2	0	0	1	1	43	1	9	33	0
Noble County	1	1	0	0	0	4	0	4	0	0
Orange County	11	0	6	2	3	6	0	6	0	0
Perry County	4	1	1	0	2	6	2	4	0	0
Pike County	10	0	2	0	8	7	0	6	1	0
Porter County	0	0	0	0	0	14	0	11	3	0
Posey County	3	0	0	0	3	10	3	7	0	0
Putnam County	3	0	2	0	1	11	1	5	5	0
Ripley County	13	0	2	1	10	42	12	28	2	0
Scott County	2	0	0	0	2	19	6	8	5	0
Shelby County	1	0	0	0	1	7	0	4	3	0
Steuben County	1	0	0	0	1	3	1	2	0	1
St. Joseph County	11	0	1	0	10	20	1	12	7	1
Sullivan County	8	0	2	0	6	6	1	5	0	1
Tippecanoe County	5	0	1	0	4	11	1	6	4	0

Table 11. Offenses Known to Law Enforcement, by Selected State, Tribal, and Other Agencies, 2017—Continued

(Number.)

State/other agency unit/office	Violent crime	Murder and nonnegligent manslaughter	Rape[1]	Robbery	Aggravated assault	Property crime	Burglary	Larceny-theft	Motor vehicle theft	Arson[2]
Tipton County	0	0	0	0	0	0	0	0	0	0
Union County	2	0	0	0	2	1	0	1	0	0
Vanderburgh County	0	0	0	0	0	14	1	13	0	0
Vermillion County	1	0	1	0	0	3	0	3	0	0
Vigo County	5	0	2	0	3	34	8	23	3	1
Wabash County	2	0	0	0	2	6	2	4	0	0
Warrick County	1	0	1	0	0	7	0	5	2	0
Washington County	12	7	1	0	4	15	5	7	3	1
Wayne County	5	0	0	1	4	9	0	7	2	0
White County	3	0	1	0	2	4	0	4	0	0
KANSAS										
State Agencies										
Kansas Alcoholic Beverage Control	0	0	0	0	0	0	0	0	0	0
Kansas Bureau of Investigation	12	3	0	1	8	2	0	2	0	1
Kansas Department of Wildlife and Parks	2	0	0	0	2	21	4	16	1	0
Kansas Highway Patrol										
Troop B	13	0	0	1	12	15	1	8	6	0
Troop D	3	0	0	0	3	3	0	1	2	0
Troop F	7	1	0	0	6	11	1	8	2	0
Troop H	0	0	0	0	0	0	0	0	0	0
Kansas Lottery Security Division	0	0	0	0	0	0	0	0	0	0
Kansas State Fire Marshall	0	0	0	0	0	1	0	1	0	20
Tribal Agencies										
Kickapoo Tribal	4	0	0	1	3	22	19	0	3	0
Sac and Fox Tribal	1	0	0	0	1	13	0	13	0	0
Other Agencies										
Johnson County Park	3	0	0	0	3	53	1	50	2	1
Shawnee Mission Public Schools	1	0	0	0	1	2	0	1	1	1
Topeka Fire Department, Arson Investigation	0	0	0	0	0	2	2	0	0	39
Unified School District	0	0	0	0	0	2	0	2	0	0
Goddard	2	0	0	0	2	14	0	14	0	1
Seaman	0	0	0	0	0	2	1	1	0	0
Shawnee Heights	0	0	0	0	0	0	0	0	0	0
KENTUCKY										
State Agencies										
Fish and Wildlife Enforcement	2	0	0	0	2	5	0	5	0	0
Motor Vehicle Enforcement	0	0	0	0	0	7	2	4	1	0
Park Security	0	0	0	0	0	9	1	8	0	1
State Police										
Ashland	51	2	31	6	12	188	73	96	19	2
Bowling Green	37	3	19	0	15	131	63	56	12	7
Campbellsburg	47	4	23	4	16	201	79	104	18	4
Columbia	60	2	47	0	11	137	66	59	12	12
Drug Enforcement Area [2]	2	0	0	0	2	3	0	1	2	0
Dry Ridge	34	1	26	3	4	184	77	84	23	3
Electronic Crimes	1	0	1	0	0	0	0	0	0	0
Elizabethtown	68	6	43	2	17	164	43	89	32	1
Frankfort	28	2	12	1	13	111	24	70	17	15
Harlan	79	2	30	4	43	267	94	131	42	7
Hazard	71	2	19	6	44	256	119	84	53	3
Henderson	29	0	15	2	12	149	52	83	14	3
London	96	14	36	2	44	251	96	103	52	10
Madisonville	47	3	29	5	10	117	41	57	19	2
Mayfield	60	1	35	3	21	212	100	97	15	4
Morehead	57	1	35	2	19	270	128	103	39	6
Pikeville	84	4	28	14	38	297	127	104	66	9
Richmond	79	8	39	1	31	303	126	137	40	11
Vehicle Investigations	0	0	0	0	0	5	0	3	2	0
West Drug Enforcement Branch	1	0	1	0	0	11	2	8	1	0
Other Agencies										
Barren County Drug Task Force	0	0	0	0	0	0	0	0	0	0
Cincinnati-Northern Kentucky International Airport	1	0	0	0	1	72	0	44	28	0
Fayette County Schools	5	0	0	0	5	71	4	66	1	1
Greater Hardin County Narcotics Task Force	0	0	0	0	0	2	0	2	0	0
Jefferson County School District	13	0	0	5	8	74	37	36	1	1
Louisville Fire Department Arson Division	0	0	0	0	0	0	0	0	0	173
Louisville Regional Airport Authority	0	0	0	0	0	41	1	18	22	0
Montgomery County School District	0	0	0	0	0	5	1	4	0	0
Northern Kentucky Drug Strike Force	0	0	0	0	0	0	0	0	0	0
Pennyrile Narcotics Task Force	0	0	0	0	0	4	0	3	1	0
South Central Kentucky Drug Task Force	0	0	0	0	0	1	0	1	0	0
LOUISIANA										
State Agencies										
Tensas Basin Levee District	1	0	0	0	1	0	0	0	0	0
Tribal Agencies										
Chitimacha Tribal	4	0	0	0	4	68	9	56	3	0
Coushatta Tribal	3	0	1	0	2	41	0	40	1	0
Tunica-Biloxi Tribal	6	0	3	0	3	128	4	122	2	0

Table 11. Offenses Known to Law Enforcement, by Selected State, Tribal, and Other Agencies, 2017—Continued

(Number.)

State/other agency unit/office	Violent crime	Murder and nonnegligent manslaughter	Rape[1]	Robbery	Aggravated assault	Property crime	Burglary	Larceny-theft	Motor vehicle theft	Arson[2]
MAINE										
State Agencies										
Bureau of Capitol Police	2	0	0	0	2	6	0	6	0	0
Drug Enforcement Agency	0	0	0	0	0	2	0	2	0	0
State Fire Marshal	0	0	0	0	0	4	2	2	0	102
State Police	147	10	36	10	91	1,214	385	759	70	1
Tribal Agencies										
Passamaquoddy Indian Township	6	0	0	0	6	23	4	19	0	2
Passamaquoddy Pleasant Point Tribal	2	0	0	0	2	15	12	2	1	0
Penobscot Nation	0	0	0	0	0	0	0	0	0	0
MARYLAND										
State Agencies										
Comptroller of the Treasury, Field Enforcement Division	0	0	0	0	0	0	0	0	0	0
Department of Public Safety and Correctional Services, Internal Investigations Unit	386	0	1	0	385	2	0	2	0	0
General Services										
Annapolis, Anne Arundel County	0	0	0	0	0	3	0	3	0	0
Baltimore City	1	0	0	1	0	22	0	22	0	0
Maryland State Police Statewide	4	0	0	0	4	9	1	8	0	0
Natural Resources Police	10	0	0	0	10	111	8	100	3	16
Springfield Hospital	0	0	0	0	0	4	0	4	0	0
State Fire Marshal	0	0	0	0	0	4	2	2	0	0
State Police										
Allegany County	39	1	4	6	28	475	100	359	16	7
Anne Arundel County	10	0	1	0	9	32	2	25	5	0
Baltimore City	3	0	0	0	3	0	0	0	0	0
Baltimore County	20	0	0	2	18	36	4	27	5	0
Calvert County	21	0	0	4	17	71	14	55	2	3
Caroline County	9	0	0	2	7	31	11	11	9	1
Carroll County	56	0	0	6	50	326	64	239	23	10
Cecil County	49	0	3	3	43	488	106	337	45	0
Charles County	3	0	0	0	3	6	0	4	2	2
Dorchester County	4	0	0	0	4	35	9	22	4	0
Garrett County	9	0	1	1	7	92	41	50	1	0
Harford County	46	0	0	10	36	199	22	167	10	20
Howard County	6	0	0	1	5	10	0	6	4	0
Kent County	3	0	0	0	3	5	0	4	1	1
Montgomery County	3	0	0	0	3	1	0	1	0	0
Prince George's County	2	0	0	0	2	27	0	11	16	1
Queen Anne's County	26	0	1	1	24	90	17	65	8	8
Somerset County	23	1	3	1	18	124	32	80	12	2
St. Mary's County	20	0	1	3	16	196	26	165	5	19
Talbot County	5	0	0	0	5	20	9	7	4	3
Washington County	23	0	0	5	18	131	33	86	12	3
Wicomico County	57	0	3	11	43	197	79	104	14	3
Worcester County	12	0	2	2	8	117	14	100	3	0
Transit Administration	67	0	0	34	33	121	0	115	6	0
Transportation Authority	32	0	0	1	31	177	6	143	28	0
Other Agencies										
Maryland-National Capital Park Police										
Montgomery County	20	0	1	11	8	110	9	99	2	2
Prince George's County	55	2	2	27	24	136	8	122	6	0
MASSACHUSETTS										
State Agencies										
Division of Law Enforcement, Environmental Police	8	0	0	1	7	13	3	8	2	1
Massachusetts Bay Transportation Authority										
Middlesex County	22	0	1	6	15	156	3	148	5	
Suffolk County	227	0	0	110	117	251	10	232	9	
State Police										
Berkshire County	1	0	0	1	0	55	27	27	1	
Bristol County	6	0	0	0	6	6	0	0	6	
Franklin County	5	0	0	0	5	0	0	0	0	
Hampden County	20	0	0	0	20	11	0	4	7	
Hampshire County	8	0	0	0	8	1	1	0	0	
Middlesex County	9	0	0	0	9	5	0	1	4	
Norfolk County	33	0	0	1	32	12	0	5	7	
Worcester County	7	0	1	0	6	0	0	0	0	
Tribal Agencies										
Wampanoag Tribe of Gay Head	0	0	0	0	0	0	0	0	0	0
Other Agencies										
Massachusetts General Hospital	8	0	0	2	6	137	5	132	0	
MICHIGAN										
State Agencies										
State Police										
Alcona County	3	0	2	0	1	20	11	9	0	0
Alger County	19	1	6	0	12	32	17	14	1	0

Table 11. Offenses Known to Law Enforcement, by Selected State, Tribal, and Other Agencies, 2017—Continued

(Number.)

State/other agency unit/office	Violent crime	Murder and nonnegligent manslaughter	Rape[1]	Robbery	Aggravated assault	Property crime	Burglary	Larceny-theft	Motor vehicle theft	Arson[2]
Allegan County	63	1	35	0	27	231	66	138	27	2
Alpena County	39	2	18	2	17	168	27	139	2	1
Antrim County	8	0	3	0	5	14	5	9	0	0
Arenac County	8	0	5	0	3	7	3	4	0	0
Baraga County	10	1	2	0	7	13	5	7	1	0
Barry County	41	0	17	1	23	163	68	85	10	6
Bay County	48	0	23	4	21	215	53	142	20	0
Benzie County	13	0	2	0	11	7	1	5	1	1
Berrien County	51	1	24	2	24	111	28	75	8	0
Branch County	43	0	12	0	31	109	44	46	19	2
Calhoun County	37	0	15	1	21	95	28	53	14	0
Cass County	8	1	7	0	0	37	5	27	5	0
Charlevoix County	5	0	4	0	1	10	2	8	0	0
Cheboygan County	11	0	3	1	7	21	6	15	0	0
Chippewa County	41	0	11	0	30	52	18	33	1	1
Clare County	17	0	15	0	2	21	9	9	3	0
Clinton County	4	0	4	0	0	31	11	20	0	0
Crawford County	11	0	9	0	2	20	8	12	0	0
Delta County	8	0	4	0	4	35	18	14	3	0
Dickinson County	5	0	4	0	1	21	5	16	0	0
Eaton County	29	0	14	0	15	83	34	44	5	1
Emmet County	15	0	11	0	4	56	8	47	1	0
Genesee County	56	1	18	3	34	91	32	51	8	2
Gladwin County	14	0	14	0	0	4	3	1	0	0
Gogebic County	5	0	1	0	4	18	2	15	1	0
Grand Traverse County	17	0	6	0	11	46	6	37	3	0
Gratiot County	23	0	14	0	9	13	2	11	0	0
Hillsdale County	32	1	17	0	14	95	34	55	6	0
Houghton County	14	0	9	0	5	78	15	60	3	1
Huron County	3	0	2	0	1	9	3	5	1	0
Ingham County	23	1	15	0	7	54	16	33	5	0
Ionia County	42	1	12	0	29	122	31	83	8	3
Iosco County	29	1	7	0	21	140	63	70	7	3
Iron County	14	0	3	1	10	26	5	19	2	1
Isabella County	28	0	23	2	3	151	40	107	4	0
Jackson County	76	5	30	0	41	147	50	78	19	2
Kalamazoo County	37	0	12	5	20	72	13	50	9	1
Kalkaska County	20	0	15	0	5	25	10	12	3	0
Kent County	27	3	13	0	11	15	4	7	4	1
Lake County	12	0	11	0	1	4	2	1	1	1
Lapeer County	27	0	10	0	17	79	21	43	15	1
Leelanau County	4	0	1	0	3	16	0	15	1	0
Lenawee County	64	0	23	1	40	77	17	52	8	0
Livingston County	51	1	20	3	27	173	28	131	14	0
Luce County	14	0	3	0	11	58	37	15	6	0
Mackinac County	6	0	3	0	3	23	4	19	0	1
Macomb County	55	1	16	1	37	56	15	35	6	1
Manistee County	23	0	11	0	12	63	18	45	0	0
Marquette County	68	0	15	0	53	146	33	98	15	3
Mason County	29	0	10	0	19	48	9	39	0	0
Mecosta County	19	0	8	0	11	45	8	36	1	0
Menominee County	10	0	5	0	5	21	9	11	1	0
Midland County	8	0	7	0	1	6	1	3	2	0
Missaukee County	5	0	1	0	4	10	5	3	2	0
Monroe County	59	0	21	1	37	154	45	86	23	3
Montcalm County	107	1	41	3	62	249	102	125	22	4
Montmorency County	3	1	2	0	0	14	5	8	1	0
Muskegon County	63	1	30	1	31	269	70	178	21	1
Newaygo County	51	0	26	0	25	134	50	75	9	2
Oakland County	93	2	23	13	55	186	42	115	29	2
Oceana County	12	0	4	0	8	89	17	68	4	0
Ogemaw County	46	0	20	2	24	132	52	69	11	2
Ontonagon County	3	0	1	0	2	7	3	4	0	0
Osceola County	28	0	16	0	12	28	18	8	2	0
Oscoda County	2	0	2	0	0	4	1	3	0	0
Otsego County	24	0	11	0	13	78	27	47	4	0
Ottawa County	2	0	1	1	0	4	0	4	0	0
Presque Isle County	6	0	3	0	3	2	1	1	0	0
Roscommon County	21	1	8	1	11	30	7	19	4	0
Saginaw County	93	2	30	4	57	107	26	67	14	4
Sanilac County	17	0	10	0	7	50	27	19	4	1
Schoolcraft County	5	0	1	0	4	43	16	27	0	1
Shiawassee County	65	3	29	2	31	223	54	151	18	0
St. Clair County	20	0	14	0	6	30	12	15	3	0
St. Joseph County	40	0	21	2	17	143	73	54	16	2
Tuscola County	33	1	13	0	19	77	32	40	5	0
Van Buren County	74	1	20	0	53	168	75	77	16	2
Washtenaw County	42	0	15	3	24	120	43	56	21	6
Wayne County	94	3	30	3	58	129	1	106	22	0
Wexford County	29	0	19	1	9	117	28	84	5	0
Tribal Agencies										
Gun Lake Tribal	1	0	0	0	1	117	1	113	3	0
Lac Vieux Desert Tribal	15	0	0	0	15	2	0	2	0	0

Table 11. Offenses Known to Law Enforcement, by Selected State, Tribal, and Other Agencies, 2017—Continued

(Number.)

State/other agency unit/office	Violent crime	Murder and nonnegligent manslaughter	Rape[1]	Robbery	Aggravated assault	Property crime	Burglary	Larceny-theft	Motor vehicle theft	Arson[2]
Little River Band of Ottawa Indians	1	0	0	0	1	24	1	23	0	0
Nottawaseppi Huron Band of Potawatomi	14	0	1	1	12	113	3	108	2	0
Other Agencies										
Bishop International Airport	1	0	0	0	1	8	0	1	7	0
Capitol Region Airport Authority	0	0	0	0	0	0	0	0	0	0
Genesee County Parks and Recreation	4	0	1	0	3	14	2	10	2	1
Gerald R. Ford International Airport	0	0	0	0	0	6	0	5	1	0
Huron-Clinton Metropolitan Authority										
Hudson Mills Metropark	0	0	0	0	0	3	0	3	0	0
Kensington Metropark	0	0	0	0	0	8	0	8	0	0
Lower Huron Metropark	1	0	0	0	1	11	0	10	1	0
Stony Creek Metropark	1	0	0	0	1	11	2	9	0	0
Wayne County Airport	2	0	0	0	2	264	0	131	133	0
MINNESOTA										
State Agencies										
Bureau of Criminal Apprehension	0	0	0	0	0	0	0	0	0	0
Capitol Security, St. Paul	0	0	0	0	0	14	0	14	0	0
Department of Natural Resources Enforcement Division	0	0	0	0	0	0	0	0	0	0
Minnesota State Patrol	0	0	0	0	0	0	0	0	0	0
State Patrol										
Brainerd	0	0	0	0	0	0	0	0	0	0
Detroit Lakes	0	0	0	0	0	0	0	0	0	0
Duluth	0	0	0	0	0	0	0	0	0	0
Golden Valley	0	0	0	0	0	0	0	0	0	0
Mankato	0	0	0	0	0	0	0	0	0	0
Marshall	0	0	0	0	0	0	0	0	0	0
Oakdale	0	0	0	0	0	0	0	0	0	0
Rochester	0	0	0	0	0	0	0	0	0	0
St. Cloud	0	0	0	0	0	0	0	0	0	0
Thief River Falls	0	0	0	0	0	0	0	0	0	0
Virginia	0	0	0	0	0	0	0	0	0	0
Tribal Agencies										
Fond du Lac Tribal	27	0	4	3	20	363	30	314	19	0
Mille Lacs Tribal	21	0	1	3	17	87	15	60	12	0
Upper Sioux Community	0	0	0	0	0	1	0	1	0	0
White Earth Tribal	23	0	4	2	17	228	44	164	20	3
Other Agencies										
Minneapolis-St. Paul International Airport	3	0	0	1	2	352	1	315	36	0
Three Rivers Park District	2	0	0	0	2	55	2	53	0	0
MISSISSIPPI										
State Agencies										
Department of Marine Resources[4]		0		0	0	1	0	1	0	0
State Capitol Police[4]		0		1	1	23	14	9	0	0
Tribal Agencies										
Choctaw Tribal	166	1	6	0	159	256	20	235	1	2
Other Agencies										
Singing River Health System[4]		0		0	0	7	0	6	1	
MISSOURI										
State Agencies										
Capitol Police	0	0	0	0	0	38	2	36	0	0
Department of Conservation	0	0	0	0	0	3	0	3	0	0
Department of Revenue, Compliance and Investigation Bureau	0	0	0	0	0	0	0	0	0	0
Department of Social Services, State Technical Assistance Team	1	0	1	0	0	0	0	0	0	0
Division of Alcohol and Tobacco Control	0	0	0	0	0	0	0	0	0	0
Gaming Commission, Enforcement Division	9	0	0	1	8	165	0	165	0	0
State Highway Patrol										
Jefferson City	8	1	1	0	6	37	1	31	5	0
Kirkwood	4	0	0	0	4	7	1	1	5	0
Lee's Summit	12	1	4	0	7	11	1	3	7	0
Macon	9	1	2	0	6	6	0	4	2	0
Poplar Bluff	9	1	1	0	7	2	2	0	0	0
Rolla	7	0	0	0	7	8	1	2	5	0
Springfield	5	2	1	0	2	54	1	34	19	0
St. Joseph	7	1	1	0	5	5	1	0	4	0
Willow Springs	4	0	0	0	4	1	0	0	1	0
State Park Rangers	0	0	0	0	0	71	3	68	0	0
Other Agencies										
Clay County Drug Task Force	0	0	0	0	0	0	0	0	0	
Clay County Park Authority	6	0	0	0	6	4	0	4	0	0
Jackson County Drug Task Force	0	0	0	0	0	0	0	0	0	0
Jackson County Park Rangers	0	0	0	0	0	3	0	3	0	0
Kansas City International Airport	4	0	0	1	3	64	2	40	22	0
Lambert-St. Louis International Airport	2	0	0	0	2	99	0	95	4	0
Platte County Multi-Jurisdictional Enforcement Group	0	0	0	0	0	0	0	0	0	0
Springfield-Branson Airport	0	0	0	0	0	9	0	5	4	0

Table 11. Offenses Known to Law Enforcement, by Selected State, Tribal, and Other Agencies, 2017—Continued

(Number.)

State/other agency unit/office	Violent crime	Murder and nonnegligent manslaughter	Rape[1]	Robbery	Aggravated assault	Property crime	Burglary	Larceny-theft	Motor vehicle theft	Arson[2]
Springfield-Greene County Park Rangers	1	0	1	0	0	11	5	5	1	0
St. Charles County Park Rangers	0	0	0	0	0	21	0	21	0	0
Terminal Railroad	0	0	0	0	0	0	0	0	0	0
Western Missouri Cyber Crimes Task Force	0	0	0	0	0	0	0	0	0	0
MONTANA										
Tribal Agencies										
Blackfeet Agency	102	2	4	36	60	94	52	0	42	0
Crow Agency	57	4	11	1	41	179	26	102	51	3
Fort Belknap Tribal	17	0	1	0	16	59	8	46	5	0
Fort Peck Assiniboine and Sioux Tribes	24	0	4	1	19	41	10	26	5	4
Northern Cheyenne Agency	76	2	13	0	61	52	12	28	12	0
Rocky Boy's Tribal	79	1	10	4	64	159	51	87	21	1
NEBRASKA										
Tribal Agencies										
Omaha Tribal	27	0	4	1	22	10	5	0	5	
Santee Tribal	11	0	1	0	10	19	8	8	3	0
Winnebago Tribal	22	0	0	0	22	21	8	7	6	2
NEVADA										
State Agencies										
Capitol Police	7	0	0	0	7	29	9	17	3	0
Department of Public Safety, Investigative Division	0	0	0	0	0	0	0	0	0	0
Highway Patrol										
Northeastern Division	0	0	0	0	0	1	0	0	1	0
Northwestern Division	3	0	0	0	3	0	0	0	0	0
Southern Division	1	0	0	0	1	15	0	2	13	0
Secretary of State Securities Division, Enforcement Section	0	0	0	0	0	0	0	0	0	0
State Fire Marshal	0	0	0	0	0	0	0	0	0	3
Tribal Agencies										
Duckwater Tribal	0	0	0	0	0	0	0	0	0	
Eastern Nevada Agency	3	1	0	0	2	0	0	0	0	0
Ely Shoshone Tribal	1	0	0	0	1	1	0	0	1	0
Fallon Tribal	12	0	0	0	12	10	1	9	0	1
Las Vegas Paiute Tribal	2	0	0	0	2	4	0	4	0	0
Lovelock Paiute Tribal	0	0	0	0	0	3	0	1	2	0
Pyramid Lake Tribal	13	0	4	0	9	38	9	16	13	4
South Fork Band Tribal	0	0	0	0	0	0	0	0	0	0
Walker River Tribal	1	0	0	0	1	7	5	2	0	0
Western Nevada Agency	2	0	0	0	2	5	2	3	0	0
Yomba Shoshone Tribal	0	0	0	0	0	0	0	0	0	0
Other Agencies										
Clark County School District	244	0	27	38	179	1,116	221	856	39	37
Las Vegas Fire and Rescue, Arson Bomb Unit	0	0	0	0	0	0	0	0	0	55
North Las Vegas Fire Department Arson Investigations	0	0	0	0	0	0	0	0	0	53
Reno Municipal Court Marshal	0	0	0	0	0	0	0	0	0	0
Reno Tahoe Airport Authority	0	0	0	0	0	52	6	37	9	0
Washoe County School District	18	0	0	2	16	129	27	102	0	2
NEW HAMPSHIRE										
State Agencies										
Liquor Commission	0	0	0	0	0	51	0	51	0	0
State Police										
Belknap County	0	0	0	0	0	2	2	0	0	0
Carroll County	4	0	1	0	3	4	0	3	1	0
Cheshire County	12	0	3	1	8	35	20	14	1	0
Coos County	8	0	4	0	4	72	28	41	3	0
Grafton County	3	0	0	0	3	62	22	36	4	0
Hillsborough County	8	0	6	0	2	3	1	0	2	0
Merrimack County	5	0	1	0	4	36	9	25	2	0
Rockingham County	3	0	0	0	3	4	0	3	1	0
Strafford County	1	0	0	0	1	0	0	0	0	0
Sullivan County	3	0	1	0	2	18	7	8	3	0
NEW JERSEY										
State Agencies										
Department of Human Services	0	0	0	0	0	0	0	0	0	
Division of Fish and Wildlife	0	0	0	0	0	0	0	0	0	
New Jersey Transit Police	43	1	0	18	24	298	0	296	2	1
Palisades Interstate Parkway	2	0	0	1	1	4	1	3	0	0
Port Authority of New York and New Jersey	22	0	0	10	12	496	14	463	19	0
State Park Police	0	0	0	0	0	0	0	0	0	
State Police										
Atlantic County	40	0	5	7	28	734	70	657	7	3
Bergen County	8	0	1	2	5	49	1	38	10	1
Burlington County	44	0	13	10	21	306	84	195	27	1
Camden County	12	0	3	0	9	27	2	21	4	0

Table 11. Offenses Known to Law Enforcement, by Selected State, Tribal, and Other Agencies, 2017—Continued

(Number.)

State/other agency unit/office	Violent crime	Murder and nonnegligent manslaughter	Rape[1]	Robbery	Aggravated assault	Property crime	Burglary	Larceny-theft	Motor vehicle theft	Arson[2]
Cape May County	20	0	7	1	12	236	57	172	7	2
Cumberland County	72	1	12	18	41	509	157	339	13	1
Essex County	11	0	0	2	9	15	0	7	8	0
Gloucester County	4	0	0	0	4	16	2	12	2	0
Hudson County	6	0	0	4	2	6	0	6	0	0
Hunterdon County	15	0	2	2	11	117	34	78	5	2
Mercer County	7	0	4	0	3	71	6	64	1	1
Middlesex County	6	0	1	1	4	26	0	22	4	1
Monmouth County	13	0	2	3	8	144	39	98	7	0
Morris County	6	0	3	0	3	15	1	11	3	0
Ocean County	6	0	2	1	3	27	8	18	1	0
Passaic County	0	0	0	0	0	11	0	6	5	0
Salem County	30	0	6	6	18	236	93	131	12	4
Somerset County	1	0	0	0	1	11	2	8	1	0
Sussex County	28	0	8	6	14	283	72	202	9	4
Union County	5	0	0	1	4	11	0	9	2	0
Warren County	8	1	1	2	4	129	33	89	7	0
Other Agencies										
Park Police										
Morris County	0	0	0	0	0	8	0	8	0	0
Union County	36	0	1	8	27	45	0	43	2	0
Prosecutor										
Atlantic County	0	0	0	0	0	0	0	0	0	0
Bergen County	0	0	0	0	0	0	0	0	0	0
Burlington County	0	0	0	0	0	0	0	0	0	0
Camden County	0	0	0	0	0	0	0	0	0	0
Cape May County	0	0	0	0	0	0	0	0	0	0
Cumberland County	0	0	0	0	0	0	0	0	0	0
Essex County	0	0	0	0	0	0	0	0	0	0
Gloucester County	0	0	0	0	0	0	0	0	0	0
Hudson County	0	0	0	0	0	0	0	0	0	0
Hunterdon County	0	0	0	0	0	0	0	0	0	0
Mercer County	0	0	0	0	0	0	0	0	0	0
Middlesex County	0	0	0	0	0	0	0	0	0	0
Monmouth County	0	0	0	0	0	0	0	0	0	0
Morris County	0	0	0	0	0	0	0	0	0	0
Ocean County	0	0	0	0	0	0	0	0	0	0
Passaic County	0	0	0	0	0	0	0	0	0	0
Salem County	0	0	0	0	0	0	0	0	0	0
Somerset County	0	0	0	0	0	0	0	0	0	0
Sussex County	0	0	0	0	0	0	0	0	0	0
Union County	0	0	0	0	0	0	0	0	0	0
Warren County	0	0	0	0	0	0	0	0	0	0
NEW MEXICO										
State Agencies										
New Mexico State Police	626	10	71	18	527	734	234	366	134	
Tribal Agencies										
Acoma Tribal	12	1	1	0	10	18	4	12	2	0
Isleta Tribal	14	0	0	0	14	1	1	0	0	0
Jemez Pueblo	14	0	0	2	12	6	3	3	0	0
Jicarilla Apache Tribal	22	0	0	0	22	1	0	0	1	0
Laguna Tribal	37	0	8	0	29	112	17	73	22	0
Mescalero Tribal	21	0	2	0	19	13	2	11	0	1
Northern Pueblos Agency	0	0	0	0	0	11	3	7	1	0
Ohkay Owingeh Tribal	20	0	1	5	14	14	4	7	3	1
Pojoaque Tribal	11	0	0	1	10	127	29	80	18	1
Ramah Navajo Tribal	19	1	0	0	18	6	6	0	0	3
Santa Ana Tribal	11	0	0	1	10	60	7	46	7	0
Santa Clara Pueblo	5	0	1	0	4	33	12	12	9	0
Southern Pueblos Agency	15	1	1	0	13	41	18	13	10	0
Taos Pueblo	2	0	0	0	2	2	1	0	1	0
Tesuque Pueblo	1	0	1	0	0	11	3	7	1	0
Zuni Tribal	17	0	1	0	16	0	0	0	0	0
NEW YORK										
State Agencies										
State Park										
Allegany Region	0	0	0	0	0	8	1	7	0	0
Central Region	0	0	0	0	0	13	0	12	1	0
Finger Lakes Region	0	0	0	0	0	18	2	16	0	0
Genesee Region	0	0	0	0	0	2	0	2	0	0
Long Island Region	5	0	1	1	3	92	0	90	2	2
New York City Region	9	0	0	2	7	75	1	73	1	0
Niagara Region	2	0	0	2	0	54	4	48	2	0
Palisades Region	0	0	0	0	0	7	2	5	0	0
Saratoga/Capital Region	4	0	0	1	3	18	0	18	0	0
Taconic Region	2	0	0	0	2	23	5	16	2	0
Thousand Island Region	0	0	0	0	0	15	1	14	0	0
State Police										
Albany County	21	0	18	1	2	164	5	155	4	0
Allegany County	54	2	32	1	19	206	49	147	10	5

Table 11. Offenses Known to Law Enforcement, by Selected State, Tribal, and Other Agencies, 2017—Continued

(Number.)

State/other agency unit/office	Violent crime	Murder and nonnegligent manslaughter	Rape[1]	Robbery	Aggravated assault	Property crime	Burglary	Larceny-theft	Motor vehicle theft	Arson[2]
Broome County	80	0	46	4	30	444	85	338	21	10
Cattaraugus County	48	0	28	3	17	219	57	154	8	3
Cayuga County	50	1	28	1	20	157	33	116	8	2
Chautauqua County	26	0	15	0	11	169	38	123	8	1
Chemung County	50	0	25	1	24	196	19	171	6	1
Chenango County	39	1	26	1	11	143	41	99	3	0
Clinton County	96	0	53	5	38	653	122	513	18	4
Columbia County	53	0	28	1	24	169	33	126	10	4
Cortland County	12	0	10	0	2	164	29	130	5	0
Delaware County	20	0	14	1	5	135	38	92	5	1
Duchess County	175	0	51	10	114	494	66	414	14	2
Erie County	37	0	20	3	14	248	19	219	10	1
Essex County	49	0	30	1	18	280	75	196	9	1
Franklin County	53	1	37	1	14	317	89	214	14	4
Fulton County	21	0	14	0	7	81	28	47	6	0
Genesee County	11	0	4	0	7	97	13	79	5	0
Greene County	109	1	33	3	72	270	67	192	11	4
Hamilton County	3	0	2	0	1	21	5	16	0	0
Herkimer County	46	1	25	0	20	199	55	127	17	3
Jefferson County	64	3	39	3	19	541	85	442	14	4
Lewis County	21	0	17	0	4	86	37	45	4	0
Livingston County	19	0	9	1	9	29	4	23	2	0
Madison County	42	0	30	4	8	188	47	134	7	0
Monroe County	16	0	12	0	4	67	2	58	7	0
Montgomery County	22	0	19	0	3	89	14	71	4	0
Nassau County	5	1	1	0	3	13	2	8	3	0
New York County	3	0	1	0	2	20	1	11	8	0
Niagara County	42	0	27	6	9	223	35	176	12	0
Oneida County	112	0	43	2	67	417	82	316	19	4
Onondaga County	73	0	40	3	30	552	68	455	29	2
Ontario County	36	0	28	1	7	228	25	192	11	
Orange County	162	0	108	15	39	658	47	592	19	2
Orleans County	12	0	5	0	7	61	8	52	1	0
Oswego County	109	1	68	2	38	582	165	380	37	3
Otsego County	42	0	30	0	12	286	45	233	8	6
Putnam County	21	0	10	2	9	100	10	79	11	3
Rensselaer County	46	0	32	3	11	383	79	289	15	1
Rockland County	13	1	7	1	4	17	2	12	3	1
Saratoga County	88	0	48	9	31	685	74	599	12	3
Schenectady County	11	0	5	2	4	43	2	37	4	0
Schoharie County	17	0	10	0	7	122	43	69	10	0
Schuyler County	9	0	9	0	0	19	10	9	0	1
Seneca County	47	0	13	1	33	147	22	125	0	1
Steuben County	79	0	52	2	25	407	86	302	19	3
St. Lawrence County	50	0	33	1	16	382	83	285	14	7
Suffolk County	33	0	16	4	13	33	2	29	2	2
Sullivan County	123	0	84	2	37	318	101	200	17	3
Tioga County	14	0	13	0	1	84	21	56	7	2
Tompkins County	53	0	34	5	14	327	56	258	13	4
Ulster County	80	0	40	2	38	326	59	252	15	4
Warren County	29	0	20	1	8	246	34	208	4	1
Washington County	24	0	13	1	10	121	14	101	6	0
Wayne County	73	1	43	5	24	431	80	333	18	
Westchester County	76	1	25	5	45	379	48	319	12	2
Wyoming County	34	0	11	0	23	12	0	11	1	0
Yates County	6	0	3	0	3	16	1	15	0	0
Tribal Agencies										
Oneida Indian Nation	10	0	0	1	9	186	3	183	0	0
St. Regis Tribal	14	0	2	0	12	31	8	22	1	0
Other Agencies										
New York City Department of Environmental Protection Police										
Ashokan Precinct	0	0	0	0	0	1	0	0	1	0
Beerston Precinct	0	0	0	0	0	0	0	0	0	0
Eastview Precinct	0	0	0	0	0	0	0	0	0	0
Gilboa Precinct	0	0	0	0	0	0	0	0	0	0
Grahamsville Precinct	0	0	0	0	0	4	0	4	0	0
Hillview Precinct	0	0	0	0	0	0	0	0	0	0
New York City Metropolitan Transportation Authority	83	0	0	38	45	521	15	498	8	0
Onondaga County Parks	0	0	0	0	0	29	0	28	1	0
NORTH CAROLINA										
State Agencies[4]										
North Carolina Highway Patrol		0		0	0	0	0	0	0	0
State Park Rangers, Raven Rcock		0		0	0	1	0	1	0	0
Tribal Agencies										
Cherokee Tribal	89	0	2	10	77	763	134	553	76	0
Other Agencies[4]	0	0		0	0	8	0	8	0	0
Raleigh-Durham International Airport		0		0	1	74	1	56	17	0
Triad Municipal Alcoholic Beverage Control Law Enforcement		0		0	0	41	0	41	0	0

Table 11. Offenses Known to Law Enforcement, by Selected State, Tribal, and Other Agencies, 2017—Continued

(Number.)

State/other agency unit/office	Violent crime	Murder and nonnegligent manslaughter	Rape[1]	Robbery	Aggravated assault	Property crime	Burglary	Larceny-theft	Motor vehicle theft	Arson[2]
NORTH DAKOTA										
State Agencies										
North Dakota Highway Patrol	3	0	0	0	3	12	0	1	11	0
Tribal Agencies										
Standing Rock Agency	83	1	10	0	72	52	17	11	24	0
Three Affiliated Tribes	13	0	1	0	12	69	8	21	40	19
Turtle Mountain Agency	147	0	13	0	134	573	214	262	97	25
OHIO										
State Agencies										
Ohio State Highway Patrol	280	3	42	6	229	209	3	157	49	4
Other Agencies										
Cleveland Metropolitan Park District	14	0	3	5	6	106	2	98	6	4
Hamilton County Park District	0	0	0	0	0	75	3	72	0	1
Lake Metroparks	2	1	0	0	1	4	0	4	0	0
Toledo Fire Department, Fire Investigation Unit	0	0	0	0	0	0	0	0	0	111
OKLAHOMA										
State Agencies										
Absentee Shawnee Tribal	5	0	0	1	4	22	4	14	4	0
Anadarko Agency	2	0	1	0	1	49	7	36	6	5
Cherokee Nation	10	0	0	0	10	32	8	16	8	0
Chickasaw Nation	23	0	3	4	16	1,092	72	938	82	2
Choctaw Nation	38	0	0	0	38	305	22	255	28	0
Citizen Potawatomi Nation	17	1	0	2	14	179	26	135	18	0
Comanche Nation	5	0	2	0	3	116	3	103	10	0
Concho Agency	9	1	1	0	7	15	1	13	1	3
Eastern Shawnee Tribal	1	0	0	0	1	79	0	78	1	0
Iowa Tribal	0	0	0	0	0	12	1	10	1	0
Kaw Tribal	0	0	0	0	0	7	1	6	0	0
Kickapoo Tribal	1	0	0	0	1	23	4	16	3	0
Miami Agency	2	0	0	0	2	20	1	17	2	0
Miami Tribal	0	0	0	0	0	1	0	1	0	0
Muscogee Nation Tribal	12	0	2	1	9	102	16	63	23	2
Osage Nation	4	0	0	2	2	90	24	45	21	0
Otoe-Missouria Tribal	3	0	0	0	3	14	5	8	1	1
Pawnee Tribal	0	0	0	0	0	3	0	3	0	0
Ponca Tribal	1	0	0	0	1	13	3	9	1	2
Quapaw Tribal	6	0	0	0	6	115	14	99	2	0
Sac and Fox Tribal	6	0	0	1	5	19	4	13	2	0
Tonkawa Tribal	7	0	0	1	6	20	5	13	2	0
Wyandotte Nation	2	0	0	0	2	14	1	12	1	1
Other Agencies										
Jenks Public Schools	0	0	0	0	0	24	0	24	0	0
Lawton Public Schools	2	0	1	0	1	34	2	32	0	0
McAlester Public Schools	1	0	1	0	0	2	0	2	0	0
Muskogee City Schools	6	0	1	1	4	2	0	2	0	0
Putnam City Campus	3	0	0	1	2	9	3	5	1	0
OREGON										
State Agencies										
Liquor Commission										
Baker County	0	0	0	0	0	0	0	0	0	0
Douglas County	0	0	0	0	0	0	0	0	0	0
Sherman County	0	0	0	0	0	0	0	0	0	0
State Police										
Baker County	1	0	0	0	1	8	1	6	1	1
Benton County	3	0	2	1	0	284	5	277	2	2
Clackamas County	19	0	1	1	17	38	0	25	13	0
Clatsop County	13	0	1	0	12	14	1	12	1	0
Columbia County	4	0	0	0	4	8	0	6	2	0
Coos County	18	0	0	1	17	38	0	32	6	0
Crook County	4	0	0	0	4	4	1	2	1	0
Curry County	6	0	0	0	6	21	0	13	8	0
Deschutes County	13	0	1	0	12	10	0	7	3	0
Douglas County	6	1	0	0	5	15	1	10	4	1
Grant County	3	0	1	0	2	3	0	3	0	0
Harney County	0	0	0	0	0	1	0	1	0	0
Hood River County	2	0	0	0	2	3	0	1	2	2
Jackson County	21	0	1	2	18	29	2	19	8	1
Jefferson County	3	0	0	0	3	3	0	3	0	1
Josephine County	60	3	9	0	48	27	3	12	12	6
Klamath County	23	1	2	0	20	26	3	13	10	0
Lake County	4	0	3	0	1	3	0	0	3	0
Lane County	14	0	0	1	13	39	4	28	7	0
Lincoln County	8	0	1	0	7	11	1	8	2	0
Linn County	10	0	0	0	10	17	1	13	3	0
Malheur County	10	0	0	0	10	4	0	3	1	1
Marion County	53	0	1	0	52	69	3	50	16	1
Multnomah County	1	0	0	0	1	15	0	8	7	0
Polk County	2	0	0	0	2	2	0	2	0	1
Tillamook County	3	0	0	0	3	20	1	17	2	0

Table 11. Offenses Known to Law Enforcement, by Selected State, Tribal, and Other Agencies, 2017—Continued

(Number.)

State/other agency unit/office	Violent crime	Murder and nonnegligent manslaughter	Rape[1]	Robbery	Aggravated assault	Property crime	Burglary	Larceny-theft	Motor vehicle theft	Arson[2]
Umatilla County	10	0	0	0	10	12	1	6	5	0
Union County	0	0	0	0	0	4	0	4	0	0
Wasco County	2	1	0	0	1	12	2	8	2	0
Washington County	0	0	0	0	0	3	0	2	1	0
Tribal Agencies										
Burns Paiute Tribal	0	0	0	0	0	2	2	0	0	0
Columbia River Inter-Tribal Fisheries Enforcement	20	0	0	0	20	7	1	5	1	0
Grand Ronde Tribal	4	0	1	0	3	90	5	82	3	0
Umatilla Tribal	22	0	5	0	17	150	29	102	19	0
Other Agencies										
Port of Portland	1	0	0	0	1	543	2	492	49	0
PENNSYLVANIA										
State Agencies										
Bureau of Forestry										
Adams County	0	0	0	0	0	0	0	0	0	1
Allegheny County	0	0	0	0	0	0	0	0	0	0
Armstrong County	0	0	0	0	0	0	0	0	0	0
Beaver County	0	0	0	0	0	0	0	0	0	0
Bedford County	0	0	0	0	0	0	0	0	0	0
Berks County	0	0	0	0	0	0	0	0	0	2
Blair County	0	0	0	0	0	0	0	0	0	0
Bradford County	0	0	0	0	0	0	0	0	0	1
Bucks County	0	0	0	0	0	0	0	0	0	2
Butler County	0	0	0	0	0	0	0	0	0	0
Cambria County	0	0	0	0	0	0	0	0	0	0
Cameron County	0	0	0	0	0	0	0	0	0	0
Carbon County	0	0	0	0	0	0	0	0	0	5
Centre County	0	0	0	0	0	0	0	0	0	3
Chester County	0	0	0	0	0	0	0	0	0	1
Clarion County	0	0	0	0	0	0	0	0	0	0
Clearfield County	0	0	0	0	0	0	0	0	0	6
Clinton County	0	0	0	0	0	0	0	0	0	0
Columbia County	0	0	0	0	0	0	0	0	0	0
Crawford County	0	0	0	0	0	0	0	0	0	0
Cumberland County	0	0	0	0	0	1	0	1	0	1
Dauphin County	0	0	0	0	0	0	0	0	0	0
Delaware County	0	0	0	0	0	0	0	0	0	0
Elk County	0	0	0	0	0	0	0	0	0	0
Erie County	0	0	0	0	0	0	0	0	0	0
Fayette County	0	0	0	0	0	0	0	0	0	1
Forest County	0	0	0	0	0	0	0	0	0	0
Franklin County	0	0	0	0	0	0	0	0	0	0
Fulton County	0	0	0	0	0	0	0	0	0	0
Greene County	0	0	0	0	0	0	0	0	0	0
Huntingdon County	0	0	0	0	0	0	0	0	0	1
Indiana County	0	0	0	0	0	0	0	0	0	0
Jefferson County	0	0	0	0	0	0	0	0	0	0
Juniata County	0	0	0	0	0	0	0	0	0	0
Lackawanna County	0	0	0	0	0	0	0	0	0	1
Lancaster County	0	0	0	0	0	0	0	0	0	0
Lawrence County	0	0	0	0	0	0	0	0	0	0
Lebanon County	0	0	0	0	0	0	0	0	0	0
Lehigh County	0	0	0	0	0	0	0	0	0	2
Luzerne County	0	0	0	0	0	0	0	0	0	20
Lycoming County	0	0	0	0	0	0	0	0	0	1
McKean County	0	0	0	0	0	0	0	0	0	0
Mercer County	0	0	0	0	0	0	0	0	0	0
Mifflin County	0	0	0	0	0	0	0	0	0	0
Monroe County	0	0	0	0	0	0	0	0	0	1
Montgomery County	0	0	0	0	0	0	0	0	0	0
Montour County	0	0	0	0	0	0	0	0	0	1
Northampton County	0	0	0	0	0	0	0	0	0	4
Northumberland County	0	0	0	0	0	0	0	0	0	2
Perry County	0	0	0	0	0	0	0	0	0	1
Philadelphia County	0	0	0	0	0	0	0	0	0	0
Pike County	0	0	0	0	0	0	0	0	0	2
Potter County	0	0	0	0	0	0	0	0	0	0
Schuylkill County	0	0	0	0	0	0	0	0	0	9
Snyder County	0	0	0	0	0	0	0	0	0	0
Somerset County	0	0	0	0	0	0	0	0	0	1
Sullivan County	0	0	0	0	0	0	0	0	0	0
Susquehanna County	0	0	0	0	0	0	0	0	0	0
Tioga County	0	0	0	0	0	0	0	0	0	0
Union County	0	0	0	0	0	0	0	0	0	0
Venango County	0	0	0	0	0	0	0	0	0	0
Warren County	0	0	0	0	0	0	0	0	0	1
Washington County	0	0	0	0	0	0	0	0	0	0
Wayne County	0	0	0	0	0	0	0	0	0	0
Westmoreland County	0	0	0	0	0	0	0	0	0	0
Wyoming County	0	0	0	0	0	0	0	0	0	1
York County	0	0	0	0	0	0	0	0	0	1

Table 11. Offenses Known to Law Enforcement, by Selected State, Tribal, and Other Agencies, 2017—Continued

(Number.)

State/other agency unit/office	Violent crime	Murder and nonnegligent manslaughter	Rape[1]	Robbery	Aggravated assault	Property crime	Burglary	Larceny-theft	Motor vehicle theft	Arson[2]
Bureau of Narcotics										
Adams County	0	0	0	0	0	0	0	0	0	0
Allegheny County	0	0	0	0	0	0	0	0	0	0
Armstrong County	0	0	0	0	0	0	0	0	0	0
Beaver County	0	0	0	0	0	0	0	0	0	0
Bedford County	0	0	0	0	0	0	0	0	0	0
Berks County	0	0	0	0	0	0	0	0	0	0
Blair County	0	0	0	0	0	0	0	0	0	0
Bradford County	0	0	0	0	0	0	0	0	0	0
Bucks County	0	0	0	0	0	0	0	0	0	0
Butler County	0	0	0	0	0	0	0	0	0	0
Cambria County	0	0	0	0	0	0	0	0	0	0
Cameron County	0	0	0	0	0	0	0	0	0	0
Carbon County	0	0	0	0	0	0	0	0	0	0
Centre County	0	0	0	0	0	0	0	0	0	0
Chester County	0	0	0	0	0	0	0	0	0	0
Clarion County	0	0	0	0	0	0	0	0	0	0
Clearfield County	0	0	0	0	0	0	0	0	0	0
Clinton County	0	0	0	0	0	0	0	0	0	0
Columbia County	0	0	0	0	0	0	0	0	0	0
Crawford County	0	0	0	0	0	0	0	0	0	0
Cumberland County	0	0	0	0	0	0	0	0	0	0
Dauphin County	0	0	0	0	0	0	0	0	0	0
Delaware County	0	0	0	0	0	0	0	0	0	0
Elk County	0	0	0	0	0	0	0	0	0	0
Erie County	0	0	0	0	0	0	0	0	0	0
Fayette County	0	0	0	0	0	0	0	0	0	0
Forest County	0	0	0	0	0	0	0	0	0	0
Franklin County	0	0	0	0	0	0	0	0	0	0
Fulton County	0	0	0	0	0	0	0	0	0	0
Greene County	0	0	0	0	0	0	0	0	0	0
Huntingdon County	0	0	0	0	0	0	0	0	0	0
Indiana County	0	0	0	0	0	0	0	0	0	0
Jefferson County	0	0	0	0	0	0	0	0	0	0
Juniata County	0	0	0	0	0	0	0	0	0	0
Lackawanna County	0	0	0	0	0	0	0	0	0	0
Lancaster County	0	0	0	0	0	0	0	0	0	0
Lawrence County	0	0	0	0	0	0	0	0	0	0
Lebanon County	0	0	0	0	0	0	0	0	0	0
Lehigh County	0	0	0	0	0	0	0	0	0	0
Luzerne County	0	0	0	0	0	0	0	0	0	0
Lycoming County	0	0	0	0	0	0	0	0	0	0
McKean County	0	0	0	0	0	0	0	0	0	0
Mercer County	0	0	0	0	0	0	0	0	0	0
Mifflin County	0	0	0	0	0	0	0	0	0	0
Monroe County	0	0	0	0	0	0	0	0	0	0
Montgomery County	0	0	0	0	0	0	0	0	0	0
Montour County	0	0	0	0	0	0	0	0	0	0
Northampton County	0	0	0	0	0	0	0	0	0	0
Northumberland County	0	0	0	0	0	0	0	0	0	0
Perry County	0	0	0	0	0	0	0	0	0	0
Philadelphia County	0	0	0	0	0	0	0	0	0	0
Pike County	0	0	0	0	0	0	0	0	0	0
Potter County	0	0	0	0	0	0	0	0	0	0
Schuylkill County	0	0	0	0	0	0	0	0	0	0
Snyder County	0	0	0	0	0	0	0	0	0	0
Somerset County	0	0	0	0	0	0	0	0	0	0
Sullivan County	0	0	0	0	0	0	0	0	0	0
Susquehanna County	0	0	0	0	0	0	0	0	0	0
Tioga County	0	0	0	0	0	0	0	0	0	0
Union County	0	0	0	0	0	0	0	0	0	0
Venango County	0	0	0	0	0	0	0	0	0	0
Warren County	0	0	0	0	0	0	0	0	0	0
Washington County	0	0	0	0	0	0	0	0	0	0
Wayne County	0	0	0	0	0	0	0	0	0	0
Westmoreland County	0	0	0	0	0	0	0	0	0	0
Wyoming County	0	0	0	0	0	0	0	0	0	0
Pennsylvania Fish and Boat Commission	1	0	0	0	1	0	0	0	0	0
State Capitol Police	1	0	0	0	1	38	2	36	0	0
State Park Rangers										
Bald Eagle	0	0	0	0	0	4	0	4	0	0
Beltzville	0	0	0	0	0	14	0	14	0	0
Ben Rush	0	0	0	0	0	0	0	0	0	0
Bendigo	0	0	0	0	0	0	0	0	0	0
Black Moshannon	0	0	0	0	0	5	2	3	0	0
Blue Knob	0	0	0	0	0	0	0	0	0	0
Caledonia	0	0	0	0	0	1	0	1	0	0
Canoe Creek	0	0	0	0	0	0	0	0	0	0
Chapman	0	0	0	0	0	2	0	2	0	0
Clear Creek	0	0	0	0	0	0	0	0	0	0
Codorus	2	1	0	1	0	15	0	15	0	0
Colonel Denning	0	0	0	0	0	0	0	0	0	0
Cook Forest	0	0	0	0	0	0	0	0	0	0

Table 11. Offenses Known to Law Enforcement, by Selected State, Tribal, and Other Agencies, 2017—Continued

(Number.)

State/other agency unit/office	Violent crime	Murder and nonnegligent manslaughter	Rape[1]	Robbery	Aggravated assault	Property crime	Burglary	Larceny-theft	Motor vehicle theft	Arson[2]
Cowans Gap	0	0	0	0	0	5	0	5	0	0
Delaware Canal	0	0	0	0	0	6	0	6	0	0
Evansburg	0	0	0	0	0	0	0	0	0	0
Fort Washington	0	0	0	0	0	0	0	0	0	0
Frances Slocum	0	0	0	0	0	6	1	5	0	0
French Creek	0	0	0	0	0	0	0	0	0	0
Gifford Pinchot	0	0	0	0	0	1	0	1	0	0
Greenwood Furnace	0	0	0	0	0	1	0	1	0	0
Hickory Run	0	0	0	0	0	0	0	0	0	1
Hills Creek	0	0	0	0	0	1	0	1	0	0
Jacobsburg Environmental Education Center	0	0	0	0	0	0	0	0	0	0
Jennings Environmental Education Center	0	0	0	0	0	0	0	0	0	0
Kettle Creek	0	0	0	0	0	0	0	0	0	0
Keystone	0	0	0	0	0	2	0	2	0	0
Kings Gap Environmental Education Center	0	0	0	0	0	0	0	0	0	0
Kooser	0	0	0	0	0	3	0	3	0	0
Lackawanna	0	0	0	0	0	0	0	0	0	0
Laurel Hill	1	0	0	0	1	4	1	3	0	0
Laurel Ridge	0	0	0	0	0	3	0	3	0	0
Leonard Harrison	0	0	0	0	0	1	0	1	0	0
Linn Run	0	0	0	0	0	0	0	0	0	0
Little Buffalo	0	0	0	0	0	2	0	2	0	0
Little Pine	0	0	0	0	0	0	0	0	0	0
Lyman Run	0	0	0	0	0	1	0	1	0	0
Marsh Creek	0	0	0	0	0	0	0	0	0	0
Maurice K. Goddard	0	0	0	0	0	1	0	1	0	0
Memorial Lake	0	0	0	0	0	0	0	0	0	0
Moraine	0	0	0	0	0	0	0	0	0	0
Mount Pisgah	0	0	0	0	0	3	3	0	0	0
Neshaminy	0	0	0	0	0	0	0	0	0	0
Nockamixon	1	0	0	0	1	3	0	3	0	0
Ohiopyle	0	0	0	0	0	1	0	1	0	0
Oil Creek	0	0	0	0	0	0	0	0	0	0
Ole Bull	0	0	0	0	0	0	0	0	0	0
Parker Dam	0	0	0	0	0	0	0	0	0	0
Pine Grove Furnace	1	0	0	0	1	0	0	0	0	0
Point	0	0	0	0	0	0	0	0	0	0
Presque Isle	0	0	0	0	0	9	0	9	0	0
Prince Gallitzin	0	0	0	0	0	5	0	5	0	0
Promised Land	1	0	1	0	0	1	0	1	0	0
Pymatuning	0	0	0	0	0	0	0	0	0	0
Raccoon Creek	0	0	0	0	0	4	0	3	1	0
Raymond B. Winter	0	0	0	0	0	1	0	1	0	0
Reeds Gap	0	0	0	0	0	1	0	1	0	0
Ricketts Glen	0	0	0	0	0	0	0	0	0	0
Ridley Creek	0	0	0	0	0	3	0	3	0	0
Ryerson Station	0	0	0	0	0	1	1	0	0	0
Samuel S. Lewis	0	0	0	0	0	0	0	0	0	0
Shawnee	0	0	0	0	0	0	0	0	0	0
Shikellamy	0	0	0	0	0	1	0	1	0	0
Sinnemahoning	0	0	0	0	0	0	0	0	0	0
Sizerville	0	0	0	0	0	0	0	0	0	0
Susquehannock	0	0	0	0	0	0	0	0	0	0
Tobyhanna	0	0	0	0	0	0	0	0	0	0
Trough Creek	0	0	0	0	0	0	0	0	0	0
Tuscarora	1	0	0	0	1	4	0	4	0	0
Tyler	0	0	0	0	0	0	0	0	0	0
White Clay	0	0	0	0	0	0	0	0	0	0
Worlds End	0	0	0	0	0	0	0	0	0	0
Yellow Creek	0	0	0	0	0	2	0	2	0	0
State Police, Bureau of Criminal Investigation										
Adams County	0	0	0	0	0	0	0	0	0	0
Allegheny County	0	0	0	0	0	1	1	0	0	0
Armstrong County	0	0	0	0	0	0	0	0	0	0
Beaver County	0	0	0	0	0	0	0	0	0	0
Bedford County	0	0	0	0	0	0	0	0	0	0
Berks County	0	0	0	0	0	4	0	4	0	0
Blair County	0	0	0	0	0	0	0	0	0	0
Bradford County	0	0	0	0	0	0	0	0	0	0
Bucks County	0	0	0	0	0	0	0	0	0	0
Butler County	0	0	0	0	0	1	1	0	0	0
Cambria County	0	0	0	0	0	4	1	3	0	0
Cameron County	0	0	0	0	0	0	0	0	0	0
Carbon County	0	0	0	0	0	0	0	0	0	0
Centre County	0	0	0	0	0	0	0	0	0	0
Chester County	0	0	0	0	0	0	0	0	0	0
Clarion County	0	0	0	0	0	0	0	0	0	0
Clearfield County	0	0	0	0	0	0	0	0	0	0
Clinton County	0	0	0	0	0	0	0	0	0	0

Table 11. Offenses Known to Law Enforcement, by Selected State, Tribal, and Other Agencies, 2017—Continued

(Number.)

State/other agency unit/office	Violent crime	Murder and nonnegligent manslaughter	Rape[1]	Robbery	Aggravated assault	Property crime	Burglary	Larceny-theft	Motor vehicle theft	Arson[2]
Columbia County	0	0	0	0	0	1	0	1	0	0
Crawford County	0	0	0	0	0	0	0	0	0	0
Cumberland County	0	0	0	0	0	0	0	0	0	0
Dauphin County	0	0	0	0	0	1	0	1	0	0
Delaware County	0	0	0	0	0	0	0	0	0	0
Elk County	0	0	0	0	0	0	0	0	0	0
Erie County	0	0	0	0	0	0	0	0	0	0
Fayette County	0	0	0	0	0	2	0	2	0	0
Forest County	0	0	0	0	0	0	0	0	0	0
Franklin County	1	0	1	0	0	0	0	0	0	0
Fulton County	0	0	0	0	0	0	0	0	0	0
Greene County	0	0	0	0	0	1	0	1	0	0
Huntingdon County	0	0	0	0	0	0	0	0	0	0
Indiana County	0	0	0	0	0	0	0	0	0	0
Jefferson County	0	0	0	0	0	0	0	0	0	0
Juniata County	0	0	0	0	0	0	0	0	0	0
Lackawanna County	7	0	7	0	0	0	0	0	0	0
Lancaster County	0	0	0	0	0	0	0	0	0	0
Lawrence County	0	0	0	0	0	0	0	0	0	0
Lebanon County	0	0	0	0	0	0	0	0	0	0
Lehigh County	0	0	0	0	0	0	0	0	0	0
Luzerne County	0	0	0	0	0	0	0	0	0	0
Lycoming County	0	0	0	0	0	0	0	0	0	0
McKean County	0	0	0	0	0	0	0	0	0	0
Mercer County	0	0	0	0	0	0	0	0	0	0
Mifflin County	0	0	0	0	0	0	0	0	0	0
Monroe County	0	0	0	0	0	0	0	0	0	0
Montgomery County	0	0	0	0	0	0	0	0	0	0
Montour County	0	0	0	0	0	0	0	0	0	0
Northampton County	0	0	0	0	0	1	0	1	0	0
Northumberland County	0	0	0	0	0	0	0	0	0	0
Perry County	0	0	0	0	0	0	0	0	0	0
Philadelphia County	0	0	0	0	0	0	0	0	0	0
Pike County	0	0	0	0	0	0	0	0	0	0
Potter County	0	0	0	0	0	0	0	0	0	0
Schuylkill County	0	0	0	0	0	0	0	0	0	0
Snyder County	0	0	0	0	0	0	0	0	0	0
Somerset County	0	0	0	0	0	0	0	0	0	0
Sullivan County	0	0	0	0	0	0	0	0	0	0
Susquehanna County	0	0	0	0	0	0	0	0	0	0
Tioga County	0	0	0	0	0	0	0	0	0	0
Union County	0	0	0	0	0	0	0	0	0	0
Venango County	0	0	0	0	0	0	0	0	0	0
Warren County	0	0	0	0	0	0	0	0	0	0
Washington County	1	0	0	0	1	0	0	0	0	0
Wayne County	0	0	0	0	0	0	0	0	0	0
Westmoreland County	0	0	0	0	0	0	0	0	0	0
Wyoming County	0	0	0	0	0	0	0	0	0	0
York County	0	0	0	0	0	1	0	1	0	0
State Police										
Adams County	75	1	16	5	53	388	91	275	22	1
Allegheny County	15	0	2	0	13	126	5	121	0	0
Armstrong County	57	2	33	6	16	246	88	147	11	2
Beaver County	39	0	13	3	23	146	54	88	4	0
Bedford County	78	2	26	8	42	424	106	297	21	2
Berks County	88	1	46	8	33	560	170	353	37	9
Blair County	33	0	20	3	10	136	32	94	10	0
Bradford County	55	0	31	0	24	465	164	272	29	1
Bucks County	29	1	11	2	15	283	39	232	12	3
Butler County	50	2	5	8	35	438	120	303	15	15
Cambria County	18	0	8	3	7	120	39	67	14	4
Cameron County	5	0	3	1	1	33	6	27	0	1
Carbon County	80	0	6	12	62	267	80	171	16	4
Centre County	50	1	21	4	24	319	66	246	7	2
Chester County	114	0	22	25	67	964	251	678	35	8
Clarion County	21	0	11	2	8	217	59	143	15	5
Clearfield County	39	2	34	3	0	388	92	278	18	1
Clinton County	38	0	5	0	33	193	50	137	6	0
Columbia County	8	0	2	0	6	125	30	90	5	2
Crawford County	55	2	15	4	34	669	274	342	53	1
Cumberland County	111	0	44	16	51	569	139	403	27	4
Delaware County	37	0	12	5	20	618	67	525	26	0
Elizabethville	255	0	67	18	170	731	133	566	32	8
Elk County	9	0	6	1	2	161	26	130	5	4
Erie County	139	6	21	10	102	1,223	178	1,005	40	5
Fayette County	219	6	56	46	111	1,586	377	1,138	71	20
Franklin County	123	0	39	15	69	925	221	670	34	13
Fulton County	28	0	10	3	15	105	32	69	4	0
Greene County	34	1	5	10	18	360	144	206	10	6
Huntingdon County	64	0	16	6	42	357	104	238	15	1
Indiana County	61	1	23	5	32	610	137	456	17	1
Jefferson County	62	0	49	1	12	264	79	172	13	1
Juniata County	14	0	7	1	6	144	43	97	4	3

Table 11. Offenses Known to Law Enforcement, by Selected State, Tribal, and Other Agencies, 2017—Continued

(Number.)

State/other agency unit/office	Violent crime	Murder and nonnegligent manslaughter	Rape[1]	Robbery	Aggravated assault	Property crime	Burglary	Larceny-theft	Motor vehicle theft	Arson[2]
Lackawanna County	23	0	7	5	11	124	53	56	15	13
Lancaster County	59	4	17	10	28	704	245	414	45	4
Lawrence County	29	2	16	2	9	157	53	89	15	4
Lebanon County	53	1	21	3	28	340	89	235	16	2
Lehigh County	37	1	6	7	23	778	110	637	31	3
Luzerne County	111	9	29	9	64	573	124	429	20	8
Lycoming County	69	0	14	4	51	426	140	277	9	0
McKean County	24	0	12	0	12	103	34	67	2	11
Mercer County	47	1	14	2	30	258	72	172	14	0
Mifflin County	28	0	8	4	16	92	28	56	8	1
Monroe County	176	1	26	24	125	1,084	298	745	41	2
Montour County	41	0	23	1	17	54	14	38	2	0
Northampton County	19	1	3	5	10	245	39	196	10	1
Northumberland County	48	0	24	4	20	203	57	122	24	0
Perry County	100	0	18	10	72	396	113	262	21	5
Philadelphia County	13	0	0	2	11	8	3	2	3	0
Pike County	38	1	12	4	21	527	172	335	20	3
Potter County	17	0	2	0	15	113	37	70	6	1
Schuylkill County	90	5	28	10	47	647	187	433	27	15
Skippack	51	1	14	10	26	363	91	253	19	19
Snyder County	29	0	8	2	19	294	44	244	6	0
Somerset County	47	3	14	5	25	407	126	268	13	6
Sullivan County	1	0	0	0	1	49	18	30	1	0
Susquehanna County	45	0	12	7	26	375	129	210	36	4
Tioga County	38	0	12	3	23	279	97	171	11	1
Tionesta	28	0	15	0	13	51	26	17	8	0
Union County	27	0	13	0	14	370	56	309	5	0
Venango County	30	2	9	3	16	238	58	173	7	0
Warren County	29	1	12	0	16	234	80	146	8	0
Washington County	85	2	15	25	43	556	138	381	37	4
Wayne County	53	0	23	6	24	465	160	285	20	3
Westmoreland County	162	2	48	22	90	1,207	293	850	64	14
Wyoming County	15	2	3	3	7	236	64	168	4	0
York County	165	0	26	17	122	569	118	433	18	7
Other Agencies										
Allegheny County Housing Authority	20	1	2	2	15	42	11	29	2	0
Allegheny County District Attorney, Criminal Investigation Division	0	0	0	0	0	50	1	49	0	0
Allegheny County Port Authority	106	0	0	14	92	43	1	41	1	0
County Detective										
Adams County	0	0	0	0	0	2	0	2	0	0
Beaver County	1	0	1	0	0	1	0	1	0	0
Berks County	92	0	1	0	91	2	0	1	1	0
Bucks County	8	0	1	0	7	1	0	1	0	0
Butler County	0	0	0	0	0	0	0	0	0	0
Chester County	13	1	3	2	7	15	0	15	0	0
Clarion County	1	0	0	0	1	2	0	2	0	0
Dauphin County	0	0	0	0	0	15	1	13	1	0
Erie County	6	0	0	0	6	1	1	0	0	0
Lackawanna County	10	0	0	0	10	0	0	0	0	0
Lancaster County	4	0	0	0	4	3	0	3	0	0
Lebanon County	2	0	2	0	0	1	0	1	0	0
Lehigh County	2	0	0	1	1	71	7	2	62	0
Luzerne County	2	0	0	0	2	1	0	1	0	0
McKean County	0	0	0	0	0	0	0	0	0	0
Monroe County	41	1	2	0	38	9	0	9	0	0
Montgomery County	4	0	0	0	4	3	0	3	0	0
Montour County	2	0	0	0	2	0	0	0	0	0
Pike County	2	0	1	0	1	0	0	0	0	0
Schuylkill County	0	0	0	0	0	0	0	0	0	0
Warren County	0	0	0	0	0	0	0	0	0	0
Wayne County	13	4	2	0	7	12	0	12	0	0
Westmoreland County	7	0	2	0	5	52	0	52	0	0
Wyoming County	3	0	2	0	1	1	0	1	0	0
York County	1	0	1	0	0	4	0	2	2	0
Delaware County District Attorney, Criminal Investigation Division	12	0	2	0	10	0	0	0	0	0
Delaware County Park	23	0	1	1	21	85	0	85	0	0
Erie Municipal Airport Authority	0	0	0	0	0	0	0	0	0	0
Fort Indiantown Gap	0	0	0	0	0	7	2	5	0	0
Harrisburg International Airport	1	0	0	0	1	4	0	1	3	0
Lehigh Valley International Airport	2	0	0	0	2	12	0	5	7	0
Westmoreland County Park	1	0	0	0	1	14	0	14	0	0
Wyoming Area School District	0	0	0	0	0	0	0	0	0	0
RHODE ISLAND										
State Agencies										
Department of Environmental Management	5	0	0	2	3	20	2	17	1	2
Rhode Island State Airport	1	0	1	0	0	28	0	19	9	0
Rhode Island State Police Headquarters	24	1	13	1	9	54	0	52	2	0
State Police										
Chepachet	8	0	3	0	5	19	2	8	9	0

Table 11. Offenses Known to Law Enforcement, by Selected State, Tribal, and Other Agencies, 2017—Continued

(Number.)

State/other agency unit/office	Violent crime	Murder and nonnegligent manslaughter	Rape[1]	Robbery	Aggravated assault	Property crime	Burglary	Larceny-theft	Motor vehicle theft	Arson[2]
Hope Valley	8	0	6	0	2	26	4	18	4	0
Lincoln	15	0	2	0	13	40	1	19	20	0
Portsmouth	0	0	0	0	0	2	0	2	0	0
Wickford	6	0	5	0	1	45	5	28	12	0
Tribal Agencies										
Narragansett Tribal	0	0	0	0	0	0	0	0	0	0
SOUTH CAROLINA										
State Agencies										
Bureau of Protective Services	0	0	0	0	0	12	2	10	0	0
Department of Mental Health	1	0	0	0	1	5	0	5	0	0
Department of Natural Resources										
Abbeville County	0	0	0	0	0	0	0	0	0	0
Aiken County	0	0	0	0	0	0	0	0	0	0
Allendale County	0	0	0	0	0	0	0	0	0	0
Anderson County	0	0	0	0	0	0	0	0	0	0
Bamberg County	0	0	0	0	0	0	0	0	0	0
Barnwell County	0	0	0	0	0	0	0	0	0	0
Beaufort County	0	0	0	0	0	0	0	0	0	0
Berkeley County	0	0	0	0	0	0	0	0	0	0
Calhoun County	0	0	0	0	0	0	0	0	0	0
Charleston County	0	0	0	0	0	0	0	0	0	0
Cherokee County	0	0	0	0	0	0	0	0	0	0
Chester County	0	0	0	0	0	0	0	0	0	0
Chesterfield County	0	0	0	0	0	0	0	0	0	0
Clarendon County	0	0	0	0	0	0	0	0	0	0
Colleton County	0	0	0	0	0	0	0	0	0	0
Darlington County	0	0	0	0	0	0	0	0	0	0
Dillon County	0	0	0	0	0	0	0	0	0	0
Dorchester County	0	0	0	0	0	0	0	0	0	0
Edgefield County	0	0	0	0	0	0	0	0	0	0
Fairfield County	0	0	0	0	0	0	0	0	0	0
Florence County	0	0	0	0	0	0	0	0	0	0
Georgetown County	0	0	0	0	0	0	0	0	0	0
Greenville County	0	0	0	0	0	0	0	0	0	0
Greenwood County	0	0	0	0	0	0	0	0	0	0
Hampton County	0	0	0	0	0	0	0	0	0	0
Horry County	0	0	0	0	0	0	0	0	0	0
Jasper County	0	0	0	0	0	0	0	0	0	0
Kershaw County	0	0	0	0	0	0	0	0	0	0
Lancaster County	0	0	0	0	0	0	0	0	0	0
Laurens County	0	0	0	0	0	0	0	0	0	0
Lee County	0	0	0	0	0	0	0	0	0	0
Lexington County	0	0	0	0	0	0	0	0	0	0
Marion County	0	0	0	0	0	0	0	0	0	0
Marlboro County	0	0	0	0	0	0	0	0	0	0
McCormick County	0	0	0	0	0	0	0	0	0	0
Newberry County	0	0	0	0	0	0	0	0	0	0
Oconee County	0	0	0	0	0	0	0	0	0	0
Orangeburg County	0	0	0	0	0	0	0	0	0	0
Pickens County	0	0	0	0	0	0	0	0	0	0
Richland County	0	0	0	0	0	0	0	0	0	0
Saluda County	0	0	0	0	0	0	0	0	0	0
Spartanburg County	0	0	0	0	0	0	0	0	0	0
Sumter County	0	0	0	0	0	0	0	0	0	0
Union County	0	0	0	0	0	0	0	0	0	0
Williamsburg County	0	0	0	0	0	0	0	0	0	0
York County	0	0	0	0	0	0	0	0	0	0
Highway Patrol	2	0	1	1	0	46	1	44	1	0
Abbeville County	0	0	0	0	0	0	0	0	0	0
Aiken County	0	0	0	0	0	4	0	0	4	0
Anderson County	0	0	0	0	0	0	0	0	0	0
Bamberg County	0	0	0	0	0	1	0	1	0	0
Barnwell County	0	0	0	0	0	0	0	0	0	0
Beaufort County	0	0	0	0	0	2	0	1	1	0
Berkeley County	1	0	0	0	1	2	0	1	1	0
Charleston County	0	0	0	0	0	2	0	2	0	0
Cherokee County	0	0	0	0	0	2	0	1	1	0
Chester County	0	0	0	0	0	0	0	0	0	0
Chesterfield County	0	0	0	0	0	0	0	0	0	0
Clarendon County	0	0	0	0	0	0	0	0	0	0
Colleton County	0	0	0	0	0	0	0	0	0	0
Darlington County	0	0	0	0	0	0	0	0	0	0
Dillon County	0	0	0	0	0	0	0	0	0	0
Dorchester County	1	1	0	0	0	1	0	0	1	0
Edgefield County	0	0	0	0	0	0	0	0	0	0
Fairfield County	1	0	0	0	1	0	0	0	0	0
Florence County	0	0	0	0	0	0	0	0	0	0
Georgetown County	0	0	0	0	0	0	0	0	0	0
Greenville County	0	0	0	0	0	0	0	0	0	0
Greenwood County	0	0	0	0	0	1	0	0	1	0
Hampton County	0	0	0	0	0	0	0	0	0	0
Horry County	0	0	0	0	0	3	0	0	3	0

Table 11. Offenses Known to Law Enforcement, by Selected State, Tribal, and Other Agencies, 2017—Continued

(Number.)

State/other agency unit/office	Violent crime	Murder and nonnegligent manslaughter	Rape[1]	Robbery	Aggravated assault	Property crime	Burglary	Larceny-theft	Motor vehicle theft	Arson[2]
Jasper County	0	0	0	0	0	0	0	0	0	0
Kershaw County	0	0	0	0	0	0	0	0	0	0
Lancaster County	0	0	0	0	0	0	0	0	0	0
Laurens County	0	0	0	0	0	0	0	0	0	0
Lee County	0	0	0	0	0	0	0	0	0	0
Lexington County	1	0	0	0	1	0	0	0	0	0
Marion County	0	0	0	0	0	0	0	0	0	0
Marlboro County	0	0	0	0	0	0	0	0	0	0
Newberry County	0	0	0	0	0	0	0	0	0	0
Oconee County	0	0	0	0	0	0	0	0	0	0
Orangeburg County	0	0	0	0	0	0	0	0	0	0
Pickens County	0	0	0	0	0	0	0	0	0	0
Richland County	0	0	0	0	0	0	0	0	0	0
Saluda County	0	0	0	0	0	0	0	0	0	0
Spartanburg County	1	0	0	0	1	2	0	2	0	0
Sumter County	0	0	0	0	0	0	0	0	0	0
Williamsburg County	0	0	0	0	0	0	0	0	0	0
York County	0	0	0	0	0	0	0	0	0	0
Santee Cooper	0	0	0	0	0	0	0	0	0	0
South Carolina School for the Deaf and Blind	0	0	0	0	0	0	0	0	0	0
State Museum	0	0	0	0	0	0	0	0	0	0
State Ports Authority	0	0	0	0	0	5	0	2	3	0
State Transport Police	0	0	0	0	0	0	0	0	0	0
Abbeville County	0	0	0	0	0	0	0	0	0	0
Aiken County	0	0	0	0	0	0	0	0	0	0
Allendale County	0	0	0	0	0	0	0	0	0	0
Bamberg County	0	0	0	0	0	0	0	0	0	0
Barnwell County	0	0	0	0	0	0	0	0	0	0
Beaufort County	0	0	0	0	0	0	0	0	0	0
Berkeley County	0	0	0	0	0	0	0	0	0	0
Calhoun County	0	0	0	0	0	0	0	0	0	0
Charleston County	0	0	0	0	0	0	0	0	0	0
Cherokee County	0	0	0	0	0	0	0	0	0	0
Chester County	0	0	0	0	0	0	0	0	0	0
Chesterfield County	0	0	0	0	0	0	0	0	0	0
Clarendon County	0	0	0	0	0	0	0	0	0	0
Colleton County	0	0	0	0	0	0	0	0	0	0
Darlington County	0	0	0	0	0	0	0	0	0	0
Dillon County	0	0	0	0	0	0	0	0	0	0
Dorchester County	0	0	0	0	0	0	0	0	0	0
Edgefield County	0	0	0	0	0	0	0	0	0	0
Fairfield County	0	0	0	0	0	0	0	0	0	0
Florence County	0	0	0	0	0	0	0	0	0	0
Georgetown County	0	0	0	0	0	0	0	0	0	0
Greenville County	0	0	0	0	0	0	0	0	0	0
Greenwood County	0	0	0	0	0	0	0	0	0	0
Hampton County	0	0	0	0	0	0	0	0	0	0
Horry County	0	0	0	0	0	0	0	0	0	0
Jasper County	0	0	0	0	0	0	0	0	0	0
Kershaw County	0	0	0	0	0	0	0	0	0	0
Lancaster County	0	0	0	0	0	0	0	0	0	0
Laurens County	0	0	0	0	0	0	0	0	0	0
Lee County	0	0	0	0	0	0	0	0	0	0
Lexington County	0	0	0	0	0	0	0	0	0	0
Marion County	0	0	0	0	0	0	0	0	0	0
Marlboro County	0	0	0	0	0	0	0	0	0	0
McCormick County	0	0	0	0	0	0	0	0	0	0
Oconee County	0	0	0	0	0	0	0	0	0	0
Orangeburg County	0	0	0	0	0	0	0	0	0	0
Pickens County	0	0	0	0	0	0	0	0	0	0
Richland County	0	0	0	0	0	0	0	0	0	0
Saluda County	0	0	0	0	0	0	0	0	0	0
Spartanburg County	0	0	0	0	0	0	0	0	0	0
Sumter County	0	0	0	0	0	0	0	0	0	0
Union County	0	0	0	0	0	0	0	0	0	0
Williamsburg County	0	0	0	0	0	0	0	0	0	0
York County	0	0	0	0	0	0	0	0	0	0
United States Department of Energy, Savannah River Plant	0	0	0	0	0	10	0	10	0	0
Other Agencies										
Charleston County Aviation Authority	2	0	0	0	2	63	0	36	27	0
Columbia Metropolitan Airport	0	0	0	0	0	13	0	7	6	0
Greenville Hospital										
Greenville	6	0	1	1	4	114	0	109	5	0
Laurens	4	0	0	0	4	1	0	1	0	0
Greenville-Spartanburg International Airport	0	0	0	0	0	4	1	2	1	0
Lexington County Medical Center	1	0	0	0	1	73	2	68	3	0
SOUTH DAKOTA										
State Agencies										
South Dakota Highway Patrol	4	0	0	0	4	12	0	7	5	0

Table 11. Offenses Known to Law Enforcement, by Selected State, Tribal, and Other Agencies, 2017—Continued

(Number.)

State/other agency unit/office	Violent crime	Murder and nonnegligent manslaughter	Rape[1]	Robbery	Aggravated assault	Property crime	Burglary	Larceny-theft	Motor vehicle theft	Arson[2]
Tribal Agencies										
Cheyenne River Tribal	341	1	7	1	332	30	24	0	6	2
Crow Creek Tribal	87	2	8	0	77	43	10	23	10	1
Flandreau Santee Sioux Tribal	0	0	0	0	0	1	1	0	0	0
Lower Brule Tribal	51	0	3	1	47	63	27	26	10	
Pine Ridge Sioux Tribal	83	0	16	1	66	146	13	91	42	
Rosebud Tribal	481	0	6	12	463	117	36	56	25	8
Sisseton-Wahpeton Tribal	22	0	2	0	20	15	5	4	6	1
Yankton Tribal	0	0	0	0	0	0	0	0	0	0
TENNESSEE										
State Agencies										
Alcoholic Beverage Commission	0	0	0	0	0	0	0	0	0	0
Department of Correction, Internal Affairs	6	0	0	1	5	0	0	0	0	0
Department of Safety	80	0	0	0	80	125	1	28	96	0
State Park Rangers										
Bicentennial Capitol Mall	1	0	0	1	0	2	1	1	0	0
Big Hill Pond	0	0	0	0	0	0	0	0	0	0
Big Ridge	0	0	0	0	0	1	0	1	0	0
Bledsoe Creek	0	0	0	0	0	2	0	2	0	0
Booker T. Washington	0	0	0	0	0	0	0	0	0	0
Burgess Falls Natural Area	1	0	0	0	1	4	0	4	0	0
Cedars of Lebanon	0	0	0	0	0	1	0	1	0	0
Chickasaw	0	0	0	0	0	1	0	1	0	0
Cordell Hull Birthplace	0	0	0	0	0	1	0	1	0	0
Cove Lake	0	0	0	0	0	0	0	0	0	0
Cumberland Mountain	1	0	0	0	1	2	0	2	0	0
Cumberland Trail	0	0	0	0	0	2	0	2	0	0
Cummins Falls	0	0	0	0	0	0	0	0	0	0
David Crockett	0	0	0	0	0	0	0	0	0	0
Davy Crockett Birthplace	0	0	0	0	0	1	0	1	0	0
Dunbar Cave Natural Area	0	0	0	0	0	2	0	2	0	0
Edgar Evins	0	0	0	0	0	0	0	0	0	0
Fall Creek Falls	0	0	0	0	0	10	0	10	0	0
Fort Loudon State Historic Park	0	0	0	0	0	0	0	0	0	0
Fort Pillow State Historic Park	0	0	0	0	0	1	0	1	0	0
Frozen Head Natural Area	0	0	0	0	0	1	0	1	0	0
Harpeth Scenic Rivers	0	0	0	0	0	5	0	5	0	0
Harrison Bay	0	0	0	0	0	2	0	1	1	0
Henry Horton	0	0	0	0	0	3	0	3	0	0
Hiwassee/Ocoee State Scenic Rivers	0	0	0	0	0	0	0	0	0	0
Indian Mountain	0	0	0	0	0	0	0	0	0	0
Johnsonville State Historic Park	0	0	0	0	0	0	0	0	0	0
Long Hunter	1	0	0	0	1	5	0	5	0	0
Meeman-Shelby Forest	0	0	0	0	0	0	0	0	0	0
Montgomery Bell	2	0	0	0	2	5	0	5	0	0
Mousetail Landing	0	0	0	0	0	1	1	0	0	0
Natchez Trace	0	0	0	0	0	2	1	1	0	0
Nathan Bedford Forrest	0	0	0	0	0	1	0	1	0	0
Norris Dam	0	0	0	0	0	0	0	0	0	0
Old Stone Fort State Archaeological Park	0	0	0	0	0	4	0	4	0	0
Panther Creek	0	0	0	0	0	7	0	7	0	1
Paris Landing	0	0	0	0	0	0	0	0	0	0
Pickett	0	0	0	0	0	0	0	0	0	0
Pickwick Landing	0	0	0	0	0	7	0	7	0	0
Pinson Mounds State Archaeological Park	0	0	0	0	0	0	0	0	0	0
Radnor Lake Natural Area	0	0	0	0	0	6	0	6	0	0
Red Clay State Historic Park	0	0	0	0	0	0	0	0	0	0
Reelfoot Lake	0	0	0	0	0	0	0	0	0	0
Roan Mountain	0	0	0	0	0	0	0	0	0	0
Rock Island	0	0	0	0	0	0	0	0	0	0
Rocky Fork	0	0	0	0	0	0	0	0	0	1
Seven Islands Birding Park	0	0	0	0	0	0	0	0	0	0
Sgt. Alvin C. York	0	0	0	0	0	1	0	1	0	0
South Cumberland Recreation Area	1	0	0	0	1	3	0	3	0	0
Standing Stone	0	0	0	0	0	1	0	1	0	0
Sycamore Shoals State Historic Park	0	0	0	0	0	0	0	0	0	0
Tim's Ford	0	0	0	0	0	2	0	2	0	0
T.O. Fuller	0	0	0	0	0	2	1	1	0	0
Warrior's Path	1	0	0	0	1	7	0	7	0	2
State Fire Marshal	0	0	0	0	0	0	0	0	0	0
TennCare Office of Inspector General	0	0	0	0	0	0	0	0	0	0
Tennessee Bureau of Investigation	6	2	0	0	4	6	0	6	0	0
Wildlife Resources Agency										
Region[1]	8	0	0	0	8	0	0	0	0	0
Region[2]	0	0	0	0	0	0	0	0	0	0
Region[3]	1	0	0	0	1	0	0	0	0	0
Region[4]	0	0	0	0	0	1	0	0	1	0
Other Agencies										
7th Judicial District Crime Task Force	0	0	0	0	0	17	0	17	0	0
Chattanooga Housing Authority	0	0	0	0	0	0	0	0	0	0

Table 11. Offenses Known to Law Enforcement, by Selected State, Tribal, and Other Agencies, 2017—Continued

(Number.)

State/other agency unit/office	Violent crime	Murder and nonnegligent manslaughter	Rape[1]	Robbery	Aggravated assault	Property crime	Burglary	Larceny-theft	Motor vehicle theft	Arson[2]
Chattanooga Metropolitan Airport	0	0	0	0	0	1	0	1	0	0
Dickson City Park Ranger Division	0	0	0	0	0	0	0	0	0	0
Drug Task Force										
1st Judicial District	0	0	0	0	0	0	0	0	0	0
2nd Judicial District	0	0	0	0	0	0	0	0	0	0
3rd Judicial District	0	0	0	0	0	1	0	1	0	0
4th Judicial District	0	0	0	0	0	1	0	1	0	0
5th Judicial District	0	0	0	0	0	0	0	0	0	0
8th Judicial District	0	0	0	0	0	0	0	0	0	0
9th Judicial District	0	0	0	0	0	3	0	3	0	0
10th Judicial District	1	0	0	0	1	0	0	0	0	0
12th Judicial District	0	0	0	0	0	0	0	0	0	0
14th Judicial District	0	0	0	0	0	0	0	0	0	0
15th Judicial District	0	0	0	0	0	1	0	1	0	0
17th Judicial District	0	0	0	0	0	0	0	0	0	0
18th Judicial District	0	0	0	0	0	0	0	0	0	0
19th Judicial District	0	0	0	0	0	0	0	0	0	0
21st Judicial District	0	0	0	0	0	0	0	0	0	0
22nd Judicial District	0	0	0	0	0	0	0	0	0	0
23rd Judicial District	2	0	0	0	2	3	0	1	2	0
24th Judicial District	1	0	0	0	1	0	0	0	0	0
25th Judicial District	0	0	0	0	0	0	0	0	0	0
27th Judicial District	0	0	0	0	0	0	0	0	0	0
31st Judicial District	1	0	0	0	1	0	0	0	0	0
Knoxville Metropolitan Airport	0	0	0	0	0	18	0	10	8	0
Memphis-Shelby County Airport Authority	0	0	0	0	0	144	1	109	34	0
Metropolitan Nashville Park Police	6	0	0	3	3	170	4	159	7	1
Nashville International Airport	1	0	0	0	1	112	0	85	27	0
Tri-Cities Regional Airport	0	0	0	0	0	5	0	0	5	0
West Tennessee Violent Crime Task Force	0	0	0	0	0	0	0	0	0	0
TEXAS										
Tribal Agencies										
Ysleta del Sur Pueblo Tribal	1	0	0	0	1	26	1	25	0	0
Other Agencies										
Amarillo International Airport	0	0	0	0	0	0	0	0	0	0
Dallas-Fort Worth International Airport	11	0	0	1	10	489	20	421	48	0
Hospital District										
Dallas County	8	0	0	2	6	348	3	339	6	0
Tarrant County	10	0	1	1	8	144	0	141	3	0
Houston Metropolitan Transit Authority	3	0	0	1	2	34	0	29	5	0
Independent School District										
Aldine[3]	12	0	0	5	7	139	31	97	11	1
Alief	89	0	0	25	64	74	8	55	11	0
Alvin	11	0	1	0	10	149	3	146	0	0
Austin	11	0	0	3	8	411	17	391	3	6
Barbers Hill[3]	1	0	0	0	1	11	1	10	0	0
Bastrop	1	0	0	0	1	13	0	13	0	0
Bay City	4	0	0	3	1	10	4	6	0	1
Brazosport	25	0	0	0	25	42	1	40	1	0
Brownsville	166	0	0	0	166	206	3	203	0	0
Columbia-Brazoria	4	0	1	0	3	7	1	6	0	0
Conroe	24	0	12	1	11	146	7	137	2	1
Corpus Christi	56	0	0	5	51	74	18	56	0	0
East Central	6	0	0	0	6	10	1	9	0	0
Ector County	90	0	0	0	90	51	13	36	2	0
Edinburg	1	0	0	1	0	95	5	90	0	0
El Paso	39	0	11	3	25	249	27	221	1	2
Farmersville	0	0	0	0	0	0	0	0	0	0
Floresville	0	0	0	0	0	11	2	9	0	0
Galveston	7	0	0	1	6	32	3	29	0	1
Hallsville	0	0	0	0	0	2	0	2	0	0
Houston	37	0	2	12	23	179	33	141	5	2
Humble	7	0	1	2	4	102	2	97	3	1
Idalou	0	0	0	0	0	1	0	1	0	0
Judson	0	0	0	0	0	99	1	97	1	0
Killeen	4	0	2	1	1	51	9	41	1	1
Klein	10	0	2	5	3	123	2	116	5	1
Lyford	0	0	0	0	0	2	1	1	0	0
Mexia	2	0	0	0	2	11	6	5	0	0
Pasadena	4	0	2	0	2	74	9	61	4	0
Pflugerville[3]	7	0	1	1	5	48	2	44	2	1
Raymondville	0	0	0	0	0	5	0	5	0	0
Rio Grande City	9	0	0	0	9	43	4	38	1	0
Santa Fe	0	0	0	0	0	20	0	20	0	0
Sealy	0	0	0	0	0	5	1	3	1	0
Socorro	4	0	0	0	4	50	5	45	0	0
Spring	50	0	5	5	40	58	1	55	2	0
Spring Branch	4	0	0	2	2	40	5	34	1	0
Taft	0	0	0	0	0	0	0	0	0	0
United	6	0	1	0	5	13	1	12	0	1
Port of Brownsville	0	0	0	0	0	14	4	10	0	0
Port of Houston Authority	2	0	0	0	2	33	0	30	3	0

Table 11. Offenses Known to Law Enforcement, by Selected State, Tribal, and Other Agencies, 2017—Continued

(Number.)

State/other agency unit/office	Violent crime	Murder and nonnegligent manslaughter	Rape[1]	Robbery	Aggravated assault	Property crime	Burglary	Larceny-theft	Motor vehicle theft	Arson[2]
UTAH										
State Agencies										
Parks And Recreation	1	0	0	0	1	21	1	18	2	1
Utah Highway Patrol	54	0	2	3	49	189	7	138	44	0
Wildlife Resources	0	0	0	0	0	12	0	10	2	0
Tribal Agencies										
Goshute Tribal	0	0	0	0	0	0	0	0	0	0
Uintah and Ouray Tribal	27	2	1	0	24	22	7	7	8	1
Other Agencies										
Cache-Rich Drug Task Force	1	0	0	1	0	0	0	0	0	0
Davis Metropolitan Narcotics Strike Force	0	0	0	0	0	0	0	0	0	0
Granite School District	15	0	0	1	14	155	7	144	4	4
Utah County Major Crimes Task Force	2	0	0	1	1	8	0	7	1	
Utah Transit Authority	33	0	1	16	16	1,309	1	1,233	75	2
Weber Morgan Narcotics Strike Force	2	0	0	0	2	1	0	1	0	0
VERMONT										
State Agencies										
Department of Motor Vehicles	0	0	0	0	0	1	0	1	0	0
Fish and Wildlife Department, Law Enforcement Division	0	0	0	0	0	0	0	0	0	0
State Police										
Derby	43	1	3	1	38	215	80	116	19	0
Middlesex	53	1	10	4	38	243	141	99	3	1
New Haven	14	0	1	0	13	122	32	81	9	1
Royalton	14	0	2	1	11	100	41	50	9	1
Rutland	24	0	4	6	14	134	46	81	7	0
Shaftsbury	12	1	0	0	11	71	23	42	6	0
St. Albans	22	0	6	1	15	201	51	132	18	3
St. Johnsbury	41	0	6	1	34	285	120	149	16	0
Westminster	21	1	7	1	12	276	130	128	18	1
Williston	19	1	2	1	15	127	42	77	8	4
Vermont State Police Headquarters, Bureau of Criminal Investigations	1	0	0	0	1	0	0	0	0	0
Other Agencies										
Chittenden Unit for Special Investigations	10	0	10	0	0	0	0	0	0	0
VIRGINIA										
State Agencies										
Alcoholic Beverage Control Commission	0	0	0	0	0	167	2	165	0	0
Department of Conservation and Recreation	0	0	0	0	0	18	0	18	0	0
Department of Game and Inland Fisheries, Enforcement Division	1	0	0	0	1	18	1	16	1	0
Department of Motor Vehicles	0	0	0	0	0	40	0	3	37	0
State Police										
Accomack County	8	2	0	0	6	11	3	8	0	3
Albemarle County	7	0	0	0	7	1	0	1	0	0
Alexandria	3	0	0	0	3	1	0	1	0	0
Alleghany County	18	0	0	0	18	4	0	3	1	1
Amelia County	1	0	0	0	1	3	0	3	0	1
Amherst County	3	0	0	0	3	3	0	3	0	1
Appomattox County	1	0	1	0	0	4	0	3	1	3
Arlington County	4	0	0	0	4	2	0	1	1	0
Augusta County	7	0	0	0	7	20	2	11	7	4
Bath County	1	0	0	0	1	4	1	3	0	1
Bedford County	1	0	0	0	1	5	0	4	1	1
Bland County	1	0	1	0	0	1	0	0	1	0
Botetourt County	5	0	0	1	4	4	0	2	2	0
Bristol	1	0	0	0	1	1	0	0	1	0
Brunswick County	1	0	0	0	1	1	0	1	0	0
Buchanan County	2	0	0	0	2	10	3	7	0	7
Buckingham County	3	1	0	0	2	0	0	0	0	1
Campbell County	1	0	0	0	1	1	1	0	0	0
Caroline County	5	0	1	0	4	16	1	8	7	0
Carroll County	5	0	0	0	5	15	1	6	8	1
Charles City County	0	0	0	0	0	2	0	0	2	0
Charlotte County	1	0	0	0	1	0	0	0	0	1
Charlottesville	2	0	2	0	0	3	1	1	1	1
Chesapeake	5	0	0	0	5	21	0	1	20	0
Chesterfield County	11	0	0	0	11	8	1	4	3	0
Clarke County	0	0	0	0	0	1	0	1	0	0
Colonial Heights	0	0	0	0	0	2	2	0	0	0
Covington	9	0	0	0	9	2	0	2	0	0
Craig County	7	0	2	0	5	0	0	0	0	1
Culpeper County	1	0	0	1	0	3	0	3	0	0
Cumberland County	0	0	0	0	0	1	0	0	1	0
Danville	2	0	0	0	2	2	0	2	0	0
Dickenson County	4	0	0	0	4	5	0	5	0	4
Dinwiddie County	4	1	0	0	3	3	0	2	1	0
Emporia	3	0	0	0	3	0	0	0	0	0
Essex County	0	0	0	0	0	1	0	0	1	0
Fairfax County	12	0	2	0	10	12	0	8	4	1

Table 11. Offenses Known to Law Enforcement, by Selected State, Tribal, and Other Agencies, 2017—Continued

(Number.)

State/other agency unit/office	Violent crime	Murder and nonnegligent manslaughter	Rape[1]	Robbery	Aggravated assault	Property crime	Burglary	Larceny-theft	Motor vehicle theft	Arson[2]
Falls Church	0	0	0	0	0	0	0	0	0	0
Fauquier County	4	0	0	0	4	2	1	1	0	0
Floyd County	0	0	0	0	0	0	0	0	0	1
Fluvanna County	1	0	0	0	1	0	0	0	0	0
Franklin	0	0	0	0	0	0	0	0	0	1
Franklin County	2	0	0	0	2	4	0	3	1	1
Frederick County	2	0	0	0	2	9	0	6	3	1
Fredericksburg	7	0	0	0	7	2	0	2	0	0
Galax	0	0	0	0	0	0	0	0	0	0
Giles County	3	1	0	0	2	2	0	2	0	0
Gloucester County	1	0	1	0	0	2	0	2	0	0
Goochland County	1	0	0	0	1	0	0	0	0	0
Grayson County	1	0	0	0	1	2	0	2	0	0
Greene County	2	0	0	0	2	1	0	1	0	1
Greensville County	7	5	0	0	2	0	0	0	0	0
Halifax County	1	0	1	0	0	4	1	2	1	0
Hampton	3	0	0	0	3	9	0	3	6	0
Hanover County	4	0	0	0	4	4	0	3	1	0
Harrisonburg	1	0	0	0	1	3	0	3	0	0
Henrico County	5	1	0	0	4	5	0	5	0	0
Henry County	2	0	0	0	2	8	0	5	3	0
Highland County	1	1	0	0	0	0	0	0	0	0
Hopewell	0	0	0	0	0	0	0	0	0	0
Isle of Wight County	0	0	0	0	0	1	0	0	1	4
James City County	1	0	0	0	1	1	0	1	0	0
King and Queen County	1	0	0	1	0	1	1	0	0	0
King George County	1	0	0	0	1	3	0	3	0	0
King William County	0	0	0	0	0	0	0	0	0	0
Lancaster County	3	0	0	0	3	0	0	0	0	0
Lee County	0	0	0	0	0	13	0	4	9	8
Loudoun County	0	0	0	0	0	0	0	0	0	1
Louisa County	5	0	1	1	3	2	0	2	0	0
Lunenburg County	3	0	0	1	2	2	0	2	0	0
Lynchburg	2	0	1	0	1	5	0	5	0	0
Madison County	1	0	0	1	0	1	1	0	0	0
Martinsville	0	0	0	0	0	2	0	2	0	0
Mathews County	1	0	0	0	1	0	0	0	0	0
Mecklenburg County	8	0	0	1	7	6	0	5	1	0
Middlesex County	0	0	0	0	0	1	0	0	1	1
Montgomery County	3	0	2	1	0	1	0	1	0	0
Nelson County	1	0	0	0	1	0	0	0	0	0
New Kent County	3	0	0	0	3	2	0	1	1	0
Newport News	4	0	0	0	4	10	0	4	6	0
Norfolk	11	0	0	0	11	4	0	2	2	0
Northampton County	3	0	0	1	2	0	0	0	0	0
Northumberland County	1	0	0	0	1	4	1	2	1	0
Norton	1	0	1	0	0	0	0	0	0	1
Nottoway County	0	0	0	0	0	6	0	6	0	0
Orange County	1	0	0	0	1	1	0	1	0	0
Page County	3	1	0	0	2	40	0	40	0	0
Patrick County	0	0	0	0	0	1	0	1	0	1
Petersburg	1	0	0	0	1	2	0	1	1	0
Pittsylvania County	1	0	0	1	0	19	1	10	8	0
Portsmouth	3	0	0	0	3	3	0	1	2	0
Powhatan County	1	0	0	0	1	2	0	2	0	0
Prince Edward County	6	0	1	1	4	1	0	1	0	0
Prince George County	2	0	0	0	2	2	0	2	0	0
Prince William County	14	0	0	0	14	13	1	11	1	2
Pulaski County	1	0	0	0	1	6	0	5	1	0
Radford	0	0	0	0	0	0	0	0	0	0
Rappahannock County	1	0	0	1	0	1	1	0	0	0
Richmond	11	4	0	0	7	15	0	6	9	0
Richmond County	0	0	0	0	0	3	0	3	0	0
Roanoke	7	2	1	1	3	8	0	3	5	0
Roanoke County	1	0	0	0	1	1	0	1	0	1
Rockbridge County	9	0	1	0	8	8	1	6	1	2
Rockingham County	11	0	2	1	8	24	0	7	17	0
Russell County	7	0	0	0	7	2	0	2	0	0
Salem	1	0	0	0	1	2	0	2	0	0
Scott County	1	0	1	0	0	6	1	3	2	4
Shenandoah County	14	0	1	0	13	5	0	1	4	2
Smyth County	7	0	3	0	4	4	0	2	2	2
Southampton County	0	0	0	0	0	0	0	0	0	0
Spotsylvania County	8	0	0	0	8	7	2	3	2	2
Stafford County	6	2	0	0	4	5	0	2	3	0
Staunton	8	0	1	0	7	0	0	0	0	0
Suffolk	1	0	0	0	1	2	0	1	1	1
Sussex County	1	0	1	0	0	2	0	1	1	0
Tazewell County	4	0	2	0	2	7	1	4	2	2
Virginia Beach	2	0	0	0	2	7	0	2	5	0
Warren County	5	0	1	0	4	5	0	3	2	0
Washington County	6	0	2	0	4	15	0	13	2	9
Waynesboro	1	0	1	0	0	0	0	0	0	0

Table 11. Offenses Known to Law Enforcement, by Selected State, Tribal, and Other Agencies, 2017—Continued

(Number.)

State/other agency unit/office	Violent crime	Murder and nonnegligent manslaughter	Rape[1]	Robbery	Aggravated assault	Property crime	Burglary	Larceny-theft	Motor vehicle theft	Arson[2]
Westmoreland County	3	1	0	0	2	0	0	0	0	0
Williamsburg	0	0	0	0	0	0	0	0	0	0
Winchester	0	0	0	0	0	0	0	0	0	0
Wise County	4	0	1	0	3	7	0	3	4	6
Wythe County	6	0	3	1	2	20	0	19	1	2
York County	2	0	0	0	2	4	0	3	1	0
Virginia State Capitol	0	0	0	0	0	18	1	17	0	0
Other Agencies										
Norfolk Airport Authority	0	0	0	0	0	88	0	67	21	0
Port Authority, Norfolk	0	0	0	0	0	1	0	1	0	0
Reagan National Airport	4	0	0	0	4	469	1	378	90	0
Richmond International Airport	0	0	0	0	0	44	0	20	24	0
WASHINGTON										
State Agencies										
State Gambling Commission, Enforcement Unit	0	0	0	0	0	21	1	20	0	0
State Insurance Commissioner, Special Investigations Unit	0	0	0	0	0	0	0	0	0	0
Washington State Patrol	0	0	0	0	0	0	0	0	0	0
Tribal Agencies										
Chehalis Tribal	26	0	2	0	24	91	10	60	21	
Hoh Tribal	1	0	0	0	1	6	2	4	0	1
Jamestown S'Klallam Tribal	0	0	0	0	0	6	0	6	0	0
Kalispel Tribal	4	2	0	1	1	155	5	132	18	0
Lummi Tribal	44	1	19	3	21	324	111	199	14	0
Makah Tribal	3	0	1	0	2	10	1	7	2	0
Nooksack Tribal	2	0	0	0	2	16	1	15	0	0
Port Gamble S'Klallam Tribal	3	0	0	0	3	13	0	11	2	0
Puyallup Tribal	87	0	10	21	56	850	207	444	199	8
Snoqualmie Tribal	0	0	0	0	0	2	0	2	0	0
Spokane Agency	39	0	0	0	39	113	17	69	27	2
Squaxin Island Tribal	14	0	1	0	13	169	11	134	24	0
Upper Skagit Tribal	3	0	0	0	3	14	2	12	0	2
Yakama Nation	45	3	30	4	8	1,086	219	557	310	37
Other Agencies										
Law Enforcement Against Drugs Task Force	0	0	0	0	0	0	0	0	0	0
Port of Seattle	9	0	1	0	8	886	30	750	106	0
Skagit County Interlocal Drug Enforcement Unit	0	0	0	0	0	0	0	0	0	0
WEST VIRGINIA										
State Agencies										
Department of Natural Resources										
Barbour County	0	0	0	0	0	1	0	1	0	0
Berkeley County	0	0	0	0	0	0	0	0	0	0
Boone County	0	0	0	0	0	0	0	0	0	0
Brooke County	0	0	0	0	0	0	0	0	0	0
Cabell County	0	0	0	0	0	0	0	0	0	0
Grant County	0	0	0	0	0	0	0	0	0	1
Hampshire County	0	0	0	0	0	0	0	0	0	0
Hancock County	0	0	0	0	0	0	0	0	0	0
Hardy County	0	0	0	0	0	0	0	0	0	0
Harrison County	0	0	0	0	0	0	0	0	0	0
Jefferson County	0	0	0	0	0	0	0	0	0	0
Kanawha County	0	0	0	0	0	0	0	0	0	0
Lincoln County	0	0	0	0	0	0	0	0	0	0
Logan County	0	0	0	0	0	0	0	0	0	0
Marion County	0	0	0	0	0	0	0	0	0	0
Marshall County	0	0	0	0	0	0	0	0	0	0
Mason County	0	0	0	0	0	0	0	0	0	0
Mineral County	0	0	0	0	0	0	0	0	0	0
Mingo County	0	0	0	0	0	0	0	0	0	0
Monongalia County	0	0	0	0	0	0	0	0	0	2
Morgan County	0	0	0	0	0	0	0	0	0	0
Ohio County	0	0	0	0	0	0	0	0	0	1
Pendleton County	0	0	0	0	0	0	0	0	0	0
Preston County	0	0	0	0	0	0	0	0	0	0
Putnam County	0	0	0	0	0	0	0	0	0	0
Taylor County	0	0	0	0	0	0	0	0	0	0
Tucker County	0	0	0	0	0	0	0	0	0	0
Wayne County	0	0	0	0	0	0	0	0	0	0
Wetzel County	0	0	0	0	0	0	0	0	0	0
Beckley	27	1	7	1	18	289	56	205	28	0
Berkeley Springs	2	0	1	0	1	61	18	38	5	0
Bridgeport	9	1	6	0	2	161	25	114	22	0
Buckhannon	8	0	5	0	3	68	19	43	6	0
Clay	33	4	2	1	26	145	48	73	24	2
Elkins	24	0	7	0	17	180	54	118	8	1
Fairmont	23	0	10	0	13	84	40	33	11	0
Franklin	10	0	0	1	9	37	16	16	5	1
Glenville	16	0	3	0	13	43	11	20	12	1

Table 11. Offenses Known to Law Enforcement, by Selected State, Tribal, and Other Agencies, 2017—Continued

(Number.)

State/other agency unit/office	Violent crime	Murder and nonnegligent manslaughter	Rape[1]	Robbery	Aggravated assault	Property crime	Burglary	Larceny-theft	Motor vehicle theft	Arson[2]
Grafton	4	0	0	0	4	11	4	5	2	0
Hamlin	78	2	19	1	56	267	79	143	45	3
Harrisville	7	0	3	0	4	60	17	37	6	0
Hinton	7	0	0	0	7	44	21	19	4	1
Huntington	42	0	19	1	22	453	103	313	37	0
Internet Crimes Against Children Unit	2	0	1	0	1	0	0	0	0	0
Jesse	6	0	0	0	6	30	6	23	1	0
Kearneysville	9	0	1	0	8	88	17	66	5	2
Keyser	23	0	10	2	11	131	38	82	11	0
Kingwood	19	0	1	1	17	83	22	52	9	1
Lewisburg	7	0	2	0	5	74	14	57	3	1
Logan	57	1	11	1	44	200	50	123	27	2
Madison	18	0	2	0	16	145	18	93	34	0
Marlinton	14	0	0	0	14	62	17	39	6	1
Martinsburg	56	1	13	4	38	335	92	223	20	5
Moorefield	11	0	3	0	8	54	18	27	9	0
Morgantown	21	0	5	2	14	286	94	168	24	1
Moundsville	6	0	3	0	3	16	5	9	2	0
New Cumberland	6	0	3	0	3	5	1	4	0	0
Oak Hill	14	0	3	0	11	59	16	30	13	0
Paden City	12	0	4	0	8	35	10	18	7	0
Parkersburg	27	0	10	0	17	174	75	83	16	1
Parsons	6	0	0	0	6	37	22	14	1	2
Petersburg	18	0	2	0	16	41	11	25	5	0
Philippi	18	1	1	1	15	73	22	40	11	0
Point Pleasant	12	0	6	0	6	47	19	21	7	0
Princeton	20	0	1	2	17	210	42	154	14	0
Quincy	26	0	4	2	20	131	22	97	12	0
Rainelle	5	0	1	0	4	65	23	35	7	0
Richwood	6	1	0	0	5	84	22	50	12	1
Ripley	2	0	0	0	2	66	16	43	7	0
Romney	8	0	2	0	6	37	6	30	1	0
South Charleston	40	1	20	0	19	434	30	382	22	2
Spencer	25	0	6	0	19	50	15	19	16	1
St. Marys	2	0	0	0	2	7	4	2	1	1
Summersville	14	0	1	0	13	73	17	46	10	0
Sutton	23	1	3	0	19	90	26	49	15	1
Union	9	0	4	0	5	38	13	22	3	0
Upperglade	32	0	1	0	31	46	17	19	10	0
Wayne	29	1	4	2	22	210	61	116	33	0
Welch	48	1	1	1	45	55	29	22	4	2
Wellsburg	12	0	6	0	6	10	1	9	0	0
Weston	5	0	3	0	2	60	12	37	11	0
West Union	11	0	1	0	10	42	16	22	4	0
Wheeling	2	0	1	0	1	8	1	7	0	0
Williamson	39	1	6	3	29	113	23	60	30	1
Winfield	4	0	3	0	1	103	9	77	17	0
State Police Bureau of Criminal Investigation										
Beckley	1	1	0	0	0	0	0	0	0	0
Bluefield	1	0	0	1	0	1	0	1	0	0
Charleston	1	0	0	0	1	4	0	3	1	0
State Police, Parkway Authority										
Fayette County	0	0	0	0	0	2	0	2	0	0
Kanawha County	1	0	1	0	0	3	0	3	0	0
Mercer County	0	0	0	0	0	1	0	0	1	0
Raleigh County	0	0	0	0	0	4	0	4	0	0
Other Agencies										
Central West Virginia Drug Task Force	0	0	0	0	0	0	0	0	0	0
Eastern Panhandle Drug and Violent Crime Task Force	0	0	0	0	0	0	0	0	0	0
Greenbrier County Drug and Violent Crime Task Force	0	0	0	0	0	0	0	0	0	0
Hancock/Brooke/Weirton Drug Task Force	0	0	0	0	0	0	0	0	0	0
Kanawha County Parks and Recreation	0	0	0	0	0	2	1	1	0	0
Logan County Drug and Violent Crime Task Force	0	0	0	0	0	0	0	0	0	0
Metropolitan Drug Enforcement Network Team	1	0	0	0	1	1	0	1	0	0
Mon Metro Drug Task Force	0	0	0	0	0	0	0	0	0	0
Ohio Valley Drug and Violent Crime Task Force	0	0	0	0	0	0	0	0	0	0
Parkersburg Narcotics and Violent Crime Task Force	1	1	0	0	0	1	0	1	0	0
Potomac Highlands Drug and Violent Crime Task Force	0	0	0	0	0	0	0	0	0	0
Three Rivers Drug and Violent Crime Task Force	0	0	0	0	0	1	0	0	1	0
WISCONSIN										
State Agencies										
Capitol Police	0	0	0	0	0	25	1	24	0	0
Department of Natural Resources	0	0	0	0	0	0	0	0	0	0

Table 11. Offenses Known to Law Enforcement, by Selected State, Tribal, and Other Agencies, 2017—Continued

(Number.)

State/other agency unit/office	Violent crime	Murder and nonnegligent manslaughter	Rape[1]	Robbery	Aggravated assault	Property crime	Burglary	Larceny-theft	Motor vehicle theft	Arson[2]
State Fair Park Police	1	0	0	0	1	45	2	43	0	1
Wisconsin State Patrol	2	0	0	0	2	0	0	0	0	0
Tribal Agencies										
Bad River Tribal	13	1	0	2	10	49	19	28	2	0
Lac Courtes Oreilles Tribal	33	0	6	3	24	70	17	46	7	0
Lac du Flambeau Tribal	23	0	1	1	21	236	18	202	16	0
Menominee Tribal	28	0	2	3	23	109	7	89	13	0
Oneida Tribal	22	1	8	0	13	88	5	75	8	2
St. Croix Tribal	2	0	0	0	2	41	4	33	4	0
WYOMING										
Tribal Agencies										
Wind River Agency	120	2	14	0	104	138	21	79	38	5
PUERTO RICO AND OTHER OUTLYING AREAS										
Guam	293	1	27	70	195	2,239	1,114	887	238	0
Puerto Rico	7,762	679	209	3,055	3,819	31,176	7,949	19,633	3,594	

1 The figures shown in this column for the offense of rape were reported using the revised Uniform Crime Reporting (UCR) definition of rape. See notes for further explanation.   2 The FBI does not publish arson data unless it receives data from either the agency or the state for all 12 months of the calendar year.   3 Because of changes in the local agency's reporting practices, figures are not comparable to previous years' data.   4 This agency/state submits rape data classified according to the legacy UCR definition; therefore the rape offense and violent crime total, which rape is a part of, is not included in this table. See the notes for further explanation.

Table 12. Crime Trends, by Population Group, 2016–2017

(Number, percent change.)

Population group	Violent crime	Murder and nonnegligent manslaughter	Rape[1]	Robbery	Aggravated assault	Property crime	Burglary	Larceny-theft	Motor vehicle theft	Arson	Number of agencies	Estimated population, 2017
Total, All Agencies												
2016	1,227,452	16,651	117,581	323,903	769,317	7,541,358	1,430,698	5,372,029	738,631	41,870		
2017	1,227,262	16,617	121,745	310,861	778,039	7,320,839	1,321,995	5,254,838	744,006	41,171	15,426	310,003,377
Percent change	*	-0.2	+3.5	-4.0	+1.1	-2.9	-7.6	-2.2	+0.7	-1.7		
Total, Cities												
2016	988,373	12,987	88,310	285,013	602,063	6,002,396	1,056,562	4,349,999	595,835	31,894		
2017	989,231	13,191	91,715	274,251	610,074	5,846,576	983,667	4,264,233	598,676	31,974	11,205	211,301,356
Percent change	+0.1	+1.6	+3.9	-3.8	+1.3	-2.6	-6.9	-2.0	+0.5	+0.3		
Group I (250,000 and over)												
2016	474,307	6,949	33,468	160,290	273,600	2,073,439	372,144	1,428,206	273,089	12,467		
2017	474,713	6,794	34,842	154,648	278,429	2,053,980	355,012	1,426,420	272,548	12,826	83	62,030,546
Percent change	+0.1	-2.2	+4.1	-3.5	+1.8	-0.9	-4.6	-0.1	-0.2	+2.9		
1,000,000 and over (Group I subset)												
2016	201,743	2,691	14,045	71,655	113,352	742,376	125,318	517,249	99,809	4,226		
2017	200,277	2,473	14,809	68,685	114,310	735,685	119,624	518,657	97,404	4,176	11	27,835,810
Percent change	-0.7	-8.1	+5.4	-4.1	+0.8	-0.9	-4.5	+0.3	-2.4	-1.2		
500,000 to 999,999 (Group I subset)												
2016	149,231	2,253	10,365	48,418	88,195	732,805	133,169	506,671	92,965	4,351		
2017	152,639	2,358	10,839	47,894	91,548	728,714	130,372	504,515	93,827	4,831	24	17,571,403
Percent change	+2.3	+4.7	+4.6	-1.1	+3.8	-0.6	-2.1	-0.4	+0.9	+11.0		
250,000 to 499,999 (Group I subset)												
2016	123,333	2,005	9,058	40,217	72,053	598,258	113,657	404,286	80,315	3,890		
2017	121,797	1,963	9,194	38,069	72,571	589,581	105,016	403,248	81,317	3,819	48	16,623,333
Percent change	-1.2	-2.1	+1.5	-5.3	+0.7	-1.5	-7.6	-0.3	+1.2	-1.8		
Group II (100,000 to 249,999)												
2016	158,660	2,137	15,152	45,781	95,590	1,054,235	189,689	745,706	118,840	5,192		
2017	158,515	2,282	15,710	43,864	96,659	1,028,358	175,848	733,964	118,546	5,095	223	33,279,937
Percent change	-0.1	+6.8	+3.7	-4.2	+1.1	-2.5	-7.3	-1.6	-0.2	-1.9		
Group III (50,000 to 99,999)												
2016	117,544	1,283	11,884	31,586	72,791	884,845	154,139	649,430	81,276	4,353		
2017	117,529	1,376	12,310	31,025	72,818	853,912	140,936	631,474	81,502	4,478	484	33,749,285
Percent change	*	+7.2	+3.6	-1.8	*	-3.5	-8.6	-2.8	+0.3	+2.9		
Group IV (25,000 to 49,999)												
2016	90,162	1,055	10,063	21,811	57,233	739,484	126,324	562,060	51,100	3,292		
2017	90,057	1,100	10,513	20,834	57,610	706,705	113,898	540,864	51,943	3,250	875	30,423,643
Percent change	-0.1	+4.3	+4.5	-4.5	+0.7	-4.4	-9.8	-3.8	+1.6	-1.3		
Group V (10,000 to 24,999)												
2016	76,670	879	8,929	15,845	51,017	673,637	117,372	515,744	40,521	2,905		
2017	76,916	868	9,285	14,905	51,858	647,140	107,002	498,276	41,862	2,811	1,798	28,686,467
Percent change	+0.3	-1.3	+4.0	-5.9	+1.6	-3.9	-8.8	-3.4	+3.3	-3.2		
Group VI (under 10,000)												
2016	71,030	684	8,814	9,700	51,832	576,756	96,894	448,853	31,009	3,685		
2017	71,501	771	9,055	8,975	52,700	556,481	90,971	433,235	32,275	3,514	7,742	23,131,478
Percent change	+0.7	+12.7	+2.7	-7.5	+1.7	-3.5	-6.1	-3.5	+4.1	-4.6		
Metropolitan Counties												
2016	190,966	2,770	20,915	36,125	131,156	1,243,670	281,127	843,894	118,649	7,468		
2017	189,421	2,613	21,628	33,967	131,213	1,190,522	250,712	820,600	119,210	6,849	1,915	74,252,901
Percent change	-0.8	-5.7	+3.4	-6.0	*	-4.3	-10.8	-2.8	+0.5	-8.3		
Nonmetropolitan Counties[2]												
2016	48,113	894	8,356	2,765	36,098	295,292	93,009	178,136	24,147	2,508		
2017	48,610	813	8,402	2,643	36,752	283,741	87,616	170,005	26,120	2,348	2,306	24,449,120
Percent change	+1.0	-9.1	+0.6	-4.4	+1.8	-3.9	-5.8	-4.6	+8.2	-6.4		
Suburban Areas[3]												
2016	333,810	4,273	38,034	68,830	222,673	2,542,241	485,703	1,851,550	204,988	13,574		
2017	332,467	4,191	39,460	65,205	223,611	2,439,671	437,162	1,795,372	207,137	12,635	8,522	134,599,243
Percent change	-0.4	-1.9	+3.7	-5.3	+0.4	-4.0	-10.0	-3.0	+1.0	-6.9		

* = Less than one-tenth of one percent.

1 The figures shown in the rape (revised definition) column include only those reported by law enforcement agencies that used the revised Uniform Crime Reporting (UCR) definition of rape. See chapter notes for more detail.   2 Includes state police agencies that report aggregately for the entire state.   3 Suburban areas include law enforcement agencies in cities with less than 50,000 inhabitants and county law enforcement agencies that are within a Metropolitan Statistical Area. Suburban areas exclude all metropolitan agencies associated with a principal city. The agencies associated with suburban areas also appear in other groups within this table.

Table 13. Crime Trends, by Suburban and Nonsuburban Cities,[1] by Population Group, 2016–2017

(Number, percent change.)

Population group	Violent crime	Murder and nonnegligent manslaughter	Rape[2]	Robbery	Aggravated assault	Property crime	Burglary	Larceny-theft	Motor vehicle theft	Arson	Number of agencies	Estimated population, 2017
Suburban Cities												
2016	142,844	1,503	17,119	32,705	91,517	1,298,571	204,576	1,007,656	86,339	6,106		
2017	143,046	1,578	17,832	31,238	92,398	1,249,149	186,450	974,772	87,927	5,786	6,607	60,346,342
Percent change	+0.1	+5.0	+4.2	-4.5	+1.0	-3.8	-8.9	-3.3	+1.8	-5.2		
Group IV (25,000 to 49,999)												
2016	55,365	610	6,607	14,335	33,813	493,625	78,185	378,789	36,651	1,999		
2017	55,658	598	6,979	14,091	33,990	474,293	70,844	366,452	36,997	1,931	690	23,776,858
Percent change	+0.5	-2.0	+5.6	-1.7	+0.5	-3.9	-9.4	-3.3	+0.9	-3.4		
Group V (10,000 to 24,999)												
2016	48,662	546	5,658	11,451	31,007	448,224	72,788	345,443	29,993	1,859		
2017	48,631	558	5,802	10,849	31,422	430,329	65,645	334,089	30,595	1,744	1,375	22,078,277
Percent change	-0.1	+2.2	+2.5	-5.3	+1.3	-4.0	-9.8	-3.3	+2.0	-6.2		
Group VI (under 10,000)												
2016	38,817	347	4,854	6,919	26,697	356,722	53,603	283,424	19,695	2,248		
2017	38,757	422	5,051	6,298	26,986	344,527	49,961	274,231	20,335	2,111	4,542	14,491,207
Percent change	-0.2	+21.6	+4.1	-9.0	+1.1	-3.4	-6.8	-3.2	+3.2	-6.1		
Nonsuburban Cities												
2016	95,018	1,115	10,687	14,651	68,565	691,306	136,014	519,001	36,291	3,776		
2017	95,428	1,161	11,021	13,476	69,770	661,177	125,421	497,603	38,153	3,789	3,808	21,895,246
Percent change	+0.4	+4.1	+3.1	-8.0	+1.8	-4.4	-7.8	-4.1	+5.1	+0.3		
Group IV (25,000 to 49,999)												
2016	34,797	445	3,456	7,476	23,420	245,859	48,139	183,271	14,449	1,293		
2017	34,399	502	3,534	6,743	23,620	232,412	43,054	174,412	14,946	1,319	185	6,646,785
Percent change	-1.1	+12.8	+2.3	-9.8	+0.9	-5.5	-10.6	-4.8	+3.4	+2.0		
Group V (10,000 to 24,999)												
2016	28,008	333	3,271	4,394	20,010	225,413	44,584	170,301	10,528	1,046		
2017	28,285	310	3,483	4,056	20,436	216,811	41,357	164,187	11,267	1,067	423	6,608,190
Percent change	+1.0	-6.9	+6.5	-7.7	+2.1	-3.8	-7.2	-3.6	+7.0	+2.0		
Group VI (under 10,000)												
2016	32,213	337	3,960	2,781	25,135	220,034	43,291	165,429	11,314	1,437		
2017	32,744	349	4,004	2,677	25,714	211,954	41,010	159,004	11,940	1,403	3,200	8,640,271
Percent change	+1.6	+3.6	+1.1	-3.7	+2.3	-3.7	-5.3	-3.9	+5.5	-2.4		

1 Suburban cities include law enforcement agencies in cities with less than 50,000 inhabitants that are within a Metropolitan Statistical Area. Suburban cities exclude all metropolitan agencies associated with a principal city. Nonsuburban cities include law enforcement agencies in cities with less than 50,000 inhabitants that are not associated with a Metropolitan Statistical Area.   2 The figures shown in the rape (revised definition) column include only those reported by law enforcement agencies that used the revised Uniform Crime Reporting (UCR) definition of rape. See chapter notes for more detail.

Table 14. Crime Trends, by Metropolitan and Nonmetropolitan Counties,[1] by Population Group, 2016–2017

(Number, percent change.)

Population group and range	Violent crime	Murder and nonnegligent manslaughter	Rape[2]	Robbery	Aggravated assault	Property crime	Burglary	Larceny-theft	Motor vehicle theft	Arson	Number of agencies	Estimated population, 2017
Metropolitan Counties												
100,000 and over												
2016	127,437	1,829	11,842	29,870	83,896	829,643	170,599	581,868	77,176	4,384		
2017	126,147	1,737	12,113	28,124	84,173	794,364	150,755	566,186	77,423	4,120	171	46,100,653
Percent change	-1.0	-5.0	+2.3	-5.8	+0.3	-4.3	-11.6	-2.7	+0.3	-6.0		
25,000 to 99,999												
2016	44,622	677	6,125	4,251	33,569	306,629	86,927	195,950	23,752	1,849		
2017	45,130	652	6,384	4,195	33,899	295,554	78,831	191,565	25,158	1,795	447	23,315,067
Percent change	+1.1	-3.7	+4.2	-1.3	+1.0	-3.6	-9.3	-2.2	+5.9	-2.9		
Under 25,000												
2016	18,630	258	2,884	1,984	13,504	105,286	23,048	64,596	17,642	1,224		
2017	17,806	221	3,028	1,637	12,920	98,481	20,536	61,414	16,531	926	1,284	4,589,724
Percent change	-4.4	-14.3	+5.0	-17.5	-4.3	-6.5	-10.9	-4.9	-6.3	-24.3		
Nonmetropolitan Counties												
25,000 and over												
2016	17,783	292	2,687	1,297	13,507	122,522	37,931	75,518	9,073	855		
2017	18,524	288	2,933	1,260	14,043	119,353	37,037	72,478	9,838	774	269	9,970,987
Percent change	+4.2	-1.4	+9.2	-2.9	+4.0	-2.6	-2.4	-4.0	+8.4	-9.5		
10,000 to 24,999												
2016	15,436	292	2,138	817	12,189	98,793	32,637	58,933	7,223	735		
2017	15,457	231	2,190	774	12,262	94,007	30,151	56,176	7,680	762	560	8,952,028
Percent change	+0.1	-20.9	+2.4	-5.3	+0.6	-4.8	-7.6	-4.7	+6.3	+3.7		
Under 10,000												
2016	10,504	190	2,378	359	7,577	52,950	16,284	31,038	5,628	672		
2017	10,068	174	2,208	311	7,375	49,650	14,432	29,290	5,928	571	1,397	4,284,517
Percent change	-4.2	-8.4	-7.1	-13.4	-2.7	-6.2	-11.4	-5.6	+5.3	-15.0		

1 Metropolitan counties include sheriffs and county law enforcement agencies associated with a Metropolitan Statistical Area. Nonmetropolitan counties include sheriffs and county law enforcement agencies that are not associated with a Metropolitan Statistical Area. The offenses from state police agencies are not included in this table.   2 The figures shown in the rape (revised definition) column include only those reported by law enforcement agencies that used the revised Uniform Crime Reporting (UCR) definition of rape. See notes for further detail.

Table 15. Crime Trends, Additional Information About Selected Offenses, by Population Group, 2016–2017

(Number, percent change.)

Population group	Rape[1] Rape by force	Rape[1] Assault to rape-attempts	Robbery Firearm	Robbery Knife or cutting instrument	Robbery Other weapon	Robbery Strong-arm	Aggravated assault Firearm	Aggravated assault Knife or cutting instrument	Aggravated assault Other weapon	Aggravated assault Hands, fists, feet, etc.
Total, All Agencies										
2016	107,478	5,472	126,840	24,476	28,583	127,117	192,335	130,554	231,438	185,727
2017	111,180	5,419	120,036	23,755	28,669	121,577	198,020	128,741	232,962	189,172
Percent change	+3.4	-1.0	-5.4	-2.9	+0.3	-4.4	+3.0	-1.4	+0.7	+1.9
Total, Cities										
2016	79,872	4,357	108,592	21,683	24,926	113,208	153,296	105,554	178,032	137,753
2017	82,940	4,272	103,210	21,140	25,084	108,252	158,392	104,871	178,898	140,723
Percent change	+3.8	-2.0	-5.0	-2.5	+0.6	-4.4	+3.3	-0.6	+0.5	+2.2
Group I (250,000 and over)										
2016	29,818	1,988	61,456	11,594	12,938	62,342	80,742	48,082	82,435	46,538
2017	31,173	1,907	58,933	11,322	13,195	59,311	83,782	48,830	82,895	47,487
Percent change	+4.5	-4.1	-4.1	-2.3	+2.0	-4.9	+3.8	+1.6	+0.6	+2.0
1,000,000 and over (Group I subset)										
2016	11,464	919	22,005	5,341	5,519	26,830	23,455	20,634	31,697	21,763
2017	12,203	844	20,893	5,186	5,351	25,368	23,696	21,247	31,344	22,588
Percent change	+6.4	-8.2	-5.1	-2.9	-3.0	-5.4	+1.0	+3.0	-1.1	+3.8
500,000 to 999,999 (Group I subset)										
2016	9,745	620	22,329	3,776	4,699	17,614	30,505	15,478	29,413	12,799
2017	10,242	597	22,235	3,746	5,053	16,860	32,359	15,671	30,397	13,121
Percent change	+5.1	-3.7	-0.4	-0.8	+7.5	-4.3	+6.1	+1.2	+3.3	+2.5
250,000 to 499,999 (Group I subset)										
2016	8,609	449	17,122	2,477	2,720	17,898	26,782	11,970	21,325	11,976
2017	8,728	466	15,805	2,390	2,791	17,083	27,727	11,912	21,154	11,778
Percent change	+1.4	+3.8	-7.7	-3.5	+2.6	-4.6	+3.5	-0.5	-0.8	-1.7
Group II (100,000 to 249,999)										
2016	14,221	604	18,964	3,685	4,357	17,866	26,433	18,195	29,314	19,295
2017	14,799	569	17,739	3,703	4,347	17,187	27,610	17,853	29,395	19,571
Percent change	+4.1	-5.8	-6.5	+0.5	-0.2	-3.8	+4.5	-1.9	+0.3	+1.4
Group III (50,000 to 99,999)										
2016	11,075	458	10,814	2,731	3,096	13,903	16,143	13,573	22,481	18,567
2017	11,380	461	10,497	2,668	3,138	13,704	16,728	13,044	22,471	18,603
Percent change	+2.8	+0.7	-2.9	-2.3	+1.4	-1.4	+3.6	-3.9	*	+0.2
Group IV (25,000 to 49,999)										
2016	8,952	399	7,904	1,732	2,159	8,779	12,639	9,985	16,528	14,805
2017	9,318	435	7,486	1,647	2,117	8,355	12,672	9,934	16,569	15,089
Percent change	+4.1	+9.0	-5.3	-4.9	-1.9	-4.8	+0.3	-0.5	+0.2	+1.9
Group V (10,000 to 24,999)										
2016	7,872	386	5,910	1,199	1,489	6,136	9,903	8,378	14,643	15,862
2017	8,192	339	5,354	1,130	1,468	5,734	10,170	8,176	14,604	16,452
Percent change	+4.1	-12.2	-9.4	-5.8	-1.4	-6.6	+2.7	-2.4	-0.3	+3.7
Group VI (under 10,000)										
2016	7,934	522	3,544	742	887	4,182	7,436	7,341	12,631	22,686
2017	8,078	561	3,201	670	819	3,961	7,430	7,034	12,964	23,521
Percent change	+1.8	+7.5	-9.7	-9.7	-7.7	-5.3	-0.1	-4.2	+2.6	+3.7
Metropolitan Counties										
2016	19,742	802	17,036	2,576	3,290	12,983	32,072	20,532	43,081	34,288
2017	20,375	811	15,697	2,413	3,252	12,376	32,370	19,424	43,616	34,546
Percent change	+3.2	+1.1	-7.9	-6.3	-1.2	-4.7	+0.9	-5.4	+1.2	+0.8
Nonmetropolitan Counties										
2016	7,864	313	1,212	217	367	926	6,967	4,468	10,325	13,686
2017	7,865	336	1,129	202	333	949	7,258	4,446	10,448	13,903
Percent change	*	+7.3	-6.8	-6.9	-9.3	+2.5	+4.2	-0.5	+1.2	+1.6
Suburban Areas[2]										
2016	34,862	1,531	28,779	5,013	6,354	26,257	48,140	35,260	68,739	64,528
2017	36,029	1,595	26,607	4,764	6,278	25,028	48,777	33,760	69,140	65,663
Percent change	+3.3	+4.2	-7.5	-5.0	-1.2	-4.7	+1.3	-4.3	+0.6	+1.8

Table 15. Crime Trends, Additional Information About Selected Offenses, by Population Group, 2016–2017 —Continued

(Number, percent change.)

Population group	Burglary			Motor vehicle theft			Arson			Number of agencies	Estimated population, 2017
	Forcible entry	Unlawful entry	Attempted forcible entry	Autos	Trucks and buses	Other vehicles	Structure	Mobile	Other		
Total, All Agencies											
2016	800,782	496,116	89,425	545,363	103,524	70,910	17,721	9,936	11,639		
2017	737,974	463,415	80,531	545,549	109,234	69,380	17,437	9,503	11,824	14,726	298,000,763
Percent change	-7.8	-6.6	-9.9	*	+5.5	-2.2	-1.6	-4.4	+1.6		
Total, Cities											
2016	588,929	359,653	69,365	447,074	81,949	48,984	13,519	7,325	8,849		
2017	547,548	338,068	63,133	444,886	87,098	47,941	13,561	7,107	9,233	10,603	201,145,014
Percent change	-7.0	-6.0	-9.0	-0.5	+6.3	-2.1	+0.3	-3.0	+4.3		
Group I (250,000 and over)											
2016	230,299	103,584	23,988	199,936	43,746	17,971	5,027	3,399	3,226		
2017	218,672	101,156	22,272	194,752	48,060	18,158	5,179	3,331	3,665	82	59,324,375
Percent change	-5.0	-2.3	-7.2	-2.6	+9.9	+1.0	+3.0	-2.0	+13.6		
1,000,000 and over (Group I subset)											
2016	74,941	29,124	6,980	65,274	16,816	6,283	1,437	1,104	1,098		
2017	70,324	29,693	6,695	58,701	20,938	6,187	1,452	909	1,301	10	25,129,639
Percent change	-6.2	+2.0	-4.1	-10.1	+24.5	-1.5	+1.0	-17.7	+18.5		
500,000 to 999,999 (Group I subset)											
2016	85,482	38,106	9,581	69,901	16,190	6,874	1,798	1,208	1,141		
2017	84,286	37,449	8,637	70,776	16,313	6,738	2,092	1,350	1,285	24	17,571,403
Percent change	-1.4	-1.7	-9.9	+1.3	+0.8	-2.0	+16.4	+11.8	+12.6		
250,000 to 499,999 (Group I subset)											
2016	69,876	36,354	7,427	64,761	10,740	4,814	1,792	1,087	987		
2017	64,062	34,014	6,940	65,275	10,809	5,233	1,635	1,072	1,079	48	16,623,333
Percent change	-8.3	-6.4	-6.6	+0.8	+0.6	+8.7	-8.8	-1.4	+9.3		
Group II (100,000 to 249,999)											
2016	106,574	66,005	13,454	91,705	16,476	9,787	2,142	1,200	1,566		
2017	98,608	61,495	12,280	91,694	16,100	9,643	2,149	1,157	1,508	217	32,439,570
Percent change	-7.5	-6.8	-8.7	*	-2.3	-1.5	+0.3	-3.6	-3.7		
Group III (50,000 to 99,999)											
2016	81,356	57,854	10,149	62,753	9,674	7,576	1,892	915	1,336		
2017	74,540	52,935	9,368	62,608	10,491	7,187	1,941	918	1,404	463	32,356,421
Percent change	-8.4	-8.5	-7.7	-0.2	+8.4	-5.1	+2.6	+0.3	+5.1		
Group IV (25,000 to 49,999)											
2016	64,653	46,886	8,283	39,255	4,882	5,227	1,309	620	1,084		
2017	58,236	42,622	7,433	40,214	4,986	4,841	1,304	579	1,031	814	28,374,921
Percent change	-9.9	-9.1	-10.3	+2.4	+2.1	-7.4	-0.4	-6.6	-4.9		
Group V (10,000 to 24,999)											
2016	58,167	46,263	6,988	30,100	4,230	4,429	1,377	501	737		
2017	52,837	42,576	6,165	31,370	4,314	4,131	1,263	503	802	1,679	26,705,583
Percent change	-9.2	-8.0	-11.8	+4.2	+2.0	-6.7	-8.3	+0.4	+8.8		
Group VI (under 10,000)											
2016	47,880	39,061	6,503	23,325	2,941	3,994	1,772	690	900		
2017	44,655	37,284	5,615	24,248	3,147	3,981	1,725	619	823	7,348	21,944,144
Percent change	-6.7	-4.5	-13.7	+4.0	+7.0	-0.3	-2.7	-10.3	-8.6		
Metropolitan Counties											
2016	158,163	102,433	16,325	82,768	17,876	17,249	2,990	2,106	2,111		
2017	140,271	92,760	14,018	83,477	18,016	16,885	2,749	1,912	1,983	1,868	72,964,323
Percent change	-11.3	-9.4	-14.1	+0.9	+0.8	-2.1	-8.1	-9.2	-6.1		
Nonmetropolitan Counties											
2016	53,690	34,030	3,735	15,521	3,699	4,677	1,212	505	679		
2017	50,155	32,587	3,380	17,186	4,120	4,554	1,127	484	608	2,255	23,891,426
Percent change	-6.6	-4.2	-9.5	+10.7	+11.4	-2.6	-7.0	-4.2	-10.5		
Suburban Areas[2]											
2016	259,836	179,407	31,119	147,687	26,403	26,582	5,678	3,292	3,823		
2017	231,821	164,363	27,151	150,040	26,780	25,476	5,294	2,999	3,619	8,053	128,974,352
Percent change	-10.8	-8.4	-12.8	+1.6	+1.4	-4.2	-6.8	-8.9	-5.3		

* = Less than one-tenth of one percent.
1 The figures shown in the rape (revised definition) column include only those reported by law enforcement agencies that used the revised Uniform Crime Reporting (UCR) definition of rape. See notes for more detail.   2 Suburban areas include law enforcement agencies in cities with less than 50,000 inhabitants and county law enforcement agencies that are within a Metropolitan Statistical Area. Suburban areas exclude all metropolitan agencies associated with a principal city. The agencies associated with suburban areas also appear in other groups within this table.

Table 16. Rate: Number of Crimes Per 100,000 Population, by Population Group, 2017

(Number, rate.)

Population group	Violent crime		Murder and nonnegligent manslaughter		Rape[1]		Robbery		Aggravated assault	
	Number of offenses known	Rate	Number of offenses known	Rate	Number of offenses known	Rate	Number of offenses known	Rate	Number of offenses known	Rate
Total, All Agencies	1,221,775	400.0	16,446	5.4	125,591	42.4	308,936	101.2	770,802	252.4
Total, Cities	981,574	469.6	12,999	6.2	94,045	46.2	272,035	130.2	602,495	288.3
Group I (250,000 and over)	472,560	768.5	6,783	11.0	35,845	59.7	154,090	250.6	275,842	448.6
1,000,000 and over (Group I subset)	200,277	719.5	2,473	8.9	14,809	53.2	68,685	246.8	114,310	410.7
500,000 to 999,999 (Group I subset)	152,876	870.0	2,358	13.4	11,076	66.5	47,894	272.6	91,548	521.0
250,000 to 499,999 (Group I subset)	119,407	742.4	1,952	12.1	9,960	64.2	37,511	233.2	69,984	435.1
Group II (100,000 to 249,999)	152,713	473.2	2,121	6.6	15,434	49.0	42,351	131.2	92,807	287.6
Group III (50,000 to 99,999)	119,145	347.9	1,386	4.0	12,730	38.2	31,337	91.5	73,692	215.1
Group IV (25,000 to 49,999)	89,414	297.8	1,068	3.6	11,032	37.6	20,451	68.1	56,863	189.4
Group V (10,000 to 24,999)	77,009	269.6	873	3.1	9,714	35.0	14,860	52.0	51,562	180.5
Group VI (under 10,000)	70,733	315.6	768	3.4	9,290	42.6	8,946	39.9	51,729	230.8
Metropolitan Counties	191,537	262.9	2,629	3.6	22,769	32.5	34,301	47.1	131,838	180.9
Nonmetropolitan Counties[2]	48,664	206.7	818	3.5	8,777	39.2	2,600	11.0	36,469	154.9
Suburban Areas[3]	335,122	252.9	4,208	3.2	41,219	32.1	65,527	49.4	224,168	169.1

Table 16. Rate: Number of Crimes Per 100,000 Population, by Population Group, 2017—Continued

(Number, rate.)

Population group	Property crime		Burglary		Larceny-theft		Motor vehicle theft		Number of agencies	Estimated population, 2017
	Number of offenses known	Rate	Number of offenses known	Rate	Number of offenses known	Rate	Number of offenses known	Rate		
Total, All Agencies	7,265,640	2,378.9	1,310,687	429.1	5,212,721	1,706.7	742,232	243.0	14,815	305,422,610
Total, Cities	5,792,834	2,771.5	972,529	465.3	4,224,859	2,021.3	595,446	284.9	10,828	209,015,851
Group I (250,000 and over)	2,034,977	3,309.4	351,565	571.7	1,412,427	2,297.0	270,985	440.7	81	61,490,148
1,000,000 and over (Group I subset)	735,685	2,642.9	119,624	429.7	518,657	1,863.3	97,404	349.9	11	27,835,810
500,000 to 999,999 (Group I subset)	728,714	4,147.2	130,372	742.0	504,515	2,871.2	93,827	534.0	24	17,571,403
250,000 to 499,999 (Group I subset)	570,578	3,547.7	101,569	631.5	389,255	2,420.3	79,754	495.9	46	16,082,935
Group II (100,000 to 249,999)	994,848	3,082.9	169,373	524.9	709,243	2,197.9	116,232	360.2	217	32,269,399
Group III (50,000 to 99,999)	868,714	2,536.3	143,162	418.0	643,254	1,878.0	82,298	240.3	491	34,251,807
Group IV (25,000 to 49,999)	695,293	2,316.1	112,415	374.5	531,582	1,770.7	51,296	170.9	864	30,020,188
Group V (10,000 to 24,999)	648,930	2,271.4	106,387	372.4	500,122	1,750.6	42,421	148.5	1,789	28,569,221
Group VI (under 10,000)	550,072	2,454.0	89,627	399.9	428,231	1,910.5	32,214	143.7	7,386	22,415,088
Metropolitan Counties	1,189,830	1,633.0	251,079	344.6	817,962	1,122.6	120,789	165.8	1,828	72,861,356
Nonmetropolitan Counties[2]	282,976	1,201.8	87,079	369.8	169,900	721.6	25,997	110.4	2,159	23,545,403
Suburban Areas[3]	2,435,027	1,837.3	437,119	329.8	1,788,884	1,349.8	209,024	157.7	8,245	132,531,489

1 The figures shown in this column for the offense of rape were reported using only the revised Uniform Crime Reporting definition of rape. See the chapter notes for further explanation.   2 Includes state police agencies that report aggregately for the entire state.   3 Suburban areas include law enforcement agencies in cities with less than 50,000 inhabitants and county law enforcement agencies that are within a Metropolitan Statistical Area. Suburban areas exclude all metropolitan agencies associated with a principal city. The agencies associated with suburban areas also appear in other groups within this table.

Table 17. Rate: Number of Crimes Per 100,000 Inhabitants, by Suburban and Nonsuburban Cities,[1] by Population Group, 2017

(Number, rate.)

Population group	Violent crime		Murder and nonnegligent manslaughter		Rape[2]		Robbery		Aggravated assault	
	Number of offenses known	Rate	Number of offenses known	Rate	Number of offenses known	Rate	Number of offenses known	Rate	Number of offenses known	Rate
Total, Suburban Cities	143,585	240.6	1,579	2.6	18,450	31.6	31,226	52.3	92,330	154.7
Group IV (25,000 to 49,999)	55,328	235.2	583	2.5	7,142	31.0	13,918	59.2	33,685	143.2
Group V (10,000 to 24,999)	49,372	224.3	575	2.6	6,082	28.3	10,963	49.8	31,752	144.2
Group VI (under 10,000)	38,885	275.2	421	3.0	5,226	37.9	6,345	44.9	26,893	190.3
Total, Nonsuburban Cities	93,571	438.6	1,130	5.3	11,586	56.3	13,031	61.1	67,824	317.9
Group IV (25,000 to 49,999)	34,086	525.0	485	7.5	3,890	61.7	6,533	100.6	23,178	357.0
Group V (10,000 to 24,999)	27,637	421.5	298	4.5	3,632	57.9	3,897	59.4	19,810	302.2
Group VI (under 10,000)	31,848	384.4	347	4.2	4,064	50.7	2,601	31.4	24,836	299.7

Population group	Property crime		Burglary		Larceny-theft		Motor vehicle theft		Number of agencies	Estimated population, 2017
	Number of offenses known	Rate	Number of offenses known	Rate	Number of offenses known	Rate	Number of offenses known	Rate		
Total, Suburban Cities	1,245,197	2,086.8	186,040	311.8	970,922	1,627.1	88,235	147.9	6,417	59,670,133
Group IV (25,000 to 49,999)	468,344	1,990.6	70,062	297.8	361,600	1,536.9	36,682	155.9	683	23,527,685
Group V (10,000 to 24,999)	434,273	1,972.8	66,059	300.1	337,072	1,531.2	31,142	141.5	1,370	22,013,097
Group VI (under 10,000)	342,580	2,424.6	49,919	353.3	272,250	1,926.8	20,411	144.5	4,364	14,129,351
Total, Nonsuburban Cities	649,098	3,042.5	122,389	573.7	489,013	2,292.1	37,696	176.7	3,622	21,334,364
Group IV (25,000 to 49,999)	226,949	3,495.6	42,353	652.3	169,982	2,618.1	14,614	225.1	181	6,492,503
Group V (10,000 to 24,999)	214,657	3,274.1	40,328	615.1	163,050	2,487.0	11,279	172.0	419	6,556,124
Group VI (under 10,000)	207,492	2,504.2	39,708	479.2	155,981	1,882.5	11,803	142.4	3,022	8,285,737

1 Suburban cities include law enforcement agencies in cities with less than 50,000 inhabitants that are within a Metropolitan Statistical Area. Suburban cities exclude all metropolitan agencies associated with a principal city. Nonsuburban cities include law enforcement agencies in cities with less than 50,000 inhabitants that are not associated with a Metropolitan Statistical Area.   2 The figures shown in this column for the offense of rape were reported using only the revised Uniform Crime Reporting definition of rape. See chapter notes for more detail.

Table 18. Rate: Number of Crimes Per 100,000 Inhabitants, by Metropolitan and Nonmetropolitan Counties,[1] by Population Group, 2017

(Number, rate.)

Population group	Violent crime		Murder and nonnegligent manslaughter		Rape (revised definition)[2]		Robbery		Aggravated assault	
	Number of offenses known	Rate	Number of offenses known	Rate	Number of offenses known	Rate	Number of offenses known	Rate	Number of offenses known	Rate
Metropolitan Counties										
100,000 and over	128,147	280.8	1,750	3.8	12,930	29.2	28,460	62.4	85,007	186.2
25,000 to 99,999	45,033	200.0	651	2.9	6,590	31.3	4,175	18.5	33,617	149.3
Under 25,000	18,357	390.3	228	4.8	3,249	69.8	1,666	35.4	13,214	280.9
Nonmetropolitan Counties										
25,000 and over	18,578	193.3	289	3.0	3,058	34.4	1,254	13.0	13,977	145.4
10,000 to 24,999	15,429	177.1	236	2.7	2,329	27.6	747	8.6	12,117	139.1
Under 10,000	9,899	248.4	169	4.2	2,226	56.7	291	7.3	7,213	181.0

Table 18. Rate: Number of Crimes Per 100,000 Inhabitants, by Metropolitan and Nonmetropolitan Counties,[1] by Population Group, 2017—Continued

(Number, rate.)

Population group	Property crime		Burglary		Larceny-theft		Motor vehicle theft		Number of agencies	Estimated population, 2017
	Number of offenses known	Rate	Number of offenses known	Rate	Number of offenses known	Rate	Number of offenses known	Rate		
Metropolitan Counties										
100,000 and over	794,253	1,740.2	151,784	332.6	564,075	1,235.9	78,394	171.8	169	45,642,167
25,000 to 99,999	295,130	1,310.8	77,921	346.1	191,449	850.3	25,760	114.4	433	22,515,711
Under 25,000	100,447	2,135.6	21,374	454.4	62,438	1,327.5	16,635	353.7	1,226	4,703,478
Nonmetropolitan Counties										
25,000 and over	118,910	1,237.4	36,619	381.1	72,511	754.6	9,780	101.8	258	9,609,655
10,000 to 24,999	93,079	1,068.7	29,836	342.6	55,636	638.8	7,607	87.3	546	8,709,847
Under 10,000	48,894	1,227.2	14,169	355.6	28,866	724.5	5,859	147.1	1,277	3,984,313

1 Metropolitan counties include sheriffs and county law enforcement agencies associated with a Metropolitan Statistical Area. Nonmetropolitan counties include sheriffs and county law enforcement agencies that are not associated with a Metropolitan Statistical Area. The offenses from state police agencies are not included in this table.   2 The figures shown in this column for the offense of rape were reported using only the revised Uniform Crime Reporting definition of rape. See the chapter notes for further explanation.

Table 19. Rate: Number of Crimes Per 100,000 Inhabitants, Additional Information About Selected Offenses, by Population Group, 2017

(Number, rate.)

Population group	Rape[1] Rape by force	Rape[1] Assault to rape-attempts	Robbery Firearm	Robbery Knife or cutting instrument	Robbery Other weapon	Aggravated assault Strong-arm	Aggravated assault Firearm	Aggravated assault Knife or cutting instrument	Aggravated assault Other weapon
Total, All Agencies									
Number of offenses known	114,793	5,649	118,745	23,710	28,555	121,126	195,194	127,897	230,469
Rate	40.4	2.0	40.5	8.1	9.7	41.3	66.5	43.6	78.5
Total, Cities									
Number of offenses known	85,114	4,424	101,850	21,057	24,942	107,643	155,606	103,970	176,309
Rate	43.9	2.3	51.2	10.6	12.5	54.1	78.2	52.3	88.6
Group I (250,000 and over)									
Number of offenses known	32,151	1,932	58,767	11,280	13,136	59,020	83,205	48,408	81,880
Rate	56.1	3.4	100.0	19.2	22.3	100.4	141.5	82.3	139.3
1,000,000 and over (Group I subset)									
Number of offenses known	12,203	844	20,893	5,186	5,351	25,368	23,696	21,247	31,344
Rate	48.6	3.4	83.1	20.6	21.3	100.9	94.3	84.5	124.7
500,000 to 999,999 (Group I subset)									
Number of offenses known	10,485	591	22,235	3,746	5,053	16,860	32,359	15,671	30,397
Rate	62.9	3.5	126.5	21.3	28.8	96.0	184.2	89.2	173.0
250,000 to 499,999 (Group I subset)									
Number of offenses known	9,463	497	15,639	2,348	2,732	16,792	27,150	11,490	20,139
Rate	61.0	3.2	97.2	14.6	17.0	104.4	168.8	71.4	125.2
Group II (100,000 to 249,999)									
Number of offenses known	14,550	542	16,731	3,665	4,262	16,805	26,062	17,420	27,836
Rate	47.5	1.8	53.2	11.7	13.6	53.5	82.9	55.4	88.6
Group III (50,000 to 99,999)									
Number of offenses known	11,788	473	10,550	2,687	3,175	13,907	16,894	13,208	22,711
Rate	36.9	1.5	32.1	8.2	9.7	42.3	51.4	40.2	69.1
Group IV (25,000 to 49,999)									
Number of offenses known	9,798	465	7,252	1,625	2,068	8,272	12,157	9,784	16,474
Rate	35.9	1.7	25.9	5.8	7.4	29.5	43.4	34.9	58.8
Group V (10,000 to 24,999)									
Number of offenses known	8,610	364	5,385	1,129	1,468	5,708	9,964	8,222	14,745
Rate	33.3	1.4	20.2	4.2	5.5	21.4	37.4	30.9	55.4
Group VI (under 10,000)									
Number of offenses known	8,217	648	3,165	671	833	3,931	7,324	6,928	12,663
Rate	39.8	3.1	14.9	3.2	3.9	18.5	34.5	32.6	59.6
Metropolitan Counties									
Number of offenses known	21,479	852	15,767	2,461	3,292	12,554	32,256	19,504	43,762
Rate	31.2	1.2	22.0	3.4	4.6	17.5	45.1	27.2	61.1
Nonmetropolitan Counties									
Number of offenses known	8,200	373	1,128	192	321	929	7,332	4,423	10,398
Rate	37.5	1.7	4.9	0.8	1.4	4.0	31.9	19.2	45.3
Suburban Areas[2]									
Number of offenses known	37,651	1,727	26,662	4,802	6,312	25,246	48,609	33,846	69,342
Rate	30.7	1.4	21.0	3.8	5.0	19.9	38.3	26.6	54.6

Table 19. Rate: Number of Crimes Per 100,000 Inhabitants, Additional Information About Selected Offenses, by Population Group, 2017—Continued

(Number, rate.)

Population group	Burglary			Motor vehicle theft				Number of agencies	Estimated population, 2017
	Hands, fists, feet, etc.	Forcible entry	Unlawful entry	Attempted forcible entry	Autos	Trucks and buses	Other vehicles		
Total, All Agencies									
Number of offenses known	188,196	730,575	460,600	79,714	544,944	108,936	68,589	14,121	293,541,938
Rate	64.1	248.9	156.9	27.2	185.6	37.1	23.4		
Total, Cities									
Number of offenses known	139,473	539,947	335,624	62,280	442,903	86,739	47,127	10,231	198,972,636
Rate	70.1	271.4	168.7	31.3	222.6	43.6	23.7		
Group I (250,000 and over)									
Number of offenses known	46,914	216,325	100,285	22,043	193,779	47,640	17,988	80	58,783,977
Rate	79.8	368.0	170.6	37.5	329.6	81.0	30.6		
1,000,000 and over (Group I subset)									
Number of offenses known	22,588	70,324	29,693	6,695	58,701	20,938	6,187	10	25,129,639
Rate	89.9	279.8	118.2	26.6	233.6	83.3	24.6		
500,000 to 999,999 (Group I subset)									
Number of offenses known	13,121	84,286	37,449	8,637	70,776	16,313	6,738	24	17,571,403
Rate	74.7	479.7	213.1	49.2	402.8	92.8	38.3		
250,000 to 499,999 (Group I subset)									
Number of offenses known	11,205	61,715	33,143	6,711	64,302	10,389	5,063	46	16,082,935
Rate	69.7	383.7	206.1	41.7	399.8	64.6	31.5		
Group II (100,000 to 249,999)									
Number of offenses known	19,259	94,543	59,455	11,910	89,853	16,085	9,185	211	31,429,032
Rate	61.3	300.8	189.2	37.9	285.9	51.2	29.2		
Group III (50,000 to 99,999)									
Number of offenses known	18,907	75,718	53,908	9,443	63,428	10,496	7,158	470	32,858,943
Rate	57.5	230.4	164.1	28.7	193.0	31.9	21.8		
Group IV (25,000 to 49,999)									
Number of offenses known	15,081	57,225	42,367	7,266	39,762	4,942	4,703	804	28,011,704
Rate	53.8	204.3	151.2	25.9	141.9	17.6	16.8		
Group V (10,000 to 24,999)									
Number of offenses known	16,273	52,313	42,763	6,111	31,915	4,436	4,110	1,673	26,638,355
Rate	61.1	196.4	160.5	22.9	119.8	16.7	15.4		
Group VI (under 10,000)									
Number of offenses known	23,039	43,823	36,846	5,507	24,166	3,140	3,983	6,993	21,250,625
Rate	108.4	206.2	173.4	25.9	113.7	14.8	18.7		
Metropolitan Counties									
Number of offenses known	35,062	140,531	92,775	14,141	84,954	18,090	16,918	1,783	71,592,146
Rate	49.0	196.3	129.6	19.8	118.7	25.3	23.6		
Nonmetropolitan Counties									
Number of offenses known	13,661	50,097	32,201	3,293	17,087	4,107	4,544	2,107	22,977,156
Rate	59.5	218.0	140.1	14.3	74.4	17.9	19.8		
Suburban Areas[2]									
Number of offenses known	66,132	231,851	164,479	27,186	151,938	26,841	25,472	7,780	127,025,777
Rate	52.1	182.5	129.5	21.4	119.6	21.1	20.1		

1 The figures shown in this column for the offense of rape were reported using only the revised Uniform Crime Reporting definition of rape. See the chapter notes for further explanation.   2 Suburban areas include law enforcement agencies in cities with less than 50,000 inhabitants and county law enforcement agencies that are within a Metropolitan Statistical Area. Suburban areas exclude all metropolitan agencies associated with a principal city. The agencies associated with suburban areas also appear in other groups within this table.

Table 20. Murder, by Selected State, Territory, and Type of Weapon, 2017

(Number.)

State/territory	Total murders[1]	Total firearms	Handguns	Rifles	Shotguns	Firearms (type unknown)	Knives or cutting instruments	Other weapons	Hands, fists, feet, etc.[2]
Alabama[3]	2	1	0	0	0	1	0	1	0
Alaska	62	37	7	3	3	24	13	8	4
Arizona	404	249	162	8	9	70	50	93	12
Arkansas	250	168	92	11	4	61	23	52	7
California	1,830	1,274	886	37	34	317	258	195	103
Colorado	218	137	88	7	4	38	37	22	22
Connecticut	102	72	30	0	1	41	11	9	10
Delaware	52	44	20	0	1	23	3	4	1
District of Columbia	116	90	89	0	0	1	15	5	6
Georgia	672	542	490	15	5	32	37	85	8
Hawaii	39	4	1	1	0	2	9	10	16
Idaho	28	13	8	4	1	0	6	3	6
Illinois[3]	814	693	596	24	3	70	53	50	18
Indiana	360	291	147	14	6	124	20	39	10
Iowa	100	57	25	1	5	26	18	18	7
Kansas	129	79	44	4	7	24	16	26	8
Kentucky	263	192	128	6	6	52	25	33	13
Louisiana	566	460	216	23	12	209	46	42	18
Maine	23	12	4	0	0	8	3	4	4
Maryland	475	370	339	5	3	23	44	50	11
Massachusetts	170	99	34	0	0	65	36	29	6
Michigan	567	381	185	13	12	171	55	101	30
Minnesota	113	69	58	1	2	8	14	23	7
Mississippi	149	111	90	4	3	14	12	20	6
Missouri	596	514	224	22	8	260	25	48	9
Montana	41	17	10	2	1	4	12	5	7
Nebraska	43	31	27	2	2	0	4	5	3
Nevada	270	201	16	58	0	127	28	30	11
New Hampshire	14	7	4	0	1	2	5	1	1
New Jersey	324	242	175	7	4	56	42	29	11
New Mexico	113	71	20	2	0	49	20	19	3
New York	547	292	233	6	9	44	113	91	51
North Carolina	547	413	279	9	26	99	33	64	37
North Dakota	9	5	2	1	0	2	1	2	1
Ohio	682	485	226	5	11	243	46	128	23
Oklahoma	239	163	131	5	5	22	25	32	19
Oregon	100	58	34	2	2	20	17	22	3
Pennsylvania	735	567	452	11	8	96	63	73	32
Rhode Island	20	8	1	0	0	7	4	5	3
South Carolina	387	312	183	11	8	110	29	36	10
South Dakota	21	8	6	0	0	2	7	2	4
Tennessee	525	407	271	19	11	106	42	64	12
Texas	1,364	1,012	594	40	26	352	156	131	65
Utah	73	46	32	0	3	11	7	12	8
Vermont	14	6	1	0	0	5	6	1	1
Virginia	453	338	156	11	11	160	44	54	17
Washington	228	134	75	1	1	57	36	40	18
West Virginia	79	45	25	4	4	12	8	23	3
Wisconsin	186	149	111	4	2	32	11	17	9
Wyoming	14	6	5	0	0	1	3	3	2
Guam	1	0	0	0	0	0	0	1	0

1 Total number of murders for which supplemental homicide data were received.   2 Pushed is included in hands, fists, feet, etc.   3 Limited supplemental homicide data were received.

Table 21. Robbery, by State and Type of Weapon, 2017

(Number.)

State	Total robberies[1]	Firearms	Knives or cutting instruments	Other weapons	Strong-arm	Agency count	Population
Alabama	3,190	1,895	137	376	782	242	4,175,710
Alaska	949	294	88	134	433	32	736,205
Arizona	7,312	3,115	826	782	2,589	97	6,732,019
Arkansas	1,813	968	104	161	580	265	2,774,792
California	56,590	15,343	5,276	6,502	29,469	729	39,379,687
Colorado	3,734	1,615	326	434	1,359	202	5,221,193
Connecticut	2,813	936	308	263	1,306	106	3,569,335
Delaware	1,082	488	96	82	416	61	961,939
District of Columbia	2,623	946	209	187	1,281	3	693,972
Florida	18,584	7,724	1,174	1,706	7,980	603	20,971,216
Georgia	9,640	5,690	327	858	2,765	484	9,793,925
Hawaii	1,077	167	114	122	674	4	1,427,538
Idaho	182	61	30	24	67	82	1,533,625
Illinois[2]	427	217	22	45	143	1	146,770
Indiana	5,913	3,000	292	536	2,085	206	4,497,992
Iowa	1,204	532	95	132	445	200	2,839,614
Kansas	1,345	657	113	119	456	226	2,325,762
Kentucky	2,946	1,332	231	333	1,050	331	4,330,642
Louisiana	5,213	2,816	236	382	1,779	185	4,439,478
Maine	249	56	30	30	133	135	1,335,907
Maryland	11,125	5,002	1,047	958	4,118	146	5,810,386
Massachusetts	4,788	1,227	875	1,012	1,674	328	6,646,961
Michigan	6,449	2,992	367	576	2,514	619	9,803,009
Minnesota	3,619	1,199	251	571	1,598	387	5,539,575
Mississippi	1,264	806	49	121	288	69	1,482,371
Missouri	6,314	3,725	335	430	1,824	560	5,993,489
Montana	295	72	27	48	148	107	1,048,283
Nebraska	670	403	47	37	183	54	764,921
Nevada	4,841	2,154	443	561	1,683	57	2,998,039
New Hampshire	409	82	53	42	232	176	1,292,643
New Jersey	7,895	2,718	665	502	4,010	576	9,005,644
New Mexico	3,617	1,916	410	351	940	115	1,858,425
New York	19,946	3,806	2,391	1,952	11,797	525	19,173,006
North Carolina	7,161	4,018	469	624	2,050	277	7,655,991
North Dakota	182	41	24	30	87	106	749,938
Ohio	10,869	3,395	462	801	6,211	458	9,718,364
Oklahoma	2,995	1,449	257	231	1,058	394	3,872,459
Oregon	2,333	515	280	323	1,215	145	3,751,984
Pennsylvania	11,707	4,816	865	731	5,295	1,452	12,586,674
Rhode Island	474	125	87	51	211	49	1,059,639
South Carolina	3,378	1,946	241	252	939	350	4,075,266
South Dakota	224	68	25	31	100	76	732,566
Tennessee	7,823	4,489	419	956	1,959	458	6,609,070
Texas	31,526	17,752	2,201	2,554	9,019	951	26,883,394
Utah	1,448	438	202	151	657	122	2,956,234
Vermont	91	22	17	14	38	71	597,819
Virginia	3,774	1,968	343	297	1,166	394	8,118,165
Washington	5,161	1,289	518	659	2,695	237	7,259,162
West Virginia	460	161	50	70	179	183	1,321,158
Wisconsin	4,337	2,274	253	400	1,410	430	5,739,270
Wyoming	75	25	3	11	36	55	550,712

1 The number of robberies from agencies that submitted 12 months of data in 2017 for which breakdowns by type of weapon were included.   2 Limited data were received.

Table 22. Aggravated Assault, by State and Type of Weapon, 2017

(Number.)

State	Total aggravated assaults[1]	Firearms	Knives or cutting instruments	Other weapons	Personal weapons	Agency count	Population
Alabama	15,072	2,872	1,589	9,182	1,429	242	4,175,710
Alaska	4,236	1,015	712	1,314	1,195	32	736,205
Arizona	22,279	5,410	3,214	5,203	8,452	97	6,732,019
Arkansas	11,822	4,311	1,555	2,536	3,420	265	2,774,792
California	104,181	19,143	17,111	36,546	31,381	729	39,379,687
Colorado	12,237	3,919	2,950	2,997	2,371	202	5,221,193
Connecticut	4,424	700	1,000	1,544	1,180	106	3,569,335
Delaware	2,891	953	569	1,070	299	61	961,939
District of Columbia	3,791	937	1,048	1,327	479	3	693,972
Florida	57,986	17,697	10,415	20,289	9,585	603	20,971,216
Georgia	22,130	7,907	3,132	5,815	5,276	484	9,793,925
Hawaii	1,894	180	448	652	614	4	1,427,538
Idaho	2,735	508	459	774	994	82	1,533,625
Illinois[2]	1,773	1,036	146	260	331	1	146,770
Indiana	14,364	3,372	1,452	3,998	5,542	206	4,497,992
Iowa	6,160	921	946	1,279	3,014	200	2,839,614
Kansas	7,107	2,484	1,315	1,884	1,424	226	2,325,762
Kentucky	5,141	1,861	730	1,772	778	331	4,330,642
Louisiana	17,410	5,690	2,546	4,539	4,635	185	4,439,478
Maine	872	79	143	257	393	135	1,335,907
Maryland	16,528	2,933	3,552	6,384	3,659	146	5,810,386
Massachusetts	16,887	1,856	3,643	7,464	3,924	328	6,646,961
Michigan	30,457	8,591	5,314	10,182	6,370	619	9,803,009
Minnesota	7,091	1,640	1,229	1,793	2,429	387	5,539,575
Mississippi	2,650	996	327	620	707	69	1,482,371
Missouri	22,213	8,810	2,453	5,590	5,360	560	5,993,489
Montana	3,003	453	387	1,065	1,098	107	1,048,283
Nebraska	2,143	715	402	714	312	54	764,921
Nevada	9,651	2,579	2,025	2,954	2,093	57	2,998,039
New Hampshire	1,521	368	341	347	465	176	1,292,643
New Jersey	10,880	2,204	2,132	3,634	2,910	576	9,005,644
New Mexico	10,855	2,568	1,739	2,816	3,732	115	1,858,425
New York	43,350	4,608	10,837	13,292	14,613	525	19,173,006
North Carolina	18,990	8,676	2,822	3,984	3,508	277	7,655,991
North Dakota	1,430	46	178	414	792	106	749,938
Ohio	15,191	5,991	2,856	4,263	2,081	458	9,718,364
Oklahoma	12,443	2,786	1,991	4,156	3,510	394	3,872,459
Oregon	6,627	1,033	1,184	2,169	2,241	145	3,751,984
Pennsylvania	23,144	4,751	3,240	5,119	10,034	1,452	12,586,674
Rhode Island	1,521	298	417	490	316	49	1,059,639
South Carolina	15,666	6,725	2,433	3,741	2,767	350	4,075,266
South Dakota	2,697	217	451	586	1,443	76	732,566
Tennessee	32,148	12,019	5,689	11,476	2,964	458	6,609,070
Texas	71,942	22,234	14,195	22,760	12,753	951	26,883,394
Utah	3,992	760	974	1,176	1,082	122	2,956,234
Vermont	701	64	132	85	420	71	597,819
Virginia	9,244	2,854	1,501	2,453	2,436	394	8,118,165
Washington	13,254	2,871	2,073	3,842	4,468	237	7,259,162
West Virginia	4,187	1,191	485	937	1,574	183	1,321,158
Wisconsin	11,873	3,247	1,279	2,530	4,817	430	5,739,270
Wyoming	972	115	136	195	526	55	550,712

1 The number of aggravated assaults from agencies that submitted 12 months of data in 2017 for which breakdowns by type of weapon were included.   2 Limited data were received.

Table 23. Offense Analysis, Number and Percent Change, 2016–2017

(Number, percent, dollars; 14,254 agencies; 2017 estimated population 291,413,377.)

Classification	Number of offenses, 2017	Percent change from 2016	Percent distribution[1]	Average value (dollars)
Murder	15,094	-11.8	NA	X
Rape[2]	106,854	+3.7	NA	X
Robbery	280,507	-4.3	100.0	$1,373
By location				
Street/highway	104,277	-8.1	37.2	1,202
Commercial house	43,445	+0.1	15.5	1,284
Gas or service station	8,402	+3.3	3.0	1,087
Convenience store	18,416	+5.6	6.6	957
Residence	44,850	-7.3	16.0	1,732
Bank	4,761	-7.1	1.7	3,483
Miscellaneous	56,356	-1.2	20.1	1,474
Burglary	1,250,983	-7.4	100.0	2,416
By location				
Residence (dwelling)	841,283	-12.0	67.2	2,368
Residence, night	255,524	-8.2	20.4	1,995
Residence, day	424,886	-11.8	34.0	2,383
Residence, unknown	160,873	-11.6	12.9	2,924
Nonresidence (store, office, etc.)	409,700	+1.2	32.8	2,514
Nonresidence, night	179,859	+1.9	14.4	2,337
Nonresidence, day	140,921	+0.5	11.3	2,211
Nonresidence, unknown	88,920	-4.3	7.1	3,353
Larceny-theft (except motor vehicle theft)	4,917,272	-2.5	100.0	1,007
By type				
Pocket-picking	27,673	+0.7	0.6	648
Purse-snatching	19,588	-5.0	0.4	564
Shoplifting	1,021,226	-3.9	20.8	260
From motor vehicles (except accessories)	1,318,007	+0.5	26.8	879
Motor vehicle accessories	363,035	-1.1	7.4	505
Bicycles	155,914	-6.1	3.2	477
From buildings	523,223	-6.7	10.6	1,381
From coin-operated machines	10,716	-5.7	0.2	538
All others	1,477,890	-2.6	30.1	1,700
By value				
Over $200	2,256,303	-1.9	45.9	2,137
$50 to $200	1,043,225	-4.2	21.2	105
Under $50	1,617,744	-2.4	32.9	13
Motor Vehicle Theft	705,254	+0.5	NA	7,708

NA = Not available.
X = Not applicable.
* = Less than one-tenth of one percent.
1 Because of rounding, the percentages may not add to 100.0.   2 The rape figure in this table is an aggregate total of the data submitted using both the revised and legacy Uniform Crime Reporting definitions. See the chapter notes for further explanation.

Table 23. Offense Analysis, Number and Percent Change, 2016–2017—Continued

(Number, percent, dollars; 14,254 agencies; 2017 estimated population 291,413,377.)

Classification	Number of offenses, 2017	Percent change from 2016	Percent distribution[1]	Average value (dollars)
Murder	15,094	-11.8	NA	X
Rape[2]	106,854	+3.7	NA	X
Robbery	280,507	-4.3	100.0	$1,373
By location				
Street/highway	104,277	-8.1	37.2	1,202
Commercial house	43,445	+0.1	15.5	1,284
Gas or service station	8,402	+3.3	3.0	1,087
Convenience store	18,416	+5.6	6.6	957
Residence	44,850	-7.3	16.0	1,732
Bank	4,761	-7.1	1.7	3,483
Miscellaneous	56,356	-1.2	20.1	1,474
Burglary	1,250,983	-7.4	100.0	2,416
By location				
Residence (dwelling)	841,283	-12.0	67.2	2,368
Residence, night	255,524	-8.2	20.4	1,995
Residence, day	424,886	-11.8	34.0	2,383
Residence, unknown	160,873	-11.6	12.9	2,924
Nonresidence (store, office, etc.)	409,700	+1.2	32.8	2,514
Nonresidence, night	179,859	+1.9	14.4	2,337
Nonresidence, day	140,921	+0.5	11.3	2,211
Nonresidence, unknown	88,920	-4.3	7.1	3,353
Larceny-theft (except motor vehicle theft)	4,917,272	-2.5	100.0	1,007
By type				
Pocket-picking	27,673	+0.7	0.6	648
Purse-snatching	19,588	-5.0	0.4	564
Shoplifting	1,021,226	-3.9	20.8	260
From motor vehicles (except accessories)	1,318,007	+0.5	26.8	879
Motor vehicle accessories	363,035	-1.1	7.4	505
Bicycles	155,914	-6.1	3.2	477
From buildings	523,223	-6.7	10.6	1,381
From coin-operated machines	10,716	-5.7	0.2	538
All others	1,477,890	-2.6	30.1	1,700
By value				
Over $200	2,256,303	-1.9	45.9	2,137
$50 to $200	1,043,225	-4.2	21.2	105
Under $50	1,617,744	-2.4	32.9	13
Motor Vehicle Theft	705,254	+0.5	NA	7,708

NA = Not available.
X = Not applicable.
* = Less than one-tenth of one percent.
1 Because of rounding, the percentages may not add to 100.0.   2 The rape figure in this table is an aggregate total of the data submitted using both the revised and legacy Uniform Crime Reporting definitions. See the chapter notes for further explanation.

Table 24. Property Stolen and Recovered, by Type and Value, 2017

(Dollars, percent; 13,681 agencies; 2017 estimated population 282,407,733.)

Type of property	Value of property (dollars)		Percent recovered
	Stolen	Recovered	
Total	$13,505,923,310	$3,938,510,699	29.2
Currency, notes, etc.	1,366,020,962	26,879,881	2.0
Jewelry and precious metals	1,213,092,968	43,196,761	3.6
Clothing and furs	376,921,356	37,029,432	9.8
Locally stolen motor vehicles	5,562,733,246	3,289,374,602	59.1
Office equipment	451,608,653	24,186,462	5.4
Televisions, radios, stereos, etc.	394,508,873	24,585,471	6.2
Firearms	151,910,488	22,230,563	14.6
Household goods	266,677,409	10,389,743	3.9
Consumable goods	134,257,875	13,128,523	9.8
Livestock	18,251,205	2,755,916	15.1
Miscellaneous	3,569,940,275	444,753,345	12.5

SECTION III

OFFENSES CLEARED

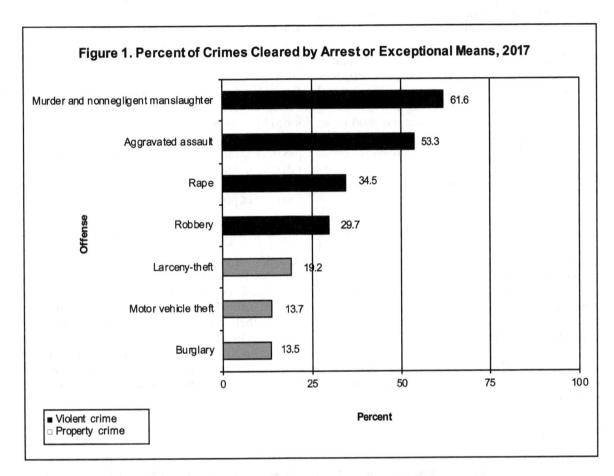

Figure 1. Percent of Crimes Cleared by Arrest or Exceptional Means, 2017

Law enforcement agencies that report crime to the Federal Bureau of Investigation (FBI) can clear, or "close," offenses in one of two ways: by arrest or by exceptional means. However, the administrative closing of a case by a local law enforcement agency does not necessarily mean that the agency can clear an offense for Uniform Crime Reporting (UCR) purposes. To clear an offense within the program's guidelines, the reporting agency must adhere to certain criteria, which are outlined in this section. (*Note:* The UCR program does not distinguish between offenses cleared by arrest and those cleared by exceptional means in its data presentations. The distinction is made solely for the purpose of a definition and not for data collection and publication.) See Appendix I for information on the UCR program's statistical methodology.

Important Note: Rape Data

In 2016, the FBI UCR Program initiated the collection of rape data within the Summary Reporting System under a revised definition. The changes bring uniformity to the offense in both the Summary Reporting System (SRS) and the National Incident-Based Reporting System

(NIBRS) by capturing data (1) without regard to gender, (2) including penetration of any bodily orifice by any object or body part, and (3) including offenses where physical force is not involved. The term "forcible" was removed, and the definition changed to the revised UCR definition below.

- Legacy UCR definition of rape: The carnal knowledge of a female forcibly and against her will. This definition ceased to be used as of January 1, 2017.

- Revised UCR definition of rape: Penetration, no matter how slight, of the vagina or anus with any body part or object, or oral penetration by a sex organ of another person, without the consent of the victim. This is the definition currently in use; unless specified otherwise, "rape" refers to this definition.

Cleared by Arrest

In the UCR program, a law enforcement agency reports that an offense is cleared by arrest, or solved for crime reporting purposes, when at least one person is arrested, charged with the commission of the offense, and turned over to the court for prosecution (whether following arrest, court summons, or police notice). To qualify as a clearance, *all* of these conditions must be met.

In its calculations, the UCR program counts the number of offenses that are cleared, not the number of arrestees. Therefore, the arrest of one person may clear several crimes, and the arrest of many persons may clear only one offense. In addition, some clearances recorded by an agency during a particular calendar year, such as 2017, may pertain to offenses that occurred in previous years.

Cleared by Exceptional Means

In certain situations, elements beyond law enforcement's control prevent the agency from arresting and formally charging the offender. When this occurs, the agency can clear the offense *exceptionally*. There are four UCR program requirements that law enforcement must meet in order to clear an offense by exceptional means. The agency must have:

- Identified the offender

- Gathered enough evidence to support an arrest, make a charge, and turn over the offender to the court for prosecution

- Identified the offender's exact location so that the suspect could be taken into custody immediately

- Encountered a circumstance outside the control of law enforcement that prohibits the agency from arresting, charging, and prosecuting the offender

Examples of exceptional clearances include, but are not limited to, the death of the offender (e.g., suicide or justifiably killed by a law enforcement officer or a citizen), the victim's refusal to cooperate with the prosecution after the offender has been identified, or the denial of extradition because the offender committed a crime in another jurisdiction and is being prosecuted for that offense. In the UCR program, the recovery of property does not clear an offense.

National Clearances

A review of the data for 2017 revealed law enforcement agencies in the United States cleared 45.6 percent of violent crimes (murder, rape, robbery, and aggravated assault) and 17.6 percent of property crimes (burglary, larceny-theft, and motor vehicle theft) brought to their attention. In addition, law enforcement cleared 21.7 percent of arson offenses, which are reported in a slightly different manner than the other property crimes. (Table 25) More details concerning this offense are furnished in the arson text in this section.

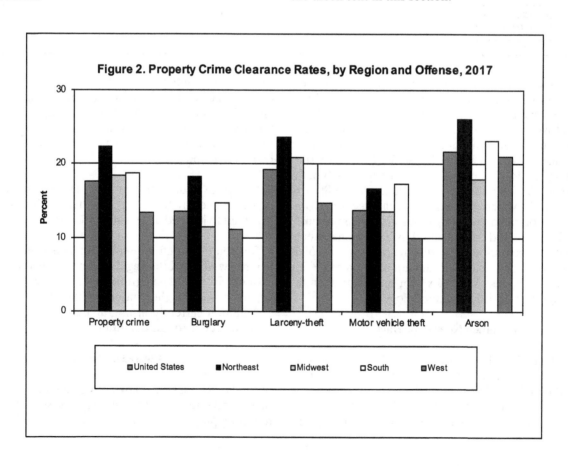

Figure 2. Property Crime Clearance Rates, by Region and Offense, 2017

As in most years, law enforcement agencies cleared a higher percentage of violent crimes than property crimes in 2017. As a rule, clearance rates generally rise due to the more vigorous investigative efforts put forth for violent crimes. In addition, violent crimes more often involve victims and/or witnesses who are able to identify the perpetrators.

A breakdown of the clearances for violent crimes for 2017 revealed that the nation's law enforcement agencies cleared 61.6 percent of murder offenses, 53.3 percent of aggravated assault offenses, 34.5 percent of rape offenses, and 29.7 percent of robbery offenses. (Table 25)

For property crime offenses in 2017, law enforcement agencies throughout the nation collectively 13.5 percent of burglary offenses, 19.2 percent of larceny-theft offenses, and 13.7 percent of motor vehicle theft offenses (up more than two percentage points from 2016). (Table 25)

Regional Clearances

The UCR program divides the nation into four regions: the Northeast, the Midwest, the South, and the West. (See Appendix III for further details.) A review of clearance data for 2017 by region showed that agencies in the Northeast cleared the greatest proportion of their violent crime offenses (53.9 percent). Law enforcement agencies in the South cleared 45.0 percent of their violent crimes, while agencies in the West and Midwest cleared 44.6 percent and 41.4 percent of their violent crimes, respectively. (Table 26)

For murder and nonnegligent manslaughter in 2017, the West cleared 65.6 percent of offenses, followed by the South (63.4 percent). The Northeast cleared 62.1 percent and the Midwest cleared 51.6 percent of these offenses. Rape offenses were cleared 38.9 percent of the time in the South, 36.4 percent of the time in the Northeast, 31.4 percent of the time in the Midwest, and 30.1 percent of the time in the West. For robbery, the Northeast had the highest clearance rate, at 37.0 percent. The Northeast also had the highest proportion of clearances for aggravated assault (64.5 percent). (Table 26)

Clearance data for 2017 showed that, among the regions, law enforcement agencies in the Northeast cleared the highest percentage of their property crimes (22.4 percent). Agencies in the South and Midwest cleared 18.7 percent and 18.5 percent, respectively. Agencies in the West cleared 13.4 percent of their property crimes. (Table 26)

Agencies in the Northeast cleared the highest percentage of burglary offenses at 18.3 percent, followed by the

South at 14.7 percent, the Midwest at 11.5 percent, and the West at 11.1 percent. For larceny-theft, the Northeast (23.7 percent) was followed by the Midwest at 20.9 percent, the South at 20.0 percent, and the West at 14.7 percent. The South and Northeast cleared the highest proportion of motor vehicle thefts at 17.3 and 16.6 percent, respectively, followed by the Midwest at 13.6 percent and the West at 9.9 percent. The Northeast cleared the greatest percentage of arson offenses (26.0 percent), followed by the South (23.2 percent). (Table 26)

Clearances by Population Groups

The UCR program uses the following population group designations in its data presentations: cities (grouped according to population size) and counties (classified as either metropolitan or nonmetropolitan counties). A breakdown of these classifications is furnished in Appendix III.

CITIES

In 2017, the clearance data collected showed that law enforcement agencies in the nation's cities cleared 43.4 percent of their violent crime offenses. Among the city population groups and subsets, agencies in the smallest cities, those with fewer than 10,000 inhabitants, cleared the greatest proportion of their violent crime offenses (54.2 percent), and law enforcement in cities with 500,000 to 999,999 inhabitants cleared the smallest proportion of their violent crime offenses (35.2 percent). (Table 25)

The clearance data for murder showed that among the city population groups and subsets, cities with populations of more than 1,000,000 inhabitants cleared the greatest percentage of their murders (69.1 percent). Law enforcement agencies in cities with 250,000 to 499,999 inhabitants cleared the lowest percentage of their murders (53.3 percent). For rape, cities with 500,000 to 999,999 inhabitants cleared the largest percentage of offenses at 35.2 percent, while cities with under 10,000 inhabitants cleared the lowest percentage of offenses at 31.3 percent. Cities with under 10,000 inhabitants cleared the greatest percentage of their robbery offenses at 37.7 percent, and cities with 500,000 to 999,999 inhabitants cleared the lowest proportion of their robbery offenses at 22.9 percent. For aggravated assault, cities with fewer than 10,000 inhabitants cleared the highest proportion of offenses (61.0 percent); cities with 500,000 to 999,999 inhabitants cleared the lowest percentage of offenses (41.0 percent). (Table 25)

In 2017, agencies in the nation's cities collectively cleared 17.4 percent of their property crime offenses. Law enforcement in cities with 10,000 to 24,999 inhabitants cleared the highest proportion of the property crimes (24.7 percent) brought to their attention; cities with 500,000 to

999,999 inhabitants cleared the smallest proportion of their property crimes (10.4 percent). (Table 25)

Law enforcement agencies in cities cleared 12.8 percent of burglaries, 19.2 percent of larceny-thefts, 12.4 percent of motor vehicle thefts, and 20.7 percent of arsons in 2017. For burglaries, cities with fewer than 10,000 inhabitants cleared the largest percentage of their offenses at 17.9 percent, while cities with 500,000 to 999,999 inhabitants cleared the smallest percentage of their offenses at 9.1 percent. Cities with 10,000 to 24,999 inhabitants cleared the greatest percentage of their larceny-theft offenses (27.0 percent), and cities with 500,000 to 999,999 inhabitants cleared the lowest proportion of larceny-theft offenses (11.1 percent). For motor vehicle theft, cities with fewer than 10,000 inhabitants cleared the highest percentages of their offenses at 24.2 percent. Cities with under 10,000 inhabitants also cleared the greatest percentage of their arson offenses, at 28.4 percent. (Table 25)

METROPOLITAN AND NONMETROPOLITAN COUNTIES

In 2017, law enforcement agencies in metropolitan counties cleared 52.5 percent of their violent crime offenses.

Of the violent crimes made known to law enforcement agencies in metropolitan counties, murder offenses had the highest proportion of clearance (64.7 percent), followed by aggravated assaults (59.4 percent), rapes (39.6 percent), and robberies (33.3 percent). Law enforcement agencies in metropolitan counties cleared 17.9 percent of their total property crimes, 15.3 percent of burglaries, 18.7 percent of larceny-thefts, 17.4 percent of motor vehicle thefts, and 23.8 percent of their arsons. (Table 25)

Like their counterparts in metropolitan counties, nonmetropolitan counties collectively cleared a greater proportion of their violent crimes than did the nation as a whole in 2017. Nonmetropolitan counties cleared 56.6 percent of their violent crime offenses and 19.6 percent of property crimes. Of the violent crimes known to them, law enforcement in nonmetropolitan counties had the highest number of clearances for murder (71.2 percent), with 36.7 percent of rapes, 42.8 percent of robberies, and 62.1 percent of aggravated assaults being cleared. Agencies in nonmetropolitan counties reported clearing 19.4 percent of property crimes, including 17.0 percent of their burglaries, 19.8 percent of their larceny-thefts, 25.6 percent of their motor vehicle thefts, and 27.5 percent of their arsons. (Table 25)

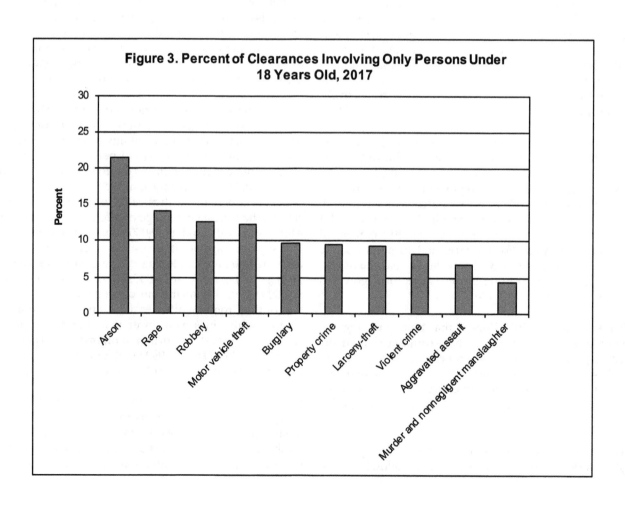

Figure 3. Percent of Clearances Involving Only Persons Under 18 Years Old, 2017

Clearances by Classification Group and Type

For rape, by classification group and type, law enforcement agencies cleared 37.7 percent of assault-to-rape attempts and 33.6 percent of rapes by force in 2017. Cleared robbery offenses included 33.1 percent of offenses involving strong-arm tactics, 33.5 percent of offenses involving knives or other cutting instruments, 31.5 percent of offenses involving other weapons, and 24.1 percent of offenses involving firearms. For aggravated assaults, agencies cleared 62.2 percent of offenses involving knives or other cutting instruments; 61.5 percent of offenses involving hands, feet, fists, etc.; 54.6 percent of offenses involving other weapons; and 36.6 percent of offenses involving firearms. (Table 27)

For property crime clearances grouped by classification and type, data showed that the highest percentage of burglary clearances in the nation in 2017 (15.0 percent) were of offenses that involved unlawful entry. Law enforcement agencies cleared 12.3 percent each of burglaries involving forcible entry and attempted forcible entry. For motor vehicle theft, agencies cleared 14.0 percent of motor vehicle theft offenses involving automobiles and 10.7 percent of motor vehicle theft offenses involving trucks and buses. (Table 27)

In 2017, 26.0 percent of structural arson offenses were cleared by arrest or exceptional means, while 10.3 percent of mobile arson offenses and 23.3 percent of other arson crimes were cleared. (Table 27)

CLEARANCES AND JUVENILES

When an offender under 18 years of age is cited to appear in juvenile court or before other juvenile authorities, the UCR program considers the incident for which the juvenile is being held responsible to be cleared by arrest, although a physical arrest may not have occurred. In addition, according to program definitions, clearances that include both adult and juvenile offenders are classified as clearances for crimes committed by adults. Therefore, the juvenile clearance data are limited to those clearances involving juveniles only, and the figures in this publication should not be used to present a definitive picture of juvenile involvement in crime.

Of the clearances for violent crimes that were reported in the nation in 2017, 8.3 percent involved only juveniles. In the nation's cities, collectively, 8.3 percent of violent crime clearances also involved only juveniles, with juveniles in cities exclusively involved in 4.4 percent of murder clearances, 14.2 percent of rape clearances, 12.7 percent of robbery clearances, and 6.8 percent of aggravated assault clearances. Of the nation's city population groups and subsets, cities with under 10,000 inhabitants had the highest percentage of overall clearances for violent crime only involving juveniles (9.3 percent); cities with 100,000 to 249,999 inhabitants and cities with 250,000 to 499,999 inhabitants had the lowest percentage, 7.9 percent. (Table 28)

Law enforcement agencies in metropolitan counties reported that 8.4 percent of their violent crime clearances—including 3.7 percent of their murder clearances, 18.4 percent of their rape clearances, 12.2 percent of their robbery clearances, and 6.9 percent of their aggravated assault clearances—involved only juveniles. Agencies in nonmetropolitan counties reported that 6.3 percent of their clearances for violent crime involved only juveniles, including 2.6 percent of their murder clearances, 17.6 percent of their rape clearances, 4.7 percent of their robbery clearances, and 2.8 percent of their aggravated assault clearances. (Table 28)

In 2017, 9.4 percent of clearances for property crime involved only juveniles. In cities collectively, 9.5 percent of the clearances for property crime, 9.7 percent of clearances for burglary, 9.3 percent of clearances for larceny-theft, 12.2 percent of clearances for motor vehicle theft, and 21.5 percent of clearances for arson involved juveniles only. Among the population groups and subsets labeled *city*, the percentages of clearances involving only juveniles for overall property crime ranged from a low of 8.4 percent in cities with more than 1,000,000 inhabitants to a high of 10.4 percent in cities with populations of 100,000 to 249,999. (Table 28)

Metropolitan counties reported that 9.6 percent of all property crime clearances, 9/0 percent of burglary clearances, 9.7 percent of larceny-theft clearances, 10.5 percent of motor vehicle theft clearances, and 19.4 percent of arson clearances involved persons under 18 years of age. In nonmetropolitan counties, 6.2 percent of property crime clearances, 6.1 percent of burglary clearances, 5.8 percent of larceny-theft clearances, 8.3 percent of motor vehicle theft clearances, and 12.6 percent of arson clearances involved juveniles exclusively. In suburban areas, 24.0 percent of arson clearances involved only juveniles. (Table 28)

Table 25. Number and Percent of Offenses Cleared by Arrest or Exceptional Means, by Population Group, 2017

(Number, percent.)

Population group	Violent crime	Murder and nonnegligent manslaughter	Rape[1]	Robbery	Aggravated assault	Property crime	Burglary	Larceny-theft	Motor vehicle theft	Arson[2]	Number of agencies	Estimated population, 2017
Total, All Agencies												
Offenses known	1,177,632	15,657	121,084	293,160	747,731	7,074,399	1,281,083	5,072,970	720,346	40,416	14,975	297,646,423
Percent cleared by arrest	45.6	61.6	34.5	29.7	53.3	17.6	13.5	19.2	13.7	21.7		
Total Cities												
Offenses known	942,624	12,288	90,329	257,523	582,484	5,646,734	951,113	4,113,790	581,831	31,105	10,968	202,173,273
Percent cleared by arrest	43.6	60.3	33.0	29.1	51.4	17.4	12.8	19.2	12.4	20.7		
Group I (250,000 and over)												
Offenses known	443,507	6,188	34,061	142,364	260,894	1,953,831	339,700	1,354,430	259,701	12,493	81	59,068,040
Percent cleared by arrest	39.0	59.6	33.6	26.5	46.0	11.9	10.0	12.9	9.2	15.1		
1,000,000 and over (Group I subset)												
Offenses known	170,598	1,878	13,047	56,798	98,875	647,361	106,712	454,823	85,826	3,662	10	25,129,639
Percent cleared by arrest	44.0	69.1	34.7	31.0	52.1	11.8	10.1	12.8	8.8	14.1		
500,000 to 999,999 (Group I subset)												
Offenses known	152,876	2,358	11,076	47,894	91,548	728,714	130,372	504,515	93,827	4,831	24	17,571,403
Percent cleared by arrest	35.2	57.1	35.2	22.9	41.0	10.4	9.1	11.1	8.5	15.5		
250,000 to 499,999 (Group I subset)												
Offenses known	120,033	1,952	9,938	37,672	70,471	577,756	102,616	395,092	80,048	4,000	47	16,366,998
Percent cleared by arrest	36.7	53.3	30.5	24.3	43.8	13.7	10.8	15.1	10.5	15.6		
Group II (100,000 to 249,999)												
Offenses known	152,832	2,162	15,091	42,443	93,136	993,919	168,996	707,837	117,086	4,811	213	31,855,061
Percent cleared by arrest	42.3	58.8	31.9	28.5	49.8	15.7	12.0	17.2	12.3	23.2		
Group III (50,000 to 99,999)												
Offenses known	115,050	1,322	12,256	30,104	71,368	840,693	138,454	621,712	80,527	4,429	469	32,747,541
Percent cleared by arrest	48.2	63.4	34.2	32.9	56.9	18.6	13.1	20.5	13.0	22.1		
Group IV (25,000 to 49,999)												
Offenses known	85,734	1,015	10,548	19,837	54,334	680,453	109,920	519,732	50,801	3,068	828	28,843,794
Percent cleared by arrest	48.1	63.5	32.0	34.1	56.0	22.2	14.5	24.5	15.4	23.9		
Group V (10,000 to 24,999)												
Offenses known	74,858	845	9,291	14,031	50,691	636,078	104,476	489,861	41,741	2,776	1,715	27,384,738
Percent cleared by arrest	51.9	63.3	33.9	36.4	59.2	24.7	16.4	27.0	18.8	26.4		
Group VI (under 10,000)												
Offenses known	70,643	756	9,082	8,744	52,061	541,760	89,567	420,218	31,975	3,528	7,662	22,274,099
Percent cleared by arrest	54.2	58.3	31.3	37.7	61.0	24.5	17.9	25.9	24.2	28.4		
Metropolitan Counties												
Offenses known	186,998	2,556	22,162	32,995	129,285	1,149,484	243,886	792,143	113,455	6,989	1,857	71,893,861
Percent cleared by arrest	52.5	64.7	39.6	33.3	59.4	17.9	15.3	18.7	17.4	23.8		
Nonmetropolitan Counties												
Offenses known	48,010	813	8,593	2,642	35,962	278,181	86,084	167,037	25,060	2,322	2,150	23,579,289
Percent cleared by arrest	56.6	71.2	36.7	42.8	62.1	19.4	17.0	19.8	25.6	27.5		
Suburban Areas[3]												
Offenses known	324,524	4,036	39,641	62,504	218,343	2,353,692	424,177	1,729,649	199,866	12,613	8,189	128,800,806
Percent cleared by arrest	52.1	63.9	37.1	34.5	59.6	20.4	15.5	21.9	17.1	24.6		

1 The figures shown in the rape column include only those reported by law enforcement agencies that used the revised Uniform Crime Reporting definition of rape. See chapter notes for more detail.   2 Not all agencies submit reports for arson to the FBI. As a result, the number of reports the FBI uses to compute the percent of offenses cleared for arson is less than the number it uses to compute the percent of offenses cleared for all other offenses.   3 Suburban area includes law enforcement agencies in cities with less than 50,000 inhabitants and county law enforcement agencies that are within a Metropolitan Statistical Area. Suburban area excludes all metropolitan agencies associated with a principal city. The agencies associated with suburban areas also appear in other groups within this table.

Table 26. Number and Percent of Offenses Cleared by Arrest or Exceptional Means, by Region and Geographic Division, 2017

(Number, percent.)

Geographic region/division	Violent crime	Murder and nonnegligent manslaughter	Rape[1]	Robbery	Aggravated assault	Property crime	Burglary	Larceny-theft	Motor vehicle theft	Arson[2]	Number of agencies	Estimated population, 2017
Total, All Agencies												
Offenses known	1,177,632	15,657	121,084	293,160	747,731	7,074,399	1,281,083	5,072,970	720,346	40,416	14,975	297,646,423
Percent cleared by arrest	45.6	61.6	34.5	29.7	53.3	17.6	13.5	19.2	13.7	21.7		
Northeast												
Offenses known	169,624	1,931	16,625	48,281	102,787	860,362	126,156	678,346	55,860	4,160	3,452	55,376,980
Percent cleared by arrest	53.9	62.1	36.4	37.0	64.5	22.4	18.3	23.7	16.6	26.0		
New England												
Offenses known	39,296	333	4,703	8,686	25,574	223,677	36,210	169,848	17,619	1,020	904	14,510,335
Percent cleared by arrest	49.6	54.7	24.9	28.1	61.3	18.3	15.7	19.4	13.5	24.0		
Middle Atlantic												
Offenses known	130,328	1,598	11,922	39,595	77,213	636,685	89,946	508,498	38,241	3,140	2,548	40,866,645
Percent cleared by arrest	55.2	63.6	40.9	39.0	65.6	23.9	19.3	25.1	18.1	26.7		
Midwest												
Offenses known	195,822	2,822	25,587	42,182	125,231	1,169,400	217,934	840,793	110,673	8,003	3,698	51,194,388
Percent cleared by arrest	41.4	51.6	31.4	23.9	49.0	18.5	11.5	20.9	13.6	18.0		
East North Central												
Offenses known	120,881	1,812	16,118	28,350	74,601	675,263	132,695	481,209	61,359	5,135	1,851	30,938,578
Percent cleared by arrest	37.9	46.2	29.6	22.3	45.5	16.9	10.6	19.4	11.2	16.5		
West North Central												
Offenses known	74,941	1,010	9,469	13,832	50,630	494,137	85,239	359,584	49,314	2,868	1,847	20,255,810
Percent cleared by arrest	46.9	61.2	34.6	27.2	54.2	20.6	12.9	22.9	16.6	20.8		
South												
Offenses known	489,912	7,461	44,547	115,014	322,890	3,007,175	576,124	2,172,813	258,238	13,464	5,798	115,159,534
Percent cleared by arrest	45.0	63.4	38.9	29.0	51.2	18.7	14.7	20.0	17.3	23.2		
South Atlantic												
Offenses known	231,554	3,702	18,030	57,511	152,311	1,494,461	269,389	1,105,039	120,033	6,145	2,694	59,852,966
Percent cleared by arrest	48.3	64.3	44.6	32.8	54.3	20.5	17.5	21.4	18.6	26.6		
East South Central												
Offenses known	80,926	1,325	6,735	15,898	56,968	466,860	98,469	325,242	43,149	2,276	1,261	17,181,666
Percent cleared by arrest	44.5	60.2	39.1	28.2	49.3	21.6	15.5	23.3	22.8	25.0		
West South Central												
Offenses known	177,432	2,434	19,782	41,605	113,611	1,045,854	208,266	742,532	95,056	5,043	1,843	38,124,902
Percent cleared by arrest	40.9	64.0	33.6	24.0	47.9	14.9	10.8	16.3	13.2	18.4		
West												
Offenses known	322,274	3,443	34,325	87,683	196,823	2,037,462	360,869	1,381,018	295,575	14,789	2,027	75,915,521
Percent cleared by arrest	44.6	65.6	30.1	29.4	53.5	13.4	11.1	14.7	9.9	21.0		
Mountain												
Offenses known	103,289	1,197	13,474	21,609	67,009	648,287	116,834	452,579	78,874	3,495	868	23,307,076
Percent cleared by arrest	43.3	68.6	24.9	24.8	52.6	17.2	11.4	19.8	10.9	26.5		
Pacific												
Offenses known	218,985	2,246	20,851	66,074	129,814	1,389,175	244,035	928,439	216,701	11,294	1,159	52,608,445
Percent cleared by arrest	45.1	64.0	33.5	30.9	53.9	11.5	11.0	12.2	9.5	19.3		

1 The figures shown in the rape column include only those reported by law enforcement agencies that used the revised Uniform Crime Reporting definition of rape. See chapter notes for more detail.   2 Not all agencies submit reports for arson to the FBI. As a result, the number of reports the FBI uses to compute the percent of offenses cleared for arson is less than the number it uses to compute the percent of offenses cleared for all other offenses.

Table 27. Number and Percent of Offenses Cleared by Arrest or Exceptional Means, Additional Information About Selected Offenses, by Population Group, 2017

(Number, percent.)

Population group	Rape[1] Rape by force	Rape[1] Assault to rape-attempts	Robbery Firearm	Robbery Knife or cutting instrument	Robbery Other weapon	Robbery Strong-arm	Aggravated assault Firearm	Aggravated assault Knife or cutting instrument	Aggravated assault Other weapon	Aggravated assault Hands, fists, feet, etc.
Total, All Agencies										
Offenses known	108,015	5,410	111,555	22,632	26,915	113,859	179,615	118,605	212,194	180,939
Percent cleared by arrest	33.6	37.7	24.1	33.5	31.5	33.1	36.6	62.2	54.6	61.5
Total Cities										
Offenses known	82,072	4,309	97,868	20,358	23,891	103,108	147,974	99,060	168,430	136,699
Percent cleared by arrest	32.5	38.1	23.9	33.0	31.0	32.6	33.8	61.0	52.8	61.5
Group I (250,000 and over)										
Offenses known	31,100	1,878	56,904	11,051	12,822	57,723	79,239	46,704	79,274	46,141
Percent cleared by arrest	32.8	38.1	21.4	30.4	27.9	30.3	29.6	58.7	48.6	56.6
1,000,000 and over (Group I subset)										
Offenses known	12,203	844	20,893	5,186	5,351	25,368	23,696	21,247	31,344	22,588
Percent cleared by arrest	34.1	42.8	23.0	34.2	33.7	36.4	31.5	62.0	53.9	62.1
500,000 to 999,999 (Group I subset)										
Offenses known	9,966	572	21,365	3,676	4,917	16,560	30,320	15,089	29,514	13,000
Percent cleared by arrest	34.2	37.9	19.2	26.1	21.5	27.1	29.2	55.2	41.9	50.2
250,000 to 499,999 (Group I subset)										
Offenses known	8,931	462	14,646	2,189	2,554	15,795	25,223	10,368	18,416	10,553
Percent cleared by arrest	29.6	29.9	22.5	28.5	27.9	24.0	28.4	57.0	50.4	52.6
Group II (100,000 to 249,999)										
Offenses known	13,738	509	16,331	3,498	3,959	15,891	25,404	16,472	27,359	18,285
Percent cleared by arrest	31.6	41.1	24.0	32.2	31.2	31.7	33.2	59.8	52.3	59.4
Group III (50,000 to 99,999)										
Offenses known	10,917	442	9,483	2,467	2,875	12,375	14,780	11,920	19,958	17,976
Percent cleared by arrest	34.2	41.6	27.5	35.2	35.8	35.6	38.8	64.3	59.2	66.3
Group IV (25,000 to 49,999)										
Offenses known	9,567	462	7,046	1,561	2,007	7,768	11,646	9,265	14,911	14,639
Percent cleared by arrest	31.5	38.1	29.2	37.8	35.6	37.6	39.2	63.4	57.6	63.1
Group V (10,000 to 24,999)										
Offenses known	8,547	364	5,036	1,098	1,415	5,476	9,725	7,793	13,996	16,046
Percent cleared by arrest	33.5	35.2	31.6	44.4	37.4	39.9	44.1	65.6	59.0	66.2
Group VI (under 10,000)										
Offenses known	8,203	654	3,068	683	813	3,875	7,180	6,906	12,932	23,612
Percent cleared by arrest	30.6	34.9	32.0	40.6	39.4	40.4	49.9	65.4	57.1	64.9
Metropolitan Counties										
Offenses known	17,927	744	12,612	2,081	2,685	9,851	24,676	15,352	33,852	31,466
Percent cleared by arrest	37.3	39.8	25.4	37.2	35.2	37.3	46.9	68.9	61.9	61.5
Nonmetropolitan Counties										
Offenses known	8,016	357	1,075	193	339	900	6,965	4,193	9,912	12,774
Percent cleared by arrest	36.5	28.3	36.1	50.3	40.4	47.2	58.5	66.8	60.7	61.8
Suburban Areas[3]										
Offenses known	33,585	1,615	22,803	4,304	5,536	21,628	39,602	28,664	57,618	61,606
Percent cleared by arrest	35.6	37.1	27.4	39.5	36.8	38.9	46.1	68.1	60.7	63.8

Table 27. Number and Percent of Offenses Cleared by Arrest or Exceptional Means, Additional Information About Selected Offenses, by Population Group, 2017—Continued

(Number, percent.)

Population group	Burglary			Motor vehicle theft			Arson[2]			Number of agencies	Estimated population, 2017
	Forcible entry	Unlawful entry	Attempted forcible entry	Autos	Trucks and buses	Other vehicles	Structure	Mobile	Other		
Total, All Agencies											
Offenses known	690,503	431,109	73,082	517,327	99,694	61,612	17,025	9,395	11,952	14,404	277,152,623
Percent cleared by arrest	12.3	15.0	12.3	14.0	10.7	10.4	26.0	10.3	23.3		
Total Cities											
Offenses known	522,927	322,119	58,123	430,295	81,615	43,548	13,365	7,034	9,385	10,662	192,305,575
Percent cleared by arrest	11.5	14.6	11.9	13.0	9.7	9.0	24.9	9.5	22.7		
Group I (250,000 and over)											
Offenses known	208,498	96,672	21,049	189,048	45,947	17,014	5,076	3,292	3,710	76	56,778,339
Percent cleared by arrest	8.8	11.8	10.6	9.7	7.3	6.1	18.7	6.4	17.4		
1,000,000 and over (Group I subset)											
Offenses known	70,324	29,693	6,695	58,701	20,938	6,187	1,452	909	1,301	10	25,129,639
Percent cleared by arrest	8.7	12.5	14.9	10.0	6.0	7.0	22.1	6.4	10.7		
500,000 to 999,999 (Group I subset)											
Offenses known	80,205	36,008	8,513	69,217	15,170	6,515	2,021	1,350	1,260	23	16,676,765
Percent cleared by arrest	8.1	10.8	8.4	8.6	7.9	4.7	17.6	6.1	21.0		
250,000 to 499,999 (Group I subset)											
Offenses known	57,969	30,971	5,841	61,130	9,839	4,312	1,603	1,033	1,149	43	14,971,935
Percent cleared by arrest	10.0	12.3	8.9	10.6	9.1	7.0	16.9	6.8	21.0		
Group II (100,000 to 249,999)											
Offenses known	92,091	56,062	10,554	87,801	14,581	8,162	2,033	1,104	1,445	197	29,500,128
Percent cleared by arrest	11.4	12.7	11.5	12.6	11.2	8.2	25.7	10.6	28.7		
Group III (50,000 to 99,999)											
Offenses known	70,431	49,785	8,149	58,913	9,519	6,249	1,867	901	1,450	436	30,481,898
Percent cleared by arrest	11.9	14.9	11.3	13.4	11.0	8.8	25.3	9.5	25.0		
Group IV (25,000 to 49,999)											
Offenses known	55,846	41,155	6,890	38,952	4,478	4,490	1,269	566	1,030	791	27,474,766
Percent cleared by arrest	13.4	15.9	11.9	15.7	13.6	11.0	27.8	13.3	25.0		
Group V (10,000 to 24,999)											
Offenses known	51,499	41,710	5,860	31,459	4,140	3,877	1,267	510	846	1,648	26,285,968
Percent cleared by arrest	15.5	17.5	14.7	19.9	15.3	12.5	30.5	15.1	26.7		
Group VI (under 10,000)											
Offenses known	44,562	36,735	5,621	24,122	2,950	3,756	1,853	661	904	7,514	21,784,476
Percent cleared by arrest	16.7	19.3	15.6	25.4	21.0	18.1	34.8	15.1	25.1		
Metropolitan Counties											
Offenses known	118,580	78,139	11,737	70,713	14,216	13,757	2,550	1,865	1,967	1,661	61,831,313
Percent cleared by arrest	13.7	16.2	13.5	17.4	13.9	12.4	29.2	12.0	25.7		
Nonmetropolitan Counties											
Offenses known	48,996	30,851	3,222	16,319	3,863	4,307	1,110	496	600	2,081	23,015,735
Percent cleared by arrest	16.7	16.7	14.8	28.2	21.0	17.3	31.5	16.1	25.2		
Suburban Areas[3]											
Offenses known	206,642	146,657	23,968	135,910	22,085	21,671	5,052	2,962	3,670	7,781	116,232,117
Percent cleared by arrest	14.1	16.8	13.2	17.3	13.8	12.4	30.4	12.0	25.9		

1 The figures shown in the rape column include only those reported by law enforcement agencies that used the revised Uniform Crime Reporting definition of rape. See chapter notes for more detail.   2 Not all agencies submit reports for arson to the FBI. As a result, the number of reports the FBI uses to compute the percent of offenses cleared for arson is less than the number it uses to compute the percent of offenses cleared for all other offenses.   3 Suburban area includes law enforcement agencies in cities with less than 50,000 inhabitants and county law enforcement agencies that are within a Metropolitan Statistical Area. Suburban area excludes all metropolitan agencies associated with a principal city. The agencies associated with suburban areas also appear in other groups within this table.

Table 28. Number of Offenses Cleared by Arrest or Exceptional Means and Percent Involving Persons Under 18 Years of Age, by Population Group, 2017

(Number, percent.)

Population group	Violent crime	Murder and nonnegligent manslaughter	Rape[1]	Robbery	Aggravated assault	Property crime	Burglary	Larceny-theft	Motor vehicle theft	Arson[2]	Number of agencies	Estimated population, 2017
Total, All Agencies												
Offenses known	494,742	9,005	38,331	80,730	366,676	1,149,647	158,241	901,686	89,720	8,407	14,404	277,152,623
Percent under 18 years	8.3	4.2	15.2	12.6	6.7	9.4	9.3	9.2	11.6	20.4		
Total Cities												
Offenses known	389,918	7,073	28,318	71,091	283,436	931,083	113,959	749,548	67,576	6,277	10,662	192,305,575
Percent under 18 years	8.3	4.4	14.2	12.7	6.8	9.5	9.7	9.3	12.2	21.5		
Group I (250,000 and over)												
Offenses known	166,660	3,563	10,930	36,652	115,515	220,644	32,036	165,921	22,687	1,835	76	56,778,339
Percent under 18 years	8.1	4.2	13.0	14.0	5.8	9.4	8.8	9.1	12.4	16.4		
1,000,000 and over (Group I subset)												
Offenses known	74,979	1,298	4,528	17,612	51,541	76,700	10,825	58,326	7,549	518	10	25,129,639
Percent under 18 years	8.1	4.5	12.7	15.4	5.3	8.4	6.5	8.6	10.3	16.8		
500,000 to 999,999 (Group I subset)												
Offenses known	51,585	1,288	3,621	10,605	36,071	71,826	11,092	53,279	7,455	728	23	16,676,765
Percent under 18 years	8.2	4.0	12.7	12.9	6.4	9.6	10.8	8.6	14.4	19.1		
250,000 to 499,999 (Group I subset)												
Offenses known	40,096	977	2,781	8,435	27,903	72,118	10,119	54,316	7,683	589	43	14,971,935
Percent under 18 years	7.9	3.9	13.7	12.5	6.0	10.2	9.2	10.1	12.4	12.7		
Group II (100,000 to 249,999)												
Offenses known	60,522	1,211	4,552	11,309	43,450	145,437	18,863	113,186	13,388	1,082	197	29,500,128
Percent under 18 years	7.9	5.4	14.3	11.4	6.4	10.4	10.4	10.1	13.1	19.7		
Group III (50,000 to 99,999)												
Offenses known	50,711	759	3,921	8,910	37,121	143,002	16,696	116,812	9,494	949	436	30,481,898
Percent under 18 years	8.6	5.0	14.5	11.9	7.2	10.6	9.9	10.6	11.9	21.7		
Group IV (25,000 to 49,999)												
Offenses known	38,352	619	3,187	6,282	28,264	143,756	14,826	121,718	7,212	715	791	27,474,766
Percent under 18 years	8.7	4.4	14.9	10.5	7.7	9.3	9.3	9.1	12.9	27.0		
Group V (10,000 to 24,999)												
Offenses known	36,572	503	2,993	4,792	28,284	149,359	16,144	125,841	7,374	705	1,648	26,285,968
Percent under 18 years	8.7	3.6	16.1	10.0	7.7	8.9	9.6	8.7	11.3	27.5		
Group VI (under 10,000)												
Offenses known	37,101	418	2,735	3,146	30,802	128,885	15,394	106,070	7,421	991	7,514	21,784,476
Percent under 18 years	9.3	3.6	15.7	13.6	8.3	8.5	10.8	8.0	10.1	24.2		
Metropolitan Counties												
Offenses known	79,411	1,383	6,986	8,592	62,450	167,219	30,475	120,754	15,990	1,518	1,661	61,831,313
Percent under 18 years	8.4	3.7	18.4	12.2	6.9	9.6	9.0	9.7	10.5	19.4		
Nonmetropolitan Counties												
Offenses known	25,413	549	3,027	1,047	20,790	51,345	13,807	31,384	6,154	612	2,081	23,015,735
Percent under 18 years	6.3	2.6	17.6	4.7	4.8	6.2	6.1	5.8	8.3	12.6		
Suburban Areas[3]												
Offenses known	145,197	2,240	12,548	18,386	112,023	425,919	56,915	339,785	29,219	2,916	7,781	116,232,117
Percent under 18 years	9.0	3.9	17.2	12.0	7.7	9.3	9.5	9.2	11.0	24.0		

1 The figures shown in the rape column include only those reported by law enforcement agencies that used the revised Uniform Crime Reporting definition of rape. See chapter notes for more detail.   2 Not all agencies submit reports for arson to the FBI. As a result, the number of reports the FBI uses to compute the percent of offenses cleared for arson is less than the number it uses to compute the percent of offenses cleared for all other offenses.   3 Suburban area includes law enforcement agencies in cities with less than 50,000 inhabitants and county law enforcement agencies that are within a Metropolitan Statistical Area. Suburban area excludes all metropolitan agencies associated with a principal city. The agencies associated with suburban areas also appear in other groups within this table.

SECTION IV

PERSONS ARRESTED

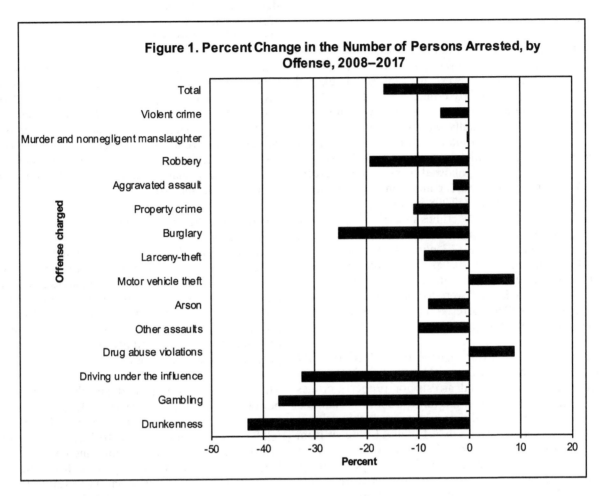

Figure 1. Percent Change in the Number of Persons Arrested, by Offense, 2008–2017

In the Uniform Crime Reporting (UCR) program, one arrest is counted for each separate instance in which an individual is arrested, cited, or summoned for criminal acts in Part I and Part II crimes. (See Appendix I for additional information concerning Part I and Part II crimes.) One person may be arrested multiple times during the year; as a result, the arrest figures in this section should not be taken as the total number of individuals arrested. Instead, it provides the number of *arrest occurrences* reported by law enforcement. Information regarding the UCR program's statistical methodology and table construction can be found in Appendix I.

Important Note: Rape Data

In 2013, the FBI UCR Program initiated the collection of rape data within the Summary Reporting System under a revised definition. The changes bring uniformity to the offense in both the Summary Reporting System (SRS) and the National Incident-Based Reporting System (NIBRS) by capturing data (1) without regard to gender, (2) including penetration of any bodily orifice by any object or body part, and (3) including offenses where

physical force is not involved. The term "forcible" was removed, and the definition changed to the revised UCR definition below.

- Legacy UCR definition of rape: The carnal knowledge of a female forcibly and against her will. This definition has been discontinued.

- Revised UCR definition of rape: Penetration, no matter how slight, of the vagina or anus with any body part or object, or oral penetration by a sex organ of another person, without the consent of the victim. Unless otherwise specified, this is the definition to which "rape" refers.

Data Collection: Juveniles

The UCR Program considers a juvenile to be an individual under 18 years of age regardless of state definition. The program does not collect data regarding police contact with a juvenile who has not committed an offense, nor does it collect data on situations in which police take a juvenile into custody for his or her protection, e.g., neglect cases.

319

National Volume, Trends, and Rates

VOLUME

The FBI estimated that approximately 10,554,985 arrests occurred in 2017 for all offenses (except traffic violations). Of these arrests, 518,617 were for violent crimes, and 1,249,757 were for property crimes. UCR does not collect data for traffic violations. Of the total violent crimes in 2017, aggravated assaults accounted for nearly 75.0 percent of the violent crime total, or 388,927 incidents. Robbery had the next highest proportion with 18.1 percent, or 94,046 incidents; followed by rape at 4.5 percent (23,436 incidents) and murder and non-negligent manslaughter, at 2.4 percent (12,208 incidents). Of the estimated arrests for property crimes in 2017, 950,357 (76.0 percent) were for larceny-theft, 199,266 (15.9 percent) were for burglary, 91,023 (7.3 percent) were for motor vehicle theft, and 9,111 (0.7 percent) were for arson. Outside of these categories, the most frequent identifiable arrests made in 2017 were for drug abuse violations (estimated at 1,632,921 arrests). These arrests comprised 15.5 percent of the total number of all arrests. (Table 29)

A comparison of arrest figures from 2016 to 2017 revealed a 0.8 percent decrease. Arrests for violent crimes increased 0.8 percent and arrests for property crimes decreased 6.7 percent over this time period. An examination of the 5-year and 10-year arrest trends showed that the total number of arrests in 2017 fell 8.1 percent from the 2013 total. Arrests for violent crimes showed a 2.3 percent increase from 2013 to 2017 and property crimes showed a 21,1 percent decrease. In the 10-year trend data (2008 to 2017), the number of arrests decreased 22.4 percent. For violent crimes, the number of arrests fell 11.7 percent, while arrests for property crimes decreased 24.3 percent. (Tables 32, 34, and 36)

TRENDS

The number of adults arrested for violent crime (arrestees age 18 years and over) increased 0.8 percent from 2016 to 2017, increased 3.3 percent from 2013 to 2017, and decreased 5.6 percent from 2008 to 2017. The number of juveniles arrested for violent crime (arrestees under 18 years of age) increased 0.9 percent from 2016 to 2017, decreased 6.1 percent from 2013 to 2017, and decreased 44.6 percent from 2008 to 2017. (Tables 32, 34, and 36)

The trend data for murder and nonnegligent manslaughter showed that the number of arrests for this offense increased 3.1 percent from 2016 to 2017, increased 11.5 percent from 2013 to 2017, and decreased 2.7 percent from 2008 to 2017. The number of adults arrested for murder increased 3.1 percent from 2016 to 2017, increased 11.5 percent from 2013 to 2017, and fell 0.2 percent from 2008 to 2017. The number of juveniles arrested for murder increased 3.3 percent from 2016 to 2017, increased 12.1 percent from 2013 to 2017, and fell 26.0 percent from 2008 to 2017. (Tables 32, 34, and 36)

For rape, the trend data showed that arrests decreased 0.3 percent from 2016 to 2017, with adult arrests decreasing 1.6 percent and juvenile arrests rising 6.3 percent. The five-year data (2013 to 2017) shows arrests increasing 19.1 percent overall, with adult arrests increasing 18.0 percent and juvenile arrests increasing 18.0 percent. The 10-year trend data percentages were not calculated due to the program changes in the classification of rape data. (Tables 32, 34, and 36)

For robbery, the data showed that arrests decreased 2.3 percent from 2016 to 2017, with adult arrests decreasing 2.9 percent and juvenile arrests falling 0.1 percent. The 5-year trend data showed that total robbery arrests fell 6.6 percent from 2013 to 2017; adult arrests decreased 7.0 percent and juvenile arrests dropped 4.8 percent during this period. The 10-year trend data showed that arrests fell 26.4 percent from 2008 to 2017, with adult arrests dropping 19.3 percent and juvenile arrests falling by 45.9 percent. (Tables 32, 34, and 36)

The aggravated assault trend data showed that the number of arrests for this offense rose 1.6 percent from 2016 to 2017, increased 3.5 percent from 2013 to 2017, and fell 8.8 percent from 2008 to 2017. The number of adults arrested for aggravated assault increased 1.7 percent from 2016 to 2017, rose 4.7 percent from 2013 to 2017, and decreased 3.1 percent from 2008 to 2017. The number of juveniles arrested for aggravated assault increased 0.7 percent from 2016 to 2017, fell 10.3 percent from 2013 to 2017, and dropped 48.0 percent from 2008 to 2017. (Tables 32, 34, and 36)

The 2-year, 5-year, and 10-year trend data showed that the number of arrests for property crime decreased 6.7 percent from 2016 to 2017, decreased 21.1 percent from 2013 to 2017, and decreased 24.3 percent from 2008 to 2017. The number of adults arrested for property crime offenses (arrestees age 18 years and over) decreased 6.6 percent from 2016 to 2017, decreased 19.0 percent from 2013 to 2017, and decreased 10.8 percent from 2008 to 2017. The number of juveniles arrested for property crime (arrestees under 18 years of age) decreased 7.5 percent from 2016 to 2017, decreased 32.5 percent from 2013 to 2017, and decreased 61.6 percent from 2008 to 2017. (Tables 32, 34, and 36)

The trend data for burglary showed that the number of arrests for this offense decreased 3.8 percent from 2016 to 2017, decreased 23.8 percent from 2013 to 2017, and decreased 35.6 percent from 2008 to 2017. The number of adults arrested for burglary fell 3.8 percent from 2016 to 2017, fell 22.7 percent from 2013 to 2017, and decreased 25.4 percent from 2008 to 2017. The number of juveniles arrested for burglary decreased 3.5 percent from 2016 to 2017, decreased 29.0 percent from 2013 to 2017, and fell 63.0 percent from 2008 to 2017. (Tables 32, 34, and 36)

For larceny-theft, the 2-year trend data showed that arrests fell 8.4 percent from 2016 to 2017, with adult arrests decreasing 8.1 percent and juvenile arrests decreasing 9.8 percent. The 5-year trend data showed that total larceny-theft arrests decreased 23.3 percent from 2013 to 2017; adult arrests fell 21.0 percent, while juvenile arrests dropped by 36.5 percent during this period. The 10-year trend data showed that larceny-theft arrests fell 23.0 percent from 2008 to 2017, with adult arrests decreasing by 8.8 percent and juvenile arrests falling by 63.0 percent. (Tables 32, 34, and 36)

For motor vehicle theft, the 2-year trend data showed that arrests rose 5.5 percent from 2016 to 2017, with adult arrests increasing 5.9 percent and juvenile arrests increasing 3.7 percent. The 5-year trend data showed that total motor vehicle theft arrests rose 30.5 percent from 2013 to 2017; juvenile arrests increased 24.7 percent and adult arrests increased 31.7 percent during this period. The 10-year trend data showed that arrests dropped 2.0 percent from 2008 to 2017, with adult arrests rising 8.6 percent and juvenile arrests dropping 34.2 percent. (Tables 32, 34, and 36)

The arson trend data showed that the number of arrests for this offense increased 0.5 percent from 2016 to 2017, fell 12.5 percent from 2013 to 2017, and fell 35.4 percent from 2008 to 2017. The number of adults arrested for arson rose 3.3 percent from 2016 to 2017, increased 2.5 percent from 2013 to 2017, and fell 7.9 percent from 2008 to 2017. The number of juveniles arrested for arson dropped 7.3 percent from 2016 to 2017, dropped 38.7 percent from 2013 to 2017, and dropped 65.1 percent from 2008 to 2017. (Tables 32, 34, and 36)

RATES

The rate of arrests was estimated at 3,251.5 arrests per 100,000 inhabitants in 2017. The arrest rate for violent

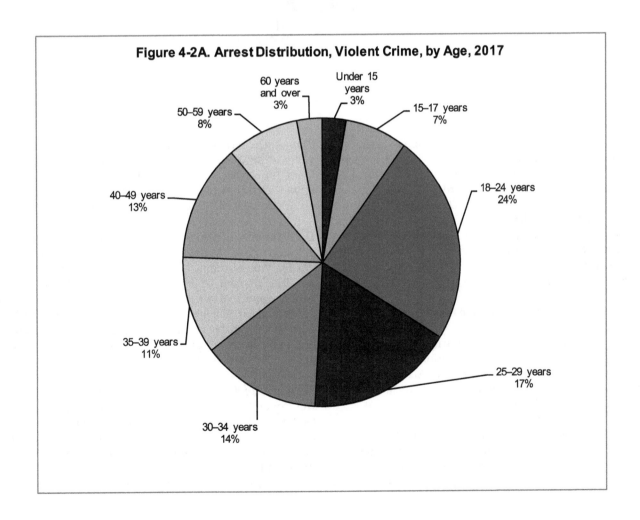

Figure 4-2A. Arrest Distribution, Violent Crime, by Age, 2017

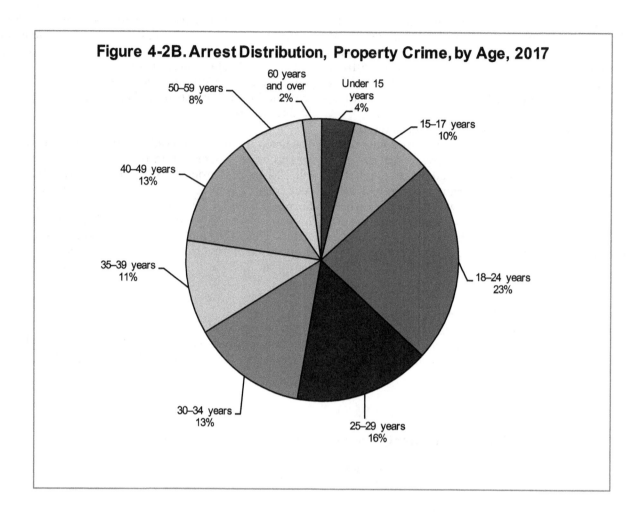

Figure 4-2B. Arrest Distribution, Property Crime, by Age, 2017

- 60 years and over 2%
- 50–59 years 8%
- 40–49 years 13%
- 35–39 years 11%
- 30–34 years 13%
- 25–29 years 16%
- 18–24 years 23%
- 15–17 years 10%
- Under 15 years 4%

crime was 160.7 arrests per 100,000 inhabitants, and the arrest rate for property crime was 388.7 arrests per 100,000 inhabitants. Law enforcement agencies throughout the nation reported 3.8 murder arrests, 7.2 rape arrests, 29.3 robbery arrests, and 120.4 aggravated assault arrests per 100,000 inhabitants in 2017. Law enforcement agencies throughout the nation reported 61.7 burglary arrests, 296.0 larceny-theft arrests, 28.2 motor vehicle theft arrests, and 2.8 arson arrests per 100,000 inhabitants in 2017. (Table 30)

By Age, Sex, and Race

Law enforcement agencies that contributed arrest data to the UCR program reported information on the age, sex, and race of the persons they arrested. According to the data for 2017, adults accounted for 92.3 percent of arrestees nationally. (Table 38)

A review of arrest data by age from 2016 to 2017 showed that arrests of adults decreased 0.5 percent during this period, with a 0.8 percent increase in arrests for violent crime and a 6.6 percent drop in arrests for property

crimes. The arrest total for juveniles (those under 18 years of age) decreased 4.5 percent from 2016 to 2017. Over the 2-year period, arrests of juveniles for violent crimes rose 0.9 percent; juvenile arrests for property crimes decreased 7.5 percent. (Table 36)

By sex, males accounted for 73.0 percent of all persons arrested in 2017. Males represented 79.5 percent of arrestees for violent crime, 87.5 percent of arrestees for murder, 97.2 percent of arrestees for rape, 85.4 percent for robbery, and 76.7 percent for aggravated assault. Females accounted for 20.5 percent of violent crime arrestees, 12.5 percent of murder arrestees, 2.8 percent of rape arrestees, 14.6 percent of robbery arrestees, and 23.3 percent of aggravated assault arrestees. (Table 42)

Most arrestees for property crime in 2017 (86.6 percent) were over 18 years of age. By sex, males accounted for 64.2 percent of arrestees for property crime, 81.2 percent of arrestees for burglary, 59.2 percent of arrestees for larceny-theft, 77.7 percent of arrestees for motor vehicle theft, and 80.0 percent of arrestees for arson. Females accounted for 35.8 percent of property crime arrestees.

Of the four property crimes, larceny-theft had the highest proportion of female arrestees at 40.8 percent. (Tables 38 and 42)

In 2017, 68.9 percent of all persons arrested were White, 27.2 percent were Black, and the remaining 3.9 percent were of other races (American Indian or Alaskan Native, Asian, and Native Hawaiian or Pacific Islander). Of all arrestees for violent crimes, 58.5 percent were White, 37.5 percent were Black, and 3.9 percent were of other races. For murder, 44.2 percent of arrestees were White, 53.1 percent were Black, and 2.6 percent were of other races. For rape, 67.5 percent of arrestees were White, 28.7 percent were Black, and 3.9 percent of arrestees were of other races. For robbery, 43.6 percent of arrestees were White, 54.3 percent of arrestees were Black, and 2.2 percent of arrestees were of other races. For aggravated assault, 62.1 percent of arrestees were White, 33.5 percent of arrestees were Black, and 4.4 percent were of other races. (Table 43)

Of all arrestees for property crimes in 2017, 67.6 percent were White, 29.3 percent were Black, and 3.1 percent were of other races. For burglary, 67.5 percent of arrestees were White, 29.8 percent were Black, and 2.7 percent were of other races. For larceny-theft, 67.7 percent of arrestees were White, 29.1 percent were Black, and 3.2

percent were of other races. For motor vehicle theft, 66.0 percent of arrestees were White, 30.3 percent of arrestees were Black, and 3.7 percent were of other races. For arson, 71.3 percent of arrestees were White, 25.2 percent of arrestees were Black, and 3.5 percent were of other races. (Table 43)

Outside of the scope of violent and property crimes, White adults were most commonly arrested for drug abuse violations (889,030 arrests) and driving under the influence (617,443 arrests). Black adults were most frequently arrested for drug abuse violations (342,513 arrests) and other assaults (258,542 arrests). (Table 43)

Regional Arrest Rates

The UCR program divides the United States into four regions: the Northeast, the Midwest, the South, and the West. (Appendix III provides more information about the regions.) Law enforcement agencies in the Northeast had an overall arrest rate of 2,767.5 arrests per 100,000 inhabitants, below the national rate (3,251.5 arrests per 100,000 inhabitants). In this region, the arrest rate for violent crimes was 127.0 arrests per 100,000 inhabitants, and for property crime, the arrest rate was 352.4 arrests per 100,000 inhabitants. In the Midwest, law enforcement agencies reported an arrest rate of 3,184.5 arrests

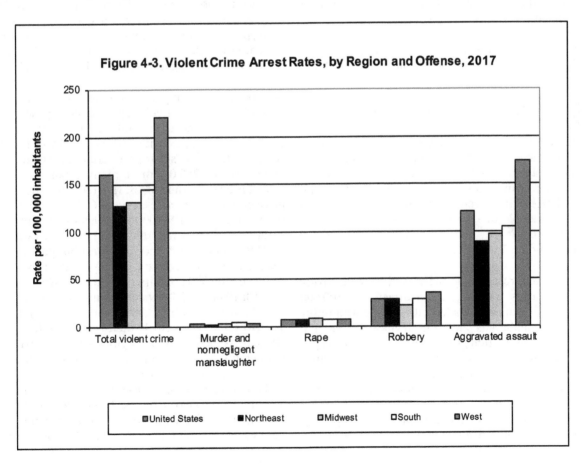

Figure 4-3. Violent Crime Arrest Rates, by Region and Offense, 2017

per 100,000 inhabitants. The arrest rate for violent crimes was 131.7 and the arrest rate for property crime was 403.1. Law enforcement agencies in the South, the nation's most populous region, reported an arrest rate of 3,578.3 per 100,000 inhabitants. Arrests for violent crime occurred at a rate of 144.7 arrests per 100,000 residents, and for property crime, the arrest rate was 425.6 arrests per 100,000 inhabitants. In the West, law enforcement agencies reported an overall arrest rate of 3,211.8 arrests per 100,000 inhabitants. The region's violent crime arrest rate was 220.3, the highest of the regions, while its property crime arrest rate was 357.9. (Table 30)

The regional murder arrest rates were 2.3 in the Northeast, 3.5 in the Midwest, 4.9 in the South, and 3.5 in the West. For rape, the regional arrest rates were 7.1 in the Northeast, 8.4 in the Midwest, 6.8 in the South, and 6.9 in the West. Regional arrest rates for robbery were 29.1 in the Northeast, 22.4 in the Midwest, 28.3 in the South, and 35.3 in the West. For aggravated assault, the regional arrest rates were 88.5 in the Northeast, 97.3 in the Midwest, 104.6 in the South, and 174.6 in the West. (Table 30)

The regional burglary arrest rates were 46.4 in the Northeast, 44.7 in the Midwest, 65.4 in the South, and 78.3 in the West. For larceny-theft, the regional arrest rates were 289.0 in the Northeast, 327.9 in the Midwest, 333.8 in the South, and 234.0 in the West. Regional arrest rates for motor vehicle theft were 14.7 in the Northeast, 27.9 in the Midwest, 23.8 in the South, and 41.9 in the West. For arson, the regional arrest rates were 2.3 in the Northeast, 2.5 in the Midwest, 2.5 in the South, and 3.7 in the West. (Table 30)

Population Groups: Trends and Rates

The national UCR program aggregates data by various population groups, which include cities, metropolitan counties, and nonmetropolitan counties. Definitions of these groups can be found in Appendix III. The total number of arrests in U.S. cities fell 1.0 percent from 2016 to 2017. The number of arrests for violent crimes rose 0.9 percent and arrests for property crimes decreased 7.0 percent during the 2-year time frame. (Table 44)

In 2017, law enforcement agencies in cities collectively recorded an arrest rate of 3,251.5 arrests per 100,000 inhabitants. The nation's smallest cities, those with fewer than 10,000 inhabitants, had the highest arrest rate among the city population groups with 4,996.2 arrests per 100,000 inhabitants. Law enforcement agencies in cities with 250,000 or more inhabitants recorded the lowest rate, 2,904.2. In the nation's metropolitan counties, law enforcement agencies reported an arrest rate of 2,826.4 per 100,000 inhabitants. Agencies in nonmetropolitan counties reported an arrest rate of 3,225.2. (Table 31)

By population group, law enforcement agencies in the nation's cities collectively reported 178.4 violent crime arrests per 100,000 inhabitants in 2017. In the city population groups, cities with 250,000 or more inhabitants reported the highest violent crime arrest rate (237.4) and cities with 10,000 to 24,999 inhabitants reported the lowest violent crime arrest rate (122.4). Cities reported an overall murder arrest rate of 4.0 per 100,000 inhabitants; cities with 250,000 or more inhabitants had the highest murder arrest rate (6.6) and cities with under 10,000 inhabitants had the lowest murder arrest rate (2.1). The collective city rape arrest rate was 7.4 per 100,000 inhabitants, with the highest rate in cities with 250,000 or more inhabitants (9.0) and the lowest rate in cities with 10,000 to 24,999 inhabitants (6.1). The overall robbery arrest rate for cities was 35.9 per 100,000 inhabitants; cities with 250,000 or more inhabitants had the highest robbery arrest rate (57.9) and cities with fewer than 10,000 inhabitants had the lowest robbery arrest rate (16.8). For aggravated assault, the collective city arrest rate was 131.0 per 100,000 inhabitants, with the greatest arrest rate in cities with 250,000 or more inhabitants (164.0) and the lowest arrest rate in cities with 10,000 to 24,999 inhabitants (94.4). (Table 31)

Agencies in metropolitan counties reported a violent crime arrest rate of 128.1 per 100,000 inhabitants, with arrest rates of 3.3 for murder, 6.2 for rape, 17.7 for robbery, and 100.8 for aggravated assault. Agencies in nonmetropolitan counties reported arrest rates of 101.0 for violent crime, 2.9 for murder, 8.0 for rape, 19.5 for robbery, and 96.0 for aggravated assault. (Table 31)

By population group, law enforcement agencies in the nation's cities collectively reported 453.6 property crime arrests per 100,000 inhabitants in 2017. In the city population groups, cities with 10,000 to 24,999 inhabitants reported the highest property crime arrest rate (517.3) and cities with 250,000 or more inhabitants reported the lowest property crime arrest rate (365.9). Cities reported an overall burglary arrest rate of 65.7 per 100,000 inhabitants; cities with 100,000 to 249,999 inhabitants had the highest burglary arrest rate (73.9) and cities with 10,000 to 24,999 inhabitants had the lowest burglary arrest rate (60.3). The collective city larceny-theft arrest rate was 354.6 per 100,000 inhabitants, with the highest rate in cities with 10,000 to 24,999 inhabitants (434.4) and the lowest rate in cities with 250,000 or more inhabitants (259.2). The overall motor vehicle theft arrest rate for cities was 30.2 per 100,000 inhabitants; cities with 100,000 to 249,999 inhabitants had the highest motor vehicle theft arrest rate (39.5), and cities with 10,000 to 24,999 inhabitants had the lowest motor vehicle theft arrest rate (19.9). For arson, the collective city arrest rate was 3.1 per 100,000 inhabitants, with the greatest arrest rate in cities with less than 10,000 inhabitants (4.2) and the lowest arrest rate in cities with more than 10,000 to 24,999 inhabitants (2.7). (Table 31)

Agencies in metropolitan counties reported a property crime arrest rate of 259.0 per 100,000 inhabitants, with arrest rates of 51.0 for burglary, 181.5 for larceny-theft, 24.3 for motor vehicle theft, and 2.2 for arson. Agencies in nonmetropolitan counties reported arrest rates of 198.6 for property crime, 57.2 for burglary, 117.6 for larceny-theft, 21.4 for motor vehicle theft, and 2.4 for arson. (Table 31)

In suburban areas, the rates per 100,000 inhabitants for violent crime and property crime were 124.2 and 364.0, respectively. The rate for murder was 2.7; for rape, 6.0; for robbery, 19.5; and for aggravated assault, 96.0. Specific property crime rates included 53.6 for burglary, 285.8 for larceny-theft, 22.1 for motor vehicle theft, and 2.6 for arson. (Table 31)

Community Types

In 2017, law enforcement agencies in the nation's cities reported that 91.5 percent of arrests in their jurisdictions were of adults and 8.5 percent of arrests were of juveniles. Adults accounted for 89.5 percent of arrestees for violent crimes, while juveniles accounted for 10.5 percent of these arrests. Adults made up 86.2 percent of the arrestees for property crimes, and juveniles accounted for the remaining 13.8 percent. Of all arrests in the nation's cities in 2017, 32.0 percent were of individuals under 25 years of age. In metropolitan counties, 28.7 percent of arrests were of individuals under 25 years of age. In nonmetropolitan counties, 25.6 percent of persons arrested were of individuals under 25 years of age. (Tables 46, 47, 53, and 59)

Males accounted for 72.7 percent and females accounted for 27.3 percent of arrestees in the nation's cities in 2017. In metropolitan counties, males comprised 73.6 percent of arrestees, and in nonmetropolitan counties, males represented 73.4 percent of all arrestees. (Tables 48, 54, and 60)

By race, 66.5 percent of arrestees in the nation's cities in 2017 were White, 29.3 percent were Black, and 4.2 percent were of other races (American Indian or Alaska Native and Asian or Pacific Islander). Whites accounted for 72.1 percent of arrestees in metropolitan counties in 2017, Blacks made up 25.5 percent of arrestees, and persons of other races made up 2.4 percent of the total. In nonmetropolitan counties, Whites made up 83.3 percent of arrestees, Blacks accounted for 12.6 percent of arrestees, and other races made up 4.2 percent of the total. (Tables 49, 55, and 61)

Table 29. Estimated Number of Arrests, United States, 2015

(Number.)

Offense	Arrests
Total[1]	10,797,088
Violent crime[2]	505,681
Murder and nonnegligent manslaughter	11,092
Rape[3]	22,863
Robbery	95,572
Aggravated assault	376,154
Property crime[2]	1,463,213
Burglary	216,010
Larceny-theft	1,160,390
Motor vehicle theft	77,979
Arson	8,834
Other assaults	1,081,019
Forgery and counterfeiting	55,333
Fraud	133,138
Embezzlement	15,909
Stolen property; buying, receiving, possessing	88,576
Vandalism	191,015
Weapons; carrying, possessing, etc.	145,358
Prostitution and commercialized vice	41,877
Sex offenses (except forcible rape and prostitution)	51,388
Drug abuse violations	1,488,707
Gambling	4,825
Offenses against the family and children	94,837
Driving under the influence	1,089,171
Liquor laws	266,250
Drunkenness	405,880
Disorderly conduct	386,078
Vagrancy	25,151
All other offenses	3,218,880
Suspicion	1,389
Curfew and loitering law violations	44,802

1 Does not include suspicion.   2 Violent crimes are offenses of murder and nonnegligent manslaughter, rape, robbery, and aggravated assault. Property crimes are offenses of burglary, larceny-theft, motor vehicle theft, and arson.   3 The rape figures in this table are an aggregate total of the data submitted using both the revised and legacy Uniform Crime Reporting definitions.

Table 30. Number and Rate of Arrests, by Geographic Region, 2017

(Number, rate per 100,000 inhabitants.)

Offense charged	United States total (12,606 agencies; population 253,634,894)		Northeast (3,233 agencies; population 45,428,011)		Midwest (3,082 agencies; population 49,278,965)		South (4,502 agencies; population 86,203,577)		West (1,789 agencies; population 72,724,341)	
	Total	Rate	Total	Rate	Total	Rate	Total	Rate	Total	Rate
Total[1]	8,246,901	3,251.5	1,257,202	2,767.5	1,569,268	3,184.5	3,084,662	3,578.3	2,335,769	3,211.8
Violent crime[2]	407,496	160.7	57,707	127.0	64,884	131.7	124,694	144.7	160,211	220.3
Murder and nonnegligent manslaughter	9,576	3.8	1,066	2.3	1,742	3.5	4,259	4.9	2,509	3.5
Rape[3]	18,289	7.2	3,221	7.1	4,162	8.4	5,865	6.8	5,041	6.9
Robbery	74,340	29.3	13,223	29.1	11,026	22.4	24,391	28.3	25,700	35.3
Aggravated assault	305,291	120.4	40,197	88.5	47,954	97.3	90,179	104.6	126,961	174.6
Property crime[2]	985,847	388.7	160,109	352.4	198,631	403.1	366,855	425.6	260,252	357.9
Burglary	156,465	61.7	21,099	46.4	22,020	44.7	56,384	65.4	56,962	78.3
Larceny-theft	750,750	296.0	131,267	289.0	161,587	327.9	287,753	333.8	170,143	234.0
Motor vehicle theft	71,452	28.2	6,682	14.7	13,771	27.9	20,542	23.8	30,457	41.9
Arson	7,180	2.8	1,061	2.3	1,253	2.5	2,176	2.5	2,690	3.7
Other assaults	833,396	328.6	143,010	314.8	160,928	326.6	321,278	372.7	208,180	286.3
Forgery and counterfeiting	43,534	17.2	7,775	17.1	7,737	15.7	18,294	21.2	9,728	13.4
Fraud	96,948	38.2	19,418	42.7	18,044	36.6	41,515	48.2	17,971	24.7
Embezzlement	12,532	4.9	1,367	3.0	2,383	4.8	6,621	7.7	2,161	3.0
Stolen property; buying, receiving, possessing	77,474	30.5	10,967	24.1	12,732	25.8	25,494	29.6	28,281	38.9
Vandalism	147,959	58.3	32,400	71.3	27,565	55.9	38,140	44.2	49,854	68.6
Weapons; carrying, possessing, etc.	129,210	50.9	15,608	34.4	26,392	53.6	45,379	52.6	41,831	57.5
Prostitution and commercialized vice	28,490	11.2	4,313	9.5	3,224	6.5	8,918	10.3	12,035	16.5
Sex offenses (except forcible rape and prostitution)	37,850	14.9	5,980	13.2	6,807	13.8	10,846	12.6	14,217	19.5
Drug abuse violations	1,275,812	503.0	228,158	502.2	232,060	470.9	477,504	553.9	338,090	464.9
Gambling	2,510	1.0	350	0.8	675	1.4	998	1.2	487	0.7
Offenses against the family and children	72,229	28.5	14,965	32.9	15,804	32.1	30,413	35.3	11,047	15.2
Driving under the influence	764,569	301.4	125,609	276.5	149,100	302.6	237,517	275.5	252,343	347.0
Liquor laws	161,277	63.6	20,672	45.5	56,259	114.2	42,387	49.2	41,959	57.7
Drunkenness	289,608	114.2	30,363	66.8	22,236	45.1	150,064	174.1	86,945	119.6
Disorderly conduct	276,987	109.2	72,124	158.8	84,750	172.0	73,728	85.5	46,385	63.8
Vagrancy	18,542	7.3	1,330	2.9	3,248	6.6	4,020	4.7	9,944	13.7
All other offenses (except traffic)	2,560,932	1,009.7	297,618	655.1	470,861	955.5	1,053,738	1,222.4	738,715	1,015.8
Suspicion	690	0.3	10	*	115	0.2	178	0.2	387	0.5
Curfew and loitering law violations	23,699	9.3	7,359	16.2	4,948	10.0	6,259	7.3	5,133	7.1

* = Less than one-tenth of one percent.
1 Does not include suspicion.   2 Violent crimes are offenses of murder and nonnegligent manslaughter, rape, robbery, and aggravated assault. Property crimes are offenses of burglary, larceny-theft, motor vehicle theft, and arson.   3 The rape figures in this table are aggregate totals of the data submitted based on both the legacy and revised Uniform Crime Reporting definitions.

Table 31. Number and Rate of Arrests, by Population Group, 2017

(Number, rate per 100,000 inhabitants.)

Offense charged	Total (12,606 agencies; population 253,634,894)		Total cities (9,289 cities; population 175,386,806)		Group I (70 cities, 250,000 and over; population 48,476,285)		Group II (187 cities, 100,000 to 249,999; population 27,988,967)		Group III (418 cities, 50,000 to 99,999; population 29,355,914)	
	Total	Rate	Total	Rate	Total	Rate	Total	Rate	Total	Rate
Total[2]	8,246,901	3,251.5	5,953,330	3,394.4	1,407,872	2,904.2	913,617	3,264.2	956,043	3,256.7
Violent crime[3]	407,496	160.7	312,819	178.4	115,089	237.4	55,908	199.8	49,858	169.8
Murder and nonnegligent manslaughter	9,576	3.8	7,058	4.0	3,188	6.6	1,357	4.8	916	3.1
Rape[4]	18,289	7.2	13,036	7.4	4,344	9.0	2,092	7.5	2,018	6.9
Robbery	74,340	29.3	62,927	35.9	28,066	57.9	10,931	39.1	9,485	32.3
Aggravated assault	305,291	120.4	229,798	131.0	79,491	164.0	41,528	148.4	37,439	127.5
Property crime[3]	985,847	388.7	795,597	453.6	177,370	365.9	127,825	456.7	135,310	460.9
Burglary	156,465	61.7	115,300	65.7	31,267	64.5	20,679	73.9	20,264	69.0
Larceny-theft	750,750	296.0	621,866	354.6	125,672	259.2	95,212	340.2	106,411	362.5
Motor vehicle theft	71,452	28.2	53,010	30.2	19,001	39.2	11,046	39.5	7,772	26.5
Arson	7,180	2.8	5,421	3.1	1,430	2.9	888	3.2	863	2.9
Other assaults	833,396	328.6	629,727	359.1	180,582	372.5	103,272	369.0	101,610	346.1
Forgery and counterfeiting	43,534	17.2	32,362	18.5	6,099	12.6	4,772	17.0	5,637	19.2
Fraud	96,948	38.2	68,407	39.0	12,527	25.8	9,932	35.5	11,456	39.0
Embezzlement	12,532	4.9	9,910	5.7	2,903	6.0	1,401	5.0	1,672	5.7
Stolen property; buying, receiving, possessing	77,474	30.5	57,682	32.9	16,289	33.6	9,259	33.1	10,843	36.9
Vandalism	147,959	58.3	114,103	65.1	29,201	60.2	17,712	63.3	19,484	66.4
Weapons; carrying, possessing, etc.	129,210	50.9	98,876	56.4	38,567	79.6	16,139	57.7	13,937	47.5
Prostitution and commercialized vice	28,490	11.2	24,853	14.2	16,093	33.2	3,860	13.8	2,014	6.9
Sex offenses (except forcible rape and prostitution)	37,850	14.9	26,831	15.3	8,179	16.9	3,973	14.2	4,477	15.3
Drug abuse violations	1,275,812	503.0	906,754	517.0	204,052	420.9	146,835	524.6	150,684	513.3
Gambling	2,510	1.0	1,789	1.0	968	2.0	200	0.7	202	0.7
Offenses against the family and children	72,229	28.5	37,793	21.5	5,701	11.8	6,562	23.4	5,194	17.7
Driving under the influence	764,569	301.4	442,122	252.1	88,409	182.4	58,336	208.4	68,250	232.5
Liquor laws	161,277	63.6	127,086	72.5	17,468	36.0	13,500	48.2	16,506	56.2
Drunkenness	289,608	114.2	252,852	144.2	39,064	80.6	40,650	145.2	43,351	147.7
Disorderly conduct	276,987	109.2	228,822	130.5	36,161	74.6	26,532	94.8	36,481	124.3
Vagrancy	18,542	7.3	16,388	9.3	6,567	13.5	3,478	12.4	2,484	8.5
All other offenses (except traffic)	2,560,932	1,009.7	1,746,599	995.9	396,875	818.7	261,456	934.1	274,132	933.8
Suspicion	690	0.3	541	0.3	4	*	0	0.0	7	*
Curfew and loitering law violations	23,699	9.3	21,958	12.5	9,708	20.0	2,015	7.2	2,461	8.4

Table 31. Number and Rate of Arrests, by Population Group, 2017—Continued

(Number, rate per 100,000 inhabitants.)

Offense charged	Group IV (731 cities, 25,000 to 49,999; population 25,358,946)		Group V (1,536 cities, 10,000 to 24,999; population 24,416,036)		Group VI (6,347 cities, under 10,000; population 19,790,658)		Metropolitan counties (1,458 agencies; population 57,699,058)		Nonmetropolitan counties (1,859 agencies; population 20,549,030)		Suburban areas[1] (7,047 agencies; population 113,235,593)	
	Total	Rate	Total	Rate	Total	Rate	Total	Rate	Total	Rate	Total	Rate
Total[2]	822,289	3,242.6	864,722	3,541.6	988,787	4,996.2	1,630,821	2,826.4	662,750	3,225.2	3,530,649	3,118.0
Violent crime[3]	33,026	130.2	29,884	122.4	29,054	146.8	73,918	128.1	20,759	101.0	140,609	124.2
Murder and nonnegligent manslaughter	622	2.5	562	2.3	413	2.1	1,917	3.3	601	2.9	3,028	2.7
Rape[4]	1,561	6.2	1,484	6.1	1,537	7.8	3,602	6.2	1,651	8.0	6,816	6.0
Robbery	6,318	24.9	4,801	19.7	3,326	16.8	10,229	17.7	1,184	5.8	22,101	19.5
Aggravated assault	24,525	96.7	23,037	94.4	23,778	120.1	58,170	100.8	17,323	84.3	108,664	96.0
Property crime[3]	125,750	495.9	126,304	517.3	103,038	520.6	149,439	259.0	40,811	198.6	412,185	364.0
Burglary	15,339	60.5	14,720	60.3	13,031	65.8	29,411	51.0	11,754	57.2	60,693	53.6
Larceny-theft	104,486	412.0	106,065	434.4	84,020	424.5	104,711	181.5	24,173	117.6	323,577	285.8
Motor vehicle theft	5,183	20.4	4,849	19.9	5,159	26.1	14,046	24.3	4,396	21.4	25,021	22.1
Arson	742	2.9	670	2.7	828	4.2	1,271	2.2	488	2.4	2,894	2.6
Other assaults	82,386	324.9	81,174	332.5	80,703	407.8	148,967	258.2	54,702	266.2	321,445	283.9
Forgery and counterfeiting	5,052	19.9	5,290	21.7	5,512	27.9	8,775	15.2	2,397	11.7	20,114	17.8
Fraud	10,445	41.2	10,986	45.0	13,061	66.0	20,799	36.0	7,742	37.7	44,857	39.6
Embezzlement	1,551	6.1	1,264	5.2	1,119	5.7	2,135	3.7	487	2.4	5,056	4.5
Stolen property; buying, receiving, possessing	8,268	32.6	7,157	29.3	5,866	29.6	15,784	27.4	4,008	19.5	32,942	29.1
Vandalism	16,352	64.5	15,672	64.2	15,682	79.2	25,455	44.1	8,401	40.9	59,610	52.6
Weapons; carrying, possessing, etc.	10,244	40.4	9,466	38.8	10,523	53.2	23,315	40.4	7,019	34.2	46,348	40.9
Prostitution and commercialized vice	1,403	5.5	909	3.7	574	2.9	3,443	6.0	194	0.9	5,941	5.2
Sex offenses (except forcible rape and prostitution)	3,312	13.1	3,368	13.8	3,522	17.8	8,202	14.2	2,817	13.7	15,725	13.9
Drug abuse violations	128,806	507.9	125,309	513.2	151,068	763.3	266,029	461.1	103,029	501.4	568,349	501.9
Gambling	47	0.2	137	0.6	235	1.2	590	1.0	131	0.6	751	0.7
Offenses against the family and children	5,142	20.3	5,872	24.0	9,322	47.1	25,730	44.6	8,706	42.4	36,905	32.6
Driving under the influence	63,876	251.9	75,990	311.2	87,261	440.9	202,119	350.3	120,328	585.6	366,970	324.1
Liquor laws	15,729	62.0	22,374	91.6	41,509	209.7	21,746	37.7	12,445	60.6	73,340	64.8
Drunkenness	32,614	128.6	35,480	145.3	61,693	311.7	25,656	44.5	11,100	54.0	97,792	86.4
Disorderly conduct	34,305	135.3	41,502	170.0	53,841	272.1	32,777	56.8	15,388	74.9	121,552	107.3
Vagrancy	1,788	7.1	1,022	4.2	1,049	5.3	1,949	3.4	205	1.0	5,236	4.6
All other offenses (except traffic)	239,680	945.1	262,884	1,076.7	311,572	1,574.3	572,506	992.2	241,827	1,176.8	1,147,843	1,013.7
Suspicion	27	0.1	18	0.1	485	2.5	86	0.1	63	0.3	350	0.3
Curfew and loitering law violations	2,513	9.9	2,678	11.0	2,583	13.1	1,487	2.6	254	1.2	7,079	6.3

* = Less than one-tenth of one percent.
1 Suburban areas include law enforcement agencies in cities with less than 50,000 inhabitants and county law enforcement agencies that are within a Metropolitan Statistical Area. Suburban areas exclude all metropolitan agencies associated with a principal city. The agencies associated with suburban areas also appear in other groups within this table.   2 Does not include suspicion.   3 Violent crimes are offenses of murder and nonnegligent manslaughter, forcible rape, robbery, and aggravated assault. Property crimes are offenses of burglary, larceny-theft, motor vehicle theft, and arson.   4 The rape figures in this table are aggregate totals of the data submitted based on both the legacy and revised Uniform Crime Reporting definitions.

Table 32. Ten-Year Arrest Trends, 2008 and 2017

(Number, percent change; 9,983 agencies; 2017 estimated population 211,303,234; 2008 estimated population 197,634,622.)

Offense charged	Number of persons arrested								
	Total, all ages			Under 18 years of age			18 years of age and over		
	2008	2017	Percent change	2008	2017	Percent change	2008	2017	Percent change
Total[1]	8,867,758	6,878,929	-22.4	1,283,505	538,333	-58.1	7,584,253	6,340,596	-16.4
Violent crime[2]	377,743	333,604	-11.7	59,171	32,785	-44.6	318,572	300,819	-5.6
Murder and nonnegligent manslaughter	7,544	7,342	-2.7	716	530	-26.0	6,828	6,812	-0.2
Rape[3]	13,598	14,759	-	2,042	2,482	NA	11,556	12,277	NA
Robbery	77,452	57,018	-26.4	20,608	11,152	-45.9	56,844	45,866	-19.3
Aggravated assault	279,149	254,485	-8.8	35,805	18,621	-48.0	243,344	235,864	-3.1
Property crime[2]	1,106,503	837,773	-24.3	293,060	112,498	-61.6	813,443	725,275	-10.8
Burglary	202,929	130,615	-35.6	55,319	20,461	-63.0	147,610	110,154	-25.4
Larceny-theft	835,771	643,853	-23.0	218,758	80,944	-63.0	617,013	562,909	-8.8
Motor vehicle theft	58,356	57,203	-2.0	14,442	9,507	-34.2	43,914	47,696	+8.6
Arson	9,447	6,102	-35.4	4,541	1,586	-65.1	4,906	4,516	-7.9
Other assaults	825,595	690,444	-16.4	149,218	81,635	-45.3	676,377	608,809	-10.0
Forgery and counterfeiting	59,792	37,230	-37.7	1,803	834	-53.7	57,989	36,396	-37.2
Fraud	155,657	83,654	-46.3	5,139	2,766	-46.2	150,518	80,888	-46.3
Embezzlement	14,477	10,501	-27.5	863	372	-56.9	13,614	10,129	-25.6
Stolen property; buying, receiving, possessing	75,402	66,036	-12.4	14,456	6,902	-52.3	60,946	59,134	-3.0
Vandalism	186,293	127,131	-31.8	70,977	25,822	-63.6	115,316	101,309	-12.1
Weapons; carrying, possessing, etc.	110,133	102,571	-6.9	24,967	11,639	-53.4	85,166	90,932	+6.8
Prostitution and commercialized vice	34,487	18,132	-47.4	749	148	-80.2	33,738	17,984	-46.7
Sex offenses (except forcible rape and prostitution)	48,889	31,007	-36.6	9,368	5,746	-38.7	39,521	25,261	-36.1
Drug abuse violations	1,044,058	1,077,640	+3.2	112,037	64,203	-42.7	932,021	1,013,437	+8.7
Gambling	2,431	1,440	-40.8	276	83	-69.9	2,155	1,357	-37.0
Offenses against the family and children	74,321	56,777	-23.6	3,568	2,558	-28.3	70,753	54,219	-23.4
Driving under the influence	974,968	654,775	-32.8	10,664	4,104	-61.5	964,304	650,671	-32.5
Liquor laws	410,755	137,829	-66.4	90,052	23,943	-73.4	320,703	113,886	-64.5
Drunkenness	410,144	230,361	-43.8	10,984	2,743	-75.0	399,160	227,618	-43.0
Disorderly conduct	439,410	232,936	-47.0	123,160	42,305	-65.7	316,250	190,631	-39.7
Vagrancy	16,039	13,953	-13.0	1,088	407	-62.6	14,951	13,546	-9.4
All other offenses (except traffic)	2,438,997	2,119,016	-13.1	240,241	100,721	-58.1	2,198,756	2,018,295	-8.2
Suspicion	805	201	-75.0	152	42	-72.4	653	159	-75.7
Curfew and loitering law violations	61,664	16,119	-73.9	61,664	16,119	-73.9	NA	NA	NA

NA = Not available.

1 Does not include suspicion.   2 Violent crimes are offenses of murder and nonnegligent manslaughter, rape, robbery, and aggravated assault. Property crimes are offenses of burglary, larceny-theft, motor vehicle theft, and arson.   3 The 2008 rape figures are based on the legacy definition, and the 2017 rape figures are aggregate totals based on both the legacy and revised Uniform Crime Reporting definitions. For this reason, a percent change is not provided.

Table 33. Ten-Year Arrest Trends, by Age and Sex, 2008 and 2017

(Number, percent change; 9,983 agencies; 2017 estimated population 211,303,234; 2008 estimated population 197,634,622.)

Offense charged	Male						Female					
	Total			Under 18			Total			Under 18		
	2008	2017	Percent change	2008	2017	Percent change	2008	2017	Percent change	2008	2017	Percent change
Total[1]	6,684,673	5,006,416	-25.1	911,744	380,337	-58.3	2,183,085	1,872,513	-14.2	371,761	157,996	-57.5
Violent crime[2]	307,768	264,829	-14.0	48,737	26,517	-45.6	69,975	68,775	-1.7	10,434	6,268	-39.9
Murder and nonnegligent manslaughter	6,727	6,407	-4.8	662	488	-26.3	817	935	+14.4	54	42	-22.2
Rape[3]	13,445	14,341	-	2,014	2,390	-	153	418	NA	28	92	NA
Robbery	68,320	48,568	-28.9	18,716	9,986	-46.6	9,132	8,450	-7.5	1,892	1,166	-38.4
Aggravated assault	219,276	195,513	-10.8	27,345	13,653	-50.1	59,873	58,972	-1.5	8,460	4,968	-41.3
Property crime[2]	714,043	533,252	-25.3	185,954	77,744	-58.2	392,460	304,521	-22.4	107,106	34,754	-67.6
Burglary	172,133	105,800	-38.5	48,260	17,996	-62.7	30,796	24,815	-19.4	7,059	2,465	-65.1
Larceny-theft	485,729	378,305	-22.1	121,620	50,722	-58.3	350,042	265,548	-24.1	97,138	30,222	-68.9
Motor vehicle theft	48,194	44,239	-8.2	12,082	7,668	-36.5	10,162	12,964	+27.6	2,360	1,839	-22.1
Arson	7,987	4,908	-38.6	3,992	1,358	-66.0	1,460	1,194	-18.2	549	228	-58.5
Other assaults	612,453	491,125	-19.8	98,121	51,063	-48.0	213,142	199,319	-6.5	51,097	30,572	-40.2
Forgery and counterfeiting	36,845	24,342	-33.9	1,199	659	-45.0	22,947	12,888	-43.8	604	175	-71.0
Fraud	86,861	52,167	-39.9	3,332	1,826	-45.2	68,796	31,487	-54.2	1,807	940	-48.0
Embezzlement	6,948	5,201	-25.1	502	187	-62.7	7,529	5,300	-29.6	361	185	-48.8
Stolen property; buying, receiving, possessing	59,620	51,469	-13.7	11,650	5,828	-50.0	15,782	14,567	-7.7	2,806	1,074	-61.7
Vandalism	154,800	98,927	-36.1	61,575	21,276	-65.4	31,493	28,204	-10.4	9,402	4,546	-51.6
Weapons; carrying, possessing, etc.	101,938	92,702	-9.1	22,675	10,377	-54.2	8,195	9,869	+20.4	2,292	1,262	-44.9
Prostitution and commercialized vice	11,333	7,705	-32.0	195	73	-62.6	23,154	10,427	-55.0	554	75	-86.5
Sex offenses (except forcible rape and prostitution)	45,409	28,773	-36.6	8,469	5,082	-40.0	3,480	2,234	-35.8	899	664	-26.1
Drug abuse violations	843,915	813,824	-3.6	93,476	48,663	-47.9	200,143	263,816	+31.8	18,561	15,540	-16.3
Gambling	2,035	1,083	-46.8	259	70	-73.0	396	357	-9.8	17	13	-23.5
Offenses against the family and children	55,945	39,753	-28.9	2,293	1,603	-30.1	18,376	17,024	-7.4	1,275	955	-25.1
Driving under the influence	763,493	488,769	-36.0	8,041	3,090	-61.6	211,475	166,006	-21.5	2,623	1,014	-61.3
Liquor laws	293,557	94,685	-67.7	55,777	14,105	-74.7	117,198	43,144	-63.2	34,275	9,838	-71.3
Drunkenness	342,258	182,844	-46.6	8,273	1,934	-76.6	67,886	47,517	-30.0	2,711	809	-70.2
Disorderly conduct	322,117	163,874	-49.1	82,845	27,063	-67.3	117,293	69,062	-41.1	40,315	15,242	-62.2
Vagrancy	12,512	10,594	-15.3	862	315	-63.5	3,527	3,359	-4.8	226	92	-59.3
All other offenses (except traffic)	1,869,437	1,549,710	-17.1	176,123	72,074	-59.1	569,560	569,306	*	64,118	28,647	-55.3
Suspicion	623	150	-75.9	124	31	-75.0	182	51	-72.0	28	11	-60.7
Curfew and loitering law violations	41,386	10,788	-73.9	41,386	10,788	-73.9	20,278	5,331	-73.7	20,278	5,331	-73.7

NA = Not available.
1 Does not include suspicion.   2 Violent crimes are offenses of murder and nonnegligent manslaughter, rape, robbery, and aggravated assault. Property crimes are offenses of burglary, larceny-theft, motor vehicle theft, and arson.   3 The 2008 rape figures are based on the legacy definition, and the 2017 rape figures are aggregate totals based on both the legacy and revised Uniform Crime Reporting definitions. For this reason, a percent change is not provided.

Table 34. Five-Year Arrest Trends, by Age, 2013 and 2017

(Number, percent change; 10,561 agencies; 2017 estimated population 218,341,582; 2013 estimated population 212,249,163.)

Offense charged	Total, all ages			Under 18 years of age			18 years of age and over		
	2013	2017	Percent change	2013	2017	Percent change	2013	2017	Percent change
Total[1]	7,713,977	7,088,331	-8.1	727,655	545,420	-25.0	6,986,322	6,542,911	-6.3
Violent crime[2]	330,719	338,485	+2.3	34,894	32,777	-6.1	295,825	305,708	+3.3
Murder and nonnegligent manslaughter	6,767	7,547	+11.5	478	536	+12.1	6,289	7,011	+11.5
Rape[3]	12,783	15,230	+19.1	2,061	2,577	+25.0	10,722	12,653	+18.0
Robbery	62,556	58,445	-6.6	11,723	11,165	-4.8	50,833	47,280	-7.0
Aggravated assault	248,613	257,263	+3.5	20,632	18,499	-10.3	227,981	238,764	+4.7
Property crime[2]	1,076,095	848,594	-21.1	169,180	114,243	-32.5	906,915	734,351	-19.0
Burglary	175,831	134,031	-23.8	29,366	20,855	-29.0	146,465	113,176	-22.7
Larceny-theft	849,570	651,332	-23.3	129,815	82,489	-36.5	719,755	568,843	-21.0
Motor vehicle theft	43,867	57,255	+30.5	7,524	9,382	+24.7	36,343	47,873	+31.7
Arson	6,827	5,976	-12.5	2,475	1,517	-38.7	4,352	4,459	+2.5
Other assaults	755,019	716,439	-5.1	99,293	82,433	-17.0	655,726	634,006	-3.3
Forgery and counterfeiting	41,814	38,137	-8.8	722	851	+17.9	41,092	37,286	-9.3
Fraud	96,273	84,446	-12.3	3,139	2,824	-10.0	93,134	81,622	-12.4
Embezzlement	11,223	11,150	-0.7	286	468	+63.6	10,937	10,682	-2.3
Stolen property; buying, receiving, possessing	66,787	67,437	+1.0	7,378	6,979	-5.4	59,409	60,458	+1.8
Vandalism	137,091	129,316	-5.7	32,316	25,800	-20.2	104,775	103,516	-1.2
Weapons; carrying, possessing, etc.	91,434	104,943	+14.8	13,236	11,628	-12.1	78,198	93,315	+19.3
Prostitution and commercialized vice	29,044	20,528	-29.3	500	182	-63.6	28,544	20,346	-28.7
Sex offenses (except forcible rape and prostitution)	39,259	32,872	-16.3	7,008	5,927	-15.4	32,251	26,945	-16.5
Drug abuse violations	1,016,496	1,120,121	+10.2	78,397	65,233	-16.8	938,099	1,054,888	+12.4
Gambling	2,259	1,754	-22.4	178	133	-25.3	2,081	1,621	-22.1
Offenses against the family and children	68,097	62,951	-7.6	1,992	2,471	+24.0	66,105	60,480	-8.5
Driving under the influence	799,032	682,771	-14.6	5,327	4,259	-20.0	793,705	678,512	-14.5
Liquor laws	238,043	141,109	-40.7	43,056	24,015	-44.2	194,987	117,094	-39.9
Drunkenness	325,493	242,478	-25.5	5,460	2,843	-47.9	320,033	239,635	-25.1
Disorderly conduct	314,330	236,027	-24.9	63,549	43,283	-31.9	250,781	192,744	-23.1
Vagrancy	17,653	16,581	-6.1	678	518	-23.6	16,975	16,063	-5.4
All other offenses (except traffic)	2,230,169	2,175,563	-2.4	133,419	101,924	-23.6	2,096,750	2,073,639	-1.1
Suspicion	431	155	-64.0	51	22	-56.9	380	133	-65.0
Curfew and loitering law violations	27,647	16,629	-39.9	27,647	16,629	-39.9	NA	NA	NA

NA = Not available.

1 Does not include suspicion.   2 Violent crimes are offenses of murder and nonnegligent manslaughter, rape, robbery, and aggravated assault.   Property crimes are offenses of burglary, larceny-theft, motor vehicle theft, and arson.   3 The 2013 rape figures are based on the legacy definition, and the 2017 rape figures are aggregate totals based on both the legacy and revised Uniform Crime Reporting definitions. For this reason, a percent change is not provided.

Table 35. Five-Year Arrest Trends, by Age and Sex, 2013 and 2017

(Number, percent change; 10,561 agencies; 2017 estimated population 218,341,582; 2013 estimated population 212,249,163.)

Offense charged	Male						Female					
	Total			Under 18			Total			Under 18		
	2013	2017	Percent change	2013	2017	Percent change	2013	2017	Percent change	2013	2017	Percent change
Total[1]	5,642,583	5,149,770	-8.7	513,166	384,986	-25.0	2,071,394	1,938,561	-6.4	214,489	160,434	-25.2
Violent crime[2]	263,794	268,617	+1.8	28,286	26,579	-6.0	66,925	69,868	+4.4	6,608	6,198	-6.2
Murder and nonnegligent manslaughter	5,944	6,563	+10.4	423	493	+16.5	823	984	+19.6	55	43	-21.8
Rape[3]	12,507	14,793	+18.3	1,969	2,481	+26.0	276	437	+58.3	92	96	+4.3
Robbery	53,930	49,664	-7.9	10,595	9,938	-6.2	8,626	8,781	+1.8	1,128	1,227	+8.8
Aggravated assault	191,413	197,597	+3.2	15,299	13,667	-10.7	57,200	59,666	+4.3	5,333	4,832	-9.4
Property crime[2]	665,395	540,099	-18.8	110,664	78,766	-28.8	410,700	308,495	-24.9	58,516	35,477	-39.4
Burglary	144,673	108,216	-25.2	25,759	18,327	-28.9	31,158	25,815	-17.1	3,607	2,528	-29.9
Larceny-theft	480,111	382,827	-20.3	76,604	51,606	-32.6	369,459	268,505	-27.3	53,211	30,883	-42.0
Motor vehicle theft	35,053	44,248	+26.2	6,184	7,536	+21.9	8,814	13,007	+47.6	1,340	1,846	+37.8
Arson	5,558	4,808	-13.5	2,117	1,297	-38.7	1,269	1,168	-8.0	358	220	-38.5
Other assaults	544,344	509,010	-6.5	63,191	51,753	-18.1	210,675	207,429	-1.5	36,102	30,680	-15.0
Forgery and counterfeiting	25,929	24,951	-3.8	507	670	+32.1	15,885	13,186	-17.0	215	181	-15.8
Fraud	57,801	52,616	-9.0	2,109	1,865	-11.6	38,472	31,830	-17.3	1,030	959	-6.9
Embezzlement	5,835	5,626	-3.6	186	271	+45.7	5,388	5,524	+2.5	100	197	+97.0
Stolen property; buying, receiving, possessing	52,348	52,367	*	6,167	5,846	-5.2	14,439	15,070	+4.4	1,211	1,133	-6.4
Vandalism	109,448	100,303	-8.4	27,229	21,211	-22.1	27,643	29,013	+5.0	5,087	4,589	-9.8
Weapons; carrying, possessing, etc.	83,229	94,642	+13.7	11,915	10,402	-12.7	8,205	10,301	+25.5	1,321	1,226	-7.2
Prostitution and commercialized vice	9,845	7,846	-20.3	105	75	-28.6	19,199	12,682	-33.9	395	107	-72.9
Sex offenses (except forcible rape and prostitution)	36,148	30,349	-16.0	6,190	5,226	-15.6	3,111	2,523	-18.9	818	701	-14.3
Drug abuse violations	795,219	844,106	+6.1	63,429	49,465	-22.0	221,277	276,015	+24.7	14,968	15,768	+5.3
Gambling	1,671	1,295	-22.5	137	97	-29.2	588	459	-21.9	41	36	-12.2
Offenses against the family and children	50,265	44,527	-11.4	1,211	1,560	+28.8	17,832	18,424	+3.3	781	911	+16.6
Driving under the influence	597,845	506,712	-15.2	4,039	3,208	-20.6	201,187	176,059	-12.5	1,288	1,051	-18.4
Liquor laws	167,695	97,360	-41.9	26,093	14,144	-45.8	70,348	43,749	-37.8	16,963	9,871	-41.8
Drunkenness	264,165	192,144	-27.3	3,954	2,004	-49.3	61,328	50,334	-17.9	1,506	839	-44.3
Disorderly conduct	224,683	165,317	-26.4	41,449	27,501	-33.7	89,647	70,710	-21.1	22,100	15,782	-28.6
Vagrancy	13,986	12,779	-8.6	520	406	-21.9	3,667	3,802	+3.7	158	112	-29.1
All other offenses (except traffic)	1,654,352	1,587,983	-4.0	97,199	72,816	-25.1	575,817	587,580	+2.0	36,220	29,108	-19.6
Suspicion	336	115	-65.8	44	19	-56.8	95	40	-57.9	7	3	-57.1
Curfew and loitering law violations	18,586	11,121	-40.2	18,586	11,121	-40.2	9,061	5,508	-39.2	9,061	5,508	-39.2

* = Less than one-tenth of one percent.
1 Does not include suspicion.   2 Violent crimes are offenses of murder and nonnegligent manslaughter, rape, robbery, and aggravated assault. Property crimes are offenses of burglary, larceny-theft, motor vehicle theft, and arson.   3 The 2013 rape figures are based on the legacy definition, and the 2017 rape figures are aggregate totals based on both the legacy and revised Uniform Crime Reporting definitions.

Table 36. Current Year Over Previous Year Arrest Trends, 2016–2017

(Number, percent change; 11,889 agencies; 2017 estimated population 245,794,668; 2016 estimated population 244,059,561.)

Offense charged	Number of persons arrested											
	Total, all ages			Under 15 years of age			Under 18 years of age			18 years of age and over		
	2016	2017	Percent change	2016	2017	Percent change	2016	2017	Percent change	2016	2017	Percent change
Total[1]	8,057,300	7,990,795	-0.8	180,936	176,559	-2.4	649,211	620,264	-4.5	7,408,089	7,370,531	-0.5
Violent crime[2]	391,723	394,928	+0.8	10,827	11,021	+1.8	39,519	39,862	+0.9	352,204	355,066	+0.8
Murder and nonnegligent manslaughter	8,899	9,177	+3.1	66	58	-12.1	663	685	+3.3	8,236	8,492	+3.1
Rape[3]	17,827	17,765	-0.3	1,135	1,148	+1.1	2,812	2,989	+6.3	15,015	14,776	-1.6
Robbery	73,298	71,599	-2.3	2,792	2,824	+1.1	14,711	14,703	-0.1	58,587	56,896	-2.9
Aggravated assault	291,699	296,387	+1.6	6,834	6,991	+2.3	21,333	21,485	+0.7	270,366	274,902	+1.7
Property crime[2]	1,025,497	956,839	-6.7	38,693	37,252	-3.7	140,060	129,488	-7.5	885,437	827,351	-6.6
Burglary	157,814	151,840	-3.8	7,290	7,425	+1.9	24,433	23,569	-3.5	133,381	128,271	-3.8
Larceny-theft	794,517	728,141	-8.4	27,654	25,846	-6.5	101,730	91,715	-9.8	692,787	636,426	-8.1
Motor vehicle theft	66,228	69,888	+5.5	2,664	2,983	+12.0	12,022	12,466	+3.7	54,206	57,422	+5.9
Arson	6,938	6,970	+0.5	1,085	998	-8.0	1,875	1,738	-7.3	5,063	5,232	+3.3
Other assaults	804,819	799,265	-0.7	37,144	36,996	-0.4	96,293	94,010	-2.4	708,526	705,255	-0.5
Forgery and counterfeiting	42,884	42,361	-1.2	109	132	+21.1	946	941	-0.5	41,938	41,420	-1.2
Fraud	96,571	94,916	-1.7	722	728	+0.8	3,468	3,646	+5.1	93,103	91,270	-2.0
Embezzlement	12,234	12,061	-1.4	41	38	-7.3	499	494	-1.0	11,735	11,567	-1.4
Stolen property; buying, receiving, possessing	72,133	76,013	+5.4	1,789	1,661	-7.2	8,330	8,060	-3.2	63,803	67,953	+6.5
Vandalism	146,436	143,337	-2.1	11,759	11,353	-3.5	29,382	28,130	-4.3	117,054	115,207	-1.6
Weapons; carrying, possessing, etc.	118,396	125,051	+5.6	4,549	4,173	-8.3	14,635	14,088	-3.7	103,761	110,963	+6.9
Prostitution and commercialized vice	28,451	26,618	-6.4	48	30	-37.5	393	207	-47.3	28,058	26,411	-5.9
Sex offenses (except forcible rape and prostitution)	37,818	36,652	-3.1	3,078	3,235	+5.1	6,392	6,469	+1.2	31,426	30,183	-4.0
Drug abuse violations	1,183,896	1,233,598	+4.2	11,214	10,813	-3.6	73,810	72,334	-2.0	1,110,086	1,161,264	+4.6
Gambling	2,791	2,460	-11.9	24	28	+16.7	198	209	+5.6	2,593	2,251	-13.2
Offenses against the family and children	67,385	69,108	+2.6	1,096	958	-12.6	2,879	2,814	-2.3	64,506	66,294	+2.8
Driving under the influence	766,954	743,538	-3.1	87	88	+1.1	4,879	4,593	-5.9	762,075	738,945	-3.0
Liquor laws	174,484	156,573	-10.3	2,909	2,981	+2.5	27,744	25,580	-7.8	146,740	130,993	-10.7
Drunkenness	294,270	283,471	-3.7	458	420	-8.3	3,757	3,333	-11.3	290,513	280,138	-3.6
Disorderly conduct	284,037	269,318	-5.2	19,466	18,924	-2.8	50,883	48,293	-5.1	233,154	221,025	-5.2
Vagrancy	19,012	18,007	-5.3	140	140	0.0	583	547	-6.2	18,429	17,460	-5.3
All other offenses (except traffic)	2,460,814	2,483,220	+0.9	29,107	28,688	-1.4	117,866	113,705	-3.5	2,342,948	2,369,515	+1.1
Suspicion	590	588	-0.3	22	12	-45.5	70	50	-28.6	520	538	+3.5
Curfew and loitering law violations	26,695	23,461	-12.1	7,676	6,900	-10.1	26,695	23,461	-12.1	NA	NA	NA

NA = Not available.

* = Less than one-tenth of 1 percent.

1 Does not include suspicion.   2 Violent crimes are offenses of murder and nonnegligent manslaughter, rape, robbery, and aggravated assault. Property crimes are offenses of burglary, larceny-theft, motor vehicle theft, and arson.   3 The rape figures in this table are aggregate totals of the data submitted based on both the legacy and revised Uniform Crime Reporting definitions.

Table 37. Current Year Over Previous Year Arrest Trends, by Age and Sex, 2016–2017

(Number, percent change; 11,889 agencies; 2017 estimated population 245,794,668; 2016 estimated population 244,059,561.)

Offense charged	Male						Female					
	Total			Under 18			Total			Under 18		
	2016	2017	Percent change	2016	2017	Percent change	2016	2017	Percent change	2016	2017	Percent change
Total[1]	5,882,996	5,826,858	-1.0	457,722	440,159	-3.8	2,174,304	2,163,937	-0.5	191,489	180,105	-5.9
Violent crime[2]	311,840	313,803	+0.6	32,294	32,498	+0.6	79,883	81,125	+1.6	7,225	7,364	+1.9
Murder and nonnegligent manslaughter	7,866	8,043	+2.3	604	635	+5.1	1,033	1,134	+9.8	59	50	-15.3
Rape[3]	17,360	17,333	-0.2	2,689	2,877	+7.0	467	432	-7.5	123	112	-8.9
Robbery	62,780	61,160	-2.6	13,162	13,175	+0.1	10,518	10,439	-0.8	1,549	1,528	-1.4
Aggravated assault	223,834	227,267	+1.5	15,839	15,811	-0.2	67,865	69,120	+1.8	5,494	5,674	+3.3
Property crime[2]	645,644	613,482	-5.0	93,213	89,958	-3.5	379,853	343,357	-9.6	46,847	39,530	-15.6
Burglary	128,265	123,128	-4.0	21,537	20,803	-3.4	29,549	28,712	-2.8	2,896	2,766	-4.5
Larceny-theft	460,063	430,454	-6.4	60,264	57,504	-4.6	334,454	297,687	-11.0	41,466	34,211	-17.5
Motor vehicle theft	51,827	54,323	+4.8	9,810	10,167	+3.6	14,401	15,565	+8.1	2,212	2,299	+3.9
Arson	5,489	5,577	+1.6	1,602	1,484	-7.4	1,449	1,393	-3.9	273	254	-7.0
Other assaults	576,747	569,227	-1.3	60,881	58,916	-3.2	228,072	230,038	+0.9	35,412	35,094	-0.9
Forgery and counterfeiting	27,717	27,773	+0.2	691	737	+6.7	36,374	35,552	-2.3	1,099	1,195	+8.7
Fraud	60,197	59,364	-1.4	2,369	2,451	+3.5	6,005	5,954	-0.8	188	212	+12.8
Embezzlement	6,229	6,107	-2.0	311	282	-9.3	15,502	16,745	+8.0	1,327	1,292	-2.6
Stolen property; buying, receiving, possessing	56,631	59,268	+4.7	7,003	6,768	-3.4	32,174	32,238	+0.2	5,012	5,043	+0.6
Vandalism	114,262	111,099	-2.8	24,370	23,087	-5.3						
Weapons; carrying, possessing, etc.	107,498	113,401	+5.5	12,998	12,612	-3.0	10,898	11,650	+6.9	1,637	1,476	-9.8
Prostitution and commercialized vice	10,800	10,424	-3.5	107	82	-23.4	17,651	16,194	-8.3	286	125	-56.3
Sex offenses (except forcible rape and prostitution)	34,926	33,924	-2.9	5,578	5,718	+2.5	2,892	2,728	-5.7	814	751	-7.7
Drug abuse violations	905,672	934,038	+3.1	56,863	55,112	-3.1	278,224	299,560	+7.7	16,947	17,222	+1.6
Gambling	2,106	1,940	-7.9	173	171	-1.2	685	520	-24.1	25	38	+52.0
Offenses against the family and children	47,613	48,490	+1.8	1,751	1,775	+1.4	19,772	20,618	+4.3	1,128	1,039	-7.9
Driving under the influence	572,551	553,322	-3.4	3,623	3,458	-4.6	194,403	190,216	-2.2	1,256	1,135	-9.6
Liquor laws	122,325	108,320	-11.4	16,633	15,076	-9.4	52,159	48,253	-7.5	11,111	10,504	-5.5
Drunkenness	236,212	225,064	-4.7	2,658	2,329	-12.4	58,058	58,407	+0.6	1,099	1,004	-8.6
Disorderly conduct	201,664	189,350	-6.1	32,597	30,695	-5.8	82,373	79,968	-2.9	18,286	17,598	-3.8
Vagrancy	14,510	13,673	-5.8	431	430	-0.2	4,502	4,334	-3.7	152	117	-23.0
All other offenses (except traffic)	1,809,174	1,818,321	+0.5	84,500	81,536	-3.5	651,640	664,899	+2.0	33,366	32,169	-3.6
Suspicion	461	444	-3.7	55	38	-30.9	129	144	+11.6	15	12	-20.0
Curfew and loitering law violations	18,678	16,468	-11.8	18,678	16,468	-11.8	8,017	6,993	-12.8	8,017	6,993	-12.8

1 Does not include suspicion.   2 Violent crimes are offenses of murder and nonnegligent manslaughter, rape, robbery, and aggravated assault.   Property crimes are offenses of burglary, larceny-theft, motor vehicle theft, and arson.   3 The rape figures in this table are aggregate totals of the data submitted based on both the legacy and revised Uniform Crime Reporting definitions.

Table 38. Arrests, Distribution by Age, 2017

(Number, percent; 12,606 agencies; 2017 estimated population 253,634,894.)

Offense charged	Total, all ages	Ages under 15	Ages under 18	Ages 18 and over	Under 10	10–12	13–14	15	16	17	18	19	20
Total	8,247,591	180,638	634,535	7,613,056	4,068	41,120	135,450	118,535	151,827	183,535	247,740	269,926	269,446
Total percent distribution[1]	100.0	2.2	7.7	92.3	*	0.5	1.6	1.4	1.8	2.2	3.0	3.3	3.3
Violent crime[2]	407,496	11,371	41,184	366,312	213	2,614	8,544	7,834	10,194	11,785	13,400	13,565	13,517
Violent crime percent distribution[1]	100.0	2.8	10.1	89.9	0.1	0.6	2.1	1.9	2.5	2.9	3.3	3.3	3.3
Murder and nonnegligent manslaughter	9,576	67	717	8,859	0	8	59	105	210	335	479	532	482
Rape[3]	18,289	1,163	3,030	15,259	25	313	825	515	667	685	764	778	630
Robbery	74,340	2,925	15,282	59,058	16	387	2,522	3,172	4,287	4,898	5,171	4,550	3,861
Aggravated assault	305,291	7,216	22,155	283,136	172	1,906	5,138	4,042	5,030	5,867	6,986	7,705	8,544
Property crime[2]	985,847	38,071	132,525	853,322	744	8,230	29,097	26,432	32,126	35,896	40,381	36,076	31,824
Property crime percent distribution[1]	100.0	3.9	13.4	86.6	0.1	0.8	3.0	2.7	3.3	3.6	4.1	3.7	3.2
Burglary	156,465	7,607	24,223	132,242	197	1,647	5,763	5,093	5,573	5,950	6,841	6,126	5,571
Larceny-theft	750,750	26,396	93,738	657,012	479	5,867	20,050	18,044	22,856	26,442	30,195	27,070	23,734
Motor vehicle theft	71,452	3,058	12,798	58,654	10	377	2,671	2,983	3,435	3,322	3,127	2,710	2,357
Arson	7,180	1,010	1,766	5,414	58	339	613	312	262	182	218	170	162
Other assaults	833,396	37,971	96,523	736,873	942	10,582	26,447	18,696	20,357	19,499	18,521	19,881	21,289
Forgery and counterfeiting	43,534	133	957	42,577	3	33	97	130	252	442	1,208	1,761	1,974
Fraud	96,948	738	3,714	93,234	8	101	629	638	994	1,344	1,904	2,639	2,865
Embezzlement	12,532	38	499	12,033	0	7	31	57	142	262	660	673	665
Stolen property; buying, receiving, possessing	77,474	1,692	8,243	69,231	15	214	1,463	1,724	2,281	2,546	3,340	3,058	2,834
Vandalism	147,959	11,632	28,842	119,117	463	3,295	7,874	5,253	5,936	6,021	5,519	5,460	5,114
Weapons; carrying, possessing, etc.	129,210	4,240	14,384	114,826	113	1,123	3,004	2,488	3,370	4,286	5,309	5,429	5,202
Prostitution and commercialized vice	28,490	30	218	28,272	0	7	23	27	57	104	672	984	1,189
Sex offenses (except forcible rape and prostitution)	37,850	3,336	6,644	31,206	120	827	2,389	1,127	1,064	1,117	1,099	1,079	964
Drug abuse violations	1,275,812	11,111	74,088	1,201,724	76	1,637	9,398	11,207	19,430	32,340	56,274	59,879	56,539
Gambling	2,510	28	213	2,297	0	2	26	33	61	91	110	120	120
Offenses against the family and children	72,229	982	2,895	69,334	60	240	682	606	630	677	861	902	1,050
Driving under the influence	764,569	90	4,692	759,877	15	11	64	236	1,107	3,259	9,243	13,975	17,083
Liquor laws	161,277	3,055	26,107	135,170	21	304	2,730	4,131	7,013	11,908	23,774	25,043	21,057
Drunkenness	289,608	432	3,395	286,213	14	31	387	520	850	1,593	4,456	5,700	6,224
Disorderly conduct	276,987	19,227	49,041	227,946	369	4,929	13,929	9,838	10,375	9,601	8,627	8,054	7,829
Vagrancy	18,542	151	583	17,959	1	18	132	126	151	155	336	383	367
All other offenses (except traffic)	2,560,932	29,317	116,023	2,444,909	763	5,615	22,939	21,934	29,051	35,721	52,027	65,245	71,723
Suspicion	690	17	66	624	0	7	10	18	9	22	19	20	17
Curfew and loitering law violations	23,699	6,976	23,699	NA	128	1,293	5,555	5,480	6,377	4,866	NA	NA	NA

Table 38. Arrests, Distribution by Age, 2017—Continued

(Number, percent; 12,606 agencies; 2017 estimated population 253,634,894.)

Offense charged	21	22	23	24	25–29	30–34	35–39	40–44	45–49	50–54	55–59	60–64	65 and over
Total	271,068	275,879	284,341	291,223	1,425,012	1,175,300	947,455	635,335	539,644	436,109	300,274	145,888	98,416
Total percent distribution[1]	3.3	3.3	3.4	3.5	17.3	14.3	11.5	7.7	6.5	5.3	3.6	1.8	1.2
Violent crime[2]	13,841	13,912	14,413	14,371	69,925	55,997	44,677	29,215	24,320	19,829	13,677	6,549	5,104
Violent crime percent distribution[1]	3.4	3.4	3.5	3.5	17.2	13.7	11.0	7.2	6.0	4.9	3.4	1.6	1.3
Murder and nonnegligent manslaughter	463	428	454	428	1,770	1,204	878	556	404	326	226	115	114
Rape[3]	605	505	495	528	2,266	2,123	1,917	1,333	1,079	877	627	381	351
Robbery	3,179	2,957	2,844	2,682	11,591	7,825	5,332	3,179	2,509	1,854	1,033	336	155
Aggravated assault	9,594	10,022	10,620	10,733	54,298	44,845	36,550	24,147	20,328	16,772	11,791	5,717	4,484
Property crime[2]	29,720	29,494	30,285	31,339	158,257	134,250	106,125	68,404	58,917	46,314	29,721	13,474	8,741
Property crime percent distribution[1]	3.0	3.0	3.1	3.2	16.1	13.6	10.8	6.9	6.0	4.7	3.0	1.4	0.9
Burglary	5,097	5,103	5,149	5,323	25,990	21,179	16,442	9,901	8,013	5,877	3,570	1,367	693
Larceny-theft	22,155	21,815	22,537	23,349	118,732	102,171	81,631	53,785	47,373	38,178	24,872	11,609	7,806
Motor vehicle theft	2,317	2,403	2,451	2,500	12,647	10,079	7,348	4,245	3,078	1,907	997	349	139
Arson	151	173	148	167	888	821	704	473	453	352	282	149	103
Other assaults	24,188	25,381	26,938	28,064	137,949	116,080	95,966	66,394	55,702	44,849	29,879	14,432	11,360
Forgery and counterfeiting	1,441	1,462	1,478	1,573	8,193	7,367	5,722	3,661	2,855	1,909	1,186	507	280
Fraud	2,711	3,039	3,046	3,359	17,731	15,834	12,979	8,695	7,176	5,151	3,293	1,653	1,159
Embezzlement	587	560	507	434	2,140	1,619	1,370	910	782	517	341	170	98
Stolen property; buying, receiving, possessing	2,666	2,722	2,840	2,791	14,420	11,727	9,013	5,381	3,777	2,525	1,360	521	256
Vandalism	5,190	5,226	5,275	5,198	23,599	18,126	13,566	8,469	6,760	5,300	3,412	1,672	1,231
Weapons; carrying, possessing, etc.	5,813	5,764	5,779	5,593	24,183	17,076	12,415	7,462	5,340	4,214	2,787	1,352	1,108
Prostitution and commercialized vice	1,149	1,273	1,162	1,221	5,665	4,249	3,102	2,310	2,003	1,528	869	508	388
Sex offenses (except forcible rape and prostitution)	909	837	864	824	4,158	3,915	3,744	2,864	2,650	2,436	2,005	1,367	1,491
Drug abuse violations	52,608	52,388	52,170	51,428	238,608	183,084	139,996	86,830	68,422	51,370	32,511	13,618	5,999
Gambling	88	89	79	91	376	229	218	187	175	149	115	74	77
Offenses against the family and children	1,302	1,498	1,759	2,131	13,306	13,863	12,133	7,841	5,662	3,703	1,950	797	576
Driving under the influence	27,384	29,179	30,435	30,927	142,447	109,980	88,958	66,019	60,148	51,929	41,058	23,197	17,915
Liquor laws	3,813	2,767	2,253	2,157	9,046	7,898	7,296	5,969	6,624	6,834	5,828	3,033	1,778
Drunkenness	9,385	8,967	8,722	8,822	43,104	39,076	34,390	27,088	28,204	26,688	20,247	9,693	5,447
Disorderly conduct	9,748	9,032	8,484	8,469	39,593	31,836	26,282	18,224	16,630	14,827	10,839	5,459	4,013
Vagrancy	338	379	425	447	2,260	2,192	2,329	1,746	1,922	1,836	1,696	850	453
All other offenses (except traffic)	78,171	81,904	87,395	91,965	469,956	400,800	327,078	217,610	181,527	144,165	97,471	46,951	30,921
Suspicion	16	6	32	19	96	102	96	56	48	36	29	11	21
Curfew and loitering law violations	NA	NA	NA	NA	NA	NA	NA	NA	NA	NA	NA	NA	NA

NA = Not available.
* = Less than one-tenth of one percent.
1 Because of rounding, the percentages may not sum to 100 percent.   2 Violent crimes are offenses of murder and nonnegligent manslaughter, rape, robbery, and aggravated assault.   Property crimes are offenses of burglary, larceny-theft, motor vehicle theft, and arson.   3 The rape figures in this table are aggregate totals of the data submitted based on both the legacy and revised Uniform Crime Reporting definitions.

Table 39. Male Arrests, Distribution by Age, 2017

(Number, percent; 12,606 agencies; 2017 estimated population 253,634,894.)

Offense charged	Total, all ages	Ages under 15	Ages under 18	Ages 18 and over	Under 10	10–12	13–14	15	16	17	18	19	20
Total	6,016,739	126,203	450,360	5,566,379	3,301	29,742	93,160	82,756	108,143	133,258	181,628	197,100	196,129
Total percent distribution[1]	100.0	2.1	7.5	92.5	0.1	0.5	1.5	1.4	1.8	2.2	3.0	3.3	3.3
Violent crime[2]	323,768	8,912	33,556	290,212	177	2,092	6,643	6,323	8,358	9,963	11,162	11,131	10,824
Violent crime percent distribution[1]	100.0	2.8	10.4	89.6	0.1	0.6	2.1	2.0	2.6	3.1	3.4	3.4	3.3
Murder and nonnegligent manslaughter	8,383	57	660	7,723	0	6	51	96	195	312	434	481	428
Rape[3]	17,781	1,103	2,918	14,863	23	290	790	489	652	674	745	765	614
Robbery	63,470	2,573	13,692	49,778	13	354	2,206	2,824	3,821	4,474	4,571	4,014	3,330
Aggravated assault	234,134	5,179	16,286	217,848	141	1,442	3,596	2,914	3,690	4,503	5,412	5,871	6,452
Property crime[2]	632,834	27,682	92,134	540,700	601	6,175	20,906	18,583	21,963	23,906	26,224	22,983	20,234
Property crime percent distribution[1]	100.0	4.4	14.6	85.4	0.1	1.0	3.3	2.9	3.5	3.8	4.1	3.6	3.2
Burglary	127,010	6,701	21,389	105,621	178	1,456	5,067	4,478	4,928	5,282	5,832	5,189	4,640
Larceny-theft	444,542	17,709	58,792	385,750	362	4,122	13,225	11,410	13,978	15,695	17,574	15,457	13,639
Motor vehicle theft	55,535	2,412	10,443	45,092	9	305	2,098	2,422	2,833	2,776	2,630	2,186	1,825
Arson	5,747	860	1,510	4,237	52	292	516	273	224	153	188	151	130
Other assaults	594,132	23,816	60,430	533,702	780	7,055	15,981	11,278	12,724	12,612	12,377	13,173	14,224
Forgery and counterfeiting	28,529	105	748	27,781	1	22	82	110	212	321	854	1,206	1,266
Fraud	60,639	487	2,496	58,143	6	68	413	445	670	894	1,293	1,715	1,856
Embezzlement	6,381	33	284	6,097	0	7	26	43	81	127	348	345	344
Stolen property; buying, receiving, possessing	60,443	1,377	6,928	53,515	7	185	1,185	1,436	1,934	2,181	2,797	2,472	2,275
Vandalism	114,670	9,704	23,673	90,997	414	2,780	6,510	4,349	4,797	4,823	4,437	4,198	3,924
Weapons; carrying, possessing, etc.	117,151	3,665	12,878	104,273	103	941	2,621	2,224	3,054	3,935	4,952	5,047	4,797
Prostitution and commercialized vice	11,124	12	84	11,040	0	3	9	10	29	33	112	178	221
Sex offenses (except forcible rape and prostitution)	35,019	2,919	5,877	29,142	106	735	2,078	987	935	1,036	1,018	1,006	879
Drug abuse violations	966,121	7,867	56,440	909,681	58	1,142	6,667	8,357	15,040	25,176	43,903	46,241	43,471
Gambling	1,977	17	174	1,803	0	2	15	26	53	78	101	105	104
Offenses against the family and children	50,652	600	1,829	48,823	43	148	409	385	390	454	592	574	628
Driving under the influence	569,148	69	3,538	565,610	14	5	50	172	812	2,485	7,147	10,580	12,853
Liquor laws	111,935	1,508	15,375	96,560	14	141	1,353	2,194	4,209	7,464	15,154	16,695	14,289
Drunkenness	229,760	277	2,369	227,391	10	21	246	322	593	1,177	3,404	4,421	4,818
Disorderly conduct	194,953	12,046	31,203	163,750	305	3,320	8,421	6,122	6,620	6,415	5,991	5,552	5,386
Vagrancy	14,071	118	452	13,619	1	14	103	88	128	118	234	243	247
All other offenses (except traffic)	1,876,286	20,181	83,213	1,793,073	566	3,937	15,678	15,442	21,093	26,497	39,513	49,220	53,476
Suspicion	518	14	51	467	0	6	8	13	6	18	15	15	13
Curfew and loitering law violations	16,628	4,794	16,628	NA	95	943	3,756	3,847	4,442	3,545	NA	NA	NA

Table 39. Male Arrests, Distribution by Age, 2017—Continued

(Number, percent; 12,606 agencies; 2017 estimated population 253,634,894.)

Offense charged	21	22	23	24	25–29	30–34	35–39	40–44	45–49	50–54	55–59	60–64	65 and over
Total	199,332	202,785	207,736	211,442	1,027,342	840,271	680,801	461,154	398,816	330,942	235,631	116,674	78,596
Total percent distribution[1]	3.3	3.4	3.5	3.5	17.1	14.0	11.3	7.7	6.6	5.5	3.9	1.9	1.3
Violent crime[2]	10,958	10,976	11,240	11,329	54,516	43,817	35,097	23,104	19,314	15,776	11,136	5,450	4,382
Violent crime percent distribution[1]	3.4	3.4	3.5	3.5	16.8	13.5	10.8	7.1	6.0	4.9	3.4	1.7	1.4
Murder and nonnegligent manslaughter	415	388	393	388	1,525	1,049	755	459	332	279	191	104	102
Rape[3]	584	490	481	515	2,210	2,054	1,849	1,296	1,060	862	614	375	349
Robbery	2,700	2,524	2,385	2,244	9,603	6,374	4,352	2,630	2,124	1,585	900	304	138
Aggravated assault	7,259	7,574	7,981	8,182	41,178	34,340	28,141	18,719	15,798	13,050	9,431	4,667	3,793
Property crime[2]	18,982	18,845	19,352	19,967	99,993	83,349	65,742	42,389	38,087	30,504	19,954	8,711	5,384
Property crime percent distribution[1]	3.0	3.0	3.1	3.2	15.8	13.2	10.4	6.7	6.0	4.8	3.2	1.4	0.9
Burglary	4,191	4,134	4,213	4,227	20,522	16,444	12,776	7,692	6,392	4,728	2,971	1,132	538
Larceny-theft	12,865	12,745	13,131	13,730	69,516	58,801	46,756	31,006	28,876	23,932	15,897	7,179	4,646
Motor vehicle theft	1,793	1,819	1,876	1,879	9,272	7,491	5,680	3,341	2,472	1,568	858	286	116
Arson	133	147	132	131	683	613	530	350	347	276	228	114	84
Other assaults	16,634	17,742	18,939	19,721	98,707	84,201	70,760	49,072	41,296	33,570	22,944	11,319	9,023
Forgery and counterfeiting	938	1,014	973	1,044	5,260	4,626	3,525	2,302	1,924	1,374	861	397	217
Fraud	1,750	1,991	1,955	2,078	10,868	9,593	7,839	5,255	4,430	3,378	2,231	1,152	759
Embezzlement	303	288	271	215	1,153	809	635	435	385	266	155	91	54
Stolen property; buying, receiving, possessing	2,099	2,138	2,158	2,095	10,846	8,741	6,810	4,154	3,031	2,111	1,136	430	222
Vandalism	3,996	3,968	4,044	3,884	17,875	13,673	10,354	6,478	5,156	4,023	2,663	1,380	944
Weapons; carrying, possessing, etc.	5,354	5,279	5,323	5,112	21,943	15,288	11,104	6,702	4,763	3,786	2,525	1,265	1,033
Prostitution and commercialized vice	231	290	286	321	1,852	1,756	1,388	1,173	1,008	868	597	409	350
Sex offenses (except forcible rape and prostitution)	844	767	787	753	3,839	3,608	3,471	2,660	2,504	2,293	1,936	1,326	1,451
Drug abuse violations	40,473	40,364	39,817	39,149	178,705	134,962	103,267	64,567	51,623	39,969	26,382	11,546	5,242
Gambling	81	83	69	84	318	166	165	139	112	104	71	52	49
Offenses against the family and children	845	911	1,103	1,322	8,559	9,360	8,790	6,010	4,525	2,994	1,575	614	421
Driving under the influence	20,131	21,347	22,337	22,902	105,801	82,054	66,171	48,766	43,835	38,224	31,135	17,989	14,338
Liquor laws	2,744	2,074	1,649	1,587	6,772	5,935	5,465	4,448	5,092	5,518	4,924	2,667	1,547
Drunkenness	7,411	7,168	7,010	6,977	33,829	30,257	26,767	20,913	22,323	21,760	17,125	8,362	4,846
Disorderly conduct	7,001	6,621	6,038	6,017	28,011	22,603	18,650	12,849	12,009	11,003	8,442	4,395	3,182
Vagrancy	261	275	308	346	1,692	1,611	1,697	1,321	1,450	1,453	1,416	689	376
All other offenses (except traffic)	58,286	60,638	64,054	66,527	336,733	283,792	233,030	158,374	135,913	111,940	78,396	38,420	24,761
Suspicion	10	6	23	12	70	70	74	43	36	28	27	10	15
Curfew and loitering law violations	NA	NA	NA	NA	NA	NA	NA	NA	NA	NA	NA	NA	NA

NA = Not available.

1 Because of rounding, the percentages may not sum to 100 percent.   2 Violent crimes are offenses of murder and nonnegligent manslaughter, rape, robbery, and aggravated assault. Property crimes are offenses of burglary, larceny-theft, motor vehicle theft, and arson.   3 The rape figures in this table are aggregate totals of the data submitted based on both the legacy and revised Uniform Crime Reporting definitions.

Table 40. Female Arrests, Distribution by Age, 2017

(Number, percent; 12,606 agencies; 2017 estimated population 253,634,894.)

Offense charged	Total, all ages	Ages under 15	Ages under 18	Ages 18 and over	Under 10	10–12	13–14	15	16	17	18	19
Total	2,230,852	54,435	184,175	2,046,677	767	11,378	42,290	35,779	43,684	50,277	66,112	72,826
Total percent distribution[1]	100.0	2.4	8.3	91.7	*	0.5	1.9	1.6	2.0	2.3	3.0	3.3
Violent crime[2]	83,728	2,459	7,628	76,100	36	522	1,901	1,511	1,836	1,822	2,238	2,434
Violent crime percent distribution[1]	100.0	2.9	9.1	90.9	*	0.6	2.3	1.8	2.2	2.2	2.7	2.9
Murder and nonnegligent manslaughter	1,193	10	57	1,136	0	2	8	9	15	23	45	51
Rape[3]	508	60	112	396	2	23	35	26	15	11	19	13
Robbery	10,870	352	1,590	9,280	3	33	316	348	466	424	600	536
Aggravated assault	71,157	2,037	5,869	65,288	31	464	1,542	1,128	1,340	1,364	1,574	1,834
Property crime[2]	353,013	10,389	40,391	312,622	143	2,055	8,191	7,849	10,163	11,990	14,157	13,093
Property crime percent distribution[1]	100.0	2.9	11.4	88.6	*	0.6	2.3	2.2	2.9	3.4	4.0	3.7
Burglary	29,455	906	2,834	26,621	19	191	696	615	645	668	1,009	937
Larceny-theft	306,208	8,687	34,946	271,262	117	1,745	6,825	6,634	8,878	10,747	12,621	11,613
Motor vehicle theft	15,917	646	2,355	13,562	1	72	573	561	602	546	497	524
Arson	1,433	150	256	1,177	6	47	97	39	38	29	30	19
Other assaults	239,264	14,155	36,093	203,171	162	3,527	10,466	7,418	7,633	6,887	6,144	6,708
Forgery and counterfeiting	15,005	28	209	14,796	2	11	15	20	40	121	354	555
Fraud	36,309	251	1,218	35,091	2	33	216	193	324	450	611	924
Embezzlement	6,151	5	215	5,936	0	0	5	14	61	135	312	328
Stolen property; buying, receiving, possessing	17,031	315	1,315	15,716	8	29	278	288	347	365	543	586
Vandalism	33,289	1,928	5,169	28,120	49	515	1,364	904	1,139	1,198	1,082	1,262
Weapons; carrying, possessing, etc.	12,059	575	1,506	10,553	10	182	383	264	316	351	357	382
Prostitution and commercialized vice	17,366	18	134	17,232	0	4	14	17	28	71	560	806
Sex offenses (except forcible rape and prostitution)	2,831	417	767	2,064	14	92	311	140	129	81	81	73
Drug abuse violations	309,691	3,244	17,648	292,043	18	495	2,731	2,850	4,390	7,164	12,371	13,638
Gambling	533	11	39	494	0	0	11	7	8	13	9	15
Offenses against the family and children	21,577	382	1,066	20,511	17	92	273	221	240	223	269	328
Driving under the influence	195,421	21	1,154	194,267	1	6	14	64	295	774	2,096	3,395
Liquor laws	49,342	1,547	10,732	38,610	7	163	1,377	1,937	2,804	4,444	8,620	8,348
Drunkenness	59,848	155	1,026	58,822	4	10	141	198	257	416	1,052	1,279
Disorderly conduct	82,034	7,181	17,838	64,196	64	1,609	5,508	3,716	3,755	3,186	2,636	2,502
Vagrancy	4,471	33	131	4,340	0	4	29	38	23	37	102	140
All other offenses (except traffic)	684,646	9,136	32,810	651,836	197	1,678	7,261	6,492	7,958	9,224	12,514	16,025
Suspicion	172	3	15	157	0	1	2	5	3	4	4	5
Curfew and loitering law violations	7,071	2,182	7,071	NA	33	350	1,799	1,633	1,935	1,321	NA	NA

Table 40. Female Arrests, Distribution by Age, 2017—Continued

(Number, percent; 12,606 agencies; 2017 estimated population 253,634,894.)

Offense charged	20	21	22	23	24	25–29	30–34	35–39	40–44	45–49	50–54	55–59	60–64	65 and over
Total	73,317	71,736	73,094	76,605	79,781	397,670	335,029	266,654	174,181	140,828	105,167	64,643	29,214	19,820
Total percent distribution[1]	3.3	3.2	3.3	3.4	3.6	17.8	15.0	12.0	7.8	6.3	4.7	2.9	1.3	0.9
Violent crime[2]	2,693	2,883	2,936	3,173	3,042	15,409	12,180	9,580	6,111	5,006	4,053	2,541	1,099	722
Violent crime percent distribution[1]	3.2	3.4	3.5	3.8	3.6	18.4	14.5	11.4	7.3	6.0	4.8	3.0	1.3	0.9
Murder and nonnegligent manslaughter	54	48	40	61	40	245	155	123	97	72	47	35	11	12
Rape[3]	16	21	15	14	13	56	69	68	37	19	15	13	6	2
Robbery	531	479	433	459	438	1,988	1,451	980	549	385	269	133	32	17
Aggravated assault	2,092	2,335	2,448	2,639	2,551	13,120	10,505	8,409	5,428	4,530	3,722	2,360	1,050	691
Property crime[2]	11,590	10,738	10,649	10,933	11,372	58,264	50,901	40,383	26,015	20,830	15,810	9,767	4,763	3,357
Property crime percent distribution[1]	3.3	3.0	3.0	3.1	3.2	16.5	14.4	11.4	7.4	5.9	4.5	2.8	1.3	1.0
Burglary	931	906	969	936	1,096	5,468	4,735	3,666	2,209	1,621	1,149	599	235	155
Larceny-theft	10,095	9,290	9,070	9,406	9,619	49,216	43,370	34,875	22,779	18,497	14,246	8,975	4,430	3,160
Motor vehicle theft	532	524	584	575	621	3,375	2,588	1,668	904	606	339	139	63	23
Arson	32	18	26	16	36	205	208	174	123	106	76	54	35	19
Other assaults	7,065	7,554	7,639	7,999	8,343	39,242	31,879	25,206	17,322	14,406	11,279	6,935	3,113	2,337
Forgery and counterfeiting	708	503	448	505	529	2,933	2,741	2,197	1,359	931	535	325	110	63
Fraud	1,009	961	1,048	1,091	1,281	6,863	6,241	5,140	3,440	2,746	1,773	1,062	501	400
Embezzlement	321	284	272	236	219	987	810	735	475	397	251	186	79	44
Stolen property; buying, receiving, possessing	559	567	584	682	696	3,574	2,986	2,203	1,227	746	414	224	91	34
Vandalism	1,190	1,194	1,258	1,231	1,314	5,724	4,453	3,212	1,991	1,604	1,277	749	292	287
Weapons; carrying, possessing, etc.	405	459	485	456	481	2,240	1,788	1,311	760	577	428	262	87	75
Prostitution and commercialized vice	968	918	983	876	900	3,813	2,493	1,714	1,137	995	660	272	99	38
Sex offenses (except forcible rape and prostitution)	85	65	70	77	71	319	307	204	273	146	143	69	41	40
Drug abuse violations	13,068	12,135	12,024	12,353	12,279	59,903	48,122	36,729	22,263	16,799	11,401	6,129	2,072	757
Gambling	16	7	6	10	7	58	63	53	48	63	45	44	22	28
Offenses against the family and children	422	457	587	656	809	4,747	4,503	3,343	1,831	1,137	709	375	183	155
Driving under the influence	4,230	7,253	7,832	8,098	8,025	36,646	27,926	22,787	17,253	16,313	13,705	9,923	5,208	3,577
Liquor laws	6,768	1,069	693	604	570	2,274	1,963	1,831	1,521	1,532	1,316	904	366	231
Drunkenness	1,406	1,974	1,799	1,712	1,845	9,275	8,819	7,623	6,175	5,881	4,928	3,122	1,331	601
Disorderly conduct	2,443	2,747	2,411	2,446	2,452	11,582	9,233	7,632	5,375	4,621	3,824	2,397	1,064	831
Vagrancy	120	77	104	117	101	568	581	632	425	472	383	280	161	77
All other offenses (except traffic)	18,247	19,885	21,266	23,341	25,438	133,223	117,008	94,048	59,236	45,614	32,225	19,075	8,531	6,160
Suspicion	4	6	0	9	7	26	32	22	13	12	8	2	1	6
Curfew and loitering law violations	NA	NA	NA	NA	NA	NA	NA	NA	NA	NA	NA	NA	NA	NA

NA = Not available.

* = Less than one-tenth of one percent.

1 Because of rounding, the percentages may not sum to 100 percent.   2 Violent crimes are offenses of murder and nonnegligent manslaughter, rape, robbery, and aggravated assault. Property crimes are offenses of burglary, larceny-theft, motor vehicle theft, and arson.   3 The rape figures in this table are aggregate totals of the data submitted based on both the legacy and revised Uniform Crime Reporting definitions.

Table 41. Arrests of Persons Under 15, 18, 21, and 25 Years of Age, 2017

(Number, percent; 12,606 agencies; 2017 estimated population 253,634,894.)

Offense charged	Total, all ages	Number of persons arrested				Percent of total all ages			
		Under 15	Under 18	Under 21	Under 25	Under 15	Under 18	Under 21	Under 25
Total	8,247,591	180,638	634,535	1,421,647	2,544,158	2.2	7.7	17.2	30.8
Violent crime[1]	407,496	11,371	41,184	81,666	138,203	2.8	10.1	20.0	33.9
Murder and nonnegligent manslaughter	9,576	67	717	2,210	3,983	0.7	7.5	23.1	41.6
Rape[2]	18,289	1,163	3,030	5,202	7,335	6.4	16.6	28.4	40.1
Robbery	74,340	2,925	15,282	28,864	40,526	3.9	20.6	38.8	54.5
Aggravated assault	305,291	7,216	22,155	45,390	86,359	2.4	7.3	14.9	28.3
Property crime[1]	985,847	38,071	132,525	240,806	361,644	3.9	13.4	24.4	36.7
Burglary	156,465	7,607	24,223	42,761	63,433	4.9	15.5	27.3	40.5
Larceny-theft	750,750	26,396	93,738	174,737	264,593	3.5	12.5	23.3	35.2
Motor vehicle theft	71,452	3,058	12,798	20,992	30,663	4.3	17.9	29.4	42.9
Arson	7,180	1,010	1,766	2,316	2,955	14.1	24.6	32.3	41.2
Other assaults	833,396	37,971	96,523	156,214	260,785	4.6	11.6	18.7	31.3
Forgery and counterfeiting	43,534	133	957	5,900	11,854	0.3	2.2	13.6	27.2
Fraud	96,948	738	3,714	11,122	23,277	0.8	3.8	11.5	24.0
Embezzlement	12,532	38	499	2,497	4,585	0.3	4.0	19.9	36.6
Stolen property; buying, receiving, possessing	77,474	1,692	8,243	17,475	28,494	2.2	10.6	22.6	36.8
Vandalism	147,959	11,632	28,842	44,935	65,824	7.9	19.5	30.4	44.5
Weapons; carrying, possessing, etc.	129,210	4,240	14,384	30,324	53,273	3.3	11.1	23.5	41.2
Prostitution and commercialized vice	28,490	30	218	3,063	7,868	0.1	0.8	10.8	27.6
Sex offenses (except forcible rape and prostitution)	37,850	3,336	6,644	9,786	13,220	8.8	17.6	25.9	34.9
Drug abuse violations	1,275,812	11,111	74,088	246,780	455,374	0.9	5.8	19.3	35.7
Gambling	2,510	28	213	563	910	1.1	8.5	22.4	36.3
Offenses against the family and children	72,229	982	2,895	5,708	12,398	1.4	4.0	7.9	17.2
Driving under the influence	764,569	90	4,692	44,993	162,918	*	0.6	5.9	21.3
Liquor laws	161,277	3,055	26,107	95,981	106,971	1.9	16.2	59.5	66.3
Drunkenness	289,608	432	3,395	19,775	55,671	0.1	1.2	6.8	19.2
Disorderly conduct	276,987	19,227	49,041	73,551	109,284	6.9	17.7	26.6	39.5
Vagrancy	18,542	151	583	1,669	3,258	0.8	3.1	9.0	17.6
All other offenses (except traffic)	2,560,932	29,317	116,023	305,018	644,453	1.1	4.5	11.9	25.2
Suspicion	690	17	66	122	195	2.5	9.6	17.7	28.3
Curfew and loitering law violations	23,699	6,976	23,699	23,699	23,699	29.4	100.0	100.0	100.0

* = Less than one-tenth of one percent.
1 Violent crimes in this table are offenses of murder and nonnegligent manslaughter, rape, robbery, and aggravated assault. Property crimes are offenses of burglary, larceny-theft, motor vehicle theft, and arson.   2 The rape figures in this table are aggregate totals of the data submitted based on both the legacy and revised Uniform Crime Reporting definitions.

Table 42. Arrests, Distribution by Sex, 2017

(Number, percent; 12,606 agencies; 2017 estimated population 253,634,894.)

Offense charged	Number of persons arrested			Percent male	Percent female	Percent distribution[1]		
	Total	Male	Female			Total	Male	Female
Total	8,247,591	6,016,739	2,230,852	73.0	27.0	100.0	100.0	100.0
Violent crime[2]	407,496	323,768	83,728	79.5	20.5	4.9	5.4	3.8
Murder and nonnegligent manslaughter	9,576	8,383	1,193	87.5	12.5	0.1	0.1	0.1
Rape[3]	18,289	17,781	508	97.2	2.8	0.2	0.3	*
Robbery	74,340	63,470	10,870	85.4	14.6	0.9	1.1	0.5
Aggravated assault	305,291	234,134	71,157	76.7	23.3	3.7	3.9	3.2
Property crime[2]	985,847	632,834	353,013	64.2	35.8	12.0	10.5	15.8
Burglary	156,465	127,010	29,455	81.2	18.8	1.9	2.1	1.3
Larceny-theft	750,750	444,542	306,208	59.2	40.8	9.1	7.4	13.7
Motor vehicle theft	71,452	55,535	15,917	77.7	22.3	0.9	0.9	0.7
Arson	7,180	5,747	1,433	80.0	20.0	0.1	0.1	0.1
Other assaults	833,396	594,132	239,264	71.3	28.7	10.1	9.9	10.7
Forgery and counterfeiting	43,534	28,529	15,005	65.5	34.5	0.5	0.5	0.7
Fraud	96,948	60,639	36,309	62.5	37.5	1.2	1.0	1.6
Embezzlement	12,532	6,381	6,151	50.9	49.1	0.2	0.1	0.3
Stolen property; buying, receiving, possessing	77,474	60,443	17,031	78.0	22.0	0.9	1.0	0.8
Vandalism	147,959	114,670	33,289	77.5	22.5	1.8	1.9	1.5
Weapons; carrying, possessing, etc.	129,210	117,151	12,059	90.7	9.3	1.6	1.9	0.5
Prostitution and commercialized vice	28,490	11,124	17,366	39.0	61.0	0.3	0.2	0.8
Sex offenses (except forcible rape and prostitution)	37,850	35,019	2,831	92.5	7.5	0.5	0.6	0.1
Drug abuse violations	1,275,812	966,121	309,691	75.7	24.3	15.5	16.1	13.9
Gambling	2,510	1,977	533	78.8	21.2	*	*	*
Offenses against the family and children	72,229	50,652	21,577	70.1	29.9	0.9	0.8	1.0
Driving under the influence	764,569	569,148	195,421	74.4	25.6	9.3	9.5	8.8
Liquor laws	161,277	111,935	49,342	69.4	30.6	2.0	1.9	2.2
Drunkenness	289,608	229,760	59,848	79.3	20.7	3.5	3.8	2.7
Disorderly conduct	276,987	194,953	82,034	70.4	29.6	3.4	3.2	3.7
Vagrancy	18,542	14,071	4,471	75.9	24.1	0.2	0.2	0.2
All other offenses (except traffic)	2,560,932	1,876,286	684,646	73.3	26.7	31.1	31.2	30.7
Suspicion	690	518	172	75.1	24.9	*	*	*
Curfew and loitering law violations	23,699	16,628	7,071	70.2	29.8	0.3	0.3	0.3

* = Less than one-tenth of 1 percent.
1 Because of rounding, the percentages may not sum to 100.   2 Violent crimes in this table are offenses of murder and nonnegligent manslaughter, rape, robbery, and aggravated assault. Property crimes are offenses of burglary, larceny-theft, motor vehicle theft, and arson.   3 The rape figures in this table are aggregate totals of the data submitted based on both the legacy and revised Uniform Crime Reporting definitions.

Table 43. Arrests, Distribution by Race, 2017

(Number, percent; 12,599 agencies; 2017 estimated population 253,405,839.)

Offense charged	Total arrests						Percent distribution[1]						Arrests under 18					
	Total	White	Black	American Indian or Alaskan Native	Asian	Native Hawaiian or Other Pacific Islander	Total	White	Black	American Indian or Alaskan Native	Asian	Native Hawaiian or Other Pacific Islander	Total	White	Black	American Indian or Alaskan Native	Asian	Native Hawaiian or Other Pacific Islander
Total	8,162,849	5,626,140	2,221,697	196,908	97,049	21,055	100.0	68.9	27.2	2.4	1.2	0.3	625,099	385,298	218,048	12,912	6,998	1,843
Violent crime[2]	404,236	236,590	151,744	8,640	5,979	1,283	100.0	58.5	37.5	2.1	1.5	0.3	40,761	18,940	20,758	555	382	126
Murder and nonnegligent manslaughter	9,468	4,188	5,025	108	127	20	100.0	44.2	53.1	1.1	1.3	0.2	708	267	429	5	5	2
Rape[3]	18,063	12,187	5,182	322	307	65	100.0	67.5	28.7	1.8	1.7	0.4	2,975	1,970	925	38	36	6
Robbery	73,764	32,128	40,024	679	664	269	100.0	43.6	54.3	0.9	0.9	0.4	15,149	4,810	10,086	66	130	57
Aggravated assault	302,941	188,087	101,513	7,531	4,881	929	100.0	62.1	33.5	2.5	1.6	0.3	21,929	11,893	9,318	446	211	61
Property crime[2]	973,219	657,574	285,080	16,630	11,576	2,359	100.0	67.6	29.3	1.7	1.2	0.2	130,243	73,204	52,551	2,204	1,876	408
Burglary	154,970	104,671	46,227	1,968	1,710	394	100.0	67.5	29.8	1.3	1.1	0.3	23,880	13,401	9,795	384	241	59
Larceny-theft	740,546	501,231	215,650	13,242	8,770	1,653	100.0	67.7	29.1	1.8	1.2	0.2	92,110	52,879	35,872	1,559	1,490	310
Motor vehicle theft	70,617	46,621	21,415	1,308	980	293	100.0	66.0	30.3	1.9	1.4	0.4	12,522	5,665	6,455	242	127	33
Arson	7,086	5,051	1,788	112	116	19	100.0	71.3	25.2	1.6	1.6	0.3	1,731	1,259	429	19	18	6
Other assaults	822,671	534,188	258,542	17,062	10,371	2,508	100.0	64.9	31.4	2.1	1.3	0.3	94,994	54,941	37,367	1,550	833	303
Forgery and counterfeiting	43,203	28,130	13,980	386	619	88	100.0	65.1	32.4	0.9	1.4	0.2	945	545	379	7	13	1
Fraud	95,997	63,908	29,556	1,256	1,174	103	100.0	66.6	30.8	1.3	1.2	0.1	3,671	1,695	1,874	58	40	4
Embezzlement	12,437	7,441	4,683	96	190	27	100.0	59.8	37.7	0.8	1.5	0.2	492	272	204	5	9	2
Stolen property; buying, receiving, possessing	76,477	48,607	25,585	1,034	940	311	100.0	63.6	33.5	1.4	1.2	0.4	8,093	3,281	4,588	101	86	37
Vandalism	145,934	99,818	40,861	3,265	1,681	309	100.0	68.4	28.0	2.2	1.2	0.2	28,335	19,664	7,877	529	222	43
Weapons; carrying, possessing, etc.	128,009	68,787	56,143	1,357	1,400	322	100.0	53.7	43.9	1.1	1.1	0.3	14,249	7,629	6,238	158	198	26
Prostitution and commercialized vice	28,229	15,812	10,605	116	1,610	86	100.0	56.0	37.6	0.4	5.7	0.3	217	98	114	2	3	0
Sex offenses (except forcible rape and prostitution)	37,518	26,615	9,355	691	741	116	100.0	70.9	24.9	1.8	2.0	0.3	6,524	4,659	1,666	75	100	24
Drug abuse violations	1,262,660	889,030	342,513	15,038	13,691	2,388	100.0	70.4	27.1	1.2	1.1	0.2	72,978	54,199	16,167	1,356	996	260
Gambling	2,493	955	1,294	20	183	41	100.0	38.3	51.9	0.8	7.3	1.6	208	44	159	3	2	0
Offenses against the family and children	71,656	46,926	20,106	4,067	534	23	100.0	65.5	28.1	5.7	0.7	*	2,878	1,675	792	389	17	5
Driving under the influence	755,726	617,443	105,585	15,950	14,294	2,454	100.0	81.7	14.0	2.1	1.9	0.3	4,593	4,066	304	154	60	9
Liquor laws	157,285	122,929	22,095	9,705	2,347	209	100.0	78.2	14.0	6.2	1.5	0.1	25,538	22,319	1,521	1,302	347	49
Drunkenness	287,985	212,908	41,073	30,632	2,931	441	100.0	73.9	14.3	10.6	1.0	0.2	3,358	2,616	283	417	35	7
Disorderly conduct	273,664	172,098	87,094	11,832	2,232	408	100.0	62.9	31.8	4.3	0.8	0.1	48,455	26,340	20,672	1,072	317	54
Vagrancy	18,453	12,609	5,148	473	209	14	100.0	68.3	27.9	2.6	1.1	0.1	579	304	262	7	5	1
All other offenses (except traffic)	2,540,842	1,750,366	700,984	57,979	24,046	7,467	100.0	68.9	27.6	2.3	0.9	0.3	114,436	75,630	34,722	2,529	1,163	392
Suspicion	669	250	148	258	7	6	100.0	37.4	22.1	38.6	1.0	0.9	66	21	27	18	0	0
Curfew and loitering law violations	23,486	13,156	9,523	421	294	92	100.0	56.0	40.5	1.8	1.3	0.4	23,486	13,156	9,523	421	294	92

Table 43. Arrests, Distribution by Race, 2017—Continued

(Number, percent; 12,599 agencies; 2017 estimated population 253,405,839.)

Offense charged	Percent distribution[1]						Arrests 18 and over						Percent distribution[1]					
	Total	White	Black	American Indian or Alaskan Native	Asian	Native Hawaiian or Other Pacific Islander	Total	White	Black	American Indian or Alaskan Native	Asian	Native Hawaiian or Other Pacific Islander	Total	White	Black	American Indian or Alaskan Native	Asian	Native Hawaiian or Other Pacific Islander
Total	100.0	61.6	34.9	2.1	1.1	0.3	7,537,750	5,240,842	2,003,649	183,996	90,051	19,212	100.0	69.5	26.6	2.4	1.2	0.3
Violent crime[2]	100.0	46.5	50.9	1.4	0.9	0.3	363,475	217,650	130,986	8,085	5,597	1,157	100.0	59.9	36.0	2.2	1.5	0.3
Murder and nonnegligent manslaughter	100.0	37.7	60.6	0.7	0.7	0.3	8,760	3,921	4,596	103	122	18	100.0	44.8	52.5	1.2	1.4	0.2
Rape[3]	100.0	66.2	31.1	1.3	1.2	0.2	15,088	10,217	4,257	284	271	59	100.0	67.7	28.2	1.9	1.8	0.4
Robbery	100.0	31.8	66.6	0.4	0.9	0.4	58,615	27,318	29,938	613	534	212	100.0	46.6	51.1	1.0	0.9	0.4
Aggravated assault	100.0	54.2	42.5	2.0	1.0	0.3	281,012	176,194	92,195	7,085	4,670	868	100.0	62.7	32.8	2.5	1.7	0.3
Property crime[2]	100.0	56.2	40.3	1.7	1.4	0.3	842,976	584,370	232,529	14,426	9,700	1,951	100.0	69.3	27.6	1.7	1.2	0.2
Burglary	100.0	56.1	41.0	1.6	1.0	0.2	131,090	91,270	36,432	1,584	1,469	335	100.0	69.6	27.8	1.2	1.1	0.3
Larceny-theft	100.0	57.4	38.9	1.7	1.6	0.3	648,436	448,352	179,778	11,683	7,280	1,343	100.0	69.1	27.7	1.8	1.1	0.2
Motor vehicle theft	100.0	45.2	51.5	1.9	1.0	0.3	58,095	40,956	14,960	1,066	853	260	100.0	70.5	25.8	1.8	1.5	0.4
Arson	100.0	72.7	24.8	1.1	1.0	0.3	5,355	3,792	1,359	93	98	13	100.0	70.8	25.4	1.7	1.8	0.2
Other assaults	100.0	57.8	39.3	1.6	0.9	0.3	727,677	479,247	221,175	15,512	9,538	2,205	100.0	65.9	30.4	2.1	1.3	0.3
Forgery and counterfeiting	100.0	57.7	40.1	0.7	1.4	0.1	42,258	27,585	13,601	379	606	87	100.0	65.3	32.2	0.9	1.4	0.2
Fraud	100.0	46.2	51.0	1.6	1.1	0.1	92,326	62,213	27,682	1,198	1,134	99	100.0	67.4	30.0	1.3	1.2	0.1
Embezzlement	100.0	55.3	41.5	1.0	1.8	0.4	11,945	7,169	4,479	91	181	25	100.0	60.0	37.5	0.8	1.5	0.2
Stolen property; buying, receiving, possessing	100.0	40.5	56.7	1.2	1.1	0.5	68,384	45,326	20,997	933	854	274	100.0	66.3	30.7	1.4	1.2	0.4
Vandalism	100.0	69.4	27.8	1.9	0.8	0.2	117,599	80,154	32,984	2,736	1,459	266	100.0	68.2	28.0	2.3	1.2	0.2
Weapons; carrying, possessing, etc.	100.0	53.5	43.8	1.1	1.4	0.2	113,760	61,158	49,905	1,199	1,202	296	100.0	53.8	43.9	1.1	1.1	0.3
Prostitution and commercialized vice	100.0	45.2	52.5	0.9	1.4	0.0	28,012	15,714	10,491	114	1,607	86	100.0	56.1	37.5	0.4	5.7	0.3
Sex offenses (except forcible rape and prostitution)	100.0	71.4	25.5	1.1	1.5	0.4	30,994	21,956	7,689	616	641	92	100.0	70.8	24.8	2.0	2.1	0.3
Drug abuse violations	100.0	74.3	22.2	1.9	1.4	0.4	1,189,682	834,831	326,346	13,682	12,695	2,128	100.0	70.2	27.4	1.2	1.1	0.2
Gambling	100.0	21.2	76.4	1.4	1.0	0.0	2,285	911	1,135	17	181	41	100.0	39.9	49.7	0.7	7.9	1.8
Offenses against the family and children	100.0	58.2	27.5	13.5	0.6	0.2	68,778	45,251	19,314	3,678	517	18	100.0	65.8	28.1	5.3	0.8	*
Driving under the influence	100.0	88.5	6.6	3.4	1.3	0.2	751,133	613,377	105,281	15,796	14,234	2,445	100.0	81.7	14.0	2.1	1.9	0.3
Liquor laws	100.0	87.4	6.0	5.1	1.4	0.2	131,747	100,610	20,574	8,403	2,000	160	100.0	76.4	15.6	6.4	1.5	0.1
Drunkenness	100.0	77.9	8.4	12.4	1.0	0.2	284,627	210,292	40,790	30,215	2,896	434	100.0	73.9	14.3	10.6	1.0	0.2
Disorderly conduct	100.0	54.4	42.7	2.2	0.7	0.1	225,209	145,758	66,422	10,760	1,915	354	100.0	64.7	29.5	4.8	0.9	0.2
Vagrancy	100.0	52.5	45.3	1.2	0.9	0.2	17,874	12,305	4,886	466	204	13	100.0	68.8	27.3	2.6	1.1	0.1
All other offenses (except traffic)	100.0	66.1	30.3	2.2	1.0	0.3	2,426,406	1,674,736	666,262	55,450	22,883	7,075	100.0	69.0	27.5	2.3	0.9	0.3
Suspicion	100.0	31.8	40.9	27.3	0.0	0.0	603	229	121	240	7	6	100.0	38.0	20.1	39.8	1.2	1.0
Curfew and loitering law violations	100.0	56.0	40.5	1.8	1.3	0.4	NA	NA	NA	NA	NA	NA	NA	NA	NA	NA	NA	NA

NA = Not available.
* = Less than one-tenth of one percent.
1 Because of rounding, the percentages may not sum to 100.   2 Violent crimes are offenses of murder and nonnegligent manslaughter, rape, robbery, and aggravated assault. Property crimes are offenses of burglary, larceny-theft, motor vehicle theft, and arson.   3 The rape figures in this table are aggregate totals of the data submitted based on both the legacy and revised Uniform Crime Reporting definitions.

Table 43A. Arrests, Distribution by Ethnicity, 2017

(Number, percent; 12,599 agencies; 2017 estimated population 253,405,839.)

Offense charged	Total arrests			Percent distribution[1]			Arrests under 18		
	Total[2]	Hispanic or Latino	Not Hispanic or Latino	Total[2]	Hispanic or Latino	Not Hispanic or Latino	Total[2]	Hispanic or Latino	Not Hispanic or Latino
Total	6,584,533	1,190,671	5,393,862	100.0	18.1	81.9	466,450	101,762	364,688
Violent crime[3]	335,792	79,078	256,714	100.0	23.5	76.5	31,866	7,651	24,215
Murder and nonnegligent manslaughter	7,031	1,462	5,569	100.0	20.8	79.2	478	123	355
Rape[4]	14,025	3,787	10,238	100.0	27.0	73.0	2,214	489	1,725
Robbery	59,680	12,722	46,958	100.0	21.3	78.7	11,570	2,673	8,897
Aggravated assault	255,056	61,107	193,949	100.0	24.0	76.0	17,604	4,366	13,238
Property crime[3]	748,347	119,392	628,955	100.0	16.0	84.0	89,662	19,066	70,596
Burglary	123,671	24,873	98,798	100.0	20.1	79.9	16,643	4,379	12,264
Larceny-theft	563,359	78,921	484,438	100.0	14.0	86.0	63,503	12,220	51,283
Motor vehicle theft	55,723	14,525	41,198	100.0	26.1	73.9	8,217	2,187	6,030
Arson	5,594	1,073	4,521	100.0	19.2	80.8	1,299	280	1,019
Other assaults	658,243	118,922	539,321	100.0	18.1	81.9	74,414	15,779	58,635
Forgery and counterfeiting	34,659	5,333	29,326	100.0	15.4	84.6	725	115	610
Fraud	75,632	8,836	66,796	100.0	11.7	88.3	2,887	376	2,511
Embezzlement	10,189	1,248	8,941	100.0	12.2	87.8	418	124	294
Stolen property; buying, receiving, possessing	58,425	11,351	47,074	100.0	19.4	80.6	5,782	1,330	4,452
Vandalism	117,580	21,549	96,031	100.0	18.3	81.7	21,299	4,548	16,751
Weapons; carrying, possessing, etc.	101,538	23,125	78,413	100.0	22.8	77.2	11,186	3,425	7,761
Prostitution and commercialized vice	24,578	5,093	19,485	100.0	20.7	79.3	183	28	155
Sex offenses (except forcible rape and prostitution)	31,424	7,632	23,792	100.0	24.3	75.7	5,312	1,279	4,033
Drug abuse violations	1,019,770	201,858	817,912	100.0	19.8	80.2	54,532	14,474	40,058
Gambling	1,558	382	1,176	100.0	24.5	75.5	127	21	106
Offenses against the family and children	57,018	6,674	50,344	100.0	11.7	88.3	2,232	321	1,911
Driving under the influence	627,315	140,918	486,397	100.0	22.5	77.5	3,741	868	2,873
Liquor laws	117,267	15,704	101,563	100.0	13.4	86.6	19,437	2,915	16,522
Drunkenness	267,218	57,521	209,697	100.0	21.5	78.5	2,847	1,023	1,824
Disorderly conduct	201,451	24,687	176,764	100.0	12.3	87.7	34,965	5,860	29,105
Vagrancy	15,017	2,195	12,822	100.0	14.6	85.4	390	108	282
All other offenses (except traffic)	2,061,185	335,002	1,726,183	100.0	16.3	83.7	84,539	18,322	66,217
Suspicion	468	44	424	100.0	9.4	90.6	48	2	46
Curfew and loitering law violations	19,859	4,127	15,732	100.0	20.8	79.2	19,858	4,127	15,731

Table 43A. Arrests, Distribution by Ethnicity, 2017—Continued

(Number, percent; 12,599 agencies; 2017 estimated population 253,405,839.)

Offense charged	Percent distribution[1]			Arrests 18 and over			Percent distribution[1]		
	Total[2]	Hispanic or Latino	Not Hispanic or Latino	Total[2]	Hispanic or Latino	Not Hispanic or Latino	Total[2]	Hispanic or Latino	Not Hispanic or Latino
Total	100.0	21.8	78.2	6,118,082	1,088,909	5,029,173	100.0	17.8	82.2
Violent crime[3]	100.0	24.0	76.0	303,926	71,427	232,499	100.0	23.5	76.5
Murder and nonnegligent manslaughter	100.0	25.7	74.3	6,553	1,339	5,214	100.0	20.4	79.6
Rape[4]	100.0	22.1	77.9	11,811	3,298	8,513	100.0	27.9	72.1
Robbery	100.0	23.1	76.9	48,110	10,049	38,061	100.0	20.9	79.1
Aggravated assault	100.0	24.8	75.2	237,452	56,741	180,711	100.0	23.9	76.1
Property crime[3]	100.0	21.3	78.7	658,685	100,326	558,359	100.0	15.2	84.8
Burglary	100.0	26.3	73.7	107,028	20,494	86,534	100.0	19.1	80.9
Larceny-theft	100.0	19.2	80.8	499,856	66,701	433,155	100.0	13.3	86.7
Motor vehicle theft	100.0	26.6	73.4	47,506	12,338	35,168	100.0	26.0	74.0
Arson	100.0	21.6	78.4	4,295	793	3,502	100.0	18.5	81.5
Other assaults	100.0	21.2	78.8	583,829	103,143	480,686	100.0	17.7	82.3
Forgery and counterfeiting	100.0	15.9	84.1	33,934	5,218	28,716	100.0	15.4	84.6
Fraud	100.0	13.0	87.0	72,745	8,460	64,285	100.0	11.6	88.4
Embezzlement	100.0	29.7	70.3	9,771	1,124	8,647	100.0	11.5	88.5
Stolen property; buying, receiving, possessing	100.0	23.0	77.0	52,643	10,021	42,622	100.0	19.0	81.0
Vandalism	100.0	21.4	78.6	96,281	17,001	79,280	100.0	17.7	82.3
Weapons; carrying, possessing, etc.	100.0	30.6	69.4	90,352	19,700	70,652	100.0	21.8	78.2
Prostitution and commercialized vice	100.0	15.3	84.7	24,395	5,065	19,330	100.0	20.8	79.2
Sex offenses (except forcible rape and prostitution)	100.0	24.1	75.9	26,112	6,353	19,759	100.0	24.3	75.7
Drug abuse violations	100.0	26.5	73.5	965,238	187,384	777,854	100.0	19.4	80.6
Gambling	100.0	16.5	83.5	1,431	361	1,070	100.0	25.2	74.8
Offenses against the family and children	100.0	14.4	85.6	54,786	6,353	48,433	100.0	11.6	88.4
Driving under the influence	100.0	23.2	76.8	623,574	140,050	483,524	100.0	22.5	77.5
Liquor laws	100.0	15.0	85.0	97,830	12,789	85,041	100.0	13.1	86.9
Drunkenness	100.0	35.9	64.1	264,371	56,498	207,873	100.0	21.4	78.6
Disorderly conduct	100.0	16.8	83.2	166,486	18,827	147,659	100.0	11.3	88.7
Vagrancy	100.0	27.7	72.3	14,627	2,087	12,540	100.0	14.3	85.7
All other offenses (except traffic)	100.0	21.7	78.3	1,976,646	316,680	1,659,966	100.0	16.0	84.0
Suspicion	100.0	4.2	95.8	420	42	378	100.0	10.0	90.0
Curfew and loitering law violations	100.0	20.8	79.2	NA	NA	NA	NA	NA	NA

NA = Not available.
1 Because of rounding, the percentages may not sum to 100.   2 The ethnicity totals are representative of those agencies that provided ethnicity breakdowns. Not all agencies provide ethnicity data; therefore, the race and ethnicity totals will not be equal.   3 Violent crimes are offenses of murder and nonnegligent manslaughter, rape, robbery, and aggravated assault. Property crimes are offenses of burglary, larceny-theft, motor vehicle theft, and arson.   4 The rape figures in this table are aggregate totals of the data submitted based on both the legacy and revised Uniform Crime Reporting definitions.

Table 44. Arrest Trends, Cities, 2016–2017

(Number, percent change; 8,756 agencies; 2017 estimated population 169,545,459; 2016 estimated population 168,654,911.)

Offense charged	Number of persons arrested								
	Total, all ages			Under 18 years of age			18 years of age and over		
	2016	2017	Percent change	2016	2017	Percent change	2016	2017	Percent change
Total[1]	5,800,182	5,739,525	-1.0	517,141	492,100	-4.8	5,283,041	5,247,425	-0.7
Violent crime[2]	299,347	302,075	+0.9	31,735	31,825	+0.3	267,612	270,250	+1.0
Murder and nonnegligent manslaughter	6,428	6,749	+5.0	516	537	+4.1	5,912	6,212	+5.1
Rape[3]	12,451	12,603	+1.2	2,005	2,102	+4.8	10,446	10,501	+0.5
Robbery	61,922	60,508	-2.3	12,739	12,651	-0.7	49,183	47,857	-2.7
Aggravated assault	218,546	222,215	+1.7	16,475	16,535	+0.4	202,071	205,680	+1.8
Property crime[2]	828,075	770,257	-7.0	116,471	107,085	-8.1	711,604	663,172	-6.8
Burglary	115,766	111,663	-3.5	19,138	18,351	-4.1	96,628	93,312	-3.4
Larceny-theft	657,861	601,503	-8.6	86,017	77,124	-10.3	571,844	524,379	-8.3
Motor vehicle theft	49,398	51,854	+5.0	9,837	10,206	+3.8	39,561	41,648	+5.3
Arson	5,050	5,237	+3.7	1,479	1,404	-5.1	3,571	3,833	+7.3
Other assaults	602,510	599,153	-0.6	72,390	70,699	-2.3	530,120	528,454	-0.3
Forgery and counterfeiting	31,599	31,338	-0.8	720	755	+4.9	30,879	30,583	-1.0
Fraud	67,337	66,809	-0.8	2,786	2,997	+7.6	64,551	63,812	-1.1
Embezzlement	9,641	9,457	-1.9	428	435	+1.6	9,213	9,022	-2.1
Stolen property; buying, receiving, possessing	53,621	56,483	+5.3	7,016	6,722	-4.2	46,605	49,761	+6.8
Vandalism	112,743	110,021	-2.4	23,041	21,755	-5.6	89,702	88,266	-1.6
Weapons; carrying, possessing, etc.	90,681	95,563	+5.4	12,046	11,466	-4.8	78,635	84,097	+6.9
Prostitution and commercialized vice	24,945	23,297	-6.6	335	176	-47.5	24,610	23,121	-6.1
Sex offenses (except forcible rape and prostitution)	26,346	25,876	-1.8	4,513	4,597	+1.9	21,833	21,279	-2.5
Drug abuse violations	837,493	870,491	+3.9	56,521	54,983	-2.7	780,972	815,508	+4.4
Gambling	1,868	1,746	-6.5	162	156	-3.7	1,706	1,590	-6.8
Offenses against the family and children	34,571	35,911	+3.9	2,107	2,227	+5.7	32,464	33,684	+3.8
Driving under the influence	438,600	425,335	-3.0	3,095	2,903	-6.2	435,505	422,432	-3.0
Liquor laws	134,874	122,936	-8.9	20,042	18,534	-7.5	114,832	104,402	-9.1
Drunkenness	255,492	247,137	-3.3	3,245	2,918	-10.1	252,247	244,219	-3.2
Disorderly conduct	234,535	222,346	-5.2	42,465	40,158	-5.4	192,070	182,188	-5.1
Vagrancy	16,046	15,897	-0.9	476	458	-3.8	15,570	15,439	-0.8
All other offenses (except traffic)	1,674,992	1,685,653	+0.6	92,681	89,507	-3.4	1,582,311	1,596,146	+0.9
Suspicion	389	439	+12.9	42	18	-57.1	347	421	+21.3
Curfew and loitering law violations	24,866	21,744	-12.6	24,866	21,744	-12.6	NA	NA	NA

NA = Not available.

1 Does not include suspicion.   2 Violent crimes are offenses of murder and nonnegligent manslaughter, rape, robbery, and aggravated assault.   Property crimes are offenses of burglary, larceny-theft, motor vehicle theft, and arson.   3 The rape figures in this table are aggregate totals of the data submitted based on both the legacy and revised Uniform Crime Reporting definitions.

Table 45. Arrest Trends, Cities, by Age and Sex, 2016–2017

(Number, percent change; 8,756 agencies; 2017 estimated population 169,545,459; 2016 estimated population 168,654,911.)

Offense charged	Male						Female					
	Total			Under 18			Total			Under 18		
	2016	2017	Percent change	2016	2017	Percent change	2016	2017	Percent change	2016	2017	Percent change
Total[1]	4,223,061	4,173,173	-1.2	363,555	348,198	-4.2	1,577,121	1,566,352	-0.7	153,586	143,902	-6.3
Violent crime[2]	237,465	238,988	+0.6	25,986	25,999	+0.1	61,882	63,087	+1.9	5,749	5,826	+1.3
Murder and nonnegligent manslaughter	5,741	5,974	+4.1	471	498	+5.7	687	775	+12.8	45	39	-13.3
Rape[3]	12,151	12,306	+1.3	1,916	2,016	+5.2	300	297	-1.0	89	86	-3.4
Robbery	53,123	51,721	-2.6	11,405	11,317	-0.8	8,799	8,787	-0.1	1,334	1,334	0.0
Aggravated assault	166,450	168,987	+1.5	12,194	12,168	-0.2	52,096	53,228	+2.2	4,281	4,367	+2.0
Property crime[2]	514,406	487,828	-5.2	76,413	73,575	-3.7	313,669	282,429	-10.0	40,058	33,510	-16.3
Burglary	93,743	90,490	-3.5	16,781	16,161	-3.7	22,023	21,173	-3.9	2,357	2,190	-7.1
Larceny-theft	377,959	352,847	-6.6	50,316	47,845	-4.9	279,902	248,656	-11.2	35,701	29,279	-18.0
Motor vehicle theft	38,698	40,322	+4.2	8,042	8,369	+4.1	10,700	11,532	+7.8	1,795	1,837	+2.3
Arson	4,006	4,169	+4.1	1,274	1,200	-5.8	1,044	1,068	+2.3	205	204	-0.5
Other assaults	430,928	425,148	-1.3	45,491	43,921	-3.5	171,582	174,005	+1.4	26,899	26,778	-0.4
Forgery and counterfeiting	20,430	20,691	+1.3	530	594	+12.1	11,169	10,647	-4.7	190	161	-15.3
Fraud	42,385	42,012	-0.9	1,906	2,014	+5.7	24,952	24,797	-0.6	880	983	+11.7
Embezzlement	4,854	4,776	-1.6	271	250	-7.7	4,787	4,681	-2.2	157	185	+17.8
Stolen property; buying, receiving, possessing	42,204	44,038	+4.3	5,896	5,688	-3.5	11,417	12,445	+9.0	1,120	1,034	-7.7
Vandalism	87,645	85,031	-3.0	19,122	17,884	-6.5	25,098	24,990	-0.4	3,919	3,871	-1.2
Weapons; carrying, possessing, etc.	82,671	87,050	+5.3	10,789	10,340	-4.2	8,010	8,513	+6.3	1,257	1,126	-10.4
Prostitution and commercialized vice	9,203	8,678	-5.7	87	66	-24.1	15,742	14,619	-7.1	248	110	-55.6
Sex offenses (except forcible rape and prostitution)	24,290	23,880	-1.7	3,920	4,029	+2.8	2,056	1,996	-2.9	593	568	-4.2
Drug abuse violations	647,227	665,759	+2.9	43,684	42,092	-3.6	190,266	204,732	+7.6	12,837	12,891	+0.4
Gambling	1,589	1,461	-8.1	152	144	-5.3	279	285	+2.2	10	12	+20.0
Offenses against the family and children	22,317	23,116	+3.6	1,323	1,393	+5.3	12,254	12,795	+4.4	784	834	+6.4
Driving under the influence	325,533	314,954	-3.2	2,282	2,149	-5.8	113,067	110,381	-2.4	813	754	-7.3
Liquor laws	95,224	85,528	-10.2	12,017	10,937	-9.0	39,650	37,408	-5.7	8,025	7,597	-5.3
Drunkenness	205,944	197,027	-4.3	2,289	2,048	-10.5	49,548	50,110	+1.1	956	870	-9.0
Disorderly conduct	166,679	156,216	-6.3	27,204	25,346	-6.8	67,856	66,130	-2.5	15,261	14,812	-2.9
Vagrancy	12,237	12,114	-1.0	352	361	+2.6	3,809	3,783	-0.7	124	97	-21.8
All other offenses (except traffic)	1,232,356	1,233,493	+0.1	66,367	63,983	-3.6	442,636	452,160	+2.2	26,314	25,524	-3.0
Suspicion	301	333	+10.6	34	14	-58.8	88	106	+20.5	8	4	-50.0
Curfew and loitering law violations	17,474	15,385	-12.0	17,474	15,385	-12.0	7,392	6,359	-14.0	7,392	6,359	-14.0

1 Does not include suspicion.   2 Violent crimes are offenses of murder and nonnegligent manslaughter, rape, robbery, and aggravated assault. Property crimes are offenses of burglary, larceny-theft, motor vehicle theft, and arson.   3 The rape figures in this table are aggregate totals of the data submitted based on both the legacy and revised Uniform Crime Reporting definitions.

Table 46. Arrests, Cities, Distribution by Age, 2017

(Number, percent; 9,289 agencies; 2017 estimated population 175,386,806.)

Offense charged	Total, all ages	Ages under 15	Ages under 18	Ages 18 and over	Under 10	10–12	13–14	15	16	17	18	19	20
Total	5,953,871	146,842	504,495	5,449,376	3,124	33,094	110,624	95,720	120,272	141,661	187,745	201,592	198,131
Total percent distribution[1]	100.0	2.5	8.5	91.5	0.1	0.6	1.9	1.6	2.0	2.4	3.2	3.4	3.3
Violent crime[2]	312,819	9,091	32,987	279,832	146	2,017	6,928	6,390	8,240	9,266	10,619	10,723	10,526
Violent crime percent distribution[1]	100.0	2.9	10.5	89.5	*	0.6	2.2	2.0	2.6	3.0	3.4	3.4	3.4
Murder and nonnegligent manslaughter	7,058	57	561	6,497	0	7	50	83	166	255	375	408	375
Rape[3]	13,036	813	2,132	10,904	9	206	598	406	462	451	521	535	424
Robbery	62,927	2,619	13,167	49,760	13	351	2,255	2,750	3,670	4,128	4,371	3,825	3,221
Aggravated assault	229,798	5,602	17,127	212,671	124	1,453	4,025	3,151	3,942	4,432	5,352	5,955	6,506
Property crime[2]	795,597	31,866	109,711	685,886	608	6,816	24,442	21,919	26,539	29,387	32,553	29,144	25,584
Property crime percent distribution[1]	100.0	4.0	13.8	86.2	0.1	0.9	3.1	2.8	3.3	3.7	4.1	3.7	3.2
Burglary	115,300	5,967	18,839	96,461	155	1,261	4,551	4,050	4,348	4,474	4,936	4,499	4,142
Larceny-theft	621,866	22,528	78,971	542,895	399	4,981	17,148	15,169	19,176	22,098	25,070	22,454	19,554
Motor vehicle theft	53,010	2,553	10,470	42,540	6	315	2,232	2,449	2,799	2,669	2,404	2,065	1,774
Arson	5,421	818	1,431	3,990	48	259	511	251	216	146	143	126	114
Other assaults	629,727	29,179	72,916	556,811	682	8,101	20,396	14,062	15,165	14,510	14,172	15,358	16,544
Forgery and counterfeiting	32,362	122	771	31,591	2	32	88	108	207	334	903	1,333	1,516
Fraud	68,407	609	3,062	65,345	3	83	523	555	826	1,072	1,447	2,045	2,227
Embezzlement	9,910	38	440	9,470	0	7	31	51	123	228	537	564	556
Stolen property; buying, receiving, possessing	57,682	1,459	6,881	50,801	14	176	1,269	1,465	1,901	2,056	2,625	2,355	2,187
Vandalism	114,103	9,332	22,392	91,711	358	2,652	6,322	4,107	4,468	4,485	4,145	4,244	3,980
Weapons; carrying, possessing, etc.	98,876	3,375	11,707	87,169	88	871	2,416	2,067	2,801	3,464	4,354	4,430	4,168
Prostitution and commercialized vice	24,853	26	185	24,668	0	5	21	22	51	86	597	902	1,052
Sex offenses (except forcible rape and prostitution)	26,831	2,395	4,727	22,104	81	586	1,728	798	764	770	724	736	669
Drug abuse violations	906,754	9,000	56,569	850,185	50	1,357	7,593	8,987	14,935	23,647	40,732	42,558	39,546
Gambling	1,789	19	160	1,629	0	1	18	24	48	69	89	96	96
Offenses against the family and children	37,793	795	2,272	35,521	50	192	553	493	470	514	617	645	718
Driving under the influence	442,122	68	2,981	439,141	8	9	51	156	707	2,050	5,544	8,207	9,989
Liquor laws	127,086	2,362	18,993	108,093	15	237	2,110	3,124	5,015	8,492	18,596	19,611	16,228
Drunkenness	252,852	376	2,976	249,876	13	24	339	459	743	1,398	3,846	4,980	5,434
Disorderly conduct	228,822	16,297	40,786	188,036	280	4,163	11,854	8,162	8,481	7,846	7,256	6,895	6,623
Vagrancy	16,388	118	469	15,919	1	15	102	100	116	135	303	335	327
All other offenses (except traffic)	1,746,599	23,770	91,518	1,655,081	604	4,517	18,649	17,606	22,793	27,349	38,071	46,416	50,151
Suspicion	541	12	34	507	0	6	6	10	4	8	15	15	10
Curfew and loitering law violations	21,958	6,533	21,958	NA	121	1,227	5,185	5,055	5,875	4,495	NA	NA	NA

Table 46. Arrests, Cities, Distribution by Age, 2017—Continued

(Number, percent; 9,289 agencies; 2017 estimated population 175,386,806.)

Offense charged	21	22	23	24	25–29	30–34	35–39	40–44	45–49	50–54	55–59	60–64	65 and over
Total	198,292	200,540	205,941	209,771	1,017,444	829,347	663,783	444,951	382,885	314,027	218,710	106,704	69,513
Total percent distribution[1]	3.3	3.4	3.5	3.5	17.1	13.9	11.1	7.5	6.4	5.3	3.7	1.8	1.2
Violent crime[2]	10,798	10,892	11,289	11,324	54,151	42,579	33,534	21,977	18,129	14,829	10,079	4,826	3,557
Violent crime percent distribution[1]	3.5	3.5	3.6	3.6	17.3	13.6	10.7	7.0	5.8	4.7	3.2	1.5	1.1
Murder and nonnegligent manslaughter	358	330	351	327	1,313	869	618	385	271	229	149	75	64
Rape[3]	430	374	350	386	1,654	1,532	1,368	978	784	648	443	255	222
Robbery	2,669	2,483	2,367	2,260	9,716	6,538	4,518	2,723	2,179	1,593	874	294	129
Aggravated assault	7,341	7,705	8,221	8,351	41,468	33,640	27,030	17,891	14,895	12,359	8,613	4,202	3,142
Property crime[2]	23,933	23,640	24,398	25,135	126,318	107,039	84,536	55,170	47,701	37,793	24,596	11,211	7,135
Property crime percent distribution[1]	3.0	3.0	3.1	3.2	15.9	13.5	10.6	6.9	6.0	4.8	3.1	1.4	0.9
Burglary	3,777	3,752	3,813	3,866	18,749	15,104	11,800	7,245	5,978	4,402	2,809	1,070	519
Larceny-theft	18,315	17,953	18,654	19,306	97,766	84,050	67,090	44,545	39,217	31,784	20,892	9,791	6,454
Motor vehicle theft	1,735	1,808	1,818	1,836	9,142	7,260	5,126	3,026	2,173	1,349	690	240	94
Arson	106	127	113	127	661	625	520	354	333	258	205	110	68
Other assaults	18,903	19,987	21,189	21,831	106,764	88,270	71,277	48,697	40,643	32,908	21,802	10,488	7,978
Forgery and counterfeiting	1,093	1,083	1,114	1,207	6,115	5,398	4,290	2,667	2,095	1,366	861	362	188
Fraud	2,019	2,271	2,204	2,505	12,893	11,058	8,953	5,720	4,679	3,423	2,147	1,041	713
Embezzlement	466	456	425	365	1,731	1,257	1,060	669	586	374	248	109	67
Stolen property; buying, receiving, possessing	2,013	2,080	2,148	2,107	10,589	8,416	6,443	3,812	2,696	1,810	969	376	175
Vandalism	4,098	4,090	4,071	4,077	18,516	13,903	10,405	6,431	5,117	3,951	2,534	1,252	897
Weapons; carrying, possessing, etc.	4,624	4,606	4,616	4,409	18,656	12,753	9,071	5,381	3,752	2,924	1,846	899	680
Prostitution and commercialized vice	1,006	1,114	1,042	1,071	4,964	3,696	2,683	1,979	1,715	1,328	748	429	342
Sex offenses (except forcible rape and prostitution)	649	559	622	571	2,968	2,777	2,665	2,036	1,864	1,767	1,493	995	1,009
Drug abuse violations	36,748	36,694	36,675	36,278	168,755	129,855	98,712	61,533	48,731	36,565	23,001	9,683	4,119
Gambling	75	74	64	66	296	157	145	122	107	89	65	46	42
Offenses against the family and children	884	1,001	1,121	1,334	7,220	6,909	5,602	3,401	2,527	1,699	1,031	463	349
Driving under the influence	16,311	17,338	17,814	18,124	82,249	63,207	51,210	38,000	34,401	29,589	23,462	13,399	10,297
Liquor laws	3,084	2,206	1,799	1,663	7,133	6,339	5,878	4,903	5,528	5,866	5,091	2,639	1,529
Drunkenness	8,308	7,956	7,679	7,663	37,394	33,788	29,624	23,559	24,785	23,470	17,928	8,658	4,804
Disorderly conduct	8,422	7,657	7,185	7,135	32,910	25,979	21,414	14,708	13,441	11,998	8,820	4,458	3,135
Vagrancy	298	318	348	384	1,929	1,916	2,065	1,585	1,742	1,655	1,538	772	404
All other offenses (except traffic)	54,552	56,514	60,114	62,505	315,816	263,967	214,133	142,557	122,605	100,593	70,423	34,590	22,074
Suspicion	8	4	24	17	77	84	83	44	41	30	28	8	19
Curfew and loitering law violations	NA	NA	NA	NA	NA	NA	NA	NA	NA	NA	NA	NA	NA

NA = Not available.
* = Less than one-tenth of one percent.
1 Because of rounding, the percentages may not sum to 100.   2 Violent crimes are offenses of murder and nonnegligent manslaughter, rape, robbery, and aggravated assault. Property crimes are offenses of burglary, larceny-theft, motor vehicle theft, and arson.   3 The rape figures in this table are aggregate totals of the data submitted based on both the legacy and revised Uniform Crime Reporting definitions.

Table 47. Arrests, Cities, Persons Under 15, 18, 21, and 25 Years of Age, 2017

(Number; percent; 9,289 agencies; 2017 estimated population 175,386,806.)

Offense charged	Total, all ages	Number of persons arrested				Percent of total of all ages			
		Under 15	Under 18	Under 21	Under 25	Under 15	Under 18	Under 21	Under 25
Total	5,953,871	146,842	504,495	1,091,963	1,906,507	2.5	8.5	18.3	32.0
Violent crime[1]	312,819	9,091	32,987	64,855	109,158	2.9	10.5	20.7	34.9
Murder and nonnegligent manslaughter	7,058	57	561	1,719	3,085	0.8	7.9	24.4	43.7
Rape[2]	13,036	813	2,132	3,612	5,152	6.2	16.4	27.7	39.5
Robbery	62,927	2,619	13,167	24,584	34,363	4.2	20.9	39.1	54.6
Aggravated assault	229,798	5,602	17,127	34,940	66,558	2.4	7.5	15.2	29.0
Property crime[1]	795,597	31,866	109,711	196,992	294,098	4.0	13.8	24.8	37.0
Burglary	115,300	5,967	18,839	32,416	47,624	5.2	16.3	28.1	41.3
Larceny-theft	621,866	22,528	78,971	146,049	220,277	3.6	12.7	23.5	35.4
Motor vehicle theft	53,010	2,553	10,470	16,713	23,910	4.8	19.8	31.5	45.1
Arson	5,421	818	1,431	1,814	2,287	15.1	26.4	33.5	42.2
Other assaults	629,727	29,179	72,916	118,990	200,900	4.6	11.6	18.9	31.9
Forgery and counterfeiting	32,362	122	771	4,523	9,020	0.4	2.4	14.0	27.9
Fraud	68,407	609	3,062	8,781	17,780	0.9	4.5	12.8	26.0
Embezzlement	9,910	38	440	2,097	3,809	0.4	4.4	21.2	38.4
Stolen property; buying, receiving, possessing	57,682	1,459	6,881	14,048	22,396	2.5	11.9	24.4	38.8
Vandalism	114,103	9,332	22,392	34,761	51,097	8.2	19.6	30.5	44.8
Weapons; carrying, possessing, etc.	98,876	3,375	11,707	24,659	42,914	3.4	11.8	24.9	43.4
Prostitution and commercialized vice	24,853	26	185	2,736	6,969	0.1	0.7	11.0	28.0
Sex offenses (except forcible rape and prostitution)	26,831	2,395	4,727	6,856	9,257	8.9	17.6	25.6	34.5
Drug abuse violations	906,754	9,000	56,569	179,405	325,800	1.0	6.2	19.8	35.9
Gambling	1,789	19	160	441	720	1.1	8.9	24.7	40.2
Offenses against the family and children	37,793	795	2,272	4,252	8,592	2.1	6.0	11.3	22.7
Driving under the influence	442,122	68	2,981	26,721	96,308	*	0.7	6.0	21.8
Liquor laws	127,086	2,362	18,993	73,428	82,180	1.9	14.9	57.8	64.7
Drunkenness	252,852	376	2,976	17,236	48,842	0.1	1.2	6.8	19.3
Disorderly conduct	228,822	16,297	40,786	61,560	91,959	7.1	17.8	26.9	40.2
Vagrancy	16,388	118	469	1,434	2,782	0.7	2.9	8.8	17.0
All other offenses (except traffic)	1,746,599	23,770	91,518	226,156	459,841	1.4	5.2	12.9	26.3
Suspicion	541	12	34	74	127	2.2	6.3	13.7	23.5
Curfew and loitering law violations	21,958	6,533	21,958	21,958	21,958	29.8	100.0	100.0	100.0

* = Less than one-tenth of one percent.
1 Violent crimes are offenses of murder and nonnegligent manslaughter, rape, robbery, and aggravated assault. Property crimes are offenses of burglary, larceny-theft, motor vehicle theft, and arson.   2 The rape figures in this table are aggregate totals of the data submitted based on both the legacy and revised Uniform Crime Reporting definitions.

Table 48. Arrests, Cities, Distribution by Sex, 2017

(Number, percent; 9,289 agencies; 2017 estimated population 175,386,806.)

Offense charged	Number of persons arrested			Percent male	Percent female	Percent distribution[1]		
	Total	Male	Female			Total	Male	Female
Total	5,953,871	4,330,425	1,623,446	72.7	27.3	100.0	100.0	100.0
Violent crime[2]	312,819	247,452	65,367	79.1	20.9	5.3	5.7	4.0
Murder and nonnegligent manslaughter	7,058	6,243	815	88.5	11.5	0.1	0.1	0.1
Rape[3]	13,036	12,663	373	97.1	2.9	0.2	0.3	*
Robbery	62,927	53,743	9,184	85.4	14.6	1.1	1.2	0.6
Aggravated assault	229,798	174,803	54,995	76.1	23.9	3.9	4.0	3.4
Property crime[2]	795,597	504,474	291,123	63.4	36.6	13.4	11.6	17.9
Burglary	115,300	93,534	21,766	81.1	18.9	1.9	2.2	1.3
Larceny-theft	621,866	365,405	256,461	58.8	41.2	10.4	8.4	15.8
Motor vehicle theft	53,010	41,218	11,792	77.8	22.2	0.9	1.0	0.7
Arson	5,421	4,317	1,104	79.6	20.4	0.1	0.1	0.1
Other assaults	629,727	447,335	182,392	71.0	29.0	10.6	10.3	11.2
Forgery and counterfeiting	32,362	21,358	11,004	66.0	34.0	0.5	0.5	0.7
Fraud	68,407	43,013	25,394	62.9	37.1	1.1	1.0	1.6
Embezzlement	9,910	5,041	4,869	50.9	49.1	0.2	0.1	0.3
Stolen property; buying, receiving, possessing	57,682	44,990	12,692	78.0	22.0	1.0	1.0	0.8
Vandalism	114,103	88,182	25,921	77.3	22.7	1.9	2.0	1.6
Weapons; carrying, possessing, etc.	98,876	90,015	8,861	91.0	9.0	1.7	2.1	0.5
Prostitution and commercialized vice	24,853	9,251	15,602	37.2	62.8	0.4	0.2	1.0
Sex offenses (except forcible rape and prostitution)	26,831	24,738	2,093	92.2	7.8	0.5	0.6	0.1
Drug abuse violations	906,754	693,098	213,656	76.4	23.6	15.2	16.0	13.2
Gambling	1,789	1,494	295	83.5	16.5	*	*	*
Offenses against the family and children	37,793	24,269	13,524	64.2	35.8	0.6	0.6	0.8
Driving under the influence	442,122	327,469	114,653	74.1	25.9	7.4	7.6	7.1
Liquor laws	127,086	88,714	38,372	69.8	30.2	2.1	2.0	2.4
Drunkenness	252,852	201,393	51,459	79.6	20.4	4.2	4.7	3.2
Disorderly conduct	228,822	160,917	67,905	70.3	29.7	3.8	3.7	4.2
Vagrancy	16,388	12,481	3,907	76.2	23.8	0.3	0.3	0.2
All other offenses (except traffic)	1,746,599	1,278,804	467,795	73.2	26.8	29.3	29.5	28.8
Suspicion	541	407	134	75.2	24.8	*	*	*
Curfew and loitering law violations	21,958	15,530	6,428	70.7	29.3	0.4	0.4	0.4

* = Less than one-tenth of 1 percent.
1 Because of rounding, the percentages may not sum to 100.   2 Violent crimes are offenses of murder and nonnegligent manslaughter, rape, robbery, and aggravated assault. Property crimes are offenses of burglary, larceny-theft, motor vehicle theft, and arson.   3 The rape figures in this table are aggregate totals of the data submitted based on both the legacy and revised Uniform Crime Reporting definitions.

Table 49. Arrests, Cities, Distribution by Race, 2017

(Number, percent; 9,282 agencies; 2017 estimated population 175,157,751.)

Offense charged	Total arrests						Percent distribution[1]						Arrests under 18					
	Total	White	Black	American Indian or Alaskan Native	Asian	Native Hawaiian or Other Pacific Islander	Total	White	Black	American Indian or Alaskan Native	Asian	Native Hawaiian or Other Pacific Islander	Total	White	Black	American Indian or Alaskan Native	Asian	Native Hawaiian or Other Pacific Islander
Total	5,889,629	3,914,125	1,725,803	164,798	72,333	12,570	100.0	66.5	29.3	2.8	1.2	0.2	496,652	300,304	178,512	11,127	5,561	1,148
Violent crime[2]	310,041	171,119	125,828	7,150	4,995	949	100.0	55.2	40.6	2.3	1.6	0.3	32,616	14,631	17,121	438	327	99
Murder and nonnegligent manslaughter	6,960	2,701	4,074	80	89	16	100.0	38.8	58.5	1.1	1.3	0.2	553	190	353	4	4	2
Rape[3]	12,860	8,028	4,298	242	254	38	100.0	62.4	33.4	1.9	2.0	0.3	2,093	1,301	735	21	31	5
Robbery	62,389	26,633	34,367	581	591	217	100.0	42.7	55.1	0.9	0.9	0.3	13,046	4,180	8,634	58	122	52
Aggravated assault	227,832	133,757	83,089	6,247	4,061	678	100.0	58.7	36.5	2.7	1.8	0.3	16,924	8,960	7,399	355	170	40
Property crime[2]	784,460	522,410	236,018	14,824	9,607	1,601	100.0	66.6	30.1	1.9	1.2	0.2	107,652	60,061	43,778	1,956	1,569	288
Burglary	114,025	73,242	37,602	1,493	1,431	257	100.0	64.2	33.0	1.3	1.3	0.2	18,526	10,008	7,992	281	202	43
Larceny-theft	612,791	412,828	179,222	12,169	7,335	1,237	100.0	67.4	29.2	2.0	1.2	0.2	77,511	44,668	29,908	1,457	1,251	227
Motor vehicle theft	52,309	32,653	17,734	1,074	751	97	100.0	62.4	33.9	2.1	1.4	0.2	10,217	4,370	5,531	200	102	14
Arson	5,335	3,687	1,460	88	90	10	100.0	69.1	27.4	1.6	1.7	0.2	1,398	1,015	347	18	14	4
Other assaults	620,816	382,950	213,481	13,969	8,537	1,879	100.0	61.7	34.4	2.3	1.4	0.3	71,646	40,958	28,546	1,249	658	235
Forgery and counterfeiting	32,094	20,687	10,569	302	463	73	100.0	64.5	32.9	0.9	1.4	0.2	761	438	307	7	9	0
Fraud	67,731	43,553	22,192	995	920	71	100.0	64.3	32.8	1.5	1.4	0.1	3,025	1,292	1,642	52	35	4
Embezzlement	9,837	5,731	3,843	90	152	21	100.0	58.3	39.1	0.9	1.5	0.2	433	244	175	5	7	2
Stolen property; buying, receiving, possessing	56,829	34,297	20,600	826	815	291	100.0	60.4	36.2	1.5	1.4	0.5	6,745	2,603	3,942	86	79	35
Vandalism	112,394	74,231	33,778	2,755	1,398	232	100.0	66.0	30.1	2.5	1.2	0.2	21,957	14,993	6,302	450	178	34
Weapons; carrying, possession, etc.	97,870	49,387	46,137	1,018	1,115	213	100.0	50.5	47.1	1.0	1.1	0.2	11,583	6,114	5,144	131	171	23
Prostitution and commercialized vice	24,603	13,859	9,259	101	1,311	73	100.0	56.3	37.6	0.4	5.3	0.3	184	82	97	2	3	0
Sex offenses (except forcible rape and prostitution)	26,574	17,840	7,430	587	628	89	100.0	67.1	28.0	2.2	2.4	0.3	4,635	3,193	1,277	56	88	21
Drug abuse violations	897,294	616,405	258,099	11,305	9,981	1,504	100.0	68.7	28.8	1.3	1.1	0.2	55,726	40,908	12,763	1,167	734	154
Gambling	1,775	560	1,107	17	87	4	100.0	31.5	62.4	1.0	4.9	0.2	155	17	136	2	0	0
Offenses against the family and children	37,362	22,895	10,289	3,808	352	18	100.0	61.3	27.5	10.2	0.9	*	2,256	1,213	657	367	14	5
Driving under the influence	437,373	353,615	62,935	11,370	7,942	1,511	100.0	80.8	14.4	2.6	1.8	0.3	2,925	2,560	202	120	37	6
Liquor laws	123,970	94,292	18,828	8,853	1,859	138	100.0	76.1	15.2	7.1	1.5	0.1	18,615	15,983	1,225	1,126	263	18
Drunkenness	251,391	181,807	36,706	29,951	2,554	373	100.0	72.3	14.6	11.9	1.0	0.1	2,941	2,253	235	414	33	6
Disorderly conduct	225,976	138,246	74,989	10,633	1,864	244	100.0	61.2	33.2	4.7	0.8	0.1	40,281	21,813	17,228	935	271	34
Vagrancy	16,307	11,020	4,614	459	201	13	100.0	67.6	28.3	2.8	1.2	0.1	466	254	199	7	5	1
All other offenses (except traffic)	1,732,651	1,147,106	519,836	45,127	17,329	3,253	100.0	66.2	30.0	2.6	1.0	0.2	90,259	58,748	28,343	2,137	863	168
Suspicion	524	180	77	256	6	5	100.0	34.4	14.7	48.9	1.1	1.0	34	11	5	18	0	0
Curfew and loitering law violations	21,757	11,935	9,188	402	217	15	100.0	54.9	42.2	1.8	1.0	0.1	21,757	11,935	9,188	402	217	15

Table 49. Arrests, Cities, Distribution by Race, 2017—Continued

(Number, percent; 9,282 agencies; 2017 estimated population 175,157,751.)

Offense charged	Percent distribution[1]						Arrests 18 and over						Percent distribution[1]					
	Total	White	Black	American Indian or Alaskan Native	Asian	Native Hawaiian or Other Pacific Islander	Total	White	Black	American Indian or Alaskan Native	Asian	Native Hawaiian or Other Pacific Islander	Total	White	Black	American Indian or Alaskan Native	Asian	Native Hawaiian or Other Pacific Islander
Total	100.0	60.5	35.9	2.2	1.1	0.2	5,392,977	3,613,821	1,547,291	153,671	66,772	11,422	100.0	67.0	28.7	2.8	1.2	0.2
Violent crime[2]	100.0	44.9	52.5	1.3	1.0	0.3	277,425	156,488	108,707	6,712	4,668	850	100.0	56.4	39.2	2.4	1.7	0.3
Murder and nonnegligent manslaughter	100.0	34.4	63.8	0.7	0.7	0.4	6,407	2,511	3,721	76	85	14	100.0	39.2	58.1	1.2	1.3	0.2
Rape[3]	100.0	62.2	35.1	1.0	1.5	0.2	10,767	6,727	3,563	221	223	33	100.0	62.5	33.1	2.1	2.1	0.3
Robbery	100.0	32.0	66.2	0.4	0.9	0.4	49,343	22,453	25,733	523	469	165	100.0	45.5	52.2	1.1	1.0	0.3
Aggravated assault	100.0	52.9	43.7	2.1	1.0	0.2	210,908	124,797	75,690	5,892	3,891	638	100.0	59.2	35.9	2.8	1.8	0.3
Property crime[2]	100.0	55.8	40.7	1.8	1.5	0.3	676,808	462,349	192,240	12,868	8,038	1,313	100.0	68.3	28.4	1.9	1.2	0.2
Burglary	100.0	54.0	43.1	1.5	1.1	0.2	95,499	63,234	29,610	1,212	1,229	214	100.0	66.2	31.0	1.3	1.3	0.2
Larceny-theft	100.0	57.6	38.6	1.9	1.6	0.3	535,280	368,160	149,314	10,712	6,084	1,010	100.0	68.8	27.9	2.0	1.1	0.2
Motor vehicle theft	100.0	42.8	54.1	2.0	1.0	0.1	42,092	28,283	12,203	874	649	83	100.0	67.2	29.0	2.1	1.5	0.2
Arson	100.0	72.6	24.8	1.3	1.0	0.3	3,937	2,672	1,113	70	76	6	100.0	67.9	28.3	1.8	1.9	0.2
Other assaults	100.0	57.2	39.8	1.7	0.9	0.3	549,170	341,992	184,935	12,720	7,879	1,644	100.0	62.3	33.7	2.3	1.4	0.3
Forgery and counterfeiting	100.0	57.6	40.3	0.9	1.2	0.0	31,333	20,249	10,262	295	454	73	100.0	64.6	32.8	0.9	1.4	0.2
Fraud	100.0	42.7	54.3	1.7	1.2	0.1	64,706	42,261	20,550	943	885	67	100.0	65.3	31.8	1.5	1.4	0.1
Embezzlement	100.0	56.4	40.4	1.2	1.6	0.5	9,404	5,487	3,668	85	145	19	100.0	58.3	39.0	0.9	1.5	0.2
Stolen property; buying, receiving, possessing	100.0	38.6	58.4	1.3	1.2	0.5	50,084	31,694	16,658	740	736	256	100.0	63.3	33.3	1.5	1.5	0.5
Vandalism	100.0	68.3	28.7	2.0	0.8	0.2	90,437	59,238	27,476	2,305	1,220	198	100.0	65.5	30.4	2.5	1.3	0.2
Weapons; carrying, possessing, etc.	100.0	52.8	44.4	1.1	1.5	0.2	86,287	43,273	40,993	887	944	190	100.0	50.2	47.5	1.0	1.1	0.2
Prostitution and commercialized vice	100.0	44.6	52.7	1.1	1.6	0.0	24,419	13,777	9,162	99	1,308	73	100.0	56.4	37.5	0.4	5.4	0.3
Sex offenses (except forcible rape and prostitution)	100.0	68.9	27.6	1.2	1.9	0.5	21,939	14,647	6,153	531	540	68	100.0	66.8	28.0	2.4	2.5	0.3
Drug abuse violations	100.0	73.4	22.9	2.1	1.3	0.3	841,568	575,497	245,336	10,138	9,247	1,350	100.0	68.4	29.2	1.2	1.1	0.2
Gambling	100.0	11.0	87.7	1.3	0.0	0.0	1,620	543	971	15	87	4	100.0	33.5	59.9	0.9	5.4	0.2
Offenses against the family and children	100.0	53.8	29.1	16.3	0.6	0.2	35,106	21,682	9,632	3,441	338	13	100.0	61.8	27.4	9.8	1.0	*
Driving under the influence	100.0	87.5	6.9	4.1	1.3	0.2	434,448	351,055	62,733	11,250	7,905	1,505	100.0	80.8	14.4	2.6	1.8	0.3
Liquor laws	100.0	85.9	6.6	6.0	1.4	0.1	105,355	78,309	17,603	7,727	1,596	120	100.0	74.3	16.7	7.3	1.5	0.1
Drunkenness	100.0	76.6	8.0	14.1	1.1	0.2	248,450	179,554	36,471	29,537	2,521	367	100.0	72.3	14.7	11.9	1.0	0.1
Disorderly conduct	100.0	54.2	42.8	2.3	0.7	0.1	185,695	116,433	57,761	9,698	1,593	210	100.0	62.7	31.1	5.2	0.9	0.1
Vagrancy	100.0	54.5	42.7	1.5	1.1	0.2	15,841	10,766	4,415	452	196	12	100.0	68.0	27.9	2.9	1.2	0.1
All other offenses (except traffic)	100.0	65.1	31.4	2.4	1.0	0.2	1,642,392	1,088,358	491,493	42,990	16,466	3,085	100.0	66.3	29.9	2.6	1.0	0.2
Suspicion	100.0	32.4	14.7	52.9	0.0	0.0	490	169	72	238	6	5	100.0	34.5	14.7	48.6	1.2	1.0
Curfew and loitering law violations	100.0	54.9	42.2	1.8	1.0	0.1	NA	NA	NA	NA	NA	NA	NA	NA	NA	NA	NA	NA

NA = Not available.
* = Less than one-tenth of one percent.
1 Because of rounding, the percentages may not sum to 100.   2 Violent crimes are offenses of murder and nonnegligent manslaughter, rape, robbery, and aggravated assault.   Property crimes are offenses of burglary, larceny-theft, motor vehicle theft, and arson.   3 The rape figures in this table are aggregate totals of the data submitted based on both the legacy and revised Uniform Crime Reporting definitions.

Table 49A. Arrests, Cities, Distribution by Ethnicity, 2017

(Number, percent; 9,282 agencies; 2017 estimated population 175,157,751.)

Offense charged	Total arrests			Percent distribution[1]			Arrests under 18		
	Total[2]	Hispanic or Latino	Not Hispanic or Latino	Total[2]	Hispanic or Latino	Not Hispanic or Latino	Total[2]	Hispanic or Latino	Not Hispanic or Latino
Total	4,822,947	936,402	3,886,545	100.0	19.4	80.6	375,472	88,858	286,614
Violent crime[3]	262,329	65,701	196,628	100.0	25.0	75.0	25,981	6,711	19,270
Murder and nonnegligent manslaughter	5,293	1,122	4,171	100.0	21.2	78.8	376	98	278
Rape[4]	10,318	3,069	7,249	100.0	29.7	70.3	1,623	411	1,212
Robbery	51,038	11,320	39,718	100.0	22.2	77.8	10,021	2,422	7,599
Aggravated assault	195,680	50,190	145,490	100.0	25.6	74.4	13,961	3,780	10,181
Property crime[3]	610,846	104,398	506,448	100.0	17.1	82.9	75,207	16,947	58,260
Burglary	93,871	21,507	72,364	100.0	22.9	77.1	13,310	3,867	9,443
Larceny-theft	471,626	70,504	401,122	100.0	14.9	85.1	54,173	10,958	43,215
Motor vehicle theft	41,109	11,481	29,628	100.0	27.9	72.1	6,675	1,876	4,799
Arson	4,240	906	3,334	100.0	21.4	78.6	1,049	246	803
Other assaults	500,164	100,106	400,058	100.0	20.0	80.0	56,345	13,671	42,674
Forgery and counterfeiting	26,454	4,205	22,249	100.0	15.9	84.1	589	94	495
Fraud	54,297	6,969	47,328	100.0	12.8	87.2	2,423	327	2,096
Embezzlement	8,081	1,093	6,988	100.0	13.5	86.5	370	117	253
Stolen property; buying, receiving, possessing	44,628	9,038	35,590	100.0	20.3	79.7	4,917	1,119	3,798
Vandalism	91,056	18,373	72,683	100.0	20.2	79.8	16,615	3,996	12,619
Weapons; carrying, possessing, etc.	78,471	18,784	59,687	100.0	23.9	76.1	9,139	3,022	6,117
Prostitution and commercialized vice	21,720	4,548	17,172	100.0	20.9	79.1	161	24	137
Sex offenses (except forcible rape and prostitution)	22,819	5,950	16,869	100.0	26.1	73.9	3,884	1,067	2,817
Drug abuse violations	740,893	158,896	581,997	100.0	21.4	78.6	42,483	12,336	30,147
Gambling	1,058	209	849	100.0	19.8	80.2	79	7	72
Offenses against the family and children	29,109	3,875	25,234	100.0	13.3	86.7	1,794	223	1,571
Driving under the influence	368,230	86,537	281,693	100.0	23.5	76.5	2,415	650	1,765
Liquor laws	93,701	12,850	80,851	100.0	13.7	86.3	14,457	2,435	12,022
Drunkenness	233,663	50,219	183,444	100.0	21.5	78.5	2,490	933	1,557
Disorderly conduct	168,275	21,881	146,394	100.0	13.0	87.0	29,439	5,400	24,039
Vagrancy	13,399	1,951	11,448	100.0	14.6	85.4	341	100	241
All other offenses (except traffic)	1,434,697	256,799	1,177,898	100.0	17.9	82.1	67,599	15,695	51,904
Suspicion	339	38	301	100.0	11.2	88.8	27	2	25
Curfew and loitering law violations	18,718	3,982	14,736	100.0	21.3	78.7	18,717	3,982	14,735

Table 49A. Arrests, Cities, Distribution by Ethnicity, 2017—Continued

(Number, percent; 9,282 agencies; 2017 estimated population 175,157,751.)

Offense charged	Percent distribution[1]			Arrests 18 and over				Percent distribution[1]	
	Total[2]	Hispanic or Latino	Not Hispanic or Latino	Total[2]	Hispanic or Latino	Not Hispanic or Latino	Total[2]	Hispanic or Latino	Not Hispanic or Latino
Total	100.0	23.7	76.3	4,447,474	847,544	3,599,930	100.0	19.1	80.9
Violent crime[3]	100.0	25.8	74.2	236,348	58,990	177,358	100.0	25.0	75.0
Murder and nonnegligent manslaughter	100.0	26.1	73.9	4,917	1,024	3,893	100.0	20.8	79.2
Rape[4]	100.0	25.3	74.7	8,695	2,658	6,037	100.0	30.6	69.4
Robbery	100.0	24.2	75.8	41,017	8,898	32,119	100.0	21.7	78.3
Aggravated assault	100.0	27.1	72.9	181,719	46,410	135,309	100.0	25.5	74.5
Property crime[3]	100.0	22.5	77.5	535,639	87,451	448,188	100.0	16.3	83.7
Burglary	100.0	29.1	70.9	80,561	17,640	62,921	100.0	21.9	78.1
Larceny-theft	100.0	20.2	79.8	417,453	59,546	357,907	100.0	14.3	85.7
Motor vehicle theft	100.0	28.1	71.9	34,434	9,605	24,829	100.0	27.9	72.1
Arson	100.0	23.5	76.5	3,191	660	2,531	100.0	20.7	79.3
Other assaults	100.0	24.3	75.7	443,819	86,435	357,384	100.0	19.5	80.5
Forgery and counterfeiting	100.0	16.0	84.0	25,865	4,111	21,754	100.0	15.9	84.1
Fraud	100.0	13.5	86.5	51,874	6,642	45,232	100.0	12.8	87.2
Embezzlement	100.0	31.6	68.4	7,711	976	6,735	100.0	12.7	87.3
Stolen property; buying, receiving, possessing	100.0	22.8	77.2	39,711	7,919	31,792	100.0	19.9	80.1
Vandalism	100.0	24.1	75.9	74,441	14,377	60,064	100.0	19.3	80.7
Weapons; carrying, possessing, etc.	100.0	33.1	66.9	69,332	15,762	53,570	100.0	22.7	77.3
Prostitution and commercialized vice	100.0	14.9	85.1	21,559	4,524	17,035	100.0	21.0	79.0
Sex offenses (except forcible rape and prostitution)	100.0	27.5	72.5	18,935	4,883	14,052	100.0	25.8	74.2
Drug abuse violations	100.0	29.0	71.0	698,410	146,560	551,850	100.0	21.0	79.0
Gambling	100.0	8.9	91.1	979	202	777	100.0	20.6	79.4
Offenses against the family and children	100.0	12.4	87.6	27,315	3,652	23,663	100.0	13.4	86.6
Driving under the influence	100.0	26.9	73.1	365,815	85,887	279,928	100.0	23.5	76.5
Liquor laws	100.0	16.8	83.2	79,244	10,415	68,829	100.0	13.1	86.9
Drunkenness	100.0	37.5	62.5	231,173	49,286	181,887	100.0	21.3	78.7
Disorderly conduct	100.0	18.3	81.7	138,836	16,481	122,355	100.0	11.9	88.1
Vagrancy	100.0	29.3	70.7	13,058	1,851	11,207	100.0	14.2	85.8
All other offenses (except traffic)	100.0	23.2	76.8	1,367,098	241,104	1,125,994	100.0	17.6	82.4
Suspicion	100.0	7.4	92.6	312	36	276	100.0	11.5	88.5
Curfew and loitering law violations	100.0	21.3	78.7	NA	NA	NA	NA	NA	NA

NA = Not available.
1 Because of rounding, the percentages may not sum to 100.   2 The ethnicity totals are representative of those agencies that provided ethnicity breakdowns. Not all agencies provide ethnicity data; therefore, the race and ethnicity totals will not be equal.   3 Violent crimes are offenses of murder and nonnegligent manslaughter, rape, robbery, and aggravated assault. Property crimes are offenses of burglary, larceny-theft, motor vehicle theft, and arson.   4 The rape figures in this table are aggregate totals of the data submitted based on both the legacy and revised Uniform Crime Reporting definitions.

Table 50. Arrest Trends, Metropolitan Counties, 2016–2017

(Number, percent change; 1,377 agencies; 2017 estimated population 56,271,230; 2016 estimated population 55,438,912.)

Offense charged	Number of persons arrested								
	Total, all ages			Under 18 years of age			18 years of age and over		
	2016	2017	Percent change	2016	2017	Percent change	2016	2017	Percent change
Total[1]	1,618,230	1,601,565	-1.0	104,167	100,895	-3.1	1,514,063	1,500,670	-0.9
Violent crime[2]	72,063	72,681	+0.9	6,580	6,731	+2.3	65,483	65,950	+0.7
Murder and nonnegligent manslaughter	1,891	1,846	-2.4	121	117	-3.3	1,770	1,729	-2.3
Rape[3]	3,746	3,542	-5.4	574	589	+2.6	3,172	2,953	-6.9
Robbery	10,047	9,961	-0.9	1,883	1,960	+4.1	8,164	8,001	-2.0
Aggravated assault	56,379	57,332	+1.7	4,002	4,065	+1.6	52,377	53,267	+1.7
Property crime[2]	156,578	146,928	-6.2	19,682	18,827	-4.3	136,896	128,101	-6.4
Burglary	30,441	28,838	-5.3	4,030	3,974	-1.4	26,411	24,864	-5.9
Larceny-theft	111,782	103,095	-7.8	13,721	12,841	-6.4	98,061	90,254	-8.0
Motor vehicle theft	12,950	13,734	+6.1	1,635	1,742	+6.5	11,315	11,992	+6.0
Arson	1,405	1,261	-10.2	296	270	-8.8	1,109	991	-10.6
Other assaults	148,173	146,947	-0.8	19,431	18,775	-3.4	128,742	128,172	-0.4
Forgery and counterfeiting	8,851	8,666	-2.1	201	155	-22.9	8,650	8,511	-1.6
Fraud	21,238	20,555	-3.2	576	534	-7.3	20,662	20,021	-3.1
Embezzlement	2,047	2,121	+3.6	63	51	-19.0	1,984	2,070	+4.3
Stolen property; buying, receiving, possessing	14,848	15,620	+5.2	1,114	1,114	0.0	13,734	14,506	+5.6
Vandalism	25,417	25,162	-1.0	4,984	4,989	+0.1	20,433	20,173	-1.3
Weapons; carrying, possessing, etc.	21,255	22,613	+6.4	2,277	2,276	*	18,978	20,337	+7.2
Prostitution and commercialized vice	3,264	3,128	-4.2	49	30	-38.8	3,215	3,098	-3.6
Sex offenses (except forcible rape and prostitution)	8,444	8,027	-4.9	1,349	1,411	+4.6	7,095	6,616	-6.8
Drug abuse violations	250,618	262,166	+4.6	13,671	13,597	-0.5	236,947	248,569	+4.9
Gambling	753	584	-22.4	29	50	+72.4	724	534	-26.2
Offenses against the family and children	24,385	24,684	+1.2	414	488	+17.9	23,971	24,196	+0.9
Driving under the influence	210,001	199,786	-4.9	1,031	992	-3.8	208,970	198,794	-4.9
Liquor laws	26,347	21,428	-18.7	5,037	4,481	-11.0	21,310	16,947	-20.5
Drunkenness	27,180	25,454	-6.4	355	303	-14.6	26,825	25,151	-6.2
Disorderly conduct	33,742	31,772	-5.8	6,432	6,171	-4.1	27,310	25,601	-6.3
Vagrancy	2,794	1,906	-31.8	103	84	-18.4	2,691	1,822	-32.3
All other offenses (except traffic)	558,656	559,873	+0.2	19,213	18,372	-4.4	539,443	541,501	+0.4
Suspicion	150	86	-42.7	28	28	0.0	122	58	-52.5
Curfew and loitering law violations	1,576	1,464	-7.1	1,576	1,464	-7.1	NA	NA	NA

NA = Not available.
* = Less than one-tenth of one percent.
1 Does not include suspicion.   2 Violent crimes in this table are offenses of murder and nonnegligent manslaughter, rape, robbery, and aggravated assault. Property crimes are offenses of burglary, larceny-theft, motor vehicle theft, and arson.
3 The rape figures in this table are aggregate totals of the data submitted based on both the legacy and revised Uniform Crime Reporting definitions.

Table 51. Arrest Trends, Metropolitan Counties, by Age and Sex, 2016–2017

(Number, percent change; 1,377 agencies; 2017 estimated population 55,438,912; 2016 estimated population 56,271,230.)

Offense charged	Male Total 2016	2017	Percent change	Male Under 18 2016	2017	Percent change	Female Total 2016	2017	Percent change	Female Under 18 2016	2017	Percent change
Total[1]	1,189,415	1,177,033	-1.0	74,090	72,427	-2.2	428,815	424,532	-1.0	30,077	28,468	-5.3
Violent crime[2]	57,834	58,388	+1.0	5,315	5,425	+2.1	14,229	14,293	+0.4	1,265	1,306	+3.2
Murder and nonnegligent manslaughter	1,645	1,599	-2.8	110	109	-0.9	246	247	+0.4	11	8	-27.3
Rape[3]	3,631	3,453	-4.9	549	574	+4.6	115	89	-22.6	25	15	-40.0
Robbery	8,558	8,500	-0.7	1,684	1,772	+5.2	1,489	1,461	-1.9	199	188	-5.5
Aggravated assault	44,000	44,836	+1.9	2,972	2,970	-0.1	12,379	12,496	+0.9	1,030	1,095	+6.3
Property crime[2]	102,733	97,919	-4.7	13,704	13,581	-0.9	53,845	49,009	-9.0	5,978	5,246	-12.2
Burglary	25,055	23,511	-6.2	3,630	3,532	-2.7	5,386	5,327	-1.1	400	442	+10.5
Larceny-theft	66,476	62,661	-5.7	8,506	8,418	-1.0	45,306	40,434	-10.8	5,215	4,423	-15.2
Motor vehicle theft	10,099	10,710	+6.1	1,327	1,397	+5.3	2,851	3,024	+6.1	308	345	+12.0
Arson	1,103	1,037	-6.0	241	234	-2.9	302	224	-25.8	55	36	-34.5
Other assaults	106,418	105,292	-1.1	12,379	12,025	-2.9	41,755	41,655	-0.2	7,052	6,750	-4.3
Forgery and counterfeiting	5,786	5,660	-2.2	145	118	-18.6	3,065	3,006	-1.9	56	37	-33.9
Fraud	13,276	12,958	-2.4	393	359	-8.7	7,962	7,597	-4.6	183	175	-4.4
Embezzlement	1,109	1,101	-0.7	35	27	-22.9	938	1,020	+8.7	28	24	-14.3
Stolen property; buying, receiving, possessing	11,627	12,220	+5.1	944	910	-3.6	3,221	3,400	+5.6	170	204	+20.0
Vandalism	19,980	19,625	-1.8	4,102	4,050	-1.3	5,437	5,537	+1.8	882	939	+6.5
Weapons; carrying, possessing, etc.	18,985	20,198	+6.4	1,930	1,965	+1.8	2,270	2,415	+6.4	347	311	-10.4
Prostitution and commercialized vice	1,478	1,640	+11.0	14	15	+7.1	1,786	1,488	-16.7	35	15	-57.1
Sex offenses (except forcible rape and prostitution)	7,804	7,496	-3.9	1,187	1,283	+8.1	640	531	-17.0	162	128	-21.0
Drug abuse violations	188,262	195,149	+3.7	10,530	10,290	-2.3	62,356	67,017	+7.5	3,141	3,307	+5.3
Gambling	391	391	0.0	17	25	+47.1	362	193	-46.7	12	25	+108.3
Offenses against the family and children	19,119	19,087	-0.2	233	319	+36.9	5,266	5,597	+6.3	181	169	-6.6
Driving under the influence	156,869	148,600	-5.3	772	772	0.0	53,132	51,186	-3.7	259	220	-15.1
Liquor laws	17,985	14,521	-19.3	3,027	2,663	-12.0	8,362	6,907	-17.4	2,010	1,818	-9.6
Drunkenness	21,547	20,022	-7.1	264	197	-25.4	5,633	5,432	-3.6	91	106	+16.5
Disorderly conduct	23,918	22,374	-6.5	4,052	3,990	-1.5	9,824	9,398	-4.3	2,380	2,181	-8.4
Vagrancy	2,149	1,405	-34.6	77	66	-14.3	645	501	-22.3	26	18	-30.8
All other offenses (except traffic)	411,077	412,055	+0.2	13,902	13,415	-3.5	147,579	147,818	+0.2	5,311	4,957	-6.7
Suspicion	118	63	-46.6	21	20	-4.8	32	23	-28.1	7	8	+14.3
Curfew and loitering law violations	1,068	932	-12.7	1,068	932	-12.7	508	532	+4.7	508	532	+4.7

* = Less than one-tenth of one percent.
1 Does not include suspicion. 2 Violent crimes are offenses of murder and nonnegligent manslaughter, rape, robbery, and aggravated assault. Property crimes are offenses of burglary, larceny-theft, motor vehicle theft, and arson. 3 The rape figures in this table are aggregate totals of the data submitted based on both the legacy and revised Uniform Crime Reporting definitions.

Table 52. Arrests, Metropolitan Counties, Distribution by Age, 2017

(Number, percent; 1,458 agencies; 2017 estimated population 57,699,058.)

Offense charged	Total, all ages	Ages under 15	Ages under 18	Ages 18 and over	Under 10	10–12	13–14	15	16	17	18	19	20
Total	1,630,907	27,079	102,325	1,528,582	667	6,313	20,099	18,494	24,816	31,936	43,115	48,757	51,032
Total percent distribution[1]	100.0	1.7	6.3	93.7	*	0.4	1.2	1.1	1.5	2.0	2.6	3.0	3.1
Violent crime[2]	73,918	1,877	6,865	67,053	52	470	1,355	1,254	1,653	2,081	2,291	2,308	2,461
Violent crime percent distribution[1]	100.0	2.5	9.3	90.7	0.1	0.6	1.8	1.7	2.2	2.8	3.1	3.1	3.3
Murder and nonnegligent manslaughter	1,917	6	125	1,792	0	0	6	19	37	63	87	101	94
Rape[3]	3,602	245	595	3,007	11	72	162	78	127	145	154	153	153
Robbery	10,229	298	2,023	8,206	3	34	261	408	594	723	744	655	582
Aggravated assault	58,170	1,328	4,122	54,048	38	364	926	749	895	1,150	1,306	1,399	1,632
Property crime[2]	149,439	5,095	19,162	130,277	86	1,104	3,905	3,885	4,725	5,457	6,221	5,589	4,962
Property crime percent distribution[1]	100.0	3.4	12.8	87.2	0.1	0.7	2.6	2.6	3.2	3.7	4.2	3.7	3.3
Burglary	29,411	1,226	4,102	25,309	22	260	944	845	947	1,084	1,315	1,180	1,044
Larceny-theft	104,711	3,354	12,986	91,725	55	743	2,556	2,566	3,238	3,828	4,282	3,883	3,432
Motor vehicle theft	14,046	365	1,803	12,243	1	40	324	423	502	513	566	500	455
Arson	1,271	150	271	1,000	8	61	81	51	38	32	58	26	31
Other assaults	148,967	7,223	18,991	129,976	190	2,031	5,002	3,797	4,133	3,838	3,214	3,285	3,508
Forgery and counterfeiting	8,775	7	155	8,620	0	0	7	18	35	95	260	354	403
Fraud	20,799	104	537	20,262	4	18	82	66	141	226	346	467	504
Embezzlement	2,135	0	51	2,084	0	0	0	4	17	30	111	97	95
Stolen property; buying, receiving, possessing	15,784	198	1,135	14,649	0	32	166	219	323	395	601	584	536
Vandalism	25,455	1,749	5,025	20,430	69	469	1,211	904	1,169	1,203	1,005	943	868
Weapons; carrying, possessing, etc.	23,315	762	2,323	20,992	18	219	525	375	488	698	802	847	812
Prostitution and commercialized vice	3,443	4	32	3,411	0	2	2	5	6	17	72	76	131
Sex offenses (except forcible rape and prostitution)	8,202	715	1,453	6,749	27	178	510	247	225	266	270	241	209
Drug abuse violations	266,029	1,707	13,716	252,313	19	210	1,478	1,804	3,525	6,680	11,355	12,605	12,261
Gambling	590	9	50	540	0	1	8	9	13	19	15	20	20
Offenses against the family and children	25,730	155	522	25,208	9	42	104	101	137	129	164	179	218
Driving under the influence	202,119	14	1,000	201,119	3	2	9	45	228	713	2,146	3,454	4,360
Liquor laws	21,746	472	4,498	17,248	3	45	424	665	1,244	2,117	3,095	3,171	2,907
Drunkenness	25,656	39	303	25,353	1	2	36	42	82	140	378	470	558
Disorderly conduct	32,777	2,298	6,284	26,493	66	603	1,629	1,273	1,421	1,292	938	793	833
Vagrancy	1,949	32	109	1,840	0	2	30	24	33	20	31	42	37
All other offenses (except traffic)	572,506	4,246	18,599	553,907	113	831	3,302	3,369	4,784	6,200	9,797	13,229	15,344
Suspicion	86	5	28	58	0	1	4	7	5	11	3	3	5
Curfew and loitering law violations	1,487	368	1,487	NA	7	51	310	381	429	309	NA	NA	NA

Table 52. Arrests, Metropolitan Counties, Distribution by Age, 2017—Continued

(Number, percent; 1,458 agencies; 2017 estimated population 57,699,058.)

Offense charged	21	22	23	24	25–29	30–34	35–39	40–44	45–49	50–54	55–59	60–64	65 and over
Total	52,405	54,806	56,860	58,874	293,488	244,053	197,787	131,573	109,556	84,972	55,995	26,449	18,860
Total percent distribution[1]	3.2	3.4	3.5	3.6	18.0	15.0	12.1	8.1	6.7	5.2	3.4	1.6	1.2
Violent crime[2]	2,476	2,434	2,505	2,404	12,412	10,381	8,487	5,396	4,669	3,764	2,658	1,276	1,131
Violent crime percent distribution[1]	3.3	3.3	3.4	3.3	16.8	14.0	11.5	7.3	6.3	5.1	3.6	1.7	1.5
Murder and nonnegligent manslaughter	84	78	73	76	358	251	193	126	90	73	52	28	28
Rape[3]	131	97	106	91	422	406	388	234	201	163	123	93	92
Robbery	468	415	426	370	1,642	1,117	692	391	282	230	134	33	25
Aggravated assault	1,793	1,844	1,900	1,867	9,990	8,607	7,214	4,645	4,096	3,298	2,349	1,122	986
Property crime[2]	4,604	4,623	4,714	4,867	24,903	20,782	16,316	10,070	8,735	6,817	4,094	1,756	1,224
Property crime percent distribution[1]	3.1	3.1	3.2	3.3	16.7	13.9	10.9	6.7	5.8	4.6	2.7	1.2	0.8
Burglary	963	926	991	1,050	5,249	4,194	3,143	1,846	1,422	1,111	540	217	118
Larceny-theft	3,166	3,191	3,183	3,284	16,784	14,381	11,365	7,246	6,541	5,230	3,271	1,437	1,049
Motor vehicle theft	443	473	517	505	2,704	2,075	1,678	893	692	402	232	74	34
Arson	32	33	23	28	166	132	130	85	80	74	51	28	23
Other assaults	3,977	4,012	4,277	4,577	23,001	20,004	17,692	12,494	10,770	8,450	5,613	2,821	2,281
Forgery and counterfeiting	297	289	298	277	1,654	1,507	1,088	735	606	417	246	120	69
Fraud	543	612	641	669	3,664	3,477	2,798	2,080	1,793	1,229	768	403	268
Embezzlement	105	86	75	59	337	289	260	185	147	101	72	44	21
Stolen property; buying, receiving, possessing	532	517	556	529	3,087	2,617	1,999	1,216	835	567	302	117	54
Vandalism	840	865	912	845	3,827	3,112	2,300	1,512	1,223	982	652	316	228
Weapons; carrying, possessing, etc.	967	915	913	922	4,333	3,265	2,483	1,523	1,130	866	656	291	267
Prostitution and commercialized vice	137	157	116	144	657	518	400	317	274	187	113	74	38
Sex offenses (except forcible rape and prostitution)	186	197	186	193	879	858	779	625	606	497	407	280	336
Drug abuse violations	11,400	11,512	11,342	11,112	50,813	38,098	29,248	17,705	13,918	10,450	6,588	2,690	1,216
Gambling	8	10	12	21	65	47	65	52	56	51	43	25	30
Offenses against the family and children	277	342	455	552	4,552	5,191	4,882	3,342	2,447	1,533	699	233	142
Driving under the influence	7,069	7,776	8,170	8,430	39,514	30,013	23,745	17,305	15,697	13,318	10,236	5,585	4,301
Liquor laws	453	374	313	341	1,305	1,117	1,014	739	760	699	521	283	156
Drunkenness	784	728	762	845	4,063	3,689	3,212	2,405	2,344	2,279	1,677	707	452
Disorderly conduct	895	985	879	910	4,507	3,798	3,146	2,278	2,083	1,915	1,302	653	578
Vagrancy	35	56	71	58	305	250	233	142	167	161	139	70	43
All other offenses (except traffic)	16,814	18,316	19,659	21,117	109,601	95,029	77,637	51,448	41,294	30,685	19,208	8,705	6,024
Suspicion	6	0	4	2	9	11	3	4	2	4	1	0	1
Curfew and loitering law violations	NA	NA	NA	NA	NA	NA	NA	NA	NA	NA	NA	NA	NA

NA = Not available.

* = Less than one-tenth of one percent.

1 Because of rounding, the percentages may not sum to 100.   2 Violent crimes are offenses of murder and nonnegligent manslaughter, rape, robbery, and aggravated assault. Property crimes are offenses of burglary, larceny-theft, motor vehicle theft, and arson.   3 The rape figures in this table are aggregate totals of the data submitted based on both the legacy and revised Uniform Crime Reporting definitions.

Table 53. Arrests, Metropolitan Counties, Persons Under 15, 18, 21, and 25 Years of Age, 2017

(Number, percent; 1,458 agencies; 2017 estimated population 57,699,058.)

Offense charged	Total, all ages	Number of persons arrested				Percent of total all ages			
		Under 15	Under 18	Under 21	Under 25	Under 15	Under 18	Under 21	Under 25
Total	1,630,907	27,079	102,325	245,229	468,174	1.7	6.3	15.0	28.7
Violent crime[1]	73,918	1,877	6,865	13,925	23,744	2.5	9.3	18.8	32.1
Murder and nonnegligent manslaughter	1,917	6	125	407	718	0.3	6.5	21.2	37.5
Rape[2]	3,602	245	595	1,055	1,480	6.8	16.5	29.3	41.1
Robbery	10,229	298	2,023	4,004	5,683	2.9	19.8	39.1	55.6
Aggravated assault	58,170	1,328	4,122	8,459	15,863	2.3	7.1	14.5	27.3
Property crime[1]	149,439	5,095	19,162	35,934	54,742	3.4	12.8	24.0	36.6
Burglary	29,411	1,226	4,102	7,641	11,571	4.2	13.9	26.0	39.3
Larceny-theft	104,711	3,354	12,986	24,583	37,407	3.2	12.4	23.5	35.7
Motor vehicle theft	14,046	365	1,803	3,324	5,262	2.6	12.8	23.7	37.5
Arson	1,271	150	271	386	502	11.8	21.3	30.4	39.5
Other assaults	148,967	7,223	18,991	28,998	45,841	4.8	12.7	19.5	30.8
Forgery and counterfeiting	8,775	7	155	1,172	2,333	0.1	1.8	13.4	26.6
Fraud	20,799	104	537	1,854	4,319	0.5	2.6	8.9	20.8
Embezzlement	2,135	0	51	354	679	0.0	2.4	16.6	31.8
Stolen property; buying, receiving, possessing	15,784	198	1,135	2,856	4,990	1.3	7.2	18.1	31.6
Vandalism	25,455	1,749	5,025	7,841	11,303	6.9	19.7	30.8	44.4
Weapons; carrying, possessing, etc.	23,315	762	2,323	4,784	8,501	3.3	10.0	20.5	36.5
Prostitution and commercialized vice	3,443	4	32	311	865	0.1	0.9	9.0	25.1
Sex offenses (except forcible rape and prostitution)	8,202	715	1,453	2,173	2,935	8.7	17.7	26.5	35.8
Drug abuse violations	266,029	1,707	13,716	49,937	95,303	0.6	5.2	18.8	35.8
Gambling	590	9	50	105	156	1.5	8.5	17.8	26.4
Offenses against the family and children	25,730	155	522	1,083	2,709	0.6	2.0	4.2	10.5
Driving under the influence	202,119	14	1,000	10,960	42,405	*	0.5	5.4	21.0
Liquor laws	21,746	472	4,498	13,671	15,152	2.2	20.7	62.9	69.7
Drunkenness	25,656	39	303	1,709	4,828	0.2	1.2	6.7	18.8
Disorderly conduct	32,777	2,298	6,284	8,848	12,517	7.0	19.2	27.0	38.2
Vagrancy	1,949	32	109	219	439	1.6	5.6	11.2	22.5
All other offenses (except traffic)	572,506	4,246	18,599	56,969	132,875	0.7	3.2	10.0	23.2
Suspicion	86	5	28	39	51	5.8	32.6	45.3	59.3
Curfew and loitering law violations	1,487	368	1,487	1,487	1,487	24.7	100.0	100.0	100.0

* = Less than one-tenth of one percent.

1 Violent crimes are offenses of murder and nonnegligent manslaughter, rape, robbery, and aggravated assault. Property crimes are offenses of burglary, larceny-theft, motor vehicle theft, and arson.   2 The rape figures in this table are aggregate totals of the data submitted based on both the legacy and revised Uniform Crime Reporting definitions.

Table 54. Arrests, Metropolitan Counties, Distribution by Sex, 2017

(Number, percent; 1,458 agencies; 2017 estimated population 57,699,058.)

Offense charged	Number of persons arrested			Percent male	Percent female	Percent distribution[1]		
	Total	Male	Female			Total	Male	Female
Total	1,630,907	1,199,640	431,267	73.6	26.4	100.0	100.0	100.0
Violent crime[2]	73,918	59,422	14,496	80.4	19.6	4.5	5.0	3.4
Murder and nonnegligent manslaughter	1,917	1,658	259	86.5	13.5	0.1	0.1	0.1
Rape[3]	3,602	3,513	89	97.5	2.5	0.2	0.3	*
Robbery	10,229	8,745	1,484	85.5	14.5	0.6	0.7	0.3
Aggravated assault	58,170	45,506	12,664	78.2	21.8	3.6	3.8	2.9
Property crime[2]	149,439	99,770	49,669	66.8	33.2	9.2	8.3	11.5
Burglary	29,411	23,997	5,414	81.6	18.4	1.8	2.0	1.3
Larceny-theft	104,711	63,776	40,935	60.9	39.1	6.4	5.3	9.5
Motor vehicle theft	14,046	10,953	3,093	78.0	22.0	0.9	0.9	0.7
Arson	1,271	1,044	227	82.1	17.9	0.1	0.1	0.1
Other assaults	148,967	106,818	42,149	71.7	28.3	9.1	8.9	9.8
Forgery and counterfeiting	8,775	5,727	3,048	65.3	34.7	0.5	0.5	0.7
Fraud	20,799	13,121	7,678	63.1	36.9	1.3	1.1	1.8
Embezzlement	2,135	1,107	1,028	51.9	48.1	0.1	0.1	0.2
Stolen property; buying, receiving, possessing	15,784	12,364	3,420	78.3	21.7	1.0	1.0	0.8
Vandalism	25,455	19,854	5,601	78.0	22.0	1.6	1.7	1.3
Weapons; carrying, possessing, etc.	23,315	20,854	2,461	89.4	10.6	1.4	1.7	0.6
Prostitution and commercialized vice	3,443	1,766	1,677	51.3	48.7	0.2	0.1	0.4
Sex offenses (except forcible rape and prostitution)	8,202	7,667	535	93.5	6.5	0.5	0.6	0.1
Drug abuse violations	266,029	198,278	67,751	74.5	25.5	16.3	16.5	15.7
Gambling	590	394	196	66.8	33.2	*	*	*
Offenses against the family and children	25,730	19,956	5,774	77.6	22.4	1.6	1.7	1.3
Driving under the influence	202,119	150,427	51,692	74.4	25.6	12.4	12.5	12.0
Liquor laws	21,746	14,776	6,970	67.9	32.1	1.3	1.2	1.6
Drunkenness	25,656	20,182	5,474	78.7	21.3	1.6	1.7	1.3
Disorderly conduct	32,777	23,140	9,637	70.6	29.4	2.0	1.9	2.2
Vagrancy	1,949	1,435	514	73.6	26.4	0.1	0.1	0.1
All other offenses (except traffic)	572,506	421,573	150,933	73.6	26.4	35.1	35.1	35.0
Suspicion	86	63	23	73.3	26.7	*	*	*
Curfew and loitering law violations	1,487	946	541	63.6	36.4	0.1	0.1	0.1

* = Less than one-tenth of one percent.
1 Because of rounding, the percentages may not sum to 100.   2 Violent crimes are offenses of murder and nonnegligent manslaughter, rape, robbery, and aggravated assault. Property crimes are offenses of burglary, larceny-theft, motor vehicle theft, and arson.   3 The rape figures in this table are aggregate totals of the data submitted based on both the legacy and revised Uniform Crime Reporting definitions.

Table 55. Arrests, Metropolitan Counties, Distribution by Race, 2017

(Number, percent; 1,536 agencies; 2015 estimated population 56,900,141.)

Offense charged	Total arrests						Percent distribution[1]						Arrests under 18					
	Total	White	Black	American Indian or Alaskan Native	Asian	Native Hawaiian or Other Pacific Islander	Total	White	Black	American Indian or Alaskan Native	Asian	Native Hawaiian or Other Pacific Islander	Total	White	Black	American Indian or Alaskan Native	Asian	Native Hawaiian or Other Pacific Islander
Total	1,620,841	1,168,771	413,868	14,694	19,106	4,402	100.0	72.1	25.5	0.9	1.2	0.3	101,419	63,533	35,635	802	1,120	329
Violent crime[2]	73,645	49,120	22,842	619	859	205	100.0	66.7	31.0	0.8	1.2	0.3	6,835	3,363	3,368	46	40	18
Murder and nonnegligent manslaughter	1,911	1,080	790	10	31	0	100.0	56.5	41.3	0.5	1.6	0.0	124	58	64	1	1	0
Rape[3]	3,568	2,748	749	24	42	5	100.0	77.0	21.0	0.7	1.2	0.1	587	419	164	1	3	0
Robbery	10,203	4,785	5,263	59	65	31	100.0	46.9	51.6	0.6	0.6	0.3	2,015	602	1,394	6	8	5
Aggravated assault	57,963	40,507	16,040	526	721	169	100.0	69.9	27.7	0.9	1.2	0.3	4,109	2,284	1,746	38	28	13
Property crime[2]	148,429	101,048	44,520	777	1,720	364	100.0	68.1	30.0	0.5	1.2	0.2	19,005	10,456	8,142	78	268	61
Burglary	29,289	21,631	7,223	134	233	68	100.0	73.9	24.7	0.5	0.8	0.2	4,086	2,477	1,562	10	29	8
Larceny-theft	103,903	68,114	33,775	548	1,280	186	100.0	65.6	32.5	0.5	1.2	0.2	12,858	6,834	5,709	57	215	43
Motor vehicle theft	13,971	10,342	3,250	87	185	107	100.0	74.0	23.3	0.6	1.3	0.8	1,792	954	795	11	22	10
Arson	1,266	961	272	8	22	3	100.0	75.9	21.5	0.6	1.7	0.2	269	191	76	0	2	0
Other assaults	147,896	106,249	38,548	1,252	1,561	286	100.0	71.8	26.1	0.8	1.2	0.2	18,823	10,632	7,886	135	144	26
Forgery and counterfeiting	8,731	5,473	3,063	48	138	9	100.0	62.7	35.1	0.5	1.7	0.1	155	83	68	0	4	0
Fraud	20,654	14,128	6,161	124	230	11	100.0	68.4	29.8	0.6	1.2	0.1	531	307	215	4	5	0
Embezzlement	2,122	1,299	786	3	34	0	100.0	61.2	37.0	0.1	1.6	0.0	51	23	27	0	1	0
Stolen property; buying, receiving, possessing	15,708	11,069	4,394	113	114	18	100.0	70.5	28.0	0.7	0.8	0.1	1,125	526	585	5	7	2
Vandalism	25,260	18,629	6,152	219	242	18	100.0	73.7	24.4	0.9	1.0	0.1	4,977	3,481	1,421	36	35	4
Weapons; carrying, possessing, etc.	23,229	14,196	8,589	140	229	75	100.0	61.1	37.0	0.6	1.3	0.3	2,318	1,282	989	19	25	3
Prostitution and commercialized vice	3,433	1,807	1,311	13	296	6	100.0	52.6	38.2	0.4	8.8	0.2	32	15	17	0	0	0
Sex offenses (except forcible rape and prostitution)	8,150	6,348	1,655	41	91	15	100.0	77.9	20.3	0.5	1.3	0.2	1,433	1,063	350	10	10	0
Drug abuse violations	264,395	189,888	69,573	1,589	2,835	510	100.0	71.8	26.3	0.6	1.3	0.2	13,588	10,210	3,025	92	205	56
Gambling	587	304	160	3	88	32	100.0	51.8	27.3	0.5	20.4	5.5	50	25	22	1	2	0
Offenses against the family and children	25,658	16,768	8,592	137	157	4	100.0	65.4	33.5	0.5	0.6	*	521	367	132	19	3	0
Driving under the influence	200,494	164,499	29,806	1,372	4,289	528	100.0	82.0	14.9	0.7	2.4	0.3	981	880	73	10	17	1
Liquor laws	21,353	17,874	2,685	368	382	44	100.0	83.7	12.6	1.7	2.0	0.2	4,401	4,015	244	60	63	19
Drunkenness	25,558	21,291	3,623	246	340	58	100.0	83.3	14.2	1.0	1.6	0.2	302	260	39	1	2	0
Disorderly conduct	32,575	21,714	10,160	393	273	35	100.0	66.7	31.2	1.2	0.9	0.1	6,241	3,123	3,018	70	28	2
Vagrancy	1,941	1,433	493	7	7	1	100.0	73.8	25.4	0.4	0.4	0.1	108	45	63	0	0	0
All other offenses (except traffic)	569,460	404,577	150,378	7,228	5,154	2,123	100.0	71.0	26.4	1.3	1.3	0.4	18,435	12,346	5,604	214	194	77
Suspicion	84	35	49	0	0	0	100.0	41.7	58.3	0.0	0.0	0.0	28	9	19	0	0	0
Curfew and loitering law violations	1,479	1,022	328	2	67	60	100.0	69.1	22.2	0.1	8.6	4.1	1,479	1,022	328	2	67	60

Table 55. Arrests, Metropolitan Counties, Distribution by Race, 2017—Continued

(Number, percent; 1,536 agencies; 2015 estimated population 56,900,141.)

Offense charged	Percent distribution[1]						Arrests 18 and over						Percent distribution[1]					
	Total	White	Black	American Indian or Alaskan Native	Asian	Native Hawaiian or Other Pacific Islander	Total	White	Black	American Indian or Alaskan Native	Asian	Native Hawaiian or Other Pacific Islander	Total	White	Black	American Indian or Alaskan Native	Asian	Native Hawaiian or Other Pacific Islander
Total	100.0	62.6	35.1	0.8	1.1	0.3	1,519,422	1,105,238	378,233	13,892	17,986	4,073	100.0	72.7	24.9	0.9	1.2	0.3
Violent crime[2]	100.0	49.2	49.3	0.7	0.6	0.3	66,810	45,757	19,474	573	819	187	100.0	68.5	29.1	0.9	1.2	0.3
Murder and nonnegligent manslaughter	100.0	46.8	51.6	0.8	0.8	0.0	1,787	1,022	726	9	30	0	100.0	57.2	40.6	0.5	1.7	0.0
Rape[3]	100.0	71.4	27.9	0.2	0.5	0.0	2,981	2,329	585	23	39	5	100.0	78.1	19.6	0.8	1.3	0.2
Robbery	100.0	29.9	69.2	0.3	0.4	0.2	8,188	4,183	3,869	53	57	26	100.0	51.1	47.3	0.6	0.7	0.3
Aggravated assault	100.0	55.6	42.5	0.9	0.7	0.3	53,854	38,223	14,294	488	693	156	100.0	71.0	26.5	0.9	1.3	0.3
Property crime[2]	100.0	55.0	42.8	0.4	1.4	0.3	129,424	90,592	36,378	699	1,452	303	100.0	70.0	28.1	0.5	1.1	0.2
Burglary	100.0	60.6	38.2	0.2	0.7	0.2	25,203	19,154	5,661	124	204	60	100.0	76.0	22.5	0.5	0.8	0.2
Larceny-theft	100.0	53.1	44.4	0.4	1.7	0.3	91,045	61,280	28,066	491	1,065	143	100.0	67.3	30.8	0.5	1.2	0.2
Motor vehicle theft	100.0	53.2	44.4	0.6	1.2	0.6	12,179	9,388	2,455	76	163	97	100.0	77.1	20.2	0.6	1.3	0.8
Arson	100.0	71.0	28.3	0.0	0.7	0.0	997	770	196	8	20	3	100.0	77.2	19.7	0.8	2.0	0.3
Other assaults	100.0	56.5	41.9	0.7	0.8	0.1	129,073	95,617	30,662	1,117	1,417	260	100.0	74.1	23.8	0.9	1.1	0.2
Forgery and counterfeiting	100.0	53.5	43.9	0.0	2.6	0.0	8,576	5,390	2,995	48	134	9	100.0	62.8	34.9	0.6	1.6	0.1
Fraud	100.0	57.8	40.5	0.8	0.9	0.0	20,123	13,821	5,946	120	225	11	100.0	68.7	29.5	0.6	1.1	0.1
Embezzlement	100.0	45.1	52.9	0.0	2.0	0.0	2,071	1,276	759	3	33	0	100.0	61.6	36.6	0.1	1.6	0.0
Stolen property; buying, receiving, possessing	100.0	46.8	52.0	0.4	0.6	0.2	14,583	10,543	3,809	108	107	16	100.0	72.3	26.1	0.7	0.7	0.1
Vandalism	100.0	69.9	28.6	0.7	0.7	0.1	20,283	15,148	4,731	183	207	14	100.0	74.7	23.3	0.9	1.0	0.1
Weapons; carrying, possessing, etc.	100.0	55.3	42.7	0.8	1.1	0.1	20,911	12,914	7,600	121	204	72	100.0	61.8	36.3	0.6	1.0	0.3
Prostitution and commercialized vice	100.0	46.9	53.1	0.0	0.0	0.0	3,401	1,792	1,294	13	296	6	100.0	52.7	38.0	0.4	8.7	0.2
Sex offenses (except forcible rape and prostitution)	100.0	74.2	24.4	0.7	0.7	0.0	6,717	5,285	1,305	31	81	15	100.0	78.7	19.4	0.5	1.2	0.2
Drug abuse violations	100.0	75.1	22.3	0.7	1.5	0.4	250,807	179,678	66,548	1,497	2,630	454	100.0	71.6	26.5	0.6	1.0	0.2
Gambling	100.0	50.0	44.0	2.0	4.0	0.0	537	279	138	2	86	32	100.0	52.0	25.7	0.4	16.0	6.0
Offenses against the family and children	100.0	70.4	25.3	3.6	0.6	0.0	25,137	16,401	8,460	118	154	4	100.0	65.2	33.7	0.5	0.6	*
Driving under the influence	100.0	89.7	7.4	1.0	1.7	0.1	199,513	163,619	29,733	1,362	4,272	527	100.0	82.0	14.9	0.7	2.1	0.3
Liquor laws	100.0	91.2	5.5	1.4	1.4	0.4	16,952	13,859	2,441	308	319	25	100.0	81.8	14.4	1.8	1.9	0.1
Drunkenness	100.0	86.1	12.9	0.3	0.7	0.0	25,256	21,031	3,584	245	338	58	100.0	83.3	14.2	1.0	1.3	0.2
Disorderly conduct	100.0	50.0	48.4	1.1	0.4	*	26,334	18,591	7,142	323	245	33	100.0	70.6	27.1	1.2	0.9	0.1
Vagrancy	100.0	41.7	58.3	0.0	0.0	0.0	1,833	1,388	430	7	7	1	100.0	75.7	23.5	0.4	0.4	0.1
All other offenses (except traffic)	100.0	67.0	30.4	1.2	1.1	0.4	551,025	392,231	144,774	7,014	4,960	2,046	100.0	71.2	26.3	1.3	0.9	0.4
Suspicion	100.0	32.1	67.9	0.0	0.0	0.0	56	26	30	0	0	0	100.0	46.4	53.6	0.0	0.0	0.0
Curfew and loitering law violations	100.0	69.1	22.2	0.1	4.5	4.1	NA	NA	NA	NA	NA	NA	NA	NA	NA	NA	NA	NA

NA = Not available.
* = Less than one-tenth of one percent.
1 Because of rounding, the percentages may not sum to 100.   2 Violent crimes are offenses of murder and nonnegligent manslaughter, rape, robbery, and aggravated assault. Property crimes are offenses of burglary, larceny-theft, motor vehicle theft, and arson.   3 The rape figures in this table are an aggregate total of the data submitted using both the revised and legacy Uniform Crime Reporting definitions.

Table 55A. Arrests, Metropolitan Counties, Distribution by Ethnicity, 2017

(Number, percent; 1,458 agencies; 2017 estimated population 57,699,058.)

Offense charged	Total arrests			Percent distribution[1]			Arrests under 18		
	Total[2]	Hispanic or Latino	Not Hispanic or Latino	Total[2]	Hispanic or Latino	Not Hispanic or Latino	Total[2]	Hispanic or Latino	Not Hispanic or Latino
Total	1,281,749	218,302	1,063,447	100.0	17.0	83.0	72,998	11,370	61,628
Violent crime[3]	58,362	12,250	46,112	100.0	21.0	79.0	5,033	885	4,148
Murder and nonnegligent manslaughter	1,338	313	1,025	100.0	23.4	76.6	78	24	54
Rape[4]	2,648	626	2,022	100.0	23.6	76.4	412	68	344
Robbery	7,884	1,356	6,528	100.0	17.2	82.8	1,504	248	1,256
Aggravated assault	46,492	9,955	36,537	100.0	21.4	78.6	3,039	545	2,494
Property crime[3]	109,330	13,455	95,875	100.0	12.3	87.7	12,461	1,935	10,526
Burglary	21,946	2,963	18,983	100.0	13.5	86.5	2,673	464	2,209
Larceny-theft	74,916	7,540	67,376	100.0	10.1	89.9	8,310	1,166	7,144
Motor vehicle theft	11,453	2,807	8,646	100.0	24.5	75.5	1,272	276	996
Arson	1,015	145	870	100.0	14.3	85.7	206	29	177
Other assaults	118,187	16,407	101,780	100.0	13.9	86.1	14,865	1,881	12,984
Forgery and counterfeiting	6,539	995	5,544	100.0	15.2	84.8	115	17	98
Fraud	15,729	1,608	14,121	100.0	10.2	89.8	396	49	347
Embezzlement	1,809	141	1,668	100.0	7.8	92.2	43	7	36
Stolen property; buying, receiving, possessing	11,035	2,104	8,931	100.0	19.1	80.9	743	188	555
Vandalism	20,396	2,840	17,556	100.0	13.9	86.1	3,747	498	3,249
Weapons; carrying, possessing, etc.	18,309	3,938	14,371	100.0	21.5	78.5	1,799	384	1,415
Prostitution and commercialized vice	2,762	536	2,226	100.0	19.4	80.6	22	4	18
Sex offenses (except forcible rape and prostitution)	6,539	1,544	4,995	100.0	23.6	76.4	1,115	202	913
Drug abuse violations	206,209	36,861	169,348	100.0	17.9	82.1	9,676	1,889	7,787
Gambling	403	134	269	100.0	33.3	66.7	46	13	33
Offenses against the family and children	21,079	2,412	18,667	100.0	11.4	88.6	361	91	270
Driving under the influence	174,911	47,471	127,440	100.0	27.1	72.9	784	168	616
Liquor laws	15,435	2,169	13,266	100.0	14.1	85.9	3,164	361	2,803
Drunkenness	23,516	6,039	17,477	100.0	25.7	74.3	254	77	177
Disorderly conduct	23,329	2,193	21,136	100.0	9.4	90.6	4,148	345	3,803
Vagrancy	1,437	221	1,216	100.0	15.4	84.6	46	8	38
All other offenses (except traffic)	445,429	64,858	380,571	100.0	14.6	85.4	13,228	2,245	10,983
Suspicion	71	3	68	100.0	4.2	95.8	19	0	19
Curfew and loitering law violations	933	123	810	100.0	13.2	86.8	933	123	810

Table 55A. Arrests, Metropolitan Counties, Distribution by Ethnicity, 2017—Continued

(Number, percent; 1,458 agencies; 2017 estimated population 57,699,058.)

Offense charged	Percent distribution[1]				Arrests 18 and over			Percent distribution[1]	
	Total[2]	Hispanic or Latino	Not Hispanic or Latino	Total[2]	Hispanic or Latino	Not Hispanic or Latino	Total[2]	Hispanic or Latino	Not Hispanic or Latino
Total	100.0	15.6	84.4	1,208,751	206,932	1,001,819	100.0	17.1	82.9
Violent crime[3]	100.0	17.6	82.4	53,329	11,365	41,964	100.0	21.3	78.7
Murder and nonnegligent manslaughter	100.0	30.8	69.2	1,260	289	971	100.0	22.9	77.1
Rape[4]	100.0	16.5	83.5	2,236	558	1,678	100.0	25.0	75.0
Robbery	100.0	16.5	83.5	6,380	1,108	5,272	100.0	17.4	82.6
Aggravated assault	100.0	17.9	82.1	43,453	9,410	34,043	100.0	21.7	78.3
Property crime[3]	100.0	15.5	84.5	96,869	11,520	85,349	100.0	11.9	88.1
Burglary	100.0	17.4	82.6	19,273	2,499	16,774	100.0	13.0	87.0
Larceny-theft	100.0	14.0	86.0	66,606	6,374	60,232	100.0	9.6	90.4
Motor vehicle theft	100.0	21.7	78.3	10,181	2,531	7,650	100.0	24.9	75.1
Arson	100.0	14.1	85.9	809	116	693	100.0	14.3	85.7
Other assaults	100.0	12.7	87.3	103,322	14,526	88,796	100.0	14.1	85.9
Forgery and counterfeiting	100.0	14.8	85.2	6,424	978	5,446	100.0	15.2	84.8
Fraud	100.0	12.4	87.6	15,333	1,559	13,774	100.0	10.2	89.8
Embezzlement	100.0	16.3	83.7	1,766	134	1,632	100.0	7.6	92.4
Stolen property; buying, receiving, possessing	100.0	25.3	74.7	10,292	1,916	8,376	100.0	18.6	81.4
Vandalism	100.0	13.3	86.7	16,649	2,342	14,307	100.0	14.1	85.9
Weapons; carrying, possessing, etc.	100.0	21.3	78.7	16,510	3,554	12,956	100.0	21.5	78.5
Prostitution and commercialized vice	100.0	18.2	81.8	2,740	532	2,208	100.0	19.4	80.6
Sex offenses (except forcible rape and prostitution)	100.0	18.1	81.9	5,424	1,342	4,082	100.0	24.7	75.3
Drug abuse violations	100.0	19.5	80.5	196,533	34,972	161,561	100.0	17.8	82.2
Gambling	100.0	28.3	71.7	357	121	236	100.0	33.9	66.1
Offenses against the family and children	100.0	25.2	74.8	20,718	2,321	18,397	100.0	11.2	88.8
Driving under the influence	100.0	21.4	78.6	174,127	47,303	126,824	100.0	27.2	72.8
Liquor laws	100.0	11.4	88.6	12,271	1,808	10,463	100.0	14.7	85.3
Drunkenness	100.0	30.3	69.7	23,262	5,962	17,300	100.0	25.6	74.4
Disorderly conduct	100.0	8.3	91.7	19,181	1,848	17,333	100.0	9.6	90.4
Vagrancy	100.0	17.4	82.6	1,391	213	1,178	100.0	15.3	84.7
All other offenses (except traffic)	100.0	17.0	83.0	432,201	62,613	369,588	100.0	14.5	85.5
Suspicion	100.0	0.0	100.0	52	3	49	100.0	5.8	94.2
Curfew and loitering law violations	100.0	13.2	86.8	NA	NA	NA	NA	NA	NA

NA = Not available.
1 Because of rounding, the percentages may not sum to 100. 2 The ethnicity totals are representative of those agencies that provided ethnicity breakdowns. Not all agencies provide ethnicity data; therefore, the race and ethnicity totals will not be equal. 3 Violent crimes are offenses of murder and nonnegligent manslaughter, rape, robbery, and aggravated assault. Property crimes are offenses of burglary, larceny-theft, motor vehicle theft, and arson. 4 The rape figures in this table are an aggregate total of the data submitted using both the revised and legacy Uniform Crime Reporting definitions.

Table 56. Arrest Trends, Nonmetropolitan Counties, 2016–2017

(Number, percent change; 1,756 agencies; 2017 estimated population 19,977,979; 2016 estimated population 19,965,738.)

Offense charged	Number of persons arrested								
	Total, all ages			Under 18 years of age			18 years of age and over		
	2016	2017	Percent change	2016	2017	Percent change	2016	2017	Percent change
Total[1]	638,888	649,705	+1.7	27,903	27,269	-2.3	610,985	622,436	+1.9
Violent crime[2]	20,313	20,172	-0.7	1,204	1,306	+8.5	19,109	18,866	-1.3
Murder and nonnegligent manslaughter	580	582	+0.3	26	31	+19.2	554	551	-0.5
Rape[3]	1,630	1,620	-0.6	233	298	+27.9	1,397	1,322	-5.4
Robbery	1,329	1,130	-15.0	89	92	+3.4	1,240	1,038	-16.3
Aggravated assault	16,774	16,840	+0.4	856	885	+3.4	15,918	15,955	+0.2
Property crime[2]	40,844	39,654	-2.9	3,907	3,576	-8.5	36,937	36,078	-2.3
Burglary	11,607	11,339	-2.3	1,265	1,244	-1.7	10,342	10,095	-2.4
Larceny-theft	24,874	23,543	-5.4	1,992	1,750	-12.1	22,882	21,793	-4.8
Motor vehicle theft	3,880	4,300	+10.8	550	518	-5.8	3,330	3,782	+13.6
Arson	483	472	-2.3	100	64	-36.0	383	408	+6.5
Other assaults	54,136	53,165	-1.8	4,472	4,536	+1.4	49,664	48,629	-2.1
Forgery and counterfeiting	2,434	2,357	-3.2	25	31	+24.0	2,409	2,326	-3.4
Fraud	7,996	7,552	-5.6	106	115	+8.5	7,890	7,437	-5.7
Embezzlement	546	483	-11.5	8	8	0.0	538	475	-11.7
Stolen property; buying, receiving, possessing	3,664	3,910	+6.7	200	224	+12.0	3,464	3,686	+6.4
Vandalism	8,276	8,154	-1.5	1,357	1,386	+2.1	6,919	6,768	-2.2
Weapons; carrying, possessing, etc.	6,460	6,875	+6.4	312	346	+10.9	6,148	6,529	+6.2
Prostitution and commercialized vice	242	193	-20.2	9	1	-88.9	233	192	-17.6
Sex offenses (except forcible rape and prostitution)	3,028	2,749	-9.2	530	461	-13.0	2,498	2,288	-8.4
Drug abuse violations	95,785	100,941	+5.4	3,618	3,754	+3.8	92,167	97,187	+5.4
Gambling	170	130	-23.5	7	3	-57.1	163	127	-22.1
Offenses against the family and children	8,429	8,513	+1.0	358	99	-72.3	8,071	8,414	+4.2
Driving under the influence	118,353	118,417	+0.1	753	698	-7.3	117,600	117,719	+0.1
Liquor laws	13,263	12,209	-7.9	2,665	2,565	-3.8	10,598	9,644	-9.0
Drunkenness	11,598	10,880	-6.2	157	112	-28.7	11,441	10,768	-5.9
Disorderly conduct	15,760	15,200	-3.6	1,986	1,964	-1.1	13,774	13,236	-3.9
Vagrancy	172	204	+18.6	4	5	+25.0	168	199	+18.5
All other offenses (except traffic)	227,166	237,694	+4.6	5,972	5,826	-2.4	221,194	231,868	+4.8
Suspicion	51	63	+23.5	0	4		51	59	+15.7
Curfew and loitering law violations	253	253	0.00	253	253	0.00	NA	NA	NA

NA = Not available.

1 Does not include suspicion.　2 Violent crimes are offenses of murder and nonnegligent manslaughter, rape, robbery, and aggravated assault.　Property crimes are offenses of burglary, larceny-theft, motor vehicle theft, and arson.　3 The rape figures in this table are aggregate totals of the data submitted based on both the legacy and revised Uniform Crime Reporting definitions.

Table 57. Arrest Trends, Nonmetropolitan Counties, by Age and Sex, 2016–2017

(Number, percent; 1,756 agencies; 2017 estimated population 19,977,979; 2016 estimated population 19,965,738.)

Offense charged	Male						Female					
	Total			Under 18			Total			Under 18		
	2016	2017	Percent change	2016	2017	Percent change	2016	2017	Percent change	2016	2017	Percent change
Total[1]	470,520	476,652	+1.3	20,077	19,534	-2.7	168,368	173,053	+2.8	7,826	7,735	-1.2
Violent crime[2]	16,541	16,427	-0.7	993	1,074	+8.2	3,772	3,745	-0.7	211	232	+10.0
Murder and nonnegligent manslaughter	480	470	-2.1	23	28	+21.7	100	112	+12.0	3	3	0.0
Rape[3]	1,578	1,574	-0.3	224	287	+28.1	52	46	-11.5	9	11	+22.2
Robbery	1,099	939	-14.6	73	86	+17.8	230	191	-17.0	16	6	-62.5
Aggravated assault	13,384	13,444	+0.4	673	673	0.0	3,390	3,396	+0.2	183	212	+15.8
Property crime[2]	28,505	27,735	-2.7	3,096	2,802	-9.5	12,339	11,919	-3.4	811	774	-4.6
Burglary	9,467	9,127	-3.6	1,126	1,110	-1.4	2,140	2,212	+3.4	139	134	-3.6
Larceny-theft	15,628	14,946	-4.4	1,442	1,241	-13.9	9,246	8,597	-7.0	550	509	-7.5
Motor vehicle theft	3,030	3,291	+8.6	441	401	-9.1	850	1,009	+18.7	109	117	+7.3
Arson	380	371	-2.4	87	50	-42.5	103	101	-1.9	13	14	+7.7
Other assaults	39,401	38,787	-1.6	3,011	2,970	-1.4	14,735	14,378	-2.4	1,461	1,566	+7.2
Forgery and counterfeiting	1,501	1,422	-5.3	16	25	+56.3	933	935	+0.2	9	6	-33.3
Fraud	4,536	4,394	-3.1	70	78	+11.4	3,460	3,158	-8.7	36	37	+2.8
Embezzlement	266	230	-13.5	5	5	0.0	280	253	-9.6	3	3	0.0
Stolen property; buying, receiving, possessing	2,800	3,010	+7.5	163	170	+4.3	864	900	+4.2	37	54	+45.9
Vandalism	6,637	6,443	-2.9	1,146	1,153	+0.6	1,639	1,711	+4.4	211	233	+10.4
Weapons; carrying, possessing, etc.	5,842	6,153	+5.3	279	307	+10.0	618	722	+16.8	33	39	+18.2
Prostitution and commercialized vice	119	106	-10.9	6	1	-83.3	123	87	-29.3	3	0	-100.0
Sex offenses (except forcible rape and prostitution)	2,832	2,548	-10.0	471	406	-13.8	196	201	+2.6	59	55	-6.8
Drug abuse violations	70,183	73,130	+4.2	2,649	2,730	+3.1	25,602	27,811	+8.6	969	1,024	+5.7
Gambling	126	88	-30.2	4	2	-50.0	44	42	-4.5	3	1	-66.7
Offenses against the family and children	6,177	6,287	+1.8	195	63	-67.7	2,252	2,226	-1.2	163	36	-77.9
Driving under the influence	90,149	89,768	-0.4	569	537	-5.6	28,204	28,649	+1.6	184	161	-12.5
Liquor laws	9,116	8,271	-9.3	1,589	1,476	-7.1	4,147	3,938	-5.0	1,076	1,089	+1.2
Drunkenness	8,721	8,015	-8.1	105	84	-20.0	2,877	2,865	-0.4	52	28	-46.2
Disorderly conduct	11,067	10,760	-2.8	1,341	1,359	+1.3	4,693	4,440	-5.4	645	605	-6.2
Vagrancy	124	154	+24.2	2	3	+50.0	48	50	+4.2	2	2	0.0
All other offenses (except traffic)	165,741	172,773	+4.2	4,231	4,138	-2.2	61,425	64,921	+5.7	1,741	1,688	-3.0
Suspicion	42	48	+14.3	0	4		9	15	+66.7	0	0	
Curfew and loitering law violations	136	151	+11.0	136	151	+11.0	117	102	-12.8	117	102	-12.8

1 Does not include suspicion.   2 Violent crimes are offenses of murder and nonnegligent manslaughter, rape, robbery, and aggravated assault. Property crimes are offenses of burglary, larceny-theft, motor vehicle theft, and arson.   3 The rape figures in this table are aggregate totals of the data submitted based on both the legacy and revised Uniform Crime Reporting definitions.

Table 58. Arrests, Nonmetropolitan Counties, Distribution by Age, 2017

(Number, percent; 1,859 agencies; 2017 estimated population 20,549,030.)

Offense charged	Total, all ages	Ages under 15	Ages under 18	Ages 18 and over	Under 10	10–12	13–14	15	16	17	18	19	20
Total	662,813	6,717	27,715	635,098	277	1,713	4,727	4,321	6,739	9,938	16,880	19,577	20,283
Total percent distribution[1]	100.0	1.0	4.2	95.8	*	0.3	0.7	0.7	1.0	1.5	2.5	3.0	3.1
Violent crime[2]	20,759	403	1,332	19,427	15	127	261	190	301	438	490	534	530
Violent crime percent distribution[1]	100.0	1.9	6.4	93.6	0.1	0.6	1.3	0.9	1.4	2.1	2.4	2.6	2.6
Murder and nonnegligent manslaughter	601	4	31	570	0	1	3	3	7	17	17	23	13
Rape[3]	1,651	105	303	1,348	5	35	65	31	78	89	89	90	53
Robbery	1,184	8	92	1,092	0	2	6	14	23	47	56	70	58
Aggravated assault	17,323	286	906	16,417	10	89	187	142	193	285	328	351	406
Property crime[2]	40,811	1,110	3,652	37,159	50	310	750	628	862	1,052	1,607	1,343	1,278
Property crime percent distribution[1]	100.0	2.7	8.9	91.1	0.1	0.8	1.8	1.5	2.1	2.6	3.9	3.3	3.1
Burglary	11,754	414	1,282	10,472	20	126	268	198	278	392	590	447	385
Larceny-theft	24,173	514	1,781	22,392	25	143	346	309	442	516	843	733	748
Motor vehicle theft	4,396	140	525	3,871	3	22	115	111	134	140	157	145	128
Arson	488	42	64	424	2	19	21	10	8	4	17	18	17
Other assaults	54,702	1,569	4,616	50,086	70	450	1,049	837	1,059	1,151	1,135	1,238	1,237
Forgery and counterfeiting	2,397	4	31	2,366	1	1	2	4	10	13	45	74	55
Fraud	7,742	25	115	7,627	1	0	24	17	27	46	111	127	134
Embezzlement	487	0	8	479	0	0	0	2	2	4	12	12	14
Stolen property; buying, receiving, possessing	4,008	35	227	3,781	1	6	28	40	57	95	114	119	111
Vandalism	8,401	551	1,425	6,976	36	174	341	242	299	333	369	273	266
Weapons; carrying, possessing, etc.	7,019	103	354	6,665	7	33	63	46	81	124	153	152	222
Prostitution and commercialized vice	194	0	1	193	0	0	0	0	0	1	3	6	6
Sex offenses (except forcible rape and prostitution)	2,817	226	464	2,353	12	63	151	82	75	81	105	102	86
Drug abuse violations	103,029	404	3,803	99,226	7	70	327	416	970	2,013	4,187	4,716	4,732
Gambling	131	0	3	128	0	0	0	0	0	3	6	4	4
Offenses against the family and children	8,706	32	101	8,605	1	6	25	12	23	34	80	78	114
Driving under the influence	120,328	8	711	119,617	4	0	4	35	172	496	1,553	2,314	2,734
Liquor laws	12,445	221	2,616	9,829	3	22	196	342	754	1,299	2,083	2,261	1,922
Drunkenness	11,100	17	116	10,984	0	5	12	19	25	55	232	250	232
Disorderly conduct	15,388	632	1,971	13,417	23	163	446	403	473	463	433	366	373
Vagrancy	205	1	5	200	0	1	0	2	2	0	2	6	3
All other offenses (except traffic)	241,827	1,301	5,906	235,921	46	267	988	959	1,474	2,172	4,159	5,600	6,228
Suspicion	63	0	4	59	0	0	0	1	0	3	1	2	2
Curfew and loitering law violations	254	75	254	NA	NA	15	60	44	73	62	NA	NA	NA

Table 58. Arrests, Nonmetropolitan Counties, Distribution by Age, 2017—Continued

(Number, percent; 1,859 agencies; 2017 estimated population 20,549,030.)

Offense charged	21	22	23	24	25–29	30–34	35–39	40–44	45–49	50–54	55–59	60–64	65 and over
Total	20,371	20,533	21,540	22,578	114,080	101,900	85,885	58,811	47,203	37,110	25,569	12,735	10,043
Total percent distribution[1]	3.1	3.1	3.2	3.4	17.2	15.4	13.0	8.9	7.1	5.6	3.9	1.9	1.5
Violent crime[2]	567	586	619	643	3,362	3,037	2,656	1,842	1,522	1,236	940	447	416
Violent crime percent distribution[1]	2.7	2.8	3.0	3.1	16.2	14.6	12.8	8.9	7.3	6.0	4.5	2.2	2.0
Murder and nonnegligent manslaughter	21	20	30	25	99	84	67	45	43	24	25	12	22
Rape[3]	44	34	39	51	190	185	161	121	94	66	61	33	37
Robbery	42	59	51	52	233	170	122	65	48	31	25	9	1
Aggravated assault	460	473	499	515	2,840	2,598	2,306	1,611	1,337	1,115	829	393	356
Property crime[2]	1,183	1,231	1,173	1,337	7,036	6,429	5,273	3,164	2,481	1,704	1,031	507	382
Property crime percent distribution[1]	2.9	3.0	2.9	3.3	17.2	15.8	12.9	7.8	6.1	4.2	2.5	1.2	0.9
Burglary	357	425	345	407	1,992	1,881	1,499	810	613	364	221	80	56
Larceny-theft	674	671	700	759	4,182	3,740	3,176	1,994	1,615	1,164	709	381	303
Motor vehicle theft	139	122	116	159	801	744	544	326	213	156	75	35	11
Arson	13	13	12	12	61	64	54	34	40	20	26	11	12
Other assaults	1,308	1,382	1,472	1,656	8,184	7,806	6,997	5,203	4,289	3,491	2,464	1,123	1,101
Forgery and counterfeiting	51	90	66	89	424	462	344	259	154	126	79	25	23
Fraud	149	156	201	185	1,174	1,299	1,228	895	704	499	378	209	178
Embezzlement	16	18	7	10	72	73	50	56	49	42	21	17	10
Stolen property; buying, receiving, possessing	121	125	136	155	744	694	571	353	246	148	89	28	27
Vandalism	252	271	292	276	1,256	1,111	861	526	420	367	226	104	106
Weapons; carrying, possessing, etc.	222	243	250	262	1,194	1,058	861	558	458	424	285	162	161
Prostitution and commercialized vice	6	2	4	6	44	35	19	14	14	13	8	5	8
Sex offenses (except forcible rape and prostitution)	74	81	56	60	311	280	300	203	180	172	105	92	146
Drug abuse violations	4,460	4,182	4,153	4,038	19,040	15,131	12,036	7,592	5,773	4,355	2,922	1,245	664
Gambling	5	5	3	4	15	25	8	13	12	9	7	3	5
Offenses against the family and children	141	155	183	245	1,534	1,763	1,649	1,098	688	471	220	101	85
Driving under the influence	4,004	4,065	4,451	4,373	20,684	16,760	14,003	10,714	10,050	9,022	7,360	4,213	3,317
Liquor laws	276	187	141	153	608	442	404	327	336	269	216	111	93
Drunkenness	293	283	281	314	1,647	1,599	1,554	1,124	1,075	939	642	328	191
Disorderly conduct	431	390	420	424	2,176	2,059	1,722	1,238	1,106	914	717	348	300
Vagrancy	5	5	6	5	26	26	31	19	13	20	19	8	6
All other offenses (except traffic)	6,805	7,074	7,622	8,343	44,539	41,804	35,308	23,605	17,628	12,887	7,840	3,656	2,823
Suspicion	2	2	4	0	10	7	10	8	5	2	0	3	1
Curfew and loitering law violations	NA	NA	NA	NA	NA	NA	NA	NA	NA	NA	NA	NA	NA

NA = Not available.

* = Less than one-tenth of one percent.

1 Because of rounding, the percentages may not sum to 100.   2 Violent crimes are offenses of murder and nonnegligent manslaughter, rape, robbery, and aggravated assault. Property crimes are offenses of burglary, larceny-theft, motor vehicle theft, and arson.   3 The rape figures in this table are aggregate totals of the data submitted based on both the legacy and revised Uniform Crime Reporting definitions.

Table 59. Arrests, Nonmetropolitan Counties, Persons under 15, 18, 21, and 25 Years of Age, 2017

(Number, percent; 1,859 agencies; 2017 estimated population 20,549,030.)

Offense charged	Total, all ages	Number of persons arrested				Percent of total all ages			
		Under 15	Under 18	Under 21	Under 25	Under 15	Under 18	Under 21	Under 25
Total	662,813	6,717	27,715	84,455	169,477	1.0	4.2	12.7	25.6
Violent crime[1]	20,759	403	1,332	2,886	5,301	1.9	6.4	13.9	25.5
Murder and nonnegligent manslaughter	601	4	31	84	180	0.7	5.2	14.0	30.0
Rape[2]	1,651	105	303	535	703	6.4	18.4	32.4	42.6
Robbery	1,184	8	92	276	480	0.7	7.8	23.3	40.5
Aggravated assault	17,323	286	906	1,991	3,938	1.7	5.2	11.5	22.7
Property crime[1]	40,811	1,110	3,652	7,880	12,804	2.7	8.9	19.3	31.4
Burglary	11,754	414	1,282	2,704	4,238	3.5	10.9	23.0	36.1
Larceny-theft	24,173	514	1,781	4,105	6,909	2.1	7.4	17.0	28.6
Motor vehicle theft	4,396	140	525	955	1,491	3.2	11.9	21.7	33.9
Arson	488	42	64	116	166	8.6	13.1	23.8	34.0
Other assaults	54,702	1,569	4,616	8,226	14,044	2.9	8.4	15.0	25.7
Forgery and counterfeiting	2,397	4	31	205	501	0.2	1.3	8.6	20.9
Fraud	7,742	25	115	487	1,178	0.3	1.5	6.3	15.2
Embezzlement	487	0	8	46	97	0.0	1.6	9.4	19.9
Stolen property; buying, receiving, possessing	4,008	35	227	571	1,108	0.9	5.7	14.2	27.6
Vandalism	8,401	551	1,425	2,333	3,424	6.6	17.0	27.8	40.8
Weapons; carrying, possessing, etc.	7,019	103	354	881	1,858	1.5	5.0	12.6	26.5
Prostitution and commercialized vice	194	0	1	16	34	0.0	0.5	8.2	17.5
Sex offenses (except forcible rape and prostitution)	2,817	226	464	757	1,028	8.0	16.5	26.9	36.5
Drug abuse violations	103,029	404	3,803	17,438	34,271	0.4	3.7	16.9	33.3
Gambling	131	0	3	17	34	0.0	2.3	13.0	26.0
Offenses against the family and children	8,706	32	101	373	1,097	0.4	1.2	4.3	12.6
Driving under the influence	120,328	8	711	7,312	24,205	*	0.6	6.1	20.1
Liquor laws	12,445	221	2,616	8,882	9,639	1.8	21.0	71.4	77.5
Drunkenness	11,100	17	116	830	2,001	0.2	1.0	7.5	18.0
Disorderly conduct	15,388	632	1,971	3,143	4,808	4.1	12.8	20.4	31.2
Vagrancy	205	1	5	16	37	0.5	2.4	7.8	18.0
All other offenses (except traffic)	241,827	1,301	5,906	21,893	51,737	0.5	2.4	9.1	21.4
Suspicion	63	0	4	9	17	0.0	6.3	14.3	27.0
Curfew and loitering law violations	254	75	254	254	254	29.5	100.0	100.0	100.0

* = Less than one-tenth of one percent.
1 Violent crimes are offenses of murder and nonnegligent manslaughter, rape, robbery, and aggravated assault. Property crimes are offenses of burglary, larceny-theft, motor vehicle theft, and arson.   2 The rape figures in this table are aggregate totals of the data submitted based on both the legacy and revised Uniform Crime Reporting definitions.

Table 60. Arrests, Nonmetropolitan Counties, Distribution by Sex, 2017

(Number, percent; 1,859 agencies; 2017 estimated population 20,549,030.)

Offense charged	Number of persons arrested			Percent male	Percent female	Percent distribution[1]		
	Total	Male	Female			Total	Male	Female
Total	662,813	486,674	176,139	73.4	26.6	100.0	100.0	100.0
Violent crime[2]	20,759	16,894	3,865	81.4	18.6	3.1	3.5	2.2
Murder and nonnegligent manslaughter	601	482	119	80.2	19.8	0.1	0.1	0.1
Rape[3]	1,651	1,605	46	97.2	2.8	0.2	0.3	*
Robbery	1,184	982	202	82.9	17.1	0.2	0.2	0.1
Aggravated assault	17,323	13,825	3,498	79.8	20.2	2.6	2.8	2.0
Property crime[2]	40,811	28,590	12,221	70.1	29.9	6.2	5.9	6.9
Burglary	11,754	9,479	2,275	80.6	19.4	1.8	1.9	1.3
Larceny-theft	24,173	15,361	8,812	63.5	36.5	3.6	3.2	5.0
Motor vehicle theft	4,396	3,364	1,032	76.5	23.5	0.7	0.7	0.6
Arson	488	386	102	79.1	20.9	0.1	0.1	0.1
Other assaults	54,702	39,979	14,723	73.1	26.9	8.3	8.2	8.4
Forgery and counterfeiting	2,397	1,444	953	60.2	39.8	0.4	0.3	0.5
Fraud	7,742	4,505	3,237	58.2	41.8	1.2	0.9	1.8
Embezzlement	487	233	254	47.8	52.2	0.1	*	0.1
Stolen property; buying, receiving, possessing	4,008	3,089	919	77.1	22.9	0.6	0.6	0.5
Vandalism	8,401	6,634	1,767	79.0	21.0	1.3	1.4	1.0
Weapons; carrying, possessing, etc.	7,019	6,282	737	89.5	10.5	1.1	1.3	0.4
Prostitution and commercialized vice	194	107	87	55.2	44.8	*	*	*
Sex offenses (except forcible rape and prostitution)	2,817	2,614	203	92.8	7.2	0.4	0.5	0.1
Drug abuse violations	103,029	74,745	28,284	72.5	27.5	15.5	15.4	16.1
Gambling	131	89	42	67.9	32.1	*	*	*
Offenses against the family and children	8,706	6,427	2,279	73.8	26.2	1.3	1.3	1.3
Driving under the influence	120,328	91,252	29,076	75.8	24.2	18.2	18.8	16.5
Liquor laws	12,445	8,445	4,000	67.9	32.1	1.9	1.7	2.3
Drunkenness	11,100	8,185	2,915	73.7	26.3	1.7	1.7	1.7
Disorderly conduct	15,388	10,896	4,492	70.8	29.2	2.3	2.2	2.6
Vagrancy	205	155	50	75.6	24.4	*	*	*
All other offenses (except traffic)	241,827	175,909	65,918	72.7	27.3	36.5	36.1	37.4
Suspicion	63	48	15	76.2	23.8	*	*	*
Curfew and loitering law violations	254	152	102	59.8	40.2	*	*	*

* = Less than one-tenth of 1 percent.
1 Because of rounding, the percentages may not sum to 100.   2 Violent crimes are offenses of murder and nonnegligent manslaughter, rape, robbery, and aggravated assault. Property crimes are offenses of burglary, larceny-theft, motor vehicle theft, and arson.   3 The rape figures in this table are aggregate totals of the data submitted based on both the legacy and revised Uniform Crime Reporting definitions.

Table 61. Arrests, Nonmetropolitan Counties, Distribution by Race, 2017

(Number, percent; 1,859 agencies; 2017 estimated population 20,549,030.)

Offense charged	Total arrests						Percent distribution[1]						Arrests under 18					
	Total	White	Black	American Indian or Alaskan Native	Asian	Native Hawaiian or Other Pacific Islander	Total	White	Black	American Indian or Alaskan Native	Asian	Native Hawaiian or Other Pacific Islander	Total	White	Black	American Indian or Alaskan Native	Asian	Native Hawaiian or Other Pacific Islander
Total	652,379	543,244	82,026	17,416	5,610	4,083	100.0	83.3	12.6	2.7	0.9	0.6	27,028	21,461	3,901	983	317	366
Violent crime[2]	20,550	16,351	3,074	871	125	129	100.0	79.6	15.0	4.2	0.6	0.6	1,310	946	269	71	15	9
Murder and nonnegligent manslaughter	597	407	161	18	7	4	100.0	68.2	27.0	3.0	1.2	0.7	31	19	12	0	0	0
Rape[3]	1,635	1,411	135	56	11	22	100.0	86.3	8.3	3.4	0.7	1.3	295	250	26	16	2	1
Robbery	1,172	710	394	39	8	21	100.0	60.6	33.6	3.3	0.7	1.8	88	28	58	2	0	0
Aggravated assault	17,146	13,823	2,384	758	99	82	100.0	80.6	13.9	4.4	0.6	0.5	896	649	173	53	13	8
Property crime[2]	40,330	34,116	4,542	1,029	249	394	100.0	84.6	11.3	2.6	0.6	1.0	3,586	2,687	631	170	39	59
Burglary	11,656	9,798	1,402	341	46	69	100.0	84.1	12.0	2.9	0.4	0.6	1,268	916	241	93	10	8
Larceny-theft	23,852	20,289	2,653	525	155	230	100.0	85.1	11.1	2.2	0.6	1.0	1,741	1,377	255	45	24	40
Motor vehicle theft	4,337	3,626	431	147	44	89	100.0	83.6	9.9	3.4	1.0	2.1	513	341	129	31	3	9
Arson	485	403	56	16	4	6	100.0	83.1	11.5	3.3	0.8	1.2	64	53	6	1	2	2
Other assaults	53,959	44,989	6,513	1,841	273	343	100.0	83.4	12.1	3.4	0.5	0.6	4,525	3,351	935	166	31	42
Forgery and counterfeiting	2,378	1,970	348	36	18	6	100.0	82.8	14.6	1.5	0.8	0.3	29	24	4	0	0	1
Fraud	7,612	6,227	1,203	137	24	21	100.0	81.8	15.8	1.8	0.3	0.3	115	96	17	2	0	0
Embezzlement	478	411	54	3	4	6	100.0	86.0	11.3	0.6	0.8	1.3	8	5	2	0	1	0
Stolen property; buying, receiving, possessing	3,940	3,241	591	95	11	2	100.0	82.3	15.0	2.4	0.3	0.1	223	152	61	10	0	0
Vandalism	8,280	6,958	931	291	41	59	100.0	84.0	11.2	3.5	0.5	0.7	1,401	1,190	154	43	9	5
Weapons; carrying, possessing, etc.	6,910	5,204	1,417	199	56	34	100.0	75.3	20.5	2.9	0.8	0.5	348	233	105	8	2	0
Prostitution and commercialized vice	193	146	35	2	3	7	100.0	75.6	18.1	1.0	1.6	3.6	1	1	0	0	0	0
Sex offenses (except forcible rape and prostitution)	2,794	2,427	270	63	22	12	100.0	86.9	9.7	2.3	0.8	0.4	456	403	39	9	2	3
Drug abuse violations	100,971	82,737	14,841	2,144	875	374	100.0	81.9	14.7	2.1	0.9	0.4	3,664	3,081	379	97	57	50
Gambling	131	91	27	0	8	5	100.0	69.5	20.6	0.0	6.1	3.8	3	2	1	0	0	0
Offenses against the family and children	8,636	7,263	1,225	122	25	1	100.0	84.1	14.2	1.4	0.3	*	101	95	3	3	0	0
Driving under the influence	117,859	99,329	12,844	3,208	2,063	415	100.0	84.3	10.9	2.7	1.8	0.4	687	626	29	24	6	2
Liquor laws	11,962	10,763	582	484	106	27	100.0	90.0	4.9	4.0	0.9	0.2	2,522	2,321	52	116	21	12
Drunkenness	11,036	9,810	744	435	37	10	100.0	88.9	6.7	3.9	0.3	0.1	115	103	9	2	0	1
Disorderly conduct	15,113	12,138	1,945	806	95	129	100.0	80.3	12.9	5.3	0.6	0.9	1,933	1,404	426	67	18	18
Vagrancy	205	156	41	7	1	0	100.0	76.1	20.0	3.4	0.5	0.0	5	5	0	0	0	0
All other offenses (except traffic)	238,731	198,683	30,770	5,624	1,563	2,091	100.0	83.2	12.9	2.4	0.7	0.9	5,742	4,536	775	178	106	147
Suspicion	61	35	22	2	1	1	100.0	57.4	36.1	3.3	1.6	1.6	4	1	3	0	0	0
Curfew and loitering law violations	250	199	7	17	10	17	100.0	79.6	2.8	6.8	4.0	6.8	250	199	7	17	10	17

Table 61. Arrests, Nonmetropolitan Counties, Distribution by Race, 2017—Continued

(Number, percent; 1,859 agencies; 2017 estimated population 20,549,030.)

Offense charged	Percent distribution[1]						Arrests 18 and over						Percent distribution[1]					
	Total	White	Black	American Indian or Alaskan Native	Asian	Native Hawaiian or Other Pacific Islander	Total	White	Black	American Indian or Alaskan Native	Asian	Native Hawaiian or Other Pacific Islander	Total	White	Black	American Indian or Alaskan Native	Asian	Native Hawaiian or Other Pacific Islander
Total	100.0	79.4	14.4	3.6	1.2	1.4	625,351	521,783	78,125	16,433	5,293	3,717	100.0	83.4	12.5	2.6	0.8	0.6
Violent crime[2]	100.0	72.2	20.5	5.4	1.1	0.7	19,240	15,405	2,805	800	110	120	100.0	80.1	14.6	4.2	0.6	0.6
Murder and nonnegligent manslaughter	100.0	61.3	38.7	0.0	0.0	0.0	566	388	149	18	7	4	100.0	68.6	26.3	3.2	1.2	0.7
Rape[3]	100.0	84.7	8.8	5.4	0.7	0.3	1,340	1,161	109	40	9	21	100.0	86.6	8.1	3.0	0.7	1.6
Robbery	100.0	31.8	65.9	2.3	0.0	0.0	1,084	682	336	37	8	21	100.0	62.9	31.0	3.4	0.7	1.9
Aggravated assault	100.0	72.4	19.3	5.9	1.5	0.9	16,250	13,174	2,211	705	86	74	100.0	81.1	13.6	4.3	0.5	0.5
Property crime[2]	100.0	74.9	17.6	4.7	1.1	1.6	36,744	31,429	3,911	859	210	335	100.0	85.5	10.6	2.3	0.6	0.9
Burglary	100.0	72.2	19.0	7.3	0.8	0.6	10,388	8,882	1,161	248	36	61	100.0	85.5	11.2	2.4	0.3	0.6
Larceny-theft	100.0	79.1	14.6	2.6	1.4	2.3	22,111	18,912	2,398	480	131	190	100.0	85.5	10.8	2.2	0.6	0.9
Motor vehicle theft	100.0	66.5	25.1	6.0	0.6	1.8	3,824	3,285	302	116	41	80	100.0	85.9	7.9	3.0	1.1	2.1
Arson	100.0	82.8	9.4	1.6	3.1	3.1	421	350	50	15	2	4	100.0	83.1	11.9	3.6	0.5	1.0
Other assaults	100.0	74.1	20.7	3.7	0.7	0.9	49,434	41,638	5,578	1,675	242	301	100.0	84.2	11.3	3.4	0.5	0.6
Forgery and counterfeiting	100.0	82.8	13.8	0.0	0.0	3.4	2,349	1,946	344	36	18	5	100.0	82.8	14.6	1.5	0.8	0.2
Fraud	100.0	83.5	14.8	1.7	0.0	0.0	7,497	6,131	1,186	135	24	21	100.0	81.8	15.8	1.8	0.3	0.3
Embezzlement	100.0	62.5	25.0	0.0	12.5	0.0	470	406	52	3	3	6	100.0	86.4	11.1	0.6	0.6	1.3
Stolen property; buying, receiving, possessing	100.0	68.2	27.4	4.5	0.0	0.0	3,717	3,089	530	85	11	2	100.0	83.1	14.3	2.3	0.3	0.1
Vandalism	100.0	84.9	11.0	3.1	0.6	0.4	6,879	5,768	777	248	32	54	100.0	83.8	11.3	3.6	0.5	0.8
Weapons; carrying, possessing, etc.	100.0	67.0	30.2	2.3	0.6	0.0	6,562	4,971	1,312	191	54	34	100.0	75.8	20.0	2.9	0.8	0.5
Prostitution and commercialized vice	100.0	100.0	0.0	0.0	0.0	0.0	192	145	35	2	3	7	100.0	75.5	18.2	1.0	1.6	3.6
Sex offenses (except forcible rape and prostitution)	100.0	88.4	8.6	2.0	0.4	0.7	2,338	2,024	231	54	20	9	100.0	86.6	9.9	2.3	0.9	0.4
Drug abuse violations	100.0	84.1	10.3	2.6	1.6	1.4	97,307	79,656	14,462	2,047	818	324	100.0	81.9	14.9	2.1	0.8	0.3
Gambling	100.0	66.7	33.3	0.0	0.0	0.0	128	89	26	0	8	5	100.0	69.5	20.3	0.0	6.3	3.9
Offenses against the family and children	100.0	94.1	3.0	3.0	0.0	0.0	8,535	7,168	1,222	119	25	1	100.0	84.0	14.3	1.4	0.3	*
Driving under the influence	100.0	91.1	4.2	3.5	0.9	0.3	117,172	98,703	12,815	3,184	2,057	413	100.0	84.2	10.9	2.7	1.8	0.4
Liquor laws	100.0	92.0	2.1	4.6	0.8	0.5	9,440	8,442	530	368	85	15	100.0	89.4	5.6	3.9	0.9	0.2
Drunkenness	100.0	89.6	7.8	1.7	0.0	0.9	10,921	9,707	735	433	37	9	100.0	88.9	6.7	4.0	0.3	0.1
Disorderly conduct	100.0	72.6	22.0	3.5	0.9	0.9	13,180	10,734	1,519	739	77	111	100.0	81.4	11.5	5.6	0.6	0.8
Vagrancy	100.0	100.0	0.0	0.0	0.0	0.0	200	151	41	7	1	0	100.0	75.5	20.5	3.5	0.5	0.0
All other offenses (except traffic)	100.0	79.0	13.5	3.1	1.8	2.6	232,989	194,147	29,995	5,446	1,457	1,944	100.0	83.3	12.9	2.3	0.6	0.8
Suspicion	100.0	25.0	75.0	0.0	0.0	0.0	57	34	19	2	1	1	100.0	59.6	33.3	3.5	1.8	1.8
Curfew and loitering law violations	100.0	79.6	2.8	6.8	4.0	6.8	NA	NA	NA	NA	NA	NA	NA	NA	NA	NA	NA	NA

NA = Not available.
* = Less than one-tenth of one percent.
1 Because of rounding, the percentages may not sum to 100.   2 Violent crimes are offenses of murder and nonnegligent manslaughter, rape, robbery, and aggravated assault. Property crimes are offenses of burglary, larceny-theft, motor vehicle theft, and arson.   3 The rape figures in this table are aggregate totals of the data submitted based on both the legacy and revised Uniform Crime Reporting definitions.

Table 61A. Arrests, Nonmetropolitan Counties, Distribution by Ethnicity, 2017

(Number, percent; 1,859 agencies; 2017 estimated population 20,549,030.)

Offense charged	Total arrests			Percent distribution[1]			Arrests under 18		
	Total[2]	Hispanic or Latino	Not Hispanic or Latino	Total[2]	Hispanic or Latino	Not Hispanic or Latino	Total[2]	Hispanic or Latino	Not Hispanic or Latino
Total	479,837	35,967	443,870	100.0	7.5	92.5	17,980	1,534	16,446
Violent crime[3]	15,101	1,127	13,974	100.0	7.5	92.5	852	55	797
Murder and nonnegligent manslaughter	400	27	373	100.0	6.8	93.3	24	1	23
Rape[4]	1,059	92	967	100.0	8.7	91.3	179	10	169
Robbery	758	46	712	100.0	6.1	93.9	45	3	42
Aggravated assault	12,884	962	11,922	100.0	7.5	92.5	604	41	563
Property crime[3]	28,171	1,539	26,632	100.0	5.5	94.5	1,994	184	1,810
Burglary	7,854	403	7,451	100.0	5.1	94.9	660	48	612
Larceny-theft	16,817	877	15,940	100.0	5.2	94.8	1,020	96	924
Motor vehicle theft	3,161	237	2,924	100.0	7.5	92.5	270	35	235
Arson	339	22	317	100.0	6.5	93.5	44	5	39
Other assaults	39,892	2,409	37,483	100.0	6.0	94.0	3,204	227	2,977
Forgery and counterfeiting	1,666	133	1,533	100.0	8.0	92.0	21	4	17
Fraud	5,606	259	5,347	100.0	4.6	95.4	68	0	68
Embezzlement	299	14	285	100.0	4.7	95.3	5	0	5
Stolen property; buying, receiving, possessing	2,762	209	2,553	100.0	7.6	92.4	122	23	99
Vandalism	6,128	336	5,792	100.0	5.5	94.5	937	54	883
Weapons; carrying, possessing, etc.	4,758	403	4,355	100.0	8.5	91.5	248	19	229
Prostitution and commercialized vice	96	9	87	100.0	9.4	90.6	0	0	0
Sex offenses (except forcible rape and prostitution)	2,066	138	1,928	100.0	6.7	93.3	313	10	303
Drug abuse violations	72,668	6,101	66,567	100.0	8.4	91.6	2,373	249	2,124
Gambling	97	39	58	100.0	40.2	59.8	2	1	1
Offenses against the family and children	6,830	387	6,443	100.0	5.7	94.3	77	7	70
Driving under the influence	84,174	6,910	77,264	100.0	8.2	91.8	542	50	492
Liquor laws	8,131	685	7,446	100.0	8.4	91.6	1,816	119	1,697
Drunkenness	10,039	1,263	8,776	100.0	12.6	87.4	103	13	90
Disorderly conduct	9,847	613	9,234	100.0	6.2	93.8	1,378	115	1,263
Vagrancy	181	23	158	100.0	12.7	87.3	3	0	3
All other offenses (except traffic)	181,059	13,345	167,714	100.0	7.4	92.6	3,712	382	3,330
Suspicion	58	3	55	100.0	5.2	94.8	2	0	2
Curfew and loitering law violations	208	22	186	100.0	10.6	89.4	208	22	186

Table 61A. Arrests, Nonmetropolitan Counties, Distribution by Ethnicity, 2017—Continued

(Number, percent; 1,859 agencies; 2017 estimated population 20,549,030.)

Offense charged	Percent distribution[1]				Arrests 18 and over			Percent distribution[1]	
	Total[2]	Hispanic or Latino	Not Hispanic or Latino	Total[2]	Hispanic or Latino	Not Hispanic or Latino	Total[2]	Hispanic or Latino	Not Hispanic or Latino
Total	100.0	8.5	91.5	461,857	34,433	427,424	100.0	7.5	92.5
Violent crime[3]	100.0	6.5	93.5	14,249	1,072	13,177	100.0	7.5	92.5
Murder and nonnegligent manslaughter	100.0	4.2	95.8	376	26	350	100.0	6.9	93.1
Rape[4]	100.0	5.6	94.4	880	82	798	100.0	9.3	90.7
Robbery	100.0	6.7	93.3	713	43	670	100.0	6.0	94.0
Aggravated assault	100.0	6.8	93.2	12,280	921	11,359	100.0	7.5	92.5
Property crime[3]	100.0	9.2	90.8	26,177	1,355	24,822	100.0	5.2	94.8
Burglary	100.0	7.3	92.7	7,194	355	6,839	100.0	4.9	95.1
Larceny-theft	100.0	9.4	90.6	15,797	781	15,016	100.0	4.9	95.1
Motor vehicle theft	100.0	13.0	87.0	2,891	202	2,689	100.0	7.0	93.0
Arson	100.0	11.4	88.6	295	17	278	100.0	5.8	94.2
Other assaults	100.0	7.1	92.9	36,688	2,182	34,506	100.0	5.9	94.1
Forgery and counterfeiting	100.0	19.0	81.0	1,645	129	1,516	100.0	7.8	92.2
Fraud	100.0	0.0	100.0	5,538	259	5,279	100.0	4.7	95.3
Embezzlement	100.0	0.0	100.0	294	14	280	100.0	4.8	95.2
Stolen property; buying, receiving, possessing	100.0	18.9	81.1	2,640	186	2,454	100.0	7.0	93.0
Vandalism	100.0	5.8	94.2	5,191	282	4,909	100.0	5.4	94.6
Weapons; carrying, possessing, etc.	100.0	7.7	92.3	4,510	384	4,126	100.0	8.5	91.5
Prostitution and commercialized vice	100.0			96	9	87	100.0	9.4	90.6
Sex offenses (except forcible rape and prostitution)	100.0	3.2	96.8	1,753	128	1,625	100.0	7.3	92.7
Drug abuse violations	100.0	10.5	89.5	70,295	5,852	64,443	100.0	8.3	91.7
Gambling	100.0	50.0	50.0	95	38	57	100.0	40.0	60.0
Offenses against the family and children	100.0	9.1	90.9	6,753	380	6,373	100.0	5.6	94.4
Driving under the influence	100.0	9.2	90.8	83,632	6,860	76,772	100.0	8.2	91.8
Liquor laws	100.0	6.6	93.4	6,315	566	5,749	100.0	9.0	91.0
Drunkenness	100.0	12.6	87.4	9,936	1,250	8,686	100.0	12.6	87.4
Disorderly conduct	100.0	8.3	91.7	8,469	498	7,971	100.0	5.9	94.1
Vagrancy	100.0	0.0	100.0	178	23	155	100.0	12.9	87.1
All other offenses (except traffic)	100.0	10.3	89.7	177,347	12,963	164,384	100.0	7.3	92.7
Suspicion	100.0	0.0	100.0	56	3	53	100.0	5.4	94.6
Curfew and loitering law violations	100.0	10.6	89.4	NA	NA	NA	NA	NA	NA

NA = Not available.
1 Because of rounding, the percentages may not sum to 100.   2 The ethnicity totals are representative of those agencies that provided ethnicity breakdowns. Not all agencies provide ethnicity data; therefore, the race and ethnicity totals will not be equal.   3 Violent crimes are offenses of murder and nonnegligent manslaughter, rape, robbery, and aggravated assault. Property crimes are offenses of burglary, larceny-theft, motor vehicle theft, and arson.   4 The rape figures in this table are aggregate totals of the data submitted based on both the legacy and revised Uniform Crime Reporting definitions.

Table 62. Arrest Trends, Suburban Areas,[1] 2016–2017

(Number, percent change; 6,553 agencies; 2017 estimated population 106,103,846; 2016 estimated population 105,016,859.)

	Number of persons arrested								
	Total, all ages			Under 18 years of age			18 years of age and over		
Offense charged	2016	2017	Percent change	2016	2017	Percent change	2016	2017	Percent change
Total[2]	3,216,993	3,196,082	-0.7	255,500	248,483	-2.7	2,961,493	2,947,599	-0.5
Violent crime[3]	127,612	128,232	+0.5	13,094	13,237	+1.1	114,518	114,995	+0.4
Murder and nonnegligent manslaughter	2,670	2,680	+0.4	187	171	-8.6	2,483	2,509	+1.0
Rape[4]	6,379	6,277	-1.6	1,052	1,104	+4.9	5,327	5,173	-2.9
Robbery	20,136	19,795	-1.7	3,833	3,821	-0.3	16,303	15,974	-2.0
Aggravated assault	98,427	99,480	+1.1	8,022	8,141	+1.5	90,405	91,339	+1.0
Property crime[3]	389,976	367,777	-5.7	50,580	48,382	-4.3	339,396	319,395	-5.9
Burglary	57,988	55,329	-4.6	8,714	8,677	-0.4	49,274	46,652	-5.3
Larceny-theft	307,461	286,849	-6.7	37,810	35,509	-6.1	269,651	251,340	-6.8
Motor vehicle theft	21,792	23,038	+5.7	3,239	3,451	+6.5	18,553	19,587	+5.6
Arson	2,735	2,561	-6.4	817	745	-8.8	1,918	1,816	-5.3
Other assaults	294,523	289,911	-1.6	39,754	38,120	-4.1	254,769	251,791	-1.2
Forgery and counterfeiting	18,568	18,313	-1.4	472	467	-1.1	18,096	17,846	-1.4
Fraud	41,757	40,830	-2.2	1,331	1,303	-2.1	40,426	39,527	-2.2
Embezzlement	4,442	4,520	+1.8	137	145	+5.8	4,305	4,375	+1.6
Stolen property; buying, receiving, possessing	28,858	30,350	+5.2	2,786	2,865	+2.8	26,072	27,485	+5.4
Vandalism	54,092	53,225	-1.6	11,928	11,806	-1.0	42,164	41,419	-1.8
Weapons; carrying, possessing, etc.	40,469	42,254	+4.4	5,141	4,898	-4.7	35,328	37,356	+5.7
Prostitution and commercialized vice	5,280	5,139	-2.7	94	66	-29.8	5,186	5,073	-2.2
Sex offenses (except forcible rape and prostitution)	15,019	14,533	-3.2	2,700	2,868	+6.2	12,319	11,665	-5.3
Drug abuse violations	496,336	523,886	+5.6	33,999	33,969	-0.1	462,337	489,917	+6.0
Gambling	972	711	-26.9	46	71	+54.3	926	640	-30.9
Offenses against the family and children	33,537	33,813	+0.8	959	979	+2.1	32,578	32,834	+0.8
Driving under the influence	359,190	346,455	-3.5	2,125	1,986	-6.5	357,065	344,469	-3.5
Liquor laws	73,329	65,687	-10.4	13,302	12,579	-5.4	60,027	53,108	-11.5
Drunkenness	90,155	85,265	-5.4	1,513	1,329	-12.2	88,642	83,936	-5.3
Disorderly conduct	110,337	106,192	-3.8	21,349	20,950	-1.9	88,988	85,242	-4.2
Vagrancy	4,982	4,220	-15.3	235	244	+3.8	4,747	3,976	-16.2
All other offenses (except traffic)	1,020,922	1,028,499	+0.7	47,318	45,949	-2.9	973,604	982,550	+0.9
Suspicion	334	338	+1.2	50	38	-24.0	284	300	+5.6
Curfew and loitering law violations	6,637	6,270	-5.5	6,637	6,270	-5.5	NA	NA	NA

NA = Not available.
1 Suburban areas include law enforcement agencies in cities with less than 50,000 inhabitants and county law enforcement agencies that are within a Metropolitan Statistical Area. Suburban areas exclude all metropolitan agencies associated with a principal city.   2 Does not include suspicion.   3 Violent crimes are offenses of murder and nonnegligent manslaughter, rape, robbery, and aggravated assault.   Property crimes are offenses of burglary, larceny-theft, motor vehicle theft, and arson.
4 The rape figures in this table are aggregate totals of the data submitted based on both the legacy and revised Uniform Crime Reporting definitions.

Table 63. Arrest Trends, Suburban Areas[1], by Age and Sex, 2016–2017

(Number, percent change; 6,553 agencies; 2017 estimated population 106,103,846; 2016 estimated population 105,016,859.)

Offense charged	Male						Female					
	Total			Under 18			Total			Under 18		
	2016	2017	Percent change	2016	2017	Percent change	2016	2017	Percent change	2016	2017	Percent change
Total[2]	2,335,277	2,317,272	-0.8	180,748	176,844	-2.2	881,716	878,810	-0.3	74,752	71,639	-4.2
Violent crime[3]	101,758	102,238	+0.5	10,603	10,620	+0.2	25,854	25,994	+0.5	2,491	2,617	+5.1
Murder and nonnegligent manslaughter	2,321	2,328	+0.3	167	161	-3.6	349	352	+0.9	20	10	-50.0
Rape[4]	6,212	6,107	-1.7	1,017	1,071	+5.3	167	170	+1.8	35	33	-5.7
Robbery	17,143	16,835	-1.8	3,460	3,447	-0.4	2,993	2,960	-1.1	373	374	+0.3
Aggravated assault	76,082	76,968	+1.2	5,959	5,941	-0.3	22,345	22,512	+0.7	2,063	2,200	+6.6
Property crime[3]	244,720	233,797	-4.5	33,976	33,934	-0.1	145,256	133,980	-7.8	16,604	14,448	-13.0
Burglary	47,613	45,221	-5.0	7,770	7,677	-1.2	10,375	10,108	-2.6	944	1,000	+5.9
Larceny-theft	177,958	168,630	-5.2	22,906	22,834	-0.3	129,503	118,219	-8.7	14,904	12,675	-15.0
Motor vehicle theft	16,960	17,848	+5.2	2,603	2,775	+6.6	4,832	5,190	+7.4	636	676	+6.3
Arson	2,189	2,098	-4.2	697	648	-7.0	546	463	-15.2	120	97	-19.2
Other assaults	210,654	206,426	-2.0	25,681	24,439	-4.8	83,869	83,485	-0.5	14,073	13,681	-2.8
Forgery and counterfeiting	12,106	12,140	+0.3	335	364	+8.7	6,462	6,173	-4.5	137	103	-24.8
Fraud	26,023	25,601	-1.6	892	851	-4.6	15,734	15,229	-3.2	439	452	+3.0
Embezzlement	2,299	2,308	+0.4	78	74	-5.1	2,143	2,212	+3.2	59	71	+20.3
Stolen property; buying, receiving, possessing	22,443	23,510	+4.8	2,362	2,366	+0.2	6,415	6,840	+6.6	424	499	+17.7
Vandalism	42,673	41,758	-2.1	9,954	9,756	-2.0	11,419	11,467	+0.4	1,974	2,050	+3.9
Weapons; carrying, possessing, etc.	36,100	37,664	+4.3	4,460	4,289	-3.8	4,369	4,590	+5.1	681	609	-10.6
Prostitution and commercialized vice	2,283	2,523	+10.5	38	38	0.0	2,997	2,616	-12.7	56	28	-50.0
Sex offenses (except forcible rape and prostitution)	13,845	13,494	-2.5	2,336	2,541	+8.8	1,174	1,039	-11.5	364	327	-10.2
Drug abuse violations	374,194	390,791	+4.4	25,981	25,707	-1.1	122,142	133,095	+9.0	8,018	8,262	+3.0
Gambling	562	483	-14.1	30	38	+26.7	410	228	-44.4	16	33	+106.3
Offenses against the family and children	25,042	24,989	-0.2	567	638	+12.5	8,495	8,824	+3.9	392	341	-13.0
Driving under the influence	265,855	255,930	-3.7	1,578	1,499	-5.0	93,335	90,525	-3.0	547	487	-11.0
Liquor laws	49,928	44,275	-11.3	7,999	7,476	-6.5	23,401	21,412	-8.5	5,303	5,103	-3.8
Drunkenness	70,900	66,287	-6.5	1,053	906	-14.0	19,255	18,978	-1.4	460	423	-8.0
Disorderly conduct	78,037	74,410	-4.6	13,986	13,741	-1.8	32,300	31,782	-1.6	7,363	7,209	-2.1
Vagrancy	3,868	3,221	-16.7	185	196	+5.9	1,114	999	-10.3	50	48	-4.0
All other offenses (except traffic)	747,471	751,253	+0.5	34,138	33,197	-2.8	273,451	277,246	+1.4	13,180	12,752	-3.2
Suspicion	256	249	-2.7	39	28	-28.2	78	89	+14.1	11	10	-9.1
Curfew and loitering law violations	4,516	4,174	-7.6	4,516	4,174	-7.6	2,121	2,096	-1.2	2,121	2,096	-1.2

1 Suburban areas include law enforcement agencies in cities with less than 50,000 inhabitants and county law enforcement agencies that are within a Metropolitan Statistical Area. Suburban areas exclude all metropolitan agencies associated with a principal city.   2 Does not include suspicion.   3 Violent crimes are offenses of murder and nonnegligent manslaughter, rape, robbery, and aggravated assault. Property crimes are offenses of burglary, larceny-theft, motor vehicle theft, and arson.
4 The rape figures in this table are aggregate totals of the data submitted based on both the legacy and revised Uniform Crime Reporting definitions.

Table 64. Arrests, Suburban Areas,[1] Distribution by Age, 2017

(Number, percent; 7,047 agencies; 2017 estimated population 113,235,593.)

Offense charged	Total, all ages	Ages under 15	Ages under 18	Ages 18 and over	Under 10	10–12	13–14	15	16	17	18	19	20
Total	3,530,999	76,017	274,676	3,256,323	1,769	17,290	56,958	49,857	65,824	82,978	117,466	124,119	121,089
Total percent distribution[2]	100.0	2.2	7.8	92.2	0.1	0.5	1.6	1.4	1.9	2.3	3.3	3.5	3.4
Violent crime[3]	140,609	4,251	14,661	125,948	98	1,025	3,128	2,716	3,528	4,166	4,777	4,790	4,645
Violent crime percent distribution[2]	100.0	3.0	10.4	89.6	0.1	0.7	2.2	1.9	2.5	3.0	3.4	3.4	3.3
Murder and nonnegligent manslaughter	3,028	13	200	2,828	0	2	11	26	63	98	146	181	149
Rape[4]	6,816	442	1,184	5,632	12	126	304	180	256	306	350	317	257
Robbery	22,101	744	4,310	17,791	6	90	648	873	1,215	1,478	1,609	1,435	1,193
Aggravated assault	108,664	3,052	8,967	99,697	80	807	2,165	1,637	1,994	2,284	2,672	2,857	3,046
Property crime[3]	412,185	14,999	54,084	358,101	291	3,303	11,405	10,527	13,211	15,347	17,515	15,553	13,461
Property crime percent distribution[2]	100.0	3.6	13.1	86.9	0.1	0.8	2.8	2.6	3.2	3.7	4.2	3.8	3.3
Burglary	60,693	2,940	9,581	51,112	59	628	2,253	2,000	2,153	2,488	2,819	2,464	2,203
Larceny-theft	323,577	10,759	39,913	283,664	208	2,398	8,153	7,528	9,882	11,744	13,500	12,068	10,406
Motor vehicle theft	25,021	839	3,786	21,235	4	117	718	862	1,056	1,029	1,072	941	783
Arson	2,894	461	804	2,090	20	160	281	137	120	86	124	80	69
Other assaults	321,445	16,555	42,025	279,420	433	4,565	11,557	8,166	8,910	8,394	7,526	7,718	8,126
Forgery and counterfeiting	20,114	75	506	19,608	1	20	54	66	122	243	619	868	843
Fraud	44,857	266	1,448	43,409	4	41	221	208	392	582	889	1,176	1,287
Embezzlement	5,056	5	168	4,888	0	0	5	11	59	93	287	247	266
Stolen property; buying, receiving, possessing	32,942	648	3,163	29,779	7	92	549	639	874	1,002	1,413	1,279	1,212
Vandalism	59,610	5,140	13,073	46,537	196	1,440	3,504	2,301	2,806	2,826	2,607	2,434	2,150
Weapons; carrying, possessing, etc.	46,348	1,847	5,418	40,930	56	536	1,255	925	1,142	1,504	1,847	1,886	1,717
Prostitution and commercialized vice	5,941	8	73	5,868	0	3	5	11	20	34	107	128	202
Sex offenses (except forcible rape and prostitution)	15,725	1,507	3,115	12,610	57	351	1,099	546	512	550	557	498	441
Drug abuse violations	568,349	5,068	36,808	531,541	36	709	4,323	5,285	9,674	16,781	30,019	31,028	28,212
Gambling	751	16	75	676	0	1	15	14	20	25	24	31	24
Offenses against the family and children	36,905	339	1,095	35,810	23	81	235	219	259	278	361	388	452
Driving under the influence	366,970	34	2,124	364,846	8	4	22	92	473	1,525	4,179	6,359	8,003
Liquor laws	73,340	1,436	13,491	59,849	6	128	1,302	1,996	3,637	6,422	13,441	12,852	10,082
Drunkenness	97,792	176	1,412	96,380	7	10	159	212	352	672	1,836	2,250	2,307
Disorderly conduct	121,552	8,951	23,611	97,941	162	2,231	6,558	4,714	5,073	4,873	4,359	3,818	3,695
Vagrancy	5,236	84	294	4,942	0	4	80	64	75	71	146	142	112
All other offenses (except traffic)	1,147,843	12,681	50,914	1,096,929	359	2,482	9,840	9,327	12,663	16,243	24,943	30,666	33,840
Suspicion	350	10	39	311	0	3	7	11	6	12	14	8	12
Curfew and loitering law violations	7,079	1,921	7,079	-	25	261	1,635	1,807	2,016	1,335	NA	NA	NA

Table 64. Arrests, Suburban Areas,[1] Distribution by Age, 2017—Continued

(Number, percent; 7,047 agencies; 2017 estimated population 113,235,593.)

Offense charged	21	22	23	24	25–29	30–34	35–39	40–44	45–49	50–54	55–59	60–64	65 and over
Total	118,854	119,783	121,958	124,787	607,966	499,735	402,491	267,769	227,430	179,665	122,153	58,956	42,102
Total percent distribution[2]	3.4	3.4	3.5	3.5	17.2	14.2	11.4	7.6	6.4	5.1	3.5	1.7	1.2
Violent crime[3]	4,775	4,679	4,774	4,705	23,136	19,156	15,485	10,222	8,587	6,993	4,880	2,323	2,021
Violent crime percent distribution[2]	3.4	3.3	3.4	3.3	16.5	13.6	11.0	7.3	6.1	5.0	3.5	1.7	1.4
Murder and nonnegligent manslaughter	124	135	126	119	556	384	302	186	134	114	79	47	46
Rape[4]	269	197	193	176	800	741	672	449	367	317	226	147	154
Robbery	989	886	872	823	3,490	2,336	1,530	930	711	529	300	94	64
Aggravated assault	3,393	3,461	3,583	3,587	18,290	15,695	12,981	8,657	7,375	6,033	4,275	2,035	1,757
Property crime[3]	12,438	12,265	12,562	13,021	66,391	56,452	44,522	28,333	24,745	19,147	12,237	5,551	3,908
Property crime percent distribution[2]	3.0	3.0	3.0	3.2	16.1	13.7	10.8	6.9	6.0	4.6	3.0	1.3	0.9
Burglary	1,944	1,893	1,998	1,998	10,175	8,315	6,226	3,804	3,019	2,228	1,259	487	280
Larceny-theft	9,633	9,462	9,620	10,099	51,264	44,250	35,209	22,835	20,361	16,099	10,470	4,861	3,527
Motor vehicle theft	786	842	886	860	4,606	3,605	2,817	1,522	1,207	697	409	144	58
Arson	75	68	58	64	346	282	270	172	158	123	99	59	43
Other assaults	9,014	9,152	9,623	10,052	49,971	43,169	36,772	25,804	22,470	17,753	11,716	5,743	4,811
Forgery and counterfeiting	668	673	688	699	3,789	3,327	2,593	1,657	1,314	892	589	247	142
Fraud	1,264	1,426	1,396	1,534	8,154	7,350	5,963	4,083	3,572	2,408	1,548	811	548
Embezzlement	229	207	183	179	850	635	590	384	332	221	145	84	49
Stolen property; buying, receiving, possessing	1,091	1,124	1,174	1,150	6,161	5,093	3,940	2,320	1,663	1,136	630	260	133
Vandalism	2,105	2,025	2,068	1,925	8,766	6,767	5,048	3,299	2,634	2,110	1,380	698	521
Weapons; carrying, possessing, etc.	1,985	1,953	1,904	1,840	8,232	6,051	4,562	2,806	2,138	1,657	1,195	617	540
Prostitution and commercialized vice	207	245	224	246	1,139	940	687	535	465	323	200	138	82
Sex offenses (except forcible rape and prostitution)	394	357	368	359	1,636	1,570	1,450	1,122	1,056	924	755	511	612
Drug abuse violations	25,276	24,604	23,957	23,489	105,173	77,913	58,972	35,108	27,577	20,101	12,511	5,304	2,297
Gambling	15	14	19	26	96	64	71	71	63	54	45	26	33
Offenses against the family and children	506	615	766	900	6,697	7,234	6,525	4,376	3,222	2,056	1,042	382	288
Driving under the influence	12,990	13,968	14,480	14,702	68,674	52,700	42,677	31,983	29,327	25,443	19,874	11,013	8,474
Liquor laws	1,570	1,162	950	930	3,650	2,964	2,600	2,010	2,126	2,169	1,806	932	605
Drunkenness	3,552	3,105	3,015	3,101	14,516	12,912	11,519	8,931	8,943	8,650	6,759	3,112	1,872
Disorderly conduct	4,242	4,018	3,529	3,610	16,432	13,250	10,968	7,607	7,229	6,397	4,613	2,298	1,876
Vagrancy	116	131	154	126	752	655	598	421	495	415	387	187	105
All other offenses (except traffic)	36,408	38,057	40,108	42,178	213,706	181,481	146,901	96,672	79,448	60,803	39,829	18,715	13,174
Suspicion	9	3	16	15	45	52	48	25	24	13	12	4	11
Curfew and loitering law violations	NA	NA	NA	NA	NA	NA	NA	NA	NA	NA	NA	NA	NA

NA = Not available.

1 Suburban areas include law enforcement agencies in cities with less than 50,000 inhabitants and county law enforcement agencies that are within a Metropolitan Statistical Area Suburban areas exclude all metropolitan agencies associated with a principal city.   2 Because of rounding, the percentages may not sum to 100.   3 Violent crimes are offenses of murder and nonnegligent manslaughter, rape, robbery, and aggravated assault. Property crimes are offenses of burglary, larceny-theft, motor vehicle theft, and arson.   4 The rape figures in this table are aggregate totals of the data submitted based on both the legacy and revised Uniform Crime Reporting definitions.

Table 65. Arrests, Suburban Areas,[1] Persons Under 15, 18, 21, and 25 Years of Age, 2017

(Number, percent; 7,047 agencies; 2017 estimated population 113,235,593.)

Offense charged	Total, all ages	Number of persons arrested				Percent of total all ages			
		Under 15	Under 18	Under 21	Under 25	Under 15	Under 18	Under 21	Under 25
Total	3,530,999	76,017	274,676	637,350	1,122,732	2.2	7.8	18.1	31.8
Violent crime[2]	140,609	4,251	14,661	28,873	47,806	3.0	10.4	20.5	34.0
Murder and nonnegligent manslaughter	3,028	13	200	676	1,180	0.4	6.6	22.3	39.0
Rape[3]	6,816	442	1,184	2,108	2,943	6.5	17.4	30.9	43.2
Robbery	22,101	744	4,310	8,547	12,117	3.4	19.5	38.7	54.8
Aggravated assault	108,664	3,052	8,967	17,542	31,566	2.8	8.3	16.1	29.0
Property crime[2]	412,185	14,999	54,084	100,613	150,899	3.6	13.1	24.4	36.6
Burglary	60,693	2,940	9,581	17,067	24,900	4.8	15.8	28.1	41.0
Larceny-theft	323,577	10,759	39,913	75,887	114,701	3.3	12.3	23.5	35.4
Motor vehicle theft	25,021	839	3,786	6,582	9,956	3.4	15.1	26.3	39.8
Arson	2,894	461	804	1,077	1,342	15.9	27.8	37.2	46.4
Other assaults	321,445	16,555	42,025	65,395	103,236	5.2	13.1	20.3	32.1
Forgery and counterfeiting	20,114	75	506	2,836	5,564	0.4	2.5	14.1	27.7
Fraud	44,857	266	1,448	4,800	10,420	0.6	3.2	10.7	23.2
Embezzlement	5,056	5	168	968	1,766	0.1	3.3	19.1	34.9
Stolen property; buying, receiving, possession	32,942	648	3,163	7,067	11,606	2.0	9.6	21.5	35.2
Vandalism	59,610	5,140	13,073	20,264	28,387	8.6	21.9	34.0	47.6
Weapons; carrying, possessing, etc.	46,348	1,847	5,418	10,868	18,550	4.0	11.7	23.4	40.0
Prostitution and commercialized vice	5,941	8	73	510	1,432	0.1	1.2	8.6	24.1
Sex offenses (except forcible rape and prostitution)	15,725	1,507	3,115	4,611	6,089	9.6	19.8	29.3	38.7
Drug abuse violations	568,349	5,068	36,808	126,067	223,393	0.9	6.5	22.2	39.3
Gambling	751	16	75	154	228	2.1	10.0	20.5	30.4
Offenses against the family and children	36,905	339	1,095	2,296	5,083	0.9	3.0	6.2	13.8
Driving under the influence	366,970	34	2,124	20,665	76,805	*	0.6	5.6	20.9
Liquor laws	73,340	1,436	13,491	49,866	54,478	2.0	18.4	68.0	74.3
Drunkenness	97,792	176	1,412	7,805	20,578	0.2	1.4	8.0	21.0
Disorderly conduct	121,552	8,951	23,611	35,483	50,882	7.4	19.4	29.2	41.9
Vagrancy	5,236	84	294	694	1,221	1.6	5.6	13.3	23.3
All other offenses (except traffic)	1,147,843	12,681	50,914	140,363	297,114	1.1	4.4	12.2	25.9
Suspicion	350	10	39	73	116	2.9	11.1	20.9	33.1
Curfew and loitering law violations	7,079	1,921	7,079	7,079	7,079	27.1	100.0	100.0	100.0

* = Less than one-tenth of one percent.
1 Suburban areas include law enforcement agencies in cities with less than 50,000 inhabitants and county law enforcement agencies that are within a Metropolitan Statistical Area. Suburban areas exclude all metropolitan agencies associated with a principal city.   2 Violent crimes are offenses of murder and nonnegligent manslaughter, rape, robbery, and aggravated assault. Property crimes are offenses of burglary, larceny-theft, motor vehicle theft, and arson.   3 The rape figures in this table are aggregate totals of the data submitted based on both the legacy and revised Uniform Crime Reporting definitions.

Table 66. Arrests, Suburban Areas,[1] Distribution by Sex, 2017

(Number, percent; 7,047 agencies; 2017 estimated population 113,235,593.)

Offense charged	Number of persons arrested			Percent male	Percent female	Percent distribution[2]		
	Total	Male	Female			Total	Male	Female
Total	3,530,999	2,556,900	974,099	72.4	27.6	100.0	100.0	100.0
Violent crime[3]	140,609	112,110	28,499	79.7	20.3	4.0	4.4	2.9
Murder and nonnegligent manslaughter	3,028	2,637	391	87.1	12.9	0.1	0.1	*
Rape[4]	6,816	6,637	179	97.4	2.6	0.2	0.3	*
Robbery	22,101	18,833	3,268	85.2	14.8	0.6	0.7	0.3
Aggravated assault	108,664	84,003	24,661	77.3	22.7	3.1	3.3	2.5
Property crime[3]	412,185	261,372	150,813	63.4	36.6	11.7	10.2	15.5
Burglary	60,693	49,664	11,029	81.8	18.2	1.7	1.9	1.1
Larceny-theft	323,577	189,978	133,599	58.7	41.3	9.2	7.4	13.7
Motor vehicle theft	25,021	19,375	5,646	77.4	22.6	0.7	0.8	0.6
Arson	2,894	2,355	539	81.4	18.6	0.1	0.1	0.1
Other assaults	321,445	228,719	92,726	71.2	28.8	9.1	8.9	9.5
Forgery and counterfeiting	20,114	13,276	6,838	66.0	34.0	0.6	0.5	0.7
Fraud	44,857	28,064	16,793	62.6	37.4	1.3	1.1	1.7
Embezzlement	5,056	2,554	2,502	50.5	49.5	0.1	0.1	0.3
Stolen property; buying, receiving, possessing	32,942	25,532	7,410	77.5	22.5	0.9	1.0	0.8
Vandalism	59,610	46,586	13,024	78.2	21.8	1.7	1.8	1.3
Weapons; carrying, possessing, etc.	46,348	41,366	4,982	89.3	10.7	1.3	1.6	0.5
Prostitution and commercialized vice	5,941	2,813	3,128	47.3	52.7	0.2	0.1	0.3
Sex offenses (except forcible rape and prostitution)	15,725	14,585	1,140	92.8	7.2	0.4	0.6	0.1
Drug abuse violations	568,349	423,999	144,350	74.6	25.4	16.1	16.6	14.8
Gambling	751	517	234	68.8	31.2	*	*	*
Offenses against the family and children	36,905	27,033	9,872	73.3	26.7	1.0	1.1	1.0
Driving under the influence	366,970	271,051	95,919	73.9	26.1	10.4	10.6	9.8
Liquor laws	73,340	49,851	23,489	68.0	32.0	2.1	1.9	2.4
Drunkenness	97,792	76,135	21,657	77.9	22.1	2.8	3.0	2.2
Disorderly conduct	121,552	84,973	36,579	69.9	30.1	3.4	3.3	3.8
Vagrancy	5,236	3,989	1,247	76.2	23.8	0.1	0.2	0.1
All other offenses (except traffic)	1,147,843	837,442	310,401	73.0	27.0	32.5	32.8	31.9
Suspicion	350	256	94	73.1	26.9	*	*	*
Curfew and loitering law violations	7,079	4,677	2,402	66.1	33.9	0.2	0.2	0.2

* = Less than one-tenth of one percent.
1 Suburban areas include law enforcement agencies in cities with less than 50,000 inhabitants and county law enforcement agencies that are within a Metropolitan Statistical Area. Suburban areas exclude all metropolitan agencies associated with a principal city.   2 Because of rounding, the percentages may not sum to 100.   3 Violent crimes are offenses of murder and nonnegligent manslaughter, rape, robbery, and aggravated assault. Property crimes are offenses of burglary, larceny-theft, motor vehicle theft, and arson.   4 The rape figures in this table are aggregate totals of the data submitted based on both the legacy and revised Uniform Crime Reporting definitions.

Table 67. Arrests, Suburban Areas,[1] Distribution by Race, 2017

(Number, percent; 7,043 agencies; 2017 estimated population 113,235,382.)

Offense charged	Total arrests						Percent distribution[2]						Arrests under 18					
	Total	White	Black	American Indian or Alaskan Native	Asian	Native Hawaiian or Other Pacific Islander	Total	White	Black	American Indian or Alaskan Native	Asian	Native Hawaiian or Other Pacific Islander	Total	White	Black	American Indian or Alaskan Native	Asian	Native Hawaiian or Other Pacific Islander
Total	3,499,848	2,519,094	901,211	35,099	38,843	5,601	100.0	72.0	25.8	1.0	1.1	0.2	271,205	178,105	87,210	2,586	2,840	464
Violent crime[3]	139,707	90,664	45,819	1,296	1,648	280	100.0	64.9	32.8	0.9	1.2	0.2	14,532	7,416	6,877	110	105	24
Murder and nonnegligent manslaughter	3,014	1,580	1,364	24	46	0	100.0	52.4	45.3	0.8	1.5	0.0	197	82	112	2	1	0
Rape[4]	6,740	5,039	1,544	56	95	6	100.0	74.8	22.9	0.8	1.4	0.1	1,164	857	293	2	12	0
Robbery	21,951	10,324	11,348	103	136	40	100.0	47.0	51.7	0.5	0.6	0.2	4,272	1,411	2,822	12	20	7
Aggravated assault	108,002	73,721	31,563	1,113	1,371	234	100.0	68.3	29.2	1.0	1.3	0.2	8,899	5,066	3,650	94	72	17
Property crime[3]	406,807	280,451	118,603	3,014	4,247	492	100.0	68.9	29.2	0.7	1.0	0.1	53,242	30,591	21,519	393	653	86
Burglary	60,271	43,417	15,872	330	539	113	100.0	72.0	26.3	0.5	0.9	0.2	9,501	5,820	3,530	58	74	19
Larceny-theft	318,816	216,850	95,938	2,398	3,370	260	100.0	68.0	30.1	0.8	1.1	0.1	39,197	22,149	16,182	281	529	56
Motor vehicle theft	24,854	18,030	6,148	263	298	115	100.0	72.5	24.7	1.1	1.2	0.5	3,752	2,031	1,618	49	43	11
Arson	2,866	2,154	645	23	40	4	100.0	75.2	22.5	0.8	1.4	0.1	792	591	189	5	7	0
Other assaults	317,789	223,823	86,855	3,304	3,407	400	100.0	70.4	27.3	1.0	1.1	0.1	41,419	24,888	15,784	375	323	49
Forgery and counterfeiting	19,989	12,791	6,777	128	278	15	100.0	64.0	33.9	0.6	1.4	0.1	504	306	186	2	10	0
Fraud	44,425	30,288	13,352	255	501	29	100.0	68.2	30.1	0.6	1.1	0.1	1,428	827	574	8	19	0
Embezzlement	5,018	3,145	1,795	15	60	3	100.0	62.7	35.8	0.3	1.2	0.1	164	93	69	0	2	0
Stolen property; buying, receiving, possessing	32,616	21,779	10,226	294	287	30	100.0	66.8	31.4	0.9	0.9	0.1	3,117	1,397	1,660	34	23	3
Vandalism	58,985	43,159	14,614	603	574	35	100.0	73.2	24.8	1.0	1.0	0.1	12,864	9,303	3,327	133	94	7
Weapons; carrying, possessing, etc.	46,041	27,940	17,236	303	468	94	100.0	60.7	37.4	0.7	1.0	0.2	5,386	3,157	2,123	38	61	7
Prostitution and commercialized vice	5,855	3,432	1,909	22	485	7	100.0	58.6	32.6	0.4	8.3	0.1	73	43	30	0	0	0
Sex offenses (except forcible rape and prostitution)	15,585	11,847	3,358	112	244	24	100.0	76.0	21.5	0.7	1.6	0.2	3,065	2,301	709	17	36	2
Drug abuse violations	562,972	408,248	144,540	3,594	5,884	706	100.0	72.5	25.7	0.6	1.0	0.1	36,342	28,312	7,165	301	477	87
Gambling	743	376	237	9	89	32	100.0	50.6	31.9	1.2	12.0	4.3	70	30	37	1	2	0
Offenses against the family and children	36,713	25,033	10,838	587	250	5	100.0	68.2	29.5	1.6	0.7	*	1,093	756	292	38	7	0
Driving under the influence	363,810	301,725	51,416	3,162	6,864	643	100.0	82.9	14.1	0.9	1.9	0.2	2,092	1,878	147	34	32	1
Liquor laws	72,288	59,799	9,860	1,211	1,330	88	100.0	82.7	13.6	1.7	1.8	0.1	13,263	11,977	813	237	215	21
Drunkenness	97,367	81,060	13,599	1,582	999	127	100.0	83.3	14.0	1.6	1.0	0.1	1,403	1,236	130	21	16	0
Disorderly conduct	120,709	80,987	36,852	1,758	1,039	73	100.0	67.1	30.5	1.5	0.9	0.1	23,447	12,936	10,117	228	151	15
Vagrancy	5,220	3,685	1,473	27	33	2	100.0	70.6	28.2	0.5	0.6	*	290	138	148	1	3	0
All other offenses (except traffic)	1,139,863	803,643	309,978	13,750	10,041	2,451	100.0	70.5	27.2	1.2	0.9	0.2	50,360	35,478	13,722	559	500	101
Suspicion	334	192	117	17	4	4	100.0	57.5	35.0	5.1	1.2	1.2	39	15	24	0	0	0
Curfew and loitering law violations	7,012	5,027	1,757	56	111	61	100.0	71.7	25.1	0.8	1.6	0.9	7,012	5,027	1,757	56	111	61

Table 67. Arrests, Suburban Areas,[1] Distribution by Race, 2017—Continued

(Number, percent; 7,043 agencies; 2017 estimated population 113,235,382.)

Offense charged	Percent distribution[2]						Arrests 18 and over						Percent distribution[2]					
	Total	White	Black	American Indian or Alaskan Native	Asian	Native Hawaiian or Other Pacific Islander	Total	White	Black	American Indian or Alaskan Native	Asian	Native Hawaiian or Other Pacific Islander	Total	White	Black	American Indian or Alaskan Native	Asian	Native Hawaiian or Other Pacific Islander
Total	100.0	65.7	32.2	1.0	1.0	0.2	3,228,643	2,340,989	814,001	32,513	36,003	5,137	100.0	72.5	25.2	1.0	1.1	0.2
Violent crime[3]	100.0	51.0	47.3	0.8	0.7	0.2	125,175	83,248	38,942	1,186	1,543	256	100.0	66.5	31.1	0.9	1.2	0.2
Murder and nonnegligent manslaughter	100.0	41.6	56.9	1.0	0.5	0.0	2,817	1,498	1,252	22	45	0	100.0	53.2	44.4	0.8	1.6	0.0
Rape[4]	100.0	73.6	25.2	0.2	1.0	0.0	5,576	4,182	1,251	54	83	6	100.0	75.0	22.4	1.0	1.5	0.1
Robbery	100.0	33.0	66.1	0.3	0.5	0.2	17,679	8,913	8,526	91	116	33	100.0	50.4	48.2	0.5	0.7	0.2
Aggravated assault	100.0	56.9	41.0	1.1	0.8	0.2	99,103	68,655	27,913	1,019	1,299	217	100.0	69.3	28.2	1.0	1.3	0.2
Property crime[3]	100.0	57.5	40.4	0.7	1.2	0.2	353,565	249,860	97,084	2,621	3,594	406	100.0	70.7	27.5	0.7	1.0	0.1
Burglary	100.0	61.3	37.2	0.6	0.8	0.2	50,770	37,597	12,342	272	465	94	100.0	74.1	24.3	0.5	0.9	0.2
Larceny-theft	100.0	56.5	41.3	0.7	1.3	0.1	279,619	194,701	79,756	2,117	2,841	204	100.0	69.6	28.5	0.8	1.0	0.1
Motor vehicle theft	100.0	54.1	43.1	1.3	1.1	0.3	21,102	15,999	4,530	214	255	104	100.0	75.8	21.5	1.0	1.2	0.5
Arson	100.0	74.6	23.9	0.6	0.9	0.0	2,074	1,563	456	18	33	4	100.0	75.4	22.0	0.9	1.6	0.2
Other assaults	100.0	60.1	38.1	0.9	0.8	0.1	276,370	198,935	71,071	2,929	3,084	351	100.0	72.0	25.7	1.1	1.1	0.1
Forgery and counterfeiting	100.0	60.7	36.9	0.4	2.0	0.0	19,485	12,485	6,591	126	268	15	100.0	64.1	33.8	0.6	1.4	0.1
Fraud	100.0	57.9	40.2	0.6	1.3	0.0	42,997	29,461	12,778	247	482	29	100.0	68.5	29.7	0.6	1.1	0.1
Embezzlement	100.0	56.7	42.1	0.0	1.2	0.0	4,854	3,052	1,726	15	58	3	100.0	62.9	35.6	0.3	1.2	0.1
Stolen property; buying, receiving, possessing	100.0	44.8	53.3	1.1	0.7	0.1	29,499	20,382	8,566	260	264	27	100.0	69.1	29.0	0.9	0.9	0.1
Vandalism	100.0	72.3	25.9	1.0	0.7	0.1	46,121	33,856	11,287	470	480	28	100.0	73.4	24.5	1.0	1.0	0.1
Weapons; carrying, possessing, etc.	100.0	58.6	39.4	0.7	1.1	0.1	40,655	24,783	15,113	265	407	87	100.0	61.0	37.2	0.7	1.0	0.2
Prostitution and commercialized vice	100.0	58.9	41.1	0.0	0.0	0.0	5,782	3,389	1,879	22	485	7	100.0	58.6	32.5	0.4	8.4	0.1
Sex offenses (except forcible rape and prostitution)	100.0	75.1	23.1	0.6	1.2	0.1	12,520	9,546	2,649	95	208	22	100.0	76.2	21.2	0.8	1.7	0.2
Drug abuse violations	100.0	77.9	19.7	0.8	1.3	0.2	526,630	379,936	137,375	3,293	5,407	619	100.0	72.1	26.1	0.6	1.0	0.1
Gambling	100.0	42.9	52.9	1.4	2.9	0.0	673	346	200	8	87	32	100.0	51.4	29.7	1.2	12.9	4.8
Offenses against the family and children	100.0	69.2	26.7	3.5	0.6	0.0	35,620	24,277	10,546	549	243	5	100.0	68.2	29.6	1.5	0.7	*
Driving under the influence	100.0	89.8	7.0	1.6	1.5	*	361,718	299,847	51,269	3,128	6,832	642	100.0	82.9	14.2	0.9	1.9	0.2
Liquor laws	100.0	90.3	6.1	1.8	1.6	0.2	59,025	47,822	9,047	974	1,115	67	100.0	81.0	15.3	1.7	1.9	0.1
Drunkenness	100.0	88.1	9.3	1.5	1.1	0.0	95,964	79,824	13,469	1,561	983	127	100.0	83.2	14.0	1.6	1.0	0.1
Disorderly conduct	100.0	55.2	43.1	1.0	0.6	0.1	97,262	68,051	26,735	1,530	888	58	100.0	70.0	27.5	1.6	0.9	0.1
Vagrancy	100.0	47.6	51.0	0.3	1.0	0.0	4,930	3,547	1,325	26	30	2	100.0	71.9	26.9	0.5	0.6	*
All other offenses (except traffic)	100.0	70.4	27.2	1.1	1.0	0.2	1,089,503	768,165	296,256	13,191	9,541	2,350	100.0	70.5	27.2	1.2	0.9	0.2
Suspicion	100.0	38.5	61.5	0.0	0.0	0.0	295	177	93	17	4	4	100.0	60.0	31.5	5.8	1.4	1.4
Curfew and loitering law violations	100.0	71.7	25.1	0.8	1.6	0.9	NA	NA	NA	NA	NA	NA	NA	NA	NA	NA	NA	NA

NA = Not available.
* = Less than one-tenth of one percent.
1 Suburban areas include law enforcement agencies in cities with less than 50,000 inhabitants and county law enforcement agencies that are within a Metropolitan Statistical Area. Suburban areas exclude all metropolitan agencies associated with a principal city.   2 Because of rounding, the percentages may not sum to 100.   3 Violent crimes are offenses of murder and nonnegligent manslaughter, rape, robbery, and aggravated assault. Property crimes are offenses of burglary, larceny-theft, motor vehicle theft, and arson.   4 The rape figures in this table are aggregate totals of the data submitted based on both the legacy and revised Uniform Crime Reporting definitions.

Table 67A. Arrests, Suburban Areas,[1] Distribution by Ethnicity, 2017

(Number, percent; 7,043 agencies; 2017 estimated population 113,235,382.)

Offense charged	Total arrests			Percent distribution[2]			Arrests under 18		
	Total[3]	Hispanic or Latino	Not Hispanic or Latino	Total[3]	Hispanic or Latino	Not Hispanic or Latino	Total[3]	Hispanic or Latino	Not Hispanic or Latino
Total	2,899,300	447,730	2,451,570	100.0	15.4	84.6	207,332	37,066	170,266
Violent crime[4]	114,008	23,125	90,883	100.0	20.3	79.7	11,068	2,223	8,845
Murder and nonnegligent manslaughter	2,121	449	1,672	100.0	21.2	78.8	124	34	90
Rape[5]	5,288	1,221	4,067	100.0	23.1	76.9	883	157	726
Robbery	16,698	2,832	13,866	100.0	17.0	83.0	3,085	600	2,485
Aggravated assault	89,901	18,623	71,278	100.0	20.7	79.3	6,976	1,432	5,544
Property crime[4]	315,198	38,209	276,989	100.0	12.1	87.9	36,285	6,091	30,194
Burglary	47,693	7,419	40,274	100.0	15.6	84.4	6,489	1,381	5,108
Larceny-theft	244,310	25,608	218,702	100.0	10.5	89.5	26,438	3,969	22,469
Motor vehicle theft	20,899	4,846	16,053	100.0	23.2	76.8	2,733	636	2,097
Arson	2,296	336	1,960	100.0	14.6	85.4	625	105	520
Other assaults	266,265	37,824	228,441	100.0	14.2	85.8	33,927	5,805	28,122
Forgery and counterfeiting	16,219	2,290	13,929	100.0	14.1	85.9	403	69	334
Fraud	35,430	3,546	31,884	100.0	10.0	90.0	1,034	143	891
Embezzlement	4,255	350	3,905	100.0	8.2	91.8	138	22	116
Stolen property; buying, receiving, possessing	23,624	3,998	19,626	100.0	16.9	83.1	2,078	434	1,644
Vandalism	49,101	6,988	42,113	100.0	14.2	85.8	10,039	1,609	8,430
Weapons; carrying, possessing, etc.	36,559	7,370	29,189	100.0	20.2	79.8	4,221	1,041	3,180
Prostitution and commercialized vice	4,436	772	3,664	100.0	17.4	82.6	55	8	47
Sex offenses (except forcible rape and prostitution)	12,843	2,821	10,022	100.0	22.0	78.0	2,461	490	1,971
Drug abuse violations	461,264	77,367	383,897	100.0	16.8	83.2	28,085	6,381	21,704
Gambling	534	154	380	100.0	28.8	71.2	57	17	40
Offenses against the family and children	31,163	3,597	27,566	100.0	11.5	88.5	907	148	759
Driving under the influence	325,714	70,637	255,077	100.0	21.7	78.3	1,829	324	1,505
Liquor laws	60,193	6,637	53,556	100.0	11.0	89.0	11,375	1,343	10,032
Drunkenness	96,435	18,603	77,832	100.0	19.3	80.7	1,357	383	974
Disorderly conduct	95,487	9,431	86,056	100.0	9.9	90.1	17,575	2,131	15,444
Vagrancy	3,280	471	2,809	100.0	14.4	85.6	158	23	135
All other offenses (except traffic)	941,495	132,371	809,124	100.0	14.1	85.9	38,636	7,243	31,393
Suspicion	188	32	156	100.0	17.0	83.0	35	1	34
Curfew and loitering law violations	5,609	1,137	4,472	100.0	20.3	79.7	5,609	1,137	4,472

Table 67A. Arrests, Suburban Areas,[1] Distribution by Ethnicity, 2017—Continued

(Number, percent; 7,043 agencies; 2017 estimated population 113,235,382.)

Offense charged	Percent distribution[2]			Arrests 18 and over			Percent distribution[2]		
	Total[3]	Hispanic or Latino	Not Hispanic or Latino	Total[3]	Hispanic or Latino	Not Hispanic or Latino	Total[3]	Hispanic or Latino	Not Hispanic or Latino
Total	100.0	17.9	82.1	2,691,968	410,664	2,281,304	100.0	15.3	84.7
Violent crime[4]	100.0	20.1	79.9	102,940	20,902	82,038	100.0	20.3	79.7
Murder and nonnegligent manslaughter	100.0	27.4	72.6	1,997	415	1,582	100.0	20.8	79.2
Rape[5]	100.0	17.8	82.2	4,405	1,064	3,341	100.0	24.2	75.8
Robbery	100.0	19.4	80.6	13,613	2,232	11,381	100.0	16.4	83.6
Aggravated assault	100.0	20.5	79.5	82,925	17,191	65,734	100.0	20.7	79.3
Property crime[4]	100.0	16.8	83.2	278,913	32,118	246,795	100.0	11.5	88.5
Burglary	100.0	21.3	78.7	41,204	6,038	35,166	100.0	14.7	85.3
Larceny-theft	100.0	15.0	85.0	217,872	21,639	196,233	100.0	9.9	90.1
Motor vehicle theft	100.0	23.3	76.7	18,166	4,210	13,956	100.0	23.2	76.8
Arson	100.0	16.8	83.2	1,671	231	1,440	100.0	13.8	86.2
Other assaults	100.0	17.1	82.9	232,338	32,019	200,319	100.0	13.8	86.2
Forgery and counterfeiting	100.0	17.1	82.9	15,816	2,221	13,595	100.0	14.0	86.0
Fraud	100.0	13.8	86.2	34,396	3,403	30,993	100.0	9.9	90.1
Embezzlement	100.0	15.9	84.1	4,117	328	3,789	100.0	8.0	92.0
Stolen property; buying, receiving, possessing	100.0	20.9	79.1	21,546	3,564	17,982	100.0	16.5	83.5
Vandalism	100.0	16.0	84.0	39,062	5,379	33,683	100.0	13.8	86.2
Weapons; carrying, possessing, etc.	100.0	24.7	75.3	32,338	6,329	26,009	100.0	19.6	80.4
Prostitution and commercialized vice	100.0	14.5	85.5	4,381	764	3,617	100.0	17.4	82.6
Sex offenses (except forcible rape and prostitution)	100.0	19.9	80.1	10,382	2,331	8,051	100.0	22.5	77.5
Drug abuse violations	100.0	22.7	77.3	433,179	70,986	362,193	100.0	16.4	83.6
Gambling	100.0	29.8	70.2	477	137	340	100.0	28.7	71.3
Offenses against the family and children	100.0	16.3	83.7	30,256	3,449	26,807	100.0	11.4	88.6
Driving under the influence	100.0	17.7	82.3	323,885	70,313	253,572	100.0	21.7	78.3
Liquor laws	100.0	11.8	88.2	48,818	5,294	43,524	100.0	10.8	89.2
Drunkenness	100.0	28.2	71.8	95,078	18,220	76,858	100.0	19.2	80.8
Disorderly conduct	100.0	12.1	87.9	77,912	7,300	70,612	100.0	9.4	90.6
Vagrancy	100.0	14.6	85.4	3,122	448	2,674	100.0	14.3	85.7
All other offenses (except traffic)	100.0	18.7	81.3	902,859	125,128	777,731	100.0	13.9	86.1
Suspicion	100.0	2.9	97.1	153	31	122	100.0	20.3	79.7
Curfew and loitering law violations	100.0	20.3	79.7	NA	NA	NA	NA	NA	NA

NA = Not available.
1 Suburban areas include law enforcement agencies in cities with less than 50,000 inhabitants and county law enforcement agencies that are within a Metropolitan Statistical Area. Suburban areas exclude all metropolitan agencies associated with a principal city.   2 Because of rounding, the percentages may not sum to 100.   3 The ethnicity totals are representative of those agencies that provided ethnicity breakdowns. Not all agencies provide ethnicity data; therefore, the race and ethnicity totals will not be equal.   4 Violent crimes are offenses of murder and nonnegligent manslaughter, rape, robbery, and aggravated assault. Property crimes are offenses of burglary, larceny-theft, motor vehicle theft, and arson.   5 The rape figures in this table are aggregate totals of the data submitted based on both the legacy and revised Uniform Crime Reporting definitions.

Table 68. Police Disposition of Juvenile Offenders Taken into Custody, 2017

(Number, percent.)

Population group	Total[1]	Handled within department and released	Referred to juvenile court jurisdiction	Referred to welfare agency	Referred to other police agency	Referred to criminal or adult court	Number of agencies	Estimated population, 2017
Total Agencies								
Number	240,536	52,901	164,028	2,010	3,218	18,379	4,806	116,625,981
Percent[2]	100.0	22.0	68.2	0.8	1.3	7.6		
Total Cities								
Number	188,075	44,067	127,075	1,449	1,817	13,667	3,711	82,312,431
Percent[2]	100.0	23.4	67.6	0.8	1.0	7.3		
Group I (250,000 and over)								
Number	49,885	13,782	34,290	469	543	801	35	22,741,422
Percent[2]	100.0	27.6	68.7	0.9	1.1	1.6		
Group II (100,000 to 249,999)								
Number	22,130	3,999	17,407	78	192	454	87	12,953,390
Percent[2]	100.0	18.1	78.7	0.4	0.9	2.1		
Group III (50,000 to 99,999)								
Number	33,045	7,567	22,573	121	355	2,429	226	15,809,143
Percent[2]	100.0	22.9	68.3	0.4	1.1	7.4		
Group IV (25,000 to 49,999)								
Number	25,580	6,240	16,126	321	277	2,616	342	11,883,635
Percent[2]	100.0	24.4	63.0	1.3	1.1	10.2		
Group V (10,000 to 24,999)								
Number	28,767	5,671	18,926	155	203	3,812	696	11,153,041
Percent[2]	100.0	19.7	65.8	0.5	0.7	13.3		
Group VI (under 10,000)								
Number	28,668	6,808	17,753	305	247	3,555	2,325	7,771,800
Percent[2]	100.0	23.7	61.9	1.1	0.9	12.4		
Metropolitan Counties								
Number	44,538	7,660	31,491	494	1,281	3,612	652	28,301,958
Percent[2]	100.0	17.2	70.7	1.1	2.9	8.1		
Nonmetropolitan Counties								
Number	7,923	1,174	5,462	67	120	1,100	443	6,011,592
Percent[2]	100.0	14.8	68.9	0.8	1.5	13.9		
Suburban Areas[3]								
Number	117,872	25,117	77,524	964	2,028	12,239	3,247	63,049,202
Percent[2]	100.0	21.3	65.8	0.8	1.7	10.4		

1 Includes all offenses except traffic and neglect cases.　2 Because of rounding, the percentages may not sum to 100.　3 Suburban areas include law enforcement agencies in cities with less than 50,000 inhabitants and county law enforcement agencies that are within a Metropolitan Statistical Area. Suburban areas exclude all metropolitan agencies associated with a principal city. The agencies associated with suburban areas also appear in other groups within this table.

Table 69. Arrests, by State, 2017

(Number)

State	Total, all classes[1]	Violent crime[2]	Property crime[2]	Murder and non-negligent man-slaughter	Rape[3]	Robbery	Aggra-vated assault	Burglary	Larceny-theft	Motor vehicle theft	Arson	Other assaults	Forgery and counter-feiting	Fraud	Embez-zlement	Stolen property; buying, receiving, possessing	Vandalism
Alabama																	
Under 18	4,707	365	1,264	18	34	116	197	323	860	71	10	782	13	29	1	134	86
Total, all ages	153,285	6,005	18,366	317	344	1,140	4,204	3,223	14,030	994	119	16,455	1,189	3,258	161	2,484	1,413
Alaska																	
Under 18	1,570	164	459	1	26	20	117	117	258	78	6	320	2	5	7	5	98
Total, all ages	29,152	2,374	3,695	46	126	289	1,913	623	2,356	694	22	4,478	113	219	77	105	1,004
Arizona																	
Under 18	22,613	1,228	4,528	30	52	450	696	761	3,364	347	56	3,677	22	74	6	156	1,754
Total, all ages	277,698	12,832	34,919	261	339	2,085	10,147	3,974	29,142	1,590	213	26,801	1,201	2,076	457	1,410	10,287
Arkansas																	
Under 18	7,878	459	1,562	15	46	101	297	386	1,083	88	5	1,443	15	29	5	144	287
Total, all ages	123,971	4,715	12,355	138	238	563	3,776	2,026	9,686	603	40	11,347	830	893	54	1,766	1,510
California																	
Under 18	51,603	7,152	10,712	98	295	2,952	3,807	4,067	4,616	1,774	255	8,483	45	175	23	1,167	2,656
Total, all ages	1,093,363	109,117	105,757	1,499	2,561	16,942	88,115	38,094	46,602	19,501	1,560	80,248	4,440	6,903	990	17,398	16,883
Colorado																	
Under 18	21,183	773	3,921	18	58	230	467	339	3,135	377	70	1,924	10	87	17	21	878
Total, all ages	234,409	7,721	27,157	176	442	1,203	5,900	2,389	21,737	2,766	265	17,009	734	2,400	126	496	5,508
Connecticut																	
Under 18	8,133	436	1,858	6	22	197	211	287	1,222	324	25	1,961	11	30	4	125	451
Total, all ages	100,211	3,844	14,074	85	190	1,082	2,487	1,998	11,076	926	74	18,621	649	912	144	693	2,188
Delaware																	
Under 18	3,360	284	661	1	18	84	181	146	462	35	18	911	0	60	4	73	154
Total, all ages	31,549	1,989	6,156	42	69	476	1,402	950	5,038	136	32	6,225	283	1,837	221	401	749
District of Columbia[5]																	
Under 18	594	80	39	0	0	60	20	0	39	0	0	79	1	2	0	9	12
Total, all ages	17,986	133	101	0	0	84	49	1	95	5	0	333	2	8	0	21	54
Florida[6,7]																	
Under 18	55,359	3,829	15,812	43	263	1,545	1,978	4,066	9,081	2,617	48	8,456	46	423	20	184	1,178
Total, all ages	713,085	36,251	91,063	635	1,873	6,398	27,345	16,483	66,033	8,306	241	78,943	2,040	11,613	1,057	1,841	6,371
Georgia																	
Under 18	19,766	1,206	5,177	46	42	396	722	996	3,697	457	27	2,712	48	110	9	373	567
Total, all ages	230,640	10,843	31,080	380	284	1,697	8,482	4,035	25,397	1,499	149	20,268	2,241	3,028	292	2,881	3,633
Hawaii																	
Under 18	3,084	135	597	2	15	56	62	60	494	36	7	440	3	2	1	48	75
Total, all ages	35,618	1,227	3,748	36	114	270	807	436	2,865	424	23	3,837	76	147	11	414	426
Idaho																	
Under 18	6,260	184	1,246	0	49	19	116	172	974	80	20	744	3	31	3	18	236
Total, all ages	51,686	1,441	5,192	10	120	70	1,241	790	4,138	220	44	4,513	127	299	43	170	756
Illinois[6]																	
Under 18	8,587	842	2,593	28	18	603	193	195	1,084	1,301	13	1,411	1	8	0	25	288
Total, all ages	64,552	3,823	11,653	272	259	1,464	1,828	882	7,599	3,113	59	13,083	108	224	1	71	2,076
Indiana																	
Under 18	11,369	842	2,724	17	48	218	559	301	2,104	294	25	1,731	15	63	7	35	349
Total, all ages	147,199	8,345	17,546	182	208	1,386	6,569	2,016	13,829	1,629	72	11,260	1,234	1,885	266	343	1,200
Iowa																	
Under 18	10,088	445	2,607	3	41	94	307	407	1,918	248	34	1,518	27	49	12	34	652
Total, all ages	94,485	4,709	12,280	53	192	341	4,123	1,594	10,029	565	92	7,296	664	743	79	212	1,995
Kansas																	
Under 18	3,948	185	683	3	17	27	138	102	490	71	20	742	4	22	8	48	243
Total, all ages	61,144	2,198	4,958	62	112	204	1,820	608	3,887	412	51	8,456	263	580	111	584	1,697
Kentucky																	
Under 18	5,273	393	1,414	26	24	212	131	326	911	171	6	1,029	13	16	8	347	164
Total, all ages	219,872	3,398	17,117	185	212	987	2,014	2,891	13,271	894	61	12,015	1,102	1,370	390	2,992	1,167
Louisiana																	
Under 18	17,571	1,149	4,603	36	95	265	753	1,173	2,914	475	41	3,124	12	33	9	258	589
Total, all ages	166,867	9,494	29,489	359	391	1,195	7,549	5,260	22,413	1,692	124	18,935	762	1,519	146	2,100	2,785
Maine																	
Under 18	3,046	57	779	0	14	12	31	131	596	28	24	505	3	11	2	10	225
Total, all ages	40,675	780	5,578	14	70	128	568	607	4,683	225	63	4,889	199	518	41	93	1,067
Maryland																	
Under 18	17,653	2,056	4,510	14	60	1,131	851	937	2,839	639	95	3,922	15	51	4	6	845
Total, all ages	165,877	9,692	21,726	286	352	3,299	5,755	4,323	15,337	1,756	310	18,261	423	893	77	73	2,332
Massachusetts																	
Under 18	6,732	793	1,179	6	23	176	588	280	780	90	29	1,562	16	17	3	134	345
Total, all ages	118,676	9,257	13,671	62	296	1,211	7,688	2,141	10,837	608	85	19,372	455	1,271	122	1,202	2,534
Michigan																	
Under 18	16,474	1,094	4,206	16	133	282	663	634	3,167	361	44	2,620	30	220	25	243	535
Total, all ages	244,417	11,798	24,692	261	750	1,306	9,481	3,190	19,983	1,280	239	27,788	650	3,931	1,174	1,806	2,815
Minnesota																	
Under 18	20,871	969	4,981	12	122	384	451	475	4,071	399	36	2,403	32	196	1	329	931
Total, all ages	143,702	5,769	26,025	120	632	1,176	3,841	2,298	22,105	1,521	101	14,363	1,465	2,664	23	1,995	3,056

Table 69. Arrests, by State, 2017—Continued

(Number)

State	Weapons; carrying, possessing, etc.	Prostitution and commercialized vice	Sex offenses (except rape and prostitution)	Drug abuse violations	Gambling	Offenses against the family and children	Driving under the influence	Liquor laws	Drunkenness[4]	Disorderly conduct	Vagrancy	All other offenses (except traffic)	Suspicion	Curfew and loitering law violations	Number of agencies	Estimated population, 2017
Alabama																
Under 18	103	0	26	196	0	29	42	212	34	338	0	1,053	0	0	223	3,737,635
Total, all ages	1,963	2	550	11,267	0	822	7,194	2,064	6,165	2,018	56	71,853	0	0		
Alaska																
Under 18	21	1	9	180	0	0	23	80	10	14	0	172	0	0	32	736,205
Total, all ages	369	5	256	1,004	0	159	3,102	653	43	757	2	10,737	0	0		
Arizona																
Under 18	258	4	218	3,096	1	182	198	1,461	78	1,424	57	3,062	3	1,126	91	6,400,872
Total, all ages	3,090	303	1,289	33,230	12	2,680	24,195	8,935	15,574	15,505	616	81,016	144	1,126		
Arkansas																
Under 18	126	0	18	876	0	6	32	205	85	609	0	1,667	0	310	264	2,760,388
Total, all ages	1,106	172	92	17,515	13	293	5,988	1,475	6,247	2,469	315	54,506	0	310		
California																
Under 18	3,081	18	1,139	3,781	11	2	455	1,107	695	1,193	103	8,607	0	998	676	39,386,220
Total, all ages	28,547	7,056	9,244	212,025	287	227	122,961	7,079	63,278	3,530	6,773	289,622	0	998		
Colorado																
Under 18	325	0	133	2,615	2	34	239	1,282	11	1,729	0	6,130	0	1,052	198	5,083,702
Total, all ages	2,309	521	471	16,626	19	3,235	23,664	8,143	485	7,284	596	108,846	7	1,052		
Connecticut																
Under 18	181	2	46	585	0	25	28	27	0	1,406	1	953	0	3	105	3,538,025
Total, all ages	1,242	183	368	9,174	7	1,500	8,228	159	5	10,579	24	27,614	0	3		
Delaware																
Under 18	82	0	37	335	1	0	0	71	3	287	0	364	0	33	62	961,939
Total, all ages	338	81	122	4,015	20	176	347	635	377	1,339	226	5,979	0	33		
District of Columbia[5]																
Under 18	15	0	0	17	0	0	0	2	0	32	0	306	0	0	2	0
Total, all ages	47	0	13	237	0	4	22	1,174	72	284	10	15,471	0	0		
Florida[6,7]																
Under 18	864	11	250	5,497	0	0	96	529	0	1	0	18,158	0	5	605	20,971,216
Total, all ages	6,306	2,468	3,001	124,487	71	4	32,727	11,739	37	33	0	303,028	0	5		
Georgia																
Under 18	412	4	313	2,127	6	129	99	260	30	1,637	129	4,080	7	331	389	8,205,589
Total, all ages	3,317	379	2,434	40,608	58	2,805	17,436	3,458	1,457	13,334	1,285	69,459	13	331		
Hawaii																
Under 18	13	0	32	436	0	0	29	76	0	87	0	893	0	217	4	1,427,538
Total, all ages	247	120	155	2,724	156	13	5,968	467	0	919	0	14,744	2	217		
Idaho																
Under 18	95	0	67	969	0	13	48	198	31	254	2	1,979	2	137	82	1,534,173
Total, all ages	276	13	188	8,432	0	636	5,458	1,010	566	1,582	15	20,826	6	137		
Illinois[6]																
Under 18	693	0	16	845	60	5	1	22	0	669	0	1,057	0	51	2	2,852,941
Total, all ages	4,290	141	235	10,915	457	277	2,357	131	0	2,988	18	11,653	0	51		
Indiana																
Under 18	207	4	123	1,391	0	209	60	653	39	597	29	2,077	4	210	201	4,267,407
Total, all ages	2,283	305	673	26,364	14	1,059	13,263	3,792	3,820	3,453	347	49,499	38	210		
Iowa																
Under 18	131	1	47	902	0	3	83	661	75	991	0	1,598	0	252	190	2,686,879
Total, all ages	900	46	125	9,645	7	1,059	10,082	3,733	5,793	3,574	17	31,274	0	252		
Kansas																
Under 18	54	0	43	701	0	6	61	353	1	156	0	638	0	0	225	1,900,556
Total, all ages	742	127	167	9,594	0	228	5,443	2,353	138	1,613	0	21,892	0	0		
Kentucky																
Under 18	94	0	39	533	0	5	41	8	44	177	0	946	0	2	330	4,329,947
Total, all ages	967	166	292	26,397	3	5,216	15,143	72	13,722	3,949	70	114,322	0	2		
Louisiana																
Under 18	398	8	168	1,361	0	114	26	191	30	2,307	32	2,909	4	246	170	3,747,239
Total, all ages	3,234	412	841	25,770	41	1,856	6,117	2,869	2,965	7,332	243	49,696	15	246		
Maine																
Under 18	6	0	35	350	0	6	39	386	4	83	0	528	0	17	135	1,335,907
Total, all ages	130	119	182	3,409	3	122	5,835	2,181	20	1,257	0	14,227	8	17		
Maryland																
Under 18	598	8	147	1,948	41	9	45	233	2	821	5	2,299	23	65	139	5,488,907
Total, all ages	3,215	748	578	28,992	117	860	14,385	3,755	29	4,202	82	55,260	112	65		
Massachusetts																
Under 18	169	1	52	215	1	45	29	231	24	447	0	1,467	0	2	321	6,522,173
Total, all ages	1,328	530	425	9,791	6	1,406	8,665	1,565	5,187	4,359	8	37,518	2	2		
Michigan																
Under 18	289	2	133	2,126	3	1	200	1,137	5	534	0	2,752	0	319	614	9,789,634
Total, all ages	4,590	233	626	33,090	42	2,766	26,558	8,729	349	5,989	139	86,333	0	319		
Minnesota																
Under 18	433	2	178	1,893	0	14	176	1,816	0	2,053	0	3,595	0	869	374	5,379,142
Total, all ages	2,208	359	1,055	19,281	16	569	19,171	7,535	2	8,665	42	28,570	0	869		

Table 69. Arrests, by State, 2017—Continued

(Number)

State	Total, all classes[1]	Violent crime[2]	Property crime[2]	Murder and non-negligent man-slaughter	Rape[3]	Robbery	Aggra-vated assault	Burglary	Larceny-theft	Motor vehicle theft	Arson	Other assaults	Forgery and counter-feiting	Fraud	Embez-zlement	Stolen property; buying, receiving, possessing	Vandalism
Mississippi																	
Under 18	3,485	138	836	5	7	75	51	180	600	50	6	449	2	9	4	76	70
Total, all ages	78,239	1,492	8,677	109	58	403	922	1,249	7,034	350	44	6,393	333	854	383	815	678
Missouri																	
Under 18	17,518	906	3,790	25	125	265	491	550	2,955	251	34	2,885	16	73	16	256	847
Total, all ages	228,042	9,371	31,387	342	551	1,553	6,925	3,815	24,973	2,473	126	21,141	1,239	1,950	290	2,876	3,868
Montana																	
Under 18	4,313	113	881	0	11	15	87	48	778	46	9	612	3	5	0	6	246
Total, all ages	30,824	1,262	4,965	19	47	91	1,105	275	4,401	252	37	4,390	106	254	30	98	931
Nebraska																	
Under 18	599	27	83	0	2	0	25	10	58	15	0	87	0	1	0	2	34
Total, all ages	5,708	161	523	1	12	5	143	53	424	44	2	617	18	67	3	35	95
Nevada																	
Under 18	7,672	924	1,159	4	54	319	547	337	700	108	14	1,720	40	31	2	166	217
Total, all ages	112,004	6,506	8,946	157	321	1,388	4,640	2,572	5,658	671	45	15,438	488	1,404	201	1,681	1,365
New Hampshire																	
Under 18	3,529	67	373	1	0	17	49	39	300	23	11	557	5	19	6	33	194
Total, all ages	47,516	896	3,642	8	52	168	668	319	3,143	152	28	5,306	292	787	120	503	1,247
New Jersey																	
Under 18	15,950	1,123	2,709	6	62	510	545	478	2,093	89	49	1,312	39	48	12	456	658
Total, all ages	281,631	8,577	24,807	149	333	2,472	5,623	3,910	20,274	494	129	20,175	1,020	3,478	269	2,511	3,297
New Mexico																	
Under 18	1,303	172	220	0	3	21	148	46	154	19	1	249	2	3	1	51	35
Total, all ages	40,552	2,708	4,340	25	43	344	2,296	613	3,546	170	11	6,223	138	230	74	1,165	684
New York[6]																	
Under 18	18,426	1,508	4,873	22	180	623	683	877	3,542	358	96	2,413	82	179	3	417	1,880
Total, all ages	259,257	12,440	43,759	264	970	3,090	8,116	5,200	36,562	1,713	284	27,397	2,616	4,086	48	3,183	13,559
North Carolina																	
Under 18	15,757	947	4,335	31	18	465	433	1,271	2,822	214	28	2,896	37	174	20	392	629
Total, all ages	240,365	11,630	34,918	464	229	2,571	8,366	7,836	25,826	1,066	190	31,024	1,326	6,720	1,185	3,356	3,958
North Dakota																	
Under 18	4,581	69	653	0	12	8	49	59	528	61	5	439	5	16	7	26	145
Total, all ages	39,944	855	3,787	6	61	69	719	352	3,128	291	16	2,943	156	421	53	311	479
Ohio																	
Under 18	22,865	870	4,203	16	78	348	428	728	3,180	222	73	4,341	33	139	2	454	960
Total, all ages	224,423	8,084	33,068	224	406	1,987	5,467	4,115	27,904	764	285	31,736	918	2,179	21	2,800	3,454
Oklahoma																	
Under 18	8,750	479	2,064	16	26	138	299	398	1,532	106	28	920	11	35	25	301	289
Total, all ages	106,731	4,820	14,352	161	179	719	3,761	2,267	11,226	713	146	8,226	607	1,489	408	2,843	1,270
Oregon																	
Under 18	8,955	349	1,833	8	24	106	211	151	1,486	141	55	1,045	12	44	2	25	678
Total, all ages	124,851	3,687	17,578	65	166	696	2,760	1,376	14,118	1,883	201	10,263	648	1,868	49	587	3,976
Pennsylvania																	
Under 18	43,800	3,049	5,821	19	238	1,071	1,721	952	4,355	426	88	5,184	64	799	20	336	1,779
Total, all ages	372,570	20,385	50,437	464	1,171	4,891	13,859	6,123	41,549	2,409	356	42,271	2,414	7,703	478	2,392	7,196
Rhode Island																	
Under 18	2,218	109	373	1	16	38	54	87	251	20	15	406	3	16	3	37	188
Total, all ages	22,707	864	2,458	10	77	150	627	533	1,773	126	26	3,638	74	425	102	287	932
South Carolina																	
Under 18	12,279	616	2,881	17	69	214	316	537	2,184	143	17	2,162	13	68	17	143	451
Total, all ages	153,573	6,500	23,848	253	378	1,133	4,736	3,149	19,592	1,006	101	14,146	1,138	3,200	358	1,952	2,552
South Dakota																	
Under 18	6,656	131	809	1	8	13	109	108	591	106	4	544	5	53	2	49	211
Total, all ages	63,625	1,748	3,283	16	79	88	1,565	445	2,512	311	15	4,931	102	731	37	225	624
Tennessee																	
Under 18	22,282	1,459	4,399	30	49	422	958	754	3,020	573	52	4,118	45	131	16	133	1,017
Total, all ages	350,912	14,682	38,394	358	351	1,839	12,134	5,143	29,649	3,422	180	32,076	1,802	5,336	664	1,496	4,571
Texas																	
Under 18	57,417	3,723	12,398	63	355	1,477	1,828	2,156	9,144	995	103	10,027	107	222	109	192	1,558
Total, all ages	745,719	30,372	78,504	839	2,247	6,519	20,767	10,570	62,387	5,093	454	90,763	4,287	5,764	794	899	7,178
Utah																	
Under 18	11,259	304	2,390	1	64	68	171	149	2,086	125	30	1,110	10	43	4	106	652
Total, all ages	104,741	2,252	14,526	48	204	404	1,596	882	13,064	519	61	7,870	746	957	32	1,225	2,364
Vermont																	
Under 18	800	51	137	0	14	1	36	33	94	6	4	145	2	4	1	6	92
Total, all ages	13,969	664	1,683	10	62	31	561	268	1,370	29	16	1,341	56	238	43	103	380
Virginia																	
Under 18	16,417	709	3,553	24	59	321	305	463	2,862	175	53	2,648	32	133	32	153	691
Total, all ages	258,878	7,068	26,582	337	430	1,633	4,668	2,698	22,662	1,032	190	30,360	1,700	4,845	1,371	994	3,621
Washington																	
Under 18	11,818	890	2,692	17	77	334	462	480	1,986	180	46	2,939	12	28	1	193	856
Total, all ages	173,344	8,472	27,055	158	515	1,887	5,912	4,723	20,526	1,637	169	25,114	862	1,056	53	3,438	5,178

Table 69. Arrests, by State, 2017—Continued

(Number)

State	Weapons; carrying, possessing, etc.	Prostitution and commercialized vice	Sex offenses (except rape and prostitution)	Drug abuse violations	Gambling	Offenses against the family and children	Driving under the influence	Liquor laws	Drunkenness[4]	Disorderly conduct	Vagrancy	All other offenses (except traffic)	Suspicion	Curfew and loitering law violations	Number of agencies	Estimated population, 2017
Mississippi																
Under 18	84	0	16	285	1	254	55	33	22	363	12	684	2	90	64	1,385,928
Total, all ages	1,110	25	198	10,268	67	2,298	7,642	971	3,888	4,070	105	27,846	36	90		
Missouri																
Under 18	277	6	265	2,266	1	88	147	707	12	1,176	4	3,136	0	644	361	5,626,134
Total, all ages	3,537	368	1,242	39,979	96	2,548	18,386	4,061	306	7,059	1,096	76,597	1	644		
Montana																
Under 18	17	0	23	385	0	40	44	575	0	398	0	659	0	306	100	1,037,591
Total, all ages	85	9	102	2,872	0	253	4,344	2,023	0	2,475	10	6,309	0	306		
Nebraska																
Under 18	4	0	3	87	0	1	19	90	12	38	0	95	0	16	54	233,437
Total, all ages	65	1	28	843	0	76	785	416	178	282	0	1,499	0	16		
Nevada																
Under 18	171	44	47	741	0	6	50	372	4	194	64	1,304	4	412	51	2,680,733
Total, all ages	1,885	2,532	695	8,923	9	702	9,470	1,950	241	1,353	1,648	45,968	187	412		
New Hampshire																
Under 18	5	0	24	507	0	10	36	371	313	133	0	865	0	11	176	1,292,643
Total, all ages	139	79	99	7,656	12	202	4,805	2,489	4,210	1,001	82	13,938	0	11		
New Jersey																
Under 18	566	9	157	3,535	30	27	76	682	0	1,281	25	2,613	0	592	490	8,521,517
Total, all ages	3,838	900	916	61,989	158	8,915	21,574	2,876	0	11,629	299	103,811	0	592		
New Mexico																
Under 18	14	1	2	99	0	11	25	31	28	41	0	318	0	0	23	823,584
Total, all ages	179	35	31	2,377	0	680	3,283	473	1,578	973	64	15,300	17	0		
New York[6]																
Under 18	330	6	322	3,344	14	24	82	198	0	504	9	2,238	0	0	510	10,121,830
Total, all ages	3,468	672	1,662	69,904	102	550	27,136	1,450	0	4,867	618	41,740	0	0		
North Carolina																
Under 18	546	6	90	1,519	2	18	190	278	0	1,173	0	2,487	0	18	213	6,457,952
Total, all ages	5,147	374	806	25,902	61	4,294	30,277	1,926	0	5,425	5	72,013	0	18		
North Dakota																
Under 18	29	2	42	476	0	171	37	554	4	706	0	1,093	0	107	106	749,938
Total, all ages	313	38	120	5,646	1	654	6,318	3,086	384	2,492	7	11,772	1	107		
Ohio																
Under 18	327	4	137	1,973	2	212	64	617	27	1,745	0	6,212	1	542	453	9,362,266
Total, all ages	3,681	1,122	516	37,022	4	1,714	15,032	5,196	4,327	12,296	208	60,497	6	542		
Oklahoma																
Under 18	145	0	42	1,280	3	20	72	111	211	538	0	1,342	0	862	389	3,789,847
Total, all ages	2,207	15	458	20,024	51	539	9,599	1,394	12,799	2,096	58	22,612	2	862		
Oregon																
Under 18	107	2	68	1,796	0	0	97	777	0	592	0	1,089	0	439	143	3,745,046
Total, all ages	2,077	364	436	15,682	0	333	13,273	3,658	18	6,594	22	43,299	0	439		
Pennsylvania																
Under 18	848	3	495	3,524	0	51	349	2,426	191	8,290	38	3,810	0	6,723	1,383	12,552,431
Total, all ages	5,056	1,755	2,211	63,306	53	2,034	45,128	9,446	20,941	35,630	298	46,713	0	6,723		
Rhode Island																
Under 18	105	0	20	111	0	27	5	68	0	422	0	314	0	11	41	943,094
Total, all ages	379	71	76	1,792	9	62	1,788	394	0	1,979	1	7,365	0	11		
South Carolina																
Under 18	435	5	56	2,090	0	8	93	297	69	1,318	0	1,525	0	32	346	3,920,047
Total, all ages	2,247	381	295	32,266	39	1,139	15,446	4,239	6,113	8,330	484	28,868	0	32		
South Dakota																
Under 18	74	0	28	979	0	653	88	804	220	576	1	1,247	11	171	75	729,800
Total, all ages	334	33	92	8,900	1	2,361	8,164	4,999	6,939	3,596	565	15,720	69	171		
Tennessee																
Under 18	408	0	133	2,591	12	47	109	532	129	1,793	0	3,996	0	1,214	449	6,505,139
Total, all ages	3,081	955	621	47,826	148	4,289	19,495	3,836	15,073	6,749	5	148,599	0	1,214		
Texas																
Under 18	858	40	459	9,997	17	190	419	1,187	783	1,284	30	11,516	0	2,301	909	25,980,682
Total, all ages	12,954	4,482	2,804	136,796	355	4,005	64,784	8,775	62,434	8,477	872	218,119	0	2,301		
Utah																
Under 18	135	10	217	1,696	0	28	143	708	66	421	18	2,842	0	356	114	2,646,000
Total, all ages	896	379	656	17,556	4	1,426	7,980	3,570	2,672	2,201	38	37,023	12	356		
Vermont																
Under 18	10	0	7	49	0	4	18	49	0	100	0	125	0	0	72	600,391
Total, all ages	28	4	41	1,137	0	174	2,450	112	0	823	0	4,692	0	0		
Virginia																
Under 18	318	5	137	2,217	1	23	70	574	75	501	0	3,804	0	741	373	7,782,044
Total, all ages	4,099	617	653	42,060	25	1,664	19,323	4,852	17,864	2,870	177	87,392	0	741		
Washington																
Under 18	225	7	123	1,224	0	9	167	683	10	190	0	1,569	0	0	222	6,678,694
Total, all ages	1,793	650	587	12,027	0	359	25,392	2,018	78	2,402	124	56,680	6	0		

Table 69. Arrests, by State, 2017—Continued

(Number)

State	Total, all classes[1]	Violent crime[2]	Property crime[2]	Murder and non-negligent man-slaughter	Rape[3]	Robbery	Aggra-vated assault	Burglary	Larceny-theft	Motor vehicle theft	Arson	Other assaults	Forgery and counter-feiting	Fraud	Embez-zlement	Stolen property; buying, receiving, possessing	Vandalism
West Virginia																	
Under 18	1,033	57	162	0	9	6	42	34	104	13	11	215	3	3	3	8	44
Total, all ages	39,296	1,832	5,077	31	103	123	1,575	751	4,018	272	36	4,320	258	486	116	410	634
Wisconsin																	
Under 18	39,393	1,067	6,140	14	212	319	522	652	4,875	555	58	2,633	31	115	27	469	1,836
Total, all ages	252,142	8,023	29,429	203	900	1,447	5,473	2,652	25,214	1,368	195	17,314	920	2,669	325	1,474	6,206
Wyoming																	
Under 18	3,046	35	449	0	6	3	26	26	379	34	10	417	1	3	5	15	150
Total, all ages	27,914	612	2,374	9	43	31	529	215	1,990	130	39	1,996	49	158	18	94	492

Table 69. Arrests, by State, 2017—Continued

(Number)

State	Weapons; carrying, possessing, etc.	Prostitution and commercialized vice	Sex offenses (except rape and prostitution)	Drug abuse violations	Gambling	Offenses against the family and children	Driving under the influence	Liquor laws	Drunkenness[4]	Disorderly conduct	Vagrancy	All other offenses (except traffic)	Suspicion	Curfew and loitering law violations	Number of agencies	Estimated population, 2017
West Virginia																
Under 18	14	0	5	120	0	1	16	24	2	30	0	317	0	9	178	1,150,294
Total, all ages	342	109	88	7,277	0	149	4,282	890	822	751	27	11,417	0	9		
Wisconsin																
Under 18	517	13	695	3,213	4	129	239	2,271	0	7,282	24	10,921	0	1,767	427	5,700,831
Total, all ages	3,449	451	1,928	30,781	37	2,493	23,541	12,228	0	32,743	809	75,555	0	1,767		
Wyoming																
Under 18	31	0	11	501	0	6	28	416	16	106	0	761	5	90	53	543,983
Total, all ages	78	48	107	4,612	0	344	3,253	1,980	2,412	810	36	8,345	6	90		

Note: Because the number of agencies submitting arrest data varies from year to year, users are cautioned about making direct comparisons between 2017 arrest totals and those published in previous years' editions of *Crime in the United States*. Further, arrest figures may vary widely from state to state because some Part II crimes are not considered crimes in some states.

1 Does not include traffic arrests.   2 Violent crimes are offenses of murder and nonnegligent manslaughter, rape, robbery, and aggravated assault. Property crimes are offenses of burglary, larceny-theft, motor vehicle theft, and arson.   3 The rape figures in this table are aggregate totals of the data submitted based on both the legacy and revised Uniform Crime Reporting definitions.   4 Drunkenness is not considered a crime in some states; therefore, the figures vary widely from state to state.   5 Includes arrests reported by the District of Columbia Fire and Emergency Medical Services: Arson Investigation Unit and the Metro Transit Police. These agencies have no population associated with them.   6 See 2017 arrest data for details.   7 The Florida arrest counts for offenses against the family and children, drunkenness, disorderly conduct, vagrancy, suspicion, and curfew and loitering law violations are included under the category All other offenses (except for the data submitted by two Bureau of Indian Affairs agencies that provided data using those specific breakdowns).

SECTION V

LAW ENFORCEMENT PERSONNEL

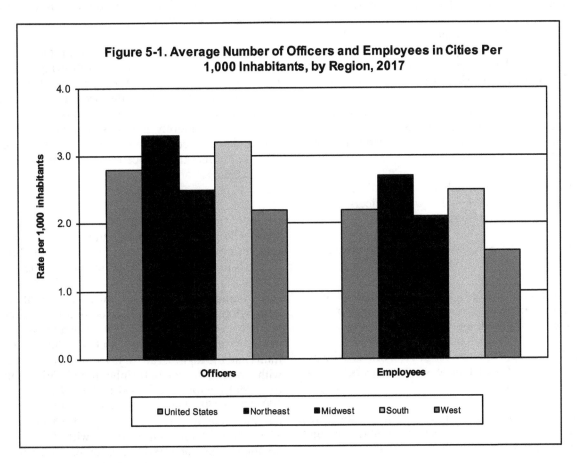

Figure 5-1. Average Number of Officers and Employees in Cities Per 1,000 Inhabitants, by Region, 2017

The Uniform Crime Reporting (UCR) program defines law enforcement officers as individuals who ordinarily carry a firearm and a badge, have full arrest powers, and are paid from government funds set aside specifically for sworn law enforcement representatives. Because of law enforcement's varied service requirements and functions, as well as the distinct demographic traits and characteristics of jurisdictions, readers should use caution when comparing staffing levels between agencies based on police employment data from the UCR program. In addition, the data presented here reflect existing staff levels and should not be interpreted as preferred officer strengths recommended by the Federal Bureau of Investigation (FBI). Also, readers should note that the totals given for sworn officers for any particular agency reflect both patrol officers on the street and officers assigned to various other duties, such as administrative and investigative positions and assignments to special teams.

Each year, law enforcement agencies across the United States report the total number of sworn law enforcement officers and civilians in their agencies as of October 31 to the UCR program. Civilian employees include personnel such as clerks, radio dispatchers, meter attendants, stenographers, jailers, correctional officers, and mechanics, (provided that they are full-time employees of the agency).

This section of *Crime in the United States* presents those data as the number and rate of law enforcement officers and civilian employees throughout the United States. In 2017, 670,279 sworn officers and 286,662 civilians provided law enforcement services to more than 281 million people nationwide. These law enforcement personnel were employed by 13,128 state, city, university/college, metropolitan/nonmetropolitan county, and other designated law enforcement agencies. Of the slightly less than 1 million law enforcement employees, 73.2 percent were male. (Table 74)

The data in this section are broken down by geographic region and division, population group, state, city, university/college, metropolitan/nonmetropolitan county, and other law enforcement agency groups. (Information about geographic regions and divisions and population groups can be found in Appendix III.) UCR program staff compute the rate of sworn officers and law enforcement employees by taking the number of employees (sworn officers only or in combination with civilians), dividing by the population for which the agency provides law enforcement service, and multiplying by 1,000.

- Tables 70 and 71 present the number and rate of law enforcement personnel per 1,000 inhabitants collectively employed by agencies, broken down by geographic region and division by population group

- Tables 72 and 73 provide a count of law enforcement agencies by population group, based on the employment rate ranges for sworn officer and civilian employees per 1,000 inhabitants

- Table 74 provides the number of total officers, the percentage of male and female sworn officers, and the civilian employees by population group

- Table 75 lists the percentage of full-time civilian law enforcement employees by population group

- Table 76 breaks down by state the number of sworn law enforcement officers and civilians employed by state law enforcement agencies

- Table 77 provides the number of total officers, the percentage of male and female sworn officers, and the civilian employees by state

- Tables 78 to 80 list the number of law enforcement employees for cities, universities and colleges, and metropolitan and nonmetropolitan counties

- Table 81 supplies employee data for those law enforcement agencies that serve selected transit systems, parks and forests, schools and school districts, hospitals, etc., in the nation

The demographic traits and characteristics of a jurisdiction affect its requirements for law enforcement service. For instance, a village between two large cities may require more law enforcement than a community of the same size with no urban center nearby. A town with legal gambling may have different law enforcement needs than a town near a military base. A city largely made up of college students may have different law enforcement needs than a city whose residents are mainly retirees.

Similarly, the functions of law enforcement agencies are diverse. Employees of these agencies patrol local streets and major highways, protect citizens in the nation's smallest towns and largest cities, and conduct investigations on offenses at the local and state levels. State police in one area may enforce traffic laws on state highways and interstates; in another area, they may be responsible for investigating violent crimes. Sheriff's departments may collect tax monies, serve as the enforcement authority for local and state courts, administer jail facilities, or carry out some combination of these duties. This has an impact on an agency's staffing levels.

Because of the differing service requirements and functions, care should be taken when drawing comparisons between and among the staffing levels of law enforcement agencies. The data in this section are not intended as recommended or preferred officer strength; they should be used merely as guides. Adequate staffing levels can be determined only after careful study of the conditions that affect the service requirements in a particular jurisdiction.

RATE

The UCR program computes these rates by taking the number of employees, dividing by the population of the agency's jurisdiction, and multiplying by 1,000.

An examination of the 2017 law enforcement employee data by population group showed that the nation's cities had a collective rate of 2.8 law enforcement employees per 1,000 inhabitants. Cities with fewer than 10,000 inhabitants had the highest rate of law enforcement employees, with a rate of 4.8 per 1,000 inhabitants. Cities with 25,000 to 49,999 inhabitants, 50,000 to 99,999 inhabitants, and 100,000 to 249,999 inhabitants all had the lowest rate of law enforcement employees (2.1 per 1,000 in population). The nation's largest cities, those with 250,000 or more inhabitants, averaged 3.4 law enforcement employees for every 1,000 inhabitants. (Table 70)

Sworn Personnel

An analysis of the 2017 data showed that law enforcement agencies in the cities in the Northeast had the highest rate of sworn officers—2.7 per 1,000 inhabitants, followed by the South (2.5), the Midwest (2.1), and the West (1.6). (Table 71)

By population group in 2017, there were 2.2 sworn officers for each 1,000 resident population. This rate remained static from 2016 to 2017. Cities with fewer than 10,000 inhabitants had the highest rate at 3.8 sworn officers per 1,000 inhabitants. The nation's largest cities, those with 250,000 or more inhabitants, averaged 2.6 officers per 1,000 inhabitants, the same as in 2016. The lowest rates were in cities with 50,000 to 99,999 inhabitants and in 100,000 to 249,999 inhabitants (1.6 per 1,000 resident population). (Table 71)

Males accounted for 87.5 percent of all full-time sworn law enforcement officers in 2017. Cities with populations of 1 million and over employed the highest percentage

(18.1 percent) of full-time female officers. Of the city population groups and subsets, cities with populations of 10,000 to 24,999 inhabitants employed the highest percentage (91.4 percent) of male officers. In metropolitan counties, 85.7 percent of officers were male, and in nonmetropolitan counties, 92.1 percent of officers were male. (Table 74)

Civilian Employees

Civilian employees provide a myriad of services to the nation's law enforcement and criminal justice agencies. Among other duties, they dispatch officers, provide administrative and record keeping support, and query local, state, and national databases.

In 2017, 30.0 percent of all law enforcement employees in the nation were civilians. Male employees accounted for 39.6 percent of all full-time civilian law enforcement employees in 2017. In cities, civilians made up 22.1 percent of law enforcement agency employees. Civilians made up 40.2 percent of law enforcement employees in metropolitan counties, 40.5 percent of law enforcement employees in nonmetropolitan counties, and 33.7 percent of law enforcement employees in suburban areas. (Table 74)

Table 70. Full-Time Law Enforcement Employees,[1] by Region and Geographic Division and Population Group, 2017

(Number, rate per 1,000 inhabitants.)

Region/geographic division	Total (10,058 cities; population 193,187,549)	Group I (79 cities, 250,000 and over; population 60,607,956)	Group II (198 cities, 100,000 to 249,999; population 29,257,403)	Group III (431 cities, 50,000 to 99,999; population 30,031,331)	Group IV (775 cities, 25,000 to 49,999; population 26,916,000)	Group V (1,609 cities, 10,000 to 24,999; population 25,660,537)	Group VI (6,966 cities, under 10,000; population 20,714,322)	Total city agencies	2017 estimated city population	County[2] (3,070 agencies; population 88,792,091)	Total city and county agencies	2017 estimated total agency population	Suburban areas[3] (7,001 agencies; population 120,076,115)
Total													
Number of employees	542,639	203,398	62,162	61,566	56,881	58,891	99,741	10,058	193,187,549	414,302	13,128	281,979,640	450,252
Average number of employees per 1,000 inhabitants	2.8	3.4	2.1	2.1	2.1	2.3	4.8			4.7			3.7
Northeast													
Number of employees	151,357	66,618	8,462	15,835	18,335	18,655	23,452	2,614	45,196,822				
Average number of employees per 1,000 inhabitants	3.3	5.6	2.9	2.4	2.2	2.1	3.7						
New England													
Number of employees	34,175	2,778	4,459	6,412	7,203	6,957	6,366	781	12,920,841				
Average number of employees per 1,000 inhabitants	2.6	4.1	3.0	2.3	2.2	2.3	3.8						
Middle Atlantic													
Number of employees	117,182	63,840	4,003	9,423	11,132	11,698	17,086	1,833	32,275,981				
Average number of employees per 1,000 inhabitants	3.6	5.6	2.9	2.4	2.2	2.0	3.6						
Midwest													
Number of employees	99,302	33,337	7,364	13,442	12,417	13,756	18,986	2,616	39,587,170				
Average number of employees per 1,000 inhabitants	2.5	3.5	2.0	1.8	1.9	2.0	3.3						
East North Central													
Number of employees	65,367	25,790	3,636	8,873	9,251	8,228	9,589	1,382	25,468,923				
Average number of employees per 1,000 inhabitants	2.6	3.8	2.0	1.9	1.9	2.0	3.1						
West North Central													
Number of employees	33,935	7,547	3,728	4,569	3,166	5,528	9,397	1,234	14,118,247				
Average number of employees per 1,000 inhabitants	2.4	2.9	2.0	1.7	1.9	2.1	3.6						
South													
Number of employees	176,083	53,827	25,431	16,884	17,314	19,607	43,020	3,427	55,419,668				
Average number of employees per 1,000 inhabitants	3.2	2.9	2.5	2.5	2.6	2.9	6.8						
South Atlantic													
Number of employees	89,454	23,853	14,310	9,661	9,288	9,854	22,488	1,606	25,229,607				
Average number of employees per 1,000 inhabitants	3.5	3.7	2.6	2.5	2.7	3.1	8.0						
East South Central													
Number of employees	27,430	6,317	2,011	2,482	3,816	3,754	9,050	738	8,207,314				
Average number of employees per 1,000 inhabitants	3.3	2.7	2.7	2.6	2.6	3.0	6.1						
West South Central													
Number of employees	59,199	23,657	9,110	4,741	4,210	5,999	11,482	1,083	21,982,747				
Average number of employees per 1,000 inhabitants	2.7	2.4	2.2	2.4	2.3	2.7	5.6						
West													
Number of employees	115,897	49,616	20,905	15,405	8,815	6,873	14,283	1,401	52,983,889				
Average number of employees per 1,000 inhabitants	2.2	2.4	1.7	1.6	1.7	2.0	6.3						
Mountain													
Number of employees	42,195	16,388	7,490	4,671	3,460	2,690	7,496	640	16,919,843				
Average number of employees per 1,000 inhabitants	2.5	2.6	1.9	1.9	1.9	2.3	6.5						
Pacific													
Number of employees	73,702	33,228	13,415	10,734	5,355	4,183	6,787	761	36,064,046				
Average number of employees per 1,000 inhabitants	2.0	2.3	1.6	1.6	1.6	1.9	6.1						

1 Full-time law enforcement employees include civilians. 2 The designation county is a combination of both metropolitan and nonmetropolitan counties. 3 Suburban areas include law enforcement agencies in cities with less than 50,000 inhabitants and county law enforcement agencies that are within a Metropolitan Statistical Area (see Data Declaration). Suburban areas exclude all metropolitan agencies associated with a principal city. The agencies associated with suburban areas also appear in other groups within this table.

Table 71. Full-Time Law Enforcement Officers, by Region, Geographic Division, and Population Group, 2017

(Number, rate per 1,000 inhabitants.)

Region/geographic division	Total (10,058 cities; population 193,187,549)	Group I (79 cities, 250,000 and over; population 60,607,956)	Group II (198 cities, 100,000 to 249,999; population 29,257,403)	Group III (431 cities, 50,000 to 99,999; population 30,031,331)	Group IV (775 cities, 25,000 to 49,999; population 26,916,000)	Group V (1,609 cities, 10,000 to 24,999; population 25,660,537)	Group VI (6,966 cities, under 10,000; population 20,714,322)	Total city agencies	2017 estimated city population	County[1] (3,070 agencies; population 88,792,091)	Total city and county agencies	2017 estimated total agency population	Suburban areas[2] (7,001 agencies; population 120,076,115)
Total													
Number of officers	422,869	155,692	47,814	47,850	45,672	47,866	77,975	10,058	193,187,549	247,410	13,128	281,979,640	298,444
Average number of officers per 1,000 inhabitants	2.2	2.6	1.6	1.6	1.7	1.9	3.8			2.8			2.5
Northeast													
Number of officers	119,962	48,868	7,188	13,201	15,436	15,893	19,376	2,614	45,196,822				
Average number of officers per 1,000 inhabitants	2.7	4.1	2.5	2.0	1.8	1.8	3.0						
New England													
Number of officers	28,038	2,205	3,831	5,409	5,985	5,628	4,980	781	12,920,841				
Average number of officers per 1,000 inhabitants	2.2	3.2	2.6	2.0	1.8	1.8	2.9						
Middle Atlantic													
Number of officers	91,924	46,663	3,357	7,792	9,451	10,265	14,396	1,833	32,275,981				
Average number of officers per 1,000 inhabitants	2.8	4.1	2.4	2.0	1.8	1.8	3.1						
Midwest													
Number of officers	82,591	28,201	6,130	10,896	10,069	11,343	15,952	2,616	39,587,170				
Average number of officers per 1,000 inhabitants	2.1	3.0	1.6	1.5	1.5	1.7	2.8						
East North Central													
Number of officers	55,403	22,440	3,127	7,232	7,554	6,862	8,188	1,382	25,468,923				
Average number of officers per 1,000 inhabitants	2.2	3.3	1.7	1.6	1.5	1.7	2.6						
West North Central													
Number of officers	27,188	5,761	3,003	3,664	2,515	4,481	7,764	1,234	14,118,247				
Average number of officers per 1,000 inhabitants	1.9	2.2	1.6	1.4	1.5	1.7	3.0						
South													
Number of officers	136,418	41,899	19,615	12,939	13,720	15,426	32,819	3,427	55,419,668				
Average number of officers per 1,000 inhabitants	2.5	2.3	1.9	1.9	2.0	2.3	5.2						
South Atlantic													
Number of officers	69,076	17,795	11,099	7,477	7,407	7,857	17,441	1,606	25,229,607				
Average number of officers per 1,000 inhabitants	2.7	2.7	2.0	2.0	2.2	2.4	6.2						
East South Central													
Number of officers	21,736	5,121	1,657	1,986	3,060	3,005	6,907	738	8,207,314				
Average number of officers per 1,000 inhabitants	2.6	2.2	2.2	2.1	2.1	2.4	4.7						
West South Central													
Number of officers	45,606	18,983	6,859	3,476	3,253	4,564	8,471	1,083	21,982,747				
Average number of officers per 1,000 inhabitants	2.1	1.9	1.7	1.8	1.8	2.0	4.2						
West													
Number of officers	83,898	36,724	14,881	10,814	6,447	5,204	9,828	1,401	52,983,889				
Average number of officers per 1,000 inhabitants	1.6	1.8	1.2	1.2	1.3	1.5	4.3						
Mountain													
Number of officers	30,266	11,612	5,493	3,300	2,618	2,077	5,166	640	16,919,843				
Average number of officers per 1,000 inhabitants	1.8	1.8	1.4	1.3	1.4	1.8	4.5						
Pacific													
Number of officers	53,632	25,112	9,388	7,514	3,829	3,127	4,662	761	36,064,046				
Average number of officers per 1,000 inhabitants	1.5	1.8	1.1	1.1	1.2	1.4	4.2						

1 The designation county is a combination of both metropolitan and nonmetropolitan counties.   2 Suburban areas include law enforcement agencies in cities with less than 50,000 inhabitants and county law enforcement agencies that are within a Metropolitan Statistical Area. Suburban areas exclude all metropolitan agencies associated with a principal city. The agencies associated with suburban areas also appear in other groups within this table.

Table 72. Full-Time Law Enforcement Employees,[1] Range in Rate, by Population Group, 2017

(Number, rate per 1,000 inhabitants.)

Rate range	Total cities[2] (8,793 cities; population 193,187,549)	Group I (79 cities, 250,000 and over; population 60,607,956)	Group II (198 cities, 100,000 to 249,999; population 29,257,403)	Group III (431 cities, 50,000 to 99,999; population 30,031,331)	Group IV (775 cities, 25,000 to 49,999; population 26,916,000)	Group V (1,609 cities, 10,000 to 24,999; population 25,660,537)	Group VI (5,701 cities, under 10,000; population 20,714,322)
Total Cities							
Number	8,793	79	198	431	775	1,609	5,701
Percent[3]	100.0	100.0	100.0	100.0	100.0	100.0	100.0
0.1–0.5							
Number	92	0	0	0	1	4	87
Percent	1.0	0.0	0.0	0.0	0.1	0.2	1.5
0.6–1.0							
Number	434	0	1	9	28	49	347
Percent	4.9	0.0	0.5	2.1	3.6	3.0	6.1
1.1–1.5							
Number	1,201	5	44	101	148	220	683
Percent	13.7	6.3	22.2	23.4	19.1	13.7	12.0
1.6–2.0							
Number	1,842	15	61	125	227	414	1,000
Percent	20.9	19.0	30.8	29.0	29.3	25.7	17.5
2.1–2.5							
Number	1,636	26	42	104	188	389	887
Percent	18.6	32.9	21.2	24.1	24.3	24.2	15.6
2.6–3.0							
Number	1,199	8	29	56	95	284	727
Percent	13.6	10.1	14.6	13.0	12.3	17.7	12.8
3.1–3.5							
Number	720	6	14	21	53	114	512
Percent	8.2	7.6	7.1	4.9	6.8	7.1	9.0
3.6–4.0							
Number	503	8	6	10	24	69	386
Percent	5.7	10.1	3.0	2.3	3.1	4.3	6.8
4.1–4.5							
Number	322	3	1	2	6	23	287
Percent	3.7	3.8	0.5	0.5	0.8	1.4	5.0
4.6–5.0							
Number	201	4	0	1	1	21	174
Percent	2.3	5.1	0.0	0.2	0.1	1.3	3.1
5.1 and over							
Number	643	4	0	2	4	22	611
Percent	7.3	5.1	0.0	0.5	0.5	1.4	10.7

1 Full-time law enforcement employees include civilians.   2 The number of agencies used to compile these figures differs from other tables that include data about law enforcement employees because agencies with no resident population are excluded from this table. Agencies not included in this table are associated with universities and colleges (see Table 79) and other agencies (see Table 81), as well as some state agencies that have concurrent jurisdiction with other local law enforcement.   3 Because of rounding, the percentages may not sum to 100.

Table 73. Full-Time Law Enforcement Officers, Range in Rate, by Population Group, 2017

(Number, rate per 1,000 inhabitants.)

Rate range	Total cities[1] (8,793 cities; population 193,187,549)	Group I (79 cities, 250,000 and over; population 60,607,956)	Group II (198 cities, 100,000 to 249,999; population 29,257,403)	Group III (431 cities, 50,000 to 99,999; population 30,031,331)	Group IV (775 cities, 25,000 to 49,999; population 26,916,000)	Group V (1,609 cities, 10,000 to 24,999; population 25,660,537)	Group VI (5,701 cities, under 10,000; population 20,714,322)
Total Cities							
Number	8,793	79	198	431	775	1,609	5,701
Percent[2]	100.0	100.0	100.0	100.0	100.0	100.0	100.0
0.1–0.5							
Number	104	0	0	1	3	4	96
Percent	1.2	0.0	0.0	0.2	0.4	0.2	1.7
0.6–1.0							
Number	683	5	34	79	77	96	392
Percent	7.8	6.3	17.2	18.3	9.9	6.0	6.9
1.1–1.5							
Number	1,817	15	69	140	265	415	913
Percent	20.7	19.0	34.8	32.5	34.2	25.8	16.0
1.6–2.0							
Number	2,199	26	48	131	241	565	1,188
Percent	25.0	32.9	24.2	30.4	31.1	35.1	20.8
2.1–2.5							
Number	1,535	13	27	57	119	317	1,002
Percent	17.5	16.5	13.6	13.2	15.4	19.7	17.6
2.6–3.0							
Number	893	7	15	14	53	125	679
Percent	10.2	8.9	7.6	3.2	6.8	7.8	11.9
3.1–3.5							
Number	540	5	4	7	13	52	459
Percent	6.1	6.3	2.0	1.6	1.7	3.2	8.1
3.6–4.0							
Number	291	2	1	0	1	22	265
Percent	3.3	2.5	0.5	0.0	0.1	1.4	4.6
4.1–4.5							
Number	188	4	0	1	0	7	176
Percent	2.1	5.1	0.0	0.2	0.0	0.4	3.1
4.6–5.0							
Number	129	1	0	1	1	1	125
Percent	1.5	1.3	0.0	0.2	0.1	0.1	2.2
5.1 and over							
Number	414	1	0	0	2	5	406
Percent	4.7	1.3	0.0	0.0	0.3	0.3	7.1

1 The number of agencies used to compile these figures differs from other tables that include data about law enforcement officers because agencies with no resident population are excluded from this table. Agencies not included in this table are associated with universities and colleges (see Table 79) and other agencies (see Table 81), as well as some state agencies that have concurrent jurisdiction with other local law enforcement.   2 Because of rounding, the percentages may not sum to 100.

Table 74. Full-Time Law Enforcement Employees, by Population Group, Percent Male and Female, 2017

(Number, percent.)

Population group	Total law enforcement employees (number)	Law enforcement employees (percent)		Total officers (number)	Officers (percent)		Civilians (number) Total civilians	Civilians (percent)		Agencies (number)	Population, 2017, estimated
		Male	Female		Male	Female		Male	Female		
Total Agencies	956,941	73.2	26.8	670,279	87.5	12.5	286,662	39.6	60.4	13,128	281,979,640
Total Cities	542,639	75.4	24.6	422,869	87.5	12.5	119,770	32.8	67.2	10,058	193,187,549
Group I (250,000 and over)	203,398	71.9	28.1	155,692	83.2	16.8	47,706	34.9	65.1	79	60,607,956
1,000,000 and over (Group I subset)	111,593	70.6	29.4	84,979	81.9	18.1	26,614	34.3	65.7	11	27,835,810
500,000 to 999,999 (Group I subset)	51,377	74.7	25.3	39,808	85.0	15.0	11,569	39.4	60.6	23	17,010,028
250,000 to 499,999 (Group I subset)	40,428	72.0	28.0	30,905	84.6	15.4	9,523	31.2	68.8	45	15,762,118
Group II (100,000 to 249,999)	62,162	73.9	26.1	47,814	88.1	11.9	14,348	26.6	73.4	198	29,257,403
Group III (50,000 to 99,999)	61,566	76.1	23.9	47,850	89.6	10.4	13,716	29.2	70.8	431	30,031,331
Group IV (25,000 to 49,999)	56,881	78.3	21.7	45,672	90.6	9.4	11,209	27.9	72.1	775	26,916,000
Group V (10,000 to 24,999)	58,891	79.5	20.5	47,866	91.4	8.6	11,025	27.7	72.3	1,609	25,660,537
Group VI (under 10,000)	99,741	79.0	21.0	77,975	90.1	9.9	21,766	39.3	60.7	6,966	20,714,322
Metropolitan Counties	299,563	69.3	30.7	179,143	85.7	14.3	120,420	44.8	55.2	1,241	67,301,047
Nonmetropolitan Counties	114,739	72.6	27.4	68,267	92.1	7.9	46,472	44.0	56.0	1,829	21,491,044
Suburban Areas[1]	450,252	72.6	27.4	298,444	87.6	12.4	151,808	43.0	57.0	7,001	120,076,115

1 Suburban areas include law enforcement agencies in cities with less than 50,000 inhabitants and county law enforcement agencies that are within a Metropolitan Statistical Area. Suburban areas exclude all metropolitan agencies associated with a principal city. The agencies associated with suburban areas also appear in other groups within this table.

Table 75. Full-Time Civilian Law Enforcement Employees, by Population Group, 2017

(Number, percent.)

Population group	Civilian employees (percent)	Agencies (number)	Population, 2017, estimated
Total Agencies	30.0	13,128	281,979,640
Total Cities	22.1	10,058	193,187,549
Group I (250,000 and over)	23.5	79	60,607,956
1,000,000 and over (Group I subset)	23.8	11	27,835,810
500,000 to 999,999 (Group I subset)	22.5	23	17,010,028
250,000 to 499,999 (Group I subset)	23.6	45	15,762,118
Group II (100,000 to 249,999)	23.1	198	29,257,403
Group III (50,000 to 99,999)	22.3	431	30,031,331
Group IV (25,000 to 49,999)	19.7	775	26,916,000
Group V (10,000 to 24,999)	18.7	1,609	25,660,537
Group VI (under 10,000)	21.8	6,966	20,714,322
Metropolitan Counties	40.2	1,241	67,301,047
Nonmetropolitan Counties	40.5	1,829	21,491,044
Suburban Areas[1]	33.7	7,001	120,076,115

1 Suburban areas include law enforcement agencies in cities with less than 50,000 inhabitants and county law enforcement agencies that are within a Metropolitan Statistical Area. Suburban areas exclude all metropolitan agencies associated with a principal city. The agencies associated with suburban areas also appear in other groups within this table.

Table 76. Full-Time State Law Enforcement Employees, by Selected State, 2017

(Number.)

State/agency	Law enforcement employees	Officers		Civilians	
		Male	Female	Male	Female
Alaska					
State Troopers	581	331	16	103	131
Arizona					
Department of Public Safety	1,976	1,118	45	334	479
Arkansas[1]					
Other state agencies	36	27	1	2	6
California					
Highway Patrol	10,737	6,934	467	1,478	1,858
Other state agencies[2]	1,278	987	178	37	76
Colorado					
State Police	1,175	739	51	148	237
Other state agencies	369	53	8	109	199
Connecticut					
State Police	1,197	883	83	92	139
Other state agencies	101	79	5	9	8
Delaware					
State Police	969	636	98	91	144
Other state agencies	780	251	31	142	356
Florida					
Highway Patrol	3,635	2,139	321	366	809
Other state agencies	3,503	1,549	247	587	1,120
Georgia					
Department of Public Safety	1,340	872	12	299	157
Other state agencies	386	156	23	86	121
Idaho					
State Police	519	272	16	66	165
Illinois					
State Police	2,698	1,457	163	457	621
Other state agencies	209	104	5	62	38
Indiana					
State Police	1,757	1,226	62	177	292
Other state agencies	86	65	14	0	7
Iowa					
Department of Public Safety	816	515	37	126	138
Kansas					
Highway Patrol	785	491	19	108	167
Other state agencies	279	60	13	75	131
Kentucky					
State Police	1,612	945	30	310	327
Other state agencies	244	197	7	11	29
Louisiana					
Other state agencies	3	2	0	0	1
Maine					
State Police	436	297	25	49	65
Other state agencies[2]	56	27	1	17	11
Maryland					
State Police	2,105	1,319	110	350	326
Other state agencies	1,474	916	124	187	247
Massachusetts					
State Police	2,614	1,970	125	191	328
Other state agencies	260	225	23	6	6
Michigan					
State Police	2,948	1,713	192	433	610
Minnesota					
State Patrol	542	453	43	13	33
Other state agencies	411	236	32	76	67
Mississippi[1]					
Other state agencies	126	97	7	4	18
Missouri					
State Highway Patrol	2,348	1,168	68	528	584
Other state agencies	475	403	43	2	27

Table 76. Full-Time State Law Enforcement Employees, by Selected State, 2017—Continued

(Number.)

State/agency	Law enforcement employees	Officers		Civilians	
		Male	Female	Male	Female
Montana					
Highway Patrol	294	223	16	14	41
Other state agencies	43	16	1	11	15
Nebraska					
State Patrol	697	419	31	84	163
Nevada					
Highway Patrol	555	427	33	42	53
Other state agencies	89	57	7	1	24
New Hampshire					
State Police	499	306	28	52	113
Other state agencies	30	14	3	3	10
New Jersey					
State Police	3,974	2,624	127	581	642
Other state agencies	576	466	45	33	32
Port Authority of New York and New Jersey[3]	1,834	1,460	191	94	89
New Mexico					
State Police	1,067	618	45	171	233
New York					
State Police	5,890	4,534	512	309	535
Other state agencies	298	247	33	7	11
North Carolina					
Highway Patrol	2,090	1,566	47	280	197
Other state agencies	1,131	715	128	116	172
North Dakota					
Highway Patrol	187	143	7	6	31
Ohio					
Highway Patrol	2,623	1,532	155	471	465
Oklahoma					
Highway Patrol	1,381	776	17	261	327
Other state agencies	122	66	6	40	10
Oregon					
State Police	1,279	644	69	200	366
Other state agencies	56	37	12	1	6
Pennsylvania					
State Police	6,269	3,959	270	1,023	1,017
Other state agencies	453	317	28	76	32
Rhode Island					
State Police	286	208	21	28	29
Other state agencies	82	59	5	9	9
South Carolina[1]					
Other state agencies	593	511	40	15	27
South Dakota					
Highway Patrol	254	167	13	41	33
Other state agencies	176	48	3	50	75
Tennessee					
Department of Safety	1,712	847	50	242	573
Other state agencies	1,140	644	174	122	200
Texas					
Department of Public Safety	9,652	3,892	295	1,905	3,560
Utah					
Highway Patrol	594	496	23	13	62
Other state agencies	134	125	6	1	2
Vermont					
State Police	348	264	33	15	36
Other state agencies	121	89	8	9	15
Virginia					
State Police	2,640	1,791	111	252	486
Other state agencies	742	448	57	100	137
Washington					
State Patrol	2,104	914	86	512	592
Other state agencies	110	45	17	14	34

Table 76. Full-Time State Law Enforcement Employees, by Selected State, 2017—Continued

(Number.)

State/agency	Law enforcement employees	Officers		Civilians	
		Male	Female	Male	Female
West Virginia					
State Patrol	1,145	689	30	170	256
Other state agencies	220	174	3	17	26
Wisconsin					
State Patrol	647	446	45	75	81
Other state agencies	388	297	52	15	24

Note: Caution should be used when comparing data from one state to that of another. The responsibilities of the various state police, highway patrol, and department of public safety agencies range from full law enforcement duties to only traffic patrol, which can impact both the level of employment for agencies as well as the ratio of sworn officers to civilians employed. Any valid comparison must take these factors and the other identified variables affecting crime into consideration.
1 Police employee data were not received from the State Police/Highway Patrol/Department of Public Safety for the state.   2 The total employee count includes employees from agencies that are not represented in other law enforcement employee tables.   3 Data reported are the number of law enforcement employees for the state of New Jersey.

Table 77. Full-Time Law Enforcement Employees, by State, 2017

(Number.)

State	Total law enforcement employees	Total officers		Total civilians		Total agencies	Population, 2017, estimated
		Male	Female	Male	Female		
Alabama	8,065	4,896	339	1,134	1,696	172	2,385,522
Alaska	1,933	1,135	112	249	437	37	739,515
Arizona	22,750	11,480	1,382	4,509	5,379	120	7,016,270
Arkansas	9,531	5,409	567	1,513	2,042	299	2,982,118
California	119,684	68,403	10,337	15,470	25,474	461	33,871,863
Colorado	16,900	9,935	1,467	1,956	3,542	228	5,303,599
Connecticut	9,380	7,045	804	624	907	107	3,588,184
Delaware	3,443	2,049	276	433	685	54	956,493
District of Columbia	4,925	3,325	903	299	398	3	693,972
Florida	72,088	37,654	6,939	10,179	17,316	320	18,257,217
Georgia	32,001	19,990	4,054	2,727	5,230	450	9,110,824
Hawaii	3,729	2,644	307	235	543	4	1,427,538
Idaho	4,506	2,647	204	341	1,314	111	1,715,911
Illinois	35,332	20,897	4,318	5,362	4,755	354	7,976,833
Indiana	9,972	7,178	616	864	1,314	97	3,550,712
Iowa	8,160	4,818	434	1,157	1,751	238	3,081,556
Kansas	9,613	6,166	708	912	1,827	322	2,765,707
Kentucky	9,811	7,151	508	885	1,267	321	4,076,207
Louisiana	20,049	12,004	3,414	1,439	3,192	182	4,458,555
Maine	2,900	2,137	185	220	358	132	1,335,392
Maryland	20,060	13,118	2,417	1,670	2,855	150	6,051,172
Massachusetts	20,119	15,045	1,466	1,534	2,074	300	6,342,223
Michigan	23,856	14,898	2,183	3,195	3,580	568	9,347,361
Minnesota	14,848	8,560	1,129	2,345	2,814	382	5,553,604
Mississippi	4,437	2,608	276	655	898	61	1,153,614
Missouri	20,492	13,197	1,491	2,274	3,530	527	6,024,515
Montana	3,034	1,787	130	491	626	109	1,042,018
Nebraska	4,852	2,954	391	513	994	135	1,704,166
Nevada	9,831	5,991	798	817	2,225	55	2,998,039
New Hampshire	3,623	2,517	247	262	597	167	1,255,077
New Jersey	40,469	28,308	3,033	3,580	5,548	534	8,708,009
New Mexico	4,208	2,646	287	472	803	99	1,022,817
New York	83,642	53,305	9,128	7,680	13,529	404	19,009,435
North Carolina	34,950	21,273	2,797	4,973	5,907	520	10,266,068
North Dakota	2,418	1,542	207	222	447	112	755,052
Ohio	17,954	12,080	1,380	1,672	2,822	293	6,713,767
Oklahoma	12,945	8,104	724	1,685	2,432	414	3,929,215
Oregon	10,729	6,056	711	1,672	2,290	206	4,083,484
Pennsylvania	30,731	23,222	2,617	1,947	2,945	1,064	9,774,479
Rhode Island	3,140	2,308	196	250	386	49	1,059,639
South Carolina	11,876	7,264	1,116	1,448	2,048	283	3,599,207
South Dakota	2,971	1,630	150	523	668	132	858,099
Tennessee	26,765	15,082	1,654	4,711	5,318	438	6,621,003
Texas	70,987	38,154	5,545	11,357	15,931	542	21,164,901
Utah	7,196	4,633	355	936	1,272	132	3,073,003
Vermont	1,506	1,084	112	106	204	85	614,709
Virginia	24,025	16,632	2,404	1,323	3,666	283	8,468,094
Washington	15,385	9,664	1,054	1,789	2,878	254	7,377,379
West Virginia	4,689	3,529	140	414	606	352	1,804,892
Wisconsin	18,406	11,149	1,721	2,342	3,194	410	5,759,066
Wyoming	2,025	1,105	138	284	498	56	551,545

Table 78. Full-Time Law Enforcement Employees, by Selected State and City, 2017

(Number.)

State/city	Population	Total law enforcement employees	Total officers	Total civilians
ALABAMA				
Adamsville	4,334	33	20	13
Addison	735	3	3	0
Albertville	21,588	69	45	24
Alexander City	14,744	68	51	17
Andalusia	8,958	43	32	11
Anniston	21,955	97	80	17
Arab	8,380	36	27	9
Ardmore	1,414	11	7	4
Arley	349	2	2	0
Ashville	2,285	9	9	0
Athens	26,004	59	48	11
Atmore	9,994	31	25	6
Attalla	5,835	27	22	5
Auburn	64,831	132	124	8
Bay Minette	9,483	27	21	6
Bayou La Batre	2,499	17	12	5
Berry	1,091	3	3	0
Bessemer	26,360	164	122	42
Boaz	9,748	36	25	11
Brent	4,916	6	6	0
Brewton	5,436	32	24	8
Bridgeport	2,325	11	7	4
Brundidge	1,955	14	9	5
Camden	1,905	11	10	1
Carrollton	974	2	2	0
Castleberry	545	2	1	1
Centreville	2,698	6	6	0
Chickasaw	5,879	27	22	5
Citronelle	3,882	9	7	2
Clanton	8,882	25	25	0
Columbiana	4,605	13	9	4
Creola	1,968	10	5	5
Cullman	15,613	72	51	21
Daleville	5,068	22	16	6
Daphne	26,669	68	43	25
Dauphin Island	1,265	27	12	15
Decatur	54,958	153	130	23
Dora	1,933	10	6	4
Dothan	68,894	237	165	72
East Brewton	2,405	10	5	5
Elberta	1,707	8	7	1
Eufaula	12,295	60	38	22
Eutaw	2,722	11	10	1
Evergreen	3,653	25	19	6
Flomaton	1,403	15	9	6
Florala	1,947	8	8	0
Florence	40,059	131	106	25
Foley	18,032	92	64	28
Fort Deposit	1,209	5	4	1
Fort Payne	14,098	40	35	5
Fultondale	9,207	32	26	6
Greensboro	2,345	10	9	1
Greenville	7,724	33	28	5
Guntersville	8,476	47	35	12
Hanceville	3,317	22	12	10
Hartford	2,640	12	8	4
Helena	18,965	28	23	5
Hoover	85,634	231	168	63
Irondale	12,362	41	34	7
Jacksonville	12,573	38	30	8
Jasper	13,940	66	46	20
Killen	974	4	4	0
Lafayette	2,963	12	11	1
Lanett	6,383	28	26	2
Leeds	11,964	33	25	8
Level Plains	1,994	5	5	0
Lexington	715	4	4	0
Lineville	2,293	13	9	4
Livingston	3,454	11	7	4
Luverne	2,831	14	13	1
Lynn	635	2	1	1
Madison	48,777	105	78	27
Margaret	4,668	1	1	0
Midland City	2,396	8	4	4
Monroeville	6,007	28	23	5
Montevallo	6,793	23	14	9
Muscle Shoals	13,939	45	35	10
New Brockton	1,159	2	2	0
Northport	25,337	85	67	18
Oneonta	6,721	19	18	1
Opelika	30,476	106	86	20
Opp	6,573	29	20	9
Orange Beach	6,073	75	51	24
Oxford	21,084	68	59	9

Table 78. Full-Time Law Enforcement Employees, by Selected State and City, 2017—Continued

(Number.)

State/city	Population	Total law enforcement employees	Total officers	Total civilians
Ozark	14,559	45	34	11
Phenix City	37,841	101	80	21
Piedmont	4,633	18	13	5
Pine Hill	904	4	4	0
Pleasant Grove	10,191	22	17	5
Priceville	3,414	5	5	0
Prichard	22,119	60	39	21
Ragland	1,707	4	4	0
Rainbow City	9,517	34	22	12
Rainsville	5,025	18	14	4
Roanoke	5,970	29	22	7
Robertsdale	6,112	26	15	11
Russellville	9,810	24	20	4
Samson	1,908	6	6	0
Sardis City	1,782	4	4	0
Satsuma	6,198	17	13	4
Scottsboro	14,660	68	43	25
Silverhill	818	5	5	0
Snead	842	4	4	0
Southside	8,630	15	11	4
Spanish Fort	8,584	25	21	4
Springville	4,280	11	11	0
Steele	1,093	4	4	0
Stevenson	1,966	7	6	1
St. Florian	630	4	4	0
Sumiton	2,390	18	10	8
Summerdale	1,314	7	7	0
Tallassee	4,748	24	18	6
Tarrant	6,249	25	20	5
Thomasville	3,971	23	18	5
Trinity	2,176	7	7	0
Troy	19,360	76	55	21
Tuscaloosa	101,124	342	264	78
Tuskegee	8,549	26	17	9
Valley	9,363	30	28	2
Vestavia Hills	34,781	91	88	3
Warrior	3,195	20	13	7
Weaver	3,081	11	8	3
Wedowee	804	8	8	0
West Blocton	1,259	3	3	0
Woodstock	1,594	4	4	0
ALASKA				
Anchorage	296,188	555	408	147
Bethel	6,426	22	11	11
Bristol Bay Borough	874	9	4	5
Cordova	2,199	9	4	5
Craig	1,235	9	4	5
Dillingham	2,369	17	6	11
Fairbanks	32,937	44	39	5
Haines	2,472	10	5	5
Homer	5,735	21	12	9
Hoonah	743	8	4	4
Juneau	32,344	72	44	28
Kenai	7,852	25	18	7
Ketchikan	8,230	32	21	11
Klawock	802	3	3	0
Kodiak	6,198	38	17	21
Kotzebue	3,251	17	10	7
Nome	3,829	15	8	7
North Pole	2,248	14	13	1
North Slope Borough	9,539	74	46	28
Palmer	7,184	25	14	11
Petersburg	3,108	14	9	5
Sand Point	1,054	3	2	1
Seward	2,806	20	10	10
Sitka	8,736	26	14	12
Skagway	1,100	10	3	7
Soldotna	4,693	16	14	2
St. Paul	498	11	4	7
Unalaska	4,449	25	12	13
Valdez	3,842	11	11	0
Wasilla	10,093	52	23	29
Whittier	213	6	5	1
Wrangell	2,395	11	5	6
ARIZONA				
Apache Junction	40,672	89	59	30
Avondale	84,041	180	122	58
Benson	4,836	22	14	8
Bisbee	5,160	15	11	4
Buckeye	67,147	119	89	30
Bullhead City	40,039	109	67	42
Camp Verde	11,299	27	18	9
Casa Grande	55,530	102	80	22

Table 78. Full-Time Law Enforcement Employees, by Selected State and City, 2017—Continued

(Number.)

State/city	Population	Total law enforcement employees	Total officers	Total civilians
Chandler	249,355	502	335	167
Chino Valley	11,324	31	24	7
Clarkdale	4,304	10	8	2
Clifton	3,817	11	5	6
Colorado City	4,818	8	6	2
Coolidge	12,645	40	28	12
Cottonwood	12,116	56	34	22
Douglas	16,443	45	33	12
Eagar	5,001	8	6	2
El Mirage	35,611	57	44	13
Eloy	17,552	36	23	13
Flagstaff	72,388	152	102	50
Florence	25,623	38	29	9
Fredonia	1,322	2	2	0
Gilbert	242,090	345	231	114
Glendale	249,273	551	423	128
Globe	7,349	18	15	3
Goodyear	79,419	139	99	40
Hayden	976	7	7	0
Holbrook	5,077	15	13	2
Huachuca City	1,725	12	5	7
Jerome	457	4	4	0
Kearny	2,096	9	6	3
Kingman	29,181	69	54	15
Lake Havasu City	53,937	112	71	41
Mammoth	1,534	5	4	1
Marana	45,123	119	91	28
Maricopa	47,466	85	65	20
Mesa	492,268	1,208	786	422
Miami	1,774	11	7	4
Nogales	19,878	65	50	15
Oro Valley	44,251	130	100	30
Page	7,632	31	19	12
Paradise Valley	14,629	45	35	10
Parker	3,022	13	10	3
Patagonia	872	3	3	0
Payson	15,504	41	26	15
Peoria	165,889	288	192	96
Phoenix	1,644,177	3,816	2,838	978
Pima	2,527	6	6	0
Pinetop-Lakeside	4,392	23	15	8
Prescott	42,975	76	65	11
Prescott Valley	43,891	93	73	20
Quartzsite	3,638	12	11	1
Safford	9,617	24	21	3
Sahuarita	29,373	46	40	6
San Luis	32,823	51	34	17
Scottsdale	251,840	623	392	231
Sedona	10,457	37	26	11
Show Low	11,163	39	29	10
Sierra Vista	42,859	87	61	26
Snowflake-Taylor	10,025	21	13	8
Somerton	15,082	29	20	9
South Tucson	5,645	20	18	2
Springerville	2,000	9	7	2
St. Johns	3,581	9	6	3
Superior	3,026	10	9	1
Surprise	135,345	191	135	56
Tempe	186,086	495	356	139
Thatcher	5,054	13	12	1
Tolleson	7,289	48	30	18
Tombstone	1,287	12	10	2
Tucson	532,323	1,174	834	340
Wellton	2,981	7	6	1
Wickenburg	6,979	26	18	8
Willcox	3,471	18	10	8
Williams	3,181	21	13	8
Winslow	9,764	35	25	10
Yuma	95,522	252	168	84
ARKANSAS				
Alexander	2,810	9	7	2
Alma	5,699	22	14	8
Amity	698	1	1	0
Arkadelphia	10,810	29	23	6
Arkansas City	316	1	1	0
Ashdown	4,433	12	11	1
Ash Flat	1,075	4	4	0
Atkins	3,065	8	7	1
Augusta	1,993	6	6	0
Austin	4,091	4	4	0
Bald Knob	2,908	9	7	2
Barling	4,820	11	11	0
Batesville	10,806	25	24	1
Bay	1,819	3	3	0

Table 78. Full-Time Law Enforcement Employees, by Selected State and City, 2017—Continued

(Number.)

State/city	Population	Total law enforcement employees	Total officers	Total civilians
Bearden	874	1	1	0
Beebe	8,258	24	17	7
Bella Vista	28,721	42	30	12
Benton	36,702	88	64	24
Bentonville	49,301	100	72	28
Berryville	5,390	13	11	2
Bethel Heights	2,564	7	6	1
Black Rock	615	1	1	0
Blytheville	14,184	41	30	11
Bono	2,304	4	4	0
Booneville	3,886	13	9	4
Bradford	759	5	4	1
Brinkley	2,740	16	11	5
Brookland	3,353	5	5	0
Bryant	20,593	53	44	9
Bull Shoals	1,944	3	3	0
Cabot	26,118	55	44	11
Caddo Valley	599	4	4	0
Camden	11,069	36	19	17
Cammack Village	742	4	3	1
Caraway	1,275	2	2	0
Carlisle	2,164	10	6	4
Cave City	1,891	4	4	0
Cave Springs	4,031	6	6	0
Cedarville	1,369	2	2	0
Centerton	13,521	23	21	2
Charleston	2,457	4	4	0
Cherokee Village	4,639	9	8	1
Cherry Valley	596	1	1	0
Clarendon	1,424	4	4	0
Clarksville	9,581	23	18	5
Clinton	2,505	8	7	1
Conway	66,299	170	127	43
Corning	3,078	12	8	4
Cotter	944	2	2	0
Crossett	5,069	27	17	10
Danville	2,450	7	6	1
Dardanelle	4,578	15	10	5
Decatur	1,803	6	6	0
Dell	201	1	1	0
De Queen	6,555	16	14	2
Dermott	2,711	12	6	6
Des Arc	1,617	4	4	0
De Valls Bluff	577	1	1	0
De Witt	3,120	15	9	6
Diamond City	787	1	1	0
Diaz	1,219	2	2	0
Dierks	1,093	3	3	0
Dover	1,404	5	5	0
Dumas	4,226	17	11	6
Dyer	864	1	1	0
Earle	2,253	2	2	0
El Dorado	18,257	68	51	17
Elkins	3,018	7	7	0
England	2,741	10	7	3
Etowah	318	1	1	0
Eudora	2,048	5	4	1
Eureka Springs	2,074	15	10	5
Fairfield Bay	2,232	17	7	10
Farmington	6,949	12	11	1
Fayetteville	85,592	175	127	48
Flippin	1,338	5	5	0
Fordyce	3,904	12	7	5
Forrest City	14,343	40	31	9
Fort Smith	88,437	174	134	40
Gassville	2,140	4	4	0
Gentry	3,777	10	8	2
Glenwood	2,128	2	1	1
Gosnell	3,175	7	7	0
Gravette	3,295	12	11	1
Greenbrier	5,488	15	9	6
Green Forest	2,784	14	11	3
Greenland	1,405	4	4	0
Greenwood	9,409	22	20	2
Greers Ferry	859	3	3	0
Gurdon	2,126	6	4	2
Guy	775	1	1	0
Hamburg	2,719	7	6	1
Hampton	1,249	4	4	0
Hardy	768	2	2	0
Harrisburg	2,315	6	5	1
Harrison	13,208	42	31	11
Haskell	4,516	8	8	0
Hazen	1,388	6	5	1
Heber Springs	7,071	25	15	10

Table 78. Full-Time Law Enforcement Employees, by Selected State and City, 2017—Continued

(Number.)

State/city	Population	Total law enforcement employees	Total officers	Total civilians
Helena-West Helena	10,609	34	18	16
Higginson	668	1	1	0
Highfill	659	3	3	0
Highland	1,071	3	3	0
Hope	9,859	36	24	12
Hot Springs	36,956	135	105	30
Hoxie	2,661	4	4	0
Hughes	1,278	3	3	0
Huntington	622	1	1	0
Jacksonville	28,540	81	69	12
Jasper	448	2	2	0
Johnson	3,681	9	8	1
Jonesboro	76,188	185	157	28
Judsonia	2,002	4	3	1
Keiser	676	1	1	0
Kensett	1,647	3	3	0
Lake City	2,462	4	4	0
Lakeview	722	2	2	0
Lake Village	2,357	15	9	6
Lamar	1,680	3	3	0
Lavaca	2,418	3	3	0
Leachville	1,800	3	2	1
Lepanto	1,818	7	3	4
Lewisville	1,134	2	2	0
Lincoln	2,455	5	5	0
Little Flock	2,842	6	6	0
Little Rock	199,314	627	509	118
Lonoke	4,234	16	11	5
Lowell	9,220	24	18	6
Luxora	1,059	2	2	0
Madison	681	4	4	0
Magnolia	11,568	24	22	2
Malvern	11,007	22	20	2
Mammoth Spring	959	2	2	0
Marianna	3,521	28	15	13
Marion	12,356	32	28	4
Marked Tree	2,496	9	5	4
Marmaduke	1,240	4	4	0
Marvell	990	7	4	3
Maumelle	18,278	46	36	10
Mayflower	2,469	9	9	0
McCrory	1,554	5	5	0
McGehee	3,839	25	12	13
McRae	663	3	2	1
Mena	5,624	15	14	1
Menifee	312	1	1	0
Mineral Springs	1,159	1	1	0
Monette	1,573	3	3	0
Monticello	9,775	28	21	7
Morrilton	6,715	26	23	3
Mountainburg	623	1	1	0
Mountain Home	12,347	34	26	8
Mountain View	2,880	10	9	1
Mulberry	1,641	3	3	0
Murfreesboro	1,571	3	3	0
Nashville	4,480	17	16	1
Newport	7,726	22	15	7
North Little Rock	66,938	225	186	39
Ola	1,227	5	4	1
Osceola	6,984	38	25	13
Ozark	3,555	12	10	2
Pangburn	602	2	2	0
Paragould	28,588	65	50	15
Paris	3,443	13	8	5
Parkin	1,035	1	1	0
Pea Ridge	5,506	15	14	1
Perryville	1,415	5	5	0
Piggott	3,574	9	8	1
Pine Bluff	43,040	155	130	25
Plainview	587	1	1	0
Plumerville	796	2	2	0
Pocahontas	6,447	16	15	1
Pottsville	3,146	8	6	2
Prairie Grove	5,511	11	11	0
Prescott	3,039	9	8	1
Quitman	730	4	4	0
Ravenden	447	1	1	0
Redfield	1,547	7	6	1
Rison	1,258	3	3	0
Rogers	66,626	141	102	39
Rose Bud	482	3	3	0
Russellville	29,786	60	53	7
Salem	1,622	4	3	1
Searcy	24,553	68	49	19
Shannon Hills	3,958	6	6	0

Table 78. Full-Time Law Enforcement Employees, by Selected State and City, 2017—Continued

(Number.)

State/city	Population	Total law enforcement employees	Total officers	Total civilians
Sheridan	4,866	29	14	15
Sherwood	30,830	89	65	24
Siloam Springs	16,680	48	35	13
Springdale	79,876	200	140	60
Stamps	1,493	3	3	0
Star City	2,131	7	6	1
St. Charles	218	1	1	0
Stuttgart	8,882	33	24	9
Sulphur Springs	534	3	3	0
Swifton	739	2	2	0
Texarkana	30,334	91	81	10
Trumann	7,104	25	18	7
Tuckerman	1,722	4	4	0
Tyronza	739	2	2	0
Van Buren	23,456	58	44	14
Vilonia	4,595	9	9	0
Waldron	3,331	10	9	1
Walnut Ridge	4,638	8	8	0
Ward	5,007	11	9	2
Warren	5,719	18	11	7
Weiner	681	1	1	0
West Fork	2,588	6	6	0
West Memphis	25,126	100	79	21
White Hall	5,009	17	15	2
Wilson	847	2	2	0
Wynne	8,033	22	20	2
CALIFORNIA				
Alameda	79,761	111	79	32
Albany	19,880	32	24	8
Alhambra	85,865	116	77	39
Alturas	2,491	7	7	0
Anaheim	353,400	602	419	183
Anderson	10,281	26	20	6
Angels Camp	3,779	7	6	1
Antioch	112,252	132	96	36
Arcadia	58,883	93	66	27
Arcata	18,054	36	23	13
Arroyo Grande	18,239	29	25	4
Arvin	21,390	26	18	8
Atascadero	30,661	37	28	9
Atherton	7,256	25	18	7
Atwater	29,442	35	25	10
Auburn	14,069	25	18	7
Avenal	12,054	19	17	2
Azusa	50,202	87	59	28
Bakersfield	381,154	514	364	150
Baldwin Park	76,636	94	69	25
Banning	31,247	38	25	13
Barstow	24,028	54	37	17
Bear Valley	5,497	6	5	1
Beaumont	46,856	56	39	17
Bell	35,925	43	27	16
Bell Gardens	42,930	72	50	22
Belmont	27,285	43	29	14
Belvedere	2,131	8	7	1
Benicia	28,370	46	30	16
Berkeley	122,687	247	162	85
Beverly Hills	34,781	216	133	83
Bishop	3,767	17	12	5
Blythe	19,572	31	21	10
Brawley	26,342	49	35	14
Brea	43,000	92	58	34
Brentwood	62,120	94	64	30
Brisbane	4,764	18	15	3
Broadmoor	4,438	9	8	1
Buena Park	83,552	128	84	44
Burbank	104,622	239	157	82
Burlingame	30,551	59	39	20
Calexico	40,499	33	20	13
California City	13,753	26	16	10
Calistoga	5,336	16	11	5
Campbell	41,192	68	44	24
Capitola	10,222	28	21	7
Carlsbad	115,344	160	115	45
Carmel	3,918	21	13	8
Cathedral City	54,506	74	51	23
Central Marin	35,060	45	40	5
Ceres	48,673	60	47	13
Chico	92,459	138	89	49
Chino	89,420	158	107	51
Chowchilla	18,174	27	18	9
Chula Vista	271,109	309	223	86
Citrus Heights	88,126	132	88	44
Claremont	36,246	60	37	23

Table 78. Full-Time Law Enforcement Employees, by Selected State and City, 2017—Continued

(Number.)

State/city	Population	Total law enforcement employees	Total officers	Total civilians
Clayton	12,173	13	11	2
Clearlake	15,018	23	17	6
Cloverdale	8,830	21	13	8
Clovis	108,419	167	100	67
Coalinga	16,371	25	17	8
Colma	1,520	25	19	6
Colton	55,127	84	50	34
Colusa	5,930	10	9	1
Concord	129,789	205	152	53
Corcoran	22,345	29	16	13
Corning	7,511	20	11	9
Corona	169,164	217	154	63
Coronado	26,294	63	43	20
Costa Mesa	113,267	183	119	64
Cotati	7,485	15	10	5
Covina	48,674	87	57	30
Crescent City	6,529	11	10	1
Culver City	39,440	145	105	40
Cypress	49,064	65	50	15
Daly City	107,355	126	98	28
Davis	68,540	91	58	33
Delano	52,639	69	48	21
Del Rey Oaks	1,694	6	6	0
Desert Hot Springs	28,717	32	24	8
Dinuba	24,387	46	36	10
Dixon	20,049	26	21	5
Dos Palos	5,291	7	6	1
Downey	113,511	154	110	44
East Palo Alto	29,933	46	35	11
El Cajon	104,447	172	116	56
El Centro	44,458	66	47	19
El Cerrito	25,704	47	40	7
Elk Grove	172,620	222	137	85
El Monte	116,168	164	118	46
El Segundo	16,932	75	58	17
Emeryville	11,971	55	41	14
Escalon	7,587	11	10	1
Escondido	152,845	214	159	55
Etna	713	3	3	0
Eureka	27,230	68	47	21
Exeter	10,533	18	16	2
Fairfax	7,623	16	11	5
Fairfield	116,372	167	111	56
Farmersville	10,760	15	14	1
Ferndale	1,372	5	5	0
Firebaugh	8,436	15	11	4
Folsom	78,155	104	72	32
Fontana	211,782	281	179	102
Fort Bragg	7,289	21	15	6
Fortuna	12,154	27	17	10
Foster City	34,808	50	36	14
Fountain Valley	56,704	71	53	18
Fowler	6,475	15	14	1
Fremont	236,368	278	178	100
Fresno	526,371	1,059	786	273
Fullerton	141,637	213	141	72
Galt	25,971	51	30	21
Gardena	60,249	116	92	24
Garden Grove	175,466	222	162	60
Gilroy	56,163	99	62	37
Glendale	202,381	327	233	94
Glendora	52,133	83	52	31
Gonzales	8,508	13	10	3
Grass Valley	12,947	27	24	3
Greenfield	17,603	23	20	3
Gridley	6,588	19	14	5
Grover Beach	13,720	26	18	8
Guadalupe	7,360	14	12	2
Gustine	5,865	11	9	2
Hanford	55,789	82	54	28
Hawthorne	88,664	139	91	48
Hayward	161,417	301	189	112
Healdsburg	11,915	27	18	9
Hemet	85,166	108	77	31
Hercules	25,570	22	20	2
Hermosa Beach	19,836	64	37	27
Hillsborough	11,531	34	27	7
Hollister	38,310	37	31	6
Huntington Beach	202,244	327	208	119
Huntington Park	59,004	81	52	29
Huron	6,973	20	13	7
Imperial	17,629	18	15	3
Indio	90,055	99	63	36
Inglewood	110,811	219	175	44
Ione	6,915	7	7	0

Table 78. Full-Time Law Enforcement Employees, by Selected State and City, 2017—Continued

(Number.)

State/city	Population	Total law enforcement employees	Total officers	Total civilians
Irvine	276,115	302	211	91
Irwindale	1,436	32	26	6
Jackson	4,683	9	8	1
Kensington	5,397	7	7	0
Kerman	14,760	24	21	3
King City	14,037	20	17	3
Kingsburg	11,874	18	15	3
Laguna Beach	23,261	88	48	40
La Habra	61,878	98	67	31
Lakeport	4,775	13	12	1
Lake Shastina	2,562	4	4	0
La Mesa	60,425	96	67	29
La Palma	15,811	24	18	6
La Verne	32,613	60	40	20
Lemoore	25,999	40	33	7
Lincoln	47,741	28	21	7
Lindsay	13,513	19	15	4
Livermore	90,485	138	90	48
Livingston	14,117	29	20	9
Lodi	65,042	95	65	30
Lompoc	43,948	65	41	24
Long Beach	471,397	1,180	799	381
Los Alamitos	11,671	26	23	3
Los Altos	30,816	46	31	15
Los Angeles	4,007,147	12,857	9,988	2,869
Los Banos	37,910	64	40	24
Los Gatos	30,720	53	36	17
Madera	64,939	75	55	20
Mammoth Lakes	7,956	13	10	3
Manhattan Beach	35,843	98	59	39
Manteca	78,564	90	62	28
Marina	22,030	33	27	6
Martinez	38,619	42	32	10
Marysville	12,275	25	18	7
McFarland	14,882	20	13	7
Mendota	11,459	13	11	2
Menlo Park	34,195	61	43	18
Merced	83,180	121	87	34
Mill Valley	14,423	27	21	6
Milpitas	79,503	99	81	18
Modesto	213,677	311	213	98
Monrovia	37,214	79	50	29
Montclair	39,318	64	46	18
Montebello	63,473	94	65	29
Monterey	28,584	69	50	19
Monterey Park	61,210	102	70	32
Moraga	17,653	14	12	2
Morgan Hill	45,277	60	39	21
Morro Bay	10,716	21	17	4
Mountain View	81,525	134	87	47
Mount Shasta	3,276	11	8	3
Murrieta	113,016	127	85	42
Napa	80,958	120	72	48
National City	61,574	119	85	34
Nevada City	3,157	13	11	2
Newark	46,360	78	56	22
Newman	11,271	14	11	3
Newport Beach	86,910	217	135	82
Novato	56,698	80	54	26
Oakdale	22,886	33	22	11
Oakland	424,915	1,037	744	293
Oceanside	176,815	282	204	78
Ontario	174,724	373	273	100
Orange	141,130	219	153	66
Orange Cove	9,674	12	11	1
Orland	7,624	13	10	3
Oroville	19,091	35	19	16
Oxnard	209,513	350	238	112
Pacifica	39,353	36	33	3
Pacific Grove	15,716	30	19	11
Palm Springs	48,193	133	94	39
Palo Alto	67,441	142	77	65
Palos Verdes Estates	13,611	37	33	4
Paradise	26,610	32	19	13
Parlier	15,289	16	16	0
Pasadena	142,891	334	229	105
Paso Robles	32,266	45	33	12
Petaluma	60,957	83	58	25
Piedmont	11,464	25	18	7
Pinole	19,449	35	22	13
Pismo Beach	8,291	33	22	11
Pittsburg	71,944	98	79	19
Placentia	52,437	69	45	24
Placerville	10,732	26	18	8
Pleasant Hill	35,136	59	44	15

Table 78. Full-Time Law Enforcement Employees, by Selected State and City, 2017—Continued

(Number.)

State/city	Population	Total law enforcement employees	Total officers	Total civilians
Pleasanton	84,440	109	76	33
Pomona	153,066	253	147	106
Porterville	59,245	85	56	29
Port Hueneme	22,374	29	22	7
Red Bluff	14,169	40	25	15
Redding	92,127	134	103	31
Redlands	71,707	116	78	38
Redondo Beach	68,051	158	99	59
Redwood City	86,353	113	85	28
Reedley	25,794	42	28	14
Rialto	103,980	137	102	35
Richmond	110,804	244	177	67
Ridgecrest	28,873	50	32	18
Rio Dell	3,414	5	5	0
Rio Vista	8,870	14	12	2
Ripon	15,659	31	22	9
Riverside	328,023	496	350	146
Rocklin	63,735	78	51	27
Rohnert Park	42,922	83	58	25
Roseville	135,028	191	125	66
Ross	2,475	8	8	0
Sacramento	499,997	925	644	281
Salinas	158,313	211	146	65
San Bernardino	217,259	378	236	142
San Bruno	43,274	64	47	17
Sand City	392	14	13	1
San Diego	1,424,116	2,282	1,752	530
San Fernando	24,899	40	28	12
San Francisco	881,255	2,935	2,332	603
San Gabriel	40,531	69	54	15
Sanger	25,126	41	37	4
San Jose	1,037,529	1,346	940	406
San Leandro	91,386	135	93	42
San Luis Obispo	47,934	80	57	23
San Marino	13,402	31	25	6
San Mateo	105,090	146	107	39
San Pablo	30,781	66	42	24
San Rafael	59,144	88	66	22
San Ramon	76,325	83	65	18
Santa Ana	335,699	537	325	212
Santa Barbara	92,508	204	140	64
Santa Clara	127,538	227	153	74
Santa Cruz	65,132	117	90	27
Santa Maria	107,424	171	115	56
Santa Monica	92,935	373	206	167
Santa Paula	30,496	34	27	7
Santa Rosa	176,361	251	173	78
Sausalito	7,155	26	20	6
Scotts Valley	11,985	27	19	8
Seal Beach	24,495	47	31	16
Seaside	34,519	43	31	12
Sebastopol	7,725	20	14	6
Selma	24,817	41	32	9
Shafter	19,284	35	25	10
Sierra Madre	11,080	20	16	4
Signal Hill	11,757	47	33	14
Simi Valley	126,635	181	123	58
Soledad	25,560	19	15	4
Sonora	4,811	16	9	7
South Gate	95,717	116	79	37
South Lake Tahoe	21,768	56	36	20
South Pasadena	25,961	43	32	11
South San Francisco	67,533	114	80	34
Stallion Springs	2,644	4	4	0
St. Helena	6,210	17	12	5
Stockton	309,566	645	441	204
Suisun City	29,738	37	25	12
Sunnyvale	154,919	273	212	61
Susanville	14,414	17	14	3
Sutter Creek	2,517	4	4	0
Taft	9,393	25	17	8
Tehachapi	12,210	24	15	9
Tiburon	9,210	14	10	4
Torrance	147,482	329	213	116
Tracy	90,263	127	85	42
Truckee	16,429	36	23	13
Tulare	63,349	109	72	37
Tulelake	988	2	2	0
Turlock	73,488	117	78	39
Tustin	81,246	138	94	44
Ukiah	15,859	51	33	18
Union City	76,311	100	76	24
Upland	77,154	88	61	27
Vacaville	99,293	155	102	53
Vallejo	122,174	148	107	41

Table 78. Full-Time Law Enforcement Employees, by Selected State and City, 2017—Continued

(Number.)

State/city	Population	Total law enforcement employees	Total officers	Total civilians
Ventura	110,006	177	134	43
Vernon	113	52	38	14
Visalia	132,143	207	139	68
Walnut Creek	69,953	122	83	39
Watsonville	54,226	92	73	19
Weed	2,605	14	9	5
West Covina	108,128	152	94	58
Westminster	91,863	113	76	37
Westmorland	2,276	6	6	0
West Sacramento	53,703	92	71	21
Wheatland	3,831	9	8	1
Whittier	87,141	166	120	46
Williams	5,201	13	11	2
Willits	4,870	14	9	5
Winters	7,235	13	11	2
Woodlake	7,678	10	9	1
Woodland	59,676	79	64	15
Yreka	7,564	21	14	7
Yuba City	67,042	85	55	30
Alamosa	10,025	28	24	4
Arvada	119,346	233	176	57
Aspen	6,906	37	28	9
Ault	1,710	6	5	1
Aurora	368,018	804	649	155
Avon	6,551	19	17	2
Basalt	3,933	11	10	1
Bayfield	2,677	9	8	1
Black Hawk	129	34	23	11
Blue River	924	1	1	0
Boulder	109,722	261	171	90
Breckenridge	4,959	27	20	7
Brighton	39,099	91	66	25
Broomfield	68,158	209	104	105
Brush	5,397	14	11	3
Buena Vista	2,815	10	9	1
Burlington	4,178	9	8	1
Calhan	797	3	3	0
Canon City	16,723	42	36	6
Carbondale	6,844	16	14	2
Castle Rock	59,337	99	72	27
Cedaredge	2,215	8	6	2
Centennial	111,416	164	126	38
Center	2,232	17	7	10
Cherry Hills Village	6,685	27	22	5
Collbran	694	1	1	0
Colorado Springs	472,958	997	707	290
Columbine Valley	1,432	8	8	0
Commerce City	56,469	118	88	30
Cortez	9,095	51	27	24
Craig	8,869	22	17	5
Crested Butte	1,626	7	7	0
Cripple Creek	1,173	22	14	8
Dacono	5,261	13	9	4
De Beque	490	4	4	0
Del Norte	1,583	5	4	1
Delta	8,925	19	16	3
Denver	706,616	1,774	1,479	295
Dillon	970	11	10	1
Durango	18,801	63	52	11
Eagle	6,780	10	9	1
Eaton	5,212	10	9	1
Edgewater	5,350	16	15	1
Elizabeth	1,400	8	7	1
Englewood	34,709	109	77	32
Erie	23,660	32	28	4
Estes Park	6,435	32	20	12
Evans	22,153	40	36	4
Fairplay	708	1	1	0
Federal Heights	12,624	35	25	10
Firestone	13,416	28	23	5
Florence	3,953	14	13	1
Fort Collins	167,633	315	205	110
Fort Lupton	8,057	18	16	2
Fort Morgan	11,347	28	22	6
Fountain	29,203	56	48	8
Fowler	1,139	3	3	0
Fraser/Winter Park	2,293	12	11	1
Frederick	12,850	21	18	3
Frisco	3,154	13	10	3
Fruita	12,971	20	17	3
Georgetown	1,064	3	3	0
Glendale	5,362	40	27	13
Glenwood Springs	10,073	30	25	5
Golden	20,948	66	45	21
Granby	1,929	7	6	1

Table 78. Full-Time Law Enforcement Employees, by Selected State and City, 2017—Continued

(Number.)

State/city	Population	Total law enforcement employees	Total officers	Total civilians
Grand Junction	62,352	186	108	78
Greeley	105,906	200	149	51
Greenwood Village	16,067	83	62	21
Gunnison	6,326	29	14	15
Gypsum	7,052	3	3	0
Haxtun	912	3	3	0
Hayden	1,887	6	4	2
Holyoke	2,195	4	4	0
Hotchkiss	912	3	3	0
Hudson	1,508	4	4	0
Hugo	748	2	2	0
Idaho Springs	1,751	9	8	1
Ignacio	728	6	6	0
Johnstown	16,552	20	18	2
Kersey	1,616	4	4	0
Kiowa	745	1	1	0
Kremmling	1,501	4	4	0
Lafayette	28,939	46	39	7
La Junta	6,900	20	14	6
Lakeside	8	5	4	1
Lakewood	156,344	432	279	153
Lamar	7,468	29	15	14
La Salle	2,153	8	8	0
La Veta	774	2	2	0
Leadville	2,711	9	8	1
Limon	1,967	5	4	1
Littleton	47,112	94	70	24
Lochbuie	5,889	10	8	2
Log Lane Village	863	3	3	0
Lone Tree	13,638	57	49	8
Longmont	93,979	214	142	72
Louisville	21,224	39	34	5
Loveland	78,671	155	101	54
Mancos	1,482	4	4	0
Manitou Springs	5,364	16	14	2
Manzanola	413	2	2	0
Meeker	2,336	6	5	1
Milliken	6,870	13	9	4
Monte Vista	4,235	15	12	3
Montrose	19,346	48	33	15
Monument	6,644	18	14	4
Morrison	437	10	9	1
Mountain View	531	8	8	0
Mountain Village	1,432	7	4	3
Mount Crested Butte	839	9	8	1
Nederland	1,548	4	3	1
New Castle	4,798	10	9	1
Northglenn	39,520	79	64	15
Oak Creek	920	3	3	0
Olathe	1,803	6	5	1
Ouray	1,038	5	5	0
Pagosa Springs	1,858	7	6	1
Palisade	2,645	9	8	1
Palmer Lake	2,672	2	2	0
Paonia	1,420	3	3	0
Parachute	1,119	5	4	1
Parker	52,179	118	72	46
Platteville	3,854	9	7	2
Pueblo	110,872	253	200	53
Rangely	2,359	10	5	5
Ridgway	994	2	2	0
Rifle	9,724	23	18	5
Rocky Ford	3,792	10	8	2
Salida	5,642	19	16	3
Sanford	862	1	1	0
Sheridan	6,103	33	30	3
Silt	3,116	6	6	0
Silverthorne	4,615	19	16	3
Simla	625	2	2	0
Snowmass Village	2,913	13	10	3
South Fork	363	2	2	0
Springfield	1,366	4	4	0
Steamboat Springs	12,799	33	23	10
Sterling	13,955	29	22	7
Stratton	653	1	1	0
Telluride	2,481	16	11	5
Thornton	139,825	287	218	69
Timnath	3,806	8	7	1
Trinidad	7,961	32	23	9
Vail	5,516	68	32	36
Walsh	506	1	1	0
Westminster	115,155	265	190	75
Wheat Ridge	31,567	103	75	28
Wiggins	885	2	2	0
Windsor	23,523	33	29	4

Table 78. Full-Time Law Enforcement Employees, by Selected State and City, 2017—Continued

(Number.)

State/city	Population	Total law enforcement employees	Total officers	Total civilians
Woodland Park	7,424	28	22	6
Wray	2,369	7	6	1
Yuma	3,593	21	6	15
Ansonia	18,647	50	43	7
Avon	18,397	39	30	9
Berlin	20,601	54	41	13
Bethel	19,796	50	37	13
Bloomfield	20,667	58	46	12
Branford	28,027	66	51	15
Bridgeport	146,110	441	388	53
Bristol	60,090	145	120	25
Brookfield	17,203	44	34	10
Canton	10,285	20	15	5
Cheshire	29,282	57	45	12
Clinton	12,915	37	27	10
Coventry	12,431	21	16	5
Cromwell	13,953	35	27	8
Danbury	85,614	144	139	5
Darien	21,910	57	49	8
Derby	12,586	36	34	2
East Hampton	12,855	18	16	2
East Hartford	50,067	159	125	34
East Haven	28,739	56	52	4
East Lyme	18,849	29	23	6
Easton	7,570	17	15	2
East Windsor	11,383	33	25	8
Enfield	44,321	113	92	21
Fairfield	61,402	108	102	6
Farmington	25,551	60	44	16
Glastonbury	34,606	77	56	21
Granby	11,241	21	16	5
Greenwich	62,531	180	153	27
Groton	9,093	35	28	7
Groton Long Point	506	5	5	0
Groton Town	29,524	68	63	5
Guilford	22,259	45	37	8
Hamden	61,042	133	107	26
Hartford	122,891	435	390	45
Ledyard	14,889	28	21	7
Madison	18,130	40	27	13
Manchester	57,808	140	109	31
Meriden	59,417	123	111	12
Middlebury	7,651	13	11	2
Middletown	46,363	128	114	14
Milford	54,265	133	115	18
Monroe	19,682	55	43	12
Naugatuck	31,310	71	60	11
New Britain	72,442	166	158	8
New Canaan	20,364	52	46	6
New Haven	129,953	476	427	49
Newington	30,402	61	50	11
New London	26,880	83	68	15
New Milford	26,993	53	42	11
Newtown	27,908	49	45	4
North Branford	14,163	27	22	5
North Haven	23,646	58	49	9
Norwalk	88,849	218	179	39
Norwich	39,393	101	84	17
Old Saybrook	10,070	25	17	8
Orange	13,904	56	46	10
Plainfield	15,011	22	18	4
Plainville	17,669	45	37	8
Plymouth	11,671	29	23	6
Portland	9,324	13	12	1
Putnam	9,293	19	15	4
Redding	9,223	23	17	6
Ridgefield	25,127	47	40	7
Rocky Hill	20,189	50	35	15
Seymour	16,555	41	39	2
Shelton	41,625	58	50	8
Simsbury	24,559	48	37	11
Southington	43,769	85	64	21
South Windsor	25,740	54	41	13
Stamford	130,189	333	283	50
Stonington	18,666	49	38	11
Stratford	52,263	111	104	7
Suffield	15,602	26	21	5
Thomaston	7,548	28	18	10
Torrington	34,372	90	80	10
Trumbull	36,265	89	78	11
Vernon	29,142	62	49	13
Wallingford	44,577	87	66	21
Waterbury	107,924	321	277	44
Waterford	19,034	50	45	5
Watertown	21,672	46	37	9

Table 78. Full-Time Law Enforcement Employees, by Selected State and City, 2017—Continued

(Number.)

State/city	Population	Total law enforcement employees	Total officers	Total civilians
West Hartford	62,812	141	122	19
West Haven	54,342	133	118	15
Weston	10,320	17	16	1
Westport	28,079	77	64	13
Wethersfield	26,116	64	48	16
Willimantic	17,768	48	43	5
Wilton	18,643	48	44	4
Winchester	10,677	26	21	5
Windsor	28,836	65	52	13
Windsor Locks	12,513	33	26	7
Wolcott	16,632	31	22	9
Woodbridge	8,816	32	24	8
DELAWARE				
Bethany Beach	1,218	11	10	1
Blades	1,404	3	3	0
Bridgeville	2,345	7	7	0
Camden	3,492	9	8	1
Cheswold	1,435	4	4	0
Dagsboro	895	3	3	0
Delaware City	1,750	5	4	1
Delmar	1,794	14	13	1
Dewey Beach	386	10	8	2
Dover	38,084	139	98	41
Ellendale	430	1	1	0
Elsmere	6,102	13	9	4
Felton	1,426	3	3	0
Fenwick Island	434	7	6	1
Georgetown	7,338	25	20	5
Greenwood	1,105	5	3	2
Harrington	3,699	14	13	1
Laurel	4,238	18	17	1
Lewes	3,131	14	13	1
Middletown	21,213	38	32	6
Milford	11,223	41	30	11
Millsboro	4,366	16	15	1
Milton	2,932	9	8	1
Newark	33,722	88	70	18
New Castle	5,362	18	17	1
Newport	1,049	9	8	1
Ocean View	2,117	10	9	1
Rehoboth Beach	1,516	28	17	11
Seaford	7,880	36	25	11
Selbyville	2,466	7	6	1
Smyrna	11,593	30	23	7
South Bethany	518	8	7	1
Wilmington	71,552	364	300	64
Wyoming	1,516	3	3	0
DISTRICT OF COLUMBIA				
Washington	693,972	4,473	3,836	637
FLORIDA				
Altamonte Springs	43,833	113	94	19
Apopka	50,833	142	104	38
Arcadia	7,992	19	15	4
Atlantic Beach	13,589	38	26	12
Atlantis	2,141	19	14	5
Auburndale	15,903	43	35	8
Aventura	38,039	121	81	40
Bal Harbour Village	3,114	37	24	13
Bartow	19,889	57	38	19
Bay Harbor Islands	6,049	28	22	6
Belleair	4,048	16	14	2
Belle Isle	6,973	17	16	1
Belleview	4,926	15	13	2
Biscayne Park	3,218	11	11	0
Blountstown	2,499	15	12	3
Boca Raton	98,069	302	205	97
Bowling Green	2,904	7	7	0
Boynton Beach	76,845	199	147	52
Bradenton	56,821	155	118	37
Bradenton Beach	1,278	10	10	0
Brooksville	8,047	28	25	3
Bunnell	2,900	10	8	2
Cape Coral	184,346	317	219	98
Carrabelle	2,742	5	5	0
Casselberry	27,218	60	51	9
Cedar Key	706	3	3	0
Chattahoochee	3,082	11	10	1
Chiefland	2,222	14	12	2
Clearwater	115,295	328	240	88
Clermont	34,412	74	68	6
Clewiston	7,735	21	13	8
Cocoa	18,265	90	62	28

Table 78. Full-Time Law Enforcement Employees, by Selected State and City, 2017—Continued

(Number.)

State/city	Population	Total law enforcement employees	Total officers	Total civilians
Coconut Creek	60,533	130	96	34
Cooper City	36,694	77	59	18
Coral Gables	51,487	252	170	82
Coral Springs	131,558	305	211	94
Cottondale	890	3	3	0
Crescent City	1,544	7	6	1
Dade City	7,214	30	23	7
Dania Beach	31,718	75	68	7
Davenport	4,201	9	8	1
Davie	103,555	248	185	63
Daytona Beach	67,564	259	225	34
Daytona Beach Shores	4,518	38	30	8
Deerfield Beach	80,552	129	122	7
Deland	32,406	79	62	17
Delray Beach	68,533	222	162	60
Dunnellon	1,815	8	7	1
Eatonville	2,297	14	12	2
Edgewater	22,301	31	26	5
Edgewood	2,914	15	12	3
Eustis	21,161	52	39	13
Fellsmere	5,608	8	7	1
Flagler Beach	5,087	18	15	3
Florida City	12,215	41	31	10
Fort Lauderdale	180,972	655	503	152
Fort Myers	79,918	235	173	62
Fort Pierce	45,858	141	114	27
Fort Walton Beach	22,413	60	44	16
Fruitland Park	6,435	17	16	1
Gainesville	132,777	398	284	114
Graceville	2,202	8	7	1
Green Cove Springs	7,800	22	19	3
Gulf Breeze	6,586	28	18	10
Gulfport	12,473	33	29	4
Gulf Stream	860	12	12	0
Haines City	23,968	57	43	14
Hallandale Beach	39,896	129	95	34
Havana	1,678	15	10	5
Hialeah	238,260	347	281	66
Hialeah Gardens	24,192	55	39	16
High Springs	6,046	16	15	1
Holly Hill	12,226	28	24	4
Hollywood	153,893	391	302	89
Holmes Beach	4,364	23	16	7
Homestead	69,276	150	116	34
Howey-in-the-Hills	1,195	6	6	0
Indialantic	2,919	14	10	4
Indian Creek Village	92	13	9	4
Indian Harbour Beach	8,649	27	20	7
Indian River Shores	4,286	24	21	3
Jacksonville	894,638	3,094	1,665	1,429
Jacksonville Beach	23,740	85	64	21
Jasper	4,156	8	7	1
Jennings	873	4	4	0
Juno Beach	3,629	18	16	2
Jupiter	65,311	145	115	30
Jupiter Inlet Colony	462	5	5	0
Jupiter Island	916	21	16	5
Kenneth City	5,125	13	12	1
Key Biscayne	13,127	47	36	11
Key Colony Beach	861	10	5	5
Key West	27,399	120	94	26
Kissimmee	71,130	202	129	73
Lady Lake	15,151	32	27	5
Lake Alfred	5,899	16	12	4
Lake Clarke Shores	3,611	12	11	1
Lake Hamilton	1,409	8	7	1
Lake Helen	2,758	6	5	1
Lakeland	107,927	336	230	106
Lake Mary	16,636	58	43	15
Lake Placid	2,272	10	8	2
Lake Wales	16,150	51	45	6
Lantana	11,322	35	27	8
Largo	83,728	185	146	39
Lauderdale-by-the-Sea	6,589	26	24	2
Lauderdale Lakes	35,144	41	39	2
Lawtey	716	2	2	0
Leesburg	22,763	88	63	25
Lighthouse Point	11,277	41	32	9
Live Oak	6,984	19	16	3
Longboat Key	7,400	21	18	3
Longwood	15,254	41	37	4
Lynn Haven	21,262	36	26	10
Madison	2,823	16	15	1
Maitland	17,830	57	49	8
Manalapan	466	11	10	1

Table 78. Full-Time Law Enforcement Employees, by Selected State and City, 2017—Continued

(Number.)

State/city	Population	Total law enforcement employees	Total officers	Total civilians
Marco Island	18,089	38	34	4
Margate	58,649	144	110	34
Marianna	9,346	25	18	7
Mascotte	5,613	13	12	1
Medley	844	48	39	9
Melbourne	82,013	210	153	57
Melbourne Beach	3,306	11	10	1
Melbourne Village	708	5	5	0
Miami	463,009	1,666	1,217	449
Miami Gardens	114,008	260	204	56
Miami Shores	10,808	45	37	8
Miami Springs	14,529	55	43	12
Midway	3,301	2	1	1
Milton	10,011	24	17	7
Miramar	141,328	293	214	79
Monticello	2,385	13	9	4
Mount Dora	14,104	47	33	14
Naples	22,244	102	70	32
Neptune Beach	7,388	28	20	8
New Port Richey	16,388	63	44	19
New Smyrna Beach	26,230	56	42	14
Niceville	15,380	33	23	10
North Bay Village	8,463	34	26	8
North Lauderdale	44,137	58	52	6
North Miami	62,543	149	114	35
North Miami Beach	44,269	136	102	34
North Palm Beach	13,160	36	31	5
North Port	65,498	120	88	32
Oakland	2,949	12	11	1
Oakland Park	44,814	95	84	11
Ocala	59,731	241	150	91
Ocean Ridge	1,946	19	15	4
Ocoee	46,501	86	74	12
Opa Locka	16,668	47	43	4
Orange City	11,478	27	21	6
Orange Park	8,848	29	22	7
Orlando	283,982	926	714	212
Ormond Beach	42,625	77	61	16
Oviedo	40,391	70	63	7
Palatka	10,439	37	31	6
Palm Bay	111,275	218	156	62
Palm Beach	8,779	95	62	33
Palm Beach Gardens	54,677	161	105	56
Palm Beach Shores	1,253	15	11	4
Palmetto	13,581	48	35	13
Palm Springs	24,300	60	43	17
Panama City Beach	12,987	78	59	19
Parker	4,667	10	9	1
Parkland	32,951	42	37	5
Pembroke Pines	170,923	327	241	86
Perry	7,051	22	20	2
Pinellas Park	52,635	125	104	21
Plantation	93,995	261	169	92
Plant City	38,798	83	66	17
Pompano Beach	111,027	235	208	27
Ponce Inlet	3,253	14	12	2
Port Orange	61,892	108	92	16
Port Richey	2,836	19	14	5
Port St. Joe	3,479	8	8	0
Port St. Lucie	188,652	297	231	66
Punta Gorda	19,181	47	31	16
Riviera Beach	34,536	139	108	31
Rockledge	27,432	69	50	19
Sanford	59,457	153	133	20
Sanibel	7,505	38	23	15
Sarasota	57,383	208	159	49
Satellite Beach	10,954	32	21	11
Sea Ranch Lakes	740	11	7	4
Sebastian	25,277	55	37	18
Sebring	10,679	38	32	6
Sewall's Point	2,212	11	10	1
Shalimar	820	4	4	0
South Daytona	12,882	34	28	6
South Miami	12,291	55	47	8
South Palm Beach	1,447	8	8	0
Springfield	9,593	23	18	5
Starke	5,413	20	19	1
St. Augustine	14,500	66	51	15
St. Cloud	49,791	123	80	43
St. Petersburg	263,712	756	556	200
Stuart	16,800	63	43	20
Surfside	5,849	34	28	6
Sweetwater	20,824	121	36	85
Tallahassee	192,455	446	375	71
Tamarac	65,988	94	77	17

Table 78. Full-Time Law Enforcement Employees, by Selected State and City, 2017—Continued

(Number.)

State/city	Population	Total law enforcement employees	Total officers	Total civilians
Tampa	384,360	1,213	956	257
Tarpon Springs	25,104	64	51	13
Tavares	16,274	28	25	3
Temple Terrace	26,854	62	45	17
Tequesta	6,049	24	19	5
Titusville	46,425	138	84	54
Umatilla	3,808	10	9	1
Valparaiso	5,081	17	12	5
Venice	22,762	56	45	11
Vero Beach	17,015	72	51	21
Village of Pinecrest	19,644	66	46	20
Virginia Gardens	2,487	7	6	1
Wauchula	4,920	17	13	4
Welaka	681	1	1	0
West Melbourne	21,808	53	43	10
West Miami	7,742	23	18	5
Weston	70,796	99	78	21
West Palm Beach	109,459	357	268	89
West Park	15,272	40	37	3
White Springs	775	4	4	0
Wildwood	7,810	46	36	10
Williston	2,758	19	12	7
Wilton Manors	12,861	46	31	15
Winter Garden	43,295	100	73	27
Winter Haven	39,859	114	85	29
Winter Park	30,602	106	78	28
Winter Springs	35,995	64	50	14
Zephyrhills	15,145	47	32	15
GEORGIA				
Abbeville	2,736	5	5	0
Acworth	22,747	59	43	16
Adairsville	4,844	15	14	1
Adel	5,359	44	20	24
Alamo	3,437	4	4	0
Albany	73,209	177	153	24
Alma	3,570	13	10	3
Alto	1,163	5	2	3
Americus	15,668	41	34	7
Aragon	1,241	12	4	8
Arcade	1,811	3	3	0
Ashburn	3,674	17	15	2
Athens-Clarke County	124,903	291	227	64
Atlanta	481,343	2,087	1,621	466
Attapulgus	429	2	1	1
Auburn	7,698	21	16	5
Austell	7,224	27	19	8
Avondale Estates	3,183	13	13	0
Bainbridge	12,208	46	40	6
Baldwin	3,308	14	9	5
Ball Ground	2,003	4	4	0
Barnesville	6,696	20	19	1
Baxley	4,752	12	11	1
Berlin	560	2	2	0
Blackshear	3,620	16	13	3
Blairsville	569	8	7	1
Bloomingdale	2,729	16	14	2
Blue Ridge	1,400	9	8	1
Blythe	689	2	2	0
Bowdon	2,106	10	8	2
Braselton	10,761	17	16	1
Braswell	391	1	1	0
Bremen	6,453	22	20	2
Brookhaven	52,973	86	67	19
Brooklet	1,547	6	5	1
Brunswick	16,500	62	58	4
Buena Vista	2,132	5	5	0
Butler	1,854	5	4	1
Byron	5,228	21	17	4
Cairo	9,558	24	21	3
Calhoun	16,557	50	43	7
Canon	804	1	1	0
Carrollton	26,951	83	67	16
Cave Spring	1,145	1	1	0
Cedartown	9,806	37	34	3
Centerville	7,689	20	17	3
Chamblee	28,558	82	62	20
Chatsworth	4,258	17	16	1
Clarkesville	1,777	7	6	1
Clarkston	12,849	22	17	5
Claxton	2,284	9	8	1
Clayton	2,285	12	12	0
Cleveland	3,912	14	13	1
Cochran	5,029	13	12	1
College Park	15,134	135	97	38

Table 78. Full-Time Law Enforcement Employees, by Selected State and City, 2017—Continued

(Number.)

State/city	Population	Total law enforcement employees	Total officers	Total civilians
Colquitt	1,896	12	9	3
Commerce	6,826	23	19	4
Conyers	16,034	82	62	20
Coolidge	529	2	1	1
Cordele	10,812	37	27	10
Covington	14,122	66	55	11
Cumming	6,365	19	12	7
Dallas	13,373	27	19	8
Dalton	34,228	98	86	12
Danielsville	588	3	3	0
Darien	1,830	13	13	0
Davisboro	1,659	1	1	0
Dawson	4,249	17	11	6
Decatur	23,378	49	38	11
Demorest	2,094	7	7	0
Dillard	336	4	3	1
Doerun	769	5	4	1
Donalsonville	2,635	13	9	4
Doraville	10,593	60	43	17
Douglasville	33,640	114	96	18
Dublin	16,086	71	61	10
Duluth	29,795	71	56	15
Dunwoody	49,321	67	54	13
East Ellijay	561	13	8	5
Eastman	5,093	13	11	2
East Point	35,740	127	84	43
Eatonton	6,568	22	15	7
Edison	1,437	6	5	1
Elberton	4,397	23	20	3
Ellaville	1,856	5	4	1
Ellijay	1,705	11	11	0
Emerson	1,579	7	7	0
Enigma	1,300	4	3	1
Eton	896	3	3	0
Euharlee	4,320	10	9	1
Fairburn	14,370	45	38	7
Fayetteville	17,749	52	44	8
Fitzgerald	8,902	34	27	7
Flowery Branch	7,317	17	15	2
Folkston	4,795	7	6	1
Forest Park	19,948	88	68	20
Forsyth	4,169	18	14	4
Fort Oglethorpe	9,935	33	31	2
Fort Valley	8,465	35	25	10
Franklin	959	8	8	0
Franklin Springs	1,160	2	2	0
Gainesville	40,836	106	93	13
Garden City	8,932	46	37	9
Glennville	5,086	15	13	2
Gordon	1,943	11	6	5
Graham	300	2	1	1
Grantville	3,226	13	12	1
Gray	3,270	13	12	1
Greensboro	3,388	22	19	3
Greenville	852	8	7	1
Griffin	22,878	91	70	21
Grovetown	13,841	28	22	6
Guyton	1,928	3	3	0
Hahira	2,968	8	7	1
Hampton	7,623	20	18	2
Hapeville	6,665	36	22	14
Harlem	3,077	7	6	1
Hartwell	4,511	25	20	5
Hazlehurst	4,178	11	11	0
Helen	547	10	9	1
Hiawassee	921	5	5	0
Hiram	3,954	17	14	3
Hoboken	525	3	2	1
Hogansville	3,157	22	15	7
Holly Springs	11,653	30	29	1
Homeland	855	7	7	0
Homerville	2,451	9	8	1
Ivey	911	2	1	1
Jackson	5,071	13	12	1
Jasper	3,841	19	17	2
Jesup	10,170	28	26	2
Johns Creek	85,048	83	75	8
Jonesboro	4,731	38	32	6
Kennesaw	34,154	67	59	8
Kingsland	16,852	35	33	2
Kingston	657	2	1	1
LaGrange	30,981	106	89	17
Lake City	2,811	17	16	1
Lakeland	3,284	10	8	2
Lake Park	724	4	4	0

Table 78. Full-Time Law Enforcement Employees, by Selected State and City, 2017—Continued

(Number.)

State/city	Population	Total law enforcement employees	Total officers	Total civilians
Lavonia	2,170	15	15	0
Lawrenceville	31,183	98	72	26
Leary	573	1	1	0
Leslie	380	4	3	1
Lilburn	12,844	37	28	9
Locust Grove	6,028	26	23	3
Loganville	11,887	32	29	3
Lookout Mountain	1,573	7	7	0
Ludowici	2,244	10	6	4
Lumber City	1,255	1	1	0
Madison	4,072	14	12	2
Manchester	4,034	17	12	5
Marietta	61,646	181	134	47
Marshallville	1,292	4	3	1
Maysville	1,901	7	3	4
McDonough	24,278	44	39	5
McIntyre	611	5	5	0
McRae-Helena	8,295	12	11	1
Metter	4,066	11	10	1
Midville	262	1	1	0
Milledgeville	19,051	67	43	24
Millen	2,853	10	10	0
Milton	39,388	43	37	6
Molena	371	2	1	1
Montezuma	3,095	11	9	2
Morrow	7,400	24	23	1
Moultrie	14,365	29	26	3
Nahunta	1,047	5	2	3
Nashville	4,849	16	13	3
Newnan	38,825	93	80	13
Norcross	17,060	57	43	14
Norman Park	968	4	2	2
Oakwood	4,200	15	13	2
Ocilla	3,630	14	14	0
Oxford	2,239	3	3	0
Palmetto	4,744	18	15	3
Patterson	758	2	2	0
Peachtree City	35,300	69	64	5
Pembroke	2,539	9	7	2
Perry	16,624	46	40	6
Pine Lake	767	4	3	1
Pine Mountain	1,385	11	9	2
Plains	727	3	3	0
Port Wentworth	8,452	35	30	5
Powder Springs	15,127	32	28	4
Quitman	3,884	15	14	1
Remerton	1,122	10	8	2
Reynolds	1,016	7	5	2
Richmond Hill	13,059	34	25	9
Rincon	10,101	23	21	2
Ringgold	4,403	11	11	0
Riverdale	16,435	49	36	13
Rochelle	1,101	8	6	2
Rockmart	4,317	20	18	2
Rome	36,366	98	88	10
Roswell	95,602	185	145	40
Sandersville	5,669	20	17	3
Sandy Springs	107,740	150	129	21
Sardis	971	5	5	0
Savannah-Chatham Metropolitan	242,941	812	620	192
Screven	778	2	2	0
Senoia	4,283	17	15	2
Shiloh	462	5	1	4
Smyrna	57,576	130	85	45
Snellville	19,982	56	44	12
Social Circle	4,490	15	14	1
Sparks	1,994	3	3	0
Sparta	1,264	14	7	7
Springfield	4,308	7	6	1
Stapleton	397	2	2	0
Statesboro	31,937	73	58	15
St. Marys	18,220	28	25	3
Stone Mountain	6,413	19	18	1
Summerville	4,337	17	15	2
Suwanee	20,186	48	37	11
Sylvania	2,514	11	9	2
Sylvester	6,042	24	18	6
Talbotton	834	4	2	2
Tallapoosa	3,189	11	10	1
Tallulah Falls	171	2	2	0
Temple	4,403	14	11	3
Tennille	1,914	4	4	0
Thomasville	18,866	54	48	6
Thunderbolt	2,710	9	8	1
Tifton	16,908	49	41	8

Table 78. Full-Time Law Enforcement Employees, by Selected State and City, 2017—Continued

(Number.)

State/city	Population	Total law enforcement employees	Total officers	Total civilians
Trenton	2,248	8	8	0
Tybee Island	3,134	34	25	9
Tyrone	7,260	17	17	0
Union City	21,160	68	55	13
Valdosta	56,729	174	147	27
Vidalia	10,743	42	32	10
Vienna	3,652	8	7	1
Villa Rica	15,398	48	40	8
Warner Robins	75,323	142	104	38
Warrenton	1,786	6	6	0
Warwick	407	6	4	2
Watkinsville	2,866	8	8	0
Waverly Hall	763	5	4	1
Waycross	13,996	73	61	12
Waynesboro	5,669	27	20	7
West Point	3,821	23	13	10
Whigham	473	3	2	1
White	735	1	1	0
Willacoochee	1,367	6	5	1
Winder	16,006	41	37	4
Winterville	1,210	2	2	0
Woodbury	892	10	7	3
Woodstock	32,293	56	52	4
Wrens	2,020	8	7	1
Zebulon	1,166	6	6	0
HAWAII				
Honolulu	990,384	2,510	2,013	497
IDAHO				
Aberdeen	1,910	7	4	3
American Falls	4,286	9	7	2
Bellevue	2,315	1	1	0
Blackfoot	11,870	30	27	3
Boise	225,677	375	290	85
Bonners Ferry	2,574	6	6	0
Buhl	4,326	8	7	1
Caldwell	54,345	78	64	14
Cascade	974	5	4	1
Chubbuck	14,754	36	22	14
Coeur d'Alene	51,364	106	87	19
Cottonwood	919	1	1	0
Emmett	6,747	13	11	2
Filer	2,757	5	5	0
Fruitland	5,205	15	9	6
Garden City	11,708	33	26	7
Gooding	3,481	9	7	2
Grangeville	3,137	6	6	0
Hagerman	878	1	1	0
Hailey	8,267	13	12	1
Heyburn	3,306	8	7	1
Homedale	2,577	6	5	1
Idaho City	441	1	1	0
Idaho Falls	60,727	127	88	39
Jerome	11,380	22	18	4
Kamiah	1,292	3	3	0
Kellogg	2,074	7	7	0
Ketchum	2,760	13	11	2
Kimberly	3,812	9	8	1
Lewiston	33,029	69	45	24
McCall	3,338	13	12	1
Meridian	99,241	123	98	25
Middleton	7,486	7	7	0
Montpelier	2,492	6	5	1
Moscow	25,576	40	34	6
Mountain Home	13,772	32	28	4
Nampa	93,064	165	113	52
Orofino	3,039	7	6	1
Osburn	1,500	2	2	0
Parma	2,101	4	4	0
Payette	7,405	16	14	2
Pinehurst	1,571	2	2	0
Pocatello	54,814	129	91	38
Ponderay	1,158	7	6	1
Post Falls	32,583	72	44	28
Preston	5,372	8	7	1
Priest River	1,780	7	5	2
Rathdrum	8,113	16	14	2
Rexburg	28,698	40	32	8
Rigby	4,078	7	6	1
Rupert	5,849	12	11	1
Salmon	3,040	8	8	0
Sandpoint	8,090	22	19	3
Shelley	4,329	8	8	0
Shoshone	1,506	5	5	0

Table 78. Full-Time Law Enforcement Employees, by Selected State and City, 2017—Continued

(Number.)

State/city	Population	Total law enforcement employees	Total officers	Total civilians
Soda Springs	2,970	7	7	0
Spirit Lake	2,207	6	5	1
St. Anthony	3,493	6	6	0
Sun Valley	1,441	11	10	1
Twin Falls	48,912	94	74	20
Weiser	5,383	14	11	3
Wendell	2,700	4	4	0
Wilder	1,697	5	5	0
ILLINOIS				
Alsip	19,137	48	39	9
Altamont	2,292	4	4	0
Amboy	2,308	4	4	0
Anna	4,244	7	7	0
Annawan	851	1	1	0
Antioch	14,242	30	27	3
Arlington Heights	75,586	130	107	23
Aroma Park	698	3	3	0
Arthur	2,265	5	5	0
Ashland	1,224	1	1	0
Assumption	1,094	1	1	0
Athens	1,944	4	4	0
Atwood	1,179	1	1	0
Aviston	2,119	1	1	0
Barrington Hills	4,221	20	16	4
Barry	1,260	1	1	0
Bartlett	41,167	69	54	15
Belleville	41,511	101	76	25
Bensenville	18,353	40	34	6
Berwyn	55,594	165	114	51
Bloomington	78,203	158	127	31
Bourbonnais	18,474	26	25	1
Bradley	15,405	46	33	13
Braidwood	6,145	19	16	3
Brookfield	18,715	34	29	5
Buffalo Grove	41,323	73	62	11
Burbank	28,876	52	43	9
Burr Ridge	10,813	31	26	5
Byron	3,604	7	6	1
Campton Hills	11,342	6	6	0
Carbondale	26,127	82	65	17
Carlinville	5,585	17	12	5
Carol Stream	40,118	90	67	23
Carpentersville	38,380	63	59	4
Carrollton	2,411	6	6	0
Carthage	2,537	3	3	0
Centreville	4,988	13	12	1
Champaign	87,543	147	124	23
Charleston	21,016	33	30	3
Chenoa	3,167	4	4	0
Cherry Valley	3,075	14	13	1
Chester	8,559	12	9	3
Chicago	2,706,171	13,566	12,383	1,183
Chicago Ridge	14,222	35	31	4
Chillicothe	6,225	11	11	0
Cicero	82,779	174	153	21
Coal City	5,409	10	9	1
Coal Valley	3,721	7	7	0
Cobden	1,119	3	3	0
Collinsville	24,487	60	42	18
Columbia	10,369	22	15	7
Cortland	4,331	5	5	0
Countryside	5,951	27	24	3
Crest Hill	21,223	32	30	2
Crete	8,151	17	16	1
Crystal Lake	40,228	70	62	8
Danvers	1,121	2	2	0
Danville	31,368	68	56	12
Decatur	72,153	181	150	31
Deer Creek	670	1	1	0
Deerfield	19,126	54	40	14
De Kalb	43,043	77	63	14
Delavan	1,625	4	4	0
De Pue	1,710	3	3	0
De Soto	1,559	4	3	1
Des Plaines	58,089	118	98	20
Downers Grove	49,563	87	71	16
Dupo	3,848	8	8	0
Du Quoin	5,808	15	11	4
Earlville	1,606	3	3	0
Edinburg	1,037	2	2	0
Effingham	12,710	40	26	14
Elburn	5,782	7	6	1
Elgin	112,767	233	182	51
Elk Grove Village	32,894	101	88	13

Table 78. Full-Time Law Enforcement Employees, by Selected State and City, 2017—Continued

(Number.)

State/city	Population	Total law enforcement employees	Total officers	Total civilians
Elmwood Park	24,581	42	35	7
Elwood	2,252	10	9	1
Energy	1,141	4	4	0
Erie	1,526	3	3	0
Eureka	5,393	6	6	0
Evanston	74,947	225	164	61
Evergreen Park	19,600	81	62	19
Fairfield	5,004	14	10	4
Fairmount	604	1	1	0
Farmington	2,293	4	4	0
Fisher	1,943	2	2	0
Flossmoor	9,347	26	21	5
Fox Lake	10,432	29	24	5
Fox River Grove	4,628	10	10	0
Freeburg	4,211	10	9	1
Freeport	24,196	62	45	17
Galena	3,229	11	10	1
Georgetown	3,286	4	4	0
Gibson City	3,372	8	7	1
Glendale Heights	34,128	70	54	16
Glenview	47,944	75	70	5
Golf	494	1	1	0
Goodfield	1,004	1	1	0
Grafton	635	2	2	0
Grandview	1,420	3	3	0
Greenfield	982	2	2	0
Greenup	1,485	3	3	0
Greenville	6,713	14	10	4
Gurnee	30,902	95	62	33
Hampshire	6,367	12	12	0
Hanover Park	38,053	84	60	24
Hartford	1,370	5	4	1
Harvard	9,067	18	16	2
Hawthorn Woods	8,234	13	12	1
Henry	2,291	5	4	1
Hickory Hills	13,980	35	28	7
Highland	9,809	27	20	7
Hillsdale	503	1	1	0
Hillside	8,066	34	27	7
Hinckley	2,055	2	2	0
Hinsdale	17,765	24	22	2
Hodgkins	1,840	23	21	2
Hoffman Estates	51,704	103	88	15
Homer	1,176	1	1	0
Hoopeston	5,106	14	10	4
Hopedale	831	1	1	0
Island Lake	8,076	15	14	1
Jacksonville	18,615	41	37	4
Jerseyville	8,315	21	15	6
Johnsburg	6,251	13	11	2
Joliet	148,342	336	267	69
Justice	12,829	29	22	7
Kansas	729	1	1	0
Kenilworth	2,522	9	8	1
Kewanee	12,386	27	21	6
Kildeer	4,072	9	8	1
Kincaid	1,405	2	2	0
Kingston	1,160	2	2	0
Kirkland	1,730	2	2	0
La Grange	15,617	30	26	4
Lake Bluff	5,664	17	15	2
Lake Villa	8,800	18	17	1
Lakewood	3,878	8	8	0
Lake Zurich	20,012	51	32	19
La Salle	9,134	23	22	1
Le Roy	3,547	7	7	0
Lincolnshire	7,259	25	22	3
Lindenhurst	14,362	15	13	2
Lockport	25,280	44	38	6
Lombard	43,885	77	66	11
Lyons	10,601	13	9	4
Machesney Park	22,772	29	28	1
Macomb	18,200	27	24	3
Manhattan	7,625	12	10	2
Marengo	7,406	14	12	2
Marissa	1,814	4	4	0
Marseilles	4,893	11	10	1
Maryville	7,968	14	13	1
Mattoon	17,942	42	37	5
McHenry	26,540	75	46	29
McLean	802	1	1	0
Mendota	7,124	17	15	2
Metropolis	6,238	18	14	4
Midlothian	14,678	29	27	2
Milledgeville	968	2	2	0

Table 78. Full-Time Law Enforcement Employees, by Selected State and City, 2017—Continued

(Number.)

State/city	Population	Total law enforcement employees	Total officers	Total civilians
Mokena	20,321	30	27	3
Moline	42,042	96	76	20
Momence	3,155	10	10	0
Monee	5,064	17	15	2
Monmouth	9,172	28	18	10
Monticello	5,591	8	7	1
Morris	14,640	28	24	4
Morrison	4,092	6	6	0
Morton	16,287	28	22	6
Mount Carmel	6,950	16	11	5
Mount Carroll	1,593	3	3	0
Mount Morris	2,829	5	4	1
Mount Olive	1,985	6	4	2
Mount Prospect	54,162	99	80	19
Mundelein	31,547	73	54	19
New Athens	1,914	4	4	0
Newton	2,780	8	7	1
Niles	29,582	68	55	13
Nokomis	2,140	6	5	1
Northfield	5,459	21	19	2
North Riverside	6,585	25	25	0
Oak Brook	8,099	43	40	3
Oak Forest	27,761	55	43	12
Oak Lawn	56,178	120	104	16
Oak Park	51,753	133	112	21
Oakwood	1,495	1	1	0
Oblong	1,414	1	1	0
O'Fallon	29,085	65	47	18
Okawville	1,382	4	4	0
Olney	8,928	14	13	1
Onarga	1,294	2	2	0
Orland Park	59,227	134	98	36
Oswego	35,273	57	48	9
Palestine	1,313	2	2	0
Palos Hills	17,396	34	31	3
Paris	8,352	23	16	7
Park Forest	21,750	47	39	8
Park Ridge	37,492	62	49	13
Peoria Heights	5,913	21	13	8
Peotone	4,132	10	9	1
Peru	9,829	25	24	1
Petersburg	2,189	6	6	0
Pittsfield	4,452	7	7	0
Plainfield	43,450	67	53	14
Plano	11,438	22	20	2
Pleasant Hill	936	1	1	0
Polo	2,209	5	4	1
Pontiac	11,813	18	17	1
Pontoon Beach	5,572	20	15	5
Posen	5,920	18	17	1
Potomac	704	1	1	0
Princeton	7,550	18	17	1
Quincy	40,506	86	73	13
Raleigh	343	1	1	0
Rantoul	12,791	36	30	6
Red Bud	3,536	6	6	0
Richmond	1,899	4	4	0
Ridge Farm	833	1	1	0
Riverdale	13,371	35	29	6
Riverton	3,429	8	8	0
Riverwoods	3,633	8	7	1
Rockford	146,770	323	284	39
Rock Island	38,079	106	79	27
Roscoe	10,478	14	13	1
Round Lake	18,382	28	24	4
Round Lake Heights	2,701	5	5	0
Roxana	1,463	8	6	2
Royalton	1,122	3	3	0
Rushville	2,875	4	4	0
San Jose	604	1	1	0
Savanna	2,827	7	7	0
Schaumburg	74,471	147	114	33
Schiller Park	11,674	36	33	3
Seneca	2,267	6	5	1
Shawneetown	1,143	3	3	0
Shorewood	17,171	31	27	4
Silvis	7,596	21	14	7
Skokie	64,167	155	115	40
Sleepy Hollow	3,333	8	7	1
Smithton	3,766	6	6	0
South Barrington	4,973	21	17	4
South Beloit	7,613	12	11	1
South Elgin	22,504	32	28	4
South Pekin	1,108	2	2	0
Springfield	115,568	267	238	29

Table 78. Full-Time Law Enforcement Employees, by Selected State and City, 2017—Continued

(Number.)

State/city	Population	Total law enforcement employees	Total officers	Total civilians
Spring Valley	5,216	11	10	1
St. Anne	1,201	2	2	0
St. Charles	32,780	64	54	10
Steger	9,436	16	15	1
St. Elmo	1,381	2	2	0
Stockton	1,747	6	5	1
Streator	13,049	26	24	2
Sycamore	17,925	32	29	3
Thornton	2,474	11	10	1
Tilton	2,562	4	4	0
Tinley Park	56,823	85	72	13
Tolono	3,433	3	3	0
Trenton	2,641	4	4	0
Vernon Hills	26,547	70	42	28
Villa Park	21,857	47	37	10
Warren	1,340	4	3	1
Warrenville	13,255	40	32	8
Waukegan	88,017	191	147	44
Westchester	16,536	34	29	5
West Chicago	27,219	49	43	6
Western Springs	13,464	24	21	3
Westmont	24,781	42	36	6
Westville	3,036	4	4	0
Wheaton	53,444	79	64	15
White Hall	2,328	7	5	2
Willowbrook	8,542	27	24	3
Willow Springs	5,645	9	6	3
Wilmette	27,242	54	41	13
Winnebago	2,986	6	6	0
Winnetka	12,451	31	26	5
Winthrop Harbor	6,777	16	10	6
Wood Dale	13,817	41	32	9
Wood River	10,187	24	18	6
Woodstock	25,127	41	37	4
Yorkville	19,155	33	30	3
INDIANA				
Albion	2,316	6	6	0
Alexandria	5,004	14	13	1
Anderson	54,959	126	105	21
Auburn	13,090	24	23	1
Aurora	3,678	11	10	1
Bargersville	7,441	13	12	1
Batesville	6,705	17	12	5
Bedford	13,330	39	30	9
Beech Grove	14,831	35	32	3
Bloomington	85,121	144	97	47
Bluffton	10,011	20	20	0
Brownsburg	26,030	49	43	6
Cannelton	1,483	2	2	0
Carmel	93,098	137	113	24
Cedar Lake	12,286	20	18	2
Clinton	4,782	9	8	1
Columbia City	8,876	19	18	1
Crawfordsville	16,011	39	34	5
Crown Point	29,399	51	45	6
Cumberland	5,649	16	14	2
Decatur	9,541	18	16	2
Dyer	15,869	35	31	4
East Chicago	28,210	95	88	7
Edinburgh	4,592	12	11	1
Ellettsville	6,682	12	11	1
Elwood	8,386	17	16	1
Evansville	119,371	304	282	22
Fairmount	2,782	7	6	1
Fishers	92,367	121	110	11
Fort Wayne	266,259	522	462	60
Franklin	25,060	52	46	6
Gary	75,808	202	178	24
Goshen	33,195	69	62	7
Greenwood	57,484	72	64	8
Hammond	76,550	237	206	31
Hartford City	5,873	11	10	1
Highland	22,577	45	38	7
Hobart	28,066	75	65	10
Huntingburg	6,143	13	12	1
Huntington	17,116	34	33	1
Indianapolis	870,788	1,834	1,625	209
Jasper	15,577	29	21	8
Jeffersonville	47,459	90	85	5
Kendallville	9,915	25	17	8
Kokomo	57,758	110	90	20
Lafayette	72,274	190	142	48
Lake Station	11,852	22	22	0
Lawrence	48,174	79	60	19

Table 78. Full-Time Law Enforcement Employees, by Selected State and City, 2017—Continued

(Number.)

State/city	Population	Total law enforcement employees	Total officers	Total civilians
Lawrenceburg	4,955	25	21	4
Linton	5,221	14	9	5
Logansport	17,700	41	40	1
Marion	28,385	78	62	16
Merrillville	34,999	55	54	1
Michigan City	31,108	91	83	8
Monticello	5,240	17	13	4
Mooresville	9,709	26	21	5
Muncie	68,814	114	100	14
Munster	22,701	45	42	3
New Haven	15,481	29	21	8
New Whiteland	6,117	9	8	1
North Vernon	6,837	20	18	2
Plainfield	32,067	51	46	5
Plymouth	9,936	24	22	2
Portage	36,447	68	61	7
Porter	4,843	14	11	3
Portland	6,154	16	12	4
Rushville	6,022	17	12	5
Sellersburg	8,836	18	16	2
Seymour	19,604	58	40	18
Shelbyville	19,047	60	44	16
South Bend	101,857	289	241	48
Speedway	12,150	49	34	15
St. John	17,128	22	20	2
Tipton	5,094	14	12	2
Valparaiso	33,329	55	50	5
Walkerton	2,283	10	6	4
Warsaw	14,850	39	34	5
Waterloo	2,250	7	7	0
West Lafayette	46,541	69	50	19
Whitestown	7,464	23	22	1
Whiting	4,805	21	19	2
Winchester	4,718	13	12	1
IOWA				
Adel	4,397	8	7	1
Albia	3,787	7	6	1
Algona	5,509	14	10	4
Altoona	18,556	30	27	3
Ames	67,461	77	54	23
Anamosa	5,411	9	8	1
Ankeny	61,090	65	57	8
Arnolds Park	1,278	6	5	1
Atlantic	6,588	13	12	1
Audubon	1,939	4	4	0
Belle Plaine	2,442	5	5	0
Belmond	2,316	5	5	0
Bettendorf	36,133	51	45	6
Bloomfield	2,643	7	6	1
Blue Grass	1,743	2	2	0
Boone	12,607	19	18	1
Buffalo	1,297	3	3	0
Burlington	25,227	49	45	4
Camanche	4,305	7	7	0
Carlisle	4,311	6	5	1
Carroll	9,920	16	15	1
Carter Lake	3,783	10	9	1
Cedar Falls	41,744	44	43	1
Cedar Rapids	131,878	274	209	65
Centerville	5,316	17	11	6
Chariton	4,171	6	5	1
Charles City	7,425	20	13	7
Cherokee	4,954	9	8	1
Clarinda	5,353	11	10	1
Clarion	2,752	8	7	1
Clear Lake	7,559	22	16	6
Clinton	25,532	48	42	6
Clive	17,913	28	24	4
Colfax	2,034	4	4	0
Coralville	20,652	38	34	4
Council Bluffs	62,549	136	115	21
Cresco	3,799	7	7	0
Creston	7,829	15	11	4
Davenport	103,063	179	160	19
Decorah	7,883	21	13	8
Denison	8,304	19	14	5
Des Moines	217,277	455	350	105
De Witt	5,218	12	11	1
Dubuque	58,674	113	107	6
Dyersville	4,217	6	6	0
Eldora	2,650	4	4	0
Eldridge	6,406	10	9	1
Emmetsburg	3,736	8	7	1
Estherville	5,877	13	13	0

Table 78. Full-Time Law Enforcement Employees, by Selected State and City, 2017—Continued

(Number.)

State/city	Population	Total law enforcement employees	Total officers	Total civilians
Evansdale	4,792	8	7	1
Fairfield	10,337	21	14	7
Forest City	3,993	8	8	0
Fort Dodge	24,331	42	39	3
Garner	3,068	5	5	0
Glenwood	5,315	11	9	2
Grinnell	9,141	15	14	1
Grundy Center	2,683	4	4	0
Hampton	4,202	8	7	1
Harlan	4,904	9	8	1
Hawarden	2,524	4	4	0
Hiawatha	7,245	14	14	0
Humboldt	4,538	7	7	0
Independence	6,027	11	11	0
Indianola	15,953	23	20	3
Iowa City	75,519	103	81	22
Iowa Falls	5,110	13	9	4
Jefferson	4,140	8	8	0
Johnston	21,816	29	27	2
Keokuk	10,376	27	24	3
Knoxville	7,233	15	14	1
Lansing	944	3	3	0
Le Claire	4,012	8	7	1
Le Mars	9,955	13	12	1
Leon	1,866	3	3	0
Lisbon	2,219	3	3	0
Manchester	5,032	15	10	5
Maquoketa	5,954	18	11	7
Marengo	2,486	4	4	0
Marion	39,050	57	45	12
Marshalltown	27,287	57	41	16
Mason City	27,327	52	47	5
Mechanicsville	1,116	1	1	0
Missouri Valley	2,635	6	6	0
Monticello	3,843	7	6	1
Mount Pleasant	8,349	16	14	2
Mount Vernon	4,436	6	6	0
Muscatine	23,940	43	40	3
Nevada	6,805	13	11	2
New Hampton	3,401	6	6	0
New Sharon	1,286	1	1	0
Newton	14,999	28	23	5
North Liberty	19,491	23	21	2
Norwalk	10,874	17	16	1
Oelwein	5,999	15	10	5
Ogden	1,989	2	2	0
Onawa	2,848	4	4	0
Orange City	6,199	7	7	0
Osage	3,623	7	6	1
Osceola	5,051	11	10	1
Oskaloosa	11,525	18	16	2
Ottumwa	24,397	44	34	10
Pella	10,240	23	17	6
Perry	7,824	19	12	7
Pleasant Hill	9,910	19	17	2
Polk City	4,616	6	6	0
Postville	2,098	4	4	0
Prairie City	1,718	3	3	0
Princeton	949	1	1	0
Red Oak	5,437	11	9	2
Rock Valley	3,788	6	6	0
Sac City	2,086	4	4	0
Sergeant Bluff	4,606	9	8	1
Sheldon	5,102	7	7	0
Sigourney	1,976	4	4	0
Sioux Center	7,578	7	7	0
Sioux City	82,879	148	126	22
Spencer	11,125	29	19	10
Spirit Lake	5,124	10	9	1
Storm Lake	10,790	23	19	4
Story City	3,406	6	6	0
Tama	2,825	5	5	0
Tipton	3,217	7	6	1
Toledo	2,163	5	5	0
Urbandale	43,637	59	50	9
Vinton	5,125	9	8	1
Walcott	1,639	3	3	0
Washington	7,451	12	11	1
Waterloo	67,855	131	122	9
Waukee	20,359	23	21	2
Waverly	10,129	17	16	1
Webster City	7,708	17	11	6
West Branch	2,365	4	4	0
West Burlington	2,935	10	10	0
West Des Moines	65,940	82	69	13

Table 78. Full-Time Law Enforcement Employees, by Selected State and City, 2017—Continued

(Number.)

State/city	Population	Total law enforcement employees	Total officers	Total civilians
West Union	2,381	5	5	0
Williamsburg	3,197	7	7	0
Windsor Heights	5,001	12	11	1
KANSAS				
Abilene	6,407	17	14	3
Alma	786	1	1	0
Altamont	1,036	4	3	1
Andale	1,003	3	3	0
Andover	13,183	34	26	8
Anthony	2,164	6	5	1
Argonia	478	1	1	0
Arkansas City	12,009	31	26	5
Assaria	406	2	2	0
Atchison	10,628	23	23	0
Attica	569	1	1	0
Atwood	1,213	2	2	0
Augusta	9,329	33	24	9
Baldwin City	4,703	11	10	1
Basehor	5,835	14	12	2
Baxter Springs	3,921	15	11	4
Bel Aire	7,819	13	12	1
Belle Plaine	1,585	4	4	0
Belleville	1,881	3	3	0
Beloit	3,761	5	5	0
Benton	875	3	3	0
Blue Rapids	963	2	2	0
Bonner Springs	7,717	28	25	3
Buhler	1,313	3	3	0
Burden	533	1	1	0
Burlingame	881	2	2	0
Burlington	2,600	9	7	2
Burrton	885	2	2	0
Caldwell	1,013	2	2	0
Caney	2,014	10	6	4
Canton	715	1	1	0
Carbondale	1,386	3	3	0
Cedar Vale	519	1	1	0
Chanute	9,143	18	16	2
Chapman	1,355	3	3	0
Cheney	2,176	6	6	0
Cherokee	712	1	1	0
Cherryvale	2,161	7	6	1
Chetopa	1,051	4	4	0
Claflin	620	1	1	0
Clay Center	4,025	7	6	1
Clearwater	2,524	7	6	1
Coffeyville	9,423	31	23	8
Colby	5,420	18	12	6
Coldwater	812	2	1	1
Columbus	3,072	9	8	1
Colwich	1,410	3	3	0
Concordia	5,144	18	11	7
Council Grove	2,041	8	7	1
Derby	23,821	56	46	10
Dodge City	27,447	61	44	17
Eastborough	759	6	6	0
Edwardsville	4,395	18	17	1
El Dorado	13,125	26	23	3
Elkhart	1,892	3	3	0
Ellinwood	2,022	5	5	0
Ellis	2,048	5	5	0
Ellsworth	3,034	7	6	1
Elwood	1,154	5	5	0
Emporia	24,804	48	41	7
Eudora	6,417	12	12	0
Fairway	3,986	11	9	2
Fort Scott	7,725	22	20	2
Fredonia	2,261	7	6	1
Frontenac	3,410	11	7	4
Galena	2,855	10	9	1
Galva	873	1	1	0
Garden City	26,728	92	63	29
Gardner	21,449	36	32	4
Garnett	3,241	7	7	0
Girard	2,741	7	6	1
Goddard	4,761	11	11	0
Goodland	4,433	10	9	1
Grandview Plaza	1,579	7	7	0
Great Bend	15,459	31	27	4
Greensburg	768	1	1	0
Halstead	2,080	6	5	1
Harper	1,361	3	3	0
Haven	1,207	3	3	0
Hays	21,110	38	33	5

Table 78. Full-Time Law Enforcement Employees, by Selected State and City, 2017—Continued

(Number.)

State/city	Population	Total law enforcement employees	Total officers	Total civilians
Haysville	11,314	28	21	7
Hesston	3,817	8	7	1
Hiawatha	3,048	9	8	1
Highland	998	2	2	0
Hill City	1,451	4	4	0
Hillsboro	2,870	5	5	0
Hoisington	2,567	7	6	1
Holcomb	2,145	4	3	1
Holton	3,278	7	7	0
Holyrood	434	1	1	0
Horton	1,690	10	6	4
Hoxie	1,170	2	2	0
Hugoton	3,819	8	6	2
Humboldt	1,831	6	5	1
Hutchinson	41,160	105	68	37
Independence	8,692	25	18	7
Inman	1,348	3	3	0
Iola	5,413	18	17	1
Junction City	24,240	63	44	19
Kansas City	152,573	431	341	90
Kechi	2,009	5	4	1
La Cygne	1,106	4	3	1
Lake Quivira	945	1	1	0
Lansing	11,941	18	17	1
Larned	3,875	8	8	0
Lawrence	96,629	173	149	24
Leavenworth	36,284	75	53	22
Leawood	35,029	80	58	22
Lenexa	53,717	122	79	43
Leon	701	1	1	0
Liberal	20,317	51	36	15
Lindsborg	3,319	7	6	1
Linn Valley	814	3	3	0
Little River	532	1	1	0
Louisburg	4,391	11	10	1
Lyndon	1,016	2	2	0
Lyons	3,658	7	6	1
Maize	4,621	13	12	1
Maple Hill	617	1	1	0
Marion	1,823	5	5	0
Marquette	606	1	1	0
Marysville	3,294	9	8	1
McLouth	842	2	2	0
McPherson	13,169	38	33	5
Meade	1,564	3	2	1
Merriam	11,278	37	32	5
Minneapolis	1,976	4	4	0
Mission	9,461	31	29	2
Mission Hills	3,616	3	3	0
Moran	511	1	1	0
Mound City	678	2	2	0
Moundridge	1,738	4	4	0
Mount Hope	806	2	2	0
Mulberry	519	1	1	0
Mulvane	6,343	21	15	6
Neodesha	2,293	7	6	1
Newton	19,095	43	38	5
North Newton	1,802	3	3	0
Norton	2,799	7	6	1
Norwich	453	1	1	0
Oakley	2,105	10	6	4
Oberlin	1,688	4	4	0
Olathe	137,070	200	171	29
Onaga	695	1	1	0
Osage City	2,820	7	7	0
Osawatomie	4,284	17	13	4
Oswego	1,729	4	4	0
Ottawa	12,307	36	29	7
Overbrook	1,018	1	1	0
Overland Park	191,566	311	251	60
Oxford	1,012	3	3	0
Paola	5,560	22	16	6
Park City	7,678	16	14	2
Parsons	9,815	33	24	9
Peabody	1,129	1	1	0
Perry	902	1	1	0
Pittsburg	20,384	72	46	26
Plainville	1,851	5	5	0
Pleasanton	1,170	2	2	0
Prairie Village	21,860	53	40	13
Pratt	6,762	22	15	7
Protection	500	1	1	0
Roeland Park	6,794	16	14	2
Rose Hill	4,029	8	7	1
Rossville	1,126	2	2	0

Table 78. Full-Time Law Enforcement Employees, by Selected State and City, 2017—Continued

(Number.)

State/city	Population	Total law enforcement employees	Total officers	Total civilians
Russell	4,497	8	7	1
Sabetha	2,587	9	5	4
Salina	47,251	98	68	30
Scott City	3,901	13	8	5
Sedan	1,021	2	2	0
Sedgwick	1,695	3	2	1
Seneca	2,056	6	6	0
Shawnee	65,683	110	92	18
Smith Center	1,569	3	3	0
South Hutchinson	2,552	10	8	2
Spearville	793	1	1	0
Spring Hill	6,293	13	12	1
Stafford	968	4	4	0
Sterling	2,253	5	5	0
St. Francis	1,289	3	2	1
St. George	1,004	2	1	1
St. John	1,202	3	3	0
St. Marys	2,669	5	5	0
Stockton	1,292	5	5	0
Tonganoxie	5,379	13	12	1
Topeka	126,624	328	274	54
Troy	964	1	1	0
Udall	723	2	2	0
Valley Center	7,431	15	14	1
Valley Falls	1,142	3	3	0
Victoria	1,223	2	2	0
Wa Keeney	1,763	4	4	0
Wathena	1,304	1	1	0
Wellington	7,845	19	16	3
Wellsville	1,806	5	4	1
Westwood	2,285	8	7	1
Wichita	391,084	819	638	181
Winfield	12,274	26	21	5
Yates Center	1,341	3	3	0
KENTUCKY				
Adairville	873	1	1	0
Albany	2,010	9	9	0
Alexandria	9,486	23	20	3
Anchorage	2,438	15	11	4
Ashland	20,927	56	52	4
Auburn	1,348	2	2	0
Audubon Park	1,511	3	3	0
Augusta	1,172	3	3	0
Barbourville	3,169	12	11	1
Bardstown	13,325	26	25	1
Beattyville	1,199	5	5	0
Beaver Dam	3,672	6	6	0
Bellefonte	855	9	9	0
Bellevue	5,826	12	11	1
Benham	452	1	1	0
Benton	4,533	7	7	0
Berea	15,406	38	36	2
Booneville	75	1	1	0
Bowling Green	66,317	153	117	36
Brandenburg	2,904	5	5	0
Brownsville	831	3	3	0
Burgin	969	2	2	0
Burkesville	1,505	6	6	0
Burnside	902	6	5	1
Butler	591	1	1	0
Cadiz	2,629	10	9	1
Calvert City	2,544	8	7	1
Campbellsville	11,486	22	20	2
Caneyville	612	1	1	0
Carlisle	1,992	10	6	4
Carrollton	3,864	17	10	7
Catlettsburg	1,794	8	8	0
Cave City	2,440	7	7	0
Centertown	446	1	1	0
Central City	5,837	12	12	0
Clinton	1,312	5	5	0
Coal Run Village	1,538	3	3	0
Cold Spring	6,276	9	9	0
Columbia	4,940	13	12	1
Corbin	7,411	28	20	8
Covington	40,845	116	108	8
Crab Orchard	830	2	1	1
Cumberland	2,032	6	6	0
Cynthiana	6,375	13	12	1
Danville	16,891	31	29	2
Dawson Springs	2,712	6	5	1
Dayton	5,423	10	9	1
Dry Ridge	2,224	5	5	0
Eddyville	2,575	5	5	0

Table 78. Full-Time Law Enforcement Employees, by Selected State and City, 2017—Continued

(Number.)

State/city	Population	Total law enforcement employees	Total officers	Total civilians
Edgewood	8,771	15	15	0
Edmonton	1,583	6	6	0
Elizabethtown	30,065	69	43	26
Elkhorn City	921	2	1	1
Elkton	2,134	7	7	0
Elsmere	8,541	14	13	1
Eminence	2,579	6	6	0
Erlanger	22,947	40	39	1
Evarts	828	3	3	0
Falmouth	2,127	8	7	1
Ferguson	942	1	1	0
Flatwoods	7,284	11	11	0
Fleming-Neon	708	2	2	0
Flemingsburg	2,866	7	7	0
Florence	32,866	68	64	4
Fort Mitchell	8,306	14	14	0
Fort Thomas	16,485	22	21	1
Fort Wright	5,780	13	13	0
Frankfort	27,975	59	56	3
Franklin	8,884	24	23	1
Fulton	2,174	9	8	1
Georgetown	34,184	77	51	26
Glasgow	14,690	34	31	3
Graymoor-Devondale	2,974	1	1	0
Grayson	4,030	12	10	2
Greensburg	2,123	5	5	0
Greenville	4,347	9	9	0
Guthrie	1,406	4	4	0
Hardinsburg	2,324	5	5	0
Harrodsburg	8,427	30	19	11
Hartford	2,787	6	6	0
Hawesville	1,020	1	1	0
Hazard	5,268	42	29	13
Henderson	28,846	81	60	21
Highland Heights	7,178	11	10	1
Hillview	8,942	14	14	0
Hodgenville	3,224	7	7	0
Hopkinsville	31,761	103	75	28
Hyden	348	2	1	1
Independence	27,400	32	30	2
Indian Hills	2,995	6	6	0
Inez	665	1	1	0
Irvine	2,385	6	6	0
Jackson	2,100	11	8	3
Jamestown	1,807	4	4	0
Jeffersontown	27,400	59	49	10
Jenkins	2,043	3	3	0
Junction City	2,308	2	2	0
La Center	982	2	2	0
La Grange	8,831	13	13	0
Lakeside Park-Crestview Hills	6,133	12	11	1
Lancaster	3,874	11	10	1
Lawrenceburg	11,211	22	14	8
Lebanon	5,656	24	15	9
Leitchfield	6,900	19	18	1
Lewisburg	793	1	1	0
Lexington	322,332	581	506	75
Livingston	224	1	1	0
London	8,184	35	32	3
Louisa	2,474	6	6	0
Louisville Metro	684,362	1,510	1,249	261
Loyall	631	2	2	0
Ludlow	4,521	12	11	1
Lynnview	948	3	3	0
Madisonville	19,316	65	46	19
Manchester	1,382	13	13	0
Marion	2,972	11	6	5
Martin	585	4	3	1
Maysville	8,841	33	25	8
Middlesboro	9,534	28	24	4
Millersburg	792	1	1	0
Monticello	6,070	12	11	1
Morehead	7,915	29	20	9
Morganfield	3,541	17	8	9
Morgantown	2,454	6	6	0
Mortons Gap	843	1	1	0
Mount Sterling	7,298	22	20	2
Mount Vernon	2,482	8	8	0
Mount Washington	14,511	19	18	1
Muldraugh	995	3	3	0
New Haven	902	1	1	0
Newport	15,202	41	39	2
Nicholasville	30,333	70	61	9
Oak Grove	7,347	20	15	5
Olive Hill	1,584	7	7	0

Table 78. Full-Time Law Enforcement Employees, by Selected State and City, 2017—Continued

(Number.)

State/city	Population	Total law enforcement employees	Total officers	Total civilians
Owensboro	59,576	136	90	46
Owingsville	1,605	5	5	0
Paducah	25,169	79	71	8
Paintsville	4,198	10	10	0
Paris	9,845	23	22	1
Park Hills	3,001	7	7	0
Pewee Valley	1,565	1	1	0
Pikeville	7,121	29	21	8
Pineville	1,739	5	5	0
Pioneer Village	2,931	5	5	0
Pippa Passes	658	6	2	4
Powderly	732	2	2	0
Prestonsburg	3,517	13	13	0
Princeton	6,084	15	14	1
Prospect	4,905	7	6	1
Providence	3,088	6	6	0
Raceland	2,380	6	6	0
Radcliff	22,473	49	35	14
Ravenna	583	2	2	0
Richmond	35,161	61	47	14
Russell	3,229	12	12	0
Russell Springs	2,573	10	9	1
Russellville	7,006	24	23	1
Salyersville	1,787	4	4	0
Scottsville	4,446	26	18	8
Sebree	1,569	1	1	0
Shelbyville	15,758	22	21	1
Shepherdsville	12,204	31	29	2
Shively	15,830	36	30	6
Silver Grove	1,119	1	1	0
Simpsonville	2,795	6	6	0
Smiths Grove	780	1	1	0
Somerset	11,531	46	40	6
Southgate	3,856	8	8	0
South Shore	1,080	1	1	0
Springfield	3,167	13	8	5
Stanford	3,654	13	13	0
Stanton	2,658	6	6	0
St. Matthews	18,163	39	33	6
Taylor Mill	6,774	11	10	1
Taylorsville	1,264	5	4	1
Tompkinsville	2,261	13	10	3
Uniontown	943	2	2	0
Vanceburg	1,421	6	6	0
Versailles	26,320	35	34	1
Villa Hills	7,494	8	8	0
Vine Grove	6,055	7	7	0
Warsaw	1,689	3	3	0
Wayland	397	1	1	0
West Buechel	1,280	11	11	0
West Point	860	4	4	0
Whitesburg	1,949	8	6	2
Wilder	3,077	12	12	0
Williamsburg	5,342	14	13	1
Williamstown	3,971	7	6	1
Wilmore	6,380	9	8	1
Woodburn	387	2	2	0
LOUISIANA				
Abbeville	12,491	36	33	3
Addis	5,117	12	11	1
Alexandria	47,860	183	150	33
Baker	13,584	32	27	5
Ball	4,011	7	5	2
Basile	1,811	10	7	3
Baton Rouge	227,403	813	641	172
Berwick	4,649	12	11	1
Blanchard	3,186	5	4	1
Bogalusa	11,865	52	33	19
Bossier City	69,632	199	159	40
Breaux Bridge	8,451	25	23	2
Broussard	12,125	32	28	4
Brusly	2,827	10	10	0
Bunkie	4,045	8	5	3
Carencro	8,944	29	27	2
Church Point	4,485	16	16	0
Clinton	1,571	22	15	7
Cottonport	1,945	6	5	1
Covington	10,571	41	36	5
Crowley	13,026	42	35	7
Denham Springs	10,329	39	31	8
De Ridder	11,116	32	26	6
Epps	825	2	1	1
Erath	2,108	11	7	4
Eunice	10,258	39	29	10

Table 78. Full-Time Law Enforcement Employees, by Selected State and City, 2017—Continued

(Number.)

State/city	Population	Total law enforcement employees	Total officers	Total civilians
Farmerville	3,841	14	14	0
Ferriday	3,300	18	14	4
Fisher	222	1	1	0
Florien	616	3	3	0
Folsom	826	5	3	2
Franklinton	3,770	26	20	6
French Settlement	1,205	2	2	0
Georgetown	326	3	2	1
Golden Meadow	2,028	7	5	2
Gonzales	11,012	49	44	5
Gramercy	3,425	8	7	1
Greenwood	3,145	10	9	1
Gretna	17,923	195	100	95
Hammond	20,712	108	81	27
Harahan	9,373	26	19	7
Haughton	3,301	13	12	1
Hodge	445	4	4	0
Houma	34,083	96	80	16
Ida	211	1	1	0
Independence	1,910	8	8	0
Iowa	3,343	17	12	5
Jena	3,440	7	6	1
Jennings	10,074	32	26	6
Kenner	67,149	221	158	63
Kentwood	2,407	12	11	1
Killian	1,347	3	3	0
Kinder	2,430	15	12	3
Lafayette	128,691	321	264	57
Lake Arthur	2,747	10	6	4
Lake Charles	77,647	186	153	33
Lake Providence	3,648	13	8	5
Leesville	6,226	32	27	5
Lutcher	3,333	3	3	0
Mamou	3,178	12	11	1
Mandeville	12,503	45	33	12
Mansfield	4,900	15	15	0
Many	2,780	11	11	0
Marion	752	1	1	0
Minden	12,497	32	31	1
Monroe	49,354	161	124	37
Montgomery	723	3	3	0
Morgan City	11,530	55	43	12
Natchitoches	18,284	70	53	17
New Orleans	397,447	1,436	1,101	335
Oak Grove	1,620	7	7	0
Oil City	982	4	4	0
Olla	1,393	2	2	0
Patterson	6,053	24	24	0
Pearl River	2,575	20	13	7
Pineville	14,473	73	64	9
Plaquemine	6,727	28	20	8
Ponchatoula	7,317	28	22	6
Port Allen	5,085	20	19	1
Port Vincent	773	3	3	0
Rayne	8,167	22	22	0
Ruston	22,438	53	39	14
Scott	8,780	27	25	2
Shreveport	193,937	608	508	100
Sibley	1,169	3	3	0
Slidell	28,163	104	81	23
Springhill	5,012	18	18	0
Sterlington	2,731	8	8	0
St. Gabriel	7,298	19	12	7
Sulphur	20,247	69	44	25
Tallulah	6,970	14	11	3
Thibodaux	14,617	68	55	13
Tickfaw	768	6	6	0
Vidalia	4,015	38	29	9
Ville Platte	7,244	48	29	19
Walker	6,447	22	18	4
Welsh	3,232	14	14	0
West Monroe	12,891	72	72	0
Westwego	8,532	38	36	2
Youngsville	13,679	29	25	4
Zachary	17,072	46	44	2
Zwolle	1,945	8	6	2
MAINE				
Ashland	1,217	2	2	0
Auburn	22,931	60	54	6
Augusta	18,394	57	45	12
Baileyville	1,433	3	3	0
Bangor	31,814	94	80	14
Bar Harbor	5,422	28	19	9
Bath	8,272	23	19	4

Table 78. Full-Time Law Enforcement Employees, by Selected State and City, 2017—Continued

(Number.)

State/city	Population	Total law enforcement employees	Total officers	Total civilians
Belfast	6,644	17	15	2
Berwick	7,627	12	11	1
Biddeford	21,378	72	50	22
Boothbay Harbor	2,188	8	7	1
Brewer	9,048	20	18	2
Bridgton	5,414	10	9	1
Brunswick	20,711	46	32	14
Bucksport	4,924	12	8	4
Buxton	8,222	12	7	5
Calais	2,940	8	8	0
Camden	4,833	10	10	0
Cape Elizabeth	9,383	14	13	1
Caribou	7,666	16	15	1
Carrabassett Valley	781	1	1	0
Clinton	3,300	4	4	0
Cumberland	7,956	12	11	1
Damariscotta	2,166	6	5	1
Dexter	3,710	5	5	0
Dixfield	2,457	3	3	0
Dover-Foxcroft	4,045	5	5	0
East Millinocket	2,943	2	2	0
Eastport	1,243	4	4	0
Eliot	6,481	9	8	1
Ellsworth	7,940	21	18	3
Fairfield	6,560	11	10	1
Falmouth	12,260	27	18	9
Farmington	7,548	24	14	10
Fort Fairfield	3,294	4	4	0
Fort Kent	3,900	9	5	4
Freeport	8,520	16	14	2
Fryeburg	3,389	6	6	0
Gardiner	5,592	12	11	1
Gorham	17,554	26	24	2
Gouldsboro	1,750	1	1	0
Greenville	1,585	3	2	1
Hallowell	2,318	5	5	0
Hampden	7,363	12	11	1
Holden	3,049	4	4	0
Houlton	5,781	19	12	7
Islesboro	565	1	1	0
Jay	4,628	7	6	1
Kennebunk	11,406	22	20	2
Kennebunkport	3,604	17	12	5
Kittery	9,669	26	20	6
Lewiston	36,067	89	78	11
Limestone	2,165	3	3	0
Lincoln	4,944	6	5	1
Lisbon	8,820	18	12	6
Livermore Falls	3,104	6	6	0
Machias	2,087	4	4	0
Madawaska	3,760	6	5	1
Mechanic Falls	2,986	3	3	0
Mexico	2,584	4	4	0
Milbridge	1,277	2	2	0
Millinocket	4,267	6	6	0
Milo	2,256	3	3	0
Monmouth	4,036	4	4	0
Newport	3,224	6	6	0
North Berwick	4,690	9	8	1
Norway	4,902	10	9	1
Oakland	6,145	10	9	1
Ogunquit	922	11	10	1
Old Orchard Beach	8,842	24	22	2
Old Town	7,466	17	16	1
Orono	11,400	16	15	1
Oxford	4,037	9	8	1
Paris	5,119	8	7	1
Phippsburg	2,246	1	1	0
Pittsfield	4,076	6	6	0
Portland	67,079	209	147	62
Presque Isle	9,016	22	17	5
Rangeley	1,159	2	2	0
Richmond	3,412	4	4	0
Rockland	7,161	18	16	2
Rockport	3,389	6	6	0
Rumford	5,692	12	12	0
Sabattus	5,038	7	6	1
Saco	19,332	44	33	11
Sanford	20,963	43	39	4
Scarborough	20,215	60	40	20
Searsport	2,638	3	3	0
Skowhegan	8,255	16	14	2
South Berwick	7,469	13	9	4
South Portland	25,679	60	53	7
Southwest Harbor	1,780	9	5	4

Table 78. Full-Time Law Enforcement Employees, by Selected State and City, 2017—Continued

(Number.)

State/city	Population	Total law enforcement employees	Total officers	Total civilians
Thomaston	2,772	5	5	0
Topsham	8,790	15	14	1
Van Buren	2,068	3	3	0
Veazie	1,827	4	4	0
Waldoboro	5,023	8	7	1
Washburn	1,558	2	2	0
Waterville	16,522	41	31	10
Wells	10,287	31	23	8
Westbrook	18,560	45	38	7
Wilton	3,944	6	6	0
Windham	18,175	30	27	3
Winslow	7,534	12	11	1
Winthrop	5,950	12	7	5
Wiscasset	3,680	3	3	0
Yarmouth	8,594	14	13	1
York	13,018	37	26	11
MARYLAND				
Aberdeen	15,720	49	39	10
Annapolis	39,596	146	114	32
Baltimore	613,217	2,937	2,516	421
Baltimore City Sheriff		201	156	45
Bel Air	10,109	41	30	11
Berlin	4,628	19	14	5
Berwyn Heights	3,300	7	7	0
Bladensburg	9,683	25	20	5
Boonsboro	3,521	5	4	1
Bowie	58,891	85	61	24
Brentwood	3,205	5	4	1
Brunswick	6,219	14	14	0
Cambridge	12,471	48	44	4
Capitol Heights	4,582	10	9	1
Centreville	4,753	12	12	0
Chestertown	5,056	15	14	1
Cheverly	6,517	15	12	3
Chevy Chase Village	2,080	17	11	6
Colmar Manor	1,474	3	2	1
Cottage City	1,378	3	3	0
Crisfield	2,616	14	11	3
Cumberland	19,842	53	50	3
Delmar	3,216	14	13	1
Denton	4,385	14	13	1
District Heights	6,064	12	11	1
Easton	16,598	54	41	13
Edmonston	1,528	7	5	2
Elkton	15,794	44	39	5
Fairmount Heights	1,579	1	1	0
Federalsburg	2,664	9	8	1
Forest Heights	2,597	6	4	2
Frederick	70,860	189	148	41
Frostburg	8,622	20	16	4
Fruitland	5,298	21	19	2
Glenarden	6,228	15	13	2
Greenbelt	24,099	60	47	13
Greensboro	1,876	1	1	0
Hagerstown	40,568	116	102	14
Hampstead	6,361	10	9	1
Hancock	1,552	5	4	1
Havre de Grace	13,610	45	36	9
Hurlock	2,019	11	10	1
Hyattsville	18,579	55	43	12
Landover Hills	1,821	5	4	1
La Plata	9,324	17	16	1
Laurel	25,997	85	64	21
Lonaconing	1,125	5	2	3
Luke	63	1	1	0
Manchester	4,820	6	6	0
Morningside	2,060	8	7	1
Mount Rainier	8,516	20	16	4
New Carrollton	12,971	26	20	6
North East	3,661	12	11	1
Oakland	1,867	2	2	0
Ocean City	6,982	123	94	29
Ocean Pines	12,263	20	16	4
Oxford	612	3	3	0
Perryville	4,432	12	11	1
Pocomoke City	4,088	24	15	9
Princess Anne	3,639	12	11	1
Ridgely	1,622	5	5	0
Rising Sun	2,800	4	4	0
Riverdale Park	7,358	28	20	8
Rock Hall	1,297	4	4	0
Salisbury	33,558	112	84	28
Seat Pleasant	4,806	20	17	3
Smithsburg	3,002	5	4	1

Table 78. Full-Time Law Enforcement Employees, by Selected State and City, 2017—Continued

(Number.)

State/city	Population	Total law enforcement employees	Total officers	Total civilians
Snow Hill	2,065	5	5	0
St. Michaels	1,039	9	8	1
Sykesville	3,940	8	7	1
Takoma Park	17,933	56	39	17
Taneytown	6,762	15	14	1
Thurmont	6,584	14	11	3
University Park	2,677	9	8	1
Upper Marlboro	672	3	3	0
Westminster	18,682	55	42	13
MASSACHUSETTS				
Abington	16,369	27	25	2
Acton	23,937	54	43	11
Acushnet	10,547	21	18	3
Agawam	28,839	65	50	15
Amesbury	17,636	41	35	6
Amherst	40,313	49	47	2
Andover	35,898	68	49	19
Aquinnah	330	4	4	0
Arlington	45,449	83	68	15
Ashburnham	6,255	16	12	4
Ashby	3,248	11	7	4
Ashland	17,878	31	25	6
Attleboro	44,607	97	82	15
Auburn	16,563	48	37	11
Avon	4,560	17	12	5
Ayer	8,240	30	20	10
Barnstable	44,142	135	117	18
Barre	5,518	10	9	1
Becket	1,744	4	4	0
Bedford	14,607	37	28	9
Belchertown	15,097	24	19	5
Bellingham	17,121	40	32	8
Belmont	26,432	67	48	19
Berkley	6,745	8	8	0
Berlin	3,175	10	9	1
Bernardston	2,082	3	3	0
Beverly	41,678	71	67	4
Billerica	43,127	79	66	13
Blackstone	9,079	18	18	0
Bolton	5,272	12	11	1
Boston	682,903	2,778	2,205	573
Bourne	19,867	53	44	9
Boxborough	5,972	18	12	6
Boxford	8,333	12	12	0
Boylston	4,610	13	9	4
Braintree	37,579	116	77	39
Brewster	9,895	28	23	5
Brockton	96,016	201	180	21
Brookfield	3,399	5	5	0
Brookline	59,233	141	102	39
Buckland	1,843	2	2	0
Burlington	26,678	73	65	8
Cambridge	111,707	311	278	33
Canton	23,551	43	43	0
Carlisle	5,313	16	11	5
Carver	11,671	20	16	4
Chatham	6,158	25	21	4
Chelmsford	35,392	65	51	14
Chelsea	40,514	114	105	9
Cheshire	3,160	1	1	0
Chicopee	56,255	138	134	4
Clinton	13,839	37	28	9
Cohasset	8,598	19	18	1
Concord	20,193	40	33	7
Dalton	6,602	12	10	2
Danvers	28,168	56	44	12
Dartmouth	34,802	85	70	15
Dedham	25,358	60	57	3
Deerfield	4,971	9	8	1
Dennis	13,976	57	47	10
Dighton	7,617	12	11	1
Douglas	8,795	18	14	4
Dover	6,053	16	16	0
Dracut	31,685	46	40	6
Dudley	11,801	14	14	0
Dunstable	3,389	9	8	1
East Bridgewater	14,573	26	22	4
Eastham	4,899	22	16	6
Easthampton	16,061	34	28	6
East Longmeadow	16,288	29	27	2
Easton	24,176	45	35	10
Egremont	1,204	4	4	0
Erving	1,763	5	5	0
Essex	3,729	9	8	1

Table 78. Full-Time Law Enforcement Employees, by Selected State and City, 2017—Continued

(Number.)

State/city	Population	Total law enforcement employees	Total officers	Total civilians
Everett	47,185	116	108	8
Fairhaven	16,188	37	31	6
Fall River	89,012	279	228	51
Falmouth	31,487	62	58	4
Fitchburg	40,445	96	77	19
Foxborough	17,636	47	35	12
Framingham	72,153	141	124	17
Franklin	33,397	53	48	5
Freetown	9,343	21	18	3
Gardner	20,491	45	33	12
Georgetown	8,715	15	11	4
Gill	1,489	2	2	0
Gloucester	29,980	64	57	7
Goshen	1,074	2	2	0
Grafton	18,763	24	20	4
Granby	6,379	13	9	4
Great Barrington	6,815	18	17	1
Greenfield	17,462	47	34	13
Groton	11,411	26	19	7
Groveland	6,838	11	10	1
Hadley	5,382	17	13	4
Hamilton	8,216	18	13	5
Hampden	5,217	14	11	3
Hanson	10,860	26	21	5
Hardwick	4,031	5	5	0
Harwich	12,150	42	33	9
Haverhill	63,244	107	94	13
Hingham	23,392	50	48	2
Holbrook	11,064	23	22	1
Holland	2,502	2	2	0
Holliston	14,736	23	19	4
Holyoke	40,451	138	119	19
Hopedale	5,959	16	12	4
Hopkinton	17,348	33	23	10
Hudson	19,963	43	33	10
Ipswich	13,951	29	24	5
Kingston	13,615	32	24	8
Lakeville	11,502	22	18	4
Lancaster	8,212	12	11	1
Lanesboro	2,951	6	6	0
Lawrence	80,890	160	135	25
Leicester	11,369	20	19	1
Lenox	4,947	10	10	0
Leominster	41,846	88	72	16
Lexington	33,768	59	44	15
Lincoln	6,860	19	13	6
Littleton	10,196	25	19	6
Longmeadow	15,848	33	27	6
Lowell	111,294	302	220	82
Ludlow	21,529	49	40	9
Lunenburg	11,477	16	15	1
Lynn	93,140	186	168	18
Malden	61,098	108	102	6
Mansfield	23,847	49	37	12
Marblehead	20,618	41	32	9
Marion	5,124	15	15	0
Marlborough	39,919	76	64	12
Marshfield	25,929	45	42	3
Mashpee	14,272	39	31	8
Mattapoisett	6,354	19	19	0
Maynard	10,756	27	21	6
Medford	57,418	108	105	3
Medway	13,407	27	22	5
Melrose	28,101	48	48	0
Mendon	6,069	17	12	5
Methuen	50,396	116	97	19
Middleboro	25,084	47	41	6
Middleton	9,788	17	15	2
Milford	28,772	57	45	12
Millbury	13,626	24	19	5
Millville	3,254	7	6	1
Montague	8,211	16	16	0
Nahant	3,500	13	12	1
Natick	36,705	71	57	14
Needham	31,054	56	47	9
New Bedford	95,107	297	247	50
Newton	89,736	180	147	33
Norfolk	11,815	24	18	6
North Adams	12,948	33	24	9
Northampton	28,458	69	63	6
North Andover	31,035	54	41	13
North Attleboro	29,158	53	40	13
Northborough	15,109	27	22	5
Northbridge	16,711	27	20	7
North Reading	15,780	33	32	1

Table 78. Full-Time Law Enforcement Employees, by Selected State and City, 2017—Continued

(Number.)

State/city	Population	Total law enforcement employees	Total officers	Total civilians
Norton	19,654	32	31	1
Norwell	11,150	28	23	5
Norwood	29,194	71	60	11
Orange	7,569	14	13	1
Orleans	5,837	28	22	6
Oxford	13,955	28	22	6
Palmer	12,136	26	19	7
Paxton	4,891	19	15	4
Peabody	52,721	115	95	20
Pelham	1,333	1	1	0
Pepperell	12,267	16	15	1
Phillipston	1,757	2	2	0
Pittsfield	42,546	110	89	21
Plymouth	59,803	137	120	17
Plympton	2,976	9	9	0
Princeton	3,472	7	6	1
Provincetown	2,993	26	19	7
Quincy	93,966	283	212	71
Randolph	33,837	62	58	4
Raynham	14,048	35	27	8
Reading	26,033	57	41	16
Rehoboth	12,153	29	24	5
Revere	53,425	111	103	8
Rochester	5,593	12	12	0
Rowley	6,378	17	12	5
Salem	43,385	107	96	11
Sandwich	20,362	36	35	1
Saugus	28,241	71	58	13
Scituate	18,687	36	34	2
Seekonk	15,521	40	38	2
Sharon	18,419	37	33	4
Sherborn	4,318	15	14	1
Shrewsbury	36,974	60	45	15
Somerset	18,239	37	33	4
Somerville	82,326	139	124	15
Southborough	10,148	22	17	5
Southbridge	16,860	43	36	7
South Hadley	17,804	31	25	6
Southwick	9,778	23	18	5
Spencer	11,920	21	17	4
Springfield	154,562	516	448	68
Stockbridge	1,919	7	6	1
Stoneham	22,077	45	38	7
Stoughton	28,678	72	60	12
Stow	7,196	10	10	0
Sturbridge	9,605	22	16	6
Sudbury	19,120	37	27	10
Sunderland	3,627	6	5	1
Sutton	9,401	20	16	4
Swampscott	15,016	32	31	1
Swansea	16,597	37	31	6
Taunton	57,047	120	114	6
Templeton	8,184	14	9	5
Tewksbury	31,245	73	58	15
Topsfield	6,604	13	12	1
Townsend	9,626	15	14	1
Truro	2,018	21	16	5
Wakefield	27,049	48	47	1
Walpole	25,312	50	42	8
Waltham	63,413	183	147	36
Wareham	22,743	55	44	11
Watertown	35,586	76	63	13
Wayland	13,976	32	23	9
Webster	16,883	31	30	1
Wellesley	29,434	59	44	15
Wellfleet	2,757	18	13	5
Wenham	5,242	11	10	1
Westborough	19,074	31	29	2
Westfield	41,735	87	82	5
Westford	24,639	46	42	4
Westminster	7,699	16	11	5
West Newbury	4,671	11	10	1
Weston	12,249	33	24	9
Westport	15,919	32	28	4
West Springfield	28,635	94	89	5
West Tisbury	2,920	10	9	1
Westwood	16,347	40	30	10
Weymouth	56,382	113	94	19
Whitman	15,000	27	26	1
Wilbraham	14,749	28	27	1
Williamsburg	2,480	1	1	0
Williamstown	7,756	15	12	3
Wilmington	23,791	50	48	2
Winchendon	10,812	19	14	5
Winchester	23,059	47	38	9

Table 78. Full-Time Law Enforcement Employees, by Selected State and City, 2017—Continued

(Number.)

State/city	Population	Total law enforcement employees	Total officers	Total civilians
Winthrop	18,319	36	35	1
Woburn	39,677	80	75	5
Worcester	185,107	505	453	52
Wrentham	11,838	22	21	1
Yarmouth	23,370	71	59	12
MICHIGAN				
Adrian	20,598	29	27	2
Akron	387	1	1	0
Albion	8,293	17	16	1
Allegan	5,085	10	9	1
Allen Park	27,062	44	40	4
Alma	9,113	14	12	2
Almont	2,780	8	7	1
Alpena	10,066	19	17	2
Ann Arbor	121,930	143	119	24
Argentine Township	6,544	6	5	1
Armada	1,742	2	2	0
Auburn Hills	23,034	53	48	5
Au Gres	848	1	1	0
Bangor	1,839	5	5	0
Bath Township	12,759	13	12	1
Battle Creek	60,852	130	108	22
Bay City	33,286	56	51	5
Beaverton	1,044	2	2	0
Belding	5,772	8	8	0
Bellaire	1,061	2	2	0
Bellevue	1,298	2	2	0
Benton Harbor	9,899	25	20	5
Benton Township	14,354	26	22	4
Berkley	15,322	34	28	6
Berrien Springs-Oronoko Township	9,039	9	8	1
Beverly Hills	10,504	24	23	1
Big Rapids	10,437	17	16	1
Birch Run	1,452	6	5	1
Birmingham	21,162	43	32	11
Blackman Township	36,908	35	34	1
Blissfield	3,229	5	5	0
Bloomfield Hills	4,021	26	23	3
Bloomfield Township	42,291	89	70	19
Breckenridge	1,296	1	1	0
Bridgeport Township	9,909	9	8	1
Bridgman	2,247	5	5	0
Brighton	7,631	19	17	2
Bronson	2,315	4	4	0
Brown City	1,246	2	2	0
Brownstown Township	31,102	39	32	7
Buchanan	4,314	10	9	1
Burton	28,439	39	36	3
Cadillac	10,473	17	15	2
Cambridge Township	5,643	4	4	0
Canton Township	90,294	119	82	37
Capac	1,834	1	1	0
Carleton	2,342	3	2	1
Caro	4,037	7	7	0
Carrollton Township	5,728	6	6	0
Carson City	1,107	3	3	0
Caspian-Gaastra	1,173	1	1	0
Cass City	2,322	4	4	0
Cassopolis	1,717	5	5	0
Center Line	8,304	25	20	5
Central Lake	929	1	1	0
Charlotte	9,053	17	16	1
Cheboygan	4,705	8	8	0
Chelsea	5,225	14	10	4
Chesterfield Township	45,212	53	40	13
Chocolay Township	5,948	5	4	1
Clare	3,058	8	8	0
Clawson	11,994	18	17	1
Clayton Township	7,113	4	4	0
Clay Township	8,845	19	16	3
Clinton	2,253	4	4	0
Clinton Township	100,999	102	93	9
Clio	2,495	4	4	0
Coldwater	10,750	20	18	2
Coleman	1,191	2	2	0
Coloma Township	6,362	11	8	3
Colon	1,150	3	3	0
Columbia Township	7,379	6	6	0
Constantine	2,042	3	3	0
Corunna	3,386	3	3	0
Covert Township	2,831	9	9	0
Croswell	2,278	6	6	0
Crystal Falls	1,380	2	2	0
Davison	4,891	7	6	1

Table 78. Full-Time Law Enforcement Employees, by Selected State and City, 2017—Continued

(Number.)

State/city	Population	Total law enforcement employees	Total officers	Total civilians
Davison Township	19,029	20	18	2
Dearborn	93,889	220	187	33
Dearborn Heights	55,454	95	83	12
Decatur	1,755	5	5	0
Denton Township	5,324	4	4	0
Detroit	670,792	3,084	2,499	585
Dewitt	4,754	7	6	1
Dewitt Township	14,799	17	16	1
Dowagiac	5,820	15	14	1
Dryden Township	4,767	4	4	0
Dundee	4,012	3	3	0
Durand	3,312	6	6	0
East Jordan	2,348	4	4	0
East Lansing	48,920	63	50	13
Eastpointe	32,712	41	37	4
Eaton Rapids	5,230	10	9	1
Eau Claire	613	1	1	0
Ecorse	9,132	18	16	2
Elk Rapids	1,610	5	5	0
Elkton	763	2	2	0
Emmett Township	11,619	15	13	2
Erie Township	4,359	4	3	1
Escanaba	12,280	41	30	11
Essexville	3,340	8	8	0
Evart	1,858	2	2	0
Fair Haven Township	1,037	1	1	0
Farmington	10,537	23	22	1
Farmington Hills	81,359	137	100	37
Fenton	11,306	22	13	9
Ferndale	20,131	48	38	10
Flat Rock	9,821	20	20	0
Flint	96,605	120	107	13
Flint Township	30,284	44	38	6
Flushing	7,972	9	9	0
Flushing Township	10,172	6	6	0
Forsyth Township	6,189	9	8	1
Fowlerville	2,922	7	6	1
Frankenmuth	5,159	7	7	0
Frankfort	1,291	3	3	0
Franklin	3,260	10	10	0
Fraser	14,645	44	34	10
Fremont	4,020	8	7	1
Fruitport Township	14,138	9	9	0
Gaines Township	6,139	1	1	0
Garden City	26,571	30	28	2
Garfield Township	812	1	1	0
Genesee Township	20,253	15	13	2
Gerrish Township	2,902	7	7	0
Gibraltar	4,472	8	7	1
Gladstone	4,767	11	10	1
Gladwin	2,865	4	4	0
Grand Beach	279	4	4	0
Grand Blanc	7,904	18	15	3
Grand Blanc Township	36,630	46	39	7
Grand Haven	11,004	36	31	5
Grand Ledge	7,809	14	14	0
Grand Rapids	197,868	335	276	59
Grandville	16,108	26	24	2
Grant	879	1	1	0
Grayling	1,830	8	8	0
Green Oak Township	18,839	17	15	2
Greenville	8,418	19	17	2
Grosse Ile Township	10,084	24	17	7
Grosse Pointe	5,151	22	22	0
Grosse Pointe Farms	9,106	41	32	9
Grosse Pointe Park	11,061	38	33	5
Grosse Pointe Shores	2,904	18	18	0
Grosse Pointe Woods	15,566	34	29	5
Hamburg Township	21,897	17	16	1
Hampton Township	9,522	9	9	0
Hamtramck	21,654	35	30	5
Hancock	4,576	8	8	0
Harbor Beach	1,602	4	4	0
Harbor Springs	1,208	6	5	1
Harper Woods	13,653	33	30	3
Hart	2,080	5	5	0
Hastings	7,272	16	14	2
Hazel Park	16,551	37	32	5
Highland Park	10,757	8	6	2
Holland	33,613	66	58	8
Home Township	1,346	1	1	0
Hopkins	609	1	1	0
Houghton	8,031	10	9	1
Howell	9,538	19	17	2
Hudson	2,225	2	2	0

Table 78. Full-Time Law Enforcement Employees, by Selected State and City, 2017—Continued

(Number.)

State/city	Population	Total law enforcement employees	Total officers	Total civilians
Huntington Woods	6,343	18	17	1
Huron Township	15,636	26	20	6
Imlay City	3,577	11	8	3
Inkster	24,324	29	25	4
Ionia	11,287	17	15	2
Iron Mountain	7,397	12	12	0
Ironwood	4,887	11	10	1
Ishpeming	6,471	11	10	1
Jackson	32,822	55	43	12
Jonesville	2,208	3	3	0
Kalamazoo	76,263	263	225	38
Kalamazoo Township	24,590	40	33	7
Kalkaska	2,043	5	4	1
Keego Harbor	3,030	4	4	0
Kentwood	52,197	77	66	11
Kingsford	5,003	17	17	0
Kinross Township	7,396	2	2	0
Laingsburg	1,284	1	1	0
Lake Angelus	297	1	1	0
Lake Linden	990	1	1	0
Lake Odessa	2,035	3	3	0
Lake Orion	3,058	5	4	1
Lakeview	1,011	2	2	0
Lansing	116,302	213	188	25
Lansing Township	8,150	16	15	1
Lapeer	8,735	22	20	2
Lathrup Village	4,126	8	8	0
Laurium	1,941	4	4	0
Lennon	498	1	1	0
Leslie	1,875	3	3	0
Lincoln Park	36,502	55	47	8
Lincoln Township	14,460	12	10	2
Linden	3,842	5	5	0
Litchfield	1,343	2	2	0
Livonia	93,603	186	147	39
Lowell	4,089	6	5	1
Ludington	8,068	15	14	1
Luna Pier	1,368	2	2	0
Mackinac Island	475	6	6	0
Mackinaw City	801	6	6	0
Madison Heights	30,152	56	45	11
Madison Township	8,470	5	5	0
Mancelona	1,359	1	1	0
Manistee	6,030	13	13	0
Manistique	2,890	8	8	0
Manton	1,438	1	1	0
Marenisco Township	1,599	1	1	0
Marine City	4,108	4	4	0
Marlette	1,762	4	4	0
Marquette	20,442	38	33	5
Marshall	7,028	14	14	0
Marysville	9,702	16	14	2
Mason	8,418	12	11	1
Mattawan	1,936	6	6	0
Melvindale	10,262	24	23	1
Mendon	854	2	2	0
Menominee	8,230	16	15	1
Meridian Township	42,878	42	37	5
Metamora Township	4,250	4	4	0
Metro Police Authority of Genesee County	20,001	28	24	4
Michiana	181	3	3	0
Midland	42,131	48	46	2
Milan	6,044	13	9	4
Milford	16,726	20	18	2
Monroe	19,868	43	38	5
Montague	2,358	5	5	0
Montrose Township	7,466	8	7	1
Morenci	2,174	2	2	0
Mount Morris Township	20,365	32	29	3
Mount Pleasant	26,366	34	28	6
Munising	2,232	4	4	0
Muskegon	38,375	82	74	8
Muskegon Heights	10,786	25	22	3
Muskegon Township	17,842	15	14	1
Napoleon Township	6,727	2	2	0
Nashville	1,644	4	4	0
Negaunee	4,576	9	9	0
Newaygo	2,045	6	5	1
New Baltimore	12,401	18	17	1
New Buffalo	1,870	6	5	1
Niles	11,202	26	17	9
Northfield Township	8,634	11	10	1
Northville	5,981	11	11	0
Northville Township	28,751	41	28	13

Table 78. Full-Time Law Enforcement Employees, by Selected State and City, 2017—Continued

(Number.)

State/city	Population	Total law enforcement employees	Total officers	Total civilians
Norton Shores	24,402	32	30	2
Norway	2,757	6	6	0
Novi	59,895	84	62	22
Oak Park	29,698	61	49	12
Olivet	1,707	2	2	0
Ontwa Township-Edwardsburg	6,487	7	7	0
Orchard Lake	2,431	9	8	1
Oscoda Township	6,831	11	10	1
Otsego	4,005	7	6	1
Ovid	1,615	2	2	0
Owosso	14,587	20	18	2
Oxford	3,548	4	4	0
Paw Paw	3,435	9	8	1
Pentwater	839	3	3	0
Petoskey	5,764	20	19	1
Pigeon	1,143	1	1	0
Pinckney	2,463	6	6	0
Pinconning	1,249	1	1	0
Pittsfield Township	39,061	57	40	17
Plainwell	3,825	9	8	1
Plymouth	9,072	17	16	1
Plymouth Township	26,779	48	30	18
Portage	48,876	74	55	19
Port Austin	628	1	1	0
Port Huron	29,092	58	49	9
Portland	3,943	6	6	0
Potterville	2,634	2	2	0
Prairieville Township	3,452	2	2	0
Quincy	1,627	3	3	0
Reading	1,046	1	1	0
Redford Township	46,867	68	60	8
Reed City	2,379	5	4	1
Richfield Township, Genesee County	8,270	11	9	2
Richfield Township, Roscommon County	3,607	6	5	1
Richmond	5,893	11	9	2
River Rouge	7,417	20	18	2
Riverview	12,045	25	23	2
Rochester	13,068	30	22	8
Rockford	6,316	11	10	1
Rockwood	3,159	6	6	0
Rogers City	2,676	6	6	0
Romeo	3,616	11	8	3
Romulus	23,174	51	39	12
Roosevelt Park	3,826	5	5	0
Roseville	47,651	72	69	3
Royal Oak	59,303	111	78	33
Saginaw	48,589	61	53	8
Saginaw Township	39,319	48	43	5
Saline	9,207	17	13	4
Sandusky	2,545	6	5	1
Sault Ste. Marie	13,630	26	24	2
Schoolcraft	1,571	3	3	0
Scottville	1,222	2	2	0
Sebewaing	1,655	3	3	0
Shelby Township	79,217	85	66	19
Shepherd	1,516	2	2	0
Somerset Township	4,556	3	3	0
Southfield	73,324	145	105	40
Southgate	28,939	39	36	3
South Haven	4,362	21	17	4
South Lyon	11,777	17	16	1
South Rockwood	1,638	2	2	0
Sparta	4,370	6	6	0
Spring Arbor Township	7,974	2	2	0
Springport Township	2,134	2	2	0
Stanton	1,415	1	1	0
St. Charles	1,925	2	2	0
St. Clair	5,350	7	7	0
St. Clair Shores	59,782	85	80	5
Sterling Heights	132,882	163	141	22
St. Ignace	2,366	6	5	1
St. Johns	7,938	12	10	2
St. Joseph Township	9,813	12	11	1
St. Louis	6,994	7	6	1
Stockbridge	1,237	2	2	0
Sturgis	10,858	23	18	5
Sumpter Township	9,215	17	14	3
Sylvan Lake	1,841	4	4	0
Tawas	4,522	6	5	1
Taylor	60,882	90	74	16
Tecumseh	8,345	14	13	1
Thomas Township	11,450	8	8	0
Three Rivers	7,695	17	15	2
Tittabawassee Township	9,776	6	5	1
Traverse City	15,617	29	28	1

Table 78. Full-Time Law Enforcement Employees, by Selected State and City, 2017—Continued

(Number.)

State/city	Population	Total law enforcement employees	Total officers	Total civilians
Trenton	18,161	35	34	1
Troy	84,086	150	106	44
Tuscarora Township	2,946	8	7	1
Ubly	811	1	1	0
Unadilla Township	3,435	3	3	0
Utica	4,960	18	14	4
Van Buren Township	27,911	55	40	15
Vassar	2,580	5	5	0
Vernon	752	1	1	0
Vicksburg	3,350	5	5	0
Walker	24,987	39	35	4
Walled Lake	7,104	6	6	0
Warren	135,303	235	196	39
Waterford Township	73,060	70	54	16
Watervliet	1,671	3	3	0
Wayland	4,228	7	6	1
Wayne	16,857	20	20	0
West Bloomfield Township	65,948	104	74	30
West Branch	2,052	6	5	1
Westland	81,158	105	81	24
White Cloud	1,372	2	2	0
Whitehall	2,726	8	8	0
White Lake Township	31,016	37	27	10
White Pigeon	1,509	4	4	0
Williamston	3,892	7	6	1
Wixom	13,801	23	20	3
Wolverine Lake	4,586	8	8	0
Woodhaven	12,397	29	27	2
Wyandotte	24,817	47	34	13
Wyoming	76,153	98	85	13
Yale	1,889	3	3	0
Ypsilanti	21,267	30	25	5
Zeeland	5,594	11	10	1
Zilwaukee	1,546	2	2	0
MINNESOTA				
Aitkin	1,987	8	7	1
Akeley	430	1	1	0
Albany	2,682	5	4	1
Albert Lea	17,608	29	26	3
Alexandria	13,756	28	24	4
Annandale	3,328	5	5	0
Anoka	17,439	39	28	11
Appleton	1,341	3	3	0
Apple Valley	52,439	59	51	8
Arlington	2,146	2	2	0
Atwater	1,118	1	1	0
Austin	24,692	37	34	3
Avon	1,550	4	3	1
Babbitt	1,513	5	5	0
Barnesville	2,578	5	5	0
Battle Lake	890	2	2	0
Baxter	8,298	15	14	1
Bayport	3,420	5	5	0
Becker	4,825	7	6	1
Belgrade/Brooten	1,516	2	2	0
Belle Plaine	7,066	11	9	2
Bemidji	15,054	35	33	2
Benson	3,080	8	7	1
Big Lake	10,730	14	12	2
Blackduck	778	2	2	0
Blaine	63,857	75	60	15
Blooming Prairie	1,986	3	3	0
Bloomington	85,704	152	123	29
Blue Earth	3,191	5	5	0
Bovey	802	2	2	0
Braham	1,774	4	4	0
Brainerd	13,307	30	24	6
Breckenridge	3,250	7	7	0
Breezy Point	2,368	7	6	1
Breitung Township	607	2	2	0
Brooklyn Center	30,989	61	49	12
Brooklyn Park	80,347	139	108	31
Brownton	730	1	1	0
Buffalo	16,206	21	17	4
Buffalo Lake	687	2	2	0
Burnsville	61,442	85	75	10
Caledonia	2,773	5	5	0
Cambridge	8,770	15	14	1
Canby	1,708	3	3	0
Cannon Falls	4,110	10	8	2
Centennial Lakes	10,956	18	16	2
Champlin	24,417	31	26	5
Chaska	26,383	28	25	3
Chisholm	4,935	13	12	1

Table 78. Full-Time Law Enforcement Employees, by Selected State and City, 2017—Continued

(Number.)

State/city	Population	Total law enforcement employees	Total officers	Total civilians
Clara City	1,316	2	2	0
Clearbrook	522	1	1	0
Cloquet	12,108	25	23	2
Cold Spring/Richmond	5,565	10	9	1
Coleraine	1,993	2	2	0
Columbia Heights	19,759	32	26	6
Coon Rapids	62,495	73	65	8
Corcoran	5,735	9	8	1
Cottage Grove	36,253	48	41	7
Crookston	7,789	17	15	2
Crosby	2,329	8	8	0
Crosslake	2,239	5	5	0
Crystal	23,173	38	33	5
Danube	454	1	1	0
Dawson/Boyd	1,564	3	3	0
Dayton	5,515	8	7	1
Deephaven	3,878	8	7	1
Deer River	932	4	4	0
Detroit Lakes	9,242	18	16	2
Dilworth	4,462	8	7	1
Duluth	86,306	168	143	25
Dundas	1,513	3	3	0
Eagan	66,805	83	70	13
Eagle Lake	3,099	2	2	0
East Grand Forks	8,713	25	23	2
East Range	3,635	9	9	0
Eden Prairie	64,429	93	69	24
Eden Valley	1,034	1	1	0
Edina	51,923	73	52	21
Elko New Market	4,714	4	4	0
Elk River	24,593	42	32	10
Ely	3,379	8	7	1
Eveleth	3,636	11	10	1
Fairfax	1,142	2	2	0
Fairmont	10,027	20	18	2
Faribault	23,713	43	35	8
Farmington	22,917	27	24	3
Fergus Falls	13,468	28	23	5
Floodwood	515	4	3	1
Foley	2,656	3	3	0
Forest Lake	19,804	27	25	2
Fridley	27,516	46	42	4
Fulda	1,218	2	2	0
Gaylord	2,221	4	4	0
Gilbert	1,789	7	7	0
Glencoe	5,478	9	8	1
Glenwood	2,563	6	5	1
Golden Valley	21,545	41	31	10
Goodhue	1,186	1	1	0
Goodview	4,116	5	4	1
Grand Rapids	11,270	23	20	3
Granite Falls	2,735	7	6	1
Hallock	922	1	1	0
Hastings	22,671	31	27	4
Hawley	2,215	4	4	0
Hector	1,047	2	2	0
Henning	799	2	2	0
Hermantown	9,455	18	15	3
Hibbing	16,051	28	25	3
Hill City	581	1	1	0
Hokah	556	1	1	0
Hopkins	18,189	39	31	8
Houston	979	2	2	0
Howard Lake	2,057	3	3	0
Hutchinson	13,846	35	23	12
International Falls	6,009	12	11	1
Inver Grove Heights	35,254	43	38	5
Isanti	5,641	10	9	1
Isle	800	3	3	0
Janesville	2,274	3	3	0
Jordan	6,261	11	9	2
Kasson	6,308	9	8	1
Keewatin	1,029	3	3	0
Kimball	782	3	3	0
La Crescent	4,816	8	7	1
Lake City	5,039	11	10	1
Lake Crystal	2,489	3	3	0
Lakefield	1,618	3	3	0
Lakes Area	9,544	15	13	2
Lake Shore	1,044	2	2	0
Lakeville	62,958	65	57	8
Lamberton	773	1	1	0
Le Center	2,436	3	3	0
Lester Prairie	1,680	3	3	0
Le Sueur	3,966	8	7	1

Table 78. Full-Time Law Enforcement Employees, by Selected State and City, 2017—Continued

(Number.)

State/city	Population	Total law enforcement employees	Total officers	Total civilians
Lewiston	1,555	2	2	0
Lino Lakes	21,147	30	27	3
Litchfield	6,634	9	8	1
Little Falls	8,665	15	14	1
Long Prairie	3,313	6	6	0
Lonsdale	3,931	9	8	1
Madelia	2,229	4	4	0
Madison Lake	1,161	2	2	0
Mankato	42,047	66	57	9
Maple Grove	70,966	79	64	15
Mapleton	1,698	3	3	0
Maplewood	40,689	57	52	5
Marshall	13,660	24	21	3
Medina	6,498	11	10	1
Melrose	3,614	6	5	1
Menahga	1,329	3	3	0
Mendota Heights	11,314	17	16	1
Milaca	2,891	7	6	1
Minneapolis	418,971	1,034	847	187
Minneota	1,357	1	1	0
Minnesota Lake	649	1	1	0
Minnetonka	52,811	69	55	14
Minnetrista	9,965	15	13	2
Montevideo	5,181	10	9	1
Montgomery	2,899	5	4	1
Moorhead	42,999	74	58	16
Moose Lake	2,834	5	4	1
Morris	5,297	10	8	2
Mounds View	13,146	22	19	3
Mountain Lake	2,101	4	4	0
Nashwauk	956	3	3	0
New Brighton	22,772	33	28	5
New Hope	20,967	44	34	10
New Prague	7,685	12	10	2
New Richland	1,198	2	2	0
New Ulm	13,316	25	22	3
New York Mills	1,232	3	3	0
North Branch	10,349	13	11	2
Northfield	20,512	27	22	5
North Mankato	13,664	15	14	1
North St. Paul	12,545	18	16	2
Oakdale	28,181	40	32	8
Oak Park Heights	4,915	11	10	1
Olivia	2,328	5	5	0
Onamia	862	3	3	0
Orono	19,923	31	27	4
Ortonville	1,815	4	4	0
Osakis	1,713	3	3	0
Osseo	2,810	6	5	1
Owatonna	25,810	38	35	3
Parkers Prairie	1,005	2	2	0
Park Rapids	3,949	11	10	1
Paynesville	2,497	5	5	0
Pequot Lakes	2,278	6	5	1
Pike Bay	1,651	3	3	0
Pine River	926	3	3	0
Plainview	3,222	8	7	1
Plymouth	78,356	92	77	15
Preston	1,302	3	3	0
Princeton	4,701	13	11	2
Prior Lake	26,374	29	26	3
Proctor	3,059	8	7	1
Ramsey	26,643	27	24	3
Red Wing	16,539	34	29	5
Redwood Falls	4,976	12	10	2
Renville	1,188	3	3	0
Rice	1,375	3	3	0
Richfield	36,087	51	43	8
Robbinsdale	14,545	29	24	5
Rochester	115,228	200	138	62
Rogers	13,021	21	18	3
Roseau	2,778	6	5	1
Rosemount	24,255	27	24	3
Roseville	36,196	58	48	10
Rushford	1,715	3	3	0
Sartell	17,353	22	19	3
Sauk Centre	4,376	7	6	1
Sauk Rapids	13,769	18	17	1
Savage	31,491	42	30	12
Sebeka	678	2	2	0
Shakopee	41,176	58	48	10
Sherburn	1,084	4	4	0
Silver Bay	1,791	5	5	0
Silver Lake	802	2	2	0
Slayton	2,017	5	4	1

Table 78. Full-Time Law Enforcement Employees, by Selected State and City, 2017—Continued

(Number.)

State/city	Population	Total law enforcement employees	Total officers	Total civilians
Sleepy Eye	3,421	7	7	0
South Lake Minnetonka	12,343	17	14	3
South St. Paul	20,235	31	28	3
Springfield	2,040	5	5	0
Spring Grove	1,290	2	2	0
Spring Lake Park	6,482	14	11	3
St. Anthony	9,159	23	20	3
Staples	2,880	7	6	1
Starbuck	1,255	4	4	0
St. Charles	3,717	5	5	0
St. Cloud	67,911	133	107	26
St. Francis	7,507	14	11	3
Stillwater	19,394	26	22	4
St. James	4,422	8	7	1
St. Joseph	6,772	10	9	1
St. Louis Park	49,355	71	56	15
St. Paul	306,696	822	645	177
St. Paul Park	5,398	8	8	0
St. Peter	11,779	19	14	5
Thief River Falls	8,824	19	17	2
Tracy	2,052	3	3	0
Tri-City	1,403	3	3	0
Trimont	700	1	1	0
Truman	1,049	2	2	0
Twin Valley	778	2	2	0
Two Harbors	3,533	9	8	1
Virginia	8,493	22	22	0
Wabasha	2,442	8	7	1
Wadena	4,142	9	8	1
Waite Park	7,455	19	16	3
Walker	931	3	3	0
Warroad	1,794	6	5	1
Waseca	9,018	18	16	2
Waterville	1,841	3	3	0
Wayzata	6,517	14	12	2
Wells	2,208	4	4	0
West Concord	771	1	1	0
West Hennepin	5,591	12	10	2
West St. Paul	19,778	34	31	3
Wheaton	1,331	3	3	0
White Bear Lake	26,065	36	29	7
Willmar	19,553	37	33	4
Windom	4,499	10	9	1
Winnebago	1,356	3	3	0
Winona	27,071	42	38	4
Winsted	2,285	4	4	0
Woodbury	69,978	82	69	13
Worthington	13,195	34	22	12
Wyoming	7,866	10	9	1
Zumbrota	3,431	6	6	0
MISSISSIPPI				
Amory	7,029	28	21	7
Batesville	7,380	52	42	10
Biloxi	46,263	177	125	52
Brandon	24,125	49	35	14
Brookhaven	12,334	46	38	8
Byram	11,549	40	29	11
Columbus	24,454	75	63	12
D'Iberville	11,852	41	37	4
Florence	4,438	25	15	10
Fulton	4,085	10	10	0
Gautier	18,451	48	37	11
Gulfport	72,792	215	162	53
Hattiesburg	47,116	147	94	53
Hernando	15,897	52	41	11
Holly Springs	7,682	27	21	6
Horn Lake	27,199	63	48	15
Iuka	2,983	11	8	3
Laurel	18,790	75	54	21
Madison	26,339	91	71	20
McComb	12,812	59	31	28
Meridian	38,778	118	94	24
Ocean Springs	17,698	51	39	12
Oxford	24,071	87	73	14
Pascagoula	21,928	92	64	28
Pass Christian	5,902	22	19	3
Petal	10,743	31	26	5
Poplarville	2,993	10	10	0
Ridgeland	24,551	86	66	20
Southaven	53,928	123	117	6
Starkville	25,852	67	57	10
Summit	1,642	6	5	1
Vicksburg	22,772	93	65	28
Waveland	6,426	18	18	0

Table 78. Full-Time Law Enforcement Employees, by Selected State and City, 2017—Continued

(Number.)

State/city	Population	Total law enforcement employees	Total officers	Total civilians
West Point	10,817	28	24	4
Wiggins	4,567	23	16	7
MISSOURI				
Adrian	1,609	4	4	0
Advance	1,368	3	3	0
Archie	1,215	4	4	0
Arnold	21,399	55	47	8
Ash Grove	1,446	4	4	0
Ashland	3,902	7	6	1
Aurora	7,508	23	17	6
Ava	2,918	12	7	5
Ballwin	30,299	60	48	12
Bates City	219	1	1	0
Battlefield	6,127	9	9	0
Bella Villa	737	4	4	0
Belle	1,504	3	3	0
Bellefontaine Neighbors	10,678	30	27	3
Bel-Nor	1,461	5	5	0
Bel-Ridge	2,679	17	16	1
Belton	23,312	63	44	19
Berkeley	8,958	28	20	8
Bernie	1,928	8	5	3
Bertrand	768	1	1	0
Bethany	3,095	4	4	0
Billings	1,101	3	3	0
Bismarck	1,482	3	3	0
Bloomfield	1,872	5	5	0
Blue Springs	54,727	140	95	45
Bolivar	10,873	29	22	7
Bonne Terre	7,185	11	11	0
Boonville	8,482	27	21	6
Bourbon	1,610	4	4	0
Bowling Green	5,541	11	8	3
Branson	11,571	61	46	15
Branson West	433	7	7	0
Braymer	849	1	1	0
Breckenridge Hills	4,655	16	15	1
Brentwood	7,991	28	26	2
Bridgeton	11,703	62	52	10
Brookfield	4,266	18	11	7
Buckner	3,052	8	7	1
Buffalo	3,043	6	5	1
Butler	4,056	13	9	4
Cabool	2,134	11	7	4
California	4,441	8	7	1
Calverton Park	1,283	8	8	0
Camdenton	3,980	18	15	3
Cameron	9,765	22	15	7
Canalou	304	1	1	0
Canton	2,377	5	4	1
Cape Girardeau	39,887	114	80	34
Carl Junction	7,822	17	12	5
Carrollton	3,574	10	10	0
Carterville	1,893	5	5	0
Carthage	14,292	37	28	9
Caruthersville	5,745	19	16	3
Cassville	3,343	13	13	0
Center	504	1	1	0
Centralia	4,220	14	9	5
Charleston	5,698	18	12	6
Chesterfield	47,687	107	94	13
Chillicothe	9,760	22	14	8
Claycomo	1,477	11	11	0
Clayton	16,743	56	47	9
Clever	2,711	4	3	1
Clinton	8,817	24	23	1
Cole Camp	1,112	3	3	0
Columbia	122,585	191	158	33
Concordia	2,375	6	6	0
Conway	776	1	1	0
Cottleville	5,612	8	8	0
Country Club Hills	1,264	8	8	0
Country Club Village	2,471	2	2	0
Crane	1,338	3	3	0
Crestwood	11,904	31	27	4
Creve Coeur	18,746	54	49	5
Crocker	1,042	4	4	0
Crystal City	4,817	23	17	6
Cuba	3,339	13	12	1
Delta	440	1	1	0
Desloge	4,910	12	11	1
De Soto	6,488	18	12	6
Des Peres	8,567	51	42	9
Dexter	7,935	23	18	5

Table 78. Full-Time Law Enforcement Employees, by Selected State and City, 2017—Continued

(Number.)

State/city	Population	Total law enforcement employees	Total officers	Total civilians
Diamond	941	2	2	0
Dixon	1,457	9	5	4
Doniphan	1,990	9	6	3
Doolittle	594	1	1	0
Drexel	958	2	2	0
Duenweg	1,295	6	6	0
Duquesne	1,725	10	9	1
East Prairie	3,094	9	5	4
Edmundson	832	12	11	1
Eldon	4,657	12	11	1
El Dorado Springs	3,575	12	7	5
Ellington	958	2	2	0
Ellisville	9,242	23	22	1
Ellsinore	449	2	2	0
Elsberry	2,002	3	3	0
Eminence	579	3	3	0
Eureka	10,588	27	23	4
Everton	302	1	1	0
Excelsior Springs	11,592	36	24	12
Fair Grove	1,456	6	6	0
Fair Play	465	1	1	0
Farmington	18,710	35	27	8
Fayette	2,697	7	7	0
Ferguson	20,789	49	41	8
Festus	12,187	32	24	8
Flordell Hills	802	9	9	0
Florissant	51,693	113	89	24
Fordland	829	3	3	0
Foristell	559	6	6	0
Forsyth	2,426	6	5	1
Fredericktown	4,108	13	12	1
Frontenac	3,859	22	21	1
Fulton	13,160	35	30	5
Galena	420	1	1	0
Gallatin	1,722	1	1	0
Garden City	1,627	3	3	0
Gerald	1,307	2	2	0
Gideon	1,011	2	2	0
Gladstone	27,390	61	45	16
Glasgow	1,089	3	3	0
Glendale	5,889	14	11	3
Goodman	1,226	2	2	0
Gower	1,494	3	3	0
Grain Valley	13,825	25	21	4
Granby	2,122	4	4	0
Grandview	25,308	65	55	10
Greenfield	1,312	3	3	0
Greenwood	5,733	9	9	0
Hallsville	1,546	3	3	0
Hamilton	1,710	4	4	0
Hannibal	17,791	49	37	12
Hardin	534	1	1	0
Harrisonville	10,043	29	24	5
Hartville	592	2	2	0
Hayti	2,684	9	8	1
Hazelwood	25,401	78	66	12
Henrietta	359	1	1	0
Herculaneum	4,050	12	11	1
Hermann	2,355	11	6	5
Higginsville	4,629	15	9	6
Hillsboro	3,178	9	7	2
Hillsdale	1,574	12	12	0
Holcomb	593	2	2	0
Holden	2,240	6	6	0
Hollister	4,499	15	9	6
Holts Summit	3,784	12	10	2
Houston	2,094	6	6	0
Howardville	359	3	1	2
Huntsville	1,508	1	1	0
Independence	117,055	260	184	76
Indian Point	512	3	3	0
Ironton	1,364	6	3	3
Jackson	15,252	31	24	7
Jasper	938	2	2	0
Jefferson City	42,989	127	89	38
Jonesburg	716	1	1	0
Joplin	52,412	134	100	34
Kahoka	1,995	2	2	0
Kansas City	484,948	1,819	1,299	520
Kearney	10,032	18	17	1
Kennett	10,505	30	23	7
Kimberling City	2,293	6	6	0
Kirksville	17,520	26	23	3
Kirkwood	27,621	76	59	17
Knob Noster	2,737	11	6	5

Table 78. Full-Time Law Enforcement Employees, by Selected State and City, 2017—Continued

(Number.)

State/city	Population	Total law enforcement employees	Total officers	Total civilians
Ladue	8,593	31	26	5
La Grange	929	5	5	0
Lake Lotawana	2,061	2	2	0
Lake Ozark	1,818	17	11	6
Lakeshire	1,412	3	3	0
Lake St. Louis	15,979	39	30	9
Lake Tapawingo	723	3	3	0
Lake Waukomis	916	2	2	0
Lake Winnebago	1,164	5	5	0
Lamar	4,338	16	14	2
La Plata	1,311	4	4	0
Lathrop	2,040	5	5	0
Laurie	932	5	5	0
Lawson	2,395	5	4	1
Leadington	510	4	4	0
Leasburg	332	1	1	0
Lebanon	14,739	42	31	11
Lee's Summit	96,855	193	140	53
Leeton	553	1	1	0
Lexington	4,560	7	6	1
Liberal	719	2	2	0
Liberty	30,850	52	40	12
Licking	3,115	5	5	0
Lincoln	1,179	3	3	0
Linn	1,424	3	3	0
Linn Creek	245	3	3	0
Lone Jack	1,179	5	5	0
Louisiana	3,269	11	5	6
Lowry City	608	1	1	0
Macon	5,360	13	11	2
Malden	4,030	17	14	3
Manchester	18,154	41	38	3
Mansfield	1,255	5	5	0
Maplewood	7,843	33	30	3
Marceline	2,112	8	8	0
Marionville	2,192	5	5	0
Marshall	12,867	32	26	6
Marshfield	7,341	11	10	1
Marston	461	1	1	0
Maryland Heights	27,083	97	78	19
Maryville	11,820	26	20	6
Matthews	614	3	3	0
Maysville	1,083	1	1	0
Memphis	1,860	2	2	0
Merriam Woods	1,770	1	1	0
Mexico	11,709	33	32	1
Milan	1,802	3	3	0
Miller	686	1	1	0
Moberly	13,838	40	29	11
Moline Acres	2,399	8	8	0
Monett	9,048	21	19	2
Monroe City	2,428	8	7	1
Montgomery City	2,692	6	6	0
Morehouse	899	2	2	0
Moscow Mills	2,620	6	6	0
Mound City	1,032	1	1	0
Mountain Grove	4,674	15	11	4
Mountain View	2,669	9	8	1
Mount Vernon	4,551	11	11	0
Neosho	12,237	27	25	2
Nevada	8,198	27	21	6
Newburg	444	1	1	0
New Florence	717	2	2	0
New Franklin	1,065	4	3	1
New Haven	2,090	7	7	0
New London	969	2	2	0
New Madrid	2,930	17	8	9
Niangua	420	1	1	0
Nixa	21,575	37	31	6
Noel	1,814	3	3	0
Normandy	7,544	32	31	1
North Kansas City	4,407	50	39	11
Northwoods	4,138	22	20	2
Oak Grove	8,019	20	19	1
Oakland	1,375	76	59	17
Oakview Village	396	3	3	0
O'Fallon	87,388	151	116	35
Old Monroe	287	2	2	0
Olivette	7,859	24	22	2
Oregon	759	1	1	0
Oronogo	2,490	6	6	0
Orrick	802	3	3	0
Osage Beach	4,474	34	22	12
Osceola	892	1	1	0
Overland	15,760	57	42	15

Table 78. Full-Time Law Enforcement Employees, by Selected State and City, 2017—Continued

(Number.)

State/city	Population	Total law enforcement employees	Total officers	Total civilians
Owensville	2,609	8	8	0
Ozark	19,688	36	32	4
Pacific	7,244	25	17	8
Pagedale	3,289	16	15	1
Palmyra	3,619	8	7	1
Park Hills	8,637	17	16	1
Parkville	6,685	15	14	1
Peculiar	5,039	10	9	1
Perry	697	1	1	0
Perryville	8,493	30	24	6
Pevely	5,748	21	14	7
Piedmont	1,931	6	6	0
Pierce City	1,298	4	4	0
Pilot Grove	762	1	1	0
Pilot Knob	699	2	2	0
Pineville	786	7	7	0
Platte City	4,900	13	12	1
Platte Woods	407	8	7	1
Plattsburg	2,280	12	12	0
Pleasant Hill	8,496	17	12	5
Pleasant Hope	613	2	2	0
Pleasant Valley	3,084	14	9	5
Polo	534	1	1	0
Poplar Bluff	17,264	60	45	15
Potosi	2,641	10	9	1
Purdy	1,102	2	2	0
Queen City	589	1	1	0
Qulin	448	1	1	0
Raymore	21,110	42	27	15
Raytown	29,224	50	38	12
Reeds Spring	857	3	2	1
Republic	16,316	28	23	5
Rich Hill	1,322	1	1	0
Richland	1,788	5	5	0
Richmond	5,540	14	12	2
Richmond Heights	8,362	42	41	1
Risco	317	1	1	0
Riverside	3,276	31	23	8
Riverview	2,795	10	10	0
Rockaway Beach	868	3	2	1
Rock Hill	4,616	12	11	1
Rock Port	1,214	3	3	0
Rogersville	3,598	9	8	1
Rolla	20,147	55	34	21
Salem	4,918	17	12	5
Salisbury	1,532	4	3	1
Sarcoxie	1,287	3	3	0
Savannah	5,136	8	7	1
Scott City	4,480	22	17	5
Sedalia	21,501	60	45	15
Seligman	831	1	1	0
Senath	1,679	5	5	0
Seneca	2,419	4	4	0
Seymour	1,997	3	3	0
Shelbina	1,610	6	5	1
Shrewsbury	6,135	21	19	2
Sikeston	16,324	78	61	17
Silex	307	1	1	0
Slater	1,797	5	4	1
Smithville	9,638	16	16	0
Southwest City	954	3	3	0
Sparta	1,883	3	3	0
Springfield	168,654	409	335	74
St. Ann	12,779	68	45	23
St. Charles	69,804	149	109	40
St. Clair	4,718	16	14	2
Steelville	1,692	6	6	0
Ste. Genevieve	4,508	9	8	1
St. James	4,102	12	11	1
St. John	6,378	22	21	1
St. Joseph	76,435	173	130	43
St. Louis	310,284	1,624	1,188	436
St. Marys	347	1	1	0
Stover	1,072	3	3	0
St. Peters	58,079	114	90	24
Strafford	2,341	7	7	0
St. Robert	6,020	25	18	7
Sugar Creek	3,298	22	18	4
Sullivan	7,132	25	18	7
Summersville	502	2	2	0
Sunset Hills	8,498	33	26	7
Sweet Springs	1,439	4	4	0
Tarkio	1,457	3	3	0
Thayer	2,208	10	6	4
Tipton	3,397	4	4	0

Table 78. Full-Time Law Enforcement Employees, by Selected State and City, 2017—Continued

(Number.)

State/city	Population	Total law enforcement employees	Total officers	Total civilians
Town and Country	11,157	32	30	2
Trenton	5,920	16	10	6
Trimble	639	2	2	0
Troy	12,079	25	23	2
Truesdale	747	1	1	0
Union	11,447	27	25	2
University City	34,601	87	70	17
Urbana	410	2	2	0
Vandalia	4,344	6	5	1
Velda City	1,382	9	9	0
Verona	602	1	1	0
Versailles	2,452	11	10	1
Vienna	588	1	1	0
Vinita Park	11,061	46	44	2
Walnut Grove	812	2	2	0
Warrensburg	20,483	40	34	6
Warrenton	8,168	22	20	2
Warsaw	2,118	5	5	0
Warson Woods	1,936	8	8	0
Washington	14,073	31	28	3
Waverly	829	2	1	1
Waynesville	5,381	12	11	1
Weatherby Lake	1,957	5	5	0
Webb City	11,259	24	20	4
Webster Groves	22,968	47	45	2
Wellsville	1,154	3	3	0
Wentzville	38,876	87	67	20
Weston	1,771	4	4	0
West Plains	12,367	34	28	6
Wheaton	693	2	2	0
Willard	5,452	11	10	1
Willow Springs	2,146	7	6	1
Winona	1,289	8	4	4
Woodson Terrace	4,043	19	17	2
Wright City	3,584	11	10	1
Wyatt	303	1	1	0
MONTANA				
Baker	2,029	5	5	0
Belgrade	8,393	25	18	7
Billings	111,317	173	150	23
Boulder	1,239	3	3	0
Bozeman	46,728	68	60	8
Bridger	736	2	2	0
Chinook	1,238	4	4	0
Colstrip	2,326	12	7	5
Columbia Falls	5,337	8	7	1
Columbus	2,050	4	4	0
Conrad	2,544	5	5	0
Cut Bank	3,031	9	8	1
Deer Lodge	2,968	6	5	1
Dillon	4,277	9	8	1
East Helena	2,084	4	4	0
Ennis	900	1	1	0
Fort Benton	1,455	4	4	0
Fromberg	446	1	1	0
Glasgow	3,379	10	8	2
Glendive	5,402	16	10	6
Great Falls	59,167	130	88	42
Hamilton	4,739	15	14	1
Havre	9,900	25	19	6
Helena	31,668	74	54	20
Hot Springs	560	2	2	0
Kalispell	23,243	51	41	10
Laurel	6,887	17	13	4
Libby	2,684	6	6	0
Livingston	7,470	14	14	0
Manhattan	1,723	3	3	0
Miles City	8,690	14	14	0
Missoula	73,304	131	106	25
Plains	1,076	3	3	0
Polson	4,821	17	16	1
Red Lodge	2,256	7	6	1
Ronan City	2,036	5	5	0
Sidney	6,814	14	13	1
Stevensville	1,985	2	2	0
St. Ignatius	827	2	2	0
Thompson Falls	1,361	4	4	0
Troy	891	3	3	0
West Yellowstone	1,367	12	6	6
Whitefish	7,446	19	16	3
Wolf Point	2,840	8	6	2
NEBRASKA				
Albion	1,591	3	3	0

Table 78. Full-Time Law Enforcement Employees, by Selected State and City, 2017—Continued

(Number.)

State/city	Population	Total law enforcement employees	Total officers	Total civilians
Alliance	8,393	23	17	6
Aurora	4,484	10	9	1
Bayard	1,122	3	3	0
Beatrice	12,311	36	22	14
Bennington	1,518	2	2	0
Blair	8,103	18	16	2
Broken Bow	3,537	7	6	1
Central City	2,900	6	5	1
Columbus	22,955	50	35	15
Cozad	3,775	8	8	0
Crete	7,071	12	11	1
Emerson	798	1	1	0
Fairbury	3,680	7	6	1
Falls City	4,196	13	9	4
Gering	8,333	18	16	2
Gordon	1,523	6	5	1
Gothenburg	3,459	7	6	1
Grand Island	51,980	101	83	18
Harvard	944	1	1	0
Hastings	24,958	50	38	12
Holdrege	5,565	16	10	6
Kearney	33,960	70	55	15
Kimball	2,385	4	4	0
La Vista	17,219	42	37	5
Lexington	9,967	23	21	2
Lincoln	284,063	466	330	136
McCook	7,498	19	14	5
Milford	2,115	4	4	0
Minatare	799	2	2	0
Minden	3,009	5	5	0
Mitchell	1,663	3	3	0
Nebraska City	7,355	15	14	1
Neligh	1,512	3	3	0
Norfolk	24,364	54	38	16
North Platte	24,011	65	42	23
Ogallala	4,512	11	10	1
Omaha	449,388	963	814	149
O'Neill	3,618	9	8	1
Plattsmouth	6,475	17	14	3
Ralston	7,564	15	13	2
Scottsbluff	16,023	37	31	6
Seward	7,259	13	11	2
Sidney	6,911	16	14	2
St. Paul	2,357	4	4	0
Superior	1,839	4	4	0
Sutton	1,396	2	2	0
Tekamah	1,715	4	4	0
Tilden	930	1	1	0
Valentine	2,815	7	6	1
Valley	2,225	5	5	0
Wahoo	4,495	6	6	0
Wayne	5,555	12	8	4
West Point	3,319	7	6	1
Wymore	1,392	3	3	0
York	7,876	23	17	6
NEVADA				
Boulder City	15,804	45	32	13
Carlin	2,299	7	5	2
Elko	20,807	39	34	5
Fallon	8,450	35	22	13
Henderson	299,285	613	364	249
Las Vegas Metropolitan Police Department	1,627,244	5,379	3,563	1,816
Lovelock	1,834	6	4	2
Mesquite	18,476	42	29	13
North Las Vegas	242,537	412	300	112
Reno	248,531	385	318	67
Sparks	99,732	153	109	44
West Wendover	4,236	20	12	8
Winnemucca	7,938	22	19	3
Yerington	3,147	7	6	1
NEW HAMPSHIRE				
Alexandria	1,620	2	2	0
Alstead	1,893	2	2	0
Alton	5,334	14	12	2
Amherst	11,250	19	18	1
Antrim	2,660	6	5	1
Ashland	2,056	5	5	0
Atkinson	6,876	7	6	1
Auburn	5,449	11	9	2
Barnstead	4,667	5	5	0
Barrington	8,981	10	9	1
Bartlett	2,755	2	2	0

Table 78. Full-Time Law Enforcement Employees, by Selected State and City, 2017—Continued

(Number.)

State/city	Population	Total law enforcement employees	Total officers	Total civilians
Bedford	22,623	49	36	13
Belmont	7,293	19	16	3
Bennington	1,485	2	2	0
Berlin	10,489	30	22	8
Bethlehem	2,560	5	5	0
Boscawen	3,977	8	7	1
Bow	7,820	14	12	2
Bradford	1,678	3	3	0
Brentwood	4,743	6	6	0
Bristol	3,057	10	9	1
Brookline	5,304	9	8	1
Campton	3,286	8	7	1
Canaan	3,894	6	6	0
Candia	3,903	7	6	1
Canterbury	2,416	3	3	0
Carroll	741	4	4	0
Center Harbor	1,098	3	3	0
Charlestown	4,971	8	5	3
Chester	5,068	8	7	1
Chesterfield	3,523	7	6	1
Claremont	12,893	31	25	6
Colebrook	2,147	4	4	0
Concord	42,942	91	79	12
Conway	9,946	32	23	9
Danville	4,471	5	5	0
Deerfield	4,465	8	7	1
Deering	1,933	2	2	0
Derry	33,382	66	53	13
Dover	31,344	74	50	24
Dublin	1,522	4	3	1
Dunbarton	2,808	4	4	0
Durham	16,751	23	20	3
East Kingston	2,396	5	5	0
Effingham	1,439	2	2	0
Enfield	4,527	8	7	1
Epping	6,978	17	16	1
Epsom	4,701	6	5	1
Exeter	14,807	34	24	10
Farmington	6,858	14	13	1
Fitzwilliam	2,316	3	3	0
Franconia	1,102	3	3	0
Franklin	8,444	26	18	8
Freedom	1,488	2	2	0
Fremont	4,737	6	5	1
Gilford	7,191	24	18	6
Gilmanton	3,746	6	5	1
Goffstown	18,057	43	30	13
Gorham	2,592	11	7	4
Grantham	2,967	5	4	1
Greenland	3,966	8	8	0
Hampstead	8,625	9	9	0
Hampton	15,524	43	34	9
Hampton Falls	2,302	3	3	0
Hancock	1,628	3	3	0
Hanover	11,443	30	17	13
Haverhill	4,542	8	7	1
Henniker	4,947	9	8	1
Hillsborough	5,954	20	14	6
Hinsdale	3,835	10	9	1
Holderness	2,090	6	6	0
Hollis	7,838	16	15	1
Hooksett	14,274	38	27	11
Hopkinton	5,629	8	7	1
Hudson	25,212	64	47	17
Jackson	814	3	3	0
Jaffrey	5,211	11	10	1
Keene	23,386	51	40	11
Kensington	2,126	5	4	1
Kingston	6,185	7	6	1
Laconia	16,616	47	37	10
Lancaster	3,288	6	5	1
Lebanon	13,577	44	31	13
Lee	4,417	7	6	1
Lincoln	1,761	16	11	5
Lisbon	1,564	3	3	0
Litchfield	8,508	13	11	2
Littleton	5,871	14	11	3
Londonderry	26,254	74	61	13
Loudon	5,506	8	7	1
Lyndeborough	1,707	1	1	0
Madison	2,523	4	4	0
Manchester	110,655	291	236	55
Marlborough	2,040	3	3	0
Meredith	6,404	18	14	4
Merrimack	25,675	49	38	11

Table 78. Full-Time Law Enforcement Employees, by Selected State and City, 2017—Continued

(Number.)

State/city	Population	Total law enforcement employees	Total officers	Total civilians
Middleton	1,810	4	4	0
Milford	15,330	32	27	5
Milton	4,592	8	7	1
Mont Vernon	2,519	3	3	0
Moultonborough	4,038	10	10	0
Nashua	88,102	235	174	61
New Boston	5,618	9	8	1
Newbury	2,198	3	3	0
New Durham	2,671	5	5	0
Newfields	1,713	3	3	0
New Hampton	2,217	6	6	0
Newington	796	10	9	1
New Ipswich	5,248	6	5	1
New London	4,590	13	8	5
Newmarket	9,003	20	13	7
Newport	6,344	17	12	5
Newton	4,963	8	7	1
Northfield	4,814	10	9	1
North Hampton	4,447	9	8	1
Northumberland	2,122	2	2	0
Northwood	4,281	7	6	1
Nottingham	5,046	8	7	1
Ossipee	4,246	10	9	1
Pelham	13,513	28	20	8
Pembroke	7,115	14	12	2
Peterborough	6,568	14	12	2
Pittsfield	4,086	6	6	0
Plainfield	2,345	3	3	0
Plaistow	7,695	26	18	8
Plymouth	6,303	18	12	6
Portsmouth	21,607	86	63	23
Raymond	10,347	26	17	9
Rindge	5,883	8	7	1
Rochester	30,441	69	56	13
Rollinsford	2,552	5	5	0
Rye	5,425	11	10	1
Salem	29,013	75	62	13
Sanbornton	2,996	6	5	1
Sandown	6,368	8	8	0
Sandwich	1,304	2	2	0
Seabrook	8,816	34	28	6
Somersworth	11,795	34	27	7
Springfield	1,319	2	2	0
Strafford	4,121	5	5	0
Stratham	7,452	12	11	1
Sugar Hill	571	2	2	0
Sunapee	3,449	5	5	0
Thornton	2,491	6	5	1
Tilton	3,556	19	16	3
Troy	2,054	3	3	0
Tuftonboro	2,327	4	4	0
Wakefield	5,613	11	10	1
Warner	2,879	5	4	1
Washington	1,108	1	1	0
Waterville Valley	245	7	6	1
Weare	8,935	10	9	1
Webster	1,906	1	1	0
Wilton	3,687	8	7	1
Winchester	4,146	8	7	1
Windham	14,686	25	19	6
Wolfeboro	6,189	18	13	5
Woodstock	1,367	6	6	0
NEW JERSEY				
Aberdeen Township	18,403	44	37	7
Absecon	8,261	32	28	4
Allendale	6,938	20	15	5
Allenhurst	486	12	9	3
Allentown	1,808	6	5	1
Alpine	1,885	12	12	0
Andover Township	5,962	17	12	5
Asbury Park	15,656	93	88	5
Atlantic City	38,601	371	253	118
Atlantic Highlands	4,281	19	14	5
Audubon	8,748	18	17	1
Avalon	1,270	29	21	8
Avon-by-the-Sea	1,775	11	11	0
Barnegat Township	22,652	47	46	1
Barrington	6,792	16	15	1
Bay Head	986	9	8	1
Bayonne	67,041	227	177	50
Beach Haven	1,181	14	13	1
Beachwood	11,296	20	18	2
Bedminster Township	8,285	18	16	2
Belleville	36,409	117	108	9

Table 78. Full-Time Law Enforcement Employees, by Selected State and City, 2017—Continued

(Number.)

State/city	Population	Total law enforcement employees	Total officers	Total civilians
Bellmawr	11,505	24	22	2
Belmar	5,666	30	23	7
Belvidere	2,589	5	5	0
Bergenfield	27,891	54	46	8
Berkeley Heights Township	13,654	34	26	8
Berkeley Township	42,036	96	70	26
Berlin	7,619	18	17	1
Berlin Township	5,560	18	17	1
Bernards Township	27,219	42	38	4
Bernardsville	7,876	26	20	6
Beverly	2,506	8	8	0
Blairstown Township	5,767	7	6	1
Bloomfield	48,928	154	129	25
Bloomingdale	8,295	18	17	1
Bogota	8,595	21	16	5
Boonton	8,421	28	23	5
Boonton Township	4,395	13	13	0
Bordentown City	3,839	13	11	2
Bordentown Township	12,216	26	25	1
Bound Brook	10,537	29	24	5
Bradley Beach	4,236	20	18	2
Branchburg Township	14,822	30	26	4
Brick Township	75,566	203	138	65
Bridgeton	24,937	78	65	13
Bridgewater Township	45,417	87	79	8
Brielle	4,708	16	15	1
Brigantine	8,976	44	34	10
Brooklawn	1,937	7	7	0
Buena	4,432	9	8	1
Burlington City	9,854	36	32	4
Burlington Township	22,772	50	41	9
Butler	7,829	17	16	1
Byram Township	7,944	14	14	0
Caldwell	8,073	21	21	0
Camden County Police Department	74,299	398	354	44
Cape May	3,483	26	21	5
Carlstadt	6,295	30	28	2
Carney's Point Township	7,729	19	18	1
Carteret	24,283	68	60	8
Cedar Grove Township	12,674	31	30	1
Chatham	9,011	23	20	3
Chatham Township	10,515	23	21	2
Cherry Hill Township	71,747	163	135	28
Chesilhurst	1,644	10	9	1
Chesterfield Township	7,451	11	10	1
Chester Township	7,961	23	22	1
Cinnaminson Township	16,696	27	27	0
Clark Township	16,084	49	38	11
Clayton	8,722	16	16	0
Clementon	4,937	13	12	1
Cliffside Park	25,166	46	44	2
Clifton	86,472	185	148	37
Clinton	2,694	10	10	0
Clinton Township	12,748	23	22	1
Closter	8,788	20	20	0
Collingswood	14,080	30	26	4
Colts Neck Township	9,936	23	22	1
Cranbury Township	3,966	18	17	1
Cranford Township	24,442	68	52	16
Cresskill	8,848	26	22	4
Deal	730	22	18	4
Delanco Township	4,528	13	12	1
Delaware Township	4,443	8	7	1
Delran Township	16,609	34	30	4
Demarest	5,034	13	13	0
Denville Township	16,811	43	33	10
Deptford Township	30,727	74	68	6
Dover	18,339	33	29	4
Dumont	18,018	38	31	7
Dunellen	7,428	16	16	0
Eastampton Township	5,962	19	18	1
East Brunswick Township	49,019	111	83	28
East Greenwich Township	10,573	18	16	2
East Hanover Township	11,284	38	34	4
East Newark	2,811	8	8	0
East Orange	65,160	255	208	47
East Rutherford	10,064	34	33	1
East Windsor Township	27,571	49	43	6
Eatontown	12,258	45	37	8
Edgewater	12,183	34	29	5
Edgewater Park Township	8,726	14	13	1
Edison Township	102,699	228	181	47
Egg Harbor City	4,182	13	12	1
Egg Harbor Township	43,515	111	83	28
Elizabeth	129,726	390	293	97

Table 78. Full-Time Law Enforcement Employees, by Selected State and City, 2017—Continued

(Number.)

State/city	Population	Total law enforcement employees	Total officers	Total civilians
Elk Township	4,140	13	12	1
Elmer	1,317	1	1	0
Elmwood Park	20,515	47	42	5
Emerson	7,747	24	21	3
Englewood	28,795	106	82	24
Englewood Cliffs	5,442	26	25	1
Englishtown	1,956	7	7	0
Essex Fells	2,135	13	13	0
Evesham Township	45,314	87	77	10
Ewing Township	36,161	102	83	19
Fairfield Township, Essex County	7,597	39	36	3
Fair Haven	5,953	13	13	0
Fair Lawn	33,759	69	60	9
Fairview	14,573	37	33	4
Fanwood	7,796	18	17	1
Far Hills	935	6	6	0
Flemington	4,627	14	14	0
Florence Township	12,755	27	25	2
Florham Park	11,818	36	32	4
Fort Lee	38,095	116	97	19
Franklin	4,773	16	15	1
Franklin Lakes	10,939	29	23	6
Franklin Township, Gloucester County	16,599	35	31	4
Franklin Township, Hunterdon County	3,223	6	6	0
Franklin Township, Somerset County	67,463	123	105	18
Freehold Borough	11,865	33	30	3
Freehold Township	35,531	71	67	4
Frenchtown	1,396	4	4	0
Galloway Township	36,672	87	57	30
Garfield	32,233	70	60	10
Garwood	4,384	20	16	4
Gibbsboro	2,253	10	10	0
Glassboro	20,134	50	44	6
Glen Ridge	7,694	29	23	6
Glen Rock	12,051	24	23	1
Gloucester City	11,366	33	31	2
Gloucester Township	64,094	151	129	22
Green Brook Township	7,273	24	23	1
Greenwich Township, Gloucester County	4,861	19	17	2
Greenwich Township, Warren County	5,501	12	12	0
Guttenberg	11,736	26	23	3
Hackensack	45,226	139	114	25
Hackettstown	9,520	19	18	1
Haddonfield	11,445	23	21	2
Haddon Heights	7,586	16	15	1
Haddon Township	14,731	27	26	1
Haledon	8,439	18	18	0
Hamburg	3,125	10	8	2
Hamilton Township, Atlantic County	26,482	70	52	18
Hamilton Township, Mercer County	88,723	203	169	34
Hammonton	14,370	37	30	7
Hanover Township	14,904	37	30	7
Harding Township	3,891	12	11	1
Hardyston Township	7,884	25	19	6
Harrington Park	4,848	11	11	0
Harrison	16,802	46	35	11
Harrison Township	13,128	21	20	1
Harvey Cedars	342	8	8	0
Hasbrouck Heights	12,286	32	30	2
Haworth	3,491	12	11	1
Hawthorne	19,041	32	31	1
Hazlet Township	19,938	50	43	7
Helmetta	2,228	4	4	0
High Bridge	3,524	7	7	0
Highland Park	14,287	34	27	7
Highlands	4,793	17	14	3
Hightstown	5,522	14	13	1
Hillsborough Township	40,369	62	51	11
Hillsdale	10,602	21	18	3
Hillside Township	22,125	79	70	9
Hi-Nella	869	13	13	0
Hoboken	55,348	155	135	20
Ho-Ho-Kus	4,169	20	16	4
Holland Township	5,113	7	6	1
Holmdel Township	16,576	48	40	8
Hopatcong	14,263	29	24	5
Hopewell Township	18,633	38	30	8
Howell Township	52,432	101	87	14
Independence Township	5,482	10	9	1
Irvington	54,728	207	151	56
Island Heights	1,659	5	5	0
Jackson Township	57,400	112	88	24
Jamesburg	6,088	18	14	4
Jefferson Township	21,505	43	35	8
Jersey City	267,906	1,038	890	148

Table 78. Full-Time Law Enforcement Employees, by Selected State and City, 2017—Continued

(Number.)

State/city	Population	Total law enforcement employees	Total officers	Total civilians
Keansburg	9,782	40	33	7
Kearny	42,527	115	109	6
Kenilworth	8,271	31	26	5
Keyport	7,062	23	17	6
Kinnelon	10,275	17	16	1
Lacey Township	28,915	58	43	15
Lakehurst	2,716	12	10	2
Lakewood Township	102,759	163	133	30
Lambertville	3,795	12	9	3
Laurel Springs	1,888	7	7	0
Lavallette	1,837	14	12	2
Lawnside	2,927	10	9	1
Lawrence Township, Mercer County	32,929	62	58	4
Lebanon Township	6,053	10	9	1
Leonia	9,273	21	18	3
Lincoln Park	10,466	28	22	6
Linden	42,948	155	124	31
Lindenwold	17,516	45	42	3
Linwood	6,859	19	18	1
Little Egg Harbor Township	21,076	53	43	10
Little Falls Township	14,479	33	28	5
Little Ferry	11,017	31	26	5
Little Silver	5,881	20	16	4
Livingston Township	29,987	81	71	10
Lodi	24,981	48	45	3
Logan Township	5,977	20	19	1
Long Beach Township	3,067	48	37	11
Long Branch	30,748	130	83	47
Long Hill Township	8,784	25	23	2
Longport	868	13	13	0
Lopatcong Township	8,298	16	15	1
Lower Alloways Creek Township	1,770	11	11	0
Lower Township	21,870	57	47	10
Lumberton Township	12,286	21	20	1
Lyndhurst Township	22,621	53	50	3
Madison	16,175	37	29	8
Magnolia	4,310	12	12	0
Mahwah Township	26,753	62	53	9
Manalapan Township	40,177	49	46	3
Manasquan	5,804	23	17	6
Manchester Township	43,916	85	68	17
Mansfield Township, Burlington County	8,593	15	14	1
Mansfield Township, Warren County	7,435	13	12	1
Mantoloking	247	9	8	1
Mantua Township	15,123	28	26	2
Manville	10,519	26	23	3
Maple Shade Township	18,797	34	30	4
Maplewood Township	24,863	73	61	12
Margate City	6,107	35	29	6
Marlboro Township	40,370	109	78	31
Matawan	8,838	23	22	1
Maywood	9,862	26	22	4
Medford Lakes	4,038	10	9	1
Medford Township	23,503	38	34	4
Mendham	5,006	13	12	1
Mendham Township	5,883	16	15	1
Merchantville	3,774	14	13	1
Metuchen	13,981	35	29	6
Middlesex Borough	13,897	34	31	3
Middle Township	18,542	66	53	13
Middletown Township	65,303	124	112	12
Midland Park	7,378	17	16	1
Millburn Township	20,421	59	53	6
Milltown	7,201	18	15	3
Millville	27,984	77	67	10
Monmouth Beach	3,213	10	9	1
Monroe Township, Gloucester County	37,174	73	66	7
Monroe Township, Middlesex County	45,722	78	60	18
Montclair	39,029	124	105	19
Montgomery Township	23,706	40	34	6
Montvale	8,653	26	24	2
Montville Township	21,818	43	37	6
Moonachie	2,815	21	18	3
Moorestown Township	20,534	38	33	5
Morris Plains	5,626	18	16	2
Morristown	19,199	61	57	4
Morris Township	22,701	45	41	4
Mountain Lakes	4,377	14	13	1
Mountainside	6,943	27	22	5
Mount Arlington	5,551	15	14	1
Mount Ephraim	4,643	14	13	1
Mount Holly Township	9,522	24	21	3
Mount Laurel Township	41,712	75	67	8
Mount Olive Township	29,410	61	52	9
Mullica Township	6,024	14	13	1

Table 78. Full-Time Law Enforcement Employees, by Selected State and City, 2017—Continued

(Number.)

State/city	Population	Total law enforcement employees	Total officers	Total civilians
Neptune City	4,725	19	17	2
Neptune Township	27,757	88	78	10
Netcong	3,247	9	9	0
Newark	283,673	1,491	1,171	320
New Brunswick	57,481	175	141	34
Newfield	1,569	5	5	0
New Hanover Township	8,264	3	3	0
New Milford	16,894	42	36	6
New Providence	12,904	21	19	2
Newton	7,874	27	22	5
North Arlington	16,009	34	27	7
North Bergen Township	63,490	125	114	11
North Brunswick Township	42,780	101	84	17
North Caldwell	6,782	20	15	5
Northfield	8,376	22	21	1
North Haledon	8,537	23	19	4
North Hanover Township	7,562	11	10	1
North Plainfield	22,255	54	46	8
Northvale	5,003	14	14	0
North Wildwood	3,856	36	29	7
Norwood	5,904	17	16	1
Nutley Township	28,833	81	69	12
Oakland	13,243	27	24	3
Oaklyn	4,002	17	16	1
Ocean City	11,281	71	57	14
Ocean Gate	2,023	10	9	1
Oceanport	5,705	15	14	1
Ocean Township, Monmouth County	26,637	78	63	15
Ocean Township, Ocean County	9,187	28	18	10
Ogdensburg	2,273	6	6	0
Old Bridge Township	67,162	117	90	27
Old Tappan	6,069	15	14	1
Oradell	8,291	24	23	1
Orange City	30,752	128	101	27
Palisades Park	21,030	45	35	10
Palmyra	7,217	19	18	1
Paramus	27,075	111	86	25
Park Ridge	8,977	20	19	1
Parsippany-Troy Hills Township	53,478	117	102	15
Passaic	71,053	188	156	32
Paterson	147,690	494	400	94
Paulsboro	5,959	20	18	2
Peapack-Gladstone	2,624	9	8	1
Pemberton Borough	1,355	9	8	1
Pemberton Township	27,506	49	44	5
Pennington	2,576	6	5	1
Pennsauken Township	36,041	84	77	7
Penns Grove	4,844	15	14	1
Pennsville Township	12,564	22	22	0
Pequannock Township	15,472	39	34	5
Perth Amboy	52,978	164	134	30
Phillipsburg	14,379	37	36	1
Pine Beach	2,170	8	7	1
Pine Hill	10,616	23	21	2
Pine Valley	11	6	6	0
Piscataway Township	58,109	108	87	21
Pitman	8,886	17	16	1
Plainfield	50,983	148	120	28
Plainsboro Township	23,569	48	36	12
Pleasantville	20,530	64	51	13
Plumsted Township	8,604	15	14	1
Pohatcong Township	3,215	14	13	1
Point Pleasant	18,696	43	33	10
Point Pleasant Beach	4,552	24	22	2
Pompton Lakes	11,176	25	21	4
Princeton	31,845	69	54	15
Prospect Park	5,944	18	17	1
Rahway	29,930	83	73	10
Ramsey	15,273	39	32	7
Randolph Township	25,950	41	35	6
Raritan	8,273	20	19	1
Raritan Township	21,918	36	33	3
Readington Township	15,834	29	23	6
Red Bank	12,135	47	39	8
Ridgefield	11,457	31	29	2
Ridgefield Park	13,166	38	31	7
Ridgewood	25,729	48	45	3
Ringwood	12,470	26	21	5
Riverdale	4,398	20	16	4
River Edge	11,744	25	22	3
Riverside Township	7,897	15	15	0
Riverton	2,704	6	6	0
River Vale Township	10,270	21	19	2
Robbinsville Township	14,446	36	27	9
Rochelle Park Township	5,714	24	20	4

Table 78. Full-Time Law Enforcement Employees, by Selected State and City, 2017—Continued

(Number.)

State/city	Population	Total law enforcement employees	Total officers	Total civilians
Rockaway	6,512	16	15	1
Rockaway Township	24,719	62	51	11
Roseland	5,916	26	26	0
Roselle	21,796	71	58	13
Roselle Park	13,747	41	34	7
Roxbury Township	23,472	45	42	3
Rumson	6,783	21	17	4
Runnemede	8,402	18	16	2
Rutherford	18,804	43	40	3
Saddle Brook Township	14,190	36	33	3
Saddle River	3,263	22	17	5
Salem	4,776	19	17	2
Sayreville	45,460	94	82	12
Scotch Plains Township	24,375	50	47	3
Sea Bright	1,375	11	11	0
Sea Girt	1,777	12	11	1
Sea Isle City	2,079	27	21	6
Seaside Heights	2,918	34	22	12
Seaside Park	1,556	14	13	1
Secaucus	20,481	82	67	15
Ship Bottom	1,146	12	11	1
Shrewsbury	4,178	21	16	5
Somerdale	5,591	15	14	1
Somers Point	10,504	37	30	7
Somerville	12,263	33	31	2
South Amboy	8,839	28	22	6
South Bound Brook	4,652	14	13	1
South Brunswick Township	46,280	111	82	29
South Hackensack Township	2,479	22	19	3
South Harrison Township	3,193	5	5	0
South Orange Village	16,407	52	45	7
South Plainfield	24,458	69	55	14
South River	16,399	42	32	10
South Toms River	3,799	13	12	1
Sparta Township	18,807	42	28	14
Spotswood	8,492	27	22	5
Springfield Township, Burlington County	3,301	11	10	1
Springfield Township, Union County	17,805	48	44	4
Spring Lake	2,958	13	13	0
Spring Lake Heights	4,597	14	14	0
Stafford Township	27,433	65	52	13
Stanhope	3,327	10	9	1
Stone Harbor	827	19	17	2
Stratford	7,024	15	15	0
Summit	22,195	51	46	5
Surf City	1,186	10	10	0
Teaneck Township	41,377	110	94	16
Tenafly	14,960	40	34	6
Tewksbury Township	5,809	12	11	1
Tinton Falls	17,761	42	41	1
Toms River Township	92,543	207	160	47
Totowa	10,964	32	28	4
Trenton	84,231	352	279	73
Tuckerton	3,406	13	12	1
Union Beach	5,479	18	15	3
Union City	70,053	205	165	40
Union Township	59,051	185	135	50
Upper Saddle River	8,385	21	17	4
Ventnor City	10,263	51	37	14
Vernon Township	22,193	41	32	9
Verona	13,584	35	30	5
Vineland	60,477	144	121	23
Voorhees Township	29,532	64	54	10
Waldwick	10,137	24	19	5
Wallington	11,794	24	23	1
Wall Township	25,956	87	69	18
Wanaque	11,925	30	25	5
Warren Township	16,264	36	29	7
Washington Township, Bergen County	9,432	22	20	2
Washington Township, Gloucester County	48,088	92	84	8
Washington Township, Morris County	18,793	32	29	3
Washington Township, Warren County	6,429	27	26	1
Watchung	6,010	36	30	6
Waterford Township	10,817	24	22	2
Wayne Township	54,903	144	117	27
Weehawken Township	15,683	71	53	18
Wenonah	2,252	6	6	0
Westampton Township	8,775	28	24	4
West Amwell Township	2,753	7	7	0
West Caldwell Township	11,013	30	25	5
West Deptford Township	21,386	46	43	3
Westfield	30,301	74	59	15
West Long Branch	7,944	22	21	1
West Milford Township	26,769	51	44	7

Table 78. Full-Time Law Enforcement Employees, by Selected State and City, 2017—Continued

(Number.)

State/city	Population	Total law enforcement employees	Total officers	Total civilians
West New York	54,156	118	107	11
West Orange	47,615	110	97	13
Westville	4,214	13	12	1
West Wildwood	563	5	5	0
West Windsor Township	28,495	60	48	12
Westwood	11,328	31	26	5
Wharton	6,610	20	19	1
Wildwood	5,087	53	43	10
Wildwood Crest	3,147	26	20	6
Willingboro Township	31,726	74	65	9
Winfield Township	1,519	10	10	0
Winslow Township	39,406	81	74	7
Woodbridge Township	102,129	239	198	41
Woodbury	9,970	31	28	3
Woodbury Heights	3,011	8	7	1
Woodcliff Lake	5,942	19	18	1
Woodland Park	12,836	29	25	4
Woodlynne	2,951	9	7	2
Wood-Ridge	8,808	25	21	4
Woodstown	3,482	10	8	2
Woolwich Township	12,798	25	24	1
Wyckoff Township	17,373	26	26	0
NEW MEXICO				
Alamogordo	31,386	83	54	29
Artesia	12,388	51	30	21
Aztec	5,836	14	12	2
Bernalillo	9,355	25	22	3
Bosque Farms	3,805	14	13	1
Capitan	1,372	3	3	0
Carlsbad	29,397	89	59	30
Carrizozo	929	4	3	1
Cimarron	881	4	3	1
Clayton	2,729	13	7	6
Clovis	39,561	78	55	23
Corrales	8,625	18	15	3
Cuba	741	5	4	1
Deming	14,428	43	39	4
Dexter	1,263	6	5	1
Edgewood	3,816	10	9	1
Estancia	1,572	10	5	5
Eunice	3,040	13	7	6
Farmington	40,940	166	125	41
Gallup	22,815	81	66	15
Grants	9,313	20	16	4
Hatch	1,585	9	6	3
Hope	107	1	1	0
Hurley	1,232	5	3	2
Jal	2,135	15	7	8
Las Cruces	102,350	261	187	74
Las Vegas	13,160	49	35	14
Logan	940	4	4	0
Lordsburg	2,415	13	9	4
Los Alamos	18,204	68	31	37
Los Lunas	15,527	43	39	4
Lovington	11,468	32	23	9
Magdalena	892	3	3	0
Mesilla	1,848	7	7	0
Milan	3,235	9	8	1
Moriarty	1,766	12	10	2
Peralta	3,548	6	5	1
Portales	11,928	27	22	5
Raton	5,983	22	14	8
Red River	477	10	4	6
Roswell	48,134	105	84	21
Ruidoso	7,729	33	23	10
Ruidoso Downs	2,543	11	7	4
Santa Clara	1,740	5	4	1
Santa Fe	84,358	215	167	48
Santa Rosa	2,652	13	8	5
San Ysidro	198	2	2	0
Socorro	8,547	25	16	9
Springer	911	4	4	0
Taos	5,771	27	20	7
Taos Ski Valley	69	3	3	0
Tatum	832	6	2	4
Texico	1,104	3	2	1
Truth or Consequences	5,949	16	11	5
Tularosa	2,920	11	6	5
NEW YORK				
Addison Town and Village	2,518	3	3	0
Akron Village	2,848	1	1	0
Albany	98,174	418	333	85
Albion Village	5,944	13	12	1

Table 78. Full-Time Law Enforcement Employees, by Selected State and City, 2017—Continued

(Number.)

State/city	Population	Total law enforcement employees	Total officers	Total civilians
Alfred Village	4,041	5	5	0
Allegany Village	1,717	1	1	0
Altamont Village	1,724	1	1	0
Amherst Town	121,150	182	152	30
Amity Town and Belmont Village	2,169	1	1	0
Amityville Village	9,492	24	23	1
Amsterdam	17,737	43	40	3
Arcade Village	1,957	5	5	0
Ardsley Village	4,663	19	19	0
Asharoken Village	647	3	3	0
Attica Village	2,435	3	3	0
Auburn	26,686	72	66	6
Avon Village	3,276	4	4	0
Baldwinsville Village	7,656	12	11	1
Ballston Spa Village	5,302	4	4	0
Batavia	14,711	31	28	3
Bath Village	5,556	11	9	2
Beacon	14,212	37	35	2
Bedford Town	17,997	43	38	5
Binghamton	45,399	150	136	14
Blooming Grove Town	11,863	12	10	2
Brant Town	2,055	1	1	0
Briarcliff Manor Village	8,064	21	21	0
Brighton Town	36,596	46	40	6
Brockport Village	8,310	16	15	1
Bronxville Village	6,420	23	21	2
Buffalo	256,169	982	781	201
Cairo Town	6,422	1	1	0
Caledonia Village	2,115	3	3	0
Cambridge Village	1,810	1	1	0
Camden Village	2,181	2	2	0
Camillus Town and Village	24,696	27	24	3
Canajoharie Village	2,132	4	4	0
Canandaigua	10,337	25	23	2
Canastota Village	4,586	5	4	1
Canisteo Village	2,171	3	3	0
Canton Village	6,557	10	9	1
Carthage Village	3,425	4	4	0
Cazenovia Village	2,849	5	4	1
Centre Island Village	408	7	7	0
Cheektowaga Town	77,576	159	122	37
Chester Town	7,970	17	17	0
Chester Village	3,960	14	13	1
Chittenango Village	4,888	3	2	1
Clarkstown Town	81,810	170	145	25
Clayton Village	1,877	3	3	0
Cobleskill Village	4,540	12	12	0
Coeymans Town	7,369	4	3	1
Cohoes	17,007	36	32	4
Colchester Town	1,988	1	1	0
Colonie Town	79,526	145	109	36
Corning	10,751	24	20	4
Cornwall-on-Hudson Village	2,915	3	3	0
Cornwall Town	9,544	12	9	3
Cortland	18,735	47	44	3
Crawford Town	9,183	10	9	1
Croton-on-Hudson Village	8,271	20	18	2
Cuba Town	3,061	4	4	0
Dansville Village	4,482	7	7	0
Deerpark Town	7,712	4	4	0
Delhi Village	3,147	4	4	0
Depew Village	15,150	34	28	6
Dewitt Town	25,405	46	42	4
Dobbs Ferry Village	11,127	28	26	2
Dolgeville Village	2,099	2	2	0
Dryden Village	2,115	5	5	0
Dunkirk	11,845	34	33	1
East Aurora-Aurora Town	13,806	20	15	5
Eastchester Town	20,052	48	46	2
East Fishkill Town	29,500	39	29	10
East Greenbush Town	16,461	31	22	9
East Hampton Town	19,937	94	69	25
East Hampton Village	1,121	26	22	4
East Rochester Village	6,613	10	9	1
Eden Town	7,644	5	4	1
Ellenville Village	4,032	11	10	1
Ellicott Town	5,093	12	12	0
Ellicottville	1,599	3	3	0
Elmira Heights Village	3,909	9	9	0
Elmira Town	5,714	4	4	0
Elmsford Village	5,072	20	20	0
Endicott Village	12,932	31	29	2
Evans Town	16,162	29	22	7
Fairport Village	5,415	11	10	1
Fallsburg Town	12,042	21	21	0

Table 78. Full-Time Law Enforcement Employees, by Selected State and City, 2017—Continued

(Number.)

State/city	Population	Total law enforcement employees	Total officers	Total civilians
Floral Park Village	15,959	48	34	14
Florida Village	2,866	1	1	0
Fort Edward Village	3,282	6	6	0
Fort Plain Village	2,212	3	3	0
Frankfort Town	4,890	1	1	0
Frankfort Village	2,466	4	4	0
Fredonia Village	10,543	18	14	4
Freeport Village	43,343	113	99	14
Garden City Village	22,579	65	52	13
Gates Town	28,723	35	31	4
Geddes Town	10,245	17	15	2
Geneseo Village	8,179	8	8	0
Geneva	12,951	33	31	2
Glen Cove	27,400	55	51	4
Glens Falls	14,268	30	28	2
Glenville Town	21,650	24	22	2
Gloversville	14,832	37	34	3
Goshen Town	8,661	9	9	0
Goshen Village	5,354	20	17	3
Gouverneur Village	3,716	9	6	3
Granville Village	2,454	5	5	0
Great Neck Estates Village	2,847	15	12	3
Greece Town	96,219	103	97	6
Greene Village	1,463	1	1	0
Greenwich Village	1,725	1	1	0
Greenwood Lake Village	3,092	6	5	1
Guilderland Town	34,098	50	36	14
Hamburg Town	46,040	65	62	3
Hamburg Village	9,617	13	12	1
Hamilton Village	4,105	5	5	0
Harriman Village	2,469	6	6	0
Harrison Town	28,480	70	60	10
Hastings-on-Hudson Village	7,987	21	21	0
Haverstraw Town	37,535	69	63	6
Hempstead Village	55,807	153	127	26
Herkimer Village	7,410	20	20	0
Highland Falls Village	3,805	10	8	2
Holley Village	1,709	2	2	0
Homer Village	3,120	6	5	1
Hoosick Falls Village	3,407	1	1	0
Hornell	8,213	23	22	1
Hudson Falls Village	7,093	11	11	0
Hunter Town	2,634	3	3	0
Huntington Bay Village	1,436	4	4	0
Ilion Village	7,801	19	17	2
Inlet Town	309	3	2	1
Irondequoit Town	50,393	64	53	11
Irvington Village	6,614	23	22	1
Ithaca	30,875	71	64	7
Jamestown	29,562	72	62	10
Johnson City Village	14,595	39	34	5
Johnstown	8,251	24	22	2
Kenmore Village	15,085	25	25	0
Kensington Village	1,179	6	6	0
Kingston	23,110	74	69	5
Kirkland Town	8,204	5	5	0
Lake Placid Village	2,424	15	12	3
Lake Success Village	3,127	28	24	4
Lakewood-Busti	7,326	11	10	1
Lancaster Town	37,458	63	48	15
Larchmont Village	6,161	29	26	3
Le Roy Village	4,227	7	7	0
Lewisboro Town	12,823	3	3	0
Lewiston Town and Village	15,974	12	11	1
Liberty Village	4,050	18	16	2
Little Falls	4,709	12	11	1
Liverpool Village	2,246	5	5	0
Lloyd Harbor Village	3,696	11	11	0
Lloyd Town	10,465	13	10	3
Lockport	20,369	49	47	2
Long Beach	33,771	87	70	17
Lowville Village	3,398	6	6	0
Lynbrook Village	19,577	57	49	8
Macedon Town and Village	8,977	8	7	1
Malone Village	5,650	13	13	0
Malverne Village	8,548	25	24	1
Mamaroneck Town	12,218	34	34	0
Mamaroneck Village	19,424	54	51	3
Manlius Town	24,550	37	37	0
Marlborough Town	8,633	10	8	2
Massena Village	10,394	25	20	5
Maybrook Village	3,513	4	4	0
Mechanicville	5,081	10	9	1
Medina Village	5,739	12	11	1
Menands Village	3,960	14	11	3

Table 78. Full-Time Law Enforcement Employees, by Selected State and City, 2017—Continued

(Number.)

State/city	Population	Total law enforcement employees	Total officers	Total civilians
Middleport Village	1,766	4	4	0
Middletown	27,607	78	65	13
Mohawk Village	2,568	4	4	0
Monroe Village	8,636	22	18	4
Montgomery Village	4,713	4	4	0
Monticello Village	6,373	25	23	2
Moriah Town	3,536	2	2	0
Mount Hope Town	6,904	3	3	0
Mount Morris Village	2,850	5	5	0
Mount Vernon	68,507	253	191	62
Newark Village	8,878	18	17	1
New Berlin Town	1,522	1	1	0
Newburgh	28,080	92	80	12
Newburgh Town	30,862	59	49	10
New Castle Town	18,189	40	38	2
New Hartford Town and Village	20,313	24	20	4
New Paltz Town and Village	14,125	25	21	4
New Rochelle	79,960	221	161	60
New Windsor Town	27,609	51	40	11
New York	8,616,333	52,079	36,378	15,701
New York Mills Village	3,278	3	3	0
Niagara Falls	48,385	176	157	19
Niagara Town	8,030	8	7	1
Niskayuna Town	22,541	29	27	2
Nissequogue Village	1,747	1	1	0
North Castle Town	12,406	30	28	2
North Greenbush Town	12,234	19	17	2
Northport Village	7,331	22	17	5
North Syracuse Village	6,796	11	10	1
North Tonawanda	30,452	52	48	4
Norwich	6,804	17	17	0
Ocean Beach Village	82	4	4	0
Ogdensburg	10,685	32	27	5
Ogden Town	20,321	14	12	2
Old Brookville Village	2,219	33	26	7
Old Westbury Village	4,747	31	26	5
Olean	13,694	39	34	5
Oneonta City	13,967	30	24	6
Orangetown Town	37,804	84	76	8
Orchard Park Town	29,725	41	32	9
Oswego City	17,510	53	47	6
Owego Village	3,774	3	2	1
Oyster Bay Cove Village	4,337	14	14	0
Palmyra Village	3,357	6	5	1
Peekskill	24,127	64	54	10
Pelham Manor Village	5,577	26	25	1
Pelham Village	7,037	26	25	1
Penn Yan Village	4,961	12	11	1
Perry Village	3,467	4	4	0
Piermont Village	2,573	8	8	0
Plattsburgh City	19,742	54	47	7
Pleasantville Village	7,172	21	21	0
Port Chester Village	29,616	62	60	2
Port Dickinson Village	1,573	5	4	1
Port Jervis	8,527	33	32	1
Port Washington	19,384	68	60	8
Poughkeepsie	30,159	122	88	34
Poughkeepsie Town	38,960	93	80	13
Pound Ridge Town	5,253	2	1	1
Quogue Village	1,006	14	13	1
Ramapo Town	94,019	121	99	22
Rensselaer City	9,331	31	26	5
Riverhead Town	33,649	106	89	17
Rochester	208,591	889	761	128
Rockville Centre Village	24,654	63	55	8
Rome	32,200	75	73	2
Rosendale Town	5,875	1	1	0
Rotterdam Town	29,586	43	40	3
Rye	16,021	40	35	5
Rye Brook Village	9,608	27	26	1
Sag Harbor Village	2,292	14	12	2
Sands Point Village	2,903	21	21	0
Saranac Lake Village	5,268	12	12	0
Saratoga Springs	27,962	80	69	11
Saugerties Town	19,033	28	24	4
Scarsdale Village	18,031	46	41	5
Schenectady	64,710	171	145	26
Schodack Town	11,685	11	10	1
Scotia Village	7,651	14	13	1
Seneca Falls Town	8,811	18	16	2
Shandaken Town	2,963	4	4	0
Shawangunk Town	14,018	5	5	0
Shelter Island Town	2,416	10	9	1
Sherrill	3,045	3	3	0
Sidney Village	3,672	8	7	1

Table 78. Full-Time Law Enforcement Employees, by Selected State and City, 2017—Continued

(Number.)

State/city	Population	Total law enforcement employees	Total officers	Total civilians
Skaneateles Village	2,493	3	3	0
Sodus Village	1,725	2	2	0
Solvay Village	6,329	15	14	1
Southampton Town	50,987	108	95	13
Southampton Village	3,309	46	31	15
South Glens Falls Village	3,567	5	5	0
South Nyack Village	3,532	6	6	0
Southold Town	19,990	71	51	20
Spring Valley Village	32,795	49	49	0
St. Johnsville Village	1,669	1	1	0
Stony Point Town	15,540	25	25	0
Syracuse	143,069	495	420	75
Tarrytown Village	11,577	35	32	3
Tonawanda	14,808	35	29	6
Tonawanda Town	57,223	151	106	45
Troy	49,644	134	123	11
Tuckahoe Village	6,636	25	22	3
Tupper Lake Village	3,521	8	8	0
Ulster Town	12,473	26	22	4
Utica	60,395	179	162	17
Vernon Village	1,163	1	1	0
Vestal Town	28,090	37	34	3
Walden Village	6,692	14	11	3
Wallkill Town	28,881	40	39	1
Walton Village	2,864	4	4	0
Wappingers Falls Village	5,510	4	1	3
Warsaw Village	3,327	5	5	0
Warwick Town	18,375	36	31	5
Washingtonville Village	5,752	14	12	2
Waterford Town and Village	8,506	8	8	0
Waterloo Village	4,996	9	8	1
Watertown	25,746	68	65	3
Watervliet	10,100	25	24	1
Watkins Glen Village	1,896	5	5	0
Waverly Village	4,151	10	9	1
Webb Town	1,811	6	6	0
Wellsville Village	4,454	11	10	1
Westfield Village	3,029	4	4	0
Westhampton Beach Village	1,774	16	14	2
West Seneca Town	45,597	78	65	13
White Plains	58,461	201	191	10
Whitesboro Village	3,651	6	6	0
Whitestown Town	9,207	6	6	0
Windham Town	1,679	1	1	0
Woodbury Town	11,017	23	19	4
Woodstock Town	5,812	10	10	0
Yonkers	201,554	689	607	82
Yorktown Town	37,142	65	56	9
Yorkville Village	2,605	3	3	0
NORTH CAROLINA				
Aberdeen	7,707	30	28	2
Ahoskie	4,970	18	17	1
Albemarle	16,022	56	47	9
Andrews	1,800	6	5	1
Angier	5,227	14	14	0
Apex	49,159	93	77	16
Archdale	11,664	31	25	6
Asheboro	26,253	82	74	8
Asheville	90,103	275	206	69
Atlantic Beach	1,491	17	16	1
Aurora	517	1	1	0
Ayden	5,215	22	18	4
Badin	1,967	4	4	0
Bailey	568	2	2	0
Bakersville	447	1	1	0
Bald Head Island	178	23	21	2
Banner Elk	1,166	8	7	1
Beaufort	4,223	17	16	1
Beech Mountain	321	14	10	4
Belhaven	1,572	8	7	1
Belmont	10,880	41	34	7
Benson	3,764	12	11	1
Bessemer City	5,586	14	13	1
Bethel	1,626	3	3	0
Beulaville	1,326	4	4	0
Biltmore Forest	1,482	14	13	1
Biscoe	1,676	9	8	1
Black Creek	762	2	2	0
Black Mountain	8,477	22	18	4
Bladenboro	1,683	6	6	0
Blowing Rock	1,297	12	11	1
Boiling Spring Lakes	6,026	13	12	1
Boiling Springs	4,715	9	9	0
Boone	19,138	47	36	11

Table 78. Full-Time Law Enforcement Employees, by Selected State and City, 2017—Continued

(Number.)

State/city	Population	Total law enforcement employees	Total officers	Total civilians
Boonville	1,201	5	5	0
Brevard	7,846	31	24	7
Bridgeton	432	1	1	0
Broadway	1,247	4	4	0
Brookford	373	1	1	0
Bryson City	1,457	9	8	1
Bunn	362	2	2	0
Burgaw	4,135	12	11	1
Burlington	52,986	157	121	36
Burnsville	1,650	8	8	0
Butner	7,718	43	36	7
Candor	831	4	4	0
Canton	4,261	19	14	5
Cape Carteret	2,080	8	8	0
Carolina Beach	6,296	30	28	2
Carrboro	21,553	38	35	3
Carthage	2,463	11	10	1
Cary	166,986	227	187	40
Caswell Beach	435	4	4	0
Chadbourn	1,758	10	9	1
Chapel Hill	59,553	120	91	29
Charlotte-Mecklenburg[1]	914,609	2,341	1,754	587
Cherryville	6,112	19	14	5
China Grove	4,226	13	13	0
Chocowinity	801	3	3	0
Claremont	1,389	10	9	1
Clayton	21,012	46	43	3
Cleveland	879	2	2	0
Clinton	8,666	31	27	4
Clyde	1,270	5	5	0
Coats	2,487	6	6	0
Columbus	979	11	10	1
Concord	91,756	189	164	25
Conover	8,354	30	28	2
Conway	744	2	2	0
Cooleemee	966	3	3	0
Cornelius	29,153	75	61	14
Cramerton	4,461	16	16	0
Creedmoor	4,563	18	14	4
Dallas	4,780	19	14	5
Davidson	12,723	20	18	2
Dobson	1,591	6	6	0
Drexel	1,872	5	5	0
Duck	386	11	10	1
Dunn	9,965	40	35	5
Durham	269,088	677	505	172
East Bend	592	2	2	0
East Spencer	1,562	10	10	0
Eden	15,321	48	44	4
Edenton	4,823	21	19	2
Elizabeth City	17,802	69	59	10
Elizabethtown	3,529	17	16	1
Elkin	4,120	21	17	4
Elon	10,283	16	15	1
Emerald Isle	3,710	19	18	1
Enfield	2,378	10	9	1
Erwin	5,017	11	10	1
Fair Bluff	899	4	3	1
Fairmont	2,680	11	9	2
Farmville	4,759	22	17	5
Fayetteville	205,432	595	438	157
Fletcher	8,237	18	17	1
Forest City	7,278	33	31	2
Four Oaks	2,118	6	6	0
Foxfire Village	1,013	3	3	0
Franklin	4,008	18	17	1
Franklinton	2,151	9	9	0
Fremont	1,279	4	4	0
Fuquay-Varina	27,429	46	40	6
Garner	29,287	73	64	9
Garysburg	941	2	2	0
Gaston	1,030	3	3	0
Gastonia	76,191	189	166	23
Gibsonville	7,131	18	17	1
Glen Alpine	1,498	4	4	0
Goldsboro	35,824	102	92	10
Graham	14,771	39	36	3
Granite Falls	4,680	17	14	3
Granite Quarry	3,006	8	8	0
Greensboro	290,051	749	656	93
Greenville	92,630	228	183	45
Grifton	2,667	5	5	0
Hamlet	6,361	21	18	3
Havelock	20,157	32	24	8
Haw River	2,467	8	8	0

Table 78. Full-Time Law Enforcement Employees, by Selected State and City, 2017—Continued

(Number.)

State/city	Population	Total law enforcement employees	Total officers	Total civilians
Henderson	15,131	50	41	9
Hendersonville	13,967	56	43	13
Hertford	2,122	8	7	1
Hickory	40,653	141	105	36
Highlands	944	13	12	1
High Point	112,368	279	232	47
Hillsborough	6,640	28	27	1
Holden Beach	656	8	8	0
Holly Ridge	2,466	11	10	1
Holly Springs	34,897	63	49	14
Hope Mills	16,325	41	36	5
Hot Springs	568	1	1	0
Hudson	3,717	15	13	2
Huntersville	56,279	95	87	8
Indian Beach	114	5	5	0
Jackson	466	1	1	0
Jacksonville	67,293	146	118	28
Jefferson	1,542	4	4	0
Jonesville	2,240	10	8	2
Kannapolis	48,754	108	81	27
Kenansville	867	3	3	0
Kenly	1,518	8	8	0
Kernersville	24,222	89	70	19
Kill Devil Hills	7,194	34	28	6
King	7,046	24	21	3
Kings Mountain	10,824	40	32	8
Kinston	20,791	71	62	9
Kitty Hawk	3,507	18	16	2
Knightdale	15,423	33	31	2
Kure Beach	2,125	13	12	1
Lake Lure	1,178	10	9	1
Lake Royale	2,701	3	3	0
Lake Waccamaw	1,440	5	5	0
Landis	3,127	10	10	0
Laurel Park	2,344	6	6	0
Laurinburg	15,398	43	41	2
Leland	19,786	36	34	2
Lenoir	17,932	66	50	16
Lewiston Woodville	486	1	1	0
Lexington	19,135	67	59	8
Liberty	2,694	11	10	1
Lilesville	496	1	1	0
Lillington	3,648	14	13	1
Lincolnton	10,823	35	30	5
Littleton	620	3	3	0
Locust	3,090	12	12	0
Long View	4,900	15	15	0
Louisburg	3,576	15	13	2
Lowell	3,727	9	9	0
Lumberton	21,484	98	87	11
Madison	2,173	17	16	1
Maggie Valley	1,316	12	11	1
Magnolia	947	2	2	0
Maiden	3,403	15	14	1
Manteo	1,421	9	8	1
Marion	7,819	26	25	1
Marshall	892	3	3	0
Mars Hill	2,239	4	4	0
Marshville	2,692	8	8	0
Matthews	32,255	70	55	15
Maxton	2,434	13	9	4
Mayodan	2,445	15	15	0
Maysville	973	3	3	0
Mebane	14,619	35	31	4
Micro	509	1	1	0
Middlesex	826	4	4	0
Mint Hill	26,868	34	31	3
Misenheimer	666	5	5	0
Mocksville	5,302	23	22	1
Monroe	35,153	95	85	10
Montreat	794	4	4	0
Mooresville	37,049	106	83	23
Morehead City	9,520	45	40	5
Morganton	16,630	88	54	34
Morrisville	25,904	40	38	2
Mount Airy	10,338	53	40	13
Mount Gilead	1,169	6	6	0
Mount Holly	14,640	40	31	9
Mount Olive	4,760	21	19	2
Murfreesboro	3,057	9	8	1
Murphy	1,648	11	9	2
Nags Head	2,943	25	23	2
Nashville	5,530	17	16	1
Navassa	1,841	2	2	0
New Bern	30,191	111	86	25

Table 78. Full-Time Law Enforcement Employees, by Selected State and City, 2017—Continued

(Number.)

State/city	Population	Total law enforcement employees	Total officers	Total civilians
Newland	682	4	4	0
Newport	4,776	8	8	0
Newton	13,059	43	35	8
Newton Grove	565	2	2	0
Norlina	1,050	5	5	0
North Topsail Beach	732	12	11	1
Northwest	783	2	2	0
North Wilkesboro	4,228	24	23	1
Norwood	2,401	9	8	1
Oakboro	1,865	6	6	0
Oak Island	7,883	25	23	2
Ocean Isle Beach	627	14	13	1
Oriental	879	1	1	0
Oxford	8,887	31	26	5
Parkton	437	1	1	0
Pembroke	3,014	18	14	4
Pikeville	695	4	4	0
Pilot Mountain	1,438	8	7	1
Pinebluff	1,491	3	3	0
Pinehurst	16,145	30	25	5
Pine Knoll Shores	1,359	7	7	0
Pine Level	1,922	5	5	0
Pinetops	1,291	6	6	0
Pineville	8,788	43	33	10
Pink Hill	520	2	2	0
Pittsboro	4,355	13	12	1
Plymouth	3,551	14	13	1
Polkton	3,461	2	2	0
Princeton	1,327	4	4	0
Raeford	5,057	16	15	1
Raleigh	468,261	869	713	156
Ramseur	1,713	6	6	0
Randleman	4,174	15	15	0
Ranlo	3,657	9	8	1
Red Springs	3,417	13	12	1
Reidsville	13,900	52	46	6
Richlands	1,702	8	8	0
Rich Square	873	1	1	0
River Bend	3,128	3	3	0
Roanoke Rapids	15,083	42	37	5
Robbins	1,189	5	5	0
Robersonville	1,402	7	7	0
Rockingham	9,005	38	33	5
Rockwell	2,148	6	6	0
Rocky Mount	55,098	198	160	38
Rolesville	7,709	19	18	1
Rose Hill	1,660	5	5	0
Rowland	1,043	7	6	1
Roxboro	8,348	32	28	4
Rutherfordton	4,134	14	13	1
Salisbury	34,085	77	71	6
Saluda	705	4	4	0
Sanford	29,295	105	81	24
Scotland Neck	1,919	9	7	2
Seagrove	229	1	1	0
Selma	6,678	26	24	2
Seven Devils	203	6	6	0
Shallotte	4,050	15	14	1
Sharpsburg	1,990	10	9	1
Shelby	20,254	83	70	13
Siler City	8,531	25	19	6
Smithfield	12,489	45	41	4
Snow Hill	1,551	5	5	0
Southern Pines	14,025	45	39	6
Southern Shores	2,919	13	12	1
Southport	3,774	11	11	0
Sparta	1,720	6	6	0
Spencer	3,315	12	11	1
Spindale	4,236	11	11	0
Spring Hope	1,313	6	6	0
Spring Lake	13,369	29	25	4
Spruce Pine	2,095	10	10	0
Stallings	15,656	26	23	3
Stanfield	1,489	5	5	0
Stanley	3,769	13	12	1
Stantonsburg	784	3	3	0
Star	867	4	4	0
Statesville	26,847	101	80	21
Stoneville	1,027	4	4	0
St. Pauls	2,402	16	11	5
Sugar Mountain	197	5	5	0
Sunset Beach	3,958	14	14	0
Surf City	2,342	19	18	1
Swansboro	3,261	12	11	1
Sylva	2,653	14	14	0

Table 78. Full-Time Law Enforcement Employees, by Selected State and City, 2017—Continued

(Number.)

State/city	Population	Total law enforcement employees	Total officers	Total civilians
Tabor City	4,225	11	10	1
Tarboro	10,924	34	28	6
Taylorsville	2,103	10	10	0
Taylortown	826	3	3	0
Thomasville	27,071	70	64	6
Topsail Beach	428	10	9	1
Trent Woods	4,162	5	5	0
Troutman	2,610	14	14	0
Troy	3,399	12	11	1
Tryon	1,618	8	6	2
Valdese	4,477	13	12	1
Vanceboro	993	2	2	0
Vass	775	4	4	0
Wadesboro	5,413	27	20	7
Wagram	795	1	1	0
Wake Forest	42,019	85	69	16
Wallace	3,946	15	11	4
Walnut Creek	867	2	2	0
Warrenton	845	5	4	1
Warsaw	3,160	16	14	2
Washington	9,793	35	28	7
Waxhaw	15,089	25	23	2
Waynesville	9,977	44	34	10
Weaverville	4,034	15	14	1
Weldon	1,563	13	12	1
Wendell	6,901	18	17	1
West Jefferson	1,305	8	8	0
Whispering Pines	3,342	9	8	1
Whitakers	718	2	2	0
White Lake	767	6	6	0
Whiteville	5,534	24	23	1
Wilkesboro	3,554	24	22	2
Williamston	5,438	20	19	1
Wilmington	119,422	345	270	75
Wilson	49,686	123	108	15
Wilson's Mills	2,597	5	5	0
Windsor	3,795	9	9	0
Wingate	3,993	7	7	0
Winston-Salem	244,278	671	511	160
Winterville	9,476	19	18	1
Woodfin	6,444	13	13	0
Woodland	717	2	2	0
Wrightsville Beach	2,574	26	24	2
Yadkinville	2,918	14	13	1
Youngsville	1,317	11	10	1
Zebulon	5,288	21	20	1
NORTH DAKOTA				
Arnegard	161	2	2	0
Belfield	1,055	4	3	1
Berthold	502	1	1	0
Beulah	3,420	6	5	1
Bismarck	74,397	151	121	30
Bowman	1,724	4	4	0
Burlington	1,215	2	2	0
Carrington	2,039	5	5	0
Cavalier	1,231	3	3	0
Devils Lake	7,344	18	16	2
Dickinson	23,967	55	36	19
Ellendale	1,269	2	2	0
Emerado	430	1	1	0
Fargo	123,430	197	174	23
Fessenden	462	1	1	0
Grafton	4,240	10	9	1
Grand Forks	58,090	103	88	15
Harvey	1,737	3	3	0
Hazen	2,424	4	4	0
Hillsboro	1,584	1	1	0
Jamestown	15,439	36	31	5
Kenmare	1,053	2	2	0
Killdeer	1,268	5	5	0
Lamoure	913	6	5	1
Lincoln	3,935	4	4	0
Lisbon	2,121	3	3	0
Mandan	22,369	40	34	6
Medora	136	2	2	0
Minot	50,118	109	81	28
Napoleon	786	1	1	0
New Town	2,642	7	6	1
Northwood	913	2	2	0
Oakes	1,769	2	2	0
Powers Lake	296	2	2	0
Ray	838	1	1	0
Rolla	1,331	3	3	0
Rugby	2,806	5	5	0

Table 78. Full-Time Law Enforcement Employees, by Selected State and City, 2017—Continued

(Number.)

State/city	Population	Total law enforcement employees	Total officers	Total civilians
Sherwood	250	1	1	0
South Heart	448	3	3	0
Stanley	2,974	4	4	0
Steele	707	1	1	0
Surrey	1,453	4	4	0
Thompson	1,016	1	1	0
Tioga	1,607	8	6	2
Valley City	6,558	13	12	1
Wahpeton	7,841	16	14	2
Watford City	8,015	27	23	4
West Fargo	36,624	68	54	14
Williston	28,748	73	52	21
Wishek	945	2	2	0
OHIO				
Ada	5,551	9	8	1
Akron	197,412	469	435	34
Alliance	21,838	50	38	12
American Township	12,208	1	1	0
Amherst	12,090	26	20	6
Ashland	20,485	36	29	7
Ashville	4,211	10	10	0
Aurora	15,932	35	28	7
Austintown	35,303	54	42	12
Avon Lake	23,839	34	29	5
Barberton	26,050	44	42	2
Bath Township, Summit County	9,678	26	20	6
Bay Village	15,327	27	23	4
Bazetta Township	5,614	8	8	0
Beavercreek	46,572	64	48	16
Beaver Township	6,427	12	9	3
Bedford	12,641	35	30	5
Bedford Heights	10,558	29	27	2
Bellbrook	7,159	13	12	1
Bellville	1,864	4	4	0
Belpre	6,466	15	10	5
Berea	18,871	28	26	2
Bethel	2,791	6	5	1
Bexley	13,773	34	30	4
Blue Ash	12,248	40	33	7
Bluffton	4,157	8	8	0
Bolivar	986	2	2	0
Boston Heights	1,293	4	4	0
Bowling Green	31,779	55	40	15
Brecksville	13,432	38	30	8
Brookville	5,896	13	12	1
Brunswick	34,838	52	40	12
Butler Township	7,799	17	17	0
Cambridge	10,391	29	23	6
Canal Fulton	5,428	10	9	1
Canfield	7,246	23	16	7
Carey	3,566	14	11	3
Carlisle	5,395	8	7	1
Carroll Township	2,085	5	5	0
Catawba Island Township	3,504	5	5	0
Celina	10,310	21	16	5
Centerville	23,782	54	39	15
Chagrin Falls	3,991	13	12	1
Cincinnati	299,116	1,274	1,025	249
Circleville	13,972	29	21	8
Clayton	13,149	21	20	1
Clearcreek Township	15,531	16	15	1
Cleveland Heights	44,525	111	101	10
Clyde	6,191	18	14	4
Coldwater	4,519	9	8	1
Colerain Township	58,996	57	52	5
Columbus	872,205	1,937	1,551	386
Copley Township	17,280	23	22	1
Cortland	6,844	9	9	0
Covington	2,637	7	6	1
Crooksville	2,491	4	3	1
Cuyahoga Falls	49,145	86	71	15
Deer Park	5,665	14	10	4
Defiance	16,594	33	30	3
Delaware	39,315	60	53	7
Delhi Township	29,619	35	33	2
Delphos	6,979	11	11	0
Eastlake	18,056	32	21	11
East Palestine	4,503	8	6	2
Elida	1,836	9	6	3
Elyria	53,586	95	81	14
Englewood	13,504	26	19	7
Evendale	2,767	23	20	3
Fairborn	33,936	65	48	17
Fairfield	42,627	78	59	19

Table 78. Full-Time Law Enforcement Employees, by Selected State and City, 2017—Continued

(Number.)

State/city	Population	Total law enforcement employees	Total officers	Total civilians
Fairfield Township	22,524	20	19	1
Fairlawn	7,467	34	26	8
Findlay	41,474	83	65	18
Forest Park	18,665	42	36	6
Fort Loramie	1,500	1	1	0
Fostoria	13,255	22	19	3
Franklin	11,779	31	24	7
Gahanna	35,243	71	56	15
Garrettsville	2,321	5	5	0
Geneva-on-the-Lake	1,199	5	5	0
Genoa Township	27,061	28	26	2
German Township, Montgomery County	2,876	5	5	0
Glenwillow	923	4	4	0
Grandview Heights	7,831	22	18	4
Greenhills	3,584	11	10	1
Green Springs	1,307	2	2	0
Greenville	12,772	30	22	8
Hamilton	62,094	131	121	10
Harrison	11,246	23	20	3
Heath	10,681	25	18	7
Highland Heights	8,434	30	23	7
Hilliard	36,144	63	53	10
Hinckley Township	7,970	10	9	1
Hiram	1,164	2	2	0
Holland	1,662	9	9	0
Hubbard	7,533	11	11	0
Huber Heights	37,996	69	50	19
Jackson Township, Mahoning County	2,018	5	5	0
Kent	30,270	55	41	14
Kenton	8,190	14	14	0
Kettering	55,152	109	82	27
Kirtland	6,759	15	10	5
Lake Township	8,287	16	15	1
Lakewood	50,151	111	94	17
Lancaster	40,026	84	67	17
Lexington	4,686	13	9	4
Lima	37,220	100	80	20
Lockland	3,427	16	15	1
Lorain	63,672	118	97	21
Lordstown	3,242	13	9	4
Loudonville	2,642	7	6	1
Lyndhurst	13,586	37	29	8
Macedonia	12,027	32	23	9
Maineville	1,070	2	2	0
Mariemont	3,435	11	10	1
Marlboro Township	4,374	5	4	1
Mason	33,406	47	43	4
Maumee	13,809	55	41	14
Medina Township	8,940	10	10	0
Mentor	46,663	110	80	30
Mentor-on-the-Lake	7,359	13	8	5
Miamisburg	19,928	39	37	2
Miami Township, Clermont County	42,352	43	40	3
Middletown	48,828	101	68	33
Mifflin Township	2,587	13	13	0
Milan	1,339	3	3	0
Milford	6,939	21	19	2
Milton Township	2,445	4	4	0
Minerva Park	1,318	10	9	1
Mogadore	3,829	7	7	0
Monroe	16,002	39	31	8
Moraine	6,360	33	25	8
Mount Healthy	6,020	11	10	1
Mount Vernon	16,553	32	29	3
Navarre	1,901	6	6	0
New Albany	10,838	28	20	8
Newark	49,389	79	68	11
New Bremen	2,966	7	7	0
New London	2,363	5	5	0
Newtown	2,679	9	8	1
Niles	18,334	39	34	5
Northfield	3,669	15	14	1
North Olmsted	31,779	59	45	14
North Ridgeville	33,586	47	37	10
Norton	11,998	17	16	1
Norwalk	16,811	30	23	7
Oak Harbor	2,731	8	5	3
Oberlin	8,321	23	16	7
Olmsted Falls	8,898	10	10	0
Orrville	8,527	15	14	1
Ottawa	4,394	8	8	0
Ottoville	975	2	2	0
Oxford Township	2,181	3	3	0
Parma	79,340	125	109	16
Pepper Pike	6,256	16	16	0

Table 78. Full-Time Law Enforcement Employees, by Selected State and City, 2017—Continued

(Number.)

State/city	Population	Total law enforcement employees	Total officers	Total civilians
Perkins Township	11,773	21	20	1
Perrysburg Township	12,784	28	23	5
Perry Township, Franklin County	3,758	12	11	1
Perry Township, Montgomery County	3,322	5	5	0
Pierce Township	11,623	17	16	1
Pioneer	1,412	3	3	0
Piqua	20,973	38	35	3
Plain City	4,379	9	9	0
Poland Township	11,921	12	12	0
Port Clinton	5,928	19	14	5
Powell	13,029	21	19	2
Reading	10,307	24	20	4
Reynoldsburg	37,704	70	54	16
Richmond Heights	10,432	27	21	6
Rittman	6,610	12	9	3
Rossford	6,609	15	14	1
Ross Township	8,755	1	1	0
Russellville	524	2	2	0
Salem	11,887	22	22	0
Sandusky	24,861	49	47	2
Seven Hills	11,668	16	15	1
Shaker Heights	27,380	89	64	25
Sharonville	13,796	49	40	9
Shawnee Hills	785	5	5	0
Shawnee Township	12,096	18	12	6
Sidney	20,466	45	35	10
Silver Lake	2,494	9	8	1
Solon	23,023	64	47	17
South Russell	3,819	9	9	0
South Zanesville	1,970	2	2	0
Springboro	18,632	30	26	4
Springfield	58,843	121	113	8
Springfield Township, Hamilton County	36,571	54	48	6
Springfield Township, Mahoning County	6,374	9	9	0
St. Clair Township	7,583	14	13	1
Steubenville	17,979	43	38	5
Stow	34,692	49	41	8
Streetsboro	16,308	36	28	8
Strongsville	44,758	85	71	14
Sugarcreek	2,222	6	6	0
Sugarcreek Township	8,300	18	16	2
Sylvania	18,908	42	35	7
Tallmadge	17,529	27	24	3
Thornville	997	1	1	0
Tiffin	17,481	40	31	9
Toledo	277,116	688	587	101
Trenton	12,906	20	15	5
Troy	25,865	45	43	2
Uhrichsville	5,372	7	7	0
Union Township, Clermont County	48,214	62	48	14
Upper Arlington	35,214	54	50	4
Upper Sandusky	6,529	18	13	5
Urbana	11,351	18	18	0
Valley View, Cuyahoga County	2,007	22	20	2
Vandalia	15,022	37	28	9
Van Wert	10,713	29	21	8
Wadsworth	23,388	39	30	9
Walton Hills	2,308	15	11	4
Warren	39,643	64	59	5
Warren Township	5,255	6	6	0
Washington Court House	14,136	26	21	5
Waterville	5,518	12	11	1
Waterville Township	1,655	5	5	0
Wauseon	7,407	19	16	3
West Carrollton	12,898	24	22	2
West Jefferson	4,347	16	12	4
West Salem	1,493	2	2	0
Whitehall	18,835	62	47	15
Whitehouse	4,622	10	10	0
Wickliffe	12,679	39	29	10
Wilmington	12,416	30	21	9
Winchester	1,025	2	2	0
Wooster	27,172	44	40	4
Worthington	14,692	43	31	12
Wyoming	8,531	20	18	2
Xenia	26,331	69	44	25
Yellow Springs	3,713	10	7	3
Yorkville	1,031	3	3	0
Youngstown	63,889	193	152	41
Zanesville	25,457	92	55	37
OKLAHOMA				
Achille	521	4	3	1
Ada	17,455	38	34	4
Allen	935	3	2	1

Table 78. Full-Time Law Enforcement Employees, by Selected State and City, 2017—Continued

(Number.)

State/city	Population	Total law enforcement employees	Total officers	Total civilians
Altus	19,054	53	40	13
Alva	5,149	10	10	0
Amber	460	2	2	0
Anadarko	6,756	21	17	4
Antlers	2,306	9	4	5
Apache	1,439	3	3	0
Ardmore	25,211	57	52	5
Arkoma	1,914	3	2	1
Atoka	3,056	16	15	1
Avant	314	1	1	0
Barnsdall	1,197	2	2	0
Bartlesville	36,788	82	61	21
Beaver	1,429	2	2	0
Beggs	1,244	5	3	2
Bernice	562	2	2	0
Bethany	19,620	41	30	11
Big Cabin	257	4	3	1
Binger	654	1	1	0
Bixby	26,131	40	32	8
Blackwell	6,765	22	16	6
Blanchard	8,649	14	9	5
Boise City	1,074	2	2	0
Bokoshe	493	1	1	0
Boley	1,183	3	3	0
Boswell	688	1	1	0
Bristow	4,251	15	11	4
Broken Arrow	108,823	184	131	53
Broken Bow	4,100	18	14	4
Burns Flat	2,001	4	4	0
Cache	2,857	6	5	1
Caddo	1,070	2	2	0
Calera	2,295	12	10	2
Caney	197	5	3	2
Canton	600	3	3	0
Carnegie	1,711	9	4	5
Carney	664	1	1	0
Cashion	860	4	4	0
Catoosa	7,129	16	15	1
Cement	499	3	3	0
Chandler	3,194	13	9	4
Chattanooga	441	3	2	1
Checotah	3,207	13	9	4
Chelsea	1,972	3	3	0
Cherokee	1,553	3	3	0
Chickasha	16,489	38	28	10
Choctaw	12,556	18	16	2
Chouteau	2,088	9	8	1
Claremore	19,147	45	37	8
Clayton	780	9	4	5
Cleveland	3,217	8	8	0
Clinton	9,455	22	14	8
Coalgate	1,850	6	6	0
Colbert	1,207	2	1	1
Colcord	814	3	3	0
Collinsville	6,836	16	11	5
Comanche	1,595	6	5	1
Commerce	2,458	5	5	0
Cordell	2,852	4	3	1
Covington	547	1	1	0
Coweta	9,718	21	15	6
Coyle	367	3	2	1
Crescent	1,564	10	5	5
Cushing	7,790	22	14	8
Cyril	1,053	1	1	0
Davenport	826	3	2	1
Davis	2,822	11	9	2
Del City	22,046	42	31	11
Depew	482	1	1	0
Dewar	865	2	2	0
Dewey	3,513	11	10	1
Dibble	846	3	3	0
Dickson	1,253	4	3	1
Drumright	2,870	5	5	0
Duncan	22,909	62	46	16
Durant	17,871	43	38	5
Earlsboro	644	2	2	0
Edmond	92,876	153	115	38
Elgin	3,164	5	5	0
Elk City	12,057	33	24	9
Elmore City	708	3	3	0
El Reno	19,133	52	32	20
Enid	51,257	125	97	28
Erick	1,034	3	3	0
Eufaula	2,971	12	8	4
Fairfax	1,335	3	1	2

Table 78. Full-Time Law Enforcement Employees, by Selected State and City, 2017—Continued

(Number.)

State/city	Population	Total law enforcement employees	Total officers	Total civilians
Fairland	1,051	3	3	0
Fairview	2,672	8	5	3
Fletcher	1,138	1	1	0
Forest Park	1,082	3	2	1
Fort Gibson	4,045	9	8	1
Fort Towson	491	1	1	0
Frederick	3,621	10	7	3
Geary	1,286	11	5	6
Glenpool	13,954	31	23	8
Goodwell	1,311	4	4	0
Gore	939	5	4	1
Grandfield	955	1	1	0
Granite	2,008	3	3	0
Grove	6,868	27	21	6
Guthrie	11,713	37	27	10
Guymon	11,733	24	15	9
Haileyville	762	4	4	0
Harrah	6,215	9	9	0
Hartshorne	1,966	5	5	0
Haskell	1,960	6	6	0
Healdton	2,757	5	4	1
Heavener	3,328	10	9	1
Hennessey	2,219	8	4	4
Henryetta	5,737	18	12	6
Hinton	3,273	5	5	0
Hobart	3,567	13	7	6
Holdenville	5,663	9	6	3
Hollis	1,886	10	6	4
Hominy	3,485	10	5	5
Hooker	1,959	3	3	0
Howe	789	2	2	0
Hugo	5,205	16	16	0
Hulbert	607	4	4	0
Hydro	959	3	3	0
Idabel	6,940	25	19	6
Jay	2,520	14	9	5
Jenks	22,693	30	22	8
Jennings	359	1	1	0
Jones	3,067	7	7	0
Kellyville	1,147	3	3	0
Kiefer	1,968	4	4	0
Kingfisher	4,931	15	12	3
Kingston	1,634	6	6	0
Kiowa	676	7	5	2
Konawa	1,267	4	3	1
Krebs	1,928	8	6	2
Lahoma	645	1	1	0
Lamont	402	1	1	0
Langley	819	3	3	0
Langston	1,857	3	2	1
Lawton	94,134	239	182	57
Lexington	2,169	11	6	5
Lindsay	2,827	14	8	6
Locust Grove	1,401	8	4	4
Lone Grove	5,252	10	7	3
Luther	1,675	8	7	1
Madill	3,937	12	11	1
Mangum	2,848	11	6	5
Mannford	3,150	11	8	3
Marietta	2,782	8	7	1
Marlow	4,520	10	10	0
Maud	1,077	2	2	0
Maysville	1,233	5	4	1
McAlester	18,181	48	45	3
McCurtain	510	2	2	0
McLoud	4,656	11	10	1
Medicine Park	447	2	2	0
Meeker	1,179	4	3	1
Miami	13,470	41	30	11
Midwest City	57,772	125	94	31
Minco	1,649	4	4	0
Moore	62,476	93	88	5
Mooreland	1,240	3	2	1
Morris	1,464	3	3	0
Mounds	1,200	3	3	0
Mountain View	759	2	2	0
Muldrow	3,250	12	7	5
Muskogee	38,199	105	87	18
Mustang	21,392	35	24	11
Nash	202	1	1	0
Newcastle	10,011	18	17	1
Newkirk	2,217	4	4	0
Nichols Hills	3,940	21	16	5
Nicoma Park	2,473	5	5	0
Ninnekah	1,033	4	3	1

Table 78. Full-Time Law Enforcement Employees, by Selected State and City, 2017—Continued

(Number.)

State/city	Population	Total law enforcement employees	Total officers	Total civilians
Noble	6,799	16	11	5
Norman	124,074	231	168	63
North Enid	922	4	4	0
Nowata	3,709	8	6	2
Oilton	1,015	2	2	0
Okarche	1,343	4	4	0
Okemah	3,239	13	8	5
Oklahoma City	648,260	1,368	1,088	280
Okmulgee	12,183	26	24	2
Olustee	576	1	1	0
Oologah	1,182	5	5	0
Owasso	36,869	75	56	19
Paoli	616	1	1	0
Pauls Valley	6,225	20	15	5
Pawhuska	3,461	14	10	4
Pawnee	2,160	7	6	1
Perkins	2,841	8	8	0
Perry	5,000	21	13	8
Piedmont	7,738	12	9	3
Pocola	4,073	12	8	4
Ponca City	24,397	69	51	18
Pond Creek	854	2	2	0
Porum	707	3	3	0
Poteau	8,913	31	25	6
Prague	2,464	13	8	5
Pryor Creek	9,517	29	22	7
Purcell	6,483	23	20	3
Quinton	987	4	4	0
Ringling	989	1	1	0
Roland	3,720	11	8	3
Rush Springs	1,271	4	4	0
Salina	1,381	5	5	0
Sallisaw	8,548	28	21	7
Sand Springs	19,977	40	29	11
Sapulpa	21,062	53	41	12
Savanna	642	7	6	1
Sawyer	312	2	2	0
Sayre	4,644	12	7	5
Seminole	7,415	15	13	2
Shady Point	995	2	2	0
Shattuck	1,333	2	2	0
Shawnee	31,725	86	63	23
Skiatook	8,018	21	17	4
Snyder	1,326	3	3	0
South Coffeyville	758	5	5	0
Spencer	4,031	6	4	2
Sperry	1,292	4	3	1
Spiro	2,184	3	3	0
Sportsmen Acres	312	1	1	0
Stigler	2,760	13	9	4
Stillwater	50,159	120	75	45
Stilwell	4,062	20	13	7
Stonewall	476	2	2	0
Stratford	1,539	4	4	0
Stringtown	401	2	2	0
Stroud	2,792	13	8	5
Sulphur	5,105	10	8	2
Tahlequah	16,905	45	36	9
Talala	278	3	2	1
Talihina	1,094	10	5	5
Tecumseh	6,699	13	12	1
Texhoma	955	3	3	0
Thackerville	478	1	1	0
The Village	9,512	29	22	7
Thomas	1,235	2	2	0
Tipton	779	2	2	0
Tishomingo	3,119	8	7	1
Tonkawa	3,077	9	6	3
Tryon	505	1	1	0
Tulsa	404,868	946	777	169
Tupelo	313	1	1	0
Tushka	301	3	3	0
Tuttle	7,140	16	11	5
Tyrone	769	2	1	1
Union City	2,053	8	8	0
Valley Brook	779	11	9	2
Valliant	737	4	4	0
Velma	602	1	1	0
Verden	527	1	1	0
Verdigris	4,488	5	4	1
Vian	1,383	4	4	0
Vici	702	3	2	1
Vinita	5,532	22	15	7
Wagoner	8,931	20	15	5
Wakita	339	1	1	0

Table 78. Full-Time Law Enforcement Employees, by Selected State and City, 2017—Continued

(Number.)

State/city	Population	Total law enforcement employees	Total officers	Total civilians
Walters	2,464	4	4	0
Warner	1,614	3	3	0
Warr Acres	10,480	33	26	7
Washington	655	3	2	1
Watonga	2,931	9	7	2
Watts	310	3	2	1
Waukomis	1,349	4	4	0
Waurika	1,960	4	4	0
Waynoka	960	3	3	0
Weatherford	12,178	38	23	15
Webbers Falls	593	4	3	1
Weleetka	981	7	5	2
West Siloam Springs	839	10	9	1
Westville	1,561	9	5	4
Wetumka	1,221	9	4	5
Wewoka	3,390	7	7	0
Wilburton	2,633	7	6	1
Wilson	1,721	4	4	0
Wister	1,067	4	3	1
Woodward	12,655	25	21	4
Wright City	733	1	1	0
Wyandotte	330	5	4	1
Wynnewood	2,227	6	5	1
Wynona	440	3	3	0
Yale	1,207	6	3	3
Yukon	26,971	63	46	17
OREGON				
Albany	53,701	97	65	32
Amity	1,676	9	2	7
Ashland	21,908	35	28	7
Astoria	9,857	23	13	10
Aumsville	4,141	7	6	1
Baker City	9,764	17	15	2
Bandon	3,146	7	7	0
Beaverton	98,897	179	139	40
Bend	93,786	123	96	27
Black Butte		7	6	1
Boardman	3,408	11	10	1
Brookings	6,560	21	14	7
Canby	17,823	28	24	4
Cannon Beach	1,710	9	7	2
Carlton	2,156	4	3	1
Central Point	18,525	31	25	6
Coburg	1,073	4	3	1
Columbia City	2,005	7	4	3
Condon	677	1	1	0
Coos Bay	16,347	32	22	10
Coquille	3,912	8	7	1
Corvallis	57,576	81	57	24
Cottage Grove	10,182	31	16	15
Dallas	16,152	26	20	6
Eagle Point	9,143	13	12	1
Enterprise	1,912	5	5	0
Eugene	168,310	307	188	119
Florence	8,857	23	16	7
Forest Grove	24,520	33	28	5
Gearhart	1,580	3	3	0
Gervais	2,710	6	5	1
Gladstone	12,220	19	17	2
Gold Beach	2,314	7	5	2
Grants Pass	38,082	87	55	32
Gresham	112,466	155	125	30
Hermiston	17,377	37	31	6
Hillsboro	107,433	177	130	47
Hood River	7,797	16	14	2
Hubbard	3,421	4	3	1
Independence	9,854	19	14	5
Jacksonville	2,917	6	5	1
John Day	1,662	10	10	0
Junction City	6,174	9	7	2
Keizer	39,397	45	38	7
King City	3,945	8	7	1
Klamath Falls	22,436	41	36	5
La Grande	13,252	31	18	13
Lake Oswego	39,318	59	43	16
Lebanon	16,826	39	27	12
Lincoln City	8,798	37	25	12
Madras	6,800	11	10	1
Malin	810	7	7	0
Manzanita	646	4	4	0
McMinnville	35,125	45	38	7
Medford	82,792	141	104	37
Milton-Freewater	7,011	17	11	6
Milwaukie	21,033	42	37	5

Table 78. Full-Time Law Enforcement Employees, by Selected State and City, 2017—Continued

(Number.)

State/city	Population	Total law enforcement employees	Total officers	Total civilians
Molalla	9,245	17	14	3
Monmouth	10,282	15	12	3
Mount Angel	3,569	9	6	3
Myrtle Creek	3,494	7	7	0
Myrtle Point	2,550	6	5	1
Newberg-Dundee	26,769	49	35	14
Newport	10,465	26	22	4
North Bend	9,806	28	21	7
North Plains	2,158	4	4	0
Nyssa	3,174	8	7	1
Oakridge	3,254	7	5	2
Ontario	10,970	25	21	4
Oregon City	36,921	54	47	7
Pendleton	16,864	28	23	5
Philomath	4,691	10	9	1
Phoenix	4,614	10	9	1
Pilot Rock	1,508	3	3	0
Portland	649,408	1,174	925	249
Port Orford	1,163	6	5	1
Prineville	10,053	28	16	12
Rainier	1,968	6	5	1
Redmond	29,870	48	40	8
Reedsport	4,106	19	10	9
Rockaway Beach	1,387	4	4	0
Rogue River	2,289	8	5	3
Roseburg	22,505	42	38	4
Salem	169,565	337	189	148
Sandy	11,249	22	18	4
Scappoose	7,236	11	10	1
Seaside	6,726	25	19	6
Sherwood	19,473	26	23	3
Silverton	10,136	18	16	2
Springfield	62,318	96	64	32
Stayton	8,148	17	13	4
St. Helens	13,611	17	15	2
Sunriver		12	11	1
Sutherlin	8,027	15	12	3
Sweet Home	9,500	22	15	7
Talent	6,558	10	8	2
The Dalles	15,670	26	23	3
Tigard	52,524	89	72	17
Tillamook	5,214	10	10	0
Toledo	3,577	13	7	6
Tualatin	27,781	46	38	8
Turner	2,061	2	2	0
Umatilla	7,009	13	11	2
Vernonia	2,199	4	3	1
Warrenton	5,545	13	12	1
West Linn	27,153	29	26	3
Winston	5,436	9	8	1
Woodburn	25,848	38	30	8
Yamhill	1,167	9	3	6
PENNSYLVANIA				
Abington Township, Montgomery County	55,578	78	61	17
Adams Township, Butler County	13,876	14	14	0
Adams Township, Cambria County	5,651	3	3	0
Akron	3,999	5	5	0
Albion	1,457	3	3	0
Alburtis	2,598	4	4	0
Aldan	4,154	5	5	0
Aleppo Township	1,887	17	14	3
Aliquippa	9,048	17	16	1
Allegheny Township, Blair County	6,602	8	7	1
Allegheny Township, Westmoreland County	8,142	10	9	1
Allentown	120,823	234	212	22
Altoona	44,366	72	64	8
Ambler	6,509	13	12	1
Ambridge	6,744	8	8	0
Amity Township	12,921	13	12	1
Annville Township	4,940	10	8	2
Archbald	6,975	18	18	0
Arnold	4,904	8	8	0
Ashland	2,694	2	2	0
Ashley	2,691	4	4	0
Aspinwall	2,726	7	6	1
Aston Township	16,714	18	16	2
Athens	3,195	4	4	0
Athens Township	5,009	11	10	1
Avalon	4,582	5	5	0
Avoca	2,606	2	2	0
Avonmore Boro	967	1	1	0
Baden	3,976	3	3	0
Baldwin Borough	19,727	23	22	1

Table 78. Full-Time Law Enforcement Employees, by Selected State and City, 2017—Continued

(Number.)

State/city	Population	Total law enforcement employees	Total officers	Total civilians
Baldwin Township	1,942	5	5	0
Bally	1,103	2	2	0
Bangor	5,179	11	10	1
Beaver	4,353	12	10	2
Beaver Falls	8,516	19	18	1
Beaver Meadows	831	1	1	0
Bedford	2,702	5	5	0
Bedminster Township	7,117	7	6	1
Bell Acres	1,392	3	3	0
Bellefonte	6,321	13	10	3
Bellevue	8,140	16	13	3
Bellwood	1,759	3	3	0
Ben Avon	1,754	17	14	3
Ben Avon Heights	375	17	14	3
Bensalem Township	60,310	127	100	27
Berlin	1,990	2	2	0
Bern Township	6,975	12	12	0
Bernville	946	2	1	1
Berwick	10,080	15	14	1
Bethel Park	31,842	44	38	6
Bethel Township, Berks County	4,122	3	3	0
Bethlehem	75,336	154	154	0
Bethlehem Township	23,973	36	35	1
Biglerville	1,207	2	2	0
Birdsboro	5,138	8	7	1
Birmingham Township	4,255	3	3	0
Blairsville	3,275	4	4	0
Blair Township	4,559	4	4	0
Blakely	6,244	6	6	0
Blawnox	1,398	3	3	0
Bloomsburg Town	14,542	23	18	5
Blossburg	1,504	2	2	0
Bonneauville	1,828	1	1	0
Boyertown	4,026	8	7	1
Brackenridge	3,167	4	4	0
Braddock Hills	1,838	2	2	0
Bradford	8,307	18	18	0
Bradford Township	4,761	5	5	0
Branch Township	1,766	2	2	0
Brecknock Township, Berks County	4,626	5	5	0
Brentwood	9,386	15	13	2
Briar Creek Township	2,989	4	4	0
Bridgeport	4,562	8	7	1
Bridgeville	5,029	9	8	1
Bridgewater	682	2	2	0
Brighton Township	8,392	8	8	0
Bristol	9,503	14	12	2
Bristol Township	53,628	69	60	9
Brockway	2,016	3	2	1
Brookhaven	8,074	9	8	1
Brookville	3,820	7	7	0
Brownsville	2,260	2	2	0
Bryn Athyn	1,394	3	3	0
Buckingham Township	20,339	24	22	2
Buffalo Township	7,276	5	5	0
Buffalo Valley Regional	12,590	16	15	1
Bushkill Township	8,494	17	16	1
Butler	13,057	24	23	1
Butler Township, Butler County	16,690	23	21	2
Butler Township, Luzerne County	9,709	12	11	1
Butler Township, Schuykill County	5,389	4	4	0
Caernarvon Township, Berks County	4,079	8	7	1
California	6,840	8	7	1
Caln Township	14,137	18	17	1
Cambria Township	5,823	4	4	0
Cambridge Springs	2,556	3	3	0
Camp Hill	7,941	13	12	1
Canonsburg	8,859	18	16	2
Canton	1,883	3	3	0
Carbondale	8,435	9	9	0
Carlisle	19,233	34	31	3
Carnegie	7,904	14	13	1
Carrolltown	804	2	2	0
Carroll Township, Washington County	5,503	3	3	0
Carroll Township, York County	6,359	12	12	0
Carroll Valley	3,949	5	4	1
Castle Shannon	8,213	15	14	1
Catasauqua	6,562	9	8	1
Catawissa	1,490	3	3	0
Cecil Township	12,605	21	20	1
Center Township	11,628	20	19	1
Centerville	3,156	2	2	0
Central Berks Regional	9,416	15	14	1
Central Bucks Regional	15,330	28	25	3
Chambersburg	20,757	36	33	3

Table 78. Full-Time Law Enforcement Employees, by Selected State and City, 2017—Continued

(Number.)

State/city	Population	Total law enforcement employees	Total officers	Total civilians
Charleroi Regional	6,556	7	7	0
Chartiers Township	7,985	12	12	0
Cheltenham Township	37,160	75	67	8
Chester	33,984	101	91	10
Cheswick	1,709	1	1	0
Chippewa Township	8,116	9	8	1
Churchill	2,946	9	9	0
Clairton	6,588	10	10	0
Clarion	5,361	9	8	1
Clarks Summit	6,294	6	6	0
Clearfield	5,940	11	7	4
Cleona	2,183	4	4	0
Clifton Heights	6,695	11	10	1
Clymer	1,283	1	1	0
Coaldale	2,172	3	3	0
Coal Township	10,349	12	11	1
Cochranton	1,101	2	2	0
Colebrookdale District	5,985	11	9	2
Collegeville	5,282	8	8	0
Collier Township	8,164	17	16	1
Collingdale	8,762	9	8	1
Colonial Regional	20,540	27	25	2
Columbia	10,352	19	16	3
Conemaugh Township, Cambria County	1,886	1	1	0
Conemaugh Township, Somerset County	6,900	6	6	0
Conewago Township, Adams County	7,184	10	9	1
Conewango Township	3,392	4	4	0
Conneaut Lake Regional	3,506	4	3	1
Connellsville	7,405	14	14	0
Conoy Township	3,483	16	14	2
Conshohocken	8,006	21	19	2
Conway	2,121	4	4	0
Conyngham	1,863	3	3	0
Coopersburg	2,494	7	7	0
Coplay	3,239	5	5	0
Coraopolis	5,513	13	9	4
Cornwall	4,318	7	6	1
Corry	6,321	11	10	1
Coudersport	2,433	4	4	0
Covington Township	2,250	4	4	0
Crafton	6,251	10	9	1
Cranberry Township	31,191	31	27	4
Crescent Township	2,574	4	4	0
Cresson	1,598	10	10	0
Cresson Township	2,574	5	4	1
Croyle Township	2,249	1	1	0
Cumberland Township, Adams County	6,225	6	6	0
Cumberland Township, Greene County	6,333	3	3	0
Cumru Township	15,341	25	24	1
Curwensville	2,443	2	1	1
Dallas	2,762	4	4	0
Dallas Township	9,252	10	10	0
Dalton	1,204	2	2	0
Danville	4,604	8	6	2
Darby	10,648	18	17	1
Darby Township	9,302	15	14	1
Decatur Township	4,804	1	1	0
Delmont	2,612	4	4	0
Derry	2,551	2	2	0
Derry Township, Dauphin County	25,082	58	39	19
Dickson City	5,794	7	7	0
Donegal Township	2,418	3	3	0
Donora	4,597	6	6	0
Dormont	8,347	14	13	1
Douglass Township, Berks County	3,584	4	4	0
Douglass Township, Montgomery County	10,534	12	11	1
Downingtown	7,907	19	16	3
Doylestown Township	17,538	22	20	2
Dublin Borough	2,157	3	2	1
Du Bois	7,504	13	13	0
Duboistown	1,200	1	1	0
Duncansville	1,186	1	1	0
Dunmore	13,047	17	17	0
Duquesne	5,507	15	14	1
Duryea	4,840	4	4	0
East Bangor	1,705	1	1	0
East Berlin	1,530	3	1	2
East Bethlehem Township	2,268	1	1	0
East Brandywine Township	8,721	16	15	1
East Coventry Township	6,738	8	7	1
East Deer Township	1,455	1	1	0
East Earl Township	6,838	8	8	0
Eastern Adams Regional	7,388	6	6	0
Eastern Pike Regional	4,607	11	10	1
East Fallowfield Township	7,539	7	7	0

Table 78. Full-Time Law Enforcement Employees, by Selected State and City, 2017—Continued

(Number.)

State/city	Population	Total law enforcement employees	Total officers	Total civilians
East Franklin Township	3,917	1	1	0
East Greenville	2,983	2	2	0
East Hempfield Township	24,504	36	32	4
East Lampeter Township	17,084	39	36	3
East Lansdowne	2,654	5	3	2
East Marlborough Township	7,310	1	1	0
East McKeesport	2,644	3	3	0
East Norriton Township	14,154	29	27	2
Easton	27,013	68	63	5
East Pennsboro Township	21,800	23	22	1
East Pikeland Township	7,360	9	9	0
East Pittsburgh	1,769	1	1	0
Easttown Township	10,609	14	13	1
East Union Township	1,593	2	2	0
East Vincent Township	7,065	7	7	0
East Whiteland Township	11,672	22	20	2
Ebensburg	3,137	4	4	0
Economy	9,338	14	13	1
Eddystone	2,397	10	9	1
Edgewood	3,026	9	9	0
Edgeworth	1,644	13	4	9
Edinboro	6,204	8	8	0
Edwardsville	4,684	5	5	0
Elizabeth	1,983	2	2	0
Elizabethtown	11,641	19	17	2
Elizabeth Township	13,079	12	12	0
Elkland	1,758	2	2	0
Ellwood City	7,476	12	10	2
Emmaus	11,424	22	20	2
Emporium	1,887	2	2	0
Emsworth	2,387	17	14	3
Ephrata	13,907	38	34	4
Erie	98,071	195	174	21
Etna	3,354	7	7	0
Evans City-Seven Fields Regional	4,554	3	3	0
Everett	1,731	3	3	0
Everson	765	1	1	0
Exeter Township, Berks County	25,830	34	32	2
Exeter Township, Luzerne County	2,344	1	1	0
Fairchance	1,904	1	1	0
Fairview Township, Luzerne County	4,479	6	6	0
Fairview Township, York County	17,393	16	13	3
Falls Township, Bucks County	33,618	60	53	7
Farrell	4,702	14	13	1
Fawn Township	2,330	1	1	0
Ferguson Township	19,630	24	22	2
Ferndale	1,524	2	2	0
Findlay Township	5,739	23	16	7
Fleetwood	4,070	6	6	0
Folcroft	6,623	12	11	1
Ford City	2,825	1	1	0
Forest City	1,742	2	2	0
Forest Hills	6,357	9	9	0
Forks Township	15,518	22	21	1
Forty Fort	4,079	4	4	0
Forward Township	3,300	1	1	0
Foster Township, McKean County	4,116	5	5	0
Fountain Hill	4,638	10	9	1
Fox Chapel	5,329	11	11	0
Frackville	3,651	5	5	0
Franconia Township	13,293	11	10	1
Franklin	6,181	23	17	6
Franklin Park	14,690	13	12	1
Franklin Township, Beaver County	3,934	3	3	0
Franklin Township, Carbon County	4,104	4	4	0
Franklin Township, Columbia County	581	4	4	0
Frazer Township	1,143	2	2	0
Freedom Township	3,385	3	3	0
Freeland	3,423	5	4	1
Freemansburg	2,619	3	3	0
Galeton	1,102	1	1	0
Gallitzin	1,807	6	6	0
Geistown	2,326	1	1	0
Gettysburg	7,716	12	11	1
Girard	2,978	4	4	0
Glassport	4,360	6	6	0
Glenolden	7,153	11	10	1
Granville Township	5,022	10	8	2
Greencastle	4,041	5	4	1
Greenfield Township, Blair County	4,035	1	1	0
Greensburg	14,356	38	28	10
Green Tree	5,020	11	10	1
Greenville	5,547	8	7	1
Grove City	8,029	12	11	1
Hamburg	4,394	7	6	1

Table 78. Full-Time Law Enforcement Employees, by Selected State and City, 2017—Continued

(Number.)

State/city	Population	Total law enforcement employees	Total officers	Total civilians
Hampden Township	29,905	26	25	1
Hampton Township	18,451	19	18	1
Hanover	15,606	28	25	3
Hanover Township, Luzerne County	10,822	17	16	1
Harmar Township	3,064	9	8	1
Harmony Township	3,066	4	4	0
Harrisburg	48,804	161	135	26
Harrison Township	10,358	21	18	3
Harveys Lake	2,770	2	2	0
Hastings	2,178	2	2	0
Hatboro	7,445	17	14	3
Hatfield Township	20,927	29	27	2
Haverford Township	49,116	82	70	12
Hazleton	24,549	42	38	4
Hegins Township	3,440	2	2	0
Heidelberg	1,215	3	3	0
Heidelberg Township, Berks County	1,739	1	1	0
Hellam Township	8,646	10	8	2
Hellertown	5,819	11	10	1
Hemlock Township	2,260	6	6	0
Hempfield Township, Mercer County	3,655	7	6	1
Hermitage	15,782	32	29	3
Highspire	2,366	13	13	0
Hilltown Township	15,278	20	17	3
Hollidaysburg	5,751	10	8	2
Homer City	1,614	2	2	0
Homestead	3,160	14	13	1
Honesdale	4,132	5	5	0
Honey Brook	1,751	1	1	0
Hooversville	607	1	1	0
Hopewell Township	12,346	16	15	1
Horsham Township	26,723	47	40	7
Houston	1,240	2	2	0
Hughesville	2,076	3	3	0
Hummelstown	4,621	7	6	1
Huntingdon	6,974	12	12	0
Independence Township, Beaver County	2,419	2	2	0
Indiana	13,984	24	22	2
Indiana Township	7,225	10	10	0
Indian Lake	386	5	5	0
Ingram	3,235	4	4	0
Irwin	3,801	4	4	0
Jackson Township, Butler County	3,834	10	8	2
Jackson Township, Cambria County	4,130	2	2	0
Jackson Township, Luzerne County	4,631	2	2	0
Jeannette	9,180	17	14	3
Jefferson Hills Borough	11,418	20	19	1
Jefferson Township, Mercer County	1,846	2	2	0
Jenkins Township	4,447	3	3	0
Jenkintown	4,421	16	14	2
Jermyn	2,065	1	1	0
Jessup	4,423	4	4	0
Jim Thorpe	4,579	8	7	1
Johnsonburg	2,313	3	3	0
Johnstown	20,946	43	38	5
Kane	3,520	3	3	0
Kenhorst	2,852	189	167	22
Kennedy Township	8,213	10	8	2
Kennett Square	6,176	16	13	3
Kennett Township	8,312	7	7	0
Kidder Township	1,929	6	6	0
Kilbuck Township	710	17	14	3
Kingston	12,809	19	19	0
Kingston Township	6,924	11	11	0
Kiskiminetas Township	4,565	9	9	0
Kittanning	3,818	9	8	1
Kline Township	1,380	2	1	1
Knox	1,076	2	2	0
Koppel	732	2	2	0
Kulpmont	2,812	1	1	0
Kutztown	5,019	14	12	2
Lake City	2,923	3	3	0
Lamar Township	2,562	2	2	0
Lancaster	59,199	163	140	23
Lancaster Township, Butler County	2,513	2	2	0
Langhorne Borough	1,583	1	1	0
Lansdale	16,561	30	23	7
Lansdowne	10,604	18	15	3
Lansford	3,740	7	7	0
Larksville	4,389	7	7	0
Latimore Township	2,604	1	1	0
Latrobe	7,950	14	13	1
Laureldale	3,868	4	4	0
Lawrence Park Township	3,793	9	8	1
Lawrence Township, Clearfield County	7,694	9	8	1

Table 78. Full-Time Law Enforcement Employees, by Selected State and City, 2017—Continued

(Number.)

State/city	Population	Total law enforcement employees	Total officers	Total civilians
Lebanon	25,771	44	41	3
Leechburg	2,033	3	3	0
Leetsdale	1,182	4	4	0
Leet Township	1,600	5	5	0
Lehighton	5,241	12	11	1
Lehigh Township, Northampton County	10,400	13	12	1
Lehman Township	3,448	3	3	0
Lewistown	8,196	11	10	1
Liberty	2,489	1	1	0
Liberty Township, Adams County	1,246	1	1	0
Ligonier	1,523	2	2	0
Ligonier Township	6,463	6	6	0
Limerick Township	19,145	27	25	2
Lincoln	1,047	3	2	1
Linesville	988	7	7	0
Lititz	9,214	16	14	2
Littlestown	4,473	9	8	1
Lock Haven	9,514	16	14	2
Locust Township	1,400	4	4	0
Logan Township	12,547	18	16	2
Lower Allen Township	19,604	25	22	3
Lower Burrell	11,303	18	17	1
Lower Chichester Township	3,468	5	5	0
Lower Frederick Township	4,901	3	3	0
Lower Gwynedd Township	11,581	19	18	1
Lower Heidelberg Township	6,143	11	10	1
Lower Makefield Township	32,779	42	38	4
Lower Merion Township	58,354	158	141	17
Lower Moreland Township	13,246	27	22	5
Lower Paxton Township	48,971	66	59	7
Lower Pottsgrove Township	12,179	19	17	2
Lower Providence Township	26,813	33	31	2
Lower Salford Township	15,487	20	18	2
Lower Saucon Township	10,818	17	15	2
Lower Southampton Township	19,120	33	30	3
Lower Swatara Township	8,855	16	14	2
Lower Windsor Township	7,500	10	9	1
Lykens	1,746	1	1	0
Macungie	3,162	4	4	0
Mahanoy City	3,981	2	2	0
Mahanoy Township	3,322	1	1	0
Mahoning Township, Carbon County	4,188	6	6	0
Mahoning Township, Lawrence County	2,910	1	1	0
Mahoning Township, Montour County	4,207	7	6	1
Malvern	3,487	6	5	1
Manheim	4,855	18	17	1
Manheim Township	40,170	74	63	11
Manor	3,334	4	4	0
Manor Township, Armstrong County	4,164	1	1	0
Manor Township, Lancaster County	20,949	21	19	2
Mansfield	3,147	5	5	0
Marcus Hook	2,388	5	4	1
Marietta	2,603	15	13	2
Marion Township, Beaver County	889	2	2	0
Marlborough Township	3,347	3	3	0
Marple Township	23,838	32	29	3
Mars	1,636	1	1	0
Martinsburg	1,884	2	2	0
Marysville	2,531	2	2	0
Masontown	3,351	5	5	0
Mayfield	1,709	2	2	0
McAdoo	2,176	3	3	0
McCandless	28,788	30	28	2
McDonald Borough	2,060	5	5	0
McKeesport	20,937	55	52	3
McKees Rocks	5,926	10	9	1
McSherrystown	3,062	4	4	0
Meadville	12,896	28	22	6
Mechanicsburg	9,012	15	14	1
Media	5,354	22	14	8
Mercer	1,896	3	3	0
Mercersburg	1,553	2	2	0
Meshoppen	1,444	2	2	0
Middleburg	1,305	3	2	1
Middlesex Township, Butler County	5,673	4	4	0
Middlesex Township, Cumberland County	7,422	10	9	1
Middletown	9,279	11	10	1
Middletown Township	45,282	63	57	6
Midland	2,523	3	3	0
Mifflinburg	3,518	10	9	1
Mifflin County Regional	16,872	14	14	0
Milford	966	2	2	0
Millbourne	1,159	1	1	0
Millcreek Township, Erie County	53,806	81	64	17

Table 78. Full-Time Law Enforcement Employees, by Selected State and City, 2017—Continued

(Number.)

State/city	Population	Total law enforcement employees	Total officers	Total civilians
Millcreek Township, Lebanon County	5,670	2	2	0
Millersburg	2,528	3	2	1
Millersville	8,419	15	13	2
Millvale	3,638	6	6	0
Milton	6,879	9	8	1
Minersville	4,185	5	5	0
Mohnton	3,044	4	4	0
Monaca	5,567	8	8	0
Monessen	7,364	12	11	1
Monongahela	4,129	8	7	1
Monroeville	27,888	55	46	9
Montgomery	1,537	10	1	9
Montgomery Township	26,369	38	35	3
Montoursville	4,497	7	6	1
Montour Township	1,302	3	3	0
Montrose	1,471	3	3	0
Moon Township	25,818	35	29	6
Moore Township	9,294	11	10	1
Moosic	5,759	10	10	0
Morris-Cooper Regional	5,514	1	1	0
Morrisville	8,523	13	11	2
Morton	2,693	5	4	1
Moscow	1,934	3	3	0
Mount Carmel	5,644	8	8	0
Mount Carmel Township	3,030	6	6	0
Mount Gretna Borough	203	7	6	1
Mount Holly Springs	2,042	2	2	0
Mount Joy	8,221	12	11	1
Mount Lebanon	32,367	54	45	9
Mount Oliver	3,308	10	10	0
Mount Pleasant	4,304	4	4	0
Mount Pleasant Township	3,497	4	4	0
Mount Union	2,385	5	5	0
Muhlenberg Township	20,150	33	31	2
Muncy	2,441	3	3	0
Muncy Township	1,081	2	2	0
Munhall	11,140	25	23	2
Murrysville	20,034	23	21	2
Nanticoke	10,144	15	14	1
Nanty Glo	2,540	1	1	0
Narberth	4,338	4	4	0
Nazareth	5,675	8	7	1
Neshannock Township	9,241	7	7	0
Nether Providence Township	13,790	16	15	1
Neville Township	1,052	17	14	3
Newberry Township	15,530	18	16	2
New Bethlehem	2,717	2	2	0
New Brighton	8,907	9	7	2
New Britain Township	11,220	13	12	1
New Cumberland	7,302	10	9	1
New Hanover Township	13,095	10	9	1
New Holland	5,443	15	14	1
New Hope	2,492	11	9	2
New Kensington	12,508	22	22	0
Newport Township	5,257	2	2	0
New Sewickley Township	7,367	11	10	1
Newtown	2,226	5	5	0
Newtown Township, Bucks County	22,903	32	28	4
Newtown Township, Delaware County	13,190	20	18	2
Newville	1,332	3	3	0
New Wilmington	2,183	5	5	0
Norristown	34,374	80	67	13
Northampton	9,854	14	12	2
Northampton Township	39,395	48	42	6
North Belle Vernon	1,871	2	2	0
North Braddock	4,721	3	3	0
North Catasauqua	2,828	5	5	0
North Cornwall Township	7,909	9	9	0
North Coventry Township	8,001	12	11	1
North East, Erie County	4,109	7	7	0
Northeastern Regional	11,728	13	12	1
Northern Berks Regional	13,282	15	14	1
Northern Cambria Borough	3,582	2	2	0
Northern Lancaster County Regional	35,500	26	24	2
Northern Regional	35,113	31	29	2
Northern York Regional	69,203	53	49	4
North Fayette Township	14,656	25	20	5
North Franklin Township	4,571	10	10	0
North Hopewell Township	2,803	2	2	0
North Huntingdon Township	30,687	32	26	6
North Lebanon Township	11,975	14	12	2
North Londonderry Township	8,525	10	9	1
North Middleton Township	11,625	11	10	1
North Sewickley Township	5,474	1	1	0
North Strabane Township	14,778	20	19	1

Table 78. Full-Time Law Enforcement Employees, by Selected State and City, 2017—Continued

(Number.)

State/city	Population	Total law enforcement employees	Total officers	Total civilians
Northumberland	3,687	5	5	0
North Versailles Township	12,193	24	19	5
North Wales	3,244	4	4	0
Northwest Lancaster County Regional	19,758	21	19	2
Norwood	5,878	7	6	1
Oakmont	6,449	7	7	0
O'Hara Township	8,514	16	15	1
Ohio Township	6,665	17	14	3
Ohioville	3,422	2	2	0
Oil City	9,931	22	16	6
Old Forge	7,949	5	5	0
Old Lycoming Township	5,014	8	8	0
Oley Township	3,760	2	2	0
Olyphant	5,075	4	4	0
Orangeville Area	1,746	1	1	0
Orwigsburg	2,979	5	5	0
Overfield Township	2,785	1	1	0
Oxford	5,447	12	11	1
Palmerton	5,253	10	9	1
Palmer Township	21,598	36	34	2
Palmyra	7,541	9	8	1
Palo Alto	988	1	1	0
Parkesburg	3,772	9	8	1
Parkside	2,328	3	3	0
Parks Township	2,603	2	2	0
Patterson Township	2,930	4	4	0
Patton	1,641	2	2	0
Patton Township	16,100	19	17	2
Penbrook	2,955	7	7	0
Penn	468	6	6	0
Penndel	2,179	1	1	0
Penn Hills	41,425	53	50	3
Pennridge Regional	10,979	15	13	2
Penn Township, Butler County	4,910	4	3	1
Penn Township, Westmoreland County	19,510	23	21	2
Penn Township, York County	16,394	24	22	2
Perkasie	8,474	19	17	2
Perryopolis	1,709	2	2	0
Peters Township	22,297	23	21	2
Philadelphia	1,575,595	7,347	6,558	789
Phoenixville	16,955	32	30	2
Pine Creek Township	3,273	2	2	0
Pine Grove	2,095	2	2	0
Pitcairn	3,202	3	3	0
Pittsburgh	305,932	903	885	18
Pittston	7,581	9	9	0
Pittston Township	3,387	4	4	0
Plains Township	9,690	19	18	1
Pleasant Hills	8,175	20	18	2
Plum	27,440	30	24	6
Plumstead Township	13,906	18	16	2
Plymouth	5,766	4	4	0
Plymouth Township, Montgomery County	17,835	52	45	7
Pocono Mountain Regional	42,213	42	37	5
Pocono Township	10,706	19	18	1
Point Township	3,670	5	5	0
Polk	782	2	2	0
Portage	2,451	2	2	0
Port Allegany	2,037	3	3	0
Port Carbon	1,794	2	2	0
Portland	509	2	2	0
Port Vue	3,693	2	2	0
Pottstown	22,706	57	44	13
Pottsville	13,645	24	24	0
Prospect Park	6,475	9	9	0
Pulaski Township, Lawrence County	3,291	2	2	0
Punxsutawney	5,790	11	8	3
Pymatuning Township	3,120	10	7	3
Quakertown	8,768	20	18	2
Quarryville	2,771	4	4	0
Raccoon Township	2,967	4	4	0
Radnor Township	31,859	46	42	4
Ralpho Township	4,279	6	6	0
Rankin	2,060	1	1	0
Reading	87,487	189	167	22
Reading Township	5,840	2	2	0
Redstone Township	4,284	3	3	0
Reilly Township	692	2	2	0
Renovo	1,216	1	1	0
Reserve Township	3,260	4	4	0
Reynoldsville	2,676	1	1	0
Rice Township	3,545	6	6	0
Richland Township, Bucks County	13,225	15	13	2
Richland Township, Cambria County	12,153	22	21	1

Table 78. Full-Time Law Enforcement Employees, by Selected State and City, 2017—Continued

(Number.)

State/city	Population	Total law enforcement employees	Total officers	Total civilians
Ridgway	3,799	6	5	1
Ridley Park	7,026	14	10	4
Ridley Township	31,082	37	32	5
Riverside	1,894	3	3	0
Roaring Brook Township	1,957	1	1	0
Roaring Creek Township	536	4	4	0
Roaring Spring	2,502	3	3	0
Robeson Township	7,379	6	5	1
Robinson Township, Allegheny County	13,777	31	29	2
Rochester	3,514	7	6	1
Rochester Township	2,699	4	4	0
Rockledge	2,535	4	4	0
Ross Township	30,684	45	43	2
Rostraver Township	11,046	15	14	1
Royalton	1,039	5	5	0
Royersford	4,761	8	7	1
Rush Township	3,305	1	1	0
Sadsbury Township, Chester County	3,934	2	2	0
Salem Township, Luzerne County	4,178	5	5	0
Salisbury Township	13,807	21	19	2
Sandy Lake	642	1	1	0
Sandy Township	10,661	11	10	1
Saxonburg	1,473	1	1	0
Saxton	696	1	1	0
Sayre	6,335	13	10	3
Schuylkill Haven	5,166	8	8	0
Schuylkill Township, Chester County	8,580	13	11	2
Scottdale	4,184	6	6	0
Scott Township, Allegheny County	16,684	23	22	1
Scott Township, Columbia County	5,035	6	6	0
Scott Township, Lackawanna County	4,789	4	4	0
Scranton	77,499	170	150	20
Selinsgrove	5,930	7	6	1
Seward	468	1	1	0
Sewickley	4,370	8	8	0
Sewickley Heights	811	4	2	2
Shaler Township	28,207	28	26	2
Shamokin	7,056	11	10	1
Shamokin Dam	1,726	3	3	0
Sharon	13,305	29	28	1
Sharon Hill	5,683	10	9	1
Sharpsburg	3,352	6	6	0
Shenandoah	4,812	4	4	0
Shenango Township, Lawrence County	7,251	7	7	0
Shenango Township, Mercer County	3,761	8	8	0
Shillington	5,241	8	7	1
Shinglehouse	1,074	1	1	0
Shippensburg	5,567	10	9	1
Shippingport	209	1	1	0
Shiremanstown	1,584	2	2	0
Shohola Township	2,308	1	1	0
Silver Lake Township	1,604	1	1	0
Silver Spring Township	17,558	25	24	1
Sinking Spring	4,100	7	6	1
Slate Belt Regional	12,398	23	23	0
Slatington	4,289	6	6	0
Slippery Rock	3,572	4	4	0
Smethport	1,552	2	2	0
Smith Township	4,391	4	4	0
Solebury Township	8,583	16	14	2
Somerset	5,945	8	7	1
Souderton	6,927	6	5	1
South Abington Township	8,995	12	11	1
South Annville Township	2,972	2	2	0
South Beaver Township	2,632	4	4	0
South Buffalo Township	2,583	2	2	0
South Centre Township	4,197	4	4	0
South Coatesville	1,447	2	2	0
South Connellsville Borough	1,905	1	1	0
Southern Chester County Regional	14,900	16	15	1
Southern Regional Lancaster County	3,867	7	7	0
Southern Regional York County	11,488	16	14	2
South Fayette Township	15,772	18	17	1
South Fork	854	2	2	0
South Greensburg	2,020	2	2	0
South Heidelberg Township	7,359	9	9	0
South Lebanon Township	9,903	8	7	1
South Londonderry Township	8,110	10	8	2
South Park Township	13,371	15	14	1
South Pymatuning Township	2,587	2	2	0
Southwestern Regional	17,764	15	14	1
Southwest Greensburg	2,052	2	2	0
Southwest Regional, Fayette County	7,619	3	3	0
South Whitehall Township	19,893	37	35	2
South Williamsport	6,206	9	7	2

Table 78. Full-Time Law Enforcement Employees, by Selected State and City, 2017—Continued

(Number.)

State/city	Population	Total law enforcement employees	Total officers	Total civilians
Spring City	3,297	3	3	0
Springdale	3,334	3	3	0
Springdale Township	1,598	3	3	0
Springettsbury Township	26,895	34	31	3
Springfield Township, Bucks County	5,030	5	5	0
Springfield Township, Delaware County	24,363	37	32	5
Springfield Township, Montgomery County	19,728	30	28	2
Spring Garden Township	13,044	21	18	3
Spring Township, Berks County	27,446	30	29	1
Spring Township, Centre County	7,712	8	7	1
State College	58,169	72	62	10
St. Clair Boro	2,855	4	4	0
Steelton	5,897	14	12	2
St. Marys City	12,413	15	14	1
Stoneboro	993	1	1	0
Stonycreek Township	2,661	3	3	0
Stowe Township	6,181	6	6	0
Strasburg	2,960	4	4	0
Stroud Area Regional	34,259	59	52	7
Sugarcreek	5,034	3	3	0
Sugarloaf Township, Luzerne County	4,029	4	4	0
Sugar Notch	963	1	1	0
Summerhill Township	2,321	2	2	0
Summit Hill	2,913	6	4	2
Sunbury	9,520	19	15	4
Susquehanna Regional	8,405	16	14	2
Susquehanna Township, Dauphin County	25,055	45	42	3
Swarthmore	6,246	9	9	0
Swatara Township	24,867	52	49	3
Sweden Township	840	1	1	0
Swissvale	8,734	14	14	0
Swoyersville	4,941	5	5	0
Sykesville	1,122	1	1	0
Tamaqua	6,748	10	9	1
Tarentum	4,401	8	7	1
Tatamy	1,131	1	1	0
Taylor	5,929	7	7	0
Telford	4,844	7	6	1
Throop	3,902	6	6	0
Tiadaghton Valley Regional	7,666	11	10	1
Tilden Township	3,575	4	4	0
Tinicum Township, Bucks County	3,936	5	5	0
Tinicum Township, Delaware County	4,105	19	17	2
Titusville	5,345	10	10	0
Towamencin Township	18,484	26	23	3
Towanda	2,839	7	7	0
Trafford	3,095	3	3	0
Trainer	1,840	4	4	0
Tredyffrin Township	29,435	48	42	6
Tremont	1,681	2	2	0
Troy	1,247	2	2	0
Tullytown	1,844	7	6	1
Tulpehocken Township	3,313	3	3	0
Tunkhannock	1,749	3	3	0
Tunkhannock Township, Wyoming County	6,212	6	6	0
Turtle Creek	5,200	5	5	0
Tyrone	5,273	14	11	3
Union City	3,167	4	3	1
Uniontown	9,875	22	21	1
Union Township, Lawrence County	4,937	8	8	0
Upland	3,243	6	5	1
Upper Allen Township	20,119	24	23	1
Upper Burrell Township	2,244	2	2	0
Upper Chichester Township	17,033	23	22	1
Upper Darby Township	82,601	145	126	19
Upper Dublin Township	26,329	46	40	6
Upper Gwynedd Township	16,042	23	20	3
Upper Leacock Township	8,904	39	36	3
Upper Macungie Township	24,535	32	30	2
Upper Makefield Township	8,425	15	14	1
Upper Merion Township	28,677	82	65	17
Upper Moreland Township	24,238	43	37	6
Upper Nazareth Township	6,891	9	8	1
Upper Perkiomen	3,870	9	8	1
Upper Pottsgrove Township	5,605	9	8	1
Upper Providence Township, Delaware County	10,497	15	15	0
Upper Providence Township, Montgomery County	24,315	31	28	3
Upper Saucon Township	16,746	22	21	1
Upper Southampton Township	15,022	25	22	3
Upper St. Clair Township	19,911	33	26	7
Upper Uwchlan Township	11,540	11	11	0

Table 78. Full-Time Law Enforcement Employees, by Selected State and City, 2017—Continued

(Number.)

State/city	Population	Total law enforcement employees	Total officers	Total civilians
Upper Yoder Township	5,158	13	13	0
Uwchlan Township	19,128	22	21	1
Valley Township	7,800	6	6	0
Vandergrift	4,945	9	8	1
Vandling	713	2	2	0
Vernon Township	5,438	2	2	0
Verona	2,410	4	3	1
Versailles	1,477	2	2	0
Walnutport	2,084	4	4	0
Warminster Township	32,423	49	44	5
Warren	9,171	21	15	6
Warrington Township	24,360	32	29	3
Warwick Township, Bucks County	14,661	20	19	1
Washington, Washington County	13,435	33	31	2
Washington Township, Fayette County	3,714	4	4	0
Washington Township, Franklin County	14,678	11	9	2
Washington Township, Northampton County	5,232	5	5	0
Washington Township, Westmoreland County	7,170	7	7	0
Watsontown	2,293	5	5	0
Waverly Township	1,699	3	3	0
Waynesboro	10,889	22	20	2
Waynesburg	3,965	9	9	0
Weatherly	2,431	4	4	0
Wellsboro	3,277	7	7	0
Wesleyville	3,170	8	7	1
West Brandywine Township	7,451	8	7	1
West Brownsville	960	1	1	0
West Caln Township	9,067	2	2	0
West Carroll Township	1,222	2	2	0
West Chester	20,183	60	47	13
West Conshohocken	1,402	12	11	1
West Cornwall Township	2,017	7	6	1
West Deer Township	11,921	12	11	1
West Earl Township	8,368	6	6	0
Western Berks Regional	4,591	6	5	1
West Fallowfield Township	2,591	2	2	0
Westfield	1,039	2	2	0
West Goshen Township	23,237	34	30	4
West Hazleton	4,452	4	3	1
West Hempfield Township	16,540	24	21	3
West Hills Regional	10,167	12	11	1
West Homestead	1,902	7	6	1
West Kittanning	1,114	2	2	0
West Lampeter Township	16,080	16	15	1
West Mahanoy Township	2,749	3	3	0
West Manchester Township	18,865	30	27	3
West Manheim Township	8,438	9	9	0
West Mead Township	5,125	2	2	0
West Mifflin	19,856	39	33	6
West Newton	2,501	2	2	0
West Norriton Township	15,780	30	27	3
West Penn Township	4,331	2	2	0
West Pikeland Township	4,092	4	4	0
West Pike Run	1,547	1	1	0
West Pittston	4,720	2	2	0
West Pottsgrove Township	3,883	8	8	0
West Reading	4,169	15	13	2
West Sadsbury Township	2,469	4	4	0
West Salem Township	3,447	8	7	1
West Shore Regional	7,736	13	12	1
Westtown-East Goshen Regional	32,299	32	29	3
West View	6,598	13	11	2
West Vincent Township	5,172	7	6	1
West Whiteland Township	18,430	27	25	2
West York	4,550	8	8	0
Whitehall	13,717	25	20	5
Whitehall Township	27,536	49	44	5
White Haven Borough	1,090	3	3	0
Whitemarsh Township	17,866	41	36	5
White Oak	7,682	13	12	1
Whitpain Township	19,377	36	28	8
Wiconisco Township	1,184	1	1	0
Wilkes-Barre	40,418	85	76	9
Wilkes-Barre Township	2,891	15	14	1
Wilkinsburg	15,530	25	23	2
Wilkins Township	6,222	12	12	0
Williamsburg	1,202	1	1	0
Williamsport	28,743	55	51	4
Willistown Township	10,965	20	18	2
Wilson	7,768	13	12	1
Windber	3,901	3	2	1
Womelsdorf	2,854	1	1	0
Woodward Township	2,389	1	1	0

Table 78. Full-Time Law Enforcement Employees, by Selected State and City, 2017—Continued

(Number.)

State/city	Population	Total law enforcement employees	Total officers	Total civilians
Wrightsville	2,280	4	4	0
Wyoming	3,001	5	5	0
Wyomissing	10,415	23	22	1
Yardley	2,455	3	3	0
Yeadon	11,499	14	13	1
York	43,857	120	105	15
York Area Regional	55,256	48	44	4
Youngsville	1,638	2	2	0
Zelienople	3,670	10	9	1
RHODE ISLAND				
Barrington	16,307	33	26	7
Bristol	22,255	48	39	9
Burrillville	16,441	27	21	6
Central Falls	19,389	48	39	9
Charlestown	7,764	25	20	5
Coventry	35,083	69	57	12
Cranston	81,337	180	149	31
Cumberland	34,973	54	43	11
East Greenwich	13,139	42	34	8
East Providence	47,502	104	86	18
Foster	4,736	13	9	4
Glocester	10,108	20	15	5
Hopkinton	8,104	19	14	5
Jamestown	5,483	19	14	5
Johnston	29,375	77	65	12
Lincoln	21,863	43	36	7
Little Compton	3,498	14	10	4
Middletown	15,993	44	40	4
Narragansett	15,556	52	39	13
Newport	24,812	99	81	18
New Shoreham	1,044	8	4	4
North Kingstown	26,069	53	44	9
North Providence	32,641	82	64	18
North Smithfield	12,447	27	26	1
Pawtucket	71,648	170	136	34
Portsmouth	17,381	39	35	4
Providence	179,854	528	431	97
Richmond	7,598	17	12	5
Scituate	10,631	25	17	8
Smithfield	21,884	55	41	14
South Kingstown	30,823	69	52	17
Tiverton	15,767	46	33	13
Warren	10,498	27	22	5
Warwick	81,617	221	169	52
Westerly	22,629	60	50	10
West Greenwich	6,167	18	13	5
West Warwick	28,790	60	48	12
Woonsocket	41,543	112	92	20
SOUTH CAROLINA				
Aiken	31,158	111	80	31
Allendale	2,983	9	9	0
Anderson	27,728	129	93	36
Bamberg	3,300	11	9	2
Barnwell	4,508	12	11	1
Batesburg-Leesville	5,462	24	20	4
Beaufort	13,612	55	51	4
Belton	4,426	12	10	2
Bennettsville	8,127	32	30	2
Blacksburg	1,894	11	10	1
Blackville	2,242	7	6	1
Bluffton	20,024	52	52	0
Bonneau	476	5	3	2
Branchville	968	4	3	1
Briarcliffe Acres	568	1	1	0
Burnettown	2,819	2	2	0
Chapin	1,599	7	7	0
Charleston	136,845	533	439	94
Cheraw	5,770	29	21	8
Chester	5,452	23	21	2
Clemson	16,442	42	31	11
Clinton	8,473	50	43	7
Clio	674	3	3	0
Clover	6,098	27	18	9
Columbia	134,957	386	301	85
Conway	23,806	57	50	7
Cowpens	2,326	6	6	0
Darlington	6,090	35	32	3
Dillon	6,568	27	24	3
Due West	1,300	5	5	0
Duncan	3,405	20	19	1
Easley	21,107	54	45	9
Edisto Beach	419	7	7	0
Ehrhardt	491	3	2	1

Table 78. Full-Time Law Enforcement Employees, by Selected State and City, 2017—Continued

(Number.)

State/city	Population	Total law enforcement employees	Total officers	Total civilians
Elgin	1,582	7	6	1
Florence	38,449	111	87	24
Forest Acres	10,563	33	26	7
Fountain Inn	8,666	29	21	8
Gaffney	12,982	39	36	3
Goose Creek	43,006	91	66	25
Greenville	68,922	244	197	47
Greenwood	23,329	63	57	6
Greer	29,585	80	55	25
Hampton	2,613	12	12	0
Hanahan	24,487	35	32	3
Hardeeville	6,328	25	23	2
Harleyville	693	6	6	0
Hartsville	7,769	31	27	4
Irmo	12,353	26	23	3
Isle of Palms	4,439	28	22	6
Iva	1,296	10	10	0
Jackson	1,794	4	4	0
Johnsonville	1,508	6	5	1
Johnston	2,342	8	8	0
Jonesville	852	5	4	1
Kingstree	3,204	10	9	1
Lake City	6,774	28	23	5
Latta	1,326	6	6	0
Lexington	21,434	59	56	3
Liberty	3,250	14	9	5
Loris	2,695	15	12	3
Lyman	3,513	11	10	1
Manning	4,031	18	17	1
Marion	6,677	21	18	3
Mauldin	25,535	59	48	11
McCormick	2,493	6	6	0
Moncks Corner	10,818	34	31	3
Mount Pleasant	87,216	168	147	21
Mullins	4,502	25	23	2
Myrtle Beach	33,167	304	219	85
Newberry	10,373	33	30	3
New Ellenton	2,160	4	4	0
North Augusta	23,198	89	64	25
North Charleston	111,305	411	339	72
North Myrtle Beach	16,422	148	82	66
Olar	234	1	1	0
Orangeburg	13,076	87	59	28
Pawleys Island	108	7	5	2
Pelion	710	3	2	1
Port Royal	13,161	23	22	1
Ridgeland	4,158	13	12	1
Ridge Spring	754	2	2	0
Ridgeville	1,751	2	2	0
Salem	149	2	2	0
Salley	424	1	1	0
Saluda	3,626	12	10	2
Scranton	861	2	1	1
South Congaree	2,427	7	6	1
Spartanburg	38,057	140	121	19
Springdale	2,817	8	8	0
Summerville	50,498	124	101	23
Sumter	40,747	179	109	70
Surfside Beach	4,488	30	20	10
Tega Cay	10,367	27	24	3
Travelers Rest	5,130	21	16	5
Union	7,940	31	28	3
Walterboro	5,275	33	26	7
Ware Shoals	2,184	9	8	1
Wellford	2,588	7	6	1
West Columbia	16,426	62	51	11
West Pelzer	934	3	3	0
Whitmire	1,480	5	4	1
Williston	2,975	10	9	1
Woodruff	4,209	10	9	1
York	8,108	38	31	7
SOUTH DAKOTA				
Aberdeen	28,800	51	42	9
Alcester	738	2	2	0
Avon	591	1	1	0
Belle Fourche	5,662	12	10	2
Beresford	1,962	4	4	0
Box Elder	9,623	12	11	1
Brandon	10,090	14	13	1
Brookings	24,198	46	34	12
Burke	583	1	1	0
Canton	3,437	6	6	0
Chamberlain	2,364	6	6	0
Clark	1,033	2	2	0

Table 78. Full-Time Law Enforcement Employees, by Selected State and City, 2017—Continued

(Number.)

State/city	Population	Total law enforcement employees	Total officers	Total civilians
Deadwood	1,262	16	13	3
Eagle Butte	1,354	3	3	0
Elk Point	1,831	4	4	0
Faith	420	2	2	0
Flandreau	2,331	7	6	1
Freeman	1,308	1	1	0
Gregory	1,237	2	2	0
Groton	1,517	4	4	0
Hot Springs	3,540	8	7	1
Huron	13,204	34	24	10
Jefferson	501	1	1	0
Kadoka	716	1	1	0
Lead	2,990	6	5	1
Lennox	2,364	4	4	0
Madison	7,584	13	12	1
Martin	1,071	2	2	0
Menno	623	1	1	0
Milbank	3,180	7	7	0
Miller	1,409	4	4	0
Mitchell	15,806	43	27	16
Mobridge	3,587	15	7	8
North Sioux City	2,766	8	7	1
Parkston	1,510	3	3	0
Philip	764	2	2	0
Pierre	14,064	43	26	17
Platte	1,280	2	2	0
Rapid City	74,986	158	126	32
Rosholt	423	1	1	0
Scotland	816	1	1	0
Sioux Falls	177,888	293	258	35
Sisseton	2,426	6	6	0
Spearfish	11,697	31	21	10
Springfield	1,945	2	2	0
Sturgis	6,868	18	15	3
Summerset	2,499	3	3	0
Tea	5,261	6	6	0
Tripp	637	1	1	0
Vermillion	10,892	20	18	2
Viborg	773	1	1	0
Wagner	1,589	6	6	0
Watertown	22,283	55	37	18
Webster	1,795	5	5	0
Whitewood	931	3	3	0
Winner	2,850	10	9	1
Yankton	14,579	28	26	2
TENNESSEE				
Adamsville	2,207	8	7	1
Alamo	2,452	5	4	1
Alcoa	10,128	48	41	7
Alexandria	974	3	3	0
Algood	4,323	11	11	0
Ardmore	1,218	13	8	5
Ashland City	4,642	16	14	2
Athens	13,783	28	26	2
Atoka	9,197	19	18	1
Baileyton	434	3	3	0
Bartlett	58,895	155	121	34
Baxter	1,413	6	6	0
Bean Station	3,090	9	8	1
Belle Meade	2,975	23	16	7
Bells	2,423	5	5	0
Benton	1,307	7	6	1
Berry Hill	536	18	14	4
Big Sandy	533	1	1	0
Blaine	1,879	2	2	0
Bluff City	1,651	8	8	0
Bolivar	5,066	22	20	2
Bradford	989	4	4	0
Brentwood	43,468	77	61	16
Brighton	2,949	7	7	0
Bristol	27,176	87	72	15
Brownsville	9,698	39	34	5
Bruceton	1,427	2	2	0
Burns	1,475	1	1	0
Calhoun	498	3	3	0
Camden	3,546	16	12	4
Carthage	2,283	11	7	4
Caryville	2,161	6	6	0
Celina	1,487	8	6	2
Centerville	3,564	24	14	10
Chapel Hill	1,481	6	6	0
Charleston	678	3	3	0
Chattanooga	178,753	558	483	75
Church Hill	6,739	11	10	1

Table 78. Full-Time Law Enforcement Employees, by Selected State and City, 2017—Continued

(Number.)

State/city	Population	Total law enforcement employees	Total officers	Total civilians
Clarksville	153,294	350	286	64
Cleveland	44,778	103	91	12
Clifton	2,653	7	7	0
Clinton	10,146	40	33	7
Collegedale	12,005	22	22	0
Collierville	49,790	137	101	36
Collinwood	963	4	4	0
Columbia	38,031	97	87	10
Cookeville	32,860	90	69	21
Coopertown	4,455	5	4	1
Cornersville	1,252	2	2	0
Covington	8,909	36	35	1
Cowan	1,678	3	3	0
Cross Plains	1,736	1	1	0
Crossville	11,555	46	43	3
Crump	1,390	2	2	0
Cumberland City	298	2	2	0
Dandridge	2,983	12	11	1
Dayton	7,262	18	18	0
Decatur	1,571	6	6	0
Decaturville	876	1	1	0
Decherd	2,426	13	12	1
Dickson	15,637	52	46	6
Dover	1,450	6	5	1
Dresden	2,825	8	7	1
Dunlap	5,185	14	12	2
Dyer	2,225	8	7	1
Dyersburg	16,612	63	55	8
Eagleville	674	2	2	0
East Ridge	21,351	48	43	5
Elizabethton	13,771	42	38	4
Elkton	541	1	1	0
Englewood	1,530	4	4	0
Erin	1,277	5	5	0
Erwin	5,894	14	14	0
Estill Springs	2,031	6	6	0
Ethridge	482	1	1	0
Etowah	3,512	10	9	1
Fairview	8,648	21	21	0
Fayetteville	7,099	28	26	2
Franklin	76,995	139	129	10
Friendship	658	1	1	0
Gainesboro	944	6	5	1
Gallatin	36,689	90	79	11
Gallaway	653	7	5	2
Gates	611	1	1	0
Gatlinburg	4,247	55	45	10
Germantown	39,086	125	99	26
Gibson	376	2	2	0
Gleason	1,381	4	4	0
Goodlettsville	17,119	54	39	15
Gordonsville	1,209	6	6	0
Grand Junction	275	2	2	0
Graysville	1,525	3	3	0
Greenbrier	6,853	16	15	1
Greeneville	15,065	55	52	3
Greenfield	2,077	7	6	1
Halls	2,148	6	5	1
Harriman	6,196	21	18	3
Henderson	6,589	15	15	0
Hendersonville	58,034	127	111	16
Henry	462	2	2	0
Hohenwald	3,666	16	15	1
Hollow Rock	685	1	1	0
Hornbeak	386	1	1	0
Humboldt	8,210	34	28	6
Huntingdon	3,899	16	12	4
Jacksboro	1,929	5	5	0
Jackson	67,031	253	211	42
Jamestown	1,964	9	9	0
Jasper	3,371	8	8	0
Jefferson City	8,351	31	29	2
Jellico	2,219	7	6	1
Johnson City	67,193	176	146	30
Jonesborough	5,378	21	16	5
Kenton	1,208	4	4	0
Kimball	1,387	9	9	0
Kingsport	52,810	154	117	37
Kingston	5,823	13	12	1
Kingston Springs	2,765	5	4	1
Knoxville	187,539	486	396	90
Lafayette	5,251	22	15	7
La Follette	6,897	34	25	9
La Vergne	35,480	69	56	13
Lawrenceburg	10,780	38	33	5

Table 78. Full-Time Law Enforcement Employees, by Selected State and City, 2017—Continued

(Number.)

State/city	Population	Total law enforcement employees	Total officers	Total civilians
Lebanon	32,248	109	86	23
Lenoir City	9,187	26	24	2
Lewisburg	11,684	29	28	1
Lexington	7,792	32	27	5
Lookout Mountain	1,892	21	16	5
Loretto	1,760	4	4	0
Loudon	5,811	16	15	1
Madisonville	4,805	20	17	3
Manchester	10,702	35	31	4
Martin	10,656	37	28	9
Maryville	28,918	61	55	6
Mason	1,574	5	4	1
Maynardville	2,348	4	4	0
McEwen	1,712	7	5	2
McKenzie	5,610	23	18	5
McMinnville	13,786	38	35	3
Medina	4,290	10	10	0
Memphis	652,765	2,501	1,972	529
Middleton	641	3	3	0
Milan	7,780	31	24	7
Millersville	6,792	13	13	0
Minor Hill	519	2	1	1
Monteagle	1,169	8	7	1
Monterey	2,867	7	6	1
Morristown	29,774	90	83	7
Moscow	524	4	4	0
Mountain City	2,431	8	8	0
Mount Carmel	5,427	8	7	1
Mount Juliet	34,888	68	55	13
Mount Pleasant	4,902	20	14	6
Munford	6,079	16	16	0
Murfreesboro	136,102	275	228	47
Nashville Metropolitan	674,942	1,725	1,394	331
Newbern	3,288	12	12	0
New Johnsonville	1,909	5	5	0
Newport	6,816	31	27	4
Niota	724	5	4	1
Nolensville	7,889	4	4	0
Norris	1,645	7	7	0
Oakland	7,884	18	17	1
Oak Ridge	29,355	77	60	17
Obion	1,064	2	2	0
Oliver Springs	3,255	14	10	4
Oneida	3,716	17	12	5
Paris	10,194	37	26	11
Parsons	2,355	8	8	0
Pigeon Forge	6,254	70	58	12
Pikeville	1,656	3	3	0
Piperton	1,725	8	8	0
Pittman Center	582	5	5	0
Plainview	2,035	1	1	0
Pleasant View	4,382	6	6	0
Portland	12,710	35	31	4
Pulaski	7,742	26	23	3
Puryear	672	1	1	0
Red Bank	11,838	26	24	2
Red Boiling Springs	1,142	4	4	0
Ridgetop	2,061	7	7	0
Ripley	8,067	29	22	7
Rockwood	5,424	16	15	1
Rocky Top	1,779	10	7	3
Rogersville	4,367	17	13	4
Rossville	848	7	7	0
Rutherford	1,101	4	4	0
Rutledge	1,201	5	5	0
Savannah	7,023	21	19	2
Scotts Hill	986	2	2	0
Selmer	4,476	18	16	2
Sevierville	16,991	72	57	15
Sharon	897	1	1	0
Shelbyville	21,618	51	41	10
Signal Mountain	8,624	17	15	2
Smithville	4,717	15	14	1
Smyrna	50,091	98	78	20
Sneedville	1,340	1	1	0
Soddy-Daisy	13,264	37	30	7
Somerville	3,139	13	12	1
South Carthage	1,348	4	4	0
South Fulton	2,238	8	7	1
South Pittsburg	3,097	7	7	0
Sparta	5,101	16	15	1
Spencer	1,634	2	2	0
Spring City	1,990	9	9	0
Springfield	16,869	38	31	7
Spring Hill	39,366	54	50	4

Table 78. Full-Time Law Enforcement Employees, by Selected State and City, 2017—Continued

(Number.)

State/city	Population	Total law enforcement employees	Total officers	Total civilians
Surgoinsville	1,785	1	1	0
Sweetwater	5,957	20	19	1
Tazewell	2,291	6	6	0
Tellico Plains	952	6	5	1
Tiptonville	4,331	7	7	0
Townsend	445	4	4	0
Trenton	4,116	23	17	6
Troy	1,275	4	4	0
Tullahoma	19,386	40	36	4
Tusculum	2,672	2	2	0
Union City	10,544	41	33	8
Vonore	1,506	9	9	0
Wartrace	658	2	1	1
Watertown	1,537	5	5	0
Waverly	4,139	14	13	1
Waynesboro	2,347	7	7	0
Westmoreland	2,328	7	6	1
White Bluff	3,483	5	5	0
White House	11,591	22	19	3
White Pine	2,270	11	10	1
Whiteville	4,481	6	6	0
Whitwell	1,720	6	6	0
Winchester	8,573	24	22	2
Woodbury	2,799	10	9	1
TEXAS				
Abernathy	2,756	5	5	0
Abilene	122,981	260	200	60
Addison	15,795	70	60	10
Alamo	19,351	41	30	11
Alamo Heights	8,507	33	20	13
Allen	101,779	184	127	57
Alpine	5,983	18	12	6
Alton	17,432	23	18	5
Alvarado	4,033	16	14	2
Andrews	14,032	20	19	1
Anna	12,716	15	14	1
Anthony	5,681	15	15	0
Aransas Pass	8,431	37	25	12
Argyle	4,145	11	10	1
Athens	12,826	32	26	6
Atlanta	5,634	17	12	5
Austin	971,949	2,366	1,808	558
Azle	12,266	34	25	9
Baird	1,516	2	2	0
Balch Springs	25,199	53	37	16
Balcones Heights	3,386	25	21	4
Bangs	1,579	3	3	0
Bayou Vista	1,625	6	6	0
Baytown	76,704	214	164	50
Beaumont	118,456	320	250	70
Bedford	49,947	130	81	49
Beeville	13,317	33	25	8
Bellville	4,304	12	11	1
Belton	21,310	48	36	12
Benbrook	23,236	48	38	10
Big Sandy	1,388	6	6	0
Big Spring	28,747	50	37	13
Bishop	3,135	9	5	4
Blue Mound	2,514	12	7	5
Bogata	1,074	4	4	0
Bovina	1,762	3	3	0
Bowie	5,131	19	15	4
Boyd	1,399	5	5	0
Brady	5,414	17	10	7
Brazoria	3,080	12	7	5
Breckenridge	5,530	17	12	5
Brenham	17,187	38	34	4
Bridge City	8,219	21	15	6
Brookside Village	1,587	4	4	0
Brownwood	19,133	53	32	21
Bryan	84,438	177	143	34
Buda	16,857	21	19	2
Bulverde	5,101	17	16	1
Burkburnett	11,142	26	19	7
Burleson	46,531	79	60	19
Cactus	3,176	11	9	2
Caddo Mills	1,587	5	5	0
Calvert	1,135	4	4	0
Carrollton	135,823	219	167	52
Castle Hills	4,533	28	21	7
Castroville	3,058	10	9	1
Cedar Hill	48,904	90	63	27
Celina	8,388	19	18	1
Cibolo	29,323	38	33	5

Table 78. Full-Time Law Enforcement Employees, by Selected State and City, 2017—Continued

(Number.)

State/city	Population	Total law enforcement employees	Total officers	Total civilians
Cisco	3,788	11	9	2
Cleburne	30,320	69	50	19
Clute	11,649	30	20	10
Cockrell Hill	4,294	19	15	4
Coleman	4,388	14	10	4
Colleyville	26,737	45	40	5
Collinsville	1,748	3	3	0
Colorado City	3,977	15	8	7
Combes	3,079	8	8	0
Commerce	9,269	22	16	6
Converse	23,510	58	39	19
Coppell	41,809	67	59	8
Copperas Cove	32,895	69	50	19
Corpus Christi	329,256	604	436	168
Corrigan	1,586	17	13	4
Corsicana	24,011	56	43	13
Crandall	3,415	17	17	0
Crowell	823	1	1	0
Crowley	15,340	36	26	10
Crystal City	7,394	15	10	5
Cuero	8,572	16	15	1
Dalhart	8,366	20	16	4
Dallas	1,338,551	3,658	3,053	605
Dalworthington Gardens	2,403	17	12	5
Dayton	7,815	31	20	11
De Kalb	1,652	5	5	0
Del Rio	35,994	77	56	21
Denison	23,814	48	43	5
Denton	136,836	232	171	61
Denver City	4,909	12	7	5
DeSoto	53,163	127	84	43
Devine	4,847	14	11	3
Diboll	5,363	19	13	6
Dickinson	20,303	48	32	16
Dilley	4,309	10	9	1
Donna	16,641	45	33	12
Driscoll	744	5	3	2
Duncanville	39,603	64	51	13
Eagle Lake	3,722	10	9	1
Early	3,026	10	8	2
Eastland	3,878	12	10	2
Edinburg	89,595	217	161	56
Electra	2,711	13	8	5
El Paso	688,667	1,269	1,043	226
Elsa	6,798	24	18	6
Ennis	19,331	44	36	8
Euless	55,345	131	87	44
Everman	6,417	18	15	3
Fairview	8,547	16	16	0
Farmersville	3,425	12	10	2
Farwell	1,309	3	3	0
Ferris	2,595	16	11	5
Floresville	7,677	19	17	2
Fort Worth	873,069	2,198	1,681	517
Friendswood	39,990	77	57	20
Frisco	172,804	267	173	94
Fulshear	8,350	18	17	1
Fulton	1,616	1	1	0
Gainesville	16,372	52	38	14
Galveston	51,021	197	142	55
Ganado	2,121	3	3	0
Garden Ridge	4,079	14	13	1
Garland	236,243	469	342	127
Georgetown	71,007	127	84	43
Gilmer	5,270	19	15	4
Gladewater	6,422	18	13	5
Glenn Heights	12,509	23	16	7
Godley	1,130	6	6	0
Gonzales	7,734	29	22	7
Grand Prairie	193,249	396	267	129
Grapevine	52,925	146	99	47
Greenville	27,434	66	50	16
Groves	15,701	24	20	4
Haltom City	44,685	85	70	15
Hamlin	2,024	8	5	3
Haskell	3,173	4	4	0
Hawkins	1,305	4	4	0
Hawley	611	1	1	0
Hedwig Village	2,681	23	17	6
Hemphill	1,224	4	4	0
Henderson	13,366	39	29	10
Hereford	14,832	33	27	6
Hewitt	14,443	35	25	10
Hickory Creek	4,413	11	11	0
Hidalgo	14,048	45	35	10

Table 78. Full-Time Law Enforcement Employees, by Selected State and City, 2017—Continued

(Number.)

State/city	Population	Total law enforcement employees	Total officers	Total civilians
Hooks	2,734	7	7	0
Houston	2,338,235	6,334	5,221	1,113
Hughes Springs	1,777	4	4	0
Hutchins	5,693	25	18	7
Indian Lake	657	3	3	0
Ingleside	10,698	21	16	5
Ingram	1,843	7	6	1
Irving	242,062	490	341	149
Jefferson	2,034	7	6	1
Jersey Village	7,938	27	25	2
Josephine	1,328	2	2	0
Joshua	6,983	14	13	1
Jourdanton	4,404	11	10	1
Junction	2,445	4	4	0
Karnes City	3,400	9	8	1
Keller	47,892	84	49	35
Kenedy	3,401	12	11	1
Kennedale	8,032	22	20	2
Kermit	6,459	19	13	6
Kerrville	23,610	66	49	17
Kilgore	15,074	48	36	12
Killeen	145,912	302	237	65
Kingsville	26,048	67	47	20
Kirby	8,746	26	13	13
Knox City	1,167	2	2	0
Kyle	41,189	63	38	25
La Feria	7,279	17	15	2
Lakeside	1,411	3	3	0
Lakeview, Harrison County	6,410	13	12	1
Lake Worth	4,921	31	23	8
La Marque	16,796	41	33	8
Lamesa	9,469	18	14	4
Lampasas	7,910	30	19	11
Laredo	260,669	549	470	79
La Vernia	1,484	7	7	0
Lavon	3,247	10	9	1
League City	105,351	155	110	45
Levelland	13,901	34	23	11
Lewisville	106,199	215	155	60
Liberty	9,308	25	19	6
Linden	1,971	6	5	1
Little Elm	46,097	53	49	4
Live Oak	16,214	46	32	14
Lone Star	1,524	7	4	3
Lytle	2,967	9	8	1
Magnolia	2,107	17	15	2
Mansfield	67,233	222	98	124
Manvel	9,756	23	18	5
Marshall	23,564	63	47	16
McAllen	144,162	413	282	131
McKinney	179,934	245	192	53
Melissa	9,270	11	11	0
Memorial Villages	12,319	43	31	12
Mercedes	16,762	38	29	9
Merkel	2,613	6	6	0
Mesquite	144,406	307	219	88
Midland	138,954	239	182	57
Midlothian	24,617	72	46	26
Mineola	4,756	17	13	4
Mineral Wells	14,534	39	28	11
Missouri City	75,863	125	97	28
Monahans	7,765	17	11	6
Montgomery	985	11	10	1
Muleshoe	5,160	14	9	5
Nassau Bay	4,073	14	13	1
Natalia	1,537	5	5	0
Navasota	7,604	26	17	9
Nederland	17,344	40	26	14
New Boston	4,667	18	12	6
Nixon	2,514	5	5	0
North Richland Hills	70,910	184	110	74
Oak Ridge	194	2	2	0
Odessa	121,194	210	160	50
Olmos Park	2,448	14	13	1
Olney	3,147	7	6	1
Omaha	993	2	2	0
Orange	19,552	59	44	15
Ovilla	4,060	10	9	1
Palacios	4,676	16	11	5
Palmer	2,081	11	10	1
Panhandle	2,358	4	4	0
Paris	24,978	81	57	24
Parker	4,541	10	9	1
Pasadena	154,000	358	263	95
Patton Village	1,953	9	8	1

Table 78. Full-Time Law Enforcement Employees, by Selected State and City, 2017—Continued

(Number.)

State/city	Population	Total law enforcement employees	Total officers	Total civilians
Pearsall	10,222	16	14	2
Pecos	9,820	45	19	26
Penitas	4,935	18	16	2
Pinehurst	2,085	8	6	2
Plainview	20,641	39	33	6
Pleasanton	10,563	29	22	7
Port Aransas	4,156	28	20	8
Port Arthur	55,583	143	113	30
Port Isabel	5,017	23	18	5
Poteet	3,476	11	10	1
Pottsboro	2,330	10	8	2
Primera	4,860	8	7	1
Princeton	9,934	17	16	1
Prosper	20,442	33	24	9
Queen City	1,464	6	6	0
Rancho Viejo	2,504	8	8	0
Ranger	2,454	4	4	0
Raymondville	11,151	24	15	9
Red Oak	12,833	25	22	3
Reno	3,324	5	5	0
Richland Hills	8,176	20	16	4
Rio Grande City	14,592	43	31	12
Rio Hondo	2,650	7	7	0
River Oaks	7,793	24	18	6
Robinson	11,653	30	22	8
Rockport	10,870	29	26	3
Roma	10,345	37	28	9
Royse City	12,599	22	19	3
Sabinal	1,711	5	4	1
Sachse	25,907	44	27	17
Saginaw	22,994	45	37	8
San Angelo	101,931	201	172	29
San Antonio	1,520,712	2,929	2,305	624
San Benito	24,503	47	39	8
Sansom Park Village	4,904	14	9	5
Santa Fe	13,347	26	20	6
Schertz	40,830	71	53	18
Seabrook	13,958	42	32	10
Seagoville	16,290	32	23	9
Seagraves	2,892	7	5	2
Seguin	29,132	72	52	20
Selma	11,117	34	30	4
Seminole	7,795	14	12	2
Seymour	2,717	7	6	1
Shallowater	2,560	5	5	0
Shavano Park	3,801	19	18	1
Shenandoah	3,019	24	23	1
Sherman	42,122	87	65	22
Shiner	2,148	7	7	0
Shoreacres	1,617	6	6	0
Sinton	5,614	12	11	1
Sour Lake	1,835	8	7	1
South Houston	17,537	42	31	11
Southlake	31,778	76	70	6
South Padre Island	2,881	35	26	9
Southside Place	1,857	12	8	4
Spearman	3,332	4	4	0
Spring Valley	4,312	24	19	5
Stafford	18,530	74	57	17
Stamford	2,961	7	6	1
Stanton	3,069	5	5	0
Stratford	2,092	3	3	0
Sullivan City	4,223	12	8	4
Sulphur Springs	16,281	38	27	11
Sunset Valley	704	14	13	1
Sweeny	3,773	8	8	0
Sweetwater	10,726	30	24	6
Terrell	17,579	58	36	22
Texarkana	37,882	101	89	12
Texas City	48,774	105	83	22
The Colony	43,484	95	62	33
Three Rivers	1,956	11	10	1
Tioga	958	2	2	0
Tool	2,284	10	6	4
Trophy Club	12,999	20	16	4
Tulia	4,673	17	9	8
Tye	1,260	5	5	0
Tyler	106,115	231	187	44
Universal City	20,668	41	31	10
University Park	25,218	53	39	14
Van Alstyne	3,700	12	8	4
Venus	3,535	12	12	0
Vernon	10,378	26	18	8
Waco	135,997	338	248	90
Waelder	1,133	4	4	0

Table 78. Full-Time Law Enforcement Employees, by Selected State and City, 2017—Continued

(Number.)

State/city	Population	Total law enforcement employees	Total officers	Total civilians
Wake Village	5,448	9	8	1
Watauga	24,814	40	32	8
Webster	11,149	67	49	18
Weimar	2,173	8	7	1
Westover Hills	714	14	10	4
West University Place	15,676	35	25	10
Wharton	8,769	35	26	9
White Oak	6,343	20	16	4
White Settlement	17,385	44	33	11
Wichita Falls	104,706	275	193	82
Willis	6,450	18	16	2
Wills Point	3,622	11	10	1
Windcrest	5,939	35	26	9
Winnsboro	3,356	14	9	5
Wylie	48,772	67	62	5
Yoakum	6,055	18	12	6
UTAH				
Alta	388	8	4	4
American Fork/Cedar Hills	39,603	45	38	7
Big Water	480	1	1	0
Blanding	4,161	6	5	1
Bluffdale	12,718	11	11	0
Bountiful	44,312	53	36	17
Brian Head	90	5	5	0
Brigham City	19,150	28	25	3
Cedar City	31,624	44	39	5
Centerville	17,635	23	18	5
Clearfield	30,994	48	33	15
Clinton	21,860	20	17	3
Cottonwood Heights	34,400	52	43	9
Draper	48,197	48	39	9
East Carbon	1,555	4	4	0
Enoch	6,691	6	4	2
Ephraim	7,240	5	5	0
Fairview	1,296	1	1	0
Farmington	24,040	22	19	3
Garland	2,500	3	3	0
Grantsville	10,731	15	13	2
Gunnison	3,323	6	4	2
Harrisville	6,512	10	9	1
Heber	15,653	25	19	6
Helper	2,077	6	5	1
Hurricane	16,592	26	23	3
Kamas	2,155	6	6	0
Kanab	4,562	7	6	1
Kaysville	31,873	28	25	3
La Verkin	4,277	3	3	0
Layton	77,048	111	78	33
Lehi	63,605	64	54	10
Lindon	11,085	17	15	2
Logan	51,059	85	54	31
Lone Peak	29,691	25	20	5
Mapleton	9,772	9	8	1
Moab	5,266	16	11	5
Monticello	2,257	3	3	0
Moroni	1,491	1	1	0
Mount Pleasant	3,380	4	4	0
Murray	49,650	86	73	13
Myton	633	1	1	0
Naples	2,203	6	5	1
Nephi	5,859	12	10	2
North Ogden	19,021	23	19	4
North Park	15,658	12	10	2
North Salt Lake	21,053	27	22	5
Ogden	87,323	181	140	41
Orem	99,045	122	88	34
Park City	8,415	34	30	4
Parowan	3,018	6	5	1
Payson	20,010	25	22	3
Perry	4,902	8	7	1
Pleasant Grove	39,666	36	28	8
Pleasant View	10,036	10	9	1
Price	8,313	19	17	2
Provo	117,540	156	105	51
Richfield	7,755	16	15	1
Riverdale	8,745	22	19	3
Roosevelt	7,057	11	10	1
Roy	38,410	42	38	4
Salem	8,086	11	10	1
Salina	2,561	5	4	1
Salt Lake City	194,968	562	450	112
Sandy	96,957	144	109	35
Santa Clara/Ivins	15,615	17	14	3
Santaquin/Genola	12,900	13	12	1

Table 78. Full-Time Law Enforcement Employees, by Selected State and City, 2017—Continued

(Number.)

State/city	Population	Total law enforcement employees	Total officers	Total civilians
Saratoga Springs	28,739	24	21	3
Smithfield	11,409	13	12	1
South Jordan	72,533	56	50	6
South Ogden	17,177	25	22	3
South Salt Lake	24,811	67	56	11
Spanish Fork	39,512	40	36	4
Springdale	577	10	8	2
Springville	33,617	37	26	11
St. George	84,007	147	104	43
Stockton	649	3	2	1
Sunset	5,246	9	8	1
Syracuse	29,114	25	23	2
Tooele	34,112	44	36	8
Tremonton	8,551	11	9	2
Washington	26,618	28	24	4
Wellington	1,596	2	2	0
West Bountiful	5,625	10	9	1
West Jordan	115,390	145	110	35
West Valley	137,762	239	197	42
Willard	1,818	3	3	0
Woods Cross	11,627	22	19	3
VERMONT				
Barre	8,655	20	20	0
Barre Town	7,768	8	7	1
Bellows Falls	2,996	10	9	1
Bennington	15,215	32	24	8
Berlin	2,789	8	7	1
Bradford	2,711	2	2	0
Brandon	3,778	7	6	1
Brattleboro	11,536	34	22	12
Brighton	1,170	1	1	0
Bristol	3,908	3	3	0
Burlington	42,230	139	98	41
Canaan	924	1	1	0
Castleton	4,528	5	5	0
Chester	3,039	6	5	1
Colchester	17,353	32	25	7
Dover	1,076	8	7	1
Essex	21,470	31	25	6
Fair Haven	2,572	4	4	0
Hardwick	2,862	8	7	1
Hartford	9,628	26	17	9
Hinesburg	4,561	5	5	0
Killington	777	2	2	0
Ludlow	1,894	9	5	4
Lyndonville	1,166	3	3	0
Manchester	4,299	13	9	4
Middlebury	8,681	17	15	2
Milton	10,825	17	16	1
Montpelier	7,484	24	16	8
Morristown	5,475	11	11	0
Newport	4,287	14	12	2
Northfield	6,014	7	6	1
Norwich	3,343	4	3	1
Pittsford	2,826	1	1	0
Randolph	4,712	5	5	0
Richmond	4,120	6	6	0
Rutland	15,462	50	38	12
Rutland Town	4,061	3	3	0
Shelburne	7,827	19	11	8
South Burlington	19,146	47	38	9
Springfield	8,993	23	17	6
St. Albans	6,772	30	23	7
St. Johnsbury	7,196	15	9	6
Stowe	4,440	13	13	0
Swanton	6,529	6	6	0
Thetford	2,576	3	3	0
Vergennes	2,593	7	7	0
Weathersfield	2,767	2	2	0
Williston	9,731	17	15	2
Wilmington	1,807	8	6	2
Windsor	3,398	9	9	0
Winhall	750	11	10	1
Winooski	7,105	20	16	4
Woodstock	2,938	9	6	3
VIRGINIA				
Abingdon	8,066	28	25	3
Alexandria	158,256	415	317	98
Altavista	3,470	13	13	0
Amherst	2,201	6	6	0
Appalachia	1,638	5	5	0
Ashland	7,722	29	26	3
Bedford	6,622	26	24	2

Table 78. Full-Time Law Enforcement Employees, by Selected State and City, 2017—Continued

(Number.)

State/city	Population	Total law enforcement employees	Total officers	Total civilians
Berryville	4,324	9	8	1
Big Stone Gap	5,334	16	15	1
Blacksburg	45,443	75	63	12
Blackstone	3,427	12	11	1
Bluefield	4,894	21	16	5
Boykins	539	1	1	0
Bridgewater	6,119	9	9	0
Bristol	16,795	72	52	20
Broadway	3,889	5	5	0
Brookneal	1,117	2	2	0
Buena Vista	6,413	17	16	1
Burkeville	402	1	1	0
Cape Charles	1,044	6	6	0
Cedar Bluff	1,049	3	3	0
Charlottesville	47,446	151	123	28
Chase City	2,268	10	9	1
Chatham	1,473	3	3	0
Chesapeake	240,119	561	379	182
Chilhowie	1,712	6	6	0
Chincoteague	2,916	14	10	4
Christiansburg	22,272	65	60	5
Clarksville	1,181	8	7	1
Clifton Forge	3,689	12	10	2
Clintwood	1,285	4	4	0
Coeburn	1,970	5	5	0
Colonial Beach	3,577	13	11	2
Colonial Heights	17,820	57	53	4
Covington	5,442	29	18	11
Crewe	2,199	6	5	1
Culpeper	18,232	51	42	9
Damascus	796	4	4	0
Danville	41,680	131	120	11
Dayton	1,621	8	7	1
Dublin	2,710	8	7	1
Dumfries	5,219	9	9	0
Elkton	2,871	6	5	1
Emporia	5,201	35	24	11
Exmore	1,438	6	6	0
Fairfax City	24,406	77	58	19
Falls Church	14,278	42	33	9
Farmville	8,127	29	27	2
Franklin	8,250	34	26	8
Fredericksburg	29,016	93	65	28
Front Royal	15,270	47	36	11
Galax	6,728	39	23	16
Gate City	1,911	4	4	0
Glade Spring	1,446	2	2	0
Glasgow	1,117	1	1	0
Glen Lyn	118	1	1	0
Gordonsville	1,599	7	7	0
Gretna	1,231	3	3	0
Grottoes	2,821	6	6	0
Grundy	949	6	6	0
Halifax	1,240	3	3	0
Hampton	134,929	361	265	96
Harrisonburg	53,717	117	99	18
Haymarket	2,001	6	6	0
Haysi	473	2	2	0
Herndon	24,561	72	56	16
Hillsville	2,643	15	14	1
Honaker	1,352	4	3	1
Hopewell	22,723	82	63	19
Hurt	1,260	2	2	0
Independence	919	2	2	0
Jonesville	948	4	4	0
Kenbridge	1,214	3	3	0
Kilmarnock	1,431	5	5	0
La Crosse	581	1	1	0
Lawrenceville	1,019	6	6	0
Lebanon	3,260	14	13	1
Leesburg	54,393	93	77	16
Lexington	7,034	20	17	3
Louisa	1,665	6	6	0
Luray	4,804	13	12	1
Lynchburg	80,890	196	171	25
Manassas	41,995	114	90	24
Manassas Park	16,158	39	30	9
Marion	5,837	21	20	1
Martinsville	13,383	50	45	5
Middleburg	856	7	6	1
Middletown	1,345	4	3	1
Mount Jackson	2,048	6	6	0
Narrows	1,963	5	5	0
New Market	2,217	5	5	0
Newport News	181,738	579	431	148

Table 78. Full-Time Law Enforcement Employees, by Selected State and City, 2017—Continued

(Number.)

State/city	Population	Total law enforcement employees	Total officers	Total civilians
Norfolk	245,190	799	713	86
Norton	3,842	25	17	8
Occoquan	1,082	1	1	0
Onancock	1,266	5	5	0
Onley	513	5	5	0
Orange	5,033	17	15	2
Parksley	841	3	3	0
Pearisburg	2,683	7	7	0
Pembroke	1,086	3	3	0
Pennington Gap	1,759	6	6	0
Petersburg	31,739	114	90	24
Poquoson	11,981	25	24	1
Portsmouth	95,100	297	222	75
Pound	945	5	5	0
Pulaski	8,799	32	28	4
Purcellville	9,779	17	15	2
Quantico	550	1	1	0
Radford	17,641	47	36	11
Remington	637	1	1	0
Rich Creek	752	1	1	0
Richlands	5,365	23	18	5
Richmond	226,236	835	695	140
Roanoke	100,027	302	254	48
Rocky Mount	4,801	21	19	2
Rural Retreat	1,480	1	1	0
Salem	25,624	86	62	24
Saltville	1,998	7	7	0
Shenandoah	2,328	6	5	1
Smithfield	8,492	23	19	4
South Boston	7,919	31	28	3
South Hill	4,449	22	20	2
Stanley	1,643	5	5	0
Staunton	24,423	62	49	13
Stephens City	1,990	4	4	0
St. Paul	899	6	6	0
Strasburg	6,613	18	17	1
Suffolk	89,922	249	188	61
Tangier	722	1	1	0
Tappahannock	2,386	10	9	1
Tazewell	4,320	15	13	2
Timberville	2,659	6	6	0
Victoria	1,663	3	3	0
Vienna	16,590	50	41	9
Vinton	8,207	24	22	2
Virginia Beach	454,353	984	805	179
Warrenton	9,901	27	25	2
Warsaw	1,483	4	3	1
Waverly	2,033	7	7	0
Waynesboro	22,004	52	42	10
Weber City	1,234	4	4	0
West Point	3,313	10	9	1
White Stone	340	2	2	0
Williamsburg	15,464	41	38	3
Winchester	27,715	80	72	8
Windsor	2,694	6	6	0
Wise	3,056	13	12	1
Woodstock	5,272	18	16	2
Wytheville	8,084	29	25	4
WASHINGTON				
Aberdeen	16,243	51	37	14
Airway Heights	8,460	19	18	1
Algona	3,177	8	7	1
Anacortes	16,838	33	26	7
Arlington	19,302	29	24	5
Asotin	1,302	3	3	0
Auburn	78,718	131	113	18
Bainbridge Island	24,635	25	22	3
Battle Ground	20,516	28	24	4
Bellevue	143,703	212	172	40
Bellingham	88,652	176	117	59
Black Diamond	4,422	10	9	1
Blaine	5,245	15	13	2
Bonney Lake	20,844	34	29	5
Bothell	45,357	84	59	25
Bremerton	41,173	67	54	13
Brewster	2,335	6	5	1
Brier	6,840	8	7	1
Buckley	5,234	11	9	2
Burien	51,479	74	52	22
Burlington	8,830	31	26	5
Camas	22,973	30	27	3
Carnation	2,032	3	2	1
Castle Rock	2,228	5	4	1
Centralia	17,048	37	28	9

Table 78. Full-Time Law Enforcement Employees, by Selected State and City, 2017—Continued

(Number.)

State/city	Population	Total law enforcement employees	Total officers	Total civilians
Chehalis	7,538	23	18	5
Cheney	12,510	21	15	6
Chewelah	2,641	6	5	1
Clarkston	7,359	16	14	2
Cle Elum	2,895	8	7	1
Clyde Hill	3,316	10	8	2
Colfax	2,913	5	5	0
College Place	9,198	13	11	2
Colville	4,805	11	9	2
Connell	5,656	7	7	0
Cosmopolis	1,593	6	5	1
Coulee Dam	1,088	3	3	0
Coupeville	1,934	2	2	0
Covington	21,001	24	18	6
Des Moines	31,415	44	34	10
Dupont	9,721	13	11	2
Duvall	7,875	12	12	0
East Wenatchee	14,097	23	20	3
Eatonville	2,994	5	4	1
Edgewood	10,984	9	9	0
Edmonds	42,197	61	52	9
Ellensburg	20,026	37	29	8
Elma	3,044	8	7	1
Enumclaw	11,745	29	15	14
Ephrata	8,086	19	16	3
Everett	110,040	231	192	39
Everson	4,217	7	6	1
Federal Way	98,014	156	127	29
Ferndale	13,757	22	19	3
Fife	10,264	40	30	10
Fircrest	6,830	9	9	0
Forks	3,822	12	6	6
Gig Harbor	9,494	21	19	2
Goldendale	3,455	8	7	1
Grand Coulee	2,051	8	8	0
Grandview	11,203	23	18	5
Granger	3,803	6	6	0
Hoquiam	8,386	25	24	1
Issaquah	38,592	65	36	29
Kalama	2,509	7	6	1
Kelso	12,070	31	27	4
Kenmore	22,673	20	16	4
Kennewick	81,499	114	99	15
Kent	128,990	201	146	55
Kettle Falls	1,609	3	2	1
Kirkland	88,898	136	99	37
Kittitas	1,452	2	2	0
La Center	3,177	9	7	2
Lacey	48,597	62	49	13
Lake Forest Park	13,375	22	19	3
Lake Stevens	32,288	37	29	8
Lakewood	61,080	114	99	15
Langley	1,111	4	4	0
Liberty Lake	9,505	13	12	1
Long Beach	1,389	8	7	1
Longview	37,424	69	57	12
Lynden	14,302	19	15	4
Lynnwood	38,469	97	68	29
Mabton	2,292	5	5	0
Maple Valley	26,214	25	20	5
Marysville	68,950	92	66	26
Mattawa	4,423	5	5	0
McCleary	1,627	4	4	0
Medina	3,293	11	9	2
Mercer Island	25,553	35	31	4
Mill Creek	20,664	31	25	6
Milton	8,121	13	13	0
Monroe	18,596	42	30	12
Montesano	3,902	9	8	1
Morton	1,149	3	3	0
Moses Lake	22,985	40	32	8
Mountlake Terrace	21,402	34	27	7
Mount Vernon	35,085	55	42	13
Moxee	4,120	6	5	1
Mukilteo	21,662	36	29	7
Napavine	1,881	2	2	0
Newcastle	11,775	13	10	3
Normandy Park	6,702	9	8	1
Oak Harbor	23,371	37	24	13
Ocean Shores	5,872	9	9	0
Odessa	863	2	2	0
Olympia	51,923	98	68	30
Omak	4,829	12	11	1
Oroville	1,673	6	5	1
Orting	7,863	12	11	1

Table 78. Full-Time Law Enforcement Employees, by Selected State and City, 2017—Continued

(Number.)

State/city	Population	Total law enforcement employees	Total officers	Total civilians
Othello	8,225	25	16	9
Pacific	7,210	13	11	2
Palouse	1,053	3	3	0
Pasco	72,146	87	78	9
Pe Ell	645	1	1	0
Port Angeles	19,964	58	31	27
Port Orchard	14,253	24	22	2
Port Townsend	9,596	17	14	3
Poulsbo	10,600	23	19	4
Prosser	6,091	14	13	1
Pullman	33,897	43	29	14
Puyallup	41,242	78	55	23
Quincy	7,488	23	16	7
Raymond	2,872	7	6	1
Reardan	567	1	1	0
Redmond	63,889	124	82	42
Renton	102,470	151	121	30
Republic	1,069	2	2	0
Richland	56,151	77	63	14
Ridgefield	7,532	11	10	1
Ritzville	1,617	4	4	0
Roy	827	2	1	1
Royal City	2,203	3	3	0
Ruston	828	3	3	0
Sammamish	64,857	40	32	8
SeaTac	29,200	62	45	17
Seattle	721,365	1,963	1,448	515
Sedro Woolley	11,545	18	15	3
Selah	7,839	18	15	3
Sequim	7,025	22	19	3
Shelton	10,000	20	18	2
Shoreline	55,703	71	52	19
Snohomish	10,045	20	18	2
Snoqualmie	13,648	26	22	4
Soap Lake	1,574	5	4	1
South Bend	1,637	5	4	1
Spokane	217,066	409	319	90
Spokane Valley	97,430	127	97	30
Stanwood	7,142	13	11	2
Steilacoom	6,364	11	10	1
Sumas	1,426	6	5	1
Sumner	10,060	22	18	4
Sunnyside	16,480	53	28	25
Tacoma	213,504	372	334	38
Tenino	1,842	5	4	1
Tieton	1,292	3	2	1
Toledo	740	5	4	1
Tonasket	1,010	5	4	1
Toppenish	8,974	17	13	4
Tukwila	20,183	93	76	17
Tumwater	22,961	35	29	6
Twisp	957	3	3	0
Union Gap	6,104	24	22	2
University Place	33,662	16	15	1
Vancouver	176,884	254	205	49
Walla Walla	32,189	77	47	30
Wapato	5,073	14	11	3
Warden	2,722	5	4	1
Washougal	15,698	25	20	5
Wenatchee	34,191	48	38	10
Westport	2,027	8	7	1
West Richland	14,603	23	19	4
White Salmon	2,495	7	6	1
Winthrop	436	3	2	1
Woodinville	12,181	19	15	4
Woodland	6,022	11	9	2
Yakima	94,375	184	138	46
Yelm	9,304	15	13	2
Zillah	3,162	9	8	1
WEST VIRGINIA				
Alderson	1,171	3	3	0
Anmoore	747	1	1	0
Ansted	1,368	3	2	1
Athens	924	1	1	0
Barboursville	4,315	24	22	2
Barrackville	1,312	3	2	1
Beckley	16,862	69	50	19
Belington	1,908	3	3	0
Belle	1,181	4	4	0
Benwood	1,332	6	6	0
Berkeley Springs	608	2	2	0
Bethlehem	2,381	5	5	0
Bluefield	10,148	33	27	6
Bradshaw	290	1	1	0

Table 78. Full-Time Law Enforcement Employees, by Selected State and City, 2017—Continued

(Number.)

State/city	Population	Total law enforcement employees	Total officers	Total civilians
Bramwell	350	2	2	0
Bridgeport	8,401	35	31	4
Buckhannon	5,610	11	10	1
Burnsville	494	2	2	0
Cameron	882	3	3	0
Capon Bridge	371	2	2	0
Cedar Grove	929	1	1	0
Ceredo	1,365	9	5	4
Chapmanville	1,161	5	5	0
Charleston	48,788	187	163	24
Charles Town	6,062	17	15	2
Chesapeake	1,469	3	3	0
Chester	2,456	6	5	1
Clarksburg	15,946	43	39	4
Clendenin	1,164	4	4	0
Danville	632	1	1	0
Davy	364	1	1	0
Delbarton	519	3	3	0
Dunbar	7,486	17	16	1
Eleanor	1,617	2	2	0
Elkins	7,188	14	12	2
Fairmont	18,604	39	33	6
Farmington	374	2	1	1
Fayetteville	2,839	10	10	0
Follansbee	2,816	7	7	0
Fort Gay	665	3	3	0
Gary	850	1	1	0
Gassaway	901	1	1	0
Gauley Bridge	580	1	1	0
Gilbert	407	2	2	0
Glasgow	865	4	4	0
Glen Dale	1,433	11	6	5
Glenville	1,512	3	3	0
Grafton	5,121	9	8	1
Grantsville	535	1	1	0
Grant Town	611	1	1	0
Granville	3,238	15	15	0
Hamlin	1,110	1	1	0
Handley	334	1	1	0
Harpers Ferry/Bolivar	1,339	3	2	1
Harrisville	1,731	1	1	0
Hartford City	589	1	1	0
Hinton	2,436	6	5	1
Huntington	47,933	100	97	3
Hurricane	6,658	18	16	2
Iaeger	261	1	1	0
Kenova	3,029	13	8	5
Kermit	366	1	1	0
Keyser	5,163	15	10	5
Kimball	170	1	1	0
Kingwood	2,959	2	2	0
Lewisburg	3,935	14	12	2
Logan	1,572	11	8	3
Lumberport	856	1	1	0
Mabscott	1,341	5	3	2
Madison	2,831	8	6	2
Man	671	3	3	0
Mannington	2,058	4	4	0
Marmet	1,417	5	5	0
Martinsburg	17,761	52	43	9
Mason	927	7	6	1
Matewan	447	2	1	1
McMechen	1,802	5	4	1
Milton	2,648	8	7	1
Monongah	1,116	1	1	0
Montgomery	1,567	4	4	0
Moorefield	2,460	10	9	1
Morgantown	31,215	89	78	11
Moundsville	8,691	20	16	4
Mount Hope	1,341	5	4	1
Mullens	1,419	4	4	0
New Cumberland	1,043	2	2	0
New Haven	1,508	1	1	0
New Martinsville	5,151	15	11	4
Nitro	6,645	19	17	2
Nutter Fort	1,565	6	6	0
Oak Hill	8,490	19	15	4
Oceana	1,263	4	4	0
Paden City	2,465	4	3	1
Parkersburg	30,475	83	70	13
Parsons	1,416	1	1	0
Paw Paw	491	2	1	1
Pennsboro	1,055	1	1	0
Petersburg	2,601	2	2	0
Philippi	3,640	6	6	0

Table 78. Full-Time Law Enforcement Employees, by Selected State and City, 2017—Continued

(Number.)

State/city	Population	Total law enforcement employees	Total officers	Total civilians
Piedmont	828	1	1	
Pineville	611	3	3	0
Point Pleasant	4,219	9	8	1
Pratt	582	3	3	0
Princeton	5,935	21	19	2
Rainelle	1,465	5	4	1
Ranson	5,303	16	15	1
Ravenswood	3,817	11	10	1
Rhodell	166	2	1	1
Richwood	1,940	3	3	0
Ridgeley	638	1	1	0
Ripley	3,243	10	9	1
Rivesville	934	1	1	0
Romney	1,746	4	3	1
Ronceverte	1,731	6	6	0
Salem	1,533	3	3	0
Shepherdstown	1,965	6	5	1
Shinnston	2,154	8	8	0
Sistersville	1,313	4	4	0
Smithers	771	2	2	0
Sophia	1,306	2	2	0
South Charleston	12,756	47	44	3
Spencer	2,136	6	6	0
St. Albans	10,476	28	26	2
Star City	2,059	7	7	0
St. Marys	1,834	4	4	0
Stonewood	1,744	2	2	0
Summersville	3,411	17	16	1
Sutton	1,040	2	2	0
Sylvester	147	1	1	0
Terra Alta	1,493	2	2	0
Triadelphia	754	1	1	0
Vienna	10,409	24	20	4
War	735	2	2	0
Wayne	1,356	3	2	1
Webster Springs	715	5	4	1
Weirton	18,870	39	35	4
Welch	1,735	6	5	1
Wellsburg	2,634	7	6	1
West Liberty	1,430	1	1	0
West Logan	383	1	1	0
West Milford	613	2	2	0
Weston	4,035	9	7	2
Westover	4,283	13	12	1
Wheeling	27,196	77	66	11
White Hall	659	4	4	0
White Sulphur Springs	2,417	7	6	1
Whitesville	459	2	2	0
Williamson	2,883	6	5	1
Williamstown	2,946	8	7	1
Winfield	2,366	6	6	0
WISCONSIN				
Adams	1,878	5	5	0
Albany	1,010	3	3	0
Algoma	3,086	8	4	4
Alma	712	1	1	0
Altoona	7,624	15	14	1
Amery	2,825	6	6	0
Antigo	7,807	18	15	3
Appleton	74,660	133	107	26
Arcadia	3,077	4	4	0
Ashland	7,915	20	19	1
Ashwaubenon	17,326	57	50	7
Athens	1,090	1	1	0
Balsam Lake	975	1	1	0
Bangor	1,487	3	3	0
Baraboo	12,191	34	29	5
Barneveld	1,226	1	1	0
Barron	3,294	6	6	0
Bayfield	473	3	3	0
Bayside	4,398	13	12	1
Beaver Dam	16,525	35	31	4
Belleville	2,438	7	6	1
Beloit	36,724	81	70	11
Beloit Town	7,648	15	13	2
Berlin	5,371	12	11	1
Big Bend	1,324	5	4	1
Birchwood	425	1	1	0
Black River Falls	3,541	6	5	1
Blair	1,384	3	3	0
Bloomer	3,503	7	6	1
Bloomfield	6,295	8	8	0
Blue Mounds	967	2	2	0
Boscobel	3,137	6	6	0

Table 78. Full-Time Law Enforcement Employees, by Selected State and City, 2017—Continued

(Number.)

State/city	Population	Total law enforcement employees	Total officers	Total civilians
Boyceville	1,099	1	1	0
Brillion	3,121	8	8	0
Brodhead	3,274	12	8	4
Brookfield	38,033	87	70	17
Brookfield Township	6,108	14	13	1
Brown Deer	12,015	34	31	3
Burlington	10,686	26	20	6
Butler	1,817	8	7	1
Caledonia	24,945	36	34	2
Campbellsport	1,971	1	1	0
Campbell Township	4,380	5	5	0
Cashton	1,100	2	2	0
Cedarburg	11,529	26	19	7
Chenequa	588	9	8	1
Chetek	2,155	5	4	1
Chilton	3,809	7	7	0
Chippewa Falls	14,141	27	23	4
Cleveland	1,455	2	2	0
Clinton	2,122	5	5	0
Clintonville	4,379	15	11	4
Colby-Abbotsford	4,079	8	7	1
Colfax	1,161	1	1	0
Columbus	5,035	11	9	2
Cornell	1,419	2	2	0
Cottage Grove	7,105	15	13	2
Crandon	1,850	4	3	1
Cross Plains	4,236	6	5	1
Cuba City	2,050	4	4	0
Cudahy	18,191	40	30	10
Cumberland	2,130	5	5	0
Darlington	2,365	5	5	0
Deforest	9,818	21	18	3
Delafield	7,563	18	16	2
Delavan	9,986	28	23	5
Delavan Town	5,333	12	11	1
De Pere	25,066	40	36	4
Dodgeville	4,737	10	10	0
Durand	1,833	3	3	0
Eagle River	1,423	7	6	1
Eagle Village	2,006	2	2	0
East Troy	4,283	7	7	0
Eau Claire	68,687	136	98	38
Edgar	1,450	1	1	0
Edgerton	5,574	11	10	1
Eleva	670	1	1	0
Elkhart Lake	965	3	3	0
Elkhorn	9,817	18	16	2
Ellsworth	3,220	5	5	0
Elm Grove	6,216	26	18	8
Elroy	1,354	3	3	0
Evansville	5,305	11	10	1
Everest Metropolitan	17,321	30	26	4
Fall Creek	1,304	2	2	0
Fall River	1,681	2	2	0
Fennimore	2,485	5	5	0
Fitchburg	29,535	62	50	12
Fond du Lac	42,929	81	73	8
Fontana	1,718	7	6	1
Fort Atkinson	12,566	25	19	6
Fox Lake	1,461	3	3	0
Fox Point	6,694	18	17	1
Fox Valley Metro	21,789	28	26	2
Franklin	36,248	75	59	16
Frederic	1,091	1	1	0
Freedom	6,132	2	2	0
Galesville	1,546	4	4	0
Geneva Town	5,049	8	7	1
Genoa City	3,019	7	6	1
Germantown	20,072	43	32	11
Gillett	1,328	3	3	0
Gilman	393	1	1	0
Glendale	12,763	49	43	6
Grafton	11,579	29	22	7
Grand Chute	22,667	36	31	5
Grand Rapids	7,392	8	6	2
Grantsburg	1,279	3	3	0
Green Bay	105,331	224	185	39
Greendale	14,242	38	29	9
Greenfield	36,882	75	57	18
Green Lake	933	3	3	0
Hales Corners	7,675	18	16	2
Hammond	1,886	4	3	1
Hartford	14,664	29	25	4
Hartland	9,229	18	16	2
Hayward	2,313	8	7	1

Table 78. Full-Time Law Enforcement Employees, by Selected State and City, 2017—Continued

(Number.)

State/city	Population	Total law enforcement employees	Total officers	Total civilians
Hazel Green	1,241	2	2	0
Highland	836	1	1	0
Hillsboro	1,423	5	5	0
Hobart-Lawrence	14,231	10	9	1
Holmen	9,714	13	12	1
Horicon	3,657	8	7	1
Hortonville	2,739	6	5	1
Hudson	13,788	28	25	3
Hurley	1,448	7	6	1
Independence	1,336	3	3	0
Iron River	1,121	2	2	0
Jackson	6,960	12	11	1
Janesville	64,257	113	99	14
Jefferson	8,033	17	14	3
Juneau	2,703	5	4	1
Kaukauna	15,969	27	26	1
Kenosha	99,671	210	199	11
Kewaskum	4,122	8	8	0
Kewaunee	2,857	6	6	0
Kiel	3,697	8	7	1
Kohler	2,102	8	7	1
Kronenwetter	7,687	8	7	1
La Crosse	52,234	114	94	20
Ladysmith	3,149	8	7	1
Lake Delton	2,982	22	20	2
Lake Geneva	7,850	34	25	9
Lake Hallie	6,678	10	9	1
Lake Mills	5,857	12	10	2
Lancaster	3,742	9	8	1
Lena	542	1	1	0
Linn Township	2,401	6	6	0
Lodi	3,060	11	5	6
Lomira	2,356	4	3	1
Luxemburg	2,562	2	2	0
Lyndon Station	476	2	1	1
Madison	255,850	593	484	109
Manawa	1,290	3	3	0
Manitowoc	32,813	74	64	10
Maple Bluff	1,342	6	5	1
Marathon City	1,505	6	3	3
Marinette	10,655	28	24	4
Marion	1,199	3	3	0
Markesan	1,400	3	3	0
Marshall Village	3,950	9	8	1
Marshfield	18,366	45	37	8
Mauston	4,368	9	8	1
Mayville	4,907	8	7	1
McFarland	8,407	18	16	2
Medford	4,336	10	9	1
Menasha	17,899	36	29	7
Menomonee Falls	36,963	68	54	14
Menomonie	16,493	33	26	7
Mequon	24,250	48	39	9
Merrill	9,154	25	22	3
Middleton	19,369	48	38	10
Milton	5,585	13	11	2
Milwaukee	595,168	2,292	1,824	468
Mineral Point	2,489	6	6	0
Minocqua	4,447	17	12	5
Mishicot	1,402	2	2	0
Mondovi	2,612	4	4	0
Monona	8,285	24	20	4
Monroe	10,709	36	26	10
Montello	1,429	3	2	1
Mosinee	4,016	8	7	1
Mount Horeb	7,518	12	11	1
Mount Pleasant	26,387	53	48	5
Mukwonago	7,898	21	14	7
Mukwonago Town	8,141	7	6	1
Muscoda	1,241	3	3	0
Muskego	25,004	45	36	9
Neenah	25,983	51	41	10
Neillsville	2,425	7	6	1
Nekoosa	2,421	6	6	0
New Berlin	39,839	86	73	13
New Glarus	2,159	2	2	0
New Holstein	3,112	7	6	1
New Lisbon	2,490	4	4	0
New London	7,150	19	17	2
New Richmond	8,987	17	16	1
Niagara	1,564	4	4	0
North Fond du Lac	5,038	10	9	1
North Hudson	3,825	5	4	1
Oak Creek	36,126	78	56	22
Oconomowoc	16,650	30	23	7

Table 78. Full-Time Law Enforcement Employees, by Selected State and City, 2017—Continued

(Number.)

State/city	Population	Total law enforcement employees	Total officers	Total civilians
Oconomowoc Lake	589	6	6	0
Oconomowoc Town	8,670	12	11	1
Oconto	4,455	10	9	1
Oconto Falls	2,825	5	5	0
Omro	3,562	7	6	1
Onalaska	18,847	31	28	3
Oregon	10,426	20	18	2
Osceola	2,510	5	4	1
Oshkosh	66,652	110	95	15
Osseo	1,695	4	4	0
Palmyra	1,768	6	6	0
Park Falls	2,266	7	7	0
Pepin	786	1	1	0
Peshtigo	3,391	6	6	0
Pewaukee Village	8,171	20	18	2
Phillips	1,359	10	5	5
Platteville	12,769	26	20	6
Pleasant Prairie	20,904	44	33	11
Plover	12,627	21	18	3
Plymouth	8,544	16	16	0
Portage	10,372	26	22	4
Port Edwards	1,739	3	3	0
Port Washington	11,702	25	20	5
Poynette	2,492	5	4	1
Prairie du Chien	5,690	13	12	1
Prescott	4,223	7	6	1
Princeton	1,169	3	3	0
Pulaski	3,544	8	7	1
Racine	77,371	223	191	32
Reedsburg	9,583	27	20	7
Rhinelander	7,560	18	15	3
Rice Lake	8,406	17	17	0
Richland Center	4,986	13	11	2
Rio	1,043	4	2	2
Ripon	7,770	21	15	6
Ripon Town	1,391	1	1	0
River Falls	15,389	26	23	3
River Hills	1,591	10	10	0
Rome Town	2,710	6	6	0
Rosendale	1,035	1	1	0
Rothschild	5,361	12	10	2
Sauk Prairie	4,652	15	13	2
Saukville	4,473	13	11	2
Seymour	3,441	6	6	0
Shawano	9,014	22	20	2
Sheboygan	48,595	100	80	20
Sheboygan Falls	7,829	16	15	1
Shiocton	918	1	1	0
Shorewood	13,405	28	24	4
Shorewood Hills	2,131	8	6	2
Shullsburg	1,205	1	1	0
Siren	774	3	2	1
Slinger	5,320	12	11	1
South Milwaukee	21,039	39	33	6
Sparta	9,721	21	19	2
Spencer	1,909	3	3	0
Spooner	2,581	8	7	1
Spring Green	1,658	4	3	1
Spring Valley	1,347	1	1	0
Stanley	3,668	5	5	0
St. Croix Falls	2,050	6	5	1
Stevens Point	26,379	49	44	5
St. Francis	9,487	22	21	1
Stoughton	13,213	28	22	6
Strum	1,114	2	2	0
Sturgeon Bay	8,876	22	20	2
Sturtevant	6,931	11	10	1
Summit	4,871	10	10	0
Sun Prairie	33,385	71	52	19
Superior	26,352	60	55	5
Theresa	1,198	2	2	0
Thiensville	3,174	8	7	1
Thorp	1,631	3	3	0
Three Lakes	2,120	5	5	0
Tomah	9,441	21	19	2
Tomahawk	3,169	9	8	1
Town of East Troy	4,113	7	6	1
Town of Madison	6,953	15	14	1
Town of Menasha	18,872	32	27	5
Trempealeau	1,633	3	3	0
Twin Lakes	6,100	17	12	5
Two Rivers	11,190	28	25	3
Verona	13,390	25	22	3
Viroqua	4,402	11	9	2
Walworth	2,842	8	7	1

Table 78. Full-Time Law Enforcement Employees, by Selected State and City, 2017—Continued

(Number.)

State/city	Population	Total law enforcement employees	Total officers	Total civilians
Washburn	2,034	5	5	0
Waterloo	3,333	9	8	1
Watertown	23,814	52	38	14
Waukesha	72,565	149	117	32
Waunakee	13,866	22	20	2
Waupaca	5,924	16	15	1
Waupun	11,332	18	17	1
Wausau	38,832	84	74	10
Wautoma	2,120	5	5	0
Wauwatosa	48,208	112	88	24
Webster	622	2	2	0
West Allis	60,043	154	125	29
West Bend	31,783	70	53	17
Westby	2,283	3	3	0
Westfield	1,226	4	2	2
West Milwaukee	4,169	25	20	5
West Salem	4,993	8	7	1
Whitefish Bay	13,952	25	24	1
Whitehall	1,609	4	4	0
Whitewater	14,538	32	22	10
Wild Rose	699	2	2	0
Williams Bay	2,598	8	7	1
Wilton	501	1	1	0
Winneconne	2,444	6	5	1
Wisconsin Dells	2,823	19	14	5
Wisconsin Rapids	17,807	39	35	4
Woodruff	1,977	6	5	1
WYOMING				
Afton	2,008	4	4	0
Buffalo	4,590	21	12	9
Casper	60,034	125	88	37
Cheyenne	64,730	124	106	18
Cody	9,885	24	22	2
Diamondville	744	4	3	1
Douglas	6,615	26	18	8
Evanston	12,044	29	23	6
Evansville	3,014	12	10	2
Gillette	32,826	77	51	26
Glenrock	2,599	12	7	5
Green River	12,289	31	26	5
Greybull	1,876	6	5	1
Hanna	808	1	1	0
Jackson	10,692	36	30	6
Kemmerer	2,792	6	6	0
Lander	7,672	19	18	1
Laramie	32,632	73	48	25
Mills	3,875	18	14	4
Moorcroft	1,072	4	3	1
Newcastle	3,537	14	6	8
Pine Bluffs	1,155	1	1	0
Powell	6,422	23	16	7
Rawlins	9,050	27	17	10
Riverton	11,028	41	27	14
Rock Springs	23,886	56	43	13
Saratoga	1,686	9	4	5
Sheridan	18,036	45	29	16
Sundance	1,294	3	3	0
Thermopolis	2,925	12	7	5
Torrington	6,729	22	15	7
Wheatland	3,602	10	9	1
Worland	5,287	12	11	1

1 The employee data presented in this table for Charlotte-Mecklenburg represent only Charlotte-Mecklenburg Police Department and exclude Mecklenburg County Sheriff's Office.

Table 79. Full-Time Law Enforcement Employees, by Selected State and University or College, 2017

(Number.)

State and university/college	Student enrollment[1]	Law enforcement employees	Officers	Civilians
ALABAMA				
Alabama A & M University	5,859	42	18	24
Alabama State University	5,318	40	29	11
Auburn University, Montgomery	4,878	21	13	8
Jacksonville State University	8,514	21	13	8
Lawson State Community College	3,128	9	8	1
Tuskegee University	2,851	24	9	15
University of Alabama				
Birmingham	19,535	165	101	64
Huntsville	8,468	29	16	13
Tuscaloosa	37,663	106	86	20
University of South Alabama	16,443	38	33	5
ALASKA				
University of Alaska				
Anchorage	16,318	18	13	5
Fairbanks	8,283	10	5	5
ARIZONA				
Arizona State University, Main Campus	97,849	148	84	64
Arizona Western College	7,569	14	9	5
Central Arizona College	5,585	8	7	1
Northern Arizona University	30,361	33	21	12
Pima Community College	24,956	51	29	22
University of Arizona	43,161	95	62	33
Yavapai College	7,282	10	9	1
ARKANSAS				
Arkansas State University				
Beebe	3,989	6	5	1
Jonesboro	14,085	23	18	5
Newport	2,735	2	2	0
Arkansas Tech University	11,894	20	17	3
Henderson State University	3,551	9	8	1
Southern Arkansas University	4,771	9	8	1
Southern Arkansas University Tech	780	3	3	0
University of Arkansas				
Fayetteville	27,194	51	35	16
Little Rock	11,746	39	26	13
Medical Sciences	2,869	67	41	26
Monticello	3,924	10	9	1
Pine Bluff	2,821	19	13	6
University of Arkansas Community College, Morrilton	2,029	3	3	0
University of Central Arkansas	11,487	36	26	10
CALIFORNIA				
Allan Hancock College	12,012	9	4	5
California State Polytechnic University				
Pomona	25,326	51	19	32
San Luis Obispo	21,306	36	20	16
California State University				
Bakersfield	9,341	22	13	9
Channel Islands	6,611	28	14	14
Chico	17,557	24	15	9
Dominguez Hills	14,731	26	19	7
East Bay	15,855	30	15	15
Fresno	24,405	40	27	13
Fullerton	40,235	44	30	14
Long Beach	37,776	39	24	15
Los Angeles	27,827	36	21	15
Monterey Bay	7,274	26	14	12
Northridge	39,916	38	22	16
Sacramento	30,510	38	22	16
San Bernardino	20,767	29	18	11
San Jose	32,154	69	27	42
San Marcos	13,144	24	19	5
Stanislaus	9,762	20	12	8
College of the Sequoias	11,959	7	6	1
Contra Costa Community College	34,487	32	21	11
Cuesta College	10,232	12	7	5
El Camino College	24,033	31	22	9
Foothill-De Anza College	37,085	22	13	9
Humboldt State University	8,503	20	12	8
Irvine Valley College	14,147	14	9	5
Marin Community College	5,621	8	6	2
Pasadena Community College	27,165	13	9	4
Riverside Community College	38,677	27	20	7
San Bernardino Community College	18,657	20	7	13
San Diego State University	34,688	49	26	23
San Francisco State University	29,045	51	27	24
San Jose/Evergreen Community College	17,213	17	7	10
Santa Rosa Junior College	21,217	26	13	13
Sonoma State University	9,323	16	12	4
State Center Community College District	39,661	22	18	4

Table 79. Full-Time Law Enforcement Employees, by Selected State and University or College, 2017—Continued

(Number.)

State and university/college	Student enrollment[1]	Law enforcement employees	Officers	Civilians
University of California				
Berkeley	40,154	123	57	66
Davis	36,460	70	45	25
Irvine	32,754	55	38	17
Los Angeles	43,548	91	56	35
Merced	7,336	25	14	11
Riverside	22,715	46	34	12
San Diego	34,979	73	38	35
San Francisco	3,145	141	50	91
Santa Barbara	24,346	58	39	19
Santa Cruz	18,783	31	20	11
Ventura County Community College District	33,976	15	14	1
West Valley-Mission College	16,131	13	9	4
COLORADO				
Adams State University	3,370	6	5	1
Arapahoe Community College	10,261	10	8	2
Auraria Higher Education Center[2]		49	31	18
Colorado School of Mines	6,069	12	11	1
Colorado State University, Fort Collins	31,856	49	35	14
Fort Lewis College	3,600	10	8	2
Pikes Peak Community College	13,154	20	18	2
Red Rocks Community College	7,738	10	6	4
University of Colorado				
Boulder	33,977	59	34	25
Colorado Springs	12,559	30	18	12
Denver	23,960	59	26	33
University of Northern Colorado	13,087	23	15	8
CONNECTICUT				
Central Connecticut State University	11,784	25	18	7
Eastern Connecticut State University	5,362	22	14	8
Southern Connecticut State University	10,320	29	23	6
University of Connecticut				
Health Center[2]		40	17	23
Storrs, Avery Point and Hartford[2]		97	77	20
Western Connecticut State University	5,721	18	12	6
Yale University	12,458	106	89	17
DELAWARE				
Delaware State University	4,328	39	15	24
University of Delaware	23,009	75	50	25
FLORIDA				
Florida A&M University	9,619	33	28	5
Florida Atlantic University	30,541	64	36	28
Florida Gulf Coast University	14,821	25	18	7
Florida International University	55,003	94	61	33
Florida Polytechnic University[2]		12	9	3
Florida SouthWestern State College	16,627	23	10	13
New College of Florida	875	19	13	6
Pensacola State College	9,643	12	10	2
Santa Fe College	15,404	23	17	6
Tallahassee Community College	12,200	26	12	14
University of Central Florida	64,088	120	73	47
University of Florida	52,367	130	80	50
University of North Florida	15,762	38	30	8
University of South Florida				
St. Petersburg	4,702	21	15	6
Tampa	42,861	68	48	20
University of West Florida	12,966	30	21	9
GEORGIA				
Abraham Baldwin Agricultural College	3,475	15	13	2
Agnes Scott College	927	15	8	7
Albany State University	3,041	39	35	4
Albany Technical College	3,251	3	3	0
Andrew College	276	2	2	0
Armstrong State University	7,157	23	18	5
Athens Technical College	4,210	2	2	0
Augusta Technical College	4,370	6	6	0
Augusta University	7,938	58	43	15
Bainbridge State College	2,468	8	5	3
Berry College	2,174	17	12	5
Chattahoochee Technical College	9,999	14	11	3
College of Coastal Georgia	3,529	14	14	0
Columbus State University	8,407	39	29	10
Dalton State College	5,188	16	13	3
East Georgia College	3,152	10	9	1
Emory University	14,067	67	50	17
Fort Valley State University	2,679	34	14	20
Georgia College and State University	6,915	22	16	6
Georgia Gwinnett College	12,052	28	23	5
Georgia Institute of Technology	26,839	104	74	30

Table 79. Full-Time Law Enforcement Employees, by Selected State and University or College, 2017—Continued

(Number.)

State and university/college	Student enrollment[1]	Law enforcement employees	Officers	Civilians
Georgia Military College	8,234	5	3	2
Georgia Southern University	20,673	70	54	16
Georgia Southwestern State University	2,954	12	12	0
Georgia State University	32,237	268	126	142
Gordon State College	3,901	13	12	1
Kennesaw State University	35,018	100	59	41
Mercer University	8,615	30	22	8
Middle Georgia State University	7,714	29	26	3
Morehouse College	2,108	23	8	15
Savannah Technical College	3,938	11	10	1
Southern Crescent Technical College	4,703	5	5	0
South Georgia State College	2,542	11	7	4
Spelman College	2,125	24	15	9
University of Georgia	36,574	104	82	22
University of North Georgia	18,219	44	35	9
University of West Georgia	13,308	42	32	10
Valdosta State University	11,375	33	25	8
Wesleyan College	676	5	5	0
West Georgia Technical College	6,743	7	7	0
Young Harris College	1,200	4	4	0
ILLINOIS				
Chicago State University	3,578	26	24	2
Elgin Community College	9,918	18	16	2
Illinois Central College	9,290	19	7	12
Illinois State University	21,039	39	29	10
John Wood Community College	1,968	5	4	1
Joliet Junior College	15,383	24	15	9
Lewis University	6,544	17	8	9
Lincoln Land Community College	5,744	15	13	2
Millikin University	2,055	17	5	12
Parkland College	7,569	15	12	3
Rend Lake College	2,489	3	3	0
Southern Illinois University				
Carbondale	15,987	54	37	17
Edwardsville	14,142	49	39	10
School of Medicine[2]		6	6	0
University of Illinois				
Springfield	5,428	22	15	7
Urbana	46,951	96	60	36
IOWA				
Iowa State University	36,350	47	35	12
University of Iowa	32,011	60	38	22
University of Northern Iowa	11,905	20	17	3
KANSAS				
Butler Community College	9,190	7	6	1
Emporia State University	5,887	10	10	0
Fort Hays State University	14,658	11	9	2
Garden City Community College	2,053	1	1	0
Kansas City Kansas Community College	5,726	16	15	1
Kansas State University	23,779	42	23	19
Pittsburg State University	7,102	16	13	3
University of Kansas, Main Campus	27,565	75	31	44
Washburn University	6,636	22	16	6
Wichita State University	14,166	40	26	14
KENTUCKY				
Eastern Kentucky University	16,881	31	24	7
Kentucky State University	1,736	13	7	6
Morehead State University	10,746	27	16	11
Murray State University	10,486	16	16	0
Northern Kentucky University	14,542	20	15	5
Transylvania University	963	11	9	2
University of Kentucky	29,781	161	55	106
University of Louisville	21,578	57	44	13
Western Kentucky University	20,271	30	21	9
LOUISIANA				
Delgado Community College	15,110	38	26	12
Dillard University	1,261	21	13	8
Grambling State University	4,863	23	10	13
Louisiana State University				
Baton Rouge	31,409	75	58	17
Health Sciences Center, New Orleans	2,758	28	28	0
Health Sciences Center, Shreveport	874	46	32	14
Shreveport	4,746	8	7	1
Louisiana Tech University	12,672	19	17	2
McNeese State University	7,621	16	10	6
Nicholls State University	6,255	11	10	1
Northwestern State University	9,819	30	24	6
Southeastern Louisiana University	14,483	26	21	5
Southern University and A&M College				
Baton Rouge	5,877	39	21	18

Table 79. Full-Time Law Enforcement Employees, by Selected State and University or College, 2017—Continued

(Number.)

State and university/college	Student enrollment[1]	Law enforcement employees	Officers	Civilians
New Orleans	2,430	20	17	3
Shreveport	3,240	6	5	1
Tulane University	12,581	99	81	18
University of Louisiana				
Lafayette	17,519	36	32	4
Monroe	9,038	24	23	1
University of New Orleans	8,037	21	18	3
MAINE				
University of Maine				
Farmington	2,000	5	4	1
Orono	11,219	26	18	8
University of Southern Maine	7,855	18	10	8
MARYLAND				
Bowie State University	5,669	28	14	14
Coppin State University	2,939	35	23	12
Frostburg State University	5,676	25	18	7
Hagerstown Community College	4,061	2	2	0
Morgan State University	7,689	56	35	21
Prince George's County Community College	12,417	18	12	6
Salisbury University	8,748	31	16	15
St. Mary's College	1,629	12	4	8
Towson University	22,343	52	39	13
University of Baltimore	5,983	29	18	11
University of Maryland				
Baltimore City	6,482	140	56	84
Baltimore County	13,640	37	26	11
College Park	39,083	131	86	45
Eastern Shore	3,904	16	12	4
MASSACHUSETTS				
Amherst College	1,849	19	14	5
Assumption College	2,607	20	15	5
Babson College	3,165	29	19	10
Becker College	2,189	18	12	6
Bentley University	5,506	31	21	10
Boston College	14,466	69	48	21
Boston University	32,695	67	51	16
Brandeis University	5,729	23	21	2
Bridgewater State University	10,998	25	22	3
Bristol Community College	8,476	8	7	1
Bunker Hill Community College	13,253	16	15	1
Clark University	3,298	14	10	4
College of the Holy Cross	2,720	23	17	6
Dean College	1,339	16	1	15
Emerson College	4,442	16	13	3
Fitchburg State University	6,763	25	20	5
Framingham State University	5,977	18	15	3
Gordon College	2,004	7	7	0
Harvard University	29,908	98	74	24
Holyoke Community College	5,890	14	14	0
Massachusetts Bay Community College	4,855	8	8	0
Massachusetts College of Art	1,982	29	10	19
Massachusetts College of Liberal Arts	1,644	13	9	4
Massachusetts Institute of Technology	11,376	65	58	7
Massasoit Community College	7,471	19	18	1
Merrimack College	4,014	18	15	3
Mount Holyoke College	2,327	60	47	13
Mount Wachusett Community College	3,961	11	10	1
Northeastern University	20,381	98	63	35
North Shore Community College	6,315	24	19	5
Quinsigamond Community College	7,696	15	12	3
Salem State University	9,001	27	22	5
Springfield College	3,144	47	18	29
Springfield Technical Community College	5,622	18	15	3
Stonehill College	2,481	21	15	6
Tufts University, Medford	11,489	89	48	41
University of Massachusetts				
Amherst	30,037	78	62	16
Dartmouth	8,647	37	26	11
Medical Center, Worcester	1,108	26	20	6
Wellesley College	2,482	17	13	4
Wentworth Institute of Technology	4,526	23	16	7
Western New England University	3,810	27	15	12
Westfield State University	6,335	23	17	6
Wheaton College	1,651	17	14	3
Worcester Polytechnic Institute	6,642	22	17	5
Worcester State University	6,471	22	16	6
MICHIGAN				
Central Michigan University	25,986	36	23	13
Delta College	9,132	8	5	3

Table 79. Full-Time Law Enforcement Employees, by Selected State and University or College, 2017—Continued

(Number.)

State and university/college	Student enrollment[1]	Law enforcement employees	Officers	Civilians
Eastern Michigan University	21,246	49	38	11
Ferris State University	14,187	17	13	4
Grand Rapids Community College	14,464	16	12	4
Grand Valley State University	25,460	22	18	4
Kalamazoo Valley Community College	8,549	8	6	2
Kellogg Community College	4,815	3	3	0
Kirtland Community College	1,529	1	1	0
Lansing Community College	13,583	15	10	5
Macomb Community College	21,734	26	22	4
Michigan State University	50,340	118	87	31
Northern Michigan University	7,865	24	21	3
Oakland Community College	18,923	23	22	1
Oakland University	20,012	28	21	7
Saginaw Valley State University	9,105	9	8	1
Schoolcraft College	11,339	15	11	4
University of Michigan				
Ann Arbor	44,718	31	19	12
Dearborn	9,131	27	13	14
Flint	8,044	31	19	12
Western Michigan University	23,227	39	32	7
MINNESOTA				
University of Minnesota				
Duluth	11,018	11	9	2
Morris	1,771	5	3	2
Twin Cities	51,579	65	53	12
MISSISSIPPI				
Coahoma Community College	2,064	10	9	1
Jackson State University	9,811	63	33	30
Mississippi State University	21,622	44	31	13
Northeast Mississippi Community College	3,521	7	7	0
University of Mississippi, Medical Center[2]		104	61	43
MISSOURI				
Jefferson College	4,692	8	8	0
Lincoln University	2,738	16	14	2
Metropolitan Community College	15,790	36	28	8
Mineral Area College	4,173	3	3	0
Missouri Southern State University	6,231	8	7	1
Missouri Western State University	5,363	9	8	1
Northwest Missouri State University	6,530	13	10	3
Southeast Missouri State University	11,978	17	16	1
St. Charles Community College	6,755	14	12	2
St. Louis Community College, Meramec	19,052	30	24	6
Truman State University	6,379	10	8	2
University of Central Missouri	13,988	33	19	14
University of Missouri				
Columbia	33,239	63	42	21
Kansas City	16,936	39	28	11
St. Louis	16,989	26	20	6
Washington University	15,047	57	37	20
MONTANA				
Montana State University	16,359	35	18	17
University of Montana	12,419	24	14	10
NEBRASKA				
University of Nebraska				
Kearney	6,788	9	7	2
Lincoln	25,897	60	32	28
NEVADA				
College of Southern Nevada	33,556	18	17	1
University of Nevada				
Las Vegas	29,702	57	41	16
Reno	21,353	40	31	9
NEW HAMPSHIRE				
University of New Hampshire	15,188	35	19	16
NEW JERSEY				
Brookdale Community College	13,165	12	12	0
Essex County College	9,596	56	11	45
Kean University	14,070	38	19	19
Middlesex County College	11,371	17	12	5
Monmouth University	6,371	49	19	30
Montclair State University	20,987	47	33	14
New Jersey Institute of Technology	11,317	68	33	35
Princeton University	8,181	102	33	69
Rowan University	17,372	89	31	58
Rutgers University				
Camden	6,475	82	19	63

Table 79. Full-Time Law Enforcement Employees, by Selected State and University or College, 2017—Continued

(Number.)

State and university/college	Student enrollment[1]	Law enforcement employees	Officers	Civilians
Newark	12,321	190	63	127
New Brunswick	50,146	141	70	71
Stevens Institute of Technology	6,617	22	20	2
Stockton University	8,728	28	18	10
The College of New Jersey	7,396	30	17	13
William Paterson University	10,583	45	32	13
NEW MEXICO				
Eastern New Mexico University	6,010	7	6	1
New Mexico Military Institute	422	5	5	0
New Mexico State University	14,852	32	17	15
University of New Mexico	26,999	55	38	17
NEW YORK				
Cornell University	22,319	72	46	26
Ithaca College	6,678	41	23	18
State University of New York Police				
Albany	17,373	59	37	22
Alfred	3,735	16	11	5
Binghamton	17,292	54	39	15
Brockport	8,243	18	16	2
Buffalo	30,184	70	57	13
Buffalo State College	9,475	36	32	4
Canton	3,205	11	10	1
Cobleskill	2,287	12	11	1
Cortland	6,900	24	18	6
Delhi	3,511	13	9	4
Downstate Medical	1,839	110	26	84
Environmental Science	2,186	13	9	4
Farmingdale	9,235	30	21	9
Fredonia	4,603	16	15	1
Geneseo	5,602	23	15	8
Morrisville	3,003	15	12	3
New Paltz	7,628	27	23	4
Oneonta	6,055	27	17	10
Optometry	401	16	6	10
Oswego	8,004	25	22	3
Plattsburgh	5,520	22	18	4
Polytechnic Institute	2,697	16	11	5
Potsdam	3,696	14	12	2
Stony Brook	25,734	143	65	78
Upstate Medical	1,491	112	20	92
NORTH CAROLINA				
Appalachian State University	18,295	44	27	17
Beaufort County Community College	1,522	2	2	0
Belmont Abbey College	1,523	2	2	0
Davidson College	1,796	10	9	1
Duke University	15,735	157	64	93
East Carolina University	28,962	71	55	16
Elizabeth City State University	1,357	21	11	10
Elon University	6,739	39	19	20
Fayetteville State University	6,223	36	19	17
Meredith College	1,981	13	3	10
Methodist University	2,446	25	10	15
North Carolina Agricultural and Technical State University	11,177	52	21	31
North Carolina Central University	8,094	53	25	28
North Carolina School of the Arts	1,040	22	15	7
North Carolina State University, Raleigh	33,755	63	47	16
Queens University	2,330	13	9	4
Saint Augustine's University	944	19	2	17
University of North Carolina				
Asheville	3,821	21	14	7
Chapel Hill	29,468	109	56	53
Charlotte	28,721	55	45	10
Greensboro	19,647	54	31	23
Pembroke	6,268	26	18	8
Wilmington	15,740	45	30	15
Wake Forest University	7,968	48	22	26
Western Carolina University	10,805	24	23	1
Winston-Salem State University	5,151	22	16	6
NORTH DAKOTA				
Bismarck State College	3,976	2	2	0
North Dakota State College of Science	3,003	4	3	1
North Dakota State University	14,432	24	15	9
University of North Dakota	14,648	17	16	1
OHIO				
Capital University	3,367	16	10	6
Lakeland Community College	7,997	15	11	4
Miami University	19,697	37	28	9
Mount St. Joseph University	2,045	7	5	2
Muskingum University	2,121	5	5	0

Table 79. Full-Time Law Enforcement Employees, by Selected State and University or College, 2017—Continued

(Number.)

State and university/college	Student enrollment[1]	Law enforcement employees	Officers	Civilians
Notre Dame College	1,985	9	8	1
Ohio State University, Columbus	59,482	60	52	8
Ohio University	29,509	37	30	7
Otterbein University	2,928	10	9	1
Sinclair Community College	18,610	23	19	4
University of Akron	21,100	42	36	6
University of Toledo	20,615	39	32	7
OKLAHOMA				
Cameron University	4,846	12	12	0
East Central University	4,160	6	5	1
Eastern Oklahoma State College	1,641	3	3	0
Langston University	2,420	17	12	5
Mid-America Christian University	2,405	4	4	0
Northeastern Oklahoma A&M College	2,077	6	6	0
Northeastern State University, Tahlequah	8,109	19	15	4
Northwestern Oklahoma State University	2,218	4	4	0
Oklahoma City Community College	12,557	33	21	12
Oklahoma City University	2,968	12	8	4
Oklahoma State University				
Main Campus	25,622	43	33	10
Okmulgee	2,396	8	7	1
Tulsa	926	8	6	2
Rogers State University	3,903	9	9	0
Seminole State College	1,729	2	2	0
Southeastern Oklahoma State University	3,725	4	3	1
Southwestern Oklahoma State University	5,320	7	6	1
Tulsa Community College	17,135	33	27	6
University of Central Oklahoma	16,428	22	15	7
University of Oklahoma				
Health Sciences Center	3,322	59	37	22
Norman	27,918	70	38	32
OREGON				
Portland State University	26,627	27	13	14
University of Oregon	23,546	34	23	11
PENNSYLVANIA				
Bloomsburg University	9,637	20	15	5
California University	7,553	21	18	3
Cheyney University	746	10	7	3
Clarion University	5,224	14	9	5
Dickinson College	2,420	20	14	6
East Stroudsburg University	6,822	15	10	5
Edinboro University	6,181	15	14	1
Indiana University	12,971	26	21	5
Kutztown University	8,513	19	16	3
Lehigh University	7,059	36	26	10
Lock Haven University	4,220	15	12	3
Mansfield University	2,180	11	8	3
Millersville University	7,914	16	14	2
Moravian College	2,426	17	14	3
Pennsylvania State University				
Abington	3,951	8	3	5
Altoona	3,491	8	7	1
Beaver	726	6	6	0
Behrend	4,566	11	7	4
Berks	2,888	8	7	1
Brandywine	1,379	3	3	0
Fayette	643	2	2	0
Greater Allegheny	550	5	5	0
Harrisburg	5,046	9	8	1
Hazleton	863	5	5	0
Mont Alto	903	5	5	0
New Kensington	686	1	1	0
Schuylkill	759	4	4	0
University Park	47,789	84	53	31
Wilkes-Barre	487	1	1	0
Worthington Scranton	1,019	3	3	0
Shippensburg University	6,972	18	16	2
Slippery Rock University	8,854	18	14	4
University of Pittsburgh				
Bradford	1,465	8	6	2
Greensburg	1,520	9	8	1
Johnstown	2,769	13	12	1
Pittsburgh	28,664	155	89	66
Titusville	332	7	6	1
West Chester University	17,005	46	25	21
RHODE ISLAND				
Brown University	9,781	86	50	36
University of Rhode Island	17,822	35	31	4
SOUTH CAROLINA				
Benedict College	2,281	23	20	3

Table 79. Full-Time Law Enforcement Employees, by Selected State and University or College, 2017—Continued

(Number.)

State and university/college	Student enrollment[1]	Law enforcement employees	Officers	Civilians
Bob Jones University	2,901	3	3	0
Clemson University	23,406	39	28	11
Coastal Carolina University	10,479	89	35	54
College of Charleston	11,294	39	26	13
Columbia College	1,588	8	6	2
Francis Marion University	3,874	14	11	3
Furman University	3,003	19	11	8
Greenville Technical College	11,932	16	9	7
Medical University of South Carolina	2,986	77	58	19
Midlands Technical College	10,749	10	10	0
Presbyterian College	1,352	8	7	1
South Carolina State University	2,905	27	11	16
Spartanburg Methodist College	737	4	4	0
The Citadel	3,602	19	16	3
Tri-County Technical College	6,094	15	11	4
Trident Technical College	13,561	28	23	5
University of South Carolina				
Beaufort	2,005	14	14	0
Upstate	5,821	14	13	1
Winthrop University	6,109	20	14	6
SOUTH DAKOTA				
South Dakota State University	12,600	18	13	5
TENNESSEE				
Austin Peay State University	10,344	27	17	10
Chattanooga State Community College	8,628	14	8	6
Christian Brothers University	2,138	20	9	11
Cleveland State Community College	3,315	4	3	1
Columbia State Community College	5,645	5	1	4
East Tennessee State University	14,022	30	22	8
Jackson State Community College	4,689	5	4	1
Lincoln Memorial University	4,254	26	9	17
Motlow State Community College	5,838	2	2	0
Northeast State Community College	6,124	8	8	0
Pellissippi State Community College	10,244	14	11	3
Roane State Community College	5,756	9	8	1
Southwest Tennessee Community College	8,327	22	18	4
Tennessee State University	8,760	90	30	60
Tennessee Technological University	10,493	22	13	9
University of Memphis	21,301	46	38	8
University of Tennessee				
Chattanooga	11,533	20	13	7
Health Science Center	3,097	56	27	29
Knoxville	28,052	90	51	39
Martin	6,705	16	12	4
University of the South	1,815	15	11	4
Vanderbilt University	12,587	261	92	169
Volunteer State Community College	8,684	12	9	3
Walters State Community College	5,951	12	10	2
TEXAS				
Abilene Christian University	4,910	15	14	1
Alamo Colleges District	56,533	90	73	17
Alvin Community College	5,677	10	9	1
Amarillo College	10,195	12	11	1
Angelo State University	9,581	16	12	4
Austin College	1,278	8	7	1
Baylor Health Care System[2]		164	57	107
Central Texas College	18,117	7	6	1
College of the Mainland	3,995	9	8	1
El Paso Community College	29,460	49	40	9
Houston Community College	57,032	109	72	37
Laredo Community College	9,176	24	22	2
Paris Junior College	4,806	5	5	0
Prairie View A&M University	8,782	19	15	4
Rice University	6,855	45	29	16
Southern Methodist University	11,739	36	29	7
Stephen F. Austin State University	12,742	51	27	24
St. Thomas University	3,247	16	8	8
Texas A&M International University	7,390	29	20	9
Texas A&M University, College Station	65,632	135	68	67
Texas Christian University	10,394	56	32	24
Texas Southern University	8,862	78	28	50
Texas State Technical College				
Harlingen[2]		13	10	3
West Texas[2]		6	6	0
Texas Woman's University	15,655	43	19	24
University of Houston, Downtown Campus	14,251	49	24	25
University of North Texas, Denton	38,145	59	39	20
University of Texas				
Arlington	45,282	109	43	66
Dallas	26,793	74	29	45
El Paso	23,922	54	26	28

Table 79. Full-Time Law Enforcement Employees, by Selected State and University or College, 2017—Continued

(Number.)

State and university/college	Student enrollment[1]	Law enforcement employees	Officers	Civilians
Health Science Center, Tyler	12	27	8	19
Permian Basin	6,673	25	14	11
Rio Grande Valley	27,560	76	36	40
Southwestern Medical School	2,316	135	44	91
Tyler	9,835	30	12	18
West Texas A&M University	9,901	24	16	8
UTAH				
Brigham Young University	34,240	43	30	13
Southern Utah University	9,299	6	5	1
University of Utah	31,860	115	35	80
Utah State University				
Eastern[2]		2	2	0
Logan	28,118	17	10	7
Utah Valley University	34,978	14	11	3
Weber State University	26,809	13	11	2
VERMONT				
University of Vermont	13,105	35	23	12
VIRGINIA				
Bridgewater College	1,882	13	7	6
Christopher Newport University	5,042	28	20	8
College of William and Mary	8,617	28	20	8
Eastern Virginia Medical School	1,130	49	21	28
Emory and Henry College	1,167	3	3	0
Ferrum College	1,294	9	9	0
George Mason University	34,909	56	41	15
Germanna Community College	6,701	7	3	4
Hampton University	4,646	52	30	22
James Madison University	21,270	39	32	7
J. Sargeant Reynolds Community College	10,375	18	13	5
Longwood University	4,884	27	17	10
Lord Fairfax Community College	6,868	4	4	0
Norfolk State University	5,421	38	24	14
Northern Virginia Community College	50,835	55	43	12
Old Dominion University	24,322	56	42	14
Radford University	9,401	30	22	8
Richard Bland College	2,409	5	4	1
Thomas Nelson Community College	8,897	12	9	3
University of Mary Washington	4,726	24	18	6
University of Richmond	4,131	35	22	13
University of Virginia	23,898	116	48	68
University of Virginia's College at Wise	2,212	10	9	1
Virginia Commonwealth University	30,872	118	90	28
Virginia Military Institute	1,713	10	9	1
Virginia Polytechnic Institute and State University	33,170	65	46	19
Virginia State University	4,584	31	16	15
Virginia Western Community College	7,719	9	9	0
WASHINGTON				
Central Washington University	11,971	16	14	2
Eastern Washington University	12,279	17	16	1
Evergreen State College	4,089	13	8	5
University of Washington	45,591	84	47	37
Washington State University				
Pullman	30,142	26	21	5
Vancouver[2]		6	3	3
Western Washington University	15,574	22	14	8
WEST VIRGINIA				
Bluefield State College	1,362	2	2	0
Concord University	2,451	9	6	3
Fairmont State University	4,049	12	9	3
Glenville State College	1,641	3	3	0
Marshall University	13,647	21	20	1
Potomac State College	1,452	7	6	1
Shepherd University	3,779	12	10	2
West Liberty University	2,317	6	6	0
West Virginia State University	3,514	9	7	2
West Virginia Tech	1,347	7	7	0
West Virginia University	28,488	71	54	17
WISCONSIN				
Marquette University	11,294	66	43	23
University of Wisconsin				
Eau Claire	10,747	11	11	0
Green Bay	7,029	12	11	1
La Crosse	10,637	19	12	7
Madison	42,582	128	59	69
Milwaukee	25,601	48	36	12
Oshkosh	13,958	16	13	3
Parkside	4,371	12	8	4
Platteville	8,779	10	8	2

Table 79. Full-Time Law Enforcement Employees, by Selected State and University or College, 2017—Continued

(Number.)

State and university/college	Student enrollment[1]	Law enforcement employees	Officers	Civilians
River Falls	5,938	7	7	0
Stevens Point	8,627	9	6	3
Stout	9,633	11	9	2
Superior	2,489	7	2	5
Whitewater	12,657	17	15	2
WYOMING				
University of Wyoming	12,366	26	15	11

1 The student enrollment figures provided by the United States Department of Education are for the 2016 school year, the most recent available. The enrollment figures include full-time and part-time students.   2 Student enrollment figures were not available.

Table 80. Full-Time Law Enforcement Employees, by Selected State Metropolitan and Nonmetropolitan Counties, 2017

(Number.)

State/county	Law enforcement employees	Officers	Civilians
ALABAMA			
Metropolitan Counties			
Autauga	69	31	38
Baldwin	296	111	185
Bibb	10	9	1
Calhoun	56	51	5
Colbert	53	34	19
Elmore	121	51	70
Etowah	156	65	91
Geneva	26	13	13
Hale	27	10	17
Henry	19	15	4
Lauderdale	46	40	6
Madison	187	130	57
Mobile	474	166	308
Montgomery	164	124	40
Pickens	31	8	23
Russell	118	41	77
Tuscaloosa	207	101	106
Nonmetropolitan Counties			
Barbour	30	13	17
Clarke	43	12	31
Clay	25	10	15
Cleburne	26	10	16
Conecuh	39	11	28
Coosa	25	11	14
Crenshaw	13	11	2
Dale	51	24	27
Dallas	49	23	26
DeKalb	72	32	40
Escambia	114	28	86
Marshall	67	32	35
Monroe	44	14	30
Pike	33	19	14
Randolph	37	20	17
Sumter	22	8	14
Talladega	97	37	60
Tallapoosa	67	26	41
ARIZONA			
Metropolitan Counties			
Cochise	181	85	96
Coconino	220	55	165
Maricopa	3,339	703	2,636
Mohave	241	81	160
Pima	1,436	483	953
Pinal	487	200	287
Yavapai	179	121	58
Yuma	304	80	224
Nonmetropolitan Counties			
Apache	82	29	53
Gila	128	45	83
Graham	77	23	54
Greenlee	46	13	33
La Paz	76	29	47
Navajo	132	49	83
Santa Cruz	88	34	54
ARKANSAS			
Metropolitan Counties			
Benton	233	118	115
Cleveland	15	8	7
Craighead	114	42	72
Crawford	71	31	40
Crittenden	142	36	106
Faulkner	160	47	113
Garland	179	50	129
Grant	18	15	3
Jefferson	124	40	84
Lincoln	27	12	15
Little River	29	12	17
Lonoke	70	33	37
Madison	19	9	10
Miller	78	26	52
Perry	23	11	12
Poinsett	45	15	30
Pulaski	487	131	356
Saline	101	51	50
Sebastian	188	46	142
Washington	284	147	137

Table 80. Full-Time Law Enforcement Employees, by Selected State Metropolitan and Nonmetropolitan Counties, 2017—Continued

(Number.)

State/county	Law enforcement employees	Officers	Civilians
Nonmetropolitan Counties			
Arkansas	12	11	1
Ashley	33	16	17
Baxter	53	33	20
Boone	56	27	29
Bradley	7	5	2
Calhoun	12	6	6
Carroll	23	20	3
Chicot	11	7	4
Clark	30	13	17
Clay	26	12	14
Cleburne	45	26	19
Columbia	38	22	16
Conway	43	21	22
Cross	39	17	22
Dallas	21	6	15
Drew	12	11	1
Franklin	24	10	14
Fulton	14	6	8
Greene	31	23	8
Hempstead	47	21	26
Hot Spring	31	16	15
Howard	22	11	11
Independence	38	34	4
Izard	34	17	17
Jackson	38	14	24
Johnson	43	17	26
Lafayette	26	8	18
Lawrence	26	12	14
Lee	10	5	5
Logan	34	14	20
Marion	20	18	2
Mississippi	90	41	49
Monroe	15	7	8
Montgomery	20	11	9
Nevada	29	23	6
Newton	18	7	11
Ouachita	46	17	29
Pike	20	7	13
Polk	27	14	13
Pope	88	35	53
Prairie	24	7	17
Randolph	11	10	1
Scott	28	8	20
Searcy	14	7	7
Sevier	36	16	20
St. Francis	39	17	22
Stone	22	11	11
Union	63	31	32
Van Buren	37	27	10
White	98	48	50
Woodruff	15	6	9
Yell	29	16	13
CALIFORNIA			
Metropolitan Counties			
Alameda	1,567	998	569
Butte	263	98	165
Contra Costa	956	628	328
El Dorado	354	161	193
Fresno	1,111	412	699
Imperial	281	189	92
Kern	1,151	812	339
Kings	278	73	205
Los Angeles	15,721	9,413	6,308
Madera	114	83	31
Marin	291	189	102
Merced	242	106	136
Monterey	446	296	150
Napa	133	101	32
Orange	3,755	1,843	1,912
Placer	538	250	288
Riverside	3,643	1,831	1,812
Sacramento	1,955	1,279	676
San Benito	56	25	31
San Bernardino	3,509	1,957	1,552
San Diego	4,290	2,601	1,689
San Francisco	1,054	862	192
San Joaquin	724	299	425
San Luis Obispo	375	270	105
San Mateo	710	341	369
Santa Barbara	626	458	168
Santa Clara	1,684	1,264	420

Table 80. Full-Time Law Enforcement Employees, by Selected State Metropolitan and Nonmetropolitan Counties, 2017—Continued

(Number.)

State/county	Law enforcement employees	Officers	Civilians
Santa Cruz	326	141	185
Shasta	184	129	55
Solano	534	124	410
Sonoma	614	229	385
Stanislaus	652	484	168
Sutter	131	106	25
Tulare	747	547	200
Ventura	1,247	767	480
Yolo	257	87	170
Yuba	156	117	39
Nonmetropolitan Counties			
Alpine	17	12	5
Amador	85	47	38
Calaveras	106	52	54
Colusa	59	39	20
Del Norte	53	23	30
Glenn	62	27	35
Humboldt	242	181	61
Inyo	63	36	27
Lake	131	47	84
Lassen	85	64	21
Mariposa	75	60	15
Mendocino	189	128	61
Modoc	29	20	9
Mono	40	22	18
Nevada	156	62	94
Plumas	66	34	32
Sierra	13	8	5
Siskiyou	98	75	23
Tehama	118	84	34
Trinity	47	35	12
Tuolumne	133	64	69
COLORADO			
Metropolitan Counties			
Adams	512	359	153
Boulder	377	201	176
Clear Creek	70	26	44
Douglas	498	319	179
Elbert	42	34	8
El Paso	781	533	248
Gilpin	56	36	20
Jefferson	784	530	254
Mesa	223	103	120
Park	54	30	24
Teller	73	45	28
Weld	364	132	232
Nonmetropolitan Counties			
Alamosa	49	28	21
Archuleta	37	17	20
Baca	12	4	8
Bent	26	11	15
Chaffee	57	21	36
Cheyenne	11	5	6
Conejos	24	8	16
Costilla	10	7	3
Crowley	14	7	7
Custer	23	10	13
Dolores	7	4	3
Eagle	74	44	30
Fremont	102	46	56
Grand	49	21	28
Gunnison	30	12	18
Hinsdale	5	4	1
Huerfano	42	21	21
Jackson	7	3	4
Kiowa	6	4	2
Kit Carson	30	7	23
Lake	25	12	13
La Plata	116	92	24
Las Animas	23	12	11
Lincoln	22	10	12
Logan	47	19	28
Mineral	7	4	3
Moffat	34	31	3
Montezuma	65	25	40
Montrose	99	46	53
Morgan	51	18	33
Otero	18	16	2
Ouray	8	7	1
Phillips	4	4	0

Table 80. Full-Time Law Enforcement Employees, by Selected State Metropolitan and Nonmetropolitan Counties, 2017—Continued

(Number.)

State/county	Law enforcement employees	Officers	Civilians
Pitkin	55	24	31
Prowers	30	10	20
Rio Blanco	28	11	17
Rio Grande	31	5	26
Routt	46	21	25
Saguache	18	8	10
San Juan	3	3	0
San Miguel	35	15	20
Sedgwick	4	3	1
Washington	31	10	21
Yuma	9	9	0
DELAWARE			
Metropolitan Counties			
New Castle County Police Department	501	379	122
FLORIDA			
Metropolitan Counties			
Alachua	830	269	561
Baker	152	48	104
Bay	275	210	65
Brevard	1,322	541	781
Broward	5,345	3,188	2,157
Charlotte	420	296	124
Citrus	340	205	135
Clay	568	276	292
Collier	881	558	323
Escambia	669	426	243
Gadsden	71	42	29
Gilchrist	39	26	13
Gulf	41	27	14
Highlands	334	146	188
Hillsborough	3,232	1,154	2,078
Indian River	470	299	171
Jefferson	51	21	30
Lee	1,561	662	899
Leon	668	251	417
Manatee	1,134	741	393
Marion	381	299	82
Martin	379	250	129
Miami-Dade	3,869	2,787	1,082
Nassau	168	121	47
Orange	2,124	1,482	642
Osceola	613	390	223
Palm Beach	3,476	1,577	1,899
Pasco	871	542	329
Pinellas	2,285	772	1,513
Polk	1,148	651	497
Sarasota	937	403	534
St. Lucie	394	277	117
Wakulla	133	92	41
Walton	385	256	129
Nonmetropolitan Counties			
Bradford	88	40	48
Calhoun	22	19	3
Columbia	183	93	90
Franklin	75	33	42
Hamilton	57	20	37
Hardee	81	60	21
Hendry	111	76	35
Holmes	36	28	8
Jackson	85	61	24
Levy	148	111	37
Monroe	480	192	288
Okeechobee	191	139	52
Putnam	208	114	94
Suwannee	108	55	53
Taylor	83	35	48
Union	15	13	2
GEORGIA			
Metropolitan Counties			
Baker	7	5	2
Barrow	183	120	63
Bartow	228	190	38
Bibb	545	453	92
Brooks	45	22	23
Bryan	68	43	25
Burke	100	65	35
Butts	93	54	39
Carroll	183	106	77
Cherokee	390	329	61

Table 80. Full-Time Law Enforcement Employees, by Selected State Metropolitan and Nonmetropolitan Counties, 2017—Continued

(Number.)

State/county	Law enforcement employees	Officers	Civilians
Clayton	412	255	157
Clayton County Police Department	447	344	103
Cobb	725	458	267
Cobb County Police Department	741	668	73
Columbia	360	280	80
Coweta	241	161	80
Crawford	33	18	15
Dade	39	24	15
Dawson	110	62	48
DeKalb	752	544	208
DeKalb County Police Department	928	718	210
Dougherty	225	213	12
Dougherty County Police Department	51	43	8
Douglas	330	291	39
Echols	9	8	1
Effingham	127	70	57
Fayette	214	195	19
Floyd	146	78	68
Floyd County Police Department	75	70	5
Forsyth	349	273	76
Fulton	933	722	211
Fulton County Police Department	142	121	21
Glynn County Police Department	124	116	8
Gwinnett County Police Department	924	681	243
Hall	414	261	153
Harris	70	68	2
Heard	34	17	17
Henry	301	289	12
Henry County Police Department	256	210	46
Houston	324	122	202
Jasper	44	26	18
Liberty	121	110	11
Long	39	35	4
Madison	67	64	3
Marion	12	6	6
McDuffie	51	34	17
McIntosh	73	46	27
Meriwether	47	27	20
Monroe	92	51	41
Murray	76	41	35
Oconee	93	58	35
Oglethorpe	43	19	24
Paulding	272	248	24
Peach	65	34	31
Pickens	95	87	8
Pulaski	34	21	13
Rockdale	275	256	19
Spalding	175	148	27
Terrell	25	21	4
Twiggs	42	21	21
Walker	117	66	51
Walton	215	187	28
Whitfield	199	168	31
Worth	40	25	15
Nonmetropolitan Counties			
Appling	54	22	32
Baldwin	118	59	59
Banks	63	60	3
Ben Hill	53	29	24
Bleckley	46	17	29
Bulloch	123	114	9
Calhoun	16	6	10
Candler	27	16	11
Charlton	31	18	13
Chattooga	43	25	18
Clay	6	5	1
Clinch	13	10	3
Coffee	112	51	61
Cook	49	28	21
Decatur	58	45	13
Dodge	49	17	32
Dooly	71	33	38
Early	47	26	21
Elbert	58	31	27
Emanuel	39	30	9
Evans	16	9	7
Fannin	51	48	3
Franklin	60	35	25
Gilmer	102	80	22
Glascock	7	6	1
Gordon	137	80	57
Grady	40	19	21

Table 80. Full-Time Law Enforcement Employees, by Selected State Metropolitan and Nonmetropolitan Counties, 2017—Continued

(Number.)

State/county	Law enforcement employees	Officers	Civilians
Habersham	73	69	4
Hancock	44	13	31
Hart	34	27	7
Irwin	22	15	7
Jackson	165	148	17
Jeff Davis	39	25	14
Jefferson	43	40	3
Laurens	111	75	36
Lumpkin	74	64	10
Miller	20	11	9
Mitchell	53	25	28
Pierce	46	18	28
Polk	76	37	39
Polk County Police Department	43	40	3
Quitman	5	4	1
Rabun	53	51	2
Schley	5	4	1
Screven	21	20	1
Seminole	30	16	14
Stephens	68	39	29
Stewart	8	5	3
Sumter	95	47	48
Taliaferro	18	13	5
Tattnall	47	20	27
Taylor	23	22	1
Thomas	87	84	3
Tift	95	51	44
Treutlen	22	11	11
Troup	81	74	7
Turner	36	19	17
Union	44	39	5
Upson	62	33	29
Ware	124	46	78
Warren	7	7	0
Washington	48	22	26
Webster	5	5	0
White	75	43	32
Wilkes	50	25	25
Wilkinson	30	17	13
HAWAII			
Metropolitan Counties			
Maui Police Department	459	358	101
Nonmetropolitan Counties			
Hawaii Police Department	567	439	128
Kauai Police Department	193	141	52
IDAHO			
Metropolitan Counties			
Ada	472	153	319
Bannock	66	42	24
Boise	18	12	6
Bonneville	107	67	40
Butte	11	4	7
Canyon	141	69	72
Franklin	15	10	5
Gem	23	13	10
Jefferson	37	21	16
Jerome	24	19	5
Kootenai	199	91	108
Nez Perce	42	23	19
Owyhee	20	13	7
Twin Falls	66	40	26
Nonmetropolitan Counties			
Adams	15	9	6
Bear Lake	14	7	7
Benewah	20	11	9
Bingham	56	35	21
Blaine	42	35	7
Bonner	58	28	30
Boundary	19	8	11
Camas	6	4	2
Caribou	14	8	6
Cassia	51	31	20
Clark	7	3	4
Clearwater	22	14	8
Custer	15	8	7
Elmore	45	23	22
Fremont	29	21	8
Gooding	21	16	5
Idaho	27	16	11

Table 80. Full-Time Law Enforcement Employees, by Selected State Metropolitan and Nonmetropolitan Counties, 2017—Continued

(Number.)

State/county	Law enforcement employees	Officers	Civilians
Latah	37	25	12
Lemhi	22	7	15
Lewis	8	5	3
Lincoln	10	8	2
Madison	35	21	14
Minidoka	30	20	10
Oneida	13	8	5
Payette	33	17	16
Power	17	9	8
Shoshone	30	18	12
Teton	16	9	7
Valley	22	11	11
Washington	20	12	8
ILLINOIS			
Metropolitan Counties			
Alexander	6	6	0
Clinton	36	16	20
Cook	5,961	1,753	4,208
DuPage	538	191	347
Ford	24	22	2
Grundy	42	28	14
Jackson	87	28	59
Kankakee	191	42	149
Macoupin	50	21	29
Madison	163	84	79
Marshall	17	8	9
McLean	135	53	82
Rock Island	149	62	87
Sangamon	198	65	133
Vermilion	96	39	57
Williamson	90	24	66
Winnebago	319	109	210
Nonmetropolitan Counties			
Brown	7	7	0
Carroll	22	9	13
Clay	16	10	6
Cumberland	16	6	10
Edgar	7	7	0
Effingham	45	19	26
Franklin	27	17	10
Fulton	40	19	.21
Gallatin	4	4	0
Greene	13	6	7
Jefferson	65	21	44
Jo Daviess	37	18	19
Mason	28	9	19
Massac	29	13	16
McDonough	23	13	10
Morgan	34	14	20
Perry	34	13	21
Pike	26	9	17
Putnam	13	8	5
Randolph	30	9	21
Saline	30	11	19
Schuyler	6	4	2
Scott	7	3	4
Shelby	30	16	14
Union	21	11	10
INDIANA			
Metropolitan Counties			
Delaware	118	44	74
Floyd	110	38	72
Lake	494	156	338
La Porte	154	131	23
Porter	79	67	12
Shelby	96	33	63
Warrick	81	40	41
Nonmetropolitan Counties			
Clinton	61	19	42
Grant	108	44	64
Miami	51	15	36
Wabash	38	34	4
Wayne	115	79	36
IOWA			
Metropolitan Counties			
Benton	31	12	19
Black Hawk	135	84	51
Dallas	64	27	37

Table 80. Full-Time Law Enforcement Employees, by Selected State Metropolitan and Nonmetropolitan Counties, 2017—Continued

(Number.)

State/county	Law enforcement employees	Officers	Civilians
Dubuque	91	77	14
Grundy	16	12	4
Guthrie	14	9	5
Harrison	11	10	1
Johnson	96	71	25
Jones	24	10	14
Linn	192	121	71
Madison	16	8	8
Mills	27	11	16
Plymouth	32	11	21
Polk	476	142	334
Pottawattamie	194	50	144
Scott	152	42	110
Story	83	29	54
Warren	37	20	17
Washington	32	17	15
Woodbury	121	40	81
Nonmetropolitan Counties			
Adair	13	5	8
Adams	11	6	5
Allamakee	19	9	10
Appanoose	16	8	8
Audubon	10	6	4
Boone	27	12	15
Buchanan	32	13	19
Buena Vista	33	13	20
Butler	18	12	6
Calhoun	11	6	5
Carroll	22	9	13
Cass	11	8	3
Cedar	36	13	23
Cerro Gordo	72	20	52
Cherokee	18	7	11
Chickasaw	16	9	7
Clarke	21	7	14
Clay	23	10	13
Clayton	27	12	15
Clinton	43	25	18
Crawford	15	10	5
Davis	16	6	10
Decatur	16	6	10
Delaware	21	14	7
Des Moines	25	21	4
Dickinson	19	9	10
Emmet	18	9	9
Fayette	35	11	24
Floyd	19	12	7
Franklin	10	7	3
Fremont	27	9	18
Greene	17	8	9
Hamilton	30	10	20
Hancock	9	8	1
Henry	29	11	18
Howard	16	9	7
Humboldt	13	9	4
Ida	16	9	7
Iowa	28	13	15
Jackson	17	10	7
Jasper	47	17	30
Jefferson	31	11	20
Keokuk	10	6	4
Kossuth	25	10	15
Lee	41	17	24
Louisa	28	11	17
Lucas	12	4	8
Lyon	24	10	14
Mahaska	26	10	16
Marion	38	16	22
Marshall	57	19	38
Mitchell	14	7	7
Monona	18	8	10
Monroe	16	5	11
Montgomery	25	9	16
Muscatine	73	22	51
O'Brien	27	9	18
Osceola	13	9	4
Page	17	9	8
Palo Alto	17	8	9
Pocahontas	15	7	8
Poweshiek	26	12	14
Ringgold	10	4	6
Sac	22	9	13

Table 80. Full-Time Law Enforcement Employees, by Selected State Metropolitan and Nonmetropolitan Counties, 2017—Continued

(Number.)

State/county	Law enforcement employees	Officers	Civilians
Shelby	15	9	6
Sioux	40	14	26
Tama	22	13	9
Taylor	14	9	5
Union	13	6	7
Van Buren	11	5	6
Wapello	42	12	30
Wayne	16	6	10
Webster	34	16	18
Winnebago	8	7	1
Winneshiek	24	11	13
Worth	25	13	12
Wright	22	10	12
KANSAS			
Metropolitan Countie			
Butler	101	61	40
Doniphan	17	8	9
Douglas	194	75	119
Harvey	25	23	2
Jackson	30	22	8
Jefferson	40	24	16
Johnson	630	480	150
Kingman	20	8	12
Leavenworth	84	63	21
Linn	31	18	13
Miami	68	36	32
Osage	43	22	21
Pottawatomie	41	28	13
Riley County Police Department	203	104	99
Sedgwick	241	184	57
Wabaunsee	19	8	11
Wyandotte	94	65	29
Nonmetropolitan Counties			
Allen	27	12	15
Anderson	9	9	0
Atchison	29	16	13
Barber	11	6	5
Barton	43	20	23
Bourbon	14	11	3
Brown	24	8	16
Chase	9	5	4
Chautauqua	15	6	9
Cherokee	45	19	26
Cheyenne	5	5	0
Clark	10	5	5
Clay	18	7	11
Cloud	9	8	1
Coffey	22	16	6
Comanche	9	4	5
Cowley	25	22	3
Crawford	51	33	18
Decatur	3	3	0
Dickinson	32	18	14
Edwards	10	6	4
Elk	10	5	5
Ellis	19	19	0
Ellsworth	19	8	11
Ford	35	25	10
Franklin	35	31	4
Gove	6	4	2
Graham	8	3	5
Grant	13	5	8
Gray	15	9	6
Greeley	3	3	0
Greenwood	22	13	9
Hamilton	10	5	5
Harper	12	6	6
Haskell	16	11	5
Hodgeman	9	4	5
Jewell	10	6	4
Kearny	20	11	9
Labette	22	18	4
Lane	11	5	6
Lincoln	12	8	4
Logan	5	5	0
Lyon	32	25	7
Marion	10	9	1
Marshall	22	9	13
McPherson	22	19	3
Mitchell	9	9	0
Morris	13	8	5

Table 80. Full-Time Law Enforcement Employees, by Selected State Metropolitan and Nonmetropolitan Counties, 2017—Continued

(Number.)

State/county	Law enforcement employees	Officers	Civilians
Morton	12	6	6
Nemaha	26	10	16
Neosho	40	16	24
Ness	13	7	6
Norton	10	5	5
Osborne	14	7	7
Ottawa	10	5	5
Pawnee	16	9	7
Phillips	14	9	5
Pratt	18	13	5
Rawlins	4	2	2
Reno	70	59	11
Republic	16	9	7
Rice	9	7	2
Rooks	11	6	5
Rush	12	7	5
Russell	12	11	1
Saline	50	38	12
Scott	4	4	0
Seward	36	14	22
Sheridan	7	3	4
Smith	5	5	0
Stafford	9	4	5
Stanton	9	4	5
Stevens	19	8	11
Trego	6	4	2
Wallace	4	3	1
Washington	12	6	6
Woodson	12	7	5
KENTUCKY			
Metropolitan Counties			
Allen	16	14	2
Boone	140	133	7
Boyd	31	27	4
Bullitt	53	38	15
Butler	8	6	2
Campbell County Police Department	33	32	1
Clark	17	13	4
Daviess	41	37	4
Edmonson	7	5	2
Fayette	81	48	33
Grant	18	16	2
Greenup	18	15	3
Hardin	44	40	4
Henry	8	7	1
Jefferson	290	238	52
Kenton	43	30	13
Kenton County Police Department	31	29	2
Larue	6	5	1
McLean	13	7	6
Meade	18	10	8
Oldham	16	12	4
Pendleton	8	7	1
Scott	35	33	2
Shelby	24	22	2
Trigg	10	7	3
Trimble	2	2	0
Warren	87	38	49
Woodford	11	8	3
Nonmetropolitan Counties			
Adair	9	7	2
Anderson	22	20	2
Ballard	17	17	0
Barren	22	17	5
Bath	8	6	2
Bell	17	12	5
Boyle	12	11	1
Breathitt	2	2	0
Breckenridge	10	7	3
Caldwell	10	8	2
Carlisle	3	2	1
Carroll	9	7	2
Carter	10	7	3
Casey	8	6	2
Clinton	6	4	2
Crittenden	5	4	1
Cumberland	6	4	2
Elliott	3	1	2
Estill	6	4	2
Fleming	7	6	1
Floyd	19	16	3

Table 80. Full-Time Law Enforcement Employees, by Selected State Metropolitan and Nonmetropolitan Counties, 2017—Continued

(Number.)

State/county	Law enforcement employees	Officers	Civilians
Franklin	28	26	2
Garrard	10	9	1
Graves	19	16	3
Grayson	11	8	3
Green	12	4	8
Harlan	21	17	4
Harrison	12	11	1
Hart	9	6	3
Hickman	3	2	1
Hopkins	20	16	4
Jackson	8	7	1
Johnson	12	10	2
Knott	9	6	3
Knox	14	9	5
Laurel	59	35	24
Lee	3	1	2
Leslie	8	6	2
Letcher	7	4	3
Lewis	7	5	2
Lincoln	8	7	1
Livingston	6	5	1
Logan	19	17	2
Lyon	5	4	1
Madison	31	28	3
Magoffin	13	10	3
Marion	10	7	3
Marshall	22	20	2
Martin	9	9	0
Mason	16	14	2
McCreary	4	3	1
Menifee	4	4	0
Mercer	9	8	1
Metcalfe	13	10	3
Monroe	4	3	1
Montgomery	17	15	2
Muhlenberg	15	13	2
Muhlenberg County Police Department	1	1	0
Nelson	30	25	5
Ohio	26	17	9
Owen	6	5	1
Perry	13	10	3
Pike	16	8	8
Powell	5	3	2
Pulaski	40	32	8
Robertson	2	1	1
Rockcastle	6	5	1
Rowan	13	11	2
Russell	11	9	2
Simpson	15	12	3
Taylor	13	10	3
Todd	5	4	1
Union	10	8	2
Washington	5	5	0
Wayne	14	12	2
Webster	9	7	2
Whitley	19	13	6
Wolfe	5	2	3
LOUISIANA			
Metropolitan Counties			
Acadia	99	57	42
Ascension	329	274	55
Bossier	379	308	71
Caddo	686	413	273
Calcasieu	831	831	0
De Soto	113	103	10
East Baton Rouge	827	706	121
East Feliciana	54	54	0
Grant	73	61	12
Iberia	254	172	82
Jefferson	1,458	1,000	458
Lafayette	769	600	169
Lafourche	331	276	55
Livingston	283	283	0
Ouachita	396	396	0
Plaquemines	228	228	0
Pointe Coupee	104	56	48
St. Bernard	270	248	22
St. Charles	382	212	170
St. Helena	42	26	16
St. James	100	60	40
St. John the Baptist	240	239	1
St. Martin	170	118	52

Table 80. Full-Time Law Enforcement Employees, by Selected State Metropolitan and Nonmetropolitan Counties, 2017—Continued

(Number.)

State/county	Law enforcement employees	Officers	Civilians
St. Tammany	661	498	163
Tangipahoa	241	115	126
Terrebonne	308	240	68
Union	48	32	16
Vermilion	145	119	26
Webster	128	107	21
West Baton Rouge	183	140	43
West Feliciana	69	69	0
Nonmetropolitan Counties			
Allen	82	82	0
Assumption	83	53	30
Avoyelles	92	62	30
Beauregard	87	68	19
Bienville	70	42	28
Catahoula	107	31	76
Claiborne	87	38	49
Concordia	232	24	208
East Carroll	41	14	27
Evangeline	32	25	7
Franklin	129	129	0
Jackson	180	44	136
Jefferson Davis	77	77	0
La Salle	49	31	18
Lincoln	79	56	23
Madison	34	34	0
Morehouse	130	130	0
Natchitoches	196	160	36
Richland	136	116	20
Sabine	86	63	23
St. Landry	201	90	111
St. Mary	150	150	0
Vernon	163	66	97
Washington	79	62	17
West Carroll	20	10	10
MAINE			
Metropolitan Counties			
Androscoggin	33	19	14
Cumberland	71	59	12
Penobscot	36	31	5
Sagadahoc	21	19	2
York	33	30	3
Nonmetropolitan Counties			
Aroostook	27	20	7
Franklin	34	19	15
Hancock	20	18	2
Kennebec	23	20	3
Knox	23	22	1
Lincoln	25	23	2
Oxford	28	25	3
Piscataquis	9	8	1
Somerset	26	22	4
Waldo	24	22	2
Washington	14	12	2
MARYLAND			
Metropolitan Counties			
Allegany	34	32	2
Anne Arundel	97	70	27
Anne Arundel County Police Department	947	707	240
Baltimore County	81	71	10
Baltimore County Police Department	2,025	1,818	207
Calvert	164	136	28
Carroll	137	108	29
Cecil	111	92	19
Charles	430	298	132
Frederick	246	185	61
Harford	386	290	96
Howard	71	53	18
Howard County Police Department	660	465	195
Montgomery	184	151	33
Montgomery County Police Department	1,748	1,249	499
Prince George's	330	247	83
Prince George's County Police Department	1,843	1,625	218
Queen Anne's	66	59	7
Somerset	24	21	3
St. Mary's	263	127	136
Washington	254	104	150
Wicomico	105	84	21
Worcester	60	52	8

Table 80. Full-Time Law Enforcement Employees, by Selected State Metropolitan and Nonmetropolitan Counties, 2017—Continued

(Number.)

State/county	Law enforcement employees	Officers	Civilians
Nonmetropolitan Counties			
Caroline	34	30	4
Dorchester	42	38	4
Garrett	56	31	25
Kent	28	25	3
Talbot	38	35	3
MICHIGAN			
Metropolitan Counties			
Barry	52	30	22
Bay	82	35	47
Berrien	158	74	84
Calhoun	179	85	94
Cass	69	32	37
Clinton	61	26	35
Eaton	127	70	57
Genesee	247	113	134
Ingham	164	91	73
Jackson	131	52	79
Kalamazoo	224	142	82
Kent	548	207	341
Lapeer	80	49	31
Livingston	168	52	116
Macomb	521	251	270
Midland	68	30	38
Monroe	154	74	80
Montcalm	42	17	25
Muskegon	107	44	63
Oakland	1,073	891	182
Ottawa	239	142	97
Saginaw	116	61	55
St. Clair	185	75	110
Washtenaw	303	128	175
Wayne	920	629	291
Nonmetropolitan Counties			
Alcona	29	12	17
Allegan	100	53	47
Alpena	27	13	14
Antrim	45	20	25
Arenac	20	11	9
Baraga	13	6	7
Benzie	33	15	18
Branch	35	14	21
Charlevoix	30	19	11
Cheboygan	37	20	17
Chippewa	30	12	18
Clare	32	26	6
Crawford	25	15	10
Delta	10	10	0
Emmet	47	25	22
Gladwin	38	15	23
Gogebic	25	17	8
Grand Traverse	113	60	53
Gratiot	26	25	1
Hillsdale	38	24	14
Houghton	28	19	9
Huron	36	20	16
Ionia	57	25	32
Iosco	22	5	17
Iron	19	10	9
Isabella	48	22	26
Keweenaw	6	6	0
Lake	76	16	60
Leelanau	21	20	1
Lenawee	104	41	63
Luce	7	6	1
Mackinac	28	13	15
Manistee	37	17	20
Marquette	61	22	39
Mason	40	20	20
Mecosta	49	21	28
Menominee	15	15	0
Montmorency	13	13	0
Newaygo	63	27	36
Oceana	36	21	15
Ogemaw	34	15	19
Ontonagon	10	6	4
Osceola	36	17	19
Oscoda	16	12	4
Otsego	28	10	18
Presque Isle	26	13	13
Roscommon	39	24	15

Table 80. Full-Time Law Enforcement Employees, by Selected State Metropolitan and Nonmetropolitan Counties, 2017—Continued

(Number.)

State/county	Law enforcement employees	Officers	Civilians
Sanilac	54	26	28
Schoolcraft	10	3	7
Shiawassee	51	21	30
St. Joseph	58	27	31
Tuscola	44	20	24
Wexford	48	23	25
MINNESOTA			
Metropolitan Counties			
Anoka	265	134	131
Benton	70	24	46
Blue Earth	76	35	41
Carlton	53	24	29
Carver	146	73	73
Chisago	83	42	41
Clay	71	34	37
Dakota	193	80	113
Dodge	37	24	13
Fillmore	30	19	11
Hennepin	809	320	489
Houston	33	13	20
Isanti	61	21	40
Le Sueur	34	19	15
Mille Lacs	86	42	44
Nicollet	44	16	28
Olmsted	177	69	108
Polk	44	32	12
Ramsey	428	215	213
Scott	125	43	82
Sherburne	289	83	206
Sibley	24	12	12
Stearns	189	64	125
St. Louis	255	102	153
Wabasha	51	17	34
Washington	252	109	143
Wright	239	138	101
Nonmetropolitan Counties			
Aitkin	47	18	29
Becker	55	21	34
Beltrami	71	29	42
Big Stone	7	5	2
Brown	36	14	22
Cass	72	42	30
Chippewa	18	8	10
Clearwater	24	10	14
Cook	20	12	8
Cottonwood	22	10	12
Crow Wing	119	38	81
Douglas	82	33	49
Faribault	27	11	16
Freeborn	79	25	54
Goodhue	107	40	67
Grant	16	10	6
Hubbard	46	18	28
Itasca	76	34	42
Jackson	26	14	12
Kanabec	49	20	29
Kandiyohi	102	32	70
Kittson	11	5	6
Koochiching	20	10	10
Lac Qui Parle	13	7	6
Lake	29	16	13
Lake of the Woods	13	7	6
Lincoln	12	6	6
Lyon	49	17	32
Mahnomen	19	12	7
Marshall	21	12	9
Martin	33	12	21
McLeod	55	24	31
Meeker	44	19	25
Morrison	51	19	32
Mower	70	22	48
Murray	18	12	6
Nobles	36	13	23
Norman	10	7	3
Otter Tail	83	36	47
Pennington	29	8	21
Pine	81	33	48
Pipestone	26	14	12
Pope	15	8	7
Red Lake	11	8	3
Redwood	29	13	16

Table 80. Full-Time Law Enforcement Employees, by Selected State Metropolitan and Nonmetropolitan Counties, 2017—Continued

(Number.)

State/county	Law enforcement employees	Officers	Civilians
Renville	40	15	25
Rice	55	29	26
Rock	17	12	5
Roseau	19	10	9
Steele	28	22	6
Stevens	15	7	8
Swift	17	8	9
Todd	33	16	17
Traverse	14	6	8
Wadena	19	10	9
Waseca	27	12	15
Watonwan	22	8	14
Wilkin	17	7	10
Winona	72	20	52
Yellow Medicine	28	10	18
MISSISSIPPI			
Metropolitan Counties			
Hancock	139	69	70
Harrison	319	114	205
Hinds	365	103	262
Jackson	192	157	35
Lamar	53	46	7
Madison	77	73	4
Rankin	210	95	115
Tunica	109	51	58
Nonmetropolitan Counties			
Choctaw	15	9	6
Claiborne	32	12	20
Grenada	14	12	2
Kemper	12	10	2
Panola	74	39	35
Scott	66	25	41
Sunflower	57	16	41
Warren	40	36	4
Washington	46	33	13
MISSOURI			
Metropolitan Counties			
Andrew	32	15	17
Bates	40	20	20
Bollinger	15	10	5
Boone	75	60	15
Buchanan	103	70	33
Caldwell	15	8	7
Callaway	27	24	3
Cape Girardeau	79	42	37
Cass	88	67	21
Christian	88	52	36
Clay	195	127	68
Clinton	27	20	7
Cole	85	52	33
Dallas	24	17	7
DeKalb	12	6	6
Franklin	131	115	16
Greene	321	134	187
Jackson	159	121	38
Jasper	133	84	49
Jefferson	209	145	64
Lafayette	53	41	12
Lincoln	116	54	62
McDonald	29	23	6
Moniteau	10	4	6
Newton	68	34	34
Osage	12	9	3
Platte	131	88	43
Polk	37	23	14
Ray	27	14	13
St. Charles	46	32	14
St. Charles County Police Department	166	133	33
St. Louis County Police Department	1,201	902	299
Warren	55	29	26
Webster	30	17	13
Nonmetropolitan Counties			
Adair	25	10	15
Atchison	11	6	5
Audrain	39	31	8
Barry	41	24	17
Benton	26	18	8
Butler	44	29	15
Camden	115	70	45

Table 80. Full-Time Law Enforcement Employees, by Selected State Metropolitan and Nonmetropolitan Counties, 2017—Continued

(Number.)

State/county	Law enforcement employees	Officers	Civilians
Carroll	8	6	2
Carter	15	9	6
Cedar	38	12	26
Chariton	14	9	5
Clark	12	6	6
Cooper	11	9	2
Crawford	33	19	14
Dade	13	7	6
Daviess	8	6	2
Dent	19	14	5
Douglas	12	7	5
Dunklin	19	10	9
Gasconade	13	12	1
Gentry	5	5	0
Grundy	14	4	10
Harrison	11	5	6
Henry	39	27	12
Hickory	14	10	4
Holt	13	6	7
Howard	11	6	5
Howell	37	28	9
Iron	15	11	4
Johnson	60	31	29
Knox	5	4	1
Laclede	35	22	13
Lawrence	33	26	7
Lewis	13	7	6
Linn	10	9	1
Livingston	8	7	1
Macon	19	9	10
Madison	10	8	2
Maries	8	7	1
Marion	40	16	24
Mercer	9	3	6
Miller	40	20	20
Mississippi	12	7	5
Monroe	9	8	1
Montgomery	20	18	2
Morgan	48	25	23
New Madrid	16	13	3
Nodaway	16	14	2
Oregon	11	7	4
Ozark	16	10	6
Pemiscot	48	18	30
Perry	39	25	14
Pettis	51	29	22
Phelps	76	33	43
Pike	30	10	20
Pulaski	54	31	23
Ralls	10	9	1
Randolph	44	26	18
Reynolds	10	9	1
Ripley	13	11	2
Saline	32	20	12
Schuyler	6	4	2
Scotland	6	3	3
Shannon	10	4	6
Shelby	8	5	3
St. Clair	69	23	46
Ste. Genevieve	65	43	22
St. Francois	70	57	13
Stoddard	31	14	17
Stone	57	46	11
Sullivan	5	4	1
Taney	54	39	15
Texas	12	11	1
Vernon	43	19	24
Washington	35	22	13
Wayne	14	5	9
Worth	4	3	1
Wright	13	7	6
MONTANA			
Metropolitan Counties			
Carbon	17	10	7
Cascade	130	29	101
Golden Valley	2	2	0
Missoula	70	53	17
Yellowstone	156	52	104
Nonmetropolitan Counties			
Beaverhead	18	7	11
Big Horn	29	20	9

Table 80. Full-Time Law Enforcement Employees, by Selected State Metropolitan and Nonmetropolitan Counties, 2017—Continued

(Number.)

State/county	Law enforcement employees	Officers	Civilians
Blaine	14	8	6
Broadwater	27	11	16
Carter	3	3	0
Chouteau	24	9	15
Custer	17	6	11
Daniels	9	2	7
Dawson	8	7	1
Deer Lodge	21	21	0
Fallon	9	4	5
Fergus	21	9	12
Flathead	116	57	59
Gallatin	110	58	52
Garfield	3	3	0
Glacier	26	13	13
Granite	10	6	4
Hill	27	12	15
Jefferson	15	13	2
Judith Basin	5	4	1
Lake	44	23	21
Lewis and Clark	79	45	34
Liberty	9	5	4
Lincoln	35	16	19
Madison	24	11	13
McCone	10	4	6
Meagher	9	3	6
Mineral	10	5	5
Musselshell	8	7	1
Park	16	14	2
Phillips	7	7	0
Pondera	8	7	1
Powder River	8	4	4
Powell	10	5	5
Prairie	4	3	1
Ravalli	73	32	41
Richland	36	11	25
Roosevelt	48	16	32
Rosebud	24	13	11
Sanders	12	12	0
Sheridan	10	8	2
Silver Bow	101	51	50
Stillwater	19	10	9
Sweet Grass	14	7	7
Teton	12	9	3
Toole	23	14	9
Treasure	1	1	0
Valley	23	8	15
Wheatland	8	8	0
Wibaux	3	3	0
NEBRASKA			
Metropolitan Counties			
Cass	73	46	27
Dixon	13	8	5
Douglas	204	127	77
Hall	41	31	10
Hamilton	19	9	10
Howard	12	5	7
Lancaster	103	77	26
Merrick	16	9	7
Sarpy	221	133	88
Saunders	22	11	11
Seward	17	15	2
Nonmetropolitan Counties			
Adams	31	16	15
Antelope	17	5	12
Arthur	1	1	0
Banner	1	1	0
Box Butte	18	5	13
Brown	8	5	3
Buffalo	48	29	19
Burt	10	5	5
Butler	25	10	15
Cedar	7	7	0
Chase	8	4	4
Cheyenne	21	9	12
Colfax	18	10	8
Cuming	6	5	1
Custer	8	7	1
Dawson	65	28	37
Dodge	21	18	3
Dundy	9	5	4
Fillmore	13	7	6

Table 80. Full-Time Law Enforcement Employees, by Selected State Metropolitan and Nonmetropolitan Counties, 2017—Continued

(Number.)

State/county	Law enforcement employees	Officers	Civilians
Franklin	8	4	4
Frontier	9	5	4
Furnas	13	7	6
Gage	30	16	14
Gosper	6	5	1
Grant	2	2	0
Harlan	8	4	4
Hayes	2	1	1
Hitchcock	8	4	4
Holt	13	6	7
Hooker	1	1	0
Jefferson	21	10	11
Johnson	11	7	4
Keith	9	8	1
Keya Paha	1	1	0
Kimball	9	4	5
Lincoln	56	23	33
Logan	2	2	0
Madison	63	34	29
McPherson	1	1	0
Morrill	14	9	5
Nance	11	7	4
Nemaha	10	10	0
Nuckolls	5	5	0
Otoe	29	15	14
Pawnee	5	4	1
Perkins	7	6	1
Phelps	25	6	19
Platte	68	20	48
Red Willow	22	7	15
Richardson	23	8	15
Rock	8	2	6
Scotts Bluff	25	18	7
Sherman	6	5	1
Stanton	9	8	1
Thayer	14	8	6
Thurston	12	9	3
Valley	6	6	0
Wayne	5	4	1
Webster	10	6	4
Wheeler	2	1	1
York	27	10	17
NEVADA			
Metropolitan Counties			
Carson City	137	95	42
Storey	22	20	2
Washoe	693	415	278
Nonmetropolitan Counties			
Churchill	47	39	8
Douglas	117	104	13
Elko	77	63	14
Esmeralda	16	12	4
Eureka	15	9	6
Humboldt	56	34	22
Lander	32	21	11
Lincoln	28	24	4
Lyon	116	83	33
Mineral	20	14	6
Nye	131	101	30
Pershing	20	13	7
White Pine	34	28	6
NEW HAMPSHIRE			
Metropolitan Counties			
Rockingham	51	26	25
Strafford	34	21	13
Nonmetropolitan Counties			
Carroll	25	11	14
Cheshire	23	10	13
Grafton	22	8	14
Merrimack	34	18	16
NEW JERSEY			
Metropolitan Counties			
Atlantic	129	106	23
Bergen	510	430	80
Burlington	88	70	18
Camden	199	167	32
Cape May	156	138	18
Cumberland	65	58	7

Table 80. Full-Time Law Enforcement Employees, by Selected State Metropolitan and Nonmetropolitan Counties, 2017—Continued

(Number.)

State/county	Law enforcement employees	Officers	Civilians
Essex	474	388	86
Gloucester	106	94	12
Hudson	398	263	135
Hunterdon	29	25	4
Mercer	190	151	39
Middlesex	226	183	43
Monmouth	659	438	221
Morris	120	89	31
Ocean	281	147	134
Passaic	672	549	123
Salem	238	199	39
Somerset	210	170	40
Sussex	159	126	33
Union	280	237	43
Warren	22	18	4
NEW MEXICO			
Metropolitan Counties			
Dona Ana	186	131	55
San Juan	127	93	34
Torrance	21	18	3
Valencia	59	48	11
Nonmetropolitan Counties			
Catron	12	8	4
Chaves	46	37	9
Cibola	30	17	13
Colfax	11	10	1
Curry	28	17	11
Guadalupe	8	7	1
Hidalgo	11	9	2
Lea	71	61	10
Lincoln	31	21	10
Luna	39	31	8
Mora	7	5	2
Otero	69	42	27
Quay	7	6	1
Rio Arriba	29	25	4
San Miguel	12	10	2
Sierra	14	12	2
Socorro	15	13	2
Taos	28	22	6
Union	7	5	2
NEW YORK			
Metropolitan Counties			
Albany	180	120	60
Broome	65	56	9
Chemung	48	43	5
Dutchess	140	104	36
Erie	188	145	43
Herkimer	18	8	10
Jefferson	59	41	18
Livingston	75	49	26
Madison	45	35	10
Monroe	317	267	50
Nassau	3,201	2,456	745
Niagara	157	107	50
Oneida	93	82	11
Onondaga	236	202	34
Ontario	112	70	42
Oswego	86	68	18
Putnam	105	86	19
Rensselaer	42	35	7
Saratoga	169	120	49
Schenectady	15	10	5
Schoharie	31	17	14
Suffolk	377	260	117
Suffolk County Police Department	3,068	2,536	532
Tioga	55	35	20
Tompkins	45	40	5
Ulster	59	56	3
Warren	101	68	33
Washington	45	39	6
Wayne	81	69	12
Westchester Public Safety	348	280	68
Yates	26	22	4
Nonmetropolitan Counties			
Allegany	46	19	27
Cattaraugus	74	48	26
Cayuga	36	32	4
Chautauqua	110	70	40

Table 80. Full-Time Law Enforcement Employees, by Selected State Metropolitan and Nonmetropolitan Counties, 2017—Continued

(Number.)

State/county	Law enforcement employees	Officers	Civilians
Clinton	39	26	13
Columbia	70	55	15
Cortland	41	38	3
Delaware	23	15	8
Franklin	6	4	2
Fulton	45	28	17
Genesee	76	49	27
Greene	27	25	2
Hamilton	7	6	1
Lewis	29	20	9
Montgomery	45	26	19
Otsego	19	17	2
Schuyler	21	18	3
Seneca	36	31	5
St. Lawrence	33	31	2
Sullivan	51	51	0
Wyoming	43	31	12
NORTH CAROLINA			
Metropolitan Counties			
Alamance	250	127	123
Alexander	71	36	35
Brunswick	284	177	107
Buncombe	394	244	150
Burke	108	89	19
Cabarrus	319	181	138
Caldwell	109	69	40
Catawba	195	147	48
Chatham	139	105	34
Craven	133	78	55
Cumberland	583	299	284
Currituck	95	61	34
Davidson	167	116	51
Davie	89	54	35
Durham	468	187	281
Edgecombe	133	54	79
Forsyth	475	197	278
Franklin	124	83	41
Gaston	211	111	100
Gaston County Police Department	221	126	95
Gates	13	12	1
Guilford	615	258	357
Haywood	123	61	62
Henderson	210	140	70
Hoke	119	63	56
Iredell	219	150	69
Johnston	187	114	73
Jones	26	18	8
Lincoln	170	117	53
Madison	42	24	18
Mecklenburg[1]	1,081	281	800
Nash	138	86	52
New Hanover	512	356	156
Onslow	264	131	133
Orange	145	98	47
Pamlico	52	23	29
Pender	115	72	43
Person	89	47	42
Pitt	315	135	180
Randolph	222	165	57
Rockingham	147	98	49
Rowan	192	124	68
Stokes	69	47	22
Union	293	205	88
Wake	946	370	576
Wayne	130	123	7
Yadkin	50	38	12
Nonmetropolitan Counties			
Alleghany	33	17	16
Anson	61	32	29
Ashe	65	32	33
Avery	50	25	25
Beaufort	89	51	38
Bertie	41	27	14
Bladen	93	55	38
Camden	19	16	3
Carteret	91	59	32
Caswell	56	36	20
Cherokee	67	32	35
Chowan	38	18	20
Clay	41	18	23
Cleveland	183	108	75

Table 80. Full-Time Law Enforcement Employees, by Selected State Metropolitan and Nonmetropolitan Counties, 2017—Continued

(Number.)

State/county	Law enforcement employees	Officers	Civilians
Columbus	108	69	39
Dare	142	63	79
Duplin	106	70	36
Graham	27	15	12
Granville	108	51	57
Greene	45	22	23
Halifax	97	65	32
Harnett	229	127	102
Hertford	58	23	35
Hyde	16	14	2
Jackson	75	51	24
Lee	105	66	39
Lenoir	117	70	47
Macon	76	49	27
Martin	39	37	2
McDowell	64	43	21
Mitchell	18	17	1
Montgomery	55	30	25
Moore	151	81	70
Northampton	45	33	12
Pasquotank	52	47	5
Perquimans	17	15	2
Polk	47	36	11
Richmond	94	60	34
Robeson	224	133	91
Rutherford	130	77	53
Sampson	130	90	40
Scotland	65	41	24
Stanly	91	49	42
Surry	101	72	29
Swain	46	27	19
Transylvania	81	61	20
Tyrrell	14	12	2
Vance	91	44	47
Warren	67	33	34
Washington	49	23	26
Watauga	72	42	30
Wilkes	129	72	57
Wilson	153	92	61
Yancey	40	19	21
NORTH DAKOTA			
Metropolitan Counties			
Burleigh	64	52	12
Cass	166	105	61
Grand Forks	39	33	6
Morton	44	35	9
Oliver	5	4	1
Sioux	1	1	0
Nonmetropolitan Counties			
Adams	6	6	0
Barnes	9	8	1
Benson	4	4	0
Billings	6	6	0
Bottineau	20	11	9
Bowman	5	4	1
Burke	5	4	1
Cavalier	12	6	6
Dickey	5	4	1
Divide	6	6	0
Dunn	17	15	2
Eddy	5	4	1
Emmons	6	5	1
Foster	2	2	0
Golden Valley	5	4	1
Grant	4	4	0
Griggs	3	3	0
Hettinger	6	5	1
Kidder	4	3	1
Lamoure	6	5	1
Logan	3	3	0
McHenry	8	8	0
McIntosh	3	3	0
McKenzie	49	30	19
McLean	42	25	17
Mercer	30	22	8
Mountrail	24	12	12
Nelson	6	5	1
Pembina	16	9	7
Pierce	37	3	34
Ramsey	8	7	1
Ransom	5	4	1

Table 80. Full-Time Law Enforcement Employees, by Selected State Metropolitan and Nonmetropolitan Counties, 2017—Continued

(Number.)

State/county	Law enforcement employees	Officers	Civilians
Renville	6	6	0
Richland	35	18	17
Rolette	16	6	10
Sargent	6	5	1
Sheridan	3	3	0
Slope	2	2	0
Stark	30	25	5
Steele	3	3	0
Stutsman	33	13	20
Towner	6	5	1
Traill	13	8	5
Walsh	18	11	7
Ward	90	35	55
Wells	4	3	1
Williams	75	37	38
OHIO			
Metropolitan Counties			
Brown	32	29	3
Carroll	35	20	15
Delaware	213	102	111
Fairfield	139	110	29
Fulton	24	22	2
Geauga	117	50	67
Greene	147	67	80
Lorain	81	74	7
Madison	41	30	11
Medina	147	57	90
Miami	110	49	61
Pickaway	84	34	50
Portage	141	57	84
Richland	128	50	78
Stark	249	125	124
Summit	405	332	73
Union	58	39	19
Warren	189	102	87
Nonmetropolitan Counties			
Ashland	79	44	35
Ashtabula	74	34	40
Athens	31	26	5
Champaign	27	24	3
Coshocton	57	42	15
Darke	65	34	31
Defiance	43	27	16
Fayette	48	24	24
Henry	23	13	10
Highland	49	28	21
Holmes	52	32	20
Knox	63	46	17
Logan	75	25	50
Marion	56	29	27
Paulding	42	27	15
Preble	51	16	35
Putnam	55	29	26
Scioto	74	39	35
Shelby	77	55	22
Washington	95	54	41
OKLAHOMA			
Metropolitan Counties			
Canadian	103	63	40
Cleveland	203	62	141
Comanche	40	29	11
Cotton	7	2	5
Creek	89	31	58
Garfield	37	26	11
Grady	33	22	11
Le Flore	19	15	4
Lincoln	32	16	16
Logan	69	36	33
McClain	35	21	14
Oklahoma	672	497	175
Okmulgee	17	15	2
Osage	71	35	36
Pawnee	25	8	17
Rogers	81	52	29
Sequoyah	25	23	2
Tulsa	624	222	402
Wagoner	66	34	32
Nonmetropolitan Counties			
Adair	8	8	0
Alfalfa	12	7	5

Table 80. Full-Time Law Enforcement Employees, by Selected State Metropolitan and Nonmetropolitan Counties, 2017—Continued

(Number.)

State/county	Law enforcement employees	Officers	Civilians
Atoka	24	9	15
Beaver	16	8	8
Beckham	40	15	25
Blaine	9	9	0
Bryan	16	13	3
Caddo	35	17	18
Carter	54	19	35
Cherokee	33	24	9
Choctaw	18	7	11
Cimarron	9	4	5
Coal	12	8	4
Craig	25	10	15
Custer	37	13	24
Delaware	46	20	26
Dewey	14	7	7
Ellis	17	8	9
Garvin	32	19	13
Grant	8	5	3
Greer	9	2	7
Harmon	4	3	1
Harper	7	4	3
Haskell	18	6	12
Hughes	17	9	8
Jackson	37	13	24
Jefferson	14	5	9
Johnston	23	7	16
Kay	24	17	7
Kingfisher	21	10	11
Kiowa	11	6	5
Latimer	14	6	8
Love	24	10	14
Major	12	6	6
Marshall	24	7	17
Mayes	55	28	27
McCurtain	23	17	6
McIntosh	25	18	7
Murray	14	6	8
Muskogee	75	29	46
Noble	22	12	10
Nowata	14	4	10
Okfuskee	20	9	11
Ottawa	36	13	23
Payne	91	34	57
Pittsburg	21	17	4
Pontotoc	37	17	20
Pottawatomie	31	28	3
Pushmataha	16	8	8
Roger Mills	13	8	5
Seminole	19	17	2
Stephens	23	19	4
Texas	35	13	22
Tillman	3	3	0
Washington	60	27	33
Washita	29	7	22
Woods	8	7	1
Woodward	36	12	24
OREGON			
Metropolitan Counties			
Benton	77	67	10
Clackamas	455	344	111
Columbia	67	54	13
Deschutes	218	161	57
Jackson	148	113	35
Josephine	61	45	16
Lane	274	64	210
Linn	170	71	99
Marion	353	96	257
Multnomah	780	133	647
Polk	35	26	9
Washington	568	405	163
Yamhill	91	76	15
Nonmetropolitan Counties			
Baker	37	37	0
Clatsop	54	25	29
Coos	89	60	29
Crook	37	16	21
Curry	41	16	25
Douglas	144	66	78
Gilliam	7	6	1
Grant	20	20	0
Harney	22	9	13

Table 80. Full-Time Law Enforcement Employees, by Selected State Metropolitan and Nonmetropolitan Counties, 2017—Continued

(Number.)

State/county	Law enforcement employees	Officers	Civilians
Hood River	53	27	26
Jefferson	55	49	6
Klamath	77	34	43
Lincoln	91	30	61
Malheur	61	27	34
Morrow	37	25	12
Sherman	7	6	1
Tillamook	52	41	11
Umatilla	109	54	55
Union	32	15	17
Wallowa	12	5	7
Wasco	30	17	13
Wheeler	5	4	1
PENNSYLVANIA			
Metropolitan Counties			
Adams	16	13	3
Allegheny	192	159	33
Allegheny County Police Department	276	217	59
Beaver	28	24	4
Berks	105	93	12
Blair	30	27	3
Bucks	68	56	12
Butler	30	27	3
Centre	19	15	4
Cumberland	30	30	0
Erie	46	39	7
Franklin	26	22	4
Lancaster	72	66	6
Lycoming	16	16	0
Mercer	19	15	4
Monroe	46	28	18
Montgomery	130	108	22
Northampton	69	64	5
Pike	24	20	4
Washington	32	29	3
Westmoreland	7	7	0
Wyoming	6	4	2
York	111	100	11
Nonmetropolitan Counties			
Bedford	11	9	2
Bradford	10	10	0
Clarion	11	8	3
Elk	6	5	1
Greene	16	9	7
Indiana	21	18	3
Jefferson	9	8	1
Lawrence	23	18	5
Northumberland	10	8	2
Schuylkill	18	14	4
Snyder	7	7	0
Tioga	9	7	2
Union	9	8	1
Warren	12	10	2
Wayne	15	12	3
SOUTH CAROLINA			
Metropolitan Counties			
Aiken	248	137	111
Beaufort	317	220	97
Berkeley	185	161	24
Calhoun	43	27	16
Charleston	714	286	428
Chester	113	60	53
Fairfield	53	45	8
Florence	229	190	39
Greenville	552	449	103
Horry	382	88	294
Lancaster	166	116	50
Lexington	433	273	160
Pickens	151	109	42
Saluda	60	21	39
Spartanburg	338	308	30
Sumter	197	105	92
Union	48	28	20
York	328	166	162
Nonmetropolitan Counties			
Allendale	16	13	3
Barnwell	82	28	54
Cherokee	101	51	50
Chesterfield	55	47	8
Clarendon	62	56	6

Table 80. Full-Time Law Enforcement Employees, by Selected State Metropolitan and Nonmetropolitan Counties, 2017—Continued

(Number.)

State/county	Law enforcement employees	Officers	Civilians
Colleton	113	48	65
Georgetown	165	75	90
Hampton	45	28	17
Marion	68	37	31
Marlboro	27	23	4
McCormick	38	17	21
Newberry	117	53	64
Oconee	168	94	74
SOUTH DAKOTA			
Metropolitan Counties			
Custer	12	10	2
Lincoln	20	18	2
McCook	8	7	1
Meade	40	18	22
Minnehaha	195	96	99
Pennington	379	97	282
Turner	10	8	2
Union	26	17	9
Nonmetropolitan Counties			
Aurora	4	3	1
Beadle	22	5	17
Bennett	4	3	1
Bon Homme	8	3	5
Brookings	23	14	9
Brown	67	18	49
Brule	10	8	2
Buffalo	1	1	0
Butte	13	5	8
Campbell	3	3	0
Charles Mix	21	7	14
Clark	3	3	0
Clay	14	8	6
Codington	29	10	19
Corson	4	4	0
Davison	9	7	2
Day	5	3	2
Deuel	6	5	1
Dewey	3	3	0
Douglas	4	4	0
Fall River	13	6	7
Faulk	13	4	9
Grant	9	4	5
Gregory	5	4	1
Haakon	2	2	0
Hamlin	9	4	5
Hand	2	1	1
Hanson	3	3	0
Harding	3	2	1
Hughes	48	6	42
Hutchinson	3	3	0
Hyde	2	2	0
Jackson	3	2	1
Jerauld	4	4	0
Jones	2	2	0
Kingsbury	6	5	1
Lake	18	6	12
Lawrence	38	15	23
Lyman	5	4	1
Marshall	10	6	4
McPherson	3	3	0
Miner	4	3	1
Moody	10	5	5
Oglala Lakota	1	1	0
Perkins	8	7	1
Potter	3	2	1
Roberts	30	5	25
Sanborn	3	3	0
Spink	14	9	5
Stanley	6	5	1
Sully	3	3	0
Todd	2	1	1
Tripp	3	3	0
Walworth	6	6	0
Yankton	32	12	20
Ziebach	2	2	0
TENNESSEE			
Metropolitan Counties			
Anderson	166	60	106
Blount	300	173	127
Bradley	218	109	109
Campbell	94	41	53
Cannon	35	16	19

Table 80. Full-Time Law Enforcement Employees, by Selected State Metropolitan and Nonmetropolitan Counties, 2017—Continued

(Number.)

State/county	Law enforcement employees	Officers	Civilians
Carter	131	57	74
Cheatham	83	41	42
Chester	48	14	34
Crockett	32	14	18
Dickson	132	63	69
Fayette	83	37	46
Grainger	46	25	21
Hamblen	106	41	65
Hamilton	421	173	248
Hartsville/Trousdale	41	19	22
Hawkins	106	59	47
Hickman	43	23	20
Jefferson	107	53	54
Knox	962	394	568
Loudon	86	48	38
Madison	277	113	164
Marion	54	26	28
Maury	162	82	80
Montgomery	351	109	242
Morgan	39	19	20
Polk	60	22	38
Roane	67	34	33
Robertson	151	58	93
Rutherford	453	233	220
Sequatchie	45	22	23
Shelby	1,811	600	1,211
Smith	60	27	33
Sullivan	288	126	162
Sumner	275	99	176
Tipton	106	62	44
Unicoi	41	24	17
Union	51	31	20
Washington	220	95	125
Williamson	271	164	107
Wilson	266	129	137
Nonmetropolitan Counties			
Bedford	93	45	48
Benton	63	17	46
Bledsoe	41	15	26
Carroll	66	26	40
Claiborne	100	38	62
Clay	21	12	9
Cocke	67	37	30
Coffee	150	45	105
Cumberland	114	48	66
Decatur	34	15	19
DeKalb	48	25	23
Dyer	97	37	60
Fentress	40	16	24
Franklin	73	43	30
Giles	60	30	30
Greene	156	60	96
Grundy	36	14	22
Hancock	34	14	20
Hardeman	72	31	41
Hardin	49	25	24
Haywood	44	17	27
Henderson	70	30	40
Henry	67	32	35
Houston	25	9	16
Humphreys	38	21	17
Jackson	48	15	33
Johnson	39	13	26
Lake	13	7	6
Lauderdale	61	23	38
Lawrence	104	58	46
Lewis	36	16	20
Lincoln	82	36	46
Marshall	56	30	26
McMinn	81	33	48
Meigs	33	18	15
Monroe	51	45	6
Moore	36	16	20
Obion	58	21	37
Overton	48	22	26
Pickett	20	11	9
Putnam	149	69	80
Rhea	56	55	1
Scott	30	30	0
Sevier	213	106	107
Stewart	48	20	28
Van Buren	19	10	9

Table 80. Full-Time Law Enforcement Employees, by Selected State Metropolitan and Nonmetropolitan Counties, 2017—Continued

(Number.)

State/county	Law enforcement employees	Officers	Civilians
Warren	99	49	50
Wayne	49	14	35
Weakley	41	21	20
White	73	33	40
TEXAS			
Metropolitan Counties			
Aransas	72	23	49
Archer	21	21	0
Armstrong	9	4	5
Austin	73	45	28
Bandera	67	29	38
Bastrop	193	77	116
Bowie	44	36	8
Brazoria	329	131	198
Brazos	243	106	137
Burleson	40	13	27
Caldwell	99	35	64
Callahan	14	6	8
Chambers	106	52	54
Clay	26	14	12
Crosby	15	6	9
Dallas	2,247	485	1,762
Denton	586	207	379
Ector	228	91	137
Ellis	229	83	146
Fort Bend	779	529	250
Grayson	160	60	100
Gregg	253	102	151
Guadalupe	219	98	121
Hardin	66	28	38
Harris	4,609	2,250	2,359
Hays	316	156	160
Hidalgo	784	276	508
Hood	147	55	92
Hunt	136	40	96
Irion	10	5	5
Jefferson	407	128	279
Jones	31	8	23
Kaufman	231	85	146
Medina	72	35	37
Midland	203	80	123
Montgomery	896	488	408
Newton	23	22	1
Parker	127	90	37
Potter	197	97	100
Robertson	30	12	18
Smith	376	164	212
Tarrant	1,399	1,219	180
Taylor	234	88	146
Travis	1,699	350	1,349
Upshur	80	45	35
Victoria	190	118	72
Waller	84	60	24
Wichita	207	76	131
Williamson	521	212	309
Wilson	74	33	41
Wise	133	61	72
Nonmetropolitan Counties			
Anderson	81	34	47
Andrews	38	13	25
Angelina	102	46	56
Baylor	8	3	5
Borden	3	2	1
Briscoe	3	3	0
Brooks	41	16	25
Brown	68	29	39
Camp	18	7	11
Cass	50	21	29
Castro	19	7	12
Cherokee	75	33	42
Childress	20	5	15
Concho	13	7	6
Crane	11	6	5
Crockett	12	9	3
Dawson	19	7	12
Deaf Smith	38	13	25
Delta	23	11	12
Dickens	5	3	2
Dimmit	65	31	34
Donley	10	6	4
Eastland	31	12	19

Table 80. Full-Time Law Enforcement Employees, by Selected State Metropolitan and Nonmetropolitan Counties, 2017—Continued

(Number.)

State/county	Law enforcement employees	Officers	Civilians
Edwards	10	4	6
Fannin	23	22	1
Fisher	12	4	8
Floyd	11	7	4
Franklin	25	11	14
Frio	24	20	4
Gaines	37	15	22
Garza	37	9	28
Gillespie	51	28	23
Gonzales	55	21	34
Gray	44	14	30
Grimes	56	29	27
Hall	9	3	6
Hansford	13	7	6
Hartley	7	6	1
Haskell	12	4	8
Hockley	30	11	19
Hopkins	62	26	36
Houston	48	20	28
Hutchinson	34	15	19
Jack	32	11	21
Jackson	36	12	24
Jasper	22	20	2
Jeff Davis	5	4	1
Jim Wells	68	31	37
Karnes	61	27	34
Kent	6	3	3
Kerr	104	49	55
Kimble	13	8	5
King	1	1	0
Kinney	6	6	0
Kleberg	75	23	52
Knox	9	3	6
Lamar	71	24	47
Lamb	29	10	19
La Salle	121	24	97
Live Oak	47	15	32
Loving	6	4	2
Madison	31	13	18
Matagorda	67	34	33
Menard	10	6	4
Nacogdoches	86	42	44
Nolan	34	12	22
Ochiltree	23	7	16
Palo Pinto	53	23	30
Panola	58	37	21
Parmer	6	5	1
Rains	26	12	14
Reagan	20	13	7
Red River	37	14	23
Runnels	27	6	21
Scurry	38	10	28
Shackelford	16	7	9
Shelby	33	15	18
Starr	91	48	43
Stephens	20	6	14
Sterling	4	4	0
Swisher	9	4	5
Terrell	9	4	5
Terry	37	10	27
Throckmorton	6	2	4
Titus	59	25	34
Upton	24	11	13
Uvalde	72	36	36
Val Verde	66	44	22
Van Zandt	72	36	36
Washington	58	30	28
Wheeler	24	10	14
Willacy	42	14	28
Winkler	24	9	15
Wood	34	25	9
Yoakum	21	8	13
UTAH			
Metropolitan Counties			
Box Elder	84	26	58
Cache	130	46	84
Davis	278	129	149
Juab	25	24	1
Morgan	13	11	2
Salt Lake County Unified Police Department	581	425	156
Tooele	86	30	56
Utah	386	149	237

Table 80. Full-Time Law Enforcement Employees, by Selected State Metropolitan and Nonmetropolitan Counties, 2017—Continued

(Number.)

State/county	Law enforcement employees	Officers	Civilians
Washington	159	44	115
Weber	75	72	3
Nonmetropolitan Counties			
Beaver	71	24	47
Carbon	53	27	26
Daggett	6	5	1
Duchesne	57	23	34
Garfield	30	17	13
Grand	30	17	13
Iron	80	35	45
Kane	47	17	30
Millard	55	31	24
Piute	3	3	0
Rich	10	4	6
San Juan	30	14	16
Sanpete	58	23	35
Sevier	24	22	2
Summit	103	61	42
Uintah	80	25	55
Wasatch	55	23	32
Wayne	7	6	1
VERMONT			
Metropolitan Counties			
Chittenden	19	17	2
Franklin	9	9	0
Grand Isle	2	2	0
Nonmetropolitan Counties			
Addison	4	4	0
Bennington	19	15	4
Caledonia	13	11	2
Essex	2	2	0
Lamoille	22	10	12
Orange	25	11	14
Orleans	9	7	2
Rutland	19	14	5
Washington	12	10	2
Windham	15	9	6
Windsor	17	16	1
VIRGINIA			
Metropolitan Counties			
Albemarle County Police Department	181	144	37
Amelia	29	17	12
Amherst	51	47	4
Appomattox	24	22	2
Arlington County Police Department	457	351	106
Augusta	77	66	11
Bedford	96	88	8
Botetourt	115	93	22
Buckingham	26	19	7
Campbell	70	61	9
Caroline	72	50	22
Charles City	20	13	7
Chesterfield County Police Department	620	517	103
Clarke	28	16	12
Craig	13	8	5
Culpeper	100	85	15
Dinwiddie	42	39	3
Fairfax County Police Department	1,619	1,411	208
Fauquier	175	128	47
Floyd	31	22	9
Fluvanna	49	34	15
Franklin	95	74	21
Frederick	144	129	15
Giles	36	24	12
Gloucester	95	76	19
Goochland	49	37	12
Greene	38	23	15
Hanover	254	236	18
Henrico County Police Department	811	620	191
Isle of Wight	54	50	4
James City County Police Department	103	97	6
King William	33	20	13
Loudoun	651	534	117
Mathews	18	11	7
Montgomery	126	114	12
Nelson	24	18	6
New Kent	49	33	16
Powhatan	47	42	5
Prince George County Police Department	74	56	18

Table 80. Full-Time Law Enforcement Employees, by Selected State Metropolitan and Nonmetropolitan Counties, 2017—Continued

(Number.)

State/county	Law enforcement employees	Officers	Civilians
Prince William County Police Department	804	664	140
Pulaski	48	46	2
Rappahannock	19	16	3
Roanoke County Police Department	151	135	16
Rockingham	79	62	17
Scott	37	37	0
Spotsylvania	245	197	48
Stafford	239	178	61
Sussex	47	43	4
Warren	71	53	18
Washington	82	61	21
York	93	87	6
Nonmetropolitan Counties			
Accomack	68	57	11
Alleghany	66	46	20
Bath	19	12	7
Bland	21	13	8
Brunswick	43	29	14
Buchanan	46	33	13
Carroll	40	34	6
Charlotte	39	36	3
Cumberland	22	17	5
Dickenson	35	20	15
Essex	21	13	8
Grayson	33	28	5
Greensville	35	21	14
Halifax	38	31	7
Henry	133	120	13
Highland	12	7	5
King and Queen	19	11	8
King George	52	37	15
Lancaster	39	30	9
Lee	34	34	0
Louisa	64	47	17
Lunenburg	18	12	6
Madison	30	19	11
Mecklenburg	52	50	2
Middlesex	39	28	11
Northampton	84	67	17
Northumberland	33	22	11
Nottoway	24	14	10
Orange	50	41	9
Page	72	54	18
Patrick	72	56	16
Pittsylvania	135	119	16
Prince Edward	31	31	0
Richmond	21	13	8
Rockbridge	41	38	3
Russell	49	34	15
Shenandoah	64	58	6
Smyth	45	38	7
Southampton	76	61	15
Surry	25	15	10
Tazewell	73	51	22
Westmoreland	40	26	14
Wise	65	49	16
Wythe	50	41	9
WASHINGTON			
Metropolitan Counties			
Asotin	30	30	0
Benton	76	63	13
Chelan	71	58	13
Clark	226	133	93
Columbia	12	10	2
Cowlitz	48	42	6
Douglas	35	29	6
Franklin	90	29	61
King	288	213	75
Kitsap	236	116	120
Pend Oreille	34	13	21
Pierce	328	273	55
Skagit	138	55	83
Skamania	19	16	3
Snohomish	341	274	67
Spokane	146	115	31
Stevens	55	26	29
Thurston	224	81	143
Walla Walla	35	26	9
Whatcom	185	84	101
Yakima	85	58	27

Table 80. Full-Time Law Enforcement Employees, by Selected State Metropolitan and Nonmetropolitan Counties, 2017—Continued

(Number.)

State/county	Law enforcement employees	Officers	Civilians
Nonmetropolitan Counties			
Adams	33	14	19
Clallam	44	36	8
Ferry	27	8	19
Garfield	14	7	7
Grant	69	52	17
Grays Harbor	79	61	18
Island	75	37	38
Jefferson	45	23	22
Kittitas	75	35	40
Klickitat	39	20	19
Lewis	107	39	68
Lincoln	30	17	13
Mason	92	50	42
Okanogan	35	30	5
Pacific	45	16	29
San Juan	32	20	12
Wahkiakum	19	8	11
Whitman	22	18	4
WEST VIRGINIA			
Metropolitan Counties			
Berkeley	68	60	8
Boone	29	23	6
Brooke	27	17	10
Cabell	52	40	12
Clay	3	3	0
Fayette	38	34	4
Hampshire	19	17	2
Hancock	33	29	4
Jefferson	39	33	6
Kanawha	128	97	31
Lincoln	7	6	1
Marshall	34	31	3
Mineral	15	13	2
Monongalia	43	40	3
Ohio	36	34	2
Preston	32	20	12
Putnam	53	41	12
Raleigh	67	51	16
Wayne	23	20	3
Wirt	3	3	0
Wood	67	37	30
Nonmetropolitan Counties			
Barbour	18	9	9
Braxton	10	8	2
Calhoun	5	3	2
Doddridge	10	8	2
Gilmer	4	4	0
Grant	8	8	0
Greenbrier	44	27	17
Hardy	12	11	1
Harrison	58	51	7
Jackson	23	15	8
Lewis	16	15	1
Logan	22	19	3
Marion	43	28	15
Mason	33	19	14
McDowell	12	11	1
Mercer	38	27	11
Mingo	19	17	2
Monroe	12	9	3
Morgan	11	10	1
Nicholas	23	20	3
Pendleton	3	3	0
Pleasants	7	6	1
Pocahontas	13	8	5
Randolph	14	13	1
Ritchie	12	8	4
Roane	11	8	3
Summers	7	6	1
Taylor	12	6	6
Tucker	6	4	2
Tyler	10	10	0
Upshur	14	12	2
Webster	7	4	3
Wetzel	15	13	2
Wyoming	26	20	6
WISCONSIN			
Metropolitan Counties			
Brown	310	158	152

Table 80. Full-Time Law Enforcement Employees, by Selected State Metropolitan and Nonmetropolitan Counties, 2017—Continued

(Number.)

State/county	Law enforcement employees	Officers	Civilians
Calumet	52	26	26
Chippewa	72	46	26
Columbia	109	41	68
Dane	553	449	104
Douglas	69	26	43
Eau Claire	104	39	65
Fond du Lac	123	55	68
Green	56	30	26
Iowa	37	19	18
Kenosha	339	118	221
Kewaunee	36	31	5
La Crosse	109	41	68
Marathon	182	68	114
Milwaukee	642	291	351
Oconto	62	27	35
Outagamie	182	73	109
Ozaukee	102	78	24
Pierce	53	39	14
Racine	310	158	152
Rock	207	97	110
Sheboygan	184	72	112
St. Croix	90	83	7
Washington	167	72	95
Waukesha	337	164	173
Winnebago	187	126	61
Nonmetropolitan Counties			
Adams	59	28	31
Ashland	33	23	10
Barron	72	29	43
Bayfield	36	20	16
Buffalo	26	11	15
Burnett	33	17	16
Clark	49	25	24
Crawford	31	25	6
Dodge	173	69	104
Door	70	56	14
Dunn	56	26	30
Florence	23	13	10
Forest	39	19	20
Grant	46	29	17
Green Lake	43	18	25
Iron	20	20	0
Jackson	48	22	26
Jefferson	115	95	20
Juneau	59	45	14
Lafayette	29	28	1
Langlade	42	18	24
Lincoln	68	30	38
Manitowoc	92	63	29
Marinette	63	31	32
Marquette	43	41	2
Menominee	11	9	2
Monroe	50	25	25
Oneida	84	35	49
Pepin	17	7	10
Polk	78	29	49
Portage	103	48	55
Price	22	20	2
Richland	26	26	0
Rusk	31	28	3
Sauk	139	47	92
Sawyer	47	25	22
Shawano	112	39	73
Taylor	42	20	22
Trempealeau	55	26	29
Vernon	48	24	24
Vilas	74	36	38
Walworth	204	82	122
Washburn	33	15	18
Waupaca	107	44	63
Waushara	56	25	31
Wood	72	40	32
WYOMING			
Metropolitan Counties			
Laramie	181	48	133
Natrona	151	60	91
Nonmetropolitan Counties			
Albany	43	40	3
Big Horn	20	14	6

Table 80. Full-Time Law Enforcement Employees, by Selected State Metropolitan and Nonmetropolitan Counties, 2017—Continued

(Number.)

State/county	Law enforcement employees	Officers	Civilians
Campbell	66	45	21
Carbon	31	17	14
Crook	21	15	6
Fremont	36	33	3
Goshen	31	9	22
Hot Springs	11	4	7
Johnson	29	28	1
Lincoln	35	19	16
Niobrara	15	4	11
Park	54	19	35
Platte	34	24	10
Sheridan	57	20	37
Sublette	71	35	36
Sweetwater	95	39	56
Uinta	47	34	13
Washakie	9	8	1
Weston	8	8	0
Sublette	37	33	4
Sweetwater	113	80	33
Uinta	52	39	13
Washakie	9	8	1
Weston	7	7	0

1 The employee data presented in this table for Mecklenburg represent only Mecklenburg County Sheriff's Office employees and exclude Charlotte-Mecklenburg Police Department employees.

Table 81. Full-Time Law Enforcement Employees, by Selected State and Agency, 2017

(Number.)

State/agency	Law enforcement employees	Officers	Civilians
ALABAMA			
Tribal Agencies			
Poarch Creek Tribal	53	46	7
Other Agencies			
Mobile Regional Airport	19	12	7
ALASKA			
Other Agencies			
Fairbanks International Airport	35	27	8
Ted Stevens Anchorage International Airport	65	52	13
ARIZONA			
Tribal Agencies			
Ak-Chin Tribal	83	24	59
Cocopah Tribal	23	15	8
Colorado River Agency	2	2	0
Colorado River Tribal	28	18	10
Fort Apache Agency	6	5	1
Fort McDowell Tribal	27	20	7
Fort Mojave Tribal	43	20	23
Gila River Indian Community	169	125	44
Hopi Tribal	43	15	28
Hualapai Tribal	21	19	2
Kaibab Paiute Tribal	2	2	0
Navajo Nation	324	222	102
Pascua Yaqui Tribal	83	28	55
Salt River Tribal	148	116	32
San Carlos Agency	4	3	1
Tonto Apache Tribal	6	6	0
Truxton Canon Agency	11	6	5
Yavapai-Apache Nation	21	16	5
Yavapai-Prescott Tribal	12	10	2
Other Agencies			
Tucson Airport Authority	36	20	16
ARKANSAS			
State Agencies			
Camp Robinson	13	7	6
State Capitol Police	23	21	2
Other Agencies			
Northwest Arkansas Regional Airport	12	9	3
CALIFORNIA			
State Agencies			
Atascadero State Hospital	165	151	14
California State Fair	5	4	1
Coalinga State Hospital	227	210	17
Department of Parks and Recreation, Capital	547	523	24
Fairview Developmental Center	14	11	3
Napa State Hospital	126	115	11
Patton State Hospital	99	83	16
Porterville Developmental Center	58	51	7
Sonoma Developmental Center	20	6	14
Tribal Agencies			
La Jolla Tribal	4	3	1
Los Coyotes Tribal	1	1	0
Sycuan Tribal	19	11	8
Table Mountain Rancheria	23	16	7
Yurok Tribal	6	5	1
Other Agencies			
East Bay Regional Park District	92	59	33
Fontana Unified School District	75	17	58
Monterey Peninsula Airport	5	5	0
Port of San Diego Harbor	167	125	42
San Bernardino Unified School District	86	25	61
San Francisco Bay Area Rapid Transit, Contra Costa County	282	187	95
Shasta County Marshal	26	20	6
Stockton Unified School District	43	31	12
Twin Rivers Unified School District	28	22	6
COLORADO			
State Agencies			
Colorado Bureau of Investigation	268	41	227
Colorado Mental Health Institute	101	20	81
Tribal Agencies			
Southern Ute Tribal	38	21	17
Ute Mountain Tribal	19	11	8
Other Agencies			
All Crimes Enforcement Team	1	1	0

Table 81. Full-Time Law Enforcement Employees, by Selected State and Agency, 2017—Continued

(Number.)

State/agency	Law enforcement employees	Officers	Civilians
CONNECTICUT			
State Agencies			
Department of Motor Vehicles	57	51	6
State Capitol Police	44	33	11
Tribal Agencies			
Mashantucket Pequot Tribal	35	25	10
Mohegan Tribal	29	28	1
Other Agencies			
Metropolitan Transportation Authority	38	37	1
DELAWARE			
State Agencies			
Alcohol and Tobacco Enforcement	19	17	2
Animal Welfare, New Castle County	33	22	11
Attorney General	82	10	72
Kent County	327	31	296
New Castle County	58	2	56
Sussex County	12	10	2
Environmental Control	30	26	4
Fish and Wildlife	18	18	0
Park Rangers	71	60	11
River and Bay Authority	82	67	15
State Capitol Police	48	19	29
State Fire Marshal			
Other Agencies			
Amtrak Police	25	18	7
Drug Enforcement Administration, Wilmington Resident Office	28	23	5
Wilmington Fire Department	16	11	5
DISTRICT OF COLUMBIA			
Other Agencies			
District of Columbia Fire and Emergency Medical Services, Arson Investigation Unit	15	15	0
Metro Transit Police	437	377	60
FLORIDA			
State Agencies			
Capitol Police	69	51	18
Department of Correction, Office of the Inspector General, Leon County	143	98	45
Department of Investigative and Forensic Services, Leon County	307	236	71
Department of Law Enforcement, Leon County, Tallahassee	1,782	473	1,309
Division of Alcoholic Beverages and Tobacco, Leon County	180	105	75
Fish and Wildlife Conservation Commission, Leon County	1,022	833	189
Tribal Agencies			
Miccosukee Tribal	60	43	17
Seminole Tribal	200	125	75
Other Agencies			
Duval County Schools	91	79	12
Florida School for the Deaf and Blind	17	9	8
Fort Lauderdale Airport	115	92	23
Jacksonville Aviation Authority	51	37	14
Lee County Port Authority	64	39	25
Melbourne International Airport	18	16	2
Miami-Dade County Public Schools	220	184	36
Northwest Florida Beaches International Airport	19	13	6
Palm Beach County School District	172	154	18
Port Everglades	77	55	22
Sarasota-Manatee Airport Authority	11	11	0
Tampa International Airport	162	65	97
Volusia County Beach Safety	52	45	7
GEORGIA			
State Agencies			
Georgia Department of Transportation, Office of Investigations	3	3	0
Georgia Forestry Commission	6	6	0
Georgia Public Safety Training Center	179	60	119
Georgia World Congress	67	18	49
Ports Authority, Savannah	121	87	34
State Board of Workers Compensation, Fraud Investigation Division	10	5	5
Other Agencies			
Appling County Board of Education	2	2	0
Atlanta Public Schools	68	65	3
Augusta Board of Education	36	33	3

Table 81. Full-Time Law Enforcement Employees, by Selected State and Agency, 2017—Continued

(Number.)

State/agency	Law enforcement employees	Officers	Civilians
Bibb County Board of Education	25	19	6
Chatham County Board of Education	54	44	10
Cherokee County Marshal	19	11	8
Cobb County Board of Education	66	64	2
Decatur County Schools	5	5	0
Dougherty County Board of Education	20	19	1
Fayette County Marshal	4	4	0
Forsyth County Fire Investigation Unit	4	4	0
Fulton County Marshal	66	50	16
Fulton County School System	68	62	6
Glynn County School System	26	26	0
Gwinnett County Public Schools	84	74	10
Hall County Marshal	21	11	10
Hartsfield-Jackson Atlanta International Airport	188	148	40
Metropolitan Atlanta Rapid Transit Authority	373	319	54
Richmond County Marshal	61	50	11
Stone Mountain Park	22	19	3
Washington County Board of Education	7	7	0
IDAHO			
Tribal Agencies			
Coeur d'Alene Tribal	14	13	1
Fort Hall Tribal	30	17	13
Nez Perce Tribal	21	16	5
ILLINOIS			
State Agencies			
Secretary of State Police	209	109	100
Other Agencies			
Alton & Southern Railway	7	7	0
Belt Railway	7	7	0
Canadian National Railway	13	12	1
Capitol Airport Authority	6	6	0
Crystal Lake Park District	1	1	0
Decatur Park District	4	4	0
Fon du Lac Park District	2	2	0
Lake County Forest Preserve	21	19	2
Kane County Forest Preserve	6	6	0
McHenry County Conservation District	11	10	1
Norfolk Southern Railway			
Cook County	41	41	0
Macon County	2	2	0
Madison County	6	6	0
Pekin Park District	1	1	0
INDIANA			
State Agencies			
Indiana State Excise Police	77	71	6
Northern Indiana Commuter Transportation District	9	8	1
KANSAS			
State Agencies			
Kansas Bureau of Investigation	279	73	206
Tribal Agencies			
Iowa Tribal	7	7	0
Kickapoo Tribal	4	4	0
Potawatomi Tribal	21	11	10
Sac and Fox Tribal	3	3	0
Other Agencies			
Blue Valley School District	8	8	0
El Dorado School District	2	2	0
Johnson County Park	25	24	1
Metropolitan Topeka Airport Authority	19	15	4
Shawnee Mission Public Schools	14	8	6
Topeka Fire Department, Arson Investigation	4	4	0
Unified School District			
Auburn-Washburn	2	2	0
Bluestem	1	1	0
Goddard	5	4	1
Kansas City	34	30	4
Seaman	3	3	0
Shawnee Heights	2	2	0
KENTUCKY			
State Agencies			
Alcohol Beverage Control			
Enforcement Division	64	29	35
Investigative Division	9	7	2
Fish and Wildlife Enforcement	119	118	1
Kentucky Horse Park	9	9	0
Park Security	43	41	2

Table 81. Full-Time Law Enforcement Employees, by Selected State and Agency, 2017—Continued

(Number.)

State/agency	Law enforcement employees	Officers	Civilians
Other Agencies			
Cincinnati-Northern Kentucky International Airport	67	48	19
Clark County School System	4	4	0
Fayette County Schools	30	26	4
Graves County Schools	2	2	0
Jefferson County School District	27	20	7
Lexington Bluegrass Airport	29	20	9
Louisville Fire Department Arson Division	8	8	0
Louisville Regional Airport Authority	46	40	6
Montgomery County School District	4	3	1
LOUISIANA			
State Agencies			
Tensas Basin Levee District	3	2	1
Tribal Agencies			
Chitimacha Tribal	15	15	0
Coushatta Tribal	31	27	4
Tunica-Biloxi Tribal	15	13	2
Other Agencies			
Tensas Basin Levee District	3	2	1
MAINE			
State Agencies			
Bureau of Capitol Police	18	13	5
Tribal Agencies			
Passamaquoddy Indian Township	9	5	4
Passamaquoddy Pleasant Point Tribal	8	8	0
Penobscot Nation	8	4	4
MARYLAND			
State Agencies			
Comptroller of the Treasury, Field Enforcement Division	54	23	31
Department of Public Safety and Correctional Services, Internal Investigations Unit	43	33	10
General Services			
Annapolis, Anne Arundel County	60	33	27
Baltimore City	134	64	70
Natural Resources Police	319	259	60
Springfield Hospital	42	6	36
State Fire Marshal	69	43	26
Transit Administration	204	153	51
Transportation Authority	549	426	123
Other Agencies			
Maryland-National Capital Park Police			
Montgomery County	103	84	19
Prince George's County	136	114	22
MASSACHUSETTS			
State Agencies			
Massachusetts Bay Transportation Authority, Suffolk County	260	248	12
Tribal Agencies			
Wampanoag Tribe of Gay Head	2	2	0
Other Agencies			
Beth Israel Deaconess Medical Center	57	14	43
Massachusetts General Hospital	145	64	81
MICHIGAN			
Tribal Agencies			
Bay Mills Tribal	11	9	2
Grand Traverse Tribal	10	9	1
Gun Lake Tribal	11	10	1
Hannahville Tribal	12	11	1
Keweenaw Bay Tribal	14	13	1
Lac Vieux Desert Tribal	9	7	2
Little River Band of Ottawa Indians	15	13	2
Little Traverse Bay Bands of Odawa Indians	18	12	6
Nottawaseppi Huron Band of Potawatomi	18	17	1
Pokagon Tribal	46	46	0
Saginaw Chippewa Tribal	33	25	8
Sault Ste. Marie Tribal	27	21	6
Other Agencies			
Bishop International Airport	8	7	1
Capitol Region Airport Authority	17	9	8
Gerald R. Ford International Airport	18	17	1
Huron-Clinton Metropolitan Authority			
Hudson Mills Metropark	3	3	0
Kensington Metropark	8	8	0
Lower Huron Metropark	9	9	0

Table 81. Full-Time Law Enforcement Employees, by Selected State and Agency, 2017—Continued

(Number.)

State/agency	Law enforcement employees	Officers	Civilians
Stony Creek Metropark	11	11	0
Wayne County Airport	104	100	4
MINNESOTA			
State Agencies			
Bureau of Criminal Apprehension	120	72	48
Capitol Security, St. Paul	89	21	68
Department of Natural Resources Enforcement Division	202	175	27
Tribal Agencies			
Fond du Lac Tribal	23	20	3
Leech Lake Band of Ojibwe	44	28	16
Lower Sioux Tribal	6	6	0
Mille Lacs Tribal	29	24	5
Nett Lake Tribal	5	5	0
Red Lake Agency	45	33	12
Upper Sioux Community	4	4	0
Other Agencies			
Minneapolis-St. Paul International Airport	151	87	64
Three Rivers Park District	14	13	1
MISSISSIPPI			
State Agencies			
Department of Marine Resources	41	34	7
State Capitol Police	85	70	15
Tribal Agencies			
Choctaw Tribal	44	41	3
MISSOURI			
State Agencies			
Capitol Police	31	28	3
Department of Conservation	201	197	4
Department of Revenue, Criminal Investigation Bureau	15	12	3
Department of Social Services, State Technical Assistance Team	10	9	1
Division of Alcohol and Tobacco Control	32	21	11
Gaming Commission, Enforcement Division	120	117	3
State Fire Marshal	24	22	2
State Park Rangers	42	40	2
Other Agencies			
Clay County Drug Task Force	4	4	0
Clay County Park Authority	6	6	0
Jackson County Drug Task Force	16	15	1
Jackson County Park Rangers	22	20	2
Kansas City International Airport	65	34	31
Lambert-St. Louis International Airport	80	63	17
Springfield-Branson Airport	11	11	0
Springfield-Greene County Park Rangers	7	7	0
St. Charles County Park Rangers	12	12	0
Terminal Railroad	6	6	0
MONTANA			
State Agencies			
Gambling Investigations Bureau	43	17	26
Tribal Agencies			
Blackfeet Agency	34	24	10
Crow Agency	14	10	4
Fort Belknap Tribal	19	12	7
Fort Peck Assiniboine and Sioux Tribes	15	13	2
Northern Cheyenne Agency	11	6	5
Rocky Boy's Tribal	23	13	10
NEBRASKA			
Tribal Agencies			
Omaha Tribal	29	9	20
Santee Tribal	5	5	0
Winnebago Tribal	24	6	18
NEVADA			
State Agencies			
Department of Public Safety, Investigative Division	48	32	16
Secretary of State Securities Division, Enforcement Section	6	6	0
State Fire Marshal	15	6	9
Tribal Agencies			
Duckwater Tribal	3	3	0
Eastern Nevada Agency	22	5	17
Ely Shoshone Tribal	2	2	0
Fallon Tribal	9	8	1
Lovelock Paiute Tribal	4	3	1
Reno-Spark Indian Colony	15	14	1

Table 81. Full-Time Law Enforcement Employees, by Selected State and Agency, 2017—Continued

(Number.)

State/agency	Law enforcement employees	Officers	Civilians
South Fork Band Tribal	1	1	0
Western Shoshone Tribal	6	6	0
Yomba Shoshone Tribal	2	1	1
Other Agencies			
Clark County School District	183	153	30
Las Vegas Fire and Rescue, Arson Bomb Unit	16	16	0
North Las Vegas Fire Department Arson Investigations	1	1	0
Reno Municipal Court Marshal	14	10	4
Reno Tahoe Airport Authority	25	24	1
Washoe County School District	43	37	6
NEW HAMPSHIRE			
State Agencies			
Liquor Commission	30	17	13
NEW JERSEY			
State Agencies			
Department of Human Services	82	82	0
Division of Fish and Wildlife	50	48	2
New Jersey Transit Police	318	263	55
Palisades Interstate Parkway	33	27	6
Port Authority of New York and New Jersey	1,834	1,651	183
State Park Police	93	91	2
Other Agencies			
Park Police			
Morris County	27	26	1
Union County	106	75	31
Prosecutor			
Atlantic County	174	77	97
Bergen County	261	103	158
Burlington County	130	42	88
Camden County	262	181	81
Cape May County	89	45	44
Cumberland County	112	39	73
Essex County	374	251	123
Gloucester County	102	37	65
Hudson County	259	97	162
Hunterdon County	56	28	28
Mercer County	176	60	116
Middlesex County	199	69	130
Monmouth County	273	77	196
Morris County	160	68	92
Ocean County	175	69	106
Passaic County	186	74	112
Salem County	48	21	27
Somerset County	124	50	74
Sussex County	56	36	20
Union County	186	76	110
Warren County	62	22	40
NEW MEXICO			
Tribal Agencies			
Acoma Tribal	25	13	12
Isleta Tribal	43	28	15
Jemez Pueblo	13	11	2
Jicarilla Apache Tribal	34	20	14
Laguna Tribal	52	38	14
Mescalero Tribal	19	10	9
Northern Pueblos Agency	13	11	2
Ohkay Owingeh Tribal	11	9	2
Pojoaque Tribal	16	9	7
Ramah Navajo Tribal	15	8	7
Santa Ana Tribal	22	20	2
Santa Clara Pueblo	14	7	7
Southern Pueblos Agency	23	14	9
Taos Pueblo	11	7	4
Tesuque Pueblo	7	3	4
Zuni Tribal	31	19	12
NEW YORK			
State Agencies			
State Park			
Allegany Region	13	12	1
Central Region	17	14	3
Finger Lakes Region	14	12	2
Genesee Region	14	13	1
Long Island Region	58	54	4
New York City Region	20	18	2
Niagara Region	29	29	0
Palisades Region	37	36	1
Saratoga/Capital Region	70	66	4
Taconic Region	12	12	0
Thousand Island Region	14	14	0

Table 81. Full-Time Law Enforcement Employees, by Selected State and Agency, 2017—Continued

(Number.)

State/agency	Law enforcement employees	Officers	Civilians
Tribal Agencies			
Oneida Indian Nation	40	34	6
St. Regis Tribal	35	29	6
Other Agencies			
New York City Department of Environmental Protection Police,			
Ashokan Precinct	221	191	30
New York City Metropolitan Transportation Authority	771	695	76
Onondaga County Parks	1	1	0
NORTH CAROLINA			
State Agencies			
Cherry Hospital	15	9	6
Department of Health and Human Resources	7	7	0
Department of Wildlife	214	201	13
Division of Alcohol Law Enforcement	112	100	12
Division of Marine Fisheries	61	51	10
North Carolina Arboretum	4	4	
North Carolina State Bureau of Investigation	397	239	158
State Capitol Police	83	52	31
State Fairgrounds	6	2	4
State Park Rangers			
Carolina Beach	6	4	2
Carvers Creek	4	3	1
Chimney Rock	8	5	3
Cliffs of the Neuse	10	3	7
Crowders Mountain	7	6	1
Dismal Swamp	3	3	0
Elk Knob	3	3	0
Eno River	5	5	0
Falls Lake Recreation Area	11	11	0
Fort Fisher	5	4	1
Fort Macon	5	4	1
Goose Creek	5	4	1
Gorges	3	2	1
Grandfather Mountain	4	3	1
Hammocks Beach	5	4	1
Hanging Rock	5	5	0
Haw River	3	3	0
Jockey's Ridge	6	5	1
Jones Lake	4	4	0
Jordan Lake State Recreation Area	13	11	2
Kerr Lake	14	10	4
Lake James	5	5	0
Lake Norman	8	5	3
Lake Waccamaw	4	4	0
Lumber River	7	4	3
Mayo River	4	2	2
Medoc Mountain	3	3	0
Merchants Millpond	5	4	1
Morrow Mountain	2	2	0
Mount Mitchell	6	4	2
New River-Mount Jefferson	8	8	0
Pettigrew	6	3	3
Pilot Mountain	5	5	0
Raven Rock	2	2	0
Singletary Lake	3	2	1
South Mountains	8	7	1
Stone Mountain	11	6	5
Weymouth Woods/Sandhills Nature Preserve	5	3	2
William B. Umstead	11	7	4
Tribal Agencies			
Cherokee Tribal	60	54	6
Other Agencies			
Asheville Regional Airport	13	13	0
Beaufort County Alcoholic Beverage Control Law Enforcement	1	1	0
Nash County Alcoholic Beverage Control Enforcement	1	1	0
Piedmont Triad International Airport	21	21	0
Raleigh-Durham International Airport	46	44	2
Triad Municipal Alcoholic Beverage Control Law Enforcement	5	4	1
University of North Carolina Hospitals	102	39	63
WakeMed Campus Police	80	47	33
Wilmington International Airport	13	9	4
NORTH DAKOTA			
Tribal Agencies			
Fort Totten Agency	22	9	13
Standing Rock Agency	42	16	26
Three Affiliated Tribes	43	28	15
Turtle Mountain Agency	27	13	14

Table 81. Full-Time Law Enforcement Employees, by Selected State and Agency, 2017—Continued

(Number.)

State/agency	Law enforcement employees	Officers	Civilians
OHIO			
Other Agencies			
Clark County Park District	1	1	0
Cleveland Metropolitan Park District	94	80	14
Hamilton County Park District	32	29	3
Holden Arboretum	2	2	0
Muskingum Watershed Conservancy District	21	21	0
Preservation Parks of Delaware County	5	5	0
Republic N&T Railroad	3	3	0
OKLAHOMA			
State Agencies			
Capitol Park Police	68	18	50
State Park Rangers	54	54	0
Tribal Agencies			
Absentee Shawnee Tribal	11	10	1
Anadarko Agency	15	9	6
Cherokee Nation	39	32	7
Chickasaw Nation	62	52	10
Choctaw Nation	40	38	2
Citizen Potawatomi Nation	43	26	17
Comanche Nation	31	23	8
Concho Agency	7	7	0
Eastern Shawnee Tribal	18	17	1
Iowa Tribal	14	8	6
Kaw Tribal	6	6	0
Kickapoo Tribal	14	13	1
Miami Agency	5	5	0
Miami Tribal	10	10	0
Muscogee Nation Tribal	43	38	5
Osage Nation	17	16	1
Otoe-Missouria Tribal	11	7	4
Pawnee Tribal	6	5	1
Ponca Tribal	4	4	0
Quapaw Tribal	14	13	1
Sac and Fox Tribal	11	11	0
Seminole Nation Lighthorse	10	9	1
Tonkawa Tribal	5	4	1
Wyandotte Nation	5	4	1
Other Agencies			
Jenks Public Schools	8	7	1
Lawton Public Schools	15	15	0
McAlester Public Schools	1	1	0
Muskogee City Schools	6	5	1
Putnam City Campus	16	12	4
OREGON			
State Agencies			
Liquor Commission			
Benton County	1	1	0
Clackamas County	1	1	0
Columbia County	1	1	0
Coos County	1	1	0
Crook County	1	1	0
Deschutes County	6	5	1
Douglas County	1	1	0
Hood River County	1	1	0
Jackson County	5	4	1
Josephine County	1	1	0
Klamath County	1	1	0
Lake County	1	1	0
Lane County	5	3	2
Lincoln County	1	1	0
Linn County	1	1	0
Malheur County	1	1	0
Marion County	3	2	1
Multnomah County	18	16	2
Polk County	1	1	0
Tillamook County	1	1	0
Umatilla County	1	1	0
Washington County	2	2	0
Yamhill County	1	1	0
Tribal Agencies			
Burns Paiute Tribal	4	3	1
Columbia River Inter-Tribal Fisheries Enforcement	20	15	5
Coos, Lower Umpqua, and Siuslaw Tribal	5	4	1
Coquille Tribal	4	4	0
Grand Ronde Tribal	9	7	2
Umatilla Tribal	25	19	6
Other Agencies			
Port of Portland	66	49	17

Table 81. Full-Time Law Enforcement Employees, by Selected State and Agency, 2017—Continued

(Number.)

State/agency	Law enforcement employees	Officers	Civilians
PENNSYLVANIA			
State Agencies			
Pennsylvania Fish and Boat Commission	88	82	6
State Capitol Police	106	99	7
State Park Rangers			
Bald Eagle	3	3	0
Beltzville	2	2	0
Bendigo	1	1	0
Ben Rush	4	2	2
Black Moshannon	2	2	0
Caledonia	1	1	0
Canoe Creek	1	1	0
Chapman	1	1	0
Codorus	11	4	7
Colonel Denning	2	1	1
Cook Forest	5	5	0
Cowans Gap	2	2	0
Delaware Canal	5	5	0
Evansburg	2	2	0
Fort Washington	2	2	0
Frances Slocum	3	3	0
French Creek	10	2	8
Gifford Pinchot	5	3	2
Greenwood Furnace	14	3	11
Hickory Run	11	11	0
Hills Creek	3	3	0
Jacobsburg Environmental Education Center	1	1	0
Jennings Environmental Education Center	6	6	0
Kettle Creek	1	1	0
Keystone	2	2	0
Kings Gap Environmental Education Center	1	1	0
Lackawanna	4	4	0
Laurel Hill	4	4	0
Leonard Harrison	3	3	0
Linn Run	1	1	0
Little Buffalo	2	2	0
Little Pine	1	1	0
Lyman Run	3	3	0
Marsh Creek	5	2	3
Maurice K. Goddard	1	1	0
Memorial Lake	1	1	0
Moraine	6	6	0
Mount Pisgah	1	1	0
Neshaminy	5	2	3
Nockamixon	3	3	0
Ohiopyle	14	3	11
Oil Creek	2	2	0
Ole Bull	1	1	0
Parker Dam	9	2	7
Pine Grove Furnace	1	1	0
Point	2	2	0
Presque Isle	6	6	0
Prince Gallitzin	15	5	10
Promised Land	1	1	0
Pymatuning	10	5	5
Raccoon Creek	14	4	10
Raymond B. Winter	1	1	0
Reeds Gap	1	1	0
Ricketts Glen	2	2	0
Ridley Creek	3	3	0
Ryerson Station	4	1	3
Samuel S. Lewis	1	1	0
Shawnee	2	2	0
Shikellamy	1	1	0
Sinnemahoning	6	1	5
Sizerville	1	1	0
Susquehannock	1	1	0
Tobyhanna	1	1	0
Tuscarora	2	2	0
Tyler	4	2	2
White Clay	4	4	0
Worlds End	7	2	5
Yellow Creek	2	2	0
Other Agencies			
Allegheny County District Attorney, Criminal Investigation Division	35	28	7
Allegheny County Housing Authority	7	6	1
Allegheny County Port Authority	58	46	12
County Detective			
Adams County	2	2	0
Beaver County	8	8	0
Berks County	37	33	4
Bucks County	23	21	2
Butler County	4	4	0

Table 81. Full-Time Law Enforcement Employees, by Selected State and Agency, 2017—Continued

(Number.)

State/agency	Law enforcement employees	Officers	Civilians
Chester County	23	19	4
Cumberland County	8	6	2
Dauphin County	12	10	2
Erie County	11	9	2
Lackawanna County	14	14	0
Lancaster County	32	30	2
Lawrence County	8	7	1
Lebanon County	7	5	2
Lehigh County	65	31	34
Luzerne County	10	10	0
McKean County	8	2	6
Monroe County	7	6	1
Montgomery County	54	39	15
Pike County	2	2	0
Schuylkill County	23	6	17
Wayne County	3	3	0
Westmoreland County	56	14	42
Wyoming County	4	4	0
York County	11	10	1
Delaware County District Attorney, Criminal Investigation Division	45	34	11
Delaware County Park	56	55	1
Erie Municipal Airport Authority	8	8	0
Fort Indiantown Gap	26	17	9
Franklin County Drug Task Force	5	3	2
Harrisburg International Airport	20	10	10
Lehigh Valley International Airport	11	11	0
Westmoreland County Park	31	30	1
Wyoming Area School District	1	1	0
RHODE ISLAND			
State Agencies			
Department of Environmental Management	42	33	9
Rhode Island State Airport	40	31	9
Tribal Agencies			
Narragansett Tribal	4	4	0
SOUTH CAROLINA			
State Agencies			
Bureau of Protective Services	62	59	3
Department of Natural Resources			
Abbeville County	3	3	0
Aiken County	4	4	0
Allendale County	3	3	0
Anderson County	6	6	0
Bamberg County	2	2	0
Barnwell County	3	3	0
Beaufort County	7	7	0
Berkeley County	6	6	0
Calhoun County	3	3	0
Charleston County	26	26	0
Cherokee County	4	4	0
Chester County	3	3	0
Chesterfield County	3	3	0
Clarendon County	4	4	0
Colleton County	4	4	0
Darlington County	2	2	0
Dillon County	3	3	0
Dorchester County	4	4	0
Edgefield County	3	3	0
Fairfield County	4	4	0
Florence County	7	7	0
Georgetown County	7	7	0
Greenville County	3	3	0
Greenwood County	4	4	0
Hampton County	3	3	0
Horry County	6	6	0
Jasper County	5	5	0
Kershaw County	3	3	0
Lancaster County	2	2	0
Laurens County	4	4	0
Lee County	2	2	0
Lexington County	5	5	0
Marion County	3	3	0
Marlboro County	3	3	0
McCormick County	3	3	0
Newberry County	4	4	0
Oconee County	4	4	0
Orangeburg County	4	4	0
Pickens County	7	7	0
Saluda County	2	2	0
Spartanburg County	3	3	0
Sumter County	4	4	0
Union County	3	3	0

Table 81. Full-Time Law Enforcement Employees, by Selected State and Agency, 2017—Continued

(Number.)

State/agency	Law enforcement employees	Officers	Civilians
Williamsburg County	6	6	0
York County	3	3	0
Department of Public Safety, Illegal Immigration Enforcement Unit	8	7	1
Forestry Commission			
Abbeville County	3	3	0
Aiken County	4	4	0
Allendale County	3	3	0
Anderson County	6	6	0
Bamberg County	2	2	0
Barnwell County	3	3	0
Beaufort County	7	7	0
Berkeley County	6	6	0
Calhoun County	3	3	0
Charleston County	26	26	0
Cherokee County	4	4	0
Chester County	3	3	0
Chesterfield County	3	3	0
Clarendon County	4	4	0
Colleton County	4	4	0
Darlington County	2	2	0
Dillon County	3	3	0
Dorchester County	4	4	0
Edgefield County	3	3	0
Fairfield County	4	4	0
Florence County	7	7	0
Georgetown County	7	7	0
Greenville County	3	3	0
Greenwood County	4	4	0
Hampton County	3	3	0
Horry County	6	6	0
Jasper County	5	5	0
Kershaw County	3	3	0
Lancaster County	2	2	0
Laurens County	4	4	0
Lee County	2	2	0
Lexington County	5	5	0
Marion County	3	3	0
Marlboro County	3	3	0
McCormick County	3	3	0
Newberry County	4	4	0
Oconee County	4	4	0
Orangeburg County	4	4	0
Pickens County	7	7	0
Saluda County	2	2	0
Spartanburg County	3	3	0
Sumter County	4	4	0
Union County	3	3	0
Williamsburg County	6	6	0
York County	3	3	0
Illegal Immigration Enforcement Unit	8	7	1
Aiken County	1	1	0
Anderson County	1	1	0
Bamberg County	1	1	0
Berkeley County	1	1	0
Cherokee County	1	1	0
Chesterfield County	3	3	0
Colleton County	1	1	0
Darlington County	2	2	0
Fairfield County	1	1	0
Florence County	2	2	0
Georgetown County	1	1	0
Horry County	1	1	0
Kershaw County	2	2	0
Laurens County	1	1	0
Lexington County	3	3	0
Marlboro County	1	1	0
Newberry County	1	1	0
Oconee County	1	1	0
Orangeburg County	1	1	0
Pickens County	1	1	0
Richland County	2	2	0
Spartanburg County	1	1	0
Sumter County	3	3	0
Williamsburg County	2	2	0
Santee Cooper	11	9	2
State Museum	4	1	3
State Ports Authority	49	32	17
State Transport Police			
Abbeville County	3	3	0
Aiken County	4	4	0
Allendale County	3	3	0
Anderson County	6	6	0
Bamberg County	2	2	0
Barnwell County	3	3	0

Table 81. Full-Time Law Enforcement Employees, by Selected State and Agency, 2017—Continued

(Number.)

State/agency	Law enforcement employees	Officers	Civilians
Beaufort County	7	7	0
Berkeley County	6	6	0
Calhoun County	3	3	0
Cherokee County	4	4	0
Chester County	3	3	0
Chesterfield County	3	3	0
Clarendon County	4	4	0
Colleton County	4	4	0
Darlington County	2	2	0
Dillon County	3	3	0
Dorchester County	4	4	0
Edgefield County	3	3	0
Fairfield County	4	4	0
Florence County	7	7	0
Georgetown County	7	7	0
Greenville County	3	3	0
Greenwood County	4	4	0
Hampton County	3	3	0
Horry County	6	6	0
Jasper County	5	5	0
Kershaw County	3	3	0
Lancaster County	2	2	0
Laurens County	4	4	0
Lee County	2	2	0
Lexington County	5	5	0
Marion County	3	3	0
Marlboro County	3	3	0
McCormick County	3	3	0
Newberry County	4	4	0
Oconee County	4	4	0
Orangeburg County	4	4	0
Pickens County	9	7	2
Saluda County	2	2	0
Spartanburg County	3	3	0
Sumter County	4	4	0
Union County	3	3	0
Williamsburg County	6	6	0
York County	5	3	2
United States Department of Energy, Savannah River Plant	52	40	12
Other Agencies			
15th Circuit Drug Enforcement Unit	4	3	1
Columbia Metropolitan Airport	18	18	0
Greenville Hospital			
Greenville	28	28	0
Laurens	4	4	0
Oconee	3	3	0
Greenville-Spartanburg International Airport	19	18	1
Lexington County Medical Center	60	22	38
SOUTH DAKOTA			
State Agencies			
Division of Criminal Investigation	176	51	125
Tribal Agencies			
Cheyenne River Tribal	26	23	3
Crow Creek Tribal	12	8	4
Flandreau Santee Sioux Tribal	2	2	0
Lower Brule Tribal	23	4	19
Pine Ridge Sioux Tribal	75	52	23
Rosebud Tribal	39	28	11
Sisseton-Wahpeton Tribal	20	12	8
Yankton Tribal	14	10	4
TENNESSEE			
State Agencies			
Alcoholic Beverage Commission	37	36	1
Department of Agricultutre, Agricultural Crime Unit	8	8	0
Department of Correction, Internal Affairs	66	25	41
State Fire Marshal	27	3	24
State Park Rangers			
Bicentennial Capitol Mall	3	3	0
Big Hill Pond	2	2	0
Big Ridge	4	4	0
Bledsoe Creek	2	2	0
Booker T. Washington	3	3	0
Burgess Falls Natural Area	4	4	0
Cedars of Lebanon	5	5	0
Chickasaw	4	4	0
Cordell Hull Birthplace	1	1	0
Cove Lake	4	4	0
Cumberland Mountain	4	4	0
Cumberland Trail	8	8	0
Cummins Falls	2	2	0
David Crockett	4	4	0

Table 81. Full-Time Law Enforcement Employees, by Selected State and Agency, 2017—Continued

(Number.)

State/agency	Law enforcement employees	Officers	Civilians
Davy Crockett Birthplace	1	1	0
Dunbar Cave Natural Area	2	2	0
Edgar Evins	4	4	0
Fall Creek Falls	9	9	0
Fort Loudon State Historic Park	4	4	0
Fort Pillow State Historic Park	2	2	0
Frozen Head Natural Area	3	3	0
Harpeth Scenic Rivers	3	3	0
Harrison Bay	4	4	0
Henry Horton	8	6	2
Hiwassee/Ocoee State Scenic Rivers	5	5	0
Indian Mountain	2	2	0
Johnsonville State Historic Park	1	1	0
Long Hunter	4	4	0
Meeman-Shelby Forest	4	4	0
Montgomery Bell	6	6	0
Mousetail Landing	3	3	0
Natchez Trace	4	4	0
Nathan Bedford Forrest	3	3	0
Norris Dam	3	3	0
Old Stone Fort State Archaeological Park	2	2	0
Panther Creek	2	2	0
Paris Landing	5	5	0
Pickett	5	5	0
Pickwick Landing	5	5	0
Pinson Mounds State Archaeological Park	1	1	0
Radnor Lake Natural Area	5	5	0
Red Clay State Historic Park	2	2	0
Reelfoot Lake	4	4	0
Roan Mountain	3	3	0
Rock Island	4	4	0
Rocky Fork	2	2	0
Seven Islands Birding Park	2	2	0
Sgt. Alvin C. York	2	2	0
South Cumberland Recreation Area	6	6	0
Standing Stone	4	4	0
Sycamore Shoals State Historic Park	2	2	0
Tim's Ford	4	4	0
T.O. Fuller	2	2	0
Warrior's Path	5	5	0
TennCare Office of Inspector General	40	14	26
Tennessee Bureau of Investigation	521	328	193
Tennessee Department of Revenue, Special Investigations Unit	53	33	20
Wildlife Resources Agency			
Region 1	48	44	4
Region 2	45	41	4
Region 3	53	50	3
Region 4	50	46	4
Other Agencies			
Chattanooga Housing Authority	6	5	1
Chattanooga Metropolitan Airport	10	10	0
Dickson Parks and Recreation	1	1	0
Drug Task Force			
1st Judicial District	4	3	1
3rd Judicial District	4	4	0
4th Judicial District	2	1	1
8th Judicial District	3	2	1
9th Judicial District	4	3	1
10th Judicial District	6	5	1
12th Judicial District	2	2	0
14th Judicial District	1	1	0
15th Judicial District	4	3	1
17th Judicial District	2	2	0
18th Judicial District	4	3	1
21st Judicial District	8	6	2
22nd Judicial District	1	1	0
23rd Judicial District	8	8	0
24th Judicial District	2	1	1
25th Judicial District	2	2	0
31st Judicial District	2	2	0
Knoxville Metropolitan Airport	46	27	19
Memphis-Shelby County Airport Authority	59	46	13
Metropolitan Nashville Park Police	18	18	0
Nashville International Airport	79	51	28
Tri-Cities Regional Airport	15	14	1
West Tennessee Violent Crime Task Force	7	6	1
TEXAS			
Tribal Agencies			
Ysleta del Sur Pueblo Tribal	10	8	2
Other Agencies			
Amarillo International Airport	13	13	0
Dallas-Fort Worth International Airport	189	175	14

Table 81. Full-Time Law Enforcement Employees, by Selected State and Agency, 2017—Continued

(Number.)

State/agency	Law enforcement employees	Officers	Civilians
Hospital District, Dallas County	159	85	74
Independent School District			
Angleton	6	4	2
Brazosport	12	11	1
Brownsville	149	38	111
East Central	12	10	2
Ector County	30	28	2
Edinburg	118	82	36
El Paso	49	36	13
Galveston	9	7	2
Hallsville	5	5	0
Idalou	1	1	0
Judson	28	27	1
Killeen	16	16	0
Klein	62	43	19
Lyford	4	4	0
Midland	18	13	5
Pasadena	41	33	8
Raymondville	9	4	5
Rio Grande City	19	15	4
Santa Fe	7	6	1
Sealy	2	2	0
Socorro	48	40	8
Spring	61	54	7
United	202	77	125
Port of Brownsville	19	12	7
UTAH			
State Agencies			
Parks and Recreation	54	53	1
Wildlife Resources	80	78	2
Tribal Agencies			
Uintah and Ouray Tribal	25	17	8
Other Agencies			
Cache-Rich Drug Task Force	5	4	1
Granite School District	38	30	8
Utah County Attorney, Investigations Division	7	5	2
Utah Transit Authority	81	68	13
Weber Morgan Narcotics Strike Force	19	17	2
VERMONT			
State Agencies			
Attorney General	4	4	0
Capitol Police	3	3	0
Department of Liquor Control, Division of Enforcement and Licensing	20	14	6
Department of Motor Vehicles	40	29	11
Fish and Wildlife Department, Law Enforcement Division	44	42	2
Secretary of State, Investigations Unit	10	5	5
VIRGINIA			
State Agencies			
Alcoholic Beverage Control Commission	143	98	45
Department of Conservation and Recreation	253	104	149
Department of Game and Inland Fisheries, Enforcement Division	179	162	17
Department of Motor Vehicles	88	75	13
Virginia State Capitol	79	66	13
Other Agencies			
Norfolk Airport Authority	45	37	8
Port Authority, Norfolk	49	36	13
Reagan National Airport	268	206	62
Richmond International Airport	36	26	10
WASHINGTON			
State Agencies			
State Gambling Commission, Enforcement Unit	100	56	44
State Insurance Commissioner, Special Investigations Unit	10	6	4
Tribal Agencies			
Chehalis Tribal	33	12	21
Colville Tribal	40	24	16
Jamestown S'Klallam Tribal	38	37	1
Kalispel Tribal	18	17	1
La Push Tribal	4	4	0
Lower Elwha Klallam Tribal	13	11	2
Lummi Tribal	24	22	2
Makah Tribal	19	10	9
Nisqually Tribal	13	12	1
Nooksack Tribal	10	9	1
Port Gamble S'Klallam Tribal	11	11	0
Puyallup Tribal	34	31	3

Table 81. Full-Time Law Enforcement Employees, by Selected State and Agency, 2017—Continued

(Number.)

State/agency	Law enforcement employees	Officers	Civilians
Quinault Indian Nation	17	10	7
Sauk-Suiattle Tribal	5	4	1
Shoalwater Bay Tribal	5	5	0
Skokomish Tribal	10	9	1
Snoqualmie Tribal	3	3	0
Spokane Agency	20	11	9
Squaxin Island Tribal	12	10	2
Stillaguamish Tribal	12	6	6
Suquamish Tribal	17	13	4
Swinomish Tribal	16	14	2
Tulalip Tribal	58	43	15
Upper Skagit Tribal	8	7	1
Yakama Nation	50	35	15
Other Agencies			
Port of Seattle	136	99	37
WEST VIRGINIA			
State Agencies			
Capitol Protective Services	50	29	21
Department of Natural Resources			
Barbour County	1	1	0
Berkeley County	1	1	0
Boone County	1	1	0
Braxton County	2	2	0
Brooke County	1	1	0
Cabell County	3	3	0
Calhoun County	2	2	0
Clay County	1	1	0
Doddridge County	2	2	0
Fayette County	2	2	0
Gilmer County	1	1	0
Grant County	2	2	0
Greenbrier County	3	3	0
Hampshire County	7	6	1
Hancock County	1	1	0
Hardy County	2	2	0
Harrison County	2	2	0
Jackson County	3	3	0
Jefferson County	1	1	0
Kanawha County	10	5	5
Lewis County	3	3	0
Lincoln County	2	2	0
Logan County	2	2	0
Marion County	5	5	0
Marshall County	2	2	0
Mason County	2	2	0
McDowell County	1	1	0
Mercer County	2	2	0
Mineral County	1	1	0
Mingo County	2	2	0
Monongalia County	2	2	0
Monroe County	1	1	0
Morgan County	1	1	0
Nicholas County	3	3	0
Ohio County	1	1	0
Pendleton County	2	2	0
Pleasants County	1	1	0
Pocahontas County	1	1	0
Preston County	3	3	0
Putnam County	7	6	1
Raleigh County	6	5	1
Randolph County	2	2	0
Ritchie County	1	1	0
Roane County	1	1	0
Summers County	2	2	0
Taylor County	1	1	0
Tucker County	1	1	0
Tyler County	1	1	0
Upshur County	4	3	1
Wayne County	2	2	0
Webster County	1	1	0
Wetzel County	1	1	0
Wirt County	1	1	0
Wood County	6	5	1
Wyoming County	4	4	0
State Fire Marshall, Kanawha County	44	32	12
Other Agencies			
Central West Virginia Drug Task Force	8	7	1
Eastern Panhandle Drug and Violent Crime Task Force	12	11	1
Greenbrier County Drug and Violent Crime Task Force	4	3	1
Hancock/Brooke/Weirton Drug Task Force	6	6	0
Harrison County Drug and Violent Crime Task Force	7	7	0
Huntington Drug and Violent Crime Task Force	4	3	1

Table 81. Full-Time Law Enforcement Employees, by Selected State and Agency, 2017—Continued

(Number.)

State/agency	Law enforcement employees	Officers	Civilians
Kanawha County Parks and Recreation	3	3	0
Logan County Drug and Violent Crime Task Force	10	9	1
Metropolitan Drug Enforcement Network Team	13	12	1
Ohio Valley Drug and Violent Crime Task Force	4	4	0
Parkersburg Narcotics and Violent Crime Task Force	8	8	0
Potomac Highlands Drug and Violent Crime Task Force	2	2	0
Southern Regional Drug and Violent Crime Task Force	5	5	0
Three Rivers Drug and Violent Crime Task Force	2	2	0
WISCONSIN			
State Agencies			
Capitol Police	44	35	9
Department of Natural Resources	344	314	30
Tribal Agencies			
Bad River Tribal	5	4	1
Lac du Flambeau Tribal	13	11	2
Menominee Tribal	29	18	11
Oneida Tribal	26	19	7
Red Cliff Tribal	5	4	1
St. Croix Tribal	14	9	5
Stockbridge Munsee Tribal	6	6	0
WYOMING			
Tribal Agencies			
Wind River Agency	27	22	5
PUERTO RICO AND OTHER OUTLYING AREAS			
Guam	355	289	66
Puerto Rico	14,234	13,461	773

SECTION VI

HATE CRIMES

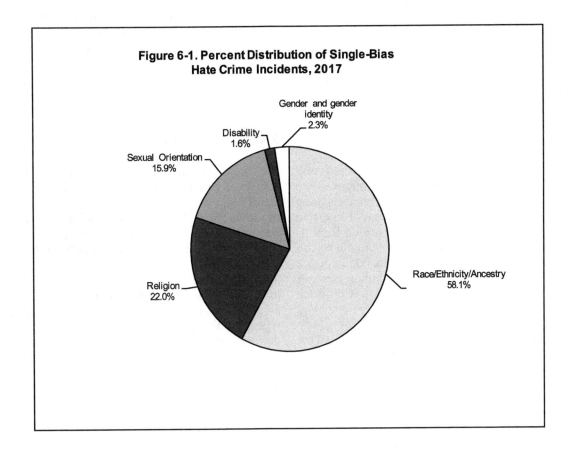

Figure 6-1. Percent Distribution of Single-Bias Hate Crime Incidents, 2017

Gender and gender identity
2.3%

Disability
1.6%

Sexual Orientation
15.9%

Religion
22.0%

Race/Ethnicity/Ancestry
58.1%

The Federal Bureau of Investigation (FBI) began the procedures for implementing, collecting, and managing hate crime data after Congress passed the Hate Crime Statistics Act in 1990. This act required the collection of data "about crimes that manifest evidence of prejudice based on race, religion, sexual orientation, or ethnicity." Beginning in 2013, law enforcement agencies could submit hate crime data in accordance with a number of program modifications. In 1994, the Hate Crime Statistics Act was amended to include bias against persons with disabilities. The Church Arson Prevention Act, which was signed into law in July 1996, removed the sunset clause from the original statute and mandated that the collection of hate crime data become a permanent part of the UCR program. In 2009, Congress further amended the Hate Crime Statistics Act by passing the Matthew Shepard and James Byrd, Jr., Hate Crime Prevention Act. The amendment includes the collection of data for crimes motivated by bias against a particular gender and gender identity, as well as for crimes committed by, and crimes directed against, juveniles. In response to the Shepard/Byrd Act, the FBI modified its data collection so that reporting

agencies could indicate whether hate crimes were committed by, or directed against, juveniles.

Definitions

Hate crimes include any crime motivated by bias against race, religion, sexual orientation, ethnicity/national origin, and/or disability. Because motivation is subjective, it is sometimes difficult to know with certainty whether a crime resulted from the offender's bias. Moreover, the presence of bias alone does not necessarily mean that a crime can be considered a hate crime. Only when law enforcement investigation reveals sufficient evidence to lead a reasonable and prudent person to conclude that the offender's actions were motivated, in whole or in part, by his or her bias should an incident be reported as a hate crime.

Data Collection

The UCR (Uniform Crime Reporting) program collects data about both single-bias and multiple-bias hate crimes. A single-bias incident is defined as an incident in which one or more offense types are motivated by the same bias. A multiple-bias incident is defined as an incident in which more than one offense type occurs and at least two offense types are motivated by different biases.

A table enumerating selected places in the United States that did not report hate crimes in 2017 is available at https://ucr.fbi.gov/hate-crime/2017/topic-pages/tables/table-14.xls/view.

Important Note: Rape

In 2013, the FBI UCR Program initiated the collection of rape data under a revised definition and removed the term "forcible" from the offense name. The changes bring uniformity to the offense in both the Summary Reporting System (SRS) and the National Incident-Based Reporting System (NIBRS) by capturing data (1) without regard to gender, (2) including penetration of any bodily orifice by any object or body part, and (3) including offenses where physical force is not involved. The UCR Program now defines rape as follows:

- **Rape (revised):** Penetration, no matter how slight, of the vagina or anus with any body part or object, or oral penetration by a sex organ of another person, without the consent of the victim. This includes the offenses of rape, sodomy, and sexual assault with an object. Unless otherwise specified, this is the definition to which "rape" refers.

- **Rape (legacy):** The carnal knowledge of a female forcibly and against her will. This definition has been discontinued.

The offenses of fondling, incest, and statutory rape are included in the Crimes Against Persons, Other category.

CRIMES AGAINST PERSONS, PROPERTY, OR SOCIETY

The UCR program's data collection guidelines stipulate that a hate crime may involve multiple offenses, victims, and offenders within one incident; therefore, the Hate Crime Statistics program is incident-based. According to UCR counting guidelines:

- One offense is counted for each victim in *crimes against persons*

- One offense is counted for each offense type in *crimes against property*

- One offense is counted for each offense type in *crimes against society*

VICTIMS

In the UCR program, the victim of a hate crime may be an individual, a business, an institution, or society as a whole.

OFFENDERS

According to the UCR program, the term *known offender* does not imply that the suspect's identity is known; rather, the term indicates that some aspect of the suspect was identified, thus distinguishing the suspect from an unknown offender. Law enforcement agencies specify the number of offenders, and when possible, the race of the offender or offenders as a group.

RACE/ETHNICITY

The UCR program uses the following racial designations in its Hate Crime Statistics program: White; Black; American Indian or Alaskan Native; Asian; Native Hawaiian or Other Pacific Islander; and Multiple Races, Group. In addition, the UCR program uses the ethnic designations of Hispanic or Latino and Not Hispanic or Latino.

The law enforcement agencies that voluntarily participate in the Hate Crime Statistics program collect details about an offender's bias motivation associated with 11 offense types already being reported to the UCR program: murder and nonnegligent manslaughter, rape, aggravated assault, simple assault, and intimidation (crimes against persons); and robbery, burglary, larceny-theft, motor vehicle theft, arson, and destruction/damage/vandalism (crimes against property). The law enforcement agencies that participate in the UCR program via the National Incident-Based Reporting System (NIBRS) collect data about additional offenses for *crimes against persons* and *crimes against property*. These data appear in the category of other. These agencies also collect hate crime data for the category called *crimes against society*, which includes drug or narcotic offenses, gambling offenses, prostitution offenses, and weapon law violations.

NATIONAL VOLUME AND PERCENT DISTRIBUTION

In 2017, 2,040 law enforcement agencies (out of 16,149 participating agencies) reported 7,175 hate crime incidents involving 8,437 offenses. Of these, 7,106 were single-bias offenses. An analysis of the single-bias incidents revealed that 58.1 percent were racially/ethnically/ancestrally motivated, 22.0 percent were motivated by religious bias, 15.9 percent resulted from sexual orientation bias, 2.3 percent were motivated by gender and gender-identity bias, and 1.6 percent were prompted by a disability bias. (Table 82)

The majority of the 4,832 hate crime offenses that were racially motivated resulted from an anti-Black or African American bias (48.8 percent) followed by an anti-White basis (17.5 percent). Bias against people of more than one race accounted for 4.4 percent of offenses, while anti-Asian bias accounted for 3.1 percent of racially motivated offenses, anti–Native Hawaiian and Other Pacific Islander accounted for 0.4 percent of these offenses, and anti–American Indian or Alaska Native bias accounted for 5.8 percent of these offenses. Approximately 10.9 percent of crimes were classified as an anti-Hispanic or Latino bias. (Table 82)

Hate crimes motivated by religious bias accounted for 1,679 offenses reported by law enforcement. A breakdown of these offenses revealed 58.1 percent were motivated by anti-Jewish bias, 18.7 percent by anti-Islamic (Muslim) bias, 3.2 percent were anti–multiple religions or groups, 4.5 percent had an anti-Catholic bias, 2.4 percent were anti-Protestant, 1.4 percent were anti—Eastern Orthodox (Russian, Greek, or other), 1.8 percent were anti—other Christian, 0.5 percent were anti-atheism/agnoticism/etc., 0.9 percent were anti-Mormon, 0.9 percent were anti-Hindu, 0.8 percent were anti—Jehovah's Witness, 0.5 percent were anti-Buddhist, 1.4 percent were anti-Sikh, and the remainder, 4.9 percent, of offenses were based on a bias against other religions—those not specified. (Table 82)

In 2017, 1,303 offenses were committed on the basis of sexual orientation bias. Of the offenses based on sexual orientation, 24.6 percent were classified as having an anti-lesbian, gay, bisexual, or transgender (mixed group) bias; 58.2 percent were classified as having an anti-gay bias; 12.2 percent had an anti-lesbian basis; 2.1 percent had an anti-bisexual bias; and 2.8 percent had an anti-heterosexual bias. (Table 82)

Hate crime offenses committed based on disability totaled 128 offenses. The majority (72.7 percent) were classified as anti-mental disability, with the rest (27.3 percent) classified as anti–physical disability. (Table 82)

Of the 131 gender identity bias offenses reported, 118 were anti-transgender and 13 were anti–gender nonconforming. Of the 53 gender bias offenses reported, 28 were anti-female and 25 were anti-male. (Table 82)

CRIMES AGAINST PERSONS

Law enforcement agencies reported 5,084 hate crime offenses against persons in 2017. Approximately 44.9 percent involved intimidation, 34.3 percent involved simple assault, and 19.5 percent involved aggravated assault. There were 12 murders and 23 rapes. (Table 83)

CRIMES AGAINST PROPERTY

In 2017, hate crime offenses against property totaled 3,115. Approximately 74.6 percent of offenses involved destruction/damage or vandalism. The remaining 25.4 percent of crimes against property consisted of robbery, burglary, larceny-theft, motor vehicle theft, arson, and other crimes. (Table 83)

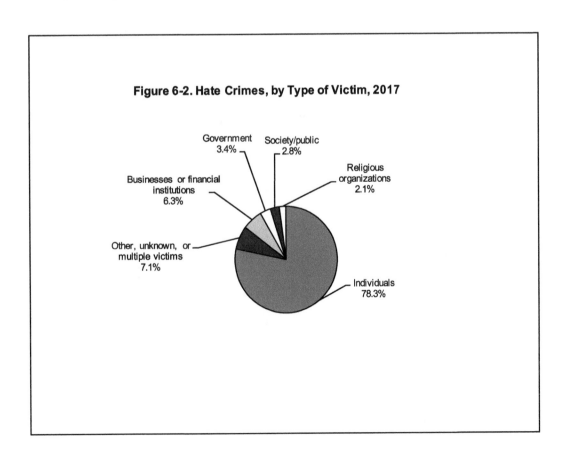

Figure 6-2. Hate Crimes, by Type of Victim, 2017

Table 82. Incidents, Offenses, Victims, and Known Offenders, by Bias Motivation, 2017

(Number.)

Bias motivation	Incidents	Offenses	Victims[1]	Known offenders[2]
Total	7,175	8,437	8,828	6,370
Single-Bias Incidents	7,106	8,126	8,493	6,307
Race/Ethnicity/Ancestry	4,131	4,832	5,060	3,747
Anti-White	741	844	864	758
Anti-Black or African American	2,013	2,358	2,458	1,742
Anti-American Indian or Alaska Native	251	281	321	228
Anti-Asian	131	152	165	108
Anti-Native Hawaiian or Other Pacific Islander	16	17	18	10
Anti-Multiple races, group	180	215	229	100
Anti-Arab	102	128	131	100
Anti-Hispanic or Latino	427	525	552	491
Anti-Other Race/Ethnicity/Ancestry	270	312	322	210
Religion	1,564	1,679	1,749	1,009
Anti-Jewish	938	976	1,017	523
Anti-Catholic	73	75	76	59
Anti-Protestant	40	40	40	15
Anti-Islamic (Muslim)	273	314	325	231
Anti-other religion	76	82	86	56
Anti-multiple religions, group	47	54	57	35
Anti-Mormon	15	15	15	8
Anti-Jehovah's Witness	7	13	13	6
Anti-Eastern Orthodox (Russian, Greek, Other)	23	23	27	14
Anti-Other Christian	27	31	32	18
Anti-Buddhist	8	9	12	10
Anti-Hindu	11	15	15	10
Anti-Sikh	20	24	26	18
Anti-atheism/agnosticism/etc.	6	8	8	6
Sexual orientation	1,130	1,303	1,338	1,250
Anti-gay (male)	679	758	774	778
Anti-lesbian	126	159	164	129
Anti-lesbian, gay, bisexual, or transgender (mixed group)	268	321	333	282
Anti-heterosexual	32	37	37	28
Anti-bisexual	25	28	30	33
Disability	116	128	160	124
Anti-physical	32	35	37	31
Anti-mental	84	93	123	93
Gender	46	53	54	40
Anti-male	22	25	26	21
Anti-female	24	28	28	19
Gender Identity	119	131	132	137
Anti-transgender	106	118	119	127
Anti-gender nonconforming	13	13	13	10
Multiple-Bias Incidents[3]	69	311	335	63

1 The term victim may refer to a person, business, institution, or society as a whole.   2 The term known offender does not imply that the identity of the suspect is known, but only that an attribute of the suspect has been identified, which distinguishes him/her from an unknown offender.   3 A multiple-bias incident is an incident in which one or more offense types are motivated by two or more biases.

Table 83. Incidents, Offenses, Victims, and Known Offenders, by Offense Type, 2017

(Number.)

Offense type	Incidents[1]	Offenses	Victims[2]	Known offenders[3]
Total	7,175	8,437	8,828	6,370
Crimes Against Persons	4,090	5,084	5,084	4,442
Murder and nonnegligent manslaughter	12	15	15	15
Rape [4]	23	23	23	30
Aggravated assault	788	990	990	1,051
Simple assault	1,433	1,745	1,745	1,725
Intimidation	1,807	2,283	2,283	1,588
Human trafficking, commercial sex acts	1	1	1	0
Other[5]	26	27	27	33
Crimes Against Property	3,115	3,115	3,506	1,933
Robbery	157	157	171	288
Burglary	145	145	185	98
Larceny-theft	326	326	379	249
Motor vehicle theft	41	41	44	25
Arson	42	42	59	34
Destruction/damage/vandalism	2,325	2,325	2,585	1,182
Other[5]	79	79	83	57
Crimes Against Society[6]	238	238	238	284

1 The actual number of incidents is 7,175. However, the column figures will not add to the total because incidents may include more than one offense type, and these are counted in each appropriate offense type category.   2 The term victim may refer to a person, business, institution, or society as a whole.   3 The term known offender does not imply the suspect's identity is known; rather, the term indicates some aspect of the suspect was identified, thus distinguishing the suspect from an unknown offender. The actual number of known offenders is 6,370. However, the column figures will not add to the total because some offenders are responsible for more than one offense type, and are, therefore, counted more than once in this table.   4 The figures shown in this row for the offense of rape include only those reported by law enforcement agencies that used the revised Uniform Crime Reporting (UCR) definition of rape.   5 Includes additional offenses collected in the National Incident-Based Reporting System.

Table 84. Offenses, Known Offender's Race and Ethnicity, by Offense Type, 2017

(Number.)

Bias motivation	Total offenses	Known offender's race							Known offender's ethnicity[1]				Unknown offender
		White	Black or African American	American Indian or Alaska Native	Asian	Native Hawaiian or Other Pacific Islander	Group of multiple races	Unknown race	Hispanic or Latino	Not Hispanic or Latino	Group of multiple ethnicities	Unknown ethnicity	
Total	8,437	3,228	1,217	58	46	3	281	1,132	350	1,294	56	3,085	2,472
Crimes Against Persons	5,084	2,491	999	49	37	3	215	445	278	1,067	50	2,064	845
Murder and nonnegligent man-slaughter	15	6	7	0	0	0	0	1	0	3	0	7	1
Rape [2]	23	13	7	0	0	0	1	1	1	4	0	17	1
Aggravated assault	990	530	262	8	8	0	64	68	107	298	11	375	50
Simple assault	1,745	840	415	23	13	2	88	151	95	388	9	729	213
Intimidation	2,283	1,084	302	18	16	1	61	223	75	370	30	914	578
Human trafficking, commercial sex acts	1	0	0	0	0	0	0	0	0	0	0	0	1
Other [3]	27	18	6	0	0	0	1	1	0	4	0	22	1
Crimes Against Property	3,115	571	178	9	8	0	55	677	62	190	5	841	1,617
Robbery	157	49	55	1	0	0	20	16	16	36	2	58	16
Burglary	145	31	12	1	0	0	3	31	1	8	1	58	67
Larceny-theft	326	102	38	1	2	0	5	46	6	14	0	165	132
Motor vehicle theft	41	12	2	0	0	0	0	6	0	1	0	19	21
Arson	42	13	1	1	1	0	1	6	1	6	0	11	19
Destruction/damage/ vandalism	2,325	336	65	4	5	0	22	565	37	115	2	496	1,328
Other [3]	79	28	5	1	0	0	4	7	1	10	0	34	34
Crimes Against Society [3]	238	166	40	0	1	0	11	10	10	37	1	180	10

1 The sum of offenses by the known offender's ethnicity does not equal the sum of offenses by the known offender's race because not all law enforcement agencies that report offender race data also report offender ethnicity data.   2 The figures shown in the rape (revised definition) row include only those reported by law enforcement agencies that used the revised Uniform Crime Reporting (UCR) definition of rape.   3 Includes additional offenses collected in the National Incident-Based Reporting System.

Table 85. Offenses, Offense Type, by Bias Motivation, 2017

(Number.)

Bias motivation	Total offenses	Crimes against persons						
		Murder and nonnegligent manslaughter	Rape[1]	Aggravated assault	Simple assault	Intimidation	Human trafficking, commercial sex acts	Other[2]
Total	8,437	15	23	990	1,745	2,283	1	27
Single-Bias Incidents	8,126	15	23	975	1,623	2,156	1	27
Race/Ethnicity/Ancestry	4,832	11	8	638	965	1,442	1	15
Anti-White	844	5	2	105	203	171	0	7
Anti-Black or African American	2,358	5	1	326	454	820	0	2
Anti-American Indian or Alaska Native	281	0	4	17	29	44	0	1
Anti-Asian	152	0	0	14	40	45	0	0
Anti-Native Hawaiian or Other Pacific Islander	17	0	0	1	2	3	1	1
Anti-Multiple Races, Group	215	0	0	8	27	65	0	2
Anti-Arab	128	0	1	24	37	37	0	2
Anti-Hispanic or Latino	525	1	0	105	124	167	0	0
Anti-Other Race/Ethnicity/Ancestry	312	0	0	38	49	90	0	0
Religion	1,679	1	1	55	184	331	0	2
Anti-Jewish	976	0	0	8	61	179	0	0
Anti-Catholic	75	0	0	1	3	4	0	0
Anti-Protestant	40	0	0	0	4	3	0	0
Anti-Islamic (Muslim)	314	0	0	28	77	110	0	0
Anti-Other Religion	82	0	0	2	10	21	0	0
Anti-Multiple Religions, Group	54	0	0	5	15	1	0	0
Anti-Mormon	15	0	0	0	0	2	0	0
Anti-Jehovah's Witness	13	0	0	1	6	2	0	0
Anti-Eastern Orthodox (Russian, Greek, Other)	23	0	0	0	2	0	0	0
Anti-Other Christian	31	0	0	1	1	1	0	0
Anti-Buddhist	9	0	0	1	1	1	0	0
Anti-Hindu	15	0	0	4	1	4	0	1
Anti-Sikh	24	1	1	4	1	3	0	0
Anti-Atheism/Agnosticism/etc.	8	0	0	0	2	0	0	1
Sexual Orientation	1,303	2	8	237	383	327	0	5
Anti-Gay (Male)	758	2	3	161	233	170	0	2
Anti-Lesbian	159	0	3	21	51	50	0	1
Anti-Lesbian, Gay, Bisexual, or Transgender (Mixed Group)	321	0	1	44	83	95	0	2
Anti-Heterosexual	37	0	0	5	8	8	0	0
Anti-Bisexual	28	0	1	6	8	4	0	0
Disability	128	1	3	12	32	23	0	2
Anti-Physical	35	1	0	4	9	5	0	0
Anti-Mental	93	0	3	8	23	18	0	2
Gender	53	0	3	5	12	8	0	3
Anti-Male	25	0	1	3	4	3	0	1
Anti-Female	28	0	2	2	8	5	0	2
Gender Identity	131	0	0	28	47	25	0	0
Anti-Transgender	118	0	0	27	43	24	0	0
Anti-Gender Non-Conforming	13	0	0	1	4	1	0	0
Multiple-Bias Incidents[3]	311	0	0	15	122	127	0	0

Table 85. Offenses, Offense Type, by Bias Motivation, 2017—Continued

(Number.)

Bias motivation	Crimes against property							Crimes against society[2]
	Robbery	Burglary	Larceny-theft	Motor vehicle theft	Arson	Destruction/ damage/ vandalism	Other[2]	
Total	157	145	326	41	42	2,325	79	238
Single-Bias Incidents	157	140	323	41	41	2,291	79	234
Race/Ethnicity/Ancestry	84	83	208	35	24	1,111	40	167
Anti-White	22	24	92	14	3	113	20	63
Anti-Black or African American	19	29	17	2	15	640	6	22
Anti-American Indian or Alaska Native	2	12	60	14	0	26	10	62
Anti-Asian	0	4	8	1	0	38	0	2
Anti-Native Hawaiian or Other Pacific Islander	1	1	4	0	0	2	1	0
Anti-Multiple Races, Group	4	4	1	0	0	102	0	2
Anti-Arab	2	1	5	2	0	16	0	1
Anti-Hispanic or Latino	29	3	12	1	3	74	2	4
Anti-Other Race/Ethnicity/Ancestry	5	5	9	1	3	100	1	11
Religion	14	35	52	3	8	938	24	31
Anti-Jewish	4	11	11	0	2	696	2	2
Anti-Catholic	0	1	6	1	2	43	3	11
Anti-Protestant	0	2	6	0	0	22	1	2
Anti-Islamic (Muslim)	6	2	6	0	0	80	5	0
Anti-Other Religion	1	3	1	1	2	36	2	3
Anti-Multiple Religions, Group	1	4	4	0	1	21	0	2
Anti-Mormon	0	4	2	0	0	2	1	4
Anti-Jehovah's Witness	0	0	1	0	0	2	0	1
Anti-Eastern Orthodox (Russian, Greek, Other)	1	2	6	0	0	3	6	3
Anti-Other Christian	0	2	2	0	1	22	0	1
Anti-Buddhist	0	0	2	0	0	4	0	0
Anti-Hindu	0	1	1	0	0	2	0	0
Anti-Sikh	0	3	2	1	0	4	3	1
Anti-Atheism/Agnosticism/etc.	1	0	2	0	0	1	0	1
Sexual Orientation	52	15	38	1	7	207	3	18
Anti-Gay (Male)	42	11	9	1	3	115	1	5
Anti-Lesbian	0	0	5	0	0	26	0	2
Anti-Lesbian, Gay, Bisexual, or Transgender (Mixed Group)	9	3	18	0	4	60	0	2
Anti-Heterosexual	1	1	4	0	0	4	1	5
Anti-Bisexual	0	0	2	0	0	2	1	4
Disability	2	2	16	0	2	8	9	16
Anti-Physical	0	0	5	0	0	2	2	7
Anti-Mental	2	2	11	0	2	6	7	9
Gender	0	2	3	2	0	13	0	2
Anti-Male	0	2	3	2	0	5	0	1
Anti-Female	0	0	0	0	0	8	0	1
Gender Identity	5	3	6	0	0	14	3	0
Anti-Transgender	4	2	4	0	0	13	1	0
Anti-Gender Non-Conforming	1	1	2	0	0	1	2	0
Multiple-Bias Incidents[3]	0	5	3	0	1	34	0	4

1 The figures shown in this column for the offense of rape include only those reported by law enforcement agencies that used the revised Uniform Crime Reporting (UCR) definition of rape.   2 Includes additional offenses collected in the National Incident-Based Reporting System.   3 A multiple-bias incident is an incident in which one or more offense types are motivated by two or more biases.

Table 86. Offenses, Known Offender's Race, by Bias Motivation, 2017

(Number.)

Bias motivation	Total offenses	Known offender's race							Known offender's ethnicity[1]				Unknown offender
		White	Black or African American	American Indian or Alaska Native	Asian	Native Hawaiian or Other Pacific Islander	Group of multiple races	Unknown race	Hispanic or Latino	Not Hispanic or Latino	Group of multiple ethnicities	Unknown ethnicity	
Total	8,437	3,228	1,217	58	46	3	281	1,132	350	1,294	56	3,085	2,472
Single-Bias Incidents	8,126	3,186	1,195	58	46	3	279	1,117	345	1,260	56	3,043	2,242
Race/Ethnicity/Ancestry	4,832	2,164	694	46	22	2	166	508	174	816	42	1,953	1,230
Anti-White	844	182	382	14	2	1	26	83	22	168	3	445	154
Anti-Black or African American	2,358	1,241	72	25	10	0	89	268	112	361	16	851	653
Anti-American Indian or Alaska Native	281	137	27	2	1	1	26	12	7	13	20	160	75
Anti-Asian	152	63	27	0	4	0	2	22	6	22	1	53	34
Anti-Native Hawaiian or Other Pacific Islander	17	7	3	0	0	0	0	0	0	3	0	4	7
Anti-Multiple Races, Group	215	76	14	0	0	0	1	29	9	25	0	67	95
Anti-Arab	128	54	30	0	2	0	5	16	4	19	0	59	21
Anti-Hispanic or Latino	525	274	107	3	0	0	9	43	6	160	2	190	89
Anti-Other Race/Ethnicity/Ancestry	312	130	32	2	3	0	8	35	8	45	0	124	102
Religion	1,679	409	87	1	13	0	25	443	40	140	2	433	701
Anti-Jewish	976	141	26	0	6	0	6	320	11	37	0	162	477
Anti-Catholic	75	28	8	0	1	0	2	16	9	6	0	30	20
Anti-Protestant	40	6	1	0	0	0	0	7	0	0	0	14	26
Anti-Islamic (Muslim)	314	139	30	0	1	0	8	44	10	48	1	120	92
Anti-Other Religion	82	18	2	0	2	0	5	19	2	8	0	30	36
Anti-Multiple Religions, Group	54	14	13	1	0	0	0	12	2	17	0	16	14
Anti-Mormon	15	6	1	0	0	0	0	1	0	2	0	6	7
Anti-Jehovah's Witness	13	11	0	0	0	0	0	1	0	6	0	6	1
Anti-Eastern Orthodox (Russian, Greek, Other)	23	9	3	0	0	0	1	0	0	7	0	6	10
Anti-Other Christian	31	10	1	0	0	0	0	8	0	3	0	11	12
Anti-Buddhist	9	3	1	0	1	0	1	2	0	2	0	4	1
Anti-Hindu	15	9	0	0	0	0	0	4	5	0	0	5	2
Anti-Sikh	24	10	1	0	1	0	2	7	1	4	1	15	3
Anti-Atheism/Agnosticism/etc.	8	5	0	0	1	0	0	2	0	0	0	8	0
Sexual Orientation	1,303	478	335	10	10	1	68	143	102	267	11	492	258
Anti-Gay (Male)	758	263	222	3	9	1	43	83	71	175	9	250	134
Anti-Lesbian	159	71	34	0	0	0	7	18	11	39	0	60	29
Anti-Lesbian, Gay, Bisexual, or Transgender (Mixed Group)	321	119	69	6	1	0	10	37	14	42	2	157	79
Anti-Heterosexual	37	10	6	0	0	0	6	2	2	6	0	12	13
Anti-Bisexual	28	15	4	1	0	0	2	3	4	5	0	13	3
Disability	128	66	28	0	0	0	2	6	4	17	0	76	26
Anti-Physical	35	18	7	0	0	0	2	1	2	6	0	19	7
Anti-Mental	93	48	21	0	0	0	0	5	2	11	0	57	19
Gender	53	28	8	0	1	0	0	8	1	3	0	41	8
Anti-Male	25	11	4	0	0	0	0	8	0	0	0	23	2
Anti-Female	28	17	4	0	1	0	0	0	1	3	0	18	6
Gender Identity	131	41	43	1	0	0	18	9	24	17	1	48	19
Anti-Transgender	118	37	40	1	0	0	17	9	22	16	1	43	14
Anti-Gender Non-Conforming	13	4	3	0	0	0	1	0	2	1	0	5	5
Multiple-Bias Incidents[2]	311	42	22	0	0	0	2	15	5	34	0	42	230

1 The total number of offenses by the known offender's ethnicity do not equal the total number of offenses by the known offender's race because not all law enforcement agencies that report offender race data also report offender ethnicity data.
2 A multiple-bias incident is an incident in which one or more offense types are motivated by two or more biases.

Table 87. Offenses, Victim Type, by Offense Type, 2017

(Number.)

Offense type	Total offenses	Victim type					
		Individual	Business/ financial institution	Government	Religious organization	Society/ public[1]	Other/ unknown/ multiple
Total	8,437	6,607	528	286	179	238	599
Crimes against persons[2]	5,084	5,084	NA	NA	NA	NA	NA
Crimes against property	3,115	1,523	528	286	179	0	599
Robbery	157	146	3	0	0	0	8
Burglary	145	94	28	3	10	0	10
Larceny-theft	326	198	101	1	8	0	18
Motor vehicle theft	41	36	3	0	0	0	2
Arson	42	31	4	0	4	0	3
Destruction/damage/vandalism	2,325	957	374	281	156	0	557
Other[2]	79	61	15	1	1	0	1
Crimes against society[2]	238	NA	NA	NA	NA	238	NA

NA = Not available.
1 The victim type society/public is collected only in the National Incident-Based Reporting System (NIBRS).   2 Includes additional offenses collected in the NIBRS.

Table 88. Victims, Offense Type, by Bias Motivation, 2017

(Number.)

Bias motivation	Total victims[1]	Total number of adult victims[2]	Total number of juvenile victims[2]	Crimes against persons						
				Murder and nonnegligent manslaughter	Rape[3]	Aggravated assault	Simple assault	Intimidation	Human trafficking, commercial sex acts	Other[4]
Total	8,828	5,125	678	15	23	990	1,745	2,283	1	27
Single-Bias Incidents	8,493	5,027	674	15	23	975	1,623	2,156	1	27
Race/Ethnicity/Ancestry	5,060	3,086	465	11	8	638	965	1,442	1	15
Anti-White	864	566	72	5	2	105	203	171	0	7
Anti-Black or African American	2,458	1,437	263	5	1	326	454	820	0	2
Anti-American Indian or Alaska Native	321	155	27	0	4	17	29	44	0	1
Anti-Asian	165	100	4	0	0	14	40	45	0	0
Anti-Native Hawaiian or Other Pacific Islander	18	11	2	0	0	1	2	3	1	1
Anti-Multiple Races, Group	229	112	18	0	0	8	27	65	0	2
Anti-Arab	131	90	12	0	1	24	37	37	0	2
Anti-Hispanic or Latino	552	430	51	1	0	105	124	167	0	0
Anti-Other Race/Ethnicity/Ancestry	322	185	16	0	0	38	49	90	0	0
Religion	1,749	732	61	1	1	55	184	331	0	2
Anti-Jewish	1,017	317	28	0	0	8	61	179	0	0
Anti-Catholic	76	20	0	0	0	1	3	4	0	0
Anti-Protestant	40	16	1	0	0	0	4	3	0	0
Anti-Islamic (Muslim)	325	219	20	0	0	28	77	110	0	0
Anti-Other Religion	86	41	4	0	0	2	10	21	0	0
Anti-Multiple Religions, Group	57	32	0	0	0	5	15	1	0	0
Anti-Mormon	15	8	0	0	0	0	0	2	0	0
Anti-Jehovah's Witness	13	9	2	0	0	1	6	2	0	0
Anti-Eastern Orthodox (Russian, Greek, Other)	27	19	1	0	0	0	2	0	0	0
Anti-Other Christian	32	7	1	0	0	1	1	1	0	0
Anti-Buddhist	12	8	1	0	0	1	1	1	0	0
Anti-Hindu	15	12	0	0	0	4	1	4	0	1
Anti-Sikh	26	20	2	1	1	4	1	3	0	0
Anti-Atheism/Agnosticism/etc.	8	4	1	0	0	0	2	0	0	1
Sexual Orientation	1,338	978	116	2	8	237	383	327	0	5
Anti-Gay (Male)	774	577	50	2	3	161	233	170	0	2
Anti-Lesbian	164	124	19	0	3	21	51	50	0	1
Anti-Lesbian, Gay, Bisexual, or Transgender (Mixed Group)	333	245	37	0	1	44	83	95	0	2
Anti-Heterosexual	37	19	0	0	0	5	8	8	0	0
Anti-Bisexual	30	13	10	0	1	6	8	4	0	0
Disability	160	104	18	1	3	12	32	23	0	2
Anti-Physical	37	22	3	1	0	4	9	5	0	0
Anti-Mental	123	82	15	0	3	8	23	18	0	2
Gender	54	38	7	0	3	5	12	8	0	3
Anti-Male	26	14	6	0	1	3	4	3	0	1
Anti-Female	28	24	1	0	2	2	8	5	0	2
Gender Identity	132	89	7	0	0	28	47	25	0	0
Anti-Transgender	119	79	6	0	0	27	43	24	0	0
Anti-Gender Non-Conforming	13	10	1	0	0	1	4	1	0	0
Multiple-Bias Incidents[5]	335	98	4	0	0	15	122	127	0	0

Table 88. Victims, Offense Type, by Bias Motivation, 2017—Continued

(Number.)

Bias motivation	Crimes against property							Crimes against society[4]
	Robbery	Burglary	Larceny-theft	Motor vehicle theft	Arson	Destruction/ damage/ vandalism	Other[4]	
Total	171	185	379	44	59	2,585	83	238
Single-Bias Incidents	171	177	375	44	58	2,531	83	234
Race/Ethnicity/Ancestry	92	111	224	38	37	1,270	41	167
Anti-White	24	25	97	15	3	124	20	63
Anti-Black or African American	20	49	18	2	25	708	6	22
Anti-American Indian or Alaska Native	2	15	67	15	0	54	11	62
Anti-Asian	0	6	8	1	0	49	0	2
Anti-Native Hawaiian or Other Pacific Islander	1	1	5	0	0	2	1	0
Anti-Multiple Races, Group	4	4	1	0	0	116	0	2
Anti-Arab	2	1	6	3	0	17	0	1
Anti-Hispanic or Latino	34	3	13	1	6	92	2	4
Anti-Other Race/Ethnicity/Ancestry	5	7	9	1	3	108	1	11
Religion	16	41	58	3	10	990	26	31
Anti-Jewish	4	11	13	0	2	735	2	2
Anti-Catholic	0	1	6	1	2	43	4	11
Anti-Protestant	0	2	6	0	0	22	1	2
Anti-Islamic (Muslim)	6	5	8	0	0	86	5	0
Anti-Other Religion	1	4	1	1	2	38	3	3
Anti-Multiple Religions, Group	2	4	4	0	3	21	0	2
Anti-Mormon	0	4	2	0	0	2	1	4
Anti-Jehovah's Witness	0	0	1	0	0	2	0	1
Anti-Eastern Orthodox (Russian, Greek, Other)	2	3	7	0	0	4	6	3
Anti-Other Christian	0	2	3	0	1	22	0	1
Anti-Buddhist	0	0	2	0	0	7	0	0
Anti-Hindu	0	1	1	0	0	2	1	0
Anti-Sikh	0	4	2	1	0	5	3	1
Anti-Atheism/Agnosticism/etc.	1	0	2	0	0	1	0	1
Sexual Orientation	56	17	39	1	9	233	3	18
Anti-Gay (Male)	45	13	9	1	3	126	1	5
Anti-Lesbian	0	0	5	0	0	31	0	2
Anti-Lesbian, Gay, Bisexual, or Transgender (Mixed Group)	10	3	18	0	6	69	0	2
Anti-Heterosexual	1	1	4	0	0	4	1	5
Anti-Bisexual	0	0	3	0	0	3	1	4
Disability	2	2	45	0	2	10	10	16
Anti-Physical	0	0	7	0	0	2	2	7
Anti-Mental	2	2	38	0	2	8	8	9
Gender	0	2	3	2	0	14	0	2
Anti-Male	0	2	3	2	0	6	0	1
Anti-Female	0	0	0	0	0	8	0	1
Gender Identity	5	4	6	0	0	14	3	0
Anti-Transgender	4	3	4	0	0	13	1	0
Anti-Gender Non-Conforming	1	1	2	0	0	1	2	0
Multiple-Bias Incidents[5]	0	8	4	0	1	54	0	4

Note: The aggregate of adult and juvenile individual victims does not equal the total number of victims because total victims include individuals, businesses, institutions, and society as a whole. In addition, the aggregate of adult and juvenile individual victims does not equal the aggregate of victims of crimes against persons because not all law enforcement agencies report the ages of individual victims.
1 A victim can be an individual, a business, an institution, or society as a whole.   2 The figures shown in this column are individual victims only.   3 The figures shown in this column for the offense of rape were reported using only the revised Uniform Crime Reporting definition of rape.   4 Includes additional offenses collected in the National Incident-Based Reporting System.   5 A multiple-bias incident is an incident in which one or more offense types are motivated by two or more biases.

Table 89. Incidents, Victim Type, by Bias Motivation, 2017

(Number.)

Bias motivation	Total incidents	Victim type					
		Individual	Business/ financial institution	Government	Religious organization	Society/ public[1]	Other/ unknown/ multiple
Total	7,175	5,373	515	282	168	220	617
Single-Bias Incidents	7,106	5,322	514	273	168	218	611
Race/Ethnicity/Ancestry	4,131	3,272	310	156	19	153	221
Religion	1,564	783	166	88	142	31	354
Sexual Orientation	1,130	1,034	20	20	6	16	34
Disability	116	89	7	2	0	16	2
Gender	46	40	3	1	0	2	0
Gender Identity	119	104	8	6	1	0	0
Multiple-Bias Incidents[2]	69	51	1	9	0	2	6

1 The victim type society/public is collected only in the National Incident-Based Reporting System.   2 A multiple-bias incident is an incident in which one or more offense types are motivated by two or more biases.

Table 90. Known Offenders,[1] by Known Offender's Race, Ethnicity, and Age, 2017

(Number.)

Race/ethnicity/age	Total
Race	
White	6,370
Black or African American	3,227
American Indian or Alaska Native	1,359
Asian	49
Native Hawaiian or Other Pacific Islander	42
Group of multiple races[2]	3
Unknown race	475
	1,215
Ethnicity[3]	
Hispanic or Latino	5,131
Not Hispanic or Latino	454
Group of multiple ethnicities[4]	1,284
Unknown ethnicity	81
	3,312
Age[3]	
Total known offenders 18 and over	4,895
Total known offenders under 18	4,062
	833

1 The term known offender does not imply the suspect's identity is known; rather, the term indicates some aspect of the suspect was identified, thus distinguishing the suspect from an unknown offender.   2 The term group of multiple races is used to describe a group of offenders of varying races.   3 The total number of known offenders by age and the total number of known offenders by ethnicity do not equal the total number of known offenders by race because not all law enforcement agencies report the age and/or ethnicity of the known offenders.   4 The term group of multiple ethnicities is used to describe a group of offenders of varying ethnicities.

Table 91. Incidents, Bias Motivation, by Location, 2017

(Number.)

Location	Total incidents	Bias motivation						Multiple-bias incidents[1]
		Race/Ethnicity/ Ancestry	Religion	Sexual orientation	Disability	Gender	Gender Identity	
Total	7,175	4,131	1,564	1,130	116	46	119	69
Abandoned/condemned structure	5	3	1	1	0	0	0	0
Air/bus/train terminal	118	84	13	15	1	0	4	1
Amusement park	3	2	0	1	0	0	0	0
Arena/stadium/fairgrounds/coliseum	7	3	0	3	1	0	0	0
ATM separate from bank	3	0	1	2	0	0	0	0
Auto dealership new/used	8	6	1	1	0	0	0	0
Bank/savings and loan	25	16	5	2	2	0	0	0
Bar/nightclub	99	52	5	37	2	0	2	1
Camp/campground	3	2	1	0	0	0	0	0
Church/synagogue/temple/mosque	292	44	234	12	0	0	1	1
Commercial office building	139	90	32	9	2	1	3	2
Community center	22	7	14	1	0	0	0	0
Construction site	25	19	3	2	1	0	0	0
Convenience store	105	71	13	14	3	1	1	2
Cyberspace	11	7	4	0	0	0	0	0
Daycare facility	6	4	0	1	1	0	0	0
Department/discount store	91	63	13	8	3	1	1	2
Dock/wharf/freight/modal terminal	3	1	1	0	0	0	1	0
Drug store/doctor's office/hospital	75	49	15	8	0	1	1	1
Farm facility	3	3	0	0	0	0	0	0
Field/woods	50	29	13	4	1	0	2	1
Gambling facility/casino/race track	3	3	0	0	0	0	0	0
Government/public building	117	78	19	17	2	1	0	0
Grocery/supermarket	75	57	11	4	1	0	2	0
Highway/road/alley/street/sidewalk	1,218	778	139	241	16	5	29	10
Hotel/motel/etc.	63	41	11	9	1	1	0	0
Industrial site	9	8	1	0	0	0	0	0
Jail/prison/penitentiary/corrections facility	59	42	3	13	1	0	0	0
Lake/waterway/beach	13	8	2	3	0	0	0	0
Liquor store	11	8	0	2	0	0	1	0
Military installation	1	1	0	0	0	0	0	0
Park/playground	128	67	33	20	1	0	1	6
Parking/drop lot/garage	419	271	62	66	7	2	4	7
Rental storage facility	14	9	4	0	1	0	0	0
Residence/home	1,971	1,133	360	366	46	24	22	20
Rest area	8	2	6	0	0	0	0	0
Restaurant	192	126	20	38	3	1	3	1
School/college[2]	199	85	87	22	3	0	2	0
School—college/university	214	129	45	29	1	1	6	3
School—elementary/secondary	340	207	67	42	7	2	9	6
Service/gas station	73	58	8	4	2	1	0	0
Shelter—mission/homeless	15	12	0	2	0	0	1	0
Shopping mall	21	10	5	3	0	0	3	0
Specialty store (TV, fur, etc.)	76	51	10	11	2	1	0	1
Other/unknown	822	381	299	115	5	1	20	1
Multiple locations	21	11	3	2	0	2	0	3

1 A *multiple-bias incident* is an incident in which one or more offense types are motivated by two or more biases.   2 The location designation school/college has been retained for agencies that have not updated their records management systems to include the new location designations of school—college/university and school—elementary/secondary, which allow for more specificity in reporting.

Table 92. Offenses, Offense Type, by Participating State, 2017

(Number.)

State	Total offenses	Crimes against persons							Crimes against property							Crimes against society[2]
		Murder and nonnegligent manslaughter	Rape[1]	Aggravated assault	Simple assault	Intimidation	Human trafficking, commercial sex acts	Other[2]	Robbery	Burglary	Larceny-theft	Motor vehicle theft	Arson	Destruction/ damage/ vandalism	Other[2]	
Total	8,437	15	23	990	1,745	2,283	1	27	157	145	326	41	42	2,325	79	238
Alabama	9	0	0	0	1	7	0	0	0	0	0	0	0	1	0	0
Alaska	4	0	0	1	1	0	0	0	0	0	0	0	0	2	0	0
Arizona	328	0	2	52	62	111	0	0	8	6	5	0	0	81	0	1
Arkansas	8	0	0	1	1	2	0	0	1	1	0	0	0	2	0	0
California	1,270	3	0	242	259	304	0	0	52	16	6	0	11	377	0	0
Colorado	136	0	1	22	30	39	0	1	3	0	3	0	1	36	0	0
Connecticut	122	0	0	3	20	41	0	0	2	1	10	2	0	39	2	2
Delaware	30	0	0	1	5	15	0	0	1	0	0	0	0	7	1	0
District of Columbia	207	0	0	30	72	40	0	0	9	0	1	0	0	55	0	0
Florida	166	0	0	37	35	22	0	0	0	2	2	1	1	66	0	0
Georgia	230	0	0	5	108	112	0	0	0	1	0	0	0	4	0	0
Idaho	61	0	0	8	22	6	0	0	0	1	5	0	0	10	2	7
Illinois	94	0	0	22	24	19	0	0	2	0	2	0	2	23	0	0
Indiana	62	3	0	5	13	14	0	0	0	1	4	0	1	12	1	8
Iowa	12	0	0	3	1	6	0	0	0	1	0	0	0	1	0	0
Kansas	83	0	0	4	20	12	0	0	0	2	8	1	2	28	1	5
Kentucky	432	0	5	9	55	102	0	9	6	20	71	11	0	67	9	68
Louisiana	30	0	0	8	14	4	0	0	0	1	0	0	0	1	1	1
Maine	40	0	0	3	10	19	0	0	0	0	0	0	0	8	0	0
Maryland	53	1	0	10	13	2	0	0	1	1	0	0	0	24	0	1
Massachusetts	486	0	0	45	89	160	0	2	1	7	8	2	0	167	5	0
Michigan	515	0	3	55	110	131	0	3	7	12	32	6	4	116	11	25
Minnesota	169	0	1	19	27	64	0	0	3	3	1	0	3	48	0	0
Mississippi	4	0	0	0	0	4	0	0	0	0	0	0	0	0	0	0
Missouri	133	0	0	45	32	23	0	0	2	2	2	0	2	24	0	1
Montana	18	0	0	5	7	0	0	0	0	0	1	0	0	5	0	0
Nebraska	46	0	0	1	5	3	0	0	0	3	2	0	0	27	1	4
Nevada	7	0	0	3	1	0	0	0	1	0	0	0	0	2	0	0
New Hampshire	16	0	0	3	7	2	0	0	0	0	0	0	0	4	0	0
New Jersey	502	0	0	6	6	310	0	0	4	0	1	0	2	173	0	0
New Mexico	14	0	0	5	7	0	0	0	1	0	0	0	0	1	0	0
New York	559	1	0	55	174	3	0	0	7	9	7	0	1	302	0	0
North Carolina	230	0	0	20	54	81	0	0	4	4	9	0	2	56	0	0
North Dakota	17	0	0	2	2	10	0	0	0	0	1	0	0	2	0	0
Ohio	449	0	3	33	66	163	0	4	8	12	45	3	2	82	4	24
Oklahoma	49	0	0	14	8	12	0	2	0	1	0	0	0	8	3	1
Oregon	169	0	2	20	25	37	0	2	1	2	5	0	0	69	3	3
Pennsylvania	93	0	0	2	20	45	0	0	1	0	1	0	3	19	1	1
Rhode Island	11	0	0	0	1	2	0	0	0	0	0	0	0	8	0	0
South Carolina	94	0	0	10	19	10	0	1	2	6	7	1	1	24	4	9
South Dakota	19	0	0	3	6	6	0	0	0	0	0	0	0	3	0	1
Tennessee	179	1	0	38	39	42	0	1	1	5	2	0	0	26	7	17
Texas	219	1	2	43	50	36	1	0	11	4	16	3	2	38	2	10
Utah	94	1	0	8	23	7	0	1	0	3	21	1	0	11	3	15
Vermont	36	0	1	1	5	3	0	0	0	0	4	0	0	18	1	3
Virginia	214	2	2	14	44	40	0	0	1	2	2	0	0	92	3	12
Washington	613	1	1	72	134	183	0	1	16	15	27	7	2	132	8	14
West Virginia	34	1	0	0	8	0	0	0	1	1	5	3	0	10	1	4
Wisconsin	48	0	0	2	9	9	0	0	0	0	10	0	0	12	5	1
Wyoming	23	0	0	0	1	20	0	0	0	0	0	0	0	2	0	0

1 The figures shown in this column for the offense of rape include only those reported by law enforcement agencies that used the revised Uniform Crime Reporting (UCR) definition of rape.   2 Includes additional offenses collected in the National Incident-Based Reporting System.

Table 93. Agency Hate Crime Reporting, by Participating State, 2017

(Number.)

State	Number of participating agencies	Population covered	Agencies submitting incident reports	Total number of incidents reported
Total	16,149	306,435,676	2,040	7,175
Alabama	334	2,918,324	3	9
Alaska	32	736,205	3	4
Arizona	87	6,755,795	20	264
Arkansas	292	2,836,240	4	7
California	730	39,529,144	232	1,094
Colorado	221	5,575,629	43	106
Connecticut	107	3,588,184	44	111
Delaware	63	961,939	11	29
District of Columbia	2	693,972	2	193
Florida	654	20,515,334	67	145
Georgia	509	8,948,013	8	27
Idaho	106	1,699,259	21	53
Illinois	741	12,270,234	32	82
Indiana	162	2,287,298	21	55
Iowa	240	3,104,739	8	11
Kansas	364	2,620,785	38	75
Kentucky	409	4,444,239	132	378
Louisiana	145	3,764,930	15	26
Maine	132	1,335,907	10	32
Maryland	154	6,052,177	18	48
Massachusetts	360	6,703,220	102	427
Michigan	624	9,928,921	177	456
Minnesota	353	5,508,515	42	146
Mississippi	28	682,046	1	1
Missouri	610	6,109,596	32	105
Montana	110	1,050,005	11	15
Nebraska	238	1,865,845	9	45
Nevada	51	2,998,039	3	5
New Hampshire	177	1,295,556	13	13
New Jersey	518	9,005,644	155	495
New Mexico	17	561,375	1	7
New York	567	19,685,625	74	552
North Carolina	527	10,271,767	44	166
North Dakota	110	754,604	8	15
Ohio	572	9,703,884	137	380
Oklahoma	412	3,916,111	27	37
Oregon	214	3,902,529	29	146
Pennsylvania	1,488	12,730,580	23	78
Rhode Island	49	1,059,639	4	11
South Carolina	438	4,996,532	46	87
South Dakota	116	799,083	10	17
Tennessee	466	6,715,984	57	136
Texas	1,009	28,096,894	75	190
Utah	126	3,056,326	27	78
Vermont	90	623,657	17	34
Virginia	413	8,467,744	65	193
Washington	243	7,396,166	72	510
West Virginia	245	1,591,058	20	31
Wisconsin	437	5,767,235	24	46
Wyoming	57	553,149	3	4

Table 94. Hate Crime Incidents Per Bias Motivation and Quarter, by Selected State and Agency, 2017

(Number.)

State/agency	Number of incidents per bias motivation						Number of incidents per quarter				Population[1]
	Race/ Ethnicity/ Ancestry	Religion	Sexual orientation	Disability	Gender	Gender Identity	1st quarter	2nd quarter	3rd quarter	4th quarter	
ALABAMA **Total**	8	1	0	0	0	0					
Cities	7	1	0	0	0	0					
Hoover	5	1	0	0	0	0	2	1	2	1	85,634
Ozark	2	0	0	0	0	0	1			1	14,559
Universities and Colleges	1	0	0	0	0	0					
Jacksonville State University	1	0	0	0	0	0			1		8,514
ALASKA **Total**	3	1	0	0	0	0					
Cities	3	0	0	0	0	0					
Anchorage	1	0	0	0	0	0	0	0	0	1	296,188
Juneau	2	0	0	0	0	0	0	0	0	2	32,344
State Police Agencies	0	1	0	0	0	0					
Alaska State Troopers	0	1	0	0	0	0	0	1			
ARIZONA **Total**	168	48	55	5	0	12					
Cities	160	47	52	5	0	12					
Avondale	0	0	1	0	0	0	0	0	0	1	84,041
Chandler	1	0	0	0	0	0	0	1	0	0	249,355
Cottonwood	1	0	0	0	0	0	0	0	0	1	12,116
El Mirage	1	0	0	0	0	0	0	1			35,611
Gilbert	2	1	0	0	0	0	0	1	1	1	242,090
Glendale	3	2	0	0	0	0	0	1	2	2	249,273
Mesa	4	1	0	0	0	0	1	0	1	3	492,268
Page	1	0	0	0	0	0	0	0	1	0	7,632
Phoenix[2]	142	41	44	4	0	12	49	57	48	65	1,644,177
Scottsdale	2	1	1	0	0	0	4	0	0	0	251,840
St. Johns	2	0	0	0	0	0	1	0	1	0	3,581
Tucson	0	1	3	1	0	0	1	2	1	1	532,323
Wickenburg	0	0	1	0	0	0	0	0	0	1	6,979
Yuma	1	0	2	0	0	0	1	0	2	0	95,522
Universities and Colleges	1	1	1	0	0	0					
University of Arizona	1	1	1	0	0	0	0	0	3		43,161
Metropolitan Counties	5	0	2	0	0	0					
Maricopa	1	0	2	0	0	0	2	0	0	1	
Mohave	1	0	0	0	0	0	0	0	1		
Pima	2	0	0	0	0	0	2			0	
Yuma	1	0	0	0	0	0	1	0	0	0	
Nonmetropolitan Counties	2	0	0	0	0	0					
Apache	2	0	0	0	0	0	0	0	0	2	
ARKANSAS **Total**	5	0	1	1	0	0					
Cities	5	0	1	0	0	0					
Benton	1	0	0	0	0	0	0	0	1	0	36,702
Fayetteville	0	0	1	0	0	0	0	0	0	1	85,592
Fort Smith	4	0	0	0	0	0	0	1	1	2	88,437
Nonmetropolitan Counties	0	0	0	1	0	0					
Boone	0	0	0	1	0	0	0	1	0	0	
CALIFORNIA **Total**	603	207	248	4	4	29					
Cities	524	187	217	4	4	26					
Adelanto	1	0	1	0	0	0	1	1	0	0	33,693
Alameda	6	1	2	1	0	0	0	0	7	3	79,761
Albany[2]	1	0	2	0	0	0	1	0	1	0	19,880
Alhambra	1	0	0	0	0	1	1	1	0	0	85,865
Aliso Viejo	1	0	0	0	0	0	1	0	0	0	51,984
Anaheim	0	0	1	0	0	0	0	0	0	1	353,400
Antioch	1	0	0	0	0	0	0	1	0	0	112,252
Apple Valley	0	1	0	0	0	0	0	0	1	0	73,105
Arcata	1	0	1	0	0	0	1	0	1	0	18,054
Atwater	1	0	0	0	0	1	1	0	1	0	29,442
Azusa	2	0	0	0	0	0	0	0	1	1	50,202
Bakersfield	4	0	3	0	0	0	0	3	0	4	381,154
Bell	0	1	0	0	0	0	0	0	0	1	35,925
Bellflower	0	1	0	0	0	0	0	0	0	1	77,984

Table 94. Hate Crime Incidents Per Bias Motivation and Quarter, by Selected State and Agency, 2017—Continued

(Number.)

State/agency	Number of incidents per bias motivation						Number of incidents per quarter				Population[1]
	Race/ Ethnicity/ Ancestry	Religion	Sexual orientation	Disability	Gender	Gender Identity	1st quarter	2nd quarter	3rd quarter	4th quarter	
Bell Gardens	1	0	0	0	0	0	0	0	1	0	42,930
Belmont	0	1	0	0	0	0	1	0	0	0	27,285
Benicia	1	0	0	0	0	0	0	1	0	0	28,370
Berkeley	13	4	6	0	0	0	7	6	4	6	122,687
Beverly Hills	2	0	0	0	0	0	0	0	1	1	34,781
Brentwood	1	0	0	0	0	1	0	1	1	0	62,120
Buena Park	1	0	0	0	0	0	0	1	0	0	83,552
Burbank	1	6	1	0	0	0	1	1	0	6	104,622
Camarillo	1	0	0	0	0	0	0	1	0	0	67,714
Capitola	1	0	0	0	0	0	0	0	0	1	10,222
Carlsbad	4	2	1	0	0	0	0	4	0	3	115,344
Carson	0	1	0	0	0	0	0	0	1	0	92,992
Central Marin	0	2	0	0	0	0	0	1	0	1	35,060
Chico	1	0	0	0	0	0	0	0	1	0	92,459
Chino	5	0	1	0	0	0	2	2	1	1	89,420
Chino Hills	1	0	0	0	0	0	1	0	0	0	79,480
Citrus Heights	1	0	1	0	0	0	1	0	1	0	88,126
Clearlake	0	1	1	0	0	0	1	1	0	0	15,018
Colma	0	0	1	0	0	0	0	1	0	0	1,520
Concord	0	0	1	0	0	0	0	0	1	0	129,789
Corcoran	1	0	0	0	0	0	0	1	0	0	22,345
Corning	1	0	0	0	0	0	0	1	0	0	7,511
Corona	1	0	1	0	0	0	0	0	2	0	169,164
Costa Mesa	2	0	0	0	0	0	1	0	0	1	113,267
Covina	0	0	1	0	0	0	0	1	0	0	48,674
Crescent City	1	0	0	0	0	0	0	0	0	1	6,529
Daly City	0	0	1	0	0	0	0	0	1	0	107,355
Davis	4	3	0	0	0	0	2	4	0	1	68,540
Desert Hot Springs	1	0	0	0	0	0	1	0	0	0	28,717
Duarte	2	0	0	0	0	0	2	0	0	0	21,877
Dublin	1	0	0	0	0	0	0	1	0	0	62,235
East Palo Alto	0	1	0	0	0	0	0	0	0	1	29,933
El Cajon	4	0	2	0	0	0	0	2	3	1	104,447
Elk Grove	4	0	0	0	0	0	0	1	2	1	172,620
El Monte	2	0	1	0	0	0	1	1	0	1	116,168
El Segundo	1	0	0	0	0	0	0	0	1	0	16,932
Escondido	5	0	0	0	0	0	3	0	1	1	152,845
Fairfield	3	0	0	0	0	0	0	1	1	1	116,372
Fontana	0	2	1	0	0	0	1	1	1	0	211,782
Fort Bragg	2	1	0	0	0	0	1	1	0	1	7,289
Foster City	0	1	0	0	0	0	1	0	0	0	34,808
Fremont	1	1	0	0	0	0	0	1	1	0	236,368
Fresno	7	1	4	0	0	1	1	3	6	3	526,371
Garden Grove	7	0	0	0	0	1	3	0	4	1	175,466
Glendora	1	0	0	0	0	0	0	0	0	1	52,133
Goleta	1	0	0	0	0	0	1	0	0	0	31,000
Gonzales	1	0	0	0	0	0	1	0	0	0	8,508
Hayward	3	1	0	0	0	0	2	1	0	1	161,417
Hesperia	3	0	0	0	0	0	2	0	0	1	94,292
Highland	1	0	0	0	0	0	1	0	0	0	55,229
Hollister	1	0	0	0	0	0	0	0	1	0	38,310
Huntington Beach	2	0	0	0	0	0	0	0	1	1	202,244
Huntington Park	1	1	0	0	0	0	1	1	0	0	59,004
Indio	1	0	0	0	0	0	0	0	1	0	90,055
Inglewood	2	0	0	0	0	0	0	1	0	1	110,811
Irvine	4	0	0	0	0	0	1	0	0	3	276,115
La Canada Flintridge	0	0	0	0	3	0	0	0	3	0	20,480
Laguna Beach	2	0	0	0	0	0	1	0	1	0	23,261
La Habra	1	0	0	0	0	0	1	0	0	0	61,878
Lake Elsinore	0	1	0	0	0	0	0	0	1	0	66,136
Lakeport	0	0	1	0	0	0	0	1	0	0	4,775
Lakewood	7	0	0	0	0	0	1	1	4	1	81,317
La Mesa	1	0	1	0	0	0	0	0	2	0	60,425
Lancaster	5	0	2	0	0	0	2	2	2	1	160,653
Lemon Grove	1	0	0	0	0	0	0	0	0	1	27,113
Livermore	2	0	0	0	0	0	0	0	2	0	90,485
Lodi	1	0	0	0	0	0	0	0	1	0	65,042
Loma Linda	1	0	0	0	0	0	1	0	0	0	24,265
Lomita	1	0	0	0	0	0	0	0	0	1	20,764
Long Beach	8	3	6	0	0	0	7	3	5	2	471,397
Los Angeles	126	43	82	0	1	11	65	72	70	56	4,007,147
Los Gatos	0	1	0	0	0	0	1	0	0	0	30,720
Malibu	2	0	0	0	0	0	1	0	1	0	12,918
Manhattan Beach	0	0	1	0	0	0	0	0	0	1	35,843
Manteca	2	2	0	0	0	0	1	0	3	0	78,564
Martinez	2	4	0	1	0	0	0	2	5	0	38,619
Marysville	3	0	0	0	0	0	0	0	3	0	12,275
Menifee	1	0	0	0	0	0	0	0	0	1	90,403
Merced	1	0	0	0	0	0	0	0	0	1	83,180
Modesto	6	1	3	0	0	0	6	1	2	1	213,677
Monterey	1	0	1	0	0	0	0	0	2	0	28,584

Table 94. Hate Crime Incidents Per Bias Motivation and Quarter, by Selected State and Agency, 2017—Continued

(Number.)

State/agency	Number of incidents per bias motivation						Number of incidents per quarter				Population[1]
	Race/Ethnicity/Ancestry	Religion	Sexual orientation	Disability	Gender	Gender Identity	1st quarter	2nd quarter	3rd quarter	4th quarter	
Monterey Park	3	1	0	0	0	0	1	0	1	2	61,210
Moreno Valley	1	0	2	0	0	0	1	0	1	1	207,418
Murrieta	1	0	0	0	0	0	0	1	0	0	113,016
National City	1	0	0	0	0	0	1	0	0	0	61,574
Newark	2	1	0	0	0	0	0	2	1	0	46,360
Newport Beach	1	0	0	0	0	0	0	0	0	1	86,910
Norco	0	1	0	0	0	0	0	1	0	0	26,654
Norwalk	1	0	1	0	0	0	0	0	1	1	106,278
Novato	2	0	0	0	0	0	1	0	1	0	56,698
Oakland	9	7	2	0	0	0	8	4	4	2	424,915
Oceanside	4	1	1	0	0	0	1	1	3	1	176,815
Ontario	1	0	0	1	0	0	1	1	0	0	174,724
Orange	1	0	0	0	0	0	0	0	0	1	141,130
Orland	1	0	0	0	0	0	0	1	0	0	7,624
Oxnard	2	4	1	0	0	0	0	2	5	0	209,513
Pacifica	1	0	1	0	0	0	1	0	1	0	39,353
Pacific Grove	0	1	0	0	0	0	0	1	0	0	15,716
Palmdale	3	0	0	0	0	0	2	1	0	0	158,094
Palm Springs	0	0	3	0	0	0	1	1	0	1	48,193
Palo Alto	2	3	0	0	0	0	4	0	1	0	67,441
Paradise	1	0	0	0	0	0	0	0	1	0	26,610
Pasadena	1	1	0	0	0	1	0	1	2	0	142,891
Petaluma	5	1	2	0	0	0	5	1	1	1	60,957
Pico Rivera	0	0	2	0	0	1	2	0	1	0	63,746
Piedmont	1	1	0	0	0	0	0	0	2	0	11,464
Placentia	1	0	0	0	0	0	0	1	0	0	52,437
Pleasant Hill	0	1	0	0	0	0	1	0	0	0	35,136
Pomona	1	1	1	0	0	0	0	2	1	0	153,066
Rancho Cordova	2	0	0	0	0	0	0	1	0	1	73,607
Red Bluff	0	0	1	0	0	0	0	0	0	1	14,169
Redding	11	0	4	0	0	0	4	3	5	3	92,127
Redlands	1	1	0	0	0	0	0	0	2	0	71,707
Redwood City	2	0	0	0	0	0	0	0	2	0	86,353
Reedley	0	1	0	0	0	0	0	0	0	1	25,794
Rialto	1	0	0	0	0	0	1	0	0	0	103,980
Richmond	3	0	2	0	0	0	1	0	2	2	110,804
Riverside	4	4	0	0	0	0	3	3	1	1	328,023
Roseville	12	6	1	0	0	0	7	6	5	1	135,028
Sacramento	2	2	0	0	0	1	1	2	1	1	499,997
Salinas	0	0	1	0	0	0	0	0	1	0	158,313
San Bernardino	4	0	4	0	0	0	4	2	2	0	217,259
San Clemente	1	0	0	0	0	0	0	1	0	0	65,596
San Diego	17	12	11	0	0	1	17	14	7	3	1,424,116
San Fernando	0	1	0	0	0	0	1	0	0	0	24,899
San Francisco	19	8	12	0	0	4	10	6	13	14	881,255
San Gabriel	1	1	0	0	0	0	1	0	0	1	40,531
San Jacinto	1	0	0	0	0	0	0	1	0	0	47,932
San Jose	26	11	7	0	0	1	10	8	16	11	1,037,529
San Leandro	6	0	3	1	0	0	3	5	1	1	91,386
San Luis Obispo	2	2	1	0	0	0	0	3	1	1	47,934
San Marcos	1	1	0	0	0	0	1	0	1	0	97,290
San Mateo	2	0	0	0	0	0	1	1	0	0	105,090
San Rafael	3	0	0	0	0	0	1	2	0	0	59,144
San Ramon	2	1	0	0	0	0	1	1	0	1	76,325
Santa Ana	1	2	0	0	0	0	0	1	1	1	335,699
Santa Clara	1	0	0	0	0	0	0	0	1	0	127,538
Santa Clarita	5	5	3	0	0	0	1	6	5	1	216,350
Santa Cruz	5	1	3	0	0	0	2	3	2	2	65,132
Santa Monica	2	0	1	0	0	0	0	0	2	1	92,935
Santa Rosa	1	0	1	0	0	0	0	1	1	0	176,361
Santee	1	0	0	0	0	0	0	1	0	0	58,563
Simi Valley	0	2	1	0	0	0	1	0	2	0	126,635
South Gate	1	0	0	0	0	0	1	0	0	0	95,717
South Lake Tahoe	1	0	4	0	0	0	4	1	0	0	21,768
South San Francisco	1	0	1	0	0	0	0	0	0	2	67,533
St. Helena	2	0	0	0	0	0	0	1	1	0	6,210
Stockton	2	3	1	0	0	0	3	0	2	1	309,566
Sunnyvale	1	0	0	0	0	1	1	1	0	0	154,919
Taft	1	0	0	0	0	0	0	0	0	1	9,393
Thousand Oaks	0	1	0	0	0	0	0	1	0	0	129,240
Torrance	4	0	1	0	0	0	2	2	0	1	147,482
Turlock	3	0	0	0	0	0	0	0	2	1	73,488
Tustin	1	0	0	0	0	0	0	0	0	1	81,246
Union City	2	0	0	0	0	0	0	0	0	2	76,311
Vacaville	2	2	0	0	0	0	2	1	0	1	99,293
Ventura	4	0	0	0	0	0	2	0	1	1	110,006
Vernon	0	1	0	0	0	0	0	0	1	0	113
Victorville	1	0	1	0	0	0	0	1	1	0	123,284
Visalia	1	0	0	0	0	0	1	0	0	0	132,143
Vista	4	1	1	0	0	0	0	3	2	1	103,004
Walnut	1	0	0	0	0	0	0	1	0	0	30,189

Table 94. Hate Crime Incidents Per Bias Motivation and Quarter, by Selected State and Agency, 2017—Continued

(Number.)

State/agency	Number of incidents per bias motivation						Number of incidents per quarter				Population[1]
	Race/ Ethnicity/ Ancestry	Religion	Sexual orientation	Disability	Gender	Gender Identity	1st quarter	2nd quarter	3rd quarter	4th quarter	
West Covina	0	3	0	0	0	0	3	0	0	0	108,128
West Hollywood	5	0	4	0	0	0	4	1	2	2	37,093
Westminster	2	2	0	0	0	0	0	2	2	0	91,863
Wildomar	1	0	0	0	0	0	0	1	0	0	36,683
Windsor	0	0	1	0	0	0	1	0	0	0	27,679
Yorba Linda	0	1	0	0	0	0	0	0	1	0	68,889
Yucca Valley	1	0	0	0	0	0	0	0	0	1	21,806
Universities and Colleges	19	7	6	0	0	0					
California State University											
Dominguez Hills	2	0	0	0	0	0	0	1	1	0	14,731
Long Beach	1	2	0	0	0	0	1	1	1	0	37,776
Monterey Bay	1	0	1	0	0	0	0	1	0	1	7,274
San Bernardino	1	0	0	0	0	0	1	0	0	0	20,767
Riverside Community College	2	0	0	0	0	0	0	0	0	2	38,677
San Diego State University	0	1	0	0	0	0	0	0	0	1	34,688
San Francisco State University	0	0	1	0	0	0	0	0	1	0	29,045
State Center Community College District	3	0	0	0	0	0	0	0	0	3	39,661
University of California											
Berkeley	3	0	2	0	0	0	3	0	1	1	40,154
Los Angeles	3	1	1	0	0	0	1	0	3	1	43,548
San Diego	0	0	1	0	0	0	0	0	0	1	34,979
San Francisco	0	2	0	0	0	0	0	2	0	0	3,145
Santa Barbara	2	0	0	0	0	0	0	2	0	0	24,346
Medical Center, Sacramento[3]	0	1	0	0	0	0	0	1	0	0	
Ventura County Community College District	1	0	0	0	0	0	0	0	1	0	33,976
Metropolitan Counties	51	12	17	0	0	3					
Alameda	1	0	1	0	0	0	0	1	1	0	
Contra Costa	1	0	0	0	0	0	0	0	0	1	
El Dorado	2	0	0	0	0	0	0	0	1	1	
Fresno	1	0	1	0	0	0	1	0	1	0	
Kern	2	0	0	0	0	0	0	1	0	1	
Los Angeles	6	5	4	0	0	0	2	5	5	3	
Marin	0	1	0	0	0	0	1	0	0	0	
Monterey	1	0	0	0	0	0	0	1	0	0	
Riverside	1	0	0	0	0	0	0	1	0	0	
Sacramento	8	1	1	0	0	1	4	0	4	3	
San Bernardino	2	1	0	0	0	0	1	2	0	0	
San Diego	7	0	7	0	0	0	3	4	4	3	
San Luis Obispo	3	0	0	0	0	0	0	1	1	1	
San Mateo	0	1	0	0	0	0	0	0	1	0	
Santa Barbara	2	0	2	0	0	0	1	3	0	0	
Santa Clara	1	0	0	0	0	2	1	1	0	1	
Santa Cruz	1	1	0	0	0	0	0	0	2	0	
Solano	1	0	0	0	0	0	0	0	0	1	
Sonoma	4	0	1	0	0	0	2	2	1	0	
Stanislaus	1	0	0	0	0	0	0	0	1	0	
Sutter	0	1	0	0	0	0	0	0	0	1	
Ventura	2	1	0	0	0	0	0	0	2	1	
Yuba	4	0	0	0	0	0	3	1	0	0	
Nonmetropolitan Counties	3	1	2	0	0	0					
Calaveras	1	0	0	0	0	0	0	0	0	1	
Lake	0	1	1	0	0	0	0	0	0	2	
Mendocino	1	0	0	0	0	0	1	0	0	0	
Nevada	0	0	1	0	0	0	0	1	0	0	
Plumas	1	0	0	0	0	0	0	0	1	0	
Other Agencies	6	0	6	0	0	0					
Department of Parks and Recreation											
Marin County	1	0	0	0	0	0	0	0	1	0	
Oceano Dunes	0	0	1	0	0	0	0	1	0	0	
Los Angeles Transportation Services Bureau	3	0	3	0	0	0	2	3	1	0	
Port of San Diego Harbor	0	0	1	0	0	0	0	0	0	1	
San Francisco Bay Area Rapid Transit											
Alameda County	1	0	0	0	0	0	0	0	0	1	
San Francisco County	1	0	1	0	0	0	1	0	1	0	
COLORADO											
Total	61	26	18	1	1	1					
Cities	49	16	13	1	1	1					
Arvada	1	0	1	0	0	0	2	0	0	0	119,346
Aspen	1	0	0	0	0	0	0	1	0	0	6,906
Aurora	14	3	1	0	0	0	8	7	2	1	368,018
Boulder	2	1	0	0	0	0	2	1	0	0	109,722
Brighton	0	0	1	0	0	0	0	0	1	0	39,099
Broomfield	1	0	0	0	0	0	1	0	0	0	68,158
Canon City	0	1	0	0	0	0	1	0	0	0	16,723

Table 94. Hate Crime Incidents Per Bias Motivation and Quarter, by Selected State and Agency, 2017—Continued

(Number.)

State/agency	Race/ Ethnicity/ Ancestry	Religion	Sexual orientation	Disability	Gender	Gender Identity	1st quarter	2nd quarter	3rd quarter	4th quarter	Population[1]
Castle Rock	2	0	0	0	0	0	0	1	0	1	59,337
Centennial	2	0	0	0	0	0	1	0	1	0	111,416
Colorado Springs	0	1	0	0	0	0	0	0	1	0	472,958
Delta[2]	0	0	0	1	1	0	0	0	0	1	8,925
Denver	9	2	6	0	0	0	4	7	1	5	706,616
Durango	0	1	0	0	0	0	0	0	1	0	18,801
Englewood	2	0	0	0	0	0	0	1	1	0	34,709
Fruita	0	0	1	0	0	0	1	0	0	0	12,971
Golden	1	0	0	0	0	0	0	0	0	1	20,948
Grand Junction	0	1	1	0	0	0	1	1	0	0	62,352
Greeley	3	0	0	0	0	0	1	0	1	1	105,906
Idaho Springs	1	0	0	0	0	0	0	0	0	1	1,751
Lafayette	0	1	0	0	0	0	0	0	1	0	28,939
Lakewood	3	0	1	0	0	0	3	1	0	0	156,344
Littleton	0	3	0	0	0	0	1	2	0	0	47,112
Longmont[2]	1	0	0	0	0	1	0	0	1	0	93,979
Loveland	1	0	1	0	0	0	0	1	1	0	78,671
Monument	1	0	0	0	0	0	1	0	0	0	6,644
Northglenn	0	1	0	0	0	0	0	1	0	0	39,520
Pueblo	2	0	0	0	0	0	0	0	1	1	110,872
Steamboat Springs	0	1	0	0	0	0	1	0	0	0	12,799
Trinidad	1	0	0	0	0	0	0	0	0	1	7,961
Windsor	1	0	0	0	0	0	0	0	0	1	23,523
Universities and Colleges	3	1	0	0	0	0					
Colorado State University, Fort Collins	3	0	0	0	0	0	0	0	0	3	31,856
University of Colorado, Boulder	0	1	0	0	0	0	1	0	0	0	33,977
Metropolitan Counties	9	8	3	0	0	0					
Adams	1	0	0	0	0	0	0	0	0	1	
Arapahoe	3	3	0	0	0	0	2	2	1	1	
Boulder	0	3	0	0	0	0	3	0	0	0	
Douglas	1	0	0	0	0	0	1	0	0	0	
El Paso	2	0	1	0	0	0	1	0	1	1	
Jefferson	1	1	1	0	0	0	1	0	1	1	
Larimer	0	1	0	0	0	0	0	1	0	0	
Mesa	1	0	1	0	0	0	0	0	0	2	
Nonmetropolitan Counties	0	1	2	0	0	0					
Garfield	0	0	1	0	0	0	0	0	0	1	
Huerfano	0	1	0	0	0	0	0	1	0	0	
Routt	0	0	1	0	0	0	0	0	1	0	
CONNECTICUT											
Total	66	23	22	0	0	1					
Cities	60	23	19	0	0	1					
Avon	1	0	0	0	0	0	1	0	0	0	18,397
Berlin	1	2	0	0	0	0	1	1	0	1	20,601
Bethel	3	0	0	0	0	0	0	0	0	3	19,796
Bloomfield	0	0	2	0	0	0	0	2	0	0	20,667
Bridgeport[2]	5	0	2	0	0	0	1	1	1	3	146,110
Brookfield	1	0	0	0	0	0	1	0	0	0	17,203
Cheshire	0	0	2	0	0	0	1	0	0	1	29,282
Clinton	1	0	0	0	0	0	0	0	1	0	12,915
Danbury	4	0	1	0	0	0	2	2	1	0	85,614
Darien	1	0	0	0	0	0	0	1	0	0	21,910
East Haven	1	0	0	0	0	0	0	1	0	0	28,739
East Windsor	1	0	0	0	0	0	0	1	0	0	11,383
Enfield	1	0	0	0	0	0	1	0	0	0	44,321
Groton	1	0	0	0	0	0	0	1	0	0	9,093
Groton Town	1	0	0	0	0	0	1	0	0	0	29,524
Guilford	0	0	1	0	0	0	0	0	1	0	22,259
Hartford	2	1	1	0	0	0	1	1	0	2	122,891
Manchester	2	0	2	0	0	0	1	2	1	0	57,808
Meriden	0	0	1	0	0	0	0	1	0	0	59,417
Middletown	5	2	1	0	0	0	2	1	3	2	46,363
New Britain	0	1	0	0	0	0	0	1	0	0	72,442
New Haven	4	2	3	0	0	1	0	4	4	2	129,953
New London	0	0	1	0	0	0	0	1	0	0	26,880
New Milford	1	0	0	0	0	0	0	0	1	0	26,993
North Branford	0	1	0	0	0	0	0	0	1	0	14,163
North Haven	0	0	1	0	0	0	0	0	0	1	23,646
Norwich	0	1	0	0	0	0	0	0	1	0	39,393
Old Saybrook	3	0	0	0	0	0	1	0	2	0	10,070
Orange	2	1	0	0	0	0	0	1	1	1	13,904
Rocky Hill	2	0	0	0	0	0	0	1	1	0	20,189
Southington	1	0	0	0	0	0	0	1	0	0	43,769
Stamford	3	3	0	0	0	0	1	0	3	2	130,189
Torrington	4	1	0	0	0	0	2	2	0	1	34,372

Table 94. Hate Crime Incidents Per Bias Motivation and Quarter, by Selected State and Agency, 2017—Continued

(Number.)

State/agency	Number of incidents per bias motivation						Number of incidents per quarter				Population[1]
	Race/ Ethnicity/ Ancestry	Religion	Sexual orientation	Disability	Gender	Gender Identity	1st quarter	2nd quarter	3rd quarter	4th quarter	
Trumbull	4	4	1	0	0	0	4	2	1	2	36,265
Waterbury	0	1	0	0	0	0	0	0	1	0	107,924
West Hartford	1	0	0	0	0	0	0	0	0	1	62,812
Westport	1	0	0	0	0	0	0	0	1	0	28,079
Willimantic	1	0	0	0	0	0	0	0	1	0	17,768
Wilton	1	2	0	0	0	0	0	0	2	1	18,643
Windsor	1	0	0	0	0	0	0	1	0	0	28,836
Woodbridge	0	1	0	0	0	0	0	1	0	0	8,816
Universities and Colleges	3	0	0	0	0	0					
Yale University	3	0	0	0	0	0	1	0	2	0	12,458
State Police Agencies	2	0	3	0	0	0					
Connecticut State Police	2	0	3	0	0	0	0	1	0	4	
Tribal Agencies	1	0	0	0	0	0					
Mohegan Tribal	1	0	0	0	0	0	0	1	0	0	
DELAWARE											
Total	14	8	6	0	0	1					
Cities	2	0	4	0	0	1					
Dewey Beach	0	0	1	0	0	0	0	1	0	0	386
New Castle	0	0	1	0	0	0	1	0	0	0	5,362
Rehoboth Beach	1	0	1	0	0	1	0	0	3	0	1,516
Wilmington	1	0	1	0	0	0	0	0	0	2	71,552
Universities and Colleges	4	1	1	0	0	0					
University of Delaware	4	1	1	0	0	0	3	0	1	2	23,009
Metropolitan Counties	2	4	0	0	0	0					
New Castle County Police Department	2	4	0	0	0	0	4	0	0	2	
State Police Agencies	4	2	0	0	0	0					
State Police											
Kent County	2	1	0	0	0	0	0	2	1	0	
New Castle County	2	1	0	0	0	0	1	1	1	0	
Other Agencies	2	1	1	0	0	0					
Fish and Wildlife	1	0	0	0	0	0	0	0	1	0	
River and Bay Authority	1	0	0	0	0	0	0	0	1	0	
State Capitol Police	0	1	1	0	0	0	1	0	1	0	
DISTRICT OF COLUMBIA											
Total	108	14	57	1	0	13					
Cities	87	12	56	1	0	13					
Washington	87	12	56	1	0	13	27	40	45	57	693,972
Other Agencies	21	2	1	0	0	0					
Metro Transit Police	21	2	1	0	0	0	6	8	3	7	
FLORIDA											
Total	70	43	32	0	0	0					
Cities	42	33	26	0	0	0					
Boca Raton	0	1	0	0	0	0	0	0	0	1	98,069
Clearwater	1	0	0	0	0	0	1	0	0	0	115,295
Cooper City	0	1	0	0	0	0	0	0	0	1	36,694
Coral Gables	1	0	0	0	0	0	0	0	0	1	51,487
Davie	4	3	0	0	0	0	3	1	1	2	103,555
Deerfield Beach	2	0	0	0	0	0	0	1	0	1	80,552
Delray Beach	0	1	0	0	0	0	1	0	0	0	68,533
Fort Lauderdale	2	2	2	0	0	0	0	2	3	1	180,972
Fort Myers	1	1	1	0	0	0	1	1	0	1	79,918
Gainesville	0	1	0	0	0	0	0	0	1	0	132,777
Hollywood	0	0	1	0	0	0	1	0	0	0	153,893
Homestead	1	1	2	0	0	0	0	1	0	3	69,276
Jacksonville	3	2	1	0	0	0	1	0	2	3	894,638
Key Biscayne	0	0	1	0	0	0	1	0	0	0	13,127
Key West	0	0	1	0	0	0	1	0	0	0	27,399
Lake City	1	0	0	0	0	0	1	0	0	0	12,326
Largo	1	2	0	0	0	0	2	0	1		83,728
Lauderdale-by-the-Sea	1	0	0	0	0	0			1		6,589
Leesburg	1	0	0	0	0	0	1	0	0	0	22,763
Mangonia Park	0	0	1	0	0	0	0	0	0	1	2,009
Miami Beach	0	7	9	0	0	0	8	6	1	1	92,571

Table 94. Hate Crime Incidents Per Bias Motivation and Quarter, by Selected State and Agency, 2017—Continued

(Number.)

State/agency	Number of incidents per bias motivation						Number of incidents per quarter				Population[1]
	Race/ Ethnicity/ Ancestry	Religion	Sexual orientation	Disability	Gender	Gender Identity	1st quarter	2nd quarter	3rd quarter	4th quarter	
Miami Gardens	0	2	0	0	0	0	2	0	0	0	114,008
New Port Richey	1	0	0	0	0	0	0	0	1	0	16,388
North Miami	1	0	0	0	0	0	1	0	0	0	62,543
Oakland Park	2	1	1	0	0	0	1	1	1	1	44,814
Ocala	0	0	1	0	0	0	1	0	0	0	59,731
Orlando	2	0	3	0	0	0	1	2	1	1	283,982
Palm Bay	1	0	1	0	0	0	0	1	1	0	111,275
Pompano Beach	2	1	0	0	0	0	0	0	1	2	111,027
Port St. Lucie	0	0	1	0	0	0	0	1	0	0	188,652
Rockledge	1	0	0	0	0	0	1	0	0	0	27,432
St. Augustine	1	0	0	0	0	0	0	1	0	0	14,500
Sunrise	1	1	0	0	0	0	0	0	0	2	95,342
Tampa	3	0	0	0	0	0	2	0	0	1	384,360
Titusville	5	0	0	0	0	0	0	0	5	0	46,425
Weston	1	2	0	0	0	0	0	0	1	2	70,796
West Palm Beach	2	0	0	0	0	0	1	1	0	0	109,459
Wilton Manors	0	3	0	0	0	0	0	1	2	0	12,861
Winter Park	0	1	0	0	0	0	0	1	0	0	30,602
Universities and Colleges	1	2	1	0	0	0					
Florida Gulf Coast University	0	1	0	0	0	0	0	0	0	1	14,821
Tallahassee Community College	0	1	0	0	0	0	0	0	1	0	12,200
University of South Florida, Tampa	1	0	0	0	0	0	1	0	0	0	42,861
University of West Florida	0	0	1	0	0	0	0	0	0	1	12,966
Metropolitan Counties	25	8	5	0	0	0					
Alachua	1	0	0	0	0	0	0	0	1	0	
Broward	1	0	0	0	0	0	1	0	0	0	
Charlotte	1	0	0	0	0	0	0	1	0	0	
Clay	1	1	0	0	0	0	0	0	0	2	
Collier	0	1	0	0	0	0	0	0	0	1	
Hillsborough	0	1	0	0	0	0	0	1	0	0	
Lake	1	0	0	0	0	0	1	0	0	0	
Lee	4	1	1	0	0	0	2	3	0	1	
Leon	1	0	0	0	0	0	1	0	0	0	
Martin	1	0	0	0	0	0	0	1	0	0	
Miami-Dade	0	0	1	0	0	0	0	0	0	1	
Okaloosa	1	0	0	0	0	0	0	1			
Orange	2	0	0	0	0	0	2	0	0	0	
Osceola	2	1	1	0	0	0	2	0	1	1	
Palm Beach	1	1	0	0	0	0	1	1	0	0	
Pasco	3	0	0	0	0	0	0	0	3	0	
Pinellas	0	1	0	0	0	0	1	0	0	0	
Santa Rosa	0	0	1	0	0	0	1	0	0	0	
Sarasota	0	1	0	0	0	0	0	0	1	0	
Seminole	1	0	1	0	0	0	0	0	1	1	
St. Johns	3	0	0	0	0	0	1	2	0	0	
Volusia	1	0	0	0	0	0	1	0	0	0	
Nonmetropolitan Counties	2	0	0	0	0	0					
Hendry	1	0	0	0	0	0	1	0	0	0	
Monroe	1	0	0	0	0	0	1	0	0	0	
GEORGIA											
Total	19	5	4	0	0	0					
Cities	5	1	3	0	0	0					
Atlanta	0	1	2	0	0	0	2	1	0	0	481,343
Columbus	3	0	1	0	0	0	1	2	1	0	198,832
Warner Robins	1	0	0	0	0	0	1	0	0	0	75,323
Woodstock	1	0	0	0	0	0	0	1	0	0	32,293
Universities and Colleges	2	0	0	0	0	0					
University of Georgia	2	0	0	0	0	0	1	0	1	0	36,574
Metropolitan Counties	12	4	1	0	0	0					
Cobb County Police Department	9	2	1	0	0	0	1	5	3	3	
Forsyth	1	0	0	0	0	0	1	0	0	0	
Gwinnett County Police Department[2]	2	2	0	0	0	0	1	2	0	0	
IDAHO											
Total	30	17	4	2	0	0					
Cities	24	15	4	2	0	0					
Boise	7	6	2	0	0	0	1	5	6	3	225,677
Bonners Ferry	0	1	0	0	0	0	0	0	1	0	2,574
Caldwell	2	0	0	0	0	0	1	1	0	0	54,345
Coeur d'Alene	2	0	0	0	0	0	0	1	1	0	51,364
Heyburn	0	1	0	0	0	0	1	0	0	0	3,306
Kimberly	2	0	0	0	0	0	0	0	1	1	3,812
Lewiston	3	0	0	0	0	0	0	1	1	1	33,029
Middleton	1	0	0	0	0	0	0	0	1	0	7,486

Table 94. Hate Crime Incidents Per Bias Motivation and Quarter, by Selected State and Agency, 2017—Continued

(Number.)

State/agency	Number of incidents per bias motivation						Number of incidents per quarter				Population[1]
	Race/ Ethnicity/ Ancestry	Religion	Sexual orientation	Disability	Gender	Gender Identity	1st quarter	2nd quarter	3rd quarter	4th quarter	
Moscow	1	0	0	0	0	0	0	1	0	0	25,576
Mountain Home	2	0	0	0	0	0	0	1	0	1	13,772
Nampa	2	1	1	0	0	0	2	1	1	0	93,064
Pocatello	0	1	0	0	0	0	1	0	0	0	54,814
Preston	0	3	0	0	0	0	1	1	1	0	5,372
Soda Springs	1	0	0	0	0	0	0	0	0	1	2,970
Spirit Lake	1	0	0	0	0	0	0	0	0	1	2,207
Twin Falls	0	2	1	2	0	0	0	1	0	4	48,912
Metropolitan Counties	0	1	0	0	0	0					
Kootenai	0	1	0	0	0	0	0	0	1	0	
Nonmetropolitan Counties	5	0	0	0	0	0					
Cassia	3	0	0	0	0	0	1	0	2	0	
Idaho	1	0	0	0	0	0	0	0	1	0	
Teton	1	0	0	0	0	0	0	0	1	0	
State Police Agencies	1	1	0	0	0	0					
Idaho State Police	1	1	0	0	0	0	0	1	1	0	
ILLINOIS											
Total	39	27	14	1	0	1					
Cities	37	23	14	1	0	1					
Aurora	2	0	0	0	0	0	1	1	0	0	201,599
Berwyn	1	1	1	0	0	0	1	0	1	1	55,594
Bloomington	1	0	0	0	0	0	0	1	0	0	78,203
Chicago	16	17	7	0	0	1	18	5	10	8	2,706,171
Decatur	1	0	0	0	0	0	0	0	1	0	72,153
De Kalb	0	1	0	0	0	0	0	0	0	1	43,043
East Peoria	1	0	0	0	0	0	1	0	0	0	22,856
Forest Park	0	0	1	0	0	0	0	0	1	0	13,950
Fox Lake	1	0	0	0	0	0	0	1	0	0	10,432
Fox River Grove	1	0	0	0	0	0	0	0	0	1	4,628
Homewood	2	0	0	0	0	0	0	1	1	0	19,150
Manhattan	1	0	0	0	0	0	0	0	0	1	7,625
Mount Prospect	0	2	0	0	0	0	0	0	2	0	54,162
New Lenox	0	0	0	1	0	0	1	0	0	0	26,529
Oak Park	1	0	0	0	0	0	0	0	1	0	51,753
Pekin	1	0	0	0	0	0	0	0	0	1	32,866
Peoria	0	0	1	0	0	0	0	1	0	0	114,157
Plainfield	0	1	0	0	0	0	0	0	1	0	43,450
Pontiac	1	0	0	0	0	0	0	1	0	0	11,813
Rockford	2	0	2	0	0	0	0	2	1	1	146,770
Sandoval	1	0	0	0	0	0	0	0	1	0	1,211
Skokie	1	0	0	0	0	0	0	1	0	0	64,167
Springfield	2	0	1	0	0	0	0	0	3	0	115,568
Urbana	1	0	0	0	0	0	0	1	0	0	42,091
West Chicago	0	0	1	0	0	0	0	0	1	0	27,219
Wheaton	0	1	0	0	0	0	0	1	0	0	53,444
Universities and Colleges	0	1	0	0	0	0					
Illinois State University	0	1	0	0	0	0	0	0	0	1	21,039
Metropolitan Counties	2	3	0	0	0	0					
Lake	0	1	0	0	0	0	1	0	0	0	
Macon	1	0	0	0	0	0	0	0	1	0	
Peoria	1	0	0	0	0	0	0	0	0	1	
Will	0	1	0	0	0	0	0	1	0	0	
Winnebago	0	1	0	0	0	0	0	0	0	1	
INDIANA											
Total	32	13	9	1	0	0					
Cities	27	4	7	0	0	0					
Bloomington	6	2	2	0	0	0	1	4	3	2	85,121
Fishers	2	0	0	0	0	0	0	0	1	1	92,367
Fort Wayne	2	0	2	0	0	0	0	2	1	1	266,259
Hammond	2	0	1	0	0	0			2	1	76,550
Lafayette	8	0	1	0	0	0	2	5		2	72,274
Lawrence	2	1	0	0	0	0	0	1	2	0	48,174
Michigan City	1	0	0	0	0	0	0	0	0	1	31,108
Plainfield	1	0	1	0	0	0	1	1	0	0	32,067
South Bend	3	0	0	0	0	0	2		0	1	101,857
Whitestown	0	1	0	0	0	0	0	0	1	0	7,464
Universities and Colleges	1	0	0	0	0	0					
Purdue University	1	0	0	0	0	0	1				41,513
Metropolitan Counties	2	0	0	0	0	0					
Vigo	2	0	0	0	0	0	0	0	1	1	

Table 94. Hate Crime Incidents Per Bias Motivation and Quarter, by Selected State and Agency, 2017—Continued

(Number.)

State/agency	Number of incidents per bias motivation						Number of incidents per quarter				Population[1]
	Race/ Ethnicity/ Ancestry	Religion	Sexual orientation	Disability	Gender	Gender Identity	1st quarter	2nd quarter	3rd quarter	4th quarter	
State Police Agencies	2	9	2	1	0	0					
State Police											
Crawford County	0	1	0	0	0	0	1	0	0	0	
Floyd County	0	1	0	0	0	0	0	0	0	1	
Marion County	1	2	1	1	0	0	1	1	3	0	
Miami County	0	1	0	0	0	0	0	0	1	0	
Monroe County	0	1	0	0	0	0	0	0	0	1	
Posey County	0	1	0	0	0	0	0	0	0	1	
Scott County	0	2	0	0	0	0	0	0	1	1	
Vanderburgh County	1	0	0	0	0	0	0	0	0	1	
Washington County	0	0	1	0	0	0	1	0	0	0	
IOWA											
Total	9	1	1	0	0	0					
Cities	9	1	1	0	0	0					
Altoona	1	0	0	0	0	0	1	0	0	0	18,556
Ames	1	0	0	0	0	0	0	0	1	0	67,461
Clinton	1	0	0	0	0	0	0	1	0	0	25,532
Dubuque	1	0	0	0	0	0	0	1	0	0	58,674
Iowa City	3	0	0	0	0	0	2	0	1	0	75,519
Marshalltown	0	1	0	0	0	0	1	0	0	0	27,287
Urbandale	1	0	0	0	0	0	0	0	0	1	43,637
Waukee	1	0	1	0	0	0	1	0	1	0	20,359
KANSAS											
Total	39	16	11	9	0	0					
Cities	28	11	9	7	0	0					
Arma	0	0	1	0	0	0	0	0	1	0	1,438
Coffeyville	1	1	0	0	0	0	1	0	0	1	9,423
Dodge City	1	3	0	1	0	0	1	0	3	1	27,447
Edwardsville	1	0	0	0	0	0	0	0	1	0	4,395
El Dorado	0	1	0	0	0	0	0	1	0	0	13,125
Emporia	1	1	0	0	0	0	2	0	0	0	24,804
Garden City	2	1	0	0	0	0	0	0	3	0	26,728
Haven	1	0	0	0	0	0	0	1	0	0	1,207
Hays	0	1	0	0	0	0	0	1	0	0	21,110
Haysville	1	0	0	0	0	0	0	1	0	0	11,314
Herington	0	0	1	0	0	0	1	0	0	0	2,336
Hutchinson	1	0	0	1	0	0	0	1	0	1	41,160
Junction City	1	0	0	0	0	0	0	1	0	0	24,240
Liberal	0	0	0	1	0	0	0	0	0	1	20,317
Lindsborg	0	0	1	1	0	0	1	0	0	1	3,319
Mulvane	1	0	0	0	0	0	1	0	0	0	6,343
Newton	2	0	0	0	0	0	2	0	0	0	19,095
Norton	1	0	1	1	0	0	3	0	0	0	2,799
Ottawa	3	1	0	0	0	0	2	1	1	0	12,307
Salina	4	1	2	1	0	0	2	2	2	2	47,251
Sedgwick	1	0	0	0	0	0	0	0	0	1	1,695
Shawnee	1	0	0	0	0	0	0	1	0	0	65,683
Tonganoxie	0	0	0	1	0	0	0	1	0	0	5,379
Topeka	1	0	0	0	0	0	1	0	0	0	126,624
Valley Center	2	0	0	0	0	0	0	2	0	0	7,431
Wichita	2	1	3	0	0	0	2	3	0	1	391,084
Universities and Colleges	1	0	0	0	0	0					
Kansas State University	1	0	0	0	0	0	1	0	0	0	23,779
Metropolitan Counties	8	2	1	1	0	0					
Doniphan	0	0	0	1	0	0	0	0	1	0	
Johnson	1	0	0	0	0	0	0	0	1	0	
Riley County Police Department	3	1	0	0	0	0	0	0	3	1	
Sedgwick	2	0	0	0	0	0	0	0	1	1	
Shawnee	2	1	1	0	0	0	0	2	0	2	
Nonmetropolitan Counties	2	3	1	0	0	0					
Barton	0	1	0	0	0	0	0	0	1	0	
Crawford	0	1	1	0	0	0	1	0	1	0	
Ford	0	1	0	0	0	0	0	0	0	1	
Labette	1	0	0	0	0	0	0	1	0	0	
Saline	1	0	0	0	0	0	0	0	0	1	
State Police Agencies	0	0	0	1	0	0					
Highway Patrol, Troop E	0	0	0	1	0	0	0	0	0	1	
KENTUCKY											
Total	283	38	27	12	16	3					
Cities	186	21	17	6	7	3					
Alexandria	1	2	0	0	0	0	1	2	0	0	9,486
Ashland	0	0	1	0	0	0	1	0	0	0	20,927

Table 94. Hate Crime Incidents Per Bias Motivation and Quarter, by Selected State and Agency, 2017—Continued

(Number.)

State/agency	Number of incidents per bias motivation						Number of incidents per quarter				Population[1]
	Race/ Ethnicity/ Ancestry	Religion	Sexual orientation	Disability	Gender	Gender Identity	1st quarter	2nd quarter	3rd quarter	4th quarter	
Barbourville	1	0	0	0	1	0	0	1	0	1	3,169
Bowling Green	18	2	2	2	1	0	3	4	10	8	66,317
Cadiz	0	0	1	0	0	0	1	0	0	0	2,629
Carrollton	2	0	0	0	0	0	1	1	0	0	3,864
Cold Spring	1	0	0	0	0	0	0	0	0	1	6,276
Corbin	2	0	0	0	0	0	0	0	0	2	7,411
Covington	4	1	1	0	0	0	1	2	0	3	40,845
Cynthiana	1	0	0	0	0	0	0	0	1	0	6,375
Danville	3	0	0	0	0	0	0	1	1	1	16,891
Dayton	2	0	0	0	0	0	0	1	0	1	5,423
Elizabethtown	4	0	0	0	0	0	0	1	2	1	30,065
Elsmere	1	1	0	0	0	0	2	0	0	0	8,541
Erlanger	1	0	0	0	1	0	0	0	2	0	22,947
Falmouth	1	0	0	0	0	0	0	0	1	0	2,127
Florence	19	1	0	0	1	0	8	6	5	2	32,866
Fort Mitchell	1	0	0	0	0	0	0	1	0	0	8,306
Frankfort	5	1	0	0	1	0	1	2	0	4	27,975
Franklin	3	0	1	0	0	0	0	2	0	2	8,884
Fulton	0	0	1	0	0	0	0	0	1	0	2,174
Georgetown	2	0	0	0	0	1	1	1	0	1	34,184
Glasgow	6	0	0	0	0	0	0	3	1	2	14,690
Greensburg	1	0	0	0	0	0	0	0	0	1	2,123
Hillview	1	0	0	0	0	0	0	1	0	0	8,942
Hopkinsville	2	0	0	0	0	0	1	0	0	1	31,761
Independence	1	0	0	0	0	0	1	0	0	0	27,400
Irvine	0	0	0	1	0	0	0	0	0	1	2,385
La Center	0	0	1	0	0	0	1	0	0	0	982
La Grange	1	0	0	0	0	0	0	0	0	1	8,831
Lawrenceburg	2	0	0	0	0	0	0	1	0	1	11,211
Leitchfield	1	0	0	0	0	0	0	0	1	0	6,900
Lexington	20	3	3	0	0	1	7	6	9	5	322,332
London	1	0	0	0	0	0	0	0	1	0	8,184
Louisville Metro	11	2	0	1	0	0	5	0	7	2	684,362
Madisonville	1	1	0	0	0	0	0	1	0	1	19,316
Mayfield	6	0	1	0	0	0	0	1	3	3	9,991
Maysville	8	0	0	0	1	0	0	3	3	3	8,841
Middlesboro	1	0	0	0	0	0	0	0	0	1	9,534
Morehead	1	0	0	0	0	0	0	0	1	0	7,915
Mount Sterling	2	0	0	0	0	0	1	0	0	1	7,298
Mount Washington	1	0	0	0	0	0	0	1	0	0	14,511
Murray	2	0	1	0	1	0	0	1	3	0	19,205
Newport	1	0	0	0	0	0	0	1	0	0	15,202
Nicholasville	4	0	0	0	0	0	1	0	1	2	30,333
Owensboro	5	1	1	0	0	0	2	0	3	2	59,576
Paducah	10	2	1	0	0	1	4	5	3	2	25,169
Paris	2	0	1	0	0	0	1	1	1	0	9,845
Park Hills	1	0	0	0	0	0	0	0	1	0	3,001
Princeton	0	1	0	0	0	0	0	0	0	1	6,084
Providence	1	0	0	0	0	0	1	0	0	0	3,088
Radcliff	3	0	0	0	0	0	0	1	0	2	22,473
Richmond	5	0	1	0	0	0	1	2	1	2	35,161
Russell Springs	1	0	0	0	0	0	0	0	0	1	2,573
Russellville	0	0	0	1	0	0	0	0	0	1	7,006
Scottsville	1	0	0	0	0	0	0	1	0	0	4,446
Shelbyville	2	0	0	1	0	0	0	1	1	1	15,758
Shively	2	0	0	0	0	0	0	1	0	1	15,830
St. Matthews	4	1	0	0	0	0	1	2	0	2	18,163
Versailles	0	1	0	0	0	0	0	1	0	0	26,320
Villa Hills	1	0	0	0	0	0	1	0	0	0	7,494
Wilmore	1	0	0	0	0	0	0	0	1	0	6,380
Winchester	1	0	0	0	0	0	0	1	0	0	18,478
Worthington	0	1	0	0	0	0	0	0	0	1	1,565
Universities and Colleges	6	2	4	0	0	0					
Eastern Kentucky University	1	0	4	0	0	0	2	2	0	1	16,881
Kentucky State University	2	0	0	0	0	0	0	1	1	0	1,736
University of Kentucky	2	2	0	0	0	0	3	1	0	0	29,781
Western Kentucky University	1	0	0	0	0	0	0	1	0	0	20,271
Metropolitan Counties	31	6	2	1	0	0					
Boone	14	1	0	0	0	0	6	3	5	1	
Boyd	0	1	0	0	0	0	0	0	0	1	
Bullitt	0	0	1	0	0	0	0	0	1	0	
Campbell County Police Department[2]	2	2	1	0	0	0	0	1	2	1	
Christian	0	1	0	0	0	0	1	0	0	0	
Clark	3	0	0	0	0	0	1	2	0	0	
Daviess	1	0	0	0	0	0	0	0	0	1	
Grant	0	1	0	0	0	0	0	0	0	1	
Greenup	1	0	0	0	0	0	0	0	1	0	
Hardin	1	0	0	0	0	0	0	1	0	0	
Jessamine	0	0	0	1	0	0	0	0	1	0	

Table 94. Hate Crime Incidents Per Bias Motivation and Quarter, by Selected State and Agency, 2017—Continued

(Number.)

State/agency	Number of incidents per bias motivation						Number of incidents per quarter				Population[1]
	Race/ Ethnicity/ Ancestry	Religion	Sexual orientation	Disability	Gender	Gender Identity	1st quarter	2nd quarter	3rd quarter	4th quarter	
Kenton County Police Department	1	0	0	0	0	0	0	0	1	0	
Oldham County Police Department	2	0	0	0	0	0	0	2	0	0	
Pendleton	1	0	0	0	0	0	0	1	0	0	
Shelby	1	0	0	0	0	0	0	1	0	0	
Trigg	1	0	0	0	0	0	0	0	0	1	
Warren	3	0	0	0	0	0	0	0	0	3	
Nonmetropolitan Counties	27	4	3	1	7	0					
Anderson	0	1	0	0	0	0	0	0	1	0	
Bell	0	1	0	0	0	0	1	0	0	0	
Boyle	2	0	0	0	0	0	2	0	0	0	
Breckinridge	1	0	0	0	0	0	0	1	0	0	
Floyd	2	0	0	0	0	0	1	1	0	0	
Franklin	1	0	0	0	0	0	1	0	0	0	
Graves	1	0	0	0	0	0	1	0	0	0	
Knott	0	1	0	0	0	0	0	0	0	1	
Knox	1	0	0	0	0	0	0	1	0	0	
Laurel	1	0	0	0	0	0	0	1	0	0	
Lincoln	1	0	0	0	0	0	1	0	0	0	
Livingston	2	0	0	0	0	0	0	0	1	1	
Madison	0	0	1	0	0	0	1	0	0	0	
Marion	1	0	0	0	0	0	0	0	0	1	
Martin	1	0	0	0	0	0	1	0	0	0	
Mason	1	0	0	0	0	0	0	1	0	0	
McCracken	6	0	0	1	7	0	1	7	1	5	
Montgomery	2	1	1	0	0	0	0	2	2	0	
Ohio	1	0	0	0	0	0	0	0	1	0	
Rockcastle	0	0	1	0	0	0	0	0	1	0	
Simpson	1	0	0	0	0	0	0	1	0	0	
Taylor	1	0	0	0	0	0	0	1	0	0	
Wolfe	1	0	0	0	0	0	0	0	0	1	
State Police Agencies	22	2	1	3	1	0					
State Police											
Ashland	0	0	0	1	0	0	0	0	0	1	
Bowling Green	1	0	0	0	0	0	0	1	0	0	
Campbellsburg	0	1	1	0	0	0	1	0	0	1	
Cannabis Suppression Section	2	0	0	0	0	0	0	0	2	0	
Dry Ridge	1	0	0	0	0	0	0	1	0	0	
Elizabethtown	1	0	0	1	0	0	1	0	0	1	
Frankfort	2	0	0	0	0	0	1	0	1	0	
Harlan	1	0	0	0	0	0	0	0	1	0	
Hazard	3	0	0	0	0	0	1	0	1	1	
Henderson	1	0	0	0	0	0	0	0	0	1	
London	1	1	0	0	0	0	0	1	0	1	
Mayfield	2	0	0	1	1	0	2	1	1	0	
Morehead	3	0	0	0	0	0	0	0	0	3	
Pikeville	2	0	0	0	0	0	1	0	1	0	
Richmond	1	0	0	0	0	0	0	0	0	1	
West Drug Enforcement Branch	1	0	0	0	0	0	0	1	0	0	
Other Agencies	11	3	0	1	1	0					
Barren County Drug Task Force	3	0	0	0	0	0	1	1	1	0	
Cincinnati-Northern Kentucky International Airport	1	0	0	0	0	0	1	0	0	0	
Clark County School System	1	0	0	0	0	0	0	0	1	0	
Fayette County Schools	0	2	0	1	0	0	1	0	1	1	
Greater Hardin County Narcotics Task Force	1	0	0	0	0	0	0	1	0	0	
Jefferson County School District	1	1	0	0	1	0	1	1	0	1	
McCracken County Public Schools	1	0	0	0	0	0	0	0	0	1	
South Central Kentucky Drug Task Force	3	0	0	0	0	0	0	0	3	0	
LOUISIANA											
Total	14	11	1	0	0	0					
Cities	4	0	0	0	0	0					
Gretna	1	0	0	0	0	0	0	0	1	0	17,923
New Orleans	1	0	0	0	0	0			0	1	397,447
Shreveport	1	0	0	0	0	0	0	0	0	1	193,937
Vidalia	1	0	0	0	0	0	0		1		4,015
Universities and Colleges	1	0	0	0	0	0					
Louisiana State University, Baton Rouge	1	0	0	0	0	0	0	0	0	1	31,409
Metropolitan Counties	6	11	1	0	0	0					
Caddo	0	1	0	0	0	0	1	0	0	0	
Calcasieu	2	0	0	0	0	0	0	1	0	1	

Table 94. Hate Crime Incidents Per Bias Motivation and Quarter, by Selected State and Agency, 2017—Continued

(Number.)

State/agency	Number of incidents per bias motivation						Number of incidents per quarter				Population[1]
	Race/Ethnicity/Ancestry	Religion	Sexual orientation	Disability	Gender	Gender Identity	1st quarter	2nd quarter	3rd quarter	4th quarter	
Jefferson	1	0	0	0	0	0	0	1	0	0	
Lafourche	1	0	0	0	0	0	0	0	0	1	
St. Charles	0	10	0	0	0	0	3	2	3	2	
St. James	1	0	0	0	0	0	0	0	0	1	
St. John the Baptist	0	0	1	0	0	0	0	0	0	1	
St. Tammany	1	0	0	0	0	0	0	1	0	0	
Nonmetropolitan Counties	3	0	0	0	0	0					
Madison	2	0	0	0	0	0	0	0	2	0	
Washington	1	0	0	0	0	0	1	0	0	0	
MAINE											
Total	17	9	4	0	0	2					
Cities	16	5	2	0	0	1					
Augusta	0	1	0	0	0	0	1	0	0	0	18,394
Biddeford	1	0	1	0	0	0	0	0	2	0	21,378
Lewiston	1	0	0	0	0	0	0	0	0	1	36,067
Old Orchard Beach	2	0	0	0	0	0	0	1	1	0	8,842
Portland	7	2	1	0	0	0	6	3	1	0	67,079
Rumford	1	0	0	0	0	0	0	0	1	0	5,692
Saco	1	2	0	0	0	0	2	1	0	0	19,332
Sanford	3	0	0	0	0	1	1	1	2	0	20,963
Universities and Colleges	1	4	2	0	0	0					
University of Southern Maine	1	4	2	0	0	0	2	3	0	2	7,855
Nonmetropolitan Counties	0	0	0	0	0	1					
Waldo	0	0	0	0	0	1	0	1	0	0	
MARYLAND											
Total	24	12	6	0	0	6					
Cities	4	1	0	0	0	1					
Aberdeen	1	0	0	0	0	0	1	0	0	0	15,720
Annapolis	1	0	0	0	0	0	0	1	0	0	39,596
Baltimore	0	0	0	0	0	1	0	0	0	1	613,217
Laurel	0	1	0	0	0	0	0	1			25,997
Taneytown	1	0	0	0	0	0	1	0			6,762
Westminster	1	0	0	0	0	0	0	1			18,682
Universities and Colleges	4	4	0	0	0	0					
University of Maryland											
Baltimore County	0	3	0	0	0	0	1	1	1	0	13,640
College Park	4	1	0	0	0	0	0	1	2	2	39,083
Metropolitan Counties	15	6	4	0	0	5					
Anne Arundel County Police Department	5	1	2	0	0	1	4	3	2	0	
Baltimore County Police Department	5	1	0	0	0	4	6	1	3	0	
Harford	1	0	0	0	0	0	1	0	0		
Howard County Police Department	0	1	0	0	0	0	1	0			
Montgomery County Police Department	2	2	2	0	0	0	0	3	2	1	
Prince George's County Police Department	1	0	0	0	0	0	0	1			
Wicomico	1	1	0	0	0	0	0	2	0	0	
State Police Agencies	0	0	1	0	0	0					
State Police, Somerset County	0	0	1	0	0	0	0	0	1	0	
Other Agencies	1	1	1	0	0	0					
State Fire Marshal	0	1	0	0	0	0	1	0	0	0	
Transit Administration	1	0	1	0	0	0	1	0	0	1	
MASSACHUSETTS											
Total	232	118	65	9	8	9					
Cities	185	110	60	9	8	9					
Acton	5	2	1	0	0	0	1	1	4	2	23,937
Agawam	1	0	0	0	0	0	1	0	0	0	28,839
Amherst[2]	1	0	1	0	2	0	0	1	1	1	40,313
Andover	1	2	0	0	0	0	0	1	0	2	35,898
Arlington	2	7	1	1	0	3	6	7	1	0	45,449
Ashburnham	1	0	0	0	0	0	0	1	0	0	6,255
Attleboro	1	0	0	0	0	0	0	1	0	0	44,607
Barnstable	2	0	0	0	0	0	0	1	0	1	44,142
Belmont	1	0	0	0	0	0	0	0	0	1	26,432
Beverly	1	0	0	0	0	0	1	0	0	0	41,678
Bolton	1	0	0	0	0	0	0	0	1	0	5,272
Boston[2]	79	28	33	0	0	1	29	42	36	33	682,903
Boxford	0	1	0	0	0	0	0	0	0	1	8,333

Table 94. Hate Crime Incidents Per Bias Motivation and Quarter, by Selected State and Agency, 2017—Continued

(Number.)

State/agency	Number of incidents per bias motivation						Number of incidents per quarter				Population[1]
	Race/ Ethnicity/ Ancestry	Religion	Sexual orientation	Disability	Gender	Gender Identity	1st quarter	2nd quarter	3rd quarter	4th quarter	
Braintree	4	1	0	0	0	2	3	3	0	1	37,579
Bridgewater	1	0	0	0	0	0	0	1	0	0	27,769
Brockton	1	0	0	0	0	0	0	0	0	1	96,016
Cambridge[2]	5	3	2	0	0	0	3	3	1	2	111,707
Chelmsford	0	1	1	0	0	0	1	0	1	0	35,392
Chelsea[2]	2	1	0	0	0	0	0	0	1	1	40,514
Concord	0	0	0	1	0	0	0	0	1	0	20,193
Danvers	0	2	0	1	0	0	0	1	0	2	28,168
Dracut	0	4	1	0	0	0	1	1	0	3	31,685
Duxbury	1	2	0	0	0	0	0	1	2	0	16,085
Edgartown	0	0	1	0	0	0	0	0	0	1	4,323
Everett	2	0	0	0	0	0	0	0	1	1	47,185
Fitchburg	1	0	0	0	0	0	1	0	0	0	40,445
Framingham	1	3	1	0	0	0	3	1	1	0	72,153
Grafton	2	0	0	0	0	0	0	1	1	0	18,763
Greenfield	1	0	0	0	0	0	0	0	0	1	17,462
Haverhill	2	1	0	0	0	0	1	0	1	1	63,244
Hingham	1	0	0	0	0	0	0	0	1	0	23,392
Holland	0	0	0	0	1	0	0	0	0	1	2,502
Hudson	0	2	0	0	0	0	0	0	1	1	19,963
Lexington	0	1	0	0	0	0	0	0	1	0	33,768
Lincoln	0	2	0	0	0	0	0	0	1	1	6,860
Lowell	0	1	1	0	0	0	0	1	1	0	111,294
Lynn[2]	5	0	2	0	0	0	4	0	1	1	93,140
Malden[2]	3	2	0	0	0	0	1	0	3	0	61,098
Manchester-by-the-Sea	0	0	0	1	0	0	1	0	0	0	5,435
Mansfield	1	0	0	0	0	0	0	0	0	1	23,847
Marblehead	0	1	0	0	0	0	0	1	0	0	20,618
Mashpee	0	1	0	0	0	0	0	0	1	0	14,272
Medford	5	1	0	1	0	0	2	3	0	2	57,418
Medway	1	0	0	0	0	0	0	0	0	1	13,407
Millbury	0	1	0	0	0	0	0	0	1	0	13,626
Milton	0	1	1	0	0	0	1	1	0	0	27,420
Nahant	0	1	0	0	0	0	0	0	1	0	3,500
Natick	0	1	0	0	0	0	1	0	0	0	36,705
New Bedford	0	0	1	0	0	0	0	1	0	0	95,107
Newburyport	0	1	0	0	0	0	0	0	1	0	18,092
Newton	3	7	2	0	0	0	5	4	1	2	89,736
North Andover	1	0	0	0	0	0	0	0	1	0	31,035
Northbridge	1	0	0	0	0	0	0	0	0	1	16,711
Northfield	0	4	4	0	0	0	0	0	0	8	2,966
Norwell	1	0	0	0	0	0	0	0	1	0	11,150
Pittsfield	0	1	0	0	0	0	1	0	0	0	42,546
Plymouth	0	1	0	0	0	0	1	0	0	0	59,803
Provincetown	1	0	1	0	0	0	0	1	0	1	2,993
Quincy[2]	8	2	1	0	0	0	2	1	4	3	93,966
Raynham	0	0	0	0	0	1	1	0	0	0	14,048
Reading	0	1	1	0	0	0	0	0	1	1	26,033
Revere	2	1	0	0	0	0	0	1	2	0	53,425
Rutland	0	1	0	0	0	0	0	0	1	0	8,687
Salem[2]	8	5	0	0	0	0	1	5	1	4	43,385
Salisbury	1	0	0	0	0	0	0	1	0	0	9,517
Saugus	1	0	0	0	0	0	1	0	0	0	28,241
Sharon	0	0	1	0	0	0	1	0	0	0	18,419
Shrewsbury	0	1	0	0	0	0	0	0	1	0	36,974
Somerville[2]	6	2	1	1	0	0	3	3	1	2	82,326
Southbridge	0	1	0	0	0	0	0	1	0	0	16,860
Springfield	5	1	1	0	0	1	4	2	1	1	154,562
Stoneham	0	0	0	1	0	0	1	0	0	0	22,077
Stoughton	0	1	0	0	0	0	0	0	0	1	28,678
Sudbury	0	1	0	0	0	0	0	0	1	0	19,120
Swampscott	0	1	0	0	1	0	2	0	0	0	15,016
Taunton	1	1	0	1	2	0	4	1	0	0	57,047
Tewksbury	1	0	0	0	0	0	0	1	0	0	31,245
Truro	1	0	0	0	0	0	0	0	0	1	2,018
Walpole	1	0	0	0	0	0	0	0	1	0	25,312
Waltham	1	1	1	1	2	0	0	3	1	2	63,413
Ware	1	0	0	0	0	0	0	0	1	0	9,907
Watertown	0	0	0	0	0	1	1	0	0	0	35,586
Webster	1	0	0	0	0	0	0	0	0	1	16,883
Westborough	0	1	0	0	0	0	0	1	0	0	19,074
Worcester[2]	5	1	0	0	0	0	2	2	0	1	185,107
Wrentham	0	1	0	0	0	0	0	0	0	1	11,838
Universities and Colleges	37	8	4	0	0	0					
Amherst College	0	0	2	0	0	0	2	0		0	1,849
Boston College	5	0	0	0	0	0	0			5	14,466
Boston University[2]	5	3	1	0	0	0	3	2	2	1	32,695
Clark University	0	2	0	0	0	0	2	0	0	0	3,298
College of the Holy Cross	0	0	1	0	0	0	0	0	0	1	2,720
Dean College	1	0	0	0	0	0	0	1	0	0	1,339

Table 94. Hate Crime Incidents Per Bias Motivation and Quarter, by Selected State and Agency, 2017—Continued

(Number.)

State/agency	Number of incidents per bias motivation						Number of incidents per quarter				Population[1]
	Race/ Ethnicity/ Ancestry	Religion	Sexual orientation	Disability	Gender	Gender Identity	1st quarter	2nd quarter	3rd quarter	4th quarter	
Framingham State University	8	0	0	0	0	0		0	0	8	5,977
Hampshire College	3	0	0	0	0	0	1	1	1	0	1,321
Harvard University	1	0	0	0	0	0	1				29,908
Massasoit Community College	0	1	0	0	0	0	1	0	0	0	7,471
Springfield Technical Community College	3	0	0	0	0	0	0	0	0	3	5,622
University of Massachusetts, Amherst	1	0	0	0	0	0	0	0	0	1	30,037
Westfield State University[2]	10	2	0	0	0	0	0	0	1	9	6,335
Other Agencies	10	0	1	0	0	0					
Massachusetts Bay Transportation Authority											
Middlesex County	1	0	0	0	0	0				1	
Suffolk County	4	0	0	0	0	0	1	1		2	
Massachusetts General Hospital	5	0	1	0	0	0			2	4	
MICHIGAN											
Total	311	78	57	2	8	0					
Cities	212	53	44	1	4	0					
Adrian	1	0	0	0	0	0	0	0	1	0	20,598
Albion	0	1	0	0	0	0	0	0	0	1	8,293
Ann Arbor	3	13	3	0	0	0	1	2	8	8	121,930
Bangor	1	0	0	0	0	0	0	1	0	0	1,839
Battle Creek	2	1	3	0	1	0	3	2	1	1	60,852
Bay City	1	0	0	0	0	0	1	0	0	0	33,286
Belleville	1	0	0	0	0	0	0	0	1	0	3,832
Benton Harbor	1	0	1	0	0	0	0	1	0	1	9,899
Berrien Springs-Oronoko Township	1	0	0	0	0	0	0	0	1	0	9,039
Birmingham	0	1	0	0	0	0	1	0	0	0	21,162
Blackman Township	23	0	0	0	0	0	1	4	3	15	36,908
Boyne City	1	1	0	0	0	0	1	1	0	0	3,741
Buena Vista Township	2	0	0	0	0	0	0	1	0	1	8,084
Burton	4	0	0	0	0	0	0	1	3	0	28,439
Cadillac	1	0	0	0	0	0	1	0	0	0	10,473
Canton Township	1	1	0	0	0	0	1	0	1	0	90,294
Carrollton Township	0	0	1	0	0	0	0	0	1	0	5,728
Center Line	2	0	0	0	0	0	1	1	0	0	8,304
Charlotte	2	0	0	0	0	0	0	0	1	1	9,053
Cheboygan	1	0	0	0	0	0	0	0	1	0	4,705
Chocolay Township	1	0	0	0	0	0	0	1	0	0	5,948
Clio	1	0	0	0	0	0	1	0	0	0	2,495
Dearborn	4	0	0	0	0	0	4	0	0	0	93,889
Dearborn Heights	1	1	1	0	0	0	1	1	0	1	55,454
Detroit	22	2	15	0	2	0	15	10	9	7	670,792
East Grand Rapids	1	0	0	0	0	0	0	0	0	1	11,812
East Lansing	2	1	0	0	0	0	0	1	2	0	48,920
Eastpointe	1	0	0	0	0	0	0	1	0	0	32,712
Ecorse	2	0	0	0	0	0	0	0	2	0	9,132
Escanaba	0	1	0	0	0	0	0	0	1	0	12,280
Farmington Hills	0	1	0	0	0	0	1	0	0	0	81,359
Ferndale	4	0	1	0	0	0	2	0	1	2	20,131
Flint	9	0	1	0	0	0	2	3	4	1	96,605
Fremont	1	0	0	0	0	0	0	0	1	0	4,020
Gaines Township	1	0	0	0	0	0	1	0	0	0	6,139
Galesburg	2	0	0	0	0	0	0	0	1	1	2,055
Gaylord	2	0	0	0	0	0	0	0	1	1	3,697
Grand Blanc	1	0	0	0	0	0	1	0	0	0	7,904
Grand Rapids	5	1	4	0	0	0	1	0	6	3	197,868
Grandville	0	2	0	0	0	0	0	1	1	0	16,108
Grosse Pointe	0	1	0	0	0	0	1	0	0	0	5,151
Grosse Pointe Farms	0	0	1	0	0	0	0	0	1	0	9,106
Hampton Township	1	0	0	0	0	0	1	0	0	0	9,522
Hamtramck	1	1	0	0	0	0	0	1	0	1	21,654
Hart	4	1	0	0	0	0	1	3	0	1	2,080
Highland Park	2	0	0	0	0	0	0	1	0	1	10,757
Holland	3	0	0	0	0	0	2	1	0	0	33,613
Huntington Woods	0	1	0	0	0	0	0	1	0	0	6,343
Huron Township	1	0	0	0	0	0	1	0	0	0	15,636
Independence Township	1	0	0	0	0	0	0	1	0	0	36,836
Inkster	1	0	0	0	0	0	1	0	0	0	24,324
Ionia	1	0	1	0	0	0	0	2	0	0	11,287
Iron River	1	0	0	0	0	0	0	0	0	1	2,838
Lansing	10	0	2	0	0	0	2	2	6	2	116,302
Lansing Township	0	0	1	0	0	0	0	1	0	0	8,150
Lapeer	0	1	0	0	0	0	1	0	0	0	8,735
Lincoln Park	2	0	0	0	0	0	0	0	2	0	36,502
Lincoln Township	1	0	0	0	0	0	1	0	0	0	14,460
Ludington	1	0	0	0	0	0	0	0	1	0	8,068
Madison Heights	1	0	0	0	0	0	1	0	0	0	30,152
Manistee	1	0	0	0	0	0	0	0	1	0	6,030

Table 94. Hate Crime Incidents Per Bias Motivation and Quarter, by Selected State and Agency, 2017—Continued

(Number.)

State/agency	Number of incidents per bias motivation						Number of incidents per quarter				Population[1]
	Race/ Ethnicity/ Ancestry	Religion	Sexual orientation	Disability	Gender	Gender Identity	1st quarter	2nd quarter	3rd quarter	4th quarter	
Meridian Township	2	1	6	0	0	0	2	0	6	1	42,878
Metro Police Authority of Genesee County	0	1	0	0	0	0	0	1	0	0	20,001
Midland	1	0	0	0	0	0	1	0	0	0	42,131
Millington	1	0	0	0	0	0	1	0	0	0	1,016
Monroe	1	0	0	0	0	0	1	0	0	0	19,868
Mount Pleasant	1	0	1	0	0	0	1	0	1	0	26,366
Muskegon	4	0	0	0	0	0	0	0	4	0	38,375
Northville Township	2	0	0	0	0	0	0	0	2	0	28,751
Oak Park	0	2	0	0	0	0	0	0	2	0	29,698
Ovid	1	0	0	0	0	0	0	0	1	0	1,615
Perry	2	0	0	0	0	0	0	2	0	0	2,094
Petoskey	1	0	0	0	0	0	0	0	1	0	5,764
Pinckney	0	0	0	1	0	0	0	0	1	0	2,463
Pittsfield Township	1	0	0	0	0	0	0	0	0	1	39,061
Pontiac	2	0	0	0	0	0	0	0	1	1	59,731
Portland	1	0	0	0	0	0	0	1	0	0	3,943
Raisin Township	1	0	0	0	0	0	1	0	0	0	7,619
Redford Township	1	0	0	0	0	0	0	1	0	0	46,867
Rochester Hills	1	2	1	0	0	0	1	0	0	3	73,827
Romulus	2	0	0	0	0	0	0	1	1	0	23,174
Roosevelt Park	0	1	0	0	0	0	0	0	1	0	3,826
Roseville	6	1	0	0	0	0	2	2	3	0	47,651
Royal Oak	1	0	0	0	0	0	0	0	1	0	59,303
Saginaw	3	0	0	0	0	0	0	0	2	1	48,589
Saginaw Township	2	0	0	0	0	0	1	0	0	1	39,319
Saline	1	0	0	0	0	0	0	0	1	0	9,207
Sault Ste. Marie	1	0	0	0	0	0	1	0	0	0	13,630
Schoolcraft	1	0	0	0	0	0	0	1	0	0	1,571
Shelby Township	4	2	0	0	0	0	2	1	2	1	79,217
Southfield	2	3	0	0	0	0	2	0	2	1	73,324
Southgate	4	0	0	0	0	0	0	0	0	4	28,939
Sparta	1	0	0	0	0	0	0	0	1	0	4,370
St. Joseph	1	0	0	0	0	0	0	0	1	0	8,276
Tawas	1	0	0	0	0	0	1	0	0	0	4,522
Taylor	3	0	0	0	0	0	0	2	1	0	60,882
Thomas Township	0	1	0	0	0	0	0	0	1	0	11,450
Traverse City	0	3	1	0	0	0	0	2	2	0	15,617
Trenton	0	1	0	0	0	0	1	0	0	0	18,161
Troy	3	0	0	0	1	0	0	2	2	0	84,086
Van Buren Township	2	0	0	0	0	0	1	0	1	0	27,911
Warren	1	0	0	0	0	0	1	0	0	0	135,303
Wayne	1	0	0	0	0	0	0	0	1	0	16,857
West Bloomfield Township	0	3	0	0	0	0	2	1	0	0	65,948
Westland	2	0	0	0	0	0	0	0	0	2	81,158
White Lake Township	1	0	0	0	0	0	0	1	0	0	31,016
Wyandotte	2	0	0	0	0	0	0	1	0	1	24,817
Wyoming	4	0	0	0	0	0	0	0	4	0	76,153
Universities and Colleges	14	5	4	0	1	0					
Eastern Michigan University	3	0	0	0	0	0	0	1	2	0	21,246
Grand Valley State University	0	0	2	0	0	0	0	0	2	0	25,460
Michigan State University	1	0	0	0	0	0	0	0	1	0	50,340
Oakland University	1	0	0	0	0	0	0	0	0	1	20,012
Saginaw Valley State University	0	0	0	0	1	0	0	0	0	1	9,105
University of Michigan											
Ann Arbor	9	4	2	0	0	0	4	0	5	6	44,718
Dearborn	0	1	0	0	0	0	0	1	0	0	9,131
Metropolitan Counties	15	10	2	0	0	0					
Eaton	1	0	0	0	0	0	0	0	1	0	
Genesee	2	2	0	0	0	0	1	1	0	2	
Jackson	0	2	0	0	0	0	0	2	0	0	
Kent	3	0	0	0	0	0	0	1	1	1	
Lapeer	0	1	0	0	0	0	0	1	0	0	
Midland	1	0	0	0	0	0	0	1	0	0	
Monroe	0	1	0	0	0	0	0	1	0	0	
Muskegon	0	0	1	0	0	0	1	0	0	0	
Ottawa	1	1	1	0	0	0	0	0	2	1	
Saginaw	0	1	0	0	0	0	0	1	0	0	
Van Buren	3	2	0	0	0	0	0	1	4	0	
Washtenaw	4	0	0	0	0	0	3	0	1	0	
Nonmetropolitan Counties	17	3	4	0	2	0					
Allegan	1	0	0	0	0	0	0	0	1	0	
Benzie	3	0	0	0	0	0	0	1	0	2	
Charlevoix	0	0	1	0	0	0	0	0	1	0	
Chippewa	1	1	1	0	0	0	0	1	1	1	
Clare	1	0	0	0	0	0	0	0	1	0	
Emmet	1	0	0	0	0	0	0	0	1	0	

Table 94. Hate Crime Incidents Per Bias Motivation and Quarter, by Selected State and Agency, 2017—Continued

(Number.)

State/agency	Number of incidents per bias motivation						Number of incidents per quarter				Population[1]
	Race/ Ethnicity/ Ancestry	Religion	Sexual orientation	Disability	Gender	Gender Identity	1st quarter	2nd quarter	3rd quarter	4th quarter	
Grand Traverse	2	0	0	0	0	0	0	1	1	0	
Gratiot	1	1	1	0	0	0	2	0	1	0	
Huron	1	0	0	0	0	0	0	1	0	0	
Mackinac	1	0	0	0	0	0	0	0	1	0	
Menominee	2	1	0	0	0	0	0	1	1	1	
Missaukee	1	0	0	0	0	0	0	0	1	0	
Newaygo	0	0	0	0	1	0	0	1	0	0	
Ontonagon	0	0	1	0	0	0	0	1	0	0	
Otsego	0	0	0	0	1	0	0	1	0	0	
Presque Isle	2	0	0	0	0	0	0	1	1	0	
State Police Agencies	50	6	3	1	1	0					
State Police											
Alpena County	2	0	0	0	0	0	0	0	2	0	
Barry County	3	0	0	0	0	0	0	0	3	0	
Bay County	2	0	1	0	0	0	0	1	2	0	
Berrien County	1	0	0	0	0	0	0	0	1	0	
Chippewa County	2	0	0	0	0	0	0	0	0	2	
Clare County	1	0	0	0	0	0	0	1	0	0	
Crawford County	1	0	0	0	0	0	0	0	0	1	
Eaton County	1	0	0	0	0	0	0	0	1	0	
Genesee County	1	0	0	0	0	0	0	0	1	0	
Gogebic County	2	0	0	0	0	0	1	0	1	0	
Isabella County	1	0	0	0	0	0	0	0	0	1	
Jackson County	3	0	1	0	0	0	1	1	1	1	
Kalamazoo County	2	0	0	0	0	0	0	1	0	1	
Kent County	3	0	0	0	0	0	0	0	1	2	
Lapeer County	1	1	0	0	0	0	0	0	1	1	
Livingston County	4	2	1	0	0	0	2	3	2	0	
Macomb County	1	0	0	0	0	0	0	0	0	1	
Mason County	0	1	0	0	0	0	0	0	0	1	
Monroe County	2	0	0	0	0	0	0	2	0	0	
Montcalm County	2	0	0	0	0	0	0	0	1	1	
Muskegon County	1	0	0	0	0	0	0	0	0	1	
Oakland County	2	0	0	1	0	0	0	2	1	0	
Oceana County	1	0	0	0	0	0	0	1	0	0	
Osceola County	1	0	0	0	0	0	0	0	1	0	
Saginaw County	2	1	0	0	0	0	0	1	1	1	
Shiawassee County	3	0	0	0	0	0	0	2	1	0	
St. Joseph County	1	0	0	0	0	0	0	1	0	0	
Van Buren County	0	1	0	0	1	0	2	0	0	0	
Washtenaw County	2	0	0	0	0	0	0	0	0	2	
Wayne County	1	0	0	0	0	0	1	0	0	0	
Wexford County	1	0	0	0	0	0	0	0	0	1	
Tribal Agencies	3	0	0	0	0	0					
Little River Band of Ottawa Indians	2	0	0	0	0	0	0	2	0	0	
Nottawaseppi Huron Band of Potawatomi	1	0	0	0	0	0	0	0	1	0	
Other Agencies	0	1	0	0	0	0					
Wayne County Airport	0	1	0	0	0	0	1	0	0	0	
MINNESOTA											
Total	92	34	22	0	0	0					
Cities	80	31	21	0	0	0					
Apple Valley	1	0	0	0	0	0	0	0	1	0	52,439
Belle Plaine	1	0	0	0	0	0	0	0	0	1	7,066
Blaine	3	0	0	0	0	0	1	1	0	1	63,857
Brooklyn Park	5	0	1	0	0	0	0	3	3	0	80,347
Burnsville	1	0	1	0	0	0	0	1	1	0	61,442
Clearbrook	1	0	0	0	0	0	0	1	0	0	522
Coon Rapids	0	1	0	0	0	0	0	0	1	0	62,495
Crookston	0	1	0	0	0	0	0	1	0	0	7,789
Duluth	1	0	1	0	0	0	1	0	1	0	86,306
Eden Prairie	1	0	0	0	0	0	0	0	0	1	64,429
Edina	0	1	0	0	0	0	0	0	1	0	51,923
Forest Lake	0	0	1	0	0	0	1	0	0	0	19,804
Fridley	0	0	1	0	0	0	0	0	1	0	27,516
Goodhue	1	0	0	0	0	0	0	0	0	1	1,186
Inver Grove Heights	4	1	0	0	0	0	0	3	0	2	35,254
Lakeville[2]	4	2	1	0	0	0	3	0	1	2	62,958
Mankato	1	0	0	0	0	0	0	0	0	1	42,047
Maple Grove	2	2	0	0	0	0	0	0	1	3	70,966
Maplewood	5	0	0	0	0	0	1	0	3	1	40,689
Minneapolis	16	7	8	0	0	0	10	9	8	4	418,971
Moorhead	2	0	1	0	0	0	3	0	0	0	42,999
New Brighton	1	0	0	0	0	0	0	0	1	0	22,772
Northfield	1	0	0	0	0	0	0	1	0	0	20,512
Oakdale	1	0	0	0	0	0	1	0	0	0	28,181

Table 94. Hate Crime Incidents Per Bias Motivation and Quarter, by Selected State and Agency, 2017—Continued

(Number.)

State/agency	Number of incidents per bias motivation						Number of incidents per quarter				Population[1]
	Race/ Ethnicity/ Ancestry	Religion	Sexual orientation	Disability	Gender	Gender Identity	1st quarter	2nd quarter	3rd quarter	4th quarter	
Plymouth	0	1	0	0	0	0	0	0	0	1	78,356
Rochester	10	3	0	0	0	0	3	3	3	4	115,228
Roseville	0	0	1	0	0	0	0	1	0	0	36,196
Sartell	0	0	1	0	0	0	0	0	1	0	17,353
Savage	1	0	1	0	0	0	1	0	1	0	31,491
Spring Lake Park	1	0	0	0	0	0	1	0	0	0	6,482
St. Anthony	1	0	0	0	0	0	0	0	0	1	9,159
St. Cloud	1	1	0	0	0	0	1	0	1	0	67,911
Stillwater	0	1	0	0	0	0	0	0	1	0	19,394
St. Louis Park[2]	3	4	2	0	0	0	3	1	2	2	49,355
St. Paul	11	5	1	0	0	0	5	8	2	2	306,696
Willmar	0	1	0	0	0	0	0	0	1	0	19,553
Universities and Colleges	3	2	0	0	0	0					
University of Minnesota, Twin Cities	3	2	0	0	0	0	2	2	1	0	51,579
Metropolitan Counties	9	0	1	0	0	0					
Benton	1	0	0	0	0	0	1	0	0	0	
Carver	5	0	0	0	0	0	1	1	2	1	
Ramsey	2	0	0	0	0	0	1	1	0	0	
Wright	1	0	1	0	0	0	1	0	0	1	
Nonmetropolitan Counties	0	1	0	0	0	0					
Otter Tail	0	1	0	0	0	0	1	0	0	0	
MISSISSIPPI											
Total	1	0	0	0	0	0					
Cities	1	0	0	0	0	0					
Gulfport	1	0	0	0	0	0	0	0	0	1	72,792
MISSOURI											
Total	79	11	13	0	1	1					
Cities	72	7	13	0	1	1					
Blue Springs	2	0	0	0	0	0	1	1	0	0	54,727
Branson	1	0	0	0	0	0	1	0	0	0	11,571
Camdenton	0	0	1	0	0	0	0	0	0	1	3,980
Cameron	3	0	0	0	0	0	0	2	0	1	9,765
Columbia	1	0	0	0	0	0	1	0	0	0	122,585
Crystal City	0	0	1	0	0	0	0	0	1	0	4,817
Festus	0	0	1	0	0	0	0	1	0	0	12,187
Gladstone	2	1	0	0	0	0	1	0	1	1	27,390
Grain Valley	2	0	0	0	0	0	0	0	1	1	13,825
Grandview	1	0	0	0	0	0	0	1	0	0	25,308
Independence	4	0	0	0	0	0	2	1	0	1	117,055
Joplin	0	0	1	0	0	0	0	0	0	1	52,412
Kansas City	34	5	6	0	1	1	6	19	16	6	484,948
Lee's Summit	1	0	0	0	0	0	1	0	0	0	96,855
Macon	1	0	0	0	0	0	0	0	1	0	5,360
Maryland Heights	1	0	0	0	0	0	0	0	0	1	27,083
Normandy	1	0	0	0	0	0	0	1	0	0	7,544
North Kansas City	1	0	0	0	0	0	0	1	0	0	4,407
Overland	1	0	0	0	0	0	0	1	0	0	15,760
Rolla	2	0	3	0	0	0	2	1	2	0	20,147
St. Louis	11	0	0	0	0	0	3	4	2	2	310,284
University City	1	0	0	0	0	0	0	1	0	0	34,601
Warrenton	1	0	0	0	0	0	0	1	0	0	8,168
Wentzville	1	0	0	0	0	0	0	1	0	0	38,876
Willard	0	1	0	0	0	0	0	1	0	0	5,452
Universities and Colleges	2	2	0	0	0	0					
St. Louis Community College, Meramec	2	1	0	0	0	0	2	0	1	0	19,052
University of Missouri, Columbia	0	1	0	0	0	0	1	0	0	0	33,239
Metropolitan Counties	3	2	0	0	0	0					
Greene	2	0	0	0	0	0	0	1	1	0	
St. Louis County Police Department	0	2	0	0	0	0	1	0	1	0	
Warren	1	0	0	0	0	0	0	0	1	0	
Nonmetropolitan Counties	2	0	0	0	0	0					
Laclede	1	0	0	0	0	0	0	0	0	1	
Taney	1	0	0	0	0	0	1	0	0	0	
MONTANA											
Total	9	4	2	0	0	0					
Cities	3	2	0	0	0	0					
Bozeman	0	2	0	0	0	0	1	0	1	0	46,728
Kalispell	2	0	0	0	0	0	0	2	0	0	23,243

Table 94. Hate Crime Incidents Per Bias Motivation and Quarter, by Selected State and Agency, 2017—Continued

(Number.)

State/agency	Number of incidents per bias motivation						Number of incidents per quarter				Population[1]
	Race/Ethnicity/Ancestry	Religion	Sexual orientation	Disability	Gender	Gender Identity	1st quarter	2nd quarter	3rd quarter	4th quarter	
Whitefish	1	0	0	0	0	0	0	0	1	0	7,446
Universities and Colleges	2	0	0	0	0	0					
Montana State University	1	0	0	0	0	0	1	0	0	0	16,359
University of Montana	1	0	0	0	0	0	0	0	0	1	12,419
Metropolitan Counties	3	1	1	0	0	0					
Cascade	1	0	0	0	0	0	1	0	0	0	
Missoula	1	1	0	0	0	0	0	0	2	0	
Yellowstone	1	0	1	0	0	0	1	1	0	0	
Nonmetropolitan Counties	1	1	1	0	0	0					
Deer Lodge	0	0	1	0	0	0	0	0	1	0	
Gallatin	1	0	0	0	0	0	0	0	1	0	
Ravalli	0	1	0	0	0	0	0	0	1	0	
NEBRASKA											
Total	34	6	4	1	0	0					
Cities	29	6	4	0	0	0					
Grand Island	1	0	1	0	0	0	0	1	0	1	51,980
Kearney	1	0	0	0	0	0	0	0	0	1	33,960
Lincoln	21	5	3	0	0	0	3	5	10	11	284,063
Norfolk	2	0	0	0	0	0	0	0	1	1	24,364
Omaha	2	1	0	0	0	0	1	1	1	0	449,388
South Sioux City	2	0	0	0	0	0	1	0	0	1	13,078
Metropolitan Counties	5	0	0	0	0	0					
Merrick	4	0	0	0	0	0	0	0	2	2	
Saunders	1	0	0	0	0	0	0	0	0	1	
Nonmetropolitan Counties	0	0	0	1	0	0					
Perkins	0	0	0	1	0	0	0	0	0	1	
NEVADA											
Total	2	0	3	0	0	0					
Cities	1	0	3	0	0	0					
Henderson	1	0	0	0	0	0	0	0	0	1	299,285
Reno	0	0	3	0	0	0	1	2	0	0	248,531
Other Agencies	1	0	0	0	0	0					
Clark County School District	1	0	0	0	0	0	0	0	1	0	
NEW HAMPSHIRE											
Total	8	4	1	0	0	0					
Cities	7	4	0	0	0	0					
Concord	1	0	0	0	0	0	0	1	0	0	42,942
Dover	1	0	0	0	0	0	1	0	0	0	31,344
Epping	0	1	0	0	0	0	1	0	0	0	6,978
Hudson	1	0	0	0	0	0	1	0	0	0	25,212
Keene	0	1	0	0	0	0	0	0	0	1	23,386
Laconia	1	0	0	0	0	0	0	1	0	0	16,616
Manchester	0	1	0	0	0	0	0	1	0	0	110,655
Pelham	1	0	0	0	0	0	0	0	1	0	13,513
Plymouth	0	1	0	0	0	0	0	0	0	1	6,303
Rye	1	0	0	0	0	0	0	1	0	0	5,425
Seabrook	1	0	0	0	0	0	0	1	0	0	8,816
Universities and Colleges	0	0	1	0	0	0					
University of New Hampshire	0	0	1	0	0	0	0	0	0	1	15,188
State Police Agencies	1	0	0	0	0	0					
State Police, Grafton County	1	0	0	0	0	0	0	1	0	0	
NEW JERSEY											
Total	260	180	51	4	0	0					
Cities	241	163	41	3	0	0					
Aberdeen Township	2	3	1	0	0	0	3	1	2	0	18,403
Belmar	0	0	1	0	0	0	0	1	0	0	5,666
Belvidere	1	0	0	0	0	0	0	0	0	1	2,589
Bergenfield	0	2	0	0	0	0	0	2	0	0	27,891
Berkeley Heights Township	1	0	0	0	0	0	0	0	1	0	13,654
Berkeley Township	0	1	0	0	0	0	0	0	1	0	42,036
Boonton	0	1	0	0	0	0	0	1	0	0	8,421
Bradley Beach	1	1	0	0	0	0	1	1	0	0	4,236
Brick Township	0	2	0	0	0	0	0	0	2	0	75,566
Bridgeton	1	0	0	0	0	0	0	1	0	0	24,937

Table 94. Hate Crime Incidents Per Bias Motivation and Quarter, by Selected State and Agency, 2017—Continued

(Number.)

State/agency	Number of incidents per bias motivation						Number of incidents per quarter				Population[1]
	Race/ Ethnicity/ Ancestry	Religion	Sexual orientation	Disability	Gender	Gender Identity	1st quarter	2nd quarter	3rd quarter	4th quarter	
Bridgewater Township	0	1	0	0	0	0	0	0	0	1	45,417
Brigantine	0	1	0	0	0	0	0	0	1	0	8,976
Burlington Township	1	0	0	0	0	0	0	1	0	0	22,772
Carteret	1	0	0	0	0	0	1	0	0	0	24,283
Chatham	0	1	0	0	0	0	0	1	0	0	9,011
Chatham Township	1	0	0	0	0	0	1	0	0	0	10,515
Cinnaminson Township	2	3	1	0	0	0	2	3	0	1	16,696
Collingswood	1	0	0	0	0	0	0	0	0	1	14,080
Colts Neck Township	2	0	0	0	0	0	2	0	0	0	9,936
Deal	0	2	0	0	0	0	0	2	0	0	730
Delanco Township	2	0	0	0	0	0	2	0	0	0	4,528
Dover	1	0	1	0	0	0	1	1	0	0	18,339
Eastampton Township	1	0	0	0	0	0	1	0	0	0	5,962
East Brunswick Township	11	13	0	0	0	0	4	13	5	2	49,019
East Hanover Township	2	1	0	0	0	0	1	2	0	0	11,284
East Orange	1	1	0	0	0	0	0	1	1	0	65,160
East Windsor Township	1	0	0	0	0	0	0	0	0	1	27,571
Eatontown	0	0	1	0	0	0	0	0	0	1	12,258
Edison Township	6	3	1	0	0	0	2	2	4	2	102,699
Egg Harbor Township	1	0	0	0	0	0	0	0	0	1	43,515
Elizabeth	0	1	0	0	0	0	1	0	0	0	129,726
Elmwood Park	1	0	0	0	0	0	0	0	0	1	20,515
Emerson	0	1	0	0	0	0	0	1	0	0	7,747
Englewood	8	1	0	0	0	0	0	1	0	8	28,795
Evesham Township	10	7	0	1	0	0	2	4	5	7	45,314
Fair Lawn	0	0	1	0	0	0	0	0	0	1	33,759
Fort Lee	1	0	1	0	0	0	0	1	1	0	38,095
Franklin Lakes	1	5	0	0	0	0	0	1	0	5	10,939
Franklin Township, Somerset County	1	0	0	0	0	0	1	0	0	0	67,463
Freehold Borough	1	0	0	0	0	0	0	0	0	1	11,865
Freehold Township	2	0	1	0	0	0	2	0	1	0	35,531
Hackensack	4	4	1	0	0	0	1	0	2	6	45,226
Hackettstown	1	0	0	0	0	0	1	0	0	0	9,520
Haddonfield	1	0	0	0	0	0	1	0	0	0	11,445
Haddon Township	2	0	0	0	0	0	1	1	0	0	14,731
Hamilton Township, Mercer County	5	0	0	0	0	0	1	1	1	2	88,723
Hanover Township	1	4	0	0	0	0	4	1	0	0	14,904
Harrison Township	0	0	1	0	0	0	0	0	0	1	13,128
Haworth	0	2	0	0	0	0	0	0	0	2	3,491
High Bridge	0	1	0	0	0	0	0	1	0	0	3,524
Highland Park	2	2	0	0	0	0	1	1	1	1	14,287
Hightstown	2	0	0	0	0	0	1	1	0	0	5,522
Hillsborough Township	3	1	0	0	0	0	1	2	0	1	40,369
Hoboken	3	3	0	0	0	0	4	1	0	1	55,348
Hopewell Township	1	0	2	0	0	0	1	2	0	0	18,633
Howell Township	7	4	0	0	0	0	4	2	4	1	52,432
Interlaken	0	0	1	0	0	0	0	1	0	0	798
Jefferson Township	1	0	0	0	0	0	1	0	0	0	21,505
Jersey City	0	0	1	0	0	0	1	0	0	0	267,906
Keansburg	8	1	1	0	0	0	0	1	7	2	9,782
Kinnelon	1	0	0	0	0	0	0	1	0	0	10,275
Lakewood Township	7	15	0	0	0	0	4	6	7	5	102,759
Lawrence Township, Mercer County	0	2	0	0	0	0	0	1	0	1	32,929
Lindenwold	0	0	1	0	0	0	0	0	0	1	17,516
Livingston Township	2	1	0	0	0	0	1	1	0	1	29,987
Lodi	2	0	3	0	0	0	3	1	0	1	24,981
Lopatcong Township	0	1	0	0	0	0	1	0	0	0	8,298
Lumberton Township	0	1	0	0	0	0	0	0	1	0	12,286
Madison	1	2	0	0	0	0	1	1	0	1	16,175
Magnolia	2	0	0	0	0	0	1	1	0	0	4,310
Manalapan Township	4	4	0	0	0	0	1	2	4	1	40,177
Manasquan	2	0	0	0	0	0	1	0	1	0	5,804
Manchester Township	1	0	0	0	0	0	1	0	0	0	43,916
Mansfield Township, Warren County	0	1	0	0	0	0	0	1	0	0	7,435
Mantua Township	1	0	0	0	0	0	0	0	0	1	15,123
Maple Shade Township	1	2	0	0	0	0	1	1	0	1	18,797
Maplewood Township	0	1	0	0	0	0	1	0	0	0	24,863
Medford Lakes	1	1	0	0	0	0	0	0	2	0	4,038
Medford Township	3	2	2	0	0	0	1	1	0	5	23,503
Metuchen	0	0	0	1	0	0	1	0	0	0	13,981
Middlesex Borough	1	1	0	0	0	0	1	0	1	0	13,897
Millburn Township	0	1	0	0	0	0	0	0	0	1	20,421
Monmouth Beach	0	1	0	0	0	0	0	0	0	1	3,213
Monroe Township, Middlesex County	0	3	0	0	0	0	0	0	0	3	45,722
Montclair	2	0	0	0	0	0	0	0	1	1	39,029
Montvale	0	1	0	0	0	0	1	0	0	0	8,653
Moorestown Township	4	1	0	0	0	0	1	2	1	1	20,534
Mount Laurel Township	0	0	1	0	0	0	1	0	0	0	41,712
Mount Olive Township	1	0	1	0	0	0	0	0	0	2	29,410
Mullica Township	1	0	0	0	0	0	0	0	0	1	6,024
Neptune Township	6	0	1	0	0	0	4	1	0	2	27,757

Table 94. Hate Crime Incidents Per Bias Motivation and Quarter, by Selected State and Agency, 2017—Continued

(Number.)

State/agency	Number of incidents per bias motivation						Number of incidents per quarter				Population[1]
	Race/ Ethnicity/ Ancestry	Religion	Sexual orientation	Disability	Gender	Gender Identity	1st quarter	2nd quarter	3rd quarter	4th quarter	
New Brunswick	1	0	2	0	0	0	2		1	1	57,481
Newton	0	1	1	0	0	0	0	0	1	1	7,874
North Bergen Township	0	1	0	0	0	0	1	0	0	0	63,490
Northfield	1	0	0	0	0	0	1	0	0	0	8,376
Oakland	0	1	0	0	0	0	0	0	0	1	13,243
Ocean Township, Monmouth County	3	3	0	0	0	0	1	3	2	0	26,637
Old Bridge Township	2	0	0	0	0	0	1	0	1	0	67,162
Old Tappan	0	1	0	0	0	0	0	0	1	0	6,069
Oradell	0	2	0	0	0	0	0	2	0	0	8,291
Palmyra	1	0	1	0	0	0	0	1	0	1	7,217
Paramus	1	1	0	0	0	0	1	0	1	0	27,075
Passaic	1	1	1	0	0	0	0	0	2	1	71,053
Paulsboro	1	0	0	0	0	0	0	0	1	0	5,959
Pennsville Township	1	0	0	0	0	0	0	0	1	0	12,564
Pequannock Township	0	1	0	0	0	0	1	0	0	0	15,472
Piscataway Township	0	1	0	0	0	0	1	0	0	0	58,109
Plainfield	0	1	0	0	0	0	1	0	0	0	50,983
Point Pleasant	0	1	0	0	0	0	1	0	0	0	18,696
Pompton Lakes	1	0	0	0	0	0	0	0	0	1	11,176
Princeton	8	7	0	0	0	0	1	6	5	3	31,845
Ramsey	1	1	0	0	0	0	0	0	1	1	15,273
Randolph Township	4	4	0	0	0	0	4	2	0	2	25,950
Ridgewood	0	4	0	0	0	0	0	0	3	1	25,729
River Edge	0	1	0	0	0	0	0	1	0	0	11,744
Robbinsville Township	3	0	0	0	0	0	1	0	2	0	14,446
Roselle Park	1	0	0	0	0	0	0	0	1	0	13,747
Shrewsbury	0	1	0	0	0	0	0	1	0	0	4,178
South Brunswick Township	1	2	1	0	0	0	2	0	1	1	46,280
South Orange Village	4	1	1	0	0	0	3	0	1	2	16,407
South Plainfield	1	0	0	0	0	0	1	0	0	0	24,458
South River	1	0	0	0	0	0	0	1	0	0	16,399
Springfield Township, Union County	1	0	0	0	0	0	1	0	0	0	17,805
Stone Harbor	0	0	2	0	0	0	0	1	1	0	827
Summit	0	1	0	0	0	0	0	1	0	0	22,195
Teaneck Township	2	1	0	0	0	0	0	1	1	1	41,377
Tenafly	0	1	0	0	0	0	0	1	0	0	14,960
Toms River Township	1	3	0	0	0	0	2	1	1	0	92,543
Trenton	0	1	0	0	0	0	1	0	0	0	84,231
Union City	1	0	0	0	0	0	0	1	0	0	70,053
Union Township	1	0	0	0	0	0	1	0	0	0	59,051
Verona	1	0	0	0	0	0	1	0	0	0	13,584
Vineland	8	0	1	0	0	0	1	0	4	4	60,477
Voorhees Township	1	0	0	0	0	0	0	0	1	0	29,532
Washington Township, Gloucester County	1	0	1	0	0	0	0	1	1	0	48,088
Washington Township, Warren County	1	0	0	0	0	0	0	1	0	0	6,429
Waterford Township	2	0	0	0	0	0	1	0	1	0	10,817
Weehawken Township	2	0	0	0	0	0	0	0	0	2	15,683
Westampton Township	2	0	0	0	0	0	0	1	1	0	8,775
West Long Branch	1	0	1	0	0	0	1	0	0	1	7,944
West New York	1	0	0	0	0	0	0	0	1	0	54,156
West Windsor Township	1	1	0	0	0	0	2	0	0	0	28,495
Wildwood	1	0	0	0	0	0	0	0	1	0	5,087
Willingboro Township	0	2	0	0	0	0	0	0	2	0	31,726
Woodbridge Township	0	2	0	0	0	0	1	0	0	1	102,129
Woodbury	27	1	4	1	0	0	4	10	14	5	9,970
Universities and Colleges	12	15	10	0	0	0					
Montclair State University	3	1	1	0	0	0	2	1	2		20,987
Princeton University	3	0	0	0	0	0				3	8,181
Rutgers University											
Newark	0	2	0	0	0	0				2	12,321
New Brunswick	4	12	9	0	0	0	6	7	3	9	50,146
Stockton University	2	0	0	0	0	0			2		8,728
Metropolitan Counties	3	1	0	0	0	0					
Bergen	1	1	0	0	0	0	2				
Cape May	1	0	0	0	0	0		1			
Warren	1	0	0	0	0	0				1	
State Police Agencies	4	1	0	1	0	0					
New Jersey State Police	4	1	0	1	0	0	4			2	
NEW MEXICO **Total**	4	2	1	0	0	0					
Cities	4	2	1	0	0	0					
Albuquerque	4	2	1	0	0	0			4	3	561,375
NEW YORK **Total**	189	284	64	1	0	14					

Table 94. Hate Crime Incidents Per Bias Motivation and Quarter, by Selected State and Agency, 2017—Continued

(Number.)

State/agency	Number of incidents per bias motivation						Number of incidents per quarter				Population[1]
	Race/ Ethnicity/ Ancestry	Religion	Sexual orientation	Disability	Gender	Gender Identity	1st quarter	2nd quarter	3rd quarter	4th quarter	
Cities	127	194	55	1	0	13					
Albany	4	0	0	0	0	0	0	0	2	2	98,174
Ardsley Village	0	1	0	0	0	0	1	0	0	0	4,663
Auburn	1	0	0	0	0	0	0	1	0	0	26,686
Brighton Town	0	1	0	0	0	0	0	0	1	0	36,596
Buffalo	6	0	2	0	0	0	2	4	2	0	256,169
Clarkstown Town	0	2	0	0	0	0	0	1	0	1	81,810
Croton-on-Hudson Village	0	0	0	1	0	0	0	1	0	0	8,271
Fishkill Town	1	0	0	0	0	0	0	1	0	0	21,532
Fulton City	1	0	0	0	0	0	0	1	0	0	11,321
Gates Town	1	0	0	0	0	0	0	0	0	1	28,723
Greenburgh Town	0	1	0	0	0	1	1	0	1	0	45,923
Hamburg Town	1	0	0	0	0	0	0	0	1	0	46,040
Hastings-on-Hudson Village	0	3	0	0	0	0	0	1	1	1	7,987
Hempstead Village	0	0	1	0	0	0	0	1	0	0	55,807
Ilion Village	1	0	0	0	0	0	0	0	1	0	7,801
Ithaca	2	0	0	0	0	0	0	1	1	0	30,875
Johnson City Village	1	0	0	0	0	0	0	0	1	0	14,595
Liberty Village	1	0	0	0	0	0	0	0	1	0	4,050
Middletown	0	1	0	0	0	0	0	0	1	0	27,607
Monroe Village	2	0	0	0	0	0	0	0	2	0	8,636
Mount Vernon	2	0	0	0	0	0	0	0	1	1	68,507
New Castle Town	1	1	0	0	0	0	2				18,189
New Paltz Town and Village	0	1	0	0	0	0	1	0	0	0	14,125
New Rochelle	4	1	0	0	0	0	2	0	1	2	79,960
New York	88	173	46	0	0	11	96	82	68	72	8,616,333
Niagara Falls	3	0	0	0	0	0	0	1	2	0	48,385
Port Jervis	0	0	1	0	0	0	0		1	0	8,527
Poughkeepsie	1	0	0	0	0	1	0	0	1	1	30,159
Ramapo Town	0	4	0	0	0	0	0	2	2	0	94,019
Rochester	1	0	2	0	0	0	0	2	1	0	208,591
Schodack Town	1	0	0	0	0	0	0	1	0	0	11,685
Scotia Village	0	0	1	0	0	0	1	0	0	0	7,651
Southampton Town	1	1	1	0	0	0	1	0	1	1	50,987
Spring Valley Village	0	1	0	0	0	0	0	1	0	0	32,795
Troy	0	0	1	0	0	0	1	0	0	0	49,644
Utica	0	1	0	0	0	0	0	0	1	0	60,395
White Plains	1	0	0	0	0	0	0	1	0	0	58,461
Yonkers	2	2	0	0	0	0	2	0	2	0	201,554
Universities and Colleges	5	7	2	0	0	0					
State University of New York Police											
Buffalo State College	0	0	1	0	0	0	1	0	0	0	9,475
Cobleskill	1	0	0	0	0	0	0	0	1	0	2,287
Delhi	0	1	0	0	0	0	0	0	0	1	3,511
Geneseo	1	0	1	0	0	0	1	0	1	0	5,602
Morrisville	2	3	0	0	0	0	0	0	1	4	3,003
New Paltz	0	2	0	0	0	0	0	0	0	2	7,628
Plattsburgh	1	1	0	0	0	0	2	0	0	0	5,520
Metropolitan Counties	18	54	3	0	0	0					
Nassau	9	28	0	0	0	0	14	9	9	5	
Putnam	1	0	0	0	0	0	1	0	0	0	
Suffolk County Police Department	7	26	3	0	0	0	10	13	10	3	
Warren	1	0	0	0	0	0	0	0	0	1	
Nonmetropolitan Counties	1	1	0	0	0	0					
Cattaraugus	1	0	0	0	0	0	0	0	0	1	
Chenango	0	1	0	0	0	0	0	0	1		
State Police Agencies	22	16	4	0	0	1					
State Police											
Albany County	2	0	0	0	0	0	1	0	0	1	
Clinton County	6	0	0	0	0	0	0	2	2	2	
Columbia County	1	0	2	0	0	0	0	3	0	0	
Duchess County	1	2	0	0	0	0	2	0	0	1	
Franklin County	1	0	0	0	0	0	0	0	0	1	
Genesee County	1	0	0	0	0	0	1	0	0	0	
Greene County	1	0	0	0	0	0	0	1	0	0	
Hamilton County	1	0	0	0	0	0	0	0	0	1	
Lewis County	1	0	0	0	0	0	0	0	1	0	
Oneida County	0	1	0	0	0	0	0	0	1	0	
Onondaga County	0	1	0	0	0	0	0	0	0	1	
Orange County	0	1	0	0	0	0	0	0	1	0	
Oswego County	0	1	0	0	0	1	1	0	0	1	
Putnam County	0	1	1	0	0	0	0	1	0	1	
Saratoga County	1	0	0	0	0	0	1	0	0	0	
Steuben County	1	0	0	0	0	0	0	0	1	0	
Sullivan County	1	2	0	0	0	0	0	2	1	0	
Tioga County	0	1	0	0	0	0	0	0	0	1	

Table 94. Hate Crime Incidents Per Bias Motivation and Quarter, by Selected State and Agency, 2017—Continued

(Number.)

State/agency	Number of incidents per bias motivation						Number of incidents per quarter				Population[1]
	Race/ Ethnicity/ Ancestry	Religion	Sexual orientation	Disability	Gender	Gender Identity	1st quarter	2nd quarter	3rd quarter	4th quarter	
Tompkins County	0	1	0	0	0	0	1	0	0	0	
Ulster County	1	1	0	0	0	0	1	0	1	0	
Wayne County	1	1	0	0	0	0	0	1	0	1	
Westchester County	2	3	1	0	0	0	4	1	0	1	
Other Agencies	16	12	0	0	0	0					
New York City Metropolitan Transportation Authority	16	12	0	0	0	0	11	1	7	9	
NORTH CAROLINA											
Total	114	24	24	4	0	0					
Cities	80	20	21	3	0	0					
Albemarle	1	0	0	0	0	0	0	1	0	0	16,022
Apex	1	1	0	0	0	0	2	0	0	0	49,159
Asheville	4	2	1	0	0	0	3	2	2	0	90,103
Benson	0	1	0	0	0	0	1	0	0	0	3,764
Chapel Hill	5	0	4	0	0	0	2	3	3	1	59,553
Charlotte-Mecklenburg	17	9	5	1	0	0	7	9	11	5	914,609
Concord	1	0	0	0	0	0	0	0	0	1	91,756
Durham	13	1	2	0	0	0	3	4	6	3	269,088
Fayetteville	3	1	2	1	0	0	2	2	1	2	205,432
Greensboro	4	1	1	0	0	0	0	1	2	3	290,051
Hertford	1	0	0	0	0	0	0	0	1	0	2,122
High Point	1	0	0	0	0	0	0	0	0	1	112,368
Jacksonville	2	0	0	0	0	0	0	0	1	1	67,293
Kannapolis	1	0	0	0	0	0	0	1	0	0	48,754
Marion	1	2	0	0	0	0	0	2	0	1	7,819
Monroe	0	0	0	1	0	0	0	0	1	0	35,153
New Bern	1	0	0	0	0	0	1	0	0	0	30,191
Raleigh	12	2	3	0	0	0	2	7	5	3	468,261
Roanoke Rapids	1	0	0	0	0	0	0	1	0	0	15,083
Salisbury	2	0	0	0	0	0	0	1	0	1	34,085
Siler City	3	0	0	0	0	0	1	0	1	1	8,531
Waynesville	1	0	0	0	0	0	0	0	1	0	9,977
Wilmington	5	0	1	0	0	0	1	1	2	2	119,422
Wilson	0	0	2	0	0	0	0	1	1	0	49,686
Universities and Colleges	3	0	1	0	0	0					
East Carolina University	1	0	1	0	0	0	0	0	0	2	28,962
North Carolina Central University	1	0	0	0	0	0	0	0	0	1	8,094
University of North Carolina, Pembroke	1	0	0	0	0	0	0	1	0	0	6,268
Metropolitan Counties	23	4	2	1	0	0					
Brunswick	1	0	0	0	0	0	1	0	0	0	
Buncombe	1	1	0	0	0	0	0	0	0	2	
Burke	3	0	0	0	0	0	0	3	0	0	
Caldwell	1	0	0	0	0	0	0	0	0	1	
Forsyth	4	0	1	0	0	0	1	1	2	1	
Franklin	0	1	0	1	0	0	1	1	0	0	
Gaston County Police Department	3	0	1	0	0	0	1	1	0	2	
Guilford	1	0	0	0	0	0	0	0	1	0	
New Hanover	2	2	0	0	0	0	0	1	3	0	
Pitt	4	0	0	0	0	0	0	1	1	2	
Randolph	1	0	0	0	0	0	0	0	1	0	
Wake	2	0	0	0	0	0	0	1	0	1	
Nonmetropolitan Counties	7	0	0	0	0	0					
Jackson	3	0	0	0	0	0	1	2	0	0	
Martin	2	0	0	0	0	0	0	0	2	0	
Surry	1	0	0	0	0	0	1	0	0	0	
Transylvania	1	0	0	0	0	0	0	1	0	0	
Other Agencies	1	0	0	0	0	0					
University of North Carolina Hospitals	1	0	0	0	0	0	1	0	0	0	
NORTH DAKOTA											
Total	8	5	2	0	0	0					
Cities	6	4	2	0	0	0					
Bismarck	2	1	1	0	0	0	0	3	1	0	74,397
Fargo	1	2	0	0	0	0	0	0	3	0	123,430
Grand Forks	2	0	0	0	0	0	0	1	1	0	58,090
Minot	1	0	1	0	0	0	0	2	0	0	50,118
Wahpeton	0	1	0	0	0	0	0	0	0	1	7,841
Metropolitan Counties	2	0	0	0	0	0					
Cass	1	0	0	0	0	0	0	1	0	0	
Morton	1	0	0	0	0	0	1	0	0	0	
Nonmetropolitan Counties	0	1	0	0	0	0					
McLean	0	1	0	0	0	0	0	0	1	0	

Table 94. Hate Crime Incidents Per Bias Motivation and Quarter, by Selected State and Agency, 2017—Continued

(Number.)

State/agency	Number of incidents per bias motivation						Number of incidents per quarter				Population[1]
	Race/ Ethnicity/ Ancestry	Religion	Sexual orientation	Disability	Gender	Gender Identity	1st quarter	2nd quarter	3rd quarter	4th quarter	
OHIO											
Total	259	35	53	31	0	2					
Cities	225	28	46	26	0	2					
Akron	10	0	0	4	0	0	4	5	4	1	197,412
Amelia	1	1	0	0	0	0	0	2	0	0	4,982
Ashland	1	0	0	0	0	0	0	0	0	1	20,485
Aurora	2	0	0	0	0	0	0	1	0	1	15,932
Austintown	1	0	0	0	0	0	0	1	0	0	35,303
Baltimore	1	0	0	0	0	0	0	0	0	1	2,973
Barberton	2	0	0	0	0	0	0	0	1	1	26,050
Beavercreek	1	0	0	0	0	0	0	0	1	0	46,572
Beaver Township	1	0	0	0	0	0	0	1	0	0	6,427
Bellefontaine	1	0	0	0	0	0	0	0	1	0	13,144
Blue Ash	1	0	0	0	0	0	0	1	0	0	12,248
Boardman	2	0	0	0	0	0	0	0	2	0	39,276
Brecksville	0	0	1	0	0	0	0	0	0	1	13,432
Butler Township	1	0	0	3	0	0	2	1	1	0	7,799
Canal Fulton	1	1	0	0	0	0	0	0	1	1	5,428
Cincinnati	31	5	4	1	0	0	6	15	13	7	299,116
Circleville	3	0	0	0	0	0	0	2	0	1	13,972
Cleveland	12	0	0	0	0	0	1	1	5	5	385,351
Colerain Township	3	1	0	0	0	0	1	3	0	0	58,996
Columbus	50	3	19	3	0	0	19	28	13	15	872,205
Copley Township	0	0	0	2	0	0	0	0	2	0	17,280
Dayton	1	0	1	0	0	0	0	1	1	0	140,171
Defiance	1	0	0	0	0	0	0	1	0	0	16,594
Englewood	0	0	1	1	0	0	1	1	0	0	13,504
Fairborn	2	0	0	0	0	0	1	1	0	0	33,936
Fairfax	1	0	0	0	0	0	0	0	0	1	1,702
Fairview Park	1	0	0	0	0	0	0	0	0	1	16,307
Findlay	2	0	1	0	0	0	0	0	2	1	41,474
Forest Park	1	0	0	0	0	0	0	0	1	0	18,665
Franklin	3	0	0	0	0	0	1	0	2	0	11,779
Gahanna	1	1	0	0	0	1	1	1	1	0	35,243
Garrettsville	1	0	0	0	0	0	0	0	0	1	2,321
Georgetown	2	0	0	0	0	0	0	0	0	2	4,356
Green Township	3	0	0	0	0	0	0	1	2	0	58,853
Grove City	1	0	0	1	0	0	1	1	0	0	40,421
Groveport	1	0	0	0	0	0	0	0	1	0	5,583
Hamilton	7	2	1	0	0	0	2	2	5	1	62,094
Hilliard	1	1	0	0	0	0	2	0	0	0	36,144
Holland	1	1	0	0	0	0	0	1	1	0	1,662
Howland Township	1	0	0	0	0	0	0	0	1	0	16,608
Huber Heights	0	0	0	1	0	0	0	0	1	0	37,996
Hudson	1	0	1	1	0	0	0	0	1	2	22,248
Ironton	1	0	0	0	0	0	0	0	0	1	10,853
Jackson	1	0	0	0	0	0	0	1	0	0	6,305
Jamestown	2	0	0	0	0	0	1	0	1	0	2,036
Lancaster	1	0	0	0	0	0	0	0	0	1	40,026
Lima	6	1	1	0	0	0	1	4	1	2	37,220
Logan	0	0	1	0	0	0	1	0	0	0	7,077
Lorain	1	1	0	0	0	0	1	1	0	0	63,672
Louisville	1	0	0	0	0	0	1	0	0	0	9,373
Loveland	1	0	0	0	0	0	0	0	0	1	12,846
Lyndhurst	2	1	0	0	0	0	0	1	1	1	13,586
Madison Township, Franklin County	0	1	0	1	0	0	1	1	0	0	18,661
Mansfield	3	0	2	0	0	0	1	2	1	1	46,507
Marietta	1	0	2	0	0	0	0	1	0	2	13,582
Marysville	0	0	1	0	0	0	1	0	0	0	23,622
Mason	3	0	0	0	0	0	1	2	0	0	33,406
Massillon	2	0	0	0	0	0	1	1	0		32,265
Medina Township	1	0	0	0	0	0	1	0	0	0	8,940
Mentor-on-the-Lake	0	1	0	0	0	0	1	0	0	0	7,359
Minster	1	0	0	0	0	0	1	0			2,866
Montgomery	0	1	0	0	0	0	0	1	0	0	10,638
Mount Healthy	1	0	0	0	0	0	0	0	0	1	6,020
Mount Vernon	0	1	0	0	0	0	0	1	0	0	16,553
New Albany	3	0	0	0	0	0	0	2	0	1	10,838
Newton Falls	0	0	1	0	0	0	1	0	0	0	4,567
North Canton	1	1	1	0	0	0	2	0	1	0	17,348
Oak Harbor	1	0	0	0	0	0	0	0	1	0	2,731
Ontario	0	0	0	1	0	0	0	1	0	0	6,058
Oxford	0	0	1	0	0	0	1	0	0	0	22,459
Parma	1	0	0	0	0	0	0	0	1	0	79,340
Perkins Township	1	0	0	0	0	0	0	1	0	0	11,773
Perry Township, Franklin County	0	1	0	0	0	0	1	0	0	0	3,758
Pickerington	0	1	0	0	0	0	0	0	0	1	20,373
Pierce Township	1	0	0	0	0	0	1	0	0	0	11,623
Portsmouth	0	0	0	1	0	0	0	1	0	0	20,451
Powell	1	0	0	0	0	0	0	0	0	1	13,029

Table 94. Hate Crime Incidents Per Bias Motivation and Quarter, by Selected State and Agency, 2017—Continued

(Number.)

State/agency	Race/ Ethnicity/ Ancestry	Religion	Sexual orientation	Disability	Gender	Gender Identity	1st quarter	2nd quarter	3rd quarter	4th quarter	Population[1]
Reading	1	0	0	0	0	0	0	0	0	1	10,307
Reynoldsburg	5	1	1	0	0	0	1	3	3	0	37,704
Rocky River	0	0	0	1	0	0	0	0	1	0	20,342
Sabina	2	0	0	0	0	0	0	2	0	0	2,534
Salem	2	0	0	0	0	0	0	1	0	1	11,887
Shelby	1	0	0	0	0	0	0	0	1	0	8,987
Sidney	0	0	1	0	0	0	0	1	0	0	20,466
South Euclid	0	0	0	1	0	0	0	0	1	0	21,628
Springfield Township, Hamilton County	1	0	2	0	0	1	0	1	0	3	36,571
Springfield Township, Summit County	1	0	0	0	0	0	1	0	0	0	14,434
St. Clair Township	0	0	0	1	0	0	0	0	0	1	7,583
Streetsboro	0	0	1	1	0	0	0	1	1	0	16,308
Sugarcreek Township	1	0	0	0	0	0	0	0	1	0	8,300
Sylvania Township	1	0	0	0	0	0	0	0	0	1	29,536
Tipp City	0	1	0	0	0	0	0	0	0	1	9,957
Toledo	2	0	0	0	0	0	1	0	0	1	277,116
Trotwood	1	0	0	0	0	0	1	0	0	0	24,308
Upper Arlington	1	0	0	0	0	0	0	1	0	0	35,214
Van Wert	1	0	0	0	0	0	0	1	0	0	10,713
Wadsworth	3	0	1	0	0	0	1	0	1	2	23,388
West Chester Township	1	0	0	0	0	0	0	1	0	0	61,386
Westerville	1	0	0	0	0	0	0	0	1	0	39,418
Whitehall	1	0	0	0	0	0	1	0	0	0	18,835
Willoughby	1	0	0	0	0	0	1	0	0	0	22,857
Wilmington	2	0	0	0	0	0	1	0	1	0	12,416
Wooster	0	0	0	1	0	0	0	1	0	0	27,172
Xenia	1	0	0	0	0	0	1	0	0	0	26,331
Zanesville	1	0	1	1	0	0	0	0	1	2	25,457
Universities and Colleges	6	1	2	0	0	0					
Bowling Green State University	2	0	0	0	0	0	2	0			17,644
Capital University	1	0	2	0	0	0	2	0	0	1	3,367
Columbus State Community College	0	1	0	0	0	0	0	0	1	0	27,109
Ohio State University, Columbus	3	0	0	0	0	0	1	0	1	1	59,482
Metropolitan Counties	14	4	2	3	0	0					
Belmont	1	0	0	0	0	0	0	0	0	1	
Butler	1	0	0	0	0	0	0	1	0	0	
Clark	1	1	0	0	0	0	0	1	1	0	
Clermont	1	0	0	0	0	0	0	0	0	1	
Fairfield	1	0	0	0	0	0	0	0	0	1	
Franklin	1	0	0	0	0	0	0	1	0	0	
Fulton	1	0	0	0	0	0	0	0	1	0	
Greene	0	1	0	0	0	0	0	0	1	0	
Hocking	0	1	0	0	0	0	0	0	0	1	
Lorain	1	0	0	0	0	0	0	0	1	0	
Lucas	2	0	0	0	0	0	0	1	1	0	
Madison	0	0	0	1	0	0	0	0	0	1	
Montgomery	3	0	2	0	0	0	1	2	0	2	
Perry	0	0	0	1	0	0	0	0	0	1	
Richland	1	0	0	0	0	0	0	0	0	1	
Stark	0	1	0	0	0	0	0	1	0	0	
Warren	0	0	0	1	0	0	0	1	0	0	
Nonmetropolitan Counties	11	2	3	1	0	0					
Ashland	3	0	0	0	0	0	2	0	1	0	
Athens	1	0	0	0	0	0	0	1	0	0	
Hardin	2	1	1	0	0	0	2	1	0	1	
Highland	1	0	0	0	0	0	0	0	1	0	
Logan	1	0	0	0	0	0	0	0	1	0	
Marion	0	0	1	1	0	0	1	1	0	0	
Ross	3	0	0	0	0	0	1	1	1	0	
Shelby	0	0	1	0	0	0	1	0	0	0	
Washington	0	1	0	0	0	0	0	1	0	0	
State Police Agencies	1	0	0	1	0	0					
Ohio State Highway Patrol	1	0	0	1	0	0	0	2	0	0	
Other Agencies	2	0	0	0	0	0					
Cleveland Metropolitan Park District	2	0	0	0	0	0	0	0	2	0	
OKLAHOMA											
Total	17	7	10	0	1	2					
Cities	10	5	7	0	1	1					
Catoosa	1	0	0	0	0	0	0	1	0	0	7,129
Chickasha	1	0	0	0	0	0	1	0	0	0	16,489
Collinsville	1	0	0	0	0	1	0	1	1	0	6,836
Fairland	0	1	0	0	0	0	1	0	0	0	1,051
Kellyville	0	0	1	0	0	0	0	0	0	1	1,147
Lawton	0	1	0	0	0	0	1	0	0	0	94,134

Table 94. Hate Crime Incidents Per Bias Motivation and Quarter, by Selected State and Agency, 2017—Continued

(Number.)

State/agency	Number of incidents per bias motivation						Number of incidents per quarter				Population[1]
	Race/ Ethnicity/ Ancestry	Religion	Sexual orientation	Disability	Gender	Gender Identity	1st quarter	2nd quarter	3rd quarter	4th quarter	
Luther	1	0	0	0	0	0	0	0	1	0	1,675
Marietta	0	1	0	0	0	0	1	0	0	0	2,782
Muldrow	1	0	1	0	0	0	0	1	1	0	3,250
Muskogee	1	0	0	0	0	0	1	0	0	0	38,199
Noble	0	0	1	0	0	0	0	0	1	0	6,799
Norman	1	0	1	0	1	0	1	0	1	1	124,074
Owasso	0	0	1	0	0	0	1	0	0	0	36,869
Sapulpa	0	1	0	0	0	0	0	0	1	0	21,062
Stillwater	0	1	1	0	0	0	0	2	0	0	50,159
Wagoner	1	0	0	0	0	0	0	0	1	0	8,931
Wewoka	1	0	1	0	0	0	0	1	0	1	3,390
Woodward	1	0	0	0	0	0	0	1	0	0	12,655
Universities and Colleges	1	0	0	0	0	1					
Langston University	0	0	0	0	0	1	0	0	0	1	2,420
Oklahoma State University, Main Campus	1	0	0	0	0	0	0	0	0	1	25,622
Metropolitan Counties	2	1	0	0	0	0					
Lincoln	1	0	0	0	0	0	0	1	0	0	
Tulsa	1	1	0	0	0	0	1	0	1	0	
Nonmetropolitan Counties	4	1	3	0	0	0					
Choctaw	0	0	1	0	0	0	0	0	0	1	
Delaware	0	1	2	0	0	0	1	1	1	0	
Kingfisher	2	0	0	0	0	0	0	1	0	1	
Marshall	1	0	0	0	0	0	0	0	1	0	
Payne	1	0	0	0	0	0	0	1	0	0	
OREGON											
Total	84	29	24	4	1	4					
Cities	79	29	20	3	1	4					
Albany	1	0	1	0	0	0	1	0	0	1	53,701
Ashland	1	1	1	0	0	0	1	0	1	1	21,908
Baker City	0	0	1	0	0	0	1	0	0	0	9,764
Beaverton	1	2	0	0	0	0	0	1	1	1	98,897
Canby	1	0	0	0	0	0	0	0	1	0	17,823
Central Point	1	0	0	0	0	0	0	1	0	0	18,525
Corvallis	3	0	1	0	0	0	0	2	1	1	57,576
Eugene	46	12	8	1	1	4	16	23	14	19	168,310
Gresham	0	0	1	1	0	0	0	1	1	0	112,466
Hillsboro	1	3	0	0	0	0	1	2	1	0	107,433
Klamath Falls	3	1	1	0	0	0	3	0	0	2	22,436
Newberg-Dundee	1	1	0	0	0	0	1	0	1	0	26,769
North Plains	1	0	0	0	0	0	0	0	1	0	2,158
Ontario	0	0	1	0	0	0	1	0	1	0	10,970
Oregon City	0	1	0	0	0	0	0	0	0	1	36,921
Portland	10	4	3	1	0	0	7	7	1	3	649,408
Salem	4	0	1	0	0	0	0	3	1	1	169,565
Sherwood	0	1	0	0	0	0	0	0	1	0	19,473
Springfield	1	0	0	0	0	0	0	0	0	1	62,318
Tigard	4	3	1	0	0	0	3	1	3	1	52,524
Universities and Colleges	0	0	1	0	0	0					
Portland State University	0	0	1	0	0	0	0	0	0	1	26,627
Metropolitan Counties	3	0	2	0	0	0					
Benton	1	0	0	0	0	0	0	0	0	1	
Columbia	1	0	0	0	0	0	0	0	1	0	
Lane	0	0	2	0	0	0	2	0	0	0	
Washington	1	0	0	0	0	0	0	1	0	0	
Nonmetropolitan Counties	0	0	1	1	0	0					
Crook	0	0	1	0	0	0	1	0	0	0	
Umatilla	0	0	0	1	0	0	1	0	0	0	
State Police Agencies	1	0	0	0	0	0					
State Police, Benton County	1	0	0	0	0	0	1	0	0	0	
Tribal Agencies	1	0	0	0	0	0					
Grand Ronde Tribal	1	0	0	0	0	0	0	1	0	0	
PENNSYLVANIA											
Total	52	17	6	0	0	3					
Cities	43	14	6	0	0	3					
Bethlehem	1	0	0	0	0	0	0	0	0	1	75,336
Carlisle	1	0	0	0	0	0	1	0	0	0	19,233
East Earl Township	1	0	0	0	0	0	0	1	0	0	6,838
Lower Windsor Township	1	0	0	0	0	0	1	0	0	0	7,500

Table 94. Hate Crime Incidents Per Bias Motivation and Quarter, by Selected State and Agency, 2017—Continued

(Number.)

State/agency	Number of incidents per bias motivation						Number of incidents per quarter				Population[1]
	Race/ Ethnicity/ Ancestry	Religion	Sexual orientation	Disability	Gender	Gender Identity	1st quarter	2nd quarter	3rd quarter	4th quarter	
Manor Township, Lancaster County	1	0	0	0	0	0	0	0	1	0	20,949
Murrysville	1	0	0	0	0	0	1	0	0	0	20,034
New Hope	0	0	1	0	0	0	0	0	0	1	2,492
Patton Township	1	0	0	0	0	0	0	0	1	0	16,100
Philadelphia	19	14	4	0	0	3	7	20	7	6	1,575,595
Pittsburgh	13	0	1	0	0	0	6	3	3	2	305,932
Richland Township, Cambria County	1	0	0	0	0	0	0	0	0	1	12,153
Selinsgrove	1	0	0	0	0	0	0	1	0	0	5,930
Washington Township, Franklin County	1	0	0	0	0	0	1	0	0	0	14,678
Wilkes-Barre	1	0	0	0	0	0	0	1	0	0	40,418
Universities and Colleges	4	2	0	0	0	0					
Elizabethtown College	1	0	0	0	0	0	0	0	0	1	1,784
Pennsylvania State University Brandywine	1	0	0	0	0	0	0	0	0	1	1,379
University Park	2	1	0	0	0	0	0	0	1	2	47,789
University of Pittsburgh, Pittsburgh	0	1	0	0	0	0	1	0	0	0	28,664
State Police Agencies	5	1	0	0	0	0					
State Police											
Centre County	1	0	0	0	0	0	0	0	1	0	
Chester County	1	0	0	0	0	0	0	1		0	
Cumberland County	1	0	0	0	0	0	0	0	1		
Erie County	1	0	0	0	0	0	0	0	1	0	
Skippack	1	1	0	0	0	0	0	1	0	1	
RHODE ISLAND											
Total	5	4	2	0	0	0					
Cities	5	4	2	0	0	0					
Coventry	1	0	0	0	0	0	0	0	1	0	35,083
East Providence	0	3	0	0	0	0	0	1	2	0	47,502
Johnston	1	0	0	0	0	0	0	1	0	0	29,375
Providence	3	1	2	0	0	0	1	2	3	0	179,854
SOUTH CAROLINA											
Total	63	11	12	1	0	0					
Cities	36	3	5	0	0	0					
Abbeville	0	0	1	0	0	0	0	0	0	1	5,153
Andrews	7	0	0	0	0	0	4	2	1	0	2,903
Beaufort	4	0	0	0	0	0	0	0	4	0	13,612
Cayce	3	0	0	0	0	0	0	3	0	0	14,434
Charleston	1	0	0	0	0	0	0	0	1	0	136,845
Chester	1	0	0	0	0	0	1	0	0	0	5,452
Denmark	3	0	0	0	0	0	0	0	0	3	2,942
Elloree	1	0	0	0	0	0	0	0	0	1	666
Greeleyville	1	0	0	0	0	0	1	0	0	0	400
Greenville	0	1	1	0	0	0	0	0	2	0	68,922
Hartsville	1	0	1	0	0	0	0	0	1	1	7,769
Irmo	1	0	0	0	0	0	0	0	1	0	12,353
Laurens	1	0	0	0	0	0	0	0	0	1	9,089
Moncks Corner	3	1	1	0	0	0	2	2	1	0	10,818
Myrtle Beach	0	0	1	0	0	0	0	0	1	0	33,167
North Charleston	1	0	0	0	0	0	0	0	0	1	111,305
Orangeburg	1	0	0	0	0	0	0	1	0	0	13,076
Pickens	1	0	0	0	0	0	0	0	1	0	3,201
St. George	1	0	0	0	0	0	0	0	1	0	2,181
Sullivans Island	0	1	0	0	0	0	0	1	0	0	1,961
Union	2	0	0	0	0	0	2	0	0	0	7,940
Westminster	1	0	0	0	0	0	0	0	0	1	2,514
Winnsboro	2	0	0	0	0	0	0	1	1	0	3,276
Universities and Colleges	4	0	0	0	0	0					
Benedict College	1	0	0	0	0	0	0	0	0	1	2,281
Clemson University	1	0	0	0	0	0	1	0	0	0	23,406
Medical University of South Carolina	1	0	0	0	0	0	1	0	0	0	2,986
The Citadel	1	0	0	0	0	0	0	1	0	0	3,602
Metropolitan Counties	5	2	4	0	0	0					
Beaufort	1	1	1	0	0	0	1	0	1	1	
Greenville	1	0	0	0	0	0	0	0	0	1	
Horry County Police Department	0	0	1	0	0	0	0	0	1	0	
Laurens	2	0	0	0	0	0	0	1	0	1	
Richland	1	1	1	0	0	0	1	0	1	1	
Sumter	0	0	1	0	0	0	1	0	0	0	
Nonmetropolitan Counties	17	6	3	1	0	0					
Abbeville	1	0	0	0	0	0	0	0	1	0	
Bamberg	0	4	0	0	0	0	2	1	0	1	
Chesterfield	4	0	0	0	0	0	1	3	0	0	

Table 94. Hate Crime Incidents Per Bias Motivation and Quarter, by Selected State and Agency, 2017—Continued

(Number.)

State/agency	Number of incidents per bias motivation						Number of incidents per quarter				Population[1]
	Race/Ethnicity/Ancestry	Religion	Sexual orientation	Disability	Gender	Gender Identity	1st quarter	2nd quarter	3rd quarter	4th quarter	
Clarendon	0	0	1	0	0	0	0	0	0	1	
Colleton	2	0	0	0	0	0	0	1	0	1	
Dillon	1	0	0	0	0	0	0	0	0	1	
Georgetown	0	1	0	0	0	0	0	0	0	1	
Greenwood	1	0	0	0	0	0	0	0	0	1	
Hampton	0	0	1	0	0	0	0	0	1	0	
Marion	0	0	1	0	0	0	0	0	0	1	
Orangeburg	7	1	0	1	0	0	3	1	2	3	
Williamsburg	1	0	0	0	0	0	1	0	0	0	
Other Agencies	1	0	0	0	0	0					
Lexington County Medical Center	1	0	0	0	0	0	0	0	0	1	
SOUTH DAKOTA											
Total	8	4	3	2	0	0					
Cities	5	2	2	0	0	0					
Brookings	2	0	0	0	0	0	0	1	0	1	24,198
Rapid City	1	0	0	0	0	0	0	1	0	0	74,986
Sioux Falls	1	2	2	0	0	0	2	2	0	1	177,888
Spearfish	1	0	0	0	0	0	1	0	0	0	11,697
Metropolitan Counties	3	0	1	1	0	0					
Custer	1	0	0	0	0	0	0	0	1	0	
McCook	0	0	1	0	0	0	0	0	0	1	
Minnehaha	1	0	0	0	0	0	1	0	0	0	
Pennington	1	0	0	0	0	0	0	0	0	1	
Union	0	0	0	1	0	0	1	0	0	0	
Nonmetropolitan Counties	0	2	0	1	0	0					
Brookings	0	2	0	1	0	0	0	0	3	0	
TENNESSEE											
Total	88	18	21	7	2	0					
Cities	61	9	21	6	2	0					
Adamsville	0	0	1	0	0	0	0	0	0	1	2,207
Alcoa	0	1	0	0	0	0	0	0	0	1	10,128
Bartlett	1	0	0	0	0	0	0	0	1	0	58,895
Bolivar	0	1	0	0	0	0	1	0	0	0	5,066
Brighton	1	0	0	0	0	0	1	0	0	0	2,949
Brownsville	1	0	0	0	0	0	1	0	0	0	9,698
Centerville	1	0	0	0	0	0	1	0	0	0	3,564
Chattanooga	3	0	1	0	0	0	2	1	1	0	178,753
Clarksville	2	0	2	0	0	0	1	1	2	0	153,294
Cleveland	7	0	0	0	0	0	0	3	0	4	44,778
Collierville	4	0	0	0	0	0	0	0	4	0	49,790
Covington	2	0	0	1	0	0	0	1	2	0	8,909
Crossville	1	0	0	0	0	0	0	1	0	0	11,555
Fairview	1	0	0	0	0	0	0	1	0	0	8,648
Germantown	1	0	0	0	1	0	0	1	0	1	39,086
Greenbrier	0	0	1	0	0	0	1	0	0	0	6,853
Greeneville	0	0	0	1	0	0	0	0	1	0	15,065
Jackson	3	0	2	0	0	0	1	3	1	0	67,031
Jamestown	0	0	1	1	0	0	1	0	1	0	1,964
Jonesborough	0	0	0	1	0	0	0	1	0	0	5,378
Knoxville	2	0	3	0	0	0	2	0	3	0	187,539
Lebanon	5	0	0	0	0	0	1	2	2	0	32,248
Manchester	1	0	0	0	0	0	0	0	0	1	10,702
McMinnville	1	1	0	0	0	0	0	1	1	0	13,786
Memphis	4	0	3	0	0	0	1	4	0	2	652,765
Milan	2	1	1	0	1	0	2	1	0	2	7,780
Millington	3	0	1	0	0	0	0	0	2	2	10,944
Morristown	3	0	0	0	0	0	0	1	2	0	29,774
Murfreesboro	0	0	0	1	0	0	1	0	0	0	136,102
Nashville Metropolitan	11	5	3	0	0	0	6	3	6	4	674,942
Ripley	0	0	1	0	0	0	0	0	1	0	8,067
Rogersville	1	0	0	0	0	0	0	0	1	0	4,367
Smyrna	0	0	1	0	0	0	0	0	0	1	50,091
White Bluff	0	0	0	1	0	0	0	1	0	0	3,483
Universities and Colleges	3	0	0	0	0	0					
Chattanooga State Community College	1	0	0	0	0	0	0	0	1	0	8,628
Tennessee Technological University	1	0	0	0	0	0	1	0	0	0	10,493
University of the South	1	0	0	0	0	0	0	0	0	1	1,815
Metropolitan Counties	10	5	0	0	0	0					
Anderson	1	0	0	0	0	0	0	1	0	0	
Cheatham	1	0	0	0	0	0	0	1	0	0	
Hamilton	1	2	0	0	0	0	0	0	3	0	
Hickman	0	1	0	0	0	0	0	0	1	0	
Knox	2	0	0	0	0	0	0	0	1	1	

Table 94. Hate Crime Incidents Per Bias Motivation and Quarter, by Selected State and Agency, 2017—Continued

(Number.)

State/agency	Number of incidents per bias motivation						Number of incidents per quarter				Population[1]
	Race/Ethnicity/Ancestry	Religion	Sexual orientation	Disability	Gender	Gender Identity	1st quarter	2nd quarter	3rd quarter	4th quarter	
Montgomery	0	1	0	0	0	0	0	0	0	1	
Rutherford	1	1	0	0	0	0	0	1	1	0	
Shelby	2	0	0	0	0	0	0	0	2	0	
Sullivan	1	0	0	0	0	0	0	0	1	0	
Washington	1	0	0	0	0	0	0	0	1	0	
Nonmetropolitan Counties	6	3	0	0	0	0					
Benton	0	2	0	0	0	0	0	0	2	0	
Claiborne	1	0	0	0	0	0	0	0	0	1	
Coffee	1	0	0	0	0	0	1	0	0	0	
Gibson	1	0	0	0	0	0	0	1	0	0	
Hardin	1	0	0	0	0	0	0	0	1	0	
McMinn	1	0	0	0	0	0	0	0	1	0	
Monroe	0	1	0	0	0	0	0	0	1	0	
Rhea	1	0	0	0	0	0	0	0	1	0	
State Police Agencies	8	1	0	0	0	0					
Department of Safety	8	1	0	0	0	0	0	2	5	2	
Other Agencies	0	0	0	1	0	0					
Tennessee Bureau of Investigation	0	0	0	1	0	0	0	0	1	0	
TEXAS											
Total	117	22	43	3	1	6					
Cities	104	20	38	3	0	6					
Abilene	3	0	0	0	0	0	0	1	2	0	122,981
Alvin	1	0	0	0	0	0	0	0	0	1	26,488
Arlington	4	2	1	0	0	0	0	1	0	6	397,377
Aubrey	0	0	1	0	0	0	1	0	0	0	3,535
Austin	10	3	4	0	0	1	5	4	4	5	971,949
Balch Springs	1	0	0	0	0	0	0	0	1	0	25,199
Beaumont	1	0	0	0	0	0	0	1	0	0	118,456
Bedford	1	0	0	0	0	0	1	0	0	0	49,947
Bellmead	1	0	0	0	0	0	0	1	0	0	10,371
Brownwood	1	0	0	0	0	0	1	0	0	0	19,133
Burkburnett	1	0	1	0	0	0	0	0	1	1	11,142
Burleson	2	0	0	0	0	0	1	0	0	1	46,531
Burnet	0	0	1	0	0	0	1	0	0	0	6,422
Cedar Park	2	0	0	0	0	0	0	1	1	0	72,143
Corsicana	0	0	1	0	0	0	0	0	0	1	24,011
Dallas	2	0	12	0	0	0	1	1	2	10	1,338,551
Decatur	1	0	0	0	0	0	0	0	0	1	6,755
Denton	1	1	2	0	0	0	0	0	3	1	136,836
Devine	3	0	0	0	0	0	0	0	0	3	4,847
Dumas	1	0	0	0	0	0	0	0	0	1	14,943
El Paso	4	0	0	0	0	0	4	0	0	0	688,667
Flower Mound	2	0	1	0	0	0	0	0	0	3	75,101
Fort Worth	7	2	4	0	0	0	2	1	7	3	873,069
Frisco	1	0	0	0	0	0	0	0	1	0	172,804
Galena Park	1	1	0	0	0	0	0	1	0	1	11,091
Galveston	2	0	1	0	0	0	0	3	0	0	51,021
Giddings	1	0	0	0	0	0	0	0	0	1	5,154
Greenville	1	0	0	0	0	0	0	0	1	0	27,434
Henderson	0	0	0	0	0	1	0	1	0	0	13,366
Hewitt	0	0	1	0	0	0	1	0	0	0	14,443
Hitchcock	1	0	0	1	0	0	0	0	0	2	7,949
Houston	2	3	1	0	0	2	2	1	2	3	2,338,235
Iowa Park	1	1	0	0	0	0	0	0	0	2	6,361
Jacksonville	1	0	0	0	0	0	0	0	0	1	14,955
Keene	2	0	0	0	0	0	1	1	0	0	6,334
Lacy-Lakeview	1	0	0	0	0	0	0	1	0	0	6,633
Lampasas	2	0	0	0	0	0	0	0	0	2	7,910
League City	3	0	0	0	0	0	1	1	0	1	105,351
Leon Valley	2	0	0	0	0	0	0	2	0	0	11,508
Longview[2]	1	2	3	0	0	1	0	3	0	3	82,303
Lubbock	2	0	0	0	0	0	0	0	0	2	256,335
Marble Falls	1	0	0	0	0	0	1	0	0	0	6,358
McKinney	4	1	0	0	0	0	2	1	2	0	179,934
Odessa	2	1	2	1	0	0	2	2	1	1	121,194
Palestine	1	0	0	0	0	0	0	0	0	1	18,316
Pampa	1	0	0	0	0	0	0	1	0	0	17,736
Pearland	1	0	0	0	0	0	0	0	0	4	117,869
Pflugerville	4	0	0	0	0	0	1	2	0	0	61,212
Plano	2	0	0	0	0	1	1	2	0	0	290,413
Rockwall	1	0	0	1	0	0	0	0	1	1	44,599
Round Rock	1	0	0	0	0	0	0	1	0	0	124,617
Rusk	2	0	0	0	0	0	0	0	1	1	5,576
Sachse	1	0	0	0	0	0	0	0	1	0	25,907
San Angelo	1	0	0	0	0	0	1	0	0	0	101,931
San Antonio	2	1	1	0	0	0	1	2	0	1	1,520,712

Table 94. Hate Crime Incidents Per Bias Motivation and Quarter, by Selected State and Agency, 2017—Continued

(Number.)

State/agency	Number of incidents per bias motivation						Number of incidents per quarter				Population[1]
	Race/ Ethnicity/ Ancestry	Religion	Sexual orientation	Disability	Gender	Gender Identity	1st quarter	2nd quarter	3rd quarter	4th quarter	
San Saba	0	1	0	0	0	0	0	0	0	1	3,071
Schulenburg	0	1	0	0	0	0	0	0	1	0	2,943
Seven Points	1	0	1	0	0	0	1	0	0	1	1,462
Silsbee	1	0	0	0	0	0	0	0	1	0	6,747
Temple	2	0	0	0	0	0	0	0	0	2	74,794
Thorndale	1	0	0	0	0	0	0	0	1	0	1,293
Victoria	1	0	0	0	0	0	0	1	0	0	68,544
Wolfforth	1	0	0	0	0	0	0	0	1	0	4,552
Universities and Colleges	0	0	2	0	0	0					
South Plains College	0	0	1	0	0	0	0	0	0	1	9,478
Texas Tech University, Lubbock	0	0	1	0	0	0			0	1	36,551
Metropolitan Counties	9	1	3	0	0	0					
Austin	1	0	0	0	0	0	0	0	1	0	
Fort Bend	3	0	0	0	0	0	1	1	0	1	
Kaufman	1	0	0	0	0	0	0	0	0	1	
Travis	2	1	3	0	0	0	2	2	0	2	
Webb	1	0	0	0	0	0	0	0	1	0	
Williamson	1	0	0	0	0	0	0	0	1	0	
Nonmetropolitan Counties	3	0	0	0	1	0					
Cherokee	1	0	0	0	0	0	0	0	1		
Floyd[2]	2	0	0	0	1	0	0	0	1	1	
Other Agencies	1	1	0	0	0	0					
Independent School District											
Austin	0	1	0	0	0	0	0	0	0	1	
Pflugerville	1	0	0	0	0	0			0	1	
UTAH											
Total	51	15	8	0	0	4					
Cities	32	10	4	0	0	2					
Bountiful	7	0	0	0	0	0	2	3	0	2	44,312
Draper	1	0	0	0	0	0	0	0	0	1	48,197
Kaysville	1	1	0	0	0	0	2	0	0	0	31,873
Layton	2	2	0	0	0	0	1	0	2	1	77,048
Logan	0	0	1	0	0	0	0	0	0	1	51,059
Moab	1	0	0	0	0	0	0	0	1	0	5,266
Ogden	2	1	1	0	0	0	1	1	2	0	87,323
Pleasant View	1	0	0	0	0	0	0	0	0	1	10,036
Price	1	1	0	0	0	2	2	2	0	0	8,313
Roosevelt	1	0	0	0	0	0	0	0	0	1	7,057
Roy	2	0	0	0	0	0	2	0	0	0	38,410
Salt Lake City	2	1	1	0	0	0	0	1	1	2	194,968
South Jordan	2	2	0	0	0	0	1	1	1	1	72,533
South Ogden	0	1	0	0	0	0	0	0	1	0	17,177
South Salt Lake	1	0	0	0	0	0	0	0	1	0	24,811
St. George	4	0	0	0	0	0	3	0	0	1	84,007
Washington	1	0	1	0	0	0	1	0	0	1	26,618
West Jordan	0	1	0	0	0	0	0	0	0	1	115,390
West Valley	3	0	0	0	0	0	0	1	2	0	137,762
Metropolitan Counties	1	3	1	0	0	0					
Davis	0	0	1	0	0	0	0	0	0	1	
Salt Lake County Unified Police Department	0	3	0	0	0	0	1	0	1	1	
Weber	1	0	0	0	0	0	0	0	1	0	
Nonmetropolitan Counties	5	1	2	0	0	0					
Carbon	0	1	1	0	0	0	0	0	0	2	
Duchesne	1	0	0	0	0	0	0	1	0	0	
Uintah	4	0	1	0	0	0	1	2	1	1	
Nonmetropolitan Counties	13	1	1	0	0	2					
Utah Transit Authority	11	1	1	0	0	2	4	5	3	3	
Weber Morgan Narcotics Strike Force	2	0	0	0	0	0	0	1	0	1	
VERMONT											
Total	18	6	8	3	0	0					
Cities	15	4	8	2	0	0					
Brattleboro[2]	2	0	1	0	0	0	1	0	1	0	11,536
Bristol	0	1	0	0	0	0	0	1	0	0	3,908
Burlington	4	1	2	0	0	0	1	1	5	0	42,230
Colchester	1	0	0	0	0	0	0	0	1	0	17,353
Dover	0	0	1	0	0	0	0	0	0	1	1,076
Essex	0	0	1	0	0	0	0	0	0	1	21,470
Hartford	1	0	0	1	0	0	0	0	1	1	9,628

Table 94. Hate Crime Incidents Per Bias Motivation and Quarter, by Selected State and Agency, 2017—Continued

(Number.)

State/agency	Number of incidents per bias motivation						Number of incidents per quarter				Population[1]
	Race/ Ethnicity/ Ancestry	Religion	Sexual orientation	Disability	Gender	Gender Identity	1st quarter	2nd quarter	3rd quarter	4th quarter	
Middlebury	1	0	0	0	0	0	0	0	0	1	8,681
Newport	0	0	1	0	0	0	0	1	0	0	4,287
Rutland	0	0	1	0	0	0	0	0	0	1	15,462
South Burlington	1	0	0	0	0	0	0	1	0	0	19,146
St. Albans	1	2	0	1	0	0	0	1	1	2	6,772
St. Johnsbury	1	0	0	0	0	0	0	1	0	0	7,196
Williston	3	0	0	0	0	0	3	0	0	0	9,731
Winooski	0	0	1	0	0	0	0	1	0	0	7,105
Universities and Colleges	2	2	0	1	0	0					
University of Vermont	2	2	0	1	0	0	1	2	1	1	13,105
Metropolitan Counties	1	0	0	0	0	0					
Franklin	1	0	0	0	0	0	0	0	0	1	
VIRGINIA											
Total	109	42	35	7	0	0					
Cities	41	10	9	1	0	0					
Alexandria	1	2	2	0	0	0	3	2	0	0	158,256
Altavista	0	0	1	0	0	0	1	0	0	0	3,470
Bedford	1	0	0	0	0	0	0	0	0	1	6,622
Blacksburg	0	1	0	0	0	0	1	0	0	0	45,443
Charlottesville	1	0	0	0	0	0	0	0	0	1	47,446
Chesapeake	6	0	0	0	0	0	1	0	1	4	240,119
Christiansburg	1	0	0	0	0	0	0	0	0	1	22,272
Emporia	1	0	0	0	0	0	1	0	0	0	5,201
Farmville	0	1	0	0	0	0	0	0	1	0	8,127
Front Royal	0	0	1	0	0	0	0	1	0	0	15,270
Hampton	3	0	0	0	0	0	0	1	1	1	134,929
Harrisonburg	2	0	0	0	0	0	0	2	0	0	53,717
Leesburg	4	2	0	0	0	0	1	3	1	1	54,393
Lynchburg	2	0	0	0	0	0	1	1	0	0	80,890
Manassas	1	0	0	0	0	0	1	0	0	0	41,995
Manassas Park	1	0	0	0	0	0	1	0	0	0	16,158
Marion	1	0	0	0	0	0	0	0	1	0	5,837
Newport News	2	1	1	0	0	0	3	0	1	0	181,738
Norfolk	1	0	1	0	0	0	0	0	1	1	245,190
Petersburg	1	0	0	0	0	0	1	0	0	0	31,739
Portsmouth	3	0	1	0	0	0	1	2	1	0	95,100
Purcellville	0	1	0	0	0	0	0	0	1	0	9,779
Richmond	2	0	0	0	0	0	1	0	0	1	226,236
Suffolk	1	0	2	0	0	0	0	1	2	0	89,922
Vienna	1	0	0	0	0	0	0	0	0	1	16,590
Vinton	0	1	0	0	0	0	0	0	1	0	8,207
Virginia Beach	5	1	0	1	0	0	2	4	1	0	454,353
Universities and Colleges	6	4	1	0	0	0					
George Mason University	3	0	0	0	0	0	0	1	2	0	34,909
Northern Virginia Community College	1	2	0	0	0	0	2	1	0	0	50,835
University of Mary Washington	0	2	1	0	0	0	1	0	2	0	4,726
Virginia Polytechnic Institute and State University	2	0	0	0	0	0	0	1	0	1	33,170
Metropolitan Counties	56	27	20	1	0	0					
Albemarle County Police Department	2	0	0	0	0	0	0	2	0	0	
Amelia	2	0	0	0	0	0	1	1	0	0	
Arlington County Police Department	2	2	0	0	0	0	1	1	2	0	
Bedford	0	0	0	1	0	0	0	1	0	0	
Chesterfield County Police Department	6	1	2	0	0	0	2	3	3	1	
Clarke	2	0	1	0	0	0	0	0	3	0	
Fairfax County Police Department	17	11	8	0	0	0	11	5	11	9	
Fauquier	3	0	0	0	0	0	1	0	1	1	
Franklin	1	0	1	0	0	0	0	0	2	0	
Frederick	2	0	0	0	0	0	0	1	0	1	
Gloucester	1	1	0	0	0	0	2	0	0	0	
Goochland	0	1	0	0	0	0	0	1	0	0	
Henrico County Police Department	1	0	0	0	0	0	1	0	0	0	
Loudoun	7	5	4	0	0	0	5	5	4	2	
Prince George County Police Department	0	0	1	0	0	0	0	0	0	1	
Prince William County Police Department	2	2	0	0	0	0	0	3	0	1	
Rockingham	1	0	1	0	0	0	0	1	1	0	
Spotsylvania	2	3	2	0	0	0	2	3	2	0	
Stafford	4	1	0	0	0	0	1	3	0	1	
York	1	0	0	0	0	0	0	1	0	0	
Nonmetropolitan Counties	4	1	1	0	0	0					
King and Queen	1	0	0	0	0	0	1	0	0	0	

Table 94. Hate Crime Incidents Per Bias Motivation and Quarter, by Selected State and Agency, 2017—Continued

(Number.)

State/agency	Number of incidents per bias motivation						Number of incidents per quarter				Population[1]
	Race/ Ethnicity/ Ancestry	Religion	Sexual orientation	Disability	Gender	Gender Identity	1st quarter	2nd quarter	3rd quarter	4th quarter	
Louisa	1	0	0	0	0	0	0	0	1	0	
Madison	0	1	0	0	0	0	1	0	0	0	
Page	2	0	0	0	0	0	1	0	0	1	
Westmoreland	0	0	1	0	0	0	1	0	0	0	
State Police Agencies	2	0	4	5	0	0					
State Police											
Amherst County	0	0	0	3	0	0	0	0	2	1	
Frederick County	0	0	1	0	0	0	0	1	0	0	
Halifax County	0	0	0	1	0	0	1	0	0	0	
Harrisonburg	0	0	1	0	0	0	0	0	0	1	
Henrico County	0	0	1	0	0	0	0	0	0	1	
Rockbridge County	1	0	0	0	0	0	1	0	0	0	
Washington County	0	0	1	0	0	0	0	1	0	0	
Westmoreland County	0	0	0	1	0	0	0	0	0	1	
Winchester	1	0	0	0	0	0	1	0	0	0	
WASHINGTON											
Total	323	88	79	1	6	16					
Cities	274	76	75	1	4	15					
Aberdeen	0	0	1	0	0	0	0	1	0	0	16,243
Arlington	1	0	0	0	0	0	0	1	0	0	19,302
Auburn	4	0	1	0	0	0	0	3	2	0	78,718
Battle Ground	1	0	0	0	0	0	1	0	0	0	20,516
Bellevue	11	4	0	0	0	1	3	3	6	4	143,703
Bellingham	9	0	1	0	1	0	0	5	3	3	88,652
Bremerton	0	0	1	0	0	0	1	0	0	0	41,173
Burien	3	0	0	0	0	0	2	0	1		51,479
Centralia	0	1	0	0	0	0	0	0	0	1	17,048
Darrington	1	0	0	0	0	0	1	0	0	0	1,391
Dupont	1	0	0	0	0	0	1	0	0	0	9,721
Edmonds	6	0	0	0	0	0	1	4	0	1	42,197
Ellensburg	0	1	0	0	0	0	0	0	0	1	20,026
Everett	5	0	1	0	0	0	2	1	2	1	110,040
Federal Way	0	1	0	0	0	0	0	0	1	0	98,014
Fife	2	0	0	0	0	0	0	1	1	0	10,264
Forks	1	0	0	0	0	0	0	0	0	1	3,822
Hoquiam	1	0	0	0	0	0	1	0	0	0	8,386
Issaquah	2	2	1	0	0	0	0	2	2	1	38,592
Kelso	1	0	0	0	0	0	0	0	0	1	12,070
Kent	13	2	0	0	0	0	5	5	3	2	128,990
Kirkland	4	1	0	0	0	0	1	2	1	1	88,898
Lacey	1	0	0	0	1	0	0	2	0	0	48,597
Lake Stevens	1	0	1	0	0	0	1	0	0	1	32,288
Lakewood	1	0	0	0	0	0	0	1	0	0	61,080
Lynnwood	1	0	0	0	0	0	1	0	0	0	38,469
Marysville	2	2	0	0	0	0	1	2	1	0	68,950
Mill Creek	0	0	1	0	0	1	0	1	0	1	20,664
Monroe	3	1	0	0	0	0	0	1	2	1	18,596
Mount Vernon	5	0	0	0	0	0	1	3	0	1	35,085
Mukilteo	0	1	0	0	0	0	0	1	0	0	21,662
Oak Harbor	1	0	0	0	0	0	0	1	0	0	23,371
Olympia	3	0	0	0	0	1	2	2	0	0	51,923
Orting	2	2	0	0	0	0	2	0	1	1	7,863
Pasco	1	0	0	0	0	0	1	0	0	0	72,146
Port Angeles	2	1	0	0	0	0	2	0	0	1	19,964
Pullman	1	0	0	0	0	0	0	0	0	1	33,897
Puyallup[2]	1	0	0	0	0	0	0	0	1	0	41,242
Redmond[2]	1	2	2	0	0	0	1	1	1	0	63,889
Renton	3	3	0	0	0	0	4	0	0	2	102,470
Richland	5	0	0	0	0	0	0	2	1	2	56,151
Seattle	120	45	57	0	1	11	46	66	63	59	721,365
Shoreline	1	0	1	0	0	0	1	0	1	0	55,703
Spokane	22	2	3	0	1	0	16	8	0	4	217,066
Spokane Valley	9	3	2	0	0	0	1	4	5	4	97,430
Tacoma	7	1	0	0	0	0	2	2	4	0	213,504
Toppenish	1	0	0	0	0	0	0	0	1	0	8,974
Tukwila	5	0	1	0	0	1	0	3	3	1	20,183
Tumwater	1	0	0	0	0	0	0	1	0	0	22,961
Union Gap	0	1	0	0	0	0	1	0	0	0	6,104
Vancouver	1	0	0	0	0	0	0	0	1	0	176,884
Walla Walla	1	0	0	0	0	0	0	1	0	0	32,189
West Richland	0	0	0	1	0	0	1	0	0	0	14,603
Yakima	6	0	1	0	0	0	3	2	1	1	94,375
Universities and Colleges	4	1	1	0	2	1					
Eastern Washington University	0	0	0	0	1	1	1	0	1	0	12,279
Evergreen State College	1	0	0	0	0	0	0	1	0	0	4,089
University of Washington	3	0	0	0	1	0	1	0	1	2	45,591

Table 94. Hate Crime Incidents Per Bias Motivation and Quarter, by Selected State and Agency, 2017—Continued

(Number.)

State/agency	Number of incidents per bias motivation						Number of incidents per quarter				Population[1]
	Race/ Ethnicity/ Ancestry	Religion	Sexual orientation	Disability	Gender	Gender Identity	1st quarter	2nd quarter	3rd quarter	4th quarter	
Washington State University, Pullman	0	0	1	0	0	0	0	1	0	0	30,142
Western Washington University	0	1	0	0	0	0	0	0	0	1	15,574
Metropolitan Counties	41	9	3	0	0	0					
Cowlitz	1	0	0	0	0	0	0	0	0	1	
King	4	0	0	0	0	0	3	1	0		
Pierce	6	1	1	0	0	0	3	0	5	0	
Skagit	1	2	0	0	0	0	2	0	1	0	
Skamania	1	0	0	0	0	0	0	1	0	0	
Snohomish	6	2	1	0	0	0	2	2	3	2	
Spokane	8	3	0	0	0	0	3	4	3	1	
Thurston	2	0	0	0	0	0	0	1	1	0	
Whatcom[2]	5	1	1	0	0	0	0	0	5	1	
Yakima	7	0	0	0	0	0	1	2	3	1	
Nonmetropolitan Counties	1	0	0	0	0	0					
Clallam	1	0	0	0	0	0	0	0	0	1	
Tribal Agencies	1	0	0	0	0	0					
Lummi Tribal	1	0	0	0	0	0	0	1	0	0	
Other Agencies	2	2	0	0	0	0					
Port of Seattle	2	2	0	0	0	0	0	1	0	3	
WEST VIRGINIA											
Total	23	6	1	1	0	0					
Cities	10	4	1	0	0	0					
Barboursville	0	1	0	0	0	0	1	0	0	0	4,315
Bridgeport	1	0	0	0	0	0	1	0	0	0	8,401
Buckhannon	1	0	0	0	0	0	0	0	0	1	5,610
Charleston	3	0	1	0	0	0	1	0	2	1	48,788
Fairmont	1	0	0	0	0	0	1	0	0	0	18,604
Huntington	0	1	0	0	0	0	0	0	0	1	47,933
Martinsburg	0	1	0	0	0	0	0	0	0	1	17,761
Oak Hill	3	0	0	0	0	0	0	3	0	0	8,490
Parkersburg	1	0	0	0	0	0	0	1	0	0	30,475
White Sulphur Springs	0	1	0	0	0	0	0	1	0	0	2,417
Universities and Colleges	2	1	0	0	0	0					
Shepherd University	2	1	0	0	0	0	1	0	0	2	3,779
Metropolitan Counties	6	0	0	0	0	0					
Berkeley	3	0	0	0	0	0	0	1	1	1	
Brooke	1	0	0	0	0	0	1	0	0	0	
Fayette	1	0	0	0	0	0	0	0	0	1	
Jefferson	1	0	0	0	0	0	0	1	0	0	
Nonmetropolitan Counties	5	1	0	1	0	0					
Braxton	1	0	0	0	0	0	1	0	0	0	
Harrison	0	1	0	0	0	0	0	1	0	0	
Lewis	1	0	0	1	0	0	0	0	1	1	
Mason	1	0	0	0	0	0	0	0	1	0	
McDowell	2	0	0	0	0	0	0	1	0	1	
WISCONSIN											
Total	15	17	13	1	0	0					
Cities	14	12	11	1	0	0					
Appleton	1	3	0	0	0	0	0	0	1	3	74,660
Beloit	0	2	0	0	0	0	2	0	0	0	36,724
Eau Claire	1	0	0	0	0	0	1	0	0	0	68,687
Fond du Lac	0	1	0	0	0	0	0	0	1	0	42,929
Hudson	1	3	8	0	0	0	2	3	6	1	13,788
Juneau	0	0	0	1	0	0	0	1	0	0	2,703
Kaukauna	0	0	1	0	0	0	0	0	1	0	15,969
La Crosse	1	0	0	0	0	0	0	0	1	0	52,234
Madison	0	1	1	0	0	0	0	1	1	0	255,850
Manitowoc	1	0	0	0	0	0	1	0	0	0	32,813
Milwaukee	4	1	0	0	0	0	3	0	0	2	595,168
North Fond du Lac	1	0	0	0	0	0	0	1	0	0	5,038
Seymour	1	0	0	0	0	0	0	0	1	0	3,441
Sheboygan	1	0	0	0	0	0	0	0	0	1	48,595
South Milwaukee	1	0	0	0	0	0	1	0	0	0	21,039
Tomahawk	0	1	0	0	0	0	0	1	0	0	3,169
West Allis	1	0	0	0	0	0	0	0	0	1	60,043
Wisconsin Rapids	0	0	1	0	0	0	0	0	1	0	17,807
Metropolitan Counties	0	4	1	0	0	0					
Calumet	0	1	0	0	0	0	0	0	0	1	
Columbia	0	1	0	0	0	0	0	1	0	0	

Table 94. Hate Crime Incidents Per Bias Motivation and Quarter, by Selected State and Agency, 2017—Continued

(Number.)

State/agency	Number of incidents per bias motivation						Number of incidents per quarter				Population[1]
	Race/ Ethnicity/ Ancestry	Religion	Sexual orientation	Disability	Gender	Gender Identity	1st quarter	2nd quarter	3rd quarter	4th quarter	
Rock	0	0	1	0	0	0	0	0	1	0	
St. Croix	0	2	0	0	0	0	1	1	0	0	
Nonmetropolitan Counties	0	1	0	0	0	0					
Burnett	0	1	0	0	0	0	0	0	1	0	
Tribal Agencies	1	0	1	0	0	0					
Lac Courtes Oreilles Tribal	1	0	1	0	0	0	1	0	1	0	
WYOMING											
Total	1	1	2	0	0	0					
Cities	0	1	2	0	0	0					
Laramie	0	1	1	0	0	0	0	0	0	2	32,632
Sheridan	0	0	1	0	0	0	0	0	1	0	18,036
Universities and Colleges	1	0	0	0	0	0					
University of Wyoming	1	0	0	0	0	0	0	1	0	0	12,366

1 Population figures are published only for the cities. The figures listed for the universities and colleges are student enrollment and were provided by the United States Department of Education for the 2016 school year, the most recent available. The enrollment figures include full-time and part-time students.   2 Includes one incident reported with more than one bias motivation.   3 Student enrollment figures were not available.

Table 95. Participation Table, Number of Participating Agencies and Population Covered, by Population Group, 2017

(Number.)

Population group	Number of participating agencies	Population covered
Total	16,149	306,435,676
Group I (cities 250,000 and over)	82	60,637,635
Group II (cities 100,000-249,999)	218	32,396,880
Group III (cities 50,000-99,999)	482	33,672,307
Group IV (cities 25,000-49,999)	868	30,072,013
Group V (cities 10,000-24,999)	1,786	28,545,233
Group VI1 (cities under 10,000)	8,290	23,637,355
Metropolitan counties[1]	1,959	73,842,621
Nonmetropolitan counties[1]	2,464	23,631,632

1 Includes universities and colleges, state police agencies, and/or other agencies to which no population is attributed.

APPENDIXES

APPENDIX

APPENDIX I. METHODOLOGY

Submitting UCR data to the FBI is a collective effort on the part of city, university/college, county, state, tribal, and federal law enforcement agencies to present a nationwide view of crime. Participating agencies throughout the country voluntarily provide reports on crimes known to the police and on persons arrested. For the most part, agencies submit monthly crime reports, using uniform offense definitions, to a centralized repository within their state. The state UCR Program then forwards the data to the FBI's UCR Program. Agencies in states that do not have a state UCR Program submit their data directly to the FBI. Staff members review the information for accuracy and reasonableness. [The FBI distributes the data presentations, special studies, and other publications compiled from the data to all who are interested in knowing about crime in the nation.] The national UCR Program is housed in the Operational Programs (OP) Branch of the FBI's Criminal Justice Information Services (CJIS) Division. Within the OP Branch, four units (the Crime Statistics Management Unit [CSMU], the CJIS Audit Unit, the Multimedia Productions Group [MPG]), and the CJIS Training and Advisory Process [CTAP] Unit), are involved in the day-to-day administration of the program.

Criteria for State UCR programs

The criteria established for state programs ensure consistency and comparability in the data submitted to the national program, as well as regular and timely reporting. These criteria are:

1. A UCR Program must conform to the FBI UCR Program's submission standards, definitions, specifications, and required deadlines.

2. A UCR Program must establish data integrity procedures and have personnel assigned to assist contributing agencies in quality assurance practices and crime reporting procedures. Data integrity procedures should include crime trend assessments, offense classification verification, and technical specification validation.

3. A UCR Program's submissions must cover more than 50 percent of the law enforcement agencies within its established reporting domain and be willing to cover any and all UCR-contributing agencies that wish to use the UCR Program from within its domain. (An agency wishing to become a UCR Program must be willing to report for all of the agencies within the state.)

4. A UCR Program must furnish the FBI UCR Program with all of the UCR data collected by the law enforcement agencies within its domain.

These requirements do not prohibit the state from gathering other statistical data beyond the national collection.

Data Completeness and Quality

National program staff members contact the state UCR program in connection with crime-reporting matters and, when necessary and approved by the state, they contact individual contributors within the state. To fulfill its responsibilities in connection with the UCR program, the FBI reviews and edits individual agency reports for completeness and quality. Upon request, they conduct training programs within the state on law enforcement record-keeping and crime-reporting procedures. The FBI conducts an audit of each state's UCR data collection procedures once every three years, in accordance with audit standards established by the federal government. Should circumstances develop in which the state program does not comply with the aforementioned requirements, the national program may institute a direct collection of data from law enforcement agencies within the state.

During a review of publication processes, the UCR Program staff analyzed Web statistics from previous editions of *Crime in the United States* (*CIUS*) to determine the tables that users access the most. Based on these criteria, the UCR Program streamlined the 2016 edition by reducing the number of tables from 81 to 29. The publication, however, still presents the major topics (offenses known, clearances, and persons arrested) that readers have come to expect. On June 30, 2017, the UCR Program launched the Crime Data Explorer (CDE), which provides law enforcement and the general public with crime data at the agency, state, and national levels. Offering multiple pathways to reported crime data, the CDE provides data visualizations of high-level trends and incident data with more detailed perspectives through downloads and a system enabling developers to create software applications. Planned enhancements to the CDE include additional tools to create dynamic data presentations, progressing beyond the static data tables of *CIUS* and the National Incident-Based Reporting System (NIBRS).

Beginning January 1, 2017, the UCR Program discontinued collecting rape data via the SRS according to the legacy definition. Therefore, the 2016 editions of *CIUS* and *Hate Crime Statistics* are the final publications which include the legacy definition of rape. Only rape data submitted under the revised definition will be published for 2017 and subsequent years. This change did not affect agencies that submit rape data via NIBRS.

Reporting Procedures

Offenses known and value of property–Law enforcement agencies tabulate the number of Part I offenses reported based on records of all reports of crime received from victims, officers who discover infractions, or other sources, and submit these reports each month to the FBI directly or through their state UCR programs. Part I offenses include murder and nonnegligent manslaughter, forcible rape, robbery, aggravated assault, burglary, larceny-theft, motor vehicle theft, and arson. Each month, law enforcement agencies also submit to the FBI the value of property stolen and recovered in connection with the offenses and detailed information pertaining to criminal homicide.

Unfounded offenses and clearances—When, through investigation, an agency determines that complaints of crimes are unfounded or false, the agency eliminates that offense from its crime tally through an entry on the monthly report. The report also provides the total number of actual Part I offenses, the number of offenses cleared, and the number of clearances that involve only offenders under the age of 18. (Law enforcement can clear crimes in one of two ways: by the arrest of at least one person who is charged and turned over to the court for prosecution or by exceptional means—when some element beyond law enforcement's control precludes the arrest of a known offender.)

Persons arrested—In addition to reporting Part I offenses each month, law enforcement agencies also provide data on the age, sex, and race of persons arrested for Part I and Part II offenses. Part II offenses encompass all crimes, except traffic violations, that are not classified as Part I offenses.

Officers killed or assaulted—Each month, law enforcement agencies also report information to the UCR program regarding law enforcement officers killed or assaulted, and each year they report the number of full-time sworn and civilian law enforcement personnel employed as of October 31.

Hate crimes—At the end of each quarter, law enforcement agencies report summarized data on hate crimes; that is specific offenses that were motivated by an offender's bias against the perceived race, religion, ethnic or national origin, sexual orientation, or physical or mental disability of the victim. Those agencies participating in the UCR program's National Incident-Based Reporting System (NIBRS) submit hate crime data monthly.

Editing Procedures

The UCR program thoroughly examines each report it receives for arithmetical accuracy and for deviations in crime data from month to month and from present to past years that may indicate errors. UCR staff members compare an agency's monthly reports with its previous submissions and with reports from similar agencies to identify any unusual fluctuations in the agency's crime count. Considerable variations in crime levels may indicate modified records procedures, incomplete reporting, or changes in the jurisdiction's geopolitical structure.

Evaluation of trends—Data reliability is a high priority of the FBI, which brings any deviations or arithmetical adjustments to the attention of state UCR programs or the submitting agencies. Typically, FBI staff members study the monthly reports to evaluate periodic trends prepared for individual reporting units. Any significant increase or decrease becomes the subject of a special inquiry. Changes in crime reporting procedures or annexations that affect an agency's jurisdiction can influence the level of reported crime. When this occurs, the FBI excludes the figures for specific crime categories or totals, if necessary, from the trend tabulations.

Training for contributors—In addition to the evaluation of trends, the FBI provides training seminars and instructional materials on crime reporting procedures to assist contributors in complying with UCR standards. Throughout the country, representatives from the national program coordinate with representatives of state programs and law enforcement personnel and hold training sessions to explain the purpose of the program, the rules of uniform classification and scoring, and the methods of assembling the information for reporting. When an individual agency has specific problems with compiling its crime statistics and its remedial efforts are unsuccessful, personnel from the FBI's Criminal Justice Information Services Division may visit the contributor to aid in resolving the problems.

UCR Handbook—The national UCR program publishes the *Uniform Crime Reporting (UCR) Handbook*, which details procedures for classifying and scoring offenses and serves as the contributing agencies' basic resource for preparing reports. The national staff also produces letters to UCR contributors, state program bulletins, and UCR newsletters as needed. These publications provide policy updates and new information, as well as clarification of reporting issues.

The final responsibility for data submissions rests with the individual contributing law enforcement agency. Although the FBI makes every effort through its editing procedures, training practices, and correspondence to ensure the validity of the data it receives, the accuracy of the statistics depends primarily on the adherence of each contributor to the established standards of reporting. Deviations from these established standards that cannot be resolved by the national UCR program may be brought to the attention of the Criminal Justice Information Systems Committees of the International Association of Chiefs of Police and the National Sheriffs' Association.

NIBRS Conversion

Thirty-three state programs are certified to provide their UCR data in the expanded National Incident-Based Reporting System (NIBRS) format. For presentation in this book, the NIBRS data were converted to the historical Summary Reporting System data. The UCR program staff constructed the NIBRS database to allow for such conversion so that UCR's long-running time series could continue.

Crime Trends

By showing fluctuations from year to year, trend statistics offer the data user an added perspective from which to study crime. Percent change tabulations in this publication are computed only for reporting agencies that provided comparable data for the periods under consideration. The FBI excludes from the trend calculations all figures except those received for common months from common agencies. Also excluded are unusual fluctuations of data that the FBI determines are the result of such variables as improved records procedures, annexations, and so on.

Caution to Users

Data users should exercise care in making any direct comparison between data in this publication and those in prior issues of *Crime in the United States*. Because of differing levels of participation from year to year and reporting problems that require the FBI to estimate crime counts for certain contributors, some data may not be comparable. In addition, this publication may contain updates to data provided in prior years' publications.

Offense Estimation

Some tables in this publication contain statistics for the entire United States. Because not all law enforcement agencies provide data for complete reporting periods, the FBI includes estimated crime numbers in these presentations. The FBI estimates data for three areas: Metropolitan Statistical Areas (MSAs), cities outside MSAs, and nonmetropolitan counties; and computes estimates for participating agencies that do not provide 12 months of complete data. For agencies supplying 3 to 11 months of data, the national UCR program estimates for the missing data by following a standard estimation procedure using the data provided by the agency. If an agency has supplied less than 3 months of data, the FBI computes estimates by using the known crime figures of similar areas within a state and assigning the same proportion of crime volumes to nonreporting agencies. The estimation process considers the following: population size covered by the agency; type of jurisdiction; for example, police department versus sheriff's office; and geographic location.

Estimation of State-Level Data

In response to various circumstances, the FBI calculates estimated offense totals for certain states. For example, some states do not provide rape figures in accordance with UCR guidelines. In addition, problems at the state level have, at times, resulted in no useable data. Also, the conversion of the National Incident-Based Reporting System (NIBRS) data to Summary data has contributed to the need for unique estimation procedures.

APPENDIX II. OFFENSE DEFINITIONS

The Uniform Crime Reporting (UCR) program divides offenses into two groups. Contributing agencies submit information on the number of Part I offenses known to law enforcement; those offenses cleared by arrest or exceptional means; and the age, sex, and race of persons arrested for each of these offenses. Contributors provide only arrest data for Part II offenses. These are definitions of offenses set forth by the UCR.

The UCR program collects data on Part I offenses to measure the level and scope of crime occurring throughout the nation. The program's founders chose these offenses because (1) they are serious crimes, (2) they occur with regularity in all areas of the country, and (3) they are likely to be reported to police.

Part I offenses include criminal homicide, forcible rape, robbery, aggravated assault, burglary, larceny-theft, motor vehicle theft, and arson.

Criminal homicide — a.) Murder and nonnegligent manslaughter: the willful (nonnegligent) killing of one human being by another. Deaths caused by negligence, attempts to kill, assaults to kill, suicides, and accidental deaths are excluded. The program classifies justifiable homicides separately and limits the definition to (1) the killing of a felon by a law enforcement officer in the line of duty; or (2) the killing of a felon, during the commission of a felony, by a private citizen. b.) Manslaughter by negligence: the killing of another person through gross negligence. Deaths of persons due to their own negligence, accidental deaths not resulting from gross negligence, and traffic fatalities are excluded.

Rape — In 2013, the FBI UCR Program initiated collection of rape data under a revised definition within the Summary Reporting System. Previously, offense data for forcible rape were collected under the legacy UCR definition: the carnal knowledge of a female forcibly and against her will. Beginning with the 2013 data year, the term "forcible" was removed from the offense title, and the definition was changed. The revised UCR definition of rape is now the only criterium measured (the legacy definition was discontinued after 2016). Rape is: penetration, no matter how slight, of the vagina or anus with any body part or object, or oral penetration by a sex organ of another person, without the consent of the victim. Attempts or assaults to commit rape are also included; however, statutory rape and incest are excluded. The UCR Program counts one offense for each victim of a rape, attempted rape, or assault with intent to rape, regardless of the victim's age. Sexual relations without the victim's consent which involves a familial offender is counted as a rape and not an act of incest. All other crimes of a sexual nature are considered to be Part II offenses; as such, the UCR Program collects only arrest data for those crimes. The offense of statutory rape, in which no force is used but the female victim is under the age of consent, is included in the arrest total for the sex offenses category.

Robbery — The taking or attempted taking of anything of value from the care, custody, or control of a person or persons by force or threat of force or violence and/or by putting the victim in fear.

Aggravated assault — An unlawful attack by one person upon another for the purpose of inflicting severe or aggravated bodily injury. This type of assault usually is accompanied by the use of a weapon or by means likely to produce death or great bodily harm. Simple assaults are excluded.

Burglary (breaking or entering) — The unlawful entry of a structure to commit a felony or a theft. Attempted forcible entry is included.

Larceny-theft (except motor vehicle theft) — The unlawful taking, carrying, leading, or riding away of property from the possession or constructive possession of another. Examples are thefts of bicycles or automobile parts and accessories, shoplifting, pocket-picking, or the stealing of any property or article that is not taken by force and violence or by fraud. Attempted larcenies are included. Embezzlement, confidence games, forgery, worthless checks, and the like, are excluded.

Motor vehicle theft — The theft or attempted theft of a motor vehicle. A motor vehicle is self-propelled and runs on land surface and not on rails. Motorboats, construction equipment, airplanes, and farming equipment are specifically excluded from this category.

Arson — Any willful or malicious burning or attempt to burn, with or without intent to defraud, a dwelling house, public building, motor vehicle, aircraft, personal property of another, and the like.

The **Part II** offenses, for which only arrest data are collected, are:

Other assaults, also known as other assaults (simple) — Assaults and attempted assaults that are not of an aggravated nature and do not result in serious injury to the victim. Included in this category are stalking, intimidation, coercion, and hazing.

Forgery and counterfeiting—The altering, copying, or imitating of something, without authority or right, with the intent to deceive or defraud by passing the copy or thing altered or imitated as that which is original or genuine; or the selling, buying, or possession of an altered, copied, or imitated thing with the intent to deceive or defraud. Attempts are included.

Fraud—The intentional perversion of the truth for the purpose of inducing another person or other entity in reliance upon it to part with something of value or to surrender a legal right. Fraudulent conversion and obtaining of money or property by false pretenses. Confidence games and bad checks, except forgeries and counterfeiting, are included.

Embezzlement—The unlawful misappropriation or misapplication by an offender of money, property, or some other thing of value entrusted to that offender's care, custody, or control.

Stolen property; buying, receiving, possessing—Buying, receiving, possessing, selling, concealing, or transporting any property with the knowledge that it has been unlawfully taken, as by burglary, embezzlement, fraud, larceny, robbery, and the like. Attempts are included.

Vandalism—To willfully or maliciously destroy, injure, disfigure, or deface any public or private property, real or personal, without the consent of the owner or person having custody or control by cutting, tearing, breaking, marking, painting, drawing, covering with filth, or any other such means as may be specified by local law. Attempts are included.

Weapons; carrying, possessing, and the like—The violation of laws or ordinances prohibiting the manufacture, sale, purchase, transportation, possession, concealment, or use of firearms, cutting instruments, explosives, incendiary devices, or other deadly weapons. Attempts are included.

Prostitution and commercialized vice—The unlawful promotion of or participation in sexual activities for profit, including attempts. To solicit customers or transport persons for prostitution purposes; to own, manage, or operate a dwelling or other establishment for the purposes of providing a place where prostitution is performed; or to otherwise assist or promote prostitution.

Sex offenses (except rape, prostitution, and commercialized vice)—Offenses against chastity, common decency, morals, and the like. Incest, indecent exposure, and statutory rape, as well as attempts are included.

Drug abuse violations—The violation of laws prohibiting the production, distribution, and/or use of certain controlled substances. The unlawful cultivation, manufacture, distribution, sale, purchase, use, possession, transportation, or importation of any controlled drug or narcotic substance. Arrests for violations of state and local laws, specifically those relating to the unlawful possession, sale, use, growing, manufacturing, and making of narcotic drugs. The following drug categories are specified: opium or cocaine and their derivatives (morphine, heroin, codeine); marijuana; synthetic narcotics—manufactured narcotics that can cause true addiction (demerol, methadone); and dangerous nonnarcotic drugs (barbiturates, benzedrine).

Gambling—To unlawfully bet or wager money or something else of value; assist, promote, or operate a game of chance for money or some other stake; possess or transmit wagering information; manufacture, sell, purchase, possess, or transport gambling equipment, devices, or goods; or tamper with the outcome of a sporting event or contest to gain a gambling advantage.

Offenses against the family and children—Unlawful nonviolent acts by a family member (or legal guardian) that threaten the physical, mental, or economic well-being or morals of another family member and that are not classifiable as other offenses, such as assault or sex offenses. Attempts are included.

Driving under the influence—Driving or operating a motor vehicle or common carrier while mentally or physically impaired as the result of consuming an alcoholic beverage or using a drug or narcotic.

Liquor laws—The violation of state or local laws or ordinances prohibiting the manufacture, sale, purchase, transportation, possession, or use of alcoholic beverages, not including driving under the influence and drunkenness. Federal violations are excluded.

Drunkenness—To drink alcoholic beverages to the extent that one's mental faculties and physical coordination are substantially impaired. Excludes driving under the influence.

Disorderly conduct—Any behavior that tends to disturb the public peace or decorum, scandalize the community, or shock the public sense of morality.

Vagrancy—The violation of a court order, regulation, ordinance, or law requiring the withdrawal of persons from the streets or other specified areas; prohibiting persons from remaining in an area or place in an idle or aimless manner; or prohibiting persons from going from place to place without visible means of support.

All other offenses—All violations of state or local laws not specifically identified as Part I or Part II offenses, except traffic violations.

Suspicion—Arrested for no specific offense and released without formal charges being placed.

Curfew and loitering laws (persons under 18 years of age)—Violations by juveniles of local curfew or loitering ordinances.

APPENDIX III. GEOGRAPHIC AREA DEFINITIONS

The program collects crime data and supplemental information that make it possible to generate a variety of statistical compilations, including data presented by reporting areas. These statistics enable data users to analyze local crime data in conjunction with those for areas of similar geographic location or population size. The reporting areas that the program uses in its data breakdowns include community types, population groups, and regions and divisions. For community types, the program considers proximity to metropolitan areas using the designations established by the U.S. Office of Management and Budget (OMB). (Generally, sheriffs, county police, and state police report crimes within counties but outside of cities; local police report crimes within city limits.) The number of inhabitants living in a locale (based on the U.S. Census Bureau's figures) determines the population group into which the program places it. For its geographic breakdowns, the program divides the United States into regions and divisions.

Regions and Divisions

The map below illustrates the nine divisions that make up the four regions of the United States. The program uses this widely recognized geographic organization when compiling the nation's crime data. The regions and divisions are as follows:

NORTHEAST

New England — Connecticut, Maine, Massachusetts, New Hampshire, Rhode Island, and Vermont

Middle Atlantic — New York, New Jersey, and Pennsylvania

MIDWEST

East North Central — Illinois, Indiana, Michigan, Ohio, and Wisconsin

West North Central — Iowa, Kansas, Minnesota, Missouri, Nebraska, North Dakota, and South Dakota

SOUTH

South Atlantic — Delaware, District of Columbia, Florida, Georgia, Maryland, North Carolina, South Carolina, Virginia, and West Virginia

East South Central — Alabama, Kentucky, Mississippi, and Tennessee

West South Central — Arkansas, Louisiana, Oklahoma, and Texas

WEST

Mountain — Arizona, Colorado, Idaho, Montana, Nevada, New Mexico, Utah, and Wyoming

Pacific — Alaska, California, Hawaii, Oregon, and Washington

Community Types

To assist data users who wish to analyze and present uniform statistical data about metropolitan areas, the program uses reporting units that represent major population centers. The program compiles data for the following three types of communities:

Metropolitan Statistical Areas (MSAs) — Each MSA contains a principal city or urbanized area with a population of at least 50,000 inhabitants. MSAs include the principal city, the county in which the city is located, and other adjacent counties that have a high degree of economic and social integration with the principal city and county (as defined by the OMB), which is measured through commuting. In the program, counties within an MSA are considered metropolitan counties. In addition, MSAs may cross state boundaries.

Some presentations in this publication refer to Metropolitan Divisions, which are subdivisions of an MSA that consists of a core with "a population of at least 2.5 million persons. A Metropolitan Division consists of one or more main/secondary counties that represent an employment center or centers, plus adjacent counties associated with the main county or counties through commuting ties," (*Federal Register* 65 [249]). Also, some tables reference suburban areas, which are subdivisions of MSAs that exclude the principal cities but include all the remaining cities (those having fewer than 50,000 inhabitants) and the unincorporated areas of the MSAs.

Because the elements that comprise MSAs, particularly the geographic compositions, are subject to change, the program discourages data users from making year-to-year comparisons of MSA data.

Cities Outside MSAs — Ordinarily, cities outside MSAs are incorporated areas. In 2013, cities outside MSAs made up 6.0 percent of the nation's population.

Nonmetropolitan Counties Outside MSAs—Most nonmetropolitan counties are composed of unincorporated areas.

Metropolitan and nonmetropolitan community types are further illustrated in the following table:

Metropolitan	Nonmetropolitan
Principal cities (50,000+ inhabitants)	Cities outside metropolitan areas
Suburban cities	
Metropolitan counties	Nonmetropolitan counties

APPENDIX IV. THE NATION'S CRIME MEASURES

The Department of Justice administers two statistical programs to measure the magnitude, nature, and impact of crime in the nation: the Uniform Crime Reporting (UCR) program and the National Crime Victimization Survey (NCVS). Each of these programs produces valuable information about aspects of the nation's crime problem. Because the UCR and NCVS programs are conducted for different purposes, use different methods, and focus on somewhat different aspects of crime, the information they produce together provides a more comprehensive panorama of the nation's crime problem than either could produce alone.

New additions to more comprehensively measure crime are being implemented into the UCR program. The most substantial, the National Incident-Based Reporting System, will soon be the FBI's sole method of data collection.

NIBRS Transition Update: Looking Toward 2021

Data collected via the National Incident-Based Reporting System (NIBRS) are the UCR Program's data standard, and by January 1, 2021, the FBI will transition to a NIBRS-only data collection. To help this effort, the FBI has intensified its engagement with law enforcement agencies across the nation. Specifically, the FBI has presented the benefits of NIBRS and called for support at several national law enforcement organizations, held conference calls with state UCR Program managers and CJIS systems officers, provided technical assistance, and held special NIBRS Train-the-Trainer sessions for state UCR Programs with limited or no NIBRS capability. It also made advancements through collaboration with tribal law enforcement agencies and those of institutions of higher education. Through its partnership with the Bureau of Justice Statistics (BJS) on the National Crime Statistics Exchange (NCS-X) Initiative, the FBI and BJS are working to increase the number of law enforcement agencies reporting data to NIBRS.

For more information about the NIBRS transition, visit www.fbi.gov/nibrs.

Uniform Crime Reporting (UCR) program

The UCR program, administered by the Federal Bureau of Investigation (FBI), was created in 1929 and collects information on the following crimes reported to law enforcement authorities: murder and nonnegligent manslaughter, rape, robbery, aggravated assault, burglary, larceny-theft, motor vehicle theft, and arson. Law enforcement agencies also report arrest data for 20 additional crime categories.

The UCR program compiles data from monthly law enforcement reports and from individual crime incident records transmitted directly to the FBI or to centralized state agencies that report to the FBI. The program thoroughly examines each report it receives for reasonableness, accuracy, and deviations that may indicate errors. Large variations in crime levels may indicate modified records procedures, incomplete reporting, or changes in a jurisdiction's boundaries. To identify any unusual fluctuations in an agency's crime counts, the program compares monthly reports to previous submissions of the agency and to those for similar agencies.

The FBI annually publishes its findings in a preliminary release in the spring of the following calendar year, followed by a detailed annual report, *Crime in the United States*, issued in the fall. (The printed copy of *Crime in the United States* is now published by Bernan.) In addition to crime counts and trends, this report includes data on crimes cleared, persons arrested (age, sex, and race), law enforcement personnel (including the number of sworn officers killed or assaulted), and the characteristics of homicides (including age, sex, and race of victims and offenders; victim-offender relationships; weapons used; and circumstances surrounding the homicides). Other periodic reports are also available from the UCR program.

The state and local law enforcement agencies participating in the UCR program are continually converting to the more comprehensive and detailed National Incident-Based Reporting System (NIBRS).

The UCR program presents crime counts for the nation as a whole, as well as for regions, states, counties, cities, towns, tribal law enforcement areas, and colleges and universities. This allows for studies among neighboring jurisdictions and among those with similar populations and other common characteristics.

National Crime Victimization Survey

The NCVS, conducted by the Bureau of Justice Statistics (BJS), began in 1973. It provides a detailed picture of crime incidents, victims, and trends. After a substantial period of research, the BJS completed an intensive methodological redesign of the survey in 1993. It conducted this redesign to improve the questions used to uncover crime, update the survey methods, and broaden the scope of crimes measured. The redesigned survey collects detailed information on the frequency and nature of the crimes of rape, sexual assault, personal robbery, aggravated and simple assault, household burglary, theft, and motor vehicle theft. It does not measure homicide or commercial crimes (such as burglaries of stores).

Twice a year, Census Bureau personnel interview household members in a nationally representative sample of approximately 90,000 households (about 160,000 people). Households stay in the sample for 3 years, and new households rotate into the sample on an ongoing basis.

The NCVS collects information on crimes suffered by individuals and households, whether or not those crimes were reported to law enforcement. It estimates the proportion of each crime type reported to law enforcement, and it summarizes the reasons that victims give for reporting or not reporting.

The survey provides information about victims (age, sex, race, ethnicity, marital status, income, and educational level); offenders (sex, race, approximate age, and victim-offender relationship); and crimes (time and place of occurrence, use of weapons, nature of injury, and economic consequences). Questions also cover victims' experiences with the criminal justice system, self-protective measures used by victims, and possible substance abuse by offenders. Supplements are added to the survey periodically to obtain detailed information on specific topics, such as school crime.

The BJS published the first data from the redesigned NCVS in a June 1995 bulletin. The publication of NCVS data includes *Criminal Victimization in the United States*, an annual report that covers the broad range of detailed information collected by the NCVS. The bureau also publishes detailed reports on topics such as crime against women, urban crime, and gun use in crime. The National Archive of Criminal Justice Data at the University of Michigan archives the NCVS data files to help researchers perform independent analyses.

Comparing the UCR program and the NCVS

Because the BJS designed the NCVS to complement the UCR program, the two programs share many similarities. As much as their different collection methods permit, the two measure the same subset of serious crimes with the same definitions. Both programs cover rape, robbery, aggravated assault, burglary, theft, and motor vehicle theft; both define rape, robbery, theft, and motor vehicle theft virtually identically. (Although rape is defined analogously, the UCR program measures the crime against women only, and the NCVS measures it against both sexes.)

There are also significant differences between the two programs. First, the two programs were created to serve different purposes. The UCR program's primary objective

is to provide a reliable set of criminal justice statistics for law enforcement administration, operation, and management. The BJS established the NCVS to provide previously unavailable information about crime (including crime not reported to police), victims, and offenders.

Second, the two programs measure an overlapping but nonidentical set of crimes. The NCVS includes crimes both reported and not reported to law enforcement. The NCVS excludes—but the UCR program includes—homicide, arson, commercial crimes, and crimes committed against children under 12 years of age. The UCR program captures crimes reported to law enforcement but collects only arrest data for simple assaults and sexual assaults other than rape.

Third, because of methodology, the NCVS and UCR have different definitions of some crimes. For example, the UCR defines burglary as the unlawful entry or attempted entry of a structure to commit a felony or theft. The NCVS, not wanting to ask victims to ascertain offender motives, defines burglary as the entry or attempted entry of a residence by a person who had no right to be there.

Fourth, for property crimes (burglary, theft, and motor vehicle theft), the two programs calculate crime rates using different bases. The UCR program rates for these crimes are per capita (number of crimes per 100,000 persons), whereas the NCVS rates for these crimes are per household (number of crimes per 1,000 households).

Because the number of households may not grow at the same annual rate as the total population, trend data for rates of property crimes measured by the two programs may not be comparable. In addition, some differences in the data from the two programs may result from sampling variation in the NCVS and from estimating for nonresponsiveness in the UCR program.

The BJS derives the NCVS estimates from interviewing a sample and are, therefore, subject to a margin of error. The bureau uses rigorous statistical methods to calculate confidence intervals around all survey estimates, and describes trend data in the NCVS reports as genuine only if there is at least a 90-percent certainty that the measured changes are not the result of sampling variation. The UCR program bases its data on the actual counts of offenses reported by law enforcement agencies. In some circumstances, the UCR program estimates its data for nonparticipating agencies or those reporting partial data. Apparent discrepancies between statistics from the two programs can usually be accounted for by their definitional and procedural differences, or resolved by comparing NCVS sampling variations (confidence intervals) of crimes said to have been reported to police with UCR program statistics.

For most types of crimes measured by both the UCR program and the NCVS, analysts familiar with the programs can exclude those aspects of crime not common to both from analysis. Resulting long-term trend lines can be brought into close concordance. The impact of such adjustments is most striking for robbery, burglary, and motor vehicle theft, whose definitions most closely coincide.

With robbery, the BJS bases the NCVS victimization rates on only those robberies reported to the police. It is also possible to remove UCR program robberies of commercial establishments, such as gas stations, convenience stores, and banks, from analysis. When users compare the resulting NCVS police-reported robbery rates and the UCR program noncommercial robbery rates, the results reveal closely corresponding long-term trends.

Each program has unique strengths. The UCR program provides a measure of the number of crimes reported to law enforcement agencies throughout the country. The program's Supplementary Homicide Reports provide the most reliable, timely data on the extent and nature of homicides in the nation. The NCVS is the primary source of information on the characteristics of criminal victimization and on the number and types of crimes not reported to law enforcement authorities.

By understanding the strengths and limitations of each program, it is possible to use the UCR program and NCVS to achieve a greater understanding of crime trends and the nature of crime in the United States. For example, changes in police procedures, shifting attitudes towards crime and police, and other societal changes can affect the extent to which people report and law enforcement agencies record crime. NCVS and UCR program data can be used in concert to explore why trends in reported and police-recorded crime may differ.

INDEX

DISTRICT OF COLUMBIA

DRIVING UNDER THE INFLUENCE

DRUG ABUSE VIOLATIONS

STUDENT ENROLLMENT

SUBURBAN AREAS

SUSPICION

TELEVISIONS, RADIOS, AND STEREOS

TENNESSEE

TEXAS

VERMONT

VICE OFFENSES

see **PROSTITUTION AND COMMERCIALIZED VICE**

VICTIMS

VIOLENT CRIME

VIRGINIA